▶ **NOTE TO
THE STUDENT**

This text was created to provide you with a high-quality educational resource. As a publisher specializing in college texts for business and economics, our goal is to provide you with learning materials that will serve you well in your college studies and throughout your career.

The educational process involves learning, retention, and the application of concepts and principles. You can accelerate your learning efforts by utilizing the supplements accompanying this text.

▶ The STUDY GUIDE, prepared by Dick Wasson of Southwestern College, is designed to help you better your performance in your managerial course. The guide includes objectives, definitions, and true/false, fill-in-the-blank, and matching questions.

▶ The WORKING PAPERS, prepared by the author, includes all forms needed to solve the end-of-chapter problems. The forms contain captions and information that you would otherwise have to copy from the text.

▶ SCOREBUILDER, prepared by Bruce Baldwin and Diane Pattison, is a set of actual examination questions used on introductory managerial accounting exams at colleges across the country. The answer to each question is given and an annotated solution tells why the answer is correct. SCOREBUILDER is specifically designed to help you prepare for and maximize your scores on exams.

These learning aids are designed to improve your performance in the course by highlighting key points in the text and providing you with assistance in mastering basic concepts. Check your local bookstore or ask the manager to place an order for you today.

We at Irwin sincerely hope that this text package will assist you in reaching your goals both now and in the future. ◀

Managerial
Accounting

Managerial Accounting

Third Edition

CALVIN ENGLER, Ph.D., CPA, CCE/A
Professor of Accounting
Iona College

IRWIN

Homewood, IL 60430
Boston, MA 02116

Sponsoring editor: Ron M. Regis
Developmental editor: Carolyn Nowak
Developmental editor, supplements: Nancy Lanum
Marketing manager: Cindy L. Ledwith
Project editor: Gladys True
Production manager: Bette K. Ittersagen
Designer: Tara Bazata
Art coordinator: Mark Malloy
Compositor: BiComp, Inc.
Typeface: 10/12 Times Roman
Printer: Von Hoffmann Press, Inc.

Library of Congress Cataloging-in-Publication Data
Engler, Cavin.
    Managerial accounting/Calvin Engler.—3rd ed.
       p.   cm.
    Includes bibliographical references and index.
    ISBN 0-256-10246-5   ISBN 0-256-11466-8 (International ed.)
    1. Managerial accounting.   I. Title.
    HF5657.4.E544   1993
    658.15'11—dc20   92–14407

Printed in the United States of America
1 2 3 4 5 6 7 8 9 0 VH 9 8 7 6 5 4 3 2

▶ To my parents and my wife, Phyllis

▶ Calvin Engler is a CPA and a Certified Cost Estimator/Analyst. He received his Ph.D. in accounting from the City University of New York. He has published numerous articles in various professional journals. In 1982 he received the Edward Kelley award for his manuscript submitted to the Westchester Chapter of the National Association of Accountants.

Professor Engler was a member of the Board of Directors of the Westchester Chapter of the National Association of Accountants. He also served as Manuscripts Director of that organization. For eight years he was the Director of the Chaykin's CPA Review Course in Westchester County where he was the principal lecturer of the Theory and Practice parts of the CPA examination. He has also prepared questions that have appeared on several CPA examinations. He is a member of Beta Alpha Psi, the national honorary accounting fraternity, and Delta Mu Delta, the national honorary fraternity in business administration.

In addition to this book, Professor Engler is the coauthor (with Leopold A. Bernstein) of *Advanced Accounting,* 2nd edition, published by Richard D. Irwin, Inc. in 1989.

▶ A knowledge of managerial accounting is essential for all aspiring accountants and managers of businesses and nonprofit entities. This text will help these individuals acquire the knowledge necessary to be successful in their chosen careers. It is presumed that students will have already completed a course on the essentials of financial accounting.

Although this text was designed for a one-semester, undergraduate course, it is sufficiently flexible to be used in a graduate course in which no prior knowledge of managerial accounting is required. This text also may be used in those schools that follow a trimester or quarter system. The instructor's manual contains suggested course outlines for each of these programs.

Managers are concerned with the five major functions of management: (1) planning, (2) organizing, (3) staffing, (4) leading, and (5) controlling. Since all of these functions deal with decision making, managers must obtain certain kinds of accounting information and then understand how to use this information. This book is designed to help aspiring managers acquire the knowledge needed to select and use the accounting information necessary for managerial decision making.

To provide students with a meaningful learning experience, the text is organized as follows:

1. At the beginning of each chapter, the stated learning objectives of that chapter tell the students what they will learn. In addition, the learning objective for each section of each chapter is identified.
2. To demonstrate the relevance of the material discussed in a chapter, the author conducted interviews with senior-level executives of large corporations and service organizations. The questions and the executives' responses appear at the beginning of the chapters immediately after the learning objectives.
3. The key terms associated with each topic are defined when the topic is introduced. All key terms in the chapter are printed in boldface type.
4. Each topic is introduced by first presenting its simplest aspects. It is then further developed by using a building block approach. When

necessary, the steps needed to prepare usable information are listed and discussed prior to the presentation of the information.

5. After a significant portion of a chapter has been covered, students are offered a series of questions as a Progress Check. These questions are designed to assist students in determining how much they have learned from reading the chapter.

6. At the end of each chapter, there is a comprehensive summary of the chapter. Most of the key terms introduced in the chapter are used in the summary and are printed in boldface type.

7. Most chapters contain one or more review problems at the end.

8. To give instructors latitude in selecting topical coverage, difficult and enriched topics are placed in appendixes at the end of the chapter. For example, FIFO process costing is covered in depth in an appendix, but weighted-average process costing is covered in the chapter. All appendixes are independent of the chapter, and there is no interruption of the chapter's continuity if an instructor chooses not to use an appendix.

9. In those chapters that require journal entries to illustrate a topic, these entries within the chapter are minimal. In general, when possible, journal entries are deferred to end-of-chapter appendixes. This allows the instructors to avoid losing the continuity of the subject matter whether or not they decide to cover the journal entries.

10. Key concepts discussed in a chapter are generally tabulated at the end of that chapter. Also shown are the uses and applications of these concepts as well as the kinds of information needed to reach a decision using the concepts.

11. All key terms appear in a glossary at the end of each chapter, and the page number on which the term is discussed in the chapter is identified. The definitions are similar to those found in the chapter. More than 400 key terms are defined in the glossaries. Each item in the glossary is included in the index at the end of the book for users wishing to refer to an alphabetical listing of the glossary terms.

12. Many chapters include a case in the end-of-chapter material that emphasizes the ethical implications of particular actions and reporting decisions. The student often is placed in a situation requiring a decision that has ethical ramifications.

13. When appropriate, a glossary of synonyms is provided at the end of a chapter.

14. Library assignments pertaining to the material covered in a chapter are provided for students who wish to enrich their understanding of the material covered in the chapter.

15. To further assist students in evaluating their understanding of the material covered, each chapter contains a self-test for students who wish to test themselves. The answers to the self-tests are provided at the end of the chapter.

16. The end-of-chapter exercises and problems contain a rich variety of material ranging from simple to challenging. Many of these problems were specifically designed to accompany the text coverage. In addition, other problems were carefully selected from problems on

professional examinations; these are identified as AICPA or CMA adapted.

17. Many other exercises and problems can be solved using Spreadsheet Applications Template Software (SPATS) developed by Minta Berry. The exercises and problems solvable with SPATS are identifed in the margin of the text with the following symbol:

▶ ORGANIZATION OF THE TEXT

The text is organized into three parts. Chapter 1 introduces these three major divisions. It also discusses the nature and objectives of management accounting. In addition, it discusses ethics for business managers and management accountants. The first division, Part 1, discusses essentials of managerial accounting and is subdivided into chapters that discuss (1) cost definitions and concepts; (2) cost behavior; (3) cost, volume, and profit analysis and relationships; (4) job order costing; and (5) process costing. The second major division, Part 2, discusses planning and control and is subdivided into chapters that discuss (1) cost accounting for the new manufacturing environment including just-in-time manufacturing, (2) cost allocation for service departments and joint products, (3) the master budget, (4) standard costing and performance evaluation for direct materials and direct labor, (5) flexible budgeting and manufacturing overhead analysis, (6) the contribution approach to segment reporting, (7) relevant data for decision making, (8) capital budgeting, (9) income tax effects on capital budgeting decisions, and (10) decentralized operations and transfer pricing. The third major division discusses selected additional topics and is subdivided into chapters that discuss (1) the statement of cash flows and (2) financial statement analysis.

▶ NEW FEATURES IN THE THIRD EDITION

1. Chapter 1 discusses ethical behavior for management accountants and business managers. This chapter and selected other chapters contain end-of-chapter cases dealing with ethical behavior for management accountants in various business situations.
2. Cost accounting for the new manufacturing environment is discussed, in depth, in a new chapter, Chapter 7. This chapter covers activity-based costing (ABC), cost drivers, and just-in-time (JIT) manufacturing.
3. Cost allocation for service departments and joint products is discussed in a new chapter, Chapter 8.
4. The discussion of cost accounting for service industries, including hospitals, has been considerably expanded. There are also many new exercises and problems dealing with these industries at the end of various chapters.
5. The material from the previous edition's Chapter 15, Selected Quantitative Methods for Managers, has been condensed and now appears as parts of other chapters. Specifically, linear programming is now Appendix 13-A, a part of Chapter 13, Selecting Relevant Data for Decision Making and Product Pricing. Inventory control including

economic order quantity and safety stock is now a part of Chapter 9, The Master Budget.

6. The author conducted interviews with senior-level executives of large corporations and service organizations. The questions and the executives' responses appear at the beginning of the chapters immediately after the learning objectives.

7. After a significant portion of a chapter has been covered, students are offered a series of questions as a Progress Check. The questions are designed to assist students in determining how much they have learned from reading the chapter.

8. When appropriate, a glossary of synonyms is provided at the end of a chapter.

9. Library assignments pertaining to the material covered in a chapter are provided for students who wish to enrich their understanding of the material covered in the chapter.

10. To further assist students in evaluating their understanding of the material covered, each chapter contains a self-test for students who wish to test themselves. The answers to the self-tests are provided at the end of the chapter.

▶ TEACHING AIDS

Various teaching aids are available to adopters of the book. In addition to the Instructor's Solutions Manual, the following are available:

1. Overhead transparencies provide instructors with a visual representation of assorted topics.

2. The Study Guide, an integral part of the teaching package, is designed to help students move above the level of the average student in the course. The material for each chapter includes an introduction to that chapter, a chapter outline, and approximately 50 questions. Depending on the chapter, these questions include true/false, multiple choice, short exercises, and some matching questions.

3. A test bank has more than 1,800 items arranged in three levels of difficulty. The first level of questions is similar to the examples in the text. The second level has more difficult questions, and the third level has questions that are AICPA or CMA adapted.

4. An instructor's lecture guide contains a chapter overview, learning objectives, a problem analysis by time and objective, a lecture outline, in-class demonstration problems, demonstration overhead transparencies, and a review quiz.

5. Spreadsheet Applications Template Software (SPATS) can be used to solve many exercises and problems. It contains innovatively designed templates based on Lotus® 1-2-3®. SPATS is available on 5.25-inch and 3.5-inch disks. Upon adoption, this package is available to instructors for classroom or laboratory use.

6. Check figures for the solution of textual material are available for instructors and students.

7. The Working Papers includes all forms needed to solve the end-of-chapter problems.

8. Irwin's computerized testing software, an improved microcomputer

version of the Test Bank, allows editing of questions; provides up to 99 different versions of each test; and allows question selection based on type of question, level of difficulty, or learning objective. Computest 3 is available on 5.25-inch and 3.5-inch disks.

9. The Richard D. Irwin Managerial/Cost Accounting video series contains six 15-minute segments covering capital budgeting, the design of a cost accounting system, process and job order costing; and service and activity based costing. Prepared by Pacific Lutheran University in Seattle, Washington, the videos are free upon adoption.

10. Ramblewood Manufacturing, by Leland Mansuetti and Keith Weidkamp, both of Sierra College, is a Managerial Accounting simulation. It is available on 5.25-inch and 3.5-inch disks.

11. The computerized tutorial, a software package prepared by Leland Mansuetti, includes true/false questions and multiple choice questions with explanations for both correct and incorrect answers. Upon adoption, this computerized tutorial is available to instructors for classroom or laboratory use and available on 5.25-inch and 3.5-inch disks.

▶ ACKNOWLEDGMENTS

Many individuals have contributed their expertise to improve the earlier editions of this book, and I am especially grateful to them. My first and foremost debt, however, is to the late University Distinguished Professor Emanuel Saxe. I was extremely privileged to have been his student, and I am most fortunate to have been able to count him as one of my dearest friends. He painstakingly read the first edition of this manuscript and made numerous suggestions for improving the initial draft. Only those individuals fortunate enough to have been exposed to his special analytical reviews can appreciate the impact of his contribution.

I am also grateful to another one of my dearest friends and coauthor on another work, Leopold A. Bernstein, for his permission to rework portions of his book, *Financial Statement Analysis*, for use in Chapters 17 and 18 of this work. His analytical review of these resulting chapters is greatly appreciated.

Numerous other individuals have made contributions to this work. I am grateful to John G. Driscoll, President of Iona College, who generously gave his time during the incubation stage of the first edition of this text and encouraged me to proceed with this project. John F. Gallagher, Provost and Vice President for Academic Affairs of Iona College, deserves special mention for his encouragement and support during this revision. Charles F. O'Donnell, Dean of the Hagan School of Business, Iona College, provided me with moral support and was instrumental in making it possible for me to have sufficient time so that I could complete all three editions of this project. I am also grateful to John L. Stancil of Cumberland College for his valuable comments and suggestions for the Instructor's Lecture Guide.

I appreciate the contributions of the many individuals who reviewed all or part of the first and second editions of this book. Many of their valuable suggestions for improvement remain in this edition. Anthony P. Curatola of Drexel Unversity deserves a special mention for his contributions to the earlier editions of this work.

I am especially grateful to the busy senior-level executives of major corporations and service organizations who took time from their schedules to be interviewed for this edition. Their contributions give it a real-world flavor of how managerial accounting is actually used in business, and I am sure that the students using this book will also appreciate their contribution. My thanks to go the following:

Michael V. Allison, Business Manager	Richard D. Irwin, Inc.
Robert L. Carleton, Senior Vice President and Controller	Pepsico, Inc.
Manuel D. Fernandes, Vice President for Finance	Iona College
John Harriott, Management Associate of Economics and Management	Manhattanville College
Lawrence J. Hoffman, Corporate Controller	AAMCO Transmissions, Inc.
Robert J. Hopper, Director of Compensation and Benefits	Reuben H. Donnelly, Dun and Bradstreet Corporation
Sheila Leonard, Tax Accountant	Ernst & Young
P. J. Lynch, Comptroller	Texaco Inc.
Angelo T. Murlo, Chief Financial Officer	Philips Laboratories Division, North American Philips Corporation
Robert Ripp, Vice President and Treasurer	International Business Machines Corporation
Joseph V. Roccosalvo, Vice President—Financial Administration	Barclays Bank PLC
E. Joseph Vellone, Vice President and Divisional Controller	Citibank—Corporate Securities
Joseph G. Whelan, President and Founder	Advantage Business Group
Vincent M. Zaccheo, Controller	ITW Minigrip, Inc., Illinois Tool Works

In the same context, I want to thank Professor Wayne G. Bremser from Villanova University for graciously agreeing to be interviewed for Chapters 7 and 8.

My colleagues at Iona College who made valuable suggestions for improving this edition are Robert Strittmatter, Ehiel Ash, and Salvatore Palestro. A special thanks goes to Ula Motekat of Old Dominion University, who assisted me in the preparation of the problem material and the solutions manual. Without her assistance, this project would not have been completed within the time constraint set by the publisher. Denis McHugh of Mercy College also assisted me with the preparation of the problem material. Dick Wasson of Southwestern College deserves a special mention for his expert development of the Instructor's Lecture Guide, the Study Guide, and the Test Bank. I am also extremely grateful to Minta Berry of Berry Publications for her development of the SPATS templates.

The following are the principal reviewers of the third edition of this work:

Terry W. Bechtell	Oklahoma City University
Wayne G. Bremser	Villanova University
Gene F. Bronson	SUNY at Albany
Robert H. Colson	Visiting Professor at the University of Michigan
Michael R. Kinney	Texas A&M University
Gary J. Mann	University of Texas—El Paso
George N. Sanderson	Moorhead State University
Mostafa H. Sarhan	University of Akron
Dick D. Wasson	Southwestern College
Michael L. Werner	University of Miami

I am extremely indebted to all of these reviewers. They made numerous suggestions for improving this work, and their suggestions were incorporated in this edition.

Others who made extremely valuable suggestions for improving this edition include Carolyn Nowak, Developmental Editor. Without the able assistance of Judith L. Besser of Richard D. Irwin, Inc., who routed all of the manuscript installments to the reviewers and then organized the reviewers' comments into logical sequences, it would have been extremely difficult for me to complete the revised manuscript within the time frame set by the publisher.

Permission has been received from the Institute of Certified Management Accountants of the Institute of Management Accountants to use questions and/or unofficial answers from past CMA examinations, and from the American Institute of Certified Public Accountants to use questions and/or unofficial answers from past CPA examinations. In addition, the Institute of Management Accountants has granted us permission to use portions of its published materials.

No work of this magnitude can be completed without enormous sacrifices by the writer's family, and this is certainly true in my case. I am fortunate that my family fully understood the demands that the writing of this manuscript made on my leisure time. In addition, my wife, Phyllis, took time away from her own busy professional pursuits to provide me with invaluable editorial and proofreading assistance throughout the development of this book. My children, Mitchell Engler and Linda and Andrew Eisen, assisted me by proofreading various portions of the text and, as college students, provided me with their reactions to the pedagogical treatment used in this book. I will always be grateful for the understanding and help my family has given me.

Of course, the work on a text is never truly complete. There is always room for polishing and revision. I welcome comments from adopters and others who can help me to improve this text in subsequent editions.

Calvin Engler

▶ When writing this book, I had three objectives in mind. First, I wanted to make your learning of managerial accounting a worthwhile experience. Toward that end, I developed the subject matter by using a building block approach. I began each new subject with the simpler concepts first and then introduced the more advanced areas of the subject. Second, I wanted to simplify your review of the subject matter when you prepared for exams. To do so, I provided you with a comprehensive review summary at the end of each chapter and a glossary of key terms with their definitions. As you read each chapter, you will notice that I provided you with progress checks to monitor your understanding of the subject matter as you read the chapter. In addition, at the end of each chapter I provided you with self-tests to test your grasp of the subject matter. You will also find one or more review problems at the end of most chapters to help reinforce your learning. A new feature of this edition are the interviews with senior-level executives of major corporations and service industries. These interviews show you how the material covered in the chapter is used in the real world. I suggest that you read the interview before you read the chapter, and then reread the interview after you have read the chapter. The interview will have more meaning to you than if you merely read the interview at the beginning of each chapter. I hope you find all of these features useful in your study of managerial accounting. And third, I hoped to prepare a book that you would find helpful as a reference resource during your professional career.

You may also wish to consider using the study guide that can be purchased in your bookstore. The study guide will help reinforce what you have learned from the book, and it will enable you to test yourself to see if you have acquired a sufficient knowledge of the subject. The study guide contains true-false, multiple choice, and computational questions together with the answers to these questions. In addition, to help you solve your homework assignments, you may wish to consider purchasing the working papers. If your bookstore does not stock these items, ask the manager of the store to order them for you.

I always invite students to write to me regarding their experiences in using this book. I find these comments useful when it comes time to prepare for the next edition. If you wish, you may contact me at Iona College, New Rochelle, N.Y. 10801. I wish you good luck in your career.

Sincerely,

Calvin Engler

CONTENTS IN BRIEF ▼

1 The Nature and Objectives of Managerial Accounting 2

▶ **PART 1 ESSENTIALS OF COST AND MANAGERIAL ACCOUNTING** **33**
2 Cost Definitions and Cost Concepts 34
3 Cost Behavior and Cost Estimation 78
4 Cost, Volume, and Profit—Analysis and Relationships 122
5 Job Order Costing 184
6 Process Costing 252
7 Cost Accounting for the New Manufacturing Environment 306
8 Cost Allocation—Service Departments and Joint Products 348

▶ **PART 2 PLANNING AND CONTROL** **391**
9 The Master Budget 392
10 Standard Costs and Performance Evaluation 472
11 Flexible Budgeting and Manufacturing Overhead Analysis 524
12 Variable-Costing and Contribution Approach to Segment Reporting 584
13 Selecting Relevant Data for Decision Making and Product Pricing 644
14 Capital Budgeting 716
15 Income Tax Effects on Capital-Budgeting Decisions 780
16 Decentralized Operations and Transfer Pricing 818

▶ **PART 3 ADDITIONAL SELECTED TOPICS** **871**
17 Statement of Cash Flows 872
18 Analysis of Financial Statements 926

Index 991

CONTENTS
▼

1 The Nature and Objectives of Managerial Accounting   2

Financial Accounting versus Managerial Accounting: *Financial Accounting. The Nature of Managerial Accounting. Differences and Similarities— Financial versus Managerial Accounting.* Information for Decision Makers: *Quantitative Information. Qualitative Information.* Goal Setting and Decision Making: *Strategic Planning—Long-Term Decision Making. Short-Term Decision Making. The Planning and Control Cycle.* Organizations and Their Structure: *Organization Charts.* Careers in Management Accounting: *Certified Management Accountant (CMA). Certified Public Accountant (CPA).* What's New? *The New Manufacturing Environment. Ethics for Business Managers.* Summary. Glossary of Key Terms. Glossary of Synonyms. Library Assignment.

▶ **PART 1 ESSENTIALS OF COST AND MANAGERIAL ACCOUNTING**   **33**

2 Cost Definitions and Cost Concepts   34

Costs and Expenses. Financial Statements for a Merchandising Firm: *Product Costs. A Merchandiser's Balance Sheet. A Merchandiser's Income Statement.* Service Businesses. Costs in a Manufacturing Firm: *Direct Costs. Indirect Costs. Product Costs. Period Costs.* Financial Statements for a Manufacturing Firm: *Inventory Classification. A Manufacturer's Balance Sheet. A Manufacturer's Income Statement. Prime Costs and Conversion Costs.* Cost Behavior: *Variable Costs. Fixed Costs.* Other Cost Concepts: *Direct versus Indirect Costs. Differential Costs. Opportunity Costs. Sunk Costs. Controllable and Noncontrollable Costs.* Cost Definitions and Cost Concepts for Service Industries: *Cost Objectives. Cost Terms for a Hospital. Summary.* Glossary of Key Terms. Glossary of Synonyms.

3 Cost Behavior and Cost Estimation   78

Cost Behavior: *Variable Costs. Fixed Costs. Mixed Costs. Curvilinear Cost Behavior.* Analyzing Mixed Costs: *Account Analysis. Engineering Cost Analysis. The High-Low Method of Analyzing Mixed Costs. Mixed Cost*

Analysis—Scatter Diagrams. Contribution Format Income Statements: *Contribution Margin. The Contribution Margin Approach to Decision Making.* Summary. Appendix 3-A: Mixed Cost Analysis—The Least Squares Method. Glossary of Key Terms. Library Assignment.

4   Cost, Volume, and Profit—Analysis and Relationships   122

Breakeven Analysis Using Equations: *Breakeven Sales. Contribution Margin per Unit Approach. Targeted Income. Special Problem—Sales Commissions or Other Variable Costs. Limiting Assumptions of Breakeven Analysis. The Margin of Safety. Breakeven Graph. Profit-Volume Graph.* Cost Structure. Operating Leverage. Cost-Volume-Profit Analysis: *Volume Changes Only. Changes in Selling Prices and Sales Volume. Changes in Variable Unit Costs.* Sales Mix: *Sales Mix Breakeven Analysis. Changes in Mix and CVP Analysis.* Summary. Glossary of Key Terms. Library Assignment.

5   Job Order Costing   184

The Uses of Product Cost Information for Manufacturing Firms. Cost Accounting Systems. Job Order Costing for Manufacturing Firms. *The Physical Flow of Production. Source Documents. Automated Systems.* Manufacturing Overhead: *The Need for a Predetermined Rate. Allocation Bases. Disposition of Overapplied or Underapplied Overhead. Payroll Fringes. Departmental Overhead Rates.* Schedules of Cost of Goods Manufactured and Cost of Goods Sold: *Schedule of Cost of Goods Manufactured. Schedule of Cost of Goods Sold.* Cost Accounting for Service Industries: *Cost Accounting for a Law Firm. Cost Accounting for a Hospital.* Summary. Glossary of Key Terms. Glossary of Synonyms. Library Assignment.

6   Process Costing   252

Firms that Use Process Cost Systems. Cost Accumulation Methods in Process Costing. The Physical Flow of Processing. Cost Accumulation in a Process System: *Direct Materials. Direct Labor. Manufacturing Overhead. Unit Costs—No Work in Process. Equivalent Production.* The Production Report: *Production Report—Initial Department. Production Report—Subsequent Department. Production Report—Beginning Work in Process Inventory. Lost Units, Normal Spoilage, and Abnormal Spoilage.* Summary. Appendix 6-A: Process Cost Accumulation—The FIFO Method. Appendix 6-B: List Units and Spoiled Units. Glossary of Key Terms. Glossary of Synonyms. Library Assignment.

7   Cost Accounting for the New Manufacturing Environment   306
Traditional Plant Layout. Traditional Application of Overhead. The New Manufacturing Environment: *Activity-Based Costing. Cost Management Systems. Nonvalue-Added Costs. Just-in-Time Production and Inventory Control. Just-in-Time Inventory Control. Elimination of Nonvalue-Added Costs. Flexible Manufacturing System. Support Services. Just-in-Time Cost Accounting.* Summary. Glossary of Key Terms. Glossary of Synonyms. Library Assignment.

8   Cost Allocation—Service Departments and Joint Products   348

Overhead Departmentalization. Allocation of Service Department Overhead to Producing Departments. Separate Cost Allocations for Fixed and Variables Costs. The New Manufacturing Environment. Joint Product Costs. Summary. Glossary of Key Terms. Library Assignment.

▶ **PART 2   PLANNING AND CONTROL   391**

9 The Master Budget   392

The Aspects of Budgeting: *Definition of Budget. The Need for Budgeting. Budget in Not-for-Profit Organizations. Advantages of Budgeting for Businesses. The Budget Time Frame.* Budget Preparation: *The Budget Committee. The Master Budget. The Sales Budget. The Production Budget. The Marketing Cost Budget. The Administrative Cost Budget. Cash Management and Cash Budgeting. The Budgeted Income Statement. The Budgeted Balance Sheet. Budget Uses.* Human Factors in Budgetary Planning and Control: *Budget Slack.* Budgeting in Not-for-Profit Organizations: *Incremental Budgeting. Zero-Base Budgeting. Budgeting for a Hospital.* Summary. Appendix 9-A: Inventory Planning and Control. Glossary of Key Terms. Glossary of Synonyms. Library Assignment.

10 Standard Costs and Performance Evaluation   472

Performance Evaluation: *Management by Exception.* Standards: *Standard Costs. Bases of Standard Costs. Uses of Standard Costs. Standards for Direct Materials. Standards for Direct Labor. Standard Quantity Allowed. Input and Output.* Variance Analysis: *Direct Materials Variance Analysis. The Diagrammatic Approach. Direct Labor Variance Analysis. Performance Reports.* Variance Investigation: *Selecting Variances for Investigation. Management Action.* Standard Costing for Service Industries: *Standard Costs for Hospitals.* Standard Costing in the New Manufacturing Environment: *New Performance Measures.* Journal Entries. Summary. Appendix 10-A: Journal Entries to Record Standard Costs for Direct Materials and Direct Labor and Recording Price Variances for Direct Materials When Quantities Purchased Differ from Quantities Used. Appendix 10-B: Joint Price and Quantity Variance. Glossary of Key Terms. Library Assignment.

11 Flexible Budgeting and Manufacturing Overhead Analysis   524

Static Budgets. Flexible Budgets: *The Importance of a Flexible Budget. Preparing a Flexible Budget.* Variable Manufacturing Overhead: *Selecting the Overhead Base. Applying Variable Overhead to Production. Analyzing Variable Overhead Variances. Preparing Performance Reports that Include Variance Analyses. Preparing Performance Reports in an Alternative Format. Interpreting Variable Overhead Variances.* Fixed Manufacturing Overhead: *Computing Predetermined Overhead Rates. Applying Fixed and Variable Overhead to Production. The Relationship between the Overhead Base and Fixed Costs. Fixed Overhead Variance Analysis. Interpreting Fixed Overhead Variances. The Graphical Solution to Fixed Overhead Variances. Journal Entries and Overhead Variances. Presenting Variances on Income Statements for Managers. The Treatment of Variances on Income Statements Prepared for External Use.* Standard Costing and the Cost Accounting Cycle. Selecting a Capacity Level for Applying Overhead. Summary. Appendix 11-A: Standard Costing and the Cost Accounting Cycle. Appendix 11-B: Selecting a Capacity Level for Applying Overhead. Glossary of Key Terms. Glossary of Synonyms. Library Assignment.

12 Variable-Costing and Contribution Approach to Segment Reporting   584

Variable Costing versus Absorption Costing: *Variable Costing—No Beginning or Ending Inventories. Absorption Costing—No Beginning or*

Ending Inventories. Variable Costing versus Absorption Costing—Beginning and Ending Inventories of Finished Goods. Segment Reporting: *The Format of Segmented Income Statements. Differentiation between Direct Fixed Costs and Common Costs. Common Costs and the Allocation Problem. Preparing Segmented Income Statements.* Uses of Segment Data: *Detecting Segments Operating at a Loss. Pinpointing the Source of a Loss. Continuing the Operations of a Segment. Cost-Volume-Profit Analysis. Altering Marketing Strategies. Evaluating and Rewarding Managerial Performance.* Summary. Glossary of Key Terms. Glossary of Synonyms. Library Assignment.

13 Selecting Relevant Data for Decision Making and Product Pricing   644

Relevant Data. Irrelevant Costs. Using Costs in Decision Making. Equipment Decisions: *Purchasing New Equipment. Replacing Existing Equipment.* Entering a Market with a New Product. Accepting Special Orders at Less than Full Cost. Making or Buying Component Parts. Joint Product Decisions: *Allocated Costs and Decision Making. Sell at Splitoff Point or Process Further.* Pricing Decisions. Allocating Scarce Resources. Recapitulation. Summary. Appendix 13-A: Linear Programming. Glossary of Key Terms. Library Assignment.

14 Capital Budgeting   716

Discounted Cash Flow Models: *Net Present Value Method. Internal Rate of Return.* Project Selection: *The Profitability Index.* Dealing with Uncertainty: *Hard Data. Soft Data. Auditing Capital-Budgeting Decisions.* Investing and Financing Decisions—Leasing versus Purchasing. Other Capital-Budgeting Techniques: *The Payback Method. The Accounting Rate of Return.* Recapitulation. Summary. Appendix 14-A: Compound Interest and Present Value. Appendix 14-B: Compound-Interest Tables. Appendix 14-C: Capital Budgeting and Inflation. Glossary of Key Terms. Glossary of Synonyms. Library Assignment.

15 Income Tax Effects on Capital-Budgeting Decisions   780

Decision Making and Income Taxes: *After-Tax Cash Flows for Capital-Budgeting Analysis. Depreciation Methods and Their Effects on Capital-Budgeting Decisions.* After-Tax Capital Budgeting: *Purchasing New or Replacement Equipment—Additional Tax Considerations. Salvage Value. The Book Value of an Existing Machine. Entering a New Market or Introducing a New Product—Additional Tax Considerations.* Summary. Glossary of Key Terms. Library Assignment.

16 Decentralized Operations and Transfer Pricing   818

Responsibility Accounting. *Responsibility Centers. Advantages and Disadvantages of Decentralization. Reporting System for Responsibility Accounting. Evaluating Performance Reports.* Evaluating a Manager's Performance Using the ROI Model: *Operating Income and Operating Assets. Analysis of the ROI Formula. Using ROI. Allocated Common Costs. Investment Center Performance Report. Residual Income. Advantages of Residual Income.* Transfer Prices: *Variable Cost. Full Cost. Cost Plus a Markup. External Market Price. Negotiated Price. Behavioral Aspects of Transfer Pricing.* Summary. Glossary of Key Terms. Library Assignment.

▶ **PART 3   ADDITIONAL SELECTED TOPICS   871**

17 Statement of Cash Flows   872

Significance and Purpose. What Is Cash Flow? Evolution of the Accounting for Cash Flows. Statement Format. Definition of Cash and Cash Equivalents. Sources and Uses of Cash: *Sources of Cash. Uses of Cash.* Gross Cash Flows versus Net Cash Flows. Noncash Exchange Transactions for Investing and Financing Activities. Cash Flow per Share. Other Disclosures. Preparation of the Statement of Cash Flows—Indirect Method: *Simple Illustration of Preparation of Statement of Cash Flows. Illustration of T Account Technique. Determining Cash Flow from Operations.* Reconstruction of Transactions: *Fixed Assets. Accumulated Depreciation. Bonds Payable. Deferred Income Taxes. Capital Stock and Paid-In-Capital. Retained Earnings. Intangibles Amortization. Investment in Marketable Securities. Accounts Receivable. Inventories. Accounts Payable.* Preparation of the Statement of Cash Flows—Direct Method: *Statement Preparation Procedures. T Account Reconstruction.* Published Statement of Cash Flows. Summary. Glossary of Key Terms. Library Assignment.

18 Analysis of Financial Statements   926

Reasons for Financial Statement Analysis. The Principal Tools of Financial Statement Analysis: *Comparative Financial Statements. Index-Number Trend Series. Common-Size Financial Statements.* Ratios: *Ratio Analysis. Interpretation of Ratios.* Illustration of Ratio Computations. Short-Term Liquidity: *Working Capital. Current Ratio. Acid-Test Ratio. Average-Accounts-Receivable-Turnover Ratio. Collection Period for Accounts Receivable. Inventory-Turnover Ratio. Days to Sell Inventory.* Capital Structure and Long-Term Solvency Ratios: *Debt-to-Equity Ratio. Times Interest Earned Ratio.* Return-on-Investment Ratios: *Return on Investment (ROI). Basic Elements of ROI.* Earnings per Share (EPS): *Primary and Fully Diluted Earnings per Share.* Market Measures: *Price-Earnings Ratio. Dividend Payout and Yield Ratios.* Summary. Appendix 18-A: Sources of Information on Financial and Operating Ratios. Glossary of Key Terms. Glossary of Key Ratios. Glossary of Synonyms. Library Assignment.

Index   991

Managerial
Accounting

The Nature and Objectives of Managerial Accounting

After reading this chapter, you should be able to:

1. List the differences between financial accounting and managerial accounting information.
2. Define the roles that planning, organizing, staffing, leading, and controlling play in an organization.
3. Differentiate between quantitative information and qualitative information.
4. Identify the kinds of decisions managers make and the information needed to make these decisions.
5. Explain why decision making is the most important managerial function.
6. Describe the importance of feedback in planning and control.
7. Construct a company organization chart.
8. Explain how lines of responsibility and delegation of authority affect an organization.
9. Differentiate between line and staff functions in organizations.
10. Explain the importance of ethics for business managers.

► **INTERVIEW**

Angelo T. Murlo
Chief Financial Officer
Philips Laboratories
Division
North American Philips
Corporation

Q. *Managers use both quantitative and qualitative information for decision-making purposes. Provide an example in your experience to indicate how both were used.*

A. Many of our research scientists travel extensively throughout the world. Like many other organizations, we centralized our business travel with one local agency. That put us in a good bargaining position with the agency to ensure that we got the most cost-effective airfare and best service for our employees. To arrange a business trip, employees notified their department secretary, who made all the arrangements with the agency.

When I found out that the best person at the agency we used had left its employ, I immediately called and asked if she wanted to work directly for our company. She agreed. I then called another agency that had been trying to get our business. We negotiated a deal and established an in-house travel service for our employees.

From a quantitative viewpoint, our in-house costs for the new travel service were more than offset by lower travel costs. More important, however, was the fact that our employees were now able to deal directly with the travel agent on site, rather than going through another person. In fact, most employees preferred it, and, because of the many changes that inevitably occur in their itineraries, it was more convenient. In addition, secretaries had more time to spend on other more productive matters, thereby increasing their efficiency. As a result, staff morale improved. Travel cost went down, since we had more travel information directly available to us for analysis.

Q. *Does obtaining the CPA and/or CMA designation provide a faster track for advancement in the corporate hierarchy? Would you recommend obtaining some form of graduate training and, if so, what kind?*

A. Without a doubt, the financial manager with the best credentials will have the greatest edge. The corporate world is highly competitive with more candidates than there are positions as one goes up the management ladder. Most people in the financial arena have the proper aptitude for the job, or they would not be there in the first place. Experience, personality, and common sense can take a candidate just so far. What enables a person to stand out from the crowd is education. The more education one has, the fewer the people in competition with that person for the position.

In my opinion, two of the major factors that allow a candidate to get his or her foot in the door are education and contacts. Of the two, only education provides the individual with the knowledge needed to sustain success in his or her career. A CPA with a CMA certainly helps. An MBA to supplement those credentials is even better.

▶ The main purpose of accounting is to provide information to decision makers. Accordingly, accounting is the process of (1) measuring—assigning dollar amounts, (2) recording, (3) classifying—grouping similar items, (4) summarizing—combining groups of items, and (5) reporting transactions and events of a financial nature and then communicating this information to users of this information. **Managerial accounting** specializes in providing information that an organization's managers find useful for internal decision making. Thus, a firm's internal accounting information system should (1) enable managers to plan for the operations of their business, (2) enable managers to assess how effectively their plans are being implemented, (3) provide the data needed to control operations, and (4) provide the data needed for decision making. Of necessity, *some* information that managers need is historical in nature, but most of it is either very recent or future oriented. ◀

▶ FINANCIAL ACCOUNTING VERSUS MANAGERIAL ACCOUNTING

Financial Accounting

While managerial accounting serves a firm's internal needs by providing recent and future-oriented information, **financial accounting** focuses primarily on historical reports. The information that financial accountants compile is intended primarily for external use by investors, creditors, potential investors, employees and their unions, government agencies, and others. The information provided to these groups usually consists of the results of operations for a period of time (an income statement), the financial position of the organization at a specific point in time (a balance sheet), and a statement of cash flows for the period of operations under examination.

L.O. 1

Financial accounting is regulated in an attempt to ensure that the resulting reports are understandable, reliable, and relatively consistent between comparable reporting periods. The principal regulatory body is the Securities and Exchange Commission (SEC). In addition, the American Institute of Certified Public Accountants (AICPA) sets ethical standards for the accounting profession, and the Financial Accounting Standards Board (FASB), an independent standard-setting body, sets procedural standards.

The FASB's pronouncements on accounting matters have come to be recognized as *generally accepted accounting principles* (*GAAP*). As a result of the FASB's, SEC's, and AICPA's efforts, all of a firm's financial statements must meet minimum standards of disclosure and show a degree of uniformity in the reporting of transactions that are the same or similar. Of necessity, the information must be summarized in the financial statements—rather than reported in full—because so many transactions occur during the course of a reporting period. However, user groups disagree on the amount and kind of information and disclosures that should be presented. To ensure adherence to GAAP, companies must hire public accounting firms to audit their financial statements. The auditing procedure is conducted in a manner that meets *generally accepted auditing standards* (*GAAS*) as developed and codified by the AICPA.

The Nature of Managerial Accounting

Because managerial accounting serves internal purposes, it is not constrained by government regulations and generally accepted accounting principles. Managerial accounting provides information for the exclusive use of managers of the firm. Our legal and regulatory systems do not regulate the nature of information one prepares for oneself. Thus, managerial accountants are free to generate any information that managers find useful. On the other hand, information prepared for use by others outside the firm is subject to regulation as discussed previously under "financial accounting."

To the extent possible, managerial accounting should provide information that will aid managers in carrying out their five basic duties:

L.O. 2
Planning, organizing, staffing, leading, and controlling

1. **Planning**—Deciding in advance what objectives to pursue and how to achieve those objectives.
2. **Organizing**—Grouping activities, assigning activities, and providing the authority to carry out the activities.
3. **Staffing**—Determining human resource needs, recruiting, selecting, training, and developing human resources.
4. **Leading**—Directing and channeling human behavior toward the accomplishment of objectives.
5. **Controlling**—Measuring actual performance against planned objectives, determining causes of deviations, and taking corrective action when necessary.[1]

These duties will be discussed in greater detail later in this chapter.

To be useful, managerial accounting information must be as reliable as possible, and when estimates are provided, they must be based on sound estimating practices. For example, a manager first may have to make an estimate of how many units of a particular product to manufacture during the coming three months and then compute an estimate of what the cost of these units will be. The management accountant starts by examining data from the same three-month period in the previous year. The accountant then modifies the data to conform to differences that are expected in the current year's three-month period. One change that must be considered is the probable demand for the product in light of current economic conditions, especially if the product is a discretionary expenditure, such as a new automobile. Probability theory would most likely be used to arrive at the number of units needed to be manufactured. Estimated changes in the costs of materials, labor, and overhead from the previous year are needed to project what the cost of these units will be this year. These calculations often entail the use of statistical theory, probability theory, mathematics, and computer applications. Thus, a management accountant must have some familiarity with these practices.

In addition to accounting information, managers use data provided by engineers, economists, mathematicians, sales and marketing specialists, psychologists, and others. The management accountant is but one member of a broad-based management team.

Differences and Similarities—Financial versus Managerial Accounting

Differences   Illustration 1-1 summarizes the differences between managerial and financial accounting.

Similarities   Although the differences noted in Illustration 1-1 are many, similarities occur because a firm uses only one management information system, and, thus, the accounting information generated for financial accounting is also used by management accountants. They start with the financial accounting information and then expand it to comply with their needs.

---

[1] Leslie W. Rue and Lloyd L. Byars, *Management: Theory and Application,* 5th ed. (Homewood, Ill.: Richard D. Irwin, 1989), p. 12.

▶ **ILLUSTRATION 1-1**   Differences—Managerial and Financial Accounting

	Managerial Accounting	**Financial Accounting**
1. Users of data	Managers and certain employees of the firm	Outsiders—stockholders, investors, creditors, financial analysts, government, and employee unions
2. Record-keeping and reporting	Useful but not mandatory	Mandatory—reporting to stockholders, regulatory commissions, and governmental agencies
3. Standards of reporting	None	Prescribed by the FASB, SEC, AICPA, and other regulatory agencies
4. Kind of information presented	Recent actual data and estimated, future-oriented data	Verifiable, typically historical data
5. Data's focus of attention	Product lines, geographic territories, and segments	Company as a whole, with *some* segmented disclosure, but not in the same detail as in managerial accounting
6. Providers of information	Managerial accountants, engineers, economists, mathematicians, sales and marketing specialists, and psychologists	Financial accountants and independent auditors
7. Data format	Any forms that managers find useful; no constraints	Some flexibility within the constraints imposed by the SEC, FASB, and AICPA

Another similarity is that management and financial accounting are both concerned with issuing financial reports about the firm's activities for a period of time. Financial accounting focuses on the firm as a whole, and management accounting focuses on smaller segments of the company.

▶ INFORMATION FOR DECISION MAKERS

L.O. 3
Quantitative and qualitative
information

Sound **decision making**—the process of searching the environment for conditions that require attention, developing and analyzing possible responses, and selecting an appropriate course of action—is crucial to the success of any enterprise. Managers of businesses and not-for-profit organizations make many decisions in the course of their duties. These decisions run the gamut from how many units of a particular product to manufacture on a particular day to the kinds of products the company should produce in the coming decades and how to produce them. For example, consider the case of a neighborhood record store. Some decisions that the manager of a record store must make are:

1. Should the store carry only records, or should it also carry audio tapes and/or compact discs?
2. Should the store specialize in a particular kind of music, such as classical music, and carry only the more popular types of other kinds of music, or should it carry a full line of all kinds of music?

3. Should the store carry audio components?
4. If the store is very successful, should the manager consider opening a branch store in another neighborhood?
5. What days and hours should the store be open?
6. Should the store use an on-line computerized cash register that automatically updates a perpetual inventory?
7. How many employees will be needed?

This list could be expanded considerably. Of course, as a business expands or enters into more complex operating activities, such as manufacturing, the decision-making process becomes more complex. As a result, the information managers require to make these decisions is varied. Much of the information is **quantitative**—that is, numerical in nature—and can be obtained either from the company's books and records or from industry statistics. Most kinds of quantitative information are estimated and may be based on statistical probability distributions or simulated models. In addition, information of a nonquantitative nature—or **qualitative information**—must be factored into decision making. Because qualitative information is difficult to include with quantitative information, the decision-making process can become complicated.

L.O. 4
Decision-making information

Quantitative Information

Most of the quantitative information that managers need can be provided by the management accountant. For example, a manager contemplating the remanufacture of a product that has not been made for a period of time will require these primary pieces of information: (1) the expected selling price and sales volume of the product and (2) the expected cost of manufacturing the product. The management accountant, a member of the management team, would consult company records and report the cost of raw materials when the product was made previously, as well as past wages, required hours, and other *relevant* historical data. **Historical data** are numerical pieces of information based on past events. In addition, the management accountant would report the present wage rates for required labor, the present—actual or estimated—cost of raw materials, and other *relevant* current information. **Current data** are numerical bits of information applicable to the immediate future. Based on these data, the management accountant would be able to calculate the estimated current cost of manufacturing the product. In addition, the sales manager would be asked to provide estimates of the product's selling price based on competition and marketing strategies. A decision would then be made about whether to proceed with manufacturing the product.

Other kinds of decisions that managers make and the kinds of quantitative information they require appear in Illustration 1-2. Although this list is not inclusive, it illustrates how managers rely heavily on management accountants to supply the information they need to make decisions that will affect their company's financial success.

Qualitative Information

Not all information needed for decision making is quantitative. Even though qualitative information cannot be reduced to numerical values, it can be very important. For example, if a manager is contemplating the installation of custom-made draperies in all executive offices, the cost can be measured quantitatively. But aside from the draperies' possible effect on the cost of

▶ **ILLUSTRATION 1-2**   Kinds of Decisions and Related Quantitative Information Needed

Kinds of Decisions	Kinds of Quantitative Information Needed
1. Purchasing new equipment	The cost of the new equipment; the costs saved by the new equipment
2. Replacing old equipment	The cost of the new equipment; the difference in operating costs between the old and the new equipment; the selling price of the old equipment
3. Entering a new market	Revenues and costs of entering the market
4. Discontinuing a product	Revenues lost and costs saved by discontinuing the product
5. Making or buying component parts	The costs of making the part; the cost of purchasing the part
6. Expanding production of an existing product	The additional revenues from expansion; the additional costs from expansion
7. Decreasing production of an existing product	The revenues lost and the costs saved by decreasing production
8. Taking special orders at less than full cost	Additional revenues and costs of the special order
9. Product pricing	Costs of producing the product; desired profit
10. Selling joint products at a splitoff point or processing further	Additional processing costs and additional revenues from further processing
11. Purchasing an existing business	Revenues generated and costs incurred as a result of the purchase

heating, the benefits the firm will derive from their installation are impossible to measure quantitatively. Assume, for instance, that based on a visit to an accounting firm's offices, a potential client decides to hire that firm. Measuring how much of the client's decision was based on the draperies and how much was based on discussions with the firm's partner is impossible. However, some weight must be assigned to such items as draperies, carpeting, and impressive furniture. If not, incurring these costs would serve no purpose when bare windows and floors and a simple desk and chair would accomplish the same result.

Other examples of qualitative information are:

1. The effect that the implementation of a pension plan has on nonunion employee productivity.
2. The effect that the automation of labor-intensive operations has on employee morale.
3. The effect that basing promotions on merit rather than on longevity has on employee morale.
4. The effect that keeping inventories low and allowing frequent stockouts to occur has on customer goodwill. (Note, however, that the lost profit on the lost sale can be measured quantitatively.)
5. The effect that the consideration of temporary layoffs has on employee morale.
6. The effect that busy telephone switchboards or asking customers to hold the line for long periods of time has on customer goodwill.
7. The effect that employees' rudeness to customers has on customer goodwill.

As the partial list suggests, managers must consider many kinds of qualitative information before making decisions.

▶ **PROGRESS CHECK**

1. Is the financial information needed by the managers of a firm the same as the information needed to prepare financial statements for external users? Explain.
2. What are the basic duties of managers?
3. The president of a company is contemplating the purchase of several original oil paintings that will be exhibited in the lobby of the executive offices of the firm. Describe the information needed to make the decision and categorize the information into quantitative and qualitative characteristics.   ◀

▶ GOAL SETTING AND DECISION MAKING

To appreciate managerial accounting, one must first appreciate the management process. One of the most important responsibilities of top management is to set overall goals to guide the firm's activities. A **goal,** or objective, is a specific statement of the end toward which a company intends to direct its efforts. Goals, once set, tend to remain relatively constant to provide purpose and direction to managers and employees alike. Without clearly defined, well-understood goals, a company's activities would become unfocused and disorganized.

Most firms give high priority to the goal of long-run profit maximization, tempered by legal and ethical constraints. In today's environment, however, this should not be an organization's only goal. Otherwise, the firm risks finding itself in conflict with employees' interests, environmental safety, and other forces that would limit its success. Thus, in addition to profit maximization, most organizations' goals address employee relations, pollution control, community involvement, charitable pursuits, and other social concerns. Although such goals may reduce short-term profits, they pay off in the long run. The amount of attention given to social responsibilities varies among organizations and is based on management's perception of the need for such action.

Another important goal pertains to the line of business the company will pursue to earn its profits. For example, a company could elect to operate a chain of retail stores specializing in both men's and women's clothing.

A company's goals form the basis for all subsequent decision making.

Strategic Planning—Long-Term Decision Making

L.O. 5
Decision making

Goal setting is the first step in the strategic planning process. **Strategic planning** is a long-term decision-making process that includes setting goals and selecting the means to attain them. Goals can be pursued in many different ways, depending on management's perceptions and preferences. The methods used to pursue goals are called **strategies.** For example, one automaker's strategy might be to manufacture only one line of automobile, such as an ultraexpensive luxury car. Another automaker's strategy might be to manufacture many lines of automobiles, ranging from subcompacts to limousines. In another strategy decision, Company A may choose to manufacture the spark plugs used in its automobiles, while Company B may prefer to purchase them from another manufacturer.

A business' strategic decision regarding the kind of business it would operate is merely one of many that make up its master strategy. A **master strategy** addresses the "entire pattern of the company's basic mission, purpose, objectives, policies, and specific resource deployment."[2] Other examples of strategic decisions that a clothing retailer would make are:

1. Should it manufacture its own line of clothing using its own label in addition to carrying other well-known designer labels?
2. Should it carry a full line of merchandise from budget sportswear to custom-tailored suits?
3. Should it have its own tailoring and alteration department, or should alterations be subcontracted?

Strategic planning decisions usually have a long-range impact on organizations. Decisions about the line of business to enter and the image the company wishes to project usually cannot be quickly reversed. For example, a business set up to manufacture clothing cannot quickly and easily shift to selling automobiles. Thus, strategic planning decisions must be carefully evaluated to avoid far-reaching negative results.

Once the master strategy is completed, managers can turn to the activities involved in short-term decision making. These can be classified as (1) short-term planning, (2) organizing, (3) staffing, (4) leading, and (5) controlling. The activities involved in each of these functions are listed in Illustration 1-3.

Short-Term Decision Making

Short-Term Planning   Short-term planning is similar to strategic planning except that it covers a shorter period of time—usually one year or less. Thus, **short-term planning** is a short-term decision-making process that includes setting objectives consistent with long-term goals and selecting the means by which the objectives will be attained. It also includes preparing the firm's operating budget for the ensuing year. For businesses that operate at more than one location, the number of employees at each location and the hours of operation must be delineated. These kinds of decisions should be periodically reevaluated, and changes should be made when needed.

Organizing   Managers must also make many day-to-day operating decisions that can be classified as organizing—the combining and arranging of human and material resources in a system of activities that will attain established goals.[3] Organizing may include deciding selling prices, determining quantities of inventory, establishing credit policies, setting hours of operation, and dividing labor among departments. These decisions can be modified over relatively short periods of time—daily, and even hourly, if necessary. This does not mean that once managers start organizing they have stopped planning. In most business situations, both activities continue side by side. For example, two new stores might be in the strategic planning stage while six other stores require short-term planning and organizing.

Staffing   **Staffing** is the process of securing and developing personnel for the jobs created during the organizing process.[4] Employees must be hired,

---

[2] George A. Steiner and John B. Miner, *Management Policy and Strategy* (New York: Macmillan, 1977), p. 20.

[3] Benjamin M. Compaine and Robert F. Litro, *Business: An Introduction* (Hinsdale, Ill.: Dryden Press, 1984), p. 79.

[4] Rue and Byars, *Management: Theory and Application*, p. 302.

▶ **ILLUSTRATION 1-3**   The Functions of Management

Planning
1. Perform self-audit—determine the present status of the organization.
2. Survey the environment.
3. Set objectives.
4. Forecast future situation.
5. State actions and resource needs.
6. Evaluate proposed actions.
7. Revise and adjust the plan in light of control results and changing conditions.
8. Communicate throughout the planning process.

Organizing
1. Identify and define work to be performed.
2. Break work down into duties.
3. Group duties into positions.
4. Define position requirements.
5. Group positions into manageable and properly related units.
6. Assign work to be performed, accountability, and extent of authority.
7. Revise and adjust the organizational structure in light of control results and changing conditions.
8. Communicate throughout the organizing process.

Staffing
1. Determine human resource needs.
2. Recruit potential employees.
3. Select from the recruits.
4. Train and develop the human resources.
5. Revise and adjust the quantity and quality of the human resources in light of control results and changing conditions.
6. Communicate throughout the staffing process.

Leading
1. Communicate and explain objectives to subordinates.
2. Assign performance standards.
3. Coach and guide subordinates to meet performance standards.
4. Reward subordinates, based on performance.
5. Praise and censure fairly.
6. Provide a motivating environment by communicating the changing situation and its requirements.
7. Revise and adjust the methods of leadership in light of control results and changing conditions.
8. Communicate throughout the leadership process.

Controlling
1. Establish standards.
2. Monitor results and compare to standards.
3. Correct deviations.
4. Revise and adjust control methods in light of control results and changing conditions.
5. Communicate throughout the control process.

SOURCE: Leslie W. Rue and Lloyd L. Byars, *Management: Theory and Application,* 6th ed. (Homewood, Ill.: Richard D. Irwin). Copyright © 1992 by Richard D. Irwin, Inc. Reprinted by permission of the publisher.

duties must be assigned, salary levels must be defined, fringe benefits must be selected, and other decisions of this type must be evaluated. Finally, a manager must motivate employees—that is, direct and channel workers' behavior to the accomplishment of company goals.

Leading   The standards of work performance must be clearly explained, and supervision must be provided to help employees meet those standards. In addition, a system of rewards should be established to encourage optimum performance. When employees are highly motivated, a manager will

▶ **ILLUSTRATION 1-4**   Planning and Control Cycle

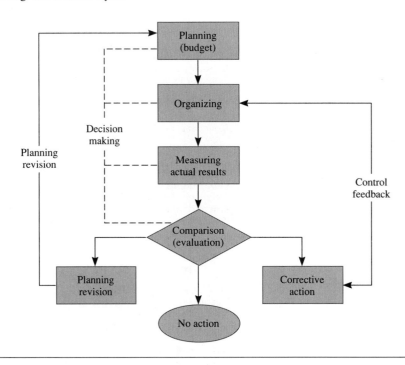

usually observe a substantial increase in performance and a significant decrease in such problems as absenteeism, tardiness, turnover, and strikes.

L.O. 6
Feedback and control

Controlling **Controlling** is the process of ensuring that a firm's operating results are proceeding according to plan. The firm's actual results are compared with its predetermined plans, the sources of any deviations are identified, and, if necessary, action is taken to correct the deviations. The information obtained by comparing actual results to predetermined plans is called **feedback.** And good control depends on accurate feedback. Examples of feedback are (1) the difference between the actual and budgeted sales volume for each of the firm's products or services and (2) the difference between the actual and budgeted costs for each cost category. Here the management accounting system plays a crucial role. It must be structured to provide the data needed to evaluate performance and derive precise and reliable feedback.

An example from daily living will help clarify the nature of control. When a heating thermostat is set at a temperature above the actual temperature in a room, it triggers a mechanism that activates the furnace and causes more heat to be produced. When the temperature of the room is approximately equal to the desired temperature, the furnace is deactivated and remains so until the room cools somewhat. Then the process is repeated. As long as the desired temperature is fairly evenly maintained, the thermostat and the heating system will not need further attention. But should the room become abnormally cool or hot, its occupant would become uncomfortable and investigate the problem to see if a repair is necessary.

In business, control operates similarly. The master strategy that includes a plan of action for an ensuing period of time, usually one year, can be viewed as the desired temperature. As the period of time progresses, actual results of the business' operations are available; these would be analogous to the actual temperature. These actual results would be considered feedback. If the feedback (actual results of operations) is fairly close to the desired plan of action or master strategy (desired temperature), no corrective action is necessary. But if comparison reveals widely disparate results, investigation by management becomes necessary. The approach to control in which a manager investigates only significant differences between planned and actual results is called **management by exception.**

The Planning and Control Cycle

In a broad sense, everything managers do involves decision making. But two managerial functions—planning and control—deserve special attention. Together they form the **planning and control cycle**—a continuous loop of planning, using feedback to evaluate results, taking corrective action if necessary, and returning to the planning stage. The actual results form the basis for any corrective action or plan revisions that may be needed. Thus, the plan provides the mechanism for evaluating performance, and the performance provides the mechanism for revising the plan, if necessary, for the next cycle.

The effect of decision making on the planning and control cycle can be demonstrated in a simple model, as shown in Illustration 1-4.

► ORGANIZATIONS AND THEIR STRUCTURE

A review of typical organizational structures can give some insight into the informational needs of management and the interrelationship of managers and management accountants. Although basic organizational principles are usually thought of in terms of profit-oriented businesses, they are equally valid for not-for-profit entities, such as hospitals, colleges, and community-service organizations.

Organization Charts

To ensure smooth operations, most firms are organized along specified lines of authority. In a very small firm, one leader can single-handedly run the company and make all necessary decisions. But as an organization grows, it becomes increasingly difficult for one individual to keep track of all pertinent information and make all decisions, and consequently it often becomes necessary for the top executives to pass on, or delegate, some authority and responsibility to lower-level employees. This is known as *decentralization*. Most business experts agree that decisions should be made by the management level closest to the situation. For example, if a decision must be made to allow some employees to work overtime on a particular day, the supervisor of that department should select the workers. The supervisor knows the affected individuals and can select those with the required skills. The president of the company would rarely participate in such decisions. Instead, the president would usually focus on decisions affecting the company as a whole. Day-to-day decision making is usually delegated to lower-level managers.

▶ **ILLUSTRATION 1-5**   Organization Chart for Heart-Marks Corporation

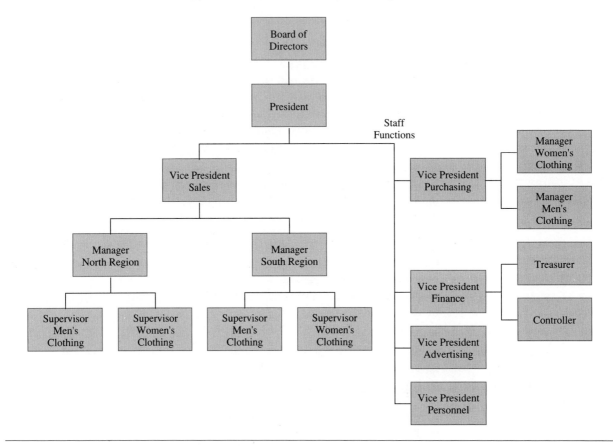

L.O. 7
Organization charts

As companies increase in size, they often construct **organization charts** to define the structure of their organization, its breakdown into departments, and the resulting lines of authority. Illustration 1-5 depicts the organization chart for the Heart-Marks Corporation, a national retail chain. The chain has two major segments, the north region and the south region. Note that the board of directors is at the top of the hierarchy. It delegates authority—the responsibility for operating the corporation—to the president, who in turn delegates specific authorities to the vice presidents, and so on down the line.

L.O. 8
Delegation of authority

Delegation of authority includes (1) assigning duties to immediate subordinates; (2) granting subordinates permission to make commitments, use resources, and take all actions necessary to perform the duties assigned; and (3) making the subordinate responsible for performing the duties in a satisfactory manner.[5]

The relatively simple organization chart shown in Illustration 1-5 merely represents one possible configuration. In contrast, an organization chart for a giant corporation may require hundreds of pages. One purpose of an orga-

---

[5] William H. Newman, *Administrative Action,* 2nd ed. (Englewood Cliffs, N.J.: Prentice Hall, 1963), pp. 185–86.

nization chart is to indicate **lines of authority,** which are the paths responsibility takes as it is passed down from managers to subordinates. The following lines of authority can be seen in Illustration 1-5:

1. There are four supervisors of clothing. One supervisor of men's clothing and one supervisor of women's clothing report to the manager of the north region. The other two supervisors report to the manager of the south region.
2. Both the manager of the north region and the manager of the south region report to the vice president of sales.
3. Both the treasurer and the controller report to the vice president of finance.
4. All five vice presidents report to the president, who in turn reports to the board of directors.

The organization chart also clarifies line and staff functions.

L.O. 9
Line and staff functions

Line Functions   Workers in **line functions** perform the primary business tasks for which the company was organized. For example, in a merchandising establishment, managers in line functions perform jobs related to selling the organization's products. In a manufacturing company, managers in line functions deal with the manufacture and sale of the organization's products.

Staff Functions   Workers in **staff functions** perform ancillary, or support, services for the people in line positions. Thus, in Illustration 1-5, purchasing, finance, advertising, and personnel are considered staff functions because they provide support services to the people involved in the actual selling of clothes. A staff function in one organization may be a line function in another organization. For example, the purchasing function is usually a staff function in most business organizations. But, in the garment industry, where there are buying offices whose business is to purchase clothing for a variety of retail stores, purchasing may be a line function. In effect, these buying offices sell their purchasing expertise. Thus, these organizations do not have a sales function. In their organization charts, the purchasing function would be substituted for the sales function shown in Illustration 1-5. Other examples of staff positions that may become line positions are managing attorneys in law firms, account executives in public accounting firms, and advertising executives in advertising agencies.

Illustration 1-6 summarizes the distinctions between line and staff functions in retailing and manufacturing organizations.

For a company to operate effectively, interaction between line and staff functions is necessary. It would be highly unusual for a company's advertising department to decide which product lines to advertise without consulting the selling department. Similarly, when prices are not fixed by the market, sales managers would not set a product's selling price without consulting with the accounting department to determine the product's costs. Thus, interaction between departments is essential.

The Treasurer and the Controller   In most companies, the treasurer and the controller provide crucial—although different—financial services. The **treasurer** is an officer of the firm, generally with a finance background, whose duties usually include (1) custodianship of the company's funds, (2) banking, (3) arranging for financing, (4) stockholder relations, (5) insurance coverage,

▶ **ILLUSTRATION 1-6**   Examples of Line and Staff Functions

Type of Firm	Line Functions	Staff Functions
1. Retailing	Vice president of sales Managers of all retail stores Sales managers Salespersons	Warehousing Advertising Purchasing Accounting Finance Legal Personnel Sanitation Security
2. Manufacturing	Vice president of manufacturing Vice president of sales Manufacturing supervisors Sales managers Production workers	Repair and maintenance Purchasing Receiving Stockroom Factory cafeteria Advertising Accounting Finance Legal Sanitation Security
3. Service (law firms, etc.)	Client partners Associates, staff attorneys Typists of legal documents	Management partners Secretaries

and (6) extension of credit. On the other hand, the **controller**, sometimes referred to as a *comptroller* and usually with an accounting background, is typically responsible for (1) designing accounting systems, management control systems, budget procedures, and performance reports; (2) preparing budgets (planning); (3) operational reporting and interpreting (feedback); (4) evaluating differences between the *budgeted amounts* and the *actual* results (variance analysis); (5) preparing tax returns and other governmental reports; (6) establishing internal control procedures to safeguard the company's assets; (7) preparing the company's external financial statements in accordance with GAAP; and (8) ensuring that the system is working according to the firm's objectives (the *internal audit function*). For example, internal control procedures established by the controller might require that the custody of assets be separate from the record-keeping of the assets and thus a cashier in the treasurer's office would take physical possession of the company's cash receipts and deposit them in the bank, while a bookkeeper in the controller's office would be responsible for recording the cash receipts.

The controller is the firm's chief accountant and a key staff member of the management team. He or she normally supplies significant portions of the data needed for decision making and, in addition, can interpret and analyze the data for his or her colleagues on the management team. In some organizations, the controller gets bogged down with everyday details, which can lessen his or her effectiveness. Ideally, controllers should delegate the details of running their offices to subordinates so that they are free to actively participate in top-level decision making.

▶ **ILLUSTRATION 1-7**   Organization Chart—Controller's Function

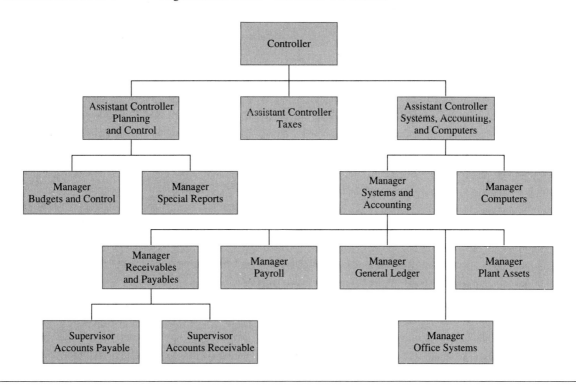

The Controller's Organization Chart   An organization chart of the controller's office is shown in Illustration 1-7. The controller's function and its many responsibilities are the major focus of managerial accounting. The chart in Illustration 1-7 would be a subset of the organization chart in Illustration 1-5.

▶ **PROGRESS CHECK**
1. Is there a difference between strategic planning and short-term planning? Explain by using examples.
2. Describe the functions of management. Give examples for each function you describe.
3. What is the planning and control cycle?
4. What is the purpose of an organization chart?
5. Do all organizations delegate authority? Why or why not?   ◀

▶ CAREERS IN MANAGEMENT ACCOUNTING

Four decades ago, all accounting students received the same training and preparation for careers as public accountants. Public accountants offer their professional services to the public for a fee, much like lawyers and doctors do. Individuals and corporations commonly call on public accountants for auditing of financial statements, accounting-related management advice, and tax services. But many accounting graduates never become public accountants. They may work in government as auditors, general accountants, or tax examiners; they may become teachers; or instead, they may enter private accounting, which means working in the accounting department of a single enterprise. Such private accountants have provided a variety of services to their companies' managers, including general accounting, cost accounting, budgeting, and internal auditing. However, as computerization advanced and became widespread, managers required more sophisticated information and reports. And private accountants naturally became involved in supplying the necessary information. This led to the growth of the management accounting field. Today, many colleges offer separate training for public accountants and management accountants.

Certified Management Accountant (CMA)

In 1972, the Institute of Management Accountants (IMA), formerly the National Association of Accountants (NAA), established the Institute of Certified Management Accountants (ICMA) to recognize the accomplishments of management accountants. It established the Certificate in Management Accounting (CMA) as a means of designating as Certified Management Accountants those management accountants who have fulfilled specified educational and experience requirements and have passed a rigorous series of examinations. The program is administered by the ICMA and requires CMA candidates to pass an examination in:

1. Economics, finance, and management.
2. Financial accounting and reporting.
3. Management reporting, analysis, and behavioral issues.
4. Decision analysis and information systems.

The purposes and objectives of the CMA program are cited from the 1988–89 Announcement of the Institute of Certified Management Accountants of the IMA:

> A **Certified Management Accountant** is well prepared to be an active participant in management. The CMA program is founded upon the dynamic role the management accountant plays in the management process. The program recognizes all aspects of business, with the focus on the development and analysis of information used in decision making. A CMA has demonstrated the knowledge and professional skills to become an influential member of the management team. . . .

The Institute of Management Accountants developed the CMA program and designation to recognize professional competence and educational attainment in the management accounting field. The objectives of the program are threefold:

1. To establish management accounting as a recognized profession by identifying the role of the management accountant and financial manager, the underlying body of knowledge, and a course of study by which such knowledge can be acquired.
2. To foster higher educational standards in the field of management accounting.
3. To establish an objective measure of an individual's knowledge and competence in the field of management accounting.

CMA Requirements   To earn the CMA and become a Certified Management Accountant, the following four steps must be completed:

1. Apply for admission to the CMA program and register for the CMA examination.
2. Pass all four parts of the Certified Management Accountant examination within a three-year period.
3. Meet the accounting experience requirement before or within seven years of passing the examination.
4. Comply with the Standards of Ethical Conduct for Management Accountants.

Certified Public Accountant (CPA)

Another highly respected designation among accounting professionals is that of Certified Public Accountant. The legislative bodies of the individual states have established the procedures and requirements necessary to obtain a **Certified Public Accountant's license.** Although educational and experience requirements differ from state to state, the required examinations are uniform for all 50 states and are prepared and graded by the AICPA. There is reciprocity among most states to qualified CPAs who meet educational and experience requirements. A CPA is licensed to practice as an independent auditor.

Many people first obtain a CPA license and then become management accountants. Thus, many management accountants are CPAs, and many of them also possess the CMA. Management accountants who possess either the CMA or the CPA are recognized as having achieved a high level of professional competency.

▶ WHAT'S NEW?

Several noteworthy developments that have occurred in managerial accounting include (1) the emergence of just-in-time (JIT) inventory control, (2) the new manufacturing environment in which computers and robots are used in the manufacture of products, and (3) a stronger emphasis on the code of ethics that management accountants are required to follow. JIT is discussed fully in Chapter 7 as well as in several later chapters. The remaining items are discussed below.

The New Manufacturing Environment

Many firms in the United States make use of **robotic technology**—having an intelligent machine perform a complete task without the use of human assistance. An example of a robotic operation would be the welding of the component parts of an automobile body and frame as they move along a conveyor belt. At various stations, an intelligent machine uses welding equipment to weld the separate parts and form them into a single component.

Considerable movement toward factory automation has been made in the United States. At one time, the manufacture of an automobile motor required manual labor to bore and machine the cylinders in an engine block. These operations are now performed by automated machines.

Firms make use of a **flexible manufacturing system (FMS)**, which is the grouping of several automated machines that can be rearranged quickly to change from one operation to another. When a firm groups a number of automated machines together, the grouping is called a *cell*. Automated firms make extensive use of **computer-integrated manufacturing (CIM),** which, through the use of computers, links material-handling equipment to flexible manufacturing system cells. An example of computer-integrated manufacturing would be the one noted earlier in which automobile frame parts move along a conveyor system and a computer-activated robotic welder moves into position and welds each seam.

Some firms have achieved a high degree of automation, requiring only a few employees for complex manufacturing operations. For example,

> . . . a manufacturer of truck axles where each axle weighs 800 pounds. The manufacturing of each axle utilizes a flexible manufacturing system (FMS) and requires 42 separate operations that include turning the axle over for some of the operations. The entire process is completed without a single employee working on the axle itself. Another example is General Motors' Vanguard plant in Saginaw, Michigan, where they expect to manufacture truck axles. They anticipate that when the plant is operational they will be able to run the plant during the night without any employees in the plant. Obviously, in operations such as these, the cost of direct labor loses most of the importance that it has occupied recently.[6]

Ethics for Business Managers

Ethics and morals have been a part of human behavior since ancient times; clearly, they can be traced to the biblical era. Most professions, including medicine, law, and public accounting, have imposed codes of ethics on its members for many years. Recent events, such as the savings and loan problems, have focused an enormous amount of attention on ethics in business.

▶ **EXAMPLE**   Michael Josephson, a former law professor at Loyola Marymount University in Los Angeles, founded the nonprofit Joseph and Edna Josephson Institute of Ethics, which specializes in offering classes in ethics for government officials and business people. Josephson ". . . encourages people to look beyond the letter of the law to such principles as honor, fairness, honesty, and justice."[7]   ◀

In 1990, California passed a state ethics-reform law that requires state legislators and their staffs to take ethics courses every two years. The following is a typical case that the Josephson Institute covers.

▶ **EXAMPLE**   A senator who is not permitted to accept an honorarium for delivering a speech in an out-of-town resort is invited to bring his family with him and the sponsoring organization agrees to pay all expenses including those for the family. Is this a violation of the honorarium rule? Although legally it would not be a violation, is this a violation from an ethical perspective? Many would say yes, but others might say no.   ◀

The Institute's classes are overflowing, and it is difficult to keep up with the demand for its lectures. The Institute predicts that ". . . the ethics movement will be to the 90s what the consumer movement was to the 60s."[8]

---

[6] Robert Cappetini and Donald K. Clancy, *Cost Accounting, Robotics, and the New Manufacturing Environment* (Sarasota, Fla.: American Accounting Association, Management Accounting Section, 1987), p. 2.8.

[7] Emily Mitchell, "Brushing up on Right and Wrong," *Time,* April 15, 1991, p. 63.

[8] Ibid.

There are common themes within the codes of ethics of the various professions. Perhaps most important is the concept of confidentiality between a professional and his or her clients (patients). This concept is sometimes referred to as *privileged information* in the legal profession. Another common theme is the concept of placing ''common good'' above self-interest, although self-interest is desirable provided it does not violate the ''common-good'' objective.

A professional who violates an applicable code of ethics is subject to sanctions from the professional organization supervising that profession's membership and the appropriate licensing authority—usually a State Board of Licensing. These sanctions vary from censure to loss of the license to practice the profession. Although CPAs are subject to these sanctions, no such sanctions apply to the behavior of businesses.

One school of thought maintains that investments in businesses that pursue profit maximization as their only goal *and* that are oblivious to ethical and moral behavior do not perform as well in the stock market as do investments in firms that pursue profits within a legal and moral constraint. Stockholders are very conscious of a firm's social goals, pollution experience, and ethical behavior. An increased emphasis is now being placed on ethical behavior in the business community. Some people believe that businesses should be bound by a special code of ethics tailored for business behavior, but others believe that there can be only one kind of ethical behavior for all situations and that businesses should abide by it. As this controversy continues, many business schools and colleges require courses in business ethics for all their majors. To acquaint you with the ethical problems you are likely to encounter in the business arena, you will find applicable ethics cases at the end of selected chapters in this book.

Ethics and Management Accountants   The Institute of Management Accountants (formerly the NAA) has been interested in the ethical behavior of its members for many years, and in 1983 it issued *Statement on Management Accounting Number 1C* (SMA 1C), ''Standards of Ethical Conduct for Management Accountants.'' These standards are reproduced below:

> Management accountants have an obligation to the organizations they serve, their profession, the public, and themselves to maintain the highest standards of ethical conduct. In recognition of this obligation, the Institute of Certified Management Accountants and the National Association of Accountants have adopted the following standards of ethical conduct for management accountants. Adherence to these standards is integral to achieving the objectives of management accounting. Management accountants shall not commit acts contrary to these standards nor shall they condone the commission of such acts by others within their organizations.
>
> **Competence**
>
> Management accountants have a responsibility to:
>
> ▶ Maintain an appropriate level of professional competence by ongoing development of their knowledge and skills.
> ▶ Perform their professional duties in accordance with relevant laws, regulations, and technical standards.
> ▶ Prepare complete and clear reports and recommendations after appropriate analyses of relevant and reliable information.

Confidentiality

Management accountants have a responsibility to:

▶ Refrain from disclosing confidential information acquired in the course of their work except when authorized, unless legally obligated to do so.
▶ Inform subordinates as appropriate regarding the confidentiality of information acquired in the course of their work and monitor their activities to assure the maintenance of that confidentiality.
▶ Refrain from using or appearing to use confidential information acquired in the course of their work for unethical or illegal advantage either personally or through third parties.

Integrity

Management accountants have a responsibility to:

▶ Avoid actual or apparent conflicts of interest and advise all appropriate parties of any potential conflict.
▶ Refrain from engaging in any activity that would prejudice their ability to carry out their duties ethically.
▶ Refuse any gift, favor, or hospitality that would influence or would appear to influence their actions.
▶ Refrain from either actively or passively subverting the attainment of the organization's legitimate and ethical objectives.
▶ Recognize and communicate professional limitations or other constraints that would preclude responsible judgement or successful performance of an activity.
▶ Communicate unfavorable as well as favorable information and professional judgements or opinions.
▶ Refrain from engaging in or supporting any activity that would discredit the profession.

Objectivity

Management accountants have a responsibility to:

▶ Communicate information fairly and objectively.
▶ Disclose fully all relevant information that could reasonably be expected to influence an intended user's understanding of the reports, comments, and recommendations presented.[9]

▶ **SUMMARY**   **Managerial accounting** is one area of accounting that specializes in providing financial information that managers will find useful for internal **decision making.** Such information may be either **quantitative** or **qualitative** and tends to be based on either **current** or future **data.** In contrast, **financial accounting** focuses on compiling financial information and reports for external users, such as investors, creditors, and government agencies. Financial accountants deal primarily with **historical information.**

---

[9] *Statements on Management Accounting Number 1C,* "Standards of Ethical Conduct for Management Accountants" (Montvale, N.J.: Institute of Management Accountants, 1983).

Organizational goals must be clearly defined for an organization to be successful. Once the goals are defined, managers must select the **strategies** that are likely to move the organization toward achieving its goals. **Strategic planning** is concerned with long-range decision making, and its outcome—the **master plan**—is not usually reversible in the short run.

In addition, managers are constantly involved in **short-term planning** and decision making. The five key functions of management are usually defined as **planning, organizing, staffing, leading,** and **controlling.** Two of these, planning and controlling, are often referred to as the **planning and control cycle,** an ongoing process essential to the success of any business. **Feedback** is a necessary ingredient of the planning and control cycle. An approach to control used in many firms is one in which a manager investigates only significant differences between planned and actual results. This approach is known as **management by exception.**

Within a company, the **controller** usually oversees managerial accounting activities, and the **treasurer** is in charge of company funds, banking, financing, stockholder relations, insurance, and extension of credit. Financial accounting is controlled by a regulatory body (the SEC) and a professional organization (the AICPA), but managerial accounting is not formally regulated. Whatever information managers find useful is acceptable in managerial accounting.

To function optimally, a management accountant needs to understand organizations and their structure. An **organization chart** helps define the **lines of authority, delegation of authority, line functions,** and **staff functions** within an organization. The controller, as a member of the management team, performs vital staff functions.

The **CMA** designation gives recognition to accountants who have met specific educational, experience, and testing requirements and confers a certain amount of status. The **CPA** license is primarily useful for professionals who practice as public accountants. Nonetheless, many management accountants also possess the CPA license and, as a result, enjoy greater distinction.

Several new things have happened in the past few years. A new manufacturing environment has emerged in which many manufacturing firms are using **robotic technology,** that is, they are using intelligent machines to perform complete tasks without human assistance. These machines are arranged in groups called a **flexible manufacturing system (FMS)** because they can be rearranged quickly to a desired configuration to perform a needed production operation. Through the use of **computer-integrated manufacturing (CIM),** these firms use computers to link material-handling equipment that moves materials into the proximity of a particular robot that then performs its designated task.

Another relatively new arrival in the United States is the use of just-in-time inventory control. This subject is fully discussed in Chapter 7 and several later chapters.

Finally, the topic of ethics for business managers and management accountants has received a significant amount of attention in the past several years. Many colleges offering degrees in business now require their students to take a course in business ethics. It is expected that this trend will continue and probably expand.

▸ **GLOSSARY OF KEY TERMS**

Certified Management Accountant (CMA)   A designation granted by the Institute of Certified Management Accountants to management accountants who have completed specific educational, experience, and testing requirements. (p. 18)

Certified Public Accountant (CPA) license   A license granted by State Boards of Accountancy, pursuant to statutory authority, generally on the completion of certain educational, experience, and testing requirements. (p. 19)

Computer-integrated manufacturing (CIM)   Through the use of computers, material-handling equipment (e.g., conveyor belts) links materials to flexible manufacturing cells. (p. 20)

Controller (comptroller)   The chief management accountant and key staff member of the management team whose duties include preparing budgets, operational reporting and interpreting, evaluating operating results and any differences from the plan, preparing income tax returns, and establishing internal control procedures to safeguard the company's assets. (p. 16)

Controlling   The process of ensuring that a firm's operating results are proceeding according to plan. The firm's actual results are compared with its predetermined plans, the sources of any deviations are identified, and, if necessary, action is taken to correct the deviations. (p. 12)

Current data   Numerical information applicable to the immediate future, such as present wage rates or expected costs of raw materials. (p. 7)

Decision making   The process of searching the environment for conditions requiring attention, developing and analyzing possible responses, and selecting an appropriate course of action. (p. 6)

Delegation of authority   Assigning duties to immediate subordinates; granting subordinates permission to make commitments, use resources, and take all actions necessary to perform the duties assigned; and making the subordinate responsible for performing the duties in a satisfactory manner. (p. 14)

Feedback   The information obtained by comparing actual results to predetermined plans. (p. 12)

Financial accounting   Area of accounting concerned with compiling the information used to prepare financial statements on a historical cost basis. Financial accounting statements are intended for external users. (p. 4)

Flexible manufacturing system (FMS)   A group of several automated machines that can be rearranged quickly to change from one operation to another one. (p. 19)

Goal   A specific statement of the end toward which a company intends to direct its efforts. (p. 9)

Historical data   Numerical information based on past events, such as former wage rates or past costs of raw materials. (p. 7)

Leading   Directing and channeling human behavior toward the accomplishment of company goals. (p. 5)

Line function   Any job related to the primary business tasks for which a company was organized. (p. 15)

Line of authority   The path responsibility takes as it is passed down from managers to subordinates. (p. 15)

Management by exception   An approach to control in which a manager investigates only those differences between planned and actual results that are considered significant. (p. 13)

Managerial accounting   The area of accounting specializing in providing information that managers find useful for internal decision making. Unlike financial accounting information, managerial accounting information is not regulated by outside agencies. (p. 4)

Master strategy   The entire pattern of a company's basic mission, purpose, objectives, policies, and specific resource deployment. (p. 10)

Organization chart   A diagram defining the structure of an organization, its breakdown into departments, and the resulting lines of authority. (p. 14)

Organizing   The combining and arranging of human and material resources in a system of activities that will attain desired goals. (p. 5)

Planning   Deciding what objectives to pursue during a future time period and what to do to achieve those objectives. (p. 5)

Planning and control cycle   A continuous loop of planning, using feedback to evaluate results, taking corrective action if necessary, and returning to the planning stage. The plan provides the mechanism for evaluating performance, and the performance provides the mechanism for revising the plan, if necessary, for the next cycle. (p. 13)

Qualitative information   Data of a nonquantitative nature. (p. 7)

Quantitative information   Data of a numerical nature. (p. 7)

Robotic technology   Having an intelligent machine perform a complete task without the use of human assistance. An example is the welding of the component parts of automobile body frames as they move along a conveyor belt. (p. 19)

Short-term planning   A short-term decision-making process that includes setting objectives consistent with long-term goals and selecting the means for attaining the objectives. It also includes preparing the firm's operating budget for the ensuing year. (p. 10)

Staff function   Any job providing ancillary, or support, services to line managers. (p. 15)

Staffing   The process of securing and developing personnel for the jobs created during the organizing process. (p. 10)

Strategic planning   A long-term decision-making process that includes setting goals and selecting the means for attaining them. (p. 9)

Strategy   The method used to pursue a goal. (p. 9)

Treasurer   A financial officer of a firm whose duties include custodianship of the company's funds, banking, arranging for financing, stockholder relations, insurance coverage, and extension of credit. (p. 15)

▶ **GLOSSARY OF SYNONYMS**

Comptroller   See **Controller.**

Objective   See **Goal.**

▶ **LIBRARY ASSIGNMENT**

Read the following:

Adams, Doug. "Paying the Price." *Management Accounting.* June 1990, pp. 43–46.

Kaplan, Jeffrey M. "Ghosts of Christmas Future." *Management Accounting.* June 1990, pp. 41–42.

Mintz, Steven M. "Ethics in the Management Accounting Curriculum." *Management Accounting.* June 1990, pp. 51–54.

Shenkir, William G. "A Perspective from Education: Business Ethics." *Management Accounting.* June 1990, pp. 30–33.

Smith, Roger B. "Ethics in Business: An Essential Element of Success." *Management Accounting.* June 1990, p. 50.

Sweeney, Robert B., and Howard L. Siers. "Survey: Ethics in Corporate America." *Management Accounting.* June 1990, pp. 34–40.

▶ **SELF-TEST**

True or False

1. Managerial accounting is not subject to any form of regulation by any governmental organization.

2. Financial accounting is concerned with preparing financial statements for external users and is therefore regulated by the Securities and Exchange Commission and the American Institute of Accounting Standards.

3. The five basic duties of managers are planning, organizing, controlling, decision making, and leading.
4. For decision-making purposes, managers find that historical information is more useful than future-oriented information.
5. Although a manager needs both quantitative and qualitative information, he or she usually finds that most often it is impossible to assign numerical values to qualitative information.
6. Strategic planning and short-term planning are used interchangeably.
7. The position of vice president for purchasing in a retail chain-store operation is a line function.
8. Although the treasurer and the controller usually have the same background, they are responsible for different functions within a firm.
9. A controller is responsible for both financial accounting and managerial accounting information.
10. Many manufacturing firms in the United States are now using CIM, which consists of using a robot to operate the computers used in the manufacturing process.

Matching

Match each of the duties of management on the left with the description of that duty.

_____ Planning   A. Recruiting, selecting, training, and developing human resources.

_____ Organizing   B. Deciding in advance what objectives to pursue.

_____ Staffing   C. Measuring actual performance against planned objectives.

_____ Leading   D. Grouping and assigning activities and providing the authority to carry them out.

_____ Controlling   E. Setting objectives that maximize goals.

    F. Directing human behavior toward the accomplishment of goals.

▶ **QUESTIONS**

1. Who are the users of financial accounting information? On what is it based?
2. Why does financial accounting have regulatory constraints? What are they?
3. Who are the users of managerial accounting information? On what is it based?
4. What quantitative information is useful for decision making? Use an example to illustrate your answer.
5. What is qualitative information? Use an example to illustrate it.
6. What should information provided to managers do?
7. What types of decisions are managers called on to make?
8. What are organizational goals?
9. What is strategic planning?
10. What is a strategy?
11. What is a master strategy?
12. What is planning?
13. What is controlling?
14. What is organizing?
15. What is staffing?
16. What is leading?
17. What is feedback?
18. What is the planning and control cycle?
19. What is a line function?
20. What is a staff function?

21. What are the duties of a treasurer?
22. What are the duties of a controller?
23. What is the CMA designation? How is it obtained? What are its objectives?
24. Several new things have occurred in the past few years that affect managerial accounting. Briefly describe each one.
25. What is robotic technology? Give an example of how it is used.
26. What is a flexible manufacturing system?
27. What is computer-integrated manufacturing?
28. Is ethics important for business managers and management accountants? Explain.
29. Assume you are in the process of starting a business organized for profit. What organizational goals other than profit would you be likely to consider important?
30. Assume that you have been appointed the president of a newly formed private college. Discuss how you would implement each of the following:
    a. College goals.
    b. Strategic planning.
    c. Planning.
    d. Organizing.
    e. Control.
31. Does a charitable organization need organizational goals, strategic planning, planning, organizing, and control? Explain.
32. Because controllership is a staff function, the controller's impact on the management function is advisory only. Thus, the controller is unimportant to the overall management process. Do you agree or disagree? Support your answer.
33. Qualitative data are nonnumerical in nature and thus more difficult to evaluate than quantitative data. However, the qualitative considerations affecting a decision may be more important than the quantitative considerations. Construct an example to illustrate such a case.

▶ **EXERCISES**   E1–1   **Staff and Line Functions**

The Interesting Toy Company is a manufacturer of toys. For each of the following, indicate which line manager or staff manager would be responsible for the costs incurred, and identify the manager as either line or staff.

1. Salaries of plastic molding employees.
2. Salaries of cafeteria employees.
3. Salaries of employees who repair and maintain the plastic molding machines.
4. Salaries of management accountants.
5. Salaries of night watchpersons.
6. Salaries of employees who package the toys.
7. Salaries of sales personnel.
8. Salaries of purchasing personnel.
9. Salaries of personnel who administer the collection and deposit of company funds.
10. Salaries of inspectors who inspect the toys prior to packaging.

E1–2   **Organization Chart**

The Makemoney Merchandising Company is a retail establishment and has the following departments:

a. Furniture.
b. Linens.
c. Electronic home video equipment.
d. Small and major appliances.

Each department has a manager in charge of the sales personnel in his or her department. The managers report to a vice president in charge of sales.

There is a vice president in charge of purchasing who supervises four purchasing managers—one for each department.

There is also a vice president for finance to whom both the treasurer and the controller report.

There are also managers for advertising and sales personnel who report to the vice president of sales.

All vice presidents report to the president, who reports to the board of directors.

Required   Prepare an organization chart for the Makemoney Merchandising Company.

E1–3   **Information for Decision Making**

For each kind of decision listed in Section I, select from Section II the kinds of information needed to arrive at that decision. Each item in Section II may be used more than once or not at all. The information needed for a decision in Section I may require more than one selection from Section II. All of the information needed for a decision may not be shown in Section II. You should limit your selections to only those items shown and select the one that is most appropriate when choices overlap.

Section I

1. _____ Purchasing new equipment.
2. _____ Replacing old equipment.
3. _____ Entering a new market.
4. _____ Discontinuing a product.
5. _____ Making or buying component parts.
6. _____ Expanding production of an existing product.
7. _____ Decreasing production of an existing product.
8. _____ Taking special orders at less than full cost.
9. _____ Product pricing.
10. _____ Selling joint products at the split-off point or processing them further.
11. _____ Purchasing an existing business.

Section II

A. The costs of making a component part.
B. The costs of making a product.
C. Revenues from the sale of a product.
D. The cost of purchasing a new machine.
E. Increased revenues generated.
F. The costs associated with operating a new machine.
G. Increased costs as a result of entering a new market.
H. Increased costs incurred.
 I. Decreased costs resulting from the use of newer equipment.
J. Decreased revenues.
K. The selling price of old equipment.
L. Decreased costs.
M. The costs associated with operating an old machine.
N. The cost of purchasing a component part.
O. Desired profit.

▶ **PROBLEMS**   P1–4   **Line and Staff Authorities**

Special Alloys Corporation is a specialized production firm that manufactures a variety of metal products for industrial use. Most of the revenues are generated by large contracts with companies that have government defense contracts. The company also develops and markets parts to the major automobile companies. The company employs many metallurgists and skilled technicians because most of its products are made from highly sophisticated alloys.

The company recently signed two large contracts; as a result, the workload of Wayne Washburn, the general manager, has become overwhelming. To relieve some of this overload, Mark Johnson was transferred from the research planning department to the general manager's office. Johnson, who had been a senior metallurgist and supervisor in the planning department, was given the title "assistant to the general manager."

Washburn assigned several responsibilities to Johnson in their first meeting. Johnson will oversee the testing of new alloys in the product planning department and have the authority to make decisions as to the use of these alloys in product development; he will also be responsible for maintaining the production schedules for one of the new contracts. In addition to these duties, he will be required to meet regularly with the supervisors of the production departments to consult with them about production problems they may be experiencing. Washburn expects that he will be able to manage the company much more efficiently with Johnson's help.

Required   *a*. Positions within organizations are often described as having (1) line authority or (2) staff authority. Describe what is meant by these two terms.

b. Of the responsibilities assigned to Mark Johnson as assistant to the general manager, which are considered line authority and which have staff authority?

c. Identify and discuss the conflicts Mark Johnson may experience in the production departments as a result of his new responsibilities.

(CMA Adapted)

P1–5   **The Role of Line and Staff Management in Strategic Planning**

One element necessary to the life of an organization is strategic planning. Strategic planning establishes an organization's long-range goals or objectives and the means to achieve them. Before a company can begin operations, its managers must develop the plan or plans necessary to determine its future. For example, these include: What products or services will the organization provide? How will the organization be financed and structured? Where will the company and its distributors be located? How will its products or services be marketed?

Line and staff management play specific roles in strategic planning. They have different responsibilities and functions in an organization. In addition, the activities of these two management groups must be coordinated.

Required   *a*. In the formulation of an organization's strategic plans, describe the contribution to be made by:

(1) The line managers.

(2) The staff groups.

In your answer, identify the types of decisions these two groups of managers make as they participate in the formulation of strategic plans.

b. In the implementation of an organization's strategic plans:

(1) State how the responsibilities of line management differ from those of staff groups.

(2) Describe how line and staff interrelate in this process.

(CMA Adapted)

P1–6   **Setting Long-Range Goals**

Successful business organizations appear to be those with clearly defined long-range goals and a well-planned strategy to reach the goals. These successful organizations understand the markets in which they do business as well as their internal strengths and weaknesses. These organizations take advantage of this knowledge to grow (through internal development or acquisitions) in a consistent and disciplined manner.

Required

a. Discuss the need for long-range goals for business organizations.

b. Discuss how long-range goals are set.

c. Define the concepts of strategic planning and management control. Discuss how they relate to each other and contribute to the attainment of long-range goals.

(CMA Adapted)

P1–7   **Decision Making Using Quantitative and Qualitative Information**

For each of the following situations, indicate whether the decision to be made requires (1) quantitative data, (2) qualitative data, or (3) both. Select a number for your choice. For each choice you make, indicate the kind of quantitative and qualitative data needed. Be as specific as you can.

Situation 1   A firm is contemplating the adoption of a company-wide major medical health plan covering all present employees. The company will pay all costs for its employees before retirement. In addition, these benefits will also be offered to retired employees at no cost to the employee if the employee has completed 25 years of service with the company at the time of retirement. For employees who have completed between 10 and 25 years of service at the time of retirement, the company will offer to pay a proportionate fraction of the amount of the insurance premiums based on the years of service as the numerator and 25 years as the denominator. Employees in this category will be asked to pay the balance of the insurance premiums if they wish to elect this coverage after their retirement. Employees with fewer than 10 years of service will not be offered this coverage option.

Situation 2   A firm presently manufactures all the component parts it uses in its manufacturing operations. It is now considering purchasing one of its component parts from an outside vendor. The portion of the factory now used to manufacture this part can be used to manufacture a new product.

Situation 3   A hospital presently performs a diagnostic test known as an angiogram for people who have heart disease. Occasionally, a patient who is undergoing this test will require immediate heart bypass surgery that the hospital does not presently perform. Such patients must be transported to another hospital on an emergency basis. The nearest hospital that performs bypass surgery is located 50 miles away, a one-hour drive by ambulance. The hospital is considering the installation of a heart bypass facility.

▶ **ETHICAL BEHAVIOR CASES**

C1–8

Victoria Addison is the assistant director of Financial Reporting for Earth Products, Inc., a large processor of ores and minerals. The Finance Department is in the final stages of compiling the financial statements for the fiscal year ended April 30, 19X7, and Addison is working late to complete the footnotes pertaining to long-term contracts. Addison has gathered several files that contain the information she needs to complete her work.

Among the contracts and other documents in the files, Addison has found a copy of a report from the procurement manager of Earth Products to the division manager of the company's coal cleaning plant regarding the procedures for disposing of plant wastes. Addison noticed some penciled calculations and notes on the bottom of the report. According to these notes, Earth Products has been using a nearby residential landfill to dump toxic coal cleaning fluid wastes, and the dump site is nearing saturation, making it necessary to locate a new disposal site for these toxic wastes. The calculations indicate that significant amounts of toxic cleaning fluids have been mixed with residential refuse over the past two years.

Determined to learn more about this situation, Addison kept the report. Uncertain how she should proceed, Addison began to ponder her options by outlining the following three alternative courses of action:

▶ Seek the advice of her boss, the director of financial reporting.
▶ Anonymously release the information to the local newspaper.
▶ Bring the information to the attention of an outside member of the board of directors with whom she was acquainted.

Required   *a.* Discuss why Victoria Addison has an ethical responsibility to take some action in the matter of Earth Products, Inc., and the dumping of toxic wastes. Refer to specific standards of **Statements on Management Accounting Number 1C (SMA 1C),** "Standards of Ethical Conduct for Management Accountants," to support your answer.

b. For each of the three alternative courses of action that Victoria Addison has outlined, explain whether or not the action is appropriate. Use **SMA 1C** to support your answer.

c. Without prejudice to your answer in requirement *b,* assume that Victoria Addison sought the advice of her superior, the director of financial reporting, and discovered that the director was involved in the dumping of toxic wastes. Describe the steps that she should take in proceeding to resolve the conflict in this situation. Use **SMA 1C** to support your answer.

(CMA Adapted)

C1–9   Allstar Brands, headquartered in Dallas, is a large, diversified manufacturer with plants located throughout the United States. The company has a strong commitment to equal opportunity employment and emphasizes this commitment in frequent communications with management and supervisory personnel. In several locations, Allstar has training programs directed at improving the skill levels of minority groups. In addition, to ensure that the corporate policy is implemented, all supervisory personnel must attend seminars on nondiscriminatory personnel practices.

Allstar's Internal Audit Department (IAD) is located at corporate headquarters. Employment with IAD is considered a management accounting career choice rather than a preparatory step to a supervisory position in another department. Roger Dixon, IAD director, has the authority to hire all departmental personnel. Dixon delegates the initial screening of all job applications and some preliminary interviews to one of his senior management accountants, Peter Foxworth. Foxworth then recommends the candidates for further consideration. This arrangement has been in place for the past year. Foxworth is concerned that, during this time, Dixon has not hired any minority applicants despite the fact that many were qualified. As a matter of fact, several minority candidates recommended by Foxworth were not even interviewed a second time. When asked why there had not been any minority applicants hired in the past year, Dixon told Foxworth to pay attention to his own responsibilities.

Foxworth believes that Dixon has intentionally discriminated against minority applicants and that Dixon's behavior should be corrected. Foxworth is uncertain about how he should proceed because Allstar Brands does not have an established policy on how to resolve this issue. Foxworth is considering following one of the three alternative courses of action listed below.

▶ Discuss Dixon's behavior with the director of personnel, one of Dixon's management peers.
▶ Informally discuss Dixon's behavior and ways to change it with a group of IAD senior management accountants.

▶ Discuss Dixon's behavior privately with the chief financial officer, Dixon's supervisor.

Required   *a.* Referring to the specific standards of competence, confidentiality, integrity, and objectivity in *Statements on Management Accounting Number 1C* **(SMA 1C),** ''Standards of Ethical Conduct for Management Accountants,'' explain why Roger Dixon's implied behavior with regard to hiring new employees is unethical.

b. For each of the three alternative courses of action that Peter Foxworth is considering, explain whether or not the action is appropriate. Refer to the specific standards in **SMA 1C** to support your answer.

c. According to **SMA 1C,** identify the steps that Peter Foxworth should take in attempting to resolve this situation.

(CMA Adapted)

C1–10   The Alert Company is a closely held investment services group that has been very successful over the past five years, consistently providing most members of the top management group with 50 percent bonuses. In addition, both the chief financial officer and the chief executive officer have received 100 percent bonuses. Alert expects this trend to continue.

Recently, the top management group of Alert, which holds 35 percent of the outstanding shares of common stock, has learned that a major corporation is interested in acquiring Alert. Alert's management is concerned that this corporation may make an attractive offer to the other shareholders and that management would be unable to prevent the takeover. If the acquisition occurs, this executive group is uncertain about continued employment in the new corporate structure. As a consequence, the management group is considering changes to several accounting policies and practices that, although not in accordance with generally accepted accounting principles, would make the company a less attractive acquisition. Management has told Roger Deerling, Alert's controller, to implement some of these changes. Deerling has also been informed that Alert's management does not intend to disclose these changes immediately to anyone outside of the immediate top management group.

Required   *a.* As a management accountant and citing the specific standards of competence, confidentiality, integrity, and/or objectivity from *Statements on Management Accounting Number 1C* **(SMA 1C),** ''Standards of Ethical Conduct for Management Accountants,'' evaluate

(1) The changes Alert Company's top management group is considering.

(2) Roger Deerling's responsibilities as a management accountant.

b. Identify all of the specific steps Roger Deerling should take to resolve the situation described above. Use **SMA 1C** to support your answer.

c. Discuss social and ethical responsibilities that a company should consider before taking defensive actions such as those described above.

(CMA Adapted)

▶ **ANSWERS TO SELF-TEST**

True-false

1. True	2. False	3. False	4. False	5. True	6. False
7. False	8. False	9. True	10. False		

Matching

Planning—B   Organizing—D   Staffing—A   Leading—F   Controlling—C

PART ▶ 1

Essentials of Cost and Managerial Accounting

2 Cost Definitions and Cost Concepts

3 Cost Behavior and Cost Estimation

4 Cost, Volume, and Profit—Analysis and Relationships

5 Job Order Costing

6 Process Costing

7 Cost Accounting for the New Manufacturing Environment

8 Cost Allocation—Service Departments and Joint Products

2 Cost Definitions and Cost Concepts

▶ **LEARNING
OBJECTIVES**

After reading this chapter, you should be able to:

1. Distinguish between a cost and an expense.
2. Explain what product cost is for a merchandising establishment.
3. Explain what product cost is for a manufacturing firm and identify the three elements that enter into a product's cost.
4. Classify costs of production according to the three elements of cost for a manufacturing firm.
5. Explain how the financial statements of a merchandising establishment differ from those of a manufacturing establishment.
6. Describe the flow of costs for merchandising and manufacturing firms.
7. Describe the differences in behavior between fixed costs and variable costs.
8. Explain the various cost classifications listed in the glossary at the end of this chapter.

▶ **INTERVIEW**

Joseph V. Roccosalvo
Vice President—Financial
Administration
Barclays Bank PLC

Q. *Do service industries have a need for cost information? If so, what cost objectives and cost information have you found to be relevant?*

A. Absolutely.

We need cost information for the tasks that employees perform in the course of carrying out their duties. We must know our costs for services rendered to our customers. Examples of our needed cost objectives include the cost of processing a check returned for insufficient funds, the cost of certifying a customer's check, the cost of processing a check drawn on a customer's account, the cost of processing a customer's deposit, the cost of processing a loan application, and the cost of processing a cash withdrawal from an automatic teller machine. This cost information enables us to determine what to charge customers for the services we render and the minimum balances that customers must maintain for the various kinds of accounts that we offer.

Q. *In classifying a cost as either controllable or noncontrollable, what criteria do you use?*

A. We classify a cost as controllable whenever a department head has the ability to influence a cost that is incurred. For example, a branch manager would be held accountable for tellers' salaries and floor personnel working at that branch. We also classify certain main-office costs as controllable when the main office performs for the branch services such as processing a loan application. However, other main-office costs are considered noncontrollable for the branch when the branch manager has no opportunity to influence the cost incurred even when the branch may benefit from the cost for items such as bank advertising. The main office, however, would consider advertising a controllable cost at the main-office level even though the branches may derive some benefit from the advertisement.

▶ For an accountant, the term *cost* can have many different definitions. At the most general level, a **cost** is the sacrifice made to acquire a good or service. Thus, in a simple transaction, the cost of an item like an adding machine is the cash paid to acquire it, regardless of whether the cash is paid at the time of the purchase or at a later time.

Costs are extremely important to accountants and managers. They are used for a variety of purposes, including (1) pricing a product for sale to customers, (2) valuing inventories when preparing an income statement, (3) evaluating the performance of groups of employees, (4) making decisions regarding alternative courses of action, and (5) budgeting for future operations. It is customary to describe costs with an adjective to signify their purpose.

For descriptive purposes, an accountant or manager may group costs in any of several ways: (1) as they relate to a specific product, (2) as they relate to a period of time rather than to a specific product, (3) by category based on behavior patterns, (4) into those needed to reach a managerial decision, and (5) into those needed for performance evaluation.

The nature of a business may also determine the way costs are described. Although manufacturing, merchandising, and service industries may incur the same kind of costs, the description of the costs may differ in each industry.

The measurement of costs is extremely important to all kinds of business entities; however, it is critical to the successful operation of a manufacturing firm. ◀

▶ COSTS AND EXPENSES

L.O. 1

Costs may be subdivided into **unexpired costs,** which are sacrifices expected to benefit future accounting periods, and **expired costs,** which are sacrifices *not* expected to benefit future accounting periods. Unexpired costs are shown as assets on the balance sheet and consist of such items as inventories; unexpired insurance; and property, plant, and equipment. Expired costs, also called **expenses,** are shown as deductions from revenues and consist of such items as the current period's rent, telephone bill, advertising charges, administrative salaries, and electric bill. They are shown as expenses because no future benefit is expected from these items. A cost is recorded as an asset if the cost's future value has not expired, but it is recorded as an expense if its future value has expired.

The distinction between whether a cost should be classified as unexpired or expired is sometimes subtle. For instance, long-lived assets, such as production equipment, do not lose all their future value at one time but rather slowly over time, through years of use. Accountants use depreciation to allocate the cost of long-lived assets to expense. For example, the purchase of a machine that costs $5,000 would also entail an expense in the form of depreciation. If the machine had an estimated useful life of five years and no salvage value, its *expense* would be $1,000 a year if straight-line depreciation were used. This amount would be considered the *expired* portion of the original cost.

The distinction between costs and expenses is relevant when preparing financial statements for external use by stockholders, investors, financial analysts, and others. Managers are concerned with *costs* and how they affect a firm's operations. Thus, we will focus on costs throughout this book and refer to expenses only in relation to external reporting.

▶ **ILLUSTRATION 2-1**

CARSON PIRIE SCOTT & CO.
Consolidated Balance Sheet
January 31, 19x1

Assets

Current assets:
Cash	$ 8,691,000
Receivables	88,325,000
Merchandise inventories	53,959,000
Supplies and prepaid expenses . . .	2,747,000
Total current assets	$153,722,000

▶ FINANCIAL STATEMENTS FOR A MERCHANDISING FIRM

For a merchandising establishment, product costs are usually easy to ascertain. Because merchandisers buy goods for resale, their product costs include the price paid for the goods purchased, shipping costs, insurance during transit, and import duties.

Product Costs

To demonstrate what is included in product cost for a merchandising firm, let us assume the Sellmore Retail Outlet Company purchased and imported some television sets that involved the following costs:

L.O. 2
Product cost for a merchandiser

1. Fifty television sets at $150 each with payment due in 30 days; a 2 percent discount would be allowed for payment within 10 days.
2. Freight and shipping costs of $300.
3. Insurance during transit costs of $150.
4. Import duties of $10 per set.

The total cost and unit cost of the television sets may be computed as follows:

Product costs
Cost of sets—50 at $150	$7,500
Import duties—50 at $10	500
Shipping costs	300
Insurance in transit	150
Subtotal	8,450
Less: Purchase discount—2% × $7,500 . . .	150
Total cost	$8,300
Unit cost—$8,300 ÷ 50	$ 166

A Merchandiser's Balance Sheet

Merchandisers have only *one* classification of inventories—finished goods for sale to customers. Because of the single classification, merchandisers customarily use the simple label *Inventories* on their balance sheets.

The current asset section of a merchandiser's balance sheet is shown in Illustration 2-1. Note that it has only one listing for inventories.

A Merchandiser's Income Statement

For merchandisers, purchases of merchandise for resale are shown as purchases (plus freight-in). The schedule of cost of goods sold for a merchandising firm is shown in Illustration 2-2.

▶ **ILLUSTRATION 2-2**

SELLMORE RETAIL OUTLET COMPANY
Schedule of Cost of Goods Sold
For the Year Ended December 31, 19x2

Cost of goods sold:

Beginning inventory		$150,000
Add: Purchases	$500,000	
Freight-in	6,000	506,000
Goods available for sale		656,000
Deduct: Ending inventory . . .		140,000
Cost of goods sold		$516,000

The remaining portion of a merchandiser's income statement is not presented but can be found in financial accounting textbooks.

▶ SERVICE BUSINESSES

Several decades ago, service firms paid little attention to costs. Their rationale was that because most of their costs were fixed costs (they had no product costs because no products were sold), and because their costs varied little based on the amount of business activity, costs could be ignored. The objective of a service firm was to concentrate on attracting customers with the expectation that profits would thereby increase. Today, service industries are very mindful of costs and are now charging their customers and clients for many services that were provided free in the past. Examples are the charges that banks now make for certifying checks and cashing bearer-bond coupons, and fees that attorneys now bill for telephone consultations.

The financial statements of service organizations are similar to those of merchandisers, except their balance sheets do not normally contain inventories and their income statements do not contain cost of goods sold.

▶ COSTS IN A MANUFACTURING FIRM

L.O. 3
Product costs

A manufacturing firm normally purchases direct materials and converts them into finished goods by combining and/or altering the direct materials. To accomplish this, a manufacturing firm usually utilizes both employees and machinery housed in some form of factory building. The resulting costs, which can be attributed specifically to products, are called **product costs** and fall into three categories: direct materials, direct labor, and manufacturing overhead.

Direct Costs

A **direct cost** is directly related, or traceable, to a cost objective. A **cost objective** is any grouping to which costs are assigned, such as an individual unit of inventory, a department, a product line, a division, or the firm itself. Indirect costs, discussed later in this chapter, are costs that relate to more than one cost objective and cannot be traced to a single objective. A cost, such as a factory supervisor's salary, may be directly traceable to a firm's product line (i.e., television receivers), but it may *not* be directly traceable to a specific receiver or model. Thus, when speaking of a direct cost, the cost objective must be specified, or else the description will suffer from an imprecision that renders it meaningless.

L.O. 4
Cost elements for
a manufacturer

Direct Materials   **Direct materials** include the cost of all materials directly traceable to a finished product that are necessary to produce the product for sale to customers. These costs can usually be calculated with a high degree of accuracy. In theory, direct materials would include every component of the finished product, including, for example, nails and glue. But in reality, most companies apply the cost-benefit rule, which states that a cost should not be incurred unless the corresponding benefit exceeds the cost. Consequently, the relatively high cost of maintaining bookkeeping records for items like nails and glue results in these items being treated as *indirect materials*—an indirect cost, which we will discuss later. Direct materials are sometimes called *raw materials*.

A manufacturer's cost of direct materials includes:

1. The invoice price of the direct materials.
2. Inbound shipping costs.
3. Import duties.
4. A reduction for any allowable discounts for prompt payment to suppliers.

Other costs associated with materials, such as insurance during transit, receiving room costs, and stockroom costs, are difficult to trace to specific units. These are known as *indirect material costs* and are treated as manufacturing overhead.

Direct Labor   **Direct labor** includes the wages paid to all employees who work directly on the transformation of direct materials into a finished product as well as the wages of inspectors who approve the product for sale to customers. Employees whose wages are not included as direct labor are (1) the factory superintendent, (2) supervisory line employees who do not work directly on the product, (3) maintenance and repair employees, (4) security guards, (5) support personnel, and (6) cleaning staff. The efforts of these workers are considered indirect labor because it is impossible to trace their salaries and wages to any specific product. Indirect labor costs are treated as manufacturing overhead.

For a manufacturer, the cost of direct materials used to manufacture a product and the cost of wages paid to employees who work on transforming direct materials into finished goods are easy to trace to a finished product.

Indirect Costs

Indirect costs (also called **common costs**) relate to more than one cost objective. If the cost objective is a particular product in a multiproduct factory, all manufacturing costs other than direct materials and direct labor are considered indirect manufacturing costs and are called manufacturing overhead.

Manufacturing Overhead   A number of terms are used to describe manufacturing overhead, including **overhead pool, overhead, burden, factory burden, factory overhead, indirect manufacturing costs, factory expenses,** and

indirect factory expenses. Whichever term is used, **manufacturing overhead** includes all *manufacturing costs* except direct materials and direct labor. The key point to remember is that *only* manufacturing costs are included in this category. For example, although factory rent is included in manufacturing overhead because the factory is essential to the production of a finished product, *office rent is excluded* because it is *not related to production*. Other examples of indirect manufacturing costs are:

Indirect materials
   Machine lubricants
   Factory janitorial supplies
   Glue used in production
   Small nails and screws used in production
Indirect labor
   Factory supervisors
   Factory cleaning staff
   Factory security guard
   Factory bookkeepers and payroll clerks
   Factory receiving room personnel
   Factory purchasing personnel
Depreciation
   Factory machinery
   Furniture used in the factory
   Office equipment (i.e., computers) used in the factory
Other factory costs
   Electricity for the factory
   Heating for the factory
   Telephones used in the factory
   Health and life insurance for factory employees
   Insurance on factory equipment
   Machinery repairs and maintenance

Product Costs

Although indirect costs cannot be traced directly to any single product, some method must be found to assign them to all products if proper dollar values are to be assigned to inventories on hand. **Assignable product costs,** usually referred to as **inventoriable costs,** include direct materials, direct labor, and all indirect manufacturing costs (overhead) necessary to produce a finished product ready for sale to customers. Once a product is in its normal salable condition at a specific location, no further costs are assignable to it.

To demonstrate what is included in product costs for a manufacturing firm, let us assume that during 19x1 the Mitchell Fabricating Corporation purchased direct materials for $500,000, incurred direct labor costs for $600,000, and incurred manufacturing overhead costs for $298,000. There are no beginning or ending inventories. The firm manufactures one product—bathroom scales—and 150,000 scales were manufactured during 19x1.

The *total product costs* for 19x1 may be summarized as follows:

Total product cost:	
Direct materials	$ 500,000
Direct labor	600,000
Manufacturing overhead . . .	298,000
Total	$1,398,000

▶ **ILLUSTRATION 2-3**   Examples of Period Costs

Type of Cost	Marketing	General and Administrative
1. Rent	Sales offices and selling showroom	General offices
2. Salaries	Sales managers and sales personnel	Corporate officers and office personnel
3. Telephone	Sales offices	General offices
4. Heat and light	Sales offices	General offices
5. Insurance	Sales offices	General offices
6. Depreciation	Sales equipment	Office equipment
7. Advertising	Sales promotion	—
8. Legal and accounting fees	—	Administrative costs

The **unit cost** per scale may be calculated by dividing the total product cost of $1,398,000 by the number of units produced, 150,000, as follows:

$$\text{Unit cost} = \frac{\$1,398,000}{150,000} = \$9.32 \text{ per scale}$$

Product costs include any costs that are associated with the manufacturing facility, in whatever guise they appear. Product costs appear as assets—inventories—until the assets are sold. When the assets are sold, they then become expired costs (expenses). In addition to product costs, firms incur other costs for marketing their products and administering day-to-day operations. These costs are referred to as *period costs*.

Period Costs

Period costs usually benefit a specific period of time and are *not related to production or product costs*. This distinguishes period costs from product costs, which are functions of production. Since product costs are associated with the manufacturing facility, we will classify as a period cost any cost that is not directly related to the manufacturing facility. Period costs are usually divided into two classifications: marketing and administrative costs. An example of a period cost would be a showroom rent cost. Since a showroom is used for sales purposes, we can determine that it does not benefit the manufactured product and is therefore a period cost. Costs to promote sales, such as renting a showroom, are known as *marketing costs*. Marketing costs include all the costs associated with finding and attracting potential customers, convincing them to purchase the firm's products, and delivering the products to customers. Had the cost been used in the performance of administrative functions, it would be classified as a general and administrative cost. Administrative costs include all costs not classified as product and marketing costs.

All period costs, whether marketing or administrative, have one common property: as the name implies, each period cost is deducted from revenues earned during the current accounting period. Illustration 2-3 lists several kinds of costs and their classifications. The illustration provides the names of common subclassifications for each cost classification.

▶ **PROGRESS**
   CHECK

1. How does a cost differ from an expense?
2. What costs are included in the product costs of a merchandising firm? What costs are included in the product costs of a manufacturing firm?
3. Differentiate a direct cost from an indirect cost.
4. Are all indirect costs factory overhead? Explain.
5. What is the difference between a product cost and a period cost?   ◀

▶ FINANCIAL STATEMENTS FOR A MANUFACTURING FIRM

Inventory Classification

Manufacturing firms generally have three classes of inventory: (1) direct materials, (2) work in process, and (3) finished goods. The value of the **work in process** inventory represents the cost of goods that have entered the production process but have not been completed. Work in process includes direct material, direct labor, and manufacturing overhead costs associated with goods still in the production stage. Work in process can be viewed as follows:

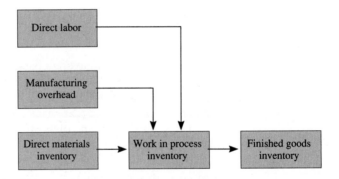

Most manufacturers have some unfinished goods at all times and thus must value this inventory at the end of an accounting period when an income statement is to be prepared. **Finished goods** are goods in finished condition awaiting sale to customers.

A Manufacturer's Balance Sheet

L.O. 5
Financial statements

The major difference between a manufacturer's and a merchandiser's balance sheets is in how inventories are presented. A merchandiser has only one class of inventory and thus merely shows one amount for merchandise inventory in the current asset section of the balance sheet. A manufacturer shows a separate amount for each of the three classes of inventory.

The Mitchell Fabricating Corporation has inventories on December 31, 19x1, as follows:

Direct materials . . .	$ 60,000
Work in process . . .	130,000
Finished goods	300,000

The firm also has cash in the bank of $100,000, accounts receivable (net of allowance for doubtful accounts) of $175,000, and prepaid costs of $20,000.

MITCHELL FABRICATING CORPORATION
Balance Sheet
December 31, 19x1

Current assets:
Cash in bank		$100,000
Accounts receivable less allowance		
for doubtful accounts		175,000
Inventories:		
Direct materials	$ 60,000	
Work in process	130,000	
Finished goods	300,000	
Total inventories		490,000
Prepaid costs		20,000
Total current assets		$785,000

The current asset section of Mitchell's balance sheet appears in Illustration 2-4.

A Manufacturer's Income Statement

As part of its management reporting system, a manufacturing firm prepares an income statement that includes both a schedule of cost of goods sold and a schedule of costs of goods manufactured. The income statement is normally prepared monthly, and it provides managers with the results of operations—net income or net loss—for the specified period of time. It is important for managers to monitor their firm's operating results frequently. This will allow them *to alter operating strategies if the results are not satisfactory*. Managers who do not monitor their firm's operating results at frequent intervals, but instead wait for the firm's annual report to assess its operations, may be placed in the position of receiving information when it is too late to take corrective action.

To prepare an income statement, it is necessary to ascertain both *beginning* and *ending inventories* for direct materials, work in process, and finished goods. Using the information previously provided for the Mitchell Fabricating Corporation, let us also assume the beginning inventories are $80,000 for direct materials, $110,000 for work in process, and $250,000 for finished goods.

Four steps are needed to prepare an income statement for a manufacturing firm.

Step 1: The Schedule of Direct Materials Used in Production   Prepare a computation of the *cost of direct materials used in production*. The cost of direct materials may be calculated using the following formula:

Direct materials used = Beginning direct materials inventory + Direct materials purchased − Ending direct materials inventory

Considering Mitchell's beginning inventory of direct materials for $80,000, the purchases of $500,000, and the ending inventory of direct mate-

▶ **ILLUSTRATION 2-5**

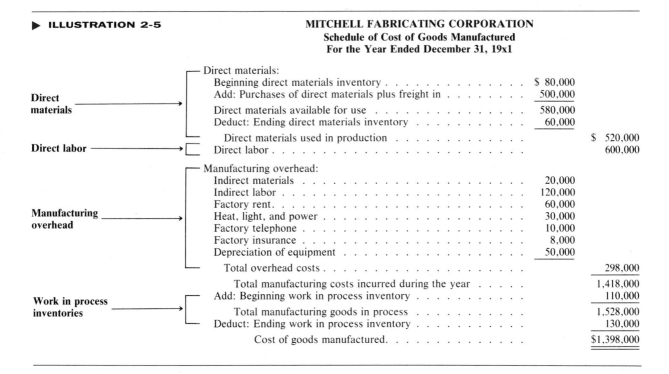

MITCHELL FABRICATING CORPORATION
Schedule of Cost of Goods Manufactured
For the Year Ended December 31, 19x1

Direct materials:

Beginning direct materials inventory	$ 80,000	
Add: Purchases of direct materials plus freight in	500,000	
Direct materials available for use	580,000	
Deduct: Ending direct materials inventory	60,000	
Direct materials used in production		$ 520,000
Direct labor		600,000

Manufacturing overhead:

Indirect materials	20,000	
Indirect labor	120,000	
Factory rent.	60,000	
Heat, light, and power	30,000	
Factory telephone	10,000	
Factory insurance	8,000	
Depreciation of equipment	50,000	
Total overhead costs		298,000
Total manufacturing costs incurred during the year		1,418,000
Add: Beginning work in process inventory		110,000
Total manufacturing goods in process		1,528,000
Deduct: Ending work in process inventory		130,000
Cost of goods manufactured.		$1,398,000

Direct materials (label pointing to direct materials section)

Direct labor (label pointing to direct labor line)

Manufacturing overhead (label pointing to overhead section)

Work in process inventories (label pointing to work in process section)

rials for $60,000, its cost of direct materials used in production may be prepared as follows:

Beginning direct materials inventory	$ 80,000
Add: Direct materials purchased plus freight in .	500,000
Direct materials available for use	580,000
Deduct: Ending direct materials inventory . . .	60,000
Direct materials used in production	$520,000

Note that this computation closely resembles the cost of goods sold section of an income statement for a merchandising firm. The computation shown above is included in the schedule of cost of goods manufactured shown in Illustration 2-5.

Step 2: The Schedule of Cost of Goods Manufactured   Cost of goods manu-factured consists of the costs of direct materials, direct labor, and manufacturing overhead associated with manufactured units that have been completed during the current accounting period. Prepare a *schedule of cost of goods manufactured* using the following formula:

Cost of goods manufactured = Beginning work in process inventory
+ Direct material used + Direct labor + Manufacturing overhead
− Ending work in process inventory

Based on the data presented so far, and adding a detailed breakdown of manufacturing overhead costs, Mitchell Fabricating Corporation's schedule of cost of goods manufactured would appear as shown in Illustration 2-5.

L.O. 6
Cost flow

It is customary to show the details of the manufacturing overhead incurred during the year. If the amount of detail makes the schedule bulky, such information may be presented in a separate schedule, with only the total overhead ($298,000) shown in the cost of goods manufactured schedule. The flow of costs that entered into the preparation of the schedule of cost of goods manufactured is shown in Illustration 2-6. Note that Illustration 2-5 contains the cost inputs noted in Illustration 2-6, namely, direct materials, direct labor, and manufacturing overhead. However, to compute the cost of goods transferred to finished goods (cost of goods manufactured), it is necessary to add the beginning work in process inventory and deduct the ending work in process. The beginning work in process inventory must be included because the manufacturing costs expended during the current period do not include the costs expended in the prior period that are contained in the beginning work in process. By including these costs, the schedule reflects all manufacturing costs expended in the current period as well as the costs expended in the prior period on *merchandise finished in the current period*. The beginning work in process becomes part of the finished goods in the current period, which must reflect both the costs expended in the prior period and the costs to finish them in the current period. Failure to include the beginning work in process costs in the schedule means they would be unaccounted for.

The ending work in process costs must be subtracted if the schedule is to reflect only the cost of goods completed. If the ending work in process inventory were not subtracted, the schedule would contain both the cost of goods completed *and* the cost of the ending work in process inventory. Clearly, this would be undesirable if only the cost of goods completed is needed. In essence, the schedule of cost of goods manufactured reflects all inputs and outputs of the Work in Process account. The relationship between the cost of goods manufactured and the cost of goods sold may be seen in Illustration 2-7.

Step 3: Schedule of the Cost of Goods Sold   The **cost of goods sold** consists of the product cost associated with goods sold during the current accounting period. Prepare a *schedule of cost of goods sold* based on the following formula:

Cost of goods sold = Beginning finished goods inventory + Cost of goods manufactured − Ending finished goods inventory

Continuing the example from Illustration 2-5, the cost of goods sold section of Mitchell's income statement would appear as in Illustration 2-7. It is assumed that the beginning finished goods inventory was $250,000 and the ending finished goods inventory was $300,000.

Step 4: The Income Statement   Using the schedule of cost of goods sold, prepare an income statement by subtracting the cost of goods sold from sales revenue to arrive at the firm's **gross margin** (or **gross profit**). From the gross margin, deduct the marketing and administrative costs. The result is the firm's **operating profit.** From this amount, a provision for income taxes may be deducted to arrive at **net income.**

▲ **ILLUSTRATION 2-6**   Mitchell Fabricating Corporation: Cost Flow for the Schedule of Cost of Goods Manufactured

Direct Material

Beginning Inventory   80,000

⊕ DM Purchases   500,000

⊖ Ending DM Inventory   60,000

Direct Labor for the Period

WIP Direct Labor   600,000

Manufacturing Overhead

Indirect Materials   20,000

⊕ Indirect Labor   120,000

⊕ Factory Rent   60,000

⊕ Heat, Light and Power   30,000

⊕ Factory Telephone   10,000

Work in Process at the Beginning of the Year

Beginning WIP Inventory   110,000

Work in Process at the End of the Year

Ending WIP Inventory   130,000

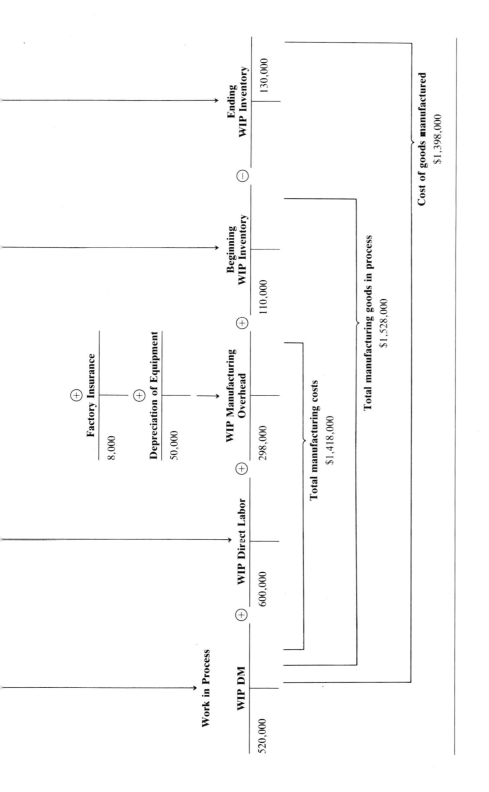

Work in Process

WIP DM	WIP Direct Labor	WIP Manufacturing Overhead	Beginning WIP Inventory	Ending WIP Inventory
520,000	600,000	298,000	110,000	130,000

Factory Insurance 8,000

Depreciation of Equipment 50,000

Total manufacturing costs $1,418,000

Total manufacturing goods in process $1,528,000

Cost of goods manufactured $1,398,000

47

▶ **ILLUSTRATION 2-7**

MITCHELL FABRICATING CORPORATION
Schedule of Cost of Goods Sold
For the Year Ended December 31, 19x1

Cost of goods sold:	
Beginning finished goods inventory	$ 250,000
Add: Cost of goods manufactured	
(from Illustration 2-5)	1,398,000
Goods available for sale	1,648,000
Deduct: Ending finished goods inventory . . .	300,000
Cost of goods sold	$1,348,000

▶ **ILLUSTRATION 2-8**

MITCHELL FABRICATING CORPORATION
Income Statement
For the Year Ended December 31, 19x1

Sales revenue	$3,000,000
Deduct: Cost of goods sold (Illustration 2-7) . . .	1,348,000
Gross margin	1,652,000
Deduct: Marketing and administrative costs . . .	700,000
Operating profit before income taxes.	952,000
Deduct: Income taxes (30%)	285,600
Net income	$ 666,400

For 19x1, Mitchell Fabricating Corporation had sales revenues of $3 million, marketing costs of $300,000, administrative costs of $400,000, and an income tax rate of 30 percent. The firm's income statement for the year is shown in Illustration 2-8.

▶ The Four Steps in Preparing a Manufacturer's Income Statement

Step 1: Prepare a *computation of the cost of direct materials used in production*. The cost of direct materials may be calculated using the following formula:

> **Direct materials used** = Beginning direct materials inventory + Direct materials purchased − Ending direct materials inventory

Step 2: Prepare a *schedule of cost of goods manufactured* using the following formula:

> **Cost of goods manufactured** = Beginning work in process inventory + Direct materials used + Direct labor + Manufacturing overhead − Ending work in process inventory

Step 3: Prepare a *schedule of cost of goods sold* based on the following formula:

> **Cost of goods sold** = Beginning finished goods inventory + Cost of goods manufactured − Ending finished goods inventory

Step 4: Using the schedule of cost of goods sold, prepare an income statement by subtracting the cost of goods sold from sales revenue to arrive at the firm's **gross margin** (or *gross profit*). From the gross margin, deduct the marketing and administrative costs. The result is the firm's **operating profit.** From this amount, a provision for income taxes may be deducted to arrive at **net income.**

Steps in Preparing a Manufacturer's Schedule of Cost of Goods Manufactured, Schedule of Cost of Goods Sold, and Income Statement

Step 2

MITCHELL FABRICATING CORPORATION
Schedule of Cost of Goods Manufactured
For the Year Ended December 31, 19x1

Step 1

Direct materials:		
Beginning direct materials inventory	$ 80,000	
Add: Purchases of direct materials plus freight in	500,000	
Direct materials available for use	580,000	
Deduct: Ending direct materials inventory	60,000	
Direct materials used in production		$ 520,000
Direct labor		600,000
Manufacturing overhead:		
Indirect materials	20,000	
Indirect labor	120,000	
Factory rent	60,000	
Heat, light, and power	30,000	
Factory telephone	10,000	
Factory insurance	8,000	
Depreciation of equipment	50,000	
Total overhead costs		298,000
Total manufacturing costs incurred during the year		1,418,000
Add: Beginning work in process inventory		110,000
Total manufacturing goods in process		1,528,000
Deduct: Ending work in process inventory		130,000
Cost of goods manufactured		$1,398,000

Step 3

MITCHELL FABRICATING CORPORATION
Schedule of Cost of Goods Sold
For the Year Ended December 31, 19x1

Cost of goods sold:		
Beginning finished goods inventory		$ 250,000
Add: Cost of goods manufactured		
(from Illustration 2-5)		1,398,000
Goods available for sale		1,648,000
Deduct: Ending finished goods inventory		300,000
Cost of goods sold		$1,348,000

Step 4

MITCHELL FABRICATING CORPORATION
Income Statement
For the Year Ended December 31, 19x1

Sales revenue	$3,000,000
Deduct: Cost of goods sold (Illustration 2-7)	1,348,000
Gross margin	1,652,000
Deduct: Marketing and administrative costs	700,000
Operating profit before income taxes	952,000
Deduct: Income taxes (30%)	285,600
Net income	$ 666,400

▶ **ILLUSTRATION 2-10**   Interrelationship between Prime Costs, Conversion Costs, and Product Costs for a Manufacturing Firm

The four steps in preparing a manufacturer's income statement are shown in Illustration 2-9.

Prime Costs and Conversion Costs

The term **prime cost** denotes the sum of direct material costs and direct labor costs—that is, the two kinds of costs directly traceable to the cost of a product. The term **conversion cost** refers to the sum of direct labor and manufacturing overhead. It stems from the notion that direct materials are *converted* into finished goods through the input of direct labor and manufacturing overhead. The interrelationships among prime cost, conversion cost, and the three elements of product cost are shown in Illustration 2-10.

▶ COST BEHAVIOR

L.O. 7

In Chapter 1, we noted that planning and controlling are important managerial duties. The cost data that managers need may not necessarily be classified in the same manner as the data used in the preparation of financial statements. For planning and control purposes, a manager is interested in how a cost behaves. **Cost behavior** relates to the way a particular cost reacts to a change in business activity. At one end of the spectrum are variable costs, which fluctuate in relation to output. At the other end are fixed costs, which do not change even if activity changes within a reasonable range. Between these extremes are mixed costs, which vary, but not in direct proportion to output. Mixed costs are discussed in Chapter 3.

Variable Costs

A **variable cost** varies *in total* directly with the number of units produced. When production is nil, the cost is nil. If production doubles, the cost doubles. For example, if the direct materials cost of a table is $20, then the variable cost of direct materials is $20 if one table is produced, $40 if two tables are produced, and so forth. The total direct materials cost can be ascertained by multiplying the number of tables produced by $20.

In this definition of variable cost, *linearity* is assumed. Thus, we assume the direct materials cost for *each table* remains $20 regardless of how many tables are produced.

Fixed Costs

Fixed costs remain constant regardless of the level of activity, so long as activity stays within a reasonable range. This range of activity is called the *relevant range.* Cost behavior is covered in detail in Chapter 3. If a firm rents a factory building in which to manufacture its products, the cost for rent is usually a fixed amount per month or year, so it is a fixed cost. Other costs that fall into this category are the factory superintendent's salary, insurance, and real estate property taxes.

It is important to recognize that a fixed cost remains fixed only for a particular range of production. For example, if the size of a factory building permits 400,000 units to be produced on any given day, its fixed cost has a range of 0 to 400,000 units per day. Whether 100,000 units or 350,000 units are produced, the cost for factory rent remains the same.

▶ OTHER COST CONCEPTS

Direct versus Indirect Costs

As noted earlier, a *direct cost* can be traced exclusively to a particular *cost objective,* such as a product, a product line, a factory, a division, or a segment of a firm's operations. An *indirect* cost is *common to more than one* cost objective and thus is *not* exclusive to any one product, product line, and so forth.

Direct costs are not limited to direct materials or direct labor. In fact, a cost can be direct in one instance and indirect in another. The *frame of reference* determines the nature of the cost. For example, a factory superintendent's salary, although classified as manufacturing overhead, can be a direct cost if a factory manufactures only one product and the cost objective is the product. On the other hand, it would be an indirect cost if the factory manufactured *several* products and the cost objective was *one* of the products. Another way of viewing this example is that in the first case, a decision to discontinue manufacturing the product would normally eliminate the need for the superintendent's services and thus eliminate his or her salary; in the second case, the discontinuance of *one* product would not necessarily change the need for the superintendent's services or the need to pay his or her salary.

It should be noted that the direct/indirect classification is not limited to product costs. Marketing and administrative costs can also be classified as direct or indirect. For example, if the Chevrolet Motor Division of General Motors placed an advertisement for its Corvette, this would be considered a direct cost if the Corvette were the cost objective. If, however, General Motors placed an advertisement extolling the virtues of its efforts to manufacture pollution-free automobiles, the advertisement would be considered an indirect cost if the cost objective were still the Corvette.

▶ **ILLUSTRATION 2-11**   Cost Analysis of Producing Delex

| Cost | Aggregate Cost Approach | | Differential Cost Approach |
	Process A	Process B	Increase (Decrease) in Cost of Process A over B
Direct materials	$ 6	$ 3	$3
Direct labor	4	5	(1)
Variable overhead	3	3	
Fixed overhead	2	2	
Totals	$15	$13	$2

Differential Costs

A **differential cost** is the difference between the costs of two alternative courses of action. This cost plays a crucial role in decision making.

When choosing among several courses of action, managers could consider either differential costs or aggregate costs. **Aggregate cost** is the total cost of a particular cost objective.

While it is possible to compute the aggregate cost for each alternative and then compare the two, this approach requires more effort than the differential cost approach. Proponents of the differential cost approach claim that considering only the *differences* between the two alternatives is clearer and more efficient.

If, for example, a firm is considering marketing a product called Delex at $20 per unit and it can manufacture Delex in two different ways, the costs can be calculated on an aggregate cost basis for each alternative or on a differential cost basis. Each method is shown in Illustration 2-11. Columns 2 and 3 illustrate the aggregate cost approach, and the last column illustrates the differential cost approach. The final decision will be based on identical results—that is, process B is favored because it costs $2 less per unit. However, the differential cost computations are much simpler than those for the aggregate cost approach. The aggregate cost approach considers all costs, even if they are the same for both processes. But the differential approach ignores identical costs and considers only the differences in costs.

Opportunity Costs

An **opportunity cost** is the value of any opportunity one gives up to engage in an alternative activity. For example, a person who chooses to attend college full time instead of entering the employment market has an opportunity cost of going to college equal to the earnings forgone during the period of study. Although opportunity cost is not presently used in financial accounting, it is an extremely important element of the managerial decision-making process.

Let us assume you have $100,000 in a savings account earning $10,000 of interest each year. You are offered an opportunity to invest the $100,000 in a business with almost no risk that will yield a yearly net income of $35,000. This business will require that you work there full time. You are presently employed full time and earning $30,000 annually for work that is similar to that required of you if you invest in the business. The opportunity costs of investing in this business may be summarized as follows:

Opportunity Costs	Amount
Employee's salary forgone . . .	$30,000
Interest income forgone	10,000
Total opportunity costs	$40,000

By comparing the opportunity costs of $40,000 with the promised net income of $35,000, it would be to your financial advantage to keep the money in the bank and continue working as an employee.

Many people have difficulty in using an opportunity cost correctly. Suppose that you need an automobile for transportation and you have looked at a compact car that would cost you $10,000. This is all you can afford right now. However, someday you would like to buy a new Corvette, but you cannot afford the $32,000 cost. As luck would have it, you are selected to appear on a game show and—you guessed it—you won a Corvette before you purchased your compact. An affluent friend has offered you $28,000 if you will sell the Corvette. Would you sell it? You probably would not. How much did the car cost you? For the moment, let us ignore the income taxes you might have to pay on winning the car. You might be tempted to say that it did not cost you anything. This answer is incorrect. The correct answer is that the car cost you $28,000. You could have had $28,000 in cash but you gave up the opportunity to receive $28,000—the opportunity cost. The car cost you $28,000 just as surely as if you sold the car and immediately repurchased it for the same price, assuming your friend agreed to it. Properly using opportunity cost is an extremely valuable tool to assist managers in arriving at correct decisions.

Sunk Costs

A **sunk cost** is any cost that has already been incurred and cannot be reversed. Except for its impact on income taxes, a sunk cost is irrelevant for all decision-making purposes. For example, assume an automobile manufacturer spent $10 million to set up an assembly line to manufacture 455-horsepower engines. Now, a month later, a gasoline shortage has developed, and the company is contemplating whether to continue manufacturing the 455-horsepower engines or produce smaller engines. The $10 million is a *sunk* cost and, as such, has no bearing on the decision except for the tax write-off it would provide. The relevant information would be the cash costs of the new assembly line and the marketing benefits of producing a smaller, more fuel-efficient engine compared with the future costs and benefits of producing the larger, gas-guzzling engine.

Controllable and Noncontrollable Costs

In the long run, all costs are controllable at some level of management. For shorter intervals, many costs are controllable, while some are not. A **controllable cost** can be altered at *a particular level of management,* and a **noncontrollable cost** cannot be influenced or altered at *a particular level of management.* For example, factory rent might be a controllable cost at the vice presidential level. If the vice president of manufacturing can make the decision to rent particular premises, she should be held accountable for their cost. Similarly, a line supervisor should be held accountable for the amount of direct labor cost expended on his assembly line. Because the supervisor has the authority to decide which employees should be used for specific

▶ **ILLUSTRATION 2-12**   Cost Classifications and Some of Their Uses

Cost Classification	Uses
Assignable product cost	Inventory valuation and budget preparation.
Conversion cost	Pricing, inventory valuation, and budget preparation.
Differential cost	Compared with differential revenue to decide on expansion or deletion of a particular product line.
Direct cost	Sum of all direct costs of a product (line) compared with revenue from product (line) to determine if product (line) is profitable.
Expired cost	Deducted from revenues of a stated period of time to compute net income for that period.
Fixed cost	Computation of breakeven sales, long-term decisions, budget preparation, and cost-volume-profit decisions.
Opportunity cost	Part of total cost to be considered for profitability decisions.
Period cost	Matched against revenue to compute net income for a period of time.
Prime cost	Inventory valuation, pricing, and budget preparation.
Sunk cost	Computation of the tax consequences when purchasing replacement equipment.
Unexpired cost	This cost, carried over into a subsequent accounting period, appears on the balance sheet at any given date.
Variable cost	Pricing, inventory valuation, budget preparation, breakeven sales, and cost-volume-profit decisions.

duties on his line, he has the ability to control the employees' performance levels and, thus, their cost. These costs would be considered controllable by the supervisor.

A second factor in examining a cost's controllability is its time frame. Certain costs may be controllable in the long term but not in the short term. Consider the cost of constructing a factory building. The size of the building and the cost of construction materials are controllable only when the building is being constructed. Once the factory is constructed, its building cost (depreciation) would be noncontrollable until it is time to raze the old building and construct a new one—far into the future. Alternatively, the cost of truck maintenance—greasing and changing the oil—is controllable in the short run. The decision can be made to do the maintenance every 4,000 miles or every 2,000 miles.

For purposes of performance evaluation, a manager should be held accountable for only those costs that are controllable at his or her level. Noncontrollable costs at one level of management are normally controllable at a higher level. A reporting system in which a cost is charged to the lowest level of management that has responsibility for it is known as **responsibility accounting,** or **activity accounting.**

L.O. 8
Explain cost classifications

A summary of this chapter's cost classifications and some of their uses appears in Illustration 2-12.

▶ **COST DEFINITIONS AND COST CONCEPTS
FOR SERVICE INDUSTRIES**

Because of the new manufacturing environment—discussed in Chapter 1—industries in the United States and many other countries have witnessed a dramatic shift away from blue-collar workers to white-collar workers. This has caused a marked increase in the need for service industries, and these

▶ **ILLUSTRATION 2-13**   Sample Listing of Cost Objectives for Service Industries

1. Airlines—flights flown, passengers processed at terminals, passenger miles.
2. Public accounting firms—audits performed, tax returns prepared, hours billed to clients.
3. Dry cleaning establishments—garments cleaned, garments pressed.
4. Hospitals—patient-days, medical procedures performed.
5. Law firms—hours billed to clients.
6. Computer processing services—hours of computer run time.
7. Word processing services—pages typed.

industries now produce a very large part of the gross national product (GNP) in the United States. Therefore, managers are now more than likely to become involved in managerial accounting for service industries.

Managerial and cost accounting was never simple for manufacturing firms. Nevertheless, there was a certain commonality in the concepts for manufacturers. Costs of production followed similar computations regardless of whether the product was a toaster, a tooth paste, or a jet engine. For service industries in general, this commonality is not presently available. However, there is a commonality within each industry, such as law firms or hospitals. Thus, because of this limitation, we will attempt to provide insight into the information needed by managers in some of the more common service industries.

Cost Objectives

One useful cost objective for a manufacturing firm is the cost of producing each unit of product. For service industries, the cost objectives are much more varied. For example Illustration 2-13 contains a sample listing of cost objectives for different service industries.

Cost Terms for a Hospital

Many of the cost terms used in this chapter for manufacturing firms are also used by hospitals. For example, the distinction between direct costs and indirect costs applies to most service industries, including hospitals. In order for this distinction to be made, it is important to define the organization's cost objective or unit of product. As noted in Illustration 2-13, a hospital's unit of product could be *patient-days* or *procedures performed*. **Patient-day** is a one-day stay for a single patient. Thus, if a hospital has 300 patients, excluding outpatients, the patient-day equivalent for that day is 300.

A direct materials cost—sometimes called *a direct supplies cost*—for a hospital could be X-ray films, disposable syringes, disposable catheters, and other nonreusable items. Direct labor costs also apply to most service industries; for a hospital, they would include salaries paid to employees whose work can be directly traced to the services provided. These direct labor costs would include the salaries of resident physicians, nurses, and laboratory technicians. The salaries of nursing supervisors and chief residents (supervisors of resident physicians) would be considered indirect labor and become part of hospital overhead. Hospital overhead is analogous to factory overhead and includes building occupancy costs (rent or depreciation of the building), electricity, heat, telephone, indirect materials, supervision, insurance, and other items.

Other manufacturing cost terms that apply to hospitals are *variable costs, fixed costs, differential costs, opportunity costs, sunk costs, controllable costs, and noncontrollable costs.*

Medicare now requires hospitals to classify patients into groups of similar procedures based on the reason for hospitalization and the treatment provided. This grouping is known as **diagnostic-related group (DRG).** Medicare pays hospitals a fixed amount for the hospital stay and procedure performed, regardless of the length of the actual stay. Thus, if a procedure calls for a five-day stay and the patient actually stays in the hospital seven days, the hospital will be paid for only five days. The reverse is also true; that is, an actual three-day stay will be reimbursed for a five-day rate if the DRG calls for five days. Non-Medicare, private patients, however, pay the hospital for the actual number of days in the hospital.

▶ **SUMMARY**

A cost is a sacrifice made to acquire a good or service. Costs can be classified in many different ways. The needs of managers and accountants govern the manner in which costs are classified.

Direct costs are directly traceable to the specific cost objective in question. **Indirect costs,** also called *common costs,* cannot be traced directly to a specific cost objective. Thus, they must be assigned on some rational basis to a specific **cost objective,** usually a specific product.

Costs that can be attributed to production are classified as **product costs,** in which case they are **assignable,** or *inventoriable.* On the other hand, noninventoriable costs are called **period costs** and are usually classified according to their functional components, such as marketing costs and administrative costs. Period costs are usually **expired costs,** or *expenses.* **Unexpired costs** are assets.

The principal difference between the financial statements of merchandising firms and manufacturing firms is in how inventories are shown. Merchandisers have only one class of inventory, merchandise inventory, which they show on their balance sheets as *Inventories.* Manufacturers, however, classify their inventories on their balance sheets into three classes: **direct materials, work in process,** and **finished goods.** In addition, manufacturers prepare a schedule of **cost of goods manufactured,** which has no counterpart in a merchandiser's financial statements. Both merchandisers and manufacturers prepare income statements that show sales revenues, **costs of goods sold, gross margins, operating profits,** and **net incomes.**

Manufacturers break down their product costs into three components: **direct materials, direct labor,** and **manufacturing overhead.** Manufacturers also consider **prime costs,** which consist of the costs for direct materials and direct labor and **conversion costs,** which consist of the costs for direct labor and manufacturing overhead. When manufacturers place direct materials into production, they become part of the work in process inventory. The addition of direct labor and manufacturing overhead transforms the work in process into finished goods inventory, which is then ready for sale. When the goods are sold, the cost of goods sold is then computed. The cost of goods sold is a cost objective that managers are interested in because it directly affects the profitability of the firm. Cost of goods sold is an **aggregate cost,** and the aggregate cost of any cost objective is its *total cost.*

Cost-behavior refers to how costs react to changes in activity levels. At one end of the spectrum are **variable costs,** whose total varies proportionately with production. At the opposite end are **fixed costs,** which are constant in total within a **relevant range** of production. In between these extremes are mixed costs, which contain both fixed and variable elements.

Costs can also be classified as **controllable** or **noncontrollable.** This distinction is useful in **responsibility accounting** and for decision-making purposes. Other classifications, also useful for decision making, are **differential costs, opportunity costs,** and **sunk costs.** The use of these classified costs in the decision-making process forms the major focus of the remainder of this book.

In recent years, there has been a sharp increase in the number of service industries. Service industries pay much attention to cost- and managerial-accounting concepts, and they utilize cost concepts that are similar to those used by manufacturing firms. However, the cost objectives that service industries use are different from those used by manufacturers. For example, hospitals use a unit of product known as **patient-days,** which is the number of patients in the hospital on any particular day. Hospital costs are also accumulated into categories of direct materials, direct labor, and hospital overhead.

Medicare now requires hospitals to classify patients into groups of similar procedures based on the reason for hospitalization and the treatment provided. This grouping is known as **diagnostic-related group (DRG).** Medicare pays hospitals a fixed amount for the hospital stay and procedure performed, regardless of the length of the actual stay.

▶ **GLOSSARY OF KEY TERMS**

Activity accounting   See **responsibility accounting.** (p. 54)

Aggregate cost   The total cost of a particular cost objective. (p. 52)

Assignable product cost   Direct materials, direct labor, and all indirect manufacturing costs (overhead) necessary to produce a finished product ready for sale to customers. (p. 40)

Burden   See **manufacturing overhead.** (p. 39–40)

Common cost   See **indirect cost.** (p. 39)

Controllable cost   A cost that can be altered at a particular level of management. (p. 53)

Conversion cost   The sum of direct labor and manufacturing overhead. (p. 50)

Cost   A sacrifice made to acquire a good or service. (p. 36)

Cost behavior   The way a cost reacts to a change in business activity. (p. 50)

Cost objective   A grouping to which costs are assigned, such as a unit of inventory, a department, a product line, a division, or the firm itself. (p. 38)

Cost of goods manufactured   The costs of direct materials, direct labor, and manufacturing overhead associated with manufactured units that have been completed during the current accounting period. (p. 44)

Cost of goods sold   The product cost associated with goods sold during the current accounting period. (p. 45)

Diagnostic-related group (DRG)   A classification that hospitals use to classify patients into similar groups based on the reason for hospitalization and the treatment provided. (p. 56)

Differential cost   The difference between the costs of two alternative courses of action. (p. 52)

Direct cost   A cost directly related, or traceable, to a single cost objective. (p. 38)

Direct labor   Wages paid to employees who work on transforming direct materials into a finished product as well as the wages of inspectors who approve the product for sale to customers. (p. 39)

Direct materials The cost of all materials directly traceable to a finished product that are necessary to produce the product for sale to customers. (p. 39)

Direct materials used Beginning direct materials inventory + Direct materials purchased − Ending direct materials inventory. (p. 43)

Expense See **expired cost.** (p. 36)

Expired cost A sacrifice not expected to benefit future accounting periods. Also called an **expense.** (p. 36)

Factory burden See **manufacturing overhead.** (p. 39–40)

Factory expenses See **manufacturing overhead.** (p. 39–40)

Factory overhead See **manufacturing overhead.** (p. 39–40)

Finished goods Goods in finished condition awaiting sale to customers. (p. 42)

Fixed cost A total cost that remains constant within a given range of activity and period of time. However, the *per-unit* cost decreases with increased output. (p. 51)

Gross margin (gross profit) On an income statement, sales revenue minus cost of goods sold. (p. 45)

Gross profit See **gross margin.** (p. 45)

Indirect cost A cost that relates to more than one cost objective. (p. 39)

Indirect factory expenses See **manufacturing overhead.** (p. 40)

Indirect manufacturing costs See **manufacturing overhead.** (p. 39–40)

Inventoriable costs See **assignable product cost.** (p. 40)

Manufacturing overhead Costs necessary to manufacture a finished product except for *direct materials* and *direct labor.* Manufacturing overhead is also called *overhead, burden, factory burden, factory expenses, indirect factory expenses, indirect manufacturing costs,* or *overhead pool.* (p. 40)

Net income Sales revenue minus cost of goods sold, marketing costs, administrative costs, and income taxes. (p. 45)

Noncontrollable cost A cost that cannot be influenced or altered at a particular level of management. (p. 53)

Operating profit Sales revenue minus cost of goods sold, marketing costs, and administrative costs. (p. 45)

Opportunity cost The value given up or the income forgone by employing a resource in an alternative use. (p. 52)

Overhead See **manufacturing overhead.** (p. 39–40)

Overhead pool See **manufacturing overhead.** (p. 39–40)

Patient-days The number of patients in the hospital on any particular day. (p. 55)

Period cost A cost related to a period of time, not to production. It is not a product cost and is classified as either a marketing cost or an administrative cost. (p. 41)

Prime cost The sum of direct material costs and direct labor. (p. 50)

Product cost A cost that can be attributed specifically to products; direct materials, direct labor, and manufacturing overhead. Also called **inventoriable cost.** (p. 38)

Relevant range The level of activity that a firm chooses for its operations. A firm normally operates within this range, although it may occasionally operate at a different level. (p. 51)

Responsibility accounting A reporting system in which a cost is charged to the lowest level of management that has responsibility for it. (p. 54)

Sunk cost A previously incurred cost that cannot be reversed. It is irrelevant for future decision making except for its tax consequences. (p. 53)

Unexpired cost A sacrifice to acquire a good or service whose benefits will expire in a subsequent accounting period. (p. 36)

Unit cost The total cost of a product divided by the number of units produced. (p. 41)

Variable cost A total cost that varies proportionately with output. However, the *per-unit* cost is constant within a given range of production. (p. 50)

Work in process   Represents the cost of goods that have entered the production process but have not been completed. Work in process includes direct material, direct labor, and manufacturing overhead costs associated with goods still in the production stage.   (p. 42)

▶ **GLOSSARY OF SYNONYMS**

Activity accounting   See responsibility accounting.

Burden   See **manufacturing overhead.**

Common cost   See **indirect cost.**

Expense   See **expired costs.**

Factory burden   See **manufacturing overhead.**

Factory expenses   See **manufacturing overhead.**

Factory overhead   See **manufacturing overhead.**

Gross profit   See **gross margin.**

Indirect factory expenses   See **manufacturing overhead.**

Indirect manufacturing costs   See **manufacturing overhead.**

Inventoriable costs   See **assignable product cost.**

Overhead   See **manufacturing overhead.**

Overhead pool   See **manufacturing overhead.**

Raw materials   See **direct materials.**

▶ **REVIEW PROBLEM**

Preparation of Cost of Goods Manufactured and Sold.

A partial trial balance of the Brown Corporation as of December 31, 19x4, follows:

Direct materials inventory, January 1	$ 68,000
Work in process inventory, January 1	45,000
Finished goods inventory, January 1	190,000
Purchases of direct materials	240,000
Direct labor	340,000
Indirect labor	60,000
Factory rent	125,000
Office rent	70,000
Depreciation—machinery	50,000
Depreciation—office equipment	12,000
Insurance—factory	28,000
Salespersons' salaries	110,000
Repairs and maintenance—machinery	18,000
Miscellaneous factory	150,000
Miscellanous office	60,000

The December 31 inventories:	
Direct materials	60,000
Work in process	50,000
Finished goods	165,000

Required   *a.* Prepare a schedule of cost of goods manufactured.

b. Prepare a schedule of cost of goods sold.

▶ **SOLUTION TO REVIEW PROBLEM**

Step 1

Prepare a computation of the cost of direct materials used in production.

Direct materials:		
Direct materials inventory, January 1	$ 68,000	
Add: Purchase of direct materials	240,000	
Total direct materials available	308,000	
Deduct: Direct materials inventory, December 31	60,000	
Direct materials used in production		$248,000

Step 2

Prepare a schedule of cost of goods manufactured using the computation prepared in step 1.

BROWN CORPORATION
Schedule of Cost of Goods Manufactured
For the Year Ended December 31, 19x4

Direct materials:		
Direct materials inventory, January 1 . . .	$ 68,000	
Add: Purchase of direct materials	240,000	
Total direct materials available	308,000	
Deduct: Direct materials inventory,		
December 31	60,000	
Direct materials used in production		$ 248,000
Direct labor.		340,000
Manufacturing overhead:		
Factory rent	125,000	
Indirect labor	60,000	
Depreciation—machinery	50,000	
Insurance—factory	28,000	
Repairs and maintenance	18,000	
Miscellaneous factory costs.	150,000	
Total manufacturing overhead		431,000
Total manufacturing costs		1,019,000
Add: Work in process, January 1		45,000
		1,064,000
Deduct: Work in process, December 31 . . .		50,000
Cost of goods manufactured		$1,014,000

Step 3

Prepare a schedule of cost of goods sold using the schedule prepared in step 2.

BROWN CORPORATION
Schedule of Cost of Goods Sold
For the Year Ended December 31, 19x4

Finished goods inventory, January 1	$ 190,000
Cost of goods manufactured	1,014,000
Goods available for sale	1,204,000
Finished goods inventory, December 31 . . .	165,000
Cost of goods sold	$1,039,000

▶ **SELF-TEST**

Matching

You are given two listings: one consists of costs incurred and the other consists of cost classifications. For each cost incurred, you are to assign one or more cost classifications to a particular cost. You may use a cost classification more than once. The firm manufactures window frames and doors.

Costs Incurred

1. Factory superintendent's salary.
2. Wood for doors.
3. Power for factory.
4. Monthly rental charge of $200 plus 3 cents per copy rental charge for photocopying machine used in the office.
5. Stockroom department salaries.

6. Glue used on windows.
7. Nails used on doors.
8. Telephone bill for office.
9. Heat for factory.
10. Salaries paid to salespersons.

Cost Classifications

A. Noncontrollable cost at the window-frame department supervisor's level.
B. Controllable cost at the window-frame department supervisor's level.
C. Direct cost.
D. Direct labor.
E. Direct materials.
F. Fixed cost.
G. Indirect cost.
H. Inventoriable cost.
I. Manufacturing cost.
J. Opportunity cost.
K. Period cost.
L. Product cost.
M. Variable cost.
N. Partly fixed and partly variable.

▶ **QUESTIONS**

1. What is an expense?
2. What is a product cost for a merchandising establishment?
3. What is cost of goods sold for a merchandising business?
4. What is a cost objective?
5. What is a direct cost?
6. What is an indirect cost?
7. What do direct materials consist of?
8. What is direct labor?
9. What is manufacturing overhead? Give some examples of what is included in manufacturing overhead.
10. What is a product cost for a manufacturing establishment?
11. How does cost of goods sold for a manufacturing business differ from that of a merchandising business?
12. How does a manufacturer's balance sheet differ from that of a merchandiser?
13. What is prime cost?
14. What is conversion cost?
15. What is a period cost?
16. What is a variable cost? Give an example of a variable cost.
17. What is a fixed cost? Give an example of a fixed cost.
18. Is a cost always direct or indirect? Can it sometimes be one and at other times be the other? Explain.
19. Contrast controllable and noncontrollable costs. Use examples to illustrate your discussion.
20. What is responsibility accounting?
21. What is meant by differential cost? Why is it used?
22. What is an opportunity cost? Why is it important for managers to use this cost concept?
23. What is a sunk cost? Is it relevant for decision making? Explain.
24. A statement was made to the effect that a fixed cost is a variable cost per unit and a variable cost is a fixed cost per unit. Do you agree? Explain your answer by using an example to prove your argument.

25. When a firm requires additional manufacturing capacity, it has several options available. What are they? How should the firm evaluate them to arrive at the optimum decision?
26. Are service industries an important part of business? Explain.
27. Do service industries use the same cost objectives as manufacturing firms? Explain.
28. Hospitals use a cost objective called *patient-days*. What does this term mean?
29. What is a diagnostic-related group?

▶ **EXERCISES**   **E2–1**   **Cost Terms**

1. The term *differential cost* refers to
   a. The difference in total costs that results from selecting one alternative instead of another.
   b. The profit forgone by selecting one alternative instead of another.
   c. A cost that does not entail any dollar outlay but is relevant to the decision-making process.
   d. A cost that continues to be incurred even though there is no activity.
   e. A cost common to all alternatives in question and not clearly or practically allocable to any of the alternatives.
2. A sunk cost is
   a. A cost that may be saved by not adopting an alternative.
   b. A cost that may be shifted to the future with little or no effect on current operations.
   c. A cost that cannot be avoided because it has already been incurred.
   d. A cost that does not entail any dollar outlay but is relevant to the decision-making process.
   e. A cost common to all alternatives in question and not clearly or practically allocable to any of the alternatives.
3. An opportunity cost is
   a. The difference in total costs that results from selecting one alternative instead of another.
   b. The profit forgone by selecting one alternative instead of another.
   c. A cost that may be saved by not adopting an alternative.
   d. A cost that may be shifted to the future with little or no effect on current operations.
   e. A cost that cannot be avoided because it has already been incurred.
4. Those costs referred to as *controllable costs* are
   a. Costs that management decides to incur in the current period to enable the company to achieve objectives other than the filling of orders placed by customers.
   b. Costs that are likely to respond to the amount of attention devoted to them by a specified manager.
   c. Costs governed mainly by past decisions that established the present levels of operating and organizational capacity and that only change slowly in response to small changes in capacity.
   d. Costs that fluctuate in total in response to small changes in the rate of utilization of capacity.
   e. Costs that will be unaffected by current managerial decisions.
5. The term *conversion costs* refers to
   a. Manufacturing costs incurred to produce units of output.
   b. All costs associated with manufacturing other than direct labor costs and raw material costs.
   c. Costs associated with marketing, shipping, warehousing, and billing activities.

    d. The sum of direct labor and all factory overhead costs.

    e. The sum of raw material costs and direct labor costs.

6. The term *prime costs* refers to

    a. Manufacturing costs incurred to produce units of output.

    b. All costs associated with manufacturing other than direct labor costs and raw material costs.

    c. Costs that are predetermined and should be attained.

    d. The sum of direct labor costs and all factory overhead costs.

    e. The sum of raw material costs and direct labor costs.

7. Costs that are inventoriable are

    a. Manufacturing costs incurred to produce units of output.

    b. All costs associated with manufacturing other than direct labor costs and raw material costs.

    c. Costs associated with marketing, shipping, warehousing, and billing activities.

    d. The sum of direct labor costs and all factory overhead costs.

    e. The sum of raw material costs and direct labor costs.

8. The term *variable costs* refers to

    a. All costs that are likely to respond to the amount of attention devoted to them by a specified manager.

    b. All costs associated with marketing, shipping, warehousing, and billing activities.

    c. All costs that do not change in total for a given period of time and relevant range but become progressively smaller on a per-unit basis as volume increases.

    d. All manufacturing costs incurred to produce units of output.

    e. All costs that fluctuate in total in response to small changes in the rate of utilization of capacity.

(CMA Adapted)

E2–2   Cost Terms and Cost Behavior

Items 1 and 2 are based on the following data:

    Roja Corporation makes aluminum fasteners. Among Roja's 19x1 manufacturing costs were the following:

Wages and salaries:	
Machine operators	$ 80,000
Factory supervisors	30,000
Machine mechanics	20,000
Materials and supplies:	
Aluminum	$400,000
Machine parts	18,000
Lubricants for machines . . .	5,000

1. Direct labor amounted to

    a. $80,000.

    b. $100,000.

    c. $110,000.

    d. $130,000.

2. Direct materials amounted to

    a. $400,000.

    b. $405,000.

    c. $418,000.

    d. $423,000.

3. Which of the following best describes an opportunity cost?

    a. It is usually relevant but is not part of traditional accounting records.

    b. It is usually not relevant but is part of traditional accounting records.

c. It is usually relevant and is part of traditional accounting records.

d. It is usually not relevant and is not part of traditional accounting records.

Items 4 and 5 are based on the following data:

Morton Company's manufacturing costs for 19x1 were as follows:

Direct materials . . .	$300,000
Direct labor	400,000
Factory overhead:	
Variable.	80,000
Fixed	50,000

4. Prime cost totaled
   a. $300,000.
   b. $380,000.
   c. $700,000.
   d. $830,000.

5. Conversion cost totaled
   a. $400,000.
   b. $480,000.
   c. $530,000.
   d. $830,000.

6. Keller Company is a manufacturer of rivets, and its 19x1 manufacturing costs were as follows:

Direct materials and direct labor . . .	$800,000
Depreciation of machines	100,000
Rent for factory building.	60,000
Electricity to run machines.	35,000

How much of these costs should be included as product cost?
   a. $800,000.
   b. $835,000.
   c. $935,000.
   d. $995,000.

(AICPA Adapted)

E2–3   Cost of Goods Manufactured and Sold

A partial trial balance of the Block Corporation as of December 31, 19x4, follows:

Direct materials inventory, January 1 . . .	$ 72,000
Work in process inventory, January 1 . . .	36,000
Finished goods inventory, January 1	160,000
Purchases of direct materials	180,000
Direct labor	264,000
Indirect labor	358,000
Factory rent.	90,000
Office rent	120,000
Depreciation—machinery	54,000
Depreciation—office equipment	60,000
Insurance—factory.	9,000
Salespersons' salaries	36,000
Repairs and maintenance—machinery . . .	40,000
Miscellaneous factory costs	28,000
Miscellaneous office costs.	144,000
The December 31 inventories:	
Direct materials	40,000
Work in process	45,000
Finished goods	150,000

Required   *a.* Prepare a schedule of cost of goods manufactured.

b. Prepare a schedule of cost of goods sold.

E2–4   **Cost Classification**

Classify the following costs as either PR (product cost) or PE (period cost).

1. Sweeping compound for the factory.
2. Light and heat for the factory.
3. Factory superintendent's salary.
4. Sales manager's travel costs.
5. Inspection salaries.
6. Receiving department salaries.
7. Salaries of stockroom personnel.
8. Salaries of finished goods warehouse personnel.
9. Payroll taxes on factory workers' salaries.
10. Night guards' salaries for factory building.
11. Telephone for factory.
12. Power.
13. Small tools—hammers, screwdrivers, etc.
14. Bookkeeping salaries to maintain customers' accounts receivable.
15. Computer rental to perform cost accounting function.
16. Computer rental to maintain finished goods inventory control system.
17. Travel cost for the vice president of manufacturing to a professional convention.
18. Salespersons' meeting cost to learn about the company's new product.

E2–5   **Cost Classification**

Classify the following costs as either V (variable), F (fixed), P (part fixed, part variable).

1. Sweeping compound for the factory.
2. Light and heat for the factory.
3. Factory superintendent's salary.
4. Factory line supervisor—two lines per supervisor.
5. Inspection salaries.
6. Receiving department salaries.
7. Salaries of stockroom personnel.
8. Salaries of finished goods warehouse personnel.
9. Payroll taxes on factory workers' salaries.
10. Night guards' salaries for factory building.
11. Telephone for factory.
12. Power.
13. Small tools—hammers, screwdrivers, etc.
14. Rental charges for machinery rented during busy periods.
15. Computer rental to perform cost accounting function.
16. Direct materials for product B.
17. Repair and maintenance of factory machinery.
18. Photocopying machine rental. The monthly charge is $300 per month plus 3 cents per copy made.
19. Salaries of management accountants.

E2–6   **Cost Classification**

Classify the following costs as either D (direct) or I (indirect). The frame of reference is product B, and the company manufactures three products: A, B, and C.

1. Sweeping compound for the factory.
2. Light and heat for the factory.
3. Factory superintendent's salary.
4. Factory line supervisor—two lines, both producing product B.
5. Inspection salaries—inspectors work only on product B.
6. Receiving department salaries.
7. Salaries of stockroom personnel.
8. Shipping cartons—product B is not commingled with A or C.
9. Payroll taxes as a percentage of direct labor for product B.
10. Night guards' salaries for factory building.
11. Telephone for factory.
12. Power.
13. Small tools—hammers, screwdrivers, etc.
14. Rental charges for machinery rented during busy periods. The machinery is used on all products.
15. Computer rental to perform cost accounting function.
16. Direct materials for product B.

E2–7   Cost of Goods Manufactured and Sold

A partial trial balance of the Brett Corporation as of December 31, 19x4, follows:

Direct materials inventory, January 1	$117,000
Work in process inventory, January 1	52,000
Finished goods inventory, January 1	210,000
Purchases of direct materials	332,000
Direct labor	403,000
Indirect labor	90,000
Factory rent	132,000
Office rent	70,000
Depreciation—machinery	60,000
Depreciation—office equipment	20,000
Insurance—factory	30,000
Salespersons' salaries	130,000
Repairs and maintenance—machinery	20,000
Miscellaneous factory costs	175,000
Miscellaneous office costs	60,000

The December 31 inventories:	
Direct materials	105,000
Work in process	60,000
Finished goods	190,000

Required   *a.* Prepare a schedule of cost of goods manufactured.

b. Prepare a schedule of cost of goods sold.

E2–8   Cost Classifications

You are given two listings; one consists of costs incurred and the other consists of cost classifications. For each cost incurred, you are to assign one or more cost classifications to a particular cost. You may use a cost classification more than once. The firm manufactures pillows and comforters.

Costs Incurred

1. Factory superintendent's salary.
2. Foam rubber for pillows.
3. Power for factory.
4. Monthly rental charge of $200 for photocopying machine used in the office.
5. Receiving department salaries.
6. Thread used to sew pillowcases.
7. Thread used to sew comforters.
8. Telephone bill for factory.

9. Electricity for office.
10. Commissions paid to salespersons.
11. Salaries of management accountants.
12. Independent accountants' audit fee.
13. Shipping cartons for pillows.
14. Factory rent.
15. Sewing machine operator's salary for pillow cases.

Cost Classifications

A. Differential cost
B. Controllable cost at the level of the vice president for manufacturing.
C. Direct cost.
D. Direct labor.
E. Direct materials.
F. Fixed cost.
G. Indirect cost.
H. Inventoriable cost.
 I. Manufacturing cost.
J. Opportunity cost.
K. Period cost.
L. Product cost.
M. Variable cost.
N. Partly fixed and partly variable.

► **PROBLEMS**   **P2–9**   **Preparation of Schedule of Cost of Goods Manufactured and Income Statement**

The president of Carter Manufacturing Company has a son who just graduated from high school and does not plan to go to college. Carter offered his son a job in the accounting department of the firm, and his son accepted. Since the son had had some bookkeeping in high school, he felt qualified to prepare the income statement for the six months ended June 30, 19x5. His prepared statement is as follows:

CARTER MANUFACTURING COMPANY
Income Statement
For the Six Months Ended June 30, 19x5

Sales		$2,320,000
Costs of goods sold:		
Beginning inventories:		
Direct materials	$ 115,000	
Work in process	47,000	
Finished goods	108,000	
Direct material purchases	615,000	
Direct labor	475,000	
Rent	318,000	
Light, heat, and power	83,000	
Telephone	31,000	
Depreciation	268,000	
Indirect labor	123,000	
Marketing and administrative salaries	156,000	
Insurance	26,000	
Miscellaneous manufacturing overhead	47,000	
Miscellaneous marketing and administrative cost . . .	27,000	
Total	$2,439,000	
Less: Ending direct materials inventory	79,000	2,360,000
Net profit (loss)		$ (40,000)

The following additional information is available:

1. The ending inventory of work in process amounted to $187,000, and the ending inventory of finished goods amounted to $309,000.
2. The following costs should be allocated:

	Manufacturing	Period
Rent	65%	35%
Light, heat, and power	55%	45%
Telephone	60%	40%
Insurance	75%	25%
Depreciation	85%	15%

Carter is concerned that his son's income statement shows a loss for the period. This is the first loss in the company's history.

Required   *a.* Prepare a schedule of cost of goods manufactured in proper format. Make any corrections that are needed.

b. Prepare a corrected income statement using the statement from part *(a)*.

P2–10   **Matching of Cost Terms**

Prentiss Company manufactures children's clothing. A number of costs are listed in column A. A number of cost terms discussed in this chapter are listed in column B.

Column A	Column B
A. Fabric	1. Variable cost
B. Thread	2. Fixed cost
C. Factory superintendent's salary	3. Product cost
D. Night guard's salary	4. Period cost
E. Direct labor	5. Direct cost
F. Factory power	6. Indirect cost
G. Factory rent	7. Prime cost
H. Heat for the office	8. Conversion cost
I. Salespersons' commissions	9. Opportunity cost
J. Bookkeeping salaries	10. Part variable, part fixed cost
K. Depreciation of office equipment	11. Marketing cost
L. Sales manager's salary	12. Administrative cost
M. The president's salary	13. Manufacturing overhead
N. Shipping cartons	
O. Factory telephone	

Required   Match cost terms from column B to each cost listed in column A. The cost objective for a direct or indirect cost is a pair of boy's denim pants. The cost terms in column B may be used more than once, and each cost listed in column A may have more than one cost term assigned to it.

P2–11   **Cost of Goods Manufactured and Income Statement**

Selected accounts from the trial balance of Powell Corporation as of December 31, 19x3, appear below:

Administrative salaries	$ 175,500
Advertising	49,500
Depreciation, machinery	76,500
Depreciation, office equipment	13,500
Depreciation, shipping equipment	18,000
Direct labor	814,500
Direct material purchases	324,000
Factory supplies used	31,500
Factory bookkeeping	36,000
Freight on direct materials	13,500
Heat and power, factory	49,500
Indirect labor	135,000
Insurance, factory	36,000

Inventories:

Direct materials, January 1	112,500
Direct materials, December 31	139,500
Work in process, January 1	49,500
Work in process, December 31	45,000
Finished goods, January 1	225,000
Finished goods, December 31	184,500
Miscellaneous factory	274,500
Office salaries	148,500
Rent, factory—80%; sales offices—10%; administrative—10%	301,500
Repairs to machinery	99,000
Sales	4,500,000
Sales discounts	63,000
Sales salaries	351,000
Superintendence, factory	148,500
Telephone, factory—50%; marketing—25%; administrative—25%	99,000

Required   *a.* Prepare a statement of cost of goods manufactured.
              b. Prepare an income statement.

P2–12   Cost of Goods Sold and Income Statement

Selected accounts from the trial balance of Colin Corporation as of December 31, 19x3, appear below:

Administrative salaries	$ 250,000
Advertising	94,500
Depreciation, office equipment	27,000
Depreciation, shipping equipment	36,000
Purchases of finished goods	650,000
Freight in on purchases	12,000
Heat and electric, marketing—40%, administrative—60% . . .	9,000
Insurance, marketing—70%, administrative—30%	24,000

Inventories:

Finished goods, January 1	112,500
Finished goods, December 31	164,500
Office salaries	48,000
Rent, sales offices—40%, administrative—60%	180,000
Sales	2,500,000
Sales discounts	63,000
Sales salaries	225,000
Telephone, marketing—60%, administrative—40%	99,000

Required   *a.* Prepare a schedule of cost of goods sold.
              b. Prepare an income statement.

P2–13   Missing Data—Cost of Goods Manufactured and Sold

Supply the missing data for each company listed below:

	Companies			
	A	**B**	**C**	**D**
Sales	$730,000	$?	$375,000	$360,000
Direct materials inventory—beginning	65,700	38,500	18,750	?
Purchases of direct materials	102,200	77,000	45,000	36,000
Direct materials inventory—ending	?	49,500	26,250	14,400
Direct labor	182,500	?	48,750	57,600
Manufacturing overhead	146,000	121,000	75,000	50,400
Work in process—beginning.	138,700	93,500	?	18,000
Work in process—ending	116,800	77,000	45,000	18,000
Finished goods—beginning	146,000	?	48,750	25,200
Finished goods—ending	167,900	115,500	?	28,800
Cost of goods manufactured.	?	308,000	202,500	?
Cost of goods sold	?	247,500	?	162,000
Gross margin	313,900	302,500	157,500	?

P2–14   Missing Data—Cost of Goods Manufactured and Sold

Supply the missing data for each company listed below:

	Companies			
	A	**B**	**C**	**D**
Sales	$300,000	$140,000	$?	$480,000
Direct materials inventory—beginning	27,000	9,800	5,500	?
Purchases of direct materials	42,000	19,600	13,200	48,000
Direct materials inventory—ending	?	12,600	7,700	19,200
Direct labor	75,000	18,200	?	76,800
Manufacturing overhead	60,000	30,800	22,000	67,200
Work in process—beginning.	57,000	?	18,700	24,000
Work in process—ending	48,000	19,600	13,200	24,000
Finished goods—beginning	60,000	18,200	?	33,600
Finished goods—ending	69,000	?	23,100	38,400
Cost of goods manufactured.	?	75,600	59,400	?
Cost of goods sold	?	?	63,800	216,000
Gross margin	129,000	77,000	46,200	?

▶ **CASE**   **C2–15   Preparation of Income Statement and Statement of Cost of Goods Manufactured from Fragmented Information**

Dataless Manufacturing Company discovered that the company's bookkeeper failed to keep any records for the first six months of 19x4. However, the firm's independent auditors and the firm had certain information in their files that enabled management to provide you with the following:

1. Sales revenues for the first six months of 19x4—$4,500,000.
2. Inventories—January 1, 19x4:

Direct materials	. . .	$223,000
Work in process	. . .	179,000
Finished goods .	. . .	531,000

3. The average percentage relationships for 19x2 and 19x3 are as follows:
   a. Gross margin as a percent of sales—45 percent.
   b. Direct labor is 40 percent of conversion cost and 75 percent of prime cost.
4. For the first half of 19x3, marketing costs amounted to $450,000 and administrative costs amounted to $560,000. An increase of 15 percent is anticipated for period costs in 19x4.
5. A physical count of all inventories was made at June 30, 19x4. The estimated dollar amounts are:

Direct materials . . .	$168,000
Work in process . . .	139,000
Finished goods	951,000

Required a. Prepare an estimated income statement for the six months ended June 30, 19x4.

b. Prepare an estimated statement of cost of goods manufactured for the six months ended June 30, 19x4. (*Hint:* First prepare the income statement using the available estimated information. Estimate the gross margin, the cost of goods sold, and, finally, the cost of goods manufactured. Second, after you have determined the cost of goods manufactured, use an algebraic equation to determine the amounts for direct materials used, direct labor, and manufacturing overhead.)

► **ETHICAL BEHAVIOR CASES**   C2–16   Ward Corporation is a manufacturer of cleaning products with three wholly owned subsidiaries that are operated as separate divisions. Ward's corporate headquarters are located in an industrial park in a Chicago suburb. The Industrial Products Division is located in the same industrial park but in its own building. The other two divisions are located in Milwaukee and Indianapolis.

The corporation's operating and financial records are maintained on a mainframe computer at corporate headquarters. Each division has a small accounting department that submits operating and financial data to corporate headquarters on a regular basis.

The Profit Planning Department at corporate headquarters is responsible for preparing special analyses and reports for Ward. To facilitate its work, the Profit Planning Department has linked a microcomputer to the mainframe to download data. The special analyses are prepared using these data and a purchased spreadsheet software package.

Beth Simons recently joined the Industrial Products Division as an accounting analyst. Simons is proficient in the use of microcomputers and spreadsheet software. She has been given an assignment to work with Doug Laird, marketing manager of the Industrial Products Division, to develop analyses and reports. One week into the assignment, she suggested that the microcomputers used in the Marketing Department for word processing could be valuable analytical tools if spreadsheet software were acquired. Laird knows little about computers, but he has received some of the special analyses prepared by the Profit Planning Department at corporate headquarters. Laird wants Simons to try her idea but has suggested that she first borrow the software from the Profit Planning Department.

Simons has approached Tom Field, manager of Profit Planning, regarding the use of the software package. Field was very sympathetic to Simons' request, but the software is used extensively in his department. Therefore, he did not want to loan the original system disk. Furthermore, the software was copy protected. However, Field did have a utility program that allowed him to make back-up copies of most copy protected software. Since there was no back-up of the spreadsheet software, Field decided to make a copy and give it to Simons for her use. Simons indicated that she planned to use the software during regular business hours.

Upon giving the copy to Simons, Field said, "This is my only copy but you may borrow it for your use only. Don't give it to anyone else. Once you have tried the software for your assignment, you must return this copy to me. Industrial Product's Accounting or Marketing Department will have to purchase its own copy."

Field did not give Simons a copy of the licensing agreement that accompanied the original software package. The license agreement reproduced below was affixed to the original sealed disk package. While Simons was not aware of the specific provisions of the licensing agreement that pertained to the borrowed software, she knew that licensing agreements accompanied computer software packages.

▶ Software License Agreement

IMPORTANT: Please read this agreement before opening the envelope. Opening the disk envelope indicates the user's acceptance of the agreement to abide by these terms.

1. The software may be used on any compatible hardware that the purchaser owns or uses.
2. Back-up copies of the software can be made provided that these copies are for exclusive use of the purchaser and only one copy of the software is in use at any one time.
3. No alterations to the software or the documentation are permitted.
4. The software may not be distributed to others on a permanent or temporary basis.
5. This license and the software may be transferred to another party provided that all copies of the software and documentation are transferred and the original party ceases to use the software after the transfer.

Required   *a.* Based on the stipulations enumerated in the license agreement for the spreadsheet software, did Tom Field violate the agreement when he
   (1) Made a copy of the software disk using the utility program?
   (2) Gave Beth Simons the copy of the software disk he had made?

Explain your answer in each case.

   b. Without prejudice to your answer in part *(a)*, assume that Tom Field did violate the license agreement when he copied the software disk and gave it to Beth Simons. Identify the alternatives that Field could have employed to determine the applicability of the spreadsheet software to the application of the Marketing Department of the Industrial Products Division without violating the license agreement.
   c. Management accountants are expected to abide by the ethical standards set forth in *Statements on Management Accounting Number 1C,* "Standards of Ethical Conduct for Management Accountants." Were any provisions of this Statement violated by
   (1) Field when he copied the software disk and gave Simons the copy for her use?
   (2) Simons when she used the copy of the software to determine its usefulness in the applications for the Marketing Department of the Industrial Products Division?

Explain your answer in each case, being sure to identify the standard(s) that is (are) violated or explaining why the statement was not violated.

(CMA Adapted)

C2–17   Belco Manufacturing builds and distributes industrial storage racks. Belco's earnings increased sharply in 19x4, and bonuses were paid to the management staff for the first time in several years. The bonuses were based in part on Belco's reported earnings.

Jim Kern, vice president of Finance, was pleased with Belco's 19x4 earnings and thought that the pressure to show financial results would ease. However, Ellen North, Belco's president, told Kern that she saw no reason why the 19x5 bonuses should not be double those of 19x4. As a result, Kern felt pressure to increase reported earnings in order to ensure increased bonuses.

Kern met with Bill Keller of Pristeel, Inc., a primary vendor of Belco's manufacturing supplies and equipment. Kern and Keller have been close business contacts for many years. Kern asked Keller to identify all of Belco's purchases (supplies and equipment) as equipment on Pristeel's sales invoices. The reason Kern gave for his request was that Belco's president had imposed stringent budget constraints on operating expenses but not on capital expenditures. Kern planned to capitalize the purchase of supplies and defer the expense recognition for these items. This procedure would increase reported earnings leading to increased bonuses. Keller agreed to do as Kern had asked.

While analyzing the second quarter financial statements, Gary Wood, Belco's controller, noticed a large decrease in supplies expense from one year ago. Wood reviewed the Supplies Expense account and noticed that only equipment but no supplies had been purchased from Pristeel, a major source for supplies. Wood, who reports to Kern, immediately brought this to Kern's attention.

Kern told Wood of President North's high expectations and of the arrangement made with Bill Keller of Pristeel. Wood told Kern that his action was an improper accounting treatment for the supplies purchased from Pristeel. Wood requested that he be allowed to correct the accounts and urged that the arrangement with Pristeel be discontinued. Kern refused the request and told Wood not to become involved in the arrangement with Pristeel.

After clarifying the situation in a confidential discussion with an objective and qualified peer within Belco, Wood arranged to meet with North, Belco's president. At the meeting, Wood disclosed the arrangement Kern had made with Pristeel.

Required
a. Explain why the use of alternative accounting methods to manipulate reported earnings is unethical.
b. Is Gary Wood, Belco's controller, correct in saying that the supplies purchased from Pristeel, Inc., were accounted for improperly? Explain your answer.
c. Without prejudice to your answer to part *(b)*, assume that Jim Kern's arrangement with Pristeel, Inc., was in violation of the Standards of Ethical Conduct for Management Accountants. Discuss whether the actions of Gary Wood, Belco's controller, were appropriate or inappropriate.

(CMA Adapted)

C2–18   Mywrite Corporation designs and builds sophisticated machinery for manufacturers of microcircuitry. The rapidity of technological advancement in this industry creates a continuing demand for highly complex, well-developed production equipment. Competition has grown in intensity in the struggle to meet market demands. Mywrite has managed to attract many bright engineers and always seems to be looking for talented people for all of its departments.

Ted Raull, cost accounting manager, has been with Mywrite for six months. He had been with a competitor previously, but that company had failed to receive sufficient contracts to stay in business. He considered himself fortunate that Mywrite happened to be looking for cost accountants and applied for the job a few months before his old company was dissolved. Raull's initial impression of Mywrite's costing procedures was that they were not as good as those used by his former employer. Thus, he thought he could contribute toward improving the costing system.

Mark Philips, human resource manager, has asked Raull to interview a job applicant for a position in Mywrite's finance area. Philips indicated that the employee who usually conducts such interviews is attending an out-of-town convention. "This applicant is an excellent prospect. You're in a better position to evaluate the candidate anyway, Ted. Who knows, you may get some good information that will help us out. He's currently employed by Vestron, our biggest competitor," said Philips.

Raull was flattered at first that he was asked to conduct the interview, but he then realized that there was no opening in the finance area. Raull asked a friend in the Human Resource Department why Mywrite had advertised for a position that did not exist. His friend said, "We do it all the time. The ads attract people from our competitors, and in the course of the employment interview, they spill all kinds of useful information trying to impress us with their capabilities. We just listen and encourage them. Sometimes we even hire one. It sure keeps us informed and keeps us abreast of the competition. Vestron apparently has a financing arrangement that we'd like to know about."

Raull's reaction was that perhaps he and others at his old company had been used. In fact, he thinks that Mywrite's actions are unethical.

Required   *a.* Explain why Mywrite Corporation's practice of interviewing people for nonexistent positions in order to obtain information is unethical.

b. Ted Raull is trying to decide what action he should take with regard to the request of Mark Philips to conduct the interview of the Vestron employee.
  (1) Identify the alternatives that would be appropriate for Raull to take in this situation.
  (2) Recommend the alternative that you identified in part *(b)*(1) that you believe Raull should take and explain why.

c. Discuss the responsibility, if any, that Ted Raull has to eliminate the practice of Mywrite's Human Resource Management Department of interviewing people for nonexistent positions.

(CMA Adapted)

C2–19   Curry Company has been a manufacturer of office machines for more than forty years. Curry was both innovative and aggressive during the era of mechanical office machines, and by the first half of its corporate life, it had a 35 percent share of its market. However, the company was slow to develop electronic office machines.

Curry's market share was reduced by one half because its competitors introduced electronic machines. This resulted in excess capacity in both of its plants and a shortage of capacity at many of its competitors.

Curry reacted to this situation by retooling both plants. The main plant has been reorganized as the Cojeen Division and now produces a line of simple, low-cost, high-quality electronic office machines. The other plant has been reorganized as the Belding Division and produces the consoles, racks, tables, and trays used with office computers and word processors. Belding Division derives 80 percent of its sales from Curry's former competitors. Top management at Curry, in addition to reorganizing the company, became extremely cost conscious and implemented a freeze on base salaries as part of its cost-reduction programs.

Ken Bender, Belding Division controller, has become aware that Susan Stans, Belding sales manager, has routinely claimed what appeared to be excessive and unsubstantiated travel expenses. The expense claims are regularly approved by Bob Porter, Belding division manager. Bender is concerned about the possible consequences to the division and asked Porter about this situation.

Porter, in the privacy of his office, told Bender that, "In the two years that Sue Stans has been the sales manager, we have not lost a single important customer. She knows our customers' business and has worked closely with them so they will remain customers. I can't authorize a salary increase because of the freeze so I told her that the company wouldn't look too closely at her expense accounts for a while."

Porter also asked Bender to help Ron Warren, production manager, ''by making whatever entries are needed to increase the gross margin percentage.'' This would increase Warren's bonus, which is based in part on gross margin percentage. Porter added, ''If these key people are not given monetary increases in some way they may leave us, something I want to avoid at all costs.''

Required
a. Ken Bender has already approached Bob Porter regarding the padded expense account of Susan Stans.
　(1) Identify other alternative courses of action Bender should consider taking.
　(2) Select the course of action you think Bender should take and explain why you selected this course of action.
b. Explain why Ken Bender should refuse the division manager's request to manipulate the gross margin percentage.
c. Assume Bob Porter insists on manipulating the gross margin percentage in order to help Ron Warren.
　(1) Identify the alternative courses of action that Ken Bender should consider taking.
　(2) Select the course of action you think Bender should take and explain why you selected this course of action.

(CMA Adapted)

C2–20 Kazunas Industries is a manufacturer of auto parts with 70 percent of its sales to the large domestic auto companies and 30 percent to auto part retailers. Kazunas' sales to retailers are increasing at a 20 percent annual rate, largely due to the increasing average age of U.S. automobiles. However, sales to domestic auto companies are decreasing because many of the parts are not compatible with new auto technology.

Domestic auto companies currently are decreasing the number of their supplies as they seek better inventory management and quality control, and Kazunas Industries is a prime candidate for deletion. Also, the sales to retailers have a built-in decline as old technology automobiles reach the end of their life cycles.

Kazunas has decided to build new production facilities and has applied for a $20 million loan from Commerce Bank to finance the modernization. Loan conditions were agreed to in a meeting between Peter Lisko, Kazunas' vice president of finance, and David Pearson, a loan officer for the bank. The loan conditions limit Kazunas' cash dividend payments to 50 percent of net income and provide for Commerce Bank's approval of several types of transactions should the current ratio fall below 1.5 : 1. The terms of the agreement were approved by Commerce Bank's Loan Committee, and Kazunas Industries received the cash on August 15, 19x3.

Joan Miraldi, Kazunas' controller, received instructions from Peter Lisko concerning the preparation of financial statements for the year ended May 31, 19x4. After reviewing the preliminary statements, Lisko instructed Miraldi to capitalize some ordinary repairs and to charge some unrelated maintenance labor cost to the installation of new equipment. Lisko also directed Miraldi not to record a May 30 purchase and to omit it from the inventory.

Miraldi met with Lisko to tell him that she believes these actions are contrary to proper accounting practice and may materially misstate the financial statements. Lisko told Miraldi that he did not think these actions violated generally accepted accounting principles and that these principles were just guidelines anyway. He explained the loan conditions to her and said, ''The loan conditions were sweeteners suggested by the bank's loan officer to get the loan application by the bank's loan committee. We are bound by the loan conditions but not by generally accepted accounting principles. Therefore, I want you to do as I told you so that these loan conditions are met!''

Required   *a.* Discuss the ethical considerations that Joan Miraldi should recognize in this situation.

b. Identify possible courses of action that are available to Joan Miraldi in this situation.

c. Recommend the course of action you would follow.

   (1) Explain the reasons for recommending this course of action.

   (2) Discuss the consequences, if any, of this course of action.

(CMA Adapted)

▶ **ANSWERS TO SELF-TEST**

1. A, F, G, H, I, L.
2. B, C, E, H, I, L, M.
3. B, G, H, I, L, M.
4. A, G, K, N.
5. A, G, H, I, L, N.
6. B, G, H, I, L, M.
7. A, G, H, I, L, M.
8. A, G, K, N.
9. A, F, G, H, I, L.
10. A, F, G, K.

Cost Behavior and Cost Estimation

After reading this chapter, you should be able to:

1. Explain why decision makers must understand cost behavior.
2. Define the three basic patterns of cost behavior: variable costs, fixed costs, and mixed costs.
3. Distinguish between semivariable costs and step-variable costs.
4. Explain why mixed costs must be separated into their fixed and variable components.
5. Use account analysis, engineering cost analysis, and the high-low method to analyze mixed costs and separate them into their fixed and variable components.
6. Use scatter diagrams to analyze mixed costs and separate them into their fixed and variable components.
7. Explain why a contribution margin income statement is more useful to managers than a traditional income statement.
8. Prepare a contribution margin income statement and use it to project future-oriented data for decision making.
9. Use the least-squares method to analyze mixed costs and separate them into their fixed and variable components.

► **INTERVIEW**

Michael V. Allison
Business Manager,
College Editorial
Richard D. Irwin, Inc.

Q. *When analyzing mixed costs, do you use the high-low method or the least-squares method? Why did you select this method?*

A. I have actually used both methods, depending on the time and resources available. For instance, when preparing the financial analysis of a major plant expansion proposal, the proposed costs would be separated into the fixed and variable components based on historical departmental costs and activity, using a computerized regression model. These results would certainly be compared to the standard cost fixed/variable "splits" and major differences reconciled.

I've limited the use of the high-low method to quick "what-if"-type situations when a computer is unavailable. These tend to be "brainstorming" sessions for which just approximations are necessary and formal plans are not developed.

Q. *Do you use a contribution format income statement? If so, for what purposes do you use it?*

A. The contribution format income statement is always used in our organization for cost analysis and decision making. A few examples are:

1. Product pricing proposals.
2. Product-line acquisitions and divestitures.
3. Make versus buy decisions.
4. Product line profitabilities.
5. Capital budgeting.

For instance, when two or more products are packaged together at sale prices, the contribution margin is analyzed to determine the incremental profitability to the company as a result of these actions. The fixed costs remain constant and are not affected by decisions to increase volume and revenue.

The contribution margin is very critical in our acquisition and divestiture analysis. We have had a number of products that have low sales volume but that require a great deal of time and resources to manage.

The contribution format helps us identify these product lines and establish action plans.

For example, once a product line is discontinued, the related contribution margin will no longer be available to help cover fixed costs. By using the contribution format, we can determine what fixed cost savings would be necessary to make this product decision viable. Without the proper analysis, these decisions could result in a lower profit margin (percent to sales) than if the product line were continued.

▶ Fixed and variable costs were discussed in the preceding chapter. These costs are explored further in this chapter because their behavior patterns affect many managerial decisions, including setting of selling prices, entering into new markets, introducing new products, eliminating existing products, investing in additional and/ or replacement plant facilities, curtailing activity, and reaching make-or-buy decisions.

Cost behavior is the way a cost reacts to a change in business activity. It is essential for managers to understand cost behavior patterns if they are to accurately predict how a cost will react to a contemplated change in business activity. The failure to project cost effects when making a decision—or incorrect projections—may have serious consequences for a firm. Of course, as with any prediction, a certain amount of error is to be expected. But fortunately, the cost-estimation techniques we will study in this chapter provide managers with reasonably accurate data for use in decision making. ◀

▶ COST BEHAVIOR

L.O. 1
Cost behavior and decision making

According to economic theory, **marginal cost**—the cost to produce one additional unit—does not increase in proportion to production or in a straight line when plotted on a graph. Rather, it increases disproportionately or as a curve on a graph. For example, consider the case of a furniture maker that is too small to afford automated equipment. If the company has only one employee, he would more than likely perform some of the cutting, planing, and sandpapering by hand. If another employee is hired and the factory is large enough to accommodate both workers, output would be doubled but costs would be less than doubled, because such costs as factory rent, heat, and light would not increase. Thus, as production increases, output increases faster than costs—a curvilinear relationship.

If the firm reaches its optimal size and the factory is fully utilized, operations that were formerly performed manually can now be performed on machinery that was unaffordable when the firm was of suboptimal size. Changes in output affect only variable costs, while fixed costs remain constant. At the optimal level of production, output increases almost proportionately with costs—an approximately linear relationship. Once the optimal size is reached, further increases in production require paying employees an overtime premium. In addition, employee fatigue may result in less than normal productivity during the overtime hours. When this occurs, output increases more slowly than the rise in costs—a curvilinear relationship. Most firms strive to operate at their optimal level of activity. Of course, it is not always possible to operate at exactly the same level. Thus, a firm will choose a span of activity levels near its optimal level called the **relevant range.** A firm usually operates within its relevant range, although production may occasionally vary from this norm.

Variable Costs

L.O. 2
Cost-behavior patterns

In Chapter 2, we defined **variable costs** as costs that vary, in total, in relation to output, although the per-unit cost is constant within a given range of activity. A key aspect of the variable cost definition is the fact that a change in a variable cost always corresponds to a change in a related item or event. An item or event that has a cause-and-effect relationship with the incurrence of a variable cost is called an **activity base.** The variable cost may then be measured in terms of its activity base. For example, in this chapter we will

▶ **ILLUSTRATION 3-1**   Variable Cost Graph

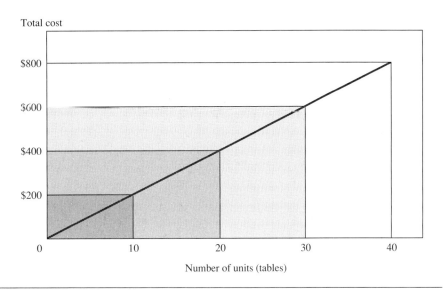

assume that a variable cost changes in direct proportion to sales volume. Therefore, if sales volume is expected to increase by 10 percent in a given period, a corresponding increase of 10 percent in variable cost is also expected. Another common activity base is units of production. Thus, if a company expects to produce 8 percent more hand-held calculators in August, it can expect its *total* cost for microchips *in August* to increase by 8 percent.

Let us assume that the cost of direct materials for manufacturing a table amounts to $20 per table. If a graph were constructed for the direct materials cost of the tables using a cost of $20 each, it would appear as in Illustration 3-1.

The graph in Illustration 3-1 may be summarized as follows:

Number of Units	Total Cost	Cost per Unit
10	$200	$20
20	400	20
30	600	20
40	800	20

The important point to remember is that *a variable cost has a constant cost per unit*. Other examples of variable costs are direct labor, electric power used to operate machinery, and commissions paid to salespeople.

The most common activity bases are sales volume and units of production, but there are also many others. For example, the variable cost of gasoline used in a delivery truck may be measured in terms of the number of miles driven. Other examples of variable costs and related activity bases are (1) clerical salaries in a college registrar's office measured by the number of students enrolled at the college, (2) nurses' salaries in a hospital measured by

▶ **ILLUSTRATION 3-2**   Fixed Cost Graph

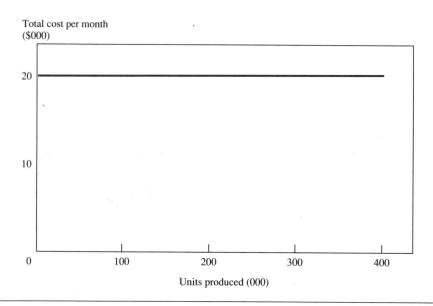

the number of patients treated, and (3) billing department salaries measured by the number of lines typed on sales invoices.

Managers must be familiar with activity bases and how they affect cost behavior. For example, managers considering the expansion of their firm's business not only must consider the increased revenues and product costs, but also must calculate the increased cost in the billing department that will result from the need to type additional invoices.

Fixed Costs

A **fixed cost** is a cost that remains constant *in total* within a given range of activity and period of time. Within the limits of an activity range, for example, 0 units to 400,000 units, per-unit fixed costs decrease with increased output. Let us assume that a firm has a factory that is capable of producing 400,000 units per month and the firm pays $20,000 per month rent for the factory premises. Illustration 3-2 presents a graph that portrays the factory rent per month within the given range of activity.

Although the monthly cost for factory rent is constant in total, it is not constant on a per-unit basis. This is shown in Illustration 3-3. As production increases, the cost per unit decreases. Managers strive to operate their firms at or near full capacity, because the fixed cost per unit is minimized at this point.

When a firm's output must be increased beyond its current capacity—in this case, beyond 400,000 units per day—several courses of action are available. A firm can (1) utilize its present workers on an overtime basis, (2) hire a new staff and begin a two-shift operation, or (3) rent an additional factory building and employ an additional staff to operate two factories concurrently. The best course of action will depend on whether increased capacity

▶ **ILLUSTRATION 3-3**   Analysis of Rent per Unit

Units Produced	Aggregate Cost per Month	Cost per Unit
1	$20,000	$20,000.00
10,000	20,000	2.00
100,000	20,000	.20
400,000	20,000	.05

is needed over a short or long period. If the need is short term, the cost of operating a second shift should be compared with the cost of operating the existing staff on an overtime basis. If the need is long term, then the cost of constructing and operating an additional factory should be compared with the cost of a second shift and the cost overtime. Other factors, such as expected productivity and employee morale, must also be considered. If the company decides to rent another factory with a capacity of 400,000 units per day, the total cost of factory rent and other fixed costs may be somewhat more or less than twice the current fixed costs, depending on the rent and other costs in the second factory. This illustrates that fixed costs remain the same only for a particular range of production. This range is usually called the **relevant range** of production. A firm has only one relevant range in a given time period and rarely, if ever, operates outside its relevant range.

Committed Costs   Fixed costs that continue for long periods of time are called **committed costs.** Once made, these costs are not reversible in the short term. An example of a committed cost would be the cost of constructing a factory building. A long-term lease for an office building would also be a committed cost, as would be the construction of a computerized extruding mill. However, if instead of constructing a factory, an equipped factory is leased for one year at a time, the rent would be a discretionary cost rather than a committed cost.

Discretionary Costs   Discretionary costs are also fixed costs, but they differ from committed costs in that they are reversible after short periods of time. Advertising would be a discretionary cost because it is usually contracted for over short periods of time. Other examples of discretionary costs include supervisory salaries and security guards' salaries. When evaluating whether to invest in expensive labor-saving equipment—a committed cost—or to perform the tasks using direct labor, the distinction between committed and discretionary costs becomes important. At present, there is a trend toward converting labor-intensive tasks to machine-intensive tasks. Such a decision may impose huge losses on a business if it must be reversed. A sudden change in consumer demand, as occurs in the automobile and steel industries, may cause a firm to have huge committed costs and idle capacity that cannot be reversed in the short term. But discretionary costs, such as direct labor, can be reversed in the short term by laying off unnecessary employees.

▶ **ILLUSTRATION 3-4**   Graph of the Semivariable Cost of Truck Rental

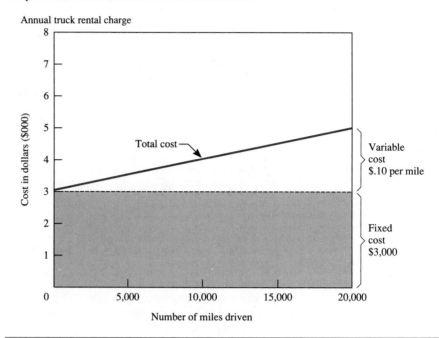

Mixed Costs

Many costs cannot be neatly classified as either fixed or variable because they show characteristics of both. Such costs, because they contain both fixed and variable elements, are called **mixed costs.** Mixed costs may be subdivided into two categories—semivariable costs and step-variable costs.

L.O. 3
Semivariable and
step-variable costs

Semivariable Costs   A **semivariable cost** is closely related to a variable cost. It consists of two components—a basic fixed charge (usually a monthly fee) and a variable charge based on the level of activity. This two-part structure often results from the way a supplier charges for its services. Among the more common semivariable costs are charges for telephone, power and lighting, photocopying, and auto and truck rentals when there is a basic charge plus a separate charge per mile.

Even when a firm purchases its own equipment, certain costs related to maintenance and repairs are semivariable costs. Some forms of maintenance are fixed costs because they must be done periodically regardless of usage. For example, the battery in a delivery truck may need to be changed every three years regardless of how many miles the truck is driven. Other maintenance activities, such as changing the oil and replacing the spark plugs, may depend directly on mileage. Thus, the total cost of the truck's repair and maintenance is a mixed cost made up of some fixed costs and some variable costs.

If the rental agreement for a truck requires a yearly charge of $3,000 plus 10 cents per mile, a graph of the annual cost would appear as shown in Illustration 3-4. Note that if 5,000 miles are driven, the total cost is $3,500 [$3,000 + ($.10 × 5,000 miles)]; if 10,000 miles are driven, the total cost is $4,000 [$3,000 + ($.10 × 10,000 miles)], and so forth.

▶ **ILLUSTRATION 3-5**   Graph of the Step-Variable Cost of Supervisors' Salaries

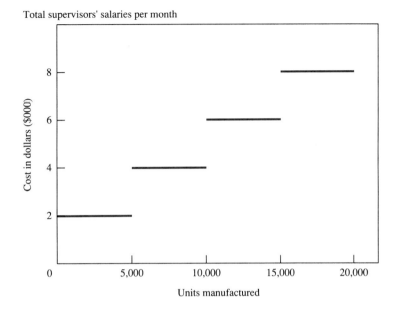

Step-Variable Costs   A **step-variable cost** consists of a series of fixed cost increments over short ranges of production within the relevant range. Thus, a step-variable cost increases in discrete jumps instead of in the continuous pattern of semivariable costs. Examples of this kind of cost are the salaries of supervisors and maintenance workers. For example, assume a plant has 10 assembly lines, 6 lines are currently operating, and one supervisor can supervise 2 lines. Under such circumstances, three supervisors would be employed. But if it becomes necessary to open a seventh line, another supervisor would have to be hired at full salary, because it is impossible to hire a fraction of a supervisor. The same is true for maintenance workers. This is quite different from direct labor, when employees can be added in small increments, on a daily or hourly basis.

A graph of the step-variable cost of hiring supervisors is shown in Illustration 3-5. Note that the supervisors' salaries hold constant over entire ranges of production—from 0 to 5,000 units, then from 5,001 to 10,000 units, and so forth. As its name implies, a step-variable cost is closely associated with variable costs because the steps, or chunks, of the cost increase over small ranges of activity, such as 0–200 units, 201–400 units, and so forth. Firms generally group this type of cost as a variable cost.

Curvilinear Cost Behavior

Illustration 3-6 presents an example of the economist's curvilinear cost relationship. Note, however, that the relevant range reflects an approximately *linear* cost relationship. Thus, for many business analysis problems, it is possible to assume linear cost behavior. Because management accountants regularly make this assumption, we will limit our discussion to linear cost-behavior problems and solutions.

▶ **ILLUSTRATION 3-6**   Economist's Total Cost Behavior Curve

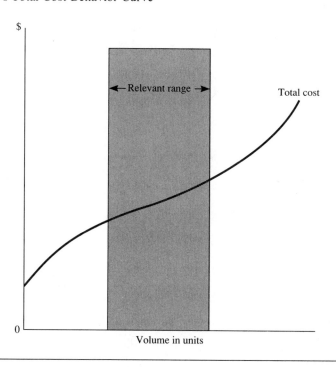

▶ **PROGRESS CHECK**

1. What is a variable cost? Create an example to demonstrate how it behaves on a per-unit basis and how it behaves in total for three different levels of activity.
2. What is a fixed cost? Create an example to demonstrate how it behaves on a per-unit basis and how it behaves in total for three different levels of activity.
3. Are committed costs and discretionary costs fixed or variable? How do these costs differ?
4. What is a mixed cost? Create an example to demonstrate how it behaves on a per-unit basis and how it behaves in total for three different levels of activity.
5. Does the economist's model of cost behavior fit the pattern of cost behavior used by management accountants? If not, how does a management accountant justify the use of a cost-behavior pattern that is different from the economist's model? ◀

▶ ANALYZING MIXED COSTS

L.O. 4

To be more useful in decision making, mixed costs should be separated into their fixed and variable cost components. Although some estimation is often necessary, accountants and managers strive ultimately to classify costs into either fixed or variable categories. This separation is vital when using numerous decision-making models that are discussed later in this text. A number of methods may be used to separate the elements of mixed costs. Among the most common are (1) account analysis, (2) engineering cost analysis, (3) the high-low method, (4) the scattergraph method, and (5) the least-squares method. The scattergraph and least-squares methods are discussed in Appendix 3-A at the end of this chapter.

Account Analysis

L.O. 5

Account analysis consists of examining the composition of the balance in a general ledger account to determine if its fixed and variable portions can be identified. For example, if a telephone company charges a fixed amount per month regardless of usage plus a specific amount for each telephone call made, the fixed and variable components of telephone costs are easily obtained by analyzing the account. However, not all mixed costs fit neatly into this pattern. Some mixed costs, such as repairs and maintenance, usually cannot be analyzed in this way, and any attempt to do so is likely to produce highly subjective, and therefore useless, results. Consequently, another method must be used in conjunction with account analysis to segregate mixed costs into their fixed and variable components.

Engineering Cost Analysis

L.O. 5

In an **engineering cost analysis,** engineers and other professionals who are familiar with the technical aspects of the process under review determine which costs are variable, or associated with variations in activity, and which costs are fixed, or incurred regardless of activity. For example, in the analysis of maintenance cost associated with corporate aircraft, an engineer can separate maintenance costs based on those that are incurred based on aircraft usage (variable) and those that are incurred due to the passage of time regardless of usage (fixed).

The High-Low Method of Analyzing Mixed Costs

L.O. 5

The High-Low Formula The **high-low method** of analyzing mixed costs is based on a linear function relationship and uses a calculation that considers *only two* observations out of a series of time periods, normally the highest and lowest levels of activity. The *difference in cost* between the two periods is then compared to the *difference in activity* to derive the variable portion of the cost. A key element of the high-low approach to mixed-cost analysis is that it uses information from the past. Thus, when the high-low method is used to predict future cost behavior, it is based on historical cost behavior.

To demonstrate the high-low method, assume the following maintenance costs for the Sonar Company:

Month	Machine-Hours	Monthly Cost
January	2,500	$ 5,000
February	2,800	5,200
March	3,000	5,300
April	3,400	5,700
May	4,000	6,100
June	5,000	7,100
July	7,000	8,500
August	9,000	10,100
September	10,000	11,000
October	6,000	7,800
November	3,000	5,300
December	2,600	5,100

▶ **ILLUSTRATION 3-7**   Sonar Company: Segregation of Fixed and Variable Costs

	Month	Machine-Hours	Monthly Cost
High	September	10,000	$11,000
Low	January	2,500	5,000
	Differences.	7,500	$ 6,000

Variable rate per hour:

$$\frac{\$6,000}{7,500} = \$.80 \text{ per machine-hour}$$

Calculation of the fixed cost:

Fixed cost (FC) = Total cost (TC) − Variable cost (VC)

September:
FC = $11,000 − (10,000 × $.80)
FC = $11,000 − $8,000
FC = $3,000

January:
FC = $5,000 − (2,500 × $.80)
FC = $5,000 − $2,000
FC = $3,000

The cost formula can be stated as:

Total cost = $3,000 + $.80 per machine-hour

The lowest month is January, with machine-hour activity of 2,500 hours, and the highest month is September, with machine-hour activity of 10,000 hours. These two months are selected and compared as shown in Illustration 3-7 to determine the variable and fixed portions of the maintenance cost. Note that:

1. The difference in cost is divided by the difference in machine-hours to arrive at the variable rate per hour.
2. The fixed cost can be determined by subtracting the variable cost from the total cost.
3. The fixed cost can be obtained by using either month. Of course, if rates for both months are computed, one can act as a check on the other.
4. The variable cost is computed by multiplying the appropriate machine-hours by the variable rate of 80 cents per hour.

The cost formula may be formally stated as:

$$Y = a + bX$$

where

Y = Total cost
a = Fixed cost
b = Variable cost per unit of activity
X = Number of units of activity

One weakness of this method is that only 2 months out of 12 are used to calculate fixed costs. The other 10 months are usually ignored. However, if

▶ **ILLUSTRATION 3-8**   Sonar Company: Graphical Segregation of Fixed and Variable Costs within the Relevant Range

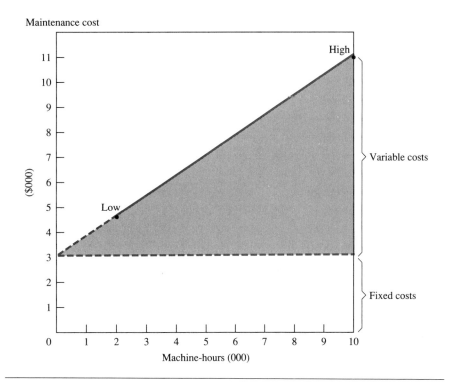

either the lowest or the highest point appears extreme, the second lowest or highest point should be selected instead. Whether the first or second points are selected, the procedure to calculate the variable rate and fixed cost remains the same.

Another weakness of this method, also true of estimation in general, is that if the computed variable cost per unit of activity is applied to any of the ignored months, the resulting fixed costs are unlikely to be the same. This can be seen by arbitrarily selecting the month of May for testing. Using the 80-cents variable rate, the calculation would be:

$$FC = \$6,100 - (4,000 \times \$.80)$$
$$= \$6,100 - \$3,200$$
$$= \$2,900$$

Of all the months other than January and September, only October results in a fixed cost of $3,000 when the variable rate of 80 cents per machine-hour is used. This could be considered a random event. Appendix 3-A covers the least-squares method of analyzing mixed costs. This method eliminates the weaknesses noted above.

The High-Low Graph   A variation on the high-low method of analyzing mixed costs is the high-low graph. A high-low graph, as shown in Illustration 3-8, is constructed as follows:

1. Plot the high point at 10,000 hours/$11,000.
2. Plot the low point at 2,500 hours/$5,000.
3. Connect the points.
4. Continue the line (extrapolate) to the maintenance cost axis. The point at which the line intersects the axis represents the fixed portion of maintenance costs, or, in this case, $3,000.

Because only two points are used to make the calculation, the result is only an approximation. Nevertheless, it is satisfactory for many cost applications.

An analysis is done for each mixed cost until all costs can be classified as either fixed or variable. Based on this grouping, a manager can begin to assess a cost's behavior and its effect on a decision to be made.

Mixed Cost Analysis—Scatter Diagrams

L.O. 6
Scatter diagrams

When a firm wishes to separate mixed costs into their fixed and variable portions based on *all* observations for a period of time instead of merely using the highest and lowest costs, it may use either the least-squares method or a scatter diagram. The discussion of the least-squares method is deferred until Appendix 3-A. All observations are used to fit a regression line so that each observation's squared deviations from the line cancel out and equal zero. The **regression line** represents the average of all of the observations. A **scatter diagram** (or **scattergraph**) is a graph on which an entire series of observations is plotted and then *visually* fitted with a regression line. The vertical distances of the points on either side of the line cancel each other out. A scatter diagram is an attempt to construct a regression line by plotting all observations on a graph and visually estimating a line representative of all the points plotted. It is not an attempt to connect any two observations, as is done in the high-low method. For example, here are the maintenance costs of the Sonar Company:

Month	Machine-Hours	Monthly Cost
January	2,500	$ 5,000
February	2,800	5,200
March	3,000	5,300
April	3,400	5,700
May	4,000	6,100
June	5,000	7,100
July	7,000	8,500
August	9,000	10,100
September . . .	10,000	11,000
October	6,000	7,800
November . . .	3,000	5,300
December . . .	2,600	5,100

The 12 points reflecting the Sonar Company's machine-hours and monthly costs are plotted in Illustration 3-9. (Only 11 points actually appear because March and November are the same.) The solid line is visually fitted, taking all the plotted points into consideration. Once the regression line is fitted, it is extrapolated (extended) to the *Y* intercept (vertical axis). The fixed cost can then be ascertained in the same way as in the high-low graphi-

▶ **ILLUSTRATION 3-9**   Sonar Company: Scatter Diagram—Maintenance Costs

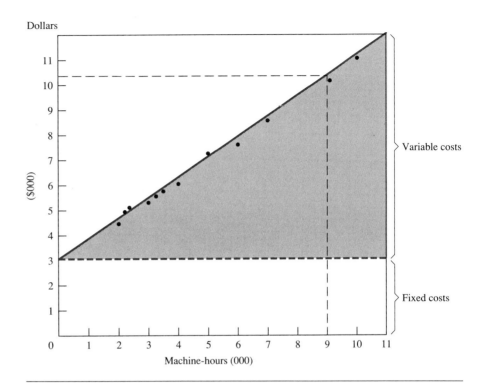

cal solution. It is the dashed horizontal line in Illustration 3-9. The variable cost for any month can be obtained by subtracting the fixed cost from the month's total cost. The fixed portion of the maintenance costs can be estimated at $2,900 per month. This solution differs somewhat from the $3,000 figure that was obtained using the high-low method, even though the same data were used. Such a discrepancy is to be expected.

The regression line in a scatter diagram may show some inaccuracy because it is visually fitted. However, the degree of inaccuracy may not be significant, and the results may be satisfactory for many business applications. This technique has two principal advantages. First, it is based on all observations rather than on only the highest and lowest costs; second, it allows the fixed cost to be easily calculated. The scatter diagram may also highlight highly unusual points that may not be obvious when the least-squares method is used.

In order to find the variable cost per unit, select two points along the regression line. A better solution is obtained by not selecting points that were plotted from the original data. Once two points have been selected, a calculation similar to the high-low method is done to calculate the variable cost per unit. The two points selected in Illustration 3-9 were zero machine-hours and 9,000 machine-hours. The costs at these points are $3,000 and $10,400, respectively. The calculation is as follows:

	Machine-Hours	Dollars
Point A	9,000	$10,400
Point B	0	3,000
Difference	9,000	$ 7,400

$$\frac{\$7,400}{9,000} = \$.8222 = \$.82 \text{ per machine hour}$$

Thus, the cost formula using the scatter diagram approach is:

$$Y = a + bX$$
$$Y = \$3,000 + \$.82X$$

Note that choosing points that are separated by a considerable distance lessens the significance of any errors in reading the graph in relation to the value differential associated with the chosen coordinates.

► **PROGRESS CHECK**

1. What is a mixed cost? Does it have to be analyzed into its components? Why?
2. What is account analysis? How is it accomplished? Use an example to explain your answer.
3. What is engineering cost analysis?
4. What is the high-low method of analyzing mixed cost? Does it provide a manager with the most sophisticated approach to analyzing mixed costs? Explain.
5. What is a scatter diagram? Is this approach more sophisticated than the high-low method? Explain your answer.   ◄

► CONTRIBUTION FORMAT INCOME STATEMENTS

L.O. 7
Contribution margin
income statement

Although it is crucial to know whether a cost is fixed or variable, such information alone will not suffice for most decision-making situations. Managers must also consider costs in terms of a larger context—that of the income statement. However, under such circumstances, a standard income statement will not suffice either. When an income statement is prepared in the traditional format, costs are grouped by functional classification—such as production, marketing, and administration—and because both fixed and variable costs appear in each category, the resulting summary may not be particularly helpful. The question is how to combine cost-behavior information with income statement information. The solution is a **contribution format income statement**—an income statement for managerial use that is classified into fixed and variable cost categories instead of into the functional categories of a traditional income statement.

Contribution Margin

The focus of a contribution format income statement is **contribution margin,** which is net sales minus variable costs (manufacturing, marketing, and administrative). It is the amount available for the recovery of fixed costs and earning income. In contrast, a standard income statement yields **gross margin,** which is net sales minus manufacturing costs of goods sold (both variable and fixed). Gross margin is not particularly useful for internal decision making because it reflects a deduction for fixed manufacturing costs, which may not change as a result of a contemplated decision, although variable manufacturing costs will change. Relying on a traditional income statement may create similar problems with marketing and administrative costs because they will not be broken down into fixed and variable portions either. A contribution format income statement is thus more suitable for internal decision making because it segregates fixed and variable costs, enabling managers to clearly assess net income changes when cost and/or volume changes occur.

The Contribution Margin Approach to Decision Making

Temar Company had sales volume in 19x2 of $900,000. Its cost of sales for the year amounted to $360,000 and consisted of $100,000 for direct materials, $160,000 for direct labor, $55,000 for variable overhead, and $45,000 for fixed overhead. Marketing costs of $100,000 for the year were also incurred, of which $18,000 were variable and $82,000 were fixed. Administrative costs—all fixed—amounted to $150,000. A traditional income statement was prepared for 19x2 and appears in Illustration 3-10.

If a manager wishes to project the effect on net income of an anticipated 20 percent increase in sales volume with no change in selling prices, a correct assessment would be impossible based on the traditional income statement in Illustration 3-10. If the manager attempts to increase sales, cost of sales, and gross margin each by 20 percent while holding the marketing and administrative costs constant, the effect on net income would be incorrect because the manufacturing overhead of $100,000 includes $45,000 of fixed costs that are not expected to change in 19x3 and, therefore, should not be increased. In addition, the marketing costs of $100,000 include $18,000 of variable costs, and these should be increased. When the income statement is prepared in the contribution format, however, these costs are easily projected.

L.O. 8
Preparation of a contribution format income statement

Preparing a Contribution Format Income Statement   As mentioned earlier, a contribution format income statement is classified into fixed and variable cost categories instead of into the functional categories used in traditional income statements. Although a contribution format income statement is not acceptable for external reporting to stockholders and other users, it is an extremely valuable management tool. As shown in Illustration 3-10, it begins with sales revenues, from which variable costs are deducted to arrive at contribution margin. Fixed costs are then deducted to arrive at net income. Occasionally, variable marketing costs are segregated from variable manufacturing costs, and an intermediate margin called *variable manufacturing margin* is shown.

If a manager wishes to assess the impact on net income of a 20 percent increase in volume and uses a contribution margin income statement, the analysis might appear as in Illustration 3-11. But in fact, once a contribution format income statement is prepared as in Illustration 3-10, the projected increase in net income may be determined through the following simple calculation:

Projected increase in net income for 19x3:

$$\text{19x2 contribution margin} = \$567,000 \times 20\% = \$113,400$$

This simplified calculation can be made only if the income statement is prepared in the contribution format.

TEMAR COMPANY
Income Statements
For the Year Ended December 31, 19x2

Traditional Format

			Percent
Sales		$900,000	100
Cost of sales:			
Direct materials.	$100,000		
Direct labor	160,000		
Manufacturing overhead . .	100,000	360,000	40
Gross margin		540,000	60
Marketing and administrative:			
Marketing costs.	100,000		
Administrative costs . . .	150,000	250,000	
Net income		$290,000	

Contribution Format

			Percent
Sales		$900,000	100
Variable manufacturing costs:			
Direct materials	$100,000		
Direct labor	160,000		
Variable overhead	55,000	315,000	35
Variable manufacturing margin . .		585,000	65
Less: Variable marketing costs . .		18,000	2
Contribution margin		567,000	63
Fixed costs:			
Manufacturing overhead . .	45,000		
Marketing	82,000		
Administrative	150,000	277,000	
Net income		$290,000	

▶ **ILLUSTRATION 3-11**

TEMAR COMPANY
Projected Increase in Net Income
Using Contribution Margin Income Statement
For the Year Ended December 31, 19x3

Sales ($900,000 × 120%)		$1,080,000
Less: Variable manufacturing costs	$315,000	
Variable marketing costs	18,000	
Total variable costs	$333,000 × 120%	399,600
Contribution margin		680,400
Less: Fixed costs		277,000
Projected net income		403,400
Less: 19x2 net income		290,000
Projected increase in net income		$ 113,400

▶ **SUMMARY**

Managers must understand **cost-behavior** patterns and cost-estimation tech-niques to effectively administer the affairs of their firms. In many cases, actual cost data may not be available for decision making, and estimated data must be used instead.

Managers use **variable costs** and **fixed costs** in different ways. In evaluat-ing proposals, managers sometimes use only variable costs, sometimes only fixed costs (which may be subdivided into **committed costs** and **discretionary costs**), and sometimes both. When considering different strategies, managers must be able to project the changes in costs that are likely to occur. Variable and fixed costs are more easily projected than are **mixed costs,** which contain some variable and some fixed costs. The fixed and variable portions of a mixed cost must be segregated for managers to make effective decisions when projections of only one kind of cost or the other are needed. Mixed costs may be classified as either **semivariable costs** or **step-variable costs.**

A semivariable cost is composed of a basic fee, usually charged per month, plus a variable charge based on activity. In contrast, a step-variable cost holds constant for a certain level of activity and then increases in discrete jumps rather than in a continuous fashion.

According to economic theory, **marginal cost** changes disproportionately to changes in production and is thus a curve when plotted on a graph. However, within the **relevant range**—the span of activity level in which a firm operates—the curve approximates a straight line. For this reason, most management accountants use a linear approach to solving business problems that require the computation of changes in costs when a contemplated change in an **activity base,** such as production, is considered.

Three common methods of dividing mixed costs into their fixed and vari-able components are **account analysis, engineering cost analysis,** and the **high-low method.** The high-low method uses the highest and lowest cost figures from a series of observations. The difference in these two costs is compared to the difference in their corresponding activity levels, and a variable cost inference is made. The fixed cost per period is then calculated.

Traditional income statements are of limited utility to managers because they are not usually classified according to fixed and variable costs. Instead, managers prefer an income statement prepared using a **contribution margin**

format. The statement starts with net sales, from which variable costs are deducted to arrive at **contribution margin.** Fixed costs are then deducted to arrive at net income. Contribution margin plays a useful role in a variety of management decisions.

► **APPENDIX 3-A**   **Mixed Cost Analysis—the Least-Squares Method**

Least-Squares Method   Some management accountants object to the use of scatter diagrams because the visual-fit approach is not precise. Instead, they employ the least-squares method to analyze mixed costs. The **least-squares method** is a *statistical analytic technique* used to separate mixed costs into their fixed and variable components. The procedure requires the simultaneous solution of two linear equations so that the squared deviations from the regression line of each of the plotted points cancel out (equal zero). Least-squares analysis measures the average change in a variable (in our example, maintenance cost) in relation to a unit of activity (here, machine-hours).

Most businesses use some form of computer processing and, accordingly, are apt to employ a more sophisticated technique to segregate mixed costs than the high-low method. The conceptual basis of the computer-applied approach is based on least-squares analysis. Even firms without computer capability may wish to use the more sophisticated least-squares method by performing the operations manually.

The equation for a linear function (straight line) with one independent variable is:

$$Y = a + bX$$

where

Y = The dependent variable
a = The constant
b = The slope of the line
X = The independent variable

The **dependent variable** is the total cost (Y) after performing the mathematical operations dictated by the equation $Y = a + bX$. The **independent variable** is the variable (unit of activity) that can take on any nonnegative value and affects the outcome of the dependent variable (the value of X in the equation $Y = a + bX$).

When an analysis is based on this equation, it is called **simple regression** because the dependent variable is based on *one* independent variable. When regression analysis has more than one independent variable, it is called **multiple regression,** which is considerably more complex. Multiple regression applications can be found in advanced cost and managerial accounting textbooks and in statistics textbooks.

The equations needed to perform the least-squares analysis are:

$$\Sigma XY = a\Sigma X + b\Sigma X^2 \tag{1}$$
$$\Sigma Y = na + b\Sigma X \tag{2}$$

▶ **ILLUSTRATION 3-12**   Solution to Least-Squares Method

Month	Machine-Hours X	Monthly Cost Y	(000) XY	(000) X^2
January	2,500	$ 5,000	$ 12,500	6,250
February	2,800	5,200	14,560	7,840
March	3,000	5,300	15,900	9,000
April	3,400	5,700	19,380	11,560
May	4,000	6,100	24,400	16,000
June	5,000	7,100	35,500	25,000
July	7,000	8,500	59,500	49,000
August	9,000	10,100	90,900	81,000
September	10,000	11,000	110,000	100,000
October	6,000	7,800	46,800	36,000
November	3,000	5,300	15,900	9,000
December	2,600	5,100	13,260	6,760
Totals	58,300	$82,200	$458,600	357,410

where

a = Fixed cost
b = Variable cost
n = Number of observations
X = Activity measure (hours, etc.)
Y = Total mixed cost

The solution to these equations, based on the same data used for the scatter diagram, is shown in Illustration 3-12. Substituting in the equations, we obtain:

$$\$458,600,000 = 58,300a + 357,410,000b \quad \textbf{(1)}$$
$$\$82,200 = 12a + 58,300b \quad \textbf{(2)}$$

Dividing Equation 1 by 1,000, we obtain:

$$\$458,600 = 58.3a + 357,410b \quad \textbf{(3)}$$
$$\$82,200 = 12a + 58,300b \quad \textbf{(2)}$$

To solve the equations simultaneously, Equation 3 is multiplied by 12 and Equation 2 is multiplied by 58.3. The results after subtracting Equation 5 from Equation 4 are:

$$[12 \times (3)] \ \$5,503,200 = 699.6a + 4,288,920b \quad \textbf{(4)}$$
$$[58.3 \times (2)] \ \underline{\$4,792,260 = 699.6a + 3,398,890b} \quad \textbf{(5)}$$
$$\$ \ 710,940 = 890,030b$$
$$\$.7988 = b$$

The variable portion of maintenance costs is $.7988 per machine-hour. The fixed portion is now calculated by substituting the value of b in either

▶ **ILLUSTRATION 3-13**   Short-Cut Approach to Least-Squares Method

Month	(1) Machine-Hours X $\overline{X} = 4{,}858$	(2) Maintenance Cost Y $\overline{Y} = \$6{,}850$	(3) X'	(4) Y'	(5) (000) X'Y'	(6) (000) X'²
January	2,500	$ 5,000	−2,358	−1,850	$ 4,362	5,560
February	2,800	5,200	−2,058	−1,650	3,396	4,235
March	3,000	5,300	−1,858	−1,550	2,880	3,452
April	3,400	5,700	−1,458	−1,150	1,677	2,126
May	4,000	6,100	− 858	− 750	644	736
June	5,000	7,100	142	250	35	20
July	7,000	8,500	2,142	1,650	3,534	4,588
August	9,000	10,100	4,142	3,250	13,462	17,156
September	10,000	11,000	5,142	4,150	21,339	26,440
October	6,000	7,800	1,142	950	1,085	1,304
November	3,000	5,300	−1,858	−1,550	2,880	3,452
December	2,600	5,100	−2,258	−1,750	3,951	5,099
Totals	58,300	$82,200	4*	−0−	$59,245	74,168

$$\text{Variable cost} = \frac{\Sigma X'Y'}{\Sigma X'^2} = \frac{\$59{,}245}{74{,}168} = \$.7988 \text{ per machine-hour.}$$

Fixed cost is computed as:

$$\overline{Y} = a + b\overline{X}$$
$$\$6{,}850 = a + \$.7988(4{,}858)$$
$$\$6{,}850 = a + \$3{,}881$$
$$\$2{,}969 = a$$

The equation for maintenance cost can be expressed as:

$$Y = \$2{,}969 + \$.7988X$$

---

* Rounding difference.

Equation 1 or Equation 2. Equation 2 is selected because it produces smaller numbers to work with. The substituted Equation 2 becomes:

$$\$82{,}200 = 12a + 58{,}300(\$.7988)$$
$$\$82{,}200 = 12a + \$46{,}570$$
$$\$82{,}200 - \$46{,}570 = 12a$$
$$\$35{,}630 = 12a$$
$$\$2{,}969 = a$$

The fixed portion of the mixed cost is thus $2,969 per month. A comparison of this amount with the amount computed using the high-low method earlier in the chapter shows that the computation of $3,000 per month for fixed costs is a good approximation of the least-squares approach. The variable rate of $.7988 per machine-hour as computed by least-squares is also close to the $.80 per machine-hour computed using the high-low method. In fact, in this case, the results obtained by high-low appear to make the least-squares approach unnecessary from a cost-benefit point of view. However, the results of the two methods may not always be so similar, and when this is the case, the least-squares method can be justified.

Short-Cut Method of Least-Squares   When performed manually, the least-squares method can become burdensome because of the large numbers involved in the multiplication operations. Fortunately, there is a **short-cut**

▶ **ILLUSTRATION 3-14**   Sonar Company: Computer Solution to Least-Squares Regression

```
DO YOU WISH TO PRINT THE DATA JUST READ IN *
?
YES
  2500.000   5000.000
  2800.000   5200.000
  3000.000   5300.000
  3400.000   5700.000
  4000.000   6100.000
  5000.000   7100.000
  7000.000   8500.000
  9000.000  10100.000
 10000.000  11000.000
  6000.000   7800.000
  3000.000   5300.000
  2600.000   5100.000

DO YOU WISH TO CHANGE SOME VALUES
?
NO

SPECIFY THE COLUMN NUMBER OF THE DEPENDENT VARIABLE
?
2

SPECIFY THE COLUMN NUMBER OF THE INDEPENDENT VARIABLE
?
1

DO YOU WISH THE REGRESSION LINE TO PASS THROUGH THE ORIGIN
?
NO

INTERCEPT................   2969.25220
REGRESSION COEFFICIENT....     0.79878
```

method based on the statistical concept of subtracting the mean $(\overline{X})$ of all the observations from each observation before proceeding with the solution to the problem. Because all observations are reduced by $\overline{X}$, the relationship of each observation to all observations remains unchanged, and all the numbers are smaller.

Using the same data from the Sonar Company, let us employ the short-cut method to determine fixed and variable costs. The first step is to compute the $\overline{X}$ of X and the $\overline{Y}$ of Y. From the least-squares computations, the sum of $X = 58,300$ and the sum of $Y = \$82,200$. Dividing both of these sums by 12 *(n)* observations, the means are:

$$\overline{X} = 58,300 \div 12 = 4,858$$
$$\overline{Y} = \$82,200 \div 12 = \$6,850$$

The solution using the short-cut approach appears in Illustration 3-13. It follows these steps:

1. Subtract the mean from each observation and record the difference as X' and Y'. The sum of X' should always equal zero, as should the sum of Y'. The sum of all deviations from a population mean must equal zero.

2. Multiply each X' by Y' and sum the results.
3. Multiply X' by itself (obtaining X'^2) and sum the results.
4. Divide the result obtained in step 2 by the result obtained in step 3. This produces the variable portion of the cost.
5. Using the equation $\overline{Y} = a + b\overline{X}$, substitute the variable portion (b) and solve for the fixed cost.

Note that the short-cut method produces the same result as the regular method of least-squares.

As mentioned earlier, much time can be saved by performing regressions on a computer. A regression solution for the Sonar Company data, prepared on a computer, is shown in Illustration 3-14. The *intercept* corresponds to the fixed cost per month, and the *regression coefficient* corresponds to the variable cost per machine-hour.

▶ **GLOSSARY OF KEY TERMS**

Account analysis   Examining the composition of the balance in a general ledger account to determine if its fixed and variable portions can be identified.   (p. 87)

Activity base   An item or event that has a cause-and-effect relationship with the incurrence of a variable cost. A variable cost may be measured in terms of its activity base.   (p. 80)

Committed cost   A fixed cost that continues for a long period of time and is not reversible in the short term.   (p. 83)

Contribution format income statement   An income statement for managerial use that is classified into fixed and variable cost categories instead of into the functional categories of a traditional income statement.   (p. 92)

Contribution margin   Sales revenues minus variable costs, and the amount available for the recovery of fixed costs and earning income.   (p. 92)

Cost behavior   The way in which a cost reacts to a change in business activity.   (p. 80)

Dependent variable*   The total cost (Y) after performing the mathematical operations dictated by the equation $Y = a + bX$.   (p. 96)

Discretionary cost   Fixed costs that are reversible after short periods of time.   (p. 83)

Engineering cost analysis   Engineers and other professionals who are familiar with the technical aspects of the process under review determine which costs are variable, or associated with variations in activity, and which costs are fixed, or incurred regardless of activity.   (p. 87)

Fixed cost   A cost that remains constant *in total* within a given range of activity and period of time. However, the *per-unit* cost decreases with increased output.   (p. 82)

Gross margin   Net sales revenue minus manufacturing cost of goods sold.   (p. 92)

High-low method   A method of analyzing mixed costs that is based on a linear function relationship and uses a calculation considering only two observations out of a series of time periods, normally the highest and lowest costs. The difference in cost between the two periods is then compared to the difference in activity to derive the variable portion of the cost.   (p. 87)

---

* Denotes a glossary term from the chapter appendix.

Independent variable* The variable (a unit of activity) that can take on any nonnegative value and affects the outcome of the dependent variable (the value of X in the equation $Y = a + bX$). (p. 96)

Least-squares method* An analytic technique used to separate mixed costs into their fixed and variable components. All observations are used in such a manner that the squared deviations from the regression line of each observation cancel out and equal zero. (See **regression line.**) (p. 96)

Marginal cost The cost to produce one additional unit. (p. 80)

Mixed cost A cost containing both fixed and variable elements. (p. 84)

Multiple regression* A method for analyzing mixed costs into their fixed and variable components that uses two or more independent variables to arrive at the dependent variable. (p. 96)

Regression line A line fitted to a series of observations plotted on a graph so that it represents the average of all the observations. (p. 90)

Relevant range The span of activity levels near its optimum level that a firm chooses for its operations. A firm usually operates within this range, although production may occasionally vary from this norm. (p. 80)

Scatter diagram A graph on which an entire series of observations are plotted and then visually fitted with a regression line. The vertical distances of the points on either side of the line cancel each other out. (p. 90)

Scattergraph See **scatter diagram.** (p. 90)

Semivariable cost A mixed cost consisting of two components—a basic fixed charge and a variable charge based on the level of activity. (p. 84)

Short-cut method of least-squares* A variation of the least-squares method in which smaller numbers are used by subtracting the mean of a series of variables from each observation. The results are identical to that produced by the least-squares method. (p. 98–99)

Simple regression* A method of analyzing mixed costs into their fixed and variable components that uses only one independent variable to arrive at the dependent variable and is based on the equation $Y = a + bX$. (p. 96)

Step-variable cost A mixed cost consisting of a series of fixed cost increments over short ranges of production within the relevant range. (p. 85)

Variable cost A total cost that varies proportionately with output. However, the *per-unit* cost is constant within a given range of production. (p. 80)

▶ REVIEW PROBLEM Kent Company provides you with the following activity levels and monthly costs for the first six months of 19x4:

Month	Units	Product Cost
January	1,000	$ 7,000
February	1,100	7,200
March	1,300	8,000
April	1,500	8,400
May	1,800	9,500
June	2,000	10,000

Required a. Compute the fixed cost per month and the variable cost per unit using the high-low method.

b. Prepare a scatter diagram to compute the fixed cost per month.

▶ **SOLUTION TO**
REVIEW PROBLEM

a.

	Month	Units	Monthly Cost
High	June	2,000	$10,000
Low	January	1,000	7,000
	Differences.	1,000	$ 3,000

Variable cost per unit:

$$\frac{\$3,000}{1,000} = \$3 \text{ per unit}$$

Calculation of the fixed cost:

Fixed cost (FC) = Total cost (TC) − Variable cost (VC)

June:
FC = $10,000 − (2,000 × $3)
FC = $10,000 − $6,000
FC = $4,000

January:
FC = $7,000 − (1,000 × $3)
FC = $7,000 − $3,000
FC = $4,000

The cost formula can be stated as:

Total cost = $4,000 + $3 per unit

b.

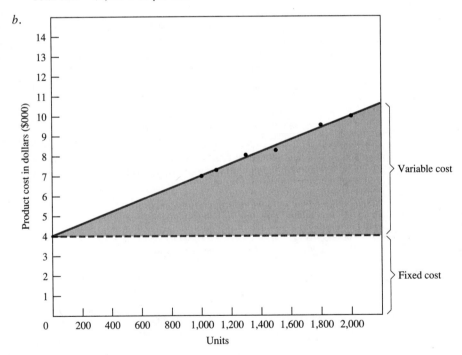

The fixed cost is approximately $4,000 per month.

▶ **LIBRARY**
ASSIGNMENT

Read the following:

Gynther, R. S. "Improving Separation of Fixed and Variable Expenses." *NAA Bulletin*, June 1963, pp. 29–38.

Nurnberg, Hugo. "The Ambiguous High-Low Method." *Issues in Accounting Education*, Spring 1986, pp. 143–47.

Pierce, Richard F. "The Importance of the Distinction between Fixed and Variable Costs." *NAA Bulletin,* May 1964, pp. 19–26.

▸ **SELF-TEST**

True or False

1. Assume a linear cost function for a variable cost; unit costs will decrease as output increases.
2. Assume a linear cost function for a fixed cost; unit costs will decrease as output increases.
3. A mixed cost is a cost that is partially a product cost and partially a period cost.
4. According to economic theory, all cost functions are curvilinear.
5. A marginal cost is any cost that increases proportionately with increases in volume.
6. A committed cost is a fixed cost; a discretionary cost is a variable cost.
7. If a firm operates at 12 different activity levels during an annual accounting period, the high-low method may be used to analyze a mixed cost by selecting any 2 activity levels.
8. For decision-making purposes, the traditional format of an income statement will usually *not* provide a manager with the needed information to reach a decision.
9. The machine-hours worked for March is 100,000 hours, and the machine maintenance cost for that month amounted to $40,000. The machine-hours worked for August is 60,000 hours, and the machine maintenance cost for that month amounted to $26,000. If these months represent the high and low activities for the year, the use of the high-low method to analyze power costs will produce a variable cost per machine-hour of $.33.
10. Using the data from question 9, the fixed cost per month would be $5,000.

▸ **QUESTIONS**

1. Is the economist's total cost-behavior pattern linear or curvilinear? Why? What does the economist's cost graph look like?
2. What is the relevant range? What is its significance?
3. Why do accountants use a linear cost assumption for solving business problems?
4. What is a mixed cost? Give an example of one and explain why it is mixed.
5. What methods may be used to analyze mixed costs into their fixed and variable components?
6. What is meant by account analysis of mixed costs? Is it useful in all cases? Explain.
7. What is meant by engineering cost analysis of mixed costs?
8. What is meant by high-low analysis of mixed costs? Describe the technique.
9. What is (are) the principal weakness(es) of the high-low method?
10. What is a scatter diagram? How is it constructed?
11. Why are traditional income statements generally not useful for decision making?
12. What statement format is better than the traditional income statement?
13. If a change in sales revenue is expected without a change in selling price or cost, and the contribution margin is known, how can this be used to project the effect of the sales revenue change on net income?

For Appendix 3–A

14. The least-squares method is a linear method based on what equation? Explain each term in the equation.
15. What is the difference between simple regression and multiple regression?

16. What are the linear equations used to solve a least-squares problem? Explain what each symbol means.
17. On what theory is the short-cut method for solving a least-squares problem based? Does it produce an identical answer to the regular least-squares method?
18. How is the short-cut least-squares method computed?

► **EXERCISES**   **E3–1**   **Missing Data—Cost Behavior**
Supply the missing data for each company listed below:

	Companies			
	A	**B**	**C**	**D**
Units produced	18,000	26,000	?	30,000
Total cost	$?	$195,000	$111,000	$?
Fixed cost	63,000	?	50,400	?
Fixed cost per unit	?	5.20	4.20	?
Variable cost per unit	6.60	?	?	4.44
Total cost per unit.	?	?	?	6.12

E3–2   **Missing Data—Cost Behavior**
Supply the missing data for each company listed below:

	Companies			
	A	**B**	**C**	**D**
Units produced	35,000	30,000	?	27,000
Total cost	$?	$135,000	$81,000	$?
Fixed cost.	26,250	?	14,400	?
Fixed cost per unit	?	2.75	2.40	?
Variable cost per unit.	4.20	?	?	4.95
Total cost per unit	?	?	?	10.35

E3–3   **Cost-Behavior Patterns**
Given here are graphical representations of various cost-behavior patterns. The vertical axis represents the total cost in dollars, and the horizontal axis represents the volume—either units produced or units sold. In addition, various types of costs are listed, and for each cost it should be assumed that the cost behaves in its normal pattern.

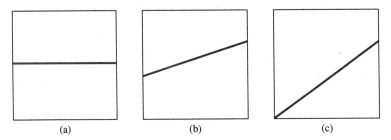

(a)   (b)   (c)

1. Advertising.
2. Depreciation—units of production method.
3. Depreciation—straight-line method.

4. Direct materials uscd.
5. Direct labor.
6. Factory supplies used.
7. Freight on direct materials.
8. Heat and power, factory.
9. Rent.
10. Repairs to machinery.
11. Sales.
12. Sales salaries.
13. Superintendence, factory.

Required   Match each cost with a particular behavior pattern. Behavior patterns may be used more than once.

E3–4   **High-Low Method**

Items 1 and 2 are based on the following information:

Maintenance costs of a company are to be analyzed for purposes of constructing a budget. Examination of past records disclosed the following costs and volume measures:

	Highest	**Lowest**
Cost per month . . .	$39,200	$32,000
Machine-hours. . . .	24,000	15,000

1. Using the high-low point method of analysis, the estimated variable cost per machine-hour is
   a. $1.25.
   b. $12.50.
   c. $.80.
   d. $.08.
2. Using the high-low technique, the estimated annual fixed cost for maintenance expenditures is
   a. $447,360.
   b. $240,000.
   c. $230,400.
   d. $384,000.

(AICPA Adapted)

E3–5   **High-Low Method**

Departmental overhead for the repair department of the X Company at the following levels of activity is as follows:

	40,000 Machine-Hours	**60,000 Machine-Hours**
Total overhead. . . .	$93,600	$117,000

The breakdown of the overhead at the 40,000-hour level is as follows:

Rent (fixed)	$39,000
Repair parts (variable) . . .	15,600
Salaries (mixed)	39,000
Total	$93,600

Required   *a.* Compute the estimated cost of repair parts at the 60,000-hour level.

b. Compute the estimated salaries cost at the 60,000-hour level.

c. Compute the fixed cost for the repair department.

d. Prepare a cost formula for the repair department.

e. Prepare an estimate of overhead costs for the repair department at the 50,000-hour level.

E3–6 Cost-Behavior Patterns for a Hospital

The management accountant for Good Samaritan Hospital prepared cost estimates for the following levels of activity (in number of X rays):

	1,000 X rays	1,500 X rays
Film	$ 2,000	$ 3,000
Developing supplies	700	950
Technicians' salaries	14,000	16,000
Depreciation of X-ray equipment . . .	5,000	5,000

Required   *a.* Compute the unit cost for each cost at each level.

b. Indicate whether the cost is V (variable), F (fixed), or M (part variable, part fixed). Explain your reasoning for each designation using your computations from part (*a*).

E3–7 High-Low Method

The Bonar Company incurred the following inspection costs for the first six months of 19x4:

Month	Units Produced	Inspection Costs
January	4,200	$14,700
February	4,800	16,200
March	2,400	9,000
April	3,000	10,800
May	6,000	19,800
June	5,400	18,300

The above cost behavior is representative of the full year.

Required   *a.* Using the high-low method, compute the fixed cost per month and the variable cost per unit.

b. Prepare the cost formula for inspection costs.

c. If the Bonar Company had an activity level of 3,000 units for the month of July 19x4, what would the expected costs be for the month?

E3–8 Scatter Diagram

Using the information provided in Exercise 3–7, construct a scatter diagram to estimate the fixed cost per month.

E3–9 Cost-Behavior Pattern Using the High-Low Method

The Donar Company had the following costs incurred for the months of June and July 19x6:

	June	July
Direct materials . . .	$ 50,000	$125,000
Direct labor	75,000	187,500
Overhead	140,000	177,500
Total costs	$265,000	$490,000
Units produced . . .	10,000	25,000

Required   a. Compute the unit costs for the months of June and July and show the breakdown for each month analyzed into direct materials, direct labor, and overhead.

b. Compute the fixed cost per month and the variable cost per unit.

c. Prepare the cost formula for the company.

d. What should the costs incurred be for August if the anticipated production is 20,000 units?

E3-10   Cost-Behavior Pattern Using the High-Low Method

Word Processing Company had the following costs incurred for the months of June and July 19x6:

	June	July
Direct materials . . .	$ 400	$ 300
Direct labor	24,000	18,000
Overhead	10,000	9,000
Total costs	$34,400	$27,300
Pages typed	40,000	30,000

Required   a. Compute the unit costs for the months of June and July and show the breakdown for each month analyzed into direct materials, direct labor, and overhead.

b. Compute the fixed cost per month and the variable cost per unit.

c. Prepare the cost formula for the company.

d. What should the costs incurred be for August if the anticipated production is 25,000 pages typed?

E3-11   Preparation of Contribution Format Income Statement

Conar Company had the following income statement prepared for the year 19x5:

CONAR COMPANY
Income Statement
For the Year Ended December 31, 19x5

Sales	$3,300,000
Cost of goods sold	2,475,000
Gross margin	825,000
Marketing and administrative costs . . .	495,000
Net income	$ 330,000

Included in the cost of goods sold are $660,000 of fixed manufacturing costs. The marketing and administrative costs include salespersons' commissions and other variable costs to the extent of $165,000. The balance of the marketing and administrative costs are fixed.

Conar Company manufactures and sells only one product at a selling price of $60 per unit.

Required Recast the income statement into a contribution format statement.

E3–12 **(Appendix 3-A) Least-Squares Method**

The controller of Connecticut Electronics Company believes the identification of the variable and fixed components of the firm's costs will enable the firm to make better planning and control decisions. Among the costs the controller is concerned about is the behavior of indirect supplies cost. He believes there is some correlation between the machine-hours worked and the amount of indirect supplies used.

A member of the controller's staff has suggested using a simple linear regression model to determine the cost behavior of the indirect supplies. The regression equation shown below was developed from 40 pairs of observations using the least-squares method of regression. The regression equation and related measures are as follows:

$$S = \$200 + \$4H$$

where

S = Total monthly costs of indirect supplies
H = Machine-hours per month

Required *a.* When a simple linear regression model is used to make inferences about a population relationship from sample data, what assumptions must be made before the inferences can be accepted as valid?

b. Assume the assumptions identified in part *(a)* are satisfied for the indirect supplies cost of Connecticut Electronics Company.
  (1) Explain the meaning of "200" and "4" in the regression equation $S = \$200 + \$4H$.
  (2) Calculate the estimated cost of indirect supplies if 900 machine-hours are to be used during the month.

(CMA Adapted)

E3–13 **(Appendix 3-A) Least-Squares Method Cost Analysis (Regular Equation Approach)**

Using the data provided in Exercise 3–7, you are asked to:

a. Compute the fixed cost per month and the variable cost per unit using the *regular least-squares method.*
b. Prepare the equation for analyzing mixed costs for Bonar Company. (Use the form $Y = a + bX$.)
c. Compute the estimated costs for August if the company is expected to produce 3,800 units during the month.

E3–14 **(Appendix 3-A) Least-Squares Method Cost Analysis (Short-Cut Approach)**

Using the data provided in Exercise 3–7, you are asked to:

a. Compute the fixed cost per month and the variable cost per unit using the *short-cut least-squares method.*
b. Prepare the equation for analyzing mixed costs for Bonar Company. (Use the form $Y = a + bX$.)

c. Compute the estimated costs for August if the company is expected to produce 3,800 units during the month.

E3–15   **(Appendix 3-A) Least-Squares Method Cost Analysis (Regular Equation Approach)**

Kent Company provides you with the following activity levels and monthly costs for the first six months of 19x4:

Month	Units	Product Cost
January	1,600	$11,000
February . . .	1,700	12,000
March	2,100	15,000
April	2,400	16,600
May	2,900	19,800
June	3,700	24,600

Required   *a.* Compute the fixed cost per month and the variable cost per unit using the *regular least-squares method.*

b. Prepare the equation for analyzing mixed costs for Kent Company. (Use the form $Y = a + bX$.)

c. Compute the estimated costs for August if the company is expected to produce 3,800 units during the month.

E3–16   **(Appendix 3-A) Least-Squares Method Cost Analysis (Short-Cut Approach)**

Kent Company provides you with the following activity levels and monthly costs for the first six months of 19x4:

Month	Units	Product Cost
January	1,600	$11,000
February . . .	1,700	12,000
March	2,100	15,000
April	2,400	16,600
May	2,900	19,800
June	3,700	24,600

Required   *a.* Compute the fixed cost per month and the variable cost per unit using the *short-cut least-squares method.*

b. Prepare the equation for analyzing mixed costs for Kent Company. (Use the form $Y = a + bX$.)

c. Compute the estimated costs for August if the company is expected to produce 3,800 units during the month.

▶ **PROBLEMS**   **P3–17**   **Fixed Cost Behavior per Unit**

Factory rent for the Brentwood Corporation is $200,000 per annum. The president of the corporation has asked you, as the company's management accountant, to analyze the effect of factory rent on the unit cost of the company's only product, Wadget.

Required   *a.* Prepare a statement showing the unit cost of factory rent at 10,000-unit intervals, starting with 10,000 and ending with 100,000 units.

b. Using your results in part *(a)*, prepare a graph showing the average unit cost on the vertical axis and the units on the horizontal axis. Is it a straight line? Why?

P3–18   **Cost-Behavior Patterns**

The management accountant for the Bern Corporation prepared cost estimates for the following levels of activity (in units):

	20,000 Units	25,000 Units
Direct materials.	$50,800	$63,500
Direct labor	42,000	52,500
Factory rent	32,000	32,000
Indirect labor.	18,000	20,000
Power	7,000	8,000
Superintendent's salary . . .	6,000	6,000
Payroll taxes	8,000	9,500

Required   *a.* Compute the unit cost for each cost at each level.

b. Indicate whether the cost is V (variable), F (fixed), or P (part variable, part fixed). Explain your reasoning for each designation using your computations from part *(a)*.

P3–19   **Identification of Cost-Behavior Patterns**

On a lined sheet of paper, number the first 10 lines from 1 through 10. Select the graph that matches the numbered factory cost or period cost data and write the letter identifying the graph on the appropriate numbered line.

The vertical axes of the graphs represent *total* dollars of cost, and the horizontal axes represent production. In each case, the zero point is at the intersection of the two axes. The graphs may be used more than once.

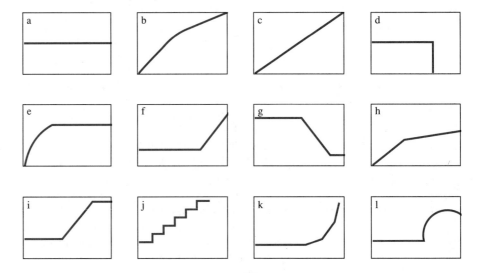

1. Depreciation of equipment, where the amount of depreciation charged is computed by the machine-hours method.

2. Electricity bill—a flat fixed charge, plus a variable cost after a certain number of kilowatt-hours are used.

3. City water bill, which is computed as follows:

First 1 million gallons or less . . .	$1,000 flat fee
Next 10,000 gallons	0.003 per gallon used
Next 10,000 gallons	0.006 per gallon used
Next 10,000 gallons	0.009 per gallon used
Etc.	

4. Cost of lubricant for machines, where cost per unit decreases with each pound of lubricant used (for example, if one pound is used, the cost is $10; if two pounds are used, the cost is $19.98; if three pounds are used, the cost is $29.94; with a minimum cost per pound of $9.25).

5. Depreciation of equipment, where the amount is computed by the straight-line method. When the depreciation rate was established, it was anticipated that the obsolescence factor would be greater than the wear-and-tear factor.

6. Rent on a factory building donated by the city, where the agreement calls for a fixed-fee payment unless 200,000 man-hours are worked, in which case no rent need be paid.

7. Salaries of repairmen, where one repairman is needed for every 1,000 hours of machine-hours or less (that is, 0 to 1,000 hours requires one repairman, 1,001 to 2,000 hours requires two repairmen, etc.).

8. Federal unemployment compensation taxes for the year, where the labor force is constant in number throughout year (average annual salary is $12,000 per worker).

9. Cost of raw material used.

10. Rent on a factory building donated by the county, where agreement calls for rent of $100,000 less $1 for each direct labor-hour worked in excess of 200,000 hours, but minimum rental payment of $20,000 must be paid.

(AICPA Adapted)

P3–20 **Scatter Diagram**

The Jonar Company provides you with the following activity levels and monthly costs for the year 19x3:

Month	Units	Product Cost
January.	600	$11,100
February	700	12,600
March	800	13,800
April	900	15,600
May	1,100	18,600
June	1,200	20,400
July	500	9,300
August	600	11,400
September . . .	1,000	16,500
October	1,600	25,800
November . . .	1,400	22,200
December. . . .	1,120	18,900

Required   Construct a scatter diagram to determine the fixed cost per month.

P3–21 **Scatter Diagram**

Fram Hospital provides you with the following activity levels and monthly costs for the year 19x3:

Month	Blood Tests Performed	Salaries and Supplies Cost
January	1,200	$ 7,400
February.	1,400	8,400
March	1,600	9,200
April	1,800	10,400
May	2,200	12,500
June.	2,400	13,600
July	1,600	9,300
August.	1,200	7,600
September	2,000	11,000
October	2,600	14,600
November	2,800	14,800
December	2,240	12,600

Required   Construct a scatter diagram to determine the fixed cost per month.

P3–22   **Preparation of Contribution Format Statement Using High-Low Analysis**

The Honar Company wishes to prepare a budgeted income statement for 19x6. The company's income statements for the two prior years are available. However, Honar wishes to experiment with an income statement prepared using the contribution format, which it plans to use for various types of decision strategies contemplated for 19x6.

The income statements for 19x5 and 19x4 are as follows:

HONAR COMPANY
Income Statement
For the Years Ended December 31, 19x5 and 19x4

	19x5	19x4
Sales	$2,400,000	$2,000,000
Cost of sales:		
Direct materials.	360,000	300,000
Direct labor	240,000	200,000
Manufacturing overhead	650,000	600,000
Total cost of sales.	1,250,000	1,100,000
Gross margin	1,150,000	900,000
Less: Marketing and administrative costs	550,000	530,000
Net income.	$ 600,000	$ 370,000

Sales for both years were at $100 per unit. Manufacturing overhead consisted of:

	19x5	19x4
Factory rent	$300,000	$300,000
Indirect labor	90,000	80,000
Utilities	71,000	60,000
Miscellaneous overhead . . .	189,000	160,000
Totals	$650,000	$600,000

Marketing and administrative costs include commissions to salespersons of 5 percent of sales. The balance of the marketing and administrative costs are fixed.

There were no beginning or ending inventories, and none are expected for 19x6.

All costs and selling prices are not expected to change for the year 19x6.

Required *a.* For each item of overhead, identify whether it is F (fixed), V (variable), or M (mixed).

b. Segregate each mixed cost into its fixed and variable components using the high-low method.

c. Prepare a cost formula for each mixed cost.

d. Prepare an income statement using the contribution format for 19x6. The projected sales volume is 26,000 units.

P3–23   **Preparation of Contribution Format Income Statement and Changes in Sales Volume**

The Shure Company had the following income statement prepared for the year 19x5:

SHURE COMPANY
Income Statement
For the Year Ended December 31, 19x5

Sales	$2,400,000
Cost of goods sold	1,800,000
Gross margin	600,000
Marketing and administrative costs . . .	360,000
Net income	$ 240,000

Included in the cost of goods sold are $940,000 of fixed manufacturing costs. The marketing and administrative costs include salespersons' commissions and other variable costs to the extent of $100,000. The balance of the marketing and administrative costs are fixed.

The Shure Company manufactures and sells only one product at a selling price of $80 per unit.

Required *a.* Recast the income statement into a contribution format statement.

b. Compute the contribution margin ratio for the company.

c. Compute the contribution margin per unit for the company.

d. During 19x5, the economy was very sluggish. For 19x6, the company president expects sales to either increase 20 percent or decrease 30 percent depending on who wins the national presidential election. In either case, the company president does not expect to change selling prices. Compute the expected change in net income for both possibilities. (You may wish to compute the expected changes using one method and then check your calculations using another method.)

P3–24   **Preparation of Traditional and Contribution Income Statements Using the High-Low Method**

Backforth Company incurred the following costs for the months of June and July 19x0:

	June	July
Direct materials	$ 315,000	$ 385,000
Direct labor	382,500	467,500
Overhead	720,000	760,000
Total costs	$1,417,500	$1,612,500
Units produced	90,000	110,000
Marketing costs	$ 700,000	$ 760,000
Administrative costs . . .	337,500	352,500

There were no opening or closing inventories for either month. The selling price of the company's single product is $30 per unit.

Required
a. Compute the unit costs for the months of June and July, showing the breakdown for each month analyzed into direct materials, direct labor, and overhead.

b. Compute the amount of fixed cost per month and the variable cost per unit separately for:
  (1) Overhead.
  (2) Marketing costs.
  (3) Administrative costs.

c. Prepare cost formulas for the following:
  (1) Overhead.
  (2) Marketing costs.
  (3) Administrative costs.

d. The sales manager predicts that 125,000 units will be sold during August. You are asked to prepare projected income statements using:
  (1) The traditional format.
  (2) The contribution format.

P3–25 **Preparation of Estimated Traditional and Contribution Income Statements Using High-Low Cost Analysis Coupled with Price Changes**

The Mountain Company closed for vacation on June 30, 19x3, and on July 4, 19x3, a fire totally destroyed the company's premises, including all of its books and records. Fortunately, independent auditors had copies of the firm's annual reports. Condensed income statements of the firm appear below.

MOUNTAIN COMPANY
Income Statements
For the Years Ended December 31, 19x2, and 19x1

	19x2	19x1
Sales revenue	$3,600,000	$3,000,000
Cost of sales:		
Direct materials	360,000	300,000
Direct labor	720,000	600,000
Manufacturing overhead . . .	888,000	840,000
Cost of sales	1,968,000	1,740,000
Gross margin	1,632,000	1,260,000
Other costs:		
Marketing.	414,000	390,000
Administrative.	516,000	480,000
Total	930,000	870,000
Net income	$ 702,000	$ 390,000

After conferring with the president and sales manager of the company, it was ascertained that:

1. The company manufactures only one product and previously sold it for $10 per unit. Effective January 1, 19x3, the price was increased by 10 percent.
2. Effective January 1, 19x3, the price of direct materials increased by 5 percent. There were no price increases in 19x1 or 19x2.
3. All of the variable marketing costs are due to salespersons' commissions. Effective January 1, 19x3, salespersons' commissions were increased by 10 percent.

4. The number of units sold for the six-month period ended June 30, 19x3, was 160,000.
5. The company had no inventories on June 30, 19x3, and December 31, 19x2.
6. Other than the information provided above, all fixed and variable costs during 19x3 were incurred in the same pattern as for 19x1 and 19x2.

Required   *a.* Prepare an estimated traditional income statement for the six months ended June 30, 19x3.
b. Recast your income statement from part *(a)* into the contribution format.

P3–26   **Preparation of Contribution Format Statement Using High-Low Analysis**
Magee Company wishes to prepare a budgeted income statement for 19x7. The company's income statements for the two prior years are available. However, Magee wishes to experiment with an income statement prepared using the contribution format that it plans to use for various types of decision strategies contemplated for 19x7.

The income statements for 19x6 and 19x5 are as follows:

MAGEE COMPANY
Income Statement
For the Years Ended December 31, 19x6 and 19x5

	19x6	19x5
Sales	$7,500,000	$6,000,000
Cost of sales:		
Direct materials	$1,650,000	$1,320,000
Direct labor	1,100,000	880,000
Manufacturing overhead	1,500,000	1,435,000
Total cost of sales	4,250,000	3,635,000
Gross margin	3,250,000	2,365,000
Less: Marketing and administrative costs	2,650,000	2,500,000
Net income (loss)	$ 600,000	$ (135,000)

Sales for both years were at $150 per unit. Manufacturing overhead consisted of:

	19x6	19x5
Factory rent	$ 585,000	$ 585,000
Indirect labor	250,000	225,000
Utilities	350,000	320,000
Miscellaneous overhead	315,000	305,000
Totals	$1,500,000	$1,435,000

Marketing and administrative costs include commissions to salespersons of 10 percent of sales. The balance of the marketing and administrative costs are fixed.
There were no beginning or ending inventories and none are expected for 19x7. All costs and selling prices are not expected to change for the year 19x7.

Required   *a.* For each item of overhead, identify whether it is (F) fixed, (V) variable, or (M) mixed.
b. Segregate each mixed cost into its fixed and variable components using the high-low method.
c. Prepare a cost formula for each mixed cost.
d. Prepare an income statement using the contribution format for 19x7. The projected sales volume is 70,000 units.

P3–27 **Preparation of Contribution Format Income Statement and Changes in Sales Volume**

Tyler Company had the following income statement prepared for the year 19x7:

TYLER COMPANY
Income Statement
For the Year Ended December 31, 19x7

Sales	$3,000,000
Costs of goods sold.	1,675,000
Gross margin	1,325,000
Marketing and administrative costs . . .	725,000
Net income	$ 600,000

Included in the cost of goods sold are $1 million of fixed manufacturing costs. The marketing and administrative costs include salespersons' commissions and other variable costs to the extent of $175,000. The balance of the marketing and administrative costs are fixed.

Tyler Company manufactures and sells only one product at a selling price of $60 per unit.

Required
a. Recast the income statement into a contribution format statement.
b. Compute the contribution margin ratio for the company.
c. Compute the contribution margin per unit for the company.
d. During 19x7, the economy was very sluggish. For 19x8, the president of the company expects sales to either increase 15 percent or decrease 30 percent depending on the outcome of the national presidential election. In either case, the company's president does not expect to change selling prices.

Required
Compute the expected change in net income for both possibilities. (You may wish to compute the expected changes using one method and check your calculations using another method.)

P3–28 **Preparation of Estimated Traditional and Contribution Income Statements Using High-Low Cost Analysis Coupled with Price Changes**

Valley Company closed for vacation on June 30, 19x5, and on July 4, 19x5, a fire totally destroyed the company's premises including all of its books and records. Fortunately, independent auditors had copies of the firm's annual reports. Condensed income statements of the firm appear below.

VALLEY COMPANY
Income Statements
For the Years Ended December 31, 19x4, and 19x3

	19x4	19x3
Sales revenue	$6,000,000	$5,000,000
Cost of sales:		
Direct materials	600,000	500,000
Direct labor	750,000	625,000
Manufacturing overhead . . .	2,050,000	1,900,000
Cost of sales	3,400,000	3,025,000
Gross margin	2,600,000	1,975,000
Other costs:		
Marketing.	625,000	575,000
Administrative.	900,000	825,000
Total	1,525,000	1,400,000
Net income	$1,075,000	$ 575,000

After conferring with the president and sales manager of the company, the following were ascertained:

1. The company manufactures only one product and previously sold it for $40 per unit. Effective January 1, 19x5, the price was increased by 20 percent.
2. Effective January 1, 19x5, the price of direct materials increased by 10 percent. There were no price increases in 19x3 or 19x4.
3. All of the variable marketing costs are due to salespersons' commissions. Effective January 1, 19x5, salespersons' commissions were increased by 5 percent.
4. The number of units sold for the six-month period ended June 30, 19x5, was 120,000.
5. The company had no inventories on June 30, 19x5, and December 31, 19x4.
6. Other than the information provided above, all fixed and variable costs during 19x5 were incurred in the same pattern as for 19x3 and 19x4.

Required   *a.* Prepare an estimated traditional income statement for the six months ended June 30, 19x5.
   b. Recast your income statement from part *(a)* into the contribution format.

P3–29   **(Appendix 3-A) Preparation of Contribution Income Statement Using Least-Squares Cost Analysis (Regular Equation Approach)**

In 19x9, Drilling Company incurred the following costs and sold the following units for the months indicated:

	Manufacturing Overhead	Marketing Costs	Units Produced and Sold
January	$ 95,520	$ 75,210	4,300
February	90,070	66,220	3,100
March	'115,220	113,710	9,800
April	102,310	89,940	6,500
May	111,220	106,790	8,800
June	106,880	98,970	7,800

The company has no inventories at the end of any month; that is, all units produced are sold in the month produced. The following additional information is available:

Direct materials cost	$5 per unit
Direct labor cost	$4 per unit
Administrative costs per month,	
all fixed	$75,000 per month
Selling price	$50 per unit

The company manufactures only one product. For July 19x9, the company estimates it will sell 8,000 units.

Required   *a.* Prepare the cost formulas for manufacturing overhead and marketing costs using the *regular equation approach* of the least-squares method.
   b. Prepare an estimated income statement for the month of July 19x9 using the contribution format.

P3–30   **(Appendix 3-A) Preparation of Contribution Income Statement Using Least-Squares Cost Analysis (Short-Cut Approach)**
Use the information provided in Problem P3–29.

Required   *a.* Prepare the cost formulas for manufacturing overhead and marketing costs using the *short-cut approach* of the least-squares method.

b. Prepare an estimated income statement for the month of July 19x9 using the contribution format.

P3–31   (Appendix 3-A) Scatter Diagram and Least-Squares Method Cost Analysis (Regular Equation Approach)

Coranda Company provides you with the following activity levels and monthly costs for the year 19x5:

Month	Units	Product Cost
January.	370	$ 6,750
February	530	9,950
March	660	12,800
April	700	11,850
May	520	10,200
June	720	12,410
July	470	8,400
August	300	6,500
September	580	11,610
October	740	13,290
November	630	12,360
December.	860	14,190

Required   *a.* Construct a scatter diagram to determine the fixed cost per month.
   b. Compute the fixed cost per month and the variable cost per unit using the *regular least-squares method.*
   c. Prepare the equation for analyzing mixed costs for Coranda Company. (Use the form $Y = a + bX$.)

P3–32   (Appendix 3-A): Scatter Diagram and Least-Squares Method Cost Analysis (Short-Cut Approach)

Use the information provided in Problem P3–31.

Required   *a.* Construct a scatter diagram to determine the fixed cost per month.
   b. Compute the fixed cost per month and the variable cost per unit using the *short-cut least-squares method.*
   c. Prepare the equation for analyzing mixed costs for Coranda Company. (Use the form $Y = a + bX$.)

P3–33   (Appendix 3-A): Least-Squares Method Cost Analysis (Regular Equation Approach)

Use the information provided in Problem P3–20.

Required   *a.* Compute the fixed cost per month and the variable cost per unit using the *regular least-squares method.*
   b. Prepare the equation for analyzing mixed costs for the Jonar Company. (Use the form $Y = a + bX$.)

P3–34   (Appendix 3-A): Least-Squares Method Cost Analysis (Short-Cut Approach)

Use the information provided in Problem P3–20.

Required   *a.* Compute the fixed cost per month and the variable cost per unit using the *short-cut approach* of the *least-squares method.*
   b. Prepare the equation for analyzing mixed costs for the Jonar Company. (Use the form $Y = a + bX$.)

P3–35 **(Appendix 3-A): Least-Squares Method Cost Analysis (Regular Equation Approach)**

Use the information provided in Problem P3–21.

Required   *a.* Compute the fixed cost per month and the variable cost per unit using the *regular least-squares method.*

  b. Prepare the equation for analyzing mixed costs for Fram Hospital. (Use the form $Y = a + bX$.)

P3–36 **(Appendix 3-A): Least-Squares Method Cost Analysis (Short-Cut Approach)**

Use the information provided in Problem P3–21.

Required   *a.* Compute the fixed cost per month and the variable cost per unit using the *short-cut approach* of the *least-squares method.*

  b. Prepare the equation for analyzing mixed costs for Fram Hospital. (Use the form $Y = a + bX$.)

P3–37 **(Appendix 3-A) Scatter Diagram and Least-Squares Method Cost Analysis (Regular Equation Approach)**

Joranda Company provides you with the following activity levels and monthly costs for the year 19x5:

Month	Units	Product Cost
January	270	$11,908
February	290	11,761
March	300	13,023
April	420	16,212
May	480	19,284
June	500	19,528
July	380	16,574
August	320	13,169
September	530	21,707
October	800	29,838
November	650	25,662
December	556	22,327

Required   *a.* Construct a scatter diagram to determine the fixed cost per month.

  b. Compute the fixed cost per month and the variable cost per unit using the *regular least-squares method.*

  c. Prepare the equation for analyzing mixed costs for Joranda Company. (Use the form $Y = a + bX$.)

P3–38 **(Appendix 3-A): Scatter Diagram and Least-Squares Method Cost Analysis (Short-Cut Approach)**

Use the information provided in Problem P3–37.

Required   *a.* Construct a scatter diagram to determine the fixed cost per month.

  b. Compute the fixed cost per month and the variable cost per unit using the *short-cut least-squares method.*

  c. Prepare the equation for analyzing mixed costs for Joranda Company. (Use the form $Y = a + bX$.)

▶ **CASE**   C3–39   **Reconstruction of Missing Data**

You are employed by Carmel Company as an assistant management accountant. You are in the process of preparing a projected income statement in the contribution format for the following year, 19x6. The statement must be available Monday morning. It is now Friday afternoon at 5 P.M., and the work is not completed. Since you have an important date for Friday evening that you do not want to cancel, you decide to take your work home with you for the weekend. Once home, you place your loose sheets of work on your desk.

Saturday afternoon you go to your desk to finish the projected income statement. You are shocked to discover that your dog somehow got your papers and tore them into pieces. You gather the pieces and try to put them together, and you wind up with a pro forma income statement that appears as follows:

CARMEL COMPANY
Projected Contribution Format Income Statement
For the Year ended December 31, 19x6

Sales		$
Variable costs:		
Direct materials.	$	
Direct labor		
Indirect labor.		
Utilities		
Miscellaneous overhead		
Total variable manufacturing costs		
Salespersons commissions	130,000	
Total variable costs		
Contribution margin.		
Fixed costs:		
Factory rent	$	
Indirect labor.		
Utilities		
Miscellaneous overhead		
Marketing and administrative.	480,000	
Total fixed costs		
Net Income		$

In a panic, you try to recall some pertinent information that will assist you in preparing your desperately needed income statement. You recall that salespersons' commissions are paid at the rate of 5 percent of sales. The firm manufactures and sells only one product for $100 each.

Because of your familiarity with the firm's costs, you are able to recall that the variable costs other than salespersons' commissions are as follows:

	Per Unit
Direct materials	$10.00
Direct labor	15.00
Indirect labor	1.70
Utilities	3.00
Miscellaneous overhead	5.30

For the year ended December 31, 19x4, you know that 24,000 units were produced. Since the firm's policy is not to carry any finished goods inventories, this also represents the amount of units sold. Fortunately, you have the following information for the year 19x4 that was safely in your briefcase.

	19x4
Factory rent	$360,000
Indirect labor	70,800
Utilities	82,000
Miscellaneous overhead.	287,200
Totals	$800,000

The firm has a 10-year lease for its premises at a fixed rent for the 10-year period.

Required Prepare the projected contribution format income statement that you need for Monday morning. Your upcoming promotion depends on your submitting this statement on your return to work.

1. False   2. True   3. False   4. True
5. False   6. False   7. False   8. True
9. False   10. True

Computations for questions 9 and 10

Month	Machine-Hours	Power Cost
March	100,000	$40,000
August.	60,000	26,000
Differences	40,000	$14,000

Variable cost per machine-hour:

$\frac{\$14,000}{40,000} = \$.35$ per machine-hour

Calculation of the fixed cost:

March:
FC = $40,000 − (100,000 × $.35)
FC = $40,000 − $35,000
FC = $5,000

Cost, Volume, and Profit—Analysis and Relationships

▶ **LEARNING OBJECTIVES**

After reading this chapter, you should be able to:

1. Compute a firm's contribution margin ratio and a product's contribution margin per unit and use them to project changes in net income.
2. Compute breakeven sales using an algebraic equation, the contribution margin ratio, and the contribution margin per unit.
3. Compute the sales needed to produce a target income.
4. Discuss breakeven's uses and limitations.
5. Compute the margin of safety and explain its significance.
6. Plot a breakeven graph and describe how it is used.
7. Plot and interpret a profit-volume graph.
8. Define the term *cost structure* and explain how a firm's choice of cost structure may affect its contribution margin and net income.
9. Explain what operating leverage is and how it affects profits.
10. Discuss how changes in selling price, cost, and volume affect profits.
11. Use comparative income statements, differential analysis, and the contribution margin approach to compute the effects that changes in selling price, cost, and volume will have on profit.
12. Compute breakeven sales and target income for a multiproduct firm and explain the role of sales mix in those computations.

▶ **INTERVIEW**

Joseph G. Whelan
President and Founder
Advantage Business
Group
(Specialists in
Accounting-Based
Management Information
Systems)
Formerly, Division
Controller—Charter Oil,
American Ultramar

Q. *Have you used breakeven analysis?*

Background Relating to the Answer

In the late 1970s, . . . huge profits were being made in shipping. A large crude carrier (oil tanker) could move 100 million gallons of crude oil over a six-week period and easily produce $2 million in profit for this single voyage.

I was employed by a company that had decided to build six ships, known as OBOs (oil, bulk, ore—the cargoes that could be carried). These ships could move crude oil to the United States and, after preparation, carry grain or coal-type cargoes on their return voyage, which normally was without cargo. Thus, the fixed charges of the return voyage could be absorbed against another billable voyage.

Economics

In world trade, every voyage in the world is recorded. Facts about the whereabouts of every ship in existence as well as the status of every ship being built, or on order, is known.

The projected revenue from the new ships was based on comprehensive and sophisticated regression analysis. The ever-increasing energy use in the 1970s was the basis of the projection of demand for oil, from which the demand for shipping was derived.

The projections, as it turned out in the middle of manufacturing the six ships, were wrong.

There were two "weak links" in the so-called chain.

1. Worldwide demand growth stopped due to recession as well as the turn to alternative fuels.
2. Crude oil was discovered in Alaska, the Gulf of Mexico, and the United Kingdom. It was closer to U.S. refineries and could be transported in days instead of weeks. There was an oversupply of tankers, almost overnight.

A. My company used breakeven analysis to get a handle on projected cash flows over the four-year period that we were building six ships. One objective was to have a "base case" scenario (i.e., "break even") at which we knew we would not have to approach the bank for additional financing. We projected breakeven for each of four years (starting in March of the second year) as follows:

Year 1—A decision was made to build six ships at a total cost of $300 million. Financing was arranged and a noncancellable contract was signed with a European shipyard.
Year 2—The shipyard commenced building two of the ships.
Year 3—The shipyard commenced building the other four ships.
Year 4—We took delivery of two of the ships.
Year 5—We took delivery of the other four ships.

Our projections in year 1 were relatively standard. However, in year 2, the market prices for shipping dropped by more than 50 percent. Our revenue assumptions, which previously were simple inflationary increases to historical prices, now had to be built from the ground up. In a short period of time, there were dozens of projections produced that could not be readily compared.

We did not use a breakeven chart. If I had it to do over again, the breakeven chart would have been a superb tool for visualizing cost behavior over the range of sales volumes that we were estimating. With hindsight, a *visual* portrayal of how fixed and variable costs behave at different volumes (in this case, the number of billable ship days), would have given a quick understanding in a simple manner.

▶ As noted in Chapter 3, managers use contribution margin in making a variety of decisions. Many managerial decisions require the evaluation of alternative courses of action involving costs, profit, and volume. These three factors are interrelated, so a change in one or more of them may well affect the others. When evaluating a particular course of action, a manager usually uses either the contribution margin ratio (CMR) or the contribution margin per unit (CMPU) to assess the effect on profit. Thus, in this chapter we will examine how the CMR and the CMPU are used in different kinds of management decisions. In particular, we will focus on **cost-volume-profit (CVP) analysis,** which measures the effects that changes in selling prices, costs, sales volume, and sales mix have on profits. CVP analysis is also useful when preparing budgets and analyzing the results of operations.

A special case of CVP is known as breakeven analysis. Because this technique is so widely used, we will examine it before we consider other techniques of CVP analysis.

In Chapter 3, we saw how useful an income statement can be when it is prepared in the contribution format. Once this information is available, there are two extensions of this concept, the contribution margin ratio and the contribution margin per unit, which provide managers with useful tools for their decision-making duties. ◀

L.O. 1
Contribution margin ratio and contribution margin per unit

Contribution Margin Ratio   A useful adjunct of the contribution margin format is the **contribution margin ratio (CMR),** which is the contribution margin divided by sales revenue. The contribution margin ratio indicates the amount of each dollar's sales available for the recovery of fixed costs and earning income. For example, once fixed costs are recovered, a contribution margin ratio of 60 percent means that for each additional dollar of sales revenue, operating income before taxes will increase 60 cents. In Illustration 3-10, the sales revenue amounted to $900,000, the variable costs were $333,000, and the contribution margin amounted to $567,000. Using this information, we can compute the contribution margin ratio as follows:

$$\text{CMR} = \frac{\text{CM}}{\text{Sales}} \qquad (1)$$

$$\text{CMR} = \frac{\$567,000}{\$900,000} = .63 = 63\%$$

It may also be computed as follows:

$$\text{CMR} = 1 - \frac{\text{Variable costs}}{\text{Sales}} = 1 - \frac{\$333,000}{\$900,000} = 1 - .37 = .63, \text{ or } 63\%$$

Contribution Margin per Unit   If Temar Company manufactured only one product and sold 50,000 units in 19x2 (see Illustration 3-10), it could also calculate the **contribution margin per unit (CMPU)** by dividing the contribution margin by the number of units sold:

$$\text{CMPU} = \frac{\text{Contribution margin}}{\text{Number of units sold}} \qquad (2)$$

$$\text{CMPU} = \frac{\$567,000}{50,000 \text{ units}} = \$11.34 \text{ per unit}$$

Thus, on each unit sold, Temar Company initially earns $11.34 toward the recovery of its fixed cost; and, once the fixed costs are recovered, each additional unit sold produces $11.34 of profit. The evolution of contribution margin stems from the fact that it initially contributes to the recovery of fixed costs, and once these are recovered, it contributes to profit.

If Temar Company anticipates a 20 percent increase in sales for 19x3, the computation of the increase in annual net income (provided the company had a net income in 19x2) is easily calculated as:

$$
\begin{aligned}
\text{Increase in net income} &= \text{Increased sales in units} \times \text{CMPU} \\
&= 50{,}000 \text{ units} \times 20\% = 10{,}000 \times \$11.34 \\
&= \$113{,}400
\end{aligned}
$$

▶ BREAKEVEN ANALYSIS USING EQUATIONS

Breakeven Sales

When managers contemplate entering a new market or starting a new product line, they often ask, "What volume of sales do we need to break even?" **Breakeven sales (BES)** is the point at which sales equals total costs, or a zero profit. The amount may be stated in dollars or in units, and it may be ascertained algebraically, arithmetically, or from a breakeven graph.

Net income may be derived from the following equation:

$$S - TC = NI \tag{3}$$

where

S = Sales
TC = Total costs
NI = Net income

Total costs may be subdivided into fixed costs (FC) and variable costs (VC). Substituting in Equation (3), we derive the following:

$$S - FC - VC = NI \tag{4}$$

Transposing, we obtain

$$S = FC + VC + NI \tag{5}$$

We can modify Equation (5) so that breakeven sales may be expressed algebraically as:

$$BES = FC + VC + NI \tag{6}$$

where

BES = Breakeven sales
FC = Fixed costs
VC = Variable costs
NI = Net income where NI is zero.

Breakeven Dollar Sales   As an example, assume that:

1. Weimar Company's fixed costs for 19x1 are expected to be $180,000.
2. The company's variable costs are 40 percent of sales. This figure, determined by dividing variable costs by sales revenue, is sometimes referred to as the **variable cost ratio (VCR).**

Inserting this information into the breakeven sales equation leads to:

$$BES = \$180{,}000 + .40BES + \$0$$

Transposing, the new equation and its solution are:

$$BES - .40BES = \$180,000$$
$$.60BES = \$180,000$$
$$BES = \frac{\$180,000}{.60}$$
$$BES = \$300,000$$

The proof of this solution would be:

		Percent
Sales	$300,000	100
Variable costs at 40 percent of sales.	120,000	40
Contribution margin	180,000	60
Fixed costs.	180,000	
Net income.	$ –0–	

Breakeven per Unit Approach   Assume Weimar Company's fixed costs are $180,000, its selling price per unit is $20, and its variable cost ratio is 40 percent. Therefore, the variable cost per unit is $8 ($20 × .40 = $8) and the contribution margin per unit (CMPU) is $12. **Breakeven units (BEU)**—the number of units that must be sold to equal total costs or yield a zero profit—may be ascertained algebraically as follows:

$$\text{Let} \quad X = \text{Breakeven units}$$
$$FC = \text{Fixed costs}$$
$$VC = \text{Variable costs}$$
$$BES = \$20X \text{ (selling price times number of units)}$$
$$VC = \$ 8X$$

Recalling the BES equation of:

$$BES = FC + VC + NI$$

it is possible to substitute for BES, VC, and zero for NI to arrive at:

$$\$20X = FC + \$8X + \$0$$

Inserting the fixed costs into the equation leads to:

$$\$20X = \$180,000 + \$8X + \$0$$

Solving the equation produces:

$$\$20X = \$180,000 + \$8X$$
$$\$20X - \$8X = \$180,000$$
$$\$12X = \$180,000$$
$$X = \frac{\$180,000}{\$12} = 15,000 \text{ units}$$

Contribution Margin per Unit Approach

Breakeven Unit Sales   The solution above eliminates the intermediate step of computing BES and then converting that dollar amount into units. It should be noted that the solution contains the following:

$$X = \frac{\$180,000}{\$12}$$

This can be stated as the **contribution margin per unit (CMPU) approach to breakeven,** or:

$$\text{Breakeven units} = \frac{FC}{CMPU} = \frac{\$180,000}{\$12} = 15,000 \text{ units}$$

This intermediate step can be used to solve CVP problems directly, thus eliminating some of the calculations required to arrive at a solution. In this approach, BEU is computed simply by dividing fixed costs by CMPU. Because of its simplicity, the CMPU approach is used in this text whenever the BEU is to be computed directly.

Breakeven Dollar Sales   In the algebraic approach to BES, note that the following step is found just prior to solving the BES equation:

$$BES = \frac{\$180,000}{.60} = \$300,000$$

As with the CMPU approach above, the **contribution margin ratio (CMR) approach to breakeven** can be used in place of the VCR equation technique as follows:

$$BES = \frac{FC}{CMR}$$

Because the CMR approach to breakeven is much simpler than the algebraic approach, this book will use the CMR in all computations requiring breakeven sales in dollars.

When the CMR approach is used to determine BES in dollars, BEU may then be computed as follows:

$$\frac{BES}{\text{Selling price}} = \frac{\$300,000}{\$20} = 15,000 \text{ units}$$

It is important to note that:

$$BEU = \frac{\$\text{Fixed costs}}{\$\text{Contribution margin } per\ unit}$$

and

$$BES = \frac{\$\text{Fixed costs}}{\text{Contribution margin } ratio}$$

Targeted Income

L.O. 3

A firm's **targeted income** is the amount of income it wishes to earn. The amount may be designated as *pre-tax operating income* or *after-tax operating income.* Our discussion will begin by considering the simpler pre-tax operating income and then conclude with the after-tax operating income. Managers must use after-tax calculations to arrive at correct decisions.

Pre-Tax Targeted Operating Income   Many managers use a targeted operating income as the starting point in deciding which marketing and pricing strategies to use. The formula to determine a specific pre-tax operating income is similar to the breakeven formula. The equation for a pre-tax operating income is:

$$S = FC + VC + PTOI \qquad\qquad (7)$$

▶ **ILLUSTRATION 4-1**

WEIMAR COMPANY
Income Statement—Contribution Format
For the Year Ended December 31, 19x2

		Percent
Sales (30,000 units at $20)	$600,000	100
Variable costs (30,000 at $8)	240,000	40
Contribution margin	360,000	60
Fixed costs	180,000	
Net income	$180,000	

where

S = Sales revenue
VC = Variable costs
FC = Fixed costs
$PTOI$ = Pre-tax targeted operating income

Let us consider the income statement of Weimar Company shown in Illustration 4-1. If Weimar Company wishes to earn a pre-tax targeted operating income of $240,000 for 19x3 based on its 19x2 operating results as shown in the illustration, the calculation of total needed sales revenue would be:

$$S = \$180,000 + .4S + \$240,000$$

Transposing .4S, the equation becomes:

$$S - .4S = \$180,000 + \$240,000$$
$$.6S = \$420,000$$

Dividing both sides of the equation by .6S, the result is:

$$S = \frac{\$420,000}{.6}$$
$$S = \$700,000$$

This solution assumes there will be no change in fixed costs and the CMR will remain at 60 percent for 19x3. The proof of the solution is:

		Percent
Sales . . . . — . .	$700,000	100
Variable costs	280,000	40
Contribution margin	420,000	60
Fixed costs.	180,000	
Net income.	$240,000	

Note that the next-to-the-last line of the solution is:

$$S = \frac{\$420,000}{.6}$$

This may also be viewed as:

$$\frac{FC + PTOI}{CMR} = \frac{\$180,000 + \$240,000}{.6} = \frac{\$420,000}{.6}$$

Thus, a simplified approach to the calculation of the sales revenue necessary to produce a pre-tax operating income is merely to add the targeted income to fixed costs and divide the total by the contribution margin ratio, as was done to compute breakeven sales.

If the answer is desired in units instead of in sales revenue, the same procedure would be used, but the division would be by the contribution margin per unit instead of by the CMR. For Weimar, the unit sales necessary to reach the pre-tax operating income of $240,000 would be:

$$\frac{FC + PTOI}{CMPU} = \frac{\$180,000 + \$240,000}{\$12} = \frac{\$420,000}{\$12} = 35,000 \text{ units}$$

After-Tax Net Income Thus far, the targeted-income problems considered only income before taxes. Because profitable companies usually pay income taxes, managers prefer CVP analysis on an after-tax basis. The amount of income a company retains after taxes can be expressed as:

$$NI = (1 - t) \text{ Income before income tax}$$

where

$$NI = \text{After-tax net income}$$
$$t = \text{The average tax rate}$$

Using the same information as before—namely, a selling price of $20 per unit, a variable cost of $12 per unit, and fixed costs of $180,000 per annum—Weimar Company now would like to earn $240,000 on an after-tax basis. Its income tax rate is 25 percent of pre-tax income.

$$\text{Let } X = \text{Sales in units}$$
$$FC = \text{Fixed costs}$$
$$VC = \text{Variable costs}$$
$$t = \text{Tax rate}$$
$$NI = \text{After-tax net income}$$

$$X = FC + VC + \frac{NI}{(1 - t)} \tag{8}$$

$$(\$20)X = \$180,000 + (\$12)X + \frac{\$240,000}{(1 - .25)}$$

$$(\$20)X - (\$12)X = \$180,000 + \frac{\$240,000}{.75}$$

$$(\$8)X = \$180,000 + \$320,000$$
$$(\$8)X = \$500,000$$
$$X = 62,500 \text{ units}$$

The proof of the above calculation is:

Sales (62,500 × $20)	$1,250,000
Variable cost (62,500 × $12).	750,000
Contribution margin	500,000
Fixed costs	180,000
Income before income taxes.	320,000
Income taxes at 25 percent	80,000
Net income	$ 240,000

Special Problem—Sales Commissions or Other Variable Costs

Targeted-income decision problems sometimes contain complexities that prohibit the use of the contribution margin ratio and contribution margin per unit approaches to cost-volume-profit analysis. Such complexities may occur, for example, when commissions on sales in excess of a specific volume are payable to salespersons. Let us now consider such a problem. For ease of presentation, we will consider the targeted income on a pre-tax basis.

Weimar Company sells portable radios at the price of $20 per unit. Its variable cost per unit is $12, and its fixed cost per annum is $180,000. In 19x4, Weimar Company wishes to earn a pre-tax targeted income of $240,000; to achieve that end, it intends to offer its sales manager an incentive of $2 per unit on sales in excess of breakeven sales. The company president wishes to know how many units must be sold to earn a pre-tax targeted income of $240,000. The problem can be solved as follows:

$$\text{Let BES} = \text{Breakeven sales in units (22,500)}$$
$$\text{PTNI} = \text{Pre-tax targeted income}$$
$$\text{VC} = \text{Variable costs}$$
$$\text{FC} = \text{Fixed costs}$$
$$\text{C} = \text{Commission}$$
$$X = \text{Sales in units}$$

$$X = \text{VC} + \text{FC} + \text{PTNI} + \text{C}$$

$$(\$20)X = (\$12)X + \$180,000 + \$240,000 + (\$2)(X - 22,500)$$
$$(\$20)X = (\$12)X + \$180,000 + \$240,000 + (\$2)X - \$45,000$$
$$(\$6)X = \$375,000$$
$$X = 62,500 \text{ units}$$

The proof of the calculation is:

Sales (62,500 × $20)	$1,250,000
Variable cost (62,500 × $12)	750,000
Subtotal	500,000
Fixed cost	180,000
Subtotal	320,000
Commission (62,500 − 22,500) × $2.	80,000
Net income.	$ 240,000

A nonalgebraic solution would be to use the contribution margin per unit approach for those units above the breakeven sales. The contribution margin per unit for sales above the breakeven mark would be $6 ($8 less the commission of $2), and the computations would be:

$$\text{Above BES} = \frac{\text{TI}}{\text{New CMPU}} = \frac{\$240,000}{\$6} = 40,000 \text{ units}$$

Add: Breakeven sales   22,500 units

Required sales   62,500 units

Limiting Assumptions of Breakeven Analysis

To avoid drawing invalid conclusions, managers must understand the assumptions on which breakeven analysis is based. In every breakeven analysis, it is assumed that:

L.O. 4
Breakeven limitations

1. All costs are classifiable as either fixed or variable.
2. Variable costs are proportional to sales volume.

3. Fixed costs are constant within the relevant range.
4. The selling price per unit will remain constant.
5. All functions—that is, sales, variable costs, and fixed costs—are linear.
6. The analysis is for either one product or a sales mix that remains constant.
7. The beginning and ending inventory levels are not significantly different.
8. There are no significant fluctuations in the efficiency of the firm's operations.
9. The only factor affecting costs is sales volume.
10. The prices of the cost factors will not change.
11. The general price level will remain relatively constant.
12. The time value of money—interest—is not significant and can be ignored.

The Margin of Safety

L.O. 5

The **margin of safety** is the amount by which a firm's actual sales revenue exceeds its breakeven sales. This is the amount of sales revenue that could be lost before the company's profit would be reduced to zero. The formula for the margin of safety is:

$$\text{Margin of safety} = \text{Sales revenue} - \text{Breakeven sales}$$

The breakeven point for Weimar Company was previously computed as $300,000, and the company's sales for 19x2 were $600,000 as shown in Illustration 4-1. The calculation of the company's margin of safety would be:

$$\text{Margin of safety} = \$600,000 - \$300,000 = \$300,000$$

What the $300,000 margin of safety means is that sales revenue would have to decrease by more than $300,000 before the company would operate at a loss. In essence, the margin of safety is a buffer before losses are incurred.

Because the breakeven point depends on a company's fixed costs and its contribution margin ratio/per unit, another company with a sales revenue of $600,000 would have a different margin of safety from that of Weimar Company. Thus, different companies have different margins of safety at any given sales revenue. When comparing two companies having the same sales level, the company having the higher breakeven point will have a smaller margin of safety and therefore a greater risk factor.

The margin of safety also may be used to assess the risk factor of a particular company. A comparison of a company's margin of safety on a year-to-year basis may shed some light on the possibility of impending difficulties.

The margin of safety may also be expressed as a percentage. The calculation is computed by dividing the margin of safety (in dollars) by the total sales (in dollars). Thus, the calculation of the margin of safety percentage is:

$$\textbf{Margin of safety percentage} = \frac{\$\text{Margin of safety}}{\$\text{Total sales}}$$

$$= \frac{\$300,000}{\$600,000} = 50\%$$

Breakeven Graph

In a **breakeven graph,** two lines—the total cost line and the total revenue line—are plotted, and their intersection indicates the breakeven point. For most managerial purposes, we can assume that both the cost line and the revenue line will be linear within the relevant range.

Constructing a Breakeven Graph To construct a breakeven graph, let us assume that:

a. One product is sold at $20 per unit.
b. The variable cost ratio is 40 percent, and the variable cost per unit is $8.
c. Fixed costs amount to $180,000 annually.

Four steps are necessary to construct a breakeven graph:

L.O 6
Plot breakeven graph

1. The cost equations developed using either the high-low method or the regression analysis covered in Appendix 3-A are used to plot the breakeven graph. To locate the slope of the variable cost line, as in Illustration 4-2, select any two random, but realistic, sales volume figures and multiply them by $8, the variable cost per unit. For example, 6,000 units multiplied by $8 equals $48,000 and 21,000 units multiplied by $8 equals $168,000 may be selected as the two points. Then, locate the point of 6,000 units on the horizontal axis (volume) that coincides with $48,000 on the vertical axis (dollars) and indicate that point with a dot. Use the same procedure to locate the point where 21,000 units coincides with $168,000. Connect and extend a straight line between the two points. If done properly, the lower extension of the line will intersect the zero point (apex). If a point other than zero is reached, one or both of the dots is misplaced. This line represents the variable costs incurred by the firm at any level of volume.
2. Locate the fixed costs, $180,000, on the vertical ($) axis. Using that point, draw a line parallel to the variable cost line drawn in step 1. The *partial area below this line and above the variable cost line* represents the firm's fixed costs of $180,000. The *total area below the line* includes both fixed costs and variable costs. Thus, this line is labeled *total costs.* This can also be seen in Illustration 4-2.

▶ **ILLUSTRATION 4-2**   Breakeven Graph

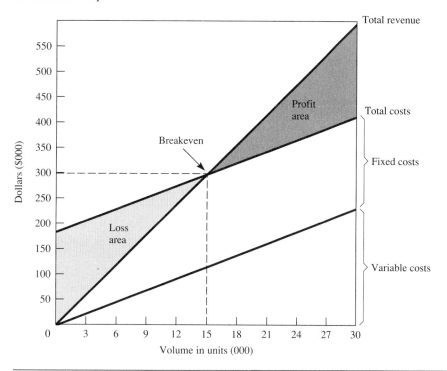

3. Again, select any two realistic sales volume figures and multiply them by $20, the selling price per unit. If the figures from step 1 are used, the results would be $120,000 for 6,000 units and $420,000 for 21,000 units. Plot the points and connect them as in step 1. When extended, the line should also intersect the zero point. This is the sales (total) revenue line, which can be seen in Illustration 4-2.

4 The breakeven point falls where the *revenue line intersects the total cost line,* because at this point total revenues equal total costs. If a perpendicular line is dropped from the breakeven point to the horizontal axis, the breakeven sales in *units* may be obtained from the horizontal axis. In Illustration 4-2, it can be seen that BEU equals 15,000 units. This amount agrees with the algebraic and CMPU calculations. A horizontal line drawn from the breakeven point to the vertical axis enables a reader of the graph to ascertain the breakeven sales in dollars. In Illustration 4-2, the amount is $300,000, which agrees with the BES calculation using the CMR approach.

Other Uses for Breakeven Graphs   Breakeven graphs can also be used to calculate profits or losses at different levels of sales volume. For example, to estimate the profit that would be realized at a volume of 21,000 units, a perpendicular is erected at that volume level. The distance between the total revenue line and the total cost line would be the profit earned. This can be seen in Illustration 4-3. The perpendicular intersects the total revenue line at $420,000 and intersects the total cost line at $348,000. The difference

▶ **ILLUSTRATION 4-3**   Profit Calculation from Breakeven Graph

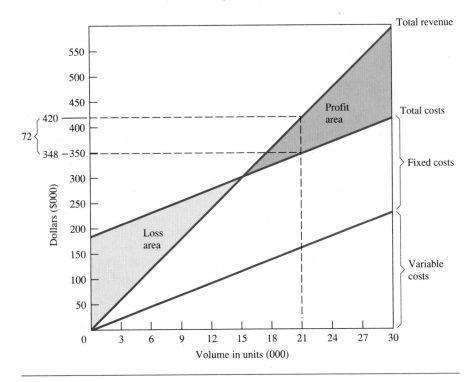

between the two, $72,000, represents the profit earned at a volume of 21,000 units.

The amount can also be determined by using the CMPU approach. The computations are:

	Per Unit
Sales price	$ 20
Variable cost	8
Contribution margin	$ 12
Contribution margin earned (21,000 × $12)	$252,000
Less: Fixed costs	180,000
Net income	$ 72,000

Profit-Volume Graph

L.O. 7

A **profit-volume graph** shows a profit and loss line for various levels of sales volume, which enables managers to examine in series the sales (revenue and/or units) required to attain different levels of targeted income. The steps needed to prepare a profit-volume graph, as shown in Illustration 4-4, are:

1. Draw a vertical line at the left of the graph.
2. Place zero profit at the center of the vertical line.
3. Plot a point below the center of the vertical line equal to the fixed costs. This shows that at a zero volume the loss equals the fixed costs.

▶ **ILLUSTRATION 4-4**   Profit-Volume Graph

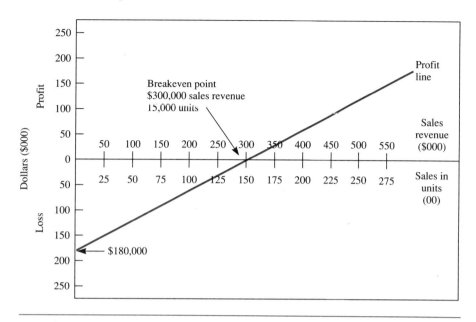

4. Draw a horizontal line at the zero point of the vertical line to the right of the vertical line. This line represents sales (revenues and units).
5. If the breakeven sales are known, indicate that point on the horizontal line and connect that point with the fixed costs point located in step 3. Extend the line above the horizontal line. If the breakeven sales are not known, any known profit point may be used instead.

For any given level of sales, the profit or loss may be obtained by (1) drawing a vertical line from the pertinent sales level to the profit line and (2) drawing a horizontal line from the intersection on the profit line to the left axis and obtaining the profit or loss from that axis. For any given level of profit or loss, the process is reversed—that is, a horizontal line is drawn from the left axis to the profit line and a vertical line is drawn from that intersection to the sales line. The required sales can then be obtained from the horizontal axis.

For example, assume a manager wanted to use this profit-volume graph to determine the sales level necessary to produce a profit of $150,000. By connecting the dotted lines as shown in Illustration 4-5, a manager can easily determine the required sales level to be $550,000 and 27,500 units.

The main advantage of a profit-volume graph is that any targeted income and its related sales figure can easily be ascertained (within the range included on the graph) without performing separate calculations for each case.

Cost Structure

L.O. 8

The relationship between a firm's fixed and variable costs is its **cost structure.** Managers constantly face trade-offs between fixed and variable costs during the decision-making process. A common example is the trade-off between a labor-intensive process (a low fixed cost structure) versus a machine-intensive process (a high fixed cost structure), which can be seen in

▶ **ILLUSTRATION 4-5**   Profit-Volume Graph

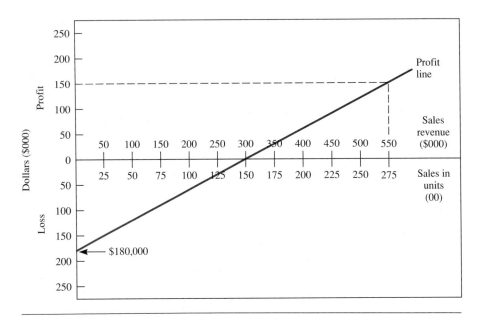

the automobile manufacturing industry. Anyone who visited an auto assembly plant 10 or more years ago would have concluded that it was very machine intensive. Nevertheless, welding and many assembly operations were performed manually. Even when Japanese auto manufacturers began using robots to perform these functions, American auto manufacturers continued to perform them manually. Why have U.S. auto manufacturers lagged behind the Japanese in robotics? The answer is complex. Some of the considerations relate to scarcity of capital, the state of robotic technology, union contracts, and cost structure.

Cost structure, assuming capital is available, is extremely important to most managers. At one extreme is a completely labor-intensive process in which all operations are performed manually. Clearly, sewing a dress or suit of clothes entirely by hand would be more costly than sewing part or all of it by machine. The advantage of a labor-intensive structure is the degree of flexibility. If there is no work due to seasonal fluctuations or economic conditions, workers can be laid off, and most costs associated with labor cease.

At the other extreme is a completely machine-intensive operation that depends on computers and robots and requires few employees. Assuming such an operation were possible and more cost efficient than using human labor, the bulk of the firm's costs would be fixed. In such cases, the cost of machines continues even during slack periods. Thus, for seasonal businesses, a completely machine-intensive operation may be more costly than a labor-intensive one. Most firms operate somewhere between the two extremes.

The choice of cost structure may have a profound effect on a firm's contribution margin and thus on its net income. A comparison of two firms

▶ **ILLUSTRATION 4-6**   Compu Company and Made–to–Order Suit Company: Comparative Cost Structures

	Compu Company		Made-to-Order Suit Company	
	Dollars	Percent	Dollars	Percent
Sales	$500,000	100	$500,000	100
Variable costs	100,000	20	300,000	60
Contribution margin.	400,000	80	200,000	40
Fixed costs	300,000		100,000	
Net income	$100,000		$100,000	

with the same net income and different cost structures will illustrate the concept. Compu Company performs computer services for other firms. It owns a computer and employs two individuals. The bulk of its costs are rent and straight-line depreciation of the computer. The firm is considered machine intensive. For the year just ended, Compu Company had $500,000 of service revenues, $100,000 of variable costs, and $300,000 of fixed costs. Its net income amounted to $100,000.

The Made-to-Order Suit Company manufactures custom-made men's suits. Some sewing is done by machine, but the bulk of the manufacturing is performed by hand. Thus, the firm is considered labor intensive. For the year just ended, its revenues were also $500,000. However, its variable costs were $300,000 and its fixed costs were $100,000. Thus, its net income also amounted to $100,000. The different cost structures are shown in Illustration 4-6.

Although both firms have the same sales and net income, they differ operationally. In periods of increased activity, Compu Company will increase its profits by 80 cents for each additional dollar of sales, assuming no changes in selling prices, unit variable costs, and fixed costs. Made-to-Order Suit Company, however, will increase its profits by only 40 cents for each dollar of increased sales. Thus, in periods of increased activity, Compu Company's cost structure would be preferable.

In periods of diminished activity, Compu Company would lose 80 cents of profit for each dollar of diminished sales activity. Made-to-Order Suit Company, on the other hand, would lose only 40 cents of profit. Thus, you can see how a firm's cost structure has significant effects on its profitability during periods of increased and diminished activity.

▶ OPERATING LEVERAGE

L.O. 9

Operating leverage is the use of fixed costs to increase profits at a faster rate than the corresponding rate of increase in sales. Thus, a firm that is labor intensive and has a low percentage of fixed costs to total costs uses less operating leverage than a machine-intensive firm that has a high percentage of fixed costs to total costs. Because fixed costs are constant within the relevant range, a machine-intensive company that has a 10 percent increase

► **ILLUSTRATION 4-7**

COMPU COMPANY AND MADE–TO–ORDER SUIT COMPANY
Projected Income Statements

	Compu Company		Made-to-Order Suit Company	
	Dollars	Percent	Dollars	Percent
Sales	$600,000	100	$600,000	100
Variable costs	120,000	20	360,000	60
Contribution margin.	480,000	80	240,000	40
Fixed costs	300,000		100,000	
Net income	$180,000		$140,000	

in sales volume will have a larger increase in profit than will a labor-intensive company with a corresponding increase in sales volume.

The **degree of operating leverage** is the measure of how a percentage change in sales volume at a *given level of sales activity* will affect profits. When a firm is operating at or near its breakeven point, the degree of operating leverage is greatest. As profitable operations move further away from the breakeven point, the degree of operating leverage is lessened. Degree of operating leverage is computed by dividing contribution margin by net income.

$$\text{Degree of operating leverage} = \frac{\text{Contribution margin}}{\text{Net income}}$$

Let us analyze the use of operating leverage at the Compu Company and the Made-to-Order Suit Company. Based on their cost structures as shown in Illustration 4-6, their degrees of operating leverage are:

$$\text{Compu:} \quad \frac{\$400,000}{\$100,000} = 4$$

$$\text{Made-to-Order:} \quad \frac{\$200,000}{\$100,000} = 2$$

The degree of operating leverage can then be used to determine what effect a change in sales will have on profits. For example, if each company is expected to experience a 20 percent increase in sales volume, the effect on profits may be calculated as:

Compu: $100,000 × 20% × 4 = $80,000
Made-to-Order: $100,000 × 20% × 2 = $40,000

This can be verified by preparing projected income statements incorporating the 20 percent increase in sales volume, as shown in Illustration 4-7. Note that the projected income statements show Compu Company's net income will increase by $80,000 ($180,000 − $100,000) and Made-to-Order Suit Company's profits will increase by $40,000 ($140,000 − $100,000)—the same results obtained by using the degree of operating leverage.

It is important to remember that the degree of operating leverage varies at different levels of sales activity. It is highest near the breakeven sales and lessens with increased sales volume. Once the breakeven point is reached, net income increases by the same amount as any increase in the contribution margin. Because both the numerator and the denominator increase by the *same* dollar amount, each resulting fraction is thereby reduced. This pattern can be clearly seen at the Compu Company. The firm's breakeven sales are:

$$\text{BES} = \frac{\text{Fixed costs}}{\text{CMR}} = \frac{\$300,000}{.80} = \$375,000$$

And its degrees of operating leverage at different levels of sales activity are:

Sales	$400,000	$450,000	$500,000	$600,000
Variable costs	80,000	90,000	100,000	120,000
Contribution margin (A)	320,000	360,000	400,000	480,000
Fixed costs	300,000	300,000	300,000	300,000
Net income (B)	$ 20,000	$ 60,000	$100,000	$180,000
Operating leverage (A) ÷ (B)	16	6	4	2.67

Operating leverage figures enable managers to quickly assess the impact on profits when either an increase or a reduction in sales activity is anticipated. For example, assume the Compu Company is presently operating at a sales level of $500,000 with a degree of operating leverage of 4. If a reduction of 20 percent in sales activity is expected, the effect on profits may be calculated as:

Effect on profits = Net income × Increase or decrease in sales
× Degree of operating leverage

Effect on profits = $100,000 × −20% × 4 = −$80,000

Thus, net income will be reduced by $80,000, resulting in a $20,000 profit. For verification, this result may be compared with the $20,000 of net income computed for the sales level of $400,000.

▶ **PROGRESS CHECK**

1. What is a breakeven graph? Explain how it can be used to obtain information other than breakeven data.
2. What is a profit-volume graph? How is it used?
3. Is a firm's cost structure important to its managers? Explain.
4. What is operating leverage? How is it used? Is a firm's operating leverage the same at all levels of activity? Explain.   ◀

▶ **COST—VOLUME—PROFIT ANALYSIS**

L.O. 10

The effects that changes in cost, volume, or selling price will have on net income can be measured by:

1. Preparing an income statement without the contemplated changes and comparing it with an income statement modified to reflect the changes.
2. Preparing a partial income statement including only those items that will change and examining the differences that would result.
3. Comparing the present contribution margin with a new contribution margin modified by the contemplated changes. The difference in contribution margins is then adjusted for any changes in fixed costs to produce the net effect that the contemplated changes would have on profits.

▶ **ILLUSTRATION 4-8**

WEIMAR COMPANY
Income Statement—Contribution Format
For the Year Ended December 31, 19x2

		Percent
Sales (30,000 units at $20)	$600,000	100
Variable costs (30,000 at $8)	240,000	40
Contribution margin	360,000	60
Fixed costs	180,000	
Net income	$180,000	

One manager may consistently rely on only one of these three methods, while another manager may prefer to use several, with one method acting as a check on another. Regardless of individual preferences, all three methods produce the same result.

Volume Changes Only

A change in the number of units sold without a change in the unit's selling price or manufacturing cost is the simplest situation to evaluate. Because neither the unit's contribution margin ratio nor its contribution margin per unit changes, both figures can be used without adjustment.

If the Weimar Company sold 30,000 units at $20 per unit in 19x2 and its variable costs were $8 per unit while its fixed costs were $180,000 per annum, its contribution income statement would appear as shown in Illustration 4-8. For 19x3, the company is considering a onetime, direct-mail sales campaign. The cost of the mailers and postage will be $5,000, and management estimates that sales volume will increase by 10 percent. At that volume, an additional supervisor will be needed at an annual salary of $35,000. All other costs are expected to behave in their normal pattern without any increases. Based on these data, the company's management accountant must prepare an analysis to aid management in deciding whether to undertake the mailing campaign. There are at least three different ways to solve this problem, and all lead to the same conclusion.

L.O. 11
Comparative income statement
approach to CVP analysis

The Comparative Income Statement Approach   One method of analyzing this decision problem is the **comparative income statement approach,** in which an income statement modified by the contemplated changes is compared to the unmodified income statement. It requires the following steps:

1. Prepare a contribution income statement without giving effect to any of the proposed changes.
2. Prepare a contribution income statement giving effect to all proposed changes. In this example, the following items must be adjusted:
   a. Sales revenue must be increased by 10 percent. Thus, sales revenue would be $600,000 × 110 percent = $660,000.
   b. Variable costs must be increased by 10 percent because of the increased volume. Variable costs should be $240,000 × 110 percent = $264,000. This amount may also be obtained by multiplying the projected sales revenue by the VCR shown in Illustration 4-8 ($660,000 × 40 percent = $264,000).

▶ **ILLUSTRATION 4-9**

WEIMAR COMPANY
Actual and Projected Income Statements—Contribution Format
For the Year Ended December 31, 19x2, 19x3

	19x2	Percent	Projected 19x3
Sales	$600,000	100	$660,000*
Variable costs	240,000	40	264,000†
Contribution margin	360,000	60	396,000
Fixed costs	180,000		220,000‡
Net income	$180,000		$176,000

* $600,000 × 110% = $660,000.
† $240,000 × 110% = $264,000, or $660,000 × 40% = $264,000.
‡ $180,000 + $5,000 + $35,000 = $220,000.

▶ **ILLUSTRATION 4-10**

WEIMAR COMPANY
Projected Differential Income for 19x3

Increase in sales volume ($600,000 × 10%)		$60,000
Less: Increase in variable costs ($60,000 × 40% CMR).		24,000
Increase in contribution margin		36,000
Less: Increase in printing and mailing	$ 5,000	
Increase in foreman's salary.	35,000	40,000
Net (loss)		$ (4,000)

　　　c. Fixed costs must be increased by the additional $5,000 for advertising and $35,000 for the new supervisor's salary.
 3. Compare the two income statements and select the one that is more advantageous to the firm—generally, the one with the higher net income.

The comparative contribution income statements for the Weimar Company are shown in Illustration 4-9.

This method has the advantage of showing both present income and projected income after additional expenditures. Based on this analysis, management should reject the mailing campaign because it will reduce net income by $4,000.

L.O. 11
Differential approach to CVP analysis

Differential (Incremental) Analysis This problem could also be solved by considering *only* the proposed changes to determine their net effect. When this approach is used, only the following items are considered:

 1. A sales revenue increase of $60,000 ($600,000 × 10 percent).
 2. The variable cost increase of $24,000 ($60,000 × 40 percent CMR).
 3. The increase in fixed costs of $40,000 ($5,000 + $35,000).

This method is usually referred to as **differential** (or **incremental) analysis** because only the differences (or increments) are used to arrive at the decision.

The differential analysis for the Weimar Company is summarized in Illustration 4-10. Note that, unlike the comparative income statement approach,

▶ **ILLUSTRATION 4-11**

WEIMAR COMPANY
Effects of Contemplated Mailing Campaign

		Per Unit
Selling price ($600,000 ÷ 30,000)		$ 20
Variable costs at 40%		8
Contribution margin		$ 12
Estimated contribution margin ($12 × 33,000)		$396,000
Present contribution margin ($12 × 30,000).		360,000
Increase in contribution margin		36,000
Less: Printing and mailing costs.	$ 5,000	
Additional foreman.	35,000	40,000
Net (loss).		$ (4,000)

differential analysis does not require the reader to compare data. Instead, the net loss of $4,000 is arrived at directly. Differential analysis is direct and succinct and allows the manager to focus on the effects of a proposal without being distracted by normal operating data. Nonetheless, some managers prefer the comparative income statement method because it enables them to better assess the relative size of the proposed changes.

L.O. 11
Contribution margin approach to CVP analysis

The Contribution Margin Approach   A third way to analyze the impact of the direct-mail campaign on Weimar's income is the **contribution margin approach.** This method requires that a new total contribution margin be computed giving effect to the contemplated changes. The difference between the new total contribution margin and the current total contribution margin reflects the expected change in that figure. The change in fixed costs is then taken into account to arrive at the net effect of the proposal. The solution using this approach is shown in Illustration 4-11.

Many managers find that the contribution margin approach is the easiest to compute and prefer it because it highlights the immediate effects of the decision to be made. They find that this approach is especially useful in complex problem-solving situations. In any event, all three methods indicate the same result (namely, a loss of $4,000); and in practice, individual preferences often dictate the form in which information is presented to managers.

Changes in Selling Prices and Sales Volume

When a change in selling price is contemplated, an additional step is required to compute its effect on net income. The contribution margin ratio and contribution margin per unit no longer apply, and a new CMR and a new CMPU must be computed. They are also needed for new breakeven computations because the previous ones are invalid.

Referring to the contribution income statement presented in Illustration 4-8, assume that:

1. Weimar is contemplating raising the selling price by 5 percent to $21.00 per unit.
2. The company expects its sales volume to decrease by 10 percent to 27,000 units.
3. All costs—fixed and variable—are expected to have the same behavior pattern they had in 19x2.

▶ **ILLUSTRATION 4-12**

WEIMAR COMPANY
Actual and Projected Income Statements—Contribution Format
For the Year Ended December 31, 19x2, 19x3

	19x2	Percent	Projected 19x3	Percent
Sales	$600,000	100	$567,000*	100
Variable costs	240,000	40	216,000†	38
Contribution margin	360,000	60	351,000	62
Fixed costs	180,000		180,000	
Net income	$180,000		$171,000	

* 27,000 × $21.00 = $567,000.
† 27,000 × $8 = $216,000.

Any one of the three approaches discussed previously may be used to solve the problem.

The Comparative Income Statement Approach　The solution to the problem using the comparative income statement approach requires the following steps:

1. Adjust sales revenues for two factors—a change in selling price and a change in sales volume. Thus, the $600,000 of sales revenue must be reduced by the volume change of 10 percent ($60,000) and the result ($540,000) increased by the selling price change of 5 percent ($27,000) for an adjusted amount of $567,000.
2. Reduce variable costs of $240,000 by 10 percent ($24,000) to $216,000 because of the reduction in sales volume.
3. Leave fixed costs unchanged.

After giving effect to the proposed changes, the comparative income statements would appear as shown in Illustration 4-12. The results indicate that Weimar should not raise its prices for 19x3 because doing so would decrease net income by $9,000. This occurs despite the increase in Weimar's contribution margin ratio from 60 percent to 62 percent and the increase in its contribution margin per unit from $12 to $13 ($21 − $8). If the company could decrease some of its fixed costs in response to the 10 percent reduction in volume, the results might be different. This is an example of the kind of decisions that managers routinely face.

Differential (Incremental) Analysis　If differential analysis were used, it would require the following steps:

1. Calculate the decrease in sales revenue due to the decrease in sales volume. This may be calculated as 10 percent × $600,000 = $60,000, *or* 30,000 units × 10 percent = 3,000 units × $20 per unit = $60,000.
2. Calculate the increase in sales revenue due to the increase in selling price. The new sales volume (27,000 units) is multiplied by the increase in selling price ($1) to arrive at the desired amount of $27,000.
3. Calculate the decrease in variable cost by multiplying the decrease in sales volume (6,000 units) by the unit cost of $8 to arrive at $24,000.

▶ **ILLUSTRATION 4-13**

WEIMAR COMPANY
Projected Differential Income for 19x3

Increase in selling price (27,000 × $1.00).	$ 27,000
Decrease in volume (3,000 × $20)	(60,000)
Net decrease in sales revenue.	(33,000)
Decrease in variable cost (3,000 × $8)	24,000
Net decrease in net income	$ (9,000)

▶ **ILLUSTRATION 4-14**

WEIMAR COMPANY
Effects of Contemplated Price Increase

	Per Unit	
Selling price contemplated	$21.00	
Variable cost	8.00	
Contribution margin	$13.00	
Effects of price reduction:		
Estimated contribution margin ($13.00 × 27,000)		$351,000
Present contribution margin ($12 × 30,000)		360,000
Loss on proposed price increase		$ (9,000)

The amount may also be calculated by multiplying the present variable cost of $240,000 by 10 percent, or $24,000.

4. Because fixed costs are unchanged, no calculation for them is necessary.
5. Prepare a summary of the changes.

A summary of the differential analysis approach to solving the problem appears in Illustration 4-13. The advantages of this solution are that it is simpler to compute than the comparative income statement approach and it focuses only on the changes expected to occur.

The Contribution Margin Approach The contribution margin method is usually the simplest to compute. When this approach is used, the following steps are helpful:

1. Calculate the present total contribution margin by multiplying the present sales volume (30,000 units) by the existing contribution margin per unit ($12), which yields $360,000.
2. Calculate the proposed contribution margin by multiplying the proposed sales volume (27,000 units) by the new contribution margin per unit ($13.00), which yields $351,000.
3. Ignore fixed costs because they are unaffected by the proposal.
4. Compare the results.

Illustration 4-14 presents the comparison of the two contribution margins and the effect of the proposal on net income. Note that the $9,000 loss indicated by this method coincides with the amounts reached by the other two methods.

The main advantage of the contribution margin approach is its simplicity. However, some managers may find the information shown in Illustra-

▶ **ILLUSTRATION 4-15**

WEIMAR COMPANY
Effects of Contemplated Upgrade in Quality

	Per Unit	Percent
Selling price contemplated	$ 30.00	100
Variable cost contemplated.	15.00	50
Contribution margin	$ 15.00	50

Effects of change:	
Estimated contribution margin ($15.00 × 27,000)	$405,000
Present contribution margin	360,000
Increase in contribution margin	45,000
Less: Increase in fixed costs	25,000
Increase in net income from expected change	$ 20,000

tion 4-14 too skimpy. For this reason, familiarity with all three methods is desirable.

Changes in Variable Unit Costs

Whenever a change in variable unit cost is contemplated, the present contribution margin ratio and contribution margin per unit must be adjusted to reflect the cost change. An exception would occur if a compensating change in the selling price were made to maintain the existing contribution margin ratio. Nonetheless, in such a case, the contribution margin per unit would still change. On the other hand, if the contribution margin per unit were maintained, the contribution margin ratio would change.

For example, assume a company's present sales are 10,000 units at $10 per unit, with variable costs of $4 per unit. The cost of the product is expected to rise 10 percent to $4.40, but the company wishes to maintain its existing contribution margin ratio. What should the product's new selling price be? Because the present variable cost ratio is 40 percent ($4 ÷ $10 = 40%), the new selling price would be $11 ($4.40 ÷ .40 = $11). However, the new CMPU would be $6.60, while the existing CMPU is $6 ($10 − $4). To maintain the CMPU at $6, the new selling price would have to be $10.40, and the new CMR would drop to 57.69 percent. It is important to remember these changes to avoid making errors in CVP analysis.

Let us return to Weimar Company's 19x2 contribution format income statement shown in Illustration 4-1. The company wishes its management accountant to evaluate the following proposal:

1. The company would like to upgrade the quality of its only product. By using more expensive direct materials and making a slight design change, the company believes it can sell the revised product at $30 per unit. However, at this price the company estimates it will sell only 27,000 units annually.
2. The increased variable costs will amount to $7 per unit for a total variable unit cost of $15 per unit.
3. A quality control inspector will have to be employed to make sure the employees maintain the higher standard of quality. The inspector will earn an annual salary of $25,000.

The contribution margin analysis for this situation is presented in Illustration 4-15. It indicates that the company should go ahead with the change in quality because net income will be increased by $20,000 if the estimates prove accurate. The same result can be obtained with the comparative income statement approach or the differential analysis approach.

Whenever there is a change in selling price, variable unit cost, or fixed cost, a new breakeven sales in dollars and units must be computed when needed. The new CMR and/or CMPU is used with the new fixed costs.

▶ SALES MIX

L.O. 12
Sales mix for a multiproduct firm

Most firms manufacture and sell more than one product. Thus, they must consider sales mix in their breakeven and CVP analyses. A firm's **sales mix** is its complete set of products classified by the relative amount that each product contributes to total sales revenue.

For example, the Yonar Company manufactures and sells three products—almond cookies, breadsticks, and croutons (hereafter referred to as A, B, and C). They are sold in the ratio of 3 : 1 : 4—that is, three cases of almond cookies are sold for each case of breadsticks and four cases of croutons are sold for each case of breadsticks. Selling prices and variable costs per case of the three products are:

	A	B	C
Selling prices	$20	$20	$10
Variable costs	13	9	6
Contribution margin	$ 7	$11	$ 4

The contribution margins of A, B, and C cannot be used in this raw form. Instead, they must be weighted by the number of cases of each product expected to be sold. The combined total of the products' adjusted contribution margins is referred to as the **weighted contribution margin per mix (WCMPM).** This figure, once computed, is used in the same way as the contribution margin per unit would be in a single-product firm. To compute the weighted contribution margin per mix:

1. Multiply each product's contribution margin by its unit sales to arrive at its contribution margin per mix.
2. Sum the individual contribution margins per mix.

For example, as shown in Illustration 4-16, the contribution margin of product A is $7 per case, and three cases of almond cookies are sold per mix. Thus, the contribution margin per mix of product A is $21. Following the same procedure, the contribution margin per mix of product B is $11, and the contribution margin per mix of product C is $16. We then sum these three figures to arrive at the WCMPM of $48.

Next, based on the WCMPM, the **contribution margin ratio per mix (CMRM)** can be derived. The contribution margin ratio of the mix is a combined weighted-average contribution margin ratio that, like the WCMPM, includes all of a firm's products. And it is used by multiproduct firms in place of the contribution margin ratio. The contribution margin ratio of the mix is determined by dividing the WCMPM by the total sales revenue

▶ **ILLUSTRATION 4-16**

YONAR COMPANY
Sales Mix and Weighted Contribution Margin per Mix

| | Product | | | |
	A	B	C	Totals
Selling price	$20	$20	$10	
Variable costs.	13	9	6	
Contribution margin	$ 7	$11	$ 4	
Units sold per mix.	3	1	4	
Contribution margin per mix	$21	$11	$16	$ 48
Sales revenue per mix	$60	$20	$40	$120

per mix. Based on Illustration 4-16, we see that Yonar's total sales revenue per mix is $120. Thus:

$$\text{Contribution margin ratio per mix} = \frac{\$48}{\$120} = 40\%$$

Sales Mix Breakeven Analysis

Although the breakeven sales calculations for a multiproduct firm are similar to those for a single-product firm, they are valid only for a particular sales mix.

Yonar Company would like to know what its breakeven sales would be in dollars and units if its estimated fixed costs are $480,000 per annum. In this case, the breakeven calculations would be the same as for a single-product firm. They are:

$$\text{BES} = \frac{\text{FC}}{\text{CMRM}} = \frac{\$480,000}{.40} = \$1,200,000$$

and

$$\text{BEU} = \frac{\text{FC}}{\text{WCMPM}} = \frac{\$480,000}{\$48} = 10,000 \text{ mixes}$$

The proof of the calculations is:

| | Product | | | |
	A	B	C	Total
Sales	$600,000*	$200,000†	$400,000‡	$1,200,000
Variable costs	390,000§	90,000‖	240,000#	720,000
Contribution margin	$210,000	$110,000	$160,000	480,000
Fixed costs				480,000
Net income				$ –0–

* 10,000 × 3 × $20.
† 10,000 × 1 × $20.
‡ 10,000 × 4 × $10.
§ 10,000 × 3 × $13.
‖ 10,000 × 1 × $9.
\# 10,000 × 4 × $6.

The breakeven sales in units are:

$$Product\ A = 10,000 \times 3 = 30,000\ units$$
$$B = 10,000 \times 1 = 10,000\ units$$
$$C = 10,000 \times 4 = 40,000\ units$$

Changes in Mix and CVP Analysis

The preceding calculations are valid only if a change in sales mix is not contemplated. However, changes in mix do occur due to variations in consumer demand; changes in costs, selling prices, and volume; and many other reasons. Any change in sales mix requires new computations for the contribution margin ratio per mix and the weighted contribution margin per mix. This is true even if the total sales revenue or number of mixes remains unchanged.

Yonar Company has reason to believe its customers are becoming very conscious of diet and are eating more salads. The company expects to sell only one third of its present sales of almond cookies and to double its sales of croutons. Breadstick sales are expected to remain unchanged. Cost-behavior patterns are expected to remain the same.

The president of Yonar Company asked the firm's management accountant to prepare calculations showing how many cases of each product must be sold and the sales revenue needed to:

1. Produce a pre-tax operating income of $240,000 if the sales mix remains unchanged.
2. Break even if the expected change in sales mix materializes.
3. Produce a pre-tax operating income of $240,000 if the change in sales mix materializes.

The targeted pre-tax operating income calculations for requirement 1 are:

$$Sales\ revenue = \frac{FC + PTOI}{CMRM} = \frac{\$480,000 + \$240,000}{.40} = \$1,800,000$$

$$Sales\ mixes = \frac{FC + PTOI}{WCMPM} = \frac{\$480,000 + \$240,000}{\$48} = 15,000\ mixes$$

The sales in units are:

$$Product\ A = 15,000 \times 3 = 45,000\ units$$
$$B = 15,000 \times 1 = 15,000\ units$$
$$C = 15,000 \times 4 = 60,000\ units$$

For requirement 2, a new weighted contribution margin per mix and a new contribution margin ratio per mix are needed. Illustration 4-17 shows the calculations for the WCMPM ($50). With the CMRM equal to 41⅔ percent ($50 ÷ $120), the new breakeven sales and breakeven units may be computed as:

$$BES = \frac{FC}{CMRM} = \frac{\$480,000}{.4167} = \$1,152,000$$

$$BEU = \frac{FC}{WCMPM} = \frac{\$480,000}{\$50} = 9,600\ mixes$$

► **ILLUSTRATION 4-17**

YONAR COMPANY
Sales Mix and Weighted Contribution Margin per Mix

	A	B	C	Totals
Selling price	$20	$20	$10	
Variable costs	13	9	6	
Contribution margin	$ 7	$11	$ 4	
Units sold per mix	1	1	8	
Contribution margin per mix	$ 7	$11	$32	$ 50
Sales mix	$20	$20	$80	$120

The proof of the calculation is:

	A	B	C	Total
Sales	$192,000*	$192,000†	$768,000‡	$1,152,000
Variable costs	124,800§	86,400‖	460,800#	672,000
Contribution margin	$ 67,200	$105,600	$307,200	480,000
Fixed costs				480,000
Net income				$ –0–

* 9,600 × 1 × $20.
† 9,600 × 1 × $20.
‡ 9,600 × 8 × $10.
§ 9,600 × 1 × $13.
‖ 9,600 × 1 × $9.
9,600 × 8 × $6.

The breakeven sales in units are:

$$\text{Product A} = 9,600 \times 1 = 9,600$$
$$\text{B} = 9,600 \times 1 = 9,600$$
$$\text{C} - 9,600 \times 8 = 76,800$$

Note that in this case, the sales revenue per sales mix remains unchanged at $120. Nevertheless, because of the change in sales mix, the weighted contribution margin per mix changed from $48 to $50, and the contribution margin ratio per mix increased from 40 percent to 41⅔ percent. Thus, the change caused by the shift in the sales mix from the less profitable cookies to the more profitable croutons may be favorable to Yonar Company because WCMPM increased by $2, and the BES decreased from $1,200,000 to $1,152,000. If the number of units (mixes) actually sold remains unchanged, then a favorable condition exists. Profits will increase by $2 multiplied by the number of mixes sold.

Generally, less profitable merchandise is easier to sell than more profitable merchandise. Thus, when a change in sales mix is contemplated, the shift should emphasize the more profitable merchandise to the greatest extent possible. A change in sales mix may increase a firm's profits when this strategy is practiced. However, a change in sales mix may also decrease

▶ **ILLUSTRATION 4-18**   Formulas and Methods for Use in Solving CVP Applications

Formula or Method	Use
1. BES = FC + VC	Algebraic method of breakeven sales in dollars
2. BES = $\dfrac{FC}{CMR}$	Contribution margin method of breakeven sales in dollars
3. $S = FC + $VC	Algebraic method of breakeven sales in units
4. BEU = $\dfrac{FC}{CMPU}$	Contribution margin method of breakeven sales in units
5. S = VC + FC + PTOI	Algebraic method of sales necessary to produce a desired pre-tax operating income
6. S = $\dfrac{FC + PTOI}{CMR}$	Contribution margin method of sales dollars necessary to produce a desired pre-tax operating income
7. S = $\dfrac{FC + PTOI}{CMPU}$	Contribution margin method of sales in units necessary to produce a desired pre-tax operating income
8. MS = S − BES	Margin of safety—the amount of sales that could be lost before a loss would result
9. MS percentage = $\dfrac{MS}{Total\ sales}$	Margin of safety percentage
10. $\dfrac{Contribution\ margin}{Net\ income}$	Operating leverage—the use of fixed costs to increase profits at a faster rate than sales revenue
11. Comparative income statement approach	Comparing the results of operations from two alternative CVP decisions by preparing an income statement for each alternative
12. Differential (incremental) analysis	Considering only the items that differ between two alternative CVP decisions
13. Contribution margin approach	Comparing the new contribution margin and any change in fixed costs with the existing contribution margin and fixed costs for a CVP decision

profits when a firm is unable to implement this strategy due to market factors.

The solution to requirement 3 for a pre-tax operating income of $240,000 is:

$$\text{Sales revenue} = \frac{FC + PTOI}{CMRM} = \frac{\$480{,}000 + \$240{,}000}{.4167} = \$1{,}728{,}000$$

$$\text{Sales mixes} = \frac{FC + PTOI}{WCMPM} = \frac{\$480{,}000 + \$240{,}000}{\$50} = 14{,}400 \text{ mixes}$$

The sales in units are:

$$\text{Product A} = 14{,}400 \times 1 = 14{,}400 \text{ units}$$
$$B = 14{,}400 \times 1 = 14{,}400 \text{ units}$$
$$C = 14{,}400 \times 8 = 115{,}200 \text{ units}$$

It is interesting to note that the number of mixes needed to produce the same targeted income of $240,000 decreases from 15,000 under the present mix to 14,400 under the expected mix. If Yonar Company can maintain a volume of 15,000 mixes after the change in mix occurs, profits will be $30,000 (15,000 × $2) higher than if the change did not occur.

A summary of the formulas and approaches used to solve CVP applications in this chapter appears in Illustration 4-18.

► **SUMMARY**

A question that managers often ask when they are about to enter a new market or make a new product is, "What volume of sales do we need to break even?" This information is helpful in assessing the risk involved in new market and new product decisions. The calculation of **breakeven sales** (in dollars and in units) may be calculated (1) algebraically, (2) by using the **contribution margin ratio,** and (3) by using the **contribution margin per unit.** Regardless of the method used, a firm's costs must be classified into two categories—fixed and variable. The variable cost per unit divided by the unit's selling price is the unit's **variable cost ratio.** Breakeven sales in dollars may be calculated by dividing a firm's fixed costs by its contribution margin ratio. Breakeven sales in units may be calculated by dividing a firm's fixed costs by its contribution margin per unit.

Breakeven sales calculations may also be used to determine the sales needed to produce a **targeted income.** The targeted income may be calculated on a pre-tax basis or on an after-tax basis, depending on the information desired. To calculate a targeted income on a pre-tax basis, fixed costs are added to the targeted income and the total is then divided either by the firm's contribution margin ratio to arrive at targeted-income sales revenue or by its contribution margin per unit to produce targeted-income sales in units.

The **margin of safety** provides managers with a measure of how much sales can decrease before the firm will operate at a loss. It is computed by subtracting the product's breakeven sales from the current sales level.

A valuable management tool is the **breakeven graph.** Managers can determine their firm's breakeven sales in dollars and in units directly from such a graph without making arithmetic calculations. A breakeven graph may also be used to determine the sales needed to produce a targeted income. The advantage of using a breakeven graph for this purpose is that any number of pre-tax targeted-income sales figures, within the range of the graph, may be determined without separate mathematical calculations. A breakeven graph may also be used to determine a firm's income for any given sales level.

A **profit-volume graph** enables managers to assess the effects that changes in sales volume will have on profits or losses. In a profit-volume graph, the profit line is plotted to intersect the sales line. Thus, it differs from a breakeven graph, in which the total cost line intersects the sales line.

Managers often must decide whether to perform certain operations manually or to automate them. Although the long-run average cost of automated operations may be less than that of the manual operations, the decision has a profound impact on a firm's **cost structure.** Automated firms have a high proportion of fixed costs to variable costs, while the reverse is true for firms that rely more on manual labor. During periods of increased activity, automated firms have a greater proportion of contribution to profit per increased sales dollar than do labor-intensive firms. During periods of decreased activity, however, automated firms have a greater diminution of contribution to profit per decreased sales dollar than do labor-intensive firms.

The use of **operating leverage** can enable a firm to increase profits at a faster rate than could be achieved through a corresponding increase in sales. The **degree of operating leverage** provides managers with a quick method of calculating the effect on profits of a contemplated change in sales revenue. It is calculated by dividing contribution margin by net income.

Through **cost-volume-profit (CVP) analysis,** managers can assess the effects that contemplated changes in marketing strategy will have on their firm's net income. The three most common forms of CVP analysis are (1) **comparative income statements,** in which current data are compared to data that reflect the contemplated changes; (2) **differential (incremental) analysis,** which considers only the items affected by the changes; and (3) the **contribution margin approach,** which compares the existing contribution margin with the contemplated contribution margin and adjusts the difference for any changes in fixed costs.

Most firms manufacture and/or sell a variety of products. In attempting to assess the effects that changes in cost, volume, and selling price will have on profits, managers of multiproduct firms must understand the concept of **sales mix**—the firm's complete set of products classified by the relative amount that each product contributes to total sales value—and the role it plays in computing **contribution margin ratio per mix** and **weighted contribution margin per mix.** A change in sales mix, with or without a change in total sales volume, may have a significant effect on a firm's profit or loss. An increase in the sales volume of one product, with a corresponding decrease in the sales volume of another product, may lead to greater profits if the product with increased volume has a higher contribution margin per unit than the product with decreased volume. Conversely, profits will decrease if the shift in sales volume favors the product with the smaller contribution margin per unit.

When calculating breakeven sales or targeted income for a change in sales mix, a new contribution margin ratio per mix and a new weighted contribution margin per mix must be computed.

► GLOSSARY OF KEY TERMS

Breakeven graph   A graph in which two lines—the total cost line and the total revenue line—are plotted, and their intersection indicates the breakeven point. (p. 132)

Breakeven sales (BES)   The amount of sales equal to total costs, or a zero profit. The amount may be stated in dollars or in units, and it may be ascertained algebraically, arithmetically, or from a breakeven graph. (p. 125)

Breakeven units (BEU)   The number of units that must be sold to equal total costs or yield a zero profit.   (p. 126)

Comparative income statement approach to CVP analysis   A method of assessing the effect on profit of contemplated changes in selling prices and/or costs and/or volume in which an income statement modified by the contemplated changes is compared to the unmodified income statement. (p. 140)

Contribution margin approach to CVP analysis   A method of assessing the effect on profit of contemplated changes in selling prices, costs, or volume in which a new total contribution margin is computed giving effect to the contemplated changes. The difference between the new total contribution margin and the current total contribution margin reflects the expected change in that figure. The change in fixed costs is then taken into account to arrive at the net effect of the proposal. (p. 142)

Contribution margin per unit (CMPU)   Contribution margin divided by the number of units sold.   (p. 124)

Contribution margin per unit (CMPU) approach to breakeven   Fixed costs are divided by the contribution margin per unit to arrive at breakeven sales in units. (p. 127)

Contribution margin ratio (CMR)   Contribution margin divided by sales revenue. (p. 124)

Contribution margin ratio (CMR) approach to breakeven   Fixed costs are divided by the contribution margin ratio to arrive at breakeven sales in dollars.   (p. 127)

Contribution margin ratio per mix   A combined, weighted-average contribution margin ratio that includes all of a firm's products and is used by multiproduct firms in the same way that the contribution margin ratio is used by single-product firms.   (p. 146)

Cost structure   The relationship between a firm's fixed and variable costs.   (p. 135)

Cost-volume-profit (CVP) analysis   The measurement of the effects that changes in selling prices, costs, volume of sales activity, and sales mix have on profits. (p. 124)

Degree of operating leverage   A measure of how a percentage change in sales volume at a given level of sales activity will affect profits. It is computed by dividing contribution margin by net income.   (p. 138)

Differential (incremental) approach to CVP analysis   A method of assessing the effect on profit of contemplated changes in selling prices and/or costs and/or volume in which only those items that are expected to change and the differences they would create are considered.   (p. 141)

Margin of safety   The amount by which a firm's actual sales revenue exceeds its breakeven sales. This is the amount of sales revenue that could be lost before the company's profits would be reduced to zero.   (p. 131)

Operating leverage   The use of fixed costs to increase profits at a faster rate than could be achieved through a corresponding increase in sales.   (p. 137)

Profit-volume graph   A graph showing a profit and loss line for various levels of sales volume, which enables managers to examine in series the sales (revenue and/or units) required to attain different levels of targeted income.   (p. 134)

Sales mix   A firm's complete set of products classified by the relative amount that each product contributes to total sales revenue.   (p. 146)

Targeted income (targeted-income sales)   The amount of income that a firm wishes to earn, designated as either pre-tax operating income or after-tax operating income.   (p. 127)

Variable cost ratio (VCR)   The relationship of variable costs to sales revenue, computed by dividing variable costs by sales revenue.   (p. 125)

Weighted contribution margin per mix   A combined weighted-average contribution margin that includes all of a firm's products and is used by multiproduct firms in the same way that the contribution margin per unit is used by single-product firms.   (p. 146)

► **REVIEW PROBLEM**   The Reg Company manufactures and sells one product at a price of $30 per unit. Its variable cost is $12 per unit, and its fixed costs for the year amount to $360,000.

Required   *a.* Calculate the breakeven sales in dollars and in units.

b. The company's sales for 19x3 were 30,000 units. What profit was earned at that level of activity?

c. For 19x4, the company is contemplating an increase in selling price by 20 percent. This is expected to cause a reduction in sales volume of 30 percent. No change is expected in the fixed costs or in the variable cost per unit. What would be the effect of the price change on net income? Would you recommend the price change?

d. What would the new breakeven sales in units and dollars be if the change in part *(c)* were implemented? Does a lowering of the breakeven point always warrant its implementation? Why?

e. As an alternative to the strategy in part *(c)*, the company is considering improving the quality of the product, which would raise the variable cost per unit to $15. In addition, advertising of the product would be required at a cost of $20,000. This amount is in addition to the fixed costs of $360,000. The selling price would be increased to $40 per unit. At this price, it is expected that sales volume would be reduced by 20 percent. What would be the effect of the proposed changes on the company's income? Prepare your analysis using three different methods.

f. Compute the breakeven sales in dollars and in units of the strategy in part *(e)*.

g. What is the margin of safety for the company in 19x3? What would it be if the strategy in part *(e)* were implemented?

Suppose that during 19x4 the company manufactures and sells two products. The selling prices and variable costs of the products are as follows:

	Blujets	Penjets
Selling prices	$20	$40
Variable costs	8	24

The sales for 19x4 were in the ratio of 3 Blujets to 1 Penjet. Sales volume for 19x4 was $1 million. Fixed costs for 19x4 amounted to $390,000.

Required

h. Compute the number of units sold in 19x4 for each product.

i. Compute the breakeven sales in dollars and in units.

j. If the sales mix were to change to two units of Blujets to one unit of Penjet, would this have any effect on the breakeven sales? If so, what would be the new breakeven sales in dollars and in units?

k. Assuming the sales volume would remain at $1 million, what net income would be generated using the sales mix in part *(j)* above? What income was generated for 19x4?

l. If the firm wishes to generate an operating income of $286,000, what sales revenue in dollars would be required to generate this income if the original mix of 3 : 1 prevailed? How many units of each product would be required to generate that operating income?

▶ **SOLUTION TO REVIEW PROBLEM**

a.

$$\text{Breakeven units} = \frac{\$360,000}{\$18} = 20,000 \text{ units}$$

$$\text{BES} = \frac{\$360,000}{.6} = \$600,000$$

b.

30,000 × $18	$540,000
Less: Fixed costs . . .	360,000
Profit.	$180,000

c.
New sales volume—21,000 × $36 . . . . $756,000
Variable cost—21,000 × $12 252,000

Contribution margin 504,000
Fixed costs 360,000

Net income—proposed for 19x4 144,000
Net income—19x3 180,000

Decrease in net income . . . . $ 36,000

or

New contribution margin 21,000 × ($36 − $12) . . . $504,000
Present contribution margin—30,000 × $18 540,000

Decrease in net income . . . . $ 36,000

No.

d.
$$\frac{\$360,000}{\$24} = 15,000 \text{ units}; \quad 15,000 \times \$36 = \$540,000$$

No. When a firm is operating above its breakeven, the breakeven should not govern any desired CVP analysis, because CVP analysis has a bearing on profits and losses. Breakeven is merely a safety measure at which point there is neither profit nor loss. The decision of price changes and volume changes is governed by its effect on profits and losses.

e. (1)

	19x3	Proposed 19x4	Difference
Sales	$900,000	$960,000*	$60,000
Variable cost	360,000	360,000†	—
Contribution margin.	540,000	600,000	60,000
Fixed costs	360,000	380,000	(20,000)
Net income	$180,000	$220,000	$40,000

* $40 × 24,000 units.
† $15 × 24,000 units.

(2)
Increase in sales revenue—($40 × 24,000 units =
$960,000) − ($30 × 30,000 units) $60,000
Change in variable costs—($3 × 24,000 units =
$72,000) − ($12 × 6,000 units) 0

Increase in contribution margin 60,000
Less: Increase in fixed costs. 20,000

Increase in net income $40,000

(3) Proposed contribution margin:

	Per Unit
Selling price	$ 40
Variable cost	15
Contribution margin	$ 25
Total proposed contribution margin (24,000 units × $25)	$600,000
Total present contribution margin (30,000 units × $18)	540,000
Increase in contribution margin	60,000
Less: Increase in fixed costs.	20,000
Increase in net income	$ 40,000

f.
$$BES = \frac{\$380,000}{.625^*} = \$608,000$$

$$BEU = \frac{\$380,000}{\$25\dagger} = 15,200 \text{ units}$$

* $600,000 \div \$960,000$ [from part *(e)* 1]
† $40 - \$15$

g.
Present margin of safety = $900,000 - \$600,000 = \$300,000$
Proposed margin of safety = $960,000 - \$608,000 = \$352,000$

h.

	Bluejets	**Penjets**	**Total**
Sales	$600,000*	$400,000*	$1,000,000
Variable costs	240,000†	240,000‡	480,000
Contribution margin	$360,000	$160,000	520,000
Fixed costs			390,000
Net income			$ 130,000

Units sold:
  Bluejets—$600,000 \div \$20 = 30,000$ units
  Penjets —$400,000 \div \$40 = 10,000$ units

		Percent
* Bluejets—3 × $20 =	$ 60	60%
Penjets —1 × $40 =	40	40
Sales per mix . . .	$100	100%

  60% × $1,000,000 = \$600,000$
  40% × 1,000,000 = \$400,000$
† $600,000 × 40% variable cost ratio
‡ $400,000 × 60% variable cost ratio

i.
$$BES = \frac{\$390,000}{1 - .48} = \frac{\$390,000}{.52} = \$750,000$$

Breakeven units:
  Bluejets—60% × $750,000 = \$450,000 \div \$20 = 22,500$ units
  Penjets —40% × $750,000 = \$300,000 \div \$40 =   7,500$ units

j. Yes.

	Dollars	**Percent**
Bluejets—2 × $20	$40	
Penjets —1 × $40	40	
Sales revenue per mix	$80	100%
Less: Variable costs		
Bluejets—2 × $8 . . . . $16		
Penjets —1 × $24 24	40	50
Contribution margin per mix	$40	50%

$$BES = \frac{\$390,000}{.50} = \$780,000$$

Breakeven units:
  Bluejets—50% × $780,000 = \$390,000 \div \$20 = 19,500$ units
  Penjets —50% × $780,000 = \$390,000 \div \$40 =   9,750$ units

k.

| | New Sales Mix | | |
	Bluejets	Penjets	Total
Sales	$500,000*	$500,000*	$1,000,000
Variable costs	200,000†	300,000‡	500,000
Contribution margin	$300,000	$200,000	500,000
Fixed costs			390,000
Net income			$ 110,000
Present sales mix [see part *(h)*]			$ 130,000

* $1,000,000 × 50%.

† $500,000 × 40%.

‡ $500,000 × 60%.

l.

$$\text{Required sales} = \frac{\$390,000 + \$286,000}{.52} = \$1,300,000$$

Sales in units:
Bluejets—60% × $1,300,000 = $780,000 ÷ $20 = 39,000 units
Penjets —40% × $1,300,000 = $520,000 ÷ $40 = 13,000 units

▶ **LIBRARY ASSIGNMENT**

Read the following:

Anderson, Lane K. "Expanded Breakeven Analysis for a Multi-Product Company." *Management Accounting,* July 1975, pp. 30–32.

Calderon, Thomas G. "A Pedagogical Note on Cost-Volume-Profit Relationships in a Multi-Product Environment." *Accounting Enquiries,* August 1991, pp. 172–182.

Morse, Wayne J., and Imogene A. Posey. "Taxes Do Make a Difference in Cost-Volume-Profit Analysis." *Management Accounting,* December 1979, pp. 20–24.

Sinclair, Kenneth P., and James A. Talbott. "Using Breakeven Analysis When Cost Behavior Is Unknown." *Management Accounting,* July 1986, pp. 52–55.

▶ **SELF-TEST**

True or False

1. A firm's contribution margin ratio is the reciprocal of its variable cost ratio.
2. The breakeven point is a firm's sales activity level at which sales revenues are exactly equal to fixed costs.
3. The breakeven point may be computed by dividing a firm's fixed costs by its variable cost ratio.
4. The sales revenue needed to produce a pre-tax targeted operating income may be computed by adding a firm's fixed costs to the desired operating income and dividing the sum by the firm's contribution margin ratio.
5. A limiting assumption of breakeven analysis is that variable costs are constant within the relevant range.
6. The margin of safety is defined as contribution margin minus breakeven sales and represents a buffer before losses are incurred.
7. A breakeven graph may be used to calculate the profit or loss that would result at a specific level of sales activity.
8. A firm that is labor intensive usually has a higher proportion of fixed costs than of variable costs.
9. A firm's contribution margin ratio is influenced by its cost structure.
10. The degree of operating leverage may be defined as net income divided by contribution margin.

Multiple Choice

1. Cost-volume-profit analysis is a technique to help management better understand the interrelationships of several factors affecting a firm's profit. As with many such techniques, the accountant oversimplifies the real world by making assumptions. Which of the following is *not* a major assumption underlying cost-volume-profit analysis?
   a. All costs incurred by a firm can be separated into their fixed and variable components.
   b. The product selling price per unit is constant at all volume levels.
   c. Operating efficiency and employee productivity are constant at all volume levels.
   d. For multiproduct situations, the sales mix can vary at all volume levels.
   e. Costs vary only with changes in volume.

The following data apply to items 2 through 4.

Laraby Company produces a single product. It sold 25,000 units last year with the following results:

Sales		$625,000
Variable costs	$375,000	
Fixed costs.	150,000	525,000
Net income before taxes.		$100,000
Income taxes (45%)		45,000
Net income		$ 55,000

In an attempt to improve its product, Laraby is considering replacing a component part in its product that has a cost of $2.50 with a new and better part costing $4.50 per unit in the coming year. A new machine would also be needed to increase plant capacity. The machine would cost $18,000 with a useful life of six years and no salvage value. The company uses straight-line depreciation on all plant assets.

2. What was Laraby Company's breakeven point in number of units last year?
   a. 6,000.
   b. 15,000.
   c. 21,000.
   d. 18,000.
   e. None of the above responses is correct.
3. If Laraby Company holds the sales price constant and makes the suggested changes, how many units of product must be sold in the coming year to break even?
   a. 15,300.
   b. 18,750.
   c. 19,125.
   d. 21,000.
   e. None of the above responses is correct.
4. If Laraby Company wishes to maintain the same contribution margin ratio, what selling price per unit of product must it charge next year to cover the increased material costs?
   a. $27.
   b. $25.
   c. $32.50.
   d. $28.33.
   e. None of the above responses is correct.

(CMA Adapted)

▶ **QUESTIONS**

1. If a change in sales revenue is expected without a change in selling price or cost, and the contribution margin is known, how can this be used to project the effect of the sales revenue change or net income?
2. What is the contribution margin ratio? How is it used?
3. What is the contribution margin per unit? How is it used?
4. Breakeven sales may be computed algebraically. Describe two different approaches to the algebraic solutions and the nature of the answers.
5. Why do some management accountants prefer the contribution margin ratio approach to breakeven analysis? How is it used? Give an example to demonstrate its use.
6. If a firm sells its only product for $20 per unit and its variable costs are 40 percent, construct the algebraic equation that is required for an answer of breakeven sales in dollars if its fixed costs are $360,000 per annum. Solve the equation.
7. How is a pre-tax targeted operating income calculated?
8. Are there any limiting assumptions to breakeven analysis? If so, what are they?
9. What is the margin of safety?
10. What is a profit-volume graph, and how is it constructed?
11. What is meant by *cost structure,* and why is it important? Use an example to demonstrate its application.
12. What is operating leverage?
13. What is the degree of operating leverage? How is it computed? Is it the same at all levels of sales activity within the relevant range? Explain.
14. A company's variable cost ratio is 40 percent, and its fixed costs are $600,000 per annum. What are its breakeven sales? Is the answer in dollars or units?
15. A firm's variable cost ratio is 30 percent, its fixed costs are $350,000, and it wishes to earn a targeted income of $140,000. Do you have enough information to compute the required sales in dollars? If so, how much sales revenue is needed to earn the targeted income? If not, what additional information is needed?
16. A firm's variable cost ratio is 35 percent, its fixed costs are $260,000 per annum, and it wishes to earn a targeted income of $130,000. Do you have enough information to compute the number of units that must be sold to earn the targeted income? If so, compute the required sales in units. If not, what additional information is needed?
17. If a firm sells its only product for $40 per unit and its variable costs are 40 percent, construct the algebraic equation that is required for an answer of breakeven sales in units if its fixed costs are $480,000 per annum. Solve the equation.
18. Three approaches have been advanced for solving CVP problems. Briefly explain each approach.
19. When there is a contemplated change in sales volume with no change in selling price or cost, what is true about the CMR and the CMPU after the change?
20. When there is a change in selling price or a change in variable cost, what is true about the CMR and the CMPU?
21. A firm has sales of $800,000 per annum. Its variable cost ratio is 40 percent, and its fixed costs are $300,000 per annum. It is contemplating increasing its selling price by 10 percent, which could result in a 12½ percent reduction in volume. Would you recommend the price increase? Why?
22. What is sales mix?
23. How are sales-mix breakeven sales computed?
24. If there is a change in the sales mix, does the CMRM normally remain unchanged? Explain.

▶ **EXERCISES**   **E4–1**   **Breakeven Analysis**

Bluebell Company manufactures one product, men's jeans. Last year, it had sales of $15 million, variable costs of $4.5 million, and fixed costs of $4.2 million.

Required   *a.* Compute the amount of sales dollars needed to break even.

b. The company is contemplating opening another factory to manufacture men's shirts. It plans to sell the shirts for $40 per unit. Variable costs are expected to be $24 per unit, and the fixed costs attributable to the new factory are expected to be $800,000 per year. Compute the amount of sales dollars needed to break even.

c. As an alternative to manufacturing men's shirts, the new factory could be used to manufacture ladies' blouses. As a result of a market survey, the company is certain it can sell 100,000 blouses for $30 each. Variable costs per blouse would be $12. At this level of sales, the company would break even on the blouse manufacturing. What would the fixed costs be if the new factory opened for this purpose?

E4–2   **Breakeven Analysis**

1. The Oliver Company plans to market a new product. Based on its market studies, Oliver estimates it can sell 5,500 units in 19x6. The selling price will be $2 per unit. Variable costs are estimated to be 40 percent of the selling price. Fixed costs are estimated to be $6,000. What is the breakeven point?
   a. 3,750 units.
   b. 5,000 units.
   c. 5,500 units.
   d. 7,500 units.

2. At a breakeven point of 400 units sold, the variable costs were $400 and the fixed costs were $200. What will the 401st unit sold contribute to profit before income taxes?
   a. $0.
   b. $.50.
   c. $1.
   d. $1.50.

3. In planning its operations for 19x1 based on a sales forecast of $6 million, Wallace, Inc., prepared the following estimated data:

| | Costs | |
	Variable	**Fixed**
Direct materials	$1,600,000	
Direct labor.	1,400,000	
Factory overhead	600,000	$ 900,000
Marketing costs	240,000	360,000
Administrative costs	60,000	140,000
Total.	$3,900,000	$1,400,000

What would be the amount of sales dollars at the breakeven point?
   a. $2,250,000.
   b. $3,500,000.
   c. $4,000,000.
   d. $5,300,000.

(AICPA Adapted)

E4–3   Breakeven and CVP Analysis

The Mystic Tie Company manufactures men's ties. Although the firm manufactures different patterns of fabric into ties, all ties sell for $9 each and have the same direct materials cost.

Fixed costs amount to $202,500 per annum. Breakeven sales for 19x3 amounted to $675,000.

Required   *a.* Compute the firm's contribution margin ratio and contribution margin per unit.

b. For 19x2, actual sales amounted to $945,000. What was the firm's net income for 19x2?

c. For 19x3, the firm is contemplating the use of a more expensive fabric, which will increase its variable costs by $1.40 per tie.

(1) What selling price would be required to maintain the same contribution margin ratio? What would the contribution margin per unit be at this selling price?

(2) As noted above, the firm plans to upgrade its fabric at a cost of $1.40 per tie, and it also plans to increase its price to $11.55 each. What would its breakeven sales in dollars be for 19x3 if it plans to spend an additional $72,500 for advertising the new ties? Would you recommend the proposal if 65,000 ties can be sold at this price? Why?

E4–4   Breakeven Graph

A breakeven chart, as illustrated below, is a useful technique for showing relationships between costs, volume, and profits.

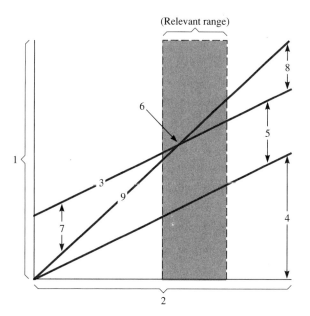

Required   *a.* Identify the numbered components of the breakeven chart.

b. Discuss the significance of the *relevant range* concept to breakeven analysis.

(AICPA Adapted)

E4–5   Construction of a Breakeven Graph

The Elnar Company manufactures one product, which it sells for $20 per unit. Variable costs amount to $8 per unit, and fixed costs amount to $600,000 per year.

Required   *a.* Construct a breakeven graph at intervals of 10,000 units on a scale of 10,000 units to 100,000 units.

b. What is the breakeven point in units and sales dollars?

E4-6   Construction of a Profit-Volume Graph

Using the information provided in Exercise 4–5, you are asked to:

a. Construct a profit-volume graph.
b. Compute the profit or loss at the following levels of activity:
    (1) 30,000 units.
    (2) 50,000 units.
    (3) 80,000 units.

E4-7   Breakeven and CVP Analysis

The following data apply to items 1 through 5.

Siberian Ski Company recently expanded its manufacturing capacity, which will now allow it to produce up to 15,000 pairs of cross-country skis of the mountaineering model or the touring model. The sales department assures management that it can sell between 9,000 and 13,000 of either product this year. Because the models are very similar, Siberian Ski will produce only one of the two models.

The following information was compiled by the accounting department:

	Model	
	Mountaineering	**Touring**
Selling price per unit	$88.00	$80.00
Variable costs per unit	52.80	52.80

Fixed costs will total $369,600 if the mountaineering model is produced but will be only $316,800 if the touring model is produced. Siberian Ski Company is subject to a 40 percent income tax rate.

1. The contribution margin rate of the touring model is
   a. 40 percent.
   b. 66 percent.
   c. 51.5 percent.
   d. 34 percent.
   e. Some amount other than those given above.
2. If the Siberian Ski Company sales department could guarantee the annual sale of 12,000 skis of either model, Siberian would
   a. Produce touring skis because they have a lower fixed cost.
   b. Be indifferent as to which model is sold because each model has the same variable cost per unit.
   c. Produce mountaineering skis because they have a lower breakeven point.
   d. Be indifferent as to which model is sold because both are profitable.
   e. Produce mountaineering skis because they are more profitable.
3. How much would the variable cost per unit of the touring model have to change before it had the same breakeven point in units as the mountaineering model?
   a. $2.68/pair increase.
   b. $4.53/pair increase.
   c. $5.03/pair decrease.

    d. $2.97/pair decrease.

    e. Some amount other than those given above.

4. If the variable cost per unit of touring skis decreases by 10 percent, and the total fixed cost of touring skis increases by 10 percent, the new breakeven point will be

    a. Unchanged from 11,648 pairs because the cost changes are equal and offsetting.

    b. 10,730 pairs.

    c. 13,007 pairs.

    d. 12,812 pairs.

    e. Some amount other than those given above.

5. Which one of the following statements is *not* an assumption made when employing a cost-volume-profit study for decision analysis?

    a. Volume is the only relevant factor affecting costs.

    b. Changes in beginning and ending inventory levels are insignificant in amount.

    c. Sales mix is variable as total volume changes.

    d. Fixed costs are constant over the relevant volume range.

    e. Efficiency and productivity are unchanged.

(CMA Adapted)

E4–8   **Breakeven and CVP Analysis**

The Piper Bear Company manufactures industrial bearings that sell for $15 each. Variable costs are $9 per unit. Fixed costs for the year just ended amounted to $189,000. Sales for the year amounted to 40,000 units.

Required   *a.* Compute the company's breakeven sales in dollars.

    b. What was the company's net income last year?

    c. For next year, variable costs are expected to increase by 10 percent. Compute to the nearest dollar:

      (1) The new breakeven sales.

      (2) The expected net income for the coming year if the company can sell 50,000 units and the fixed costs remain unchanged.

    d. If the variable costs do increase by 10 percent, what selling price would produce the same contribution margin ratio?

E4–9   **CVP Analysis for a Governmental Organization**

Manasota County has received an appropriation from the state to provide financial support for local employers who hire high school students for part-time summer jobs. The appropriation for 19x1 is $900,000, and the fixed costs for administering the program are $180,000. The county normally gives employers a supplement of $1,500 for each student hired.

Required   *a.* How many students will be hired under the program for the summer of 19x1?

    b. The county's budget appropriation has been reduced by 15 percent for 19x2. If the supplement for each student remains unchanged, how many students will be helped in 19x2? What is the percentage decrease from 19x1?

    c. The budget appropriation for 19x2 is being reduced by 15 percent as in part *(b)* above, but the county labor relations administrator does not want to reduce the number of students hired. Under these conditions, what amount of the supplement will be provided to employers for each student hired? What is the percentage decrease from 19x1?

E4–10 **Breakeven and CVP Analysis**

The Belair Company provides you with the following:

Fixed costs per annum	$ 864,000
Breakeven sales	$2,880,000
Annual sales in units	40,000
Net income	$ 480,000

Required *a.* Compute the variable cost ratio.

b. Compute the firm's sales for the year.

c. Compute the firm's variable costs for the year.

d. What is the firm's selling price per unit?

e. If the firm were able to change its variable cost ratio to 60 percent, would the breakeven sales change? If so, what would the new breakeven sales be?

f. If the firm were able to increase its sales volume by 5 percent without a change in its selling price, variable costs, or fixed costs, would this change the breakeven point? If so, by how much? If not, why not?

E4–11 **Breakeven Analysis and Net-of-Tax CVP Analysis**

The following data apply to items 1 through 5.

The statement of income for Davann Company presented below represents the operating results for the fiscal year just ended. Davann had sales of 1,800 tons of product during the current year. The manufacturing capacity of Davann's facilities is 3,000 tons of product.

DAVANN COMPANY
Statement of Income
For the Year Ended December 31, 19x0

Sales	$900,000
Variable costs:	
Manufacturing	315,000
Marketing	180,000
Total variable costs	495,000
Contribution margin	405,000
Fixed costs:	
Manufacturing	90,000
Marketing	112,500
Administration	45,000
Total fixed costs	247,500
Net income before income taxes	157,500
Income taxes (40%)	63,000
Net income after income taxes	$ 94,500

---

1. The breakeven volume in tons of product for 19x0 is
   a. 420 tons.
   b. 1,100 tons.
   c. 495 tons.
   d. 550 tons.
   e. Some amount other than those shown above.
2. If the sales volume is estimated to be 2,100 tons in the next year, and if the prices and costs stay at the same levels and amounts next year, the after-tax net income that Davann can expect for 19x1 is
   a. $135,000.
   b. $110,250.

    c. $283,500.

    d. $184,500.

    e. Some amount other than those shown above.

3. Davann plans to market its product in a new territory. Davann estimates that an advertising and promotion program costing $61,500 annually would need to be undertaken for the next two or three years. In addition, a $25-per-ton sales commission over and above the current commission to the sales force in the new territory would be required. How many tons would have to be sold in the new territory to maintain Davann's current after-tax income of $94,500?

    a. 307.5 tons.

    b. 1,095.0 tons.

    c. 273.333 tons.

    d. 1,545.0 tons.

    e. Some amount other than those shown above.

4. Davann is considering replacing a highly labor-intensive process with an automatic machine. This would result in an increase of $58,500 annually in manufacturing fixed costs. The variable manufacturing costs would decrease $25 per ton. The new breakeven volume in tons would be

    a. 990 tons.

    b. 1,224 tons.

    c. 1,854 tons.

    d. 612 tons.

    e. Some amount other than those shown above.

5. Assume Davann estimates that the per-ton selling price would decline 10 percent next year. Variable costs would increase $40 per ton, and the fixed costs would not change. What sales volume in dollars would be required to earn an after-tax net income of $94,500 next year?

    a. $1,140,000.

    b. $825,000.

    c. $1,500,000.

    d. $1,350,000.

    e. Some amount other than those shown above.

(CMA Adapted)

E4–12   Profit-Volume Graph

The following data apply to items 1 through 5.

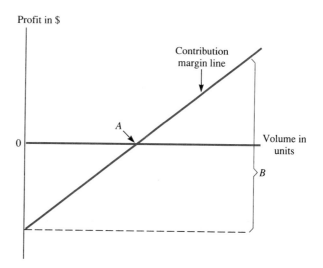

The SAB Company uses a profit-volume graph similar to the one shown above to represent the cost-volume-profit relationships of its operations. The vertical (*Y*-axis) is the profit in dollars, and the horizontal (*X*-axis) is the volume in units. The diagonal line is the contribution margin line.

1. Point *A* on the profit-volume graph represents
   a. The point where fixed costs equal sales.
   b. The point where fixed costs equal variable costs.
   c. A volume level of zero units.
   d. The point where total costs equal total sales.
   e. The point where the rate of contribution margin increases.

2. The vertical distance from the dotted line to the contribution margin line denoted as *B* on the profit-volume graph represents
   a. The total contribution margin.
   b. The contribution margin per unit.
   c. The contribution margin rate.
   d. Total sales.
   e. The sum of the variable and fixed costs.

3. If SAB Company's fixed costs were to increase,
   a. The contribution margin line would shift upward parallel to the present line.
   b. The contribution margin line would shift downward parallel to the present line.
   c. The slope of the contribution margin line would be more pronounced (steeper).
   d. The slope of the contribution margin line would be less pronounced (flatter).
   e. The contribution margin line would coincide with the present contribution margin line.

4. If SAB Company's variable costs per unit were to increase but its unit selling price stays constant,
   a. The contribution margin line would shift upward parallel to the present line.
   b. The contribution margin line would shift downward parallel to the present line.
   c. The slope of the contribution margin line would be more pronounced (steeper).
   d. The slope of the contribution margin line would be less pronounced (flatter).
   e. The slope of the contribution margin line probably would change, but how it would change is not determinable.

5. If SAB Company decided to increase its unit selling price to offset exactly the increase in the variable cost per unit,
   a. The contribution margin line would shift upward parallel to the present line.
   b. The contribution margin line would shift downward parallel to the present line.
   c. The slope of the contribution margin line would be more pronounced (steeper).
   d. The slope of the contribution margin line would be less pronounced (flatter).
   e. The contribution margin line would coincide with the present contribution margin line.

(CMA Adapted)

E4–13   CVP Analysis and Targeted Income

1. Moon Company sells product Q at $6 a unit. In 19x0, fixed costs are expected to be $200,000, and variable costs are estimated at $4 a unit. How many units of product Q must Moon sell to generate operating income of $40,000?
   a. 50,000.
   b. 60,000.
   c. 100,000.
   d. 120,000.

2. Tice Company is a medium-sized manufacturer of lamps. During the year, a new line called Horolin was made available to Tice's customers. The breakeven point for sales of Horolin is $200,000 with a contribution margin of 40 percent. Assuming the profit for the Horolin line during the year amounted to $100,000, total sales during the year would have amounted to
   a. $300,000.
   b. $420,000.
   c. $450,000.
   d. $475,000.

3. Purvis Company manufactures a product that has a variable cost of $50 per unit. Fixed costs total $1 million, allocated on the basis of the number of units produced. Selling price is computed by adding a 10 percent markup to full cost. How much should the selling price be per unit for 100,000 units?
   a. $55.
   b. $60.
   c. $61.
   d. $66.

4. Bert Company has projected cost of goods sold of $2 million, including fixed costs of $400,000, and variable costs are expected to be 75 percent of net sales. What will be the projected net sales?
   a. $2,133,333.
   b. $2,400,000.
   c. $2,666,667.
   d. $3,200,000.

5. Warfield Company is planning to sell 100,000 units of product T for $12 a unit. The fixed costs are $280,000. To realize a profit of $200,000, what would the variable costs be?
   a. $480,000.
   b. $720,000.
   c. $900,000.
   d. $920,000.

(AICPA Adapted)

E4–14   CVP Analysis for a Retirement Health Care Facility—Sales Mix

The Eastview Retirement Home accepts residents who are in good health and those who require continued medical care and supervision. The financial director of the home has developed the following estimate of costs for next year:

Variable costs . . . . . $50 per resident-day for normal-care residents and $84 per resident-day for continued-care residents
Fixed costs $7,620,000

A resident-day is defined as one resident occupying a room for one day. The ancillary activities of the home also provide contribution margins of $15 per day for each normal-care resident and $18 per day for each continued-care resident. Ancillary activities include home-sponsored entertainment activities and medical consultation and treatment for its residents.

Required   a. The home admits three times as many normal-care residents as continued-care residents. If room charges are set at $100 per day and $125 per day, respectively, how many resident-days must the home achieve to break even for the year?

b. The financial director forecasts 90,000 resident-days for normal-care residents and 25,000 resident-days for continued-care residents. He intends to set the room charges to ensure that each class of resident care provides the same contribution margin ratio. Considering this and the home's contribution margins from ancillary activities, what room charges will enable the home to earn a $4,080,000 profit?

E4–15   **CVP Analysis**

The High Flyer Company manufactures lures for sport fishing. For 19x2, the company provides the following:

Selling price per unit . . .	$ 12
Units sold	150,000
Variable costs	$900,000
Fixed costs	$600,000

A market research study indicates that the company could increase its selling price by 20 percent and its sales volume by 10 percent if it spends an additional $200,000 on advertising.

Required   a. What is the company's net income for 19x2?

b. What will the company's net income be for 19x3 if it spends the $200,000 for advertising? (Use the differential approach.) Would you recommend the increased advertising cost? Why?

c. As an alternative to the proposal for spending an additional $200,000 for advertising, the firm's sales manager believes a $80,000 increase in advertising would cause the sales volume to increase by 30 percent if there were no sales price increase. What would the firm's 19x3 income be if this proposal were adopted? (Use the contribution margin approach.) Would you recommend the $80,000 or the $200,000 advertising increase? Why?

E4–16   **CVP Analysis**

The Corvair Company provides you with the following:

Fixed costs per annum	$420,000
Sales for the year.	$900,000
Selling price per unit	$ 10
Variable cost ratio	30%

Required   a. Compute the company's breakeven sales in dollars and units using the contribution margin approach.

b. The company is planning to reduce the selling price of its only product from $10 to $9. A market survey indicates volume will increase by 20 percent at that price. At that level of production, fixed costs will increase $30,000. Prepare an analysis of the proposal using the comparative income statement approach in the contribution format. Should the company proceed with the change? Why?

c. The company expects an increase in variable costs (direct materials and direct labor) for the following year. The increase is expected to amount to 60 cents per unit. Compute the new selling price needed to:
(1) Maintain the same contribution margin per unit.
(2) Maintain the same contribution margin ratio.

E4–17   Breakeven Graph and Profit-Volume Graph

The Decair Company provides you with the following:

Fixed costs per annum	$420,000
Sales for the year	$900,000
Selling price per unit	$ 10
Variable cost per unit	$ 4

Required   *a.* Construct a breakeven graph using 10,000 intervals for units and $100,000 intervals for dollars, from 0 to 100,000 units.
b. Construct a profit-volume graph using the same intervals as in part *(a)*.
c. Compute the profit or loss from *each* graph for:
(1) 50,000 units.
(2) 80,000 units.

E4–18   Net-of-Tax CVP Analysis

The Garsombke Company manufactures and sells one product. Its income statement for 19x5 is as follows:

Sales (20,000 units)		$500,000
Less: Variable costs	$300,000	
Fixed costs	100,000	400,000
Income before income taxes		100,000
Income taxes (40 percent)		40,000
Net income		$ 60,000

Required   *a.* The company is considering a new direct material that is more durable than the one presently used. This material would cost $2 more per unit. All other costs would remain unchanged. How many units would have to be sold in 19x6 to earn a net income (after taxes) of $90,000?
b. The company is also considering a move to a more convenient location. The move would increase fixed costs by $40,000 per year. If the company goes forward with the durable direct material and the move to a new location, how many units would have to be sold in 19x6 to earn the same net income as that for 19x5?
c. If the firm has a choice of continuing with its 19x5 costs and sales of 20,000 units or implementing its direct material change for 19x6 with sales of 24,000 units, which alternative would you recommend? Why?

E4–19   Net-of-Tax CVP Analysis

All-Day Candy Company is a wholesale distributor of candy. The company services grocery, convenience, and drug stores in a large metropolitan area.

Small but steady growth in sales has been achieved by All-Day Candy Company over the past few years while candy prices have been increasing. The company is formulating its plans for the coming fiscal year. Presented below are the data used to project the current year's after-tax net income of $110,400.

Average selling price	$4.00 per box

Average variable costs:

Cost of candy	$2.00 per box
Marketing	0.40 per box
Total	$2.40 per box

Annual fixed costs:

Marketing	$160,000
Administrative	280,000
Total	$440,000

Expected annual sales volume (390,000 boxes)		$1,560,000
Tax rate		40%

Manufacturers of candy have announced that they will increase prices of their products an average of 15 percent in the coming year due to increases in direct material (sugar, cocoa, peanuts, etc.) and labor costs. All-Day Candy Company expects that all other costs will remain at the same rates or levels as the current year.

Required
a. What is All-Day Candy Company's breakeven point in boxes of candy for the current year?
b. What selling price per box must All-Day Candy Company charge to cover the 15 percent increase in the cost of candy and still maintain the current contribution margin ratio?
c. What volume of sales in dollars must All-Day Candy Company achieve in the coming year to maintain the same net income after taxes as projected for the current year if the selling price of candy remains at $4 per box and the cost of candy increases 15 percent?

(CMA Adapted)

E4–20 **Algebraic Solutions**

1. The following data apply to Frelm Corporation for a given period:

Total variable cost per unit	$ 3.50
Contribution margin ÷ Sales	30%
Breakeven sales (present volume)	$1,000,000

Frelm wants to sell an additional 50,000 units at the same selling price and contribution margin. By how much can fixed costs increase to generate a gross margin equal to 10 percent of the sales value of the additional 50,000 units to be sold?
a. $50,000.
b. $57,500.
c. $67,500.
d. $125,000.

2. The Breiden Company sells rodaks for $6 per unit. Variable costs are $2 per unit. Fixed costs are $37,500. How many rodaks must be sold to realize a profit before income taxes of 15 percent of sales?
a. 9,375 units.
b. 9,740 units.
c. 11,029 units.
d. 12,097 units.

3. Singer, Inc., sells product R for $5 per unit. The fixed costs are $210,000, and the variable costs are 60 percent of the selling price. What would be the amount of sales if Singer is to realize a profit of 10 percent of sales?
    a. $700,000.
    b. $525,000.
    c. $472,500.
    d. $420,000.

(AICPA Adapted)

E4–21 **Preparation of Contribution Format Income Statement and Use of Operating Leverage**

The Conar Company had the following income statement prepared for the year 19x5:

CONAR COMPANY
Income Statement
For the Year Ended December 31, 19x5

Sales	$3,000,000
Cost of goods sold	1,600,000
Gross margin	1,400,000
Marketing and administrative costs.	800,000
Net income	$ 600,000

Included in the cost of goods sold are $600,000 of fixed manufacturing costs. The marketing and administrative costs include salespersons' commissions and other variable costs to the extent of $200,000. The balance of the marketing and administrative costs are fixed.

Conar Company manufactures and sells only one product at a selling price of $40 per unit.

Required *a.* Recast the income statement into a contribution format statement.
b. Compute the degree of operating leverage.
c. For 19x6, the company expects sales to increase by 30 percent. Using the operating leverage you computed in part *(b)*, compute the projected net income for 19x6.

E4–22 **Sales-Mix Breakeven and Targeted Income**

The Baby Face Doll Company manufactures a doll that is sold with one set of clothing. It also sells a kit of clothing that permits the doll to be changed into different outfits. Dolls account for 60 percent of the firm's sales, and the kits account for the remainder. The variable cost ratio is 40 percent for the dolls and 65 percent for the kits. For 19x3, the fixed costs amounted to $600,000.

Required *a.* What were the breakeven sales in dollars for the year?
b. If the company's sales for the year were $1,800,000, what net income did the company earn?
c. If the company's fixed costs are expected to increase to $750,000 for 19x4 and the company wishes to earn the same net income as it earned in 19x3, what sales revenue would be required to accomplish this?

E4–23   **Sales Mix and Breakeven Sales**

The Dooley Company manufactures two products, baubles and trinkets. The following are projections for the coming year.

| | Baubles | | Trinkets | | |
	Units	Amount	Units	Amount	Totals
Sales	10,000	$10,000	7,500	$10,000	$20,000
Costs:					
Fixed.		2,000		5,600	7,600
Variable		6,000		3,000	9,000
		8,000		8,600	16,600
Income before taxes		$ 2,000		$ 1,400	$ 3,400

1. Assuming the facilities are not jointly used, the breakeven output (in units) for baubles would be
   a. 8,000.
   b. 7,000.
   c. 6,000.
   d. 5,000.
2. The breakeven volume (dollars) for trinkets would be
   a. $8,000.
   b. $7,000.
   c. $6,000.
   d. $5,000.
3. Assuming consumers purchase a mix of four baubles and three trinkets, the weighted-average unit contribution margin would be
   a. $4.40.
   b. $4.00.
   c. $1.33.
   d. $1.10.
4. If consumers purchase a mix of four baubles and three trinkets, the breakeven output for the two products would be
   a. 6,909 baubles; 6,909 trinkets.
   b. 6,909 baubles; 5,182 trinkets.
   c. 5,000 baubles; 8,000 trinkets.
   d. 5,000 baubles; 6,000 trinkets.
5. If baubles and trinkets become one-to-one complements and there is no change in the Dooley Company's cost function, the breakeven volume would be
   a. $22,500.
   b. $15,750.
   c. $13,300.
   d. $10,858.
6. If a mix is defined as one bauble and one trinket, the weighted-average contribution margin ratio would be
   a. $7/10$.
   b. $4/7$.
   c. $2/5$.
   d. $19/50$.

(AICPA Adapted)

▶ PROBLEMS   P4–24   **Breakeven and CVP Analysis**

Praxis Company manufactures and sells one product at $80 per unit. Its variable cost is $55 per unit, and its fixed costs for the year amount to $1,850,000.

Required   *a.* Calculate the breakeven sales in dollars and in units.

b. The company's sales for 19x1 were 120,000 units. What profit was earned at that level of activity?

c. For 19x2, the company is contemplating an increase in selling price by 20 percent. This is expected to cause a reduction in sales volume of 30 percent. No change is expected in the fixed costs or in the variable cost per unit. What would be the effect of the price change on net income? Would you recommend the price change?

d. What would the new breakeven sales in units and dollars be if the change in part *(c)* were implemented? Does a lowering of the breakeven point always warrant its implementation? Why?

e. As an alternative to the strategy in part *(c)*, the company is considering improving the quality of the product, which would raise the variable cost per unit to $65. In addition, advertising of the product would be required at a cost of $75,000. This amount is in addition to the fixed costs of $1,850,000. The selling price would be increased to $100 per unit. At this price, it is expected that sales volume would be reduced by 20 percent. What would be the effect on the company's income of the proposed changes? Prepare your analysis using three different methods.

f. Compute the breakeven sales in dollars and in units of the strategy in part *(e)*.

g. What is the margin of safety for the company in 19x1? What would it be if the strategy in part *(e)* were implemented?

P4–25   **Breakeven and CVP Analysis**

Starbird Company manufactures and sells one product at a price of $120 per unit. Its variable cost is $40 per unit, and it fixed costs for the year amount to $560,000.

Required   *a.* Calculate the breakeven sales in dollars and in units.

b. The company's sales for 19x1 were 25,000 units. What profit was earned at that level of activity?

c. For 19x2, the company is contemplating a decrease in selling price by 10 percent. This is expected to cause an increase in sales volume of 20 percent. No change is expected in the fixed costs or in the variable cost per unit. What would be the effect of the price change on net income? Would you recommend the price change?

d. What would be the new breakeven sales in units and in dollars if the change in part *(c)* were implemented?

e. As an alternative to the strategy in part *(c)*, the company is considering improving the quality of the product, which would raise the variable cost per unit to $60. In addition, advertising the product would be required at a cost of $74,000. This amount is in addition to the fixed costs of $560,000. The selling price would be increased to $160 per unit. At this price, sales volume is expected to be reduced by 10 percent. What would be the effect of the proposed changes on the company's income? Prepare your analysis using three different methods.

f. Compute the breakeven sales in dollars and in units of the strategy in part *(e)*.

g. What is the margin of safety for the company in 19x1? What would it be if the strategy in part *(e)* were implemented?

P4–26   **CVP Analysis**

Hartbeater Company manufactures an electronic instrument that measures pulse and blood pressure for joggers. The instrument has a sleeve that joggers wear, and the dials are attached to the jogger's clothing. A contribution income statement for 19x2 appears below:

HARTBEATER COMPANY
Contribution Format Income Statement
For the Year Ended December 31, 19x2

Sales revenue (20,000 units)	$600,000
Variable costs	200,000
Contribution margin	400,000
Fixed costs	150,000
Net income	$250,000

The director of marketing believes sales can be increased substantially by increasing the advertising budget for 19x3. She believes sales could increase as much as 25 percent.

Required   a. The president of the company is willing to increase the advertising budget provided that net income can be increased by 30 percent. What is the maximum amount of additional advertising that should be spent to achieve the president's goal assuming that the 25 percent increase in volume will occur? (Use the differential approach or the contribution margin approach.)

b. Instead of increasing the advertising budget by the amount you computed in part *(a)*, the president decided to increase the budget by $15,000. To his surprise, sales volume in 19x3 increased by 25 percent and net income increased by 30 percent.

Having met his goal for the net income increase, the president is planning to call the management team together to applaud their efforts during 19x3 and to consider some form of incentive reward. You are asked to analyze the results for 19x3 assuming that the contribution margin ratio for 19x3 is the same as that for 19x2. Would you recommend the incentive award for *both* the sales staff and the manufacturing staff? If not, indicate who should get the award and explain your reasons for giving or denying an award. (*Hint*: Prepare a comparative contribution income statement for 19x3 to determine where the inconsistent operating results, if any, are present. There were no changes in fixed administrative costs, and the only change in fixed marketing costs is the increase in advertising cost of $15,000.)

P4–27   **Breakeven Graph and Profit-Volume Graph**

The Gonar Company manufactures and sells one product at a selling price of $100 per unit. Its variable cost is $40 per unit, and its fixed costs are $900,000 per annum.

Required   a. Prepare a breakeven graph using 5,000-unit intervals from 0 to 50,000 units.
b. Prepare a profit-volume graph using the same intervals as in part *(a)*.
c. What is the breakeven point in units and in dollars?
d. Compute the profit or loss from the profit-volume graph at the following levels of sales in units:
   (1) 10,000.
   (2) 30,000.
   (3) 40,000.

P4–28   **Preparation of Contribution Format Income Statement and Use of Operating Leverage**

The Shure Company had the following income statement prepared for the year 19x5:

SHURE COMPANY
Income Statement
For the Year Ended December 31, 19x5

Sales.	$3,000,000
Cost of goods sold.	1,800,000
Gross margin	1,200,000
Marketing and administrative costs	600,000
Net income.	$ 600,000

Included in the cost of goods sold are $700,000 of fixed manufacturing costs. The marketing and administrative costs include salespersons' commissions and other variable costs to the extent of $100,000. The balance of the marketing and administrative costs are fixed.

Shure Company manufactures and sells only one product at a selling price of $50 per unit.

Required   *a.* Recast the income statement into a contribution format statement.

b. Compute the company's degree of operating leverage.

c. During 19x5, the economy was very sluggish. For 19x6, the president of the company expects sales to either increase 20 percent or decrease 30 percent depending on who wins the national presidential election. In either case, the company president does not expect to change selling prices. Compute the expected change in net income for both possibilities, using the operating leverage computed in part *(b)*.

P4–29   **Breakeven and CVP Analysis for a Hospital**

Melford Hospital operates a general hospital but rents space and beds to separately owned entities rendering specialized services such as pediatrics and psychiatric. Melford charges each separate entity for common services such as patients' meals and laundry, and for administrative services such as billings and collections. Space and bed rentals are fixed charges for the year, based on bed capacity rented to each entity.

Melford charged the following costs to pediatrics for the year ended June 30, 19x2:

	Patient-Days (Variable)	Bed Capacity (Fixed)
Dietary	$ 600,000	—
Janitorial	—	$ 70,000
Laundry.	300,000	—
Laboratory	450,000	—
Pharmacy	350,000	—
Repairs and maintenance	—	30,000
General and administrative	—	1,300,000
Rent	—	1,500,000
Billings and collections	300,000	—
Totals.	$2,000,000	$2,900,000

During the year ended June 30, 19x2, pediatrics charged each patient an average of $300 per day, had a capacity of 60 beds, and had revenue of $6,000,000 for 365 days.

In addition, pediatrics directly employed the following personnel:

	Annual Salaries
Supervising nurses.	$25,000
Nurses	20,000
Aides.	9,000

Melford has the following minimum departmental personnel requirements based on total annual patient-days:

Annual Patient-Days	Aides	Nurses	Supervising Nurses
Up to 21,900	20	10	4
21,901 to 26,000	26	13	4
26,001 to 29,200	30	15	4

These staffing levels represent full-time equivalents. Pediatrics always employs only the minimum number of required full-time equivalent personnel. Salaries of supervising nurses, nurses, and aides are therefore fixed within ranges of annual patient-days.

Pediatrics operated at 100 percent capacity on 90 days during the year ended June 30, 19x2. It is estimated that during these 90 days, the demand exceeded 20 patients more than capacity. Melford has an additional 20 beds available for rent for the year ending June 30, 19x3. Such additional rental would increase pediatrics' fixed charges based on bed capacity.

Required   *a.* Calculate the minimum number of patient-days required for pediatrics to break even for the year ending June 30, 19x3, if the additional 20 beds are not rented. Patient demand is unknown, but assume that revenue per patient-day, cost per patient-day, cost per bed, and salary rates will remain the same as for the year ended June 30, 19x2.

   b. Assume that patient demand, revenue per patient-day, cost per patient-day, cost per bed, and salary rates for the year ending June 30, 19x3, remain the same as for the year ended June 30, 19x2. Prepare a schedule of increase in revenue and increase in costs for the year ending June 30, 19x3, to determine the net increase or decrease in earnings from the additional 20 beds if pediatrics rents this extra capacity from Melford.

(AICPA Adapted)

P4–30   **Breakeven and CVP Analysis with Sales Commissions**

Marston Corporation manufactures pharmaceutical products that are sold through a network of sales agents located in the United States and Canada. The agents are currently paid an 18 percent commission on sales, and this percentage was used when Marston prepared the following pro forma income statement for the fiscal year ending June 30, 19x1.

MARSTON CORPORATION
Pro Forma Income Statement
For the Year Ending June 30, 19x1
($000 omitted)

Sales.		$26,000
Cost of goods sold		
Variable	$11,700	
Fixed	2,870	14,570
Gross profit.		11,430
Selling and administrative costs		
Commissions	$ 4,680	
Fixed advertising cost	750	
Fixed administrative cost.	1,850	7,280
Operating income		4,150
Fixed interest cost.		650
Income before income taxes		3,500
Income taxes (40%)		1,400
Net income.		$ 2,100

Since the completion of this statement, Marston has learned that its agents are requiring an increase in the commission rate to 23 percent for the upcoming year. As a result, Marston's president has decided to investigate the possibility of hiring its own sales staff in place of the network of sales agents, and has asked Tom Ross, Marston's controller, to gather information on the costs associated with this change.

Ross estimates that Marston will have to hire eight salespeople to cover the current market area, and the annual payroll cost of each of these employees will average $80,000, including fringe benefit cost. Travel and entertainment cost is expected to total $600,000 for the year, and the annual cost of hiring a sales manager and sales secretary will be $150,000. In addition to their salaries, the eight salespeople will each earn commissions at the rate of 10 percent on the first $2 million in sales and 15 percent on all sales over $2 million. For planning purposes, Ross expects that all eight salespeople will exceed the $2 million mark and that sales will be at the level previously projected. Ross believes that Marston should also increase its advertising budget by $500,000.

Required
a. Calculate Marston Corporation's breakeven point in sales dollars for the fiscal year ending June 30, 19x1, if the company hires its own sales force and increases its advertising costs.
b. If Marston Corporation continues to sell through its network of sales agents and pays the higher commission rate, determine the estimated volume in sales dollars for the fiscal year ending June 30, 19x1, that would be required to generate the same net income as projected in the pro forma income statement presented above.
c. Describe the general assumptions underlying breakeven analysis that limit its usefulness.

(CMA Adapted)

P4–31 **CVP Analysis**

The management of the Southern Cottonseed Company has engaged you to assist in the development of information to be used for managerial decisions.

The company has the capacity to process 20,000 tons of cottonseed per year. The yield of a ton of cottonseed is as follows:

Product	Average Yield per Ton of Cottonseed	Average Selling Price per Trade Unit
Oil	300 pounds	$ 0.15 per pound
Meal	600	50.00 per ton
Hulls	800	20.00 per ton
Lint	100	3.00 per cwt.
Waste	200	

A special marketing study revealed the company can expect to sell its entire output for the coming year at the listed average selling prices.

You have determined the company's costs to be as follows:

Processing costs:
Variable . . . . $ 9 per ton of cottonseed put into process
Fixed . . . . 108,000 per year

Marketing costs:
All variable. . . . . . .   20 per ton sold

Administrative costs:
All fixed . . . .   90,000 per year

From the above information, you prepared and submitted to management a detailed report on the company's breakeven point. In view of conditions in the cottonseed market, management told you they would also like to know the average maximum amount that the company can afford to pay for a ton of cottonseed.

Management has defined the average maximum amount the company can afford to pay for a ton of cottonseed as the amount that would result in the company's having losses no greater when operating than when closed down under the existing cost and revenue structure. Management states you are to assume that the fixed costs shown in your breakeven point report will continue unchanged even when the operations are shut down.

Required   Compute the average maximum amount that the company can afford to pay for a ton of cottonseed.

(AICPA Adapted)

P4–32   **Sales Mix and CVP Analysis**

The Ionar Company manufactures and sells two products. The selling prices and variable costs of the products are as follows:

	Blujets	Penjets
Selling prices	$60	$120
Variable costs	24	72

The sales for 19x2 were in the ratio of 3 Blujets to 1 Penjet. Sales volume for 19x2 was $3 million. Fixed costs for 19x2 amounted to $1,170,000.

Required   a. Compute the number of units sold in 19x2 for each product.
b. Compute the breakeven sales in dollars and in units.
c. If the sales mix were to change to two units of Blujets to one unit of Penjet, would this have any effect on the breakeven sales? If so, what would be the new breakeven sales in dollars and in units?

  d. Assuming the sales volume would remain at $3 million, what operating income would be generated using the sales mix in part *(c)*? What income was generated for 19x2?

  e. If the firm wishes to generate an operating income of $858,000, what sales revenue in dollars would be required to generate this income if the original mix of 3 : 1 prevailed? How many units of each product would be required to generate that operating income?

P4–33   **CVP Analysis and Sales Mix for a Public Accounting Firm**

The public accounting firm of Haskins, Whinney, and Mitchell performs three kinds of services: auditing, tax return preparation, and management advisory services (MAS). For 19x2, the firm's fixed costs amounted to $50.5 million and the revenue mix was as follows:

Service	Percent of Total
Auditing	60%
Tax return preparation	15%
Management advisory services	25%

For 19x2, the following information is available:

	Auditing	Tax	MAS
Fee revenue	$120,000,000	$30,000,000	$50,000,000
Variable costs . . .	72,000,000	12,000,000	15,000,000

Required   *a.* Compute the breakeven revenue in dollars.

  b. If the firm were able to change its revenue mix to 50 percent, 10 percent, and 40 percent, respectively, would this change the breakeven point? If so, what would be the new breakeven point, assuming that fixed costs remain unchanged and variable costs behave in their normal manner?

  c. What net income would be generated using the sales mix in part *(b)* assuming that fee revenue would remain at $200 million? What net income was generated for 19x2? Assuming that the firm could change the mix, would you recommend that it do so? Why?

  d. If the firm wishes to generate a net income of $75.75 million, what fee revenue would be required to generate this net income if the original mix prevailed?

  e. What fee revenue would be required to generate a net income of $75.75 million if the firm were able to adjust its mix to that indicated in part *(b)*?

▶ **CASES**   **C4–34**   **Cost Structure**

Brian and Nancy McGrew are brother and sister. Each operates the same type of business, but in two different cities. They both employ the same CPA, and there is a free exchange of information and business results between brother and sister.

Although they operate the same type of business, Brian prefers to have a great deal of flexibility in running his business. Thus, all employees are compensated on an hourly basis and all salespersons are compensated on a commission basis.

Alternatively, Nancy believes in running her business making maximum use of the latest automation. She employs very few employees, but she has a very large investment in machinery and equipment. Her employees are compensated on an annual basis and her salespeople are paid annual salaries with no commissions.

For 19x0, the condensed income statements for the McGrews were as follows:

	Brian	Nancy
Sales revenues	$1,500,000	$1,500,000
Costs	1,275,000	1,275,000
Net income	$ 225,000	$ 225,000

Their CPA provided each of them with both income statements, and they were pleased to see that they each had the same net income. The CPA also informed them of the following:

Brian's fixed costs	$150,000
Nancy's fixed costs.	$975,000

Brian notified the CPA that he expects a 40 percent increase in sales volume for 19x1, with no expected changes in selling prices or fixed costs. Nancy notified the CPA that she expects only a 20 percent increase in sales volume, and she too does not expect any changes in selling prices or fixed costs. The CPA was asked to prepare forecasted income statements for 19x1 for both businesses. Condensed versions of his forecasts for 19x1 are as follows:

	Brian	Nancy
Sales revenues	$2,100,000	$1,800,000
Costs	1,725,000	1,335,000
Net income	$ 375,000	$ 465,000

After reviewing the results, Brian had difficulty in understanding why Nancy has a projected net income that is $90,000 higher than his projected net income when he anticipates a 40 percent increase in sales volume while Nancy expects only a 20 percent increase in volume.

Required
a. Recast the 19x0 income statements into the contribution format.
b. Do the same for the 19x1 projections.
c. Write an explanation for the apparent inconsistency for Brian. You may refer to your calculations in parts *(a)* and *(b)*.
d. Nancy is delighted with her projected income statement for 19x1. However, she is concerned with the economic outlook for 19x2. She expects that a 20 percent decline in her 19x0 sales for 19x2 is a real possibility. Brian also expects a 20 percent decline in his 19x2 sales volume from that of 19x0. Prepare projected income statements for Brian and Nancy for 19x2, assuming that each will experience a 20 percent decline from 19x0 sales volume with no changes in selling prices or fixed costs. If the projection for Nancy is different from the one prepared for Brian, explain the difference. (The 19x2 projected income statements should be in the contribution format.)

C4–35   **Preparation of Contribution Format Income Statement and Use of Operating Leverage**

Solstice Company had the following income statement prepared for the year 19x2:

SOLSTICE COMPANY
Income Statement
For the Year Ended December 31, 19x2

Sales	$6,000,000
Cost of goods sold	4,000,000
Gross margin	2,000,000
Marketing and administrative costs.	750,000
Net income	$1,250,000

Included in the cost of goods sold are $2,950,000 of fixed manufacturing costs. The marketing and administrative costs include salespersons' commissions and other variable costs to the extent of $450,000. The balance of the marketing and administrative costs is fixed.

Solstice Company manufactures and sells only one product at a selling price of $80 per unit.

Required   *a.* Recast the income statement into a contribution format statement.

b. Compute the company's degree of operating leverage.

c. During 19x2, the economy was very sluggish. For 19x3, the president of the company expects sales to either increase 20 percent or decrease 30 percent, depending on the outcome of the national presidential election. In either case, the company's president does not expect to change selling prices. Compute the expected change in net income for both possibilities, using the operating leverage computed in part *(b)*.

C4–36   **CVP Analysis**

The president of Beth Corporation, which manufactures tape decks and sells them to producers of sound reproduction systems, anticipates a 10 percent wage increase on January 1 of next year to the manufacturing employees (variable labor). He expects no other changes in costs. Overhead will not change as a result of the wage increase. The president has asked you to assist him in developing the information he needs to formulate a reasonable product strategy for next year.

You are satisfied by cost analysis that volume is the primary factor affecting costs and have separated the semivariable costs into their fixed and variable segments. You also observe that the beginning and ending inventories are never materially different.

Below are the current year data assembled for your analysis:

Current selling price per unit	$ 80.00
Variable cost per unit:	
Material	$ 30.00
Labor	12.00
Overhead	6.00
Total	$ 48.00
Annual volume of sales	5,000 units
Fixed costs.	$51,000

Required   Provide the following information for the president using cost-volume-profit analysis.

    a. What increase in the selling price is necessary to cover the 10 percent wage increase and still maintain the current profit-volume-cost ratio?

    b. How many tape decks must be sold to maintain the current net income if the sales price remains at $80 and the 10 percent wage increase goes into effect?

    c. The president believes an additional $190,000 of machinery (to be depreciated at 10 percent annually) will increase present capacity (5,300 units) by 30 percent. If all tape decks produced can be sold at the present price and the wage increase goes into effect, how would the estimated net income before capacity is increased compare with the estimated net income after capacity is increased? Prepare computations of estimated net income *before* and *after* the expansion.

(AICPA Adapted)

C4–37 **Soccer Camp CVP Analysis**

Peter English, the head basketball coach at Stroud College, has been considering the possibility of establishing and operating a children's summer camp at the college. English has received a commitment from the college to provide food and lodging for the campers and to allow use of the athletic fields. However, English and the summer camp must bear the costs of hiring counselors; obtaining insurance, hats, and tee shirts for the campers; providing alternative indoor activities on rainy days; and printing and mailing brochures. Hector Rodrigues, the controller of Stroud College, assisted English in developing the following enrollment and cost estimates:

Expected enrollment.	190 campers
Average regional price per camper	$ 225.00
Costs per camper:	
Food and lodging provided by the college	125.00
Insurance, hats, and tee shirts	25.00
Movies and transportation on rainy days.	7.50
Cost per camp counselor.	500.00
Printing and mailing of brochures	2,750.00

Rodrigues informed English that it is standard procedure for the college to charge profit-oriented ventures 10 percent of gross revenues for use of its facilities. Other local coaches have told English that at least one counselor is needed to supervise every 10 children. Each camp will run for one week, Monday through Friday; normal summer weather patterns usually provide at least one weekday thunderstorm early in the afternoon. Peter English, as director of the summer camp, would retain all profits and suffer all losses from camp operations.

Required   *a.* If the expected enrollment is achieved and the price charged and costs incurred as indicated above, what would English's profit be?

    b. What price would have to be charged to permit English to earn a profit of $3,000 if only 135 campers enrolled?

    c. If summer weather were severe and each afternoon's activities rained out, what would be the effect on the profit expected in part *(a)*?

    d. What are the advantages and disadvantages to English and the college of the proposed children's summer camp?

▶ **ETHICAL BEHAVIOR CASE**   **C4–38**   You are a recent graduate of Michelin College with a major in accounting. Because you graduated with a fairly high cumulative average and you interview well, you were fortunate to get a job as a management accountant with a Fortune-500 company. This firm is one of only three electronics firms that has the capability to manufacture very sophisticated electronic equipment for the U.S. Air Force.

Your immediate supervisor has asked you to assist her in preparing cost estimates needed for the company's bid on a government contract. Not quite sure how to proceed, you decide to use the firm's bid on a previous contract as a guide in preparing the needed data. Looking through the file containing the previous bid, you find a copy of a letter marked "confidential." Thinking that this letter may have a bearing on the data you need, you read the letter, which is on a letterhead of one of the other two competing firms. The letter follows:

Dear Bill:
It was great having lunch with you and John last week. I thought the objectives we achieved were very productive. I completed my cost estimate for the bid, and we are going to come in at $500 million. John told me that his bid was going in at $510 million.

Since we agreed that this bid was yours, I trust that this information will enable you to prepare your bid. My source in Washington informs me that there won't be any problem getting this bid through at this amount. He also informed me that an invitation to bid on a new contract will be coming out in about three months. We really have a great thing going for us.

Best regards.

Required *a.* Describe your ethical responsibilities with regard to the information you have inadvertently obtained. Refer to the specific standards discussed in Chapter 1 using the "Standards of Ethical Conduct for Management Accountants." What course of action would you take?

b. As you know, whistle-blowers who perform a public service are usually fired from their jobs and are often blackballed in the business world. You may not be able to get another job if you become a whistle-blower. Would this affect the decision you reached in part *(a)*?

▶ **ANSWERS TO SELF-TEST**

True or False

1. False	2. False	3. False	4. True	5. False	6. False
7. True	8. False	9. True	10. False		

Multiple Choice

1. *d.*

2. *b.* $\dfrac{\$150,000}{(\$625,000 - \$375,000) \div 25,000 \text{ units}} = 15,000 \text{ units.}$

3. *c.* CMPU = ($625,000 − $375,000) ÷ 25,000 units = $10 BES after changes:

$$\frac{\$150,000 + (\$18,000 \div 6)}{\$10 - (\$4.50 - \$2.50)} = 19,125 \text{ units.}$$

4. *d.* $\text{CMR} = \dfrac{\$250,000}{\$625,000} = 40\%.$

$$\text{Selling price} = \frac{\text{VC}}{\text{VCR}} = \frac{\$15.00^* + \$2.00}{.6} = \$28.33.$$

---

* $375,000 ÷ 25,000 units

Job Order Costing

▶ **LEARNING OBJECTIVES**

After reading this chapter, you should be able to:

1. Discuss why product cost information and a cost accounting system are needed.
2. Differentiate between a process cost accounting system and a job order cost accounting system and identify the kinds of firms for which each would be appropriate.
3. Trace the physical flow of production and the corresponding cost flow (the cost accounting cycle).
4. Identify the different kinds of source documents and how they contribute to a job order cost system.
5. Explain what book inventories are, how they are automatically generated in a job order cost system, and how they are used.
6. Discuss why firms use estimated amounts rather than actual amounts to apply manufacturing overhead to production.
7. Calculate predetermined overhead rates using five different bases and explain the circumstances under which each base is most effective.
8. Dispose of underapplied and overapplied overhead at the end of the fiscal year.
9. Describe two different ways of assigning payroll fringes to particular batches of production.
10. Use the Direct Materials and Supplies Inventory, Work in Process, and Finished Goods accounts to prepare the schedules of cost of goods manufactured and cost of goods sold.

▶ **INTERVIEW**

Angelo T. Murlo
Chief Financial Officer
Philips Laboratories Division
North American Philips Corporation

Q. *Have you had occasion to use a job order cost accounting system? If so, did you use a full-costing (absorption system) or a contribution margin (variable costing) system? Give examples of how your system was used for external reporting purposes and how it was used for internal decision-making purposes.*

A. The job order cost accounting system we use is a full-costing, absorption system.

All our costs fall into two broad categories: direct costs, which are charged to project numbers, and indirect costs, which are identified as either overhead or general and administrative (G&A) costs.

Direct costs are tracked, and reported, in two separate ways: one in a report that reflects all costs, direct and indirect, by project number; the other

▶ in a report that reflects only direct costs, exclusive of direct labor costs. The first report is used externally to show the cost of our total operation allocated by project. This gives senior management an understanding of which projects carry the highest costs relative to the returns from those projects. The second report is used internally to track, and control, spending in each project by specific functional account (e.g. Materials, Travel, Equipment Rental, Consultants). In addition, this report identifies the net value of commitments to vendors from purchase orders after partial payments have been deducted. Those two categories (cost plus commitments) are totaled and compared to the budget for each project.

When project costs are running close to, or higher than, budgeted costs, detailed analyses are prepared to pinpoint the source of overspending. Many decisions can result from that investigation, including continuing the project (albeit, at a slower pace) or stopping it entirely, if costs are seen as getting out of hand relative to projected returns.

Q. *Did you use a predetermined overhead rate for applying overhead to production? If so, were the rates departmentalized, and what base(s) did you use for applying overhead? Why was each base chosen? If you did not use a predetermined overhead rate, what method did you use to assign overhead to product costs?*

A. Indirect costs are identified as either overhead or general and administrative (G&A). Rates are developed to allocate those costs to projects monthly. Rates are not developed by department.

Overhead costs include those that, although not directly related to a project, are just one step removed from a project. Such costs are not easily identified as tied to a specific project but nonetheless are affected by projects. Examples include energy, depreciation of project equipment, payroll-related benefits for project staff, and so on.

G&A costs include those that support all projects but are not significantly influenced by any single project. Examples include costs to maintain accounting, human resources, maintenance, and other similar support services.

The overhead rate is calculated with direct labor costs as the base. Since our projects are labor intensive, using a direct labor base was the logical way to allocate overhead costs. The G&A rate is calculated with *all* costs (except G&A) as the base. This allows us to allocate G&A costs proportionately to projects.

▶ **Cost accounting** is the subfield of accounting that records, measures, and reports information about costs. In a manufacturing setting, the cost accounting system usually focuses on product costs—that is, direct materials, direct labor, and manufacturing overhead—that can be specifically attributed to products and are part of inventory. The resulting information plays a key role in such managerial activities as valuing inventory, pricing company products, preparing financial statements, planning and control, and decision making of all kinds.

During the past several decades, the number and variety of service industries has increased significantly. As a result, adapting cost accounting applications to service businesses has become prevalent. This chapter first examines job order cost accounting applications for manufacturing firms and then highlights these applications for service industries.

The **cost accounting cycle**—the sequential recording and classifying of transactions that affect costs—usually corresponds to a firm's physical flow of operations. Based on this cycle, product costs for manufacturing firms are accumulated and assigned to units of product or departments. Because the way in which costs are accumulated and assigned can affect both the income statement and the balance sheet as well as many managerial decisions related to planning, control, and product pricing, it is crucial for managers to understand how their company's operations relate to its flow of costs and its cost accounting system.

In this chapter, we examine **absorption costing**—also called **full costing**—in which all manufacturing costs, both fixed and variable, are assigned to products and thus included in inventory. In Chapter 12, we consider a different method of costing—variable costing—in which only variable manufacturing costs are inventoried. ◀

The Uses of Product Cost Information for Manufacturing Firms

L.O. 1
The need for a cost accounting system

Inventory Valuation   Most managers and investors need financial information on a regular basis. Because inventory values are needed every time an interim or annual report is prepared, a physical count of all goods in stock—a costly and time-consuming process—would be required unless some other method could be found to calculate inventories. In addition, if the physical quantities are to be translated into dollars, some method must be found to calculate the unit cost of each item manufactured. An **integrated cost accounting system**—one that is an integral part of the firm's comprehensive record-keeping system—can provide the needed quantities and unit costs of inventories without the need for a physical count. These amounts, called **book inventories,** enable a business to prepare interim financial statements as frequently as needed without taking a physical inventory count.

The book inventory does not replace the need for a physical inventory count, however. A physical inventory count is also necessary from time to time to determine that the quantities shown in the book inventory actually exist. It is not uncommon to find differences between the book inventory and the actual physical count. These differences may be due to theft, errors in record-keeping, or both. A company that relies only on a physical count or only on a book inventory is missing an important control device because one method acts as a check on the other.

Planning and Control   A cost accounting system is extremely useful for providing the information needed to prepare a firm's budget for the next accounting period. As noted in Chapter 1, a firm must make plans for its operations in future accounting periods, and this is accomplished through the use of budgets.

Decision Making   Cost accounting is indispensable for many decisions that managers must make on a routine basis. Here are some common managerial decisions and the cost accounting information they require:

Kinds of Decisions	Cost Accounting Information Required
1. Pricing a product	Costs of producing the product
2. Discontinuing a product	Costs avoided
3. Making or buying component parts	Costs of making the part
4. Expanding production of an existing product	Additional costs due to expansion
5. Taking special orders at less than regular prices	Additional costs of the special order

Because cost accounting information is needed for (1) inventory pricing and valuation, (2) annual income statement and balance sheet preparation, (3) interim income statement and balance sheet preparation, (4) budget preparation, (5) planning and control, and (6) a variety of decisions that managers must make in carrying out their duties, a good cost accounting system is crucial to a company's success.

► COST ACCOUNTING SYSTEMS

L.O. 2
Differences between job order and process cost accounting systems

There are two basic kinds of cost accounting systems. In a **process cost accounting system,** product costs are accumulated for a specific period of time—a week or a month. The total of the accumulated costs is then divided by the number of units produced to arrive at an average unit cost for the period. This system is used primarily by firms that manufacture a homogeneous product repetitively, such as paint manufacturers, petroleum refiners, and mining firms. Firms that use this system manufacture their products repetitively, and thus, their production is continuous. Process costing is discussed further in Chapter 6.

Unlike process costing, which is used for continuously produced products on a production line, the other system, a **job order cost accounting system,** accumulates costs for a particular batch of production that is often unique or custom-made. The batch of production is referred to as a **job.** A job has a definite starting point and completion point, as would, for example, the manufacture of 1,000 coffee tables. A furniture manufacturer may start and complete a batch of coffee tables and then not make coffee tables again for a six-month period. When the coffee tables are completed, a batch of sofas may follow, and when those are completed, a batch of dining room tables may be started, and so forth. This kind of production differs sharply from that of the paint manufacturer who produces paint on a continuous basis. In many cases, the paint manufacturer may have difficulty determining when one batch of paint ends and a new one begins, but the furniture manufacturer can clearly identify when the manufacture of each batch of products begins and ends. For manufacturers like the furniture maker, it is logical to relate manufacturing costs to the batch being manufactured. Among the firms likely to use job order systems are furniture manufacturers, clothing manufacturers, tool and die manufacturers, construction contractors, and ship and missile producers.

▶ **ILLUSTRATION 5-1**   Sample Physical Flow of Production for a Manufacturing Firm

1. A decision is made to order basic direct materials. (Specialized direct materials may be ordered as needed.)
2. Direct materials and supplies are ordered from vendors.
3. Direct materials and supplies are received and placed in the storeroom.
4. A decision is made to manufacture a specific product in a product line.
5. Direct materials and supplies are issued from the storeroom and placed into production.
6. Direct-labor employees work on transforming the direct materials into work in process.
7. Other cost factors of production—the manufacturing overhead—are incurred in the process of transforming the direct materials into work in process.
8. The work in process is completed and becomes finished goods.
9. The finished goods are sold and become cost of goods sold.

▶ JOB ORDER COSTING FOR MANUFACTURING FIRMS

An interrelationship exists between (1) the physical flow of production, (2) source documents, and (3) the cost accounting cycle (cost accumulation). In a well-controlled system, a business form, or source document, known as a *production order* will be issued prior to the start of production to authorize the manufacture of a particular product. Additional source documents will be added as the production cycle progresses. In this way, source documents help the company keep track of its production process and form the basis of the journal entries that are part of its cost accounting system.

The Physical Flow of Production

L.O. 3

The **physical flow of production** is the sequence of operating activity that begins with the decision to order direct materials and ends with a finished product ready for sale to customers. Although the intervening steps may vary from firm to firm, they share a common thread that allows one general example to be adapted to particular cases. A typical physical flow of production appears in Illustration 5-1. Each step in the flow is associated with a specific source document. The source documents explained in the next section are keyed to the numerical sequence shown in Illustration 5-1.

Source Documents

Source documents are business forms used to initiate or record a firm's accounting transactions. Although the specific forms may vary among organizations, certain kinds of information are common to them all. The source documents presented here contain the essential information needed to maintain control of a firm's accounting system. In practice, a firm's source documents may contain additional information to satisfy the unique needs of its managers.

L.O. 4

1. Purchase Requisition   Most firms keep on hand a specified minimum stock of basic direct materials and supplies, such as lumber, glue, nails, and hardware. The purpose of maintaining such a minimum stock—called a **safety stock**—is to avoid the interruption of the production process that would occur if a crucial direct material were to go unexpectedly out of stock due to a delay in shipment or unusually heavy usage. A safety stock is usually maintained for all basic direct materials.

When the quantity of a direct material reaches the level at which it must be reordered, the storeroom clerk prepares a **purchase requisition,** a form

    Sample Purchase Requisition

Bettermade Furniture Company
1211 World Avenue
New York, N.Y. 10036
(212) 765-4321

Date _January 15, 19x2_   Requisition No. _422_

PURCHASE REQUISITION		
		Prepared by: L.A.B.
Quantity	Description	Date Needed
_10,000 ft._	_Clear Maple_	
	_1" x 6"_	_February 15, 19x2_

requesting the purchase of needed materials, and sends it to the purchasing department. The form usually includes:

1. The date the form was prepared.
2. A control number.
3. A description of the desired direct material.
4. The quantity needed.
5. The date when the direct material is needed.

A sample purchase requisition is shown in Illustration 5-2. *No journal entry* is required when a purchase requisition is prepared.

2. Purchase Order   A **purchase order**, a document authorizing a vendor to ship the desired merchandise ordered, is usually generated by the purchasing department. It specifies the price and terms of the order and should contain:

1. The purchaser's name, billing address, and delivery address.
2. A purchase order number.
3. The date of the purchase order.
4. The requisition number.
5. The vendor's name and address.
6. The delivery date.
7. The quantity and description of the material.
8. The price and terms of payment.
9. Shipping instructions and terms.

A sample purchase order appears in Illustration 5-3. *No journal entry* is required when direct materials are ordered.

3. Receiving Report   When the shipment arrives, the receiving department prepares a **receiving report,** which lists the descriptions and quantities of the goods received. A copy of this document is then sent to the storeroom along with the materials. The receiving report, together with a copy of the

▶ **ILLUSTRATION 5-3**   Sample Purchase Order

Bettermade Furniture Company
1211 World Avenue
New York, N.Y. 10036
(212) 765-4321

Date *January 20, 19x2*

Vendor:	Ship To:	Purchase Order No. *1344*
Alco Lumber Co. *P.O. Box 17* *New York, N.Y. 10010*	*Factory* *14-24 Corona Ave.* *Long Island City, N.Y.*	(Pleae show this number on invoice, packing slip, and correspondence.)

F.O.B. Point	Ship Via	Terms	Delivery Date	Requisition No.
Factory - LIC, N.Y.	*R.R. or Truck*	*2/10, n/60*	*Feb. 15, 19x2*	*422*

Item No.	Quantity	Unit	Description	Unit Price	Extension
1	*10,000*	*Ft.*	*Clear Maple* *1" x 6"*	*$2.00* *lineal foot*	*$20,000*

vendor's invoice, form the basis of an entry in the company's journals. If the Bettermade Furniture Company purchased lumber for $20,000, drawer hardware for $3,000, and lacquer for $4,000, the summary journal entry to record the purchases would be:

(a)

19x2
Feb. 15 Direct Materials and Supplies Inventory 27,000
              Accounts Payable   27,000
         To record the purchases of direct materials.

This entry requires posting to the general ledger account Direct Materials and Supplies Inventory and to the direct materials and supplies ledger cards in the subsidiary ledger. A separate subsidiary ledger card is kept for each form of direct material. If Bettermade's beginning inventory balances were $12,500 for lumber, $3,500 for drawer hardware, and $3,000 for lacquer, and if it also had $600 of glue in beginning inventory, the general ledger account and the subsidiary ledger cards would appear as shown in Illustration 5-4.

A sample receiving report for the lumber purchased appears in Illustration 5-5. Receiving reports would also be prepared when the drawer hardware and the lacquer are delivered.

4. Production Order   Although the use of a job order system may seem to imply that production begins only on the receipt of an order from a customer, this is not the case. Production may begin with the receipt of a customer's order, but it may also start when a firm decides to produce finished goods for stock inventory to be sold at a later time. In either case, when a decision is made to produce a batch of goods, such as 200 desks, a

▶ **ILLUSTRATION 5-4**   Materials and Supplies Inventory Ledgers

GENERAL LEDGER

Direct Materials and Supplies Inventory

19x2	
Jan. 1 Inventory at beginning 19,600	
Feb. 15 Purchases *(a)* 27,000	

SUBSIDIARY LEDGER

Clear Maple—1″ × 6″

Receipts			Amounts Issued			Balance		
	feet					19x2	feet	
Feb. 15	10,000	20,000				Jan. 1	6,250	12,500
						Feb. 15	16,250	32,500

Drawer Hardware

Receipts			Amounts Issued			Balance		
	units					19x2	units	
Feb. 15	6,000	3,000				Jan. 1	7,000	3,500
						Feb. 15	13,000	6,500

Lacquer

Receipts			Amounts Issued			Balance		
	gal.					19x2	gal.	
Feb. 15	800	4,000				Jan. 1	600	3,000
						Feb. 15	1,400	7,000

Glue

Receipts			Amounts Issued			Balance		
						19x2	gal.	
						Jan. 1	100	600

production order is prepared and approved by the manager in charge. The production order authorizes the manufacture of a product and contains:

1. A description of the product to be manufactured.
2. The quantity required.
3. A product model number.

▶ **ILLUSTRATION 5-5**   Sample Receiving Report

Bettermade Furniture Company Receiving Report			
Received from: *Alco Lumber Company*			Receiving Report No. R 1842
Freight: Ppd. ☑ Collect ☐			Purchase Order No. *1344*
Date Received: *Feb. 15, 19x2*		Received by: *Leonard*	
Quantity	Description	Weight	
		Gross	Net
10,000 lineal feet	*Clear Maple 1" x 6"*		

▶ **ILLUSTRATION 5-6**   Sample Production Order

Bettermade Furniture Company Production Order		
Date: February 19, 19x2		Job No. 456
Manufactured for: Stock _____ Customer Smith's Dept. Store		
Date needed: April 15, 19x2		
Quantity	Model Number	Description
200	D 2051	Natural maple desks

Authorized by: _____*Phyllis Tamara*_____

4. The estimated date of completion.
5. A job order number.
6. The date of the production order.
7. The authorization signature.

   No journal entries are required on the company's books when the production order is issued. A sample production order is presented in Illustration 5-6.

▶ **ILLUSTRATION 5-7**   Sample Materials Requisition Form

Materials Requisition Number 406   Date Feb. 28, 19x2
Job Number to Be Charged 456

Quantity	Description	Unit Cost	Total Cost	Classification
5,000 ft.	Clear maple 1″ × 6″	$2.00	$10,000	Direct
600	Drawer pulls	.50	300	Direct
50 gal.	Lacquer	5.00	250	Direct
5 gal.	Glue	6.00	30	Indirect
			$10,580	

L. Bern
Authorized signature

Direct materials $10,550
Indirect materials   30

---

5. Materials Requisition   Once the production order is issued, a **materials requisition** form is prepared. This source document authorizes the transfer of the necessary direct and indirect materials from the storeroom to the production line to start manufacture. The materials requisition should contain specific descriptions of the materials needed and distinguish between direct and indirect materials.

For control purposes, a storeroom clerk issues direct materials and supplies only on receipt of a properly authorized materials requisition form. As shown in Illustration 5-7, a materials requisition form should contain places for:

1. The job number for which the materials are to be issued.
2. A description of the direct materials and supplies needed.
3. The quantity of each direct material and supply needed.
4. The unit cost of each material.
5. The total cost.
6. Classification into direct materials and indirect materials.

When the materials are issued from the storeroom, the following entry is made in the company's journals:

(b)

```
19x2
Feb. 28  Work in Process . . . . . . . . . . . . . . . . . . . 10,550
           Manufacturing Overhead* . . . . . . . . . . . . .     30
             Direct Materials and Supplies Inventory. . . . . .       10,580
           To record the issuance of direct and indirect materials
           for Job No. 456.
```

* As noted in Chapter 2, glue is treated as manufacturing overhead, even though it is really direct materials.

L.O. 5
Book inventory

Journal entry *(b)* must be posted to the general ledger *and* to the subsidiary ledger cards for the direct materials and supplies inventory. After these postings, the ledgers for direct materials and supplies would appear as shown in Illustration 5-8. If a book inventory of direct materials and supplies

▶ **ILLUSTRATION 5-8**   Materials and Supplies Inventory Ledgers

GENERAL LEDGER

Direct Materials and Supplies Inventory	
19x2 Jan. 1 Inventory at beginning 19,600 Feb. 28 Purchases (a) 27,000 *Balance* *36,020*	19x2 Feb. 28 Issuances (b) 10,580

SUBSIDIARY LEDGER

Clear Maple—1″ × 6″

	Receipts			Amounts Issued			Balance	
	feet			feet		19x2	feet	
						Jan. 1	6,250	12,500
Feb. 15	10,000	20,000				Feb. 15	16,250	32,500
			Feb. 28	5,000	10,000	28	11,250	22,500

Drawer Hardware

	Receipts			Amounts Issued			Balance	
	units			units		19x2	units	
						Jan. 1	7,000	3,500
Feb. 15	6,000	3,000				Feb. 15	13,000	6,500
			Feb. 28	600	300	28	12,400	6,200

Lacquer

	Receipts			Amounts Issued			Balance	
	gal.			gal.		19x2	gal.	
						Jan. 1	600	3,000
Feb. 15	800	4,000				Feb. 15	1,400	7,000
			Feb. 28	50	250	28	1,350	6,750

Glue

	Receipts			Amounts Issued			Balance	
				gal.		19x2	gal.	
						Jan. 1	100	600
			Feb. 28	5	30	Feb. 28	95	570

is needed, the general ledger balance of $36,020 provides the information. This amount is supported by these individual balances in the subsidiary ledger:

Clear maple	$22,500
Drawer hardware	6,200
Lacquer	6,750
Glue	570
Total	$36,020

It is customary to *accumulate* the materials requisitions and *journalize* them as summary entries, either monthly or weekly depending on the frequency of the reporting system. However, *individual* materials requisitions are *posted* currently to the appropriate individual materials ledger cards. Furthermore, although entry *(b)* summarizes cost information, it also corresponds to the physical flow of production. Thus, when the materials are transferred from the storeroom to the factory, they are no longer direct materials inventory; instead, they become *work in process*. The debit to Work in Process in entry *(b)* signifies that the direct materials are in the process of becoming finished goods.

Soon after the preparation of the production order, a **job cost sheet** is prepared. Its purpose is twofold. First, it is used to break down the job's costs into the components of direct materials, direct labor, and manufacturing overhead. The total costs are then divided by the number of units produced to arrive at the unit cost. Second, the job cost sheet acts as the subsidiary ledger to the Work in Process account in the general ledger. A separate sheet is kept for each job. Thus, the details of the work in process inventory at any point in time can be found by consulting the job cost sheets. The active file of job cost sheets contains only jobs still in process. When a job is *completed,* the cost summary at the bottom of the job cost sheet is filled in and the form is transferred to a file of completed jobs. Because the volume of postings to job cost sheets is normally quite substantial, most firms use computers to perform this function, and, thus, job cost sheets are stored in computer files and printed on paper only when necessary.

The general ledger account for work in process and the related job cost sheet for a manual system are shown in Illustration 5-9.

Let us assume Jobs 457 and 458 are started on March 2, 19x2, and the direct materials and indirect materials for these jobs are as shown in journal entry *(c)*:

(c)

19x2				
Mar. 31	Work in Process	14,000	
	Manufacturing Overhead	900	
	Direct Materials and Supplies Inventory		14,900

To record the issuance of materials for Jobs 457 and 458 as follows:

	457	458	Total
Direct materials	$6,000	$8,000	$14,000
Indirect materials . . .	400	500	900
Totals	$6,400	$8,500	$14,900

The postings to the general ledger and job cost sheet would be similar to those shown for journal entry *(b)*.

6. Job Time Ticket If a cost accounting system is to operate properly, some method must be used to track the time each employee spent on each job (batch) so that direct labor can be properly costed. As most of us know, time cards are used to track the number of hours that each employee worked. Employees insert time cards into a special clock and "punch-in" to record when they begin to work, and then "punch-out" to record when they stop working. As company accountants prepare payroll checks, *time cards* are adequate for the preparation of payroll, but they do not satisfy the cost

▶ **ILLUSTRATION 5-9**   Work in Process and Job Cost Sheet

GENERAL LEDGER

Work in Process	
19x2 Feb. 28 *(b)* 10,550	

SUBSIDIARY LEDGER

JOB COST SHEET

Job Number __456__   Date __Feb. 19, 19x2__

Date Completed _____

Units __200__

Item __D 2051 Desks__

For Stock _____

For Customer __Smith's Dept. Store__

Direct Materials			Direct Labor				Manufacturing Overhead			
Date	Req. No.	Amount	Date	Clock No.	Hours	Amount	Date	DLH	Rate	Amount
19x2 Feb. 28	406	$10,550								

Cost Summary	
Direct Materials	$
Direct Labor	$
Overhead	$
Total Cost	$
Unit Cost	$

accountant's need to know specifically how much labor time was spent on each individual job. A *job time ticket* is used to provide this detailed information.

Although tracking systems vary from company to company, each depends on a **job time ticket,** a source document on which an employee records the amount of time he or she worked on a particular job. For example, time clocks may be located at each workstation, and an employee may have a supply of preprinted forms showing his or her employee number and job number. When a particular job is started, the employee inserts the form into the clock and punches in. When going to another job, the employee punches out on the first form and punches a new form for the new job. These job time

▶ **ILLUSTRATION 5-10**   Job Time Ticket

JOB TIME TICKET			
Employee's Name A. Gucci	Date March 18, 19x2		
Clock No. 613	Department Sanding		
Operation Sanding	Time Finished 11:45 A.M.		
Job No. 456	Time Started 10:15 A.M.		
Hours	Rate of Pay	Direct Labor	Comments
1½	$10.00	$15.00	

Approved _____ *P. Block* _____

tickets are then costed using the employee's rate of pay. The total of an employee's job time tickets is compared to the employee's time card for the week, and any difference between them is considered idle time unless an obvious error exists. Illustration 5-10 presents an example of a job time ticket.

Another method of accomplishing the same result is to use prepunched cards that are processed by computer, which saves a considerable amount of time. Whichever method is used, a summary entry would be made, either monthly or weekly. At Bettermade, the total of March's job tickets amounted to $12,000, idle time was $500, and indirect labor was $4,000. An analysis of the month's job time tickets showed the following:

	Direct Labor
Job 456	$ 7,500
Job 457	2,500
Job 458	2,000
Total	$12,000

The total payroll for March at Bettermade may be summarized as follows:

Direct labor	$12,000
Idle time	500
Indirect labor	4,000
Total payroll	$16,500

The journal entry to record the job time is:

(d)

```
19x2
Mar. 31  Work in Process . . . . . . . . . . . . . . . . . . . . . . . . .   12,000
             Manufacturing Overhead—Idle Time . . . . . . . . . .      500
             Manufacturing Overhead—Indirect Labor . . . . . . . .    4,000
                 Wages Payable . . . . . . . . . . . . . . . . . . .              16,500
             To record the factory payroll for the month based on an
             analysis of job time tickets.
```

Overtime Premium   During a busy period, businesses may ask employees to work overtime. Most businesses are required to pay an **overtime premium**—or increased wage rate—for all hours over 40 that an employee works. The premium is usually equal to one half of the straight-time rate. If an employee's regular rate of pay is $8 per hour and she worked 46 hours in a particular week, she would receive the following as gross pay:

40 hours at $ 8	$320
6 hours at 12	72
Total	$392

Although it may seem that the overtime premium could be identified as belonging to the same product as the regular pay rate, some companies classify it differently. If a firm regularly produces many items, the product that required overtime work may be considered a random departure from the norm. In such a case, the cost of the product would be unduly burdened if the entire overtime premium were charged to it. When this occurs, it is customary to charge the overtime premium to manufacturing overhead and thereby spread the cost across all units produced during the year, much like factory rent. The treatment changes, however, if the firm is not in its busy season and if the overtime is worked because of a customer's rush order. Then the overtime premium should be charged to the specific job, because the rush order can be said to have caused the overtime. Another reason for charging the overtime to the specific job may be that the customer will be charged a premium for rush orders and, therefore, the premiums will be matched against each other.

Idle Time   Although most managers would prefer to avoid idle time, its total absence in a business environment would be the exception rather than the rule. **Idle time**—production time lost during a machine breakdown or when material shortages occur—occurs randomly, so its cost should be absorbed by all production rather than by a particular product. This is accomplished by charging the cost of idle time to overhead.

▶ **PROGRESS CHECK**

1. Why is product cost information needed?
2. What does the term *physical flow of production* mean?
3. What are source documents? List the normal source documents used by a manufacturing firm.
4. What is the difference between a time card and a job time ticket? What is the purpose of each?
5. Is there more than one method of treating overtime premium? If so, what are the methods and what circumstances give rise to the alternate treatments? ◀

7. Manufacturing Overhead   Factors of production other than direct materials and direct labor, such as rent, power, and machinery, are necessary to transform direct materials into finished goods. Although such components of manufacturing overhead cannot be directly traced to a specific job because they are mostly fixed costs, they must be appropriately assigned to all jobs. This is not an easy task. If *actual* overhead were used, random fluctuations for items like repairs might cause overhead costs in a particular month to be distorted. And to obtain actual costs, allocation would have to be deferred until the end of the fiscal year, when all overhead costs would be known. As a result, all job cost sheets would have to remain incomplete until the end of the year, despite the fact that most jobs would be physically complete. This approach would also prevent the firm from preparing interim financial statements, because without overhead figures, the total cost of goods manufactured and sold could not be computed. For these reasons, most firms use a *predetermined overhead rate to apply manufacturing overhead to each job.*

A **predetermined overhead rate** is based on estimates of overhead costs and the applicable activity base. Thus, to compute the predetermined overhead rate, a firm must first estimate its overhead for the coming year and project figures for a base, such as direct labor-hours. For example, if in 19x1, the Bettermade Furniture Company estimates that its 19x2 overhead will approximate $800,000 and its direct labor-hours (DLH) will approximate 40,000 hours, its predetermined overhead rate (POR) would be:

$$\text{POR} = \frac{\text{Estimated overhead}}{\text{Estimated direct labor-hours}} = \frac{\$800,000}{40,000} = \$20 \text{ per DLH}$$

Bettermade can then use the POR to apply manufacturing overhead to specific jobs. It would do this by multiplying the POR by the number of direct labor-hours (the base) that a particular job required. Thus, if a job required 100 direct labor-hours, its applied manufacturing overhead would be $2,000 (100 hours × $20 POR). Manufacturing overhead will be discussed in further detail later in this chapter.

Although actual overhead costs are not assigned directly to jobs, they nevertheless are incurred and must be paid. Overhead entries are normally made as the costs are incurred. The following sample journal entry acts as a summary for the month of March 19x2:

(e)

19x2
Mar. 31　Manufacturing Overhead . . . .　22,000
　　　　　　　Accounts Payable . . . . 　　　　　22,000
　　　　　To record actual overhead incurred as follows:

Factory rent	$10,000
Utilities	3,000
Other factory costs	9,000
Total	$22,000

An analysis of Bettermade's job time tickets for March 19x2 revealed the following:

Job Number	Direct Labor-Hours
456	750
457	250
458	200

The journal entry to apply overhead to production is as follows:

(f)

19x2
Mar. 31　Work in Process . . . .　24,000
　　　　　　　Manufacturing Overhead Applied . . . . 　　　　　24,000
　　　　　To apply overhead to March's production as follows:

Job 456 ($20 × 750 DLH)	$15,000
Job 457 ($20 × 250 DLH)	5,000
Job 458 ($20 × 200 DLH)	4,000
Total	$24,000

▶ **ILLUSTRATION 5-11**   Work in Process and Job Cost Sheet

GENERAL LEDGER

Work in Process

19x2			
Feb. 28	*(b)*	10,550	
Mar. 31	*(c)*	14,000	
31	*(d)*	12,000	
31	*(e)*	24,000	
		60,550	

SUBSIDIARY LEDGER

JOB COST SHEET

Job Number 456   Date Feb. 19, 19x2

                                        Date Completed Mar. 31, 19x2

                                        Units 200

Item D 2051 Desks

For Stock _____

For Customer Smith's Dept. Store

Direct Materials			Direct Labor				Manufacturing Overhead			
Date	**Req. No.**	**Amount**	**Date**	**Clock No.**	**Hours**	**Amount**	**Date**	**DLH**	**Rate**	**Amount**
19x2 Feb. 28	406	$10,550	19x2 Mar. 31	613	190	$1,900	19x2 Mar. 31	750	$20	$15,000
				614	180	1,800				
				615	180	1,800				
				616	200	2,000				
		$10,550			750	$7,500				$15,000

Cost Summary	
Direct Materials	$10,550
Direct Labor	$ 7,500
Overhead	$15,000
Total Cost	$33,050
Unit Cost	$165.25*

* $33,050 ÷ 200 = $165.25

After posting journal entries *(c)*, *(d)*, and *(f)*, the Work in Process account and the job cost sheets would appear as shown in Illustration 5-11. Note that Job 457 is for 100 tables manufactured for stock and that Job 458 is for 400 chairs manufactured for stock. Jobs 456 and 457 are completed; thus, their cost summaries are filled in. But these two jobs have not yet been shipped to customers or transferred to the finished goods warehouse, so their total

▶ **ILLUSTRATION 5-11** *(continued)*

JOB COST SHEET

Job Number <u>457</u>

Date <u>Mar. 5, 19x2</u>

Date Completed <u>Mar, 31, 19x2</u>

Units <u>100</u>

Item <u>T 311 Tables</u>

For Stock ✓

For Customer _____

Direct Materials			Direct Labor				Manufacturing Overhead			
Date	**Req. No.**	**Amount**	**Date**	**Clock No.**	**Hours**	**Amount**	**Date**	**DLH**	**Rate**	**Amount**
19x2 Mar. 5	407	$6,000	19x2 Mar. 31	617 618	130 120	$1,300 1,200	19x2 Mar. 31	250	$20	$5,000
		$6,000			250	$2,500				$5,000

Cost Summary	
Direct Materials	$ 6,000
Direct Labor	$ 2,500
Overhead	$ 5,000
Total Cost	$13,500
Unit Cost	$135.00*

* $13,500 ÷ 100 = $135

costs are still included in the Work in Process account in the general ledger. This can be verified by totaling the costs expended on the three jobs:

Job Number	Total Costs
456	$33,050
457	13,500
458 ($8,000 + $2,000 + $4,000)	14,000
Total	$60,550

The total is then compared with the total of the general ledger account as shown in Illustration 5-11. The comparison generally proves that the journal entries posted to the Work in Process account in the general ledger have been correctly posted to the job cost sheets in the subsidiary ledger.

8. Finished Goods Inventory Ledger Card Similar to the direct materials inventory, a perpetual **finished goods inventory ledger**—one card for each different product—records all completed goods held for sale to customers.

▶ **ILLUSTRATION 5-11**   *(concluded)*

JOB COST SHEET

Job Number <u>458</u>   Date <u>Mar. 5, 19x2</u>

Date Completed _____

Units <u>400</u>

Item <u>Ch 201 Chairs</u>

For Stock <u>✓</u>

For Customer _____

Direct Materials			Direct Labor				Manufacturing Overhead			
Date	Req. No.	Amount	Date	Clock No.	Hours	Amount	Date	DLH	Rate	Amount
19x2 Mar. 5	408	$8,000	19x2 Mar. 31	619 620	100 100	$1,000 1,000	19x2 Mar. 31	200	$20	$4,000

Cost Summary	
Direct Materials	$
Direct Labor	$
Overhead	$
Total Cost	$
Unit Cost	$

The structure of this finished goods inventory ledger card is similar to the direct materials inventory ledger card presented in Illustration 5-4. When work in process from Jobs 456 and 457 is completed and transferred to the finished goods warehouse, the following journal entry is made:

(g)

19x2
Mar. 31   Finished Goods   46,550
                Work in Process   46,550
            To record the completion of Jobs 456 and 457 and their
            transfer to the finished goods warehouse as follows:

Job	Cost
456.	$33,050
457.	13,500
Total	$46,550

L.O. 5
Book inventory

After the posting of entry *(g)*, the Work in Process account would appear as shown in Illustration 5-12. The balance of $14,000 reflects the amounts shown on the job cost sheet for Job 458 (see Illustration 5-11), the only job still in process.

► **ILLUSTRATION 5-12**   Bettermade Furniture Company

GENERAL LEDGER

Work in Process

19x2			19x2		
Feb. 28	(b)	10,550	Mar. 31	(g)	46,550
Mar. 31	(c)	14,000			
31	(d)	12,000			
31	(e)	24,000			
		60,550			46,550
Balance		*14,000*			

Note that Bettermade's cost accounting system shows the firm has a book inventory of $14,000 of work in process at March 31, 19x2. Without this system, Bettermade would be obligated to take a physical inventory count each time it prepared interim income statements.

Entry (g) must also be posted to the Finished Goods account in the general ledger and to the finished goods inventory ledger cards in the subsidiary ledger. These postings and ledger cards appear in Illustration 5-13. The total of the finished goods inventory ledger cards corresponds to the Finished Goods account in the general ledger. This can be seen when the costs of the finished goods are added:

Description	Dollars
D 2051 Desks.	$33,050
T 311 Tables	13,500
Total.	$46,550

9. Cost of Goods Sold   Two more entries are necessary to complete the cost accounting cycle. These occur when Bettermade sells some of the furniture it has produced. One entry records the sale of the merchandise at its selling price, and the other records Bettermade's cost of producing the merchandise.

On March 31, Bettermade shipped the following finished goods:

Date	Item	Quantity	Unit Selling Price	Sales Revenue
19x2				
March 31	D 2051 Desks	200	$300	$60,000
31	T 311 Tables	40	275	11,000
	Total			$71,000

▶ **ILLUSTRATION 5-13**   Finished Goods Inventory Ledgers

GENERAL LEDGER

Finished Goods	
19x2 Mar. 31 (g) 46,550	

SUBSIDIARY LEDGER

Item <u>D 2051 Desks</u>   Location in Warehouse <u>Rack T 10</u>

Date	Manufactured			Sold			Balance		
	Units	Cost	Total	Units	Cost	Total	Units	Cost	Balance
19x2 Mar. 31	200	$165.25	$33,050		.		200	$165.25	$33,050

Item <u>T 311 Tables</u>   Location in Warehouse <u>Rack C 14</u>

Date	Manufactured			Sold			Balance		
	Units	Cost	Total	Units	Cost	Total	Units	Cost	Balance
19x2 Mar. 31	100	$135.00	$13,500				100	$135.00	$13,500

To record the transactions, two journal entries were made:

(h)

19x2			
Mar. 31	Accounts Receivable	71,000	
	Sales Revenue		71,000
	As per schedule (above).		

(i)

19x2			
Mar. 31	Cost of Goods Sold	38,450	
	Finished Goods		38,450
	To record the cost of goods sold as follows:		

D 2051 desks (200 at $165.25) $33,050
T 311 tables (40 at $135.00)   5,400
Total $38,450

▶ **ILLUSTRATION 5-14**　　Finished Goods Inventory Ledgers

GENERAL LEDGER

Finished Goods					
19x2			19x2		
Mar. 31	*(f)*	46,550	Mar. 31 *(g)*		38,450
Balance		*8,100*			

SUBSIDIARY LEDGER

Item <u>D 2051 Desks</u>　　　　　　　Location in Warehouse <u>Rack T 10</u>

Date	Manufactured			Sold			Balance		
	Units	Cost	Total	Units	Cost	Total	Units	Cost	Balance
19x2									
Mar. 31	200	$165.25	$33,050				200	$165.25	$33,050
31				200	$165.25	$33,050	0	—	0

Item <u>T 311 Tables</u>　　　　　　　Location in Warehouse <u>Rack C 14</u>

Date	Manufactured			Sold			Balance		
	Units	Cost	Total	Units	Cost	Total	Units	Cost	Balance
19x2									
Mar. 31	100	$135.00	$13,500				100	$135.00	$13,500
31				40	$135.00	$5,400	60	135.00	8,100

L.O. 5
Book inventory

After the posting of entry *(i),* the finished goods ledger would appear as shown in Illustration 5-14. The balance in the Finished Goods account is $8,100, which agrees with the balance shown on the finished goods ledger card for T 311 Tables, the only item of finished goods on hand.

Here, too, the cost accounting system provides a book inventory of finished goods without a physical count, and it also produces a dollar amount for cost of goods sold. Based on the book inventories and the cost of goods sold figure, the firm is able to prepare an interim income statement and balance sheet.

The complete cost accounting cycle is diagrammed in Illustration 5-15. The arrows show the movement of costs from one T account to another. A

▲ **ILLUSTRATION 5-15**   Cost Accounting Cycle

Direct Materials and Supplies Inventory

Beginning inventory	19,600	(b)	10,580
Purchases (a)	27,000	(c)	14,900
Balance	21,120		

Wages Payable

Payment	16,500	(d)	16,500

Manufacturing Overhead Applied

		(e)	24,000

Manufacturing Overhead

(b)	30
(c)	900
(d)	4,500
(f)	22,000
Balance	27,430

Work in Process

(b)	10,550	(g)	46,550
(c)	14,000		
(d)	12,000		
(e)	24,000		
Balance	14,000		

Finished Goods

(g)	46,550	(i)	38,450
Balance	8,100		

Sales Revenue

	(h)	71,000

Cost of Goods Sold

(i)	38,450

careful study of this illustration should help you understand the relationships among the T accounts that form the cost accounting cycle. The letter designations in parentheses correspond to the sample journal entries cited earlier.

The cost accounting cycle automatically yields book inventories as follows:

Direct materials and supplies	$21,120
Work in process	14,000
Finished goods	8,100

These results not only permit Bettermade to prepare financial statements (both interim and annual) without a physical count but also act as a check on physical counts whenever they are taken. This check is a crucial part of the firm's control system because it will indicate if errors in record-keeping and/ or thefts have occurred.

Automated Systems

Although it is easier to understand the cost accounting cycle by studying manually prepared forms, most businesses have computerized their cost accounting systems. In such cases, much of the data may be stored in the computer, and only certain source documents may actually be in printed form. For example, the materials requisition may be printed, while the direct materials and supplies inventory ledger, the job cost sheets (work in process inventory), and the finished goods inventory ledger are stored in the computer. The data in storage would be used for control purposes and to prepare interim or annual reports, but the detailed amounts shown in this chapter's illustrations would not be reproduced. Such details would be stored in computer memory and recalled only if necessary.

▶ **PROGRESS CHECK**

1. Why is it necessary to use a predetermined overhead rate to apply overhead to production instead of using the actual overhead for this purpose?
2. How is a predetermined overhead rate computed?
3. How is a predetermined overhead rate used to apply overhead to production?
4. What is a book inventory? Does the inventory contain only actual costs, only estimated costs, or a hybrid of the two? Explain.
5. Maintaining a job order cost accounting system is a very tedious job that requires voluminous entries and postings. How do firms cope with the volume of work? ◀

▶ MANUFACTURING OVERHEAD

L.O. 6
Applied manufacturing overhead

As noted in Chapter 2, **manufacturing overhead** encompasses all manufacturing costs other than direct materials and direct labor. It would be difficult, if not impossible, to attempt to charge each of these items to a particular product. Most manufacturing overhead items are common costs—costs shared by more than one product—and thus must be apportioned among products. Because the apportionment process used is based on predetermined estimates, it is less than exact, but its results are adequate provided the allocation base is closely related to the nature of the firm's operations.

An **allocation base** is a measurement used to assign manufacturing overhead to a cost objective (a product) in a logical manner based on the cause of the overhead and the benefits received by the product. Thus, a **labor-intensive firm**—a firm whose operations are performed manually and only incidentally by machines—should use a labor-oriented base, and a **machine-intensive firm**—a firm whose operations are highly automated—should use a machine-oriented base. The amount of estimated overhead assigned to jobs during a period of time through the use of an allocation base is called **applied manufacturing overhead.**

The Need for a Predetermined Rate

As noted earlier, if manufacturing overhead were assigned to a particular job on the basis of actual manufacturing overhead, it could be done only at the end of the fiscal year. This is highly unsatisfactory because a firm needs interim financial statements and must make timely decisions about pricing, profitability, and the like. Thus, some method must be found to assign manufacturing overhead to jobs as they progress and are completed. The most common practice is to use a predetermined rate calculation. Estimated manufacturing overhead for the coming year is used as the numerator of the calculation, and the allocation base is used as the denominator:

$$POR = \frac{\text{Estimated overhead}}{\text{Allocation base in amount}}$$

Allocation Bases

L.O. 7
Calculation of POR

In practice, a company may use any one of several different allocation bases. The choice depends on the nature of the firm's manufacturing operations. The most commonly used bases are (1) direct labor cost, (2) direct labor-hours, (3) machine-hours, (4) materials cost, and (5) prime cost. The first three are used much more extensively than the last two. However, a new manufacturing environment has evolved in the past decade. Many manufacturing firms that are highly automated are shifting toward the use of activity costing and they now use *cost drivers* for assigning overhead to production. Activity costing and cost drivers are discussed in Chapter 7.

For the purposes of our discussion, let us assume the Mitchell Fabricating Corporation estimates the following information for the coming year, 19x3:

Direct materials cost	$300,000
Direct labor cost	$600,000
Direct labor-hours	120,000
Machine-hours	60,000
Manufacturing overhead	$900,000

Direct Labor Cost Base   When a **direct labor cost base** is used to assign manufacturing overhead, the estimated amount of direct labor cost to be incurred in the coming year appears as the denominator in the POR equation. Using this base, Mitchell's POR would be calculated as:

$$\frac{\text{Estimated manufacturing overhead}}{\text{Estimated direct labor cost}} = \frac{\$900,000}{\$600,000}$$
$$= 150\% \text{ of direct labor cost}$$

This base is very popular because information about direct labor costs is readily available from the payroll records. It is most appropriate for labor-

► **ILLUSTRATION 5-16**   Assignment of Factory Rent to a Product's Cost

	Employee A	**Employee B**
Salary for 40 hours	$200	$400
Factory rent—10% of direct labor cost.	$ 20	$ 40

intensive manufacturing firms in which most employees *earn approximately the same hourly rates of pay.* On the other hand, it should be avoided when wage rates differ significantly because the resulting overhead assignments may be distorted for certain products.

For example, let us assume a firm using direct labor costs as a base estimates that its factory rent is 10 percent of its estimated direct labor for the year. If employee A earns $5 per hour, employee B earns $10 per hour, and each works 40 hours on a product, the rent would be assigned as shown in Illustration 5-16. Note that even though both employees' workstations occupy the same amount of square footage, twice as much rent is charged to a job for employee B as for employee A. This would produce a questionable assignment of cost. To avoid this problem, when wage rates differ among employees, it is best to use a direct labor-hours base.

Direct Labor-Hours Base   When a **direct labor-hours base** is used to assign manufacturing overhead, the estimated amount of direct labor-hours to be worked by employees in the coming year appears as the denominator in the POR equation. Using this base, Mitchell's POR would be calculated as follows:

$$\frac{\text{Estimated manufacturing overhead}}{\text{Estimated direct labor-hours}} = \frac{\$900,000}{120,000}$$
$$= \$7.50 \text{ per direct labor-hour}$$

Like the direct labor cost base, the direct labor-hours base is appropriate for labor-intensive manufacturers. Its advantage is that it can be used effectively *when hourly wage rates differ* as well as when hourly rates are uniform. However, because this base may have a slightly higher administrative cost, it is generally used only when the direct labor cost base is not appropriate.

When wage rates differ, the direct labor-hours base provides a better assignment of such overhead items as factory supervision and factory rent to all products. The cost of factory supervision is usually related to the number of hours worked rather than the dollar amount paid to an employee, and factory rent is related to the space occupied by an employee, not to his or her wages. Thus, because overhead should be assigned in a manner that correlates with its incurrence, direct labor cost is not a particularly useful overhead base for factory rent and factory supervision.

Using the data from Illustration 5-16 but substituting direct labor-hours (DLH) as the allocation base, the $60 of factory rent would be assigned to the product as follows:

	Employee A	Employee B
Number of hours worked	40	40
Factory rent—		
$^{60}/_{80}$ DLH = $.75 DLH	$30	$30

Thus, when direct labor-hours are used as a base, such factory overhead items as factory rent and factory supervision are not influenced by different wage rates, and their assignment to product costs is more closely related to the factors that cause the incurrence of those overhead items.

Machine-Hours Base   When a **machine-hours base** is used to assign manufacturing overhead, the denominator of the POR calculation is the estimated amount of factory activity as measured by the sum of all hours that each machine will be operated in the coming year. For example, if a factory has three machines, X, Y, and Z, and machines X and Y are each operated 40 hours per week and machine Z is operated 20 hours per week, the factory activity in machine-hours would be 100 (40 + 40 + 20) machine-hours per week and 5,000 hours per year for a 50-week year. If a particular job required machine time of 15 hours on machine X and 13 hours on machine Z, its machine-hours would be 28 hours. The computation of the Mitchell Fabricating Corporation's POR when this base is used would be:

$$\frac{\text{Estimated manufacturing overhead}}{\text{Estimated machine-hours}} = \frac{\$900,000}{60,000}$$
$$= \$15 \text{ per machine-hour}$$

Machine-intensive firms are most apt to use a machine-hours base. Although figures on machine-hours may not be as readily available in a firm's accounting system as are figures on direct labor, the additional cost of using a machine-hours base is usually justified. In fact, using direct labor cost or direct labor-hours as a base for a machine-intensive firm may lead to inaccuracies in product costing and pricing decisions that would be more costly to the firm than would be the cost of administering a machine-hours base POR.

Materials Cost Base   When a **materials cost base** is used to assign manufacturing overhead, the estimated amount of direct materials to be used in the coming year appears as the denominator of the POR equation. If Mitchell used this base, the calculation of its POR would be:

$$\frac{\text{Estimated manufacturing overhead}}{\text{Estimated direct materials cost}} = \frac{\$900,000}{\$300,000}$$
$$= 300\% \text{ of direct materials cost}$$

Few companies use materials cost as a base because very few manufacturing overhead costs are a function of materials cost. For example, a manufacturer of gold and silver rings should not use this base because the cost of gold far exceeds that of silver. If a materials cost base were used, the gold rings would absorb a much larger share of manufacturing overhead than would the silver rings, even though the overhead might be approximately the same for each.

The use of a materials cost base should be limited to firms whose direct material cost per unit of product is relatively uniform. For example, this

▶ **ILLUSTRATION 5-17**   Allocation Bases and Their Applicability

Base	Applicability
1. Direct labor cost	Labor-intensive firms where hourly wage rates are uniform; minimal administrative costs
2. Direct labor-hours	Labor-intensive firms where hourly wage rates are not uniform; slightly greater administrative costs than direct labor cost
3. Machine-hours	Machine-intensive firms; greater administrative cost than labor-oriented base
4. Materials cost	Firms where direct materials cost is uniform per unit of production or where material is fed into automatic machines at a uniform rate per hour; minimal administrative cost
5. Prime cost	Similar to materials cost

method may be used effectively when direct materials of equal cost are fed into an automatic stamping machine at a uniform rate per hour, as in the manufacture of tokens for toll booths or subway turnstiles. Under such conditions, the direct materials cost is converted into a time basis that is compatible with the way in which overhead costs are generally incurred and allocated.

Prime Cost Base   When a **prime cost base** is used, the estimated amounts of direct materials and direct labor expected to be incurred in the coming year are used as the denominator in the POR computation. When this base is used, Mitchell's POR would be calculated as:

$$\frac{\text{Estimated manufacturing overhead}}{\text{Estimated prime cost}} = \frac{\$900,000}{\$900,000}$$
$$= 100\% \text{ of prime cost}$$

Prime cost consists of direct materials cost plus direct labor cost. Thus, a prime cost base suffers from the same weakness as a direct materials cost base. Because direct labor cost is included in a prime cost base, it is a compromise method; but it offers little, if any, advantage over a direct materials cost base.

The foregoing computations were provided only for illustrative purposes. In reality, a firm would select one of these predetermined rates based on the nature of its manufacturing operations and use it consistently year after year. A summary of allocation bases and their applicability appears in Illustration 5-17.

Seasonal and Other Fluctuations   Other reasons for using a predetermined rate include uneven cost occurrences and seasonal fluctuations. Under such circumstances, if the actual, uneven overhead were applied, the same product manufactured in two different batches could have widely divergent unit costs. For example, if there were a repair cost in January of $20,000, this amount would be factored into the cost of batch A. But batch B, manufactured in March, would escape this cost if no repairs were needed in that month. When a predetermined rate is used, the $20,000 repair is spread uniformly over all batches for the year, which is reasonable because the repair benefits the production process in other months besides January.

Another problem with using actual costs stems from seasonal fluctuations. Assume factory rent is $50,000 per month. If 20,000 units were manufactured in March and only 10,000 units were manufactured in April, the unit cost for rent in March would be $2.50, while the unit cost for April would be $5. All other manufacturing overhead items would similarly affect the unit costs for the two months.

If a company made pricing decisions based on such widely fluctuating monthly costs, its prices would also widely fluctuate. Although seasonal price structures are appropriate for service industries like vacation hotels and restaurants, they are not practical for most businesses. Most customers expect the prices of the goods they buy to stay relatively stable from month to month. They would not trust a supplier whose prices constantly changed. Thus, to prevent short-term price variability, most firms use predetermined overhead rates based on long-term performance. These rates are also called *normal overhead rates*.

Normal Overhead Rates   A **normal overhead rate** is a predetermined overhead rate based on estimates for a complete business cycle—a period of three to five years—instead of for the coming year alone. Because it is an average rate for the entire business cycle, its results are more uniform from year to year than would be the case if a new POR were computed each year. Normalized overhead rates are discussed in greater detail in Chapter 11.

The use of a normal predetermined overhead rate does create one problem, however, which occurs at the end of the fiscal year: It is highly improbable that the dollar amounts of the actual overhead and the applied overhead will coincide, because the applied overhead is an estimated number. Thus, at the end of the year, there will usually be a difference between the two accounts. The difference is called **overapplied overhead** when the applied overhead is greater than the actual overhead. When the reverse is true—that is, when the actual overhead is greater than the applied overhead—the difference is referred to as **underapplied overhead.** The terms **overabsorbed overhead** and **underabsorbed overhead** are often used interchangeably with *overapplied overhead* and *underapplied overhead,* respectively.

Disposition of Overapplied or Underapplied Overhead

L.O. 8

Let us review the manufacturing overhead accounts shown in Illustration 5-15:

Manufacturing Overhead		Applied Manufacturing Overhead	
19x2		19x2	
Feb. 28 *(b)*	30	Mar. 31 *(e)* 24,000	
Mar. 31 *(c)*	900		
31 *(d)*	4,500		
31 *(f)*	22,000		
Balance	*27,430*		

Note that the actual manufacturing overhead—the debit balance of $27,430—does not equal the applied overhead of $24,000.

Any underapplied or overapplied overhead that remained at the end of one fiscal year would not be carried forward to the next year. Instead, it is normally closed to cost of goods sold as follows:

(j)

Applied Manufacturing Overhead	24,000	
Cost of Goods Sold	3,430	
Manufacturing Overhead		27,430

Such an entry is satisfactory for most business conditions if the amount of over- or underapplied overhead is relatively small.

During interim periods, it is preferable to carry forward any underapplied or overapplied overhead to the balance sheet as a deferred debit or a deferred credit, provided there is a reasonable expectation that the amount will be absorbed before the end of the fiscal year.

When the difference between the actual overhead and the applied overhead is small, most firms will expedite its disposition by closing it into cost of goods sold. However, when the amount of underapplied or overapplied overhead is large and if greater accuracy is desired, the amount may be prorated. Proration may be required for external reporting purposes and/or income tax return preparation. The Internal Revenue Service accepts normal costing as long as the underapplied or overapplied overhead is small. When the amount is large, the IRS usually insists on proration. Independent auditors have similar requirements.

The Proration Procedure   The objective of **proration** is to convert any general ledger account balance that contains estimated (applied) overhead to reflect actual overhead. To do so, the amounts of applied overhead in the Work in Process, Finished Goods, and Cost of Goods Sold accounts must be ascertained, and the relationship that each amount bears to the yearly applied overhead must be determined. The resulting percentages are then used to apportion the under- or overapplied overhead among the accounts. After proration, the overhead in the accounts reflects actual amounts instead of estimated amounts.

Consider the following information as of December 31, 19x4:

1. The balance of the Work in Process account is:

Direct materials.	$ 3,000
Direct labor	5,000
Manufacturing overhead	6,000
Total	$14,000

2. The balance in the Finished Goods inventory account consists of:

Direct materials.	$15,000
Direct labor	30,000
Manufacturing overhead	36,000
Total	$81,000

3. The balance in the Cost of Goods Sold account consists of:

Direct materials.	$125,000
Direct labor	215,000
Manufacturing overhead	258,000
Total	$598,000

▶ **ILLUSTRATION 5-18**   Proration of Underapplied Overhead

	1	2	3
	Applied	**Percent**	**Underapplied Proration**
Work in process	$ 6,000	2%*	$ 800†
Finished goods inventory	36,000	12	4,800
Cost of goods sold	258,000	86	34,400
Total	$300,000	100%	$40,000

* $6,000 ÷ $300,000 = 2%.

† 2% × $40,000 = $800.

4. The actual manufacturing overhead for 19x4 amounted to $340,000 and included expenditures that could not be anticipated prior to the last day of the year.
5. The applied overhead amounted to $300,000.
6. The underapplied overhead amounts to $40,000 ($340,000 actual minus the $300,000 applied).

To determine the appropriate prorations, the estimated overhead in each account is extracted and tabulated as shown in Illustration 5-18. First, the amount of overhead applied to each account is recorded in column 1. Note that the total of the first column equals the total amount of overhead applied for the year. The relationship that each account's applied overhead figure bears to the total yearly figure is then determined by dividing each account's overhead allocation by $300,000—the total amount of overhead applied. These percentages are entered in column 2. Finally, the prorated amount of underapplied overhead to be added to each account is calculated by multiplying $40,000—the total amount of underapplied overhead—by the corresponding percentage in column 2, and these figures are recorded in column 3.

The journal entry to close the underapplied overhead would be:

Work in Process.	800	
Finished Goods Inventory	4,800	
Cost of Goods Sold	34,400	
Manufacturing Overhead Applied	300,000	
Manufacturing Overhead		340,000

After this entry is posted, we can verify that the estimated manufacturing overhead has been converted to actual overhead by totaling the applied figures plus the prorations to ensure that they equal the actual overhead figure. This proof is shown in Illustration 5-19.

Payroll Fringes

L.O. 9

One component of overhead that requires further attention is **payroll fringes,** which generally include all payroll taxes (such as social security taxes and unemployment insurance taxes), vacation pay, holiday pay, union welfare contributions, hospitalization insurance, and other employee-related costs. Because these costs are significant—often in excess of 30 percent of the labor cost—some firms treat them differently than manufacturing overhead.

Most fringe-benefit costs are considered functions of labor cost and can thus be tacked on to direct labor. If, for example, payroll fringes amount to

▶ **ILLUSTRATION 5-19**   Proof of Conversion of Applied to Actual Overhead

	Applied	Proration	Actual
Work in process	$ 6,000 +	$ 800 =	$ 6,800
Finished goods inventory	36,000 +	4,800 =	40,800
Cost of goods sold	258,000 +	34,400 =	292,400
Total	$300,000 +	$40,000 =	$340,000

▶ **ILLUSTRATION 5-20**   Allocation Bases for Departmentalizing Overhead

Factory Overhead	Basis for Allocation
Factory rent	Square feet occupied
Repairs to factory	Square feet occupied
Repairs to machinery	Direct to department
Depreciation—machinery	Direct to department
Superintendence	Number of employees
Heat	Square feet occupied
Light and power	Horsepower/kilowatt rating
Indirect labor	Direct to department
Insurance	Investment in equipment
Payroll fringes	Payroll cost
Factory cafeteria	Number of employees
Factory hospital	Number of employees
Cost accounting	Labor-hours
Maintenance	Direct to department

30 percent of labor costs, a Payroll Fringe account can be established separately from the Manufacturing Overhead account, and payroll fringes can be assigned directly to direct labor at the rate of 30 percent. Then, if an employee who earns $6 per hour works for four hours on a particular job, the charge to that job would be:

Direct labor—4 hours at $6	$24.00
Fringes at 30%	7.20
Total direct labor cost	$31.20

Other firms may merely charge $24 to the job and charge all fringes to manufacturing overhead to be applied to the job through the predetermined overhead rate.

Departmental Overhead Rates

If a firm has at least one labor-intensive department and one machine-intensive department, a factorywide overhead rate would produce distortions in the assignment of overhead to specific jobs and could possibly provide misleading information for pricing decisions. Another reason for departmentalized overhead rates is that different jobs require different proportions of processing time in the various departments. Although it is impossible to obtain completely accurate information, a firm that desires high accuracy will likely departmentalize its overhead application. In doing so, the firm must examine each item of manufacturing overhead and allocate it to all affected departments using a specific allocation mechanism. For example, if

► **ILLUSTRATION 5-21**   Partial General Ledger

Direct Materials and Supplies Inventory				
19x2			19x2	
Jan. 1 Inventory at beginning	19,600		Feb. 28 Issuances *(b)*	10,580
Feb. 28 Purchases *(a)*	27,000			
Balance	*21,120*		Mar. 31 Issuances *(c)*	14,900

Work in Process				
19x2			19x2	
Feb. 28 *(b)*	10,550		Mar. 31 *(g)* 46,550	
Mar. 31 *(c)*	14,000			
31 *(d)*	12,000			
31 *(e)*	24,000			
	60,550		46,550	
Balance	*14,000*			

Manufacturing Overhead		
19x2		
Feb. 28 *(b)*	30	
Mar. 31 *(c)*	900	
31 *(d)*	4,500	
31 *(f)*	22,000	
Balance	*27,430*	

Applied Manufacturing Overhead		
	19x2	
	Mar. 31 *(e)* 24,000	

a firm has a machining department that is machine intensive and a finishing department that is labor intensive, the factory rent can be allocated on the basis of the square feet occupied by each department. A table of allocation bases for various forms of manufacturing overhead is presented in Illustration 5-20. Departmental overhead rates and service department costs are discussed more fully in Chapter 8.

► **SCHEDULES OF COST OF GOODS MANUFACTURED AND COST OF GOODS SOLD**

L.O. 10
Preparation of schedule of cost of goods manufactured

The Direct Materials and Supplies Inventory, Work in Process, and Manufacturing Overhead accounts provide the components for preparing the cost of goods manufactured schedule. For your reference, these accounts from the Bettermade Furniture Company are repeated in Illustration 5-21, while Bettermade's schedule of cost of goods manufactured for the three months ended March 31, 19x2, is shown in Illustration 5-22. The beginning direct materials and supplies inventory, purchases, and ending direct materials and supplies inventory may be obtained from the Direct Materials and Supplies Inventory account shown in Illustration 5-21. However, the *indirect materials* used must be deducted from the *direct materials* and *supplies* issued to

▶ **ILLUSTRATION 5-22**

BETTERMADE FURNITURE COMPANY
Schedule of Cost of Goods Manufactured
For the Three Months Ended March 31, 19x2

Direct materials:
Direct materials and supplies inventory, January 1	$19,600	
Add: Purchases of direct materials and supplies.	27,000	
Total direct materials and supplies available	46,600	
Deduct: Direct materials and supplies inventory, March 31.	21,120	
Direct materials and supplies issued	25,480	
Deduct: Indirect materials	930	
Direct materials used in production		$24,550
Direct labor.		12,000

Manufacturing overhead:
Indirect labor	$ 4,500	
Factory rent	10,000	
Utilities	3,000	
Indirect materials deducted above	930	
Miscellaneous factory costs.	9,000	
Actual overhead costs	27,430	
Less: Underapplied overhead	3,430	
Overhead applied to work in process		24,000
Total manufacturing costs		60,550
Add: Beginning work in process inventory		–0–
Total manufacturing costs in process		60,550
Deduct: Ending work in process inventory		14,000
Cost of goods manufactured at normal costing		$46,550

arrive at the *direct materials* used in production. The $930 of indirect materials issued is shown as part of the actual overhead costs. The *total manufacturing costs in process* ($60,550) should always agree with the debit side of the Work in Process account.

Schedule of Cost of Goods Manufactured

After deducting the ending work in process inventory of $14,000, the cost of goods manufactured *at normal costing* should agree with the credit side of the Work in Process account. The practice of using *actual* direct materials, *actual* direct labor, and *applied* manufacturing overhead is known as **normal costing.**

The Manufacturing Overhead account provides the information for listing the actual overhead costs incurred. Normally, a subsidiary ledger contains the details. For this example, the details may be obtained by referring to journal entries *(b), (c), (d),* and *(f).* Adjusting the total actual overhead by the $3,430 of underapplied overhead reduces it to the $24,000 of overhead applied to production, which agrees with the credit balance shown in the Applied Manufacturing Overhead account.

Schedule of Cost of Goods Sold

The Finished Goods account in Bettermade's general ledger is reproduced in Illustration 5-23. The information needed to prepare the schedule of cost of goods sold is contained in this account.

Bettermade's schedule of cost of goods sold for the three months ended March 31, 19x2, is shown in Illustration 5-24. For illustrative purposes, the

▶ **ILLUSTRATION 5-23**   Finished Goods Inventory Ledger

GENERAL LEDGER

Finished Goods			
19x2		19x2	
Mar. 31 *(g)*	46,550	Mar. 31 *(i)*	38,450
Balance	*8,100*		

▶ **ILLUSTRATION 5-24**

BETTERMADE FURNITURE COMPANY
Schedule of Cost of Goods Sold
For the Three Months Ended March 31, 19x2

Beginning finished goods inventory	$ –0–
Add: Cost of goods manufactured at normal costing	46,550
Goods available for sale	46,550
Ending finished goods inventory.	8,100
Cost of goods sold at normal costing.	38,450
Add: Underapplied overhead	3,430
Cost of goods sold at actual costing	$41,880

underapplied overhead is shown on this schedule. Usually, this is done only at the close of a company's fiscal year.

If there are no sales returns, the value of the goods available for sale should agree with the debit side of the Finished Goods account. If there was a beginning inventory of finished goods, the account and the schedule would reflect it. The cost of goods sold at normal costing should agree with the credit side of the account.

▶ COST ACCOUNTING FOR SERVICE INDUSTRIES

Because of the wide variety of service industries, such as hospitals, restaurants, law firms, accounting firms, physicians, and typing services, cost accounting systems for these industries will vary for each kind of industry. Thus, a detailed discussion of a cost accounting system for each industry is beyond the scope of this work. However, a law firm was selected as an example of a service industry whose cost accounting may be easily developed using the procedures previously demonstrated for a manufacturing firm.

Cost Accounting for a Law Firm

L.O. 11
Job cost sheet for a service firm

Direct Materials   Attorneys do not use direct materials in the course of rendering services to clients. However, they do incur out-of-pocket costs on behalf of their clients. Thus, they should use a job cost sheet for each client, and any out-of-pocket costs, such as court filing fees, long-distance telephone calls, messenger services, printing costs, and postage, should be posted to a job cost sheet in a manner similar to that used for direct materials for a manufacturer.

Direct Labor   Law firms typically have partners, associates, and typists who work on specific aspects of the services rendered to a client. Each individual should keep a time sheet showing (1) the date, (2) the client's name, (3) the nature of the task, such as "drafted a will," "typed a will," "researched a tax matter," and "held a conference with the client," (4) the beginning and ending times of the task performed for a specific client, and (5) the elapsed time for the task. The time sheet should be totaled for all of the elapsed times, and the difference between the total working day and the total elapsed time should be explained. The explanation may consist of general administrative work, attendance at professional seminars, office parties, and so on. The total times chargeable to clients should be priced out at the individual's hourly rate of pay for employees; for partners, the total times should be priced at the partner's base salary per hour, if applicable, or, if not, then the estimated share of profit for the partner may be used in place of the base salary. The amounts chargeable to a specific client can then be posted to the job cost sheet in much the same way as direct labor is posted for a manufacturing firm. The amounts priced out for nonbillable time (administrative, professional development, etc.) are charged to the appropriate administrative cost in the same manner as indirect labor is charged to overhead in a manufacturing firm. The amounts thus charged should equal an individual's total pay for the period.

Overhead   The distinction between manufacturing overhead and administrative costs is not relevant for a service industry. Recall that for a manufacturing firm, it is essential to determine what is inventoriable because ending inventories must be valued and a unit cost must be computed for each item produced. In a service industry, the valuation problems for inventories are not present. Under certain conditions, the costs assigned to a job in progress for a service industry may have to be computed. However, the overhead assigned to a job will vary from firm to firm. Thus, the usual practice is to combine all of a firm's administrative costs—sometimes referred to as *overhead*—and apply these costs to a job using a predetermined rate, such as direct labor dollars, in the same way that manufacturing firms apply overhead to production. However, some firms may choose to use only selected administrative costs for the purpose of assigning them to specific jobs, with the remaining administrative costs treated as general costs not assigned to any job.

Total Cost   The total of the items posted to the job cost sheet when a service is completed enables the firm to determine whether a profit has been earned on the job. Most law firms bill clients at an hourly rate for the number of hours worked on a particular service. When this is the case, a profit is assured, and the amount of the profit may be ascertained by comparing the amount billed to the client with the total of the job cost sheet. However, sometimes a firm will accept work at a predetermined fixed price, such as $200 for the drafting of a will, and the job cost sheet enables the firm to determine if a profit was made on that job.

Cost Accounting for a Hospital

Hospitals use both job order cost accounting systems and process cost accounting systems. Although a job order cost system provides increased managerial information, it is generally more costly to administer. These factors must be weighed when determining which system to use. Under Medicare, patients are subject to diagnostic-related groups (DRGs) for which third-party reimbursements are fixed for each kind of service rendered. Thus, the costs of caring for these patients should be averaged as a group. The same can be said when fixed allowances for services rendered to patients are paid directly to the hospital by insurance companies, such as Empire Blue Cross. Bear in mind that hospitals who participate in the Empire Blue Cross Plan have different rates for patients who are billed individually and for patients whose invoices are billed directly to Empire Blue Cross. By using a job order system for patients billed individually, an individual patient's costs can be matched against the patient's charges to determine the contribution margin or profit on each patient. This cost information is extremely useful for setting future patients' charges and for managerial control.

When a job order system is used, a job cost sheet is prepared for each patient. Of course, this is done on a computer, and the job cost sheet is merely a file in the computer's storage. Charges that would be recorded on the job cost sheet include the cost of medication, special dietary food and services, operating room usage, ancillary procedures, special nursing care, and ICU usage.[1] The assignment of materials, supplies, and direct labor to a particular patient is usually straightforward. The assignment of overhead for service industries is more complex and is covered in Chapter 8.

► **SUMMARY**

The purpose of **cost accounting** is to record, measure, and report information about product costs. An **integrated cost accounting system** provides managers with the product costs they need for inventory valuations, pricing the company's products, preparing interim financial statements, planning and control, and decision making.

Two systems of cost accounting are widely used. Firms that manufacture a few products on a repetitive basis use a **process cost system.** Firms that manufacture a variety of products, with each product manufactured in a separate batch, or job, use a **job order cost accounting system.**

Source documents are business forms serving as the basis of the journal entries that record the **cost accounting cycle.** This flow of cost accumulation usually parallels the **physical flow** of production. A **purchase requisition** authorizes the purchasing department to issue a **purchase order** for the acquisition of direct materials. A **receiving report** records the receipt of the direct materials, which are then placed in the stockroom. The stockroom always maintains a **safety stock** of both direct and indirect materials to ensure that production will not be interrupted by delayed shipments or abnormally heavy usage. A **production order** is issued when a particular product is needed for either a specific customer or inventory in the finished goods warehouse. A **materials requisition** authorizes the stockroom to transfer direct materials to the production line.

At this point, a **job cost sheet** is started to keep track of the costs of the job. As they are incurred, all elements of cost—direct materials, direct

[1] Robert N. Anthony and David W. Young, *Management Control in Nonprofit Organizations,* 4th ed. (Homewood, Ill.: Richard D. Irwin, 1988), p. 179.

labor, and manufacturing overhead—are recorded on the job cost sheet. Employees' **job time tickets** are used to arrive at the direct labor spent on the job. And through the use of a **predetermined overhead rate** based on estimated overhead for the year and an **allocation base,** such as direct labor cost or direct labor-hours, overhead is assigned. This method of costing—in which all manufacturing costs, both fixed and variable, are assigned to products and thus inventoried—is called **absorption costing.**

When a job is finished, the total on the job cost sheet is transferred to the **finished goods inventory ledger.** When goods are sold, their cost is deducted from the finished goods inventory ledger and transferred to cost of goods sold. The journal entries accompanying these events are the components of the cost accounting cycle. Subsidiary ledgers and controlling accounts provide managers with **book inventory** amounts that can be compared with periodic physical counts to control inventory and guard against errors and thefts.

The allocation base a company uses to apply manufacturing overhead to specific jobs depends on whether its operations are **labor intensive** or **machine intensive.**

The most commonly used allocation bases are **direct labor cost, direct labor-hours,** and **machine-hours.** Less frequently used bases are **materials cost** and **prime cost.** Many firms use a **normal overhead rate,** which is an average rate for an entire business cycle, rather than a rate based on the coming year's activity alone. At the end of the firm's fiscal year, the difference between the actual overhead and the amount applied to production during the year is ordinarily closed to cost of goods sold. When **applied manufacturing overhead** exceeds actual overhead, the difference is called **overapplied overhead,** and when actual overhead exceeds applied overhead, the difference is called **underapplied overhead.**

The Direct Materials and Supplies Inventory, Work in Process, and Manufacturing Overhead accounts provide the details needed to prepare the schedule of cost of goods manufactured, which is usually prepared at **normal cost.** Normal cost consists of *actual* direct materials and direct labor and applied (estimated) manufacturing overhead. The overapplied or underapplied overhead usually appears as a separate item on the cost of goods sold schedule.

During the past several decades, the number of service industries, such as hospitals, restaurants, law firms, accounting firms, physicians, and typing services, has increased significantly. As a result, increased attention is now focused on adapting cost accounting applications to these kinds of businesses. Some of the cost accounting procedures demonstrated in this chapter for manufacturing firms can be modified and applied to service industries.

▶ **GLOSSARY OF KEY TERMS**

Absorption costing   A method of assigning costs to a firm's products in which all fixed and variable manufacturing costs are inventoried.   (p. 186)

Allocation base   A measurement used to assign manufacturing overhead to a cost objective (a product) in a logical manner based on the cause of the overhead and the benefits received by the product.   (p. 208)

Applied manufacturing overhead   The amount of estimated overhead assigned to jobs during a period of time through the use of an allocation base.   (p. 208)

Book inventory   The dollar and quantity amounts generated by the records of a cost accounting system for direct materials, work in process, or finished goods, without taking a physical count.   (p. 186)

Cost accounting   A subfield of accounting that records, measures, and reports information about costs.   (p. 186)

Cost accounting cycle   The sequential recording and classifying of transactions that affect costs. The sequence usually corresponds to the firm's physical flow of operations.   (p. 186)

Direct labor cost base   A method of assigning overhead costs that uses the estimated amount of direct labor cost to be incurred in the coming year as the denominator in the POR equation.   (p. 208)

Direct labor-hours base   A method of assigning overhead costs that uses the estimated amount of direct labor-hours to be worked by employees in the coming year as the denominator in the POR equation.   (p. 209)

Finished goods inventory ledger   Perpetual inventory cards (or computer storage)—one card for each different product—that record all completed goods held for sale to customers.   (p. 201)

Full costing   See **absorption costing.**   (p. 186)

Idle time   Production time lost during a machine breakdown or when material shortages occur—manifests itself as the difference between the amount of hours shown on an employee's time card and the amount of time charged to specific jobs for that employee.   (p. 198)

Integrated cost accounting system   A cost accounting system that forms an integral part of a firm's books and reporting system.   (p. 186)

Job   A batch of production that has a definite starting point and completion point.   (p. 187)

Job cost sheet   A sheet for accumulating the cost of direct materials, direct labor, and applied manufacturing overhead during a firm's production cycle. A separate sheet is kept for each job, and the total of all costs on the uncompleted job cost sheets forms the subsidiary ledger for the Work in Process account in the general ledger.   (p. 195)

Job order cost accounting system   A method of accumulating costs by batches of production.   (p. 187)

Job time ticket   A source document on which an employee records the amount of time he or she worked on a particular job.   (p. 196)

Labor-intensive firm (department)   A firm or department in which production operations are performed principally by manual labor and only incidentally by machinery.   (p. 208)

Machine-hours base   A method of assigning overhead costs using the sum of all hours that each machine will be operated in the coming year as the denominator in the POR equation.   (p. 210)

Machine-intensive firm (department)   A firm or department in which production operations are automated, with a concomitant reduction in direct labor costs.   (p. 208)

Manufacturing overhead   All costs other than direct materials and direct labor that are necessary to manufacture a finished product.   (p. 207)

Manufacturing overhead applied   See **applied manufacturing overhead.**   (p. 208)

Materials cost base   A method of assigning overhead costs that uses the estimated amount of direct materials to be used in the coming year as the denominator in the POR equation.   (p. 210)

Materials requisition   A source document authorizing the transfer of direct and indirect materials from the storeroom to the production line to start manufacture.   (p. 193)

Normal costing   A cost accumulation system in which *actual* direct materials, *actual* direct labor, and *applied* manufacturing overhead are used for accounting and pricing purposes.   (p. 217)

Normal overhead rate   A predetermined overhead rate based on estimates for a complete business cycle—usually three to five years; as a result, it is an *average* long-term rate.   (p. 212)

Overabsorbed overhead   See **overapplied overhead.**   (p. 212)

Overapplied overhead   The amount by which actual overhead for a period of time is less than estimated overhead that was allocated to specific jobs.   (p. 212)

Overhead applied   See **applied manufacturing overhead.**   (p. 208)

Overtime premium   An increased wage rate paid for all hours over 40 that an employee works—usually equal to one half of the straight-time rate.   (p. 198)

Payroll fringes   Employee-related costs, such as social security taxes, unemployment insurance taxes, disability premiums, hospitalization insurance, vacation pay, holiday pay, and retirement benefit contributions.   (p. 214)

Physical flow of production   The sequence of operating activity that begins with the purchase of direct materials and ends with a finished product ready for sale to customers.   (p. 188)

Predetermined overhead rate (POR)   A method used to apply overhead to a job based on estimates of overhead costs and the applicable activity base.   (p. 199)

Prime cost base   A method of assigning overhead costs that uses the estimated amounts of direct materials and direct labor expected to be incurred in the coming year as the denominator in the POR equation.   (p. 211)

Process cost accounting system   A cost accounting method in which product costs are accumulated for a specific period of time and then the total cost is divided by the units produced to compute the unit cost for the period. This method is used by firms that produce relatively few products, with each product produced repetitively.   (p. 187)

Production order   A source document issued prior to the start of production that authorizes the manufacture of a particular product.   (p. 191)

Proration   A procedure used to convert estimated (applied) overhead, such as that found in the Work in Process, Finished Goods, and Cost of Goods Sold accounts, to reflect actual overhead.   (p. 213)

Purchase order   A source document authorizing a vendor to ship the ordered goods (or services) at the specified price and terms.   (p. 189)

Purchase requisition   A source document issued by the storeroom clerk requesting the firm's purchasing department to purchase needed direct materials.   (p. 188)

Receiving report   A report prepared by a firm's receiving department listing the quantities and descriptions of merchandise received from vendors.   (p. 189)

Safety stock   A specified minimum amount of direct and indirect materials inventory kept on hand at all times to provide a cushion against unusual delays in shipment and abnormally heavy usage.   (p. 188)

Source document   Any original record or business form used by a firm to initiate or record any of its transactions. Such documents help a company keep track of its production process and form the basis of the journal entries that are part of its cost accounting system.   (p. 188)

Underabsorbed overhead   See **underapplied overhead.**   (p. 212)

Underapplied overhead   The amount by which the actual overhead for a period of time exceeds the estimated overhead allocated to specific jobs.   (p. 212)

▶ **GLOSSARY OF SYNONYMS**

Estimated overhead rate   See predetermined overhead rate.

Full costing   See **absorption costing.**

Manufacturing overhead applied   See applied manufacturing overhead.

Overabsorbed overhead   See overapplied overhead.

Overhead applied   See **applied manufacturing overhead.**

Underabsorbed overhead   See underapplied overhead.

▶ **REVIEW PROBLEM**   **Individual Job Costs and the Cost Accounting Cycle**

The following information and transactions are assumed to have occurred during the month of January 19x5 for the Seneca Company:

1. The beginning inventory of direct materials consisted of:

Material A.	$ 6,720
Material B.	5,700
Material C.	8,900
Total	$21,320

2. Purchases of direct materials consisted of:

Material A.	$22,400
Material B.	28,000
Material C.	45,000
Total	$95,400

3. Issuances of direct materials consisted of:

Material A.	$20,100
Material B.	29,100
Material C.	43,700
Total	$92,900

The materials are to be charged to:

Job 101.	$30,200
Job 102.	25,700
Job 103.	37,000
Total	$92,900

4. The beginning work in process inventory consisted of:

Job 101.	$14,500
Job 102.	16,800
Job 103.	13,400
Total	$44,700

The beginning finished goods inventory consisted of:

30 desks at $170.	$5,100
40 chairs at $80	3,200
Total	$8,300

5. Payroll for the month is:

Direct labor	$67,000
Indirect labor.	16,800
Total	$83,800

The direct labor is chargeable 40 percent to Job 101, 25 percent to Job 102, and 35 percent to Job 103.

6. Manufacturing overhead is applied to production at 70 percent of direct labor cost.

7. Other manufacturing overhead for the month amounted to $33,000.
8. Jobs 101 and 102 are complete. Job 103 is not completed.
9. Job 101 was for 1,130 chairs, and Job 102 was for 500 desks. Job 103 is for 600 tables.
10. Sales for the month were as follows:
    a. 1,000 chairs at $145.
    b. 400 desks at $340.
    The company uses the first-in, first-out (FIFO) method to account for all inventories.

Required
a. Prepare all the necessary journal entries to record the above information.
b. Prepare either job cost sheets for each job or prepare a tabular summary of costs by job.
c. Compute the unit costs for Job 101 and Job 102.
d. Compute the following inventories at January 31, 19x5:
    (1) Direct materials.
    (2) Work in process.
    (3) Finished goods.
e. Prepare T accounts for Direct Materials and Supplies Inventory, Work in Process, and Finished Goods and compare your answers with your computations in part *(d)*.

▶ **SOLUTION TO REVIEW PROBLEM**

a.

Direct Materials and Supplies Inventory	95,400	
Accounts Payable		95,400
Work in Process	92,900	
Direct Materials and Supplies Inventory		92,900
Work in Process	67,000	
Manufacturing Overhead	16,800	
Accrued Wages Payable		83,800
Work in Process	46,900	
Manufacturing Overhead Applied		46,900
Manufacturing Overhead	33,000	
Sundry Credits		33,000
Finished Goods	161,235	
Work in Process		161,235

Job 101	$ 90,260*
Job 102	70,975*
	$161,235

* See part *(b)*.

Accounts Receivable	281,000	
Sales Revenue		281,000
Cost of Goods Sold	137,506	
Finished Goods		137,506

30 desks @ $170 + 370 @ $141.95* =	$ 57,621
40 chairs @ $80 + 960 @ $79.88* =	79,885
	$137,506

* See part *(c)*.

b. Job 101

Work in process	$14,500
Direct materials	30,200
Direct labor	26,800
Overhead applied (70% × $26,800)	18,760
Total	$90,260

Job 102
```
Work in process . . . . . . . . . . . . . . . . . . .    $16,800
Direct materials . . . . . . . . . . . . . . . . . . .    25,700
Direct labor . . . . . . . . . . . . . . . . . . . .      16,750
Overhead applied (70% × $16,750). . . . . . . . .         11,725
    Total . . . . . . . . . . . . . . . . . . . . .      $70,975
```

Job 103
```
Work in process . . . . . . . . . . . . . . . . . . .    $13,400
Direct materials . . . . . . . . . . . . . . . . . . .    37,000
Direct labor . . . . . . . . . . . . . . . . . . . .      23,450
Overhead applied (70% × $23,450). . . . . . . . .         16,415
    Total . . . . . . . . . . . . . . . . . . . . .      $90,265
```

c. Job 101

$$\$90,260 \div 1,130 = \$79.88$$

Job 102

$$\$70,975 \div 500 = \$141.95$$

d. (1) Direct Materials
```
    Material A ($6,720 + $22,400 − $20,100)        $ 9,020
    Material B ($5,700 + $28,000 − $29,100)          4,600
    Material C ($8,900 + $45,000 − $43,700)         10,200
        Total . . . . . . . . . . . . . . . . .     $23,820
```

(2) Work in Process
```
    Job 103 . . . . . . . . . . . . . . . . . . . .  $90,265*
* From part (b).
```

(3) Finished Goods
```
    170 chairs @ $79.88 . . . . . . . . . . . . .    $13,580
    130 desks @ $141.95 . . . . . . . . . . . . .     18,453
        Total . . . . . . . . . . . . . . . . . . .  $32,033
```

e.

Direct Materials and Supplies Inventory		Work in Process		Finished Goods	
Bal. 21,320	92,900	Bal. 44,700	161,235	Bal. 8,300	137,506
95,400		92,900		161,235	
		67,000			
		46,900			
Bal. 23,820		*Bal. 90,265*		*Bal. 32,029*	

▶ **LIBRARY ASSIGNMENT**

Read the following:

Anthony, Robert N. "The Rebirth of Cost Accounting." *Management Accounting,* October 1975, pp. 13–16.

Carbone, Frank J. "Automated Job Costing Helps Mulach Steel Stay Competitive." *Management Accounting,* June 1980, pp. 29–31.

Hunt, Rick, Linda Garrett, and C. Mike Merz. "Direct Labor Cost Not Always Relevant at H-P." *Management Accounting,* February 1985, pp. 58–62.

Sandretto, Michael J. "What Kind of Cost System Do You Need?" *Harvard Business Review,* January–February 1985, pp. 110–118.

▶ **SELF-TEST**

True or False

1. Every source document requires that a journal entry be made to record the transaction.
2. Cost accounting information is needed for pricing decisions, inventory valuation, financial statement preparation, planning and control, and a variety of business decisions, but is not needed for budget preparation.
3. When a firm orders materials from a vendor, it prepares a purchase requisition.
4. A materials requisition form is used when materials are transferred from the stockroom to the factory.
5. Job costs sheets are considered a subsidiary ledger to support the Work in Process account in the general ledger.
6. The job time ticket is used for the purpose of preparing an employee's weekly payroll.
7. When overhead is applied to production, the entry to record the application requires a debit to Manufacturing Overhead Applied.
8. The machine-hour base should be used to apply overhead to production for a firm that is highly automated.
9. A normal overhead rate is the overhead rate used when a firm's production for the period is considered normal.
10. When there is a difference between the applied overhead and the actual overhead, the difference is normally prorated between cost of goods sold and work in process.

Multiple Choice

Items 1 and 2 are based on the following information:

Hamilton Company uses job order costing. Factory overhead is applied to production at a predetermined rate of 150 percent of direct labor cost. Any over- or underapplied factory overhead is closed to the Cost of Goods Sold account at the end of each month. Additional information is available as follows:

a. Job 101 was the only job in process at January 31, 19x2, with accumulated costs as follows:

Direct materials	$4,000
Direct labor	2,000
Applied factory overhead	3,000
Total	$9,000

b. Jobs 102, 103, and 104 were started during February.
c. Direct materials requisitions for February totaled $26,000.
d. Direct labor cost of $20,000 was incurred for February.
e. Actual factory overhead was $32,000 for February.
f. The only job still in process at February 28, 19x2, was Job 104, with costs of $2,800 for direct materials and $1,800 for direct labor.

1. The cost of goods manufactured for February 19x2 was
   a. $77,700.
   b. $78,000.
   c. $79,700.
   d. $85,000.

2. Over- or underapplied factory overhead should be closed to the Cost of Goods Sold account at February 28, 19x2, in the amount of
   a. $ 700 overapplied.
   b. $1,000 overapplied.
   c. $1,700 underapplied.
   d. $2,000 underapplied.

3. Peters Company uses a flexible budget system and prepared the following information for 19x0:

	Percent of Capacity	
	80%	90%
Direct labor-hours	24,000	27,000
Variable factory overhead.	$ 48,000	$ 54,000
Fixed factory overhead	$108,000	$108,000
Total factory overhead rate per direct labor-hour	$6.50	$6

Peters operated at 80 percent of capacity during 19x0 but applied factory overhead based on the 90-percent-capacity level. Assuming actual factory overhead was equal to the budgeted amount for the attained capacity, what is the amount of overhead variance for the year?
   a. $ 6,000 overabsorbed.
   b. $ 6,000 underabsorbed.
   c. $12,000 overabsorbed.
   d. $12,000 underabsorbed.

4. Worrell Corporation has a job order cost system. The following debits (credits) appeared in the general ledger account Work in Process for the month of March 19x2:

March 1, balance	$ 12,000
March 31, direct materials	40,000
March 31, direct labor.	30,000
March 31, factory overhead . . .	27,000
March 31, to finished goods . . .	(100,000)

Worrell applies overhead to production at a predetermined rate of 90 percent based on the direct labor cost. Job 232, the only job still in process at the end of March 19x2, has been charged with factory overhead of $2,250. What was the amount of direct materials charged to Job 232?
   a. $2,250.
   b. $2,500.
   c. $4,250.
   d. $9,000.

5. Cannon Cannery, Inc., estimated its factory overhead at $510,000 for 19x1, based on a normal capacity of 100,000 direct labor-hours. Direct labor-hours for the year totaled 105,000, while the Factory Overhead account at the end of the year showed a balance of $540,000. How much was the underapplied factory overhead for 19x1?
   a. $0.
   b. $ 4,500.
   c. $27,000.
   d. $30,000.

(AICPA Adapted)

The following data apply to items 6 through 9.

Department 203–work in process—beginning of period:

Job No.	Material	Labor	Overhead	Total
1376	$17,500	$ 22,000	$33,000	$ 72,500

Department 203 costs for 19x7:

Incurred by Jobs	Material	Labor	Other	Total
1376	$ 1,000	$ 7,000	—	$ 8,000
1377	26,000	53,000	—	79,000
1378	12,000	9,000	—	21,000
1379	4,000	1,000	—	5,000
Not Incurred by Jobs				
Indirect materials and supplies	15,000	—	—	15,000
Indirect labor	—	53,000	—	53,000
Employee benefits	—	—	$23,000	23,000
Depreciation	—	—	12,000	12,000
Supervision	—	20,000	—	20,000
Total	$58,000	$143,000	$35,000	$236,000

Department 203 overhead rate for 19x7:

Budgeted overhead:	
Variable—Indirect materials	$ 16,000
Indirect labor	56,000
Employee benefits	24,000
Fixed—Supervision	20,000
Depreciation.	12,000
Total.	$128,000
Budgeted direct labor-dollars	$ 80,000
Rate per direct labor-dollar ($128,000 ÷ 80,000).	160%

6. The actual overhead for Department 203 for 19x7 was
   a. $156,000.
   b. $123,000.
   c. $70,000.
   d. $112,000.
   e. Not shown above.

7. Department 203 overhead for 19x7 was
   a. $11,000 underapplied.
   b. $11,000 overapplied.
   c. $44,000 underapplied.
   d. $44,000 overapplied.
   e. Not shown above.

8. Job 1376 was the only job completed and sold in 19x7. What amount was included in cost of goods sold for this job?
   a. $72,500.
   b. $91,700.
   c. $80,500.
   d. $19,200.
   e. Not shown above.

9. The value of work in process inventory at the end of 19x7 was
   a. $105,000.
   b. $180,600.
   c. $228,000.
   d. $205,800.
   e. Not shown above.

(CMA Adapted)

► **QUESTIONS**

1. Why is product cost information needed in connection with inventories?
2. For what purposes other than inventories is product cost information useful?
3. Explain how a process cost system differs from a job order system.
4. What is physical production flow? Is there usually a relationship between the physical flow and the cost accounting cycle? Explain.
5. What are source documents?
6. What is a purchase requisition? What basic information should it contain?
7. What is a purchase order? What basic information should it contain?
8. What is a receiving report? What information should it contain as a minimum? Should the *quantities ordered* be shown on the receiving report or should they be omitted? Present the arguments for their inclusion and omission.
9. What is a production order? Why is it used?
10. What should a materials requisition form contain? How is it used for control purposes?
11. What should a direct materials and supplies inventory ledger card contain? How is it used?
12. What is a job time ticket? How is it used?
13. What is a job cost sheet? What purpose does it serve?
14. What is a finished goods inventory ledger card? What purpose does it serve?
15. Is it usually possible to charge manufacturing overhead directly to a particular job? Why?
16. Why is it necessary to apply overhead to production through the use of a predetermined rate?
17. What allocation bases of applying overhead are usually found in practice? Are some used more than others? If so, which are they?
18. Does the use of direct labor cost as a base for applying overhead to production sometimes cause a misapplication? If so, use an example to illustrate the type of distortion. Does the use of direct labor-hours cure the distortion? Explain.
19. When should a machine-hours base be used for applying overhead? Does it cost more to use this base? Explain.
20. Is material cost widely used as a base for applying overhead? Explain.
21. How is a predetermined overhead rate computed? Use an example to demonstrate the procedure.
22. Do seasonal fluctuations and uneven cost flows impact on the use of actual overhead? Does the use of a predetermined overhead rate minimize the impact? Explain.
23. Does the use of a normal overhead rate serve any purpose other than smoothing seasonal fluctuations and uneven cost flows? Explain.
24. What are payroll fringes? Is there more than one way of treating them? Explain.
25. How is underapplied or overapplied overhead normally treated in interim reports? Are they usually treated differently in annual reports? Explain.
26. When is proration of under/overapplied overhead used? What does proration of overhead accomplish?
27. Do service industry firms use cost accounting systems? If not, why not? If so,

describe a system that such a firm might use, and explain how the system differs from one used by a manufacturing firm.

▶ **EXERCISES**   **E5–1**   **Journal Entries for the Job Order Cost Accounting Cycle**

The following information and transactions are assumed to have occurred during the year 19x3 for the Juniper Company:

a. Purchases of direct materials and supplies amounted to $700,000.
b. Issuances of direct materials and supplies amounted to $670,000 for direct materials and $6,000 for indirect materials.
c. Payroll for the year 19x3 amounted to $620,000 for direct labor and $160,000 for indirect labor.
d. Manufacturing overhead is applied to production at 70 percent of direct labor cost.
e. Other manufacturing overhead for the year 19x3 amounted to $280,000. (Credit Sundry Credits.)
f. Finished goods for the year amounted to $1,600,000.
g. Sales on account for the year were $1.3 million.
h. The cost of these sales amounted to $770,000.

Required   Journalize the transactions for the year.

E5–2   **Job Order Cost Concepts**

The following data apply to items 1 through 4.

Selected data concerning the past fiscal year's operations of the Televans Manufacturing Company are presented below (in thousands):

	Inventories	
	Beginning	**Ending**
Direct materials	$75	$ 85
Work in process	80	30
Finished goods	90	110

Other data:	
Direct materials used	$326
Total manufacturing costs charged to production during the year (includes direct materials, direct labor, and factory overhead applied at a rate of 60% of direct labor cost)	686
Cost of goods available for sale	826
Marketing and administrative costs	25

1. The cost of direct materials purchased during the year amounted to
   a. $411.
   b. $360.
   c. $316.
   d. $336.
   e. Some amount other than those shown above.
2. Direct labor costs charged to production during the year amounted to
   a. $135.
   b. $225.
   c. $360.
   d. $216.
   e. Some amount other than those shown above.

3. The cost of goods manufactured during the year was
   a. $636.
   b. $766.
   c. $736.
   d. $716.
   e. Some amount other than those shown above.
4. The cost of goods sold during the year was
   a. $736.
   b. $716.
   c. $691.
   d. $801.
   e. Some amount other than those shown above.

(CMA Adapted)

E5–3 Job Order Cost Concepts

The following data apply to items 1 through 6.

Baehr Company is a manufacturing company with a fiscal year that runs from July 1 to June 30. The company uses a job order accounting system for its production costs.

A predetermined overhead rate based on direct labor-hours is used to apply overhead to individual jobs. A budget of overhead costs was prepared for the 19x7–x8 fiscal year as shown below.

Direct labor-hours	120,000
Variable overhead costs	$390,000
Fixed overhead costs	216,000
Total overhead	$606,000

The information presented below is for November 19x7. Jobs 77–50 and 77–51 were completed during November.

Inventories November 1, 19x7:
Direct materials and supplies	$ 10,500
Work in process (Job 77–50)	54,000
Finished goods	112,500

Purchases of direct materials and supplies:
Direct materials	$135,000
Supplies	15,000

Materials and supplies requisitioned for production:
Job 77–50	$ 45,000
Job 77–51	37,500
Job 77–52	25,500
Supplies	12,000
Total	$120,000

Factory direct labor-hours:
Job 77–50	3,500 DLH
Job 77–51	3,000 DLH
Job 77–52	2,000 DLH

Labor costs:
Direct labor wages	$ 51,000
Indirect labor wages (4,000 hours)	15,000
Supervisory salaries	6,000

Building occupancy costs (heat, light, depreciation, etc.):
Factory facilities	$ 6,500
Sales offices	1,500
Administrative offices	1,000
Total	$ 9,000

Factory equipment costs:

Power.	$ 4,000
Repairs and maintenance	1,500
Depreciation.	1,500
Other	1,000
Total	$ 8,000

1. The predetermined overhead rate to be used to apply overhead to individual jobs during the 19x7–x8 fiscal year is
   a. $3.25 per DLH.
   b. $4.69 per DLH.
   c. $5.05 per DLH.
   d. $5.41 per DLH.
   e. Some rate other than those shown above.
   Note: Without prejudice to your answer to item 1, assume the predetermined overhead rate is $4.50 per direct labor-hour. Use this amount in answering items 2 through 6.

2. The total cost of Job 77–50 is
   a. $81,750.
   b. $135,750.
   c. $142,750.
   d. $146,750.
   e. Some amount other than those shown above.

3. The factory overhead costs applied to Job 77–52 during November were
   a. $9,000.
   b. $47,500.
   c. $46,500.
   d. $8,000.
   e. Some amount other than those shown above.

4. The total amount of overhead applied to jobs during November was
   a. $29,250.
   b. $38,250.
   c. $47,250.
   d. $56,250.
   e. Some amount other than those shown above.

5. Actual factory overhead incurred during November 19x7 was
   a. $38,000.
   b. $41,500.
   c. $47,500.
   d. $50,500.
   e. Some amount other than those shown above.

6. At the end of the last fiscal year (June 30, 19x7), Baehr Company had the following account balances:

Overapplied Overhead	$ 1,000
Cost of Goods Sold	980,000
Work in Process Inventory	38,000
Finished Goods Inventory	82,000

The most common treatment of the overapplied overhead would be to
   a. Prorate it between work in process inventory and finished goods inventory.
   b. Prorate it between work in process inventory, finished goods inventory, and cost of goods sold.
   c. Carry it as a deferred credit on the balance sheet.
   d. Carry it as miscellaneous operating revenue on the income statement.
   e. Credit it to cost of goods sold.

(CMA Adapted)

E5–4   **Preparation of Schedule of Cost of Goods Manufactured**

The Helper Corporation manufactures one product and accounts for costs by a job order cost system. You have obtained the following information for the year ended December 31, 19x3, from the corporation's books and records:

1. Total manufacturing cost added during 19x3 (sometimes called *cost to manufacture*) was $1 million based on actual direct material, actual direct labor, and applied factory overhead on actual direct labor-dollars.
2. Cost of goods manufactured was $970,000, also based on actual direct material, actual direct labor, and applied factory overhead.
3. Factory overhead was applied to work in process at 75 percent of direct labor-dollars. Applied factory overhead for the year was 27 percent of the total manufacturing cost.
4. Beginning work in process inventory, January 1, was 80 percent of ending work in process inventory, December 31.

Required   Prepare a formal schedule of cost of goods manufactured for the year ended December 31, 19x3, for the Helper Corporation. Use actual direct material used, actual direct labor, and applied factory overhead. Show supporting computations in good form.

(AICPA Adapted)

E5–5   **Preparation of Schedule of Cost of Goods Manufactured**

The Rebecca Corporation manufactures special machines made to customer specifications. All production costs are accumulated by means of a job order costing system. The following information is available at the beginning of the month of October 19x0:

Direct materials inventory, October 1	$16,200
Work in process, October 1	3,600

A review of the job order cost sheets revealed the composition of the work in process inventory on October 1 as follows:

Direct materials	$1,320
Direct labor (300 hours)	1,500
Factory overhead applied	780
Total	$3,600

Activity during the month of October was as follows:

1. Direct materials costing $20,000 were purchased.
2. Direct labor for job orders totaled 3,300 hours at $5 per hour.
3. Factory overhead was applied to production at the rate of $2.60 per direct labor-hour.

On October 31, inventories consisted of the following components:

Direct materials inventory	$17,000
Work in process inventory:	
Direct materials	$ 4,320
Direct labor (500 hours)	2,500
Factory overhead applied	1,300
Total	$ 8,120

Required   Prepare in good form a detailed schedule of the cost of goods manufactured for the month of October.

(AICPA Adapted)

E5–6　Job Cost Sheet and Unit Cost

The Herald Company manufactures clothing. Job 476 was started on February 14, 19x3, and completed on February 28, 19x3, and consisted of 1,000 raincoats. The following data are available:

	Week of February 14	Week of February 21
Materials purchased.	$16,000	$ 3,000
Materials used—Job 476.	12,000	4,000
Direct labor used	30,000	10,000
Actual overhead incurred	36,000	38,000

Factory overhead is applied at a rate of 80 percent of direct labor cost.

Required　*a.* Prepare a job cost sheet and compute the unit cost for Job 476.
b. What should the unit sales price be if Herald wants to earn 90 percent of cost as gross profit?

E5–7　Computation and Use of Predetermined Overhead Rates

The Uniprojector Company manufactures photographic slide projectors. The firm operates in a seasonal market where 60 percent of the firm's annual sales occur during the months of October and November. The factory operates on a cyclical basis. Production for the year amounts to 300,000 units. The firm's manufacturing overhead consists mainly of fixed costs and usually amounts to $2,160,000 yearly.

The firm's cost accountant prepares monthly cost figures based on actual costs, including actual overhead for the month. His cost calculations for the most recent three months are as follows:

	July	August	September
Direct materials	$60,000	$120,000	$ 450,000
Direct labor	96,000	192,000	720,000
Overhead.	172,000	176,000	198,000
Total costs	$328,000	$488,000	$1,368,000
Units produced	8,000	16,000	60,000
Unit cost.	$ 41.00	$ 30.50	$ 22.80

After reviewing these cost figures, the company president expressed concern about the widely fluctuating unit costs. He has heard somewhere that some firms use normal costing. The firm's direct labor for the year is estimated to be $3.6 million.

Required　Redo the cost calculations using normal costing. Use direct labor cost as the base for applying overhead to production.

E5–8　Journal Entries for Cost Accounting Cycle

The following transactions were completed during the month of March 19x4:

1. Materials in the amount of $300,000 were purchased on account.
2. Requisitions representing issues of direct materials amounted to $240,000. Indirect materials in the amount of $5,000 were issued.
3. The factory payroll for March consisted of:

Direct labor $180,000
Indirect labor 60,000

4. Factory overhead is applied to production on the basis of 90 percent of direct labor cost.
5. Overhead costs in addition to those listed above amounted to $105,000.
6. Goods worth $550,000 were completed and transferred to the stockroom.
7. Sales to customers amounted to $750,000; the cost of these goods was $400,000.

Required   *a.* Prepare journal entries to record the above information.
         b. Compute the work in process at March 31, 19x4.

E5–9   ### Using Actual Overhead versus Predetermined Overhead

Your parents are the owners of Word Processing Agency, a firm that does word processing for its customers. Because the firm has some free capacity and the workload fluctuates from month-to-month, the firm has an arrangement with Busy Word Factory, another word processing firm, that has overflow work and does not wish to move to larger quarters. Instead of billing Busy at the Word Processing Agency's normal price of $2.50 per page, your parents bill Busy at *actual* costs of material, labor, and *overhead,* plus 20 percent of total cost for profit. The actual overhead for the month is prorated based on the total number of pages typed for the month.

For the months of July, August, and September, the costs incurred, the activity, and the billings were as follows:

	July	August	September
Direct materials	$ 350	$ 400	$ 200
Direct labor	28,000	32,000	16,000
Overhead	31,500	31,000	31,000
Total costs	$59,850	$63,400	$47,200
Pages Typed			
Customers	30,000	20,000	5,000
For Busy	5,000	20,000	15,000
Total	35,000	40,000	20,000
Billings to Busy			
Typing paper @ $.01	$ 50	$ 200	$ 150
Labor @ $.80 per page	4,000	16,000	12,000
Overhead	4,500*	15,500†	23,250‡
Subtotal	8,550	31,700	35,400
Profit @ 20%	1,710	6,340	7,080
Total	$10,260	$38,040	$42,480
Cost per page	$ 2.052	$ 1.902	$ 2.832

* $\frac{5,000}{35,000} \times \$31,500 = \$4,500.$

† $\frac{20,000}{40,000} \times \$31,000 = \$15,500.$

‡ $\frac{15,000}{20,000} \times \$31,000 = \$23,250.$

After getting its invoices for the three months, Busy Word Factory expressed concern about the widely fluctuating cost per page typed. Unless it is billed at stable prices per page, it is threatening to take its overflow work to another firm. Your parents are anxious to retain the overflow work from Busy. Because you have just completed a course in managerial accounting, your parents consult you to see if you can work out a more equitable billing agreement.

You ascertain that your parents' overhead for a year is estimated at $360,000 and that their firm's normal capacity is 400,000 pages per year.

Required   Redo the cost calculations and billing for the three months using normal costing. Use typed pages as the base for applying overhead.

E5–10   Preparation of Job Cost Sheet for a Hospital

Charles Eberhart entered the Riverview Hospital for some surgery on August 19, 19x8. Eberhart is not covered by Medicare, but he has health insurance coverage with a private insurance company. Consequently, he will be billed individually by the hospital, and he will seek reimbursement from his insurance company.

The hospital uses a job order cost accounting system for its private patients. All labor charges include the actual wages paid to employees plus all fringe benefits that are applicable.

The following procedures were performed and costs incurred:

Chest X ray—cost of film	$ 4.00
—technician—½ hr. @ $20/hr.	10.00
Electrocardiogram—technician—¼ hr. @ $25/hr.	6.25
Laboratory—blood analysis—materials	10.00
—technician— 1 hr. @ $25.00	25.00
Operating room—resident physicians—9 hours @ $30.00	270.00
Operating room—OR nurses—9 hours @ $30.00	270.00
Recovery room—nurses—24 hours @ $25.00	600.00
Subsequent care—3 electrocardiograms—technician—¾ hr. @ $25/hr.	18.75
Laboratory—blood analysis—materials	10.00
—technician—1 hr. @ $25.00	25.00
Medications	125.00
Special diet food	75.00

The hospital has separate overhead pools for various functions. The operating rooms' costs are accumulated in one pool and costed out to patients on an hourly basis. The cost per hour is $400. Eberhart's surgery lasted three hours and, thus, the cost for his surgery in the operating room amounted to $1,200. Another overhead pool is for the patients' rooms and the associated ancillary services, such as floor nursing, regular meals, sanitary services, and so on. This overhead pool is allocated on the basis of patient-days. The cost per patient-day is $250 for a semipriviate room. Eberhart was discharged from the hospital on August 27, 19x8.

Eberhart was given an itemized bill in the amount of $10,000 upon his discharge.

Required   Prepare a job cost sheet for Charles Eberhart.

E5–11   Preparation of Job Cost Sheets for a Law Firm

Tort and Feaser, a law firm, provides you with the following:

Payroll for the *month* of February, 19x5:

James Tyser—Typist	$ 2,600
Mary Tyler—Associate	7,200
Harris Tweed—Partner base salary	24,000

The normal *workweek* is as follows:

Typists	40 hours
Associates	60
Partners	60

The month of February has four working weeks. During February, the following work was performed for Z Corporation, a client of the firm:

Typist	120 hours
Associate	180
Partner	40

Out-of-pocket costs paid on behalf of Z Corporation amounted to:

Court filing fees	$500
Messenger services	300
Telephone charges.	250

The firm uses a predetermined overhead rate of 200 percent of direct labor costs. The firm billed Z Corporation for an associate's hours at a rate of $150 per hour and a partner's hours at $300 per hour. Typing salaries are not billed to the client but are included in the associate's and partner's rates of billing. Out-of-pocket costs are billed to clients.

Required   *a.* Prepare a job cost sheet for the Z Corporation.
             b. Determine how much profit was made on this client engagement.

E5–12   **Computation of Predetermined Overhead Rate and Closing of Manufacturing Overhead Account**

The Mayfair Company estimates that its direct labor cost for 19x3 will amount to $1.8 million, while its overhead for the year is expected to amount to $1,350,000. During the year, its actual direct labor cost amounted to $1,920,000, and its actual overhead amounted to $1,420,000. The company uses an Applied Manufacturing Overhead account when it applies overhead to production.

Required   *a.* Compute the predetermined overhead rate that Mayfair should use for 19x3 using a direct labor cost base.
             b. Prepare the summary journal entry for 19x3 showing the application of overhead for the year.
             c. Close the Overhead and Applied Manufacturing Overhead accounts to Cost of Goods Sold.

E5–13   **Computation of Predetermined Overhead Rate and Completion of Job Cost Sheet**

The Moveover Company estimates that its direct labor cost for 19x4 will amount to $500,000, while its overhead is expected to amount to $325,000 for the year. At the end of June 19x4, the debits in the Work in Process account consisted of the following:

Direct materials	$187,500
Direct labor	281,200
Overhead.	182,780
Total debits.	$651,480

Transfers to finished goods for the six months ended June 30, 19x4, amounted to $601,560. Job 266 was the only job still in process on June 30. The direct labor for Job 266 amounted to $16,000 at June 30.

Required   *a.* Compute the predetermined overhead rate for Moveover, using direct labor cost as the base.
             b. Prepare the breakdown of direct materials, direct labor, and overhead that would appear on the job cost sheet for Job 266.

E5–14   **Computation of Predetermined Overhead Rate and Closing of Manufacturing Overhead Account**

The Sawyer Company estimates that its direct labor cost for 19x3 will amount to $500,000, while its overhead for the year is expected to amount to $575,000. During the year, its actual direct labor cost amounted to $460,000, and its actual overhead amounted to $537,500. The company uses an Applied Manufacturing Overhead account when it applies overhead to production.

Required
a. Compute the predetermined overhead rate that Sawyer should use for 19x3, using a direct labor cost base.
b. Prepare the summary journal entry for 19x3 showing the application of overhead for the year.
c. Close the Overhead and Applied Manufacturing Overhead accounts to Cost of Goods Sold.

E5–15   **Proration of Underapplied or Overapplied Manufacturing Overhead**

1. The balance of the Work in Process account on December 31, 19x4, is:

Direct materials	$ 45,000
Direct labor	90,000
Manufacturing overhead.	91,800
Total	$226,800

2. The balance in the Finished Goods Inventory account on December 31, 19x4, consists of:

Direct materials	$ 30,000
Direct labor	60,000
Manufacturing overhead.	61,200
Total	$151,200

3. The balance in the Cost of Goods Sold account on December 31, 19x4, consists of:

Direct materials	$ 420,000
Direct labor	850,000
Manufacturing overhead.	867,000
Total	$2,137,000

4. The actual manufacturing overhead for 19x4 amounted to $912,000 and included expenditures that could not be anticipated prior to December 31, 19x4.
5. The applied overhead amounted to $1,020,000.

Required
a. Prepare a schedule to prorate the under/overapplied manufacturing overhead.
b. Prepare the journal entry to close the under/overapplied overhead as prorated in part (a).
c. Prepare the journal entry to close the under/overapplied overhead if it is *not* prorated.

▶ **PROBLEMS**   **P5–16**   **Journal Entries for Cost Accounting Cycle and Preparation of Schedule of Cost of Goods Sold**

The following information and transactions are assumed to have occurred during the year 19x3 for the Humbart Company:

1. The beginning inventory of direct materials and supplies amounted to $364,000.
2. Purchases of direct materials and supplies amounted to $1,121,000.
3. Issuances of materials amounted to $1,159,000 for direct materials and $6,000 for indirect materials.

4. The beginning inventories for work in process and finished goods were:

Work in process $110,000
Finished goods 235,000

5. Payroll for the year 19x3 amounted to $773,000 for direct labor and $216,000 for indirect labor.
6. Manufacturing overhead is applied to production at 80 percent of direct labor cost.
7. Other manufacturing overhead for the year 19x3 amounted to $500,000. (Credit Sundry Credits.)
8. Cost of goods manufactured for the year amounted to $2,477,000.
9. Sales on account for the year were $4,042,000. The cost of these sales amounted to $2,388,000.
10. The company's policy is to close any underapplied or overapplied manufacturing overhead to cost of goods sold.

Required   *a.* Journalize the transactions for the year.
        b. Open T accounts for the beginning inventory balances, and post the journalized entries from part *(a)*.
        c. Prepare a schedule of cost of goods manufactured and a schedule of cost of goods sold.

P5–17   **T Account Entries for Cost Accounting Cycle and Preparation of Schedule of Cost of Goods Sold**

The following information and transactions are assumed to have occurred during the year 19x3 for the Altosax Company:

1. The beginning inventory of direct materials and supplies amounted to $317,000.
2. Purchases of direct materials and supplies amounted to $1,025,000.
3. Issuances of materials and supplies amounted to $1,039,000 for direct materials and $5,000 for indirect materials.
4. The beginning inventories for work in process and finished goods were:

Work in process $134,000
Finished goods 211,000

5. Payroll for the year 19x3 amounted to $749,000 for direct labor and $192,000 for indirect labor.
6. Manufacturing overhead is applied to production at 80 percent of direct labor cost.
7. Other manufacturing overhead for the year 19x3 amounted to $391,000. (Credit Sundry Credits.)
8. Cost of goods manufactured for the year amounted to $2,381,000.
9. Sales on account for the year were $3,898,000. The cost of these sales amounted to $2,316,000.
10. The company's policy is to close any underapplied/overapplied manufacturing overhead to cost of goods sold.

Required   *a.* Open T accounts for the beginning inventory balances, and post the above transactions directly to the necessary T accounts.
        b. Prepare a schedule of cost of goods manufactured and a schedule of cost of goods sold.

P5–18   **Cost Accounting Cycle Prepared from Schedules of Cost of Goods Manufactured and Sold**

PAUL COMPANY
Schedule of Cost of Goods Manufactured
For the Year Ended December 31, 19x2

Direct materials:		
Direct materials and supplies inventory, January 1	$ 52,700	
Add: Purchases of direct materials and supplies	104,600	
Total direct materials and supplies available	157,300	
Deduct: Direct materials and supplies inventory, December 31	86,500	
Direct materials and supplies used	70,800	
Deduct: Indirect materials used	3,300	
Direct materials used in production		$ 67,500
Direct labor		99,100
Manufacturing overhead:		
Indirect materials	3,300	
Indirect labor	61,700	
Miscellaneous factory costs	90,300	
Actual manufacturing overhead costs	155,300	
Less: Underapplied overhead	5,200	
Overhead applied to work in process		150,100
Total manufacturing costs		316,700
Add: Work in process, January 1		9,700
		326,400
Deduct: Work in process, December 31		15,800
Cost of goods manufactured at normal		$310,600

PAUL COMPANY
Schedule of Cost of Goods Sold
For the Year Ended December 31, 19x2

Finished goods inventory, January 1	$ 87,000
Cost of goods manufactured at normal	310,600
Goods available for sale	397,600
Finished goods inventory, December 31	82,200
Cost of goods sold at normal	315,400
Add: Underapplied manufacturing overhead	5,200
Cost of goods sold at actual	$320,600

The company closes its under/overapplied overhead to cost of goods sold.

Required   a. From the above schedules, you are asked to prepare all entries implicit in the cost accounting cycle that can be prepared.

b. The company uses direct labor cost as its base for applying overhead. Compute the company's predetermined overhead rate.

P5–19   **Individual Job Costs and the Cost Accounting Cycle**

The following information and transactions are assumed to have occurred during the month of January 19x5 for the Charles Nailtop Company:

1. The beginning inventory of direct materials consisted of:

Material A	$29,300
Material B	12,700
Material C	12,200
Total	$54,200

2. Purchases of direct materials consisted of:

Material A	$ 73,200
Material B	73,500
Material C	72,700
Total	$219,400

3. Issuances of direct materials consisted of:

Material A	$ 88,000
Material B	44,300
Material C	69,500
Total	$201,800

The direct materials are to be charged to:

Job 101	$ 61,400
Job 102	86,600
Job 103	53,800
Total	$201,800

4. The beginning work in process inventory consisted of:

Job 101	$ 23,100
Job 102	31,200
Job 103	46,400
Total	$100,700

The beginning finished goods inventory consisted of:

45 desks at $325	$14,625
200 chairs at $150	30,000
Total	$44,625

5. Payroll for the month is:

Direct labor	$169,000
Indirect labor	60,000
Total	$229,000

The direct labor is chargeable 30 percent to Job 101, 25 percent to Job 102, and 45 percent to Job 103.
6. Manufacturing overhead is applied to production at 80 percent of direct labor cost.
7. Other manufacturing overhead for the month amounted to $74,900.
8. Jobs 101 and 102 are complete. Job 103 is not completed.
9. Job 101 was for 1,200 chairs, and Job 102 was for 625 desks. Job 103 is for 800 tables.
10. Sales for the month were as follows:
    a. 1,300 chairs at $300.
    b. 500 desks at $650.
    The company uses the first-in, first-out (FIFO) method to account for all inventories.

Required   *a.* Prepare all of the necessary journal entries to record the above information.

b. Prepare either job cost sheets for each job or a tabular summary of costs by job. (Do not forget to include beginning inventories.)

c. Compute the unit costs for Job 101 and Job 102.

d. Compute the following inventories at January 31, 19x5:

(1) Direct materials.

(2) Work in process.

(3) Finished goods.

e. Prepare T accounts for direct materials inventory, work in process, and finished goods, and compare your answers with your computations in part *(d).*

P5–20   Journal Entries for Cost Accounting Cycle and Preparation of Schedule of Cost of Goods Sold

The following information and transactions are assumed to have occurred during the year 19x2 for the Todd Company:

1. The beginning inventory of direct materials and supplies amounted to $59,200.
2. Purchases of direct materials and supplies amounted to $230,000.
3. Issuances of materials and supplies amounted to $196,600 for direct materials and $4,400 for indirect materials.
4. The beginning inventories for work in process and finished goods were:

> Work in process $65,700
> Finished goods   41,500

5. Payroll for the year 19x2 amounted to $221,500 for direct labor and $93,800 for indirect labor.
6. Manufacturing overhead is applied to production at 80 percent of direct labor cost.
7. Other manufacturing overhead for the year 19x2 amounted to $88,800. (Credit Sundry Credits.)
8. Cost of goods manufactured for the year amounted to $523,500.
9. Sales on account for the year were $820,500. The cost of these sales amounted to $410,250.
10. The company's policy is to close any underapplied or overapplied manufacturing overhead to cost of goods sold.

Required   *a.* Journalize the transactions for the year.

b. Open T accounts for the beginning inventory balances, and post the journalized entries from part *(a).*

c. Prepare a schedule of cost of goods manufactured and a schedule of cost of goods sold.

P5–21   T Account Entries for Cost Accounting Cycle and Preparation of Schedule of Cost of Goods Sold

The following information and transactions are assumed to have occurred during the year 19x2 for the Lewist Company:

1. The beginning inventory of direct materials and supplies amounted to $99,800.
2. Purchases of direct materials and supplies amounted to $178,700.
3. Issuances of materials and supplies amounted to $222,200 for direct materials and $400 for indirect materials.
4. The beginning inventories for work in process and finished goods were:

> Work in process $31,200
> Finished goods   53,100

5. Payroll for the year 19x2 amounted to $137,900 for direct labor and $26,500 for indirect labor.

6. Manufacturing overhead is applied to production at 60 percent of direct labor cost.

7. Other manufacturing overhead for the year 19x2 amounted to $65,500. (Credit Sundry Credits.)

8. Cost of goods manufactured for the year amounted to $460,900.

9. Sales on account for the year were $894,500. The cost of these sales amounted to $405,525.

10. The company's policy is to close any underapplied or overapplied manufacturing overhead to cost of goods sold.

Required   *a.* Open T accounts for the beginning inventory balances, and post the above transactions directly to the necessary T accounts.

b. Prepare a schedule of cost of goods manufactured and a schedule of cost of goods sold.

P5–22   **Cost Accounting Cycle Prepared from Schedules of Cost of Goods Manufactured and Sold**

INVERNESS COMPANY
Schedule of Cost of Goods Manufactured
For the Year Ended December 31, 19x2

Direct materials:

Direct materials and supplies inventory, January 1	$ 54,300	
Add: Purchases of direct materials and supplies	187,300	
Total direct materials and supplies available	241,600	
Deduct: Direct materials and supplies inventory, December 31	93,600	
Direct materials and supplies used	148,000	
Deduct: Indirect materials used	970	
Direct materials used in production		$147,030
Direct labor		94,700
Manufacturing overhead:		
Indirect materials	970	
Indirect labor	35,600	
Miscellaneous factory costs	72,900	
Actual manufacturing overhead costs	109,470	
Less: Underapplied overhead	1,800	
Overhead applied to work in process		107,670
Total manufacturing costs		349,400
Add: Work in process, January 1		39,100
		388,500
Deduct: Work in process, December 31		16,000
Cost of goods manufactured at normal		$372,500

INVERNESS COMPANY
Schedule of Cost of Goods Sold
For the Year Ended December 31, 19x2

Finished goods inventory, January 1	$ 53,600
Cost of goods manufactured at normal	372,500
Goods available for sale	426,100
Finished goods inventory, December 31	31,800
Cost of goods sold at normal	394,300
Add: Underapplied manufacturing overhead	1,800
Cost of goods sold at actual	$396,100

The company closes its under/overapplied overhead to cost of goods sold.

Required
a. From the above schedules, you are asked to prepare all entries implicit in the cost accounting cycle that can be prepared.

b. The company uses direct labor cost as its base for applying overhead. Compute the company's predetermined overhead rate.

P5–23 **Individual Job Costs and the Cost Accounting Cycle**

The following information and transactions are assumed to have occurred during the month of January 19x2 for Odega Company:

1. The beginning inventory of direct materials consisted of:

Material A	$ 42,200
Material B	73,300
Material C	49,900
Total	$165,400

2. Purchases of direct materials consisted of:

Material A	$127,300
Material B	196,000
Material C	139,200
Total	$462,500

3. Issuances of direct materials consisted of:

Material A	$122,900
Material B	194,100
Material C	147,600
Total	$464,600

The direct materials are to be charged to:

Job 101	$151,000
Job 102	128,500
Job 103	185,100
Total	$464,600

4. The beginning work in process inventory consisted of:

Job 101	$ 33,300
Job 102	49,500
Job 103	41,300
Total	$124,100

The beginning finished goods inventory consisted of:

75 desks at $350	$26,250
150 chairs at $125	18,750
Total	$45,000

5. Payroll for the month is:

Direct labor.	$164,200
Indirect labor	81,300
Total.	$245,500

The direct labor is chargeable 35 percent to Job 101, 30 percent to Job 102, and 35 percent to Job 103.

6. Manufacturing overhead is applied to production at 70 percent of direct labor cost.
7. Other manufacturing overhead for the month amounted to $99,000.
8. Jobs 101 and 102 are complete. Job 103 is not completed.
9. Job 101 was for 2,300 chairs, and Job 102 was for 750 desks. Job 103 is for 1,325 tables.
10. Sales for the month were as follows:
    a. 2,400 chairs at $325.
    b. 775 desks at $700.
    The company uses the first-in, first-out (FIFO) method to account for all inventories.

Required
    a. Prepare all of the necessary journal entries to record the above information.
    b. Prepare either job cost sheets for each job or a tabular summary of costs by job. (Do not forget to include beginning inventories.)
    c. Compute the unit costs for Job 101 and Job 102.
    d. Compute the following inventories at January 31, 19x2:
       (1) Direct materials.
       (2) Work in process.
       (3) Finished goods.
    e. Prepare T accounts for direct materials inventory, work in process, and finished goods, and compare your answers with your computations in part *(d)*.

P5–24   **T Account Entries for Cost Accounting Cycle and Preparation of Schedules of Cost of Goods Manufactured and Sold**

The following information and transactions are assumed to have occurred during the year 19x2 for the Clark Company:

1. The beginning inventory of direct materials and supplies amounted to $169,800.
2. Purchases of direct materials and supplies amounted to $529,900.
3. Issuances of materials and supplies amounted to $505,300 for direct materials and $4,600 for indirect materials.
4. The beginning inventories for work in process and finished goods were:

Work in process	$93,000
Finished goods	98,900

5. Payroll for the year 19x2 amounted to $416,600 for direct labor and $90,300 for indirect labor.
6. Manufacturing overhead is applied to production at 60 percent of direct labor cost.
7. Other manufacturing overhead for the year 19x2 amounted to $178,000. (Credit Sundry Credits.)
8. Cost of goods manufactured for the year amounted to $1,142,300.
9. Sales on account for the year were $2,632,000. The cost of these sales amounted to $1,052,960.
10. The company's policy is to close any underapplied or overapplied manufacturing overhead to cost of goods sold.

Required
    a. Open T accounts for the beginning inventory balances, and post the above transactions directly to the necessary T accounts.
    b. Prepare a schedule of cost of goods manufactured and a schedule of cost of goods sold.

P5–25   **Rappim and Savin, a law firm, provides you with the following:**

Payroll for the month of February, 19x2:

John Knower, typist	$ 2,400
Bill Patterson, associate	8,400
Roger Rappim, partner base salary	18,000

The normal workweek is as follows:

Typists	40 hours
Associates	60
Partners	60

The month of February has four working weeks. During February, the following work was performed for clients of the firm and for other duties:

Typing:	
A&R Corp.	45 hours
B&S Corp.	70
C&X Corp.	25
Miscellaneous	20

Associate:	
A&R Corp.	75 hours
B&S Corp.	80
C&X Corp.	60
Seminars	25

Partner—Roger Rappim	
A&R Corp.	40 hours
B&S Corp.	55
C&X Corp.	25
Administrative	120

Out-of-pocket costs paid on behalf of clients amounted to:

Court Filing Fees:	
A&R Corp.	$ 900
B&S Corp.	700
C&X Corp.	800

Messenger Services:	
A&R Corp.	$ 100
B&S Corp.	90
C&X Corp.	20

Telephone Charges:	
A&R Corp.	$ 77
B&S Corp.	24
C&X Corp.	123

The firm uses a predetermined overhead rate of 150 percent of direct labor costs. The firm billed A&R Corporation and B&S Corporation for an associate's hours at the rate of $175 per hour and for a partner's hours at $325 per hour. Typing salaries are not billed to the client but are included in the associate's and partner's rates of billing. Out-of-pocket costs are billed to clients. The work for A&R Corporation and B&S Corporation is complete, but the work for C&X Corporation is still in process. C&X Corporation will be billed when the work is complete.

Required   *a.* Prepare job cost sheets for all jobs.

b. Determine how much profit was made on each client engagement for completed jobs.

c. How much work in process does the firm have?

P5–26   **Calculation of Predetermined Overhead and Job Costing for an Auditing Firm**

Torch and Roster, one of the world's largest public accounting firms, provides pro bono accounting and consulting services to many small business and nonprofit organizations in the major cities in which it operates. Members of the firm are selected for a period of one year to staff these engagements. The firm's managing partner developed the following budget for pro bono activities for the year 19x2:

Professional salaries:			
Managers	4 @ $65,000 =	$ 260,000	
Senior accountants	16 @ $50,000 =	800,000	
Staff accountants	48 @ $30,000 =	1,440,000	$2,500,000
Travel and other costs			618,100
Total budgeted costs			$3,118,100

The firm uses a job order costing system to cost each engagement and applies overhead costs to each engagement based on the ratio of total overhead to direct labor.

At the end of each month, members of the firm are required to submit time and expense reports. The reports must indicate the hours spent on each engagement; other time must be accounted for as nonchargeable time (NCT) and described. NCT is usually spent attending continuing education seminars or in an unassigned status and is normally expected to include about 15 percent of available time. Professional staff members are expected to work 2,000 hours per year with very limited overtime. NCT is considered part of overhead.

Required

a. Calculate the rate used to apply overhead to each engagement as a percentage of chargeable direct labor.

b. The firm has been assisting Smithville Medical Center in installing a new computer-based patient billing and financial reporting system. For April 19x2, the monthly time and expense reports for this engagement showed the following: manager time—11 hours; senior accountant's time—31 hours; staff accountant's time—144 hours. Calculate the total cost allocated to this engagement for the month.

P5–27 **Disposition of Underapplied or Overapplied Manufacturing Overhead**

1. The balance of the Work in Process account on December 31, 19x2, is:

Direct materials	$ 69,000
Direct labor	106,000
Manufacturing overhead	53,000
Total	$228,000

2. The balance in the Finished Goods Inventory account on December 31, 19x2, consists of:

Direct materials	$ 90,000
Direct labor	176,000
Manufacturing overhead	88,000
Total	$354,000

3. The balance in the Cost of Goods Sold account on December 31, 19x2, consists of:

Direct materials	$ 540,000
Direct labor	1,056,000
Manufacturing overhead	528,000
Total	$2,124,000

4. The actual manufacturing overhead for 19x2 amounted to $694,000 and included expenditures that could not be anticipated prior to December 31, 19x2.

5. The applied overhead amounted to $669,000.

Required   a. Prepare a schedule to prorate the under- or overapplied manufacturing overhead.
b. Prepare a schedule to verify that the applied overhead would be converted to actual overhead if the proration from part *(a)* is journalized.
c. Journalize the proration from part *(a)*.

▸ **CASES**   C5–28   ### Cost Accounting Cycle from Fragmentary Data

The bookkeeper of the Harold Company had a large backlog of work, and he decided to take some work home to his farm for the weekend. After tending to the chickens and goats, the bookkeeper started working on the company's books while sitting on the outdoor porch. After about an hour's work, he got drowsy and dozed off. Hearing a noise, he awakened to see a goat enjoying her lunch of the company's records. Fortunately, some scraps were left, and after the bookkeeper had assembled the scraps to the extent possible, he found the following:

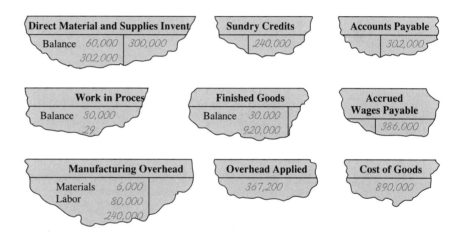

The bookkeeper seeks your advice in reconstructing the company's records. Assume the records are for the year 19x6.

Required   a. Prepare the journal entries that can be reconstructed from the scraps above. (Any under/overapplied overhead is to be closed to cost of goods sold.)
b. Compute the ending inventories for:
    (1) Direct materials.
    (2) Work in process.
    (3) Finished goods.
c. Compute the predetermined overhead rate if direct labor cost was used as the base.

▸ **ETHICAL BEHAVIOR CASE**   C5–29   Failsafe Electronics Company manufactures electronic equipment and components to order for other manufacturers. It also manufactures electronic devices for the U.S. Armed Forces. Because each item it manufactures is custom-made, the firm uses a job order accounting system.

As a recent college graduate with a degree in accounting, you have been hired by the firm as an assistant management accountant.

The firm has several contracts with the U.S. Department of Defense. One contract, Job No. 071655, was for the Signal Corps and was recently completed. Because the contract was for an item that had never been made before, the contract with the Department of Defense contained a clause allowing the government to audit the firm's costs for this contract and permitting the firm to recover all of its costs plus a reasonable amount for profit.

Failsafe previously submitted its vouchers for Job No. 071655 to the Department of Defense and had been paid for this contract. The firm has been notified that the government auditors are expected next week. Your supervisor has asked you to assist in the preparation of the job cost sheets that are to be used to substantiate the direct materials costs to the Department of Defense auditors. All purchase orders for component parts for this contract contained the notation DD132546, the Department of Defense contract number. You are told to accumulate all invoices with this notation to support the claim for the direct materials used on this job, and you find that the total direct material cost amounts to $3,150,000.

You also remember that in the course of your studies, you learned of the use of a bill of materials, which is a detailed listing of every item and quantity of direct material needed to manufacture one unit of the finished product. Being anxious not to make a mistake on your first important assignment, you reason that if you had this bill of materials available and you priced out each item on the bill of materials using the invoice prices from the invoices you just accumulated, you could determine what the direct materials cost should be for one unit. If you then multiply this unit cost by 1,000, the number of units manufactured, you would obtain a dollar amount that would act as check on the $3,150,000 you just computed. This would give you comfort in your computations. You go to the file on this contract and you find the bill of materials. After pricing it out and multiplying by 1,000 units, you wind up with an expected cost for direct materials of $2,025,000. You recheck all of your calculations and find that you made no apparent error.

You are now in a panic because you realize that there must be something wrong with your work, but you do not know what it is. Grasping at straws, you try to find the error by looking at the "big ticket" items. In the bill of materials, you notice that the finished unit calls for one transformer, which had a unit cost of $489. Looking at the purchase invoices for these transformers, you notice that the company purchased 2,000 transformers for this contract number. Believing that this could account for a substantial part of the error, you look further to see if these transformers were purchased for spare parts. You examine the contract and find that there is no provision for spare parts to be provided by Failsafe.

After some thought, you realize that these extra 1,000 transformers might have been returned to the vendor for credit. You examine the purchase returns register and see that they were returned, but the return did *not* bear the contract number DD132546. This would explain about half of the discrepancy. You proceed to look at other big-ticket items and find the same pattern (i.e., extra purchases using the contract number and returns without the number). It is apparent to you that you have uncovered a series of mistakes or an intent to defraud the Department of Defense.

You go to your supervisor with your apparent discrepancy. You are told to leave the work and you are assigned to a different project.

Several months later, you learn that the Department of Defense auditors allowed the claim of $3,150,000 for direct materials.

Required   What would you do with the information that you have? In answering this question, refer to "Standards of Ethical Conduct for Management Accountants" discussed in Chapter 1.

▶ **ANSWERS TO SELF-TEST**

True or False

1. False	2. False	3. False	4. True	5. True	6. False
7. False	8. True	9. False	10. False		

Multiple Choice

1. *a.*

Beginning inventory		$ 9,000
Add: Direct materials		26,000
Direct labor		20,000
Applied overhead—150%		30,000
		85,000
Less: Ending Inventory—		
Direct materials	$2,800	
Direct labor	1,800	
Applied overhead	2,700	7,300
		$77,700

2. *d.*

Actual overhead	$32,000
Applied overhead	30,000
Underapplied	$ 2,000

3. *d.* $48,000 + $108,000 = $156,000 - ($6.00 \times 24,000) = $12,000$ underabsorbed.

4. *c.* March 31 balance $= $9,000^* - $2,250 - \dfrac{$2,250}{.90} = $4,250$

     * $12,000 + $40,000 + $30,000 + $27,000 - $100,000 = $9,000$

5. *b.* $\dfrac{$510,000}{100,000} = 5.10 per DLH; $5.10 \times 105,000 = $535,500$

	Actual	= 540,000
	Underapplied	$ 4,500

6. *b.* ($15,000 + $53,000 + $23,000 + $12,000 + $20,000 = $123,000$).

7. *a.* $123,000 - (160\% \times $70,000) = $11,000$ underapplied.

8. *b.* ($72,500 + $8,000 + 160\% \times $7,000) = $91,700$.

9. *d.*

($79,000 + $21,000 + $5,000)	=	$105,000
+ 160\% \times ($53,000 + $9,000 + $1,000)	=	100,800
Total		$205,800

Process Costing

After reading this chapter, you should be able to:

1. Identify the manufacturing situations in which process costing is most appropriate and explain its advantages under such circumstances.
2. Differentiate between sequential processing and parallel processing and tell when each is used.
3. Explain how costs are accumulated in a process cost system.
4. Compute equivalent production (equivalent units) and explain its use in determining unit costs.
5. Prepare a production report, including the quantity of production, cost of production, and cost recapitulation sections.
6. Calculate unit costs of partially completed products and finished goods, assuming an average cost flow.
7. Account for cost in a preceding department when computing departmental costs.
8. Explain the difference between normal and abnormal spoilage, and account for lost, spoiled, and defective units.

▶ **INTERVIEW***

P. J. Lynch
Comptroller
Texaco Inc.

Q. *Have you had occasion to use a process cost accounting system? If so, did you use a full-costing absorption system, or did you use a contribution margin (variable costing) system? Give examples of how your system was used for external reporting purposes and how it was used for internal decision-making purposes.*

A. Texaco's chemical operations are currently using a process cost accounting system. The system is a full-absorption costing process with the ability to identify individual product cost and contribution margins. This system is used for the purpose of making business decisions. Additionally, the inventory is adjusted to a LIFO basis for inclusion in the consolidated financial reports of Texaco Inc. We use both the full-absorption and contribution margin methods in analyzing trend data for Texaco. The contribution margin method is used internally for the following types of decision making:

1. Pricing of products for sale.
2. Areas in which to concentrate sales efforts.

---

* The questions and answers relate to Texaco's chemical operations.

3. Unit modernization.
4. Product line expansions.
5. Acquisitions and divestitures.

The contribution margin approach is applied to help decide whether we should make a spot business transaction at less than the current established sales price. Although other business factors must be considered, the contribution margin is a vital piece of information when taken into account with total fixed and variable costs.

The full-costing absorption method is also used in the internal decision-making process in regard to the pricing of specialty products. This is a high-price, low-volume business for which we use full-costing absorption information to ensure that the gross margins being received from sales are at a level sufficient to support necessary research and technical activities and provide for an appropriate return on investment.

Q. *In the course of your work, have you used a weighted-average process cost method or a FIFO process cost method? What factors caused you to choose that particular method?*

A. Texaco's chemical operations currently use a weighted-average process cost method that is adjusted, at the division level, to a LIFO basis for external and certain internal reporting. This method has been selected because it gives a fair representation of product cost and also provides ease of calculation. Given Texaco's more than 400 chemical products, the layering required for a FIFO process cost method was not attractive.

Q. *In the course of your work, has your firm prepared process cost of production reports? If so, what time period were these reports for? To how many decimal places do you carry your unit costs? What factors influenced your decisions regarding the frequency of reporting and the number of decimal places used?*

A. We prepare monthly cost of production reports. Unit costs of production are carried out to five places to the right of the decimal point. This is done to eliminate rounding problems when working with the cost of production data.

Monthly cost of production reports are prepared as an integral part of our monthly closing cycle and our profitability reporting. These data are used in preparing monthly earnings reports to unit management. Costing is not done at less than monthly intervals due to the monthly recording of certain costs, such as payroll and billing of intercorporate services, which constitute a significant portion of our monthly costs. More frequent costing would require excessive accrual activity in order to generate accurate production costs.

▶ As noted in Chapter 5, cost information is useful for purposes of planning and control, inventory valuation, and decision making. Because the flow of costs parallels the flow of operations, a firm's production processes will influence its choice of a cost accounting system. Companies that manufacture discrete batches of different products usually prefer a job order cost accounting system, and firms that repetitively manufacture similar or homogenous products generally find a process cost accounting system more suitable for their needs. Although a job order system accumulates costs by job, a **process cost accounting system** *accumulates costs by departments* for a period of time, usually a week or two, but no longer than a month. A department's total costs are then divided by the number of units produced to compute the unit cost for the period. This chapter focuses on the kinds of firms that use a process cost accounting system and the accounting procedures such a system entails. ◀

Firms that Use Process Cost Systems

L.O. 1

When a firm manufactures products repetitively, a job order cost accounting system would be unnecessarily expensive. Because each job would consist of the same (or very similar) products, maintaining individual job cost sheets would not be advantageous. The aggregate cost and the unit cost of a batch may be computed without a job cost sheet, thereby saving the costs associated with producing such records. Among the firms that find the process cost accounting system useful are (1) paint manufacturers, (2) oil refineries, (3) sugar refineries, (4) salt producers, (5) public utilities, (6) pulp and paper mills, (7) bakeries, (8) lumber mills, (9) pen and pencil manufacturers, and (10) toothbrush manufacturers. A company's decision to use process costing is based on the number of different products and the length of the production cycle.

Cost Accumulation Methods in Process Costing

Either of two cost-flow assumptions may be used to account for inventories and unit cost computations in a process cost accounting system. The **average cost assumption** (sometimes referred to as *moving average*) is more commonly used in practice. It combines any costs assigned to the beginning work in process with the costs expended in the current period to arrive at the average costs assignable to the output in the current period. This eliminates the need to compute separate unit costs for the work in process and the current production costs because the two are combined for unit cost computations. This procedure is demonstrated in detail later.

The other cost-flow assumption is the **first-in, first-out (FIFO) method,** which assigns costs based on when the product was manufactured. Although used only occasionally in practice, you should be aware that the FIFO method regularly appears in professional certification examinations, such as the CPA and CMA examinations. For a more complete discussion of this method, refer to Appendix 6-A. Under FIFO, costs expended in a current period are accounted for separately from the costs assigned to the beginning work in process inventory. The merchandise completed and transferred is accounted for in batches, and costs are assigned to the batches according to the sequence of processing.

The Physical Flow of Processing

L.O. 2
Sequential and parallel processing

The flow of processing may follow several different patterns. In a **sequential production process,** all basic direct materials pass through *all processing centers.* For example, note in Illustration 6-1 that all direct materials go through the same three phases of production—(1) mining, (2) crushing and sizing, and (3) packaging.

▶ **ILLUSTRATION 6-1**   Sequential Processing (Salt Manufacturing)

▶ **ILLUSTRATION 6-2**   Parallel Processing (Meat Processing)

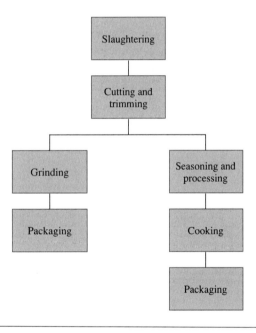

In a **parallel production process,** direct materials pass through common processing departments and are then split off into separate processing departments for further processing. For example, the physical flow of processing in a meat-packing plant might appear as in Illustration 6-2. Note that in this case, after cutting and trimming, some of the meat goes to the grinding department while other meat is sent to be seasoned and processed. Many variations of parallel processing are possible.

► COST ACCUMULATION IN A PROCESS SYSTEM

L.O. 3

In process costing, the components of manufacturing costs—direct materials, direct labor, and manufacturing overhead—are accumulated in much the same way as when job order costing is used. But they are accumulated by departments for a specific time period instead of by job. The period of time is flexible and depends on the information needs of the company. Cost accumulation is much simpler for a process cost system than for a job order cost system.

Direct Materials

In process costing, as in job order costing, materials requisitions form the basis for issuing materials to production, but far fewer requisitions are usually required. A firm that uses a process costing system may have only one product or a few products in process at any one time and thus may have just a few requisitions per month. The number of requisitions would depend on how often a batch of product is started.

The entry to record the issuance of materials for process costing is similar to the entry used for job order costing. However, because costs are accumulated by departments for a period of time, it is customary to departmentalize the Work in Process account.

The Jones Manufacturing Corporation has two departments—cutting and finishing. During the month of January 19x3, the corporation issued direct materials for production as follows:

Cutting department	$144,000
Finishing department . . .	9,000

The entry to record the issuance of direct materials would be:

(a)

Work in Process—Cutting	144,000	
Work in Process—Finishing	9,000	
Direct Materials and Supplies Inventory		153,000

Direct Labor

As with direct materials, the cost accumulation of direct labor in a process cost system is much simpler than that for job order costing. Payroll costs are accumulated by department for a specified period of time, and the departmental payroll costs can usually be taken directly from the payroll records without much additional effort. It is not necessary to have employees punch in and out every time they work on a particular job, and it is not necessary to cost out separate job time tickets. This can mean a significant amount of savings in record-keeping costs. However, if employees perform work for more than one department, they will need to keep records of the time spent in each department.

For the month of January 19x3, the Jones Manufacturing Corporation incurred the following direct labor costs:

Cutting department	$72,000
Finishing department . . .	63,700

The entry to record direct labor is:

(b)

Work in Process—Cutting	72,000	
Work in Process—Finishing	63,700	
Accrued Wages Payable		135,700

Manufacturing Overhead

A normal predetermined overhead rate, as discussed in Chapter 5, is also needed when a process cost accounting system is used. An appropriate base—direct labor cost, direct labor-hours, machine-hours—would be selected in the same manner as in job order costing, and any underapplied or overapplied overhead would be disposed of as discussed in Chapter 5.

The Jones Manufacturing Corporation uses direct labor cost (DLC) as the base for applying manufacturing overhead to production, and the rates are 80 percent of DLC for the cutting department and 110 percent of DLC for the finishing department. The entry to record overhead for January 19x3 is:

(c)

Work in Process—Cutting.	57,600	
Work in Process—Finishing	70,070	
Manufacturing Overhead Applied.		127,670

To apply manufacturing overhead as follows:
80% × $72,000 DLC = $57,600
110% ×   63,700 DLC =   70,070

Unit Costs—No Work in Process

The computation of unit costs is relatively simple when there are no work in process inventories. A cost-flow assumption—average or FIFO—is not necessary when there are no inventories. For example, unit costs for a month would be computed as follows, assuming no work in process inventories, 40,000 units of production, direct material costs of $120,000, direct labor costs of $80,000, and overhead of $48,000:

Direct materials	$120,000 ÷ 40,000 units =	$3.00 per unit
Direct labor.	80,000 ÷ 40,000	= 2.00
Overhead applied . . .	48,000 ÷ 40,000	= 1.20
Totals	$248,000	$6.20 per unit

Equivalent Production

L.O. 4

When a firm uses a process costing system, it usually manufactures one or a few items repetitively and would thus be highly likely to have work in process inventory at the end of an accounting period. Therefore, the simple calculations shown above are not likely to be sufficient. When beginning and/or ending inventories of work in process does exist, a cost-flow assumption must be made, and a method must be found to convert partially complete units into the equivalent of completed units. For example, if the 40,000 units shown above were only 60 percent complete, it would be impossible to compute unit costs for the month without further adjustments. For example, if you divided the $120,000 of materials cost by 40,000 units to arrive at a unit cost of $3, this unit cost would not be correct because the 40,000 units are only 60 percent complete. The $3 unit cost for direct materials is relevant only if the 40,000 units are complete. When production figures are adjusted to include partially completed units that have been converted into an equivalent number of completed units, the result is known as *equivalent production,* or **equivalent units.**

Computing Equivalent Production   Process costing would be quite simple except for the complicating issue of beginning and ending work in process inventories. Units in ending inventory are incomplete by definition. If they were complete, they would be transferred out as finished goods and not be part of ending work in process. If 10,000 units are in the ending work in process inventory, can we say that we have 10,000 units? The answer is

▶ **ILLUSTRATION 6-3**

JONES MANUFACTURING CORPORATION
Quantity of Production Report—Cutting Department
For the Month of January 19x3

To be accounted for:
Work in process, beginning . . . .   –0–
Started this period   30,000

    Total to be accounted for   30,000

Accounted for as follows:
Completed and transferred to finishing department   20,000
Work in process, ending. . . . .   10,000 (100% materials;
                                                   40% labor and
                                                 overhead)

    Total accounted for   30,000

clearly, "no." Because the units are incomplete, they represent fewer than 10,000 *completed* units. In an attempt to quantify the number of units in the ending work in process inventory, the concept of equivalent production emerges. **Equivalent production** represents the number of units that would have been completed if all production efforts resulted in only *completed* units (i.e., no work in process inventory). Equivalent production is calculated by multiplying the number of partially completed units produced by the percentage of completion. Thus, if the 10,000 units in the ending work in process inventory are only 40 percent complete, they are equivalent to 4,000 units that are fully complete. In other words, if we had produced only finished units with the same amount of effort, we would have produced only 4,000 units, but they would have been 100 percent complete. The adjusted figure for partial units is then added to the number of completed units to arrive at equivalent production. To compute the equivalent units at the Jones Manufacturing Corporation, we need the following additional information for the month of January 19x3:

Number of units started.   30,000
Number of units completed in the cutting department and
  transferred to the finishing department   20,000
Number of units partially complete (Ending work in process inventory)   10,000

All direct materials were added at the *beginning* of the process. Thus, the units are 100 percent complete with respect to materials. But only 40 percent of the labor and applied overhead needed to finish the 10,000 units has been used.

Unit production information is often summarized in a quantity of production report. A **quantity of production report** summarizes unit productivity for a period of time, and it is usually included as part of the production report, discussed later. Jones's quantity of production report for the month of January 19x3 appears in Illustration 6-3.

To compute equivalent production (EP) for an *average cost* assumption, the following equation is used:

$$EP_{av} = \text{Number of units completed} + [(\text{Percentage of completion})$$
$$\times (\text{Ending work in process units})]$$

where

EP = Equivalent production
av = Average cost-flow assumption

Therefore, equivalent production for January would be:

EP_{av} materials   = 20,000 + 100% (10,000)
                            = 30,000 units
EP_{av} labor and applied overhead = 20,000 + 40% (10,000)
                                      = 24,000 units

The calculation for labor and overhead reflects the fact that 10,000 units that are 40 percent complete would have the same direct labor cost as 4,000 units that were 100 percent complete. Using this calculation, it is now possible to compute unit costs because the output can be measured as equivalent to 24,000 completed units.

▶ THE PRODUCTION REPORT

L.O. 5

A **production report,** a periodic report that summarizes unit costs and costs of inventories, usually consists of three sections—a quantity of production report, a cost of production report, and a cost recapitulation. The quantity of production report, as mentioned earlier, summarizes unit production for the period. The **cost of production report** summarizes and combines cost information for the purpose of calculating unit costs and costs of inventories of partially completed and finished goods. And the **cost recapitulation section** proves that all costs have been accounted for, forms the basis of journal entries, and provides beginning inventory figures for the next production report. Customarily, a production report is prepared each month for every production department in a firm.

Production Report—Initial Department

The Jones Manufacturing Corporation production report for the cutting department for the month of January 19x3 is presented in Illustration 6-4. It is based on the production quantities provided in Illustration 6-3 and the cost data shown in journal entries *(a)*, *(b)*, and *(c)*.

The steps used to prepare the production report are:

1. Prepare the quantity of production section.
2. Calculate the equivalent production for materials and labor and overhead.
3. Insert the costs previously expended for the opening balance of the work in process (in this case, zero), as well as the costs newly incurred in the current month, and add them to arrive at the figures in the total column. Sum the total column to compute the total cost to be accounted for.

L.O. 6
Unit costs—average costing

4. Compute the unit costs of direct materials, direct labor, and applied overhead by dividing each component's total costs by the applicable equivalent production. (See footnotes *a, b,* and *c* in Step 4.) Sum the unit cost column to arrive at the *total* unit cost for the month.
5. Multiply the number of completed units by the *total* unit cost for the month to arrive at the total cost of units transferred to the next department.

▶ **ILLUSTRATION 6-4**

JONES MANUFACTURING CORPORATION
Production Report—Cutting Department
For the Month of January 19x3
Quantity of Production

Step 1.   Quantity to be accounted for:
              Work in process, beginning . . .   –0–
              Started or transferred in   30,000

                 Total to be accounted for . . .   30,000

              Accounted for as follows:
              Completed and transferred. . . .   20,000
              Work in process, ending.   10,000   (100% materials; 40% labor and overhead)

                 Total accounted for   30,000

Step 2.   Equivalent production:
              Materials = 30,000 units. Labor and overhead = 24,000 units

Cost of Production

		Work in Process +	Costs this Period =	Total Cost	Unit Cost
Step 3.	Cost in this department:				
	Direct materials.	$–0–	$144,000	$144,000	$ 4.80^a
	Direct labor	–0–	72,000	72,000	3.00^b
	Overhead	–0–	57,600	57,600	2.40^c
	Totals	$–0–	$273,600	273,600	10.20
	Total cost to be accounted for			$273,600	$10.20

Step 4.   a. $144,000 ÷ 30,000 = $4.80.
              b. $ 72,000 ÷ 24,000 = $3.
              c. $ 57,600 ÷ 24,000 = $2.40.

Cost Recapitulation

Step 5.   Accounted for as follows:
              Completed and transferred . . .   20,000 × $10.20 $204,000

              Work in process:
Step 6a.   Direct materials . . . .   10,000 × 100% × $4.80   48,000
Step 6b.   Direct labor . . . .   10,000 × 40% × 3.00   12,000
Step 6c.   Overhead . . . .   10,000 × 40% × 2.40   9,600

                 Total   69,600

Step 7.   Total accounted for $273,600

6. Compute the ending work in process inventory by:
   a. Multiplying the number of units in the ending inventory by the stage of completion of *direct materials* by the unit cost of *direct materials* to arrive at the direct materials cost in the ending inventory.
   b. Repeat step 6a, substituting the state of completion and the unit cost of *direct labor* for the direct materials amounts.
   c. Repeat step 6a, substituting the stage of completion and the unit cost of applied *overhead* for the direct materials amounts.
   Sum the three calculations to arrive at the total work in process inventory at the end of the month.

7. Add the amounts computed in steps 5 and 6, and compare the total to the total cost to be accounted for as computed in step 3. The amounts should be the same.

In Illustration 6-4, note that:

1. The quantity of production report is identical to the information provided in Illustration 6-3.
2. Because there is no beginning inventory of work in process, there are no costs in that column.
3. The costs in the current period are taken from journal entries *(a)*, *(b)*, and *(c)*.
4. The recapitulation section, showing the completed and transferred work of $204,000 and the ending work in process of $69,600, is a key element of the report. In addition to proving that all costs ($273,600) have been accounted for, these computations form the basis of journal entry *(d)*, shown below, and provide the beginning inventory figures for the February 19x3 report.

After the report is prepared, it is possible to journalize the cost of units transferred by the cutting department to the finishing department. The amount—$204,000—is obtained from the recapitulation portion of the report. The needed journal entry would be:

(d)

Work in Process—Finishing 204,000
    Work in Process—Cutting 204,000

Production Report— Subsequent Department

It is now possible to prepare a production report for the *finishing department* using the information provided in journal entries *(a)*, *(b)*, *(c)*, and *(d)* together with the following production information:

	Units
Work in process, beginning	–0–
Transferred in from cutting department.	20,000
Completed and transferred to finished goods	14,000
Work in process, ending (All materials are added at the beginning of the process. Thus, materials are 100% complete. Labor and overhead—conversion costs—are only 70% complete.)	6,000

L.O. 7
Cost in a preceding department

The steps used to prepare the production report for the finishing department are similar to the ones used to prepare the production report for the cutting department, except:

1. A new section, entitled Cost in Preceding Department, is added in the cost of production section. This section is reserved for the cost of units transferred in from a preceding department, in this case $204,000. **Transferred-in cost** is the dollar value assigned to the units transferred into a department from a preceding department. **Transferred-out cost** is the dollar value assigned to the units transferred from a department to a subsequent department or to the finished goods warehouse. In this case, the *transferred-out costs* of the cutting department *become the transferred-in costs* of the finishing department.

2. The transferred-in costs are included in the *total cost to be accounted for*.
3. The ending work in process now includes another calculation for cost in preceding department.

The production report for the finishing department is presented in Illustration 6-5. The quantity of production report for the department appears at the top. Based on its figures, the equivalent production may be computed as follows:

	Units
Materials:	
Completed and transferred	14,000
Work in process—6,000 × 100% . . .	6,000
Equivalent production	20,000
Labor and overhead:	
Completed and transferred	14,000
Work in process—6,000 × 70%	4,200
Equivalent production	18,200

The recapitulation section of the report shows the cost of the finished goods as $252,000. This forms the basis of the following journal entry:

(e)

Finished Goods 252,000
    Work in Process—Finishing Department 252,000

From Illustration 6-5, it can be seen that:

1. Because there was no work in process inventory at the beginning of the period, the spaces for these amounts show zero balances.
2. The recapitulation section of the report accounts for all costs, including the $204,000 of transferred-in costs from the cutting department.
3. The total unit cost of the finished goods is $18, which includes the $10.20 unit cost in the cutting department and the $7.80 unit cost in the finishing department.

Thus far, the illustrations have not included any work in process at the beginning of the period. If journal entries *(a)* through *(e)* were to be posted, the work in process and finished goods T accounts at the end of January 19x3 would appear as in Illustration 6-6. These balances become the beginning balances for February 19x3. Thus, beginning work in process balances would be present in the February 19x3 production reports.

The balances in the Work in Process accounts shown in Illustration 6-6 should be compared with the recapitulation sections of Illustrations 6-4 and 6-5 to verify that the work in process amounts shown in the production reports agree with the balances shown in the T accounts. A similar comparison can be made between the finished goods balance in Illustration 6-6 and the recapitulation section of Illustration 6-5.

► **ILLUSTRATION 6-5**

JONES MANUFACTURING CORPORATION
Production Report—Finishing Department
For the Month of January 19x3
Quantity of Production

Quantity to be accounted for:
Work in process, beginning . . .   –0–
Started or transferred in   20,000

    Total to be accounted for . . .   20,000

Accounted for as follows:
Completed and transferred   14,000
Work in process, ending   6,000   (100% materials; 70% conversion costs)

    Total accounted for   20,000

Equivalent production:
Materials = 20,000 units
Labor and overhead = 18,200 units

Cost of Production

	Total Cost	Unit Cost
Cost in preceding department:		
Work in process, beginning	$ –0–	$
Transferred in during the period	204,000	10.20
Totals	204,000	10.20[a]

	Work in Process +	Costs this Period =		
Cost in this department:				
Direct materials	$–0–	$ 9,000	9,000	0.45[b]
Direct labor	–0–	63,700	63,700	3.50[c]
Overhead	–0–	70,070	70,070	3.85[d]
Totals	$–0–	$142,770	142,770	7.80
Total cost to be accounted for.			$346,770	$18.00

Cost Recapitulation

Accounted for as follows:
Completed and transferred	14,000 × $18	$252,000
Work in process:		
Cost in preceding department . . .	6,000 × $10.20	61,200
Direct materials	6,000 × 100% × $ .45	2,700
Direct labor	6,000 × 70% × 3.50	14,700
Overhead	6,000 × 70% × 3.85	16,170
Total		94,770
Total accounted for.		$346,770

These costs appear in journal entries *(a)*, *(b)*, and *(c)*.
   a. $204,000 ÷ 20,000 units = $10.20.
   b. $9,000 ÷ 20,000 units = $.45.
   c. $63,700 ÷ 18,200 units = $3.50.
   d. $70,070 ÷ 18,200 units = $3.85.

JONES MANUFACTURING CORPORATION
Partial General Ledger
January 31, 19x3

Work in Process—Cutting

(a)	144,000	(d)	204,000
(b)	72,000		
(c)	57,600		
Balance	69,600		

Work in Process—Finishing

(a)	9,000	(e)	252,000
(b)	63,700		
(c)	70,070		
(d)	204,000		
Balance	94,770		

Finished Goods

(e)	252,000	
Balance	252,000	

1. What is the difference between sequential processing and parallel processing?
2. When there are no beginning or ending work in process inventories, is it possible to compute unit costs without the use of equivalent production? If so, when is it necessary to use equivalent production?
3. Assume that Catalyst Company uses process costing. In its first department of the manufacturing process, the work in process for labor and overhead on March 31, 19x1, consisted of 30,000 units that were 35 percent complete. If the firm started 100,000 units at the beginning of March and finished 70,000 units during March, what is the equivalent production for the month?
4. Assume that the firm incurred direct labor costs of $169,050 in Department 1 for the month of March. What is the unit cost for labor?
5. Is a production report prepared for all departments of a firm? What are the three main sections of a production report? ◀

Production Report—Beginning Work in Process Inventory

During the month of February 19x3, the Jones Manufacturing Corporation incurred direct material costs of $146,000 and direct labor costs of $102,080 in the cutting department. Manufacturing overhead was applied at 80 percent of direct labor cost ($81,664). The beginning inventory of work in process in the cutting department was 10,000 units (the same as the ending work in process inventory for January). In addition, 30,000 new units were started. Of the total 40,000 units in production, 32,000 units were completed and transferred to the finishing department. The remaining 8,000 units were 100 percent completed for direct materials and 60 percent completed for labor and applied overhead.

The steps needed to prepare the production report for the cutting department are similar to those used previously except for the beginning work in process column, which must now be filled in. The amounts of $48,000 for direct materials, $12,000 for direct labor, and $9,600 for applied overhead are obtained from the recapitulation section of the January production report for the cutting department.

The equivalent production computations are prepared using the equation approach and are shown in the February production report presented in Illustration 6-7.

▶ **ILLUSTRATION 6-7**

JONES MANUFACTURING CORPORATION
Production Report—Cutting Department
For the Month of February 19x3

Quantity of Production

Quantity to be accounted for:
Work in process, beginning . . .   10,000
Started or transferred in   30,000
Total to be accounted for . . .   40,000

Accounted for as follows:
Completed and transferred   32,000
Work in process, ending   8,000   (100% materials; 60% labor and overhead)
Total accounted for   40,000

Equivalent production:
EP_{av} materials $= 32{,}000 + 100\% (8{,}000) = 40{,}000$ units
EP_{av} labor and applied overhead $= 32{,}000 + 60\% (8{,}000) = 36{,}800$ units

Cost of Production

	Work in Process +	Costs this Period =	Total Cost	Unit Cost
Cost in this department:				
Direct materials.	$48,000	$146,000	$194,000	$ 4.85[a]
Direct labor	12,000	102,080	114,080	3.10[b]
Overhead	9,600	81,664	91,264	2.48[c]
Totals	$69,600	$329,744	399,344	10.43
Total cost to be accounted for			$399,344	$10.43

Cost Recapitulation

Accounted for as follows:
Completed and transferred . . . . $32{,}000 \times \$10.43$ $333,760

Work in process:
Direct materials . . . . $8{,}000 \times 100\% \times \$4.85$ 38,800
Direct labor . . . . $8{,}000 \times 60\% \times 3.10$ 14,880
Overhead . . . . $8{,}000 \times 60\% \times 2.48$ 11,904
Total   65,584
Total accounted for $399,344

---

a. $194{,}000 \div 40{,}000$ units $= \$4.85$.
b. $114{,}080 \div 36{,}800$ units $= \$3.10$.
c. $ 91{,}264 \div 36{,}800$ units $= \$2.48$.

Illustration 6-7 reveals that:

1. The quantity of production report is easily prepared by adding the beginning work in process inventory of 10,000 units to the new units started—30,000. The completed and transferred units of 32,000 combined with the 8,000 units of ending work in process comprise the bottom portion of this section.
2. The cost in preceding department section is always zero in the first department of the production cycle and is, therefore, omitted from this production report.
3. The work in process column contains the information obtained from the recapitulation section of the January production report for the cutting department (Illustration 6-4).

4. The recapitulation section contains the calculations of the cost of goods completed and transferred and the work in process inventory. The total of these two equals the total cost to be accounted for.

Also during the month of February, the Jones Manufacturing Corporation incurred direct material costs of $16,300 and direct labor costs of $115,230 in the finishing department. Overhead of $126,753 was applied at the predetermined rate of 110 percent of direct labor cost. The beginning work in process inventory amounted to 6,000 units, and 32,000 units were transferred in from the cutting department. The finishing department completed 31,000 units and transferred them to the finished goods warehouse. In addition, 7,000 units were still in process at the end of February. These units are 100 percent complete for direct materials and 80 percent complete for conversion costs.

The steps needed to prepare the February production report for the finishing department are the same as those discussed previously, except the cost in preceding department consists of two amounts—$61,200 assigned to work in process at the end of January (see the recapitulation section of Illustration 6-5) and $333,760 of transferred-in costs from the cutting department (see Illustration 6-7). Because an average cost flow is assumed, the individual unit costs of these amounts are *not* shown on the production report; instead, the average unit cost of the total of these amounts ($394,960) is used. The unitizing may be calculated as $394,960 ÷ 38,000 units (total accounted for) = $10.3937.

This result can be seen in Illustration 6-8, the production report for the finishing department for the month of February 19x3.

In Illustration 6-8, note that:

1. The work in process column of cost in this department contains the breakdown shown in the cost of recapitulation section of the January 19x3 report for the finishing department—Illustration 6-5.
2. The recapitulation section contains a rounding difference of 60 cents. This is not unusual when the number of decimal places is carried to only four places. It is rarely worth the effort to carry the unit cost calculations beyond four places. The use of fewer decimal places usually increases the rounding difference. The number of decimal places in calculations depends on the needs of the company.
3. In any department after the first, ending work in process includes costs from the preceding department. In this example, the four elements of the ending inventory have a total unit cost of $18.3487. To ensure that the proper unit costs are used in the proof, the $10.3937 + $.50 + $3.55 + $3.905 can be added to arrive at the $18.3487 used to compute the cost of the completed and transferred units.
4. The ending work in process inventory of $94,770, shown in the recapitulation section of Illustration 6-5, is divided into two sections—$61,200 is shown in the cost in preceding department section; and $2,700, $14,700, and $16,170 (total $33,570) are shown in the cost in this department section.

Lost Units, Normal Spoilage, and Abnormal Spoilage

Many manufacturing firms find that some of their direct materials evaporate during processing. This commonly happens with chemical, paint, and gasoline manufacturers. Other firms find that some of their products are spoiled during the manufacturing process. The spoilage may be usual for the

▶ **ILLUSTRATION 6-8**

JONES MANUFACTURING CORPORATION
Production Report—Finishing Department
For the Month of February 19x3
Quantity of Production

Quantity to be accounted for:
Work in process, beginning . . .   6,000
Started or transferred in   32,000
Total to be accounted for . . .   38,000

Accounted for as follows:
Completed and transferred. . . .   31,000
Work in process, ending.   7,000   (100% materials; 80% labor and overhead)
Total accounted for   38,000

Equivalent production:
EP_{av} transferred in = 6,000 + 32,000 = 38,000 units
EP_{av} materials = 31,000 + 100% (7,000) = 38,000 units
EP_{av} conversion = 31,000 + 80% (7,000) = 36,600 units

Cost of Production

	Total Cost	Unit Cost
Cost in preceding department:		
Work in process, beginning	$ 61,200	$
Transferred in during the period	333,760	
Totals	394,960	10.3937[a]

	Work in Process	+	Costs this Period	=		
Cost in this department:						
Direct materials.	$ 2,700		$ 16,300		19,000	0.5000[b]
Direct labor	14,700		115,230		129,930	3.5500[c]
Overhead	16,170		126,753		142,923	3.9050[d]
Totals	$33,570		$258,283		291,853	7.9550
Total cost to be accounted for					$686,813	$18.3487

Cost Recapitulation

Accounted for as follows:
Completed and transferred . . . . .   31,000 × $18.3487 $568,809.70

Work in process:
Cost in preceding department . . .   7,000 × $10.3937   72,755.90
Direct materials . . . .   7,000 × 100% × $ .5000   3,500.00
Direct labor . . . .   7,000 × 80% × 3.5500   19,880.00
Overhead . . . .   7,000 × 80% × 3.9050   21,868.00
                                                            118,003.90
Total accounted for. . . . . $686,813.60[e]

---

a. $394,960 ÷ 38,000 units = $10.3937.
b. $ 19,000 ÷ 38,000 units =   .5000.
c. $129,930 ÷ 36,600 units =   3.5500.
d. $142,923 ÷ 36,600 units =   3.9050.
e.   There is a rounding difference of $.60.

process, in which case it would be considered normal spoilage, or it may be unusual, in which case it would be abnormal spoilage. Accounting for lost and spoiled units is discussed in Appendix 6-B.

▶ **SUMMARY**

When a firm manufactures products repetitively, its use of a job order cost accounting system would lead to excessive bookkeeping costs. In such cases, whether the flow of processing is **sequential** or **parallel,** a **process cost accounting system** is more efficient. Instead of accumulating costs by jobs, a process cost accounting system accumulates costs by department for a specified period of time. This eliminates the need for job cost sheets and job time tickets. It also requires fewer materials requisitions.

Because costs are accumulated for a period of time, a method of measuring the output for that period must be found if unit costs are to be computed. Completed units are easily counted. However, work in process is another matter. Any uncompleted units on hand at the end of the cost-accumulation period must be converted into an equivalent number of completed units and added to the completed units to determine the **equivalent production** for the period. Unit costs for direct materials, direct labor, and overhead may then be computed. The sum of these figures equals the total unit cost for the period.

Although two cost-flow assumptions may be found in practice—**average** and **FIFO**—the average method is used most often. In such cases, the costs assigned to the beginning work in process inventory are merged with the costs expended in the current period. This results in an average of the two costs.

Most firms prepare a **production report** for each production department for a specified period of time, usually a month. The report contains three sections—a **quantity of production report,** a **cost of production report,** and a **cost recapitulation section.** The production report must account for all **transferred-in costs** and all **transferred-out costs.**

The production report provides part of the information needed to record the journal entries that comprise the cost accounting cycle. The remaining information is obtained from the firm's material requisitions and payroll records.

▶ **APPENDIX 6-A**

Process Cost Accumulation—The FIFO Method

A production report that uses the first-in, first-out (FIFO) method in place of average costing will produce different figures for equivalent production and unit cost *only when beginning work in process inventory is present.* If there is no beginning work in process inventory, the production reports for both methods will be exactly the same.

Reasons for Selecting a Particular Cost-Flow Assumption

Managers base their cost-flow assumptions on their perceptions of company objectives. During a period of significant price changes, FIFO costing retains the unit costs that were originally calculated in the month the units were produced, and these changes in unit costs are highlighted in comparative reports. On the other hand, average costing tends to lessen the effect of these price changes in comparative reports. For example, assume 1,000 units of direct materials in beginning inventory were purchased at a cost of $5 each and an additional 1,000 were purchased at $7 each. If the 2,000 units were used (or sold) during the month, the usage would be reported as:

FIFO:
1,000 units at $5 . . . . . $ 5,000
1,000 units at $7   7,000
       Total $12,000

Average:
2,000 units at $6 . . . . . $12,000

If only 1,500 units were used (or sold), they would be reported as:

FIFO:
1,000 units at $5 . . . . . $5,000
500 units at $7   3,500
       Total $8,500

Average:
1,500 units at $6 . . . . . $9,000

Thus, when all units are not used, different costs values will occur for costs per unit, the value assigned to units transferred out to the next department or to finished goods.

FIFO Equivalent Production

Recall that FIFO keeps track of, and accounts for, individual inventory layers, but average costing "mixes" both old and new costs for a single average cost. The principal difference between FIFO and average costing occurs in the computations of equivalent production and unit costs. Two different methods are used to compute FIFO equivalent production, and if both methods are used, one can act as a check on the other.

In one method, FIFO equivalent production is computed in the same way as average equivalent production except the equivalent units in the beginning work in process inventory are subtracted. The result would be the equivalent work done in the period under consideration. The equation for this approach is:

$$EP_{FIFO} = \text{Units completed} + [(\text{Percentage of completion}) \times (\text{Ending work in process units})] - [(\text{Percentage of completion}) \times (\text{Beginning work in process units})]$$

where

EP = Equivalent production
$FIFO$ = First in, first-out cost assumption

If the Jones Manufacturing Corporation were to use FIFO costing instead of average costing, its production reports for January 19x3 would be *identical* to the average costing ones shown in Illustrations 6-4 and 6-5. This would occur because there were *no* beginning work in process inventories in either department. Because there are no beginning work in process units to

▶ **ILLUSTRATION 6-9**

JONES MANUFACTURING CORPORATION
Quantity of Production Report—Cutting Department
For the Month of February 19x3

Quantity to be accounted for:
Work in process, beginning . . . . . 10,000 (100% materials; 40% labor
                                                                    and overhead)
Started or transferred in 30,000
Total to be accounted for 40,000

Accounted for as follows:
Completed and transferred 32,000
Work in process, ending . . . . . . 8,000 (100% materials; 60% labor
                                                                    and overhead)
Total accounted for 40,000

subtract, the equation for EP_{FIFO} is equal to EP_{av}. However, for February, the equations are not equal to each other, and thus the production reports are different.

The quantity of production section from Illustration 6-7 is repeated in Illustration 6-9, except the stages of completion of the beginning inventory have been inserted. The stages were obtained from the quantity of production section of the January report (see Illustration 6-4).

From Illustration 6-9, it is now possible to compute the FIFO equivalent production as follows:

$$EP_{FIFO} \text{ Materials} = 32,000 + 100\% (8,000) - 100\% (10,000)$$
$$= 30,000 \text{ units}$$
$$EP_{FIFO} \text{ Labor and Overhead} = 32,000 + 60\% (8,000) - 40\% (10,000)$$
$$= 32,800 \text{ units}$$

In essence, these calculations indicate the number of equivalent units produced during the month of February by *excluding* the portion of the equivalent units *produced during January* and completed in February, but *including* the portion of equivalent units *produced during February* on the units started in January.

The second method of determining equivalent production under a FIFO cost assumption is to compute the amount of equivalent work needed to complete the beginning work in process inventory and to add the amount of *new* equivalent work done in the period under consideration. The computation is based on a separation of the completed and transferred units into two batches—one batch equal to the beginning work in process inventory and the remainder coming from the new units started and completed in February. The calculations are shown in Illustration 6-10. This approach and the equation approach produce identical results.

FIFO Production Report

To prepare a FIFO production report, consider that:

1. When a beginning work in process inventory is present and FIFO costing is used, it is best to arrange the departmental cost in a vertical format instead of the format used for average costing because the

▶ **ILLUSTRATION 6-10**

JONES MANUFACTURING CORPORATION
Calculation of Equivalent Production—Cutting Department
For the Month of February 19x3

Materials

Completed and transferred:
  10,000—First batch:
      Beginning work in process—to complete—10,000 ×
        (100% − 100%) . . . . −0−
  22,000—Second batch:
      Started new—22,000 × 100% 22,000
  32,000   Total completed and transferred 22,000
Ending work in process—8,000 × 100% 8,000
FIFO equivalent production 30,000

Conversion

Completed and transferred:
  10,000—First batch:
      Beginning work in process—to complete—10,000 ×
        (100% − 40%) 6,000
  22,000—Second batch:
      Started new—22,000 × 100% 22,000
  32,000   Total completed and transferred 28,000
Ending work in process—8,000 × 60% 4,800
FIFO equivalent production 32,800

beginning work in process costs are not used to compute unit costs for the current period. (See Illustration 6-11.)

2. The quantity of production section includes the stage of completion for *both* the beginning and ending work in process inventories, because they are needed to compute equivalent production.

3. The beginning work in process costs are included in the total cost to be accounted for even though they are not used to compute unit costs for the month.

4. In the cost recapitulation section of the production report, the cost of the completed and transferred units are calculated in batches. The first batch consists of the units in the beginning work in process inventory. The total cost of these units consists of the beginning inventory costs carried forward from the preceding production report and the costs expended in the current month to complete the units. The sum of these costs represents the total cost of the first batch. The cost of the second batch of completed and transferred goods is merely the remainder of the units completed and transferred multiplied by the *total* unit cost for the current month.

5. The ending work in process inventory is computed in the same way as it is in average costing.

The Jones Manufacturing Corporation's February production report for the cutting department appears in Illustration 6-11. Note that:

1. Only the current period costs are unitized. No unit costs are shown for the beginning work in process. Because these costs were incurred in the prior month, they do not affect unit costs for February. However,

▶ **ILLUSTRATION 6-11**　　　　**JONES MANUFACTURING CORPORATION**
FIFO Production Report—Cutting Department
For the Month of February 19x3
Quantity of Production

Quantity to be accounted for:
　Work in process, beginning . . . . 10,000　　(100% materials; 40% labor
　　　　　　　　　　　　　　　　　　　　　　　　　　　　　　　　　　　　　and overhead)
　Started or transferred in. 30,000
　　Total to be accounted for 40,000

Accounted for as follows:
　Completed and transferred. 32,000
　Work in process, ending. . . . . 8,000　　(100% materials; 60% labor
　　　　　　　　　　　　　　　　　　　　　　　　　　　　　　　　　　　　　and overhead)
　　Total accounted for 40,000

Equivalent production:
　EP_{FIFO} Materials = 32,000 + 100% (8,000) − 100% (10,000) = 30,000 units.
　EP_{FIFO} Labor and overhead = 32,000 + 60% (8,000) − 40% (10,000) = 32,800 units.

Cost of Production

	Total Cost	Unit Cost
Cost in this department:		
Work in process, beginning:		
Direct materials	$ 48,000	
Direct labor	12,000	
Overhead	9,600	
Current period costs:		
Direct materials	146,000	$ 4.8667[a]
Direct labor	102,080	3.1122[b]
Overhead	81,664	2.4897[c]
Total costs in this department	399,344	10.4686
Total cost to be accounted for	$399,344	$10.4686

Cost Recapitulation

Accounted for as follows:
　Completed and transferred:
　First batch:

Prior period costs		$ 69,600
Costs to complete:		
Direct materials.	10,000 × 0%	–0–
Direct labor.	10,000 × 60% × $3.1122	18,673
Overhead.	10,000 × 60% × 2.4897	14,938
Total first batch		103,211
Second batch: 22,000 × $10.4686		230,309
Total completed and transferred		$333,520
Work in process, ending:		
Direct materials.	8,000 × 100% × $4.8667	38,934
Direct labor.	8,000 × 60% × 3.1122	14,939
Overhead.	8,000 × 60% × 2.4897	11,951
Total work in process		65,824
Total accounted for		$399,344

a. $146,000 ÷ 30,000 units = $4.8667.
b. $102,080 ÷ 32,800 units = $3.1122.
c. $81,664 ÷ 32,800 units = $2.4897.

these costs enter into the recapitulation calculation of the completed and transferred units.

2. In the recapitulation section, the cost of the first batch of the completed and transferred units includes the $69,600 of costs assigned to the beginning inventory plus $0 for direct materials, $18,673 for direct labor, and $14,938 for overhead. Because direct materials in the beginning inventory were 100 percent complete, no additional materials were added in February. For direct labor and overhead, the beginning inventory was only 40 percent complete. Thus, an additional 60 percent was needed to complete these units, and the $18,673 of additional direct labor and $14,938 of additional overhead reflect these additions of 60 percent.

Illustration 6-11 is based on the same information used to prepare the average costing production report shown in Illustration 6-7. A comparison of the two illustrations reveals that:

1. Unit cost differences between the two methods are less than $.02 each for direct materials, direct labor, and overhead.
2. The difference in aggregate unit cost is less than $.04—that is, $10.4686 versus $10.43.
3. The difference between the completed and transferred costs is $240, a difference of .06 percent of the total cost to be accounted for. The same $240 difference also exists for the ending work in process.

The difference in costing between average and FIFO is negligible in most cases, and thus the additional effort required for FIFO costing is usually not justified from a cost-benefit standpoint. However, it is possible for the differences to be larger, in which case the additional effort may be justified.

The procedures used to prepare the February production report for the cutting department apply equally to the preparation of the production report for the finishing department, except:

1. The cost in preceding department section of the production report should reflect each batch separately, with a separate unit cost for each batch. The unit costs are not averaged as they are in average costing.
2. In the recapitulation section, the cost of the completed and transferred units should reflect a batch treatment, as demonstrated in Illustration 6-11, but it should also include the cost from the preceding department. Thus, the first batch of completed and transferred costs would include not only $2,700 for direct materials, $14,700 for direct labor, and $16,170 of overhead (see Illustration 6-8), but also $61,200 for costs from the preceding department. It would also include the costs expended in the finishing department during February to finish the beginning work in process of 6,000 units. The next batch of completed and transferred costs would be limited to costs incurred entirely in February, but the batch must include a transferred-in cost plus the costs for direct materials, direct labor, and overhead.
3. The ending work in process inventory would also include the cost from the preceding department in addition to the costs for direct materials, direct labor, and overhead. The cost in preceding department portion would come from the most recent transferred-in costs.

▶ **APPENDIX 6-B**   **Lost Units and Spoiled Units**

Lost units should be distinguished from defective units and spoiled units. **Lost units** are goods that disappear due to evaporation, breakage, or some other function of the production process. **Defective units** are goods of inferior quality that can be repaired at an additional cost and sold as first-quality merchandise. **Spoiled units,** however, are goods of inferior quality that cannot be repaired and sold as regular quality goods; they must be sold as seconds or scrap. An example of a spoiled unit would be a shirt with a permanent oil stain on its sleeve.

Lost Units

When a certain number of lost units are inherent in a firm's production process, it is customary to spread their cost over the remaining good units. One way of doing this is through the **method of neglect,** in which equivalent production is computed in *exactly* the same way as if there were no lost units. In essence, the lost units are ignored, and the unit cost of usable units thereby includes the cost of the lost units.

For example, assume:

1. The Kenyon Company incurred $140,000 of material costs for the month of January.
2. The company put into production 40,000 units of input and got 35,000 units of output. It is customary for the company to lose 12½ percent of its input in the production process.
3. The company would like to compute its unit cost for materials for the month using both the method of neglect and a method showing the separate cost for lost units.

The computation for the method of neglect would simply be:

$$\$140,000 \div 35,000 = \$4 \text{ per unit}$$

The computations showing a separate lost unit cost would be:

Input cost:
   $140,000 ÷ 40,000 = $3.50 per unit

Lost unit cost:
   5,000 × $3.50 = $17,500
   $17,500 ÷ 35,000 units = $.50 per unit

Total unit cost:
   Input cost. $3.50
   Lost unit cost 50
      Total unit cost. $4.00

Thus, it can be seen that the input cost of $3.50 must be adjusted for the cost of the lost units ($17,500), and the cost of lost units must be spread over the output of 35,000 usable units. This amounts to $.50 per unit, which brings the total cost of each usable unit to $4. Although the method-of-neglect computation is much simpler, it does not reveal the $.50-per-unit cost of the lost units. It merely distributes the total cost over usable output without regard to units of input.

When the method of neglect is used, the computation of equivalent production is *exactly the same* as demonstrated previously. The production report is also the same except for the quantity of production section. The lost units are shown as a separate item as follows:

Quantity of Production Report

Quantity to be accounted for:
Work in process, beginning   8,000
Started or transferred in   44,000
　　Total to be accounted for.   52,000

Accounted for as follows:
Completed and transferred   36,000
Work in process, ending . . . .   12,000 (100% materials; 60% conversion costs)
Lost units.   4,000
　　Total accounted for   52,000

EP_{av} Materials = 36,000 + 100% (12,000) = 48,000 units
EP_{av} Conversion costs = 36,000 + 60% (12,000) = 43,200 units

---

Spoiled Units

L.O. 8
Normal and abnormal spoilage

When the number of units that cannot be repaired and sold as first-quality units falls within an acceptable range of production, the amount is considered **normal spoilage.** On the production report, such units are treated in the same way as lost units. Unlike lost units, however, spoiled units can usually be sold for small amounts that are treated as miscellaneous revenue. When both lost units and spoiled units occur within an acceptable range, they are usually shown separately in the quantity of production section of the production report even though the method of neglect may be used for both.

Abnormal Lost or Spoiled Units

In most production processes, a certain amount of spoilage is considered normal. However, when spoilage exceeds the normal range due to poorly trained personnel, sabotage, or other reasons, it is considered **abnormal spoilage.** When this occurs, the cost of lost or spoiled units that is considered excessive should *not* be spread over the usable units; instead, it should be charged to income as a period cost. This procedure is preferred because abnormal spoilage is unexpected and rare and, therefore, should not be built into the pricing system or inventoried. Abnormal lost or spoiled units should be treated as a loss rather than as a cost of manufacturing.

▶ **GLOSSARY OF KEY TERMS**

Abnormal spoilage* An amount of scrap or second-quality merchandise that exceeds an acceptable (normal) range of production. The cost assigned to these units should be charged as a loss to income in the period of the loss. (p. 275)

Average cost assumption A method of accounting for inventories and unit cost computations in process cost accounting in which costs assigned to the beginning

---

* Denotes a glossary term from the chapter appendix.

work in process are merged with the costs expended in the current period to compute average costs assignable to the output in the current period. (p. 254)

Cost of production report   The part of a production report that summarizes and combines cost information for the purpose of calculating unit costs and costs of inventories of partially completed and finished goods. (p. 259)

Cost recapitulation section   The part of a production report that proves all costs have been accounted for, forms the basis of journal entries, and provides beginning inventory figures for the next production report. (p. 259)

Defective units*   Merchandise of inferior quality that can be repaired at an additional cost and then sold as first-quality merchandise. (p. 274)

Equivalent production   The number of units that would have been completed if all production efforts had resulted in only *completed* units (i.e., no work in process inventory). It is calculated by multiplying the number of partially completed units produced by the percentage of completion. (p. 258)

Equivalent units   See **equivalent production.** (p. 257)

First-in, first-out (FIFO) cost assumption   A method of accounting for inventories and unit cost computations in process cost accounting in which the costs expended in a current period are unitized separately from the costs assigned to the beginning work in process inventory. The merchandise completed and transferred is accounted for in batches, and costs are assigned to the batches according to the sequence of processing. (p. 254)

Lost units*   Good that disappear through evaporation, breakage, or some other function of the production process. If the loss is within an acceptable range—not due to sabotage or negligence—the cost of these units should be absorbed by the remaining usable units. (p. 274)

Method of neglect*   An approach used to spread the cost of lost units over the remaining usable units by treating the lost units as if they never existed and using only the usable units to compute unit costs. (p. 274)

Normal spoilage*   A number of units that cannot be repaired or sold as first-quality units and that fall within an acceptable range of production. These units are treated in the same manner as lost units except for any salvage value, which is usually handled expeditiously—treated as miscellaneous revenue. (See **method of neglect.**) (p. 275)

Parallel production process   A sequence of production in which common direct materials pass through some of the same processing centers, but not all of them. (p. 255)

Process cost accounting system   A cost accounting method in which product costs are accumulated by department for a specific period of time, usually a week or two, but no longer than a month. A department's total costs are then divided by the equivalent units produced to compute the unit cost for the period. (p. 254)

Production report   A process cost accounting report that summarizes unit costs and costs of inventories. The report is usually prepared monthly and contains three sections—a quantity of production report, a cost of production report, and a cost recapitulation. (p. 259)

Quantity of production report   A report that summarizes unit productivity for a period of time, usually included as part of the production report. (p. 258)

Sequential production process   A sequence of production in which all direct materials pass through all processing centers. (p. 254)

Spoiled units*   Goods of inferior quality that cannot be repaired and sold as regular finished goods. They must either be scrapped or sold as seconds. (p. 274)

Transferred-in cost   The dollar value assigned to units transferred into a department from a preceding department. (p. 261)

Transferred-out cost   The dollar value assigned to units transferred from a department to a subsequent department or to the finished goods warehouse. (p. 261)

▶ **GLOSSARY OF SYNONYMS**

Equivalent Units   See **equivalent production.**

▶ **REVIEW PROBLEM**

Average Production Report for Two Departments—Beginning Inventory

The Pat Company has two departments, mixing and coloring. For the month of March 19x4, the company incurred the following costs:

	Mixing	Coloring
Direct materials . . .	$ 73,175	$ 12,500
Direct labor	78,940	142,600
Overhead	94,728	114,080
Totals.	$246,843	$269,180

The beginning inventory on March 1, 19x4, amounted to:

	Mixing	Coloring
Cost in preceding department . . .	$ –0–	$39,000
Direct materials	7,825	2,060
Direct labor	5,540	3,720
Overhead	6,648	2,976
Totals.	$20,013	$47,756

The quantity production statistics for the month of March 19x4 are as follows:

	Mixing	Coloring
Beginning inventory	3,000	4,000
Started new	27,000	–0–
Transferred in	–0–	22,000
Transferred out	22,000	20,000
Ending inventory:		
(100% materials; 60% conversion) . . .	8,000	
(100% materials; 40% conversion) . . .		6,000

Required

a. Prepare a production report using average costing. (Combine labor and overhead into conversion cost.)

b. Prepare all journal entries to record:
   (1) The issuance of direct materials.
   (2) The direct labor.
   (3) The applied overhead.
   (4) Finished goods.

► **SOLUTION TO**
REVIEW PROBLEM

PAT COMPANY
Production Report—Mixing Department
For the Month of March 19x4

a.   **Quantity of Production**

Quantity to be accounted for:
Work in process—beginning . . .	3,000	
Started or transferred in	27,000	
Total to be accounted for . . .	30,000	

Accounted for as follows:
Completed and transferred. . . .	22,000	
Work in process—ending	8,000	(100% materials; 60% labor and overhead)
Total accounted for	30,000	

	Materials	**Labor**	**Overhead**
Computation of equivalent units:			
Completed and transferred. . . .	22,000	22,000	22,000
Add: Equivalent units, ending work in process	8,000 (100%)	4,800 (60%)	4,800 (60%)
Equivalent units of production . .	30,000	26,800	26,800

Cost of Production

	Work in Process +	**Costs This Period** =	**Total Cost**	**Unit Cost**
Cost in this department:				
Direct materials	$ 7,825	$ 73,175	$ 81,000	$2.700[a]
Direct labor	5,540	78,940	84,480	3.152[b]
Overhead	6,648	94,728	101,376	3.783[c]
Totals	$20,013	$246,843	266,856	9.635
Total cost to be accounted for . .			$266,856	$9.635

Cost Recapitulation

Accounted for as follows:
Completed and transferred . . .	22,000 × $9.635	$211,970

Work in process:
Direct materials	8,000 × 2.70	$21,600	
Direct labor	4,800 × 3.152	15,130	
Overhead	4,800 × 3.783	18,158	54,888
Total accounted for			$266,858*

a. $81,000 ÷ 30,000 units = $2.700.

b. $84,480 ÷ 26,800 units = $3.152.

c. $101,376 ÷ 26,800 units = $3.783.

* $2 difference due to rounding.

PAT COMPANY
Production Report—Coloring Department
For the Month of March 19x4
Quantity of Production

Quantity to be accounted for:
    Work in process—beginning . . .   4,000
    Started or transferred in 22,000
       Total to be accounted for . . . 26,000

Accounted for as follows:
    Completed and transferred. . . . 20,000
    Work in process—ending . . . .   6,000 (100% materials; 40% labor and overhead)
       Total accounted for 26,000

Computation of equivalent units:	Transferred In and Materials	Labor	Overhead
Completed and transferred	20,000	20,000	20,000
Add: Equivalent units, ending work in process	6,000 (100%)	2,400 (40%)	2,400 (40%)
Equivalent units of production. . .	26,000	22,400	22,400

Cost of Production

	Total Cost	Unit Cost
Cost in preceding department:		
Work in process—beginning	$ 39,000	
Transferred in during the period	211,970	
Total	250,970	$ 9.6527[a]

Cost in this department:	Work in Process +	Costs this Period =		
Direct materials	$2,060	$ 12,500	$ 14,560	$ .5600[b]
Direct labor	3,720	142,600	146,320	6.5321[c]
Overhead	2,976	114,080	117,056	5.2257[d]
Totals.	$8,756	$269,180	277,936	12.3178
Total cost to be accounted for			$528,906	$21.9705

Cost Recapitulation

Accounted for as follows:
  Completed and transferred. . . . . . . 20,000 × $21.9705 $439,410

Work in process:
    Cost in preceding department . . . . 6,000 × $9.6527 $57,916
    Direct materials. . . . . 6,000 × .56   3,360
    Direct labor . . . . 2,400 × 6.5321 15,677
    Overhead . . . . 2,400 × 5.2257 12,542   89,495
Total accounted for $528,905*

a. $250,970 ÷ 26,000 units = $9.6527.
b. $14,560 ÷ 26,000 units = $.5600.
c. $146,320 ÷ 22,400 units = $6.5321.
d. $117,056 ÷ 22,400 units = $5.2257.
* $1 difference due to rounding.

b. Journal entries:

(1) Work in Process—Mixing 73,175
　　Work in Process—Coloring 12,500
　　　　Direct Materials and Supplies Inventory . . . . . 　　　　　85,675
　　To record the placing of materials into production.

(2) Work in Process—Mixing 78,940
　　Work in Process—Coloring 142,600
　　　　Wages Payable . . . . 　　　　　221,540
　　To record labor costs.

(3) Work in Process—Mixing 94,728
　　Work in Process—Coloring 114,080
　　　　Manufacturing Overhead Applied . . . . 　　　　　208,808
　　To record the application of overhead.

(4) Work in Process—Coloring 211,970
　　　　Work in Process—Mixing . . . . 　　　　　211,970
　　To record the transfer from mixing to coloring.

　　Finished Goods 439,410
　　　　Work in Process—Coloring . . . . 　　　　　439,410
　　To record the transfer of units to finished goods.

▶ **REVIEW PROBLEM**　　**(Appendix 6-A) FIFO Production Report for One Department**

The Oat Company has one department. For the month of March 19x4, the company incurred the following costs:

Direct materials	$ 73,175
Direct labor	78,940
Overhead	94,728
Total	$246,843

The beginning inventory on March 1, 19x4, amounted to:

Direct materials	$ 7,825
Direct labor	5,540
Overhead	6,648
Total	$20,013

The quantity of production statistics for the month of March 19x4 are as follows:

Beginning inventory (100% material; 40% conversion)	3,000
Started new	27,000
Transferred out	22,000
Ending inventory (100% materials; 60% conversion)	8,000

Required　　*a.* Prepare a production report.
　　b. Prepare all journal entries to record:
　　　　(1) The issuance of direct materials.
　　　　(2) The direct labor.
　　　　(3) The applied overhead.
　　　　(4) The transfer to finished goods.

a.

OAT COMPANY
Production Report
FIFO Basis, for the Month of March 19x4

Quantity of Production

Quantity to be accounted for:		
Work in process, beginning	3,000	(100% materials; 40% labor and overhead)
Started or transferred in	27,000	
Total to be accounted for	30,000	
Accounted for as follows:		
Completed and transferred	22,000	
Work in process—ending	8,000	(100% materials; 60% labor and overhead)
Total accounted for	30,000	

Cost of Production

	Total Cost	Unit Cost
Cost in this department:		
Work in process—beginning:		
Direct materials	$ 7,825	
Direct labor	5,540	
Overhead	6,648	
Current period costs:		
Direct materials	73,175	$ 2.710[a]
Direct labor	78,940	3.084[b]
Overhead	94,728	3.700[c]
Total cost to be accounted for	$266,856	$ 9.494

Cost Recapitulation

Accounted for as follows:			
Completed and transferred:			
First batch:			
Prior period costs		$20,013	
Costs to complete:			
Direct materials			
Direct labor	1,800 × $3.084	5,551	
Overhead	1,800 × $3.700	6,660	
Total first batch			$ 32,224
Second batch: 19,000 × $9.494			180,386
Total completed and transferred			212,610
Work in process—ending:			
Direct materials	8,000 × $2.71	21,680	
Direct labor	4,800 × $3.084	14,803	
Overhead	4,800 × $3.70	17,760	
Total work in process			54,243
Total accounted for			$266,853*

Computation of equivalent units:

	Materials	Labor	Overhead
Units transferred out	22,000	22,000	22,000
Deduct: Equivalent units beginning inventory	3,000 (100%)	1,200 (40%)	1,200 (40%)
	19,000	20,800	20,800
Add: Equivalent units ending inventory	8,000 (100%)	4,800 (60%)	4,800 (60%)
Equivalent units of production	27,000	25,600	25,600

a. $73,175 ÷ 27,000 units $2.710.

b. $78,940 ÷ 25,600 units = $3.084.

c. $94,728 ÷ 25,600 units = $3.700.

* $3 difference due to rounding.

b. Journal entries:

(1) Work in Process   73,175
          Materials and Supplies Inventory   73,175
     To record issuance of direct material.

(2) Work in Process   78,940
          Wages Payable   78,940
     To record direct labor costs.

(3) Work in Process   94,728
          Manufacturing Overhead Applied   94,728
     To record application of overhead.

(4) Finished Goods . . . : 212,610
          Work in Process   212,610
     To record the transfer of units to finished goods.

▶ **LIBRARY ASSIGNMENT**

Read the following:

Cummins, Peter. "Process Costing Calculations: An Alternative Layout." *Australian Accountant,* September 1985, pp. 69–71.

Lovata, Linda M. "Experiential Process Costing Project." *Issues in Accounting Education,* Spring 1986, pp. 148–52.

Partington, Graham H. "Teaching Process Cost Accounting." *Issues in Accounting Education,* 1984, pp. 75–80.

Siegel, Joel G., and Michael Stevens. "Reporting and Appraisal of Process Cost Data." *Accountants Record* (England), March-April 1984, pp. 10–13, 19.

▶ **SELF-TEST**

True or False

1. Passing direct materials through all processing centers may be considered an example of parallel processing.
2. The average costing method and the FIFO method produce identical results provided there are no work in process inventories.
3. When computing equivalent production under the average method, the proper amount may be obtained by adding the amount of units completed and transferred to the beginning work in process inventory multiplied by the percentage of completion of the beginning inventory.
4. The three main sections of a production report are the quantity of production, cost of production, and equivalent production sections.
5. Any department can have a transferred-in cost.
6. The cost recapitulation section of the production report acts as a proof that all costs incurred in a department for a particular period (week, month, etc.) are properly accounted for at the end the period.
7. Only a department after the first department can have a work in process inventory.
8. Only a department after the first department can have a transferred-out cost.
9. It is not necessary to compute a unit cost for transferred-in cost.
10. It is advisable to use a predetermined overhead rate for applying overhead to production, but it is not essential to use one when a firm uses process costing.

Multiple Choice

Items 1 through 3 are based on the following information.

The Jorcano Manufacturing Company uses a process cost system to account for the costs of its only product, product D. Production begins in the fabrication department, where units of direct material are molded into various connecting parts. After fabrication is complete, the units are transferred to the assembly department. There is no material added in the assembly department. After assembly is complete, the units are transferred to a packaging department where packing material is placed around the units. After the units are ready for shipping, they are sent to a shipping area.

At year-end June 30, 19x3, the following inventory of product D is on hand:

a. No unused direct material or packing material.
b. Fabrication department: 300 units, ⅓ complete as to direct material and ½ complete as to direct labor.
c. Assembly department: 1,000 units, ⅖ complete as to direct labor.
d. Packaging department: 100 units, ¾ complete as to packing material and ¼ complete as to direct labor.
e. Shipping area: 400 units.

1. The number of equivalent units of direct material in all inventories at June 30, 19x3, is
   a. 300.
   b. 100.
   c. 1,600.
   d. 925.
2. The number of equivalent units of fabrication department direct labor in all inventories at June 30, 19x3, is
   a. 1,650.
   b. 150.
   c. 300.
   d. 975.
3. The number of equivalent units of packing material in all inventories at June 30, 19x3, is
   a. 75.
   b. 475.
   c. 100.
   d. 425.

(AICPA Adapted)

Items 4 and 5 are based on the following information.

Levittown Company employs a process cost system for its manufacturing operations. All direct materials are added at the beginning of the process and conversion costs are added proportionately. Levittown's production quantity schedule for November is reproduced below.

	Units
Work-in-process on November 1, 19x6 (60% complete as to conversion costs)	1,000
Units started during November	5,000
Total units to account for	6,000
Units completed and transferred out from beginning inventory	1,000
Units started and completed during November	3,000
Work-in-process on November 30, 19x6 (20% complete as to conversion costs)	2,000
Total units accounted for.	6,000

4. Using the weighted-average method, the equivalent units for direct materials for November are
   a. 3,400 units.
   b. 4,400 units.

c. 5,000 units.

d. 6,000 units.

e. some amount other than those given above.

5. Using the weighted-average method, the equivalent units for conversion costs for November are

a. 3,400 units.

b. 3,800 units.

c. 4,000 units.

d. 4,400 units.

e. some amount other than those given above.

(CMA Adapted)

▶ **QUESTIONS**

1. What types of firms use a process cost system? Why?

2. Two methods are generally used to account for inventories and unit costs when process costing is used. Discuss each method.

3. There are generally two sequential physical flows of manufacturing processes. Discuss and illustrate each one.

4. How are costs accumulated for firms that use a process cost accounting system? How does this differ from cost accumulation under a job order cost accounting system?

5. Is it possible to compute unit costs of production when work in process exists at the end or beginning of an accounting period? How is this accomplished? Use an example to illustrate the procedure involved for average costing.

6. Is it appropriate to use a predetermined overhead rate for applying overhead to production when a process cost accounting system is used? Under what circumstances would it be acceptable to use actual overhead instead of applied overhead? When should applied overhead be used?

7. Assume a firm has two departments, cutting and finishing. Prepare sample journal entries to illustrate the cost accounting cycle for direct materials, direct labor, and applied manufacturing overhead.

8. What are the components of a cost of production report? What is the purpose of each section?

For Appendix 6-A

9. When is there a difference between the cost of production reports for average costing and FIFO costing?

10. There are two different ways to compute FIFO equivalent production. What are they? How are they computed?

For Appendix 6-B

11. What is the difference between lost units, defective units, and spoiled units?

12. There are two methods of treating normal lost units. What are they? What is true regarding the end result on unit costs when each method is used?

13. How should abnormal spoilage or abnormal lost units be treated? Why should they be treated in this manner?

▶ **EXERCISES**

E6–1   Computation of Average Equivalent Units

Compute the equivalent production for materials and conversion costs for each case. All materials are added at the beginning of the process. Use average costing.

Case A
Beginning inventory—12,000 units 60% complete.
Started or transferred in—100,000 units.
Completed and transferred out—90,000 units.
Ending inventory—70% complete.

Case B
Beginning inventory—10,000 units 70% complete.
Completed and transferred out—60,000 units.
Ending inventory—30,000 units 40% complete.

Case C
Beginning inventory—15,000 units 40% complete.
Started or transferred in—120,000 units.
Ending inventory—25,000 units 60% complete.

E6–2 **Computation of Average Equivalent Units**

The Felix Manufacturing Company uses a process cost system to account for the costs of its only product, known as Nino. Production begins in the fabrication department, where units of direct material are molded into various connecting parts. After fabrication is complete, the units are transferred to the assembly department. There is no material added in the assembly department. After assembly is complete, the units are transferred to the packaging department, where the units are packaged for shipment. At the end of this process, the units are complete and are transferred to the shipping department.

At year-end December 31, 19x7, the following inventory of Ninos is on hand:

1. No unused direct material or packing material.
2. Fabrication department: 6,000 units, 25 percent complete as to direct material and 40 percent complete as to direct labor.
3. Assembly department: 10,000 units, 75 percent complete as to direct labor.
4. Packaging department: 3,000 units, 60 percent complete as to packing material and 75 percent complete as to direct labor.
5. Shipping department: 8,000 units.

Required Prepare in proper form schedules showing the following at December 31, 19x7:

a. The number of equivalent units of direct material in all inventories.
b. The number of equivalent units of fabrication department direct labor in all inventories.
c. The number of equivalent units of packaging department material and direct labor in the packaging department inventory.

(AICPA Adapted)

E6–3 **Average Costing Equivalent Units and Quantity Started**

The Young Corporation had 12,000 units in its work in process inventory at the beginning of September 19x3. These units were 60 percent complete as to conversion costs. During September, the company completed 60,000 units; it also had 20,000 units in its work in process at the end of September. These units were 40 percent complete as to conversion costs. All materials are added at the beginning of the production process. The company uses weighted-average process costing for its cost accounting.

Required *a.* Compute the following:
(1) Equivalent units for materials for the month of September.
(2) Equivalent units for conversion costs for the month of September.
b. How many units were started in September?

E6–4 **Average Costing for a First Department**

The Edwards Company uses weighted-average process costing and provides you with the following information for the month of July 19x4:

	Materials	Conversion
Work in process, beginning.	$16,000	$11,500
Current costs	79,700	58,000
Total costs	$95,700	$69,500
Equivalent production	58,000	55,600

All materials are added at the beginning of the process. During the month of July, 50,000 were completed and transferred to finished goods; 8,000 units were in the work in process inventory at the end of July. These units were 70 percent complete as to conversion costs.

Required
a. Compute the cost of the goods completed and transferred to finished goods.
b. Compute the cost of the ending work in process, showing the costs separately for materials and conversion costs.
c. Compare your totals from parts *(a)* and *(b)* with the information given to prove the accuracy of your computations.

E6–5 **Average Costing for a First Department**

The Finer Company uses weighted-average process costing and provides you with the following information for the month of July 19x5:

	Materials	Conversion
Work in process, beginning.	$19,325	$16,300
Current costs	80,000	81,436
Total costs	$99,325	$97,736
Equivalent production	68,500	64,300

All materials are added at the beginning of the process. During the month of July, 62,500 units were completed and transferred to finished goods; 6,000 units were in the work in process inventory at the end of July. These units were 30 percent complete as to conversion costs.

Required
a. Compute the cost of the goods completed and transferred to finished goods.
b. Compute the cost of the ending work in process, showing the costs separately for materials and conversion costs.
c. Compare your totals from parts *(a)* and *(b)* with the information given to prove the accuracy of your computations.

E6–6 **Average Costing for a Second Department**

The Goodin Company uses weighted-average process costing and provides you with the following information for the month of May 19x6:

1. The finishing department is the last stage of the production process. At the beginning of May 19x6, the company had 12,000 units in its beginning inventory. These units had accumulated costs as follows:

Transferred-in costs $60,000
Materials—this department. 4,200
Conversion—this department. 3,360

2. During the month, the preceding department transferred in 24,000 units at a cost of $112,800. The finishing department incurred $8,400 of additional materials costs and $6,000 of conversion costs on these units.
3. The ending inventory consisted of 8,000 units that were 40 percent complete as to conversion costs.
4. All materials are added at the beginning of the process.

Required a. Compute the equivalent production for:
   (1) Transferred in from preceding department.
   (2) Materials.
   (3) Conversion costs.
b. Compute the unit costs for:
   (1) Transferred in from preceding department.
   (2) Materials.
   (3) Conversion costs.
c. Compute the cost of the goods completed and transferred to finished goods.
d. Compute the cost of the ending work in process, showing the costs separately for transferred-in costs, materials, and conversion costs.

E6–7 **Average Costing for a Second Department**

The Harbus Company uses weighted-average process costing and provides you with the following information for the month of April 19x7:

1. The finishing department is the last stage of the production process. At the beginning of April 19x7, the company had 18,000 units in its beginning inventory. These units had accumulated costs as follows:

Transferred-in costs $74,920
Materials—this department. 10,930
Conversion—this department. 8,640

2. During the month, the preceding department transferred in 28,000 units at a cost of $121,500. The finishing department incurred $15,750 of additional materials costs and $13,500 of conversion costs on these units.
3. The ending inventory consisted of 10,000 units that were 50 percent complete as to conversion costs.
4. All materials are added at the beginning of the process.

Required a. Compute the equivalent production for:
   (1) Transferred in from preceding department.
   (2) Materials.
   (3) Conversion costs.
b. Compute the unit costs for:
   (1) Transferred in from preceding department.
   (2) Materials.
   (3) Conversion costs.
c. Compute the cost of the goods completed and transferred to finished goods.
d. Compute the cost of the ending work in process, showing the costs separately for transferred-in costs, materials, and conversion costs.

E6–8 **Computations from Data—Average Costing**

Tasty Breadstick Company uses a process costing system and uses average costing for its cost accounting records. For the month of March 19x3, the company's cost of production report showed the following costs:

	Work in Process	Costs This Period	Total Cost	Unit Cost
Materials.	$3,850	$29,270	$33,120	$ .552
Conversion costs	6,700	66,308	73,008	1.352

The following additional information is available.

1. The number of units completed and transferred to finished goods was 45,000 cases.
2. All materials are added at the beginning of the process.
3. There was no work in process at the beginning of the month.

Required   *a.* How many units are in the ending work in process inventory?
b. What is the stage of completion for conversion costs?
c. What are the equivalent units for conversion costs?
d. Complete the following:
(1) The costs of goods completed and transferred out.
(2) The cost of the ending work in process inventory.

E6–9   **Computations from Data—Average Costing**

Eatclean China Company uses a process costing system and average costing for its cost accounting records. For the month of March 19x3, the company's cost of production report showed the following costs:

	Work in Process	Costs This Period	Total Cost	Unit Cost
Materials	$33,080	$176,920	$210,000	$ 8.40
Conversion costs	81,000	358,344	439,344	19.44

The following additional information is available.

1. The number of units completed and transferred to finished goods was 17,000 sets of china.
2. All materials are added at the beginning of the process.
3. There was no work in process at the beginning of the month.

Required   *a.* How many units are in the ending work in process inventory?
b. What is the stage of completion for conversion costs?
c. What are the equivalent units for conversion costs?
d. Compute the following:
(1) The costs of goods completed and transferred out.
(2) The cost of the ending work in process inventory.

E6–10   **(Appendix 6-A) Computation of FIFO Equivalent Units**

1. On November 1, 19x7, Yankee Company had 20,000 units of work in process in Department 1 that were 100 percent complete as to material costs and 20 percent complete as to conversion costs. During November, 160,000 units were started in Department 1, and 170,000 units were completed and transferred to Department 2. The work in process on November 30, 19x7, was 100 percent complete as to material costs and 40 percent complete as to conversion costs. By what amount would the equivalent units for conversion costs for the month of November differ if the first-in, first-out (FIFO) method were used instead of the weighted-average method?
a. 20,000 decrease.
b. 16,000 decrease.
c. 8,000 decrease.
d. 4,000 decrease.

2. A company uses the FIFO method of costing in a process costing system. Material is added at the beginning of the process in Department A, and conversion costs are incurred uniformly throughout the process. Beginning work in process inventory on April 1 in Department A consisted of 50,000 units estimated to be 30 percent complete. During April, 150,000 units were started in Department A, and 160,000 units were completed and transferred to Department B. Ending work in process inventory on April 30 in Department A was estimated to be 20 percent complete. What were the total equivalent units in Department A for April for materials and conversion costs, respectively?
   a. 150,000 and 133,000.
   b. 150,000 and 153,000.
   c. 200,000 and 133,000.
   d. 200,000 and 153,000.

3. Department 1 is the first stage of Drucker Company's production cycle. The following information is available for conversion costs for the month of April:

	Units
Work in process, beginning (40% complete)	40,000
Started in April	320,000
Completed in April and transferred to Department 2	340,000
Work in process, ending (60% complete)	20,000

Using the FIFO method, the equivalent units for the conversion cost calculation are
   a. 320,000.
   b. 336,000.
   c. 352,000.
   d. 360,000.

(AICPA Adapted)

E6–11 (Appendix 6-A) Computation of FIFO Equivalent Units

The Olds Corporation had 24,000 units in its work in process inventory at the beginning of September 19x3. These units were 40 percent complete as to conversion costs. During September, the company completed 60,000 units; it also had 30,000 units in its work in process at the end of September. These units were 60 percent complete as to conversion costs. All materials are added at the beginning of the production process. The company uses FIFO process costing for its cost accounting.

Required a. Compute the following:
   (1) Equivalent units for materials for the month of September.
   (2) Equivalent units for conversion costs for the month of September.
   b. How many units were started in September?

E6–12 (Appendix 6-A) FIFO Costing for a First Department

The Morrow Company uses FIFO process costing and provides you with the following information for the month of July 19x4:

	Materials	Conversion
Work in process, beginning	$14,400	$13,200
Current costs	72,000	85,800
Total costs	$86,400	$99,000

All materials are added at the beginning of the process. During the month of July, 25,000 were completed and transferred to finished goods; 15,000 units were in the work in process inventory at the end of July. These units were 50 percent complete as to conversion costs. The beginning inventory consisted of 6,250 units that were 80 percent complete as to conversion costs.

Required
a. Compute the cost of the goods completed and transferred to finished goods.
b. Compute the cost of the ending work in process, showing the costs separately for materials and conversion costs.
c. Compare your totals from parts (a) and (b) with the information given to prove the accuracy of your computations.

E6–13 (Appendix 6-B) Equivalent Units with Lost and Spoiled Units— Average Costing

1. *Materials are added at the start of the process* in Cedar Company's blending department, the first stage of the production cycle. The following information is available for the month of July 19x1:

	Units
Work in process, July 1 (60% complete as to conversion costs)	60,000
Started in July	150,000
Transferred to the next department	110,000
Lost in production	30,000
Work in process, July 31 (50% complete as to conversion costs)	70,000

Under Cedar's cost accounting system, the costs incurred on the lost units are absorbed by the remaining good units. Using the weighted-average method, what are the equivalent units for the materials unit cost calculation?
a. 120,000.
b. 145,000.
c. 180,000.
d. 210,000.

2. Tooker Company adds materials at the *beginning* of the process in Department A. Information concerning the materials used in April 19x2 production is as follows:

	Units
Work in process at April 1	10,000
Started during April	50,000
Completed and transferred to next department during April	36,000
Normal spoilage incurred	3,000
Abnormal spoilage incurred	5,000
Work in process at April 30	16,000

Under Tooker's cost accounting system, costs of normal spoilage are treated as a part of the costs of the good units produced. However, the costs of abnormal spoilage are charged to a loss account. Using the weighted-average method, what are the equivalent units for the materials unit cost calculation for the month of April?

a. 47,000.

b. 52,000.

c. 55,000.

d. 57,000.

3. Milton, Inc., had 8,000 units of work in process in Department M on March 1, 19x0, that were 50 percent complete as to conversion costs. Materials are introduced at the beginning of the process. During March, 17,000 units were started, 18,000 units were completed, and there were 2,000 units of normal spoilage. Milton had 5,000 units of work in process at March 31, 19x0, that were 60 percent complete as to conversion costs. Under Milton's cost accounting system, spoiled units reduce the number of units over which total costs can be spread. Using the weighted-average method, the equivalent units for March for conversion costs were

a. 17,000.

b. 19,000.

c. 21,000.

d. 23,000.

4. Read, Inc., instituted a new process in October 19x7. During October, 10,000 units were started in Department A. Of the units started, 1,000 were lost in the process, 7,000 were transferred to Department B, and 2,000 remained in work in process at October 31, 19x7. The work in process at October 31, 19x7, was 100 percent complete as to material costs and 50 percent complete as to conversion costs. Material costs of $27,000 and conversion costs of $40,000 were charged to Department A in October. What were the total costs transferred to Department B?

a. $46,900.

b. $53,600.

c. $56,000.

d. $57,120.

(AICPA Adapted)

E6–14   **(Appendix 6-B) Average Costing for a Third Department**

The following data apply to items 1 through 5.

JC Company employs a process cost system. A unit of product passes through three departments—molding, assembly, and finishing—before it is completed.

The following activity took place in the finishing department during May:

	Units
Work in process inventory, May 1	1,400
Units transferred in from the assembly department	14,000
Units spoiled	700
Units transferred out to finished goods inventory	11,200

Direct material is added at the beginning of the processing in the finishing department without changing the number of units being processed. The work in process inventory was 70 percent complete as to conversion on May 1 and 40 percent complete as to conversion on May 31. All spoilage was discovered at final inspection before the units were transferred to finished goods; 560 of the units spoiled were within the limit considered normal.

JC Company employs the weighted-average costing method. The equivalent units and the current costs per equivalent unit of production for each cost factor are as follows:

	Equivalent Units	Current Costs per Equivalent Unit
Cost of prior departments	15,400	$5
Direct materials	15,400	1
Conversion cost	13,300	3
Total		$9

1. The cost of production transferred to the finished goods inventory is
   a. $100,800.
   b. $105,840.
   c. $107,100.
   d. $102,060.
   e. Some amount other than those given above.
2. The cost assigned to the work in process inventory on May 31 is
   a. $28,000.
   b. $31,000.
   c. $25,200.
   d. $30,240.
   e. Some amount other than those given above.
3. If the total costs of prior departments included in the work in process inventory of the finishing department on May 1 amounted to $6,300, the total cost transferred in from the assembly department to the finishing department during May is
   a. $70,000.
   b. $62,300.
   c. $70,700.
   d. $63,700.
   e. Some amount other than those given above.
4. The cost associated with the abnormal spoilage is
   a. $6,300.
   b. $1,260.
   c. $560.
   d. $840.
   e. Some amount other than those given above.
5. The cost associated with abnormal spoilage ordinarily would be
   a. Charged to inventory.
   b. Charged to a material variance account.
   c. Charged to retained earnings.
   d. Charged to manufacturing overhead.
   e. Charged to a special loss account.

(CMA Adapted)

▶ **PROBLEMS**   P6–15   **Average Production Report for a First Department—No Beginning Inventory**

The Lumbar Company had the following transactions for the month of January 19x1 in its only processing department:

Costs incurred:

Materials	$310,000
Direct labor	357,000
Overhead	392,700
Total	$1,059,700

Production:

Started new	80,000	
Completed and transferred . . .	60,000	
Ending work in process	20,000	(100% materials; 40% labor and overhead)

Required   *a.* Prepare a production report.

b. Prepare the journal entries to record the issuance of materials, direct labor, applied overhead, and finished goods.

P6–16   **Average Production Report for Two Departments—No Beginning Inventory**

The Miramar Company had the following transactions for the month of January 19x2 in its two departments:

	Cutting	Finishing
Costs incurred:		
Materials	$337,500	$ 41,000
Direct labor	316,250	139,200
Overhead	253,000	125,280
Total	$906,750	$305,480
Production:		
Started new	100,000	
Completed and transferred	80,000	64,000
Ending work in process	20,000	(100% materials; 60% labor and overhead)
	16,000	(100% materials; 80% conversion)

Required   *a.* Prepare a production report.

b. Prepare all of the implicit journal entries for both departments, assuming overhead is applied to production on the basis of direct labor cost.

P6–17   **Average Production Report for a First Department—Beginning Inventory**

The Necknar Company's production process is limited to one department. For the month of March 19x4, the company incurred the following costs:

Direct materials	$292,700
Direct labor	315,760
Overhead	347,336
Total	$955,796

The beginning inventory on March 1, 19x4, amounted to:

Direct materials	$ 38,500
Direct labor	32,000
Overhead	35,200
Total	$105,700

The quantity of production statistics for the month of March 19x4 are as follows:

Beginning inventory 7,000
Started new 53,000
Transferred out 45,000
Ending inventory 15,000   (100% materials; 60% conversion)

Required   *a.* Prepare a production report using average costing. (Combine labor and overhead into conversion cost.)

b. Prepare all journal entries to record:
  (1) The issuance of direct materials.
  (2) The direct labor.

P6-18 Average Production Report for the First Department—Beginning Inventory

Collard Company's production process is limited to one department. For the month of March 19x2, the company incurred the following costs:

Direct materials . . . . . $ 51,400
Direct labor 20,100
Overhead 34,200
     Total $105,700

The beginning inventory on March 1, 19x2, amounted to:

Direct materials . . . . . $ 6,400
Direct labor 9,300
Overhead 8,800
     Total $24,500

The quantity production statistics for the month of March 19x2 are as follows:

Beginning inventory 2,100
Started new 4,800
Transferred out 4,200
Ending inventory 2,700   (100% materials; 70% conversion)

Required   *a.* Prepare a production report using average costing. (Combine labor and overhead into conversion cost.)

b. Prepare all journal entries to record:
  (1) The issuance of direct materials.
  (2) The direct labor.
  (3) The applied overhead.
  (4) Finished goods.

P6-19 Average Production Report for a First Department—No Beginning Inventory

Solare Company had the following transactions for the month of January 19x2 in its only processing department:

Costs incurred:
  Materials . . . . $ 28,400
  Direct labor 79,100
  Overhead 71,500
     Total $179,000

Production:
  Started new 39,900
  Completed and transferred 25,000
  Ending work in process . . 14,900   (100% materials; 80% labor and overhead)

Required   a. Prepare a production report.

b. Prepare the journal entries to record the issuance of materials, direct labor, applied overhead, and finished goods.

P6–20   **Average Production Report for Two Departments—No Beginning Inventory**

Handare Company had the following transactions for the month of January 19x3 in its two departments:

	Cutting	Finishing
Costs incurred:		
Materials.	$11,400	$11,100
Direct labor	28,500	12,100
Overhead	49,700	14,500
Total	$89,600	$37,700
Production:		
Started new	99,500	
Completed and transferred.	84,300	80,000
Ending work in process	15,200ᵃ	4,300ᵇ

a. 100% materials; 50% labor and overhead.
b. 100% materials; 60% conversion.

Required   a. Prepare a production report.

b. Prepare all of the implicit journal entries for both departments assuming that overhead is applied to production on the basis of direct labor cost.

P6–21   **Average Production Report for the First Department—Beginning Inventory**

Iggle Company's production process is limited to one department. For the month of March 19x2, the company incurred the following costs:

Direct materials.	$ 516,000
Direct labor	832,000
Overhead.	420,000
Total.	$1,768,000

The beginning inventory on March 1, 19x2, amounted to:

Direct materials.	$ 46,700
Direct labor	35,900
Overhead.	68,600
Total.	$151,200

The quantity production statistics for the month of March 19x2 are as follows:

Beginning inventory.	6,000
Started new	44,000
Transferred out	42,000
Ending inventory	8,000ᵃ

a. 100% materials; 60% conversion.

Required   a. Prepare a production report using average costing. (Combine labor and overhead into conversion cost.)

b. Prepare all journal entries to record:

(1) The issuance of direct materials.
(2) The direct labor.
(3) The applied overhead.
(4) Finished goods.

P6–22 **Average Production Report for Two Departments—No Beginning Inventory**

Whyte Company had the following transactions for the month of January 19x3 in its two departments:

	Cutting	Finishing
Costs incurred:		
Materials.	$ 280,000	$ 71,900
Direct labor	720,000	165,000
Overhead	938,000	140,000
Totals	$1,938,000	$376,900
Production:		
Started new	21,000	
Completed and transferred.	15,500	12,250
Ending work in process	5,500[a]	3,250[b]

a. 100% materials; 50% labor and overhead.
b. 100% materials; 75% conversion.

Required a. Prepare a production report.
b. Prepare all of the implicit journal entries for both departments assuming that overhead is applied to production on the basis of direct labor cost.

P6–23 **Average Production Report for Two Departments—Beginning Inventory**

Rowe Company has two departments, mixing and coloring. For the month of March 19x2, the company incurred the following costs:

	Mixing	Coloring
Direct materials.	$ 348,000	$ 20,400
Direct labor	364,000	40,800
Overhead.	767,000	87,800
Totals	$1,479,000	$149,000

The beginning inventory on March 1, 19x2, amounted to:

	Mixing	Coloring
Cost in preceding department	$ –0–	$78,000
Direct materials	37,210	3,350
Direct labor.	25,550	1,050
Overhead.	53,830	2,290
Totals	$116,590	$84,690

The quantity of production statistics for the month of March 19x2 are as follows:

	Mixing	Coloring
Beginning inventory.	3,000	4,000
Started new	27,000	–0–
Transferred in	–0–	22,000
Transferred out	22,000	20,000
Ending inventory	8,000[a]	6,000[b]

a. 100% materials; 50% conversion.
b. 100% materials; 60% conversion.

Required   *a.* Prepare a production report using average costing. (Combine labor and overhead into conversion cost.)

   b. Prepare all journal entries to record:
   (1) The issuance of direct materials.
   (2) The direct labor.
   (3) The applied overhead.
   (4) Finished goods.

P6–24   **Average Production Report for Two Departments—Beginning Inventory**

The Oar Company has two departments, mixing and coloring. For the month of March 19x4, the company incurred the following costs:

	Mixing	Coloring
Direct materials.	$146,350	$ 25,000
Direct labor	157,880	285,200
Overhead.	189,456	228,160
Totals	$493,686	$538,360

The beginning inventory on March 1, 19x4, amounted to:

	Mixing	Coloring
Cost in preceding department.	$ –0–	$78,000
Direct materials	$15,650	4,120
Direct labor.	11,080	7,440
Overhead.	13,296	5,952
Total.	$40,026	$95,512

The quantity of production statistics for the month of March 19x4 are as follows:

	Mixing	Coloring	
Beginning inventory.	1,500	2,000	
Started new	13,500	–0–	
Transferred in	–0–	11,000	
Transferred out	11,000	10,000	
Ending inventory	4,000		(100% materials; 60% conversion)
		3,000	(100% materials; 40% conversion)

Required   *a.* Prepare a production report using average costing. (Combine labor and overhead into conversion cost).

   b. Prepare all journal entries to record:
   (1) The issuance of direct materials.
   (2) The direct labor.
   (3) The applied overhead.
   (4) Finished goods.

P6–25   **Average Production Report for a Second Department—Beginning Inventory**

Lakeview Corporation is a manufacturer that uses the weighted-average process cost method to account for costs of production. Lakeview manufactures a product that is produced in three separate departments: molding, assembling, and finishing. The following information was obtained for the assembling department for the month of June 19x0:

Work in process, June 1—2,000 units composed of the following:

	Amount	Degree of Completion
Transferred in from the molding department	$32,000	100%
Costs added by the assembling department:		
Direct materials	$20,000	100
Direct labor	7,200	60
Factory overhead applied	5,500	50
	32,700	
Work in process, June 1.	$64,700	

The following activity occurred during the month of June:

1. 10,000 units were transferred in from the molding department at a cost of $160,000.
2. $150,000 of costs were added by the assembling department:

Direct materials	$ 96,000
Direct labor	36,000
Factory overhead applied	18,000
Total	$150,000

3. 8,000 units were completed and transferred to the finishing department.

At June 30, 4,000 units were still in work in process. The degree of completion of work in process at June 30 was as follows:

Direct materials	90%
Direct labor	70
Factory overhead applied	35

Required Prepare in good form a production report for the assembling department for the month of June. Show supporting computations in good form. The report should include:

a. Equivalent units of production.
b. Total manufacturing costs.
c. Cost per equivalent unit.
d. Dollar amount of ending work in process.
e. Dollar amount of inventory cost transferred out.

(AICPA Adapted)

P6–26 · **Average Production Report for a Single Department—Compared to Book Inventory**

You are engaged in the audit of the December 31, 19x8, financial statements of Spirit Corporation, a digital watch manufacturer. You are attempting to verify the costing of the ending inventory of work in process and finished goods, which were recorded on Spirit's books as follows:

	Units	Cost
Work in process (50% complete as to labor and overhead)	300,000	$ 660,960
Finished goods	200,000	$1,009,800

Materials are added to production at the beginning of the manufacturing process, and overhead is applied to each product at the rate of 60 percent of direct labor costs. There was no finished goods inventory on January 1, 19x8. A review of Spirit's inventory cost records disclosed the following information:

			Costs	
	Units	Materials	Labor
Work in process January 1, 19x8 (80% complete as to labor and overhead)	200,000	$ 200,000	$ 315,000
Units started in production:	1,000,000		
Material costs		$1,300,000	
Labor costs			$1,995,000
Units completed	900,000		

Required *a.* Prepare schedules as of December 31, 19x8, to compute the following:
(1) Equivalent units of production using the weighted-average method.
(2) Unit costs of production of materials, labor, and overhead.
(3) Costing of the finished goods inventory and work in process inventory.
b. Prepare the necessary journal entry to correctly state the inventory of finished goods and work in process, assuming the books have not been closed.

(AICPA Adapted)

P6–27 **(Appendix 6-A) FIFO Production Report for a Single Department**

The Rosar Company has a single-stage production process. You, the company's cost accountant, are provided with the following information for the purpose of preparing a cost of production report.

Costs for the month of April 19x5 were:

Direct materials	$292,560
Direct labor	313,480
Overhead	344,828
Total	$950,868

The costs of the beginning inventory are:

Direct materials	$ 38,500
Direct labor	32,000
Overhead	35,200
Total	$105,700

The production statistics for April 19x5 were:

> Beginning work in process:
>   Materials—7,000 units 100% complete
>   Conversion—7,000 units 70% complete
> Started new—53,000 units
> Ending work in process:
>   Materials—15,000 units 100% complete
>   Conversion—15,000 units 40% complete
> There were no lost units or increased units.

Required *a.* Prepare a production report using FIFO costing. (Combine labor and overhead into conversion cost.)

b. Prepare all journal entries to record:
   (1) The issuance of direct materials.
   (2) The direct labor.
   (3) The applied overhead.
   (4) Finished goods.

P6–28 **(Appendix 6-A) FIFO Production Report for a First Department**

Claudetta Company has a single-stage production process. You are the company's cost accountant, and you are provided with the following information for the purpose of preparing a cost of production report.

Costs for the month of April 19x2 were:

Direct materials.	$284,000
Direct labor	240,000
Overhead.	408,000
Total.	$932,000

The costs of the beginning inventory are:

Direct materials.	$ 37,300
Direct labor	24,500
Overhead.	41,600
Total.	$103,400

The production statistics for April 19x2 were:

> Beginning work in process:
>   Materials—9,000 units 100% complete
>   Conversion—9,000 units 70% complete
>   Started new—71,000 units
> Ending work in process:
>   Materials—20,000 units 100% complete
>   Conversion—20,000 units 40% complete

There were no lost units or increased units.

Required *a.* Prepare a production report using FIFO costing. (Combine labor and overhead into conversion cost.)

b. Prepare all journal entries to record:
   (1) The issuance of direct materials.
   (2) The direct labor.
   (3) The applied overhead.
   (4) Finished goods.

P6–29 **(Appendix 6-A) FIFO Production Report for One Department**

Rowe Company has one department. For the month of March 19x4, the company incurred the following costs:

Direct materials.	$ 348,000
Direct labor	364,000
Overhead.	767,000
Total.	$1,479,000

The beginning inventory on March 1, 19x4, amounted to:

Direct materials.	$ 37,210
Direct labor	25,550
Overhead.	53,830
Total.	$116,590

The quantity production statistics for the month of March 19x4 are as follows:

Beginning inventory	3,000	(100% materials; 50% conversion)
Started new	27,000	
Transferred out	22,000	
Ending inventory	8,000	(100% materials; 70% conversion)

Required *a.* Prepare a production report.
b. Prepare all journal entries to record:
   (1) The issuance of direct materials.
   (2) The direct labor.
   (3) The applied overhead.
   (4) The transfer to finished goods.

P6–30 **(Appendix 6-A) FIFO Production Report for a Second Department**

Pinkette Company has two departments, a stripping department and a finishing department. For the month of March 19x2, the finishing department incurred the following costs:

Transferred-in cost	$ 177,900
Direct materials	217,700
Direct labor	363,800
Overhead	526,500
Total	$1,285,900

The beginning inventory on March 1, 19x2, amounted to:

Cost in preceding department	$ 43,550
Direct materials	53,510
Direct labor.	55,310
Overhead.	80,050
Total.	$232,420

The quantity production statistics for the month of March 19x2 are as follows:

Beginning inventory	8,000	(100% materials; 70% conversion)
Transferred in	32,000	
Transferred out	30,400	
Ending inventory	9,600	(100% materials; 50% conversion)

Required   *a.* Prepare a production report.

         b. Prepare all journal entries to record:

           (1) The issuance of direct materials.

           (2) The direct labor.

           (3) The applied overhead.

           (4) The transfer to finished goods.

P6–31   **(Appendix 6-B) Average Production Report—Normal Spoilage and Lost Units**

Rallip Company operates a single-process manufacturing firm. For the month of March 19x4, the company incurred the following costs:

Direct materials.	$ 68,200
Direct labor	15,500
Overhead.	55,700
Total.	$139,400

The beginning inventory on March 1, 19x4, amounted to:

Direct materials.	$ 9,500
Direct labor	1,270
Overhead.	4,560
Total.	$15,330

The quantity production statistics for the month of March 19x4 are as follows:

Beginning inventory	3,500	
Started new	26,400	
Transferred out	21,100	
Ending inventory	7,100	(100% materials; 50% conversion)
Lost units—normal	?	

The lost units—all considered normal—occur evenly throughout the production cycle. The company uses the method of neglect to account for them.

Required   *a.* Prepare a production report using average costing.

         b. Prepare journal entries to record the issuance of materials, direct labor, applied overhead, and the transfer to finished goods.

P6–32   **(Appendix 6-B) Average Production Report for a Second Department—Normal Spoilage**

Falstar Company has two departments, mixing and coloring. For the month of March 19x2, the company incurred the following costs:

	Coloring
Direct materials.	$ 661,000
Direct labor	822,000
Overhead.	811,000
Total.	$2,294,000

The beginning inventory on March 1, 19x2, amounted to:

	Coloring
Cost in preceding department	$ 40,200
Direct materials	80,900
Direct labor.	82,200
Overhead.	81,100
Total	$284,400

The quantity production statistics for the month of March 19x2 are as follows:

Coloring

Beginning inventory	11,250
Transferred in	78,750
Transferred out	67,500
Ending inventory.	18,000 (100% materials; 50% conversion)
Lost units—all normal	?

The mixing department costs for the 78,750 units transferred in amounted to $277,000. The company uses the method of neglect to account for normal spoilage.

Required   Prepare a production report using average costing. (Combine labor and overhead into conversion cost.)

P6–33   **(Appendix 6-B) Average Production Report for a Single Department— with Spoilage**

West Corporation is a divisionalized manufacturing company. A product called Aggregate is manufactured in one department of the California division. Aggregate is transferred on completion at a predetermined price to the Utah division, where it is used in the manufacture of other products.

The direct material is added at the beginning of the process. Labor and overhead are added continuously throughout the process. Shrinkage of 10 to 14 percent, all occurring at the beginning of the process, is considered normal. In the California division, all departmental overhead is charged to the departments, and divisional overhead is allocated to the departments on the basis of direct labor-hours. The divisional overhead rate for 19x9 is $2 per direct labor-hour.

The following information relates to production during November 19x9:

Work in process, November 1 (4,000 pounds—75% complete):
Direct material	$22,800
Direct labor at $5 per hour	24,650
Departmental overhead	12,000
Divisional overhead.	9,860

Direct material:
Inventory, November 1 (2,000 pounds)	$10,000
Purchases, November 3 (10,000 pounds)	51,000
Purchases, November 18 (10,000 pounds)	51,500
Released to production during November (16,000 pounds)	

Direct labor costs at $5 per hour ($103,350)
Direct departmental overhead costs ($52,000)
Transferred to Utah division (15,000 pounds)
Work in process, November 30 (3,000 pounds, 33⅓% complete)

The FIFO method is used for materials inventory valuation, and the weighted-average method is used for work in process inventories.

Required   Prepare a production report for the department of the California division producing Aggregate for November 19x9 that presents:

a. The equivalent units of production by cost factor of Aggregate (e.g., direct material, direct labor, and overhead).
b. The equivalent unit costs for each cost factor of Aggregate.
c. The cost of Aggregate transferred to the Utah division.
d. The cost of abnormal shrinkage, if any.
e. The cost of the work in process inventory at November 30, 19x9.

(CMA Adapted)

▶ **CASE** C6–34 **Explanation of Difference in Weighted Average and FIFO Costing**

Forbes Company is presently using an informal cost accounting approach. It is considering the adoption of a process cost accounting system, but the company is unsure whether to use a weighted-average approach or to use FIFO. The firm's bookkeeper is somewhat familiar with process cost accounting, and he has heard that the cost results using either approach are nearly the same. The company is wondering whether or not it is worth the extra effort to adopt FIFO costing. The following information is available for the month of May 19x2:

1. The company's production process is limited to one department. All materials are added at the beginning of the process. During the current month, the following costs were incurred:

Direct materials.	$ 556,500
Direct labor	712,050
Overhead.	854,460
Total.	$2,123,010

2. The beginning inventory on May 1, 19x2, amounted to:

Direct materials.	$ 57,750
Direct labor	42,000
Overhead.	50,400
Total.	$150,150

3. The quantity production statistics for the month of May 19x2 are as follows:

Beginning inventory.	10,500	(100% materials; 60% conversion)
Started new	79,500	
Transferred out.	67,500	
Ending inventory	22,500	(100% materials; 50% conversion)

Required
a. Prepare a production report using average costing.
b. Prepare a production report using FIFO costing.
c. Write a brief report explaining any significant cost differences between the two methods. Do you think the firm should use average costing or FIFO costing? Why?

▶ **ANSWERS TO SELF-TEST**

True or False

1. False 2. True 3. False 4. False 5. False 6. True
7. False 8. False 9. False 10. True

Multiple Choice

1. *c.* Fabrication = 300 × 1/3 = 100
      Assembly   =   1,000
      Packaging =   100
      Shipping   =   400
                        1,600

2. *a.* Fabrication = 300 × 1/2 = 150
      Assembly   =   1,000
      Packaging =   100
      Shipping   =   400
                        1,650

3. *b.* Packaging = 100 × ¾ =   75
      Shipping   =   400
                              ───
                              475
                              ═══

4. *d.* Completed and transferred   4,000
      Work in process (2,000 × 100%)   2,000
                                       ─────
         Equivalent units   6,000
                                       ═════

5. *d.* Completed and transferred   4,000
      Work in process (2,000 × 20%)   400
                                        ─────
         Equivalent units   4,400
                                        ═════

CHAPTER ▶ 7

Cost Accounting for the New Manufacturing Environment

▶ **LEARNING OBJECTIVES**

After reading this chapter, you should be able to:

1. Differentiate between a traditional plant layout and a just-in-time plant layout.
2. Distinguish the traditional manner of applying manufacturing overhead to production from the manner in which it is applied when activity-based costing is used.
3. List the various kinds of cost drivers that are available to users of activity-based costing.
4. Explain the two-stage process of applying overhead to production for both the traditional method and the activity-based costing method.
5. Describe nonvalue-added costs and how they may be eliminated.
6. Explain what is meant by a just-in-time philosophy and what conditions must exist for it to function effectively.
7. Discuss why a flexible manufacturing system is more efficient than a traditional manufacturing system.

▶ **INTERVIEW**

Wayne G. Bremser
Professor of Accountancy
Villanova University

Q. *How do you explain the just-in-time philosophy to your students?*

A. Just-in-time philosophy represents the current trends used in modern factories. Companies coordinate manufacturing by raw materials processed through in small batches. A just-in-time philosophy focuses on quality control and emphasizes zero or small inventories. Goods are delivered to the customer as soon as they are finished and inventories are eliminated. Thus, high costs are eliminated because expenses for maintaining inventories are avoided.

Q. *Why is it important to explain the just-in-time philosophy to students?*

A. Modern factories are undergoing a great change. The JIT philosophy represents the latest ideas in modern manufacturing. Manufacturers have accepted the belief that work sells. Workers are now more skilled and play a large role in efficient manufacturing. Understanding the concepts of JIT helps students see how cost ties in to manufacturing. The traditional plant layout is still in existence. The just-in-time philosophy is more competitive and efficient than traditional approaches to manufacturing.

▶ As manufacturing firms have matured, new manufacturing technologies have emerged over the past several decades. This has led to radical changes in manufacturing operations. As firms increased the variety of products manufactured, the changes in manufacturing operations did not shift merely from labor-intensive operations to machine-intensive operations but also to the use of computers and robots to create a highly automated manufacturing environment. This shift has necessitated a new kind of plant layout using a flexible manufacturing system (FMS) to accommodate computer-assisted manufacturing (CAM). It has been necessary to refine the methods of assigning overhead to production to achieve more accurate cost information. As the number of factory workers employed by these manufacturing firms decreased over the past few decades, the traditional method of using labor-hours or labor cost as an overhead base began producing severe distortions of cost information. Prior to these changes in the work force, direct-labor costs were often the principal cost of manufacturing a product; today, direct-labor costs have diminished in importance as a factor of a product's cost. In fact, in some manufacturing operations direct labor ranges between 5 and 10 percent of the total manufacturing cost, overhead is somewhere around 40 percent, and direct materials account for about 50 percent.[1] Firms that used CAM found that assigning overhead to production based on an activity provided better cost information for decision making. It then became necessary to analyze how overhead was incurred, resulting in overhead being assigned to production through the use of a base called a *cost driver.*

The Japanese have been pacesetters in automated production facilities and quality control. One has merely to examine the inroads into the U.S. economy that the Japanese have made, especially in the electronics, automative, and photographic industries, to conclude that Japanese manufacturing methods must be reckoned with if one is to remain competitive in the marketplace. The Japanese have pioneered a manufacturing technique that minimizes the amount, if any, of inventories carried on hand. This technique is known as just-in-time (JIT) inventory control. ◀

Traditional Plant Layout

L.O. 1

Traditional plant layouts usually group similar activities so that these similar activities are all performed in one department. In a simple example, direct materials are received and placed into a centralized stockroom. When materials are entered into production, they must first be moved into the initial department—possibly a cutting department. Once the direct materials are cut to size, they are again moved to the next department—possibly a machining department. From there, they must again be moved to the next department—possibly a finishing department—and so on, until they become finished goods at which time they are moved to the finished goods stockroom. A simplified plant layout in the traditional format appears in Illustration 7-1.

In some manufacturing operations, the movement of direct materials through the production cycle may entail movement motion of a mile or more. Many plant managers fail to grasp the concept that moving direct materials, work in process, and finished goods incurs cost but does not add value to the product. In a later section of this chapter, we consider value-added costs and nonvalue-added costs.

[1] Robert Capettini and Donald K. Clancy, eds., *Cost Accounting, Robotics, and the New Manufacturing Environment.* (Sarasota, Fla.: American Accounting Association, 1987), p. 8.9.

▶ **ILLUSTRATION 7-1**   Traditional Plant Layout

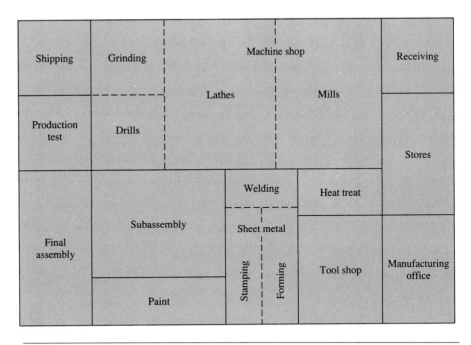

SOURCE: Robert Capettini and Donald K. Clancy, eds., *Cost Accounting, Robotics, and the New Manufacturing Environment* (Sarasota, Fla.: American Accounting Association, 1987), p. 6.3.

Traditional Application of Overhead

L.O. 2

Firms that Manufacture a Single Product   When a firm manufactures a single product, overhead allocation problems are minimized. If the cost objective is the firm's product, overhead cost allocations are not needed since all overhead costs are direct costs. Thus, overhead costs are traceable to the firm's product cost in a manner similar to direct materials and direct labor. Of course, instead of using actual overhead costs for product costing, a firm may still choose to apply overhead to production through the use of normal costing because of the seasonal fluctuations of overhead. Seasonal fluctuations of overhead were discussed in Chapter 5.

Multiproduct Firms   When a firm produces more than one product, overhead allocation becomes a necessity when product cost information is desired. Using a single plant-wide predetermined overhead rate to apply overhead would most likely provide managers with product costs that are distorted. As firms increase in size and diversify their product lines, they may produce hundreds of different products. For these firms, severe distortions of overhead allocation are likely to be encountered by using a single overhead rate. One method to improve overhead allocation procedures is to departmentalize overhead allocations and to use different overhead rates for labor-intensive and machine-intensive departments. These procedures are discussed in the next chapter, Chapter 8. However, when firms are highly automated, even labor-intensive and machine-intensive departmentalization of overhead is inadequate to arrive at proper product cost information.

▶ **ILLUSTRATION 7-2**   Compusmart Company—Volume and Cost Data

	Product X	Product Y	Product Z
Production:			
Units	20,000	30,000	12,000
Number of runs	2 runs of 10,000 each	6 runs of 5,000 each	12 runs of 1,000 each
Manufacturing costs:			
Direct materials	$30	$40	$10
Direct labor—per unit*	¼ hour	½ hour	⅓ hour

* Direct labor has a cost of $24 per hour including fringe benefits.

▶ **ILLUSTRATION 7-3**   Unit Cost Information

	Product X	Product Y	Product Z
Direct material	$30	$ 40	$10
Direct labor:			
¼ hour at $24	6		
½ hour at $24		12	
⅓ hour at $24			8
Manufacturing overhead (Applied on a basis direct labor cost)*	24	48	32
Total	$60	$100	$50

Predetermined overhead rate:

$$\frac{\text{Total overhead}}{\text{Budgeted direct labor cost}} = \frac{\$2,303,840}{\$576,000} = 400\%$$

* Budgeted direct labor cost:
Product X—20,000 units × $ 6 = $120,000
Product Y—30,000 units × $12 = 360,000
Product Z—12,000 units × $ 8 = 96,000
Total budgeted direct labor cost $576,000

Let us now consider an example[2] of the traditional approach to costing that is based on assigning overhead to products on a volume-based approach *(throughput)*, such as direct labor cost or direct labor-hours. **Throughput** is the volume of activity or production in a firm's facility, such as a factory, a department, or a machine. Compusmart Company manufactures three products, X, Y, and Z. Sales and volume data for the three products are shown in Illustration 7-2. The target selling price is computed by multiplying the product's normal cost by 150 percent.

For our present use of traditional overhead costing, it is assumed that Compusmart Company does not departmentalize overhead. Accordingly, only one overhead pool for the year is used, and it is estimated at $2,303,840. The unit cost information of Compusmart's three products appears in Illustration 7-3. Profitability information for the three products is shown in Illus-

[2] This example is based on two works by John K. Shank and Vijay Govindarajan, "The Perils of Cost Allocation Based on Production Volumes," *Accounting Horizons,* December 1988, pp. 71–79; and *Strategic Cost Analysis* (Homewood, Ill.: Richard D. Irwin, 1989), pp. 60–75.

► **ILLUSTRATION 7-4**   Compusmart's Profitability Data

	Product X	Product Y	Product Z
Normal unit cost	$60.00	$100.00	$ 50.00
Targeted selling price	$90.00	$150.00	$ 75.00
Planned gross profit	33⅓%	33⅓%	33⅓%
Actual selling price	$95.03	$134.43	$105.53
Actual gross profit	36.86%	25.61%	52.62%

tration 7-4. Note that the anticipated gross margin—based on selling price—is the same for all three products—33⅓ percent. Compusmart found that its price of product X was lower than the competition's price of its comparable product, and, thus, the company was able to increase the price of product X to the competition's price of $95.03. However, product Y's unit sales declined as a result of its targeted selling price, and Compusmart was forced to lower the selling price for product Y to meet competition. The managers of the company were perplexed as to why the competition was able to sell its products at a lower price because Compusmart's equipment was the latest in the state of the art and its direct material and direct labor costs were the same as those of the competition. The unit sales of product Z increased dramatically when it was sold at the targeted selling price, and the company was unable to supply all of the units demanded by customers. Again, the company was perplexed as to why the competition's product, comparable to product Z, was selling at a much higher price. The company raised the price of product Z until the units demanded by customers coincided with the company's capacity to produce them. Thus, the targeted selling price and the actual selling price turned out to be different for products X, Y, and Z.

Although this hit-and-miss pricing strategy eventually resulted in arriving at competitive market prices, Compusmart had lost opportunities until that point was reached. For example, product X was initially sold at $90 per unit but could have been sold at $95.03 from the outset. Product Z also suffered from this situation. For product Y, the company lost sales that it could have made until it changed the price of the product to $134.43 from $150. Incorrect pricing strategies are not without penalties to the profitability of a firm.

From the above data, you might guess that there is something wrong with the way Compusmart is determining the selling prices of its products. Since direct material costs and direct labor costs for the company and its competition are the same, the only area of suspicious costing is in overhead. Clearly, the competition must be using a different method to apply overhead to production to justify the differences in the way it prices its products and the way Compusmart prices its products. We will now consider another way to cost a company's products.

► THE NEW MANUFACTURING ENVIRONMENT

Activity-Based Costing   ***Applying Overhead to Production—Traditional Method***   Applying overhead to production is usually a two-stage process. In traditional costing, overhead costs for a multiproduct firm are first accumulated by department and then assigned to products using a base such as direct labor or machine-hours.

▶ **ILLUSTRATION 7-5**   Examples of Cost Drivers

Number of labor transactions
Number of material moves
Number of total part numbers
Number of parts received in a month
Number of products
Number of part numbers in an average product
Average number of options
Number of schedule changes
Number of accessories
Number of vendors
Number of units scrapped
Number of engineering changes
Number of process changes
Number of units reworked
Number of direct labor employees
Number of new parts introduced

Source: Robert D. McIlhattan, "How Cost Management Systems Can Support the JIT Philosophy," *Management Accounting* (IMA), September 1987, p. 22.

Departmentalized overhead approaches can be found in the next chapter, Chapter 8.

Many firms with multiple product lines use cost accounting systems that are outmoded because they apply overhead to production as if they were a single product firm. Our example of Compusmart Company may fall into this category. Recall that in Illustration 7-3, Compusmart's direct labor costs are between 10 percent and 16 percent of each product's total cost, yet the firm used direct labor cost to apply overhead to production. This approach to overhead costing probably contributed to Compusmart's problem with pricing its products.

L.O. 3
Cost drivers

Cost Drivers   A more sophisticated approach to overhead costing is to search for causal factors when overhead is incurred. For example, engineering costs are not incurred in proportion to the total activity in a firm's facility (throughput), but they are incurred by the number of engineering changes made. Thus, applying engineering costs to product costs by using direct labor as the basis can produce a severe distortion of a product's actual cost. Costs should be analyzed into separate homogeneous pools based on the factors that cause the cost to be incurred. This process results in finding **cost drivers** that are the activities that cause costs to be incurred. Examples of cost drivers are shown in Illustration 7-5.

Cost drivers also include the following:

Number of setups.
Number of direct labor-hours.
Number of machine-hours.
Number of purchase orders placed.
Number of inspections.

L.O. 2
ABC method of applying overhead

L.O. 4
Two-stage process of applying overhead

Applying Overhead to Production—Activity-Based Costing   **Activity-based costing (ABC),** also known as **transaction-based costing,** is also a two-stage costing process. In the first stage, costs are traced to the various *activities* performed by a firm. In the second stage, these costs are assigned to the

▶ **ILLUSTRATION 7-6**   Compusmart's Production Information

	Product X	**Product Y**	**Product Z**
Production:			
Units	20,000	30,000	12,000
Number of runs	2 runs of 10,000 each	6 runs of 5,000 each	12 runs of 1,000 each
Setup labor—per run*	8 hours	8 hours	8 hours
Engineering changes	10	8	30
Machine usage—per unit	½ hour	¾ hour	1 hour

* Setup labor has a cost of $24 per hour including fringe benefits.

firm's products.[3] During the first stage, overhead costs are accumulated into separate homogeneous pools using cost drivers as the bases for analyzing the overhead. Then, for each overhead pool, a rate is computed in much the same way as in traditional costing. For example, if the pool of overhead for machine setup time amounts to $50,000 and 100 setups were made, the pool rate would be $500 per setup ($50,000 ÷ 100 setups = $500 per setup). Many overhead pools are likely to be used when overhead is analyzed using ABC. The second stage is then to assign overhead to product costs using the appropriate cost driver as the base. For example, setup costs would be assigned to products on the basis of the number of setups required for each product instead of on the amount of direct labor cost as was done previously for the Compusmart Company. Similarly, engineering costs would be accumulated in an overhead pool and then a pool rate would be computed using the number of engineering changes made during the time period. Engineering costs would then be assigned to products based on the number of engineering changes for each product instead of using direct labor cost as the basis for assigning engineering overhead to product cost. Clearly, by using ABC, a firm's products should reflect more accurate costing than when traditional costing is used.

Let us now return to assigning overhead for Compusmart Company, except that we will now use ABC. The production information that is available for the company is shown in Illustration 7-6.

Recall that the first stage of ABC is to analyze overhead into cost pools using cost drivers as the base. It is now assumed that Compusmart has reanalyzed its overhead into ABC pools, and these are listed below:

Machine setup time*	$ 3,840
Receiving costs	384,000
Engineering costs	240,000
Other overhead	1,676,000
Total	$2,303,840

* Machine setup time overhead costs consist of the labor and fringe costs for employees who set up the tools and dies used to manufacture one product and then change the tools and dies to manufacture another product.

---

[3] H. Thomas Johnson and Robert S. Kaplan, *Relevance Lost: The Rise and Fall of Management Accounting* (Boston: Harvard Business School Press, 1987), p. 238. For a more extended discussion of the two-stage process, see Robin Cooper, "The Two-Stage Procedure in Cost Accounting: Part One," *Journal of Cost Management for the Manufacturing Industry,* Summer 1987, pp. 43–51; and "The Two-Stage Procedure in Cost Accounting: Part Two," *Journal of Cost Management for the Manufacturing Industry,* Fall 1987, pp. 39–45.

▶ **ILLUSTRATION 7-7**   Computation of Overhead Pool Rates

Machine Setup Time

Setups—Product X	2 setups at 8 hours	16
—Product Y	6 setups at 8 hours	48
—Product Z	12 setups at 8 hours	96
Total setup time		160

$$\text{Pool rate} = \frac{\$3,840}{160 \text{ hours}} = \$24 \text{ per setup-hour}$$

Receiving Costs

Direct material cost

Product X	20,000 units at $30 =	$ 600,000
Product Y	30,000 units at $40 =	1,200,000
Product Z	12,000 units at $10 =	120,000
Total direct materials cost		$1,920,000

$$\text{Pool rate} = \frac{\$384,000}{\$1,920,000} = \$.20 \text{ per dollar material cost}$$

Engineering Costs

Engineering changes

Product X	10
Product Y	8
Product Z	30
Total	48

$$\text{Pool rate} = \frac{\$240,000}{48 \text{ changes}} = \$5,000 \text{ per change}$$

▶ **ILLUSTRATION 7-8**   Computation of Pool Rate for Other Overhead

Budgeted Machine-Hours

Product X	20,000 units × ½ hour =	10,000 hours
Product Y	30,000 units × ¾ hour =	22,500 hours
Product Z	12,000 units × 1 hour =	12,000 hours
Total budgeted machine-hours		44,500

$$\text{Overhead rate} = \frac{\$1,676,000}{44,500 \text{ hours}} = \$37.663 \text{ per machine-hour}$$

Using the appropriate cost drivers, the pool rate for each of these pools can be computed as shown in Illustration 7-7.

The other overhead costs that cannot be assigned to specific cost drivers other than direct labor or machine-hours are allocated using machine-hours as the base since Compusmart is a machine-intensive firm. In this type of business, machine-hour is a better measure of a firm's level of activity associated with the production of different products than direct labor-hour or costs. The computation of this pool rate appears in Illustration 7-8.

We turn now to the second stage of ABC at which we assign overhead to product costs using cost drivers to allocate the overhead pools noted above. The unit cost information using ABC is shown in Illustration 7-9.

▶ **ILLUSTRATION 7-9**   Unit Cost Information Using ABC

	Product X	Product Y	Product Z
Direct material	$30.00	$40.00	$10.00
Direct labor:			
¼ hour at $24.00	6.00		
½ hour at $24.00		12.00	
⅓ hour at $24.00			8.00
Manufacturing overhead			
Machine setup time:			
Product X—16 hours			
× $24.00 per hour			
÷ 20,000 units	.02		
Product Y—48 hours			
× $24.00 per hour			
÷ 30,000 units		.04	
Product Z—96 hours			
× $24.00 per hour			
÷ 12,000 units			.19
Receiving costs:			
Product X—$600,000			
× .20 = $120,000			
÷ 20,000 units	6.00		
Product Y—$1,200,000			
× .20 = $240,000			
÷ 30,000 units		8.00	
Product Z—$120,000			
× .20 = $24,000			
÷ 12,000 units			2.00
Engineering costs:			
Product X—10 changes			
× $5,000 = $50,000			
÷ 20,000 units	2.50		
Product Y—8 changes			
× $5,000 = $40,000			
÷ 30,000 units		1.33	
Product Z—30 changes			
× $5,000 = $150,000			
÷ 12,000 units			12.50
Other overhead*	18.83	28.25	37.66
Total	$63.35	$89.62	$70.35

* Product X—½ hour × $37.663 = $18.83
  Product Y—¾ hour × $37.663 = $28.25
  Product Z—1 hour × $37.663 = $37.66

   Compare the unit costs in Illustration 7-9 when ABC is used with those computed in Illustration 7-3 when traditional costing was used. Computing costs using ABC reveals that traditional costing may give a firm misleading cost information that may cause faulty pricing strategies. Let us summarize the profitability data for Compusmart Company using ABC. The results are shown in Illustration 7-10.

   Notice that in Illustration 7-10 the actual selling prices dictated by the competition in the marketplace produces the targeted gross profit for products X, Y, and Z and that in Illustration 7-4 when traditional costing was used, the company was unable to maintain its selling prices and targeted gross profit.

▶ **ILLUSTRATION 7-10**   Profitability Data Using ABC

	Product X	**Product Y**	**Product Z**
Normal unit cost	$63.35	$ 89.62	$ 70.35
Planned gross profit	33⅓%	33⅓%	33⅓%
Targeted selling price	$95.03	$134.43	$105.53
Actual selling price	$95.03	$134.43	$105.53
Actual gross profit	33⅓%	33⅓%	33⅓%

▶ **PROGRESS CHECK**

1. Does traditional costing for overhead sometimes produce misleading cost information? Explain.
2. What is activity-based costing?
3. Applying overhead to production is a two-stage process in both traditional costing and activity-based costing, yet the methods are different. Comment on how they differ.
4. What is a cost driver? Why does the use of cost drivers for applying overhead to product costs produce more accurate costing than traditional costing?
5. How are overhead pool rates computed when using cost drivers? ◀

Cost Management Systems

In 1986, Computer Aided Manufacturing-International, Inc. (CAM-I) formed a consortium of manufacturing firms, accounting firms, and governmental agencies to explore the role of cost management in the new manufacturing environment.[4] CAM-I, based in Arlington, Texas, was concerned with the design of a cost management system (CMS). A **cost management system** is concerned with planning, managing, and reducing costs[5] and can be contrasted to a traditional cost accounting system that is historical in nature and is concerned with reporting costs that have already occurred. The following are important objectives and advantages of a CMS:

1. To identify and eliminate nonvalue-added costs. A **nonvalue-added cost** is a cost or activity that can be eliminated without any deterioration of product performance, functionality, quality, or perceived value.[6] Stated differently, a nonvalue-added cost is an activity performed within a firm that does not add any value to a product.[7]
2. To utilize activity-based costing.
3. To improve the tracing of costs to a firm's reporting objectives.
4. To measure the cost of the resources used by a firm in carrying out its activities.
5. To ascertain a firm's efficiency and effectiveness in carrying out its activities.
6. To identify and evaluate new activities that can improve the future performance of the firm.[8]

---

[4] Callie Berliner and James A. Brimson, eds., *Cost Management for Today's Advanced Manufacturing* (Boston: Harvard Business School Press, 1988), p. vii.

[5] Ibid., p. 3.

[6] Ibid., p. 242.

[7] McIlhattan, "How Cost Management Systems Can Support the JIT Philosophy," p. 20.

[8] Berliner and Brimson, *Cost Management*, pp. 3, 10.

Nonvalue-Added Costs

L.O. 5

The author of an article about a CMS under just-in-time (JIT) philosophy—JIT is discussed later in this chapter—identifies the following activities in connection with manufacturing a salable product:

1. **Process time.** The amount of time that a product is actually worked on.
2. **Inspection time.** The amount of time spent either ensuring that the product is of high quality or actually spent reworking the product to an acceptable quality level.
3. **Move time.** The time spent moving the product from one location to another.
4. **Queue time.** The amount of time the product waits before being processed, moved, inspected, or whatever.
5. **Storage time.** The amount of time a product spends in stock before further processing or shipment.[9]

The author goes on to state:

> Of these five steps, only process time actually adds value to the product. All other activities—inspection time, move time, queue time and storage time—add cost but no value to the product and therefore are deemed as *nonvalue-added* processes within the JIT philosophy.[10]

In order to eliminate nonvalue-added costs, a firm's production process must be restructured to keep a product flowing continuously through the plant. Costs such as inventory-carrying costs, storage, expediting, and production control do not improve the product in any way and should be eliminated by restructuring the manufacturing process.[11]

Lead time, the interval of time between the request for the delivery of parts and their actual arrival, may be expressed as follows:

$$\text{Lead time} = \text{Process time} + \text{Inspection time} + \text{Move time} + \text{Wait time}$$

Because only process time is a value-added cost, the equation may be modified to read as

$$\text{Lead time} = \text{Process time} + \text{Nonvalue-added time}$$

This concept, **manufacturing-cycle efficiency (MCE),** which expresses the relationship between the amount of process time and the amount of nonvalue-added time, may be expressed as

$$\text{MCE} = \frac{\text{Processing time}}{\text{Processing time} + \text{Nonvalue-added time}}$$

To illustrate the calculation of the MCE, let us assume that General Manufacturing Company determined the following for one of its products:

Process time	0.25 days
Inspection time	0.05 days
Move time	0.10 days
Queue time	1.00 days

---

[9] McIlhattan, "How Cost Management Systems Can Support the JIT Philosophy," pp. 20–21.
[10] Ibid., p. 21
[11] Berliner and Brimson, *Cost Management,* p. 4.

▶ **ILLUSTRATION 7-11**   Lead-time Reduction

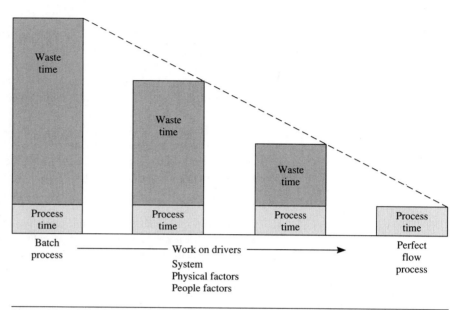

Batch process — Work on drivers → Perfect flow process
System
Physical factors
People factors

Source: Adapted from Lawrence J. Utzig, General Electric Company, in Callie Berliner and James A. Brimson, eds., *Cost Management in Today's Advanced Manufacturing* (Boston: Harvard Business School Press, 1988), p. 5.

Finished goods are shipped as soon as they are completed. The calculation of lead time would be:

Lead time = (0.25 + 0.05 + 0.10 + 1.00) days = 1.40 days

The calculation of the MCE would be:

$$\text{MCE} = \frac{0.25}{0.25 + 0.05 + 0.10 + 1.00} = 0.1786$$

A MCE of 0.1786 means that only about 18 percent of the lead time is spent on processing this particular product and that about 82 percent of the lead time is spent on nonvalue-added costs.

In many manufacturing firms today, MCE is *less than 10 percent* (0.10). In an optimal situation, MCE should be 100 percent (1.00)[12] and the equation would be:

$$\text{MCE} = \frac{\text{Processing time}}{\text{Processing time}}$$

The path leading to an MCE of 1 is shown in Illustration 7-11.

A **value-added cost** is any cost of an activity that adds value to the product at the lowest possible cost of the activity. Examples of value-added activities in the manufacture of enamel-glazed cookware include the following:

1. Receiving direct materials on a firm's premises.
2. Cutting, shaping, and forming direct materials.

---

[12] Ibid.

3. Assembling a product.
4. Painting, glazing, and coating the product.
5. Packaging finished goods for sale.

▶ JUST-IN-TIME PRODUCTION AND INVENTORY CONTROL

Just-in-Time Inventory Control

L.O. 6

One type of inventory control for the purchase of direct materials that is concerned with ordering the optimum quantity of direct materials based on *annual usage* is discussed in Appendix 9-A. This type of inventory control may be viewed as **push-it-through control** because the materials are ordered *without considering how many units are needed for the next batch of production* and the direct materials are then pushed through the production line when production is started. With this kind of inventory control, it is presumed that some inventory, such as safety stock, will usually be on hand, just in case a problem develops with the source of supply.

The Japanese consider the carrying of inventory an anathema because a firm thus incurs inventory carrying costs, which are nonvalue-added costs. Japanese manufacturers employ an inventory method known as **just-in-time (JIT),** in which inventories are zero or as near to zero as possible. When this inventory method is used, production runs are scheduled *only* when a customer's order is received, and deliveries of direct materials are made by vendors *just in time* to be used on a particular production run. When the goods are finished, they are delivered to the customer so that no finished goods inventory is carried. No finished goods inventories are carried in the finished goods warehouse, and no direct materials are carried in a direct materials stockroom. In this way, significant cost efficiencies are achieved because costs associated with carrying and maintaining inventories are avoided. This inventory control method is referred to as **pull-it-through control** because the purchase of direct materials is based on a *particular* production run, and when the direct materials are received, they are pulled through until they are completed for a particular customer.

In order for JIT to work, certain requirements must be met:

1. There must be absolutely reliable, uninterruptible supply sources of direct materials.
2. The quality of the materials must be absolute. No defective materials are permitted.
3. The production process should be repetitive and low in volume.
4. Purchase ordering costs and/or machine setup time is minimal or close to zero.
5. Machinery must be maintained in optimum operating condition to minimize downtime.
6. Employees should be classified into small groups, with each group being responsible for a production sequence.

Uninterrupted Sources of Supply   After the installation of a JIT system, business relationships with a firm's vendors are considerably changed. A firm will now usually limit its purchases of a direct material to one vendor. In exchange, the vendor must be willing to assume the responsibility for delivering the direct materials as needed, usually on a daily basis or even several times daily. In addition, the operations of the vendor itself must be free from interruptions, such as employee strikes or machine breakdowns. If this cannot be guaranteed, the vendor must be willing to carry inventories for these eventualities, and thus the vendor would be precluded from employing a JIT system in its own operations.

Absence of Defective Parts   The vendor must have a stringent quality control system that weeds out defective parts prior to delivery. Defective parts usually force the firm to stop the production line, which may have enormous cost consequences. Thus, quality control for the firm, as well as the vendor, is extremely important in achieving the benefits from a JIT system. In fact, a firm that uses JIT attempts to achieve **total quality control,** which is a philosophy of always striving toward a goal of zero defects, although this goal may never by achieved.

Repetitive Production Process   Although JIT can be used by any manufacturing firm, it appears most suitable for firms that have repetitive production runs. Because minimal machine setup time is necessary for achieving the economies of JIT, a firm that has repetitive production runs is more apt to reduce its setup time. Production volume is usually low to minimize the carrying of inventories.

Minimal Purchase Order Cost and Minimal Machine Setup Time   In a JIT environment in which a special arrangement exists with a particular vendor and the vendor knows it is the sole supplier to a firm, the vendor will enter into a special arrangement with the firm to minimize purchase order costs. The vendor will usually absorb certain costs, such as freight, in exchange for being a firm's sole supplier.

Machine Maintenance   If costly downtime is to be avoided, machine maintenance must be of the highest quality. Very often, the operator(s) of a machine is entrusted with maintenance of the equipment. In this way, the machine operator who experiences a machine breakdown is held accountable for it unless the breakdown is due to an unforeseen event. When a repair person is entrusted with a machine's maintenance, the responsibility for downtime then becomes a joint responsibility—between the maintenance person and the machine operator—and some control is lost.

Employee Groupings   Assigning small clusters of employees to a segment of a production run introduces a team spirit and fixes responsibility for that segment. Employees are trained to be part of the team, and employee morale and flexibility are enhanced. Toyota uses a JIT system called *kanban*. A kanban is a card in Japanese. Under this system, two trays follow the direct materials through the production process. At the beginning of the process, all of the cards are in the production tray; as each direct material is used, the card for that material is taken out of the production tray and put into the withdrawal tray, so that at the end of the process, all of the kanbans appear in the withdrawal tray.[13]

The JIT system enjoys its widest usage in Japan, where (1) employee strikes are relatively unknown; (2) sources of supply are relatively near the factories that use the direct materials; (3) quality control is sought, rather

---

[13] John Y. Lee, *Managerial Accounting Changes for the 1990s* (Reading, Mass.: Addison-Wesley Publishing Co., 1987), p. 20.

than shoddy workmanship allowed; and (4) employee morale is high. However, U.S. Companies like General Motors, Ford Motor Company, Warner Lambert, Brunswick, Teledyne, and Harley Davidson are also using JIT systems.

Elimination of Nonvalue-Added Costs

An important theme of the JIT philosophy is the elimination of nonvalue-added costs. Although it may not be possible to eliminate all nonvalue-added costs, a firm that uses JIT is always searching for nonvalue-added costs and then strives to eliminate them. Recall that in a traditional plant layout, the floor plan (see Illustration 7-1) is structured so that all machines of the same kind are grouped together in a department. Similarly, all direct materials that are received by the firm and stored until they are used are housed in a location other than where the machinery is located. Thus, it is necessary to move the direct materials from the stockroom into a production area and, once the materials are in process, they are moved from department to department.

Flexible Manufacturing System

L.O. 7

The plant layout in a JIT factory is radically different from the traditional plant layout shown in Illustration 7-1. Under JIT, the plant layout is such that movement of direct materials and work in process is virtually eliminated. The adjacent work stations are arranged in the order in which the materials must pass through them to be processed. The direct materials are then delivered directly to the production area adjacent to the first work station. When the direct materials are completed at the first work station, the work in process is moved to the next adjacent work station, and so on. The arrangement of work stations in this manner is called a **flexible manufacturing cell (FMC),** which is the arrangement of a group of machines and personnel in a cluster so that the cluster can receive direct materials and process them into finished goods without requiring the work in process to move to another cell for processing.

▶ **Example**   Harley-Davidson-York went from 60 forklift operators to 5.[14] The cost of operating the eliminated 55 forklifts was a nonvalue-added cost because Harley-Davidson was able to eliminate the costs of moving materials without affecting the quality of its motorcycles.   ◀

An example of a FMC can be seen in Illustration 7-12.

L.O. 1
JIT Plant Layout

An integral part of JIT production is a **flexible manufacturing system (FMS),** which is the grouping of several automated flexible manufacturing cells where the tools and dies in a FMC can be rearranged quickly to change from one operation to another. The system consists of computer-controlled machines that are used to manufacture a firm's products at low or relatively low volumes of production. **Computer-aided manufacturing (CAM)** utilizes computers to program, direct, and control production equipment in the fabrication of manufactured items.[15] Closely allied to CAM is **computer-integrated manufacturing (CIM),** which not only uses computers to direct and control production equipment but also uses them to assist manufacturing

---

[14] Capettini and Clancy, *Cost Accounting,* p. 8.12.
[15] Berliner and Brimson, *Cost Management,* p. 238.

▶ **ILLUSTRATION 7-12**   Sample Flexible Manufacturing Cell

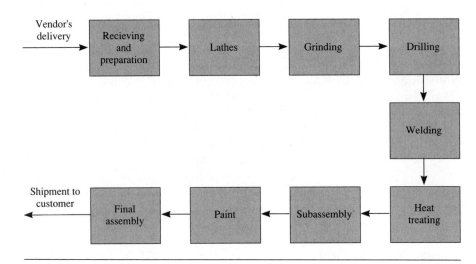

operations, such as using computers to link material-handling equipment to flexible manufacturing cells. A CIM system is a highly automated manufacturing operation that utilizes relatively few manufacturing personnel.

▶ **Example**   By implementing a JIT system, Harley-Davidson was able to reduce inventory levels by 75 percent, reduce scrap and rework by 68 percent, increase productivity by 50 percent, and reduce space requirements by 25 percent.[16]   ◀

A sample flexible manufacturing system can be seen in Illustration 7-13.

Support Services   As noted earlier regarding repairs to equipment, traditional manufacturing firms maintain centralized departments for the various kinds of support services provided by a manufacturing firm. Examples include (1) repairs to machinery, (2) machine maintenance, and (3) receiving direct materials from vendors. Under a JIT system, these support services are decentralized and each flexible manufacturing cell has personnel who can perform the manufacturing functions as well as the support services. A significant advantage of having each FMC decentralized is that each cell is responsible for the maintenance of its own equipment and if faulty maintenance causes a machine to break down, the cell cannot blame this on a maintenance department. Thus, responsibility control is maintained within each cell, which in theory should reduce the number of breakdowns. In addition, if a machine does break down, the employees who are idled by the breakdown can immediately start to repair it without waiting for someone from the repair department to do it. Thus, idle time is minimized.

A comparison of the differences between traditional and JIT manufacturing environments appears in Illustration 7-14.

---

[16] Peter C. Reid, *Well Made in America* (New York: McGraw-Hill, 1990), p. 148.

▶ **ILLUSTRATION 7-13**   Sample Flexible Manufacturing System

▶ **ILLUSTRATION 7-14**   Differences between Traditional and JIT Manufacturing Environments

Traditional	JIT
Manufacturing departments	Flexible manufacturing cells
Centralized support services	Decentralized support services
Push-it-through manufacturing	Pull-it-through manufacturing
Substantial direct materials and finished goods inventories	Zero or almost zero inventories
Some quality control	Total quality control

Just-in-Time Cost Accounting

The cost accounting cycle for a true JIT system is much simplified when compared to either a job order system or a process cost system.

Job Order Costing—Direct Materials   Recall from Chapter 5 that when direct material inventories are maintained, a direct materials inventory system—usually a perpetual inventory system—is required. This entails recording all purchases of direct materials in the inventory system. In addition, when production orders are issued, materials requisition forms are needed to authorize the issuance of direct materials from the stockroom. These requisitions are also entered into the inventory system so that the balance of direct materials on hand at any given time may be ascertained from the inventory system. It is obvious that a large amount of record-keeping is needed when a traditional job order cost accounting system is used. Conversely, if there is *no direct materials inventory on hand at any time,* there is *no need for a direct materials inventory system and no need for materials requisitions forms.* Thus, there are no journal entries to the Direct Materials Inventory account, but instead, the purchases of direct materials are debited directly to a work in process account. Because the account may include some direct materials that have not been processed yet, the account is usually called *Direct Materials and In Process Inventory.* However, the JIT system must be a true JIT system to eliminate the need for the record-keeping; a partial JIT system in which direct material inventories are maintained—albeit smaller inventories—would require similar record-keeping as in a traditional job order cost accounting system.

Job Order Costing—Direct Labor   When the cost of direct labor was a substantial part of a product's cost, the record-keeping and control of direct labor costs were very important. Now, direct labor costs are often less than 10 percent of a product's cost and, therefore, the record-keeping and control of direct labor costs are not so important. Accordingly, the cost of direct labor is no longer accounted for separately as was done in Chapter 5, but, instead, the cost of direct labor is combined with manufacturing overhead into one account. Again, record-keeping and product cost accumulation are greatly simplified. Let us reflect on this aspect. In Chapter 5, we saw that it was necessary to use a job cost sheet to track direct materials cost and direct labor costs to particular jobs. Because a particular job in an FMC has the exact amount of materials needed for that job, it is not necessary to track materials for the job. The amount of the vendor's invoice is the direct materials cost for the job. Since direct labor costs are now combined with manufacturing overhead, there is no need to track direct labor costs. *Thus, there is no need for job cost sheets.*

Job Order Costing—Conversion Costs   In a traditional job order costing system, manufacturing overhead costs are accumulated by department (see Chapter 8 for departmentalized overhead) and applied to production using an appropriate overhead base, such as direct labor cost, direct labor-hours, or machine-hours. Under JIT, activity-based costing is used, and the costs of direct labor and overhead are accumulated into pools segregated by cost drivers and then applied to production using the appropriate cost driver.

The cost accounting system for JIT is referred to as **backflush costing** because, consistent with the pull-it-through system, costs are "flushed" out of the system when production is completed. Comparatively, costs in a traditional cost accounting system, a push-it-through system, are pushed through the production cycle.

Nonvalue-Added Costs   Because of the simplified and reduced record-keeping under a JIT system, record-keeping costs are substantially reduced when JIT is used. Note how these cost savings have no effect on the quality or amount of a firm's throughput. Therefore, this is another example of how the JIT system eliminates nonvalue-added costs.

Process Costing   Recall that in Chapter 6 we discussed the two ways to calculate unit costs for a firm that uses process costing—the weighted-average method and the FIFO method. These methods produce different results whenever there are beginning work in process inventories. However, in a true JIT production process, there are no work in process inventories or, if there are any, they are negligible and may be ignored. Therefore, if there are no work in process inventories, the weighted-average and the FIFO methods produce identical results! In fact, if there are no work in process inventories, *there is no need to calculate equivalent production* because the production for any period will consist only of finished goods. Calculating unit costs would require merely dividing the cost of all direct materials, direct labor, and manufacturing overhead by the number of finished units produced during the period. This is another example of the reduced record-keeping and the elimination of nonvalue-added costs.

Example of JIT Cost Accounting Entries   Assume that Compusmart Company incurred the following costs for the month of January 19x2:

1. Purchased direct materials at a cost of $192,000.
2. Incurred direct labor costs of $57,600.
3. Incurred manufacturing overhead costs of $235,000.
4. Conversion costs applied amounted to $290,000.
5. All merchandise started during the month is completed.
6. Underapplied or overapplied manufacturing overhead is closed only to Cost of Goods Sold at the end of the company's year, which ends December 31, 19x2.

The above transactions would be recorded as follows:

1. Direct Materials and In Process Inventory 192,000
     Accounts Payable 192,000
       To record the purchase of direct materials for the month.
2. Conversion Costs Control 57,600
     Wages Payable 57,600
       To record the direct labor costs for the month.
3. Conversion Costs Control 235,000
     Accounts Payable, etc. 235,000
       To record the cost of manufacturing overhead for the month.
4. Direct Materials and In Process Inventory 290,000
     Conversion Costs Applied 290,000
       To apply conversion costs to production.
5. Cost of Goods Sold 482,000
     Direct Materials and In Process Inventory 482,000
       To transfer merchandise completed and sold to cost of goods sold.
6. No entry.

Journal entry 5 is predicated on the assumption that the finished goods were shipped directly from the FMC to the firm's customer. If the finished goods were not shipped but were instead stored in a warehouse awaiting sale, the debit in entry 5 would be to Finished Goods Inventory instead of to Cost of Goods Sold.

► **SUMMARY**

In a traditional plant layout, all similar activities are grouped into departments. Thus, direct materials are stored in a stockroom, direct materials are cut in the cutting department, and so forth. This normally entails moving the direct materials and work in process from one location to another. The activity of a department, a machine, or the entire factory is referred to as **throughput.** When overhead is applied to a firm's throughput in a traditional manufacturing environment, an overhead base, such as direct labor cost, direct labor-hours, or machine-hours, is usually used. When these methods are used, assigning overhead to production is a two-stage process. In the first stage, overhead is accumulated into one or more pools, and, in the second stage, the overhead pools are assigned to throughput using one of the bases selected. The use of only one of these bases may cause a firm to compute its unit costs in a manner that is not consistent with the way these costs are actually incurred, and, hence, incorrect decisions based on these costs may occur.

Another method to apply overhead to throughput is to use another two-stage costing process called **activity-based costing (ABC),** also known as *transaction-based costing*. In the first stage, costs are traced to the various *activities* performed by a firm, and, in the second stage, these costs are assigned to the firm's products using the activities as the base for assigning overhead to throughput. In tracing the activities performed by a firm, overhead is analyzed to search for its causal factors that are called **cost drivers.** Although this process usually results in many more overhead pools being used, it produces unit costs that are more relevant for decision making than those produced by traditional costing.

A **cost management system (CMS)** is concerned with planning, managing, and reducing costs and can be contrasted to a traditional cost accounting system that is historical in nature and is concerned with reporting on costs that have already occurred. An important objective of a CMS is to eliminate **nonvalue-added costs,** which are costs or activities that can be avoided without any deterioration of product performance, functionality, quality, or perceived value. Nonvalue-added costs include **inspection time,** which is the amount of time spent either ensuring that the product is of high quality or actually spent reworking the product to an acceptable quality level; **move time,** which is the time spent moving the product from one location to another; **queue time,** which is the amount of time the product waits before being processed, or moved, or inspected; and **storage time,** which is the amount of time a product spends in stock before further processing or shipment. Other objectives of a CMS include using activity-based costing, measuring the cost of resources used by the firm, ascertaining a firm's efficiency and effectiveness, and identifying and evaluating new opportunities for a firm.

A **value-added cost** is any cost of an activity that adds value to the product at the lowest possible cost of the activity. Ideally, it should include only **process time,** which is the amount of time that a product is actually worked on. A firm's process time is a part of **lead time,** which is the interval of time between the request for the delivery of parts and their actual delivery. Lead time may be expressed as process time plus inspection time plus move time plus wait time. A measure that expresses the relationship between the amount of process time and the amount of nonvalue-added time is the **manufacturing-cycle efficiency (MCE).**

Under the **just-in-time (JIT)** manufacturing philosophy, manufacturers strive to carry zero, or near zero, inventories. In order for this system to work, there must be reliable and uninterrupted sources of supply of direct materials; quality control must be absolute or near absolute through the use of **total quality control;** production should be repetitive and low in volume, setup time should be minimal or almost zero, permitting easy changeovers between products; and equipment must be maintained in optimum operating condition to minimize downtime. In a JIT system, employees and machines are organized into an arrangement called a **flexible manufacturing cell (FMC),** which is the arrangement of a group of machines and personnel in a cluster so that the cluster can receive direct materials and process them into finished goods without requiring the work in process to move to another cell for processing. This system of manufacturing is called a **flexible manufacturing system (FMS),** which is the grouping of several automated flexible manufacturing cells so that the tools and dies in an FMC can be rearranged quickly to change from one operation to another. The system normally employs **computer-aided manufacturing (CAM),** which utilizes computers to program, direct, and control production equipment in the fabrication of manufactured items. Closely allied to CAM is **computer-integrated manufacturing (CIM),** which not only uses computers to direct and control production equipment, but also uses them to assist manufacturing operations, such as linking material-handling equipment to flexible manufacturing cells. A CIM system is a highly automated manufacturing operation that utilizes relatively few manufacturing personnel. This FMS type of manufacturing is also referred to as **pull-it-through** manufacturing because when the direct materials arrive just-in-time to commence manufacturing operations, the direct materials are pulled through the system. This may be contrasted with **push-it-through** manufacturing, the traditional manufacturing system, in which direct materials are taken from the stockroom and then pushed through the system.

The cost accounting system for JIT is referred to as **back-flush costing** because costs are ''flushed'' out of the system when production is completed. This is compatible with JIT being a pull-it-through system. There is considerably less record-keeping in a JIT system than in a traditional manufacturing system because of the absence of inventories. Since there are no inventories, there is no need for a perpetual inventory control system and there is no need to track costs through the use of job cost sheets when a job order system is used. The costing for process costing is also greatly simplified when a JIT system is used.

▶ **GLOSSARY OF KEY TERMS**

Activity-based costing (ABC),   also known as *transaction-based costing,* is a two-stage costing process. In the first stage, costs are traced to the various *activities* performed by a firm. In the second stage, these costs are assigned to the firm's products.   (p. 312)

Backflush costing   A cost accounting method used for JIT costing in which costs are ''flushed'' out of the system when production is completed. This is compatible with JIT being a ''pull-it-through'' system.   (p. 324)

Computer-aided manufacturing (CAM)   A manufacturing system that utilizes computers to program, direct, and control production equipment in the fabrication of manufactured items.   (p. 321)

Cost drivers   The activities that cause costs to be incurred.   (p. 312)

Computer-integrated manufacturing (CIM)   A manufacturing system that not only uses computers to direct and control production equipment but also to assist manufacturing operations, such as to link material-handling equipment to flexible manufacturing cells. A CIM system is a highly automated manufacturing operation that utilizes relatively few manufacturing personnel.   (p. 321)

Cost management system (CMS)   A system concerned with planning, managing, and reducing costs, in contrast to a traditional cost accounting system that is historical in nature and is concerned with reporting costs that have already occurred. (p. 316)

Flexible manufacturing cell (FMC)   The arrangement of a group of machines and personnel in a cluster so that the cluster can receive direct materials and process them into finished goods without requiring the work in process to move to another cell for processing. (p. 321)

Flexible manufacturing system (FMS)   The grouping of several automated flexible manufacturing cells so that the tools and dies in an FMC can be rearranged quickly to change from one operation to another. This system is an integral part of a JIT production system and consists of computer-controlled machines that are used to manufacture a firm's products at low or relatively low volumes of production. (p. 321)

Inspection time   The amount of time spent either ensuring that the product is of high quality or actually spent reworking the product to an acceptable quality level. (p. 317)

Just-in-time (JIT)   An inventory control method where inventories are zero or as near to zero as possible. When this inventory method is used, production runs are scheduled *only* when a customer's order is received, and deliveries of direct materials are made by vendors *just-in-time* to be used on a particular production run. When the goods are finished, they are delivered to the customer so that no finished goods are carried. Significant cost efficiencies are achieved because no finished goods inventories are carried in the finished goods warehouse and no direct materials are carried in a direct materials stockroom, thus avoiding the costs associated with carrying and maintaining inventories. (p. 319)

Lead time   The interval of time between the request for the delivery of parts and their actual delivery. (p. 317)

Manufacturing-cycle efficiency (MCE)   The relationship between the amount of process time and the amount of nonvalue-added time. (p. 317)

Move time   The time spent moving the product from one location to another. (p. 317)

Nonvalue-added cost   A cost or activity that can be eliminated without any deterioration of product performance, functionality, quality, or perceived value. Stated differently, a nonvalue-added cost is an activity performed within a firm that does not add any value to a product. (p. 316)

Process time   The amount of time that a product is actually worked on. (p. 317)

Pull-it-through   The JIT system based on the purchase of direct materials for a *particular* production run and, when the direct materials are received, pulling them through until they are completed for a particular customer. (p. 319)

Push-it-through   A control method concerned with ordering the optimum quantity of direct materials based on *annual usage* and pushing the direct materials through the production line when production is started. (p. 319)

Queue time   The amount of time the product waits before being processed, moved, or inspected. (p. 317)

Storage time   The amount of time a product spends in stock before further processing or shipment. (p. 317)

Throughput   The volume of activity or production in a firm's facility, such as a factory, a department, or a machine. (p. 310)

Total quality control   A philosophy of always striving toward a goal of zero defects, although this goal may never be achieved. (p. 320)

Transaction-based costing   See **activity-based costing (ABC).** (p. 312)

Value-added cost   The lowest possible cost of an activity that adds value to the product. (p. 318)

▶ **GLOSSARY OF SYNONYMS**   **Transaction-based costing**   See **activity-based costing (ABC).**

▶ **REVIEW PROBLEM**   **Plant-Wide Rate versus Multiple Overhead Rates Based on Cost Drivers**

The president of Jones Company has been reading about accounting in the new manufacturing environment and is concerned that she may be pricing the company's products incorrectly. As the newly hired management accountant, you are asked by the president to prepare two cost analyses of one of the firm's products, an electronic component used in the manufacture of computer mainframes. The first analysis should be prepared using traditional costing, and the second analysis should be prepared using activity-based costing.

Currently, the firm is using a single plant-wide overhead rate using direct labor-hours as the base for applying overhead to production.

The following information is available:

Next Year's Annual Budget

Expected annual volume: . . .	637,500 DLH*
Depreciation: Building.	$ 375,000
Depreciation: Equipment . . .	187,500
Engineering	112,500
Energy	71,625
Rework costs.	303,750
Supervision	255,000
Miscellaneous overhead	243,750
Total	$1,549,125

* Direct labor-hours

Selected Cost Drivers—Estimated Annual Activity

Engineering changes . . .	1,425
Kilowatt-hours.	82,500
Units reworked	3,425
Machine-hours.	46,875

Component (Estimated Data)

Units	75
Direct labor-hours	6,500
Direct labor cost	$39,000
Direct materials	$ 9,000
Engineering changes . . .	20
Kilowatt-hours.	925
Units reworked	2
Machine-hours.	600

Required   *a.* Compute the cost of the component using a plant-wide rate with direct labor-hours as the base for applying overhead to production.

b. Compute the cost of the component using the cost drivers given above. Residual overhead is to be assigned to products using direct labor-hours as the base.

▶ **SOLUTION TO**
REVIEW PROBLEM

a. Compute the Cost of the Job Using a Plant-Wide Rate:

Direct labor	$ 39,000
Direct materials	9,000
Overhead	15,795*
Total manufacturing cost . . .	$ 63,795
÷ Number of units	75
= Unit cost	$ 850.60

*Total overhead	$ 1,549,125
÷DLH	637,500
= Overhead Rate	$2.43/DLH
× Job	6,500 DLH
= Overhead applied	$ 15,795

b. Using activity-based costing, compute the cost of the job using the cost driver information given. Any residual overhead is assigned using DLH.

Compute the cost pool rates	Cost		Driver	= Pool Rate
Depreciation: Equipment . . .	$ 187,500	÷	46,875	$ 4.00
Engineering	112,500	÷	1,425	78.95
Energy	71,625	÷	82,500	0.87
Rework costs	303,750	÷	3,425	88.69
Residual overhead	873,750	÷	637,500	1.37
Total overhead cost	$1,549,125			

Compute the job cost	Rate	× Activity =	
Direct labor			$39,000
Direct materials			9,000
Overhead:			
Depreciation: Equipment	$ 4.00	600	2,400
Engineering changes	78.95	20	1,579
Energy	0.87	925	805
Rework costs	88.69	2	177
Residual overhead	1.37	6,500	8,905
Total manufacturing cost			$61,866
÷ Number of units			75
= Unit cost			$824.88

▶ **LIBRARY**
ASSIGNMENT

Read the following:

Green, F. B., Felix Amenkhienan, and George Johnson. "Performance Measures and JIT." *Management Accounting,* February 1991, pp. 50–53.

Harr, David J. "How Activity Accounting Works in Government." *Management Accounting,* September 1990, pp. 36–40.

Howery, C. Kenneth, Earl D. Bennett, and Sarah Reed. "How Lockheed Implemented CIM." *Management Accounting,* December 1991, pp. 22–28.

Kaplan, Robert S. "The Four-Stage Model of Cost Systems Design." *Management Accounting,* February 1990, pp. 22–26.

Lee, John Y. "Activity-Based Costing at Cal Electronic Circuits." *Management Accounting,* October 1990, pp. 36–38.

Lewis, Ronald J. "Activity-Based Costing for Marketing." *Management Accounting,* November 1991, pp. 33–38.

Parker, Thornton, and Theodore Lettes. "Is Accounting Standing in the Way of Flexible Computer-Integrated Manufacturing?" *Management Accounting*, January 1991, pp. 34–38.

Phillips, Al, and Don E. Collins. "How Borg-Warner Made the Transition from Pile Accounting to JIT." *Management Accounting,* October 1990, pp. 32–35.

Raffish, Norm. "How Much Does that Product Really Co\$t?" *Management Accounting,* March 1991, pp. 36–39.

Roth, Howard P., and A. Faye Borthick. "Are You Distorting Costs by Violating ABC Assumptions?" *Management Accounting,* November 1991, pp. 39–42.

► **SELF-TEST**

True or False

1. In a traditional plant layout, similar activities are performed in departments.
2. In a traditional plant layout, overhead is usually departmentalized and applied to production using an activity base such as direct labor cost or machine-hours.
3. Throughput is the volume of activity in a particular firm. The volume of activity can be in a department, a machine, or the firm as a whole.
4. Cost drivers are activities that cause costs to be incurred and can be used only in activity-based costing.
5. Activity-based costing will always produce cost information that is more accurate than traditional costing.
6. An important objective of a cost management system is to eliminate nonvalue-added costs.
7. Inspection time, move time, process time, and storage time are all nonvalue-added costs.
8. Manufacturing-cycle efficiency is the relationship between the amount of lead time and the amount of nonvalue-added time.
9. In order for JIT to be effective, there must be uninterrupted sources of supply, the firm must strive for total quality control, setup time for changeovers should be minimal, and volume should be repetitive and low.
10. A flexible manufacturing system utilizes flexible manufacturing cells and relies heavily on computers that are integrated in the production process.

Multiple Choice

1. When using a job order costing system under JIT manufacturing, which of the following is *not* an advantage of JIT?
   a. The need for a perpetual inventory system for direct materials is eliminated.
   b. The cost of direct labor is not tracked separately, but, instead, it is combined with manufacturing overhead.
   c. The cost of manufacturing overhead is allocated to individual products using direct labor-hours as the base.
   d. The need for job cost sheets is eliminated.
2. When using a process costing system under JIT manufacturing, which of the following is *not* an advantage of JIT?
   a. The computation of equivalent production is greatly simplified.
   b. The need for a perpetual inventory system for direct materials is eliminated.
   c. The cost of direct labor is not tracked separately, but, instead, it is combined with manufacturing overhead.
   d. There is no need to decide on a cost-flow assumption since the results using weighted average and FIFO are identical.

3. A firm manufactures three products, A, B, and C. The annual volume of A is expected to be 50,000 units and will require 4 machine setups per year. The annual volume of B is expected to be 80,000 units and will require 8 machine setups per year. The annual volume of C is expected to be 60,000 units and will require 12 machine setups per year. Each setup is expected to require six hours of setup time. The estimated machine setup costs for the year are expected to be $4,320. The pool rate per setup-hour is
   a. $180.
   b. $30.
   c. $720.
   d. $.02.

4. Utilize the information provided in Question 3. Assume further that the direct materials unit costs for the three products are as follows:

Product A . . .	$10
Product B . . .	5
Product C . . .	8

The estimated materials receiving costs for the year are expected to be $345,000. The pool rate per dollar of material cost is
   a. $.18.
   b. $15,000.
   c. $2.00.
   d. $.25.

▶ **QUESTIONS**

1. How are traditional plant layouts grouped? When this plant layout is used, is there a significant amount of move time? Explain.
2. When a firm manufactures one product, are there any unusual overhead allocation problems encountered? Explain.
3. When a firm manufactures more than one product, are there any unusual overhead allocation problems encountered? Explain.
4. What is activity-based costing?
5. What is meant by the statement "applying overhead to production is a two-stage process"? Is there a difference between using this process for traditional costing and activity-based costing? Explain.
6. What is a cost driver and how is it used?
7. Are there usually more overhead pools used when activity-based costing is used than when traditional costing is used? Explain.
8. Can traditional costing produce misleading cost information? Explain.
9. What is a cost management system? What are the objectives and advantages of using a cost management system?
10. What are nonvalue-added costs? If a firm wishes to be competitive, what should the firm strive for regarding nonvalue-added costs? Explain.
11. What is lead time? What is manufacturing-cycle efficiency? How are they related? Are most firms efficient? Explain.
12. What is the difference between the push-it-through and pull-it-through philosophies? Which one is used for JIT manufacturing? Explain.
13. What conditions are needed in a firm's manufacturing operations before JIT can be used effectively?
14. What is a flexible manufacturing system and how does this interact with a flexible manufacturing cell?
15. What is the difference between computer-aided manufacturing and computer-integrated manufacturing?

16. Is there a difference in how repairs and maintenance to machinery and equipment are handled when a firm uses JIT manufacturing as opposed to traditional manufacturing? Explain.

17. When a firm uses job order costing, will the cost accounting function be the same for JIT and traditional costing? If not, which one is simpler and less costly to administer? Explain.

18. What are the differences between a firm that uses process costing under a JIT system and a firm using a traditional cost accounting system?

19. Are the journal entries different for a firm using JIT and a firm using traditional costing? Explain.

▶ **EXERCISES**   **E7–1**   ### Traditional Costing—Selecting an Appropriate Cost Driver

Howard Company manufactures two lines of men's high-quality shoes. One line of shoes is manufactured on machinery that is highly automated; the other line of shoes is manufactured primarily by hand, although some machinery is used to cut the leather and do some stitching of the welts. The firm uses the same leather for both lines of shoes.

The company has been using direct labor cost to assign manufacturing overhead to production. The company has a policy of pricing its shoes so that it earns a gross margin of 50 percent based on selling price. The president of the company, John Howard, is concerned about the accuracy of the calculation of the unit costs of the shoes by the firm's accounting department because the company's selling prices are not comparable to the selling prices charged by the firm's competitors. The selling price of the handmade shoes is higher than competitors' prices, but the selling price of the machine-made shoes is less than competitors' prices.

To keep things simple, you, a newly hired management accounting trainee, decide to focus on only two overhead items. You are requested to prepare an analysis that will help you to decide whether the basis for assigning overhead to production should be changed.

The following information for the month of January is available.

	Machine-Made	Handmade
Direct materials	$20,000	$20,000
Direct labor	$ 5,000	$35,000
Machine-hours	1 hour/pair	½ hour/pair
Units produced	1,000 pairs	1,000 pairs

The two overhead items for the year to be considered are as follows:

Factory rent	$240,000
Machine depreciation—	
straight line	360,000

The factory is occupied 75 percent by the machine-made section and 25 percent by the handmade section. The two overhead costs should each be divided by 12 to arrive at the allocated monthly cost.

Required   a. Compute the unit cost for each product using direct labor cost to assign overhead to production.

b. Compute the unit cost for each product using machine-hours to assign overhead to production.

c. Which cost driver produces better cost information? Why?

E7–2 **Classification of Manufacturing Costs under Traditional and Activity-Based Costing Systems**

You are given the following kinds of manufacturing costs for a firm that manufactures a variety of products.

1. Sweeping compound for the factory.
2. Light and heat for the factory.
3. Factory superintendent's salary.
4. Inspection salaries.
5. Receiving department salaries.
6. Salaries of stockroom personnel.
7. Direct materials.
8. Payroll taxes on factory workers' salaries.
9. Factory night guards' salaries.
10. Telephone for factory.
11. Power.
12. Small tools—hammers, screwdrivers, etc.
13. Engineering costs.
14. Rental of computer to perform cost accounting function.
15. Salaries of machine repair and maintenance staff.
16. Direct labor.
17. Factory rent.
18. Depreciation of machinery.

Required   *a.* Using a single product as the firm's cost objective, classify each of the above costs as either a direct cost (DC) or manufacturing overhead (indirect cost) (MO) if the firm uses traditional costing.

b. Using a single product as the firm's cost objective, classify each of the above costs as either a direct cost (DC), a manufacturing overhead (indirect cost) (MO), or a cost that would not be incurred (DEL) if the firm uses a JIT activity-based costing system. If you classify a cost as (MO), indicate an appropriate cost driver that would be used to allocate the overhead to production. (Select a cost driver from the table of cost drivers given in the chapter.)

E7–3 **Computation of Cost-Driver Pool Rates**

A firm manufactures three products, A, B, and C. The annual volume of A is expected to be 25,000 units and will require 5 machine setups per year. The annual volume of B is expected to be 40,000 units and will require 10 machine setups per year. The annual volume of C is expected to be 30,000 units and will require 6 machine setups per year. Each setup is expected to require five hours of setup time. Setup costs are expected to be $4,725 for the year.

The direct materials unit costs for the three products are as follows:

Product A . . . $20
Product B . . . 10
Product C . . . 8

The estimated materials handling costs for the year are expected to be $342,000. The number of engineering changes for each product is as follows:

Product A . . . 20
Product B . . . 15
Product C . . . 10

Engineering costs for the year are expected to amount to $67,500.

Required   Compute the pool overhead rate for each of the following:

a. Setup time.
b. Materials handling.
c. Engineering changes.

E7–4   **Choice of Traditional Costing or Activity-Based Costing for a Bid
on a Government Contract**

Toilet Accessories Manufacturing Company uses a traditional costing system for its
production of a variety of products. Plant-wide overhead is assigned to production on
the basis of direct labor cost. It plans to bid for a U. S. government contract on one of
its products. However, the product requires major modifications from its commercial
design in order to meet the standards required by the U.S. armed forces. You are a
third-year management accountant, and you have been asked to prepare cost estimates for this product using the traditional costing system now in place and also for
an activity-based costing system in the event the company wishes to change its
method of costing.

In order to simplify the cost calculations, the analysis is to be made using representative amounts rather than using the entire costing system of the firm. It is
believed that the amounts chosen as samples will enable the president of the firm to
prepare an accurate bid for this contract.

Pertinent costing and other data are as follows:

	Commercial	Government
Direct material	$20,000	$30,000
Direct labor	$30,000	$60,000
Units produced	10,000	1,000
Machine-hours	1 hour	1 hour
Setups	10	1
Kilowatt-hours	100	100
Material handling moves . . .	500	50

Other cost information is as follows:

Manufacturing overhead:
Straight-line
depreciation—machinery . . . $ 600,000
Machine setup costs   200,000
Power   300,000
Material handling costs   400,000
Other overhead costs.   2,500,000
  Total annual overhead . . . $4,000,000

Pool rates:
Machine setup   . . . . $200   per setup
Power . . . . $.25   per kilowatt-hour
Material handling . . . $50   per move
Other overhead . . . . $20   per machine-hour
Plant-wide overhead rate:
Total overhead . . . .   100% of direct labor cost

Required   a. Prepare cost estimates for one unit each for the government bid and the
commercial version using a plant-wide overhead rate (traditional costing).
b. Prepare cost estimates for one unit each for the government bid and the
commercial version using activity-based costing (cost drivers).
c. Compare the results. Which one do you believe provides better cost
information if the president wishes to prepare a competitive bid that has the
best chance of being successful? Why?

E7–5   **Pricing—Using Traditional Costing and Activity-Based Costing**

Midway Electronics Company manufactures electronic components for manufacturers of television receivers and VCRs. For some time, the company has been bidding on special-order electrical equipment used by state and local governments. Thus far, the company has been unsuccessful in getting any of the contracts.

The president of the company subscribes to various management magazines, and the current issue of one has a feature article on activity-based costing (ABC) and how it provides more accurate cost data. The president, Phyllis Tamara, believes that the manner in which the firm computes costs may play a role in its failure to win any of the previously submitted bids. You are employed by the company as a junior management accountant, and the president has contacted you because she believes that as a recent accounting graduate, you might be more familiar with ABC than the company's chief accountant, who has been employed by the company for the past 40 years.

You are provided with certain estimated cost information pertaining to a new bid that the president plans to submit to a state government. In addition, you have access to the firm's cost records from which you can extract information about the company's current production. Fortunately, you retained a copy of your managerial accounting textbook that contained an excellent discussion of ABC. The company uses a traditional costing system that applies a plant-wide overhead rate to production on the basis of direct labor cost (DLC). The company's policy is to accept new work provided that a minimum gross profit of 60 percent (based on total cost) is earned.

The following information is available for a component manufactured for regular customers and for the equipment needed by the state government.

	Regular	Government Bid
Direct material	$500,000	$ 40,000
Direct labor	$600,000	$100,000
Units produced	10,000	1,000
Machine-hours	2 hours	2 hours
Setups	20	2
Kilowatt-hours	400	400
Material handling moves	500	50

Other cost information is as follows:

Manufacturing overhead:

Straight-line depreciation—machinery	$ 800,000
Machine setup costs	400,000
Power	600,000
Material handling costs	400,000
Other overhead costs	2,800,000
Total annual overhead	$5,000,000

Pool rates:

Machine setup	$600 per setup
Power	$ .30 per kilowatt-hour
Material handling	$ 80 per move
Other overhead	$ 25 per machine-hour

Plant-wide overhead rate:

Total overhead	80% of DLC

Required   *a.* Prepare cost estimates for one unit each for the government bid and the commercial version using a plant-wide overhead rate (traditional costing). What price should the president bid if this costing method is used?

b. Prepare cost estimates for one unit each for the government bid and the commercial version using activity-based costing (cost drivers). What price should the president bid if this costing method is used?

c. Compare the results. Which one do you believe provides better cost information if the company wishes to prepare a competitive bid that has the best chance of being successful? Why?

E7–6   **Grouping Overhead into Pools and Computing Pool Rates for Activity-Based Costing**

Fully Automated Stamping Company manufactures metal parts for various industries. Coiled sheets of steel are fed into fully automated stamping presses, and the steel is formed into different kinds of parts to be used in a manufacturing process at a later time.

Annual overhead costs are as follows:

Depreciation—machinery	$400,000
Engineering costs	250,000
Factory rent	500,000
Sweeping compound for the factory	5,000
Light and heat for the factory	80,000
Factory superintendent's salary	70,000
Machine setup costs	100,000
Quality control salaries	120,000
Machine repairs and maintenance	240,000
Receiving department salaries	140,000
Salaries of direct materials stockroom personnel	80,000
Night guards' salaries for factory building	50,000
Telephone for factory	40,000
Power for machinery	150,000

The following information is available for the year:

Engineering changes	125
Machine setups	500
Direct materials purchases	$880,000
Kilowatt-hours	600,000
Repair and maintenance hours	10,000
Machine-hours	57,250
Number of inspections	2,400

Required   *a.* Group all of the overhead into homogeneous pools.

b. Compute the pool overhead rates using the appropriate cost driver for each pool.

E7–7   **Journal Entries for a Just-In-Time Costing System**

Lap Top Computer Company had the following transactions during the month of January 19x3:

1. Purchased direct materials at a cost of $125,000.
2. Incurred direct labor costs of $30,000.
3. Incurred manufacturing overhead costs of $200,000.
4. Conversion costs applied amounted to $240,000.
5. All merchandise started during the month is completed and sold.
6. Underapplied or overapplied manufacturing overhead is closed only to Cost of Goods Sold at the end of the company's year, which ends December 31, 19x3.

Required   *a.* Journalize the above transactions.

b. Compute the unit cost of each computer if 425 computers were manufactured during January.

E7–8   Journal Entries for a Just-In-Time Costing System

Generous Electric Appliance Company manufactures toaster ovens and had the following transactions during the month of May 19x5:

1. Purchased direct materials at a cost of $300,000.
2. Incurred direct labor costs of $60,000.
3. Incurred manufacturing overhead costs of $400,000.
4. All merchandise started during the month is completed and sold.
5. Underapplied or overapplied manufacturing overhead is closed only to Cost of Goods Sold at the end of the company's year, which ends December 31, 19x5.

During the month of May, the company produced 65,000 toaster ovens; the unit cost per oven was $12.

Required   *a.* Journalize all of the transactions that should be recorded during the month.

b. Compute the amount of under/overapplied overhead for the month of May and indicate whether it is underapplied or overapplied.

E7–9   Journal Entries for a Just-In-Time Costing System

Frigid Electric Appliance Company manufactures freezers; it had the following transactions during the month of June 19x6:

1. Purchased direct materials at a cost of $400,000.
2. Incurred direct labor costs of $80,000.
3. Incurred manufacturing overhead costs of $400,000.
4. All merchandise started during the month is completed and sold.
5. Underapplied or overapplied manufacturing overhead is closed only to Cost of Goods Sold at the end of the company's year, which ends December 31, 19x6. For the month of June, the overapplied overhead amounted to $30,000.

During the month of June, the company produced 7,000 freezers.

Required   *a.* Journalize all of the transactions that should be recorded during the month.

b. Compute the unit cost of each freezer.

► **PROBLEMS**   **P7–10**   **Plant-Wide Rate versus Multiple Overhead Rates Based on Cost Drivers**

John Jefferson, the marketing manager of the Quadstar Electronics firm, had just received an inquiry for 100 subassemblies that are used in the radar tracking systems at most large airports. The price offered was $900, which is $250 less than the normal selling price of $1,150. The firm's policy is to accept only those orders that will yield a 25 percent markup over the full manufacturing cost. He is very anxious to accept the order because he knows his firm could expect more orders from the same customer.

At the weekly manager's meeting, Jefferson made these points to the recently hired controller, Dan Kelly, CMA. Kelly was in the process of reviewing the firm's costing methods. Currently, the firm uses a single plant-wide overhead rate that was applied on the basis of direct labor-hours (DLH). Besides the normal data assembled during the annual budgeting process, Kelly had also assembled the following data on activities and cost drivers:

Next Year's Annual Budget

Expected annual volume:	850,000 DLH
Depreciation: Building	$ 500,000
Depreciation: Equipment	250,000
Engineering	150,000
Energy	95,500
Rework costs	405,000
Supervision	340,000
Miscellaneous overhead	325,000
Total	$2,065,500

Selected Cost Drivers—Estimated Annual Activity

Engineering changes	460
Kilowatt-hours.	220,000
Units reworked	3,425
Machine-hours.	125,000

Kelly wanted to use the information to develop multiple overhead rates based on activities rather than the traditional departmental-based multiple rates. Then using the information below, he would cost out the special order Jefferson had received.

Special order (Estimated data)

Subassemblies ordered	100 Units
Direct labor-hours	6,000
Direct labor cost	$48,750
Direct materials	$12,000
Engineering changes	1
Kilowatt-hours.	925
Units reworked	2
Units spoiled	–0–
Machine-hours.	750

Required
a. (1) Compute the cost of the job using a plant-wide rate.
(2) Compute the gross profit earned by the job.
(3) Would the job be accepted?
b. (1) Compute the cost of the job using the cost drivers given above. Any residual overhead will be assigned using DLH.
(2) Compute the gross profit earned by the job.
(3) Would the job be accepted?
c. Explain which approach is best for the the firm.

P7–11 **Departmental-Based (Traditional) Costing versus Activity-Based Costing—Two Production Departments, One Service Department; Two Products**

Pieto Company has two producing departments and one service department in its manufacturing process. Until last year, it produced one product called A, which is produced in sets of four. This year it added another product called B, which is also produced in sets of four. The addition of product B caused the service department's costs to increase substantially from the prior year.

	Quality Control	Department 1	Department 2
Current Year's Results			
Department cost	$950,000		
Number of inspections		7,500	2,500
Direct labor-hours (DLH)		300,000	60,000
DLH per product A.		13.33	1.00
DLH per product B		8.33	3.75

Other Information

	Prior Year	Current Year
Production:		
Product A (Sets)	15,000	15,000
Product B (Sets)	–0–	12,000
Total	15,000	27,000
Number of inspections:		
Product A.	3,400	3,400
Product B	0	6,600
Total	3,400	10,000

Required

a. Compute the amount of quality control cost that should be allocated to a set of product A and a set of product B using the traditional allocation process.

b. Compute the amount of service department cost allocated to a set of product A last year before product B was added. Quality control cost was $475,000 last year.

c. Allocate the service department's costs directly to the product lines using the cost driver for the allocation base.

d. Which method of allocating costs produces more accurate costing, the traditional approach or the activity-based approach?

P7–12 ### Traditional versus Activity-Based Costing—Pricing Strategy

Computer Components Company manufactures two components for computers, Part A and Part B. The firm has been growing rapidly. Part A is a high-volume product and Part B's sales volume is about one-third of that for Part A. Foreign competition, primarily Japanese, has been undercutting the volume of Part A.

The company has normal selling prices for $96 for Part A and $73 for Part B. A very important customer of the firm yesterday informed William Lawson, president, that he was offered Part A for $86. The customer assures Lawson that the quality of the product offered was the same as that produced by Computer Components. The customer normally uses 2,000 units of Part A each year.

Lawson calls you into his office to inform you of this problem. It is safe to assume that more of the firm's customers will get this offer. Lawson refers you to previous cost analyses that show the cost of Part A is $71.69. You are asked to recheck the cost analysis to be sure that there is no error. Lawson also informs you that the competition is charging $100 for Part B. Computer Components appears to have this part of the market to itself. You are also asked to analyze the cost allocations to Part B in case there is an error.

The following information is available:

	Part A	Part B
Production in units	85,000	30,000
Direct materials cost per unit	$40.25	$52.30
Direct labor cost per unit	$19.25	$1.50
Overhead per unit	$12.19	$0.82
Cost driver activity:		
Direct labor-hours	148,000	3,500
Machine-hours	8,000	3,000
Number machine setups	15	35
Material moves	350	650
Engineering hours	6,250	3,750
Square feet occupied	5,000	10,000
Costs incurred:		
Machine setup	$ 160,500	
Material handling	120,000	
Engineering	330,000	
Occupancy	450,000	
Total costs	$1,060,500	

Required *a.* Using direct labor-hours as the cost driver, recompute the overhead per unit for each product to determine whether an error has been made. Compute the gross margin per unit for each product.

b. Using activity-based costing, compute the overhead per unit for each product. Compute the gross margin per unit for each product.

c. Do you think that the foreign competition is engaging in "dumping" below cost? Explain your answer.

d. Do you think that the company should adjust its prices for its products? If so, how much should they charge for each product?

P7–13   **Plant-Wide Rate versus Departmental Rates: 2 Departments; Activity-Based Costing**

Given the following:

	Next Year's Budget	
	Component X	Component Z
Yearly production	20,000	300,000
Number of setups	75	25
Machine-hours	15,000	225,000
Direct labor-hours	65,000	975,000
Inspection-hours	1,100	1,600

Budgeted Departmental Data

	Cutting	Finishing
Direct labor-hours:		
Component X	60,000	5,000
Component Z	35,000	940,000
Total	95,000	945,000
Machine-hours:		
Component X	7,500	7,500
Component Z	135,000	90,000
Total	142,500	97,500
Overhead Costs:		
Setup costs	$120,000	$ 90,000
Quality control	110,000	100,000
Electricity	120,000	75,000
Maintenance	150,000	175,000
Total	$500,000	$440,000

Required

a. Using the above information, determine the overhead cost per unit. Use a plant-wide rate based on direct labor-hours.

b. For each product, determine the overhead cost per unit using departmental rates. First use machine-hours for the cutting department and direct labor-hours for the finishing department; then use direct labor-hours for the cutting department and machine-hours for the finishing department.

c. Using activity-based costing, determine the overhead cost per unit. (*Hint:* Combine the electricity with the maintenance costs and use machine-hours as the base.)

d. Which do you think would be more accurate, one plant-wide rate or departmental rates?

e. How does the accuracy of the departmental rates compare with that of the activity-based rates?

P7–14   Plant-Wide versus Multiple-Rate Activity-Based Approach

Lasertonics Company makes three specialty products, X, Y, Z, in the electronics industry. These products are facing heavy competition from foreign and domestic producers. Management is very concerned about the prices charged that are based on costs incurred. The vice president of finance, George Bosa, spoke to the company's controller, Sarah Patterson, to discuss the matter. Realizing that manufacturing overhead is a very large proportion of each product's total cost, Bosa expressed his concern that the company was using a single plant-wide overhead rate based on direct labor-hours. He requested Patterson to study the matter to see whether the method of applying overhead to production should be changed to an activity-based basis.

Patterson determined that the overhead cost for each activity was as follows:

	Overhead Costs
Materials receiving	$ 119,800
Materials moving	523,000
Machine setup	595,000
Machine maintenance and repairs	70,800
Power	94,000
Quality control	30,000
Depreciation—machinery	104,000
Occupancy and other	443,000
Total	$1,979,600

The controller also had the following data available:

	Product X	Product Y	Product Z
Units produced.	7,000	53,000	37,000
Direct labor-hours	32,500	19,500	78,000
Machine-hours	24,600	8,200	49,200
Orders received	179	128	204
Material moves.	83	132	116
Machine setups.	93	148	130
Machine maintenance and repair-hours	1,500	500	3,000
Kilowatt-hours	11,100	3,700	22,200
Inspections	70	112	98
Direct materials unit cost	$56.00	$62.00	$46.00
Direct labor unit cost	$45.25	$3.75	$21.70

Required

a. Determine the unit cost of each product using a plant-wide rate based on direct labor-hours.

b. Determine the unit cost of each product using activity-based costing. Use machine-hours as the cost driver for machine depreciation and occupancy and other overhead costs.

c. Explain how the plant-wide rate compares with the activity-based costing approach. Which do you think produces better cost information? Why?

P7–15 **Discussion of Activity-Based Costing**

Many companies now recognize that their cost systems are inadequate for today's powerful global competition. Managers in companies selling multiple products are making important product decisions based on distorted cost information because most cost systems designed in the past focused on inventory valuation. To elevate the level of management information, current literature suggests that companies should have as many as three cost systems for (1) inventory valuation, (2) operational control, and (3) activity-based costing, which is also known as *individual product cost measurement.*

Required

a. Discuss why the traditional cost system, developed to value inventory, distorts product cost information.

b. Identify the purpose and characteristics of each of the following cost systems:
   (1) Inventory valuation.
   (2) Operational control.
   (3) Activity-based costing.

c. (1) Describe the benefits that management can expect from activity-based costing.
   (2) List the steps that a company, using a traditional cost system, would take to implement activity-based costing.

(CMA Adapted)

P7–16 **Conversion to Activity-Based Costing**

Moss Manufacturing has just completed a major change in its quality control (QC) process. Previously, products had been reviewed by QC inspectors at the end of each major process, and the company's 10 QC inspectors were charged as direct labor to the operation or job. In an effort to improve efficiency and quality, a computerized video QC system was purchased for $250,000. The system consists of a minicomputer, 15 video cameras, other peripheral hardware, and software.

The new system uses cameras stationed by QC engineers at key points in the production process. Each time an operation changes or there is a new operation, the cameras are moved, and a new master picture is loaded into the computer by a QC engineer. The camera takes pictures of the units in process, and the computer compares them to the picture of a "good" unit. Any differences are sent to a QC engineer who removes the bad units and discusses the flaws with the production supervisors. The new system has replaced the 10 QC inspectors with two QC engineers.

The operating costs of the new QC system, including the salaries of the QC engineers, have been included as factory overhead in calculating the company's plant-wide factory overhead rate, which is based on direct labor dollars.

The company's president is confused. His vice president of production has told him how efficient the new system is, yet there is a large increase in the factory overhead rate. The computation of the rate before and after automation is shown below.

	Before	After
Budgeted overhead	$1,900,000	$2,100,000
Budgeted direct labor	1,000,000	700,000
Budgeted overhead rate	190%	300%

"Three hundred percent," lamented the president. "How can we compete with such a high factory overhead rate?"

Required
a. (1) Define *factory overhead*, and cite three examples of typical costs that would be included in factory overhead.
   (2) Explain why companies develop factory overhead rates.
b. Explain why the increase in the overhead rate should not have a negative financial impact on Moss Manufacturing.
c. Explain, in the greatest detail possible, how Moss Manufacturing could change its overhead accounting system to eliminate confusion over product costs.
d. Discuss how an activity-based costing system might benefit Moss Manufacturing

(CMA Adapted)

P7–17 ## Traditional Costing versus JIT Costing

Steinroad Piano Company is using a traditional cost accounting system. Due to foreign competition, the company called in management and accounting experts to advise whether the company should change its production methods and accounting system. Steinroad manufactures two kinds of pianos, the concert grand and the home spinet. The foreign competition for the concert grand is minimal because the company's reputation in this field is virtually unchallenged. However, the competition for the home spinet is fierce.

The factory is organized by departments (i.e., woodcutting, planing and sanding, gluing, stringing, and finishing). During the past year, the following transactions occurred:

1. Purchased $800,000 of direct materials.
2. Issued $600,000 of direct materials to production. Of this amount, $150,000 was for concert grands.
3. Incurred $120,000 material moving costs between departments.
4. Direct labor incurred for concert grands amounted to $100,000; direct labor for home spinets was $250,000.
5. Factory supervisory salaries—one for each line of business—amounted to $50,000 each for a total of $100,000.
6. Straight-line depreciation of machinery and equipment amounted to $200,000.
7. Factory occupancy costs—rent, heating, lighting, and so on—amounted to $250,000.
8. Power for machinery amounted to $60,000.
9. Engineering costs amounted to $80,000.

10. Repair and maintenance to machinery amounted to $130,000.
11. Direct material storage costs amounted to $60,000.
12. Other miscellaneous overhead amounted to $260,000.
13. There was no over/underapplied overhead for the year.
14. There were no beginning inventories. Ending inventories of work in process were negligible and may be ignored.
15. Manufacturing overhead is applied to production at 360 percent of direct labor cost.

The management and accounting consultants have surveyed and analyzed the firm's operations, and they were able to ascertain the following:

1. Production for the year amounted to 122 concert grands and 1,600 home spinets.
2. Material moves were 800 for concert grands and 1,600 for home spinets.
3. Machine-hours were 40,000 for concert grands and 60,000 for home spinets.
4. Kilowatt-hours were 80,000 for concert grands and 120,000 for home spinets.
5. Engineering-hours were 1,200 for concert grands and 800 for home spinets.

Required
a. Compute the unit costs of production for each product for last year.
b. Using each product as a cost objective, identify each cost above as either a direct cost (D) or an indirect cost (I) under the traditional costing system.
c. Assume that the company intends to change its operations to a JIT system organized into two flexible manufacturing cells, one for concert grands, the other for home spinets. Using each product as a cost objective, identify each cost above as a direct cost (D), an indirect cost (I), or a nonvalue-added cost (NV) under the JIT costing system.
d. Compute the unit cost for each product using all of the possible pools that can be used from the cost drivers given, assuming that the firm had used JIT last year. All overhead that cannot be otherwise classified into a specific pool should be combined into one pool, and that pool should be applied to overhead using machine hours as the cost driver.
e. What can you say about the use of JIT compared to traditional costing in view of the fierce competition on home spinets?

P7–18 Journal Entries for JIT Costing

Utilizing the information provided in Problem 7–17, prepare the journal entries for the year assuming that the firm had used JIT costing for that year. (*Hint:* Some of the costs incurred in that problem would not be incurred if the firm had used JIT. Be sure that these costs are not included in your journal entries.)

P7–19 Traditional Costing versus JIT Costing

Smart Electronics Company is using a traditional cost accounting system. Due to foreign competition, the company called in management and accounting experts to advise whether the company should change its production methods and accounting system. Smart manufactures high-quality automated photocopiers for the high end of the market and fax machines. The foreign competition for the photocopiers is not so intense as the competition for the fax machines because the company enjoys a high reputation in the photocopying field.

The factory is organized by departments (i.e., receiving, stockroom, and assembling). During the past year, the following transactions occurred:

1. Purchased $1,600,000 of direct materials.
2. Issued $1,400,000 of direct materials to production. Of this amount, $800,000 was for photocopiers.
3. Incurred $200,000 of material moving costs between departments.
4. Direct labor incurred for photocopiers amounted to $200,000, while direct labor for faxes was $500,000.

5. Factory supervisory salaries—one for each line of business—amounted to $60,000 each for a total of $120,000.
6. Straight-line depreciation of machinery and equipment amounted to $500,000.
7. Factory occupancy costs—rent, heating, lighting, and so forth—amounted to $600,000.
8. Power for machinery amounted to $130,000.
9. Engineering costs amounted to $300,000.
10. Repair and maintenance to machinery amounted to $250,000.
11. Direct material storage costs amounted to $100,000.
12. Other miscellaneous overhead amounted to $600,000.
13. There was no over/underapplied overhead for the year.
14. There were no beginning inventories. Ending inventories of work in process were negligible and may be ignored.
15. Manufacturing overhead is applied to production at 400 percent of direct labor cost.

The management and accounting consultants surveyed and analyzed the firm's operations, and they were able to ascertain the following:

1. Production for the year amounted to 30 photocopiers and 15,500 faxes.
2. Material moves were 400 for photocopiers and 600 for faxes.
3. Machine-hours were 20,000 for photocopiers and 30,000 for faxes.
4. Kilowatt-hours were 208,000 for photocopiers and 312,000 for faxes.
5. Engineering-hours were 7,000 for photocopiers and 3,000 for faxes.

Required
a. Compute the unit costs of production for each product for last year.
b. Using each product as a cost objective, identify each cost above as either a direct cost (D) or an indirect cost (I) under the traditional costing system.
c. Assume that the company intends to change its operations to a JIT system organized into two flexible manufacturing cells, one for photocopiers, the other for faxes. Using each product as a cost objective, identify each cost above as a direct cost (D), an indirect cost (I), or a nonvalue-added cost (NV) under the JIT costing system.
d. Compute the unit cost for each product using all of the possible pools that can be used from the cost drivers given, assuming that the firm had used JIT last year. All overhead that cannot be otherwise classified into a specific pool should be combined into one pool, and that pool should be applied to overhead using machine-hours as the cost driver.
e. What can you say about the use of JIT compared to traditional costing in view of the competition on faxes?

P7–20 **Journal Entries for JIT Costing**
Utilizing the information provided in Problem 7–19, prepare the journal entries for the year assuming that the firm had used JIT costing for that year. (*Hint:* Some of the costs incurred in that problem would not be incurred if the firm had used JIT. Be sure that these costs are not included in your journal entries.)

▶ **ETHICAL BEHAVIOR CASE**

C7–21 **Activity Costing and Ethical Behavior**
Custom Electronics Company manufactures electrical equipment, such as transformers used in power transmission lines, for electric public utilities. Because of the maturity of the industry, sales have fallen, and the firm is planning to expand into other businesses. Thus far, the firm has not sought any work from government agencies, but it recently subscribed to government publications and trade newspapers that invite firms to bid on government contracts. The firm is now interested in a

government contract to manufacture special custom-made transformers for the U.S. Army. Because this product has never been manufactured before, the government is inviting bids with a price-redetermination clause in the contract. This clause permits the government to audit the contractor's books at the conclusion of the contract when all of the transformers are delivered. The terms of the contract specify that the government will allow the contractor to recover the price specified in the bid provided that this amount is not greater than the total costs incurred by the contractor plus a reasonable profit based on the firm's normal profit percentage. If the price charged exceeds this amount, such excess must be refunded to the government. Thus, this clause is intended to prevent contractors from making exorbitant profits from the government by deliberately bidding unusually high prices on contracts for custom-made products.

The firm is now using activity-based costing with cost pools that have the following cost drivers:

1. Number of material moves.
2. Number of parts received.
3. Number of units reworked.
4. Number of engineering changes.
5. Number of machine setups.
6. Number of inspections.
7. Number of machine-hours.

The controller of the company has asked you, a recently hired management accountant, to do sensitivity analysis of the cost drivers. Specifically, the controller has asked you to work with the budgeted commercial production for next year and has given you the expected commercial production. To this you are to add the government contract as if the contract were awarded to the firm. You are to prepare a cost analysis of how much overhead would be applied to government production and how much would be applied to commercial production using the existing cost drivers. You are then to prepare similar analyses by eliminating one cost pool and combining that cost driver's costs with another cost pool. You are expected to do this for all possible combinations. In addition, you are also to prepare similar analyses using single plant-wide rates with machine-hours, direct labor costs, and direct labor-hours as the cost drivers. Needless to say, each of these analyses produced results with different amounts of overhead assigned to commercial production and government production. After you performed these tedious tasks, the controller called you into his office and told you what a great job you had done.

A few months later, you are happy to learn that your hard work had paid off and that the firm had been awarded the government contract. However, to your dismay, you find that the firm had changed the method of assigning its overhead to production and that the method chosen was the one that assigns the most overhead to government production and the least amount of overhead to commercial production.

Required   Discuss your position in this matter considering the legal, moral, and ethical implications. Indicate what steps, if any, you are prepared to take to bring this matter to an ethical conclusion. (You may wish to refer to Chapter 1, which discussed these issues.)

▶ **ANSWERS TO SELF-TEST**

True or False

1. True	2. True	3. True	4. False	5. False	6. True
7. False	8. False	9. True	10. True		

Multiple Choice

1. *c.*   2. *a.*   3. *b.*   4. *d.*

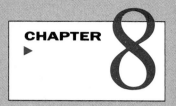

CHAPTER
▶

Cost Allocation— Service Departments and Joint Products

▶ **LEARNING OBJECTIVES**

After reading this chapter, you should be able to:

1. Explain why it may be necessary to departmentalize overhead.
2. Allocate service department overhead to producing departments.
3. Describe the different methods used to allocate service department overhead to the producing departments and discuss the advantages and disadvantages of each.
4. Explain why many firms prefer to allocate overhead separately for the fixed and variable portions.
5. Describe what is meant by joint product costs and explain why it is necessary to allocate them.
6. Discuss the different methods used to allocate joint product costs and when it is appropriate to use each one.

Q. *How does the chapter describe what is meant by joint product costs? Can you explain why it is necessary to allocate them? (Learning Objective 5)*

A. The explanation of joint product costs and the necessity to allocate them is accomplished with the discussion of the cattle example.

Q. *In the course of reviewing this chapter, what would you consider the basic strengths of the chapter? Please give examples that help best explain the topic of cost allocation to your students.*

A. The basic strength of this chapter is that it covers the standard material that professors are looking for in a chapter like this. Another strength might be that the author uses an adequate number of examples.

Q. *In the course of your work, have you taught the different methods used to allocate service department overhead to the producing departments? Give examples of methods that you use in your classroom discussion.*

A. I don't believe too many professors bother with the reciprocal approach. Instead, if they're going beyond the stepdown method, it will be the mathematical (matrix) approach. I personally do not have the students do calculations with the mathematical approach because I do not use a spreadsheet in the management accounting class for this type of a problem.

▶ The method used to allocate costs can often unduly influence decision making. For example, we saw in Chapter 5 that the amount of overhead assigned to a particular job could be different depending on the choice of the overhead base used, direct labor cost or direct labor-hours. Thus, all overhead cost allocations are somewhat arbitrary, and management accountants usually seek ways to refine their cost-allocation methods to minimize the distortions that may arise from the use of a particular method of cost allocation.

More sophisticated cost allocations may be achieved by departmentalizing overhead instead of using one overhead pool for all factory overhead. When this method is used, departmentalization usually results in separate overhead pools for each producing department and service department. A **producing department** is any department, such as machining and finishing, in which employees work on converting direct materials into finished goods; a **service department** is one in which employees perform such ancillary functions as making repairs, operating the factory cafeteria, and maintaining personnel and payroll records. Once the overhead is departmentalized, each service department's overhead must then be allocated to the producing departments. This allocation may be achieved through the use of different allocation methods, depending on the degree of sophistication desired. Once this allocation is completed, the resulting producing departments' overheads are then assigned to the products manufactured in the departments. Similar allocation procedures are used for service departments in service industries.

These allocations may be for overhead in total without any separation for fixed and variable overhead. Although, this approach is simpler than using separate allocations for fixed and variable overhead, distortions may arise from the use of this approach. To reduce such distortions, many firms make separate allocations for fixed and variable overhead.

Very often, a firm uses one direct material, such as livestock, to manufacture several different products, such s steaks, salami, and dog food. The cost of the direct material must be allocated to the separable products in order to determine inventory valuations of any products remaining on hand at the end of an accounting period. Recall that it is necessary to value work in process and finished goods inventories so that financial statements at the end of an accounting period may be prepared. ◀

Overhead Departmentalization

L.O. 1

If a firm has at least one labor-intensive department and one machine-intensive department, a factorywide overhead rate would produce distortions in the assignment of overhead to specific jobs and could possibly provide misleading information for pricing decisions. Another reason for departmentalized overhead rates is that different jobs require different proportions of processing time in the various departments. Although it is impossible to obtain completely accurate information, a firm that desires high accuracy will likely departmentalize its overhead application. In doing so, the firm must examine each item of manufacturing overhead and allocate it to all affected departments using a specific allocation mechanism. For example, if a firm has a machining department that is machine intensive and a finishing department that is labor intensive, the factory rent can be allocated on the basis of the square feet occupied by each department. A table of allocation bases for various forms of manufacturing overhead is presented in Illustration 8-1.

In departmentalizing overhead, the first step is to prepare a factory survey, by department, of square feet occupied, number of employees, labor cost, and machinery horsepower ratings. Then, each item of overhead is allocated to a department using the bases suggested in Illustration 8-1. Next,

▶ **ILLUSTRATION 8-1**   Allocation Bases for Departmentalizing Overhead

Factory Overhead	Basis for Allocation
Factory rent	Square feet occupied
Repairs to factory	Square feet occupied
Repairs to machinery	Direct to department
Depreciation—machinery	Direct to department
Superintendence	Number of employees
Heat	Square feet occupied
Light and power	Horsepower/kilowatt rating
Indirect labor	Direct to department
Insurance	Investment in equipment
Payroll fringes	Payroll cost
Factory cafeteria	Number of employees
Factory hospital	Number of employees
Cost accounting	Labor-hours
Maintenance	Direct to department

▶ **ILLUSTRATION 8-2**   Factory Survey

Department	Basis			
	Square Feet	No. of Employees	Payroll Cost	Horse-Power
Producing Department A	16,000	20	$ 300,000	40,000
Producing Department B	9,000	80	900,000	5,000
Maintenance service	5,000	10	120,000	3,500
Factory cafeteria.	6,000	10	90,000	1,000
Factory hospital	4,000	5	90,000	500
Totals.	40,000	125	$1,500,000	50,000

the service departments' costs are allocated to the producing departments. Because production passes only through *producing* departments, only *their* time is used to apply overhead to production. Finally, the total for each producing department is divided by an appropriate base to arrive at a predetermined rate for each producing department.

Illustrations 8-2 and 8-3 show a sample factory survey and the allocation of overhead to all departments. In addition,

1. The service log indicates that maintenance was done in accordance with the following schedule:

   Producing Department A . . .   70%
   Producing Department B . . .   20
   Factory cafeteria.   5
   Factory hospital   5

2. Producing Department A is machine intensive and is estimated to operate at 40,000 machine-hours for the year.
3. Producing Department B is labor intensive and is estimated to operate at 160,000 labor-hours for the year. The predetermined rate will be based on labor-hours.

▶ **ILLUSTRATION 8-3**   Departmental Overhead Allocation

Cost Item	Total	Producing Departments		Service Departments		
		A	B	Maintenance	Factory Cafeteria	Factory Hospital
Payroll fringes	$ 500,000	$100,000	$300,000	$ 40,000	$ 30,000	$ 30,000
Indirect labor	360,000	30,000	30,000	120,000	90,000	90,000
Superintendence	50,000	8,000	32,000	4,000	4,000	2,000
Factory rent	100,000	40,000	22,500	12,500	15,000	10,000
Light and power	75,000	60,000	7,500	5,250	1,500	750
Heat	20,000	8,000	4,500	2,500	3,000	2,000
Repairs to machinery	40,000	35,000	4,000	1,000	—	—
Depreciation of machinery.	100,000	80,000	15,000	2,000	1,000	2,000
Totals	$1,245,000	$361,000	$415,500	$187,250	$144,500	$136,750

Allocation of Service Department Overhead to Producing Departments

L.O. 2

L.O. 3

There are many approaches to the allocation of service department costs to producing departments. The most accurate is the mathematical approach, which uses complex equations that are best solved by computers or matrix inversion. Less sophisticated methods that yield approximate results make use of simple decision rules. Allocation problems arise when one service department renders service to another service department. It must then be determined which department's overhead should be allocated first, which should be allocated next, and so on.

Aside from a mathematical solution, one of three different approaches may be used: (1) the direct method, (2) the step-down method, and (3) the reciprocal, or redistribution, method.

The Direct Method   The simplest method to implement is the **direct method** because it ignores the services rendered between service departments and allocates all service department costs to producing departments only. It is also the least accurate of the three methods because it ignores the interdepartmental activities between service departments. Nonetheless, if the service departments' overhead is small in relation to the producing departments' overhead, the direct method may be used without causing wide distortions in overhead allocation. This method is shown in Illustration 8-4.

Although the maintenance log indicates that the factory cafeteria and the factory hospital each required 5 percent of the maintenance department's services, this aspect is *ignored* when the direct method is used, and the maintenance department's costs of $187,250 are assigned only to departments A and B in the ratio of 70 : 20 instead of 70 : 20 : 5 : 5, as noted in the service log. Similarly, even though the maintenance department has 10 employees and the factory hospital has 5 employees, the two departments are ignored when allocating the factory cafeteria's costs of $144,500. These costs are allocated only to the producing departments in proportion to their number of employees (20 : 80). The factory hospital's costs are also allocated on the basis of the number of employees (20 : 80), and its services to the

▶ **ILLUSTRATION 8-4**   Departmental Overhead Allocation: Direct Allocation Method

Cost Item	Total	Producing Departments		Service Departments		
		A	B	Maintenance	Factory Cafeteria	Factory Hospital
Payroll fringes	$ 500,000	$100,000	$300,000	$ 40,000	$ 30,000	$ 30,000
Indirect labor	360,000	30,000	30,000	120,000	90,000	90,000
Superintendence	50,000	8,000	32,000	4,000	4,000	2,000
Factory rent	100,000	40,000	22,500	12,500	15,000	10,000
Light and power	75,000	60,000	7,500	5,250	1,500	750
Heat	20,000	8,000	4,500	2,500	3,000	2,000
Repairs to machinery	40,000	35,000	4,000	1,000	—	—
Depreciation of machinery.	100,000	80,000	15,000	2,000	1,000	2,000
Totals.	$1,245,000	$361,000	$415,500	$187,250	$144,500	$136,750
Maintenance (7:2)*.	–0–	145,639	41,611	(187,250)		
Factory cafeteria (2:8)†	–0–	28,900	115,600		(144,500)	
Factory hospital (2:8)†	–0–	27,350	109,400			(136,750)
Totals.	$1,245,000	$562,889	$682,111	$ –0–	$ –0–	$ –0–
Basis.		40,000 machine-hours				
Basis			160,000 labor-hours			
Predetermined rate for allocating producing department overhead		$14.072 per machine-hour	$4.263 per labor-hour			

* From the maintenance log, 70% and 20%.
† Based on the number of employees—Department A, 20 employees; and Department B, 80 employees.

maintenance department and the factory cafeteria are ignored. Although the maintenance department allocation was completed first, the sequence of allocation is not relevant when the direct method is used. Any sequence of allocation would produce the same result.

When the allocations are completed, the predetermined rates are computed as follows:

Department A

$$\frac{\$562,889}{40,000 \text{ machine-hours}} = \$14.072 \text{ per machine-hour}$$

Department B

$$\frac{\$682,111}{160,000 \text{ labor-hours}} = \$4.263 \text{ per labor-hour}$$

L.O. 3

The Step-Down Method   The **step-down method** is more sophisticated than the direct method and, therefore, produces a more accurate result. This approach recognizes services provided to other service departments and sequentially allocates overhead to each department. A popular set of decision rules for selecting the sequence of service department allocation is:

1. Begin with the department that services the largest number of other service departments. If it is impossible to select one department that meets this criterion, select the one with the largest dollar amount of overhead. The purpose is to distribute as much service department overhead as possible to other service departments before turning to the producing departments.
2. When rule 1 can no longer be applied, allocate the department that services the largest number of other departments including producing departments. When it is no longer possible to use this criterion, select the one with the largest dollar amount of overhead.
3. When all service department overhead accounts have been closed, the allocation procedure is complete.

When the step-down method is used, it is important to remember that *once a service department's overhead account is closed, it is not reopened.* The next service department is selected, and the process is repeated until all service department accounts are closed. This method is shown in Illustration 8-5.

This example makes use of the basic step-down decision rules. Because all three service departments rendered services to the other two and were thus all tied for the first allocation, the one with the largest dollar amount of overhead—the maintenance department—was allocated first. This time, the ratio noted in the service log, $70:20:5:5$, was used. The second allocation would be from the department that had the largest dollar amount of over head *after* the allocation from the maintenance department. In this case, the dollar amount of overhead for the cafeteria was larger than that for the hospital *both before and after* the allocation from the maintenance department, but this need not be the case. The allocation ratio became $20:80:5$ instead of $20:80:10:5$ because the maintenance department's overhead account was closed once it was allocated. Finally, the factory hospital's overhead is allocated using the ratio $20:80$ because both the maintenance department and the factory cafeteria have been omitted.

When the allocations are completed, the predetermined rates are computed as follows:

Department A

$$\frac{\$552,070}{40,000 \text{ machine-hours}} = \$13.802 \text{ per machine-hour}$$

Department B

$$\frac{\$692,930}{160,000 \text{ labor-hours}} = \$4.331 \text{ per labor-hour}$$

L.O. 3

Reciprocal (Redistribution) Method   The **reciprocal method** is similar to the step-down method except service department overhead accounts are reopened after each iteration, and the process is repeated until the amounts reallocated to a closed service department account are negligible (usually less than $100). Each round of closing and reopening produces succeedingly

▶ **ILLUSTRATION 8-5**   Departmental Overhead Allocation: Step-Down Allocation Method

Cost Item	Total	Producing Departments		Service Departments		
		A	B	Maintenance	Factory Cafeteria	Factory Hospital
Payroll fringes	$ 500,000	$100,000	$300,000	$ 40,000	$ 30,000	$ 30,000
Indirect labor	360,000	30,000	30,000	120,000	90,000	90,000
Superintendence	50,000	8,000	32,000	4,000	4,000	2,000
Factory rent	100,000	40,000	22,500	12,500	15,000	10,000
Light and power	75,000	60,000	7,500	5,250	1,500	750
Heat . . . . `.` . . .	20,000	8,000	4,500	2,500	3,000	2,000
Repairs to machinery	40,000	35,000	4,000	1,000	—	—
Depreciation of machinery.	100,000	80,000	15,000	2,000	1,000	2,000
Totals	$1,245,000	$361,000	$415,500	$187,250	$144,500	$136,750
Maintenance (70 : 20 : 5 : 5)*	–0–	131,075	37,450	(187,250)	9,363	9,362
Factory cafeteria (20 : 80 : 5)†.	–0–	29,307	117,229		(153,863)	7,327
Factory hospital (20 : 80)†	–0–	30,688	122,751			(153,439)
Totals	$1,245,000	$552,070	$692,930	$ –0–	$ –0–	$ –0–
Basis.	40,000 machine-hours					
Basis		160,000 labor-hours				
Predetermined rate for allocating producing department overhead	$13.802 per machine-hour	$4.331 per labor-hour				

* From the maintenance log.
† Number of employees.

smaller numbers until the negligible amount is closed in the last iteration without reopening any service department account.

Illustration 8-6 shows the first and second cycles of the closing and reopening process. For the maintenance department, the first cycle closing amounted to $187,250, and after the reopening, $26,112 was reallocated from the factory cafeteria and the factory hospital. In the second cycle, the $26,112 was again closed, and after the reopening, $1,381 remained. After several more cycles, the reopened balance was closed without any further reopenings.

It is interesting to note that the predetermined overhead rates in Illustration 8-6 ($14.160 and $4.241) are closer to those calculated with the direct method (Illustration 8-4) than they are to those calculated with the step-down method. This need not be the usual case.

L.O. 3   ***Mathematical Approach***   When the greatest degree of accuracy in allocating service department costs is desired, a **mathematical approach** must be used. In this approach, the information is set into mathematical equations that are solved either simultaneously or by substitution.

▶ **ILLUSTRATION 8-6**   Departmental Overhead Allocation: Reciprocal (Redistribution) Method

Cost Item	Total	Producing Departments		Service Departments		
		A	B	Maintenance	Factory Cafeteria	Factory Hospital
Payroll fringes	$ 500,000	$100,000	$300,000	$ 40,000	$ 30,000	$ 30,000
Indirect labor	360,000	30,000	30,000	120,000	90,000	90,000
Superintendence	50,000	8,000	32,000	4,000	4,000	2,000
Factory rent	100,000	40,000	22,500	12,500	15,000	10,000
Light and power	75,000	60,000	7,500	5,250	1,500	750
Heat	20,000	8,000	4,500	2,500	3,000	2,000
Repairs to machinery	40,000	35,000	4,000	1,000	—	—
Depreciation of machinery.	100,000	80,000	15,000	2,000	1,000	2,000
Totals	$1,245,000	$361,000	$415,500	$187,250	$144,500	$136,750
Maintenance (70 : 20 : 5 : 5)	–0–	131,075	37,450	(187,250)	9,363	9,362
Factory cafeteria (20 : 80 : 10 : 5)	–0–	26,759	107,035	13,379	(153,863)	6,690
Factory hospital (20 : 80 : 10 : 10)	–0–	25,467	101,868	12,733	12,734	(152,802)
Subtotal, first cycle	$1,245,000	$544,301	$661,853	$ 26,112	$ 12,734	$ –0–
Second cycle:						
Maintenance (70 : 20 : 5 : 5)	–0–	18,278	5,222	(26,112)	1,306	1,306
Factory cafeteria (20 : 80 : 10 : 5)	–0–	2,442	9,767	1,221	(14,040)	610
Factory hospital (20 : 80 : 10 : 10)	–0–	319	1,277	160	160	(1,916)
Subtotal, second cycle	$1,245,000	$565,340	$678,119	$ 1,381	$ 160	$ –0–
Totals	$1,245,000	$566,381	$678,619	$ –0–	$ –0–	$ –0–
Basis		40,000 machine-hours				
Basis			160,000 labor-hours			
Predetermined rate for allocating producing department overhead		$14.160 per machine-hour	$4.241 per labor-hour			

For example, assume a firm has two producing departments, A and B, and two service departments, C and D. Their allocated overheads are:

Department A	. . .	$100,000
Department B	. . .	200,000
Department C	. . .	80,000
Department D	. . .	50,000
Total	. . . . .	$430,000

Departments C and D render the following services:

Department C	. . .	30% to A
		50% to B
		20% to D
Department D	. . .	60% to A
		30% to B
		10% to C

The equations can be solved by substitution and would be set up as:

$$A = \$100,000 + .3C + .6D$$
$$B = \$200,000 + .5C + .3D$$
$$C = \$\ 80,000 + \qquad .1D$$
$$D = \$\ 50,000 + .2C$$

The solution can start with Equation C and substitute for D, or it can start with Equation D and substitute for C. Starting with Equation C, the solution proceeds as follows:

$$C = \$80,000 + .1D$$

By substitution:

$$C = \$80,000 + .1(\$50,000 + .2C)$$
$$C = \$80,000 + \$5,000 + .02C$$
$$C = \$85,000 + .02C$$
$$.98C = \$85,000$$
$$C = \$86,735$$

Therefore:

$$D = \$50,000 + .2C$$
$$D = \$50,000 + .2(\$86,735)$$
$$D = \$50,000 + \$17,347$$
$$D = \$67,347$$

And:

$$A = \$100,000 + .3C + .6D$$
$$A = \$100,000 + .3(\$86,735) + .6(\$67,347)$$
$$A = \$100,000 + \$26,020 + \$40,408$$
$$A = \$166,428$$

And:

$$B = \$200,000 + .5C + .3D$$
$$B = \$200,000 + .5(\$86,735) + .3(\$67,347)$$
$$B = \$200,000 + \$43,368 + \$20,204$$
$$B = \$263,572$$

The proof of the above calculations would be:

Total overhead . . .	$430,000
Department A. . . .	$166,428
Department B. . . .	263,572
Total.	$430,000

The results of the mathematical solution, which are technically accurate, can be compared with the results obtained by the step-down method shown in Illustration 8-7.

Although the difference in results between the mathematical solution and the step-down method is not large in this case, the results can be materially different, especially when increasingly more departments are involved. As the number of departments increases, the mathematical approach becomes

▶ **ILLUSTRATION 8-7**   Step-Down Overhead Allocation Method

	Total	Producing Departments		Service Departments	
		A	B	C	D
Allocated overhead.	$430,000	$100,000	$200,000	$80,000	$50,000
Department C—3 : 5 : 2	–0–	24,000	40,000	(80,000)	16,000
Department D—6 : 3	–0–	44,000	22,000		(66,000)
Totals.	$430,000	$168,000	$262,000	$ –0–	$ –0–

▶ **PROGRESS CHECK**

1. What is the difference between a producing department and a service department?
2. Why is it important to departmentalize overhead?
3. What is the major advantage of using the direct method for allocating service department costs? The major disadvantage?
4. What are the major differences between the direct method, the step-down method, and the reciprocal (redistribution) methods?
5. Which method of service cost allocation is the most accurate? Is this method easy to use when the allocation is performed manually and the number of departments is many (more than five)? If not, what can you use to assist you to lessen the amount of work involved? ◀

unwieldy to perform manually, and the use of a computer becomes preferable.

Separate Cost Allocations for Fixed and Variable Costs

L.O. 4

Thus far, all service department allocations have treated fixed and variable costs as a single total amount. This procedure is acceptable for the first year that a service department is established. However, when budgeting for years after the first year, the use of this method may result in unintended distortions in the allocation of budgeted costs. As we will see, these distortions occur because variable costs are incurred based on usage for any given period of time, but fixed costs are incurred based on the capacity provided whether or not the capacity is used.

To understand this, let us reconsider the case in which a firm operates a factory cafeteria for its employees. In most cases, the charges for food consumed by employees is charged at prices less than the prices charged by food establishments outside the factory. Very often, the factory cafeteria operates at a loss, both to provide employees with a fringe benefit and to save employees the time they would spend traveling to an outside establishment. In some cases, food is even provided to employees free of charge for the convenience of the firm. The cost of food is a variable cost that varies with the number of employees eating at the cafeteria; the cost of cooks would be considered a fixed cost, as would the cost of ovens and cooking furnishings because the cooks' salaries are fairly constant within a given relevant range. To simplify our example, we will assume that the food is

▶ **ILLUSTRATION 8-8**   Allocation of Total Cafeteria Costs—19x2

Cutting department—	40/200 × $200,000 =	$ 40,000
Finishing department—	160/200 × $200,000 =	160,000
Total allocated		$200,000

provided to employees free of charge. Let us assume that the actual costs for 19x2 are as follows:

Factory Cafeteria Costs

Variable costs	$ 50,000
Fixed costs.	150,000
Total costs	$200,000

Producing Departments' Employees

Cutting department	40
Finishing department . . .	160
Total	200

The total cafeteria costs would be allocated as shown in Illustration 8-8.

Let us now prepare the budget for 19x3 to determine the predetermined overhead rate for 19x3. The finishing department is automating part of its operations, and, accordingly, it anticipates temporarily reducing the number of its employees to 120 (a reduction of 40 employees). This reduction will be short-term since these employees, or other similar employees, are expected to be rehired in a later year when the demand for the company's products expands. The cutting department's operations are expected to remain unchanged, and, thus, the department will continue to employ 40 employees. We will assume that there are no price changes anticipated for 19x3. Thus, the budgeted costs for the cafeteria and number of employees for 19x3 are as follows:

Factory Cafeteria Costs

Variable costs	$ 40,000*
Fixed costs.	150,000
Total costs	$190,000

Producing Departments' Employees

Cutting department	40
Finishing department . . .	120
Total	160

* 160/200 × $50,000

The allocation of cafeteria costs using the budgeted 19x3 total costs would be as shown in Illustration 8-9.

When comparing Illustration 8-8 and Illustration 8-9, you will notice that when we allocated the cafeteria costs by using the single total amount, the

▶ **ILLUSTRATION 8-9**   Allocation of Total Cafeteria Costs—19x3

> Cutting department—   40/160 × $190,000 = $ 47,500
> Finishing department—120/160 × $190,000 =   142,500
> Total allocated $190,000

cutting department's budgeted cafeteria costs for 19x3 increased by $7,500 (19x2—$40,000, 19x3—$47,500). This increase occurred even though there were no price changes and the number of cutting department employees was expected to remain the same. However, the finishing department's budgeted cafeteria costs for 19x3 decreased by $7,500 (19x2—$150,000, 19x3—$142,500). Let us see why this happened by analyzing only the fixed costs. The allocation of fixed costs for 19x2 is as follows:

> Cutting department (40/200 × $150,000). . . . . $ 30,000
> Finishing department (160/200 × $150,000) . . .   120,000

For 19x3, using the new employee ratio to allocate fixed costs would give the following:

> Cutting department (40/160 × $150,000). . . . . $ 37,500
> Finishing department (120/160 × $150,000) . . .   112,500

From the above, it can be seen that because the finishing department reduced its staff by 40 employees, it would be able to shift $7,500 of the cafeteria's fixed costs to the cutting department. The manager of the cutting department could make a strong argument that the department is being unfairly penalized by the action of another department manager, especially because the reduction in staff is expected to be short-term.

The manager would be correct. When it is necessary to consider allocations for future years, variable costs should be allocated using a short-term rate based on consumption. In this case, the rate would be the percentage of departmental employees (departmental employees divided by total employees) multiplied by the variable costs incurred.

Fixed costs should be treated differently because they do not depend on the short-term fluctuations in the number of employees using the service department. When a service department is established, certain capacities are provided to accommodate the departments it services. The initial establishment of capacities requires a long-term commitment of fixed costs. Therefore, it follows that the producing department that causes this long-term commitment of fixed costs should be charged for its incurrence regardless of short-term fluctuations of usage. Thus, the allocation to each consuming department of the fixed costs of a service department should remain constant from year to year if the total fixed costs of the service department remain unchanged. Only if there is a permanent change in a department's utilization should the capacity of the service department be examined to see whether some of the fixed costs may be eliminated.

If 19x2 costs are allocated separately for the fixed and variable costs, the results would be as shown in Illustration 8-10.

▶ **ILLUSTRATION 8-10**   Allocation of Variable and Fixed Cafeteria Costs—19x2

Factory Cafeteria Costs

Variable costs . . . . $ 50,000
Fixed costs 150,000
  Total costs $200,000

Cutting Department

Variable costs (40/200 × $50,000) $10,000
Fixed costs (40/200 × $150,000) 30,000
  Total allocated costs $40,000

Finishing Department

Variable costs (160/200 × $50,000) . . . $ 40,000
Fixed costs (160/200 × $150,000) 120,000
  Total allocated costs $160,000

▶ **ILLUSTRATION 8-11**   Allocation of Variable and Fixed Cafeteria Costs—19x3

Factory Cafeteria Costs

Variable costs . . . . $ 40,000
Fixed costs 150,000
  Total costs. $190,000

Cutting Department

Variable costs (40/160 × $40,000). . . . $10,000
Fixed costs (based on 19x2 formula) . . . 30,000
  Total allocated costs $40,000

Finishing Department

Variable costs (120/160 × $40,000) . . . . $ 30,000
Fixed costs (based on 19x2 formula) . . . 120,000
  Total allocated costs $150,000

The allocation of budgeted costs for 19x3 using the separate cost-allocation approach appears in Illustration 8-11.

Notice that this method of allocation charges the cutting department in 19x3 for the same amount ($40,000) as shown in Illustration 8-10 for 19x2.

Expanded Example for Service Industry   Let us now consider an expanded example of allocating service department costs for a service business by allocating variable and fixed costs separately.

The following information is provided for a taxi and limousine service that departmentalizes its operations separately for taxis and limousines. The firm has three service departments, a maintenance department, a building occupancy department, and a payroll department. The kinds of costs and the bases of allocation for the year 19x1, the first year of operations, are as follows:

Department	Cost Type	Basis for Allocation
Maintenance	Grease and oil change	$.008 per mile
	Tire rotation and repair	$.004 per mile
	Normal maintenance	$50 per vehicle
	Building occupancy costs	Number of vehicles
Building	Occupancy costs	Square feet occupied
Payroll	Salaries	Number of employees
	Building occupancy costs	Number of employees

In addition, the costs associated with the operation of the building are to be allocated to the various departments based on each department's square feet occupied.

The behaviors of the various costs are as follows:

Department	Cost Type	Behavior
Maintenance	Grease and oil change	Variable
	Tire rotation and repair	Variable
	Normal maintenance	Variable
	Building occupancy costs	Fixed
Building	Occupancy costs	Fixed
Payroll	Salaries	Fixed
	Building occupancy costs	Fixed

A survey of the expected operations for 19x1 reveals the following:

Department	Number of Employees	Miles Driven (000)	Square Feet Occupied
Maintenance	10	—	12,000
Building	3	—	—
Payroll	1	—	3,000
Taxis	125	12,500	30,000
Limousines	50	2,500	15,000
Totals	189	15,000	60,000

For 19x2, economic activity is expected to be less than that for 19x1 due to a temporary recession. Accordingly, the survey of the expected operations for 19x2 reveals the following:

Department	Number of Employees	Miles Driven (000)	Square Feet Occupied
Maintenance	9	—	12,000
Building	3	—	—
Payroll	1	—	3,000
Taxis	125	12,500	30,000
Limousines	20	1,000	6,000
Totals	158	13,500	51,000

The number of taxis and limousines used by the firm is the same as the number of employees (i.e., only one taxi or limousine is used by an em-

▶ **ILLUSTRATION 8-12**   Cost Data, 19x1

	Maintenance	Building	Payroll	Taxis	Limousines
Variable costs:					
Fuel	$ —	$ —	$ —	$1,080,000	$ 250,000
Salaries	160,000	—	—	3,750,000	750,000
Supplies	28,750	—	—	—	—
Tires	—	—	—	12,500	2,500
Miscellaneous	—	—	—	10,000	2,000
Repairs	—	—	—	62,500	25,000
Total	188,750	—	—	4,915,000	1,029,500
Fixed costs:					
Utilities	—	60,000	—	—	—
Salaries	—	30,000	25,000	100,000	80,000
Miscellaneous	—	280,000	2,200	80,000	50,000
Depreciation	—	330,000	1,000	1,250,000	500,000
Total	—	700,000	28,200	1,430,000	630,000
Total costs	$188,750	$700,000	$28,200	$6,345,000	$1,659,500

▶ **ILLUSTRATION 8-13**   Budgeted Cost Data, 19x2

	Maintenance	Building	Payroll	Taxis	Limousines
Variable costs:					
Fuel	$ —	$ —	$ —	$1,080,000	$100,000
Salaries	144,000	—	—	3,750,000	300,000
Supplies	25,875	—	—	—	—
Tires	—	—	—	12,500	1,000
Miscellaneous	—	—	—	10,000	800
Repairs	—	—	—	62,500	10,000
Total	169,875	—	—	4,915,000	411,800
Fixed costs:					
Utilities	—	60,000	—	—	—
Salaries	—	30,000	25,000	100,000	80,000
Miscellaneous	—	280,000	2,200	80,000	50,000
Depreciation	—	330,000	1,000	1,250,000	200,000
Total	—	700,000	28,200	1,430,000	330,000
Total costs	$169,875	$700,000	$28,200	$6,345,000	$741,800

ployee). For 19x2, the number of limousines not in use will be sold; new ones will be purchased when economic conditions improve.

The actual costs for 19x1 appear in Illustration 8-12.

The 19x2 cost patterns are expected to remain unchanged from those that appeared in 19x1. Stated differently, the fixed costs are not expected to change for 19x2, except for the depreciation of the limousines, nor are the variable costs per mile driven, per vehicle, and per employee expected to change. The budgeted costs for 19x2 that appear in Illustration 8-13 were prepared by using variable cost formulas discussed in Chapter 3; fixed costs remain unchanged from 19x1 costs except for the depreciation of limousines. For example, the 19x2 variable cost for maintenance was estimated at 90 percent of 19x1 costs because the number of maintenance employees was reduced from 10 to 9 employees. The estimations are as follows:

$$19x2 \text{ salaries—19x1 salaries of } \quad \$160{,}000 \times .9 = \$144{,}000$$
$$19x2 \text{ supplies—19x1 supplies of } \quad 28{,}750 \times .9 = \quad 25{,}875$$

The 19x2 variable costs for limousines are 40 percent of 19x1 costs because the number of limousines for 19x2 is estimated at 40 percent of 19x1 limousines ($50 \times 0.40 = 20$).

The preparation of the departmental overhead allocation report may be done by either the direct-allocation method or the step-down method. For our example, we chose the step-down method. Recall that when the step-down method is used, a service department's costs may be allocated to another service department, but once a service department is closed, no further allocations to it are permitted. The departmental overhead allocation report appears in Illustration 8-14. The report should be studied in conjunction with the notes following the illustration.

Notes to Illustration 8-14.

1. The building department's costs are allocated first because its costs affect the most other departments—all four other departments—*and* its costs are higher than the costs of the other department that affects four departments—the payroll department. The departmental costs are allocated using the 19x1 square feet occupied, not the 19x2 square feet. As discussed earlier, the capacity (50 limousines) rather than the budgeted number of limousines (20) is used for allocating fixed costs.
2. The payroll department is allocated next because its costs affect the most remaining departments. Here, too, the 19x1 capacity of 50 employees for limousines is used rather than the 19x2 budgeted number of employees (20).
3. The maintenance department is closed last because its costs affect only the revenue-producing departments. The per-mile costs for grease and oil changes ($.008) and tire rotation and repair ($.004) were combined into one amount ($.012). The fixed costs for the maintenance department amounted to $143,416 ($140,000 + $3,416) and were allocated using the 19x1 capacities of the revenue departments.

The New Manufacturing Environment

Although firms that use the JIT manufacturing philosophy also incur service department costs that must be allocated to producing departments, these firms usually have fewer costs to allocate than do firms that do not use this philosophy. The reason for this is that firms that use flexible manufacturing systems (FMS) usually train a cell's employees to perform repairs and maintenance for the equipment used in the cell. Thus, in these situations, repairs and maintenance are performed by the same employees who manufacture the firm's products, and so these costs are direct costs. In fact, one objective of FMS is to have as many tasks as possible performed within a particular cell without using outside services. This approach minimizes the movement of resources—personnel and equipment—and produces indirect costs that must be allocated. However, it is not possible to eliminate all indirect costs, and, therefore, some allocation of service department costs is still required by the most sophisticated flexible manufacturing systems.

▶ **ILLUSTRATION 8-14**   Departmental Overhead Allocation: Step-Down Method—19x2

		Revenue Departments		Service Departments		
	Total	**Taxis**	**Limousines**	**Maintenance**	**Building**	**Payroll**
Variable costs:						
Fuel	1,180,000	1,080,000	100,000	—	—	—
Salaries	4,194,000	3,750,000	300,000	144,000	—	—
Supplies	25,875	—	—	25,875	—	—
Tires	13,500	12,500	1,000	—	—	—
Miscellaneous	10,800	10,000	800	—	—	—
Repairs	72,500	62,500	10,000	—	—	—
Total	5,496,675	4,915,000	411,800	169,875	—	—
Fixed costs:						
Utilities	60,000	—	—	—	60,000	—
Salaries	235,000	100,000	80,000	—	30,000	25,000
Miscellaneous	412,200	80,000	50,000	—	280,000	2,200
Depreciation	1,781,000	1,250,000	200,000	—	330,000	1,000
Total	2,488,200	1,430,000	330,000	—	700,000	28,200
Total costs	7,984,875	6,345,000	741,800	169,875	700,000	28,200
Allocations:						
Building:						
Maintenance (12,000/60,000) × $700,000 . .				140,000	(140,000)	
Payroll (3,000/60,000) × $700,000					(35,000)	35,000
Taxis (30,000/60,000) × $700,000		350,000			(350,000)	
Limousines (15,000/60,000) × $700,000 . . .			175,000		(175,000)	
Payroll:						
Maintenance (10/185) × $63,200				3,416		(3,416)
Taxis (125/185) × $63,200		42,703				(42,703)
Limousines (50/185) × $63,200			17,081			(17,081)
Maintenance:						
Taxis 12,500,000 miles × $.012		150,000		(150,000)		
Limousines 1,000,000 miles × $.012			12,000	(12,000)		
Taxis 125 vehicles × $50.00		6,250		(6,250)		
Limousines 20 vehicles × $50.00			1,000	(1,000)		
Taxis (125/175) × $14		102,886		(102,886)		
Limousines 50/175 × $14			41,155	(41,155)		
Totals	$7,984,875	$6,996,839	$988,036	$ –0–	$ –0–	$ –0–

Departmental overhead rates:
Taxis   ($6,996,839 ÷ 12,500,000 miles)
$0.5597 per mile.
Limousines ($ 988,036 ÷ 1,000,000 miles) $.9880 per mile.

Joint Product Costs

L.O. 5

Often a firm manufactures several different products from the same direct material. For example, an oil refinery may process crude petroleum into gasoline and petrolatum. Such products produced from a common input and a common production process are called **joint products.** The point in the production process at which the joint products are separated is known as the **splitoff point.** At the splitoff point, a product may either be sold or treated to further processing. The costs of acquiring and processing a common direct material up to the splitoff point are **joint product costs,** and the costs of further processing after the splitoff point are **separable costs.** The relationships among joint products and their costs at a beef-processing plant are shown in Illustration 8-15.

▶ **ILLUSTRATION 8-15**   Relationships between Joint Products and Their Costs

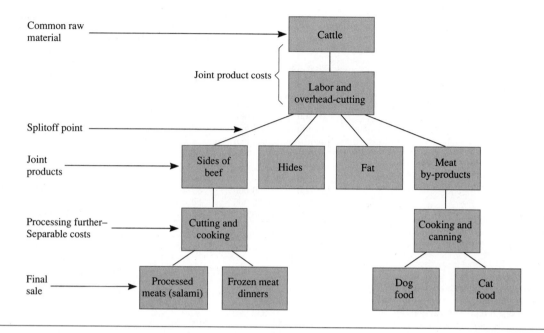

▶ **ILLUSTRATION 8-16**   Data for Dig-It-Out Mining Company, 19x2

Cost of 500,000 tons of ore mined . . . $10,000,000

Production for the year:
   Copper . . . .   4,000,000 pounds
   Silver . . . .   100,000 pounds
   Gold . . . .   10,000 pounds

Ending inventories:
   Copper . . . .   200,000 pounds
   Silver . . . .   1,000 pounds
   Gold . . . .   200 pounds

At the splitoff point, management must often decide whether it is more advantageous to sell the joint products as is or to process them further. When such a choice is available, managers must be familiar with the relevant cost and revenue data to reach a correct conclusion.

Allocated Costs and Inventory Valuation   Income statements and balance sheets cannot be prepared without valuing inventories at a dollar amount. Thus, when joint products are on hand at the end of an accounting period, some value must be assigned to them. To do so, joint product costs must be allocated to specific units of inventory. For example, let us assume that Dig-It-Out Mining Company had joint production costs, production yields, and ending inventories for the year 19x2 as shown in Illustration 8-16.

When mining ore, it is important to note that all three metal ores must be mined because the same ore contains all three metals. Let us also assume

▶ **ILLUSTRATION 8-17**   Joint Cost Allocation and Ending Inventories—Physical Units Method

Joint Cost Allocation

	Pounds	Percent of Total	Allocated Joint Cost	Unit Cost
Copper.	4,000,000	97.324	$ 9,732,400*	$2.433†
Silver	100,000	2.433	243,300‡	2.433§
Gold	10,000	.243	24,300‖	2.433#
Total.	4,110,000	100.000	$10,000,000	

Ending Inventories

Copper.	(200,000 pounds × $2.433)	$486,600
Silver	(1,000 pounds × 2.433)	2,433
Gold	(200 pounds × 2.433)	487
Total.		$489,520

* $10,000,000 × 0.97324.
† $9,732,400/4,000,000.
‡ $10,000,000 × 0.02433.
§ $243,300/100,000.
‖ $10,000,000 × 0.00243.
\# $24,300/10,000.

that copper sells for $.50 per pound; silver sells for $3 per ounce, or $48 per pound; and gold sells for $300 per ounce, or $4,800 per pound.

Several acceptable methods are used when allocating joint costs. Three methods found in practice depend on the nature of the joint costs and the products produced. They are the physical-units method, the relative-sales-value method, and the net-realizable-sales-value method.

L.O. 6

Physical-Units Method Because the **physical-units method** allocates joint production costs on the basis of the physical units of output without any regard to the selling prices of the joint products, it is most appropriate for industries in which each product of output has the same (or almost the same) selling price per unit. The allocation of the joint cost and the ending inventory valuations using the physical-units method for Dig-It-Out Mining Company are shown in Illustration 8-17.

Because the different values of the metals were ignored in the allocation, the unit costs of copper, silver, and gold are all the same. Using this method results in a severe distortion of cost allocation. For example, copper sells at $.50 per pound, yet the cost of the copper is shown as $2.433. If the management of the firm were to use the unit cost of $2.433 for decision making, they would wrongly conclude that they were losing money on the production of copper. In addition, if the $2.433 were used to value the copper inventories, the copper inventories would be severely overstated and would require a write-down to reflect their net realizable values. Decision making involving joint products is discussed further in Chapter 13.

L.O. 6

Relative-Sales-Value Method The obvious distortions produced by the physical-units method in the above example can be corrected by using the relative-sales-value method. The **relative-sales-value method** is essentially a weighted average method using both the physical units produced and the selling prices of the individual products. The joint product cost is allocated

▶ **ILLUSTRATION 8-18**   Joint Cost Allocation and Ending Inventories—Relative-Sales-Value Method

Joint Cost Allocation

Product	Physical Units-Pounds	Sales Price per Pound	Sales Value	Percent of Total Sales Value	Allocated Joint Cost	Unit Cost
Copper	4,000,000	$ .50	$ 2,000,000	3.650*	$ 365,000†	$ .091‡
Silver	100,000	48.00	4,800,000	8.759§	875,900‖	8.759#
Gold	10,000	4,800.00	48,000,000	87.591**	8,759,100††	875.910‡‡
Total			$54,800,000	100.000	$10,000,000	

Ending Inventories

Copper	(200,000 pounds × $	0.091)	$ 18,200
Silver	(1,000 pounds ×	8.759)	8,759
Gold	(200 pounds ×	875.910)	175,182
Total			$202,141

* $2,000,000 ÷ $54,800,000 = 3.650%.
† 10,000,000 × 0.03650 = $365,000.
‡ $365,000 ÷ 4,000,000 pounds = $.091.
§ $4,800,000 ÷ $54,800,000 = 8.759%.
‖ $10,000,000 × 0.08759 = $875,900.
\# $875,900 ÷ 100,000 pounds = $8.759.
** $48,000,000 ÷ $54,800,000 = 87.591%.
†† $10,000,000 × 0.87591 = $8,759,100.
‡‡ $8,759,100 ÷ 10,000 pounds = $875.910.

to the individual products on the basis of their relative sales values. The use of this method is very appropriate when the individual selling prices of the joint products are different. The allocation of the joint cost and the ending inventory valuations using the relative-sales-value method for Dig-It-Out Mining Company is shown in Illustration 8-18.

Notice the difference in the results for Illustration 8-17 and Illustration 8-18. In Illustration 8-17, copper is the most valuable item in the ending inventory, accounting for 99.4 percent of the total inventory, and gold is a mere 1/10 of 1 percent of the total inventory. It should be noted that even if the physical-units method of allocation were to be used, generally accepted accounting principles (GAAP) would mandate that the ending inventory of copper be reduced from $2.433 per pound to the net realizable value of $.50 per pound, a sizable reduction. The reason for this is that GAAP require that inventories be valued at the lower of cost or market for external reporting purposes.

In Illustration 8-18, gold is the most valuable item in the ending inventory, accounting for 86.7 percent of the total inventory, and copper is 9 percent of the total inventory. Using the relative-sales-value method of allocation, copper is valued in the inventory at $.091 per pound and, therefore, no reduction in inventory values would be necessary to comply with GAAP requirements.

L.O. 6

Net-Realizable-Sales-Value Method   The **net-realizable-sales-value method** is a variation of the relative-sales-value method and is especially useful when there is no market for a firm's products at the splitoff point, but instead, these products must be processed further in order to be sold in the marketplace. If this occurs, these products are called **intermediate products.** An example of an intermediate product would be the ingots that an ore processor produces but cannot sell in the marketplace until they are rolled into

▶ **ILLUSTRATION 8-19**   Data for Process Further Mining Company, 19x2

Cost of 300,000 tons of ore mined . . . $6,000,000

Production for the year:
Product A . . . . 4,000,000 pounds
Product B . . . . 2,000,000 pounds
Product C . . . . 4,000,000 pounds

Further processing costs:
Product A $4,000,000
Product B 2,000,000
Product C 4,000,000

Selling price of finished product—per pound:
Product A $4
Product B 3
Product C 5

▶ **ILLUSTRATION 8-20**   Joint Cost Allocation and Unit Costs—Net-Realizable-Sales-Value Method

Joint Cost Allocation

Product	Physical Unit— Pounds	Selling Price per Pound	Sales Value	Further Processing Costs	Theoretical Sales Value at Splitoff	Percent of Total	Allocated Joint Cost	Unit Total Cost
A	4,000,000	$4	$16,000,000	$ 4,000,000	$12,000,000*	37.5†	$2,250,000‡	$1.5625§
B	2,000,000	3	6,000,000	2,000,000	4,000,000‖	12.5#	750,000**	1.375 ††
C	4,000,000	5	20,000,000	4,000,000	16,000,000‡‡	50.0§§	3,000,000‖‖‖	1.75 ##
Total . . .			$42,000,000	$10,000,000	$32,000,000	100.0	$6,000,000	

* $16,000,000 − $4,000,000 = $12,000,000.
† $12,000,000 ÷ $32,000,000 = 37.5%.
‡ $6,000,000 × 0.375 = $2,250,000.
§ $2,250,000 + $4,000,000 separable costs = $6,250,000 ÷ 4,000,000 lbs. = $1.5625.
‖ $10,000,000 − $6,000,000 = $4,000,000.
$4,000,000 ÷ $32,000,000 = 12.5%.
** $6,000,000 × 0.125 = $750,000.
†† $750,000 + $2,000,000 separable costs = $2,750,000 ÷ 2,000,000 lbs. = $1.375.
‡‡ $20,000 − $4,000,000 = $16,000,000.
§§ $16,000,000 ÷ $32,000,000 = 50.0%.
‖‖‖ $6,000,000 × 0.500 = $3,000,000.
$3,000,000 + $4,000,000 separable costs = $7,000,000 ÷ 4,000,000 lbs. = $1.75.

sheets. In such a case, the relative-sales-value method could not be used because there is no selling price for the ingots. However, since there is a market for the firm's rolled sheets, the selling price of the sheets is used as the gross selling price. The cost of rolling the ingots into sheets—a separable cost—is then deducted from the gross selling price of sheets to arrive at a theoretical sales value at splitoff point. This value is called the *net-realizable-sales-value* and is used as the surrogate value of an ingot's selling price at the splitoff point. Once this value is determined, the allocation of joint costs proceeds in the same manner as discussed in the relative-sales-value method.

To illustrate this method, let us assume the data as shown in Illustration 8-19.

The cost allocations and unit costs appear in Illustration 8-20.

► **SUMMARY**

When a firm uses a single overhead pool and a single overhead rate to allocate overhead to its output, the process may cause distortions in the overhead assigned to a particular product. Thus, firms usually departmentalize overhead into separate overhead pools for **producing departments** and **service departments.** A producing department is concerned with producing a firm's goods or services; a service department is concerned with producing services needed by the producing departments and/or other service departments.

There are four methods of allocating service department overhead: the direct method, the step-down method, the reciprocal (redistribution) method, and the mathematical approach. The **direct method** allocates service department overhead to producing departments only and ignores services rendered by service departments to other service departments. The **step-down method** allocates service department overhead to all departments serviced, including other service departments. However, once a service department's overhead account is closed, it is not reopened for any other interservice department overhead allocation. The **reciprocal (redistribution) method** allocates service department overhead to all departments serviced, including other service departments. This method differs from the step-down method in that it permits a service department's overhead account to be reopened after it has been closed and then the allocation procedure is repeated until the successive closings and reopenings of a service department's overhead account produces a small balance in the account. The small balance (usually less than $100) is disposed of expeditiously. The **mathematical approach** is the most accurate method and assigns service department costs to producing departments through the use of mathematical equations that are usually solved by a computer.

In addition to departmentalizing overhead, many firms analyze each department's overhead into its fixed and variable portions. Rather than allocating a service department's overhead in total, these firms prefer to allocate the department's overhead separately for the fixed and variable portions. A service department's variable overhead should be allocated to a consuming department based on the consuming department's usage, while the service department's fixed overhead should be allocated using the capacity provided to the consuming department whether or not the capacity was fully used. This kind of allocation produces more accurate costs than allocating a service department's overhead in total and is also fairer to department managers when their performance is evaluated.

Service department costs are usually less in the new manufacturing environment than in the traditional environment. The reason for this is that when a flexible manufacturing system is used, employees of a particular cell are trained to repair and service the equipment the cell uses. Therefore, the cost of services, such as repairs and maintenance, become direct costs instead of indirect costs that must be allocated.

A firm often manufactures several products from a common direct material. These products are called **joint products.** The cost of a common direct material and the processing costs up to the **splitoff point**—the point at which a common direct material is separated into separate products—are called **joint product costs.** If the products are processed further, the additional costs are referred to as **separable costs.** Since a firm cannot prepare financial statements without assigning costs to its inventories, it is necessary for a firm to allocate its joint product costs to the separate products produced in order to value its inventories. Three methods may be used to accomplish the cost allocation. The **physical-units method** allocates joint product costs on the basis of the physical units of output without any regard to the selling prices of the joint products. This method is most appropriate for industries in which each product of output has the same, or almost the same, selling price per unit. The **relative-sales-value method** considers both the physical units produced and the selling prices of the individual products. This method is a weighted average of both factors and is appropriate when the selling prices of the joint products are different. The **net-realizable-sales-value method** is especially useful when there is no market for the **intermediate product** at the splitoff point. Thus, the products must be processed further. Since there is no selling price for the intermediate product, a surrogate price for that product is obtained by subtracting the separable costs from the selling price of the final product to compute the net realizable value. This surrogate selling price is then used as in the relative-sales-value method.

▶ **GLOSSARY OF KEY TERMS**

Direct method   A procedure for allocating service department overhead to producing departments only by ignoring the services rendered to other service departments. (p. 352)

Intermediate product   A product at the splitoff point that cannot be sold without further processing. (p. 368)

Joint product   Two or more products produced from a common direct material and a common production process. (p. 365)

Joint product costs   The costs of acquiring and processing a single direct material up to the splitoff point of the joint products. (p. 365)

Mathematical approach   A highly accurate method of assigning service department costs to producing departments that makes use of mathematical equations that may be solved simultaneously, by substitution, or by computer. (p. 355)

Net-realizable-sales-value method   An allocation method that is especially useful when there is no market for the intermediate product at the splitoff point. Thus, the products must be processed further. Since there is no selling price for the intermediate product, a surrogate price for that product is obtained by subtracting the separable costs from the selling price of the final product to compute the net realizable value. This surrogate selling price is then used as in the relative-sales-value method. (p. 368)

Physical-units method   An allocation method that allocates joint product costs on the basis of the physical units of output without any regard to the selling prices of the joint products. This method is most appropriate for industries in which each product of output has the same, or almost the same, selling price per unit. (p. 367)

Producing department   A segment of a manufacturing firm whose employees actually work on transforming direct materials into finished goods. (p. 350)

Reciprocal (redistribution) method   A sequential allocation procedure used to assign service department costs to producing departments that recognizes services provided to other service departments. The interservice department allocations are continued in each iteration until they are relatively small (usually less than $100), at which time they are allocated expeditiously. (p. 354)

Relative-sales-value method   An allocation method that allocates joint product costs on the basis of both the physical units produced and the selling prices of the individual products. This method is a weighted average of both factors and is appropriate when the selling prices of the joint products are different. (p. 367)

Separable costs The costs of further processing joint products after the splitoff point. (p. 365)

Service department A segment of a manufacturing firm whose employees provide support services to a producing department. (p. 350)

Splitoff point The stage in the production process at which joint products are separated. (p. 365)

Step-down method A sequential approach used to assign service department costs to producing departments that recognizes services provided to other service departments. Once a service department's overhead account is closed, it is not reopened for an allocation of interservice department services. (p. 353)

▶ **REVIEW PROBLEM (A)**

Allocation of Service Department Overhead to Producing Departments

Best Manufacturing Company has two production departments (fabrication and assembly) and three service departments (general factory administration, factory maintenance, and factory cafeteria). A summary of costs and other data for each department prior to allocation of service department costs for the year ended June 30, 19x8, appears below.

	Fabrication	Assembly	General Factory Administration	Factory Maintenance	Factory Cafeteria
Manufacturing overhead costs	$577,600	$664,800	$218,800	$299,600	$231,200
Direct labor-hours	80,000	200,000	—	—	—
Number of employees.	40	100	20	20	20
Square footage occupied	24,000	13,500	6,000	7,500	9,000

The costs of the general factory administration department, factory maintenance department, and factory cafeteria are allocated on the basis of direct labor-hours, square footage occupied, and number of employees, respectively.

Round all final calculations to the nearest dollar.

Required Using the step-down method for allocating service department overhead, calculate the predetermined overhead rates per direct labor-hour for the fabrication and assembly departments. (*Hint:* Since the factory cafeteria renders services to the other service departments, allocate this department's overhead costs first.)

▶ **SOLUTION TO**
REVIEW PROBLEM
(A)

	Fabrication	Assembly	General Factory Administration	Factory Maintenance	Factory Cafeteria
Manufacturing overhead costs	$577,600	$ 664,800	$218,800	$299,600	$231,200
Factory cafeteria:					
Fabrication 40/180.	51,378				(51,378)
Assembly 100/180		128,444			(128,444)
General factory administration 20/180			25,689		(25,689)
Factory maintenance 20/180				25,689	(25,689)
Subtotal	628,978	793,244	244,489	325,289	$ –0–
Factory maintenance:					
Fabrication 24,000/37,500.	208,185			(208,185)	
Assembly 13,500/37,500		117,104		(117,104)	
Subtotal	837,163	910,348	244,489	$ –0–	
General factory administration:					
Fabrication 80,000/280,000	69,854		(69,854)		
Assembly 200,000/280,000		174,635	(174,635)		
Total.	$907,017	$1,084,983	$ –0–		

Predetermined rates:
  Fabrication ($ 907,017 ÷ 80,000 DLH) = $11.338 per DLH
  Assembly ($1,084,983 ÷ 200,000 DLH) = $ 5.425 per DLH

▶ **REVIEW PROBLEM**   **Joint Product Cost Allocation**
   (B)
Breakup Company produced three products that had joint production costs and
production yields as follows:

Cost of 500,000 pounds of direct materials . . . $1,000,000

Production for the year:
  Product A. . . . .   320,000 pounds
  Product B. . . . .   100,000 pounds
  Product C. . . . .   80,000 pounds

The selling prices of each of the products are as follows:

Product A $10
Product B   16
Product C   20

Required   Using the relative-sales-value method, compute the unit costs of direct materials for
products A, B, and C.

► **SOLUTION TO REVIEW PROBLEM (B)**

Product:	Physical Units-Pounds	Sales Price per Pound	Sales Value	Percent of Total Sales Value	Allocated Joint Cost	Unit Cost
A . . .	320,000	$10	$3,200,000	50*	500,000†	$1.5625‡
B . . .	100,000	16	1,600,000	25§	250,000‖	2.5000#
C . . .	80,000	20	1,600,000	25**	250,000††	3.1250‡‡
Total . . .	500,000		$6,400,000	100	$1,000,000	

* $3,200,000 ÷ $6,400,000.
† $1,000,000 × 0.50.
‡ $500,000 ÷ 320,000 pounds.
§ $1,600,000 ÷ $6,400,000.
‖ $1,000,000 × 0.25.
\# $250,000 ÷ 100,000 pounds.
** $1,600,000 ÷ $6,400,000.
†† $1,000,000 × 0.25.
‡‡ $250,000 ÷ 80,000 pounds.

► **LIBRARY ASSIGNMENT**

Read the following:

Cats-Baril, William L., James F. Gatti, and D. Jacque Grinnell. "Joint Product Costing in the Semiconductor Industry." *Management Accounting,* February 1986, pp. 28–31, 34–35.

Lowenthal, Franklin. "Multiple Splitoff Points." *Issues in Accounting Education,* Fall 1986, pp. 302–8.

Schiff, Jonathan B. "Allocation of Service and Administrative Costs." *Management Accounting,* September 1985, pp. 54–60.

► **SELF-TEST**

True or False

1. Direct labor-hours is a logical basis for allocating a factory hospital's costs to a producing department.

2. When the direct method of cost allocation is used, no service department's costs are allocated to another service department even if the service departments rendered interdepartment services.

3. When the step-down method of cost allocation is used, no service department's costs are allocated to another service department even if the service departments rendered interdepartment services.

4. Of all the methods used to allocate service department costs to producing departments, the reciprocal (redistribution) method is the most accurate.

5. More accurate results are usually achieved when fixed and variable costs of service departments are allocated separately to producing departments.

6. Fixed costs of a service department should normally be allocated to a producing department on the basis of the services rendered to the producing department.

7. The allocation of service department costs to producing departments is generally less important in the new manufacturing environment than in the traditional environment.

8. The physical-units method of allocating joint product costs is most appropriate when the selling prices of the firm's separated products are the same or nearly the same.

9. The relative-sales-value method of allocating joint product costs is most appropriate when there is no market for the firm's separated products.

10. The net-realizable-sales-value method of allocating joint product costs is most appropriate when the selling prices of the firm's separated products are significantly different from each other.

Multiple Choice

Items 1 through 4 are based on the following information.

The Parker Manufacturing Company has two production departments (fabrication and assembly) and three service departments (general factory administration, factory maintenance, and factory cafeteria). A summary of costs and other data for each department prior to allocation of service department costs for the year ended June 30, 19x3, appears below, items 1 through 4.

The costs of the general factory administration department, factory maintenance department, and factory cafeteria are allocated on the basis of direct labor-hours, square footage occupied, and number of employees, respectively.

Round all final calculations to the nearest dollar.

1. Assuming Parker elects to distribute service department costs directly to production departments without interservice department cost allocation, the amount of factory maintenance department costs that would be allocated to the fabrication department would be
   a. $0.
   b. $111,760.
   c. $106,091.
   d. $91,440.
2. Assuming the same method of allocation as in item 1, the amount of general factory administration department costs that would be allocated to the assembly department would be
   a. $0.
   b. $63,636.
   c. $70,000.
   d. $90,000.
3. Assuming Parker elects to distribute service department costs to other service departments (starting with the service department with the greatest total costs) as well as the production departments, the amount of factory cafeteria department costs that would be allocated to the factory maintenance department would be which of the following? (*Note:* Once a service department's costs have been reallocated, no subsequent service department costs are recirculated back to it.)
   a. $0.
   b. $96,000.
   c. $3,840.
   d. $6,124.
4. Assuming the same method of allocation as in item 3, the amount of factory maintenance department costs that would be allocated to the factory cafeteria would be
   a. $0.
   b. $5,787.
   c. $5,856.
   d. $148,910.

	Fabrication	Assembly	General Factory Administration	Factory Maintenance	Factory Cafeteria
Direct labor costs	$1,950,000	$2,050,000	$90,000	$82,100	$87,000
Direct material costs	$3,130,000	$ 950,000	—	$65,000	$91,000
Manufacturing overhead costs	$1,650,000	$1,850,000	$70,000	$56,100	$62,000
Direct labor-hours.	562,500	437,500	31,000	27,000	42,000
Number of employees	280	200	12	8	20
Square footage occupied	88,000	72,000	1,750	2,000	4,800

(AICPA Adapted)

▶ **QUESTIONS**

1. Why would a firm want to departmentalize its overhead?
2. What is the difference between a producing department and a service department?
3. What steps are necessary to departmentalize overhead?
4. What methods are in general usage for allocating service department overhead to producing departments?
5. What is the direct method of allocating service department overhead to producing departments? When should it be used?
6. What is the step-down method of allocating service department overhead to producing departments? Are there any problems with using this method? Explain.
7. What is the reciprocal (redistribution) method of allocating service department overhead to producing departments? Is it an efficient method to achieve accuracy? Explain.
8. Do firms often allocate service department costs separately for fixed and variable portions? If so, why?
9. When a firm does allocate service department costs separately for fixed and variable portions, is there a difference in the way each is allocated? If so, explain the difference.
10. Is the allocation of service department costs as important in the new manufacturing environment as it is in the traditional manufacturing environment? Explain.
11. What is a joint product cost? Why is it important to allocate this cost?
12. How is a joint product cost allocated when the physical-units method is used? When is it appropriate to use this method?
13. How is a joint product cost allocated when the relative-sales-value method is used? When is it appropriate to use this method?
14. How is a joint product cost allocated when the net-realizable-sales-value method is used? When is it appropriate to use this method?

▶ **EXERCISES**

E8–1 **Calculation of Departmental Overhead Rates**

The Samuel Company uses a job order cost accounting system. It plans to use a normalized predetermined overhead rate on a departmentalized basis. For Department A, it plans to use a direct labor-hours basis; and for Department B, it plans to use a machine-hours basis. Prior to 19x5, the company estimated the following for 19x5:

	Department A	Department B
Direct labor-hours	100,000	20,000
Machine-hours	10,000	80,000
Manufacturing overhead cost	$400,000	$144,000

In addition, assume the job cost sheet for Job 152 contains the following:

	Department A	Department B
Materials requisitioned	$100,000	$40,000
Direct labor cost	$200,000	$40,000
Direct labor-hours	20,000	4,000
Machine-hours	1,000	15,000

Required   *a.* Compute the predetermined overhead rate to be used in each department.

b. Compute the total cost of Job 152, and compute the unit cost if 100,000 units were produced.

E8–2   Departmental Overhead Allocation

1. Tillman Corporation uses a job order cost system and has two production departments, M and A. Budgeted manufacturing costs for 19x0 are as follows:

	Department M	Department A
Direct materials	$700,000	$100,000
Direct labor	200,000	800,000
Manufacturing overhead	600,000	400,000

The actual material and labor costs charged to Job 432 during 19x0 were as follows:

Direct material		$25,000
Direct labor:		
Department M	$ 8,000	
Department A	12,000	20,000

Tillman applies manufacturing overhead to production orders on the basis of direct labor cost, using departmental rates predetermined at the beginning of the year based on the annual budget. The total manufacturing cost associated with Job 432 for 19x0 should be

a. $50,000.
b. $55,000.
c. $65,000.
d. $75,000.

2. Hartwell Company distributes the service department overhead costs directly to producing departments without allocation to the other service department. Information for the month of January 19x2 is as follows:

	Service Departments	
	Maintenance	Utilities
Overhead costs incurred	$18,700	$9,000
Service provided to:		
Maintenance department	—	10%
Utilities department	20%	—
Producing Department A	40	30
Producing Department B	40	60
Total	100%	100%

The amount of utilities department costs distributed to producing Department B for January 19x2 should be

a. $3,600.
b. $4,500.
c. $5,400.
d. $6,000.

(AICPA Adapted)

E8–3 **Direct Method of Allocating Service Department Costs**

Ace Printing Company has two producing departments, engraving and printing. These departments are serviced by the repairs and maintenance department and the payroll and accounting department.

The budgeted overhead for the producing departments exclusive of any allocations from the service departments is as follows:

Department	Budgeted Overhead
Engraving	$600,000
Printing	900,000

The services rendered by the service departments and their budgeted overheads are as follows:

Consuming Department	Services Rendered Repairs and Maintenance	Services Rendered Payroll and Accounting
Repairs and maintenance	—	10%
Payroll and accounting	—	—
Engraving	30%	40%
Printing	70%	50%
Budgeted overhead	$300,000	$100,000

Required   Using the direct method of allocating service department overhead to producing departments, prepare an allocation schedule of the budgeted overhead for the producing departments to be used for the calculation of each department's predetermined overhead rate.

E8–4 **Step-Down Method of Allocating Service Department Costs**

Use the information provided in Exercise 8–3.

Required   Using the step-down method of allocating service department overhead to producing departments, prepare an allocation schedule of the budgeted overhead for the producing departments to be used for the calculation of each department's predetermined overhead rate.

E8–5 **Direct Method of Allocating Service Department Costs**

A-One Diagnostic Center has two producing departments, radiology and ultrasound. These departments are serviced by the machine maintenance department and the patients' records department.

The budgeted overhead for the producing departments exclusive of any allocations from the service departments is as follows:

Department	Budgeted Overhead
Radiology	$150,000
Ultrasound	100,000

The services rendered by the service departments and their budgeted overheads are as follows:

	Services Rendered	
Consuming Department	**Machine Maintenance**	**Patients' Records**
Machine maintenance	—	10%
Patients' records	—	—
Radiology	60%	70%
Ultrasound.	40%	20%
Budgeted overhead	$120,000	$100,000

Required   Using the direct method of allocating service department overhead to producing departments, prepare an allocation schedule of the budgeted overhead for the producing departments to be used for the calculation of each department's predetermined overhead rate.

E8–6   Step-Down Method of Allocating Service Department Costs

Use the information provided in Exercise 8–5.

Required   Using the step-down method of allocating service department overhead to producing departments, prepare an allocation schedule of the budgeted overhead for the producing departments to be used for the calculation of each department's predetermined overhead rate.

E8–7   Direct Method of Allocating Service Department Costs

Best Made Company has two producing departments and three service departments. Budgeted overhead and selected other data for the departments are as follows:

	Service Departments			Producing Departments		
	A	**B**	**C**	**X**	**Y**	**Total**
Overhead costs	$112,350	$86,700	$82,050	$216,600	$249,300	$747,000
Number of employees	8	4	8	16	64	100
Square feet of space occupied	4,000	4,800	3,200	12,800	7,200	32,000
Machine-hours	—	—	—	18,000	12,000	30,000

Department B allocates its overhead using number of employees, C allocates its overhead using space occupied, and A allocates its overhead using machine-hours. The sequence of allocation is to allocate the service department that services the most service departments first, and so forth. When two or more service departments are tied for a position, the greatest dollar amount of overhead is used for sequence purposes.

Required   Using the direct method of allocating service department overhead to producing departments, prepare an allocation schedule of the budgeted overhead for the producing departments to be used for the calculation of each department's predetermined overhead rate.

E8–8   **Step-Down Method of Allocating Service Department Costs**
Use the information provided in Exercise 8–7.

Required   Using the step-down method of allocating service department overhead to producing departments, prepare an allocation schedule of the budgeted overhead for the producing departments to be used for the calculation of each department's predetermined overhead rate.

E8–9   **Direct Method of Allocating Service Department Costs**
Better Made Company has two producing departments and three service departments. Budgeted overhead and selected other data for the departments are as follows:

	Service Departments			Producing Departments		
	D	E	F	V	W	Total
Overhead costs	$134,820	$104,040	$98,460	$259,900	$299,180	$896,400
Number of employees	10	6	10	30	50	106
Square feet of space occupied.	5,000	4,000	6,000	40,000	55,000	110,000
Labor-hours.	—	—	—	80,000	120,000	200,000

Department D allocates its overhead using space occupied, E allocates its overhead using number of employees, and F allocates its overhead using labor-hours. The sequence of allocation is to allocate the service department that services the most service departments first, and so on. When two or more service departments are tied, the greatest dollar amount of overhead is used for sequence purposes.

Required   Using the direct method of allocating service department overhead to producing departments, prepare an allocation schedule of the budgeted overhead for the producing departments to be used for the calculation of each department's predetermined overhead rate.

E8–10   **Step-Down Method of Allocating Service Department Costs**
Use the information provided in Exercise 8–9.

Required   Using the step-down method of allocating service department overhead to producing departments, prepare an allocation schedule of the budgeted overhead for the producing departments to be used for the calculation of each department's predetermined overhead rate.

E8–11   **Joint Cost Allocation—Physical-Units Method**
All-Purpose Lumber Mill harvests trees and cuts them into lumber. Two main products are produced from the joint direct material, clear pine and common grade. Other by-products such as pulp and sawdust may be ignored. For 19x3, the company had joint product costs amounting to $3,000,000. The physical yields were as follows:

Clear pine . . . . . . 4,000,000 board feet
Common pine. . . . . 8,000,000 board feet

Clear pine sells for $.80 per board feet while common pine sells for $.40 per board foot.

Inventories at December 31, 19x3 were 500,000 board feet of clear pine and 800,000 board feet of common pine.

Required   a. Allocate the joint product costs using the physical-units method.
b. Calculate the cost of the closing inventories for 19x3.

E8–12   Joint Cost Allocation—Relative-Sales-Value Method

Use the information presented in Exercise 8–11.

Required   *a.* Allocate the joint product costs using the relative-sales-value method.

b. Calculate the cost of the closing inventories for 19x3.

E8–13   Joint Cost Allocation—Net-Realizable-Sales-Value Method

1. Gilbert Manufacturing Company manufactures two products, Alt and Bat. Initially, they are processed from the same raw material and then, after splitoff, they are further processed separately. Additional information is as follows:

	Alt	Bat	Total
Final sales price	$9,000	$6,000	$15,000
Joint costs prior to splitoff point	?	?	6,600
Costs beyond splitoff point	3,000	3,000	6,000

Using the net-realizable-sales-value approach, what are the assigned joint costs of Alt and Bat, respectively?

a. $3,300 and $3,300.

b. $3,960 and $2,640.

c. $4,400 and $2,200.

d. $4,560 and $2,040.

Items 2 and 3 are based on the following information:

Forward, Inc., manufactures products P, Q, and R from a joint process. Additional information is as follows:

	Product			
	P	Q	R	Total
Units produced.	4,000	2,000	1,000	7,000
Joint cost	$36,000	?	?	$ 60,000
Sales value at splitoff	?	?	$15,000	$100,000
Additional costs if processed further . . .	$ 7,000	$ 5,000	$ 3,000	$ 15,000
Sales value if processed further	$70,000	$30,000	$20,000	$120,000

2. Assuming that joint costs are allocated using the net-realizable-sales-value at splitoff approach, what were the joint costs allocated to products Q and R?

a. $12,000 for Q and $12,000 for R.

b. $14,400 for Q and $9,600 for R.

c. $15,000 for Q and $9,000 for R.

d. $16,000 for Q and $8,000 for R.

3. Assuming that joint costs are allocated using the net-realizable-sales-value at splitoff approach, what was the sales value at splitoff for product P?

a. $58,333.

b. $59,500.

c. $60,000.

d. $63,000.

▶ **PROBLEMS   P8–14   Departmentalized Overhead**

Upton, Inc., manufactures a line of home furniture. The company's single manufacturing plant consists of the cutting, assembly, and finishing departments. Upton uses departmental rates for applying manufacturing overhead to production and maintains separate manufacturing overhead control and manufacturing overhead applied accounts for each of the three production departments.

The following predetermined departmental manufacturing overhead rates were calculated for Upton's fiscal year ending May 31, 19x6.

Department	Rate
Cutting	$2.40 per machine-hour
Assembly.	5.00 per direct labor-hour
Finishing	1.60 per direct labor-dollar

Information regarding actual operations for Upton's plant for the six months ended November 30, 19x5, is presented below.

	Department		
	Cutting	**Assembly**	**Finishing**
Manufacturing overhead costs	$22,600	$56,800	$98,500
Machine-hours	10,800	2,100	4,400
Direct labor-hours	6,800	12,400	16,500
Direct labor-dollars	$40,800	$62,000	$66,000

Based on this experience and updated projections for the last six months of the fiscal year, Upton revised its operating budget. Projected data regarding manufacturing overhead and operating activity for each department for the six months ending May 31, 19x6, are presented below.

	Department		
	Cutting	**Assembly**	**Finishing**
Manufacturing overhead costs	$23,400	$57,500	$96,500
Machine-hours	9,200	2,000	4,200
Direct labor-hours	6,000	13,000	16,000
Direct labor-dollars	$36,000	$65,000	$64,000

Diane Potter, Upton's controller, plans to develop revised departmental manufacturing overhead rates that will be more representative of efficient operations for the current fiscal year ending May 31, 19x6. She had decided to combine the actual results for the first six months of the fiscal year with the projections for the next six months to develop the revised departmental application rates. She then plans to adjust the manufacturing overhead applied accounts for each department through November 19x5 to recognize the revised application rates. The analysis presented below was prepared by Potter from general ledger account balances as of November 30, 19x5.

Account	Direct Material	Direct Labor	Manufacturing Overhead	Account Balance
Work in Process Inventory	$ 53,000	$ 95,000	$ 12,000	$ 160,000
Finished Goods	96,000	176,000	48,000	320,000
Cost of Goods Sold	336,000	604,000	180,000	1,120,000
Total.	$485,000	$875,000	$240,000	$1,600,000

Required   *a.* Determine the balance of the manufacturing overhead applied accounts as of November 30, 19x5, before any revision for the:
  (1) Cutting department.
  (2) Assembly department.
  (3) Finishing department.

b. Calculate the revised departmental manufacturing overhead rates that Upton should use for the remainder of the fiscal year ending May 31, 19x6.

c. Prepare an analysis that shows how the manufacturing overhead applied account for each production department of Upton should be adjusted as of November 30, 19x5, and prepare the adjusting entry to correct all affected general ledger accounts.

(CMA Adapted)

P8–15   **Direct Method and Step-Down Method of Allocating Service Department Costs—Single Allocation of Total Costs**

Framsonite Company manufactures plastic parts for use by automobile manufacturers. The company has two producing departments, the molding department and the assembly department. In addition, the company has three service departments, maintenance, personnel, and cafeteria.

The budgeted overhead for 19x5 for the producing departments exclusive of any allocations from the service departments is as follows:

| Department | Budgeted Overhead | |
	Variable	Fixed
Molding	$200,000	$300,000
Assembly	400,000	400,000

The budgeted overhead for 19x5 for the service departments exclusive of any allocations from the other service departments is as follows:

| Department | Budgeted Overhead | |
	Variable	Fixed
Maintenance . . .	$100,000	$200,000
Personnel	50,000	150,000
Cafeteria	150,000	250,000

Selected data for 19x5 for the producing and service departments are presented below.

| Department | Survey for 19x5 | |
	Hours of Maintenance	Number of Employees
Maintenance	—	10
Personnel	—	10
Cafeteria	2,000	20
Molding	10,000	150
Assembly	8,000	240

The company combines the variable and fixed overhead for allocation purposes and uses only one allocation for both costs.

Maintenance allocates its overhead using hours of maintenance; personnel and cafeteria allocate overhead using the number of employees. The sequence of allocation is to allocate the service department that services the most service departments first, and so on. When two or more service departments are tied for a position, the greatest dollar amount of overhead is used for sequence purposes.

Required   *a.* Using the direct method of allocating service department overhead to producing departments, prepare an allocation schedule of the budgeted overhead for the producing departments to be used for the calculation of each department's predetermined overhead rate.

   b. Using the step-down method of allocating service department overhead to producing departments, prepare an allocation schedule of the budgeted overhead for the producing departments to be used for the calculation of each department's predetermined overhead rate.

P8–16   Reciprocal (Redistribution) Method of Allocating Service Department Costs—Single Allocation of Total Costs

Use the information provided in Problem 8–15.

Required   Using the reciprocal (redistribution) method of allocating service department overhead to producing departments, prepare an allocation schedule of the budgeted overhead for the producing departments to be used for the calculation of each department's predetermined overhead rate.

P8–17   Direct Method and Step-Down Method of Allocating Service Department Costs—Separate Allocation of Variable and Fixed Costs

Use the information provided in Problem 8–15, except that fixed and variable budgeted costs for 19x5 are to be allocated separately. The long-term capacities established in 19x1 are as follows:

	Survey for 19x1	
Department	**Hours of Maintenance**	**Number of Employees**
Maintenance	—	10
Personnel	—	10
Cafeteria	2,000	20
Molding	10,000	150
Assembly	13,000	340

Required   *a.* Using the direct method of allocating service department overhead to producing departments, prepare an allocation schedule of the budgeted overhead for the producing departments to be used for the calculation of each department's predetermined overhead rate.

   b. Using the step-down method of allocating service department overhead to producing departments, prepare an allocation schedule of the budgeted overhead for the producing departments to be used for the calculation of each department's predetermined overhead rate.

P8–18   Calculation of Departmental Overhead Rates Using the Direct Method and the Reciprocal Method

Barrylou Corporation is developing departmental overhead rates based upon direct labor-hours for its two production departments—molding and assembly. Molding employs 20 people, and assembly employs 80 people. Each person in these two departments work 2,000 hours per year. The production-related overhead costs for molding are budgeted at $200,000, and the costs for assembly are budgeted at $320,000. Two service departments—repair and power—directly support the two production departments and have budgeted costs of $48,000 and $250,000, respectively. The production departments' overhead rates cannot be determined until the service departments' costs are properly allocated. The following schedule reflects the use of output by the various departments.

| | Department | | | |
	Repair	Power	Molding	Assembly
Repair-hours.	–0–	1,000	1,000	8,000
Kilowatt-hours.	240,000	–0–	840,000	120,000

Required   *a.* Calculate the overhead rates per direct labor-hour for the molding and assembly departments using the direct allocation method to charge the production departments for service department cost.

b. Calculate the overhead rates per direct labor-hour for the molding and assembly departments using the reciprocal distribution method (sometimes called *algebraic method*) to charge service department costs to each other and to the production department.

c. Explain the difference between the methods and indicate the arguments that are generally presented to support the reciprocal method over the direct allocation method.

(CMA Adapted)

P8–19   Calculation of Departmental Overhead Rates Using Direct Method with Separate Calculations for Fixed and Variable Costs

MumsDay Corporation manufactures a complete line of fiberglass attache cases and suitcases. MumsDay has three manufacturing departments—molding, component, and assembly—and two service departments—power and maintenance.

The sides of the cases are manufactured in molding. The frames, hinges, locks, and so on are manufactured in the component department. The cases are completed in the assembly department. Varying amounts of materials, time, and effort are required for each of the various cases. The power and maintenance departments provide services to the three manufacturing departments.

MumsDay has always used a plant-wide overhead rate. Direct labor-hours are used to assign the overhead to its product. The predetermined rate is calculated by dividing the company's total estimated overhead by the total estimated direct labor-hours to be worked in the three manufacturing departments.

Whit Portlock, manager of Cost Accounting, has recommended that MumsDay use departmental overhead rates. The planned operating costs and expected levels of activity for the coming year have been developed by Portlock and are presented by department in the schedules shown below (thousands omitted).

	Manufacturing Departments		
	Molding	**Component**	**Assembly**
Departmental activity measures			
Direct labor-hours	500	2,000	1,500
Machine-hours	875	125	–0–
Departmental costs			
Direct materials	$12,400	$30,000	$ 1,250
Direct labor	3,500	20,000	12,000
Variable overhead	3,500	10,000	16,500
Fixed overhead	17,500	6,200	6,100
Total departmental costs	$36,900	$66,200	$35,850
Use of service departments			
Maintenance			
Estimated usage in labor-hours for coming year	90	25	10
Power (in kilowatt-hours)			
Estimated usage for coming year	360	320	120
Maximum allotted capacity	500	350	150

	Service Departments	
	Power	**Maintenance**
Departmental activity measures		
Maximum capacity	1,000 KWH	Adjustable
Estimated usage in coming year	800 KWH	125 hours
Departmental costs		
Materials and supplies	$ 5,000	$1,500
Variable labor	1,400	2,250
Fixed overhead	12,000	250
Total service department costs	$18,400	$4,000

Required

a. Calculate the plant-wide overhead rate for MumsDay Corporation for the coming year using the same method as used in the past.

b. Whit Portlock has been asked to develop departmental overhead rates for comparison with the plant-wide rate. The following steps are to be followed in developing the departmental rates.
   (1) Maintenance department costs should be allocated to the three manufacturing departments using the direct method.
   (2) Power department costs should be allocated to the three manufacturing departments using the dual method (i.e., the fixed costs allocated according to long-term capacity and the variable costs according to planned usage).
   (3) Calculate departmental overhead rates for the three manufacturing departments using a machine-hour base for molding and a direct labor-hour base for the component and assembly departments.

c. Should MumsDay Corporation use a plant-wide rate or departmental rates to assign overhead to its products? Explain your answer.

(CMA Adapted)

P8–20   **Allocation of Joint Product Costs Using the Relative-Sales-Value Method**

Multiproduct Corporation is a chemical manufacturer that produces two main products (Pepco-1 and Repke-3) and a by-product (SE-5) from a joint process. If Multiproduct had the proper facilities, it could process SE-5 further into a main product. The ratio of output quantities to input quantity of direct material used in the joint process remains consistent with the processing conditions and activity level.

Multiproduct currently uses the physical method of allocating joint costs to the main products. The FIFO (first-in, first-out) inventory method is used to value the main products. The by-product is inventoried at its net realizable value, and the net realizable value of the by-product is used to reduce the joint production costs before the joint costs are allocated to the main products.

Jim Simpson, Multiproduct's controller, wants to implement the relative-sales-value method of joint cost allocation. He believes that inventoriable costs should be based on each product's ability to contribute to the recovery of joint production costs. The net realizable value of the by-product would be treated in the same manner as with the physical method.

Data regarding Multiproduct's operations for November 19x6 are presented below. The joint cost of production amounted to $2,640,000 for November 19x6.

	Main Products		By-Product
	Pepco-1	**Repke-3**	**SE-5**
Finished goods inventory in gallons on November 1, 19x6.	20,000	40,000	10,000
November sales in gallons	800,000	700,000	200,000
November production in gallons	900,000	720,000	240,000
Sales value per gallon at splitoff point.	$2.00	$1.50	$.55*
Additional processing costs after splitoff . . .	$1,800,000	$720,000	—
Final sales value per gallon	$5.00	$4.00	—

* Disposal and selling costs of $.05 per gallon will be incurred to sell the by-product.

Required   a. Describe the relative sales value method and explain how it accomplishes Simpson's objective.

b. Assuming that Multiproduct Corporation adopts the relative-sales-value method for internal reporting purposes
  (1) Calculate how the joint production cost for November 19x6 would be allocated.
  (2) Determine the dollar values of the finished goods inventories for Pepco-1, Repke-3, and SE-5 as of November 30, 19x6.

c. Multiproduct Corporation plans to expand its production facilities to enable the further processing of SE-5 into a main product. Discuss how the allocation of the joint production costs under the relative-sales-value method would change when SE-5 becomes a main product.

(CMA Adapted)

P8–21   **Allocation of Joint Product Costs Using the Net-Realizable-Sales-Value Method**

Alderon Industries is a manufacturer of chemicals for various purposes. One of the processes used by Alderon produces SPL-3, a chemical used in swimming pools; PST-4, a chemical used in pesticides; and RJ-5, a by-product that is sold to fertilizer manufacturers. Alderon uses the net-realizable value of its main products to allocate joint production costs, and the first-in, first-out (FIFO) inventory method to value the main products. The by-product is inventoried at its net realizable value, and this value is used to reduce the joint production costs before the joint costs are allocated to the main products. The ratio of output quantities to input quantities of direct material used in the joint process remains consistent from month to month.

Data regarding Alderon's operations for the month of November 19x9 are presented below. During this month, Alderon incurred joint production costs of $1,702,000 in the manufacture of SPL-3, PST-4, and RJ-5.

	November 19x9 Operations		
	SPL-3	PST-4	RJ-5
Finished goods inventory in gallons (11/1/x9). . . .	18,000	52,000	3,000
November sales in gallons	650,000	325,000	150,000
November production in gallons	700,000	350,000	170,000
Sales value per gallon at splitoff	None	$3.80	$.70*
Additional processing costs	$874,000	$816,000	None
Final sales value per gallon	$4.00	$6.00	None

* Disposal costs of $.10 per gallon will be incurred to sell the by-product.

Required
a. Determine Alderon Industries' allocation of joint production costs for the month of November 19x9. Be sure to present appropriate supporting calculations.

b. Determine the dollar values of the finished goods inventories for SPL-3, PST-4, and RJ-5 as of November 30, 19x9.

(CMA Adapted)

P8–22 Allocation of Joint Product Costs Using the Net-Realizable-Sales-Value Method

Doe Corporation grows, processes, cans, and sells three main pineapple products—sliced pineapple, crushed pineapple, and pineapple juice. The outside skin is cut off in the cutting department and processed as animal feed. The skin is treated as a by-product. Doe's production process is as follows:

▶ Pineapples first are processed in the cutting department. The pineapples are washed and the outside skin is cut away. Then the pineapples are cored and trimmed for slicing. The three main products (sliced, crushed, juice) and the by-product (animal feed) are recognizable after processing in the cutting department. Each product is then transferred to a separate department for final processing.

▶ The trimmed pineapples are forwarded to the slicing department where the pineapples are sliced and canned. Any juice generated during the slicing operation is packed in the cans with the slices.

▶ The pieces of pineapple trimmed from the fruit are diced and canned in the crushing department. Again, the juice generated during this operation is packed in the can with the crushed pineapple.

▶ The core and surplus pineapple generated from the cutting department are pulverized into a liquid in the juicing department. An evaporation loss equal to 8 percent of the weight of the good output produced in this department occurs as the juices are heated.

▶ The outside skin is chopped into animal feed in the feed department.

Doe Corporation uses the net-realizable-value method to assign costs of the joint process to its main products. The by-product is inventoried at its market value.

A total of 270,000 pounds were entered into the cutting department during May. The schedule presented below shows the costs incurred in each department, the proportion by weight transferred to the four final processing departments, and the selling price of each end product.

	Processing Data and Costs—May 19x1		
Department	**Costs Incurred**	**Proportion of Product by Weight Transferred to Departments**	**Selling Price per Pound of Final Product**
Cutting	$60,000	—	none
Slicing	4,700	35%	$.60
Crushing	10,580	28	.55
Juicing	3,250	27	.30
Animal feed	700	10	.10
Total	$79,230	100%	

Required   Doe Corporation uses the net-realizable-value method to determine inventory values for its main products and by-products. Calculate the following:

a. The pounds of pineapple that result as output for pineapple slices, crushed pineapple, pineapple juice, and animal feed.
b. The net realizable value at the splitoff point of the three main products.
c. The amount of the cost of the cutting department assigned to each of the three main products and to the by-product in accordance with corporate policy.

(CMA Adapted)

► **CASE**   **C8–23**   **Departmentalized Manufacturing Overhead**

Rose Bach has recently been hired as controller of Empco, Inc., a sheet metal manufacturer. Empco has been in the sheet metal business for many years and is currently investigating ways to modernize its manufacturing process. At the first staff meeting Bach attended, Bob Kelley, chief engineer, presented a proposal for automating the drilling department. Kelley recommended that Empco purchase two robots that would have the capability to replace the eight direct labor workers in the department. The cost savings outlined in Kelley's proposal included the elimination of direct labor cost in the drilling department plus a reduction of manufacturing overhead cost in the department to zero because Empco charges manufacturing overhead on the basis of direct labor dollars using a plant-wide rate.

The president of Empco was puzzled by Kelley's explanation of cost savings, believing it made no sense. Bach agreed, explaining that as firms become more automated, they should rethink their manufacturing overhead systems. The president then asked Bach to look into the matter and to prepare a report for the next staff meeting.

To refresh her knowledge, Bach reviewed articles on manufacturing overhead allocation for an automated factory and discussed the matter with some of her peers. Bach also gathered the historical data presented below on the manufacturing overhead rates experienced by Empco over the years. Bach also wanted to have some departmental data to present at the meeting and, using Empco's accounting records, was able to estimate the annual averages presented below for each manufacturing department in the 1980s.

Historical Data

Date	Average Annual Direct Labor Cost	Average Annual Manufacturing Overhead Cost	Average Manufacturing Overhead Application Rate
1940s	$1,000,000	$ 1,000,000	100%
1950s	1,200,000	3,000,000	250
1960s	2,000,000	7,000,000	350
1970s	3,000,000	12,000,000	400
1980s	4,000,000	20,000,000	500

Annual Averages

	Cutting Department	Grinding Department	Drilling Department
Direct labor	$ 2,000,000	$1,750,000	$ 250,000
Manufacturing overhead . . .	11,000,000	7,000,000	2,000,000

Required　*a.* Disregarding the proposed use of robots in the drilling department, describe the shortcomings of the system for applying overhead that is currently used by Empco, Inc.

b. Explain the misconceptions underlying Kelley's statement that the manufacturing overhead cost in the drilling department would be reduced to zero if the automation proposal was implemented.

c. Recommend ways to improve Empco's method for applying overhead by describing how it should revise its overhead accounting system
(1) In the cutting and grinding departments.
(2) To accommodate the automation of the drilling department.

(CMA Adapted)

▶ **ANSWERS TO SELF-TEST**

True-False

1. False　　2. True　　3. False　　4. False　　5. True　　6. False
7. True　　8. True　　9. False　　10. False

Multiple Choice

1. *b.* $\frac{88,000}{160,000} \times \$203,200 = \$111,760.$

2. *c.* $\frac{437,500}{1,000,000} \times \$160,000 = \$70,000.$

3. *c.* $\frac{8}{500} \times \$240,000 = \$3,840.$

4. *a.* None, since the factory-cafeteria costs are closed first, and once a service department is closed, it is not reopened.

Planning and Control

9 The Master Budget

10 Standard Costs and Performance Evaluation

11 Flexible Budgeting and Manufacturing Overhead Analysis

12 Variable-Costing and Contribution Approach to Segment Reporting

13 Selecting Relevant Data for Decision Making and Product Pricing

14 Capital Budgeting

15 Income Tax Effects on Capital-Budgeting Decisions

16 Decentralized Operations and Transfer Pricing

The Master Budget

▶ **LEARNING OBJECTIVES**

After reading this chapter, you should be able to:

1. Explain why budgets are needed and how they are used.
2. Describe the difference between long-term and short-term planning.
3. Identify the duties of the budget committee and list its members.
4. Discuss what role the management accountant plays in budget preparation.
5. Explain the structure of the master budget and the nature of its subunits.
6. Prepare a sales budget, a production budget, a direct materials budget, a direct labor budget, a manufacturing overhead budget, an ending inventories budget, a marketing cost budget, an administrative cost budget, a cash budget, a budgeted income statement, and a budgeted balance sheet.
7. Discuss the human factors in budgeting.
8. Explain the difference between incremental budgeting and zero-base budgeting.
9. Compute the economic order quantity (EOQ) for purchasing inventory using the tabular solution, the graphical solution, and the formula solution. (Appendix 9-A)
10. Adapt the EOQ formula for use in solving economic production run problems. (Appendix 9-A)
11. Determine the reorder point using a given lead time under conditions of usage with certainty. (Appendix 9-A)
12. Compute the safety stock needed to normally avoid stockouts when usage is uncertain and determine the reorder point when safety stock is provided for. (Appendix 9-A)

▶ **INTERVIEW**

Manuel D. Fernandes
Vice President for Finance
Iona College

Q. *In the course of your work, have you had an occasion to prepare a master budget for a not-for-profit organization? If so, how did this type of budget differ from a master budget for a manufacturing firm?*

A. A master budget for a not-for-profit organization differs from that of a manufacturing firm only in form. The objectives are similar: to provide an operating plan for the year or other fiscal period. The desired results for the two types of organizations differ in accordance with the stated purpose or mission.

The manufacturing firm has an obligation to generate profits for the owners/stockholders as the incentive to attract their investment. In this environment, the master budget serves as a profit plan.

In the not-for-profit organization, the operating budget serves to plan the most cost-efficient way to deliver services. The process of preparing this type of budget must be disciplined and accurate. Since most not-for-profit organizations offer personal services to the public, their operations are both labor and capital intensive. This requires careful planning of human resources as well as facilities. Once the plan is in place, there is little flexibility to effect changes since cost of facilities is usually of a fixed nature and personnel usually work under annual contracts. Therefore, a not-for-profit budget must be prepared with utmost discipline and thoroughness. Profit is not an object of this type of budget, but sufficient flexibilities must be built into the plan to prevent deficits. In fact, some level of a net margin of revenues over expenditures should be part of the budget plan. This net margin is used to build reserve funds to meet unanticipated future needs or to offset unanticipated deficits.

The following is a brief listing of the components of a master budget for a college.

College Master Budget Components:

- ▶ Enrollments.
- ▶ Faculty.
- ▶ Libraries.
- ▶ Instructional supplies.
- ▶ Facilities.
- ▶ Marketing (recruitment/admissions).
- ▶ Administrative.

Since ultimately all expenditures and disbursements require a cash flow, a companion plan to not-for-profit budgets is the cash budget. The preparation of a cash flow plan is similar for all types of organizations.

▶ At the root of any firm's financial success is careful planning. **Planning** is the process of deciding what objectives to pursue during a future time period and what to do to achieve those objectives. **Profit planning** is the preparation of budgets to achieve the objectives that have been set. The budgeting process serves several purposes. First, it provides a financial blueprint that enables a firm to coordinate all its activities. Using budgets, managers can project outcomes and adjust strategies, where needed, before operations begin, thus avoiding costly errors. Second, the budgeting process forces managers to reexamine past performance, which may enable them to discover and correct inefficient, outmoded methods of operation. Third, budgets enable managers to implement the *planning and control* function discussed in Chapter 1. In **controlling,** managers measure their firm's performance against established objectives, determine the causes of deviations, and take corrective action where necessary. Without a budget, controlling would be extremely difficult because managers would lack a plan against which to measure performance. ◀

▶ THE ASPECTS OF BUDGETING

Definition of Budget

A **budget** is a financial plan that sets forth the resources necessary to carry out activities and meet financial goals for a future period of time. A **master budget** presents a company's overall financial plan for the coming year or other planning period. Among a master budget's usual components are an operating budget and a cash budget. The **operating budget,** which summarizes the firm's operating plans for the period, consists of a sales budget, a production budget, a direct materials budget, an ending inventories budget, a direct labor budget, a manufacturing overhead budget, a marketing cost budget, and an administrative cost budget. The **cash budget** is a summary of projected cash balances based on expected cash receipts from operations, cash payments for operations, and cash receipts and payments from financing and investing activities. The master budget also contains a complete set of projected financial statements for the ensuing period. Thus, it is future oriented and composed of estimated data rather than historical data, although the estimates may be based on past operating results.

The Need for Budgeting

L.O. 1

Almost everyone uses some form of cash budgeting to handle personal finances. Whether it be a written plan for how much to spend for rent, food, clothing, entertainment, travel, and the like, or a mental plan for what to do on a Saturday night date, most individuals use some form of financial planning. Only rare individuals *consistently* buy everything they need on impulse.

Businesses must also plan ahead. Random business behavior is undesirable. Instead, a firm must set forth its goals and delineate how it expects to achieve them. A vital goal of a profit-oriented firm that wishes to remain viable is *long-range profitability*. To achieve this, firms—except very small ones—prepare written budgets setting forth their operating and financial plans for each ensuing accounting period, normally one year.

Budget in Not-for-Profit Organizations

It is difficult to envision a government—whether on the federal, state, city, town, or village level—operating without a budget. In fact, most legislatures require governmental units to budget for control purposes. Although the need for governmental budgeting is similar to that of businesses, the governmental budgeting process differs somewhat from that of commercial organizations. A government budgets from the "bottom up," meaning department heads of units (such as police, fire fighting, and sanitation) prepare operating budgets for their respective departments that are then combined into a master budget. The government decides how much revenue can be raised from various kinds of taxes and then levies the taxes. Thus, a government first determines its expenditure requirements for an ensuing year and then determines its revenue needs from its expenditure budget. The process is reversed for businesses (i.e., a firm's revenue estimates are determined first, and its expense budgets are based on its revenue budget).

Advantages of Budgeting for Businesses

The managers of firms that do not budget offer a variety of reasons to support their claims that budgeting is not suitable for their firms. The most popular ones are (1) the firm is too small, (2) the manager is in control and therefore does not need a budget for control purposes, and (3) budgeting does not adapt well to their kind of business. These reasons are tenuous at best and probably fallacious. Although the preparation of formal budgets is time consuming and expensive, the cost of not budgeting is usually far greater and may ultimately lead to a firm's failure.

Budgeting has several advantages. The more notable ones are:

1. By incorporating a firm's goals into a formalized plan for the coming year, managers refine their operational and financial objectives and thereby remove many unforeseen pitfalls. The formalized plan forces coordination and communication between the functional areas within the company.
2. A formalized budget provides employees with a target to reach. They therefore know what is expected from them prior to performing their duties, rather than being notified after the fact—when it is too late—that their performance was not in accordance with the firm's expectations.
3. A budget provides the firm with a plan against which an employee's performance may be measured. Without such a plan, it is difficult to measure *and* pinpoint unsatisfactory performance.

1. Unforeseen Pitfalls   In the course of preparing a budget, a firm often finds that the budgeting process indicates areas where corrective action might be needed prior to a pitfall's occurrence. *Examples:* (1) When a budget is prepared, the required purchases of direct materials and supplies for each month are computed. This enables a firm to plan for its purchases so that a shortage of direct materials does not occur. Otherwise, the firm might experience a shortage due to improper planning for purchases from suppliers. This is especially important when a firm has seasonal fluctuations in production. (2) By preparing a cash budget, a firm may find that a severe cash shortage is projected. It then might wish to issue additional shares of its stock or issue bonds to cover the shortfall. Because the budget indicates when a cash shortage is likely to occur, the required advance planning can be accomplished and the cash shortage avoided.

2. Performance Target for Employees   If a budget is prepared properly, employees know what standard of performance is expected from them before they begin their duties. Ideally, a budget should be prepared from the "bottom up" (i.e., having employees participate in the preparation of the budget). This kind of budget is known as a **participative budget,** and is also sometimes referred to as a *self-imposed budget.* Once the level of activity for the coming year is determined, employees should be invited to prepare their shares of the budget using the estimates of performance they are comfortable with. The level of operating activity is based on sales estimates and involves complexities discussed later in this chapter.

The alternative, preparing a budget from the "top down" (a department's budget prepared by a manager at a level higher than the manager of that department), usually suffers from the fact that employees might refuse to accept a budget imposed on them from above. They may resent it because they feel the budget has unrealistic expectations. When a budget is prepared from the bottom up, it must be reviewed by upper management to determine if the budget is too lax. If this condition arises, the upper-level manager should review the budget with the employee who prepared it, and they should negotiate their differences rather than have the budget imposed by fiat.

Human factors play an important role in the budgeting process. These factors are discussed later in this chapter.

3. Measurement of Employee Performance   If a budget is not used, there is no standard against which actual results can be measured. Comparison of a current year's actual results with the actual results of a prior year is an ineffective control mechanism. Because it is impossible to determine if a prior year's actual results were satisfactory—they may contain severe inefficiencies—any comparison may contain misleading conclusions. *Examples:* (1) The prior year's operating level may differ from this year's operating level, and hence a comparison is invalid. (2) The prior year's actual results contain inefficiencies and unusual conditions, such as a union-ordered work slowdown, and comparing this year's actual results with last year's might show a favorable condition when, in fact, the condition is still unfavorable.

By preparing a budget for the current year's operating level, the firm has a standard by which to evaluate employee performance and pinpoint troublesome areas. Further, a budget permits the firm to make frequent comparisons between budgeted amounts and actual results. The frequency of comparison varies from firm to firm. Usually comparison periods vary from one week to one month and, in many cases, are dictated by the availability of the data. With present-day computer capabilities, very frequent comparisons are possible at a negligible incremental cost. The author was associated with a steel fabricating firm where comparisons between budgeted and actual data were made daily. In planning for profits, managers must consider two time horizons: the short term and the long term.

The Budget Time Frame

L.O. 2
Short-term versus long-term planning

Short-Term Planning   **Short-term planning** is the process of deciding what objectives to pursue during a short, near-future period, usually one year, and what to do to achieve those objectives. For example, a firm must decide which units and what quantities to produce and sell during the next year. These decisions cannot be left to chance. Thus, a short-term plan must be compiled to give employees instructions for carrying out the firm's goals.

The typical short-term budget covers one year and is broken down into monthly or quarterly units. When quarterly units are used, the first quarter's budget is further subdivided into monthly segments. Then, toward the end of each succeeding quarter, the next quarter's budget is also divided into months. Postponing the division of quarters into months leads to more accurate results because more recent data are available by the time the monthly figures are prepared.

Another method frequently used to prepare a short-term budget is the **continuous budget,** which is also known as a *perpetual budget*. This kind of budget starts with an annual budget broken down into 12 monthly units. As each month arrives, it is dropped from the plan and replaced by a new month so that at any given time, the next 12 months are always shown. Thus, in a budgetary period covering January through December 19x4, when January 19x4 arrives, it would be dropped from the plan and replaced by January 19x5, thus creating a new budgetary period covering February 19x4 through January 19x5. Using this technique, a firm always has guidance for the full following year. When a continuous budget is not used, a firm will have guidance for only a month or two as it approaches the end of its budgetary period. A continuous budget helps to keep the budgeting workload constant throughout the year rather than having a spurt in workload once each year.

Long-Term Planning   **Long-term planning,** also known as *strategic planning,* is the process of setting long-term goals and determining the means to attain them. Short-term planning is concerned with operating details for the next accounting period, but long-term planning addresses broader issues, such as new product development, plant and equipment replacement, and other matters that require years of advance planning. For example, short-term planning in the automotive industry would be concerned with which and how many of the current year's models to manufacture, while long-range planning would focus on new model development and major design changes, equipment replacements, and construction of additional plant capacity to accommodate future increases in demand for the firm's products. The time frame for long-range planning may extend as far as 20 years in the future, but its usual range is from 2 to 10 years. An important part of long-term planning is the preparation of the **capital budget,** which details plans for the acquisition and replacement of major portions of property, plant, and equipment.

▶ BUDGET PREPARATION

The Budget Committee

L.O. 3

Responsibility for preparing the budget is usually assigned to several high-level managers. In most large firms, this group is referred to as the **budget committee.** The committee then calls on managers throughout the company for help in the budgeting process. Budgeting is a collective effort rather than the responsibility of one individual because if a budget is to be an effective tool of control, it must be accepted by the people responsible for its implementation. When managers and employees are given a voice in the preparation of the budget, they feel a greater stake in its success. Thus, budget preparation should be delegated to the lowest possible level of authority, subject to review and adjustment by superiors.

The budget committee generally consists of representatives from:

1. The president's office.
2. The upper levels of management.
3. Sales and marketing.

4. Production and manufacturing.
5. Purchasing.
6. The controller's office.

Members of the budget committee are usually assistants, but they keep superiors up to date on their deliberations and actively involve the senior executives when upper-level decisions are needed.

Duties of the Budget Committee The budget committee's duties usually consist of:

1. Selecting budget policies compatible with organizational goals and objectives.
2. Reviewing budget estimates submitted by section heads.
3. Revising budget estimates when necessary.
4. Approving budget estimates.
5. Analyzing budget reports and recommending changes.
6. Establishing the budget timetable.

L.O. 4
Role of the
management accountant

The Role of the Management Accountant The controller occupies a special place on the budget committee. Although the sales, production, and purchasing managers provide input regarding how much can be sold, how much can be manufactured, and how much production will cost, the controller's office usually bears responsibility for collecting such data and transforming them into coherent financial statements with appropriate supporting schedules. In effect, the management accountant—the representative from the controller's office—provides support to the production and sales functions by transforming their data into reports that will be useful for both planning and control.

▶ **PROGRESS CHECK**

1. What is a budget for a business firm?
2. Why does a business firm or a not-for-profit institution prepare a master budget?
3. What is the difference between short-term and long-term planning? Use examples to illustrate the kinds of decisions that would be appropriate for each type of planning.
4. What is a budget committee and who participates in it?
5. What are the duties of the budget committee?   ◀

The Master Budget

L.O. 5

The master budget is an operational, short-term business plan. In reality, it is an amalgamation of smaller, specialized budgets, each based on information provided by the appropriate manager. For example, the information for the sales budget would come from the sales department's manager and related support personnel, such as management accountants and economists. Similarly, the purchasing department's manager would supply estimated costs for direct materials.

The subunits of the master budget may be classified as:

A. The operating budget.
   1. Sales budget.
   2. Production budget.
      a. Direct materials.

    b. Ending inventories.

    c. Direct labor.

    d. Manufacturing overhead.

  3. Marketing cost budget.

  4. Administrative cost budget.

  5. Budgeted income statement.

B. The financial budget.

  1. Capital budget.

  2. Cash budget.

  3. Budgeted balance sheet.

  4. Budgeted statement of cash flows.[1]

Some subunits of the master budget are interdependent. For example, the sales forecast is influenced by the amount spent for advertising and promotion, and these expenditures, in turn, depend on the sales forecast. The interrelationships of the elements of the master budget are shown in Illustration 9-1.

The Sales Budget

L.O. 6
Sales forecast and sales budget

The preparation of the master budget must begin with the sales budget. A **sales budget** is a formal plan that sets forth a firm's anticipated sales—in quantities and in dollars—for the coming year based on the sales forecast. A **sales forecast** is a formal prediction of the quantities expected to be sold in the coming year based on such factors as past sales, economic and seasonal conditions, pricing policies, and market research studies. Without forecasts of expected sales for the planning period, a firm would not know how many units to produce and could easily manufacture too many units or too few. Besides leading to overstocks or lost sales, the lack of reliable sales projections can lead to costly mistakes in purchasing materials and hiring employees. Thus, the sales budget and its forecasts provide a crucial foundation on which the preparation of all other components of the master budget depends.

Sales-forecasting techniques can vary from simple estimates based on past experience to sophisticated statistical approaches and computer models. Whichever method is used, some prediction must be made regarding how many of each product can be sold in the forthcoming year and at what prices they can be sold.

The elements that enter into the preparation of the sales forecast are:

1. Prior periods' sales broken down by product line, types of customers, territories, and seasonal variations.
2. Present market share modified by future expectations.
3. Pricing policies modified by CVP adjustments.
4. General economic conditions.
5. Economic conditions of the particular industry.
6. Disposable income of consumers.
7. Advertising and promotion.
8. New product entries.
9. Market research studies.
10. Competition and the likely entry of new producers.
11. Backlog of unfilled orders.

---

[1] Chapter 17 is devoted to the preparation of this statement.

▶ **ILLUSTRATION 9-1**   Master Budget Relationships

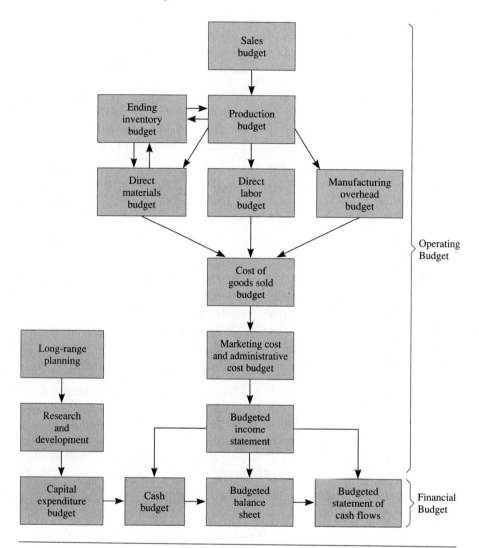

Once estimates of unit sales are selling prices have been derived, the sales budget is well on its way. The actual figures are computed by multiplying the expected unit sales for each product by its selling price and then aggregating the results.

To demonstrate, let us assume the Fiber Company manufactures a single product, powdered hand soap. The Fiber Company's sales forecast for 19x2 and the first two quarters of 19x3 appears in Illustration 9-2, and its sales budget is presented in Illustration 9-3. Note how estimates of unit sales and prices are multiplied and totaled to arrive at budgeted sales revenue.

The Production Budget

L.O. 6

Once the sales forecast and the sales budget are completed, the next phase, the production budget, can be started. A **production budget** is a formal plan quantifying in units the required production for the coming year based on

▶ **ILLUSTRATION 9-2**

FIBER COMPANY
Sales Forecast
For the Year Ended December 31, 19x2

Quarter	Number of Units	Price
19x2:		
First	10,000	$12
Second	12,000	12
Third	18,000	12
Fourth	30,000	13
19x3:		
First	12,000	13
Second	15,000	13

▶ **ILLUSTRATION 9-3**

FIBER COMPANY
Sales Budget
For the Year Ended December 31, 19x2

Quarter	Number of Units	× Price =	Budgeted Sales Revenue
19x2:			
First	10,000	$12	$120,000
Second	12,000	12	144,000
Third	18,000	12	216,000
Fourth	30,000	13	390,000
Total			$870,000

budgeted sales and the budgeted inventories of finished goods. Without the guidance of a production budget, a firm might not manufacture enough to meet sales requirements, or it might produce goods that are not needed. A firm must budget both required production and desired ending inventory. To do so, it must take into account the goods on hand from the beginning inventory. The production budget in units may be calculated as follows:

Expected sales + Desired ending finished goods inventory
    = Total needs
    − Beginning finished goods inventory
    = Required production

At Fiber Company, the manufacture of a carton of powdered hand soap requires two pounds of tetraborate, which is expected to cost 20 cents per pound, and one pound of sodium soap at 15 cents per pound. The beginning inventories at January 1, 19x2, are estimated as:

Finished goods:
    Powdered soap . . . . . 3,000 units at $5.30 per unit

Direct materials:
    Tetraborate . . . . . . 6,000 pounds at $.20 per pound
    Sodium soap . . . . . . 3,000 pounds at $.15 per pound

The company's policy is to maintain inventories equal to 30 percent of its needs for the following quarter. This applies to both direct materials and finished goods. The company has no work in process inventories.

▶ **ILLUSTRATION 9-4**

FIBER COMPANY
Production Budget in Units
For the Year Ended December 31, 19x2

	First Quarter	Second Quarter	Third Quarter	Fourth Quarter	Year
Sales	10,000	12,000	18,000	30,000	70,000
Add: Ending inventory	3,600	5,400	9,000	3,600	3,600*
Total needs.	13,600	17,400	27,000	33,600	73,600
Less: Beginning inventory	3,000	3,600	5,400	9,000	3,000
Required production.	10,600	13,800	21,600	24,600	70,600

* 30% × 12,000 units from the second quarter 19x3.

To prepare the production budget, the required production must be determined for each quarter and for the year as a whole. The following are the steps necessary to determine the required production for each quarter:

Step 1
Record the sales forecast for the quarter as determined by management.

Step 2
Compute the ending inventory for the first quarter by taking 30 percent of the second quarter's sales (12,000 units × 30% = 3,600).

Step 3
Add the amount from step 1 to the sales for the first quarter (10,000 units) for a subtotal of 13,600. Subtract the beginning inventory of 3,000 units (given information) to arrive at the required production of 10,600 units.

Step 4
Repeat steps 1 and 2 for the remaining three quarters. Note that the beginning inventory for any quarter after the first is the ending inventory for the preceding quarter. This relationship can be seen by the arrows shown in Illustration 9-4.

When the required production for each quarter has been determined, the required production for the year can be determined as in the following steps:

Step 1
Total the sales of the four quarters to get the year's sales.
10,000 + 12,000 + 18,000 + 30,000 = ... 70,000

Step 2
Maintain 30 percent of the next quarter's projected sales in ending inventory (see Illustration 9-2). Naturally, this figure should be the same as the ending inventory for the fourth quarter.
12,000 × .30 = ... 3,600

Step 3
Add the ending inventory to the projected sales to find the total needs.
70,000 + 3,600 = ... 73,600

Step 4
The beginning inventory for the year is the beginning inventory for the first quarter. (Recall that this was taken from the ending inventory of 19x1)
. . . . 3,000

Step 5

Subtract the year's beginning inventory from the total needs for the year to find the required production for the year.

$73,600 - 3,000 = \ldots\ldots\ldots\ldots\ldots\ldots\ldots\ldots\ldots\ldots\ldots\ldots\ldots$ <u>70,600</u>

The Fiber Company's production budget appears as Illustration 9-4.

L.O. 6
Direct materials budget

The Direct Materials Budget   The **direct materials budget** is a formal plan indicating the quantities and dollar amounts of direct material purchases for the coming year based on required production and the budgeted direct materials inventories. Without the guidance of a direct materials budget, a firm may have to shut down production due to insufficient quantities of direct materials or may carry a larger inventory of direct materials than it actually needs. In either case, the failure to plan properly for the purchase of direct materials would cause the firm to incur extra costs if the production line is shut down or if funds and stockroom space are tied up in unnecessary inventory.

The direct materials budget requires computations similar to those used for required production. It may be calculated as:

> Required production + Required ending direct materials inventory
> = Total needs
> − Beginning direct materials inventory
> = Required purchases of direct materials

Using the required production amounts from Illustration 9-4, the direct materials budget may be prepared as follows:

Step 1

Multiply the required quarterly production figures from Illustration 9-4 by the direct materials per unit to determine the required direct materials. The sum of the quarterly amounts is the yearly requirement. This is done separately for each direct material.

Step 2

Prepare a schedule similar to Illustration 9-4, but use the required direct materials from step 1 instead of budgeted sales. The computations for beginning and ending inventories and yearly totals follow the same pattern as those in Illustration 9-4. The inventory relationships are highlighted by arrows in Illustration 9-5.

Step 3

Multiply the required purchases in pounds by the respective prices per pound to compute the dollar value of the direct materials purchases.

The Fiber Company's direct materials budget appears in Illustration 9-5. A review of Illustration 9-5 shows that:

1. The *direct materials purchases* are computed in the same manner as the required production. The required ending inventory is added to the production in pounds as computed in the upper portion of Illustration 9-5, and the beginning inventory is deducted from that subtotal to arrive at the required purchases of direct materials.

FIBER COMPANY
Direct Materials Budget
For the Year Ended December 31, 19x2
Direct Materials Required

Tetraborate:
Quarter:

First	10,600 × 2 pounds =	21,200 pounds
Second	13,800 × 2 pounds =	27,600
Third	21,600 × 2 pounds =	43,200
Fourth	24,600 × 2 pounds =	49,200
Yearly total needed . . .		141,200 pounds

Sodium soap:
Quarter:

First	10,600 × 1 pound =	10,600 pounds
Second	13,800 × 1 pound =	13,800
Third	21,600 × 1 pound =	21,600
Fourth	24,600 × 1 pound =	24,600
Yearly total needed . . .		70,600 pounds

Direct Materials Purchases (in pounds)

	First Quarter	Second Quarter	Third Quarter	Fourth Quarter	Yearly Total
Tetraborate:					
Production	21,200 →30%→	27,600	43,200	49,200	141,200
Add: Ending inventory	8,280 ←	12,960	14,760	7,740	7,740*
Total needs	29,480	40,560	57,960	56,940	148,940
Less: Beginning inventory	6,000	8,280	12,960	14,760	6,000
Required purchases	23,480	32,280	45,000	42,180	142,940
Sodium soap:					
Production	10,600 →30%→	13,800	21,600	24,600	70,600
Add: Ending inventory	4,140 ←	6,480	7,380	3,870	3,870†
Total needs	14,740	20,280	28,980	28,470	74,470
Less: Beginning inventory	3,000	4,140	6,480	7,380	3,000
Required purchases	11,740	16,140	22,500	21,090	71,470

Direct Materials Purchases (in dollars)
Pounds × Price per Pound = Dollars

	Pounds	Price per Pound	Dollars
Tetraborate:			
First quarter	23,480	$.20	$ 4,696
Second quarter	32,280	.20	6,456
Third quarter	45,000	.20	9,000
Fourth quarter	42,180	.20	8,436
Subtotals	142,940		28,588
Sodium soap:			
First quarter	11,740	.15	1,761
Second quarter	16,140	.15	2,421
Third quarter	22,500	.15	3,375
Fourth quarter	21,090	.15	3,164
Subtotals	71,470		10,721
Total			$39,309

---

* Production for the first quarter 19x3:

Budgeted sales	12,000
Add: Required inventory—30% × 15,000 (second quarter)	4,500
Total needs	16,500
Less: Ending inventory for the fourth quarter 19x2—see Illustration 9-4	3,600
Required production	12,900

Required ending inventory:
12,900 × 2 pounds = 25,800 pounds × 30% = 7,740 pounds.

† Required production—from (*)—12,900 × 1 pound × 30% = 3,870 pounds.

404

2. The ending inventory for any quarter is 30 percent of the production of the following quarter in pounds. This can be seen by examining the arrow relationships. The *ending inventory for the year* must be computed by first computing the required production in pounds for the first quarter of 19x3 and then multiplying this amount by 30 percent. This calculation is shown in the footnotes at the end of the illustration.

3. The beginning inventory of one period is merely the ending inventory of the preceding period. This is demonstrated by the arrows in the illustration.

▶ **PROGRESS CHECK**

The Eastern Hat Company manufactures ladies' hats and is preparing its production budget for the first three months of 19x2. The sales budget in units is as follows:

Month	Units
January	6,000
February	4,500
March	12,000
April	30,000
May	9,000

The December 31, 19x1, inventory is estimated as 1,200 units. The company normally maintains an inventory at the end of each month equal to 20 percent of the following month's sales. However, due to the surge of sales in April, the company normally maintains an inventory on March 31 equal to 40 percent of the anticipated sales for April.

The company's capacity is limited to 18,000 hats per month. If the production requirement exceeds this amount, the production is scheduled in the next preceding month in which production capacity is available. Thus, if the required production for April cannot be met, it is produced in March if production is available, and if not, it is produced in February.

Required   Prepare the production requirements for the months of January, February, and March. Use a total column to indicate the production requirement for the first quarter of 19x2.

Check Figures
Required production:
  January   5,700;   February   9,600;   March   18,000   ◀

L.O. 6
Direct labor budget

Direct Labor Budget   A **direct labor budget** is a quantitative calculation and listing of planned expenditures for direct labor costs for the coming budget period. Like the direct materials budget, the direct labor budget is based on the required production. To ease the complexities of computing this portion of the budget when multiple wage rates exist, a uniform wage rate is assumed. At the Fiber Company, the budgeted uniform rate, based on previous experience, is $8 per hour, and the required time per unit, based on previous experience, is 15 minutes per unit.

Preparation of the direct labor budget starts with the required production as computed in Illustration 9-4. This figure is then multiplied by the required time per unit, which yields the required time in hours. This amount is then multiplied by the hourly rate to arrive at the direct labor amount in dollars. The direct labor budget for the Fiber Company appears as Illustration 9-6.

▶ **ILLUSTRATION 9-6**

FIBER COMPANY
Direct Labor Budget
For the Year Ended December 31, 19x2

	First Quarter	Second Quarter	Third Quarter	Fourth Quarter	Yearly Total
Required production*	10,600	13,800	21,600	24,600	70,600
Required direct labor time in hours per unit	× ¼	× ¼	× ¼	× ¼	× ¼
Total direct labor in hours	2,650	3,450	5,400	6,150	17,650
Hourly rate	× $8	× $8	× $8	× $8	× $8
Budgeted direct labor cost	$21,200	$27,600	$43,200	$49,200	$141,200

* From Illustration 9-4.

The direct labor budget provides management with an approximate schedule of its labor needs and helps the company plan for seasonal fluctuations in direct labor requirements. From Illustration 9-6, it can be seen that the third and fourth quarters of 19x2 will require a significant amount of additional direct labor over that needed for the first two quarters.

L.O. 6
Manufacturing overhead budget

Manufacturing Overhead Budget A **manufacturing overhead budget** is a quantitative listing of each type of planned cost classified as manufacturing overhead, such as factory rent, factory supervision, and repairs, segregated into fixed and variable categories. Fixed costs are estimated by using last year's costs and modifying them by any expected changes. Variable costs are estimated by multiplying the rate per unit by the required production. Mixed costs are estimated by using the cost formula $Y = a + bX$, as discussed in Chapter 3. A predetermined overhead rate is then computed and used to apply overhead to production during the budget period. This procedure is demonstrated in Chapter 5.

The manufacturing overhead budget enables a firm to prepare the budgeted cost of goods manufactured and sold, which is needed for the budgeted income statement. In addition, the overhead budget provides needed information for the firm's cash budget, because the items in the overhead budget require an outlay of cash. Although depreciation of machinery and factory equipment are needed to compute the predetermined overhead rate, it must be remembered that depreciation does not require a cash outlay and should not be used when preparing the cash budget.

The Fiber Company's manufacturing overhead budget is shown in Illustration 9-7. All information it presents is assumed, except for the direct labor cost, which is based on Illustration 9-6.

L.O. 6
Ending inventory budget

Ending Inventory Budget Inventory planning and control is a very important part of a manager's responsibility because it can save a company from costly errors. A company that practices good inventory planning and control orders sufficient quantities of direct materials and supplies at the best prices available without carrying excessive quantities, and it has sufficient quantities available to meet production requirements. It also carries sufficient quantities of finished goods to meet customers' demands but avoids maintaining a wasteful excess. Without careful planning and control, firms would accumulate inventories on a haphazard basis. This could result in an overinvestment in inventories as well as increased costs for storage, interest on

▶ **ILLUSTRATION 9-7**

FIBER COMPANY
Manufacturing Overhead Budget
For the Year Ended December 31, 19x2

	First Quarter	Second Quarter	Third Quarter	Fourth Quarter	Yearly Total
Budgeted direct labor cost	$21,200	$27,600	$43,200	$49,200	$141,200
Variable overhead at 80% of above	$16,960	$22,080	$34,560	$39,360	$112,960
Fixed overhead	20,000	20,000	20,000	20,000	80,000
Totals	$36,960	$42,080	$54,560	$59,360	$192,960

Schedule of Overhead

	Fixed	Variable	Total
Superintendence	$30,000		$ 30,000
Indirect labor.	10,000	$ 20,000	30,000
Rent.	24,000		24,000
Repairs	2,000	12,000	14,000
Light and power	1,000	15,000	16,000
Maintenance	3,000	3,000	6,000
Payroll fringes		42,360	42,360
Miscellaneous	1,000	20,600	21,600
Depreciation of machinery	9,000		9,000
Totals	$80,000	$112,960	$192,960

Variable rate per direct labor cost:
$112,960 ÷ $141,200 = 80% per direct labor-dollar

invested capital, and insurance. In addition, obsolete merchandise would be more likely to accumulate, causing losses at the time of its disposal. Poor inventory planning and control can also cause shortages of direct materials, which would lead to assembly line shutdowns and lost sales for lack of finished goods. Thus, managers recognize the crucial importance of budgeting for ending inventories. Inventory planning and control is discussed more fully in Appendix 9-A at the end of this chapter.

An **ending inventory budget** is a quantitative calculation, in units and dollars, of the coming year's planned ending inventories for direct materials, work in process, and finished goods. Illustration 9-8 contains the Fiber Company's ending inventory budget for finished goods. Without this budget, it would be impossible to prepare a budgeted income statement.

The Marketing Cost Budget

L.O. 6

A **marketing cost budget** is a quantitative listing of each planned marketing cost for the coming year, such as salespersons' salaries and commissions. A significant portion of this budget is dictated by the sales budget; thus, the two are usually prepared in conjunction with each other.

Like all other budgets, the marketing cost budget is useful for control purposes. A comparison between this budget and the actual costs at the end of an accounting period is likely to disclose differences, and if the differences are significant, managers should investigate the reasons for them and take the necessary corrective action. In addition, this budget is needed to prepare a budgeted income statement and a cash budget.

Illustration 9-9 presents the Fiber Company's marketing cost budget. All dollar amounts are assumed, except the salespersons' commissions, which are based on the information provided in the sales budget in Illustration 9-3.

▶ **ILLUSTRATION 9-8**

FIBER COMPANY
Ending Finished Goods Inventory Budget
For the Year Ended December 31, 19x2

Powdered Hand Soap

Cost per unit:
  Direct materials:
    Tetraborate—2 pounds at $.20* . . . . $ .40
    Sodium soap—1 pound at $.15* 15

  Direct labor:
    ¼ hour at $8 (from Illustration 9-6) 2.00

  Overhead:
    Variable—80% of direct labor cost (from
      Illustration 9-7) 1.60
    Fixed—$80,000 ÷ $141,200 = 56.66% of
      direct labor cost (from Illustration 9-7) 1.13
        Total cost per unit. $5.28

Ending finished goods inventory:
  Hand soap—3,600 units† × $5.28 = $19,008

---

* From Illustration 9-5.
† From Illustration 9-4.

Note: There is a rounding difference on the fixed overhead as follows:

Powdered hand soap:
  Production of 70,600 × $1.13 = $79,778
  Budgeted fixed costs   80,000
      Rounding difference . . . . $ 222

▶ **ILLUSTRATION 9-9**

FIBER COMPANY
Marketing Cost Budget
For the Year Ended December 31, 19x2

	First Quarter	Second Quarter	Third Quarter	Fourth Quarter	Yearly Total
Variable cost:					
Sales commissions*	$ 3,600	$ 4,320	$ 6,480	$11,700	$26,100
Miscellaneous	1,200	1,440	2,160	3,900	8,700
Subtotal	4,800	5,760	8,640	15,600	34,800
Fixed cost:					
Sales salaries	5,000	5,000	5,000	5,000	20,000
Advertising.	575	575	575	575	2,300
Travel	2,000	2,000	2,000	2,000	8,000
Rent.	1,500	1,500	1,500	1,500	6,000
Utilities	1,000	1,000	1,000	1,000	4,000
Miscellaneous	2,000	2,000	2,000	2,000	8,000
Subtotal	12,075	12,075	12,075	12,075	48,300
Total	$16,875	$17,835	$20,715	$27,675	$83,100

---

* 3% of sales per Illustration 9-3.

The Administrative Cost Budget

L.O. 6

An **administrative cost budget** is a quantitative listing of each planned administrative cost for the coming year, such as office rent and office salaries. The budget is constructed in the same way as the marketing cost budget and is useful for the same control purposes. Also, like the marketing cost budget, the information provided by the administrative cost budget is needed to prepare the budgeted income statement and cash budget.

▶ **ILLUSTRATION 9-10**

FIBER COMPANY
Administrative Cost Budget
For the Year Ended December 31, 19x2

	First Quarter	Second Quarter	Third Quarter	Fourth Quarter	Yearly Total
Variable cost:					
Bad debts cost*	$ 1,200	$ 1,440	$ 2,160	$ 3,900	$ 8,700
Fixed cost:					
Administrative salaries	$20,000	$20,000	$20,000	$20,000	$ 80,000
Rent	2,000	2,000	2,000	2,000	8,000
Utilities	1,000	1,000	1,000	1,000	4,000
Insurance	1,500	1,500	1,500	1,500	6,000
Professional fees	2,000	2,000	2,000	2,000	8,000
Payroll fringes	6,000	6,000	6,000	6,000	24,000
Miscellaneous	5,000	5,000	5,000	5,000	20,000
Subtotal	37,500	37,500	37,500	37,500	150,000
Totals	$38,700	$38,940	$39,660	$41,400	$158,700

* 1% of sales in Illustration 9-3.

A sample administrative cost budget appears in Illustration 9-10. All dollar amounts are assumed.

Cash Management and Cash Budgeting

L.O. 6

The cash budget is an extremely important cash management tool because it enables a firm to plan ahead for its day-to-day cash needs. Without a cash budget, a firm could suddenly find itself strapped for cash and scrambling to pay its bills. Lack of cash can lead to the loss of purchase discounts, poor credit ratings, and many lost opportunities.

Cash Management Several decades ago, when interest rates hovered in the range of 2 percent to 4 percent, little attention was paid to cash management. But today, when interest rates are close to double-digit figures, cash management and the cash budget have become crucial parts of a firm's planning process. The goal of **cash management** is to plan a firm's cash position so that cash is available when it is needed and all available idle cash is invested to provide maximum income, taking into account the amount of risk the firm is willing to assume.

For example, to make sure customers' payments are put to work as quickly as possible, many firms collect their bills through lockboxes. In such cases, customers send their payments directly to the firm's bank, where the checks are immediately entered as deposits. The bank then transmits a list of the deposited checks to the firm for the updating of its accounts receivable. Without a lockbox system, a firm would have to do the bookkeeping first and then deposit the funds. Such delays in depositing funds can be very costly when interest rates are significant.

To ensure that all available funds are optimally invested, some firms, in cooperation with their banks, maintain a zero balance in their bank accounts and fully invest all cash in government securities or money market funds. Each day that a firm's deposits exceed its cleared checks, the bank invests the excess in approved securities. And when cleared checks exceed deposits, the bank sells securities to cover the shortfall. As a result, on any given day all available cash is fully invested and earning interest. This procedure may still be used when a bank requires a firm to maintain a minimum balance by substituting the minimum balance for the zero balance.

The Cash Budget The cash budget is broken down into sections showing (1) cash receipts, (2) cash disbursements, (3) cash surplus or deficiency, and (4) financing activities—bank loans, other borrowings, and repayments. This system enables a firm to plan and time such discretionary payouts as dividend payments and equipment purchases. It also facilitates the arrangement of financing activities, such as bank borrowing, well in advance of actual need, thus avoiding the costs and inefficiencies of crisis financing.

The cash budget for the Fiber Company is based on all previously discussed elements of the master budget plus the following additional information:

1. Past experience has shown that the company collects its accounts receivable as follows:

During the quarter of the sale . . .	80%
In the quarter following the quarter of the sale.	19
Not collected	1

2. Salaries and wages are paid in the current quarter.
3. All purchases of direct materials are paid 80 percent in the current quarter and 20 percent in the quarter following their incurrence. Overhead, period costs, and equipment purchases are paid currently.
4. Income taxes are estimated at $60,000 for the year, with 25 percent of this total being paid each quarter.
5. The company has a line of credit with its bank through which it can borrow at the beginning of any quarter at the simple interest rate of 12 percent per annum. The bank computes interest at the rate of 1 percent per month.
6. The company's policy is to maintain a minimum cash balance of $30,000. At the beginning of each quarter, the company will borrow a sufficient amount to maintain that balance and will repay any loans on the last day of a quarter whenever the balance exceeds $30,000.
7. Equipment is to be purchased as follows:

First quarter	$ 10,000
Second quarter . . .	30,000
Third quarter	100,000
Fourth quarter . . .	20,000

   Payment for the equipment is in accordance with the payment schedule in item 3 above.
8. Dividends are to be paid in the amount of $2,000 per quarter.
9. During the first quarter of 19x2, the company collected $75,000 of accounts receivable from the prior year. The balance of the opening accounts receivable as shown in Illustration 9-11 is not considered collectible and will be written off.
10. The entire balance of accounts payable on December 31, 19x1 (see Illustration 9-11), is to be paid in the first quarter of 19x2.

   Some of the information required to prepare the cash budget is taken from the Fiber Company's estimated balance sheet as of the beginning of the year, January 1, 19x2, which appears in Illustration 9-11.

▶ **ILLUSTRATION 9-11**

FIBER COMPANY
Budgeted Balance Sheet
January 1, 19x2

Assets

Current assets:			
Cash		$ 40,000	
Accounts receivable	$77,000		
Less: Allowance for uncollectibles	2,500	74,500	
Inventories.			
Direct materials	1,650		
Finished goods.	15,900	17,550	
Total current assets.			$132,050
Plant assets:			
Equipment.		50,000	
Less: Accumulated depreciation		20,000	30,000
Total assets			$162,050

Liabilities and Stockholders' Equity

Current liabilities:			
Accounts payable		$ 5,000	
Total current liabilities			$ 5,000
Stockholders' equity:			
Common stock.		100,000	
Retained earnings		57,050	
Total stockholders' equity.			157,050
Total liabilities and stockholders' equity			$162,050

The steps used to prepare a cash budget, as shown in Illustration 9-12, are:

Step 1

Prepare a quarterly schedule of cash receipts from accounts receivable by calculating 80 percent of each quarter's sales and 19 percent of the prior quarter's sales. For the first quarter, the amount of $75,000 is used in place of the 19 percent of the prior quarter's sales, as instructed in item 9. (See Schedule A of Illustration 9-12.)

Step 2

Enter the beginning cash balance ($40,000 from Illustration 9-11) in the first quarter column of the cash budget.

Step 3

Enter the cash receipts computed in step 1 for each quarter. The yearly column may also be completed, for both the yearly cash collections and the beginning cash balance of $40,000.

Step 4

Prepare a schedule of cash payments for materials by taking 80 percent of the current quarter's purchases and 20 percent of the prior quarter's purchases (purchases are found in Illustration 9-5). For the first quarter, $5,000 (the opening balance of the accounts payable) is used in accordance with item 10. (See Schedule B of Illustration 9-12.)

▶ **ILLUSTRATION 9-12**

FIBER COMPANY
Cash Budget
For the Year Ended December 31, 19x2

	See Illustration or Schedule	First Quarter	Second Quarter	Third Quarter	Fourth Quarter	Yearly Total
Cash balance, beginning		$ 40,000	$ 63,549	$ 30,000	$ 30,000	$ 40,000
Add: Receipts from customers	(A)	171,000	138,000	200,160	353,040	862,200
Subtotal		211,000	201,549	230,160	383,040	902,200
Deduct disbursements:						
Direct materials	(B)	10,166	8,393	11,675	11,755	41,989
Direct labor	(9-6)	21,200	27,600	43,200	49,200	141,200
Manufacturing overhead	(9-7)	34,710*	39,830	52,310	57,110	183,960
Marketing.	(9-9)	16,875	17,835	20,715	27,675	83,100
Administrative.	(9-10)	37,500†	37,500	37,500	37,500	150,000
Equipment		10,000	30,000	100,000	20,000	160,000
Dividends.		2,000	2,000	2,000	2,000	8,000
Income taxes		15,000	15,000	15,000	15,000	60,000
Subtotal		147,451	178,158	282,400	220,240	828,249
Excess (deficiency) of cash		63,549	23,391	(52,240)	162,800	73,951
Financing:						
Borrowing			6,813	84,994		91,807
Repayment					(91,807)	(91,807)
Interest			(204)	(2,754)	(2,754)	(5,712)
Total financing		–0–	6,609	82,240	(94,561)	(5,712)
Cash balance, ending.		$ 63,549	$ 30,000	$ 30,000	$ 68,239	$ 68,239

* Because depreciation does not require any cash outflow, each quarter's overhead was reduced by the depreciation per quarter ($9,000 ÷ 4 = $2,250).

† Because the provision for bad debts does not require any cash outflow, each quarter's administrative cost was reduced by the amount of the bad debt provision.

Step 5

Enter the payments for direct materials in the disbursements section. Enter the amounts for direct labor, manufacturing overhead, marketing costs, and administrative costs from Illustrations 9-6, 9-7, 9-9, and 9-10. However, the amounts for manufacturing overhead must be reduced by the depreciation, and the administrative costs must be reduced by the bad debts, because depreciation and bad debts do not require any cash payments. They are costs created by bookkeeping entries rather than by cash outflows.

Step 6

Enter the disbursements for equipment purchases, dividend payments, and estimated income tax payments. Add the totals of the disbursements for each quarter and for the year. For the first quarter, calculate the excess (or deficiency) of cash.

Step 7

Whenever the excess cash is greater than $30,000 (as in the first quarter), enter the ending cash balance as the beginning cash balance of the next quarter. When the excess cash is less than $30,000, or when a deficiency is

▶ **ILLUSTRATION 9-12**   *(concluded)*   **FIBER COMPANY**
Supporting Schedules
to Illustration 9-12

Schedule 9-12A—Cash Receipts from Accounts Receivable

	First Quarter	Second Quarter	Third Quarter	Fourth Quarter
19x2:				
Balance from accounts receivable, 1/1/x2	$ 75,000			
Sales from first quarter*:				
80% × $120,000	96,000			
19% × $120,000		$ 22,800		
Sales from second quarter*:				
80% × $144,000		115,200		
19% × $144,000			$ 27,360	
Sales from third quarter*:				
80% × $216,000			172,800	
19% × $216,000				$ 41,040
Sales from fourth quarter*:				
80% × $390,000				312,000
Cash collections	$171,000	$138,000	$200,160	$353,040

Schedule 9-12B—Cash Payments for Materials

	First Quarter	Second Quarter	Third Quarter	Fourth Quarter
19x2:				
Balance from accounts payable, 1/1/x2	$ 5,000			
Payments from first quarter[†]:				
80% × ($4,696 + $1,761)	5,166			
20% × ($4,696 + $1,761)		$1,291		
Payments from second quarter[†]:				
80% × ($6,456 + $2,421)		7,102		
20% × (same)			$ 1,775	
Payments from third quarter[†]:				
80% × ($9,000 + $3,375)			9,900	
20% × (same)				$ 2,475
Payments from fourth quarter[†]:				
80% × ($8,436 + $3,164)				9,280
Cash payments.	$10,166	$8,393	$11,675	$11,755

* From Illustration 9-3.

† From Illustration 9-5.

present, calculate the deficiency from $30,000 and divide the result by 97 percent to allow for three months' interest (1% × 3 months), because any needed borrowings are to be made at the *beginning of the quarter*. For the second quarter, the borrowing may be calculated as $30,000 minus the excess cash of $23,391 = $6,609, which amount is then divided by .97 = $6,813. The interest for the second quarter would then be $6,813 × .03 = $204 and a cash balance of $30,000 would be maintained. The same procedure is used for the third quarter, except the $204 of interest must be added to the cash deficiency. Thus, the calculation would be $52,240 deficiency + $30,000 cash balance + $204 of second-quarter interest that must be paid for in the third quarter = $82,444 ÷ .97 = $84,994. The interest for the third quarter is calculated as 3 percent of the second- and third-quarter loans, or ($84,994 + $6,813 = $91,807 × .03 = $2,754). For the fourth quarter, there is sufficient cash to liquidate the loans and pay the interest of $2,754, which is the same as in the third quarter, because the loan is paid at the *end* of the quarter.

A review of Illustration 9-12 reveals that:

1. The cash balance at the beginning of the first quarter is $40,000, which is the amount shown in Illustration 9-11, the beginning budgeted balance sheet.
2. The cash receipts from accounts receivable are computed in the supporting schedules (Schedule A).
3. The cash disbursements are either computed in the supporting schedules or in the previously discussed subsidiary budgets, except for the equipment payments, dividends, and income taxes, which are given in items 4, 7, and 8 of the additional information provided on page 410.
4. Because the estimated cash balance at the end of the first quarter exceeds the minimum balance of $30,000, no borrowing is necessary. However, borrowings are required in the second and third quarters.
5. The computations for interest are shown in step 7 following the cash budget.
6. The cash budget enables the firm to plan for needed borrowing in the second and third quarters and for repayment in the fourth quarter. A cash budget would also indicate if borrowing were needed but repayment impossible in the current year. Under such circumstances, the company might consider alternative forms of long-term borrowing.

The Budgeted Income Statement

L.O. 6

It is now possible to prepare the **budgeted income statement,** which is a projected income statement based on the various units of the operating budget. This statement is extremely important because it indicates how profitable the firm is expected to be. Each segment of the operating budget enhances planning and control, but it is the budgeted income statement that informs managers, *in advance,* whether the firm's operations for the coming year are expected to be profitable and how much the profit or loss is expected to be. If the projected operations are not satisfactory to management, altered strategies may be adopted to try to improve the results. Without a budgeted income statement, managers would discover unsatisfactory results after they had occurred, when it would be too late to make necessary adjustments. In addition, managers can compare the budgeted income statement to the actual income statement to determine if significant variances exist and whether corrective action is warranted.

The only additional information needed to prepare the budgeted income statement is the income tax rate. In our example, the Fiber Company pays income taxes at an average rate of 23.75 percent of pre-tax income.

The steps needed to prepare a budgeted income statement, as shown in Illustration 9-13, are:

Step 1
Use the sales from the sales budget (Illustration 9-3).

► **ILLUSTRATION 9-13**

FIBER COMPANY
Budgeted Income Statement
For the Year Ended December 31, 19x2

	From Illustration	
Sales.	9-3	$870,000
Cost of goods sold*.		369,882
Gross margin		500,118
Marketing and administrative costs:		
Marketing costs.	9-9	83,100
Administrative costs.	9-10	158,700
Total marketing and administrative		241,800
Operating income before income taxes		258,318
Less: Interest cost	9-12	5,712
Income before income taxes		252,606
Income taxes at 23.75%		59,994
Net income		$192,612

---

* Cost of goods sold:			
Beginning inventories:			
Finished goods (3,000 × $5.30)	9-11		$ 15,900
Direct materials	9-11		1,650
Purchases of direct materials	9-5		39,309
Direct labor	9-6		141,200
Manufacturing overhead	9-7		192,960
Subtotal			391,019
Less: Ending inventories:			
Finished goods	9-8	$19,008	
Direct materials—Tetraborate (7,740 × $.20)	9-5	1,548	
—Sodium soap (3,870 × $.15)	9-5	581	21,137
Cost of goods sold			$369,882

Step 2

Compute the cost of goods sold using the inventories of finished goods and direct materials from the budgeted balance sheet (Illustration 9-11). To these inventories, add the direct material purchases from the direct materials budget (Illustration 9-5), the direct labor from the direct labor budget (Illustration 9-6), and the manufacturing overhead from the manufacturing overhead budget (Illustration 9-7). Add them for a subtotal and then deduct the closing inventories from the ending finished goods inventory budget and the direct materials budget (Illustrations 9-8 and 9-5) to arrive at the cost of goods sold. The calculation may be seen at the bottom of the budgeted income statement shown in Illustration 9-13. Deduct the cost of goods sold from the sales to compute the gross margin for the year.

Step 3

Deduct the marketing costs shown in the marketing cost budget (Illustration 9-9) and the administrative costs shown in the administrative cost budget (Illustration 9-10) from the gross margin to arrive at operating income before income taxes. Next, deduct the interest cost shown on the cash budget (Illustration 9-12) to derive income before income taxes. Finally, multiply this amount by 23.75 percent, which is the Fiber Company's income tax rate, and deduct the result to arrive at the net income for the year.

FIBER COMPANY
Budgeted Balance Sheet
December 31, 19x2
Assets

Current assets:
Cash . . . . $ 68,239*
Accounts receivable. . . . . $82,800†
Less: Allowance for uncollectibles . . .   9,200‡   73,600

Inventories:
Direct materials. . . . .   2,129§
Finished goods . . . .   19,008‖   21,137
Prepaid income taxes   6
        Total current assets $162,982

Plant assets:
Equipment . . . .   210,000#
Less: Accumulated depreciation 29,000**   181,000
Total assets $343,982

Liabilities and Stockholders' Equity

Current liabilities:
Accounts payable . . . . $ 2,320††
        Total current liabilities . . . . . . $ 2,320

Stockholders' equity:
Common stock   100,000
Retained earnings . . . .   241,662‡‡
        Total stockholders' equity   341,662
Total liabilities and stockholders' equity $343,982

---

* Per cash budget, Illustration 9-12.
† Beginning balance, Illustration 9-11 . . . . $ 77,000
  Add: Sales, Illustration 9-3   870,000
  Less: Collections, Illustration 9-12 . . . .   (862,200)
  Less: Bad debts written off. . . . .   (2,000)

  Ending balance . . . . $ 82,800

‡ Beginning balance, Illustration 9-11 . . . . $ 2,500
  Add: Bad debts provision (1% × $870,000),
    Illustration 9-10   8,700
  Less: Bad debts written off. . . . .   (2,000)

  Ending balance . . . . $ 9,200

§ Tetraborate, (Illustration 9-13, footnote) . . . . $ 1,548
  Sodium soap, (Illustration 9-13, footnote)   581

  Total. . . . . $ 2,129

‖ From Illustration 9-8.
Beginning balance, Illustration 9-11 . . . . $ 50,000
  Add: Purchases, Illustration 9-12   160,000

  Ending balance . . . . $ 210,000

** Beginning balance, Illustration 9-11 . . . . $ 20,000
  Add: Depreciation, Illustration 9-7   9,000

  Ending balance . . . . $ 29,000

†† Beginning balance, Illustration 9-11 . . . . $ 5,000
  Add: Purchases, Illustration 9-5.   39,309
  Less: Payments for materials, Illustration 9-12 . . . . .   (41,989)

  Ending balance . . . . $ 2,320

‡‡ Beginning balance, Illustration 9-11 . . . . $ 57,050
  Add: Net income, Illustration 9-13   192,612
  Less: Dividends paid, Illustration 9-12. . . . .   (8,000)

  Ending balance . . . . $ 241,662

▶ **ILLUSTRATION 9-15**

FIBER COMPANY
Manufacturing Overhead Performance Report—Partial Report
For the Year Ended December 31, 19x2

	Budgeted Amounts	Actual Amounts	Over (Under) Budget	Explanation
Superintendence	$ 30,000	$ 30,000	$ –0–	
Indirect labor	30,000	32,000	2,000	Salary increase
Rent	24,000	24,000	–0–	
Repairs	14,000	26,000	12,000	Unexpected
Light and power	16,000	20,000	4,000	Rate increase
Maintenance	6,000	5,500	(500)	
Payroll fringes	42,360	42,960	600	
Miscellaneous	21,600	19,600	(2,000)	
Depreciation of machinery	9,000	10,000	1,000	New equipment
Totals	$192,960	$210,060	$17,100	

The Budgeted Balance Sheet

L.O. 6

A **budgeted balance sheet** is a projected statement of financial position that reflects the expected balances in the accounts at the end of the planning period. It is prepared by starting with the firm's balance sheet at the beginning of a year and adjusting each figure for all of the expected transactions shown in the operating and cash budgets. The budgeted balance sheet provides managers with the firm's expected financial position at the end of an accounting period. Based on this information, management may be able to predict potential trouble spots in liquidity and/or operating efficiency and take corrective action to prevent their occurrence.

The Fiber Company's budgeted balance sheet is presented in Illustration 9-14. The calculations of the individual amounts are detailed in the notes that accompany the illustration.

Budget Uses

Performance Reports So far we have emphasized the use of a master budget to plan and guide a firm's operations for the coming year. But a master budget also serves another important function: it provides a basis of comparison against which actual results can be measured to determine if an organization is in control of its operations. A firm should monitor its actual results and compare them with its planned results to determine if any unusual variations warrant investigation. This can be accomplished by preparing a **performance report** that contains four columns: one column for budgeted data, one for actual data, one showing the difference between budget and actual and whether the difference is over or under budget, and one for explanations of the differences. The differences are of primary interest. Illustration 9-15 contains a sample performance report for the Fiber Company. The unexpected repairs of $12,000 merit investigation. Performance reports are discussed more fully in Chapters 10 and 11 of this book.

▶ HUMAN FACTORS IN BUDGETARY PLANNING AND CONTROL

In a tight budget, maximum revenues and minimum costs are combined to produce an ideal budget. This type of budget could theoretically be achieved, but it does not allow for the human factors that normally prevent the achievement of perfection. Although some individuals attempt to work at optimal levels, most people do not; thus, a very tight budget is considered unattainable. For this reason, such a budget is not an effective device for motivating employees. When employees realize that a budget is unattainable and that, as a result, they cannot possibly achieve any rewards for attainment, they will tend to rationalize, saying to themselves, ''If we are going to miss the target, we might as well miss it by a mile as by an inch because the penalty and/or reward is the same for either one.'' Thus, they reject the budget.

On the other hand, a lax budget is equally unacceptable as a control device. When a sales budget is set so low that anyone can attain the required sales, or a production budget is set so low that employees can attain the required output with a minimum of effort, the result is a reward system that encourages unacceptable performance. Conscientious employees are likely to resent this type of budget because they receive the same rewards as employees who exert a minimum amount of effort. Consequently, too lax a budget may make a firm cost inefficient in the long run and possibly even spell its demise.

Ultimately, the desired goal should be a budget that is fair to both the firm and its employees. A certain amount of lost efficiency due to human factors, such as illness, personal problems, and reasonable coffee breaks, is to be expected and should be built into the budgeting process. A budget that is reasonable to both employees and the firm can operate as an effective control mechanism that rewards exemplary performance and identifies mediocre performance.

Budget Slack

Budget slack occurs when an employee or manager prepares a lax budget for the purpose of making company objectives easily attainable. Much has been written in organizational behavior and management journals about the existence of slack in business organizations. One authority maintains that managers want to satisfy both their own goals and those of their firm. Because in many cases the two sets of goals are not perfectly congruent, a slack environment provides the best opportunity for satisfying both.[2] This is especially true at the lower levels of management. Upper-level managers enjoy great freedom in carrying out their duties and receive many perquisites—stock options, chauffeured limousines, corporate jets, and so on—while lower-level managers are usually less privileged. Thus, lower-level managers often use budget slack as one means of satisfying personal goals.

Other authorities have found that managers tend to satisfy personal goals by using slack in good years and converting slack into profits in bad years.[3] In effect, they keep the wolf away from the door by using the slack to satisfy the firm's goals when times are bad, but they use the slack for themselves once the firm's goals have been satisfied. This approach also ensures that the firm will not increase its expectations in future years. If the manager continued to use the slack to benefit the firm once its goals were satisfied, the firm would raise its goals for subsequent years, thereby taking control of the slack away from the manager.

[2] O. E. Williamson, *The Economics of Discretionary Behavior: Managerial Objectives in a Theory of the Firm* (Englewood Cliffs, N.J.: Prentice Hall, 1964), pp. 28–37.

[3] Michael Schiff and Arie Y. Lewin, ''Where Traditional Budgeting Fails,'' *Financial Executive* 36 (May 1968), pp. 50–52 ff.

Schiff and Lewin maintain that in *a decentralized company, slack is concentrated at the divisional level,* and in *a centralized company, slack extends throughout the entire company.*[4] They estimate that slack may compose as much as 25 percent of a division's operating cost budget.[5]

Budget slack is also encountered when a participative budget is used. When an employee is asked to prepare a budget for the coming year, there is a tendency for the employee to build in some budget slack because he or she may fear that management will likely cut the budget to tighten it. Management, suspecting that employees are deliberately inflating budget estimates to allow for budget slack, then cut the budget estimates. This can result in a vicious cycle in which employees build in slack and managers cut budget estimates. Managers should recognize that slack is an ever-present problem in budget construction. It is probably impossible to eliminate all slack, but managers should attempt to determine an acceptable level and try to control its abuse. This can be accomplished to some extent through the use of engineering estimates adjusted for an acceptable amount of slack.

▶ BUDGETING IN NOT-FOR-PROFIT ORGANIZATIONS

Not-for-profit organizations, such as governments, hospitals, welfare organizations, schools, and colleges, make extensive use of budgets. In fact, budgets are usually required of these organizations by such regulatory authorities as legislatures, boards of trustees, and administrative agencies. Although not-for-profit organizations rarely manufacture products and therefore do not start with a sales forecast as profit-oriented businesses do, they do provide services to their users. Consequently, they must prepare a forecast of the services to be rendered during the planning period (usually one year) to provide a starting point for the rest of the master budget.

Incremental Budgeting

L.O. 7
Incremental budgeting

Many organizations make use of the incremental approach when preparing budgets. When **incremental budgeting** is used, *the previous period's budget is accepted as a base,* and those figures are either increased or decreased depending on whether the organization wishes to increase or decrease its output during the coming period.

The major advantage of using this approach is that the preparer starts with a budget—albeit last year's—already prepared and merely has to add or subtract to arrive at the next year's budget. Thus, the work is greatly simplified.

The greatest disadvantage of using this approach is that the prior years' inefficiencies are automatically perpetuated and included in the current year's budget. In addition, the effectiveness of the programs remains unchallenged and perpetuated. Thus, programs continue in force through inertia.

Zero-Base Budgeting

L.O. 7
Zero-base budgeting

Zero-base budgeting has recently attracted increasing attention. Unlike incremental budgeting, which begins with the previous period's figures as a base, **zero-base budgeting** starts with a base of zero. Each program with its cost is then ranked, starting with the one most vital to the organization. In

---

[4] Michael Schiff and Arie Y. Lewin, "The Impact of People on Budgets," *The Accounting Review* 55, no. 2 (April 1970), p. 264.

[5] Ibid., p. 263.

this manner, managers can choose to fund programs on the basis of merit, without preconceived notions about what must be included.

The major advantage of zero-base budgeting is that every year, every program and its cost must be justified before it can be included in the budget. In the process, weak programs and inefficiencies tend to be weeded out. Zero-base budgeting requires a great deal more effort and cost than incremental budgeting, but in the long run it may be more efficient.

Zero-Base Budgeting Applications to Businesses In most cases, a business's master budget starts with a sales forecast, which is based, in part, on the previous year's sales. Thus, incremental budgeting is used for products that the firm is already producing and selling. But when a firm brings out a new product, it uses zero-base budgeting because the product lacks a sales history. Even with existing products, a firm uses zero-base budgeting when evaluating whether to continue making them. Thus, businesses make use of both incremental and zero-base budgeting. Although several budgeting experts have written books advocating the extensive use of zero-base budgeting in business, few firms have put these experts' ideas into practice. Nevertheless, the concept is a useful one.

Budgeting for a Hospital

Participative Budgeting Participative budgeting is appropriate not only for profit-oriented businesses but also for the not-for-profit sector. Motivation of employees working in a critical sector, such as the health-care industry, is extremely important.

▶ **EXAMPLE** A considerable amount of patient care depends upon using highly sophisticated equipment. Also, because of the nature of hospital organization, flexibility, innovation, and the capacity to deal with unanticipated difficulties are important. In addition, if individuals are allowed to participate in decision making, the hospital will realize a greater economic payoff than it would were it to resort to more authoritarian styles. Numerous studies support the notion that sophisticated and advanced technologies influence organizational behavior in the direction of more participative approaches to management. Therefore, it would seem reasonable that enlightened management would not only allow, but would require, considerable participation in the budget process by department directors and first-line supervisors. At University Community Hospital, we do use participative budgeting to a considerable degree within the general guidelines established. . . .

The degree of participation as well as the rank of those participating in the budget process generally will correlate with how closely the budget purpose has been achieved. Studies have shown that managers are more productive and satisfied with both their job and colleagues when they are working within a situation where they have had significant input in formulating the operational plan. Therefore, we may well conclude that allowing participation of managers and employees in the budgeting process can do much to increase their acceptance of the budget, their subsequent involvement with and commitment to it as well as the quality of the budget as an aid to decision making.

The degree of effectiveness of managers and first-line supervisors at our hospital—or any hospital, for that matter—depends upon many personality traits. One of the most important of these traits is the ability to be motivated by being involved. This trait is essential because the degree of decentralization typical in a hospital setting requires individuals to make timely quality decisions within the scope of established general guidelines. Furthermore, the various departments tend to be so diverse and complex that the department director is the "expert" who must relate to the vice president, a "generalist," in developing and executing a plan of operation. Therefore, the hospital setting is ideal for a high degree of participative budgeting given the diverse departments and individuals and groups of differing ranks.

The participative approach to budgeting has proven very successful at University Community Hospital. Our budget projections have proven to be extremely accurate because of a combination of good forecasting and willingness to cooperate in taking corrective action to overcome adverse variances. In fact, our overall projections have generally been so close to our actual experience that our finance committee of the board has jokingly suggested the budget was prepared after the fact. It would be difficult to envision our budget effort being accomplished in an effective manner without the participative approach.[6]   ◀

Revenue Budget   A hospital has a capacity of beds that is often measured in patient-days. Thus, it is possible to partially project revenues based on previous rates of occupancy. This is done by using the coming year's prices and projected usage to adjust the current year's revenues from operating room usage, procedures (such as X rays, electrocardiograms, and laboratory analysis), and outpatient services. Recall that a hospital's revenues are subject to different charges depending on who is paying for the procedures performed. Rates can vary among Medicare, Medicaid, insurance companies (such as Empire Blue Cross/Shield), employees of the hospital, and private patients, often referred to as *self-pay*.

It is customary to show revenues at their expected gross amounts at the normal rates and then deduct the allowances for the expected payers noted previously to arrive at the expected net revenues. This additional step permits the managers of a hospital to see what amounts are allowed to third-party payers and employees. It also provides useful information for performance reports in which actual amounts are compared with budgeted amounts. This comparison provides a measure of control that would not be available if the revenues were shown only at the net amounts.

Separate revenue reports are prepared for each unit in a hospital. For example, departments include radiology, pediatrics, obstetrics and gynecology, cardiac care, thoracic surgery, vascular surgery, neurology, burn units, dermatology, anesthesiology, physical therapy, and pharmacy, depending upon the degree of specialization in a particular hospital. Budgets are prepared by each individual department of the organization, and these individual budgets are then combined into a master budget for the organization as a whole. This process results in a **bottom-up budget.**

A sample revenue budget appears in Illustration 9-16.

---

[6] Marvin A. Feldbush, "Participative Budgeting in a Hospital Setting," *Management Accounting,* September 1981, pp. 43–46.

▶ **ILLUSTRATION 9-16**   Master Revenue Budget

VENTURA HOSPITAL
Master Revenue Budget
For the Year Ended December 31, 19x3
(in $thousands)

	Gross Revenues	Allowances and Deductions	Net Revenues
Inpatient revenues:			
Nursing services			
Operating room	$ 1,848	$ 490	$ 1,358
Recovery room	860	94	766
Emergency room	945	234	711
Daily patient care	10,980	2,670	8,310
Total	14,633	3,488	11,145
Other services			
Radiology	2,431	592	1,839
Pediatrics	1,968	368	1,600
Obstetrics and gynecology	2,866	622	2,244
Cardiac care	3,792	849	2,943
Pulmonary care	1,658	349	1,309
Thoracic surgery	1,423	372	1,051
Neurology	2,341	489	1,852
Anesthesiology	1,994	267	1,727
Physical therapy	1,350	326	1,024
Pharmacy	1,932	168	1,764
Total	21,755	4,402	17,353
Outpatient services:			
Nursing services			
Operating room	938	257	681
Recovery room	432	86	346
Emergency room	6,430	1,520	4,910
Total	7,800	1,863	5,937
Other services			
Radiology	2,982	539	2,443
Pediatrics	1,674	268	1,406
Dermatology	964	126	838
Anesthesiology	841	95	746
Physical therapy	1,675	340	1,335
Pharmacy	992	120	872
Total	9,128	1,488	7,640
Total revenues	$53,316	$11,241	$42,075

An additional schedule would be required to set forth the details of the allowances and deductions from revenues. A sample schedule for one kind of revenue appears in Illustration 9-17. Clearly, the schedule would be structured so that the allowances and deductions for all types of revenue would be shown.

Cost Budget   Each functional department is required to prepare a cost budget. These individual budgets are then combined into a master cost budget. Each department's cost budget is deducted from the department's revenue budget to arrive at its projected results of operations. Similarly, the

▶ ILLUSTRATION 9-17   Sample Allowances and Deductions from Revenue Budget

VENTURA HOSPITAL
Allowances and Deductions from Revenue Budget
For the Year Ended December 31, 19x3
(in $thousands)

Inpatient revenues:
  Nursing services
    Operating room

Medicare	$132
Medicaid	60
Empire Blue Cross	225
Employee discounts . . .	22
Bad debts	51
Total	$490

▶ ILLUSTRATION 9-18   Sample Departmental Cost Budget

VENTURA HOSPITAL
Cost Budget—Pediatric Department
For the Year Ended December 31, 19x3
(in $thousands)

Description	Cost
Salaries—management . . .	$ 50
Salaries—MDs	150
Salaries—RNs	150
Salaries—LPNs	80
Salaries—aides	60
Salaries—clerical staff . . .	50
Medical supplies	40
Other supplies	10
Repairs and maintenance . .	100
Telephone	110
Utilities	80
Payroll fringes	200
Other costs	110
Total	$1,190

master cost budget is subtracted from the master revenue budget to determine the hospital's expected results of operations. A sample departmental cost budget appears in Illustration 9-18.

▶ SUMMARY

To ensure coherence and continuity, businesses must plan their operations and profit goals. During the **planning** process, a company sets goals, chooses strategies for attaining them, and quantifies its decisions. The result is a **master budget,** which provides an overall plan of operations for future periods.

Profit planning is best accomplished with a formalized master budget. A master budget presents a company's overall financial plan for the coming period, usually one year. A master budget falls within the realm of **short-term planning.** As part of their planning processes, an increasing number of firms are using **continuous budgeting,** which starts with a full year's budget broken down into 12 monthly units. As each month arrives, it is dropped from the plan and replaced with a new month so that at any given time, the next 12 months are always shown. **Long-term planning,** also known as *strategic planning,* is concerned with long-term goals, such as new product development, plant and equipment replacement, and other matters that require years of advance planning. An important part of long-term planning is the preparation of the **capital budget.** The prime responsibility for coordinating the master budget's preparation is given to the **budget committee,** which is made up of representatives from various high-level managers' offices. The master budget usually includes an **operating budget,** a cash budget, and projected financial statements.

The foundation of the master budget is the **sales forecast,** which is based on such factors as the firm's market share, economic and seasonal conditions, competitive factors, and prices. From the sales forecast, the **sales budget** can be constructed. It is then possible to prepare a **production budget,** which contains as subunits a **direct materials budget,** a **direct labor budget,** a **manufacturing overhead budget,** and an **ending inventories budget.** In addition, the master budget contains a **marketing cost budget,** an **administrative cost budget,** and a **cash budget.** These budgets in turn provide the information necessary to prepare budgeted financial statements—a **budgeted income statement,** a **budgeted balance sheet,** and a budgeted statement of cash flows.

When interest rates are significant, cash management is an increasingly important part of a financial manager's duties. **Cash management** is the planning of a firm's cash position so that cash is available when needed and all available idle cash is invested to provide maximum income, taking into account the amount of risk the firm is willing to assume. The cash budget plays a key role in cash management because it enables a firm to plan and time financing activities and discretionary payouts.

Human factors play a very important part of the budgeting process. Wherever possible, **participative budgeting** should be used. Participative budgeting is the process in which budgets are prepared at the lowest levels, or departments, and then these individual budgets prepared by employees are combined into a master budget for the firm as a whole. This type of budgeting is referred to as **bottom-up budgeting.** When employees prepare budgets for themselves, they are more apt to accept those budgets and adhere to them rather than they are to adhere to budgets prepared by management from the top down. Participative budgeting is not without risk. Employees may be tempted to build **slack,** or padding, into the budgets, although a certain amount of slack is unavoidable. It can be kept to a reasonable level when managers and employees work together.

There are two basic approaches to budgeting. When the **incremental approach** is used, the previous year's budget is taken as the starting point and adjusted upward or downward to reflect anticipated changes for the coming year. With **zero-base budgeting,** each year a new budget is started from zero and all programs must be justified as if they were entirely new. This approach requires more effort than incremental budgeting, but its proponents claim the effort is justified from a cost-benefit viewpoint.

Planning is the predecessor to the **control** function. As part of the control function, **performance reports** are used to compare the actual results of operations to the planned results to determine if there are any significant variations from the plan and, if so, whether further investigation is necessary.

Not-for-profit organizations must budget as carefully as for-profit organizations because they are normally subject to control by legislatures, boards of directors, and other regulatory bodies.

▶ **APPENDIX 9-A**   **Inventory Planning and Control**

In inventory planning and control, the two basic questions to be resolved are "When should an order for inventory be placed?" and "How much should be ordered?" Through **inventory planning and control,** a firm attempts to ensure that an optimum level of inventory will be maintained so that the costs of carrying and ordering inventories will be minimized and sufficient quantities will be on hand to avoid production interruptions due to stockouts (not having a needed material on hand). **Inventory carrying costs** include storage costs, insurance, interest on funds invested in inventories, personal property taxes, and obsolescence and deterioration. **Inventory ordering costs** include the costs associated with placing a purchase order, transportation costs, and receiving and handling costs. Carrying costs and ordering costs conflict with each other. At one extreme, a firm could order a full year's supply of direct materials, which would require only one purchase order, one transportation cost, and one receiving report. As a result, ordering costs would be relatively small. However, carrying costs would be unnecessarily high because of the large inventory needed to accommodate a full year's production requirements. At the other extreme, a purchase order could be placed 250 times (50 weeks × 5 days) per year. This would result in insignificant carrying costs because inventories would be very small, but it would produce 250 purchase orders, 250 transportation costs, and 250 receiving reports. Somewhere between these two extremes lies an optimum ordering quantity at which the sum of carrying and ordering costs would be less than at any other ordering quantity.

Unfortunately, accounting systems do not normally provide the data needed to measure carrying and ordering costs per se. Interest on investment in inventories is an opportunity cost not reflected in accounting records. The cost to place an order is normally not detailed in a firm's accounting system, although purchasing department salaries are shown in total. Thus, cost studies are usually required to arrive at the appropriate amounts to use when considering the effects of carrying and ordering costs on inventory planning and control.

Economic Order Quantity (EOQ)

L.O. 8

The **economic order quantity (EOQ)** is the amount of materials that should be ordered to minimize the total of the inventory carrying costs and the inventory ordering costs. EOQ is based on four assumptions:

1. The demand (usage) rate is constant over a period of time, such as one year, and the rate is known with certainty.

2. The carrying costs are proportional to the number of units carried in inventory—a linear variable cost (a constant cost per unit).
3. The order costs are fixed per order—a declining cost per unit as order size increases.
4. The purchase price per unit of inventory is fixed.

There are three ways to calculate EOQ. One method is to prepare a tabulation of the total relevant costs at various order sizes until the order size with the lowest cost is reached. The other two methods, a graphical solution and a mathematical formula, arrive at the optimum solution directly.

Let us assume the Martin Company uses 5,000 units of direct material Beta annually. Each unit of Beta costs $20, and the inventory carrying costs are 12 percent of the unit's cost, or $2.40 per unit. The inventory ordering costs are $24 per purchase order placed.

The EOQ Table

The steps needed to prepare a tabulation to determine the EOQ are:

Step 1

Select a series of approximately six order sizes that are likely to be near the EOQ. Because the EOQ is unknown, the selection of the order sizes is done through trial and error. A possible beginning is to take the annual demand (usage)—in this case, 5,000 units—and divide it by 10. Then use either 50-unit or 100-unit intervals below and above the 500 units (5,000 ÷ 10).

Step 2

For each order size selected in step 1, compute the average inventory by dividing the order size by 2. The reason for this computation is that the carrying costs are applied to the *average* amount of units carried in inventory and not to the order size. Because the total amount ordered is carried in inventory only at the beginning of the ordering cycle and the inventory may be reduced by usage until it reaches zero, the average inventory may be computed as:

$$\text{Average inventory} = \frac{\text{Order size} + 0}{2}$$

Step 3

Compute the number of purchase orders per annum for each order size. This step may be computed as:

$$\text{Number of purchase orders} = \frac{\text{Annual usage}}{\text{Order size}}$$

Step 4

Compute the annual carrying costs for each order size by multiplying the average inventory in units by the carrying cost per unit.

$$\text{Annual carrying costs} = \text{Carrying cost per unit} \left(\frac{\text{Order size}}{2}\right)$$

► **ILLUSTRATION 9-19**

THE MARTIN COMPANY
Determining Economic Order Quality
Tabulation of Total Relevant Costs for Ordering Inventory

Steps	Symbols*		250	300	400	500	600	1,000
Step 1		Order Size in Units	250	300	400	500	600	1,000
Step 2	OS/2	Average inventory in units.	125	150	200	250	300	500
Step 3	A/OS	Number of purchase orders	20	16⅔	12½	10	8⅓	5
Step 4	C(OS/2)	Annual carrying cost at $2.40 per unit	$300	$360	$480	$600	$720	$1,200
Step 5	P(A/OS)	Annual purchase order cost at $24 per order.	480	400	300	240	200	120
Step 6	TC	Total annual costs	$780	$760	$780	$840	$920	$1,320

* OS = Order size in units.
  A = Annual usage in units.
  C = Annual cost of carrying one unit in inventory.
  P = Cost of placing a purchase order.
 TC = Total cost.

► **ILLUSTRATION 9-20**

THE MARTIN COMPANY
Tabulation of Selected Total Relevant Costs
for Ordering Inventory

Symbols	Order Size in Units	200	800
OS/2	Average inventory in units	100	400
A/OS	Number of purchase orders	25	6¼
C(OS/2)	Annual carrying cost of $2.40 per unit	$240	$ 960
P(A/OS)	Annual purchase order cost at $24 per order	600	150
TC	Total annual costs	$840	$1,110

Step 5

Compute the annual purchase ordering costs for each order size by multiplying the number of purchase orders computed in step 3 by the cost of placing a purchase order (in this case, $24).

$$\text{Annual order costs} = \text{Cost per order} \left(\frac{\text{Annual usage}}{\text{Order size}} \right)$$

Step 6

Total the carrying and ordering costs to arrive at the total annual costs for each order size.

The tabulation is shown in Illustration 9-19. The order size that minimizes total annual costs is approximately 300 units; thus, the firm should order approximately 300 units each time it orders material Beta.

The EOQ Graph

The graphical solution may be prepared from the tabular solution. If different order sizes are desired for the graphical solution, their total costs would be computed as shown in Illustration 9-19. The calculations for the additional order sizes of 200 and 800 units of Beta are shown in Illustration 9-20. The annual carrying costs for order sizes of 200, 400, 600, 800, and 1,000 units of Beta are plotted on the graph in Illustration 9-21. Note that this line

▶ **ILLUSTRATION 9-21**   Graphical Solution to Determining Economic Order Quantity

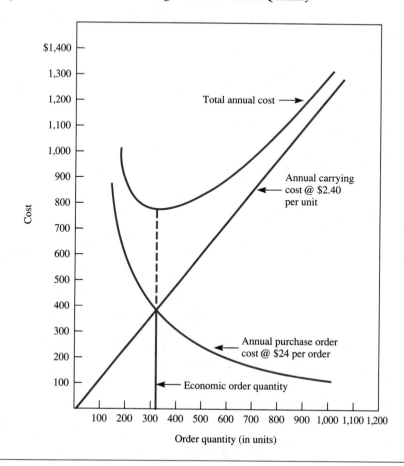

is a linear function. The annual purchase order costs for these five different order sizes are similarly plotted in the same illustration. Note that this is a curvilinear function. The total costs for these same order sizes are also plotted, and this, too, is a curvilinear function. By dropping a perpendicular line from where the annual carrying costs intersect the annual purchase order costs, the optimum solution may be obtained from the purchase order axis. The solution indicates an amount slightly above 300 units. When the perpendicular is extended to the total cost function, as shown by the dotted line in Illustration 9-21, it hits the lowest point on the total cost line, thus indicating that total costs are at a minimum.

Although the optimum solution is slightly greater than 300 units, the firm would probably round its order size to 300 units because suppliers prefer to deal in round lots.

The EOQ Formula

The economic order quantity may also be determined by using a mathematical formula. This formula, derived by calculus, is:

$$EOQ = \sqrt{\frac{2AP}{C}}$$

where

EOQ = Economic order quantity
A = Annual usage in units
P = The cost of placing an order
C = The annual cost of carrying one unit in inventory

Using this formula and the information about the Martin Company's orders of Beta, the mathematical computation of EOQ would be:

$$EOQ = \sqrt{\frac{2(5000)(\$24)}{\$2.40}} = \sqrt{100,000} = 316$$

Although the mathematical solution is the simplest to compute, it does not provide as much information as the tabular and graphical solutions. Firms prefer to find a range that produces minimum costs rather than a single precise point. Ranges of costs for order sizes from 250 to 500 units can be obtained from either the table or the graph, but information about only a single order size—316 units—is obtained from the formula. The range provides greater flexibility in ordering.

Production Runs

The EOQ formula is also suitable for computing an optimum production run when a firm must change its machinery setup to accommodate a particular product's manufacturing requirements. The cost of setting up the machinery is used in place of the purchase order cost, and the remainder of the items in the equation are treated the same as for ordering materials. An **economic production run in units** is the number of units to produce to minimize the total of inventory carrying costs and production setup costs.

L.O. 9
Economic production run

The Brooke Company manufactures a variety of belt buckles. All of the buckles are made on a punch press, but the die (a form used to shape metal) must be changed for each style. The cost of carrying the western buckle in inventory is 25 cents per buckle per annum. Annual sales of this buckle are 60,000 units, and the cost of setting up the punch press for a production run is $300 per setup.

The mathematical formula for computing the optimal size production run is:

$$EPR = \sqrt{\frac{2AR}{C}}$$

where

EPR = Economic production run in units
A = Annual production in units
R = Setup cost for each change in production runs
C = The annual cost of carrying one unit in inventory

Inserting the information about the western buckle into the equation provides the following economic production run in units:

$$EPR = \sqrt{\frac{2(60,000)(\$300)}{\$.25}} = \sqrt{144,000,000} = 12,000 \text{ units}$$

The optimum production run is 12,000 units, or five production runs per year.

▶ **ILLUSTRATION 9-22**   Determining the Reorder Point under Conditions of Certainty (*Graphical Solution*)

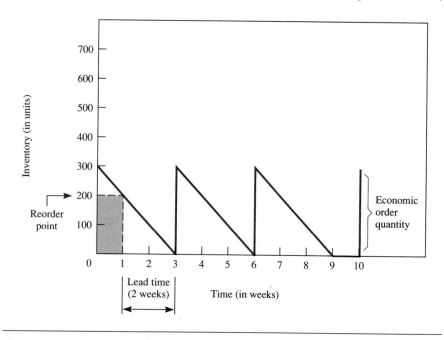

Reordering Point

Thus far, we have addressed the problem *how much* to order. The remaining discussion of inventory planning and control is concerned with determining *when* to place the order. In making this determination, an essential ingredient is the lead time. **Lead time** is the interval of time between the placing of an order and the receipt of the ordered merchandise on the purchaser's premises. Another key ingredient is the usage rate. The amount used per period (daily or weekly) may be known with certainty; or, it may fluctuate, in which case a firm may prefer to carry extra inventory to accommodate sudden spurts in demand for the material.

L.O. 10
Reorder point—conditions of certainty

Reordering Point under Conditions of Certainty   The **reorder point** is the point in time when depleted inventory must be reordered. When the usage rate is known with certainty, it may be expressed as:

$$\text{Reorder point} = \text{Lead time} \times \text{Usage rate}$$

If the Martin Company uses 100 units of Beta per week (5,000 units per year ÷ 50 weeks) and the lead time is two weeks, the reorder point would be:

$$\text{Reorder point} = 2 \text{ weeks} \times 100 \text{ units} = 200 \text{ units}$$

Therefore, whenever the inventory of Beta falls to 200 units, the company will place an order for 300 units (computed earlier as EOQ). This calculation is shown graphically in Illustration 9-22.

Reordering Point under Conditions of Uncertainty   Although firms would like to be certain about their usage rates, it is usually not possible. In reality, most firms operate under conditions in which usage rates are likely to fluctuate. In such cases, ordering as shown in Illustration 9-22 is likely to produce

L.O. 11
Reorder point with safety stock

a stockout whenever a sudden spurt in usage occurs. Therefore, firms are likely to provide for this contingency by carrying a safety stock. **Safety stock** is the amount of inventory carried to accommodate the difference between the maximum expected usage and the average usage of materials during the lead time.

Safety stock also accommodates differences between expected and actual delivery times. Thus, it is possible to use safety stock for a situation in which delivery time averages three days but may take as long as seven days. In addition, being out of stock for certain critical items may be more expensive for some products than for others. When this condition is present, it must be factored into safety stock considerations.

▶ **Example**   A hospital is often called upon to administer a blood-clot dissolving drug, such as streptokinase or TPA, to a patient who has suffered a heart attack within the past hour or two. Being out of stock of this kind of medicine may cause a patient to die or suffer serious heart damage, which the administration of the drug would have avoided. Obviously, being out of stock of a medicine, such as Tylenol, is far less critical.   ◀

Recall that the Martin Company always uses 100 units of Beta per week and reorders 300 units (EOQ) with two weeks of lead time. Let us now assume that instead of always using 100 units per week, the company uses an average of 100 units per week with usage in some weeks reaching as high as 125 units. The highest amount, 125 units, is referred to as the *maximum usage*. To provide for reasonable maximum usage, firms normally provide for a safety stock calculated as follows:

	Units
Maximum usage per week.	125
Average usage per week	100
Excess usage	25
Lead time	× 2 weeks
Safety stock	50

The equation to compute safety stock is:

$$\text{Safety stock} = \text{Lead time} \times (\text{Maximum usage} - \text{Average usage})$$

To calculate the reorder point when safety stock is needed, add the safety stock to the reorder point as computed under conditions of certainty. The equation used to compute the reorder point under conditions of uncertainty may be stated as:

$$\text{Reorder point} = (\text{Lead time} \times \text{Average usage}) + \text{Safety stock}$$

Inserting the data for the Martin Company into the equation, the result is:

$$\text{Reorder point} = (2 \text{ weeks} \times 100 \text{ units}) + 50 \text{ units} = 250 \text{ units}$$

The graphical approach to computing the reorder point under conditions of uncertainty is shown in Illustration 9-23. Note how the *expected average usage* line descends to the safety stock of 50 units when the new shipment

▶ **ILLUSTRATION 9-23**   Determining the Reorder Point under Conditions of Uncertainty (*Graphical Solution*)

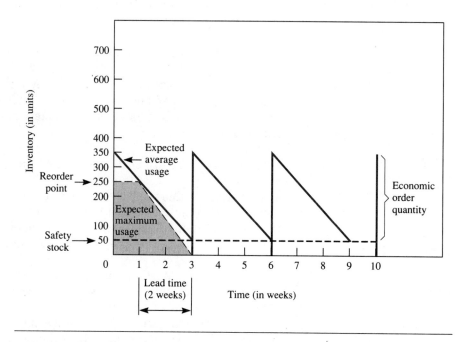

arrives, and *only* the *expected maximum usage* line descends to zero when the new shipment arrives.

▶ **GLOSSARY OF KEY TERMS**

Administrative cost budget   A quantitative listing of each planned administrative cost for the coming year, such as office rent and office salaries. (p. 408)

Bottom-up budget   A budget that is prepared by each individual department of an organization; these individual budgets is then combined into a master budget for the organization as a whole. (p. 421)

Budget   A financial plan that sets forth the resources necessary to carry out activities and meet financial goals for a future period of time. (p. 394)

Budgeted balance sheet   A projected statement of financial position that reflects the expected balances in the accounts at the end of the planning period. It is prepared by starting with a firm's balance sheet at the beginning of a year and adjusting each figure for all of the expected transactions shown in the operating and cash budgets. (p. 417)

Budget committee   Representatives from various high-level managers' offices who have the primary responsibility for, and participate in, the preparation of the budget. (p. 397)

Budget slack   Occurs when an employee or manager deliberately causes a firm's sales revenues to be less than they could have been, causes actual costs to be more than they should have been, or both. (p. 418)

Budgeted income statement   A projected income statement based on the various units of the operating budget that informs managers in advance whether the firm's operations are expected to be profitable and how much the profit or loss is expected to be. (p. 414)

Capital budget   The planned amounts to be spent for the acquisition and replacement of major portions of property, plant, and equipment. (p. 397)

Cash budget   A summary of projected cash balances based on expected cash receipts from operations, cash payments for operations, and cash receipts and payments from financing and investing activities. (p. 394)

Cash management   The planning of a firm's cash position so that cash is available when it is needed and all available idle cash is invested to provide maximum income, taking into account the amount of risk the firm is willing to assume. (p. 409)

Continuous budget   An annual budget broken down into 12 monthly units. As each month arrives, it is dropped from the plan and replaced by a new month so that at any given time, the next 12 months are always shown. (p. 397)

Controlling   The process of measuring performance against the firm's objectives, determining the causes of deviations, and taking corrective action where necessary. (p. 394)

Direct labor budget   A quantitative calculation and listing of planned expenditures for direct labor costs for the coming budget period. (p. 405)

Direct materials budget   A formal plan indicating the quantities and dollar amounts of direct material purchases for the coming year based on required production and the budgeted direct materials inventories. (p. 403)

Economic order quantity (EOQ)*   The amount of materials that should be ordered to minimize the total of inventory carrying costs and inventory ordering costs. (p. 425)

Economic production run in units*   The number of units to produce to minimize the total of inventory carrying costs and production setup costs. (p. 429)

Ending inventory budget   A quantitative calculation, in units and dollars, of the coming year's planned ending inventories for direct materials, work in process, and finished goods. (p. 407)

Incremental budgeting   A planning system that starts with the previous period's budget as a base and either increases or decreases those figures depending on whether the organization wishes to increase or decrease its output during the coming period. (p. 419)

Inventory carrying costs*   Storage costs, insurance, interest on funds invested in inventories, personal property taxes, and obsolescence and deterioration. (p. 425)

Inventory ordering costs*   Costs associated with placing a purchase order, transportation costs, and receiving and handling costs. (p. 425)

Inventory planning and control*   Techniques used to ensure that an optimum level of inventory will be maintained so that the costs of carrying and ordering inventories will be minimized and sufficient quantities will be on hand to avoid production interruptions due to stockouts (not having a needed material on hand). (p. 425)

Lead time*   The interval of time between the placing of an order and the receipt of the ordered merchandise on the purchaser's premises. (p. 430)

Long-term planning   The process of setting long-term goals and determining the means by which they will be attained. The time frame for long-term planning may extend as far as 20 years into the future, but its usual range is from 2 to 10 years. (p. 397)

Manufacturing overhead budget   A quantitative listing of each type of planned cost classified as manufacturing overhead, such as factory rent, factory supervision, and repairs, segregated into fixed and variable categories. (p. 406)

Marketing cost budget   A quantitative listing of each planned marketing cost for the coming year, such as salespersons' salaries and commissions. (p. 407)

---

* Denotes a glossary term from the chapter appendix.

Master budget   A company's overall financial plan for the coming year or other planning period, which usually includes an operating budget, a cash budget, and projected financial statements.   (p. 394)

Operating budget   A firm's operating plans for the coming year consisting of a sales budget, a production budget, a direct materials budget, an ending inventories budget, a direct labor budget, a manufacturing overhead budget, a marketing cost budget, and an administrative cost budget.   (p. 394)

Participative budget   A budget prepared from the bottom up (i.e., having employees participate in its the preparation). This type of budget is sometimes referred to as a *self-imposed budget*.   (p. 396)

Performance report   A report that compares actual results to planned results using four columns: one column for budgeted data, one for actual data, one showing the difference between budget and actual and whether the difference is over or under budget, and one for explanations of the difference.   (p. 417)

Planning   The process of deciding what objectives to pursue during a future time period and what to do to achieve those objectives.   (p. 394)

Production budget   A formal plan quantifying in units the required production for the coming year based on the budgeted sales and the budgeted inventories of finished goods.   (p. 400)

Profit planning   The preparation of budgets to achieve the objectives that have been set.   (p. 394)

Reorder point*   The point in time when depleted inventory must be reordered. When the usage rate is known with certainty, it is computed by multiplying the lead time by the usage rate.   (p. 430).

Safety stock*   The amount of inventory carried to accommodate the difference between the maximum expected usage and the average usage of materials during the lead time.   (p. 431)

Sales budget   A formal plan setting forth a firm's anticipated sales—in quantities and in dollars—for the coming year based on the sales forecast.   (p. 399)

Sales forecast   A formal prediction of the quantities expected to be sold in the coming year based on such factors as past sales, economic and seasonal conditions, pricing policies, and market research studies.   (p. 399)

Short-term planning   The process of deciding what objectives to pursue during a short, near-future period, usually one year, and what to do to achieve those objectives.   (p. 396)

Slack   See **budget slack.**

Zero-base budgeting   A method of budgeting that starts with a base of zero and ranks each program and its cost, starting with the one most vital to the organization. In this manner, managers can choose to fund programs on the basis of merit, without preconceived notions about what must be included.   (p. 419)

---

* Denotes a glossary term from the chapter appendix.

▶ **GLOSSARY OF SYNONYMS**

Perpetual budget   See **continuous budget.**

Self-imposed budget   See **participative budget.**

Slack   See **budgetary slack.**

Strategic planning   See **long-term planning.**

▶ **REVIEW PROBLEM**   The Best Company manufactures one product, Stepon. The sales forecast for 19x3 and expected selling prices of Stepon are as follows:

Quarter	Number of Units	Price
19x3:		
First	15,000	$24
Second . . .	14,000	24
Third	18,000	25
Fourth . . .	21,000	26
19x4:		
First	13,000	27
Second . . .	15,000	27

Stepon requires two pounds of Purest at $1.20 per pound. The beginning inventories at January 1, 19x3, are estimated as follows:

Stepon . . . 2,800 units at $10.50 each
Purest . . . 6,000 pounds at $1.20 per pound

The company's policy is to carry as inventories 20 percent of its needs for the following quarter. This applies to both direct materials and finished goods. The company has no work in process inventories.

Stepon requires an average of 15 minutes (¼ of an hour) of direct labor to manufacture. Wage rates are fixed at $18 per hour.

Manufacturing overhead is applied to production at 90 percent of direct labor cost and consists of the following:

	Fixed	Variable	Total
Superintendence	$ 60,000	—	$ 60,000
Indirect labor.	30,000	$ 30,000	60,000
Rent.	30,000	—	30,000
Repairs and maintenance	4,000	18,000	22,000
Light and power	2,000	18,000	20,000
Payroll fringes	9,550	44,040	53,590
Miscellaneous	2,000	12,000	14,000
Depreciation of machinery	15,000	—	15,000
Totals	$152,550	$122,040	$274,590

Overhead rate per direct labor cost:
$274,590 ÷ $305,100 = 90% per direct labor-dollar.

The information needed to prepare the marketing and administrative cost budgets is as follows:

BEST COMPANY
Partial Marketing Cost Budget
For the Year Ended December 31, 19x3

	First Quarter	Second Quarter	Third Quarter	Fourth Quarter	Yearly Total
Sales salaries	$10,000	$10,000	$10,000	$10,000	$40,000
Sales commissions*	?	?	?	?	?
Advertising.	2,500	2,500	3,500	3,500	12,000
Travel	2,000	2,000	2,000	2,000	8,000
Rent.	3,000	3,000	3,000	3,000	12,000
Utilities	1,000	1,000	1,000	1,000	4,000
Miscellaneous	2,500	2,500	2,500	2,500	10,000
Totals	$?	$?	$?	$?	$?

* 3% of sales.

BEST COMPANY
Partial Administrative Cost Budget
For the Year Ended December 31, 19x3

	First Quarter	Second Quarter	Third Quarter	Fourth Quarter	Yearly Total
Administrative salaries	$45,000	$45,000	$45,000	$45,000	$180,000
Rent	6,000	6,000	6,000	6,000	24,000
Utilities	1,000	1,000	1,000	1,000	4,000
Insurance	1,000	1,000	1,000	1,000	4,000
Professional fees	4,000	4,000	4,000	4,000	16,000
Bad debts cost*	?	?	?	?	?
Payroll fringes	10,000	10,000	10,000	10,000	40,000
Miscellaneous	5,000	5,000	5,000	5,000	20,000
Totals	$?	$?	$?	$?	$?

* 1% of sales.

Income taxes are expected to average 30 percent for the year, and estimated income taxes are $140,000, payable $35,000 each quarter. Any difference between the estimated taxes of $140,000 and the provision required on the income statement is to be shown on the balance sheet as either a current liability or a current asset, depending on whether the difference is a debit or a credit.

Accounts receivable are collected as follows:

	Percent
During the quarter of sale . . .	90
The subsequent quarter	9
Uncollectible	1

Payments are made as follows:

Direct materials purchases	80% in the quarter purchased, 20% in the following quarter
Direct labor	100% in the quarter incurred
Manufacturing overhead	90% in the quarter incurred, 10% in the following quarter
Marketing and administrative costs . . .	100% in the quarter incurred

Accounts receivable on January 1, 19x3, is expected to contain the following:

From sales made in the fourth quarter, 19x2	$50,000
From sales made prior to the fourth quarter, 19x2 . . .	10,000
Total	$60,000

The accounts payable on January 1, 19x3, is expected to amount to $15,400. This includes $9,200 for direct materials purchases and $6,200 for manufacturing overhead.

Administrative costs include a provision for bad debts equal to 1 percent of sales. The balance of administrative costs are fixed costs.

Equipment is to be purchased and paid for as follows:

Quarter	Amount
First	$15,000
Second . . .	90,000
Third	25,000
Fourth . . .	15,000

Dividends of $20,000 are paid on the last day of each quarter.

The cash balance on January 1, 19x3, is expected to be $50,000, and the company wishes to maintain a minimum cash balance of $50,000 at the end of each quarter.

The company has an arrangement with its bank to borrow money at a 12 percent interest rate. Borrowings, if needed, are made on the last day of the quarter, and maximum repayments are made on the last day of the quarter when the cash balance exceeds $50,000.

During the year, $10,000 of accounts receivable are expected to be written off against the allowance for uncollectibles.

The company's budgeted balance sheet at January 1, 19x3, is as follows:

BEST COMPANY
Budgeted Balance Sheet
January 1, 19x3
Assets

Current assets:			
Cash.			$ 50,000
Accounts receivable . . .		$60,000	
Less: Allowance for uncollectibles . . .		7,000	53,000
Inventories:			
Direct materials. . . .		7,200	
Finished goods		29,400	36,600
Total current assets . . .			$139,600
Plant assets:			
Equipment		160,000	
Less: Accumulated depreciation . . .		60,000	100,000
Total assets. . . .			$239,600

Liabilities and Stockholders' Equity

Current liabilities:			
Accounts payable . . .		$ 15,400	
Total current liabilities . . .			$ 15,400
Stockholders' equity:			
Common stock . . .		100,000	
Retained earnings . . .		124,200	
Total stockholders' equity . . .			224,200
Total liabilities and stockholders' equity . . .			$239,600

Required
a. Prepare quarterly budgets with a total column for the year for:
   (1) Sales in dollars.
   (2) Production in units.
   (3) Direct material purchases in units and in dollars.
   (4) Marketing costs.
   (5) Administrative costs.
b. Prepare year-end inventories budgets for direct materials and finished goods.
c. Prepare a budgeted income statement.

d. Prepare a cash budget for each quarter of 19x3 and include a total column for the year.

e. Prepare a budgeted balance sheet at December 31, 19x3. (Show all computations.)

▶ **SOLUTION TO REVIEW PROBLEM**

a. (1) *Sales Budget:*

	1st	2nd	3rd	4th	Year
Budgeted sales in units	15,000	14,000	18,000	21,000	68,000
Budgeted selling price	× $24	× $24	× $25	× $26	
Budgeted sales in dollars	$360,000	$336,000	$450,000	$546,000	$1,692,000

(2) *Production Budget:*

	1st	2nd	3rd	4th	Year
Expected sales units	15,000	14,000	18,000	21,000	68,000
Add: Desired ending inventory*	2,800	3,600	4,200	2,600	2,600
Total needs	17,800	17,600	22,200	23,600	70,600
Less: Beginning inventory	2,800	2,800	3,600	4,200	2,800
Required production	15,000	14,800	18,600	19,400	67,800

* 20% of following quarter's sales

(3) *Direct Materials Budget:*

	1st	2nd	3rd	4th	Total
Required production in units	15,000	14,800	18,600	19,400	67,800
Direct material requirements per unit	× 2	× 2	× 2	× 2	× 2
Total production needs (lbs.)	30,000	29,600	37,200	38,800	135,600
Add: Desired ending inventory (lbs.)	5,920	7,440	7,760	5,360*	5,360
Total needs lbs.	35,920	37,040	44,960	44,160	140,960
Less: Beginning inventory (lbs.)	6,000	5,920	7,440	7,760	6,000
Budgeted purchases—lbs.	29,920	31,120	37,520	36,400	134,960
Cost per lb.	× $1.20	× $1.20	× $1.20	× $1.20	× $1.20
Budgeted purchases—dollars	$35,904	$37,344	$45,024	$43,680	$161,952

* 20% of following quarter's needs:

```
        13,000  19x4 1st quarter sales
         3,000  (15,000 × 20%)
        16,000
        −2,600  ending inventory
        13,400  required production

13,400 × 2 lbs. =  26,800  lbs.
                  ×  20%
                    5,360
```

(4) *Marketing Cost Budget:*

	1st	2nd	3rd	4th	Total
Sales salaries	$10,000	$10,000	$10,000	$10,000	$40,000
Sales commissions*	10,800	10,080	13,500	16,380	50,760
Advertising	2,500	2,500	3,500	3,500	12,000
Travel	2,000	2,000	2,000	2,000	8,000
Rent	3,000	3,000	3,000	3,000	12,000
Utilities	1,000	1,000	1,000	1,000	4,000
Miscellaneous	2,500	2,500	2,500	2,500	10,000
Totals	$31,800	$31,080	$35,500	$38,380	$136,760

* 3% of sales

(5) *Administrative Cost Budget:*

	1st	2nd	3rd	4th	Total
Administrative salaries	$45,000	$45,000	$45,000	$45,000	$180,000
Rent	6,000	6,000	6,000	6,000	24,000
Utilities	1,000	1,000	1,000	1,000	4,000
Insurance	1,000	1,000	1,000	1,000	4,000
Professional fees	4,000	4,000	4,000	4,000	16,000
Bad debts*	3,600	3,360	4,500	5,460	16,920
Payroll fringes	10,000	10,000	10,000	10,000	40,000
Miscellaneous	5,000	5,000	5,000	5,000	20,000
Totals	$75,600	$75,360	$76,500	$77,460	$304,920

* 1% of sales

b. *Ending Finished Goods Inventory Budget:*

Item	Quantity	Cost	Total
Variable production cost per unit:			
Direct material—Purest	2 lbs.	$ 1.20	$ 2.40
Direct labor	.25 hr.	$18.00	4.50
Manufacturing overhead	.25 hr.	$16.20	4.05
			$10.95

Budgeted Finished Goods Inventory:
Ending finished goods inventory in units 2,600
Total production cost per unit . . . . × $10.95
Ending finished goods inventory in dollars $28,470

Ending Direct Materials Inventories Budget:
Ending direct materials inventory in lbs. 5,360
Total cost per lb . . . . × $ 1.20
Ending direct materials inventory in dollars . . . . $ 6,432

c. *Budgeted Income Statement:*

68,000
units sold

Sales (see sales budget) $1,692,000

Cost of goods manufactured and sold:
Beginning inventories—Direct materials and finished goods (beginning balance sheet) . . $ 36,600
Add: Direct material purchases (materials budget) 161,952
Direct labor (production of 67,800 units at $4.50 per unit) 305,100
Manufacturing overhead (given) 274,590
Subtotal 778,242
Deduct: Ending inventories (from part b.)
($28,470 + $6,432) 34,902   743,340
Gross margin 948,660
Less marketing and administrative costs:
Marketing costs 136,760
Administrative costs 304,920
Total 441,680
Operating income before income taxes 506,980
Less interest 1,254
Income before income taxes 505,726
Provision for income taxes (30%) 151,718
Net income $354,008

d.   *Schedule of Cash Collections:*

	1st	2nd	3rd	4th	Total
From accounts receivable*.	$ 45,000				$ 45,000
From 1st quarter sales:					
90% × $360,000.	324,000				324,000
9% × $360,000.		$ 32,400			32,400
From 2nd quarter sales:					
90% × $336,000.		302,400			302,400
9% × $336,000.			$ 30,240		30,240
From 3rd quarter sales:					
90% × $450,000.			405,000		405,000
9% × $450,000.				$ 40,500	40,500
From 4th quarter sales:					
90% × $546,000.				491,400	491,400
Total.	$369,000	$334,800	$435,240	$531,900	$1,670,940

* ($50,000 + .10) × .09 = $45,000

Schedule of Direct Materials Payable:

	1st	2nd	3rd	4th	Total
From accounts payable	$ 9,200				$ 9,200
From 1st quarter purchases:					
80% × $35,904	28,723				28,723
20% × $35,904		$ 7,181			7,181
From 2nd quarter purchases:					
80% × $37,344		29,875			29,875
20% × $37,344			$ 7,469		7,469
From 3rd quarter purchases:					
80% × $45,024			36,019		36,019
20% × $45,024				$ 9,005	9,005
From 4th quarter purchases:					
80% × $43,680				34,944	34,944
Totals	$37,923	$37,056	$43,488	$43,949	$162,416

Schedule of Manufacturing Overhead Payable:

Overhead rate per direct labor cost (less depreciation)
$259,590 ÷ $305,100 = .85084 = 85.084% DLC

Quarters	1st	2nd	3rd	4th	Total
Direct labor cost	$67,500	$66,600	$83,700	$87,300	$305,100
Overhead rate.	× .85084	× .85084	× .85084	× .85084	× .85084
Total manufacturing overhead.	$ 57,432	$ 56,666	$ 71,215	$ 74,278	$259,591

Payments:

	1st	2nd	3rd	4th	Total
From accounts payable	$ 6,200				$ 6,200
From 1st quarter:					
90% × $57,432	51,689				51,689
10% × $57,432		$ 5,743			5,743
From 2nd quarter:					
90% × $56,666		50,999			50,999
10% × $56,666			$ 5,667		5,667
From 3rd quarter:					
90% × $71,215			64,093		64,093
10% × $71,215				$ 7,121	7,121
From 4th quarter:					
90% × $74,278				66,850	66,850
Total	$57,889	$56,742	$69,760	$73,971	$258,362

Cash Budget:

	1st	2nd	3rd	4th	Total
Cash beginning balance.	$ 50,000	$ 81,888	$ 50,000	$ 57,748	$ 50,000
Add receipts:					
Collections from customers	369,000	334,800	435,240	531,900	1,670,940
Total available.	419,000	416,688	485,240	589,648	1,720,940
Less Disbursements:					
Direct materials purchases	37,923	37,056	43,488	43,949	162,416
Direct labor*	67,500	66,600	83,700	87,300	305,100
Manufacturing overhead†	57,889	56,742	69,760	73,971	258,362
Marketing costs	31,800	31,080	35,500	38,380	136,760
Administrative costs	72,000	72,000	72,000	72,000	288,000
Estimated income taxes	35,000	35,000	35,000	35,000	140,000
Equipment purchases.	15,000	90,000	25,000	15,000	145,000
Dividends.	20,000	20,000	20,000	20,000	80,000
Total	337,112	408,478	384,448	385,600	1,515,638
Excess (deficiency) of receipts over disbursements	81,888	8,210	100,792	204,048	205,302
Financing:					
Borrowings	—	41,790	—	—	41,790
Repayments	—	—	(41,790)	—	(41,790)
Interest	—	—	(1,254)‡		(1,254)
Total	$ 81,888	$ 50,000	$ 57,748	$204,048	$ 204,048

* Required production × Direct labor cost per unit.
† See manufacturing overhead schedule.
‡ $41,790 × 12% × ³⁄₁₂ = $1,254.

e.   *Budgeted Balance Sheet:*

Assets

Current assets:		
Cash (cash budget)		$204,048
Accounts receivable		
($60,000 + $1,692,000 − $1,670,940 − $10,000).	$ 71,060	
Less: Allowance for uncollectibles		
($7,000 + $16,920 − $10,000).	13,920	57,140
Inventories:		
Direct materials (direct materials budget)	6,432	
Finished goods (finished goods budget)	28,470	34,902
Total current assets		296,090
Plant assets:		
Equipment ($160,000 + $145,000).	305,000	
Less: Accumulated depreciation		
($60,000 + $15,000)	75,000	230,000
Total assets		$526,090

Liabilities and Stockholders' Equity

Current liabilities:		
Accounts payable*	$ 16,164	
Income tax payable	11,718	
Total current liabilities		$ 27,882
Stockholders' equity:		
Common stock	$100,000	
Retained earnings		
($124,200 + $354,008 − $80,000)	398,208	
Total stockholders' equity		498,208
Total liabilities and stockholders' equity		$526,090

* $8,736 (20% × $43,680) + $7,428 (10% × $74,278).

► **LIBRARY ASSIGNMENT**

Read the following:

Chandler, John S., and Thomas N. Trone. " 'Bottom-Up' Budgeting and Control." *Management Accounting,* February 1982, pp. 37–41.

Finch, Gerald L. "Improving the Bottom Line with Budget Incentive Programs." *Management Accounting,* October 1987, pp. 42–43, 46–47.

Merchant, Kenneth A. "How Challenging Should Profit Budget Targets Be?" *Management Accounting,* November 1990, pp. 46–48.

Pasewark, William R., and Kelly S. McCabe. "Preparing and Maintaining a Budget Manual." *Management Accounting,* May 1988, pp. 33–36.

Schiff, Michael, and Arie Y. Lewin. "Where Traditional Budgeting Fails." *Financial Executive,* May 1968, pp. 50–52, 55–56, 61–62.

————. "The Impact of People on Budgets." *The Accounting Review,* April 1970, pp. 259–268.

Shelton, Fred A., and Jack C. Bailes. "How to Create an Electronic Spreadsheet Budget." *Management Accounting,* July 1986, pp. 40–47.

Umapathy, Srinivasan. "How Successful Firms Budget." *Management Accounting,* February 1987, pp. 25–27.

► **SELF-TEST**

True or False

1. A budget has only one distinct advantage—planning for a firm's operations for the coming year.
2. A participative budget is one in which all of a firm's upper levels of management, such as the controller and the executive vice presidents, prepare the firm's budget for the coming year.
3. The budget committee's duties consist of selecting budget policies, reviewing budget estimates, revising budget estimates, approving the budget, preparing the firm's performance reports, and establishing the budget timetable.
4. The master budget contains three subdivisions, the operating budget, the production budget, and the financial budget.
5. A production budget is a formal plan quantifying in units the required production for the coming year based on budgeted sales and the budgeted inventories of finished goods, work in process, and direct materials.
6. The main purpose of preparing a cash budget is to project the cash balance at the end of the coming year so that a budgeted balance sheet can be prepared.
7. A budgeted income statement is a projected income statement based on the various units of the operating budget.
8. A firm can monitor its actual results and compare them with its planned results to determine whether any unusual variations warrant investigation.
9. Budget slack occurs when lower-level employees are asked to participate in the preparation of the firm's budget and they deliberately underestimate the amount of time it will take them to perform their duties.
10. Zero-base budgeting is a concept that is most useful for a not-for-profit organization but should not be used by a profit-oriented business.
11. Although a hospital grants certain discounts and allowances to third-party payers, it is best to prepare the hospital's revenue budget showing the anticipated gross revenues and then deducting these discounts and allowances to arrive at the net revenues.

Multiple Choice

The January 31, 19x6, balance sheet of Shelpat Corporation follows:

Assets

Cash	$ 8,000
Accounts receivable (net of allowance for uncollectible accounts of $2,000) . . .	38,000
Inventory.	16,000
Property, plant, and equipment (net of allowance for accumulated depreciation of $60,000).	40,000
Total assets.	$102,000

Liabilities and Stockholders' Equity

Accounts payable	$ 82,500
Common stock	50,000
Retained earnings (deficit)	(30,500)
Total liabilities and stockholders' equity	$102,000

Additional information:

a. Sales are budgeted as follows:

February.	$110,000
March	120,000

b. Collections are expected to be 60 percent in the month of sale, 38 percent the next month, and 2 percent uncollectible.

c. The gross margin is 25 percent of sales. Purchases each month are 75 percent of the next month's projected sales. The purchases are paid in full the following month.

d. Other costs for each month, paid in cash, are expected to be $16,500. Depreciation each month is $5,000.

1. What are the budgeted cash collections for February 19x6?
   a. $63,800.
   b. $66,000.
   c. $101,800.
   d. $104,000.
2. What is the budgeted income (loss) before income taxes for February 19x6?
   a. ($3,700).
   b. ($1,500).
   c. $3,800.
   d. $6,000.
3. What is the projected balance in accounts payable on February 29, 19x6?
   a. $82,500.
   b. $86,250.
   c. $90,000.
   d. $106,500.
4. Fields Corporation projects the following transactions for 19x1, its first year of operations:

Proceeds from issuance of common stock . . .	$1,000,000
Sales on account	2,200,000
Collections of accounts receivable.	1,800,000
Cost of goods sold.	1,400,000
Disbursements for purchases of merchandise and other costs	1,200,000
Disbursements for income taxes	250,000
Disbursements for purchase of fixed assets	800,000
Depreciation on fixed assets	150,000
Proceeds from borrowings	700,000
Payments on borrowings	80,000

The projected cash balance at December 31, 19x1, is
a. $1,170,000.
b. $1,220,000.
c. $1,370,000.
d. $1,820,000.

5. In preparing its budget for July 19x2, Robinson Company has the following accounts receivable information available:

Accounts receivable at June 30, 19x2 . . .	$350,000
Estimated credit sales for July	400,000
Estimated collections in July for credit sales in July and prior months	320,000
Estimated write-offs in July for uncollectible credit sales	16,000
Estimated provision for doubtful accounts for credit sales in July	12,000

What is the projected balance of accounts receivable at July 31, 19x2?
a. $402,000.
b. $414,000.
c. $426,000.
d. $430,000.

(AICPA Adapted)

▶ **QUESTIONS**

1. What is the difference between planning and profit planning?
2. Why are budgets needed for control purposes?
3. What is a master budget?
4. What is the difference between short-term planning and long-term planning?
5. What is a continuous budget? What are its advantages?
6. What is a budget committee? Evaluate the statement, "An effective budget committee dictates the budget policies of the firm and prepares the ensuing budget with as little help from nonmembers as possible."
7. What role does the management accountant play in the development of the master budget? Use examples to explain your discussion.
8. What are the subunits of a master budget?
9. What factors enter into the preparation of the sales budget?
10. What is sales forecasting?
11. What is a production budget? What is required production?
12. Is it important to budget for ending inventories? Why?
13. How is the manufacturing overhead budget prepared?
14. What is the difference between cash management and cash budgeting?
15. What purpose does a budgeted income statement serve?
16. What is a performance report? How is it used?
17. Do human factors enter into the preparation of a budget? Explain.
18. What is budget slack? Is it usually present in budgets? Explain.
19. What is incremental budgeting? Why is it used?
20. What is zero-base budgeting? What are its advantages? Disadvantages?
21. What is a participative budget? Should it be used in a hospital budget? Why?
22. How should a revenue budget be prepared for a hospital?
23. How should a cost budget be prepared for a hospital?

For Appendix 9–A

24. What is inventory planning and control? Why is it important?
25. What are inventory carrying costs? Are they normally a linear function or a curvilinear function? Explain.

26. What are inventory purchasing costs? Are they normally a linear function or a curvilinear function? Explain.
27. Why do inventory carrying costs and inventory purchasing costs pull in opposite directions?
28. What is EOQ? Describe the different ways it can be computed.
29. What is lead time in relation to inventory purchasing? How is it used by managers?
30. What is safety stock? Why is it important?

▶ **EXERCISES**   **E9–1**   **Budgeted Cash Collections, Inventory, Purchases, and Payments for Merchandise**

The Russon Corporation is a retailer whose sales are all made on credit. Sales are billed twice monthly, on the 10th of the month for the last half of the prior month's sales and on the 20th of the month for the first half of the current month's sales. The terms of all sales are 2/10, net 30. Based on past experience, the collection experience of accounts receivable is as follows:

Within the discount period	80%
On the 30th day	18
Uncollectible	2

The sales value of shipments for May 19x0 and the forecast for the next four months are:

May (actual)	$500,000
June	600,000
July	700,000
August	700,000
September	400,000

Russon's average markup on its products is 20 percent of the sales price.

Russon purchases merchandise for resale to meet the current month's sales demand and to maintain a desired monthly ending inventory for 25 percent of the next month's sales. All purchases are on credit with terms of net 30. Russon pays for one half of a month's purchases in the month of purchase and the other half in the month following the purchase.

All sales and purchases occur uniformly throughout the year.

1. How much cash can Russon Corporation plan to collect from accounts receivable collections during July 19x0?
   a. $574,000.
   b. $662,600.
   c. $619,000.
   d. $608,000.
   e. None of the above answers is correct.
2. How much cash can Russon plan to collect in September from sales made in August 19x0?
   a. $337,400.
   b. $343,000.
   c. $400,400.
   d. $280,000.
   e. None of the above answers is correct.
3. The budgeted dollar value of Russon's inventory on August 31, 19x0, will be
   a. $110,000.
   b. $80,000.
   c. $112,000.

    d. $100,000.

    e. Some amount other than those given above.

  4. How much merchandise should Russon plan to purchase during June 19x0?

    a. $520,000.

    b. $460,000.

    c. $500,000.

    d. $580,000.

    e. None of the above answers is correct.

  5. The amount Russon should budget in August 19x0 for the payment of merchandise is

    a. $560,000.

    b. $500,000.

    c. $667,000.

    d. $600,000.

    e. None of the above answers is correct.

(*Note:* 2/10, net 30, means that a cash discount of 2 percent is allowed if paid within 10 days. The full amount is payable within 30 days.)

(CMA Adapted)

E9–2 Production Budget

The Eastern Hat Company manufactures ladies' hats and is preparing its production budget for the first three months of 19x2. The sales budget in units is as follows:

Month	Units
January	9,000
February	6,500
March	18,000
April.	45,000
May	13,000

    The December 31, 19x1, inventory is estimated as 1,800 units. The company normally maintains an inventory at the end of each month equal to 20 percent of the following month's sales. However, due to the surge of sales in April, the company normally maintains an inventory on March 31 equal to 40 percent of the anticipated sales for April.

    The company's capacity is limited to 27,000 hats per month. If the production requirement exceeds this amount, the production is scheduled in the next preceding month in which production capacity is available. Thus, if the required production for April cannot be met, it is produced in March if production is available, and if not, it is produced in February.

Required Prepare the production requirements for the months of January, February, and March. Use a total column to indicate the production requirement for the first quarter of 19x2.

E9–3 Direct Materials Budget

The Western Desk Company manufactures desks. Each desk manufactured requires an average of 30 board feet of lumber. Normally, the company maintains an inventory of 15 percent of its needs for the following quarter. The firm's production budget is as follows:

Quarter	Units
19x3:	
First	6,400
Second	7,600
Third	5,100
Fourth	9,000
19x4:	
First	7,000

The projected beginning inventory on January 1, 19x3, is 29,000 board feet of lumber. The price of lumber is expected to be relatively stable for 19x3 at an average price of 90 cents per board foot.

Required   *a.* Prepare a direct materials purchases budget for the company's lumber needs in board feet for each quarter and for the year.

         b. Translate the board-feet requirements into dollar purchases for each quarter and for the year.

E9–4   **Budgeted Cash Disbursements**

Wipers Company provides you with the following information for the month of March 19x2:

Sales	$2,200,000
Estimated beginning inventory	240,000
Estimated cost of goods sold	1,320,000
Estimated ending inventory	270,000
Unpaid accounts payable for inventories—March 1, 19x2	360,000

Marketing and administrative costs are estimated at 20% of sales plus $300,000. These costs are paid 80% in the month incurred and 20% in the following month. The unpaid balance from the prior month is $90,000. Included in $300,000 of fixed costs is $45,000 of depreciation.

Purchases for inventories are paid 70% in the month of purchase and 30% in the following month.

Required   *a.* Compute the estimated cash payments made during the month of March 19x2 for the purchase of inventories.

         b. Compute the purchase of inventories for the month of February 19x2.

         c. Compute the estimated cash payments for all costs other than the payments for purchases of inventories.

E9–5   **Budgeted Cash Receipts**

The Roxy Company's budgeted sales for the first quarter of 19x4 are as follows:

January	$ 480,000
February	385,000
March	575,000
Total	$1,440,000

Credit sales are normally collected as follows:

	Percent
In the month of sale	50
The month following the sale	25
The second month following the month of the sale	22
Bad debts, not collected	3

The firm's beginning balance of accounts receivable is $360,000 and is composed of the following:

From December 19x3 sales	$120,000
From November 19x3 sales.	144,000
From prior sales	96,000
Total.	$360,000

The company offers a 2 percent cash discount to its wholesale customers who pay their bills within the month of sale.

Required   *a.* Compute the amount of sales for November and December.
b. Prepare a cash budget of cash collections for each month of the first quarter of 19x4 and a total for the quarter.
c. Calculate the balance of accounts receivable at March 31, 19x4.
d. Calculate the cash discounts taken during the first quarter of 19x4.

E9–6   Cash Receipts Budget

The Epoxy Hardware Company sells hardware at the wholesale and retail levels. Its retail sales are for cash, and its wholesale sales are on credit.

The budgeted sales for the first quarter of 19x4 are as follows:

Month	Wholesale	Retail	Total
January	$310,000	$ 62,000	$ 372,000
February.	248,000	56,000	304,000
March	372,000	78,000	450,000
Total	$930,000	$196,000	$1,126,000

Credit sales are normally collected as follows:

	Percent
In the month of sale	70
The month following the sale	10
The second month following the month of the sale	18
Bad debts, not collected	2

The firm's beginning balance of accounts receivable is $300,000 and is composed of the following:

From December 19x3 sales	$186,000
From November 19x3 sales.	93,000
From prior sales	21,000
Total.	$300,000

The company offers a 2 percent cash discount to its wholesale customers who pay their bills within the month of sale.

Required   *a.* Compute the amount of sales for November and December.
b. Prepare a cash budget of cash collections for each month of the first quarter of 19x4 and a total for the quarter.
c. Calculate the balance of accounts receivable at March 31, 19x4.
d. Calculate the cash discounts taken during the first quarter of 19x4.

E9–7   Cash Payments Budget

The All-Natural Bakery Company bakes a variety of bread and rolls for sale to retail food stores. The budgeted direct material purchases for the first quarter of 19x5 are:

Month	Purchases
January	$ 68,000
February	85,000
March	102,000
Total	$255,000

Budgeted direct labor for the months of January, February, and March are $340,000, $374,000, and $425,000, respectively. Manufacturing overhead for the same three months is budgeted at $306,000, $337,000, and $382,000, respectively.

Budgeted marketing costs for the quarter are $204,000, and administrative costs are budgeted at $306,000 for the quarter. Both occur uniformly on a monthly basis.

Equipment costing $170,000 is expected to arrive at the company's factory in February. The payment for the equipment is due 30 days, net, after its delivery.

Dividends of $34,000 per quarter are paid on the last day of the quarter.

The company takes advantage of all cash discounts offered. Past experience shows that 80 percent of the firm's direct materials vendors offer a 2 percent cash discount if paid in the month of purchase. The remaining 20 percent of the purchases are paid in the month following the purchase. The beginning balance of accounts payable on January 1, 19x5, is expected to be $20,000.

Straight-line depreciation for the year is expected to be $408,000. This amount is allocated 85 percent to manufacturing overhead, 5 percent to marketing costs, and 10 percent to administrative costs, and these amounts are included in the respective amounts provided above for each category.

The first payment for estimated income taxes is due April 15, 19x5, and amounts to $68,000.

Required   Prepare a cash payments budget for each month and for the quarter, using a separate column for each month and a total column for the quarter.

E9–8   Production and Direct Materials Purchases Budgets

The Richard Company manufactures wooden cabinets. Its sales budget in units for part of 19x6 is as follows:

Month	Budgeted Sales in Units
January	18,000
February	22,000
March	16,500
April	27,500
May	14,000

Each cabinet requires 10 board feet of clear oak wood, which costs $3 per board foot. Glue and nails are ordered in bulk quantities and may be ignored.

The firm's policy is to maintain a finished goods inventory equal to 30 percent of the following month's sales and to maintain an inventory of direct materials equal to 40 percent of the production requirements for the following month.

The beginning inventories of finished goods and lumber are expected to be equal to the 30 percent and 40 percent respective requirements.

Required   *a.* Prepare a production budget for each of the months in the first quarter and in total for the quarter.

   b. Prepare a direct materials purchases budget, in board feet and in dollars, for the quarter in total and for each month of the quarter.

E9–9   **Budgeted Purchases, Inventory, Payments for Purchases, Sales Discounts, and Cash Collections**

The Dilly Company marks up all merchandise at 25 percent of gross purchase price. All purchases are made on account with terms of 1/10, net 60. Purchase discounts, which are recorded as miscellaneous income, are always taken. Normally, 60 percent of each month's purchases are paid for in the month of purchase, and the other 40 percent are paid during the first 10 days of the first month after purchase. Inventories of merchandise at the end of each month are kept at 30 percent of the next month's projected cost of goods sold.

Terms for sales on account are 2/10, net 30. Cash sales are not subject to discount. Fifty percent of each month's sales on account are collected during the month of sale, 45 percent are collected in the succeeding month, and the remainder are usually uncollectible. Seventy percent of the collections in the month of sale are subject to discount, and 10 percent of the collections in the succeeding month are subject to discount.

Projected sales data for selected months follow:

Month	Sales on Account—Gross	Cash Sales
December.	$1,900,000	$400,000
January	1,500,000	250,000
February	1,700,000	350,000
March	1,600,000	300,000

1. Projected gross purchases for January are
   a. $1,400,000.
   b. $1,470,000.
   c. $1,472,000.
   d. $1,248,000.
   e. None of the above.
2. Projected inventory at the end of December is
   a. $420,000.
   b. $441,600.
   c. $552,000.
   d. $393,750.
   e. None of the above.
3. Projected payments to suppliers during February are
   a. $1,551,200.
   b. $1,535,688.
   c. $1,528,560.
   d. $1,509,552.
   e. None of the above.
4. Projected sales discounts to be taken by customers making remittances during February are
   a. $5,250.
   b. $15,925.

c. $30,500.
d. $11,900.
e. None of the above.
5. Projected total collections from customers during February are
a. $1,875,000.
b. $1,861,750.
c. $1,511,750.
d. $1,188,100.
e. None of the above.

(Note: 2/10, net 30, means that a cash discount of 2 percent is allowed if paid within 10 days. The full amount is payable within 30 days. 1/10, net 60, is treated in a similar manner.)

(AICPA Adapted)

E9–10   Production and Direct Materials Purchases Budgets

The Seymour Picture Frame Company manufactures wooden picture frames. Its sales budget in units for part of 19x6 is as follows:

Month	Budgeted Sales in Units
January	18,000
February	21,800
March	16,400
April	27,000
May	14,500

Each picture frame requires three lineal feet of wood molding, which costs 40 cents per foot. Glue and nails are ordered in bulk quantities and may be ignored.

The firm's policy is to maintain a finished goods inventory equal to 30 percent of the following month's sales and to maintain an inventory of direct materials equal to 40 percent of the production requirements for the following month.

The beginning inventories of finished goods and lumber are expected to equal the 30 percent and 40 percent respective requirements.

Required   *a.* Prepare a production budget for each of the months in the first quarter and in total for the quarter.
b. Prepare a direct materials purchases budget, in lineal feet and in dollars, for the quarter in total and for each month of the quarter.

E9–11   Production and Direct Materials Budgets from Missing Data

The Sealess Picture Frame Company manufactures wooden picture frames. Each picture frame requires one board foot of wood, which costs 80 cents per board foot. Glue and nails are negligible and may be ignored.

The firm's policy is to maintain a finished goods inventory equal to 20 percent of the following month's sales and to maintain an inventory of direct materials equal to 30 percent of the production requirements for the following month.

The company's incomplete budgets, in units, are as follows for the first quarter of 19x6:

SEALESS PICTURE FRAME COMPANY
Partial Direct Materials Purchases and Production Budgets
For the First Quarter of 19x6

	January	February	March	Total
Direct materials purchases (in board feet):				
Production	?	?	?	?
Add: Ending inventory	?	?	?	?
Subtotal	43,584	48,192	47,968	?
Less: Beginning inventory	9,792	10,944	11,712	?
Required purchases	33,792	37,248	36,256	?
Production budget (in units):				
Budgeted sales	?	?	?	?
Add: Ending inventory	?	?	?	?
Subtotal	?	?	?	?
Less: Beginning inventory	6,400	7,040	8,320	?
Required production	?	?	?	?

Required

a. Supply the missing data and complete the direct materials purchases budget and the production budget. (*Hint:* Complete the direct materials purchases budget first.)

b. Compute the budgeted sales for April and May.

E9–12 **Budgetary Slack**

The following data apply to items 1–5.

Research has shown that having several levels of management participate in the budgetary process is beneficial to both the company and the employees. However, there are certain behavioral problems encountered in this process, one of which is the use of budgetary slack.

1. Budgetary slack can **best** be described as
   a. The elimination of certain expenses to enhance budgeted income.
   b. The planned overestimation of budgeted expenses.
   c. A "plug" number used to achieve a preset level of operating income.
   d. The planned underestimation of budgeted expenses.
   e. An inflation factor used to bring historic costs to current levels.

2. The use of budgetary slack does **not** allow the preparer to
   a. Be flexible under unexpected circumstances.
   b. Project actual expenses.
   c. Increase the probability of achieving budgeted performance.
   d. Use the budget to control subordinate performance.
   e. Blend personal goals with organizational goals.

3. From the perspective of corporate management, the use of budgetary slack
   a. Increases the probability that budgets will not be achieved.
   b. Increases the effectiveness of the corporate planning process.
   c. Increases the ability to identify potential budget weaknesses.
   d. Encourages the use of effective corrective actions.
   e. Increases the likelihood of inefficient resource allocation.

4. All of the following are characteristics of the strategic planning process *except* the
   a. Emphasis on both the short and long run.
   b. Analysis and review of departmental budgets.
   c. Review of the attributes and behavior of the organization's competition.
   d. Analysis of external economic factors.
   e. Analysis of consumer demand.

5. The operating budget process usually begins with the
   a. Financial budget.
   b. Balance sheet.
   c. Income statement.
   d. Cash budget.
   e. Sales budget.

(CMA Adapted)

E9–13 **Direct Materials and Direct Labor Budget for an X ray Laboratory**

You have been asked to prepare a direct materials budget and a direct labor budget for the coming six months for the Pathology X ray Laboratory. The following information is available for the current year:

Month	Usable X rays Taken
January	20,000
February	22,000
March	21,000
April	25,000
May	24,000
June	26,000
July	28,000

For the coming year, the laboratory expects the numbers of X rays taken to remain the same. In addition, it has a contract with a nearby health maintenance organization (HMO). The HMO estimates that it will need approximately 5,000 usable X rays per month, and the laboratory has agreed to charge the HMO a reduced fee.

The laboratory wishes to have an inventory of film on hand at the beginning of each month that will equal 25 percent of that month's needs. Thus, the needed inventory must be purchased in the immediately preceding month. The expected inventory to be on hand on January 1, 19x5—the beginning of the coming year—is 5,200 plates.

The laboratory purchases only one size of X-ray film. Past experience has shown that a certain amount of X rays have to be retaken before a usable one is obtained. In the past, approximately 5 percent of X rays have to be retaken. Thus, for every 100 usable X rays, 105 must be taken. This pattern is expected to continue. X-ray film purchased during the current year has averaged $1.90 per plate. For the coming year, the laboratory has been notified that the new price of film will be $1.95 per plate.

The firm employs X-ray technicians on a full-time basis at $30,000 per year each. Payroll fringes amount to approximately 30 percent of the direct labor cost. If necessary, the laboratory can hire additional technicians on a daily basis at the same rate of pay. The average X ray requires approximately 3 minutes. The firm also employs two office workers at $20,000 per annum each and a physician at an annual salary of $120,000, all exclusive of payroll fringes. Payroll fringes are also estimated at 30 percent of these salaries.

Required a. Prepare a monthly direct materials budget for the first six months of 19x5. You may ignore chemicals, such as developer, and other supplies, such as patients' records and manila envelopes used to store X rays in the files.

b. Prepare a monthly direct labor budget and an indirect labor budget for the first six months of 19x5.

E9–14 **Zero-Base Budgeting**

There has been much recent publicity about a budgeting system called *zero-base budgeting*. The system can be applied in governmental, not-for-profit, and profit-making organizations. Its proponents believe it represents a significant change in the budgeting process for most types of organizations and thus leads to more effective use of limited resources.

Required
a. Describe the zero-base budgeting system.
b. Explain how the proponents of zero-base budgeting say it differs from the traditional budgeting process.
c. Identify the advantages and disadvantages of the zero-base budgeting system.

(CMA Adapted)

E9–15 **(Appendix 9-A) Economic Order Quantity (EOQ)**

The Gender Company uses 10,000 units of LS–6 per annum. The cost of placing a purchase order and receiving the merchandise is $90 per order. The cost of insurance, property taxes, and interest on the investment in inventory is $2.50 per unit per annum.

Required Compute the economic order quantity. Use the formula method.

E9–16 **(Appendix 9-A) Economic Order Quantity (EOQ)**

The Marcus Company uses 15,000 units of MT–3 per annum. The costs of placing an order and carrying a unit in inventory annually consist of the following:

Interest on investment	$ 1.20 per unit
Receiving department costs	15.00 per order
Purchasing department costs	75.00 per order
Insurance	.20 per unit
Property taxes	.60 per unit

Required Compute the economic order quantity. Use the formula method.

E9–17 **(Appendix 9-A) Economic Order Quantity (EOQ)**

A firm computed its economic order quantity for Part 22 as 848.5281. Its purchase order costs are $80, and its carrying costs are $4 per unit per annum.

Required Compute the firm's annual usage for Part 22.

E9–18 **(Appendix 9-A) Economic Order Quantity (EOQ)**

The Gemset Company uses 50,000 units of RH–5 per annum. The cost of placing an order is $90 per order, and the annual carrying cost in inventory is $3 per unit.

Required
a. Compute the economic order quantity. Use the formula method.
b. The firm has been purchasing RH–5 in 5,000-order-size lots. How much will the firm save annually if it will now purchase in the order size computed in part *(a)*?

E9–19 **(Appendix 9-A) Optimal Production Run (EOQ)**

1. Politan Company manufactures bookcases. Setup costs are $2. Politan manufactures 4,000 bookcases evenly throughout the year. Using the economic order quantity approach, the optimal production run would be 200 when the cost of carrying one bookcase in inventory for one year is
   a. $.05.
   b. $.10.
   c. $.20.
   d. $.40.

2. Pierce Incorporated has to manufacture 10,000 blades for its electric lawn mower division. The blades will be used evenly throughout the year. The setup cost every time a production run is made is $80, and the cost to carry a blade in inventory for the year is 40 cents. Pierce's objective is to produce the blades at the lowest cost possible. Assuming each production run will be for the same number of blades, how many production runs should Pierce make?
   a. 3.
   b. 4.
   c. 5.
   d. 6.

3. The following information relates to the Gerald Company:

Optimal production run	500
Average inventory in units.	250
Number of production runs	10
Cost per unit produced	$5
Desired annual return on	
inventory investment	10%
Setup costs per production run	$10

   Assuming the units will be required evenly throughout the year, what are the total annual relevant costs using the economic order quantity approach?
   a. $225.
   b. $350.
   c. $1,350.
   d. $2,625.

(AICPA Adapted)

E9-20   **(Appendix 9-A) Economic Order Quantity (EOQ)**

Items 1 and 2 are based on the following information:
   Expected annual usage of a particular direct material is 2 million units, and the standard order size is 10,000 units. The invoice cost of each unit is $500, and the cost to place one purchase order is $80.

1. The average inventory is
   a. 1 million units.
   b. 5,000 units.
   c. 10,000 units.
   d. 7,500 units.

2. The estimated annual order cost is
   a. $16,000.
   b. $100,000.
   c. $32,000.
   d. $50,000.

3. The Aron Company requires 40,000 units of product Q for the year. The units will be required evenly throughout the year. It costs $60 to place an order and $10 to carry a unit in inventory for the year. What is the economic order quantity?
   a. 400.
   b. 490.
   c. 600.
   d. 693.

4. The following data refer to various annual costs relating to the inventory of a single-product company:

	Cost per Unit
Transportation-in on purchases.	$ .20
Storage	.12
Insurance	.10

	Total per Year
Interest that could have been earned on alternate investment of funds	$ 800
Units required	10,000

What is the annual carrying cost per unit?

a. $.22.
b. $.30.
c. $.42.
d. $.50.

(AICPA Adapted)

E9–21 **Optimal Production Run (EOQ)**

The Surefire Fabricating Company sells 60,000 units of product W per annum. The product is formed on a hydraulic press using a forming die. The cost of setting up the die is $160 each time it is set up. The annual carrying cost of carrying one unit in inventory is $4.

Required Compute the optimal size production run.

E9–22 **(Appendix 9-A) Safety Stock and Reorder Point**

The Ferret Company provides you with the following information:

Economic order quantity	1,000 units
Lead time	4 weeks
Average weekly usage	200 units
Maximum weekly usage	260 units

Required a. Compute the safety stock.
b. Compute the reorder point using the safety stock computed in part *(a)*.
c. Assume the average weekly usage is known with certainty (i.e., there is no maximum weekly usage). Compute the reorder point.

▶ **PROBLEMS** **P9–23** **Preparation of Operating Budget**

The Scarborough Corporation manufactures and sells two products. Thingone and Thingtwo. In July 19x7, Scarborough's budget department gathered the following data to project sales and budget requirements for 19x8.

19x8 Projected Sales		
Product	Units	Price
Thingone	60,000	$ 70
Thingtwo	40,000	100

19x8 Inventories (in units)		
Product	Expected January 1, 19x8	Desired December 31, 19x8
Thingone	20,000	25,000
Thingtwo	8,000	9,000

To produce one unit of Thingone and Thingtwo, the following direct materials are used:

		Amount Used per Unit	
Direct Material	**Unit**	**Thingone**	**Thingtwo**
A	pounds	4	5
B	pounds	2	3
C	each		1

Projected data for 19x8 with respect to direct materials is as follows:

Direct Material	**Anticipated Purchase Price**	**Expected Inventories January 1, 19x8**	**Desired Inventories December 31, 19x8**
A	$8	32,000 pounds	36,000 pounds
B	5	29,000 pounds	32,000 pounds
C	3	6,000 each	7,000 each

Projected direct labor requirements for 19x8 and rates are as follows:

Product	**Hours per Unit**	**Rate per Hour**
Thingone	2	$3
Thingtwo	3	4

Overhead is applied at the rate of $2 per direct labor-hour.

Required Based on the above projections and budget requirements for 19x8 for Thingone and Thingtwo, prepare the following budgets for 19x8:

a. Sales budget (in dollars).
b. Production budget (in units).
c. Direct materials purchase budget (in quantities).
d. Direct materials purchase budget (in dollars).
e. Direct labor budget (in dollars).
f. Budgeted finished goods inventory at December 31, 19x8 (in dollars).

(AICPA Adapted)

P9–24 **Procedures Used to Develop the Annual Budget**

Arment Company has sales in the range of $25 million to $30 million, has one manufacturing plant, and employs 700 people, including 15 national account salespeople and 80 traveling sales representatives. The home office and plant are in Philadelphia, and the product is distributed east of the Mississippi River. The product is a line of pumps and related fittings used at construction sites, in homes, and in processing plants. The company has total assets equal to 80 percent of sales. Its capitalization is as follows: accruals and current liabilities, 30 percent; long-term debt, 15 percent; and shareholders' equity, 55 percent. In the last two years, sales have increased 7 percent each year, and income after tax has amounted to 5 percent of sales.

Required a. Strategic decisions by top management on a number of important topics serve as a basis for the annual profit plan. What are these topics, and why are they important?

b. What specific procedures will be followed each year in developing the annual profit plan?

(CMA Adapted)

P9–25 **Production Budget, Direct Materials Budget, and Direct Labor Budget**

The Wyoming Division of Reid Corporation produces an intricate component part used in Reid's major product line. The division manager has been concerned recently by a lack of coordination between purchasing and production personnel and believes a monthly budgeting system would be better than the present system.

Wyoming's division manager has decided to develop budget information for the third quarter of the current year as a trial before the budget system is implemented for an entire fiscal year. In response to the division manager's request for data to use to develop budget information, the division controller accumulated the following data:

Sales

Sales through June 30, 19x7, the first six months of the current year, are 24,000 units. Actual sales in units for May and June and estimated unit sales for the next four months are detailed as follows:

May (actual)	4,000
June (actual)	4,000
July (estimated).	5,000
August (estimated)	6,000
September (estimated).	7,000
October (estimated)	7,000

Wyoming Division expects to sell 60,000 units during the year ending December 31, 19x7.

Direct Material

Data regarding the materials used in the component are shown in the schedule below. The desired monthly ending inventory for all direct materials is to have sufficient materials on hand to produce the next month's estimated sales.

Direct Material	Units of Direct Materials per Finished Component	Cost per Unit	Inventory Level 6/30/x7
#101	6	$2.40	35,000 units
211	4	3.60	30,000
242	2	1.20	14,000

Direct Labor

Each component must pass through three different processes to be completed. Data regarding the direct labor are presented below.

Process	Direct Labor-Hours per Finished Component	Cost per Direct Labor-Hour
Forming	.80	$8.00
Assembly.	2.00	5.50
Finishing	.25	6.00

Finished Goods Inventory

The desired monthly ending inventory in units of completed components is 80 percent of the next month's estimated sales. There are 5,000 finished units in the inventory on June 30, 19x7.

Required *a.* Prepare a production budget in units for the Wyoming Division for the third quarter ending September 30, 19x7.

b. Without prejudice to your answer in part *(a),* assume the Wyoming Division plans to produce 18,000 units during the third quarter ending September 30, 19x7, and 60,000 units for the year ending December 31, 19x7.
  (1) Prepare a direct material purchase budget in units and dollars for the third quarter ending September 30, 19x7.
  (2) Prepare a direct labor budget in hours and dollars for the third quarter ending September 30, 19x7.

(CMA Adapted)

P9–26 **Preparation of a Cash Budget**

The Ace Corporation ends its fiscal year on December 31. You have been asked to assist in making a cash budget or forecast early in January 19x3. The following information is available from the company's records and interviews:

1. Management feels that the sales pattern for 19x2 is a reasonable basis for budgeting the sales for 19x3. Sales for 19x2 were as follows:

January	$ 360,000
February	420,000
March	600,000
April	540,000
May	480,000
June	400,000
July	350,000
August	550,000
September	500,000
October	400,000
November	600,000
December	800,000
Total	$6,000,000

2. The accounts receivable at December 31, 19x2, totaled $380,000. Sales collections are generally made as follows:

	Percent
During month of sale	60
In first subsequent month	30
In second subsequent month	9
Uncollectible	1

3. Cost of goods purchased averages 60 percent of the selling price. The cost of the inventory on hand December 31, 19x2, is $840,000, of which $30,000 is obsolete. Arrangements have been made to sell the obsolete inventory in January at half its normal selling price on a COD basis.

The company wishes to maintain the inventory as of the first of each month at a level of three months' sales as determined by the sales forecast for the next three months. All purchases are paid for by the 10th of the following month. Accounts payable at December 31, 19x2, were $370,000.

4. Recurring fixed costs amount to $120,000 *per month,* of which $20,000 is for depreciation. For accounting purposes, the company apportions the recurring fixed costs to the various months in the same proportion as the month's estimated sales bears to the total estimated annual sales. Variable costs amount to 10 percent of the sales. Payments are made as follows:

	During Month Incurred	Following Month
Fixed costs	55%	45%
Variable costs	70	30

5. Annual property taxes amount to $50,000 and are paid in two equal installments on December 31 and March 31. These taxes are in addition to the costs in item 4.
6. It is anticipated that a cash dividend of $20,000 will be paid on the 15th day of the third month in each quarter.
7. In addition to the costs indicated in item 4 above, unusual advertising will require cash payments in February of $10,000 and in March of $15,000.
8. Equipment replacements are made at the rate of $3,000 per month. The equipment has an average estimated life of six years.
9. At December 31, 19x2, the company had a bank loan with an unpaid balance of $280,000. The loan requires a principal payment of $20,000 on the last day of each month, plus interest at ½ percent per month on the unpaid balance at the first of the month. The entire balance is due March 31, 19x3.
10. The cash balance on December 31, 19x2, is $100,000.

Required Prepare a cash budget for each month of the first three months of 19x3. The budget should show the amount of cash on hand (or deficiency of cash) at the end of each month. (Include a total column for the quarter.)

(AICPA Adapted)

P9–27 **Preparation of Operating Budget and Budgeted Income Statement**
The Realistic Company manufactures one product, Destro. The sales forecast for 19x3 and expected selling prices of Destro are as follows:

Quarter	Number of Units	Price
19x3:		
First	52,000	$25
Second	63,000	25
Third	97,000	25
Fourth	42,000	30
19x4:		
First	70,000	30
Second	50,000	30

Destro requires three pounds of Prest at 75 cents per pound and four pounds of Sisal at $1.25 per pound. The beginning inventories at January 1, 19x3, are estimated as follows:

Prest	36,000 pounds at $.75 per pound
Sisal	48,000 pounds at $1.25 per pound
Destro	20,000 units at $19.50 per unit

The company's policy is to carry as inventories 40 percent of its needs for the following quarter. This applies to both direct materials and finished goods. The company has no work in process inventories. Thus, the required beginning inventory of Destro is 40 percent of the first quarter's expected sales of 52,000 units, or 20,800 (40 percent × 52,000) units. The ending inventories of each item are computed in this manner.

Destro requires an average of 20 minutes ($\frac{1}{3}$ of an hour) of direct labor to manufacture. Wage rates are fixed at $21 per hour.

Manufacturing overhead is applied to production at 75 percent of direct labor cost.

The information needed to prepare the marketing and administrative cost budgets is as follows:

REALISTIC COMPANY
Partial Marketing Cost Budget
For the Year Ended December 31, 19x3

	First Quarter	Second Quarter	Third Quarter	Fourth Quarter	Yearly Total
Sales salaries	$12,000	$12,000	$12,000	$12,000	$48,000
Sales commissions* . . .	?	?	?	?	?
Advertising	9,000	9,000	9,000	12,000	39,000
Travel	5,000	5,000	5,000	5,000	20,000
Rent	4,500	4,500	4,500	4,500	18,000
Utilities.	3,500	3,500	3,500	3,500	14,000
Miscellaneous	7,000	7,000	8,000	8,000	30,000
Totals	$?	$?	$?	$?	$?

* 5% of sales.

REALISTIC COMPANY
Partial Administrative Cost Budget
For the Year Ended December 31, 19x3

	First Quarter	Second Quarter	Third Quarter	Fourth Quarter	Yearly Total
Administrative salaries . . .	$50,000	$50,000	$50,000	$50,000	$200,000
Rent	5,000	5,000	5,000	5,000	20,000
Utilities	3,000	3,000	3,000	3,000	12,000
Insurance	4,500	4,500	4,500	4,500	18,000
Professional fees	5,500	5,500	5,500	5,500	22,000
Bad debts cost*	?	?	?	?	?
Payroll fringes	12,500	12,500	12,500	12,500	50,000
Miscellaneous	15,000	15,000	15,000	15,000	60,000
Totals.	$?	$?	$?	$?	$?

* 1% of sales.

Income taxes are expected to average 30 percent for the year.

Required a. Prepare quarterly budgets with a total column for the year for:
   (1) Sales in dollars.
   (2) Production in units.
   (3) Direct material purchases in units and in dollars.
   (4) Marketing costs.
   (5) Administrative costs.
  b. Prepare year-end inventories budgets for direct materials and finished goods.
  c. Prepare a budgeted income statement.

P9–28   **Preparation of Cash Budget**

The Surrey Company has already prepared its operating budget for 19x4 and now wishes to have a cash budget prepared. The following budgeted information is available (all in dollars):

	First Quarter	Second Quarter	Third Quarter	Fourth Quarter	Yearly Total
Sales	$187,000	$250,000	$300,000	$375,000	$1,112,000
Direct materials purchases . . .	19,000	25,000	30,000	38,000	112,000
Direct labor	37,000	50,000	60,000	75,000	222,000
Manufacturing overhead	45,000	47,000	56,000	58,000	206,000
Marketing costs	29,000	30,000	31,000	32,000	122,000
Administrative costs	40,000	40,000	45,000	45,000	170,000
Estimated income taxes	25,000	25,000	25,000	25,000	100,000

Accounts receivable are collected as follows:

	Percent
During the quarter of sale	90
The subsequent quarter	8
Uncollectible.	2

Payments are made as follows:

Direct materials purchases. . . . .   75% in the quarter purchased, 25% in the following quarter

Direct labor . . . .   100% in the quarter incurred

Manufacturing overhead. . . . .   80% in the quarter incurred, 20% in the following quarter

Marketing and administrative costs . . . . .   100% in the quarter incurred

Accounts receivable on January 1, 19x4, is expected to contain the following:

From sales made in the fourth quarter, 19x3	$38,000
From sales made prior to the fourth quarter, 19x3	12,000
Total	$50,000

The accounts payable on January 1, 19x4, is expected to amount to $20,000. This includes $7,500 for direct materials purchases and $12,500 for manufacturing overhead.

Manufacturing overhead includes $12,500 per quarter for depreciation.

Administrative costs include a provision for bad debts equal to 2 percent of sales. The balance of administrative costs are fixed costs.

Equipment is to be purchased and paid for as follows:

Quarter	Amount
First	$ 6,300
Second	62,500
Third	12,500
Fourth	4,000

Dividends of $6,000 are paid on the last day of each quarter.

The cash balance on January 1, 19x4, is expected to be $50,000, and the company wishes to maintain a minimum cash balance of $40,000 at the end of each quarter.

The company has an arrangement with its bank to borrow money at a 10 percent interest rate. Borrowings, if needed, are made on the last day of the quarter, and maximum repayments are made on the last day of the quarter when the cash balance exceeds $40,000.

Required   Prepare a cash budget for each quarter of 19x4 and include a total column for the year.

P9–29 **Cash Budget for a Court Club**

Prime Time Court Club (PTCC) has been in business for five years. The club has experienced cash flow problems each year, especially in the summer when court use is quite low and new membership sales are insignificant. Temporary loans have been obtained from the local bank to cover the summer shortages. Additional permanent capital has also been invested by the owners.

The owners and the bank have decided that some action needs to be taken at this time to improve PTCC's net cash flow position. They would like to review a quarterly cash budget based upon a revised fee structure that it is hoped will increase club revenues. The purpose of the cash budget is to better anticipate both the timing and amounts of the probable cash flow of the club and to determine whether the club can survive.

John Harper, club manager, recommended that the membership dues be increased and that the hourly court time fees be replaced with a monthly charge for unlimited court use. He believes that this plan will increase membership and reduce the cash flow and timing problem. The proposed fee schedule, which is consistent with rates at other clubs, is presented below. In his opinion, the proportions of the different membership categories should not change, but the total number of members should increase by 10 percent. Court use should also increase an estimated 20 percent as a result of this new program. The pattern of use throughout the year is not expected to change.

The present fee structure, the distribution among membership categories, and the projected 19x3 operating data including membership status, court usage, and estimated operating costs are presented below. The projected operating data presented in the table were based on the present fee structure before Harper's proposed fee schedule was recommended.

Proposed Fee Schedule

Membership Category	Annual Membership Fees	Monthly Court Charges
Individual	$ 75	$10
Youth	45	8
Family	150	18

Present Fee Structure

Annual membership dues	
Individual	$ 45
Youth	30
Family	100
Court time fees	
Prime	$10 per hour
Regular	6 per hour

Membership Distribution

Individual	50%
Youth	20
Family	30
	100%

Projected Operating Data

Quarter	Membership Renewal or New Memberships	Court Time in Hours		Costs	
		Prime	Regular	Fixed Costs*	Variable Costs
1	600	5,500	6,000	$ 56,500	$ 57,500
2	200	2,000	4,000	56,500	30,000
3	200	1,000	2,000	56,500	15,000
4	600	5,500	6,000	56,500	57,500
	1,600			$226,000	$160,000

* Includes a quarterly depreciation charge of $12,500.

Required *a.* Construct a quarterly cash budget for one year for PTCC assuming that the new fee structure is adopted and that Harper's estimates of increases in membership and court use occur. Assume that the transition from the old to the new fee structure is immediate and complete when preparing the budget.

b. Will Harper's proposal solve the summer cash shortfall problem? Explain your answer.

c. Will Harper's proposal support a conclusion that the club can become profitable and survive in the long run? Explain your answer.

(CMA Adapted)

P9–30 Cash Budget for a Hospital

Voorhees Hospital provides a wide range of health services in its community. Voorhees' board of directors has authorized the following capital expenditures.

Inter-aortic balloon pump	$1,100,000
CT scanner	700,000
X-ray equipment	600,000
Laboratory equipment.	1,400,000
	$3,800,000

The expenditures are planned for October 1, 19x4, and the board wishes to know the amount of borrowing, if any, necessary on that date. Marc Kelly, hospital controller, has gathered the following information to be used in preparing an analysis of future cash flows.

▶ Billings, made in the month of service, for the first six months of 19x4 are listed below.

Month	Actual Amount
January	$4,400,000
February.	4,400,000
March	4,500,000
April	4,500,000
May	5,000,000
June	5,000,000

Ninety percent of Voorhees' billings are made to third parties such as Blue Cross, federal or state governments, and private insurance companies. The remaining 10 percent of the billings are made directly to patients. Historical patterns of billing collections are presented below.

	Third Party Billings	Direct Patient Billings
Month of service	20%	10%
Month following service	50	40
Second month following service	20	40
Uncollectible	10	10

Estimated billings for the last six months of 19x4 are listed at the top of the next column. The same billing and collection patterns that have been experienced during the first six months of 19x4 are expected to continue during the last six months of the year.

Month	Estimated Amount
July.	$4,500,000
August	5,000,000
September.	5,500,000
October	5,700,000
November.	5,800,000
December	5,500,000

▶ The purchases that have been made during the past three months and the planned purchases for the last six months of 19x4 are presented in the following schedule.

Month	Amount
April	$1,100,000
May	1,200,000
June	1,200,000
July.	1,250,000
August	1,500,000
September.	1,850,000
October	1,950,000
November.	2,250,000
December	1,750,000

All purchases are made on account, and accounts payable are remitted in the month following the purchase.
▶ Salaries for each month during the remainder of 19x4 are expected to be $1,500,000 per month plus 20 percent of that month's billings. Salaries are paid in the month of service.
▶ Voorhees' monthly depreciation charges are $125,000.
▶ Voorhees incurs interest charges of $150,000 per month and makes interest payments of $450,000 on the last day of each calendar quarter.
▶ Endowment fund income is expected to continue to total $175,000 per month.
▶ Voorhees has a cash balance of $300,000 on July 1, 19x4, and has a policy of maintaining a minimum end-of-month cash balance of 10 percent of the current month's purchases.
▶ Voorhees Hospital employs a calendar-year reporting period.

Required   *a.* Prepare a budgeted schedule of cash receipts by month for the third quarter of 19x4.

b. Prepare a budgeted schedule of cash disbursements by month for the third quarter of 19x4.

c. Determine the amount of borrowing, if any, necessary on October 1, 19x4, to acquire the capital items totaling $3,800,000.

(CMA Adapted)

P9–31   Preparation of Budgeted Balance Sheet

The Fringe Company has prepared its budgeted income statement and its cash budget, which are presented below. Its budgeted balance sheet at January 1, 19x3, is also presented below.

FRINGE COMPANY
Budgeted Income Statement
For the Year Ended December 31, 19x3

Sales	$600,000
Cost of goods sold	270,000
Gross margin	330,000
Marketing and administrative costs:	
Marketing costs	90,000
Administrative costs	65,000
Total marketing and administrative costs	155,000
Operating income before income taxes	175,000
Income taxes	70,000
Net income	$105,000

FRINGE COMPANY
Cash Budget
For the Year Ended December 31, 19x3

Cash balance, beginning	$ 25,000
Add: Receipts from customers.	590,000
Subtotal.	615,000
Deduct disbursements:	
Direct materials	75,000
Direct labor	95,000
Manufacturing overhead	86,000
Marketing	90,000
Administrative	47,000
Equipment	60,000
Dividends	45,000
Income taxes	70,000
Subtotal.	568,000
Excess (deficiency) of cash	47,000
Financing:	
Borrowing.	–0–
Repayment	–0–
Interest	–0–
Total financing.	–0–
Cash balance, ending	$ 47,000

FRINGE COMPANY
Budgeted Balance Sheet
January 1, 19x3
Assets

Current assets:		
Cash		$25,000
Accounts receivable	$32,000	
Less: Allowance for uncollectibles	3,500	28,500
Inventories:		
Direct materials	3,000	
Finished goods	12,000	15,000
Total current assets		$ 68,500
Plant assets:		
Equipment	55,000	
Less: Accumulated depreciation	15,500	39,500
Total assets		$108,000

Liabilities and Stockholders' Equity

Current liabilities:		
Accounts payable	$32,500	
Total current liabilities		$ 32,500
Stockholders' equity:		
Common stock	30,000	
Retained earnings	45,500	
Total stockholders' equity		75,500
Total liabilities and stockholders' equity		$108,000

The following additional information is available:

1. The company provides for bad debts at 3 percent of sales.
2. During the year, $15,000 of accounts receivable were written off against the allowance for uncollectibles.
3. Depreciation for the year amounted to $17,000.
4. Inventories at December 31, 19x3, are expected to consist of:

Direct materials	$ 4,500
Finished goods	13,500

Required Prepare a budgeted balance sheet at December 31, 19x3. (Show all computations.)

► **CASE**   **C9–32** **Preparation of Master Budget**

The Best Company manufactures one product, Stepon. The sales forecast for 19x3 and expected selling prices of Stepon are as follows:

Quarter	Number of Units	Price
19x3:		
First	17,000	$27
Second	13,000	27
Third	19,000	28
Fourth	20,000	28
19x4:		
First	16,000	29
Second	18,000	29

Stepon requires three pounds of Purest at $1.50 per pound. The beginning inventories at January 1, 19x3, are estimated as follows:

Stepon . . . . .   3,000 units at $12.00 each
Purest . . . . .   8,000 pounds at $1.50 per pound

The company's policy is to carry as inventories 25 percent of its needs for the following quarter. This applies to both direct materials and finished goods. The company has no work in process inventories.

Stepon requires an average of 30 minutes (½ of an hour) of direct labor to manufacture. Wage rates are fixed at $15 per hour.

Manufacturing overhead is applied to production at 50 percent of direct labor cost and consists of the following:

	Fixed	Variable	Total
Superintendence	$ 64,000	—	$ 64,000
Indirect labor	39,000	$24,500	63,500
Rent	25,000	—	25,000
Repairs and maintenance	5,000	20,000	25,000
Light and power	3,000	15,000	18,000
Payroll fringes	12,000	20,000	32,000
Miscellaneous	3,000	12,000	15,000
Depreciation of machinery	20,000	—	20,000
Totals	$171,000	$91,500	$262,500

Overhead rate per direct labor cost:
$262,500 ÷ $525,000 = 50% per direct labor-dollar.

The information needed to prepare the marketing and administrative cost budgets is as follows:

BEST COMPANY
Partial Marketing Cost Budget
For the Year Ended December 31, 19x3

	First Quarter	Second Quarter	Third Quarter	Fourth Quarter	Yearly Total
Sales salaries	$12,000	$12,000	$12,000	$12,000	$48,000
Sales commissions* . . .	?	?	?	?	?
Advertising	4,000	4,000	6,000	7,000	21,000
Travel	2,500	2,500	2,500	3,000	10,500
Rent	4,000	4,000	4,000	4,000	16,000
Utilities	1,500	1,500	1,500	1,500	6,000
Miscellaneous	3,000	3,500	4,000	4,500	15,000
Totals	$?	$?	$?	$?	$?

* 4% of sales.

BEST COMPANY
Partial Administrative Cost Budget
For the Year Ended December 31, 19x3

	First Quarter	Second Quarter	Third Quarter	Fourth Quarter	Yearly Total
Administrative salaries . . .	$50,000	$50,000	$50,000	$50,000	$200,000
Rent	5,000	5,000	5,000	5,000	20,000
Utilities	1,500	1,500	1,500	1,500	6,000
Insurance	2,000	2,000	2,000	2,000	8,000
Professional fees	5,000	5,000	5,000	5,000	20,000
Bad debts cost*	?	?	?	?	?
Payroll fringes	11,000	11,000	11,000	11,000	44,000
Miscellaneous	5,500	5,500	5,500	5,500	22,000
Totals.	$?	$?	$?	$?	$?

* 2% of sales.

Income taxes are expected to average 35 percent for the year, and estimated income taxes are $80,000, payable $20,000 each quarter. Any difference between the estimated taxes of $80,000 and the provision required on the income statement is to be shown on the balance sheet as either a current liability or a current asset, depending on whether the difference is a debit or a credit.

Accounts receivable are collected as follows:

	Percent
During the quarter of sale	90
The subsequent quarter	8
Uncollectible	2

Payments are made as follows:

Direct materials purchases.	75% in the quarter purchased, 25% in the following quarter
Direct labor	100% in the quarter incurred
Manufacturing overhead.	85% in the quarter incurred, 15% in the following quarter
Marketing and administrative costs.	100% in the quarter incurred

Accounts receivable on January 1, 19x3, is expected to contain the following:

From sales made in the fourth quarter, 19x2	$58,100
From sales made prior to the fourth quarter, 19x2.	12,000
Total	$70,100

The accounts payable on January 1, 19x3, is expected to amount to $21,900. This includes $13,700 for direct materials purchases and $8,200 for manufacturing overhead.

Administrative costs include a provision for bad debts equal to 2 percent of sales. The balance of administrative costs are fixed costs.

Equipment is to be purchased and paid for as follows:

Quarter	Amount
First	$ 5,000
Second	55,000
Third	15,000
Fourth	15,000

Dividends of $5,000 are paid on the last day of each quarter.

The cash balance on January 1, 19x3, is expected to be $35,000, and the company wishes to maintain a minimum cash balance of $30,000 at the end of each quarter.

The company has an arrangement with its bank to borrow money at a 12 percent interest rate. Borrowings, if needed, are made on the last day of the quarter, and maximum repayments are made on the last day of the quarter when the cash balance exceeds $30,000.

During the year, $12,000 of accounts receivable are expected to be written off against the allowance for uncollectibles.

The company's budgeted balance sheet at January 1, 19x3, is as follows:

BEST COMPANY
Budgeted Balance Sheet
January 1, 19x3
Assets

Current assets:		
Cash		$ 35,000
Accounts receivable	$70,100	
Less: Allowance for uncollectibles	7,000	63,100
Inventories:		
Direct materials	12,000	
Finished goods	36,000	48,000
Total current assets		$146,100
Plant assets:		
Equipment	185,000	
Less: Accumulated depreciation.	70,000	115,000
Total assets		$261,100

Liabilities and Stockholders' Equity

Current liabilities:		
Accounts payable	$ 21,900	
Total current liabilities		$ 21,900
Stockholders' equity:		
Common stock	110,000	
Retained earnings	129,200	
Total stockholders' equity		239,200
Total liabilities and stockholders' equity		$261,100

Required *a.* Prepare quarterly budgets with a total column for the year for:

(1) Sales in dollars.
(2) Production in units.
(3) Direct material purchases in units and in dollars.
(4) Marketing costs.
(5) Administrative costs.

b. Prepare year-end inventories budgets for direct materials and finished goods.
c. Prepare a budgeted income statement.
d. Prepare a cash budget for each quarter of 19x3 and include a total column for the year.
e. Prepare a budgeted balance sheet at December 31, 19x3. (Show all computations.)

▶ **ANSWERS TO SELF-TEST**

True or False

1. False	2. False	3. False	4. False	5. False	6. False
7. True	8. True	9. False	10. False	11. True	

Multiple Choice

1. *d.* Balance of accounts receivable . . . . $ 38,000
Add: 60% × $110,000.   66,000
$ 104,000

2. *c.* 25% × $110,000 . . . . $ 27,500
Less:
Other costs . . . . $ 16,500
Depreciation.   5,000
Bad debts (2% × $110,000)   2,200   23,700
$ 3,800

3. *c.* 75% × $120,000 . . . . $ 90,000

4. *a.* Proceeds from sale of stock $1,000,000
Collections of accounts receivable   1,800,000
Proceeds from borrowings.   700,000
Subtotal   3,500,000
Deduct:
Disbursements for purchases $1,200,000
Disbursements for income taxes   250,000
Disbursements for fixed assets.   800,000
Payments on borrowings   80,000   2,330,000
Total $1,170,000

5. *b.* Balance—6/30/x2 . . . . $ 350,000
Sales—July   400,000
Subtotal   750,000
Deduct:
July collections . . . . $ 320,000
July write-offs   16,000   336,000
Balance—7/31/x2 . . . . $ 414,000

Standard Costs and Performance Evaluation

▶ **LEARNING OBJECTIVES**

After reading this chapter, you should be able to:

1. Discuss why businesses need standard costs.
2. Explain the difference between effectiveness and efficiency.
3. Explain the difference between standard costs, budgeted costs, and actual costs.
4. List the members of the standards committee and discuss how standards are set.
5. Differentiate between ideal standards and practical standards.
6. List and discuss the uses of standard costs.
7. Compute standard costs for direct materials and direct labor.
8. Analyze a variance between actual and total standard costs to determine the price variance and the quantity variance.
9. Prepare a performance report.
10. List the criteria used to select variances for investigation.
11. Discuss the function of standard costing in the new manufacturing environment.
12. Prepare the journal entries needed when standard costs are part of a firm's cost accounting system (Appendix 10-A).

Q. *Have you had occasion to use standard costs in your work? If so, what procedures were used to establish the standards?*

A. Yes. When determining standards for a service industry, we studied particular tasks that employees performed in the course of carrying out their duties. Once the task was identified, we were able to compute the average time required to perform it and then we used the employee's rate of pay to price its cost. When an employee performed more than one kind of task, separate calculations were made for each kind of task. Through the use of this procedure, we were able to compute the standard hours allowed for the work done and the total standard cost for each task during our reporting periods. For each accounting period, we were able to compare the total standard cost for the period to the actual results for the period to determine the amount and the extent of any variances. Any significant variances were then investigated to determine whether corrective action was needed.

Q. *What criteria do you use to determine when a variance is significant and should be investigated by a manager?*

A. The main criterion that we use is the dollar amount of the variance. We generally consider a variance significant if the variance—especially an unfavorable one—is more than 10 percent of the total standard cost for the period. If it is smaller than this amount, it is usually not investigated. However, we keep cumulative records of variances and if a variance is consistently unfavorable and the cumulative amount of the variances becomes significant, the variances will then be investigated. Sometimes it becomes necessary to reexamine our standard costs allowed and revise them when our investigation proves that circumstances regarding the task have changed and the variances are not due to employees' performance.

▶ Standards, the expected levels of performance, play an important part in our daily lives. When attending high school or college, a student must perform at a certain level of scholarship to graduate and earn a diploma or a degree. When dining in a restaurant, a patron expects a certain level of quality in the food served, and when purchasing a product, a consumer demands a certain level of dependability and service. Thus, standards pervade all areas of human activity, including, as we shall see, the field of management, where it is vital that clear and quantitative standards be used to measure performance.

L.O. 1
Need for standard costs

A firm is usually concerned with producing its product at the lowest possible cost consistent with the quality it wishes to maintain. Thus, the firm will monitor the prices it pays for its direct materials, direct labor, and manufacturing overhead. Not only must it monitor these items, it must also control the quantities of these factors used in its production process. Because of the volume of transactions that a firm has in an accounting period, such as one month, it is extremely impractical and costly to monitor every transaction during the period. Thus, firms group large numbers of similar transactions and then compare the grouping to a norm set in advance of the actual occurrence of the transactions. The setting of norms to be used for the controlling of costs is known as *standard costing*. This chapter is concerned with the setting of predetermined (standard) costs and their use in a firm's accounting system, the identification of the differences between a firm's actual costs and standard costs, the analysis of these differences, and their interpretation. The use of standard costs is not a cost accounting system in and of itself; rather, standard costs are used in conjunction with job order costs (discussed in Chapter 5) or process costs (discussed in Chapter 6).

Actual costs vary from predetermined costs for two reasons: the actual price paid for a good or service may differ from its estimated price, and the quantity consumed may differ from the amount predicted. These differences may be classified as favorable when the price paid or the quantity consumed is less than expected, or they may be classified as unfavorable when the reverse is true. For cost-control purposes, managers need timely performance reports showing the differences between standard costs and actual costs with analyses showing the causes of the differences and whether the differences are favorable or unfavorable. ◀

▶ PERFORMANCE EVALUATION

Management by Exception

Very often, one person may expect a standard of behavior from another person, but the actual behavior is different from the expectation. For example, you may expect an easy exam from a certain professor, but when you take the exam, it is more difficult than you expected. In the same manner, the actual performance of an employee, machine, or a product is usually different from its expected performance. Differences between actual performance and expected performance can range in size from infinitesimal to extremely large. Since it is quite likely that a variance will occur between actual performance and expected performance, should a manager investigate every variance? It is obvious that the answer is "no." Thus, a manager of a firm must decide what variances should be investigated. When management chooses to investigate and take action on only those variances that depart significantly from prescribed standards, their approach is called **management by exception.** The critical aspect of management by exception lies in the choice of variances to investigate. Thus, each firm must develop decision rules for selecting which variances to investigate. Practices vary from firm to firm. The criteria used in selecting variances to investigate are discussed later in this chapter.

L.O. 2
Effectiveness versus efficiency

Everyone at one time or another is evaluated on his or her performance. Terms like *effective* and *efficient* are often used to rate favorable performance, while *ineffective* and *inefficient* are used to rate unfavorable performance. **Effectiveness** relates to whether an objective is achieved. **Efficiency,** on the other hand, is a measure of the means by which an objective is achieved—that is, whether it is achieved with the least amount of effort and the least possible cost. For example, if a sales representative is required to make a trip from New York to Florida to attend a sales convention, she may choose a direct flight from New York to Florida, which would be both efficient and effective. Alternatively, she could take a flight from New York to California and then take another flight from California to Florida. Although this route would be effective—the objective is to attend a sales convention in Florida—the means by which it is achieved is inefficient. Evaluating the effectiveness and efficiency of an employee's performance requires the setting of expected levels of performance, or standards.

▶ STANDARDS

A *standard* is an established criterion used to measure the quality of performance. Unless a firm develops standards for measuring employee performance, a manager's evaluations are likely to be biased, subjective, and ineffective. Moreover, if employees are not told what level of performance is expected, they cannot be expected to take their manager's evaluations seriously. On the other hand, when an appropriate level of performance is clearly defined and when that level is reasonable and fair to both the employer and the employee, companies should give rewards for superior performance and penalties for inferior performance. Thus, it is important for managers to clearly define the levels of performance they expect of employees. These levels should be relatively free from bias and scientifically determined, when possible.

Standards may be developed to measure both effectiveness and efficiency. If a firm's factory is capable of producing 10,000 units of product per month and the firm's objective is to produce the full 10,000 units, this would be a standard of effectiveness. If 10,000 units are actually produced, then production is effective. If only 9,500 are produced, then production is ineffective. An efficiency standard relates to the *cost* of the units produced. If a particular task should take five hours of direct labor to perform and the rate of pay is $8 per hour, the cost of this task for direct labor is expected to be $40. However, if an employee works at a slower pace than normal and takes seven hours to complete the task, the cost for direct labor is $56 (7 hours × $8), and performance is inefficient. In effect, seven hours of direct labor were put into production and only five hours of output were received, leading to a waste of two hours at a cost of $8 per hour, or $16 of inefficiency. Efficiency standards are usually referred to as *standard costs*.

Standard Costs

L.O. 3
Standard, budgeted, and actual costs

A **standard cost** is a carefully predetermined cost used in evaluating performance. Because budgeted costs are also predetermined costs, one may ask, "What is the difference between standard costs and budgeted costs?" The answer is relatively simple. Standard cost applies to *one unit of output* efficiently produced, and budgeted cost relates to *total output* for a period of time. If the standard cost for one unit of production is multiplied by the expected number of units to be produced during a period of time, the result is the **budgeted cost** for the period.

Because the setting of standards tends to extend beyond the scope of any individual, companies usually have a committee to set standards in accordance with the firms' goals and objectives.

L.O. 4
Standards committee

The Standards Committee   A company's **standards committee** normally includes its controller, industrial engineer, purchasing manager, management accountants, marketing manager, factory superintendent, and line supervisors. Each member provides needed information within his or her area of expertise. The committee is directly responsible for the setting of standards.

Setting Standards   Standard costs are determined for direct materials, direct labor, and manufacturing overhead (discussed in Chapter 11). For standard costs to be an effective control mechanism, they must reflect what *future* costs should be and *not* what *past* costs were. Past costs may contain inefficiencies, and if they are automatically used as a starting point for the current year, the inefficiencies will be perpetuated. Furthermore, standard costs must be kept current. Even if the previous year's standard costs contain little or no inefficiencies, they may still be useless for the current year if there have been changes in prices, product quality, or operating practices and procedures. Firms use standards to control the behavior of their employees.

When setting the standard cost for direct materials, the committee must consider both the *quantity* of each direct material and its price. The quantities of direct materials needed for one unit may be determined by having the firm's engineering staff prepare a bill of materials. A **bill of materials** is a detailed listing, right down to the smallest bolt and nut (although nuts and bolts are often classified as indirect materials for reasons discussed in Chapter 5) of every item and quantity of direct material needed to manufacture one unit of finished product. The bill of materials is then priced out by asking the firm's purchasing department to quote the best prices available for each item, multiplying the quantities by the prices, and summarizing the results to obtain the total standard cost for direct materials.

A similar procedure may be used to obtain the standard cost for direct labor. However, although the quantities of direct labor may be obtained from engineering estimates, line supervisors can corroborate the estimates by observing and timing employees performing the task. The company's wage rates are then used to price out the standard direct labor cost for a unit of product.

Many firms now construct computer models of the operations to be performed, and through simulation studies, the standards committee can obtain additional corroboration of what standard costs should be.

Once standard costs are determined by the standards committee, managers and employees responsible for operating efficiency usually accept them as reasonable.

**Bases of
Standard Costs**

Ideal Standards versus Practical Standards   Standard costs may be used to motivate employees to achieve organizational goals. However, when standards are selected, great care must be given to evaluating their attainability. If standards are too tight, they will discourage employee performance. If they are too loose, they will lead to inefficient operations. An **ideal standard**

L.O. 5
Ideal versus practical standards

is a measurement for evaluating performance that is theoretically possible but impractical to attain because it does not allow for machine breakdowns, rest periods, and the like, and requires employees to work at a constant rate of peak performance without any interruptions. In contrast, **practical (attainable) standards** are set high enough to motivate employees and low enough to allow for normal interruptions.

Some firms mistakenly use ideal standards so that employees will always have something to strive for. However, when employees realize it is impossible to reach the ideal, they usually lose both faith and interest in the system. Instead of being motivated, they become cynical and disgruntled. Consequently, most firms use practical standards that set realistic demands and reward employees for desired levels of performance.

After the standards committee has decided the question of attainability, it can turn to setting specific standards.

Uses of Standard Costs

L.O. 6

Managers utilize standard costs in a variety of ways. Among the most important uses are:

1. Control through performance reports.
2. Critical cost analysis when setting standards.
3. Pricing.
4. Inventory valuation.
5. Budget preparation.
6. Simplified record-keeping.

1. Control through Performance Reports   By comparing actual performance results with planned operations, managers are able to monitor subordinates' results. When employees know their performance is being monitored, they are more likely to recognize the importance of meeting specified standards. When performance reports are prepared fairly and humanely, they should not be offensive to employees who understand the need for control.

2. Critical Cost Analysis When Setting Standards   When setting or updating standards each year, the standards committee reexamines prior costs, which should lead to increased efficiencies. In many cases, the setting of proper standards is an extremely difficult task.

3. Pricing   Many firms believe setting a long-run, stable selling price based on what costs should be (normal costs) is superior to constantly adjusting prices to reflect fluctuations in actual costs. Proponents of this strategy believe customers prefer to purchase their goods knowing that in the foreseeable future the price will remain unchanged and that they will not obtain a better price by waiting. General Motors, Ford, and Chrysler have been practicing this strategy for many years. Occasionally, the automobile manufacturers have been known to offer rebates on certain slow-selling models, but their overall policy has been to price their products using long-run standard costs rather than actual costs.

4. Inventory Valuation   If a firm does not use standard costs, it must price its inventories at actual costs. This necessitates the use of a cost-flow assumption (such as FIFO, LIFO, or average) and the maintenance of a record-keeping system for inventories and cost of goods sold that is unnecessarily complex. With standard costs, all inventories (with the possible exception of direct materials) and cost of goods sold are priced at standard, and thus all units of the same kind are priced the same regardless of their actual costs. As a result, the need for a cost-flow assumption is obviated, and the record-keeping for inventories and cost of goods sold is simplified.

5. Budget Preparation   When standard costs are used as part of a firm's accounting system, standard costs are also used for budget preparation. Instead of basing the coming year's budget on the preceding year's costs, standard costs for the expected level of activity are used. In this manner, the budget is based on *what costs should be* rather than on *what they were in the past.* From a control standpoint, comparing actual costs to standard costs is superior to comparing actual costs to estimated costs based on a previous year's actual results because, as noted earlier, built-in inefficiencies tend to be weeded out when standard costs are used.

6. Simplified Record-Keeping   When actual costs are used, records like materials requisitions must be priced out using a cost-flow assumption. This entails using the actual purchase prices, which differ over time, on material requisitions for the same item. Clearly, a different cost for direct materials will be used whenever the price of a direct material changes and the firm uses FIFO, LIFO, or average unit costs for its direct materials prices on material requisitions. When standard costs are used, only one price—the standard unit price—is used even if the materials are issued from two batches purchased at different prices. In fact, the materials requisitions may have the prices preprinted on them, because only one price is used until a new standard price is adopted.

Standards for Direct Materials

L.O. 7

Each amount of material listed in the bill of materials prepared by the engineering department must be adjusted to account for normal spoilage, waste, shrinkage, and the like. For example, if a firm is manufacturing wooden bookcases, the amount of lumber required must be adjusted to account for saw cuts, trimming of ends, and random defects, such as knots, planing, and sanding. The bill of materials plus the sum of all such adjustments for each direct material equal the **standard quantity of direct materials.**

When the prices of direct materials are obtained from the purchasing department, they must be adjusted for such items as freight-in, insurance while in transit, cash discounts allowed, and import duties. After adjustment, the prices equal the **standard price of direct materials.**

The **standard cost of direct materials** per unit may be expressed as:

> Standard quantity of direct material per unit
> × Standard price per unit of direct material
> = Standard cost of direct material per unit

If a bookcase requires 30 board feet (bd. ft.) of clear pine lumber and the lumber's standard cost is $1 per board foot, the standard cost for direct materials is $30 (30 feet × $1).

Normally, a tabulation is prepared by listing the quantity, price, and total cost of the required direct materials, as shown in Illustration 10-1.

▶ **ILLUSTRATION 10-1**

FOREMOST FURNITURE COMPANY
Standard Cost of Direct Materials and Direct Labor
Product: Pine unfinished bookcase

Description	Quantity	Price or Rate	Total
Direct materials—1″ clear pine*.	30 board feet	$1	$30
Direct labor.	1 hour	8	8
Total.			$38

* Although glue is also used, it is not listed here because it is considered an indirect material.

Standards for Direct Labor

L.O. 7

The estimates of required direct labor-hours obtained from engineers and factory supervisors must be adjusted for reasonable personal needs, coffee breaks, machine breakdowns and maintenance, and the like. If the required time to manufacture a bookcase is 55 minutes and the adjustment for personal needs and the like is 40 minutes per eight-hour day, the **standard quantity of direct labor** is 60 minutes ($55 + {}^{40}\!/_8 = 60$ minutes).

If an employee who works on bookcases earns $8 per hour, the standard direct labor rate is $8 per hour. A **standard direct labor rate** is the normal rate of pay per hour paid to employees for a particular kind of work. The **standard cost of direct labor** per unit may be expressed as:

$$\text{Standard quantity of direct labor per unit}$$
$$\times \text{ Standard direct labor rate}$$
$$= \text{ Standard cost of direct labor per unit}$$

Using the one-hour quantity and the $8 rate, the standard cost of direct labor at Foremost Furniture would be $8 (1 hour $\times$ $8), as summarized in Illustration 10-1.

The determination of standard overhead is discussed in the next chapter.

Once the standard cost per unit is decided upon, work may proceed toward the construction of a budget.

Standard Quantity Allowed

As noted previously, a standard cost refers to only *one unit* of product. Because firms usually manufacture their products in batches, the standard cost per unit must be converted into budgeted data. This is accomplished by multiplying the expected number of units to be produced in an accounting period by the standard cost per unit. For example, the standard cost of direct materials for the Foremost Furniture Company's bookcase is $30 per unit. If the company expects to manufacture 100 bookcases for the month of January 19x1, its budgeted cost for direct materials is $3,000 (100 units $\times$ $30). A budgeted cost may be computed by multiplying the *estimated* production by the standard cost per unit:

$$\text{Budgeted cost} = \text{Estimated units} \times \text{Standard cost per unit} \qquad \textbf{(1)}$$

The budgeted cost for direct materials is useful for planning purposes. It provides a measure of the expected activity and how much direct materials will be needed for the month. However, it may not be useful for controlling purposes. In this case, if exactly 100 bookcases are produced in January, then the $3,000 budgeted amount is useful for comparing the actual materials cost with the estimated cost to determine if the actual cost is higher than it should be (an unfavorable event) or lower than it should be (a favorable event). For example, if the actual direct materials cost for the bookcases during January is $3,200 and 100 bookcases were manufactured, then the actual cost is $200 greater than it should be—an unfavorable event. But if 110 bookcases were *actually* produced and the direct materials cost amounted to $3,200, a manager's conclusion that the additional cost of $200 is unfavorable might be erroneous. Before a conclusion can be reached about the $3,200 actual cost, it is necessary to adjust the budgeted cost of $3,000 to reflect the *actual* number of units produced. This is accomplished by computing the **standard quantity allowed** using the formula:

$$\text{Standard quantity allowed} = \text{Standard quantity of one unit} \times \text{Actual number of units produced} \tag{2}$$

If 110 bookcases were manufactured, the standard quantity allowed for materials would be 3,300 board feet (110 units × 30 bd. ft. per unit).

The standard quantity allowed, sometimes called the *flexible budget quantity,* is then used to compute the total standard cost. The formula to find the **total standard cost** for direct materials is:

$$\text{Total standard cost}_{dm} = \text{Standard quantity allowed} \times \text{Standard unit price of direct material} \tag{3}$$

Because Foremost normally pays $1 per board foot of lumber, its total standard cost for direct materials would be $3,300 (3,300 bd. ft. × $1). The same result may be achieved by multiplying the number of units produced by the standard cost per unit (110 units × $30 = $3,300). Although this calculation of the total standard cost is simpler to compute than the standard-quantity-allowed approach, we will see later that the standard quantity allowed provides some useful information for control purposes that is not found in this simpler calculation. However, the simpler calculation may be used as a check on the standard-quantity-allowed calculations.

It is now possible to make a valid comparison between the actual cost of $3,200 for direct materials and the total standard cost of $3,300. This comparison indicates that a favorable cost difference exists, instead of the unfavorable one indicated by the comparison of the budgeted cost with the actual cost. Thus, whenever actual production differs from estimated production, it is necessary to first compute the total standard cost for comparison with the actual cost. The budgeted cost should only be used for comparison when actual production coincides with estimated production.

Similar equations are used for analyzing direct labor, except direct labor is substituted for direct materials. Therefore, Equation 3 for direct labor becomes:

$$\text{Total standard cost}_{dl} = \text{Standard quantity allowed} \times \text{Standard rate per direct labor-hour} \tag{4}$$

Using Equation 2 for direct labor, the standard quantity allowed is 110 hours (110 units × 1 hour), and the total standard cost, using Equation 4, is $880 (110 hours × $8 per hour). This amount should be used for comparison with the actual cost to determine if a favorable or unfavorable condition occurred during January 19x1.

When comparing actual costs with total standard costs, it is important for managers to recognize that a difference between the two costs is really composed of two factors, a quantity-used factor and a price factor. The individuals responsible for each factor are normally different, and thus it is necessary to analyze these factors to attribute the cause of a difference to the individual(s) responsible for it.

Input and Output

Input is a quantity of goods or services entered into production that is expected to yield a certain quantity of finished goods, and **output** is all completed units (or equivalent completed units) of product. Suppose that at Foremost, the input of 4,000 board feet of lumber and 130 direct labor-hours were used to produce the output of 110 bookcases. Based on standard quantity allowed, the 4,000 board feet of lumber should have produced 133 bookcases (4,000 bd. ft. ÷ 30 bd. ft.). Thus, the fact that only 110 bookcases were produced indicates that management should investigate the reason(s) for the difference. Similarly, 130 hours of direct labor should produce 130 units of output (130 hours ÷ 1 hour), so this difference, too, requires investigation.

▶ **PROGRESS CHECK**

1. Why do firms use standard cost accounting?
2. What is meant by *management by exception*? Why is it used?
3. What is the difference between effectiveness and efficiency?
4. How are standards for direct materials and direct labor determined?
5. What is the difference between an ideal standard and a practical standard?
6. For what purposes do managers use standard costs?
7. How is the standard cost of direct materials computed?
8. How is the standard cost of direct labor computed?
9. What does the *standard quantity allowed* mean?   ◀

▶ VARIANCE ANALYSIS

In **variance analysis**, the difference between an actual cost and its budgeted, or standard, counterpart is segregated into price and quantity components. As noted before, these components are needed to properly assess responsibility. For example, responsibility for a direct materials price variance should rest with the manager of the purchasing department; and responsibility for a direct labor quantity variance, sometimes called an *efficiency variance,* should lie with the line supervisor whose employees created the variance. A **favorable variance** occurs when *output exceeds input* or when the price paid for a good or service is less than expected. An **unfavorable variance** arises when *output is less than input* or when the price paid for a good or service is greater than expected. Although an unfavorable variance is generally unsatisfactory, this is not always the case. An example of an unfavorable variance that is not unsatisfactory appears in the next three paragraphs.

If your roommates went to the supermarket to buy two cans of tuna fish that normally cost $1.25 each, you would expect them to spend $2.50. If you discover that they spent $3.00 on tuna fish, you might conclude that this was an unfavorable transaction, because an extra $.50 was actually expended. Your mental analysis would be:

Actual cost	$3.00
Planned (budgeted) cost	2.50
Unfavorable	$ .50

However, on questioning your roommates you may learn that the tuna fish was on sale for $.75 per can and that they bought four cans instead of the two you requested. Having completed a course in managerial accounting, your roommates then explain how important it is to analyze a seemingly unfavorable result before rushing to a conclusion that may be wrong. To help you understand the results, they present the following analysis:

Price difference:
4 cans at $.50 ($1.25 − $.75) . . . . . $2.00 favorable

Quantity difference:
2 additional cans at $1.25 . . . . . . 2.50 unfavorable
Net difference expended . . . . . $ .50 unfavorable

However, although the net difference in the amount spent is unfavorable, a proper analysis shows that there was a savings of 50 cents per can on the two originally requested and that you actually received two additional cans at a unit cost savings of 50 cents.

A manager who compares only actual and total standard costs without segregating them into their quantity and price components may also come to a wrong conclusion. Therefore, formulas have been developed to compare the components of actual and total standard costs so that managers can determine if a variance is detrimental or beneficial to their firm.

Direct Materials Variance Analysis

The Foremost Furniture Company's budgeted costs, total standard costs, and actual costs for direct materials and direct labor for the bookcases are summarized in Illustration 10-2. The actual data are assumed, and 110 units are produced. Under these circumstances, the total standard cost for direct materials amounts to $3,300 (30 budgeted board feet × $1 budgeted cost per board foot × 110 bookcases). Now let us assume the actual cost of direct materials is $3,200 (4,000 board feet at 80 cents per board foot). A comparison of the actual with the total standard cost indicates a savings of $100, an apparently favorable condition. However, this figure does not provide Foremost's managers with all the information they need to control their firm's operations. To be optimally helpful, the **total variance**—the difference between the actual cost and the total standard cost—needs to be broken down into price and quantity segments. A **price variance** is the actual quantity of a good or service used multiplied by the difference between the actual and standard prices. For direct materials, the price variance may be stated as:

L.O. 8
Price and quantity variances

$$\text{Price variance}_{dm} = \text{Actual quantity of direct material} \times (\text{Actual price per unit} - \text{Standard price per unit}) \tag{5}$$

A **quantity variance** is the difference between the input quantity of a good or service and the corresponding output quantity (standard quantity al-

▶ **ILLUSTRATION 10-2**   Foremost Furniture Company

Budgeted Data

Direct materials—100 units × 30 bd. ft. × $1.00 =	$3,000
Direct labor —100 units × 1 hour × 8.00 =	800
Total	$3,800

Total Standard Cost

Direct materials—110 units × 30 bd. ft. × $1.00 =	$3,300
Direct labor —110 units × 1 hour × 8.00 =	880
Total	$4,180

Actual Cost

Direct materials—4,000 bd. ft. × $0.80 =	$3,200
Direct labor —130 hours × 8.10 =	1,053
Total	$4,253

lowed) multiplied by the standard price per unit of input. For direct materials, the quantity variance may be stated as:

$$\text{Quantity variance}_{dm} = \text{Standard price} \\ \times (\text{Actual quantity} - \text{Standard quantity allowed}) \tag{6}$$

Inserting Foremost's numbers, the results are:

Direct materials price variance:
4,000 bd. ft. × ($.80 − $1) . . . . $800 favorable

Direct materials quantity variance:
$1 × (4,000 bd. ft. − 3,300 bd. ft.) . . . .   700 unfavorable

Net variance . . . . $100 favorable

The combined $100 favorable variance assumes new importance when it is analyzed into price and quantity components. On investigation, Foremost's general manager found that the purchasing agent bought a lower grade of lumber at 20 cents per board foot below the clear pine price. Because this grade of lumber has occasional knots, significant amounts of lumber were wasted to avoid flaws in the finished shelves. A lower grade of direct materials may also affect the amount of direct labor used.

The Diagrammatic Approach

Another format for analyzing variances into price and quantity components is shown in Illustration 10-3. Referred to as the *diagrammatic approach,* it is extremely useful for analyzing variances because it is systematic and highlights the relationships of the data to be analyzed. The **diagrammatic approach** shows the actual cost at the extreme left arrow, the total standard cost at the extreme right arrow, and the actual quantity of inputs at the standard price per input in the center. The price variance is computed by subtracting the actual cost of inputs from the dollar amount above the center arrow. If the actual cost is less than the center amount, the price variance is favorable; otherwise, it is unfavorable. A similar subtraction is made between the total standard cost and the amount above the center arrow. If the

▶ **ILLUSTRATION 10-3**   Analysis of Direct Materials Variances

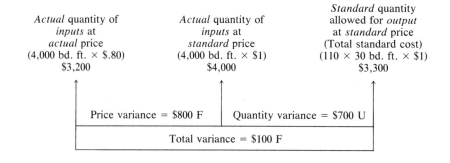

Actual quantity of inputs at *actual* price (4,000 bd. ft. × $.80) $3,200	*Actual* quantity of inputs at *standard* price (4,000 bd. ft. × $1) $4,000	*Standard* quantity allowed for *output* at *standard* price (Total standard cost) (110 × 30 bd. ft. × $1) $3,300

Price variance = $800 F | Quantity variance = $700 U

Total variance = $100 F

total standard cost is less than the center amount, the variance is unfavorable; otherwise, it is favorable.

Under certain conditions, a firm may wish to analyze its direct materials variance into three components, which includes a joint price-quantity variance. This approach is discussed in Appendix 10-B at the end of this chapter.

Direct Labor Variance Analysis

When analyzing direct labor variances into their price and quantity components, most accountants, including this author, prefer to use the terms *rate variance* in place of *price variance* and *efficiency variance* in place of *quantity variance*. The reason for this is that employees earn a *rate* of pay and are either *efficient* or inefficient. The **direct labor rate variance** is computed in the same way as the material price variance and may be stated as:

$$\text{Rate variance}_{dl} = \text{Actual number of direct labor-hours} \times (\text{Actual rate per hour} - \text{Standard rate per hour}) \tag{7}$$

The **direct labor efficiency variance** is the standard rate of pay per direct labor-hour multiplied by the difference between the input number of direct labor-hours and the corresponding output (standard quantity allowed). It may be stated as follows:

$$\text{Efficiency variance}_{dl} = \text{Standard rate per hour} \times (\text{Actual number of hours} - \text{Standard quantity allowed}) \tag{8}$$

Using the information provided in Illustration 10-2, the direct labor rate and efficiency variances for the Foremost Furniture Company are:

Direct labor rate variance:
130 hours × ($8.10 − $8.00) . . . . $ 13 unfavorable

Direct labor efficiency variance:
$8 × (130 hours − 110 standard allowed hours) . . .   160 unfavorable

Total labor variance . . . . $173 unfavorable

Although the variances themselves do not provide specific information, they do indicate when and where to investigate further. In this case, the rate

▶ **ILLUSTRATION 10-4**   Analysis of Direct Labor Variances

variance of $13 would not require investigation or action because it is too small to warrant further attention. On the other hand, the $160 efficiency variance is worthy of investigation because it represents an 18 percent deviation ($160 ÷ $880) from the total standard direct labor cost.

On investigation, Foremost found that the additional 20 hours of direct labor were spent on screening the lumber for knots and deciding where saw cuts should be made to minimize materials waste. Also, because 700 extra board feet of lumber were used due to the knots, additional cutting was needed to complete the 110 bookcases.

Based on the results of his investigation, the general manager concluded that the $800 saved by purchasing lower-grade lumber was not beneficial to the company as a whole because there was $700 of wasted material and $160 of wasted direct labor, or a total of $860 of additional costs, attributable to the attempt to save on direct materials. Moreover, the extra 20 hours of direct labor would normally require that additional variable manufacturing overhead costs be incurred. What may have at first seemed a smart move by the purchasing agent turned out to be an added cost for the firm as a whole.

The diagrammatic approach to isolating direct labor rate and efficiency variances appears in Illustration 10-4. Note that it is similar to Illustration 10-3 except direct labor costs are substituted for direct materials costs.

Performance Reports

L.O. 9

A **performance report** is a detailed comparison of *budgeted*, or *total standard, costs* with *actual costs*. Variances between the two are segregated into price and quantity components, and when a variance is significant, its source is explained. Although performance reports may differ in format from firm to firm, their purpose remains the same. They provide information and, when possible, explanations to assist managers in deciding what, if any, remedial action is needed when a significant unfavorable variance occurs. The remedial action should be taken as soon as possible after the triggering event. Otherwise, the negative situation is likely to continue and grow more costly. Furthermore, as time passes, people may forget details about the problem, making a solution more difficult to formulate.

As shown in Illustration 10-5, a performance report typically contains standard cost data, actual data, the difference between the two segregated

▶ **ILLUSTRATION 10-5**

FOREMOST FURNITURE COMPANY
Performance Report
For the Month of January 19x1

Description	Standard Quantity Allowed	Actual Quantity	Standard Price	Actual Price	Variance F—Favorable U—Unfavorable	Explanation
Direct materials:						
Quantity variance	3,300 bd. ft.	4,000 bd. ft.	$1		$700 U	Inferior materials— waste
Price variance		4,000	1	$ .80	800 F	Cheaper grade of material
Total direct materials variance					$100 F	
Direct labor:						
Efficiency variance	110 hours	130 hours	8		$160 U	Inferior materials— extra cutting
Rate variance		130	8	$8.10	13 U	
Total direct labor variance					$173 U	

into price and quantity components, and explanations of the variances, if they are available. The steps needed to prepare a performance report are:

Step 1
Compute the standard quantity allowed for direct materials and direct labor. Insert these amounts in the first column.

Step 2
Enter the actual quantities for direct materials and direct labor in the second column and place the respective standard prices in the third column.

Step 3
Determine the actual price for direct materials and the actual rate of pay for direct labor and insert these amounts in column 4.

Step 4
Compute the direct materials price variance using Equation 5, the direct materials quantity variance using Equation 6, the direct labor rate variance using Equation 7, and the direct labor efficiency variance using Equation 8. (The variances may also be computed using the diagrammatic approach instead of the equations.) Insert the variances in the fifth column and label each F (if favorable) or U (if unfavorable).

Step 5
Investigate the reasons for the significant variances and report the findings in the final column.

▶ **VARIANCE INVESTIGATION**

Selecting Variances for Investigation

L.O. 10

The cost/benefit rule controls variance investigation. An attempt to determine the cause of a variance will be made only if the cost of such investigation does not exceed the benefits to be gained from eliminating the variance. Thus, each firm must develop decision rules for selecting which variances to investigate. Although practices vary from firm to firm, the following factors should be considered:

1. Size of variance.
2. Frequency of occurrence.
3. Nature of item.
4. Kind of variance (unfavorable versus favorable).

1. Size of Variance   When assessing the significance of the size of a variance, two measures are usually used—a specified dollar amount and a specified percentage of standard (or budgeted) cost. For example, if total standard cost is $50 and a $10 unfavorable variance occurs, the difference would amount to 20 percent of standard. Although 20 percent is a significant variation, $10 is not a significant amount of money, so investigation would not be justified. To avoid such unjustifiable investigations, a percentage cutoff point is usually used in conjunction with a dollar value. Let us assume, for example, that a variance must exceed both 2 percent and $300. Then, if the total standard cost of an item is $50,000 and the variance is $1,100 (that is, 2.2 percent), the variance should be investigated. On the other hand, if the variance is $500 (1 percent), the item should not be investigated. In practice, many firms prefer to investigate any dollar variance greater than a set amount, regardless of its percentage of total standard cost. In such cases, the decision rule would be to investigate any variance that is at least $300 *or* at least 2 percent of total standard cost, whichever is smaller. This decision rule may be illustrated as follows:

Case 1

Total standard cost is $10,000, and variance is $150. *Action:* Do not investigate. The rationale for this decision might be that a variance of 1.5 percent is a normal variance—one that is expected and due to random events. The manager's conclusion might be that there is nothing wrong and that $150 is too small an amount to worry about.

Case 2

Total standard cost is $20,000, and variance is $350. *Action:* Investigate. The rationale for this decision might be that although the variance, at 1.75 percent, is below the 2 percent threshold, $350 is a significant amount of money and justifies a manager's time to investigate. Through further study, the manager might find a control mechanism that would prevent the recurrence of this kind of unfavorable variance in the future.

Case 3

Total standard cost is $5,000, and variance is $150. *Action:* Investigate. Here the manager might decide that although $150 is not a significant amount of money, because it amounts to 3 percent of total standard cost the deviation might not be normal or random. In such a case, the manager should take corrective action before the condition becomes more serious and a significant amount of money is lost.

2. Frequency of Occurrence   This author was associated with a steel fabricating firm where daily performance reports were prepared by computer. One particular supervisor's performance report was an ongoing concern for the firm's accountants. The report consistently showed an unfavorable direct labor efficiency variance, but the amount was always lower than the firm's investigative cutoff point. When such a condition exists, management may wish to investigate and take corrective action even though the variances are below the specified cutoff point. The fact that the variances are always unfavorable may be symptomatic of leadership problems or wasteful practices. The cumulative effect of consistently small unfavorable variances may be just as damaging to a firm's cost efficiency as an occasional large one. The supervisor in this steel fabricating firm was ultimately replaced when it became clear that the unfavorable variances were likely to continue despite his attempts to correct them.

3. Nature of Item   Some variances require closer surveillance than others. For example, a supervisor may have an unfavorable variance due to unexpected repairs to machinery and may attempt to compensate for it by forgoing required maintenance. Although this tactic may temporarily negate the unfavorable variance, the forgone maintenance may cause more expensive repairs in the future that could have been avoided. Thus, favorable repair variances in one time period may lead to unfavorable repair variances in a subsequent period.

Another critical variance is light and power. If an unfavorable variance is due to a utility company's rate increase, it is uncontrollable and must be accepted. However, if the variance is due to an unreasonable number of kilowatt-hours having been consumed, it is possible that machines were left running when not in use. Other variances that require close surveillance are (1) the direct materials price variance, (2) the direct materials quantity variance, and (3) the direct labor efficiency variance.

4. Kind of Variance (Unfavorable versus Favorable)   Significant unfavorable variances require a manager's attention, but favorable variances should not be ignored. Significant favorable variances, on investigation, may reveal outdated standards, inferior direct materials, inferior workmanship, neglected maintenance or research and development, or exemplary performance. Thus, both favorable and unfavorable variances should be investigated when indicated by size, frequency of occurrence, and kind of item.

Once managers determine which variances are significant and warrant investigation, they must decide which variances require action and what kind of action to take.

Management Action

Based on the performance report shown in Illustration 10-5, the manager in charge of the purchasing department should investigate the reasons for the purchase of lower-grade lumber. The purchasing agent might have erroneously believed the $800 savings in price would more than compensate for the waste of $700 and the firm would receive $100 in overall savings. If so, he should be made aware of the additional $160 in labor-hours that was spent. Another possibility is that clear pine lumber was not available from the firm's suppliers at the time of purchase. The manager should determine if the reasons are excusable. If they are, the variances are not charged to anyone. If the variances are due to errors in judgment by the purchasing agent, the resulting efficiency variance for direct labor should be charged to the purchasing department and *not* to the line supervisors in charge of direct labor.

► STANDARD COSTING FOR SERVICE INDUSTRIES

Service industries also use standard cost accounting. For example, a word processing business can have a standard direct materials cost for its paper supplies and a standard direct labor cost per typewritten page. Similarly, a public accounting firm can have a standard direct labor cost for each of the different kinds of tax returns prepared, and a law firm can have standard costs for each of the different kinds of wills and trust agreements prepared by staff attorneys. Automobile repair service centers very often charge customers for the services performed by using a standard amount of allotted time per service performed, rather than the actual time used to perform the service. These standard times are published by Chilton. Hospitals also use standard costs.

Standard Costs for Hospitals

Hospitals use standard costs in a manner similar to manufacturing firms, but there are significant differences. For certain procedures, such as laboratory tests and X rays, hospitals use a concept called a **relative value unit,** which is a weighted-average measurement based on the time used to perform a task, the degree of skill needed, and the resources used. In a variety of functions performed by hospitals, standards can be developed for direct materials and direct labor. Examples of these standards include (1) patients' meals; (2) diagnostic procedures, such as X rays, CAT scans, and MRIs; (3) blood tests; (4) hospital laundry; and (5) nursing services. Once the standards are computed, the analysis of the variances into price and efficiency components is prepared in the same manner as for manufacturing firms.

► STANDARD COSTING IN THE NEW MANUFACTURING ENVIRONMENT

L.O. 11
New manufacturing environment

As discussed in Chapter 7, the manufacturing environment is undergoing dynamic changes. Standard costs and their analyses, while still relevant, are not so important in the new manufacturing environment as they are in the traditional manufacturing environment. In a highly automated manufacturing environment, labor costs are significantly reduced and replaced with large infusions of automated machinery and computers. Primary manufacturing costs now consist of direct materials cost—a variable cost—and large amounts of fixed costs. Thus, for firms in this new manufacturing environment, standard costs for direct materials are now more important than direct labor standard costs. Because of the shift in cost structure from a predominantly variable cost structure to a predominantly fixed cost structure, highly automated firms now pay greater attention to manufacturing overhead costs. These costs are discussed in the next chapter.

New Performance Measures

As discussed in Chapter 7, highly automated firms have developed new performance measures in place of traditional ones. Since firms strive for a zero-defects process, quality control is now accorded a higher performance measure. In addition, nonvalue-added costs, such as those assigned to inspection time, move time, and wait time, are always reviewed with an eye to minimizing or eliminating them. The performance measure used to evaluate the measure of success the firm has achieved with regard to nonvalue-added costs is the manufacturing cycle efficiency (MCE). Firms that are moving in the direction of the new manufacturing environment rely more heavily on these newer performance measures and less on the traditional standard costing ones. Nevertheless, Hewlett-Packard, a firm that has adopted the JIT philosophy in its manufacturing operations, continues to use some standard cost accounting in its accounting system.

▶ **EXAMPLE**   For both planning and product costing, much of the accounting activity at (POD) [HP Personal Office Computer Division] was organized within two six-month cycles comprising the October 31 fiscal year. POD used a standard cost system *together with other target systems* to formulate a six-month operating budget; the six-month target production volume implied a total standard production cost, which, when combined with period cost targets, yielded a semi-annual net income goal. Monthly production plans provided intermediate targets from which monthly variance reports were generated (emphasis added).[1]   ◀

▶ JOURNAL ENTRIES

The journal entries associated with standard costs appear in Appendix 10-A at the end of this chapter.

▶ SUMMARY

For control purposes, managers employ the principle of **management by exception,** which means they investigate only significant variances of actual costs compared with standard (or budgeted) costs. The factors that influence a manager's decision to investigate a variance are the size of the variance, the frequency of its occurrence, the kind of item creating the variance, and the kind of variance. Some items, such as machine maintenance, require more scrutiny than others, such as direct labor, which may vary only slightly due to union contracts and/or employment policies.

Estimated costs are based on historical costs and thus may contain inefficiencies based on past performance. When estimated historical costs are adjusted to eliminate inefficiencies, they become **standard costs,** which are carefully predetermined to reflect what costs *ought* to be rather than what they were in prior periods. Because the setting of standards extends beyond any one department, standard costs are determined by a **standards committee** composed of engineers, management accountants, and various managers who base their decisions on **bills of materials,** prices of direct materials, time-and-motion studies, and direct labor wage rates.

Using standard costs, a firm can evaluate the efficiency of each segment's operations. **Efficiency** is a measure of whether an objective was accomplished with a minimum amount of effort and cost. Standard costs are especially suited for measuring efficiency, but they may also help in measuring **effectiveness**—that is, whether an objective was actually achieved.

Standard costs are used for (1) controlling through the use of performance reports, (2) critical cost analysis when the standards are set, (3) pricing, (4) inventory valuation, (5) budget preparation, and (6) simplified record-keeping.

---

[1] James M. Patell, "Cost Accounting, Process Control, and Product Design: A Case Study of the Hewlett-Packard Personal Office Computer Division," *The Accounting Review,* October 1987, p. 823.

In setting standards, managers must consider both **ideal standards,** which are theoretically possible but impractical to attain because they fail to allow for machine breakdowns, rest periods, and the like, and **practical standards,** which are set high enough to motivate employees and low enough to allow for normal, predictable interruptions and rest periods. If standards are to be useful, they must be both current and practical.

The **standard quantity of direct material** must allow for normal amounts of waste and scrap, and the **standard price of direct material** includes the cash price paid for the material plus the cost of freight-in, insurance during transit, and import duties. The **standard cost of direct material** equals the standard quantity of direct materials multiplied by the standard price of direct materials.

The **standard quantity of direct labor** is the required time to manufacture one unit of product adjusted for normal interruptions, and the **standard direct labor rate** is the normal hourly rate paid to employees for a particular kind of work. The **standard cost of direct labor** is obtained by multiplying the standard quantity of direct labor by the standard direct labor rate.

A standard cost refers to the cost of one unit of product. In contrast, a **budgeted cost** is the estimated number of units to be produced multiplied by the standard cost. Budgeted costs are useful for planning, but they are only useful for controlling when the actual production is exactly as anticipated. Because actual production usually differs from anticipated production, the **standard quantity allowed** must be used instead. The standard quantity allowed is the standard quantity for one unit multiplied by the actual number of units produced. This figure must then be converted to the **total standard cost,** which is the standard quantity allowed multiplied by the standard unit price of direct material or direct labor.

Efficiency may be measured by comparing an **input,** which is a commodity put into production, with its **output,** which is the completed units of product.

Comparing an actual cost for direct materials or direct labor with its total standard cost merely indicates that a **variance** exists. It does not explain why the variance arose or where its source might lie. Through **variance analysis,** a **total variance** is segmented into its **price (rate)** and **quantity (efficiency)** components, which when classified as either **favorable** or **unfavorable** can provide the additional information managers need to decide where potential problems may lie and what action may be needed. Variance analysis may be performed using either equations or the **diagrammatic approach.** Based on their variance analyses and related studies, management accountants usually prepare a **performance report** for use by managers. The report presents the total standard costs, the actual costs, the variances analyzed into their components, and explanations for significant variances.

Service industries also use standard cost accounting. Firms such as a word processing business, a public accounting firm, a law firm, and an automobile repair service center can use a standard cost accounting system. Hospitals also use standard costs in a manner somewhat similar to manufacturing firms but with significant differences. For certain procedures, such as laboratory tests and X rays, hospitals use a concept called a **relative value unit,** which is a weighted-average measurement based on the time used to perform a task, the degree of skill needed, and the resources used. Standard costs can be used for (1) patients' meals, (2) diagnostic procedures, (3) blood tests, (4) hospital laundry, and (5) nursing services.

The new manufacturing environment uses standard costs less and in different ways. In a highly automated manufacturing environment, labor costs are significantly reduced and, therefore, direct labor standard costs are less important. Thus, the primary manufacturing costs now consist of direct materials cost—a variable cost—and large amounts of fixed costs.

Highly automated firms have developed new performance measures in place of traditional ones. These firms strive for a zero-defects process, and thus quality control is accorded a higher performance measure. In addition, nonvalue-added costs, such as those assigned to inspection time, move time, and wait time, are always reviewed with an eye to minimizing or eliminating them. The performance measure used to evaluate the measure of success the firm has achieved with regard to nonvalue-added costs is the manufacturing cycle efficiency (MCE).

▸ **APPENDIX 10-A**

L.O. 12
Journal entries

Journal Entries to Record Standard Costs for Direct Materials and Direct Labor and Recording Price Variances for Direct Materials When Quantities Purchased Differ from Quantities Used

Direct Materials

Management accountants use two different methods to record direct materials price variances. Some record the price variance when the materials are issued, and others record the price variance at the time of purchase.

Variances Recorded at the Time of Use   When variances are recorded at the time that direct materials are issued for use, no variances are entered at the date of purchase and the Direct Materials Inventory account indicates *actual cost*. Thus, if the Foremost Furniture Company purchased 10,000 board feet of pine lumber at 80 cents per board foot, the entry to record the purchase would be:

(1a)

Direct Materials Inventory	8,000	
Accounts Payable		8,000
(10,000 board feet at 80 cents)		

As long as this material remains in the stockroom, the price variance remains hidden in this account. Furthermore, if only part of the materials are used, only the portion of the price variance on the quantity used finds its way into the reporting system. At the Foremost Furniture Company, where the standard cost is $1 per board foot and 4,000 board feet of pine lumber were issued to the factory for manufacture into 110 bookcases, the standard quantity per bookcase is 30 board feet. The entry to record the price and quantity variances is:

(2a)

Work in Process (110 × 30 bd. ft. × $1)	3,300	
Materials Quantity Variance (4,000 bd. ft.		
− 3,300 bd. ft. = 700 bd. ft. × $1).	700	
Materials Price Variance ($1 − $.80		
= $.20 × 4,000 bd. ft.)		800
Direct Materials Inventory (4,000 bd. ft. ×		
$.80 actual price)		3,200

Note the following:

1. The debit to Work in Process is always at the standard quantity allowed (110 × 30 = 3,300 board feet) multiplied by the standard price. *The Work in Process account is always stated at standard (budgeted) cost.*
2. The materials quantity variance is the difference between the actual quantity (4,000 board feet) and the standard quantity allowed (3,300 board feet) multiplied by the standard price ($1). Because the quantity variance is *unfavorable,* the variance appears as a *debit.*
3. The materials price variance is the quantity *used* (4,000 board feet) multiplied by the difference between the standard price and the actual price ($1 − $.80 = $.20). *Favorable variances appear as credits.*
4. The credit to the Direct Materials Inventory account is made at the actual quantity issued at the *actual* price paid.

The main disadvantage of using this approach is that only $800 of the variance is reported and, if a performance report is prepared at this time, only this portion is shown. The additional $1,200 (10,000 board feet × $.20 = $2,000 − $800) remains in the Direct Materials Inventory account until subsequent issuances of the material to the factory. Thus, the $2,000 price variance is reflected on performance reports in a piecemeal fashion and often long after its occurrence.

Variance Recorded at the Time of Purchase   Price variances may also be recorded at the time of purchase. When this approach is used, the Direct Materials Inventory account is carried at *standard cost,* and all issuances are at that price. This is compatible with the use of standard costs because the work in process inventory, the finished goods inventory, and cost of goods sold are all carried at standard cost regardless of which method is used to reflect the price variance. Thus, when the price variance is recorded at the time of purchase, all inventory accounts are carried at standard cost.

An additional advantage of this method is that the entire price variance is reported currently regardless of when the direct materials are used. This is highly desirable for controlling large variances and for reporting the variances quickly to the managers who can take appropriate remedial action.

The journal entries to record the purchase and issuance of direct materials are:

(1b)

Direct Materials Inventory (10,000 bd. ft. × $1)	10,000	
Materials Price Variance (10,000 bd. ft. × $.20).		2,000
Accounts Payable (10,000 bd. ft. × $.80).		8,000

(2b)

Work in Process (110 × 30 bd. ft. × $1)	3,300	
Materials Quantity Variance [same as in entry *(2a)*]	700	
Direct Materials Inventory (4,000 bd. ft.		
× $1 standard cost)		4,000

A comparison of entries *(1b)* and *(2b)* with entries *(1a)* and *(2a)* indicates that:

1. The accounts payable, the materials quantity variance, and the work in process are the same for both methods.

▶ **ILLUSTRATION 10-6**   Partial General Ledger

	(a) (Price variance recorded when materials are *used*)			*(b)* (Price variance recorded when materials are *purchased*)	

Direct Materials Inventory

(1)	8,000	(2)	3,200
Balance	*4,800*		

Materials Price Variance

		(2)	800

Direct Materials Inventory

(1)	10,000	(2)	4,000
Balance	*6,000*		

Materials Price Variance

(1)	2,000

2. The Material Price Variance and the Direct Materials Inventory accounts are different. The price variance under *(a)* is based on materials *used,* while under *(b)* it is based on materials *purchased.* Direct materials inventory is carried at *actual* cost under *(a)* and at *standard* cost under *(b).* These differences appear in the corresponding ledger accounts shown in Illustration 10-6.

Direct Labor

Recall that the Foremost Furniture Company incurred $1,053 (130 hours × $8.10) of direct labor costs, and the budgeted cost for 110 bookcases was $880 (110 × 1 hour × $8). The entry to record the direct labor costs, based on the variance analysis shown in Illustration 10-4, is:

(3)

Work in Process (110 × $8)	880	
Labor Rate Variance (130 hours × $.10).	13	
Labor Efficiency Variance (20 hours × $8).	160	
Wages Payable (130 hours × $8.10)		1,053

From entry 3 it can be seen that:

1. The debit to Work in Process is at standard cost.
2. Both the rate variance and the efficiency variance are unfavorable and hence are debits.
3. Wages payable are always the actual hours worked at the actual rate per hour.

▶ **APPENDIX 10-B**   **Joint Price and Quantity Variance**

When responsibility is assigned for unfavorable variances, the analysis of a variance into its price and quantity components may sometimes cause dissension among managers.

Let us assume, for example, that the Foremost Furniture Company manufactured a batch of 200 unfinished pine bookcases in February 19x1. The purchasing agent is no longer interested in buying inferior lumber. In fact, he

▶ **ILLUSTRATION 10-7**   Graphical Analysis of Direct Materials Variances

is now extra careful to insist on premium-grade clear pine and has to pay $1.05 per board foot. However, the line supervisor experienced some employee turnover, and, as a result, a less experienced employee wasted lumber. The purchasing agent originally bought 6,000 board feet of clear pine for this batch but had to purchase an extra 800 board feet because there was not enough lumber to finish the 200 bookcases. Thus, the actual direct materials cost amounted to $7,140 (6,800 board feet × $1.05), while the total standard cost is $6,000 (200 units × 30 board feet × $1). The resulting total variance amounted to $1,140 ($7,140 − $6,000) unfavorable, and the usual analysis would produce the following:

Price variance:
  6,800 bd. ft. × ($1.05 − $1.00) . . . . $ 340 unfavorable

Quantity variance:
  $1 × (6,800 bd. ft. − 6,000 bd. ft.) . . . . <u>800</u> unfavorable
    Total variance . . . . <u>$1,140</u> unfavorable

Based on this analysis, the purchasing agent would be held responsible for $340 and the line supervisor would be held responsible for $800. The purchasing agent objects to this analysis, however, and as evidence of his position offers the analysis shown in Illustration 10-7. The agent maintains that the $40 shown in the joint price-quantity variance should also be charged to the line supervisor because he hired the inexperienced person who caused the extra lumber to be used. Thus, the purchasing agent believes only $300 (6,000 bd. ft. × $.05) should be charged to him and $840 should be charged to the line supervisor. Due to such potential problems, some firms prefer to analyze variances as shown in Illustration 10-7. The joint price-quantity portion of the price variance is then assigned only after the general manager reaches a conclusion about who is responsible for it.

▶ **GLOSSARY OF KEY TERMS**

Bill of materials   A detailed listing of every item and quantity of direct material needed to manufacture one unit of finished product. (p. 476)

Budgeted cost   The estimated production multiplied by the standard cost per unit. (p. 476)

Diagrammatic approach   A method of analyzing variances in which the actual cost is shown at the extreme left, the total standard cost is shown at the extreme right, and the actual quantity of inputs at the standard price per input is shown in the center. The price and quantity variances are found by subtracting each end figure from the center figure. (p. 483)

Direct labor efficiency variance   The standard rate of pay per direct labor-hour multiplied by the difference between the input number of direct labor-hours and the corresponding output (standard quantity allowed). (p. 484)

Direct labor rate variance   The actual number of direct labor-hours multiplied by the difference between the actual rate of pay per hour and the standard rate of pay per hour. (p. 484)

Effectiveness   A measure of whether an objective is achieved. (p. 475)

Efficiency   A measure of the means by which an objective is achieved—that is, whether it is achieved with the least amount of effort and the least possible cost. (p. 475)

Favorable variance   A case in which output exceeds input or the price paid for a good or service is less than expected. (p. 481)

Ideal standard   A measurement for evaluating performance that is theoretically possible but impractical to attain because it does not allow for machine breakdowns, rest periods, and the like, and requires employees to work at a constant rate of peak performance without interruptions. (p. 476)

Input   A quantity of goods or services entered into production that is expected to yield a certain quantity of manufactured finished goods. (p. 481)

Management by exception   An approach in which management chooses to investigate and take action on only those variances that depart significantly from prescribed standards. (p. 474)

Output   All completed units (or equivalent completed units) of product. (p. 481)

Performance report   A detailed comparison of budgeted, or total standard, costs with actual costs. Variances between the two are segregated into price and quantity components, and when a variance is significant, its source is explained. (p. 485)

Practical (attainable) standard   A measurement for evaluating performance that is set high enough to motivate employees and low enough to allow for normal machine breakdowns, rest periods, and the like. (p. 477)

Price variance   The actual quantity of a good or service used multiplied by the difference between the actual and standard prices. (p. 482)

Quantity variance   The difference between the input quantity of direct materials and the corresponding output quantity (standard quantity allowed) multiplied by the standard price per unit of input. (p. 482)

Relative value unit A weighted-average measurement used by hospitals. It is based on the time used to perform a task, the degree of skill needed, and the resources used. (p. 489)

Standard cost A carefully predetermined cost, usually per unit, used to evaluate performance. (p. 475)

Standard cost of direct labor The standard quantity of direct labor multiplied by the standard direct labor rate. (p. 479)

Standard cost of direct materials The standard quantity of direct materials multiplied by the standard price per unit of direct materials. (p. 478)

Standard direct labor rate The normal rate of pay per hour paid to employees for a particular kind of work. (p. 479)

Standard price of direct materials The price of a direct material quoted by the purchasing department and adjusted for such items as freight-in, insurance during transit, cash discounts allowed, and import duties. (p. 478)

Standard quantity allowed The standard quantity of one unit multiplied by the actual number of units produced. (p. 480)

Standard quantity of direct labor The estimated required direct labor-hours provided by engineers and factory supervisors adjusted for reasonable personal needs, coffee breaks, machine breakdowns, and the like. (p. 479)

Standard quantity of direct materials The required direct material listed in the bill of materials adjusted for normal spoilage, waste, shrinkage, and the like. (p. 478)

Standards committee A committee directly responsible for the setting of standards, composed of the company's controller, industrial engineer, purchasing manager, management accountants, factory superintendent, and the line supervisors. (p. 476)

Total standard cost The standard quantity allowed multiplied by the standard price of direct material or direct labor. (p. 480)

Total variance The difference between the actual cost and the total standard cost. (p. 482)

Unfavorable variance A case in which output is less than input or the price paid for a good or service is greater than expected. (p. 481)

Variance analysis Segregating the difference between an actual cost and its budgeted counterpart into price (rate) and quantity (efficiency) components. (p. 481)

► **REVIEW PROBLEM**   **Computation of Price and Quantity Variances**

The Mercer Company manufactures redwood window boxes. Each box requires the following direct materials and direct labor:

	Standard Quantity	Price (Rate)	Standard Cost
1″ clear redwood	5 bd. ft.	$ 1.10 per bd. ft.	$5.50
Direct labor	.5 hour	10.00 per hour	5.00

During January 19x2, the following transactions occurred:

1. Purchases of lumber amounted to $27,540. The price paid was $1.08 per board foot. There was no direct materials inventory at the beginning or end of the month.
2. The direct labor cost was $28,050. The hourly rate of pay was $10.20.
3. There was no work in process inventory on January 31, 19x2, and 5,000 window boxes were manufactured.

Required   Using *both* the formula and diagrammatic approaches, compute the appropriate price (rate) and quantity (efficiency) variances, and indicate if they are favorable or unfavorable.

▶ **SOLUTION TO REVIEW PROBLEM**

Formula approach—Direct materials:

MPV = AQ(AP − SP)
Materials price variance—25,500($1.08 − $1.10) . . . . $510 F
MQV = SP(AQ − SQ)
Materials quantity variance—$1.10(25,500* − 25,000†) . . . . 550 U

* $27,540 ÷ $1.08 = 25,500 bd. ft.
† 5,000 units × 5 bd. ft. = 25,000 bd. ft.

Diagrammatic approach—Direct materials:

Actual Quantity of Inputs, at Actual Price (AQ × AP) (25,500 × $1.08) $27,540		Actual Quantity of Inputs, at Standard Price (AQ × SP) (25,500 × $1.10) $28,050		Standard Quantity Allowed for Output, at Standard Price (SQ × SP) (25,000 × $1.10) $27,500
	Price Variance, $510 F		Quantity Variance, $ 550 U	
		Total Variance, $40 U		

Formula approach—Direct labor:

LRV = AH(AR − SR)
Labor rate variance—2,750($10.20 − $10.00) . . . . $ 550 U
LEV = SR(AH − SH)
Labor efficiency variance—$10.00(2,750‡ − 2,500§) . . . . 2,500 U

‡ $28,050 ÷ $10.20 = 2,750 DLH.
§ 5,000 units × .5 hr. = 2,500 DLH.

Diagrammatic approach—Direct labor:

Actual Hours of Input, at the Actual Rate (AH × AR) (2,750 × $10.20) $28,050		Actual Hours of Input, at the Standard Rate (AH × SR) (2,750 × $10.00) $27,500		Standard Hours Allowed for Output, at the Standard Rate (SH × SR) (2,500 × $10.00) $25,000
	Rate Variance, $550 U		Efficiency Variance, $2,500 U	
		Total Variance, $3,050 U		

▶ **LIBRARY ASSIGNMENT**

Read the following:

Calvasina, Richard V., and Eugene J. Calvasina. "Standard Costing Games that Managers Play." *Management Accounting,* March 1984, pp. 49–51, 77.

Foster, Jeremy, and Alan Scott. "Standard Costing in a Manufacturing Environment." *Management Accounting* (England), April 1984, pp. 36–38.

Laudeman, Max, and F. W. Schaeberle. ''Cost Accounting Practices of Firms Using Standard Costs.'' *Cost and Management* (Canada), July-August 1983, pp. 21–25.

Messmer, Victor C. ''Standard Cost Accounting: Methods that Can Be Applied to DRG Classifications.'' *Healthcare Financial Management,* January 1984, pp. 44–45, 48.

Mister, William G. ''Note on the Interpretation of Standard Cost Variances.'' *Journal of Accounting Education,* Fall 1983, pp. 51–56.

▸ **SELF-TEST**

True or False

1. A manager choosing to investigate only the significant variances between standard and actual costs is practicing management by exception.

2. A supervisor of a production line had to have the line work overtime to meet a rush order and was successful in getting the order out on time. In this instance, the supervisor was efficient.

3. Standard costs are really budgeted costs that are carefully predetermined.

4. The reason that a standards committee is used is that the preparation of standards requires input from individuals with different abilities.

5. Standard costs are used for a variety of reasons, but the most important one is that it helps managers better understand the firm's record-keeping.

6. A standard bill of materials is a listing of the most important components of the product being manufactured.

7. The difference between a standard cost and an actual cost for direct materials can be analyzed into price and quantity components.

8. The standard quantity allowed is the standard units multiplied by the standard cost per unit.

9. The difference between a standard cost and an actual cost for direct labor can be analyzed into rate and efficiency components.

10. A performance report is used to summarize favorable and unfavorable variances and the reasons for their occurrence.

11. It is never necessary to investigate unfavorable variances as long as they are less than the cutoff point established for variance investigation.

12. Firms that use the new performance measures in the new manufacturing environment have no need for standard costs.

Multiple Choice

1. Home Company manufactures tables with vinyl tops. The standard material cost for the vinyl used per type R table is $7.80 based on six square feet of vinyl at a cost of $1.30 per square foot. A production run of 1,000 tables in January 19x0 resulted in usage of 6,400 square feet of vinyl at a cost of $1.20 per square foot, a total cost of $7,680. The quantity variance resulting from the above production run was
   a. $120 favorable.
   b. $480 unfavorable.
   c. $520 unfavorable.
   d. $640 favorable.

Items 2 and 3 are based on the following information.
   Data on Goodman Company's direct labor costs are given below:

Standard direct labor-hours	30,000
Actual direct labor-hours	29,000
Direct labor usage (efficiency) variance—favorable	$4,000
Direct labor rate variance—favorable	$5,800
Total payroll	$110,200

2. What was Goodman's actual direct labor rate?
   a. $3.60.
   b. $3.80.
   c. $4.00.
   d. $5.80.

3. What was Goodman's standard direct labor rate?
   a. $3.54.
   b. $3.80.
   c. $4.00.
   d. $5.80.

4. Perkins Company, which has a standard cost system, had 500 units of direct material X in its inventory at June 1, 19x2, purchased in May for $1.20 per unit and carried at a standard cost of $1. The following information pertains to direct material X for the month of June 19x2:

Actual number of units purchased	1,400
Actual number of units used	1,500
Standard number of units allowed for actual production	1,300
Standard cost per unit	$1.00
Actual cost per unit	$1.10

   The unfavorable materials purchase price variance for direct material X for June was
   a. $0.
   b. $130.
   c. $140.
   d. $150.

5. Information on Kennedy Company's direct material costs is as follows:

Standard unit price	$3.60
Actual quantity purchased	1,600
Standard quantity allowed for actual production	1,450
Materials purchase price variance—favorable	$240

   What was the actual purchase price per unit, rounded to the nearest penny?
   a. $3.06.
   b. $3.11.
   c. $3.45.
   d. $3.75.

   (AICPA Adapted)

▶ **QUESTIONS**

1. What is management by exception?
2. What is the difference between effectiveness and efficiency? Use an example to demonstrate each.
3. What standards are used by businesses?
4. What is a standard for efficiency? Give an example to illustrate its use.
5. What is a standards committee, and why do firms generally use one?
6. What are some of the uses of standard costs? Explain each one.
7. Explain the difference between ideal standards and practical standards. Which one would you use? Why?
8. What is the difference between a budgeted cost and a standard cost?
9. What is the standard quantity allowed? How is it used?
10. Differentiate input and output. Use an example to illustrate their use.
11. What is a quantity (efficiency) variance? How is it computed? Is it important? Why?
12. What is a price (rate) variance? How is it computed? Is it important? Why?

13. What is a performance report? What purpose docs it serve?
14. Are all variances investigated? If not, how do managers select which variances to investigate?
15. Do service industries use standard costs? If so, explain how they are used.
16. What is a relative value unit? How is it used by hospitals?
17. Does the new manufacturing environment use standard costs? If so, do firms in this environment limit their performance measures to standard costs? Explain.

For Appendix 10-A

18. There are two different approaches for recording material price variances. What are they? Explain the essential differences between them.

For Appendix 10-B

19. What is the joint price and quantity variance? Is it usually shown alone? If not, where is it usually shown? Why? Describe the circumstances when it might be important to compute the joint price-quantity variance.

▶ **EXERCISES** **E10–1** **Computations of Variances**

The Martin Company manufactures tables with glass tops. Each table requires the following direct materials for glass and direct labor:

	Standard Quantity	Price (Rate)	Standard Cost
¼″ plate glass.	10 sq. ft.	$ 4 per sq. ft.	$40
Direct labor	2 hours	14 per hour	28

During January 19x2, the following transactions occurred:

1. Purchases of plate glass amounted to $6,510. The amount of glass purchased was 1,550 square feet. There was no direct materials inventory at the beginning or end of the month.
2. The direct labor cost was $4,560. The hourly rate of pay was $14.25.
3. There was no work in process inventory on January 31, 19x2, and 150 tables were manufactured.

Required Using *both* the formula and diagrammatic approaches, compute the appropriate price (rate) and quantity (efficiency) variances, and indicate if they are favorable or unfavorable.

E10–2 **Computation of Data from Variances**

The Crest Company manufactures redwood umbrella stands. Each stand requires the following direct materials and direct labor:

	Standard Quantity	Price (Rate)	Standard Cost
2″ clear redwood.	12 bd. ft.	$ 2.10 per bd. ft.	$25.20
Direct labor	1.5 hours	14.00 per hour	21.00

During March 19x2, the following was determined:

1. There was no work in process or direct materials inventory at the beginning or end of March, and 6,000 stands were manufactured.

2. The total direct materials variance was $6,180 unfavorable, and the materials quantity variance was $2,520 unfavorable.
3. The direct labor cost for the month amounted to $127,875, and the direct labor rate variance was $2,325 favorable.
4. Bolts and screws are considered indirect materials.

Required   *a.* How many board feet of lumber were purchased?
 b. What was the price paid per board foot?
 c. What was the actual cost of the direct materials purchased?
 d. How many hours were actually worked?
 e. What was the hourly rate of pay?

E10–3 Standard Process Costs with Equivalent Production

The following data apply to items 1 through 6.

Dash Company adopted a standard cost system several years ago. The standard costs for the prime costs of its single product are as follows:

Material (8 kilograms at $5 per kilogram) $40.00
Labor (6 hours at $8.20 per hour) 49.20

The following operating data were taken from the records for November:

In-process beginning inventory . . . . . None
In-process ending inventory . . . . . . 800 units, 75% complete as to labor; material is issued at the beginning of processing
Units completed . . . . 5,600 units
Budgeted output . . . . 6,000 units
Purchases of materials . . . . 50,000 kilograms
Total actual labor costs $300,760
Actual hours of labor . . . . 36,500 hours
Material usage variance . . . . $1,500 unfavorable
Total material variance . . . . $750 unfavorable

1. The labor rate variance for November is
   a. $1,460 U.
   b. $1,460 F.
   c. $4,120 U.
   d. $4,120 F.
   e. Some amount other than those shown above.
2. The labor efficiency variance for November is
   a. $4,100 U.
   b. $5,740 F.
   c. $15,580 F.
   d. $23,780 U.
   e. Some amount other than those shown above.
3. The actual kilograms of material used in the production process during November are
   a. 45,100 kg.
   b. 49,900 kg.
   c. 50,000 kg.
   d. 51,500 kg.
   e. Some amount other than those shown above.
4. The actual price paid per kilogram of material during November is
   a. $4.495.
   b. $4.985.
   c. $5.015.
   d. $5.135.
   e. Some amount other than those shown above.

5. The total amounts of material and labor cost transferred to the finished goods account for November is
   a. $499,520.
   b. $535,200.
   c. $550,010.
   d. $561,040.
   e. Some amount other than those shown above.
6. The total amount of material and labor cost in the ending balance of work in process inventory at the end of November is
   a. $0.
   b. $9,840.
   c. $61,520.
   d. $71,360.
   e. Some amount other than those shown above.

(CMA Adapted)

E10–4   **Computation of Price and Quantity Variances**

Stackum Company manufactures cedar storage boxes. Each box requires the following direct materials and direct labor:

	Standard Quantity	Price (Rate)	Standard Cost
1″ clear cedar	10 bd. ft.	$ 1.20 per bd. ft.	$12
Direct labor	1 hour	12.00 per hour	12

During January 19x2, the following transactions occurred:

1. Purchases of lumber amounted to $100,500. The price paid was $1.25 per board foot. There was no direct materials inventory at the beginning or end of the month.
2. The direct labor cost was $99,225. The hourly rate of pay was $12.25.
3. There was no work in process inventory on January 31, 19x2, and 8,000 storage boxes were manufactured.

Required   Using *both* the formula and diagrammatic approaches, compute the appropriate price (rate) and quantity (efficiency) variances, and indicate if they are favorable or unfavorable.

E10–5   **Computation of Data from Variances**

The Broome Company manufactures redwood flowerpots. Each flowerpot requires the following direct materials and direct labor:

	Standard Quantity	Price (Rate)	Standard Cost
1″ clear redwood	3 bd. ft.	$ 1.20 per bd. ft.	$3.60
Direct labor	.5 hour	12.00 per hour	6.00

During March 19x2, the following was determined:

1. There was no work in process or direct materials inventory at the beginning or end of March, and 6,000 flowerpots were manufactured.

2. The total direct materials variance was $555 favorable, and the materials quantity variance was $360 unfavorable.
3. The direct labor cost for the month amounted to $37,975, and the direct labor rate variance was $775 unfavorable.

Required

   a. How many board feet of lumber were purchased?
   b. What was the price paid per board foot?
   c. What was the actual cost of the direct materials purchased?
   d. How many hours were actually worked?
   e. What was the hourly rate of pay?

E10–6   **Computation of Standard Cost per Unit from Variances and Actual Data**

The Prince Company manufactures redwood outdoor furniture sets. The direct material consists of one item, 2″ × 4″ redwood. Screws and bolts may be ignored.

The following information is available for the month of April 19x3:

1. Two thousand sets of furniture were produced. There are no beginning or ending inventories.
2. The actual cost of lumber purchased amounted to $285,200 for 184,000 board feet of redwood. The materials price variance amounted to $9,200 unfavorable, and the materials quantity variance amounted to $6,000 unfavorable.
3. The direct labor payroll for the month amounted to $121,520, and the labor rate variance was $3,920 unfavorable. The labor efficiency variance was $2,400 favorable. The actual hours worked were 9,800.

Required   Compute the following:

   a. The standard cost of one board foot of lumber.
   b. The standard quantity of board feet per one set of furniture.
   c. The actual cost per board foot.
   d. The standard rate per hour of direct labor.
   e. The standard quantity of hours needed per one set of furniture.
   f. The actual labor rate per hour.

E10–7   **Computation of Price and Quantity Variances for an X Ray Lab**

The X-Tra Careful X ray Lab is an X-ray laboratory. Each chest X ray requires the following direct materials and direct labor:

	Standard Quantity	Price (Rate)	Standard Cost
X-ray film	2 exposures	$ 2 per film	$4
Direct labor.	.25 hour	20 per hour	5

During January 19x2, the following transactions occurred:

1. Purchases of film amounted to $4,290. The price paid was $1.95 per X-ray film. There was no direct materials inventory at the beginning or end of the month.
2. The direct labor cost was $5,460. The hourly rate of pay was $21 per hour.
3. There was no work in process inventory on January 31, 19x2, and 1,000 chest X rays were taken during the month. (Each X ray requires two exposures.)

Required   Using *both* the formula and diagrammatic approaches, compute the appropriate price (rate) and quantity (efficiency) variances, and indicate if they are favorable or unfavorable.

E10–8   Computation of Variances and Information from Variances

1. The following information pertains to Bates Company's direct labor for March 19x2:

Standard direct labor-hours	21,000
Actual direct labor-hours	20,000
Favorable direct labor rate variance	$8,400
Standard direct labor rate per hour	$6.30

What was Bates's total actual direct labor cost for March 19x2?
   a. $117,600.
   b. $118,000.
   c. $134,000.
   d. $134,400.

2. Throop Company had budgeted 50,000 units of output using 50,000 units of direct materials at a total material cost of $100,000. Actual output was 50,000 units of product requiring 45,000 units of direct materials at a cost of $2.10 per unit. The direct material price variance and usage variance were

	Price	Quantity (Usage)
a.	$ 4,500 unfavorable	$10,000 favorable
b.	$ 5,000 favorable	$10,500 unfavorable
c.	$ 5,000 unfavorable	$10,500 favorable
d.	$10,000 favorable	$ 4,500 unfavorable

3. Lab Corporation uses a standard cost system. Direct labor information for product CER for the month of October is as follows:

Standard rate	$6 per hour
Actual rate paid	$6.10 per hour
Standard hours allowed for actual production	1,500 hours
Labor efficiency variance	$600 unfavorable

What are the actual hours worked?
   a. 1,400.
   b. 1,402.
   c. 1,598.
   d. 1,600.

(AICPA Adapted)

E10–9   Computation of Price and Quantity Variances

The Marder Company manufactures shoeshine boxes. Each box requires the following direct materials and direct labor:

	Standard Quantity	Price (Rate)	Standard Cost
1″ clear oak	3 bd. ft.	$ 2 per bd. ft.	$6
Direct labor	.4 hour	12 per hour	4

During January 19x2, the following transactions occurred:

1. Purchases of lumber amounted to $38,220. The price paid was $2.10 per board foot. There was no direct materials inventory at the beginning or end of the month.

2. The direct labor cost was $30,625. The hourly rate of pay was $12.25.
3. There was no work in process inventory on January 31, 19x2, and 6,000 shoeshine boxes were manufactured.

Required Using *both* the formula and diagrammatic approaches, compute the appropriate price (rate) and quantity (efficiency) variances, and indicate if they are favorable or unfavorable.

E10–10 **Computation of Variances with Possible Explanations for Their Occurrence**

The Saxonel Company manufactures draperies with the following standard costs:

Direct materials (20 yards at $2.40 per yard) . . . $48
Direct labor (4 hours at $12 per hour) 48

The following transactions occurred during the month of July 19x2:

1. Production of finished goods amounted to 5,000 pairs.
2. There were no beginning or ending inventories of direct materials or work in process.
3. Purchases of direct materials were 101,000 yards at $2.50 per yard.
4. The direct labor cost was for 20,500 hours at $13 per hour.

Required a. Compute the materials price and quantity variances, and indicate if they are favorable or unfavorable.
 b. Compute the labor rate and efficiency variances, and indicate if they are favorable or unfavorable.
 c. Write a brief explanation of why the labor efficiency variance is unfavorable.

E10–11 **Computation of Data from Variances**

The Brisk Company manufactures redwood picnic tables. Each table requires the following direct materials and direct labor:

	Standard Quantity	Price (Rate)	Standard Cost
2″ clear redwood	14 bd. ft.	$ 1.10 per bd. ft.	$15.40
Direct labor	1 hour	10.00 per hour	10.00

During March 19x2, the following was determined:

1. There was no work in process or direct materials inventory at the beginning or end of March, and 8,000 tables were manufactured.
2. The total direct materials variance was $3,500 favorable, and the materials quantity variance was $2,200 unfavorable.
3. The direct labor cost for the month amounted to $81,340, and the direct labor rate variance was $1,660 favorable.
4. Bolts and screws are considered indirect materials.

Required a. How many board feet of lumber were purchased?
 b. What was the price paid per board foot?
 c. What was the actual cost of the direct materials purchased?
 d. How many hours were actually worked?
 e. What was the hourly rate of pay?

E10–12   **Computation of Variances with Possible Explanations for Their Occurrence**

The Chambers Company manufactures a product with the following standard costs:

> Direct materials (20 yards at $2 per yard) . . . $40
> Direct labor (2 hours at $16 per hour)   32

The following transactions occurred during the month of July 19x2:

1. Production of finished goods amounted to 4,000 units.
2. There were no beginning or ending inventories of direct materials or work in process.
3. Purchases of direct materials were 86,000 yards at $1.70 per yard.
4. The direct labor cost was for 9,000 hours at $15 per hour.

Required   *a.* Compute the materials price and quantity variances, and indicate if they are favorable or unfavorable.

b. Compute the labor rate and efficiency variances, and indicate if they are favorable or unfavorable.

c. Write a brief explanation of why the labor efficiency variance is unfavorable.

E10–13   **Setting Standards for Direct Materials**

Danson Company is a chemical manufacturer that supplies industrial users. The company plans to introduce a new chemical solution and needs to develop a standard product cost for it.

The new chemical solution is made by combining a chemical compound (nyclyn) and a solution (salex), boiling the mixture, adding a second compound (protet), and bottling the resulting solution in 10-liter containers. The initial mix, which is 10 liters in volume, consists of 12 kilograms of nyclyn and 9.6 liters of salex. A 20 percent reduction in volume occurs during the boiling process. The solution is then cooled slightly before five kilograms of protet are added; the addition of protet does not affect the total liquid volume.

The purchase prices of the direct materials used in the manufacture of this new chemical solution are as follows:

> Nyclyn . . . . . $1.30 per kilogram
> Salex . . . . . .   1.80 per liter
> Protet . . . . .   2.40 per kilogram

Required   Determine the standard quantity for each of the direct materials needed to produce a 10-liter container of Danson Company's new chemical solution and the standard materials cost of a 10-liter container of the new product.

(CMA Adapted)

E10–14   **Computations of Variances**

The following information pertains to the month of June 19x1:

1. Pyle Company manufactures a product with the following standard costs:

> Direct materials (30 yards at $1.35 per yard) . . . $40.50
> Direct labor (6 hours at $11 per hour) 66.00

2. Direct materials purchased were $39,200 (28,000 yards at $1.40 per yard).
3. There was no beginning direct materials inventory.
4. The ending direct materials inventory amounted to 3,000 yards.
5. Direct labor was $56,000 (5,000 hours at $11.20 per hour).

6. During the month of June, 800 units were manufactured. There was no work in process at the beginning or end of the month.

Required   Compute the following:

a. Materials price variance (based on purchases).
b. Materials quantity variance.
c. Labor rate variance.
d. Labor efficiency variance.

E10–15   **Computation of Variances**

The Carberg Corporation manufactures and sells a single product. The company uses a standard cost system. The standard cost per unit of product is shown below:

Material (one pound plastic at $2) . . . $2.00
Direct labor (1.6 hours at $4) 6.40

The charges to the manufacturing department for November, when 5,000 units were produced, are given below:

Material (5,300 pounds at $2). $10,600
Direct labor (8,200 hours at $4.10) . . .   33,620

The purchasing department normally buys about the same quantity as is used in production during a month. In November, 5,200 pounds were purchased at a price of $2.10 per pound.

Required   *a.* Calculate the following variances from standard costs for the data given:
(1) Materials purchase price.
(2) Materials quantity.
(3) Direct labor wage rate.
(4) Direct labor efficiency.
b. The company has divided its responsibilities such that the purchasing department is responsible for the price at which materials and supplies are purchased. The manufacturing department is responsible for the quantities of materials used. Does this division of responsibilities solve the conflict between price and quantity variances? Explain your answer.

(CMA Adapted)

E10–16   **Computation of Variances with Two Direct Materials**

Eastern Company manufactures special electrical equipment and parts. Eastern employs a standard cost accounting system with separate standards established for each product.

A special transformer is manufactured in the transformer department. Production volume is measured by direct labor-hours in this department.

Standard costs for the special transformer are determined annually in September for the coming year. The standard cost of a transformer for 19x7 was computed as shown below:

Direct materials:
   Iron . . . .   5 sheets at $2 $10
   Copper . . . .   3 spools at $3   9
   Direct labor . . . . . .   4 hours at $7   28

During October 19x7, 800 transformers were produced. This was below expectations because a work stoppage occurred during contract negotiations with the labor force. Once the contract was settled, the department scheduled overtime in an attempt to catch up to expected production levels.

The following costs were incurred in October 19x7:

Direct Material	Direct Materials Purchased	Materials Used
Iron	5,000 sheets at $2 per sheet	3,900 sheets
Copper.	2,200 spools at $3.10 per spool	2,600 spools

Direct labor:
Regular time	2,000 hours at $7.00	
	1,400 hours at $7.20	
Overtime.	600 of the 1,400 hours were subject to overtime premium. The total overtime premium of $2,160 is included in variable overhead in accordance with company accounting practices.	

Answer the following items:

1. The total material quantity variation is
   a. $200 favorable.
   b. $400 favorable.
   c. $600 favorable.
   d. $400 unfavorable.
   e. Some amount other than those shown above.
2. The labor rate (price) variation is
   a. $280 unfavorable.
   b. $340 unfavorable.
   c. $1,680 unfavorable.
   d. $2,440 unfavorable.
   e. None of the above responses is correct.

(CMA Adapted)

E10–17   (Appendix 10-A) Journal Entries for Standard Costs

Tolbert Manufacturing Company uses a standard cost system in accounting for the cost of production of its only product, product A. The standards for the production of one unit of product A are as follows:

Direct materials	10 feet of item 1 at $.75 per foot and 3 feet of item 2 at $1 per foot
Direct labor.	4 hours at $3.50 per hour

There was no inventory on hand at July 1, 19x2. Following is a summary of costs and related data for the production of product A during the year ended June 30, 19x3.

1. 100,000 feet of item 1 were purchased at $.78 per foot.
2. 30,000 feet of item 2 were purchased at $.90 per foot.
3. 8,000 units of product A were produced, which required 78,000 feet of item 1; 26,000 feet of item 2; and 31,000 hours of direct labor at $3.60 per hour.
4. 6,000 units of product A were sold.

At June 30, 19x3, there are 22,000 feet of item 1; 4,000 feet of item 2; and 2,000 completed units of product A on hand. All purchases and transfers are "charged in" at standard.

1. For the year ended June 30, 19x3, the total debits to the Direct Materials account for the purchase of item 1 would be
   a. $75,000.
   b. $78,000.

    c. $58,500.
    d. $60,000.

2. For the year ended June 30, 19x3, the total debits to the Work in Process account for direct labor would be
    a. $111,600.
    b. $108,500.
    c. $112,000.
    d. $115,100.

3. The balance in the Material Quantity Variance account for item 2 was
    a. $1,000 credit.
    b. $2,600 debit.
    c. $600 debit.
    d. $2,000 debit.

(AICPA Adapted)

E10–18   **(Appendix 10-A) Journal Entries for Standard Costs**

The Canal Company manufactures wooden umbrella stands. Each stand requires the following direct materials and direct labor (glue and nails may be ignored):

	Standard Quantity	Price (Rate)	Standard Cost
1″ clear oak	3 bd. ft.	$ 1.80 per bd. ft.	$ 5.40
Direct labor	1 hour	12.00 per hour	12.00

During January 19x5, the following transactions occurred:

1. Purchases of lumber amounted to $133,000. The price paid was $1.90 per board foot.
2. The direct labor cost was $137,500. The hourly wage rate was $11.
3. There was no work in process inventory at the beginning or end of the month.
4. The January 31, 19x5, inventory of direct materials consisted of 33,000 board feet of lumber.
5. Production amounted to 12,000 units.

Required   *a.* Prepare the journal entries to record the above transactions. Assume the firm records material price variances at the time of purchase.
  b. Redo the direct materials journal entries, assuming the firm keeps its direct materials inventory at actual cost.

E10–19   **(Appendix 10-A) Reconstruction of Journal Entries from Missing Data**

The Clinton Company's bookkeeper was working on the company's general ledger. Disliking working on the pages in a binder, he left them loose on his desk, which was near an open window. Because it was a warm day and he was thirsty, the bookkeeper went to the water fountain for a drink of water. While he was gone, the person sitting at a desk nearby turned on the room's oscillating fan. When the bookkeeper returned, he was surprised to find his desk clear of all papers. Wondering what had happened to the firm's general ledger, he looked out into the street and saw it scrambled on the pavement. He hastily retrieved the loose sheets; but to his chagrin, some sheets were missing.

Some of the available T accounts are reproduced as follows:

Direct Materials Inventory		Accounts Payable	
19x1	19x1		19x1
Jan. 31 69,000	Jan. 31 44,850		Jan. 31 75,000

Work in Process—Materials		Wages Payable	
19x1			19x1
Jan. 31 43,700			Jan. 31 66,300

Work in Process—Direct Labor		Labor Rate Variance	
19x1		19x1	
Jan. 31 62,500		Jan. 31 2,500	

Required
a. Prepare all of the journal entries, in journal entry form, that must have been prepared for direct materials and direct labor. The company uses a standard cost job order system, and material price variances are recorded at the time of purchase. There are no beginning inventories.
b. If the company uses only one direct material in pounds, and the standard cost per pound is $1.15, compute the following:
   (1) The number of pounds purchased.
   (2) The number of pounds put into production (input).
   (3) The standard quantity allowed in pounds (output).
   (4) The actual price paid per pound.

E10–20   **(Appendix 10-A) Journal Entries for Standard Costs**

The Hall Company manufactures wooden telephone stands. Each stand requires the following direct materials and direct labor (glue and nails may be ignored):

	Standard Quantity	Price (Rate)	Standard Cost
1″ clear pine	4 bd. ft.	$ 1.40 per bd. ft.	$ 5.60
Direct labor	1 hour	13.00 per hour	13.00

During January 19x5, the following transactions occurred:

1. Purchases of lumber amounted to $105,000. The price paid was $1.50 per board foot.
2. The direct labor cost was $139,125. The hourly wage rate was $13.25.
3. There was no work in process inventory at the beginning or end of the month.
4. The January 31, 19x5, inventory of direct materials consisted of 28,000 board feet of lumber.
5. Production amounted to 10,000 units.

Required
a. Prepare the journal entries to record the above transactions. Assume the firm records material price variances at the time of purchase.
b. Redo the direct materials journal entries, assuming the firm keeps its direct materials inventory at actual cost.

▶ **PROBLEMS**   **P10–21**   **Computation of Variances with Equivalent Production**

The Lafayette Company manufactures men's jeans of one quality. The standard costs of direct materials and direct labor per dozen are:

> Direct materials (40 yards at $2) $80
> Direct labor (5 hours at $10)   50

Thread, zippers, and labels may be ignored.

During the month of September 19x4, the company started two batches of 1,500 dozen jeans each. One batch, Lot 606, is complete. The other batch, Lot 607, is 100 percent complete as to materials and 80 percent complete as to direct labor. There was no work in process inventory at the beginning of the month.

On September 1, 19x4, the company's direct materials inventory consisted of 12,000 yards of fabric. Material price variances are recorded at the time of purchase.

The following transactions occurred during September:

1. Two batches of fabric were purchased as follows:

> 55,000 yards at $2.15
> 80,000 yards at 1.60

2. The quantities of fabric used were as follows:

Lot 606 . . . . .   12,000 yards from the beginning inventory, and 48,550 yards from the first batch purchased
Lot 607 . . . . .   6,450 yards from the first batch, and 52,950 yards from the second batch

3. Direct labor was incurred as follows:

> Lot 606 . . . . .   7,400 hours at $10.20 per hour
> Lot 607 . . . . .   6,150 hours at 9.90 per hour

Required   *a.* Compute each of the following variances separately for each lot and in total for both lots:
  (1) Materials quantity variance.
  (2) Labor rate variance.
  (3) Labor efficiency variance.
b. Compute the materials price variance separately for each purchase and in total for the month.
c. When preparing performance reports, would you recommend that one report be prepared for the entire month, or would you recommend that separate reports be prepared for each lot? Why?
d. Write a brief explanation of the possible reasons for the wide disparity in the price of fabric between the first and second purchases. Might any other side effects have occurred as a result of this disparity? Explain.

P10–22   **Computation of Variances and Preparation of Performance Report**

The Fulton Company manufactures men's dress shirts of one quality. The standard costs of direct materials and direct labor per dozen are:

> Direct materials (32 yards at $2.25) . . . $72
> Direct labor (5 hours at $11)   55

Thread, buttons, and labels may be ignored.

During the month of September 19x5, the company started and completed one batch of 3,000 dozen shirts.

There were no direct materials or work in process inventories at the beginning or end of the month.

The following transactions occurred during September:

1. Two batches of fabric were purchased as follows:

    18,000 yards at $2.75
    80,000 yards at 2.00

2. Direct labor was incurred as follows:

    15,400 hours at $10.25 per hour

Required   *a.* Compute each of the following variances:
  (1) Materials price variance.
  (2) Materials quantity variance.
  (3) Labor rate variance.
  (4) Labor efficiency variance.

  b. Prepare a performance report showing the materials price variance separately for each purchase. Where possible, indicate explanations for any variance that is, in your opinion, significant.

P10–23   Setting Direct Labor Standards

The Alton Company is going to expand its punch press department. It is about to purchase three new punch presses from Equipment Manufacturers, Inc. Equipment Manufacturers' engineers report that their mechanical studies indicate that for Alton's intended use, the output rate for one press should be 1,000 pieces per hour. Alton has very similar presses now in operation. At the present time, production from these presses averages 600 pieces per hour.

A study of the Alton experience shows the average is derived from the following individual outputs:

Worker	Daily Output
L. Jones.	750
J. Green.	750
R. Smith	600
H. Brown	500
R. Alters	550
G. Hoag.	450
Total	3,600
Average	600

Alton's management also plans to institute a standard cost accounting system in the very near future. The company engineers are supporting a standard based on 1,000 pieces per hour, the accounting department is arguing for 750 pieces per hour, and the department supervisor is arguing for 600 pieces per hour.

Required   *a.* What arguments would each proponent be likely to use to support his or her case?

  b. Which alternative best reconciles the needs of cost control and the motivation of improved performance? Explain why you made that choice.

(CMA Adapted)

P10–24   Computation of Variances with Equivalent Production

Vogue Fashions, Inc., manufactures ladies' blouses of one quality, produced in lots to fill each special order from its customers, which are department stores located in various cities. Vogue sews the particular store's labels on the blouses. The standard costs for a dozen blouses are:

Direct materials (24 yards at $1.10) . . . $26.40
Direct labor (3 hours at $4.90). 14.70

During June 19x0, Vogue worked on three orders, for which the month's job cost records disclose the following:

Lot No.	Units in Lot (dozens)	Material Used (yards)	Hours Worked
22.	1,000	24,100	2,980
23.	1,700	40,440	5,130
24.	1,200	28,825	2,890

The following information is also available:

1. Vogue purchased 95,000 yards of material during June at a cost of $106,400. The materials price variance is recorded when goods are purchased. All inventories are carried at standard cost.
2. Direct labor during June amounted to $55,000. According to payroll records, production employees were paid $5 per hour.
3. There was no work in process at June 1. During June, Lots 22 and 23 were completed. All material was issued for Lot 24, which was 80 percent completed as to direct labor.

Required   a. Prepare a schedule showing the computation of the standard cost of Lots 22, 23, and 24 for June 19x0.
   b. Prepare a schedule showing the computation of the materials price variance for June 19x0. Indicate whether the variance is favorable or unfavorable.
   c. Prepare a schedule showing, for each lot produced during June 19x0, computations of the:
   (1) Materials quantity variance in yards.
   (2) Labor efficiency variance in hours.
   (3) Labor rate variance in dollars.
   Indicate whether each variance is favorable or unfavorable.

(AICPA Adapted)

P10–25   **Computation of Variances with Equivalent Production**
The Lombard Company manufactures men's pants of one quality. The standard costs of direct materials and direct labor per dozen are:

Direct materials (33 yards at $6) . . . $198
Direct labor (5 hours at $12) 60

Thread, zippers, and labels may be ignored.

During the month of September 19x4, the company started two batches of 2,000 dozen pants each. One batch, Lot 901, is complete. The other batch, Lot 902, is 100 percent complete as to materials and 75 percent complete as to direct labor. There was no work in process inventory at the beginning of the month.

On September 1, 19x4, the company's direct materials inventory consisted of 30,000 yards of fabric. Material price variances are recorded at the time of purchase.

The following transactions occurred during September:

1. Two batches of fabric were purchased as follows:

40,000 yards at $6.20
80,000 yards at $5.90

2. The quantities of fabric used were as follows:

Lot 901 . . . . . 30,000 yards from the beginning inventory, and 36,200 yards from the first batch purchased

Lot 902 . . . . . 3,800 yards from the first batch, and 62,600 yards from the second batch

3. Direct labor was incurred as follows:

Lot 901 . . . . . 10,400 hours at $12.30 per hour
Lot 902 . . . . . 7,100 hours at $12.10 per hour

Required   *a.* Compute each of the following variances separately for each lot and in total for both lots:

(1) Materials quantity variance.
(2) Labor rate variance.
(3) Labor efficiency variance.

b. Compute the materials price variance separately for each purchase and in total for the month.

c. When preparing performance reports, would you recommend that one report be prepared for the entire month, or would you recommend that separate reports be prepared for each lot? Why?

P10–26   **Computation of Standard Cost per Unit from Variances and Actual Data, and Preparation of Performance Report**

The Worth Company manufactures redwood outdoor furniture sets. The direct material consists of one item, 2″ × 4″ redwood. Screws and bolts may be ignored.

The following information is available for the month of April 19x3:

1. Six thousand sets of furniture were produced. There are no beginning or ending inventories.
2. The actual cost of lumber purchased amounted to $410,850 for 249,000 board feet of redwood. The materials price variance amounted to $12,450 favorable, and the materials quantity variance amounted to $15,300 unfavorable.
3. The direct labor payroll for the month amounted to $313,650, and the labor rate variance was $6,150 favorable. The labor efficiency variance was $7,800 unfavorable. The actual hours worked were 24,600.

Required   *a.* Compute the following:

(1) The standard cost of one board foot of lumber.
(2) The standard quantity of board feet per one set of furniture.
(3) The actual cost per board foot.
(4) The standard rate per hour of direct labor.
(5) The standard quantity of hours needed per one set of furniture.
(6) The actual labor rate per hour.

b. Prepare a performance report and insert any possible explanations that seem reasonable for the variances.

P10–27   **Computation of Variances**

The Terry Company manufactures a commercial solvent used for industrial maintenance. This solvent is sold by the drum and generally has a stable selling price. Due to a decrease in demand for this product, Terry produced and sold 60,000 drums in December 19x6, which is 50 percent of normal capacity.

The following information is available regarding Terry's operations for the month of December 19x6:

1. Standard costs per drum of product manufactured were as follows:

Materials:
10 gallons of direct material $20
1 empty drum 1
Total materials. $21

Direct labor:
1 hour . . . . $ 7

2. Costs incurred during December 19x6 were as follows:

Direct materials . . . . . 600,000 gallons purchased at a cost of $1,150,000
700,000 gallons used
Empty drums . . . . . . 85,000 drums purchased at a cost of $85,000
60,000 drums used
Direct labor . . . . . . 65,000 hours worked at a cost of $470,000

Required Prepare a schedule computing the following variances for the month of December 19x6:

a. Materials price variance (computed at time of purchase).
b. Materials quantity variance.
c. Labor rate variance.
d. Labor usage (efficiency) variance.
Indicate whether each variance was favorable or unfavorable.

(AICPA Adapted)

P10–28 **Computation of Variances for a Hospital**
Mountain View Hospital has adopted a standard cost accounting system for evaluation and control of nursing labor. Diagnosis related groups (DRGs), instituted by the U.S. government for health insurance reimbursement, are used as the output measure in the standard cost system A DRG is a patient classification scheme that perceives hospitals to be multiproduct firms in which inpatient treatment procedures are related to the numbers and types of patient ailments treated. Mountain View Hospital has developed standard nursing times for the treatment of each DRG classification, and nursing labor hours are assumed to vary with the number of DRGs treated within a time period.

The nursing unit on the fourth floor treats patients with four DRG classifications. The unit is staffed with registered nurses (RNs), licensed practical nurses (LPNs), and aides. The standard nursing hours and salary rates are as follows.

| | Fourth Floor Nursing Unit Standard Hours | | |
DRG Classification	RN	LPN	Aide
1	6	4	5
2	26	16	10
3	10	5	4
4	12	7	10

Standard Hourly Rates

RN	$12
LPN	8
Aide	6

For the month of May 19x9, the results of operations for the fourth floor nursing unit are presented below.

Actual Number of Patients	
DRG 1	250
DRG 2	90
DRG 3	240
DRG 4	140
	720

	RN	LPN	Aide
Actual hours	8,150	4,300	4,400
Actual salary	$100,245	$35,260	$25,300
Actual hourly rate	$12.30	$8.20	$5.75

The accountant for Mountain View Hospital calculated the following standard times for the fourth floor nursing unit for May 19x9.

DRG Classification	No. of Patients	Standard Hrs/DRG RN	Standard Hrs/DRG LPN	Standard Hrs/DRG Aide	Total Standard Hrs RN	Total Standard Hrs LPN	Total Standard Hrs Aide
1	250	6	4	5	1,500	1,000	1,250
2	90	26	16	10	2,340	1,440	900
3	240	10	5	4	2,400	1,200	960
4	140	12	7	10	1,680	980	1,400
					7,920	4,620	4,510

The hospital calculates labor variances, using a flexible budgeting approach, for each reporting period by labor classification (RN, LPN, Aide) since the hospital does not have data to calculate variances by DRG.

Required   Calculate the total budget variance for the fourth floor nursing unit of Mountain View Hospital for May 19x9, indicating how much of this variance is attributed to

a. Labor efficiency.
b. Rate differences.

(CMA Adapted)

P10–29   Revising Standards

NuLathe Co. produces a turbo engine component for jet aircraft manufacturers. A standard cost system has been used for years with good results.

Unfortunately, NuLathe has recently experienced production problems. The source for its direct material went out of business. The new source produces a similar but higher-quality material. The price per pound from the original source averaged $7.00; the price from the new source is $7.77. The use of the new material results in a reduction in scrap. This scrap reduction reduces the actual consumption of direct material from 1.25 to 1.00 pounds per unit. In addition, direct labor is reduced from 24 to 22 minutes per unit because there is less scrap labor and machine setup time.

The direct material problem was occurring at the same time that labor negotiations resulted in an increase of more than 14 percent in hourly direct labor costs. The average rate rose from $12.60 per hour to $14.40 per hour. Production of the main product requires a high level of labor skill. Because of a continuing shortage in that skill area, an interim wage agreement had to be signed.

NuLathe started using the new direct material on April 1, the same date that the new labor agreement went into effect. NuLathe has been using standards that were set at the beginning of the calendar year. The direct material and direct labor standards for the turbo engine component are as follows:

Direct materials	1.2 lbs. at $6.80/lb.	$ 8.16
Direct labor	20 min. at $12.30/DLH	4.10
Standard prime cost per unit		$12.26

Howard Foster, cost accounting supervisor, had been examining the performance report shown below that he had prepared at the close of business on April 30. Jane Keene, assistant controller, came into Foster's office, and Foster said, "Jane, look at this performance report. Direct material price increased 11 percent and the labor rate increased more than 14 percent during April. I expected greater variances, yet prime costs decreased more than 5 percent from the $13.79 we experienced during the first quarter of this year. The proper message just isn't coming through."

"This has been an unusual period," said Keene. "With all the unforeseen changes, perhaps we should revise our standards based on current conditions and start over."

Foster replied, "I think we can retain the current standards but expand the variance analysis. We could calculate variances for the specific changes that have occurred to direct material and direct labor before we calculate the normal price and quantity variances. What I really think would be useful to management right now is to determine the impact the changes in direct material and direct labor had in reducing our prime costs per unit from $13.79 in the first quarter to $13.05 in April—a reduction of $.74."

NULATHE CO.
Analysis of Prime Costs

Standard Cost Variance Analysis for April 19x5

	Standard	Price Variance		Quantity Variance		Actual
Direct materials	$ 8.16	($.97 × 1.0)	$.97 U	($6.80 × .2)	$1.36 F	$ 7.77
Direct labor	4.10	$\left(\$2.10 \times \frac{22}{60}\right)$	.77 U	$\left(\$12.30 \times \frac{2}{60}\right)$	.41 U	5.28
	$12.26					$13.05

Comparison of 19x5 Actual Costs

	First Quarter Costs	April Costs	Percentage Increase (Decrease)
Direct materials	$ 8.75	$ 7.77	(11.2)%
Direct labor	5.04	5.28	4.8 %
	$13.79	$13.05	(5.4)%

Required a. Discuss the advantages of
   (1) Immediately revising the standards.
   (2) Retaining the current standards and expanding the analysis of variances.
 b. Prepare an analysis that reflects the impact that the new direct material and new labor contract had on reducing NuLathe Co.'s prime costs per unit from $13.79 in the first quarter to $13.05 in April. The analysis should show the changes in prime costs per unit that are due to the
   (1) Use of new direct material.
   (2) New labor contract.
   This analysis should be in sufficient detail to identify the changes due to

▸ Direct material price.
▸ Direct labor rate.

▸ The effect of direct material quality on direct material usage.

▸ The effect of direct material quality on direct labor usage.

(CMA Adapted)

P10–30   **Setting Standards**

Mark-Wright, Inc. (MWI), is a specialty frozen food processor located in the midwestern states. Since its founding in 19x2, MWI has enjoyed a loyal local clientele willing to pay premium prices for the high-quality frozen foods it prepares from specialized recipes. In the last two years, the company has experienced rapid sales growth in its operating region and has had many inquiries about supplying its products on a national basis. To meet this growth, MWI expanded its processing capabilities, which resulted in increased production and distribution costs. Furthermore, MWI has been encountering pricing pressure from competitors outside its normal marketing region.

Because MWI desires to continue its expansion, Jim Condon, CEO, has engaged a consulting firm to assist MWI in determining its best course of action. The consulting firm concluded that, although premium pricing is sustainable in some area, MWI must make some price concessions if sales growth is to be achieved. Also, in order to maintain profit margins, cost must be reduced and controlled. The consulting firm recommended the institution of a standard cost system that would also facilitate a flexible budgeting system to better accommodate the changes in demand that can be expected when serving an expanding market area.

Condon met with his management team and explained the recommendations of the consulting firm. Condon then assigned the task of establishing standard costs to the management team. After discussing the situation with their respective staffs, the management team met to review the matter.

Jane Morgan, purchasing manager, advised that meeting expanded production would necessitate obtaining basic food supplies from other than MWI's traditional sources. This would entail increased direct material and shipping costs and may result in lower-quality supplies. Consequently, these increased costs would need to be made up by the processing department if current cost levels are to be maintained or reduced.

Stan Walters, processing manager, countered that the need to accelerate processing cycles to increase production, coupled with the possibility of receiving lower-grade supplies, can be expected to result in a slip in quality and a greater product rejection rate. Under these circumstances, per-unit labor utilization cannot be maintained or reduced, and forecasting future unit labor content becomes very difficult.

Tom Lopez, production engineer, advised that if the equipment is not properly maintained and thoroughly cleaned at prescribed daily intervals, it can be anticipated that the quality and unique taste of the frozen food products will be affected. Jack Reid, vice president of sales, stated that if quality cannot be maintained, MWI cannot expect to increase sales to the levels projected.

When Condon was apprised of the problems encountered by the management team, he advised members that if agreement could not be reached on appropriate standards, he would arrange to have them set by the consulting firm and everyone would have to live with the results.

Required   a. (1) List the major advantages of using a standard cost system.

        (2) List disadvantages that can result from using a standard cost system.

      b. (1) Identify those who should participate in setting standards and describe the benefits of their participation in the standard-setting process.

        (2) Explain the general features and characteristics associated with the introduction and operation of a standard cost system that make it an effective tool for cost control.

c. What could be the consequences if Condon has the standards set by the outside consulting firm?

(CMA Adapted)

P10–31   **(Appendix 10-B) Graphical Solution for Joint Price-Quantity Variance**
The Ideal Frame Company manufactures wooden picture frames for sale to specialty stores. For the month of January 19x2, a batch of 2,000 frames was manufactured. All of the frames were the same size (8″ × 10″) and made from oak wood. The standard cost for one frame is:

Direct materials (3.2 lineal feet of oak molding at $1.25 per ln. ft.)	$4.00
Direct labor (.5 hours at $9 per direct labor-hour).	4.50
Total	$8.50

The purchasing agent was unable to secure the oak molding from the firm's normal source of supply and had to purchase the molding elsewhere at a price of $1.75 per lineal foot. She purchased 6,400 lineal feet on January 2, 19x2. On January 6, she learned that the employee who was cutting the 45-degree miter had cut the molding for 300 frames before he found that the miter saw was set at 60 degrees instead of 45. The molding for the 300 frames will be recut next month for use in making 5″ × 7″ frames. However, the purchasing agent was instructed to purchase an additional 960 lineal feet of oak molding, which she did at $1.75 per lineal foot.

Required   *a.* Prepare a graphical solution for the price and quantity variances showing the joint price-quantity variance.
b. How much of the price variance should be charged to the purchasing agent? Explain your answer.

▶ **CASES**   C10–32   **Discussion and Development of Standard Costs**
Ogwood Company is a small manufacturer of wooden household items. Al Rivkin, corporate controller, plans to implement a standard cost system for Ogwood. Rivkin has information from several co-workers that will assist him in developing standards for Ogwood's products.

One of Ogwood's products is a wooden cutting board. Each cutting board requires 1.25 board feet of lumber and 12 minutes of direct labor time to prepare and cut the lumber. The cutting boards are inspected after they are cut. Because the cutting boards are made of a natural material that has imperfections, one board is normally rejected for every five that are accepted. Four rubber foot pads are attached to each good cutting board. A total of 15 minutes of direct labor time is required to attach all four foot pads and finish each cutting board. The lumber for the cutting boards costs $3 per board foot, and each foot pad costs $.05. Direct labor is paid at the rate of $8 per hour.

Required   *a.* Develop the standard cost for the direct cost components of the cutting board. For each direct cost component of the cutting board, the standard cost should identify the:
(1) Standard quantity.
(2) Standard rate.
(3) Standard cost per unit.
b. Identify the advantages of implementing a standard cost system.
c. Explain the role of each of the following persons in developing standards.
(1) Purchasing manager.

(2) Industrial engineer.

(3) Cost accountant.

(CMA Adapted)

C10–33   **(Appendix 10-A) Journal Entries and Computations from Fragmentary Data**
The Exchange Company manufactures one grade of ladies' slacks. The firm's book-keeper was working on the general ledger when he decided to have a cup of coffee. As luck would have it, he stumbled over a tear in the carpeting near his desk, and the coffee was spilled over the general ledger, obliterating parts of it.

The legible portion of selected T accounts appears as follows:

Direct Materials Inventory				Accounts Payable		
19x3		19x3			19x3	
Jan. 1 Bal. 6,720		Jan. 31 140			Jan. 1 Bal. 8,000	
					31 86,400	

Work in Process—Materials		Material Quantity Variance	
19x3		19x3	
Jan. 31 69,300		Jan. 31 40	

Work in Process—Direct Labor		Labor Rate Variance	
19x3		19x3	
Jan. 31 64,680		Jan. 31 00	

Labor Efficiency Variance		Wages Payable	
	19x3		19x3
	Jan. 31 80		Jan. 31 65,000

The following additional information is available:

1. The standard direct materials cost for one dozen slacks is 30 yards at $1.40 per yard.
2. The standard time of direct labor is four hours per dozen.
3. The purchase of direct materials was made at four cents above the standard price.
4. The material quantity variance was partially obliterated. However, the bookkeeper remembers that it was less than $1,000.
5. The labor rate variance was at the rate of 20 cents per hour.

Required   *a.* Compute the following:

(1) The price paid per yard of material.
(2) The quantity of yards purchased in January.
(3) The number of slacks manufactured in January (in dozens).
(4) The actual quantity of yards used.
(5) The standard direct labor rate per hour.
(6) The actual direct labor rate per hour.
(7) The actual number of hours worked.
(8) The standard quantity of direct labor-hours allowed.

b. Reconstruct the journal entries made by the bookkeeper as of January 31, 19x3.

▶ **ANSWERS TO SELF-TEST**

True or False

1. True	2. False	3. True	4. True	5. False	6. False
7. True	8. False	9. True	10. True	11. False	12. False

Multiple Choice

1. *c.* MQV = SP(AQ − SQ)
   MQV = $1.30(6,400 − 6,000)
   MQV = $520 U
2. *b.* $110,200 ÷ 29,000 hours = $3.80
3. *c.* $5,800 ÷ 29,000 = $.20 + $3.80 = $4.00
4. *c.* 1,400($1.10 − $1.00) = $140
5. *c.* $3.60 − ($240 ÷ 1,600) = $3.45

Flexible Budgeting and Manufacturing Overhead Analysis

▶ **LEARNING OBJECTIVES**

After reading this chapter, you should be able to:

1. Explain the difference between a flexible budget and a static budget.
2. Prepare a flexible budget for manufacturing overhead.
3. Explain why certain activity bases are preferable to others when applying overhead to production.
4. Analyze and interpret variable and fixed overhead variances.
5. Prepare performance reports that include variance analyses.
6. Discuss why some of the efficiency variance in variable overhead may be included in the variable overhead spending variance.
7. Apply overhead to production when separate predetermined rates are used for variable and fixed overhead.
8. Prepare the closing entries for actual and applied manufacturing overhead and set up the overhead variances on a firm's books and records.
9. Prepare an income statement for management's use when standard cost variances are separately disclosed.
10. Explain how to treat standard cost variances in financial statements prepared for external use.
11. Select one of four capacity levels that is most consistent with a firm's objective when applying fixed overhead to production (Appendix 11-B).

▶ **INTERVIEW**

Vincent M. Zaccheo
Controller
ITW Minigrip,
Inc.—Subsidiary of
Illinois Tool Works
President—New York
State Society of
CPAs—Westchester
Chapter

Q. *Have you ever used flexible budgeting for manufacturing overhead analysis, and if so, how was it used?*

A. The flexible budget and its planning, preparation, and use are integral parts of our overall operating plan and budget at ITW Minigrip, Inc. Since labor and manufacturing overhead represent 60 percent of the total cost of manufacturing, the flexible budget is crucial in controlling costs and product pricing.

In the preparation and use of any budget, it is important to understand the cost elements and their behavior differences and assumptions. Operations are broken into three major processes: extrusion, printing, and bag conversion. Since cost components vary, separate budgets are prepared for each of the production departments.

Although direct labor can be traceable to a given process, it cannot be traceable to a given item or job order. Because of this difficulty, direct labor is combined with indirect labor and thus treated as manufacturing overhead.

► Within departments, labor is controlled by the following:

- ► Step-variable labor costs in extrusion.
- ► Variable labor costs in print.
- ► In bag conversion 50 percent of labor costs are step-variable and 50 percent are variable.

Since manufacturing is machine intensive, both labor and overhead are applied to production based on machine-hours and then further by units of output per machine-hour as illustrated below:

Extrusion
Total extrusion overhead per M* feet of film =
Overhead rate per extrusion hour/M feet of output per hour

Total overhead rate per extrusion hour =
Total departmental costs/Total number of machines budgeted

Printing
Total printing overhead per M feet of film =
Overhead rate per printing hour/M feet of output per hour

Total overhead rate per printing hour =
Total departmental costs/Total number of machines budgeted

Bag Conversion
Total bag conversion overhead per M bags =
Overhead rate per hour/M bags of output per hour

Total overhead rate per hour =
Total departmental costs/Total number of machines budgeted

Since manufacturing overhead, as illustrated above, is applied to production based on budgeted machine-hours, selecting a capacity level is critical. Of the four possible capacity levels—(1) ideal capacity, (2) practical capacity, (3) normal capacity, and (4) expected capacity—both expected capacity and practical capacity are used. Expected capacity is used for product pricing, while practical capacity is used to determine plant underutilization:

To ensure that the flexible budget remains a key management tool, it is reviewed and updated quarterly.

* M = thousand.

▶ The control of manufacturing overhead is not as straightforward as the control of direct materials and direct labor. In Chapter 10, we discussed only the variable costs associated with direct materials and direct labor, and it was a relatively simple matter to compute the standard quantity allowed and total standard cost for such items. Also, by analyzing variances, it was usually simple to assign responsibility for the components of the variances associated with these costs. Manufacturing overhead does not fit into such neat compartments, however.

Manufacturing overhead has some variable costs, but it also has fixed costs and mixed costs. As a result, the analysis of variable overhead is similar to the method introduced in Chapter 10, but the assignment of responsibility for the variances may require further analysis than has been demonstrated thus far. Furthermore, the analysis of fixed overhead variances differs from that of variable costs. Fixed manufacturing overhead is made up of many different kinds of costs, such as factory rent, machinery repairs, and factory telephone. Thus, instead of a few managers being responsible for large chunks of costs, as is the case for direct materials and direct labor, many managers are responsible for many different costs. These factors compound the problems of the general manager when it is time to assign responsibility for unfavorable variances from manufacturing overhead.

The starting point for controlling overhead costs is the firm's budget. The expected overhead stated in the budget provides a measure against which the actual overhead can be compared.

▶ STATIC BUDGETS

L.O. 1

A **static budget** is a budget prepared for a single level of activity. As such, it is useful for planning purposes because, in effect, it provides the firm with a road map of where to travel during the next accounting period. However, because the firm's actual results usually differ from the expected level, the static budget may not be useful for control. In fact, a static budget's usefulness in control is limited to cases in which the *actual level* of operations *coincides with the planned (budgeted) level.*

For example, assume you were planning a 200-mile round trip by automobile and started your trip with a full tank of gasoline. To evaluate your automobile's efficiency, you intended to fill the tank again when you returned and then compute the rate of miles per gallon for the entire trip. However, after you drove 25 miles, there was a sudden change in the weather and you decided to return home. You stopped to fill the tank again and found that the tank took only two gallons of gasoline. Obviously, the miles per gallon for the shortened trip is 25 (50 miles ÷ 2 gallons) and not 100 (200 miles ÷ 2 gallons). While the original plan to drive 200 miles was useful in preparing for the trip and would have been used for evaluation if the trip had been completed, once the trip was shortened, the actual miles driven (50 miles) had to be used in your calculations. Using the planned mileage of 200 miles and arriving at a figure of 100 miles per gallon would yield false information about your car's efficiency.

Similarly, although performance reports based on the expected results presented in budgets can provide managers with much needed information, a manager would get a false idea of a firm's efficiency if performance reports were based solely on static budgets.

▶ ILLUSTRATION 11-1

BLOCK MANUFACTURING COMPANY
Manufacturing Overhead Static Budget
For the Month of January 19x2

Production in units.	90,000
Variable overhead:	
Power	$ 2,700
Repairs	4,500
Payroll fringes	63,000
Miscellaneous	9,000
Total variable overhead.	79,200
Fixed overhead:	
Superintendence	8,000
Factory rent	10,000
Maintenance.	3,000
Indirect labor	5,000
Depreciation of equipment	12,000
Miscellaneous	4,000
Total fixed overhead	42,000
Total overhead	$121,200

▶ FLEXIBLE BUDGETS

L.O. 1

A **flexible budget** is a series of static budgets for different levels of activity within a firm's relevant range. For example, if a factory has a relevant range of 70,000 units to 100,000 units per month and it expects to produce an average of 90,000 units per month, its accountants might prepare budgets for 80,000, 85,000, 90,000, and 95,000 units. Although flexible budgeting applies to all components of the budgeted income statement, we will focus only on manufacturing overhead. Nonetheless, the reader should bear in mind that the limitations of a static budget and the importance of a flexible budget carry over to all components of the statement.

The Importance of a Flexible Budget

The Block Manufacturing Company prepared a budget for manufacturing overhead at a level of 90,000 units, as shown in Illustration 11-1. At the end of the month, it was determined that only 80,000 units were produced. Using the static budget shown in Illustration 11-1 as the basis for comparison, the Block Manufacturing Company prepared the performance report shown in Illustration 11-2.

In evaluating this performance report, managers would first compare the actual production to the budgeted production to determine if there is a difference and, if so, why the difference occurred. During January, the company produced 10,000 fewer units than anticipated. This might have been a planned reduction due to an unexpected reduction in sales, or it might have been a production shortfall due to problems in the factory. If the former is the case, no management action is required; if the latter occurred, management action may be indicated because of the failure in *effectiveness*.

Next, management would want to examine cost control, or *efficiency*. Unfortunately, this performance report would be useless for this purpose.

▶ **ILLUSTRATION 11-2**

BLOCK MANUFACTURING COMPANY
Manufacturing Overhead Performance Report
For the Month of January 19x2

	Budget	Actual	Variance
Units	90,000	80,000	10,000
Variable overhead:			
Power.	$ 2,700	$ 2,500	$ 200 F
Repairs	4,500	4,200	300 F
Payroll fringes	63,000	56,800	6,200 F
Miscellaneous	9,000	8,500	500 F
Total variable overhead	79,200	72,000	7,200 F
Fixed overhead:			
Superintendence	8,000	8,500	500 U
Factory rent	10,000	10,000	–0–
Maintenance.	3,000	2,500	500 F
Indirect labor	5,000	5,200	200 U
Depreciation of equipment	12,000	12,000	–0–
Miscellaneous	4,000	4,300	300 U
Total fixed overhead	42,000	42,500	500 U
Total overhead.	$121,200	$114,500	$6,700 F

F = Favorable.
U = Unfavorable.

Problems arise because even though the variable overhead variances are all favorable, they do not necessarily imply efficiency. Erroneous conclusions may be drawn because the actual results of 80,000 units are compared with the budget for 90,000 units. This comparison is analogous to the earlier example of computing miles per gallon by using the *actual* gallons used (2 gallons) and the budgeted mileage (200 miles). A proper conclusion must be made with a budget of 80,000 units, not 90,000 units. Illustration 11-3 contains the proper performance report based on a budget for 80,000 units.

From Illustration 11-3, it can be seen that the variances for variable overhead are really unfavorable, although Illustration 11-2 indicated they were favorable. A performance report based on a static budget that is not adjusted to the actual level of production is worse than no report, because managers may draw incorrect conclusions from it.

It is highly unlikely that, for any given time period, actual production will coincide exactly with budgeted production. Thus, a single static budget is usually useful for planning but not for controlling. In anticipation of this, some firms find that constructing a series of budgets at budget preparation time is easier than waiting to construct a new budget every time a performance report must be prepared. Other firms prefer to wait until the level of production is known and then prepare a flexible budget for that level.

Preparing a Flexible Budget

L.O. 2

The steps to construct a flexible budget are as follows:

1. Analyze the firm's costs and divide them into fixed, mixed, and variable categories. This topic was discussed in detail in Chapter 3.
2. Ascertain the per-unit amounts for sales and variable costs. Per-unit

▶ **ILLUSTRATION 11-3**

BLOCK MANUFACTURING COMPANY
Manufacturing Overhead Performance Report
For the Month of January 19x2

	Budgeted Costs per Unit	Budget	Actual	Variance
Units.		80,000	80,000	–0–
Variable overhead:				
Power	$.03	$ 2,400	$ 2,500	$ 100 U
Repairs	.05	4,000	4,200	200 U
Payroll fringes	.70	56,000	56,800	800 U
Miscellaneous	.10	8,000	8,500	500 U
Total variable overhead.		70,400	72,000	1,600 U
Fixed overhead:				
Superintendence		8,000	8,500	500 U
Factory rent.		10,000	10,000	–0–
Maintenance.		3,000	2,500	500 F
Indirect labor		5,000	5,200	200 U
Depreciation of equipment		12,000	12,000	–0–
Miscellaneous		4,000	4,300	300 U
Total fixed overhead		42,000	42,500	500 U
Total overhead.		$112,400	$114,500	$2,100 U

amounts may be stated, or, if not, they can be calculated by dividing the total dollar amount given by the corresponding number of units. For example, if the given variable miscellaneous costs are $9,000 with budgeted units of 90,000, the per-unit amount is $.10 ($9,000 ÷ 90,000 units).

3. Determine the desired budget activity level and multiply the per-unit amounts in (2) above by the number of units in the desired activity level. For example, if we desired a flexible budget for a production level of 80,000 units, variable miscellaneous costs would be 80,000 units multiplied by $.10, or $8,000.

4. Because fixed costs remain constant in total, per unit amounts are not required. Rather, fixed costs would be the same for every level of activity as long as the activity stays within the firm's relevant range. *Relevant range* refers to a firm's normal range of operating activity and is discussed in detail in Chapter 3. For example, budgeted fixed miscellaneous costs are the same regardless of whether 90,000 units or 80,000 units are produced.

Consider the information shown in Illustration 11-4. Applying the above steps, we can compute the following:

1. Costs are already separated into fixed and variable components.
2. Calculate the per-unit amounts:

Sales	$100,000 ÷ 50,000 units	= $2.00
Variable costs	$ 60,000 ÷ 50,000 units	= $1.20
Contribution margin	$ 40,000 ÷ 50,000 units	= $ .80

▶ **ILLUSTRATION 11-4**   Sample Flexible Budget

	Total	Per Unit	Total
Sales—in units	50,000		60,000
Sales	$100,000	$2.00	$120,000
Variable costs	60,000	1.20	72,000
Contribution margin	40,000	$ .80	48,000
Fixed costs	30,000		30,000
Net income	$ 10,000		$ 18,000

▶ **ILLUSTRATION 11-5**

BLOCK MANUFACTURING COMPANY
Manufacturing Overhead Flexible Budget
For the Month of January 19x2

	Budgeted Costs per Unit	Level of Activity Units				
Units		75,000	80,000	85,000	90,000	95,000
Variable overhead:						
Power	$.03	$ 2,250	$ 2,400	$ 2,550	$ 2,700	$ 2,850
Repairs	.05	3,750	4,000	4,250	4,500	4,750
Payroll fringes	.70	52,500	56,000	59,500	63,000	66,500
Miscellaneous	.10	7,500	8,000	8,500	9,000	9,500
Total variable overhead	$.88	66,000	70,400	74,800	79,200	83,600
Fixed overhead:						
Superintendence		8,000	8,000	8,000	8,000	8,000
Factory rent		10,000	10,000	10,000	10,000	10,000
Maintenance		3,000	3,000	3,000	3,000	3,000
Indirect labor		5,000	5,000	5,000	5,000	5,000
Depreciation of equipment		12,000	12,000	12,000	12,000	12,000
Miscellaneous		4,000	4,000	4,000	4,000	4,000
Total fixed overhead		42,000	42,000	42,000	42,000	42,000
Total overhead		$108,000	$112,400	$116,800	$121,200	$125,600

3. Multiply the amounts per unit by the desired budgeted activity of 60,000 units sold.

Sales	60,000 units × $2.00 =	$120,000
Variable costs	60,000 units × $1.20 =	72,000
Contribution margin	60,000 units × $ .80 =	48,000

4. Within the relevant range, fixed costs are $30,000 regardless of the units sold.

Extending Illustration 11-3, the following is assumed:

1. The relevant range of operations for the Block Manufacturing Company is from 70,000 to 100,000 units per month.
2. Based on the firm's production budget, the most likely operating levels are 80,000 and 90,000 units per month.

3. Management decided to prepare a flexible budget using operating levels of 75,000, 80,000, 85,000, 90,000, and 95,000 units per month.

Block's flexible budget appears in Illustration 11-5. It was prepared using the budgeted variable costs per unit shown in the first column of Illustration 11-3.

Returning to Illustration 11-3, we can see that the budgeted activity level of 80,000 units agrees with that level of activity disclosed in the flexible budget shown in Illustration 11-5. Had the actual production been 75,000, 85,000, 90,000, or 95,000 units, that level of activity would have been extracted from Illustration 11-5, and a performance report similar to the one shown in Illustration 11-3 would have been prepared.

Once the flexible budget is prepared and compared with the actual results, the total variance for each item of overhead is computed. It is then possible for managers to further analyze the variances for variable manufacturing overhead. However, care must be exercised in selecting a proper overhead application base if the analysis is to be meaningful.

▶ VARIABLE MANUFACTURING OVERHEAD

Selecting the Overhead Base

L.O. 3

An **overhead application base** is a measure of activity, such as direct labor cost, direct labor-hours, and machine-hours, used in the calculation of a predetermined overhead rate. The discussion of these overhead bases was covered in Chapter 5, and the discussion of other cost drivers was discussed in Chapter 7. When selecting a base for use in the application and analysis of overhead, managers should select the one that has the strongest cause-and-effect relationship with overhead cost behavior. Thus, in a labor-intensive firm or department, the base should be direct labor; and in a machine-intensive firm or department, the base should be machine-hours or a more appropriate cost driver. Although either direct labor cost or direct labor-hours may be used as a direct labor base, direct labor-hours usually produces a more accurate application and analysis of overhead for a labor-intensive firm.

Applying Variable Overhead to Production

Manufacturing overhead is rarely applied to production on a per-unit basis; instead, one of the bases noted above is usually used. Thus far, we have presented variable overhead on a per-unit basis, as shown in Illustration 11-5. But if the Block Manufacturing Company uses direct labor-hours to apply overhead to production, and if each unit requires one fourth of an hour of direct labor, the variable overhead per unit from Illustration 11-5 may be restated in direct labor-hours, as shown in Illustration 11-6. Thus, the predetermined variable overhead rate is $3.52 per direct labor-hour.

Let us assume 22,500 direct labor-hours (DLH) were budgeted for January 19x2. This means 90,000 units (22,500 DLH ÷ .25 = 90,000 units) should have been produced. If only 80,000 units of output were produced, the standard hours allowed are 20,000 (80,000 units × .25 DLH).

Before proceeding with the analysis for controlling variable overhead, it is necessary to compute the total standard cost for variable overhead. The **total standard variable overhead cost** represents the standard hours allowed

▶ **ILLUSTRATION 11-6**

BLOCK MANUFACTURING COMPANY
Budgeted Variable Manufacturing Overhead per Unit
and per Direct Labor-Hour

Overhead Cost	(1) Budgeted Cost per Unit	(2) Direct Labor-Hours per Unit	(3) Budgeted Cost per DLH (1) ÷ (2)
Power	$.03	.25	$ .12
Repairs	.05	.25	.20
Payroll fringes*	.70	.25	2.80
Miscellaneous	.10	.25	.40
Total	$.88		$3.52

* The company has uniform wage rates. Thus, payroll fringes per direct labor-hour do not distort this example.

multiplied by the variable overhead rate. In equation format, Equation (1) may be stated as:

$$\text{Total standard variable overhead cost} = \text{Standard hours allowed} \times \text{Variable overhead rate} \quad (1)$$

The total standard variable overhead cost for the Block Manufacturing Company for January is $70,400 (20,000 standard hours allowed × $3.52). This is also the amount of variable overhead applied to production. It is now possible to consider the controlling of variable overhead costs through the analysis of the variable overhead variance.

Analyzing Variable Overhead Variances

L.O. 4

In Chapter 10, a direct labor variance was analyzed into its rate and efficiency components. The analysis of a variable overhead variance is very similar, except the portion that corresponds to a *rate* variance is usually called a *spending* variance instead.

The **variable overhead spending variance** is the actual number of hours of activity used in production multiplied by the difference between the actual and the standard rates of variable overhead per hour. The amount is derived using Equation (2):

$$\text{Variable overhead spending variance} = \text{Actual hours} \times (\text{Actual rate per hour} - \text{Standard rate per hour}) \quad (2)$$

The variable overhead efficiency variance is also very similar to its counterpart in direct labor. The **variable overhead efficiency variance** is the standard variable overhead rate per hour multiplied by the difference between the actual hours worked and the standard hours allowed. It may be derived from Equation (3):

$$\text{Variable overhead efficiency variance} = \text{Standard rate per hour} \times (\text{Actual hours} - \text{Standard hours allowed}) \quad (3)$$

Bear in mind that Equation (3) is an efficiency variance and is very *similar* to the direct labor efficiency variance. In fact, it is triggered because of the direct labor efficiency variance. However, it is an *overhead variance*. Thus, there are two efficiency variances, one for direct labor and one for variable overhead.

▶ ILLUSTRATION 11-7

BLOCK MANUFACTURING COMPANY
Calculation of Actual Variable Overhead Rates
For January 19x2

Overhead Cost	Actual Cost	Actual DLH worked	Rate per DLH
Power	$ 2,500	20,500	$ .12195
Repairs.	4,200	20,500	.20488
Payroll fringes	56,800	20,500	2.77073
Miscellaneous.	8,500	20,500	.41463
Total.	$72,000		$3.51219

Firms usually find that calculations of the total spending variance and the total efficiency variance do not provide adequate information for control purposes. They need a more detailed analysis because variable overhead consists of many items, and a favorable variance of one item, such as power, may mask an unfavorable variance of another item, such as repairs. Therefore, it is customary to prepare a variance report similar to the one shown in Illustration 11-3, except the variances are further segregated into their spending and efficiency components. To do this, a starting point is to compute the *actual rate per direct labor-hour* for each item of variable overhead. Assuming the actual number of hours (inputs) is 20,500 and using the actual variable overhead costs shown in Illustration 11-3, it is possible to compute the actual rates per direct labor-hour for each item, as shown in Illustration 11-7.

▶ **PROGRESS CHECK**

1. Under what circumstances would a business be able to use a static budget effectively?
2. Why is a flexible budget used for most business purposes when a budget is needed?
3. What steps are used to prepare a flexible budget?
4. What components are used to analyze variable overhead? What information does each component provide to a manager?
5. What is a performance report and how does it assist managers in carrying out their duties? ◀

Preparing Performance Reports that Include Variance Analyses

Using the budgeted costs per direct labor-hour, it is now possible to prepare a performance report suitable for segregating variances into their spending and efficiency components. Each cost must be analyzed separately using either the equation or the diagrammatic approach. The calculation of the spending and efficiency variances is shown in Illustration 11-8, and the performance report based on the variances computed in Illustration 11-8 is presented in Illustration 11-9.

L.O. 5

Preparing Performance Reports in an Alternative Format

It is possible to avoid the use of the equation and diagrammatic approaches to analyzing variances by inserting another column in the performance report for *budgeted costs* at the *actual* number of hours. The spending variance is then computed by subtracting the budgeted cost at the actual hours

▶ **ILLUSTRATION 11-8**   Analysis of Variable Overhead Variances

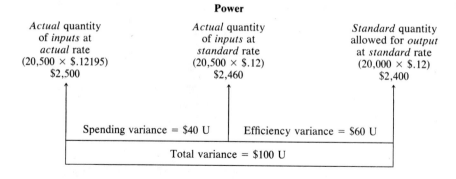

Power

| *Actual* quantity of *inputs* at *actual* rate (20,500 × $.12195) $2,500 | *Actual* quantity of *inputs* at *standard* rate (20,500 × $.12) $2,460 | *Standard* quantity allowed for *output* at *standard* rate (20,000 × $.12) $2,400 |

Spending variance = $40 U   Efficiency variance = $60 U

Total variance = $100 U

Repairs

| *Actual* quantity of *inputs* at *actual* rate (20,500 × $.20488) $4,200 | *Actual* quantity of *inputs* at *standard* rate (20,500 × $.20) $4,100 | *Standard* quantity allowed for *output* at *standard* rate (20,000 × $.20) $4,000 |

Spending variance = $100 U   Efficiency variance = $100 U

Total variance = $200 U

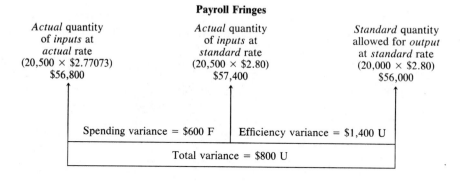

Payroll Fringes

| *Actual* quantity of *inputs* at *actual* rate (20,500 × $2.77073) $56,800 | *Actual* quantity of *inputs* at *standard* rate (20,500 × $2.80) $57,400 | *Standard* quantity allowed for *output* at *standard* rate (20,000 × $2.80) $56,000 |

Spending variance = $600 F   Efficiency variance = $1,400 U

Total variance = $800 U

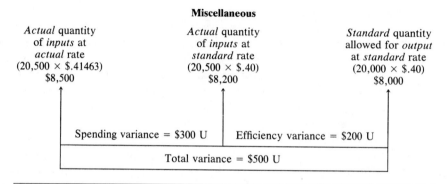

Miscellaneous

| *Actual* quantity of *inputs* at *actual* rate (20,500 × $.41463) $8,500 | *Actual* quantity of *inputs* at *standard* rate (20,500 × $.40) $8,200 | *Standard* quantity allowed for *output* at *standard* rate (20,000 × $.40) $8,000 |

Spending variance = $300 U   Efficiency variance = $200 U

Total variance = $500 U

▶ **ILLUSTRATION 11-9**

BLOCK MANUFACTURING COMPANY
Variable Manufacturing Overhead Performance Report
For the Month of January 19x2

Direct labor-hours:	
Actual	20,500
Standard allowed	20,000
Variance—efficiency.	500 U
Units produced	80,000
Units budgeted	90,000
Variance—effectiveness	10,000 U

	Budgeted Cost per DLH	Total Standard Costs	Actual Costs	Total Variance	Spending Variance	Efficiency Variance
Variable overhead:						
Power.	$ .12	$ 2,400	$ 2,500	$ 100 U	$ 40 U	$ 60 U
Repairs	.20	4,000	4,200	200 U	100 U	100 U
Payroll fringes	2.80	56,000	56,800	800 U	600 F	1,400 U
Miscellaneous	.40	8,000	8,500	500 U	300 U	200 U
Total	$3.52	$70,400	$72,000	$1,600 U	$160 F	$1,760 U

from the actual cost, and the efficiency variance is computed by subtracting the total standard cost from the budgeted cost at the actual number of hours.

Based on the information for power usage shown in Illustration 11-9, the total variance of $100 unfavorable may be analyzed as follows:

Actual cost.	$2,500
Total standard cost	2,400
Total variance	$ 100 U

Budgeted cost at the actual number of hours—	
20,500 hours × $.12	$2,460
Total standard cost	2,400
Efficiency variance	$ 60 U

Actual cost.	$2,500
Budgeted cost at actual hours	2,460
Spending variance.	$ 40 U

The performance report using this approach is shown in Illustration 11-10.

Interpreting Variable Overhead Variances

L.O. 6
Efficiency variance as part of spending variance

Spending Variance Illustration 11-9 provides a great deal more information about the composition of the variable overhead variances than does Illustration 11-3, where the spending component is not shown. Normally, a price variance is composed of price differences exclusively. However, when it comes to variable overhead, the variance is commonly called a *spending variance* because it may be caused by a combination of the prices that deviate from expected prices, and the differences between the anticipated and actual usage of a particular variable overhead item.

When it comes to variable overhead, it is not unusual for a portion of an efficiency variance to find its way into the spending variance. This may occur because the efficiency variance computation for variable overhead is

▶ **ILLUSTRATION 11-10**

BLOCK MANUFACTURING COMPANY
Variable Manufacturing Overhead Performance Report
For the Month of January 19x2

Direct labor-hours:
Actual 20,500
Standard allowed 20,000
 Variance—efficiency. . . . . 500 U

Units produced 80,000
Units budgeted 90,000
 Variance—effectiveness . . . . . . 10,000 U

Variable overhead:	Budgeted Cost per DLH	(1) Total Standard Costs	(2) Actual Costs	(3) Budgeted Costs at Actual Hours	Total Variance (2) − (1)	Spending Variance (2) − (3)	Efficiency Variance (3) − (1)
Power	$ .12	$ 2,400	$ 2,500	$ 2,460	$ 100 U	$ 40 U	$ 60 U
Repairs	.20	4,000	4,200	4,100	200 U	100 U	100 U
Payroll fringes.	2.80	56,000	56,800	57,400	800 U	600 F	1,400 U
Miscellaneous	.40	8,000	8,500	8,200	500 U	300 U	200 U
Total	$3.52	$70,400	$72,000	$72,160	$1,600 U	$160 F	$1,760 U

▶ **ILLUSTRATION 11-11**

BLOCK MANUFACTURING COMPANY
Analysis of Power Costs
For the Month of January 19x2

Total variance . . . . $100 U

Efficiency variances:
500 extra direct labor-hours at 12 cents . . . . . . $ 60 U
333 extra kilowatt-hours at 12 cents . . . . 40 U
 Total efficiency variance . . . . $100 U

based on *direct labor or machine-hours* and *not* on a base that is part of overhead. To illustrate the problem, let us assume each hour of direct labor used by the Block Manufacturing Company consumes one kilowatt-hour (kwhr) of power and the *budgeted cost of power is 12 cents per kilowatt-hour.* Using the analysis of variances for power shown in Illustration 11-8 and the assumption that the *actual cost* of power for January 19x2 was 20,833 kilowatt-hours *at 12 cents* per kilowatt-hour for a total of $2,500, a different analysis may appear, as shown in Illustration 11-11.

The analysis presented in Illustration 11-11 should not be surprising because the *budgeted and actual prices of kilowatt-hours are the same,* and, theoretically, no spending (price) variance should be expected. The analysis in Illustration 11-8 is faulty because the cost of the extra usage of 333 kilowatt-hours has found its way into the spending variance, but only the portion that is based on direct labor-hours is labeled as the efficiency variance. Although this condition may occur for other variable overhead costs, the problem is not usually burdensome. When the spending variance merits management investigation, it is usually a simple matter to analyze items, such as kilowatt-hours used or indirect materials used, and reach the proper conclusions about spending versus efficiency variances.

Efficiency Variance   The variable overhead efficiency variance has little to do with the efficient utilization of overhead. Rather, it results from the efficient or inefficient use of direct labor-hours or machine-hours. It represents the amount of variable overhead costs saved or wasted because of saved or wasted direct labor. As production employees work, they cause an increase in variable overhead costs by using machinery and by consuming factory supplies and electricity, and so on. Therefore, as direct labor-hours increase, variable overhead costs increase as well, usually in a more or less proportionate manner. Therefore, if a firm's employees operate inefficiently, more variable overhead will be incurred and will contribute to the exacerbation of the efficiency variance. The variable overhead efficiency variance is a measure of the variable overhead cost caused by the efficient or inefficient use of direct labor time. In theory, the variable overhead efficiency variance should be grouped with the direct labor efficiency variance; but in practice, its use as a separate variance is deeply ingrained. Consequently, managers must understand how it is used. As noted in the discussion of the interpretation of the spending variance, portions of the efficiency variance for overhead costs are often included as part of the spending variance. Thus, when managers evaluate a direct labor efficiency variance, they should also consider the variable overhead efficiency caused by direct labor. They should also analyze significant spending variances to determine how much of these are caused by price factors and how much are caused by efficiency factors, as demonstrated in the analysis of power costs for the Block Manufacturing Company.

▶ FIXED MANUFACTURING OVERHEAD

The analysis of fixed overhead variances differs substantially from the analysis of variable overhead variances. Although the base used to apply overhead to production is the same for both, the behavior of fixed costs is markedly different from that of variable costs. For variable costs, there is a cause-and-effect relationship between the activity base, such as direct labor-hours, and the incurrence of costs. But for fixed costs within the relevant range, there is no cause-and-effect relationship between the activity base and the incurrence of costs. Fixed costs are constant within the relevant range regardless of how many machine-hours or direct labor-hours are worked, yet fixed costs are applied to production at a fixed amount per direct labor-hour (or machine-hour), as is done for variable costs. Thus, in a sense, fixed costs are treated as variable costs when they are applied to production, but they must be analyzed differently if the variances are to be useful to managers. To properly analyze fixed overhead variances, a manager must understand how the predetermined fixed overhead rate is computed and how fixed overhead is applied to production.

Computing Predetermined Overhead Rates   Chapter 5 explained the computation of a single predetermined overhead rate with no distinction between variable and fixed costs. The procedure used to compute a single rate may be extended to compute separate rates, as follows:

$$\text{Predetermined variable overhead rate} = \frac{\text{Estimated variable overhead}}{\begin{array}{c}\text{Direct labor-hours}\\ \text{(or machine-hours)}\end{array}}$$

$$\text{Predetermined fixed overhead rate} = \frac{\text{Estimated fixed overhead}}{\begin{array}{c}\text{Direct labor-hours}\\ \text{(or machine-hours)}\end{array}}$$

If for 19x2 the Block Manufacturing Company estimated that its variable overhead would be $788,480, its fixed overhead would be $504,000, and its direct labor-hours would be 224,000, its predetermined overhead rates would be calculated as:

$$\text{Predetermined variable overhead rate} = \frac{\$788,480}{224,000 \text{ DLH}} = \$3.52 \text{ per DLH}$$

$$\text{Predetermined fixed overhead rate} = \frac{\$504,000}{224,000 \text{ DLH}} = \$2.25 \text{ per DLH}$$

Although Block could use the combined predetermined overhead rate of $5.77 ($3.52 + $2.25) if it did not wish to segregate overhead variances—and did not mind sacrificing some control—most firms prefer to segregate overhead variances and thus use separate predetermined overhead rates for fixed and variable costs.

Applying Fixed and Variable Overhead to Production

L.O. 7

In Chapter 10, we considered standard cost applications for direct materials and direct labor, but overhead must also be included to arrive at a firm's total standard cost for a unit of finished product. At the Block Manufacturing Company, the total standard cost of manufacturing one tie rack is as shown in Illustration 11-12.

If 80,000 units are manufactured during the month of January 19x2, the journal entry to apply manufacturing overhead to production would be:

(a)

```
19x2
Jan. 31  Work in Process . . . . . . . . . . . . . . . . .   115,400
                 Applied Manufacturing Overhead—Variable. . . .          70,400
                 Applied Manufacturing Overhead—Fixed . . . . .          45,000
             To apply overhead to production:
             Variable—80,000 × ¼ hour = 20,000 DLH × $3.52 = $70,400
             Fixed    —80,000 × ¼ hour = 20,000 DLH ×  2.25 =  45,000
```

Throughout the year, similar entries would be made. In addition, these entries would be posted to the job cost sheets, if a job order cost accounting system is used.

The Relationship between the Overhead Base and Fixed Costs

Ideally, a firm's overhead base should be strongly related to variable overhead costs, but such a relationship does not exist between the base and fixed costs. Nevertheless, the same base is used to apply fixed overhead to production as in journal entry *(a)*. This base is usually referred to as the **denominator activity** because it is the denominator when the predetermined fixed overhead rate is calculated. The base is also referred to as the **volume** or **capacity level,** all of which refer to the firm's expected level of activity. Recall from Chapter 5 that the *base* is used to calculate the predetermined overhead rate. Applied overhead, however, is a function of the *standard hours allowed for actual production.*

▶ **ILLUSTRATION 11-12**

BLOCK MANUFACTURING COMPANY
Standard Cost Sheet

Product ___Oak tie racks___

Description	Quantity	Price or Rate	Total
Direct materials—1″ clear oak	2 bd. ft.	$1.00	$2.0000 .
Direct labor	¼ hour	8.00	2.0000
Variable overhead	¼ hour	3.52	.8800
Fixed overhead.	¼ hour	2.25	.5625
Total			$5.4425

▶ **ILLUSTRATION 11-13**

BLOCK MANUFACTURING COMPANY
Flexible Budget for Fixed Manufacturing Overhead
For the Year Ended December 31, 19x2

Fixed overhead:	
Superintendence	$ 96,000
Factory rent	120,000
Maintenance	36,000
Indirect labor	60,000
Depreciation of equipment	144,000
Miscellaneous	48,000
Total fixed overhead	$504,000

▶ **ILLUSTRATION 11-14**

BLOCK MANUFACTURING COMPANY
Actual Fixed Manufacturing Overhead
For the Month of January 19x2

Fixed overhead:	
Superintendence	$ 8,500
Factory rent	10,000
Maintenance	2,500
Indirect labor	5,200
Depreciation of equipment	12,000
Miscellaneous	4,300
Total fixed overhead	$42,500

Fixed Overhead Variance Analysis

To demonstrate the analysis of fixed overhead variances, we will assume the Block Manufacturing Company uses the capacity of 224,000 direct labor-hours to compute its predetermined fixed overhead rate of $2.25 per direct labor-hour, as shown earlier. Block's flexible budget for 19x2's fixed costs is shown in Illustration 11-13, and its actual fixed overhead for January 19x2 is shown in Illustration 11-14.

Variance Computations The total fixed overhead variance for the month of January 19x2 amounts to $2,500 favorable, calculated as follows:

Actual fixed overhead (Illustration 11-14)	$42,500
Applied fixed overhead [journal entry *(a)*]	45,000
Total fixed overhead variance	$ 2,500 F

This total variance is usually segregated into two components: the spending variance and the volume variance. The **fixed overhead spending variance,** sometimes referred to as the *budget variance,* is the difference between the budgeted fixed overhead and the actual fixed overhead. The **fixed overhead volume variance,** also called the **fixed overhead capacity variance, fixed overhead denominator variance,** or **fixed overhead production volume variance,** is the difference between the budgeted fixed overhead and the applied fixed overhead.

The equations for calculating these variances are:

$$\text{Fixed overhead spending variance} = \text{Actual overhead} - \text{Budgeted fixed overhead} \qquad (4)$$

$$\text{Fixed overhead volume variance} = \text{Budgeted fixed overhead} - (\text{Standard hours allowed} \times \text{Fixed overhead rate})^* \qquad (5)$$

* This is the applied fixed overhead.

The calculations of the variances at Block Manufacturing are:

Fixed overhead spending variance:

Actual overhead (Illustration 11-14)	$42,500
Flexible budget (Illustration 11-5)*	42,000
Spending variance	$ 500 U

Fixed overhead volume variance:

Flexible budget (Illustration 11-5)	$42,000
Applied fixed overhead (20,000 DLH × $2.25)	45,000
Volume variance	$ 3,000 F

* Also, $504,000 (Illustration 11-13) ÷ 12 months = $42,000.

The fixed overhead volume variance may be verified by another calculation, as follows:

Budgeted hours at normal capacity:	
224,000 DLH ÷ 12 months.	18,666⅔ DLH
Standard hours allowed (80,000 units × ¼ DLH). . . .	20,000 DLH
DLH worked in excess of budget.	1,333⅓ DLH
Fixed overhead rate.	× $2.25
Favorable volume variance	$ 3,000

The volume variance is favorable because the number of direct labor-hours worked was greater than anticipated. Thus, the fixed costs are spread over a greater number of units than expected, a favorable condition. When the reverse is true (that is, when the fixed costs must be spread over fewer units), the variance is unfavorable.

The total variance, $2,500 favorable, may also be segregated into its components through the use of the diagrammatic approach. This method is shown in Illustration 11-15.

Illustration 11-15 demonstrates the analysis of variances for the *total* fixed overhead. In practice, however, this kind of analysis is applied to *each item* of fixed overhead, as was demonstrated for variable overhead in Illustration 11-8. Otherwise, a variance in one item, such as factory supervision, may mask a variance in another item, such as maintenance. In addition, the performance report for fixed overhead should be prepared using a format

▶ **ILLUSTRATION 11-15**   Analysis of Fixed Overhead Variances

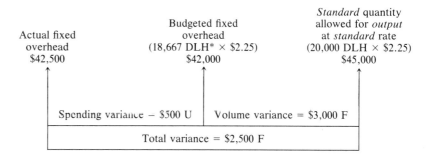

* Normal capacity of 224,000 DLH ÷ 12 months = 18,666⅔ DLH.

similar to that used in Illustration 11-9. The performance report for fixed overhead is usually shown in the same report used for variable overhead.

Once the fixed overhead variances have been analyzed, managers must discover why they occurred.

Interpreting Fixed Overhead Variances

Spending Variance The spending variance usually results from price changes in the items included in fixed overhead. For example, there may have been a personnel change in the indirect labor category, and the new employee may be paid at a different rate than that of the former employee. Variances may also stem from other personnel-related price changes, such as bonuses in profitable times and voluntary salary reductions during difficult times, both of which occurred in the automobile industry in the early 1980s. In addition, the spending variance is often caused by poor budget preparation rather than by price changes. Poor budgeting estimates should be reported separately from changes in price. Other unexpected price changes may occur in real estate taxes on the factory building, heating fuel, and the like.

The spending variance may also reflect changed costs due to changed quantities. Although this does not usually occur when production approximates the projected quantity, a sudden significant change may require the hiring of an additional supervisor or the laying off of a supervisor included in the budget. Thus, the spending variance may contain both a change in price and a change in quantity. Care must be exercised to disclose the makeup of the individual items in the spending variance. The variance should be further analyzed between price and quantity changes and separately disclosed in the performance report for fixed overhead.

Volume (Denominator) Variance Conclusions should never be based on only one month's or several months' volume variance. Seasonal fluctuations may cause distortions in the volume variance for a particular month that will be averaged out over the course of the year.

It should be remembered that although Block Manufacturing charges fixed overhead to production at the rate of $2.25 per direct labor-hour, the fixed overhead is not incurred in this manner. The factory rent is $120,000 per year regardless of how many units are produced (or direct labor-hours

▶ **ILLUSTRATION 11-16**

BLOCK MANUFACTURING COMPANY
Graphical Analysis of Fixed Overhead Variances
For the Month of January 19x2

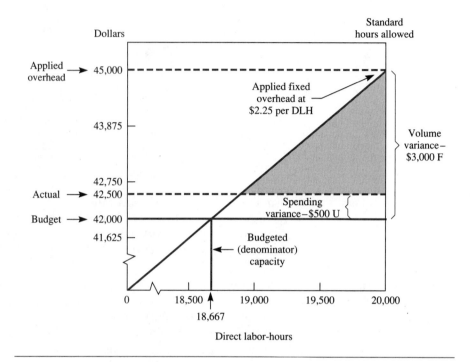

worked). Thus, when fewer direct labor-hours are worked than anticipated, less overhead is charged to production and an unfavorable volume variance occurs. This provides a measure of the underutilization of the factory compared to the planned amount, but it may not necessarily be unfavorable for the firm as a whole. Continuing to produce merchandise as planned when a sudden downward shift in the demand for a product occurs may later cause the firm to lose money due to excess inventories and the related high warehouse costs and/or selling below cost. Curtailing production, with a concomitant unfavorable volume variance, may be preferable if it produces smaller losses (or greater profits) for the firm than would the production of merchandise as planned.

The Graphical Solution to Fixed Overhead Variances

Further insight into fixed overhead variances may be gained through graphs. The graphical solution to fixed overhead variances at Block Manufacturing is shown in Illustration 11-16. This illustration indicates that:

1. The applied overhead of $45,000 is based on 20,000 standard hours allowed at $2.25 per direct labor-hour.
2. The budgeted overhead of $42,000 is based on the budgeted normal capacity of 18,667 direct labor-hours.
3. The difference between the applied overhead and the budgeted overhead gives rise to the volume variance (in this case, favorable). Had applied and budgeted overhead coincided, one line would have

▶ **ILLUSTRATION 11-17**

BLOCK MANUFACTURING COMPANY
Graphical Analysis of Fixed Overhead Volume Variance
For the Month of January 19x2

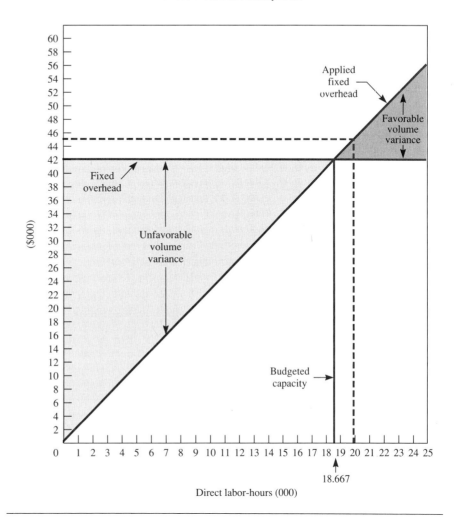

been superimposed on the other, and no volume variance would have been created.

An alternative form of graph, shown in Illustration 11-17, helps clarify why a volume variance arises. Here, the fixed overhead is plotted as a horizontal line, and the applied overhead is plotted as a function of activity (direct labor-hours). The lines intersect at the firm's budgeted denominator capacity, 18,667 direct labor-hours (224,000 direct labor-hours ÷ 12 months). The area to the left of the intersection and beneath the fixed cost line ($42,000) represents the area of unfavorable volume variances because the firm's plant utilization was at a level below the budgeted denominator capacity. The area to the right of the intersection and above the fixed cost line represents the area of favorable volume variances because the firm's plant utilization was at a level higher than the budgeted denominator capacity. The size of the

▶ **ILLUSTRATION 11-18**

BLOCK MANUFACTURING COMPANY
Selected T Account Balances
January 31, 19x2

Variable Manufacturing Overhead	Fixed Manufacturing Overhead
72,000	42,500

Applied Variable Overhead	Applied Fixed Overhead
70,400	45,000

variance may be obtained by (1) erecting a perpendicular line from the number of direct labor-hours worked to the applied overhead line and then drawing a horizontal line from that point to the left scale and (2) subtracting the budgeted fixed overhead from the dollar amount indicated by the scale.

Journal Entries and Overhead Variances

L.O. 8

The actual manufacturing overhead and applied manufacturing overhead accounts for the Block Manufacturing Company for the month of January 19x2 are shown in Illustration 11-18. These accounts are based on the data presented in Illustrations 11-9 and 11-15.

The actual and applied overhead accounts are *not normally* closed at the end of each month. Instead, they are carried forward, as they appear in Illustration 11-18, with additional amounts posted for each month until the end of the firm's fiscal year, at which time they are closed to Cost of Goods Sold. As discussed in Chapter 5, the manufacturing overhead application process smooths the effect of fluctuations in both factory overhead costs and production volume. If the over/underapplied manufacturing overhead balances were closed monthly, the smoothing benefit would be lost since each month's actual overhead costs would be closed to production, resulting in widely fluctuating monthly unit costs.

By not closing the over/underapplied manufacturing overhead each month, the over/underapplied manufacturing overhead may increase in one month but decrease in another month and will likely result in a small amount of over/underapplied manufacturing overhead to be closed by the year's end.

For the sake of demonstration, however, let us assume the Block Manufacturing Company wishes to close the accounts and record the variances at the end of January 19x2. The entries are:

(b)

Applied Variable Overhead	70,400	
Variable Overhead Efficiency Variance	1,760	
Variable Overhead Spending Variance		160
Variable Manufacturing Overhead		72,000

As per variance analysis in Illustrations 11-8 and 11-9.

(c)

Applied Fixed Overhead	45,000	
Fixed Overhead Spending Variance	500	
Fixed Overhead Volume Variance		3,000
Fixed Manufacturing Overhead		42,500

As per variance analysis in Illustration 11-15.

Presenting Variances on Income Statements for Managers

L.O. 9
Income statement for managerial use

Although these variances are usually closed to Cost of Goods Sold at the end of a firm's fiscal year, they are shown separately from cost of goods sold on income statements prepared for managerial use. For example, for the month of January 19x2, the Block Manufacturing Company's books and records reflect the following variances for direct materials and direct labor:

Direct materials price variance	$2,000 U
Direct materials quantity variance	800 U
Direct labor rate variance	1,000 U
Direct labor efficiency variance	4,000 U

The following items have also been recorded:

Sales (80,000 × $10)	$800,000
Standard cost of goods sold (80,000 × $5.4425) (see Illustration 11-12)	435,400
Marketing and administrative costs	180,000
Income taxes	80,000

An income statement for managerial use differs somewhat from one issued to stockholders and other external users. The statement for managers contains a section for standard cost of goods sold. The **standard cost of goods sold** is the number of units sold in an accounting period multiplied by the standard cost per unit. The managerial income statement also contains a **standard gross margin,** which is the sales revenue in an accounting period minus the standard cost of goods sold for the period. An income statement prepared for external use contains *only* the *actual* cost of goods sold and the *actual* gross margin.

The variances noted for direct materials and direct labor, together with the overhead variances shown in Illustrations 11-9 and 11-15, are deducted or added to adjust the standard cost of goods sold to actual cost of goods sold. The remainder of the income statement is prepared in the same format as that used for external reporting and discussed in Chapter 2.

The Block Manufacturing Company's income statement prepared for managerial use appears in Illustration 11-19.

The Treatment of Variances on Income Statements Prepared for External Use

L.O. 10

When income statements are prepared for external use, it is customary to combine all variances with cost of goods sold and show cost of goods sold as a single amount, net of variances. An exception to this approach may pertain to the fixed overhead volume variance. If this variance is due to a seasonal fluctuation that will probably be countered by a future variance, it may be carried forward on the balance sheet and not offset against cost of goods sold.

If the Block Manufacturing Company were to prepare an income statement for external use based on Illustration 11-19 and the volume variance is *not* due to a seasonal fluctuation, it might appear as shown in Illustration 11-20.

If the fixed overhead volume variance were due to a seasonal variation that is expected to be countered in subsequent months, cost of goods sold would be $3,000 higher and gross margin, operating income before income taxes, and net income would each be $3,000 lower. The balance sheet would reflect a *deferred credit* of $3,000 between liabilities and stockholders' equity.

▶ ILLUSTRATION 11-19

BLOCK MANUFACTURING COMPANY
Income Statement for Managerial Use
For the Month of January 19x2

Sales (80,000 at $10)		$800,000
Standard cost of goods sold		
(80,000 at $5.4425)		435,400
Standard gross margin		364,600
Less: Variances from standard cost:		
Direct materials price variance	$2,000 U	
Direct materials quantity variance	800 U	
Direct labor rate variance	1,000 U	
Direct labor efficiency variance	4,000 U	
Variable overhead spending variance	(160) F	
Variable overhead efficiency variance	1,760 U	
Fixed overhead spending variance	500 U	
Fixed overhead volume variance	(3,000) F	
Total variances from standard		6,900 U
Actual gross margin		357,700
Marketing and administrative costs		180,000
Operating income before income taxes		177,700
Provision for income taxes		80,000
Net income		$ 97,700

▶ ILLUSTRATION 11-20

BLOCK MANUFACTURING COMPANY
Income Statement
For the Month of January 19x2

Sales	$800,000
Cost of goods sold	442,300
Gross margin	357,700
Marketing and administrative costs	180,000
Operating income before income taxes	177,700
Provision for income taxes	80,000
Net income	$ 97,700

▶ STANDARD COSTING AND THE COST ACCOUNTING CYCLE

Appendix 11-A reviews the material covered in both chapters 10 and 11 by showing the journal entries used to record the standard costing of direct materials, direct labor, and manufacturing overhead.

▶ SELECTING A CAPACITY LEVEL FOR APPLYING OVERHEAD

To calculate the predetermined overhead rate, managers must normally select a capacity level. Depending on the objectives of their firm, they may choose an ideal capacity, a practical capacity, a normal capacity, or an expected capacity. The factors that influence management's decision when selecting a capacity level are discussed in Appendix 11-B.

▶ SUMMARY

A budget prepared for a single level of activity, a **static budget,** is useful for planning purposes but cannot usually be used for controlling operations because, in most cases, a firm will not actually operate at an exact planned level. For comparison and control purposes, the actual level of operations must be compared to a budget prepared for that specific level. Many firms, therefore, prepare a **flexible budget** consisting of a series of static budgets within the firm's relevant range. Other firms wait until the level of production is known and then prepare a flexible budget for that level.

A firm's **overhead application base** should reflect a strong cause-and-effect relationship with variable overhead cost behavior. Thus, for a labor-intensive firm, the base should be direct labor, preferably direct labor-hours; and for a machine-intensive firm, the base should be machine-hours.

Each *element* of variable overhead should be analyzed separately into **spending** and **efficiency variances.** The spending variance usually measures the changes in the prices of the costs classified as variable overhead. However, the variable overhead spending variance often includes a usage variance as well. Consequently, the spending variance is usually a combination of price and usage variances. The variable manufacturing overhead efficiency variance measures the variation in variable manufacturing overhead cost caused by the efficient or inefficient use of direct labor and/or machine hours. Analyzing *total* variable overhead variances would yield unreliable results because an unfavorable variance in one element, such as indirect labor, could be masked by a favorable variance in another element, such as maintenance.

Each element of fixed overhead should also be analyzed into two components, which are usually called the **spending (budget) variance** and the **volume (capacity) variance.** The volume variance measures the difference between a firm's budgeted plant capacity and its actual level of operations, and the spending variance measures the changes in the prices of the inputs classified as fixed overhead from the prices budgeted for these items.

Income statements prepared for management's use separately disclose each variance for direct materials, direct labor, variable overhead, and fixed overhead. When income statements are prepared for external use, these variances are not disclosed separately but are netted against cost of goods sold. The other principal difference is that an income statement prepared for a manager's use contains a section for **standard cost of goods sold** and **standard gross margin,** while an income statement for external use contains only actual cost of goods sold and actual gross margin.

▶ **APPENDIX 11-A**　**Standard Costing and the Cost Accounting Cycle**

To see how standard costing is reflected throughout the cost accounting cycle, let us assume the Mentor Company manufactures butcher block tables. Each table requires the following direct materials, direct labor, and overhead:

	Standard Quantity	Price (Rate)	Standard Cost
2″ clear maple.	12 bd. ft.	$1 per bd. ft.	$12
Direct labor.	2 hours	$9 per hour	18
Variable overhead.	2 hours	$2.50 per hour	5
Fixed overhead	2 hours	$2 per hour	4
Total.			$39

During January 19x2, the following transactions occurred:

1. Purchases of lumber amounted to $63,525. The price paid was $1.05 per board foot. There was no direct materials inventory at the beginning or end of the month. (The price variance is recorded at the time of purchase.)
2. The direct labor cost was $96,075. The hourly rate of pay was $9.15.
3. There was no work in process inventory on January 31, 19x2, and 5,000 tables were manufactured.
4. The actual overhead incurred amounted to:

> Variable $27,000
> Fixed 24,500

The budgeted capacity *for the year* is 72,000 units, or 144,000 direct labor-hours (72,000 units × 2 direct labor-hours = 144,000 direct labor-hours). The company's policy is to record all variances and close them to Cost of Goods Sold at the end of each month.

Sales for the month were 4,500 tables at a price of $100 per table. All sales are made on account.

The journal entries to record all transactions at the Mentor Company for January 19x2 would be:

19x2   (a)
Jan. 31 Direct Materials Inventory   60,500
         Materials Price Variance*   3,025
             Accounts Payable   63,525
             To record the purchase of direct materials—$63,525 ÷
             $1.05 = 60,500 bd. ft.—60,500 bd. ft. × $1 = $60,500
             standard cost.

* 60,500 bd. ft. × ($1.05 − $1) = $3,025.

                                          (b)
         Work in Process   60,000
         Materials Quantity Variance*   500
             Direct Materials Inventory   60,500
             To record the issuance of direct materials to
             production—5,000 units × 12 bd. ft. × $1 = $60,000
             total standard cost.

* (60,500 bd. ft. − 60,000 bd. ft.) × $1 = $500.

                                          (c)
         Work in Process   90,000
         Labor Rate Variance*   1,575
         Labor Efficiency Variance†   4,500
             Wages Payable   96,075
             To record monthly payroll—5,000 units × 2 hours ×
             $9 = $90,000 total standard cost.

* 10,500 direct labor-hours × ($9.15 − $9) = $1,575.
† $9 × (10,500 direct labor-hours − 10,000 direct labor-hours) = $4,500.

                                          (d)
         Work in Process   45,000
             Applied Overhead—Variable   25,000
             Applied Overhead—Fixed   20,000
             Variable—5,000 units × 2 hours × $2.50 =
             $25,000.
             Fixed—5,000 units × 2 hours × $2 = $20,000.

(e)

Manufacturing Overhead Control—Variable	27,000	
Manufacturing Overhead Control—Fixed	24,500	
Accounts Payable, Cash, etc..		51,500

    To record the actual overhead incurred.

(f)

Finished Goods.	195,000	
Work in Process		195,000

    To record completed goods—5,000 units × $39 = $195,000.

(g)

Accounts Receivable	450,000	
Sales Revenue		450,000

    To record sales—4,500 units × $100 = $450,000.

(h)

Cost of Goods Sold	175,500	
Finished Goods		175,500

    To record the cost of units sold at standard cost—4,500 units × $39 = $175,500.

(i)

Applied Overhead—Variable	25,000	
Variable Overhead Spending Variance*	750	
Variable Overhead Efficiency Variance†	1,250	
Manufacturing Overhead Control—Variable		27,000

    To record variances for variable overhead.

* $27,000 − (10,500 direct labor-hours × $2.50) = $750.

† (10,500 direct labor-hours − 10,000 direct labor-hours = 500 direct labor-hours) × $2.50 = $1,250.

(j)

Applied Overhead—Fixed	20,000	
Fixed Overhead Volume Variance*	4,000	
Fixed Overhead Spending Variance†	500	
Manufacturing Overhead Control—Fixed		24,500

    To record variances for fixed overhead.

* Monthly budget = $24,000 (72,000 units × 2 hours × $2 = $288,000 ÷ 12 months = $24,000). Budget − Applied overhead = $24,000 − $20,000 = $4,000.

† $24,500 actual − $24,000 budget = $500.

(k)

Cost of Goods Sold	16,100	
Materials Price Variance.		3,025
Materials Quantity Variance		500
Labor Rate Variance		1,575
Labor Efficiency Variance		4,500
Variable Overhead Spending Variance.		750
Variable Overhead Efficiency Variance		1,250
Fixed Overhead Volume Variance		4,000
Fixed Overhead Spending Variance		500

    To close variances to cost of goods sold.

The ending inventory of 500 tables is valued at the standard cost of $19,500 (500 units × $39). This is also the balance in the Finished Goods account, which may be computed by subtracting entry *(h)* from entry *(f)* ($195,000 − $175,500 = $19,500).

Selecting a Capacity Level for Applying Overhead

L.O. 11
Capacity levels

In Chapter 10, two levels of standards were discussed: ideal standards and practical standards. These levels also apply to the amount of activity that is used in calculating the predetermined fixed overhead rate. Two other activity levels are also used in practice. Thus, the four possible activity levels are (1) ideal capacity, (2) practical capacity, (3) normal capacity, and (4) expected capacity. In choosing one of these activity levels as the basis for applying overhead, managers must consider the objectives of their firm.

Ideal Capacity

As noted in Chapter 10, ideal standards are of limited usefulness. Because an **ideal capacity** level does not allow for machine breakdowns, rest periods, and personal needs, it is attainable in only the rarest circumstances. When ideal capacity is used to calculate predetermined overhead rates, the applied overhead will invariably be less than the actual overhead, and underapplied overhead will be common. This is a questionable control mechanism, because standard costs and budgeted costs will be less than they should be, and incorrect management decisions may result. To illustrate the problems that may arise, let us assume the Block Manufacturing Company's ideal capacity is 252,000 direct labor-hours and its estimated fixed overhead is $504,000. Its fixed predetermined overhead rate (POR) would therefore be:

$$\text{Predetermined fixed overhead rate} = \frac{\$504,000}{252,000 \text{ DLH}} = \$2 \text{ per DLH}$$

This rate should be compared with the previously computed rate of $2.25. At the $2 rate, each unit will have a cost of $.25 less than it should have, and if the firm actually operates at 224,000 direct labor-hours, an underapplied overhead of $56,000 will result. This can be seen in Illustration 11-21.

Because this base almost always produces an unfavorable volume variance, it is not often used. When used, it is with the understanding that an unfavorable volume variance is expected.

Practical Capacity

As noted in Chapter 10, practical standards allow for machine breakdowns, rest periods, and personal needs. **Practical capacity** is similar in that it is essentially ideal capacity minus an allowance for predictable interruptions. This capacity level presumes a firm can sell all of its output, although in reality few firms sell 100 percent of their practical-capacity production over long periods of time. In fact, most U.S. industries have some idle capacity at various phases of our business and economic cycles. This is especially true for firms in the steel, automobile, and farm machinery industries. When practical capacity is used to compute predetermined overhead rates, it is extremely likely that underapplied overhead will prevail during periods of idle capacity. Nevertheless, some firms find this level useful, because the underapplied overhead provides some indication that the plant is being underutilized.

▶ **ILLUSTRATION 11-21**

BLOCK MANUFACTURING COMPANY
Projected Results of Activity Levels
For the Year Ended December 31, 19x2

		$2.00 Rate	$2.25 Rate
Direct labor-hours worked	(a)	224,000	224,000
Overhead rate	(b)	$ 2.00	$ 2.25
Applied fixed overhead—(a) × (b)		$448,000	$504,000
Actual fixed overhead		504,000	504,000
Underapplied fixed overhead		$ 56,000	$ –0–

Normal Capacity

Manufacturing firms often use **normal capacity** in computing POR. It is the average number of units that a firm expects to sell annually over the course of a complete business cycle, usually three to six years. Normal capacity is superior to practical capacity because it *spreads idle-capacity fixed costs* over all units produced during the cycle. In contrast, when practical capacity is used, costs are charged to Cost of Goods Sold in the period they occur. To demonstrate, let us assume Block's expected and actual fixed costs are $504,000 per year, its practical capacity is 240,000 direct labor-hours, and its normal capacity is 224,000 direct labor-hours. Normal capacity is the average of the expected annual production for each year during a projected business cycle. Thus, at Block, the normal capacity of 224,000 direct labor-hours is based on an assumed three-year cycle of 224,000 direct labor-hours for 19x2, 240,000 direct labor-hours for 19x3, and 208,000 direct labor-hours for 19x4. The projected results of the two capacities are shown in Illustration 11-22.

The data indicate that:

1. The company operated at 100 percent of the practical capacity (240,000 direct labor-hours) in only one year, 19x3.
2. The amount of fixed overhead charged to production is $2.25 per unit when normal capacity is used and $2.10 per unit when practical capacity is used. Thus, if the practical-capacity cost of $2.10 is used for inventory valuation and pricing decisions, the cost per unit will be $.15 less than if normal capacity were used.
3. When the $2.25 fixed cost per unit is used, there is no underapplied overhead in 19x2, there is an overapplied overhead of $36,000 in 19x3, and there is an underapplied overhead of $36,000 in 19x4. For the three-year cycle, overapplied and underapplied overhead cancel each other, and *all overhead* for the three years is charged to production. Thus, at a cost of $2.25 per unit, the entire fixed overhead for the three years is averaged over all units produced during those three years.
4. When the $2.10 fixed cost per unit is used, there is an underapplied overhead of $33,600 in 19x2, none in 19x3, and an underapplied overhead of $67,200 in 19x4, for a total underapplied overhead of $100,800 for the three-year period. Each amount is charged off in the

▶ **ILLUSTRATION 11-22**

BLOCK MANUFACTURING COMPANY
Projected Results of Activity Levels
For the Years Ended December 31, 19x2, 19x3, and 19x4

Calculation of predetermined fixed overhead rate:

$$\text{Practical capacity rate} = \frac{\$504,000}{240,000 \text{ DLH}} = \$2.10 \text{ per DLH}$$

$$\text{Normal capacity rate} = \frac{\$504,000}{224,000 \text{ DLH}} = \$2.25 \text{ per DLH}$$

		Normal Capacity	Practical Capacity
19x2:			
Actual DLH worked	(a)	224,000	224,000
Overhead rate	(b)	$ 2.25	$ 2.10
Applied fixed overhead—(a) × (b)		$504,000	$470,400
Actual fixed overhead		504,000	504,000
Charged to cost of goods sold (underapplied overhead)		$ –0–	$ 33,600
19x3:			
Actual DLH worked	(c)	240,000	240,000
Overhead rate	(d)	$ 2.25	$ 2.10
Applied fixed overhead—(c) × (d)		$540,000	$504,000
Actual fixed overhead		504,000	504,000
Credited to cost of goods sold (overapplied overhead)		$ 36,000	$ –0–
19x4:			
Actual DLH worked	(e)	208,000	208,000
Overhead rate	(f)	$ 2.25	$ 2.10
Applied fixed overhead—(e) × (f)		$468,000	$436,800
Actual fixed overhead		504,000	504,000
Charged to cost of goods sold (underapplied overhead)		$ 36,000	$ 67,200

year it is incurred. Thus, these amounts are *not* applied to the units produced in the three-year period but are written off without being inventoried.

Because it is not economically feasible to reduce the firm's plant capacity below 240,000 direct labor-hours—the capacity is needed in some years—it is difficult to justify the concept of "wasted plant capacity," which is normally written off as a loss. Rather, the 240,000 direct labor-hours is needed capacity in some years and *benefits all years* within the complete business cycle. Thus, the cost of the benefit should be allocated to all years benefited—that is, the complete cycle. The normal capacity is the one that accomplishes this objective.

When normal capacity is used, the same predetermined rate is maintained for the duration of the business cycle unless there is a change in the factors used in its calculation. Therefore, unless the firm's fixed costs or anticipated direct labor-hours change, the same rate would remain in use until the business cycle is completed. Shortly before that time, a new predetermined rate would be computed using the best estimates available at that time.

Expected Capacity

Expected capacity is the level of activity at which a firm expects to operate for the coming year. Because this capacity is concerned with the coming year only, a new predetermined rate is computed for each year in a business cycle. Using the same data for the three years in Illustration 11-22, Block's predetermined rates using expected capacity would be:

$$19\text{x}2 = \frac{\$504{,}000}{224{,}000 \text{ DLH}} = \$2.25 \text{ per DLH}$$

$$19\text{x}3 = \frac{\$504{,}000}{240{,}000 \text{ DLH}} = \$2.10 \text{ per DLH}$$

$$19\text{x}4 = \frac{\$504{,}000}{208{,}000 \text{ DLH}} = \$2.42 \text{ per DLH}$$

When expected capacity is used, the objective is to assign a given year's fixed overhead only to the units produced in that year. No attempt is made to allocate idle-capacity fixed costs to any year other than the current one. The use of this method produces different inventoriable costs in each year of Block's three-year cycle even though each year's total fixed costs are the same. When the actual direct labor-hours in any year equal the anticipated direct labor-hours, there is no underapplied or overapplied overhead.

Many firms believe a change in unit costs should be made only when total costs change, and when there is no change in total costs, unit costs should not be changed. The use of expected capacity is not compatible with this view. In a sense, when expected capacity is used, part of a unit's cost is determined by the number of units produced even though there is no change in the total fixed overhead during the three-year cycle. That is, when 224,000 direct labor-hours are worked, inventory values include $2.25 per unit for fixed overhead; when 208,000 direct labor-hours are worked, inventory values include $2.42 per unit for fixed overhead; and when 240,000 direct labor-hours are worked, inventory values include $2.10 per unit for fixed overhead. Many managers find this objectionable.

▶ **GLOSSARY OF KEY TERMS**

Capacity level   The volume of activity, expressed in direct labor-hours, machine-hours, or units, that a firm is capable of producing. (p. 538)

Denominator activity   See **capacity level.** (p. 538)

Expected capacity*   The level of activity at which a firm expects to operate for the coming year. (p. 553)

Fixed overhead capacity variance   See **fixed overhead volume variance.** (p. 540)

Fixed overhead denominator variance   See **fixed overhead volume variance.** (p. 540)

Fixed overhead spending variance   The difference between the budgeted fixed overhead and the actual fixed overhead. (p. 540)

Fixed overhead volume variance   The difference between the budgeted fixed overhead and the applied fixed overhead. (p. 540)

Flexible budget   A series of static budgets for different levels of activity within a firm's relevant range. (p. 527)

---

* Denotes a glossary term from Appendix 11-B.

Ideal capacity* A theoretical level of activity that does not allow for machine breakdowns, rest periods, employees' personal needs, and the like. It is attainable only in the rarest circumstances. (p. 550)

Normal capacity* A level of activity consisting of the average number of units that a firm expects to sell annually over the course of a complete business cycle, usually three to six years. (p. 551)

Overhead application base A measure of activity, such as direct labor-hours or machine-hours, used in the calculation of a predetermined overhead rate. (p. 531)

Practical capacity* A level of activity that allows for machine breakdowns, rest periods, employees' personal needs, etc., and assumes a firm can sell all of the output it is capable of producing. (p. 550)

Production volume variance See **fixed overhead volume variance.** (p. 540)

Standard cost of goods sold The number of units sold in an accounting period multiplied by the standard cost per unit. (p. 545)

Standard gross margin Sales revenue in an accounting period minus the standard cost of goods sold for the period. (p. 545)

Static budget A budget prepared for a single level of activity. (p. 526)

Total standard variable overhead cost The standard hours allowed multiplied by the variable overhead rate. (p. 531)

Variable overhead efficiency variance The standard variable overhead rate per hour multiplied by the difference between the actual hours worked and the standard hours allowed. (p. 532)

Variable overhead spending variance The actual number of hours of activity used in production multiplied by the difference between the actual and the standard rates of variable overhead per hour. (p. 532)

Volume level See **capacity level.** (p. 538)

▶ **GLOSSARY OF SYNONYMS**

Denominator activity See **capacity level.**

Fixed overhead capacity variance See **fixed overhead volume variance.**

Fixed overhead denominator variance See **fixed overhead volume variance.**

Production volume variance See **fixed overhead volume variance.**

Volume level See **capacity level.**

▶ **REVIEW PROBLEM** **Calculation of Variances and Preparation of a Performance Report**

The Melon Company hired a new factory superintendent at the beginning of 19x2. Under the terms of their employment agreement, the superintendent is to receive a year-end bonus of 20 percent of his annual salary if his performance report for the year shows that costs under his control are equal to, or less than, the standard costs allowed for the year. The superintendent provides you with the following performance report to support his claim that he is entitled to receive the year-end bonus:

Activity	60,000 units	
	Budget	**Actual**
Sales.	$900,000	$900,000
Cost of goods sold at standard cost ($6)	360,000	360,000
Gross margin—standard cost	540,000	540,000
Total variance from standard cost—favorable	—	12,000
Gross margin—actual cost	540,000	552,000
Marketing and administrative costs	200,000	205,000
Operating income before income taxes.	340,000	347,000
Provision for income taxes	136,000	138,800
Net income	$204,000	$208,200

To evaluate the superintendent's claim, you are able to ascertain the following:

1. The company manufactures only one product, and its standard cost sheet consists of the following:

Direct materials, two pounds at $.10	$ .20
Direct labor, ¼ hour at $8 per hour	2.00
Variable overhead, ¼ hour at $6.80 per hour	1.70
Fixed overhead, ¼ hour at $8.40 per hour	2.10
Standard cost per unit	$6.00

2. The normal activity for applying overhead to production is 12,500 direct labor-hours.

3. Actual costs for the year are:

Direct materials, 130,000 pounds at $.11.	$ 14,300
Direct labor, 15,300 hours at $8.10	123,930
Variable overhead.	104,499
Fixed overhead	105,271

Required   *a.* Calculate the spending (price, rate) variances and efficiency (quantity) or volume variances for:

(1) Direct materials.
(2) Direct labor.
(3) Variable overhead.
(4) Fixed overhead.

b. Recast the performance report to the format used in the chapter, showing each of the variances you have calculated. Limit your report to costs only (i.e., exclude sales, gross margin, marketing and administrative costs, provision for income taxes, and net income).

c. Write a brief report to the president of the company, explaining your position regarding the superintendent's claim that he is entitled to the bonus.

▶ **SOLUTION TO**
REVIEW PROBLEM

a. (1) *Direct Materials Variances:*

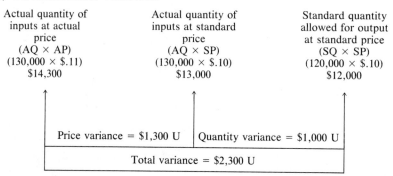

Actual quantity of inputs at actual price (AQ × AP) (130,000 × $.11) $14,300	Actual quantity of inputs at standard price (AQ × SP) (130,000 × $.10) $13,000	Standard quantity allowed for output at standard price (SQ × SP) (120,000 × $.10) $12,000

Price variance = $1,300 U | Quantity variance = $1,000 U

Total variance = $2,300 U

(2) *Direct Labor Variances:*

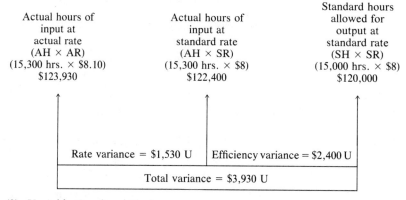

Actual hours of input at actual rate (AH × AR) (15,300 hrs. × $8.10) $123,930	Actual hours of input at standard rate (AH × SR) (15,300 hrs. × $8) $122,400	Standard hours allowed for output at standard rate (SH × SR) (15,000 hrs. × $8) $120,000

Rate variance = $1,530 U | Efficiency variance = $2,400 U

Total variance = $3,930 U

(3) *Variable Overhead Variances:*

Actual hours of input at actual rate (AH × AR) $104,499	Actual hours of input at standard rate (AH × SR) (15,300 hrs. × $6.80) $104,040	Standard hours allowed for output at standard rate (SH × SR) (15,000 hrs. × $6.80) $102,000

Spending variance = $459 U | Efficiency variance = $2,040 U

Total variance = $2,499 U

(4) *Fixed Overhead Variances:*

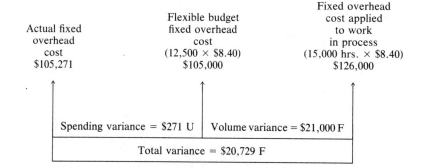

Actual fixed overhead cost $105,271	Flexible budget fixed overhead cost (12,500 × $8.40) $105,000	Fixed overhead cost applied to work in process (15,000 hrs. × $8.40) $126,000

Spending variance = $271 U | Volume variance = $21,000 F

Total variance = $20,729 F

b.

MELON COMPANY
Performance Report
For the Year Ended December 31, 19x2

	Cost per Unit	Budgeted for 60,000 Units	Actual for 60,000 Units	Total Variance	Price (Rate) Spending Variance	Quantity (Efficiency) Variance	Volume Variance
Direct materials	$ .20	$ 12,000	$ 14,300	$ 2,300 U	$1,300 U	$1,000 U	—
Direct labor	2.00	120,000	123,930	3,930 U	1,530 U	2,400 U	—
Variable overhead . . .	1.70	102,000	104,499	2,499 U	459 U	2,040 U	—
Fixed overhead	2.10	126,000	105,271	20,729 F	271 U	—	21,000 F
Total	$6.00	$360,000	$348,000	$12,000 F	$3,560 U	$5,440 U	$21,000 F

c. By all indications, the superintendent is not entitled to a year-end bonus. The bonus is an incentive that is contingent on his performance in keeping costs under his control equal to, or below, the standard allowed for the year. The recast performance report clearly shows that the superintendent did not keep the costs under his control below the standard allowed. The main fault of the superintendent's performance report is the application of fixed overhead based on the normal activity of 12,500 DLH when the actual hours worked were much higher. This results in a favorable volume variance offsetting all the other variances that proved to be unfavorable. The volume variance should not be used in determining the bonus as it is not under the superintendent's control.

▶ **LIBRARY ASSIGNMENT**

Read the following:

Carman-Stone, Marie Sandra. "Unabsorbed Overhead: What to Do When Contracts Are Canceled." *Management Accounting,* April 1987, pp. 55–57.

Chen, Kung H. "Impurity of Variable Factory Overhead Variances." *Journal of Accounting Education,* Spring 1985, pp. 189–196.

Cornick, Michael, William Cooper, and Susan Wilson. "How Do Companies Analyze Overhead?" *Management Accounting,* June 1988, pp. 41–43.

Martin, James R., and Eugene J. Laughlin. "A Graphic Approach to Variance Analysis Emphasizes Concepts Rather than Mechanics." *Issues in Accounting Education,* Fall 1988, pp. 351–364.

▶ **SELF-TEST**

True or False

1. For purposes of managerial control, the most meaningful review of actual results is to compare them to a static budget provided there is a change in the actual operating level of activity from the budgeted level of activity.

2. A flexible budget is a series of static budgets for different levels of operating activity.

3. The variable overhead spending variance principally consists of the differences between the actual prices and the budgeted prices of the variable overhead costs incurred, but it may also include quantity differences between actual and budgeted amounts.

4. The variable overhead efficiency variance is caused by the efficient or inefficient use of the overhead base, such as direct labor or machine-hours.

5. Fixed manufacturing overhead does not have an efficiency variance.

6. The fixed overhead spending variance occurs because the actual level of operations is different from the budgeted level of operations.
7. An unfavorable direct labor efficiency variance will always cause the variable overhead efficiency variance to be unfavorable.
8. The main reason for not closing the under/overapplied overhead to Cost of Goods Sold at the end of each month is the additional work involved in preparing the monthly entries.
9. Income statements prepared for internal (managerial) use and external use should contain a section for disclosing variances from standards costs.
10. The selection of an overhead base, or cost driver, for applying overhead to production should be a base (cost driver) that has a strong cause-and-effect relationship to the manufacturing overhead costs incurred.

Multiple Choice

King Company estimates that it will operate its manufacturing facilities at 800,000 direct labor-hours for the year. The estimate for total budgeted overhead is $2 million. The standard variable overhead rate is estimated to be $2 per direct labor-hour or $6 per unit. The actual data for the year are presented below:

Actual finished units	250,000
Actual direct labor-hours	764,000
Actual variable overhead	$1,610,000
Actual fixed overhead	$ 392,000

1. The variable overhead spending variance for the year is
   a. $2,000 F.
   b. $10,000 U.
   c. $82,000 U.
   d. $110,000 U.
   e. Some amount other than those shown above.
2. The variable overhead efficiency variance for the year is
   a. $28,000 U.
   b. $100,000 U.
   c. $110,000 U.
   d. Determined from information other than that given above.
   e. Some response other than those shown above.
3. The fixed overhead spending variance for the year is
   a. $8,000 F.
   b. $10,000 U.
   c. $17,000 U.
   d. $74,000 U.
   e. Some amount other than those shown above.
4. The fixed overhead volume variance for the year is
   a. $7,000 U.
   b. $25,000 U.
   c. $41,667 U.
   d. $18,000 F.
   e. Some amount other than those shown above.

(CMA Adapted)

▶ **QUESTIONS**

1. What is a static budget? Is it useful for planning? Controlling? Explain.
2. What is a flexible budget? Is it more useful than a static budget? Why?
3. How is a flexible budget prepared?
4. If you were given a static budget, the level of activity for the budget, and no other

information, would it be possible to prepare a flexible budget from the information given? Explain why or why not.

5. Is it important to use care in selecting the overhead base for applying overhead to production? Why?

6. What variances are computed for variable overhead? Explain what each one normally contains.

7. Should the variances for variable overhead be computed only for the total variable overhead? Why or why not?

8. Spending (rate) variances for direct labor consist of the difference between the actual and standard rates of pay per hour multiplied by the number of hours worked. Is the same always true for the spending variance for variable overhead? Explain.

9. Fixed costs are incurred in large indivisible amounts, and variable costs are incurred in proportion to the number of units produced. When applying overhead to production, is fixed overhead applied differently than variable overhead? Why?

10. What variances are computed for fixed overhead? What do the variances contain?

11. When preparing a performance report for fixed overhead, should separate variances be computed for each item? Why?

12. What is a denominator variance? Why is it referred to in this manner?

13. When a significant unfavorable volume variance exists after one or a few months of a firm's fiscal year, is it always cause for concern? Discuss.

14. How should variances be treated in interim income statements prepared for management's use? Would the treatment be different if the income statement were for a full 12 months? Why?

15. How should variances be treated in interim income statements prepared for external use? Does this treatment differ from that used for internal use? Why?

16. When a significant volume variance exists, how should it be treated in interim income statements prepared for external use? Would your answer be different for annual income statements prepared for external use? Discuss.

For Appendix 11-B

17. When computing a predetermined overhead rate, one of four different activity levels must be selected for the computation. What are the four levels? For each level, discuss the factors that may influence your selection of the activity level.

► **EXERCISES**   **E11–1**   **Flexible Budgeting**

1. A static budget
   a. Drops the current month or quarter and adds a future month or a future quarter as the current month or quarter is completed.
   b. Presents a statement of expectations for a period of time but does not present a firm commitment.
   c. Presents the plan for only one level of activity and does not adjust to changes in the level of activity.
   d. Presents the plan for a range of activity so that the plan can be adjusted for changes in activity levels.
   e. Divides the activities of individual responsibility centers into a series of packages that are ranked ordinally.

2. A flexible budget
   a. Classifies budget requests by activity and estimates the benefits arising from each activity.
   b. Presents a statement of expectations for a period of time but does not present a firm commitment.

c. Presents the plan for only one level of activity and does not adjust to changes in the level of activity.

d. Presents the plan for a range of activity so that the plan can be adjusted for changes in activity levels.

e. Divides the activities of individual responsibility centers into a series of packages that are ranked ordinally.

(CMA Adapted)

3. Dean Company is preparing a flexible budget for 19x2, and the following maximum-capacity estimates for Department M are available:

	At Maximum Capacity
Direct labor-hours	60,000
Variable factory overhead	$150,000
Fixed factory overhead	$240,000

Assume Dean's normal capacity is 80 percent of maximum capacity. What would be the total factory overhead rate, based on direct labor-hours, in a flexible budget at normal capacity?

a. $6.00.

b. $6.50.

c. $7.50.

d. $8.13.

(AICPA Adapted)

E11–2   Flexible Budgeting and Computation of the Differences between Actual Costs and the Flexible Budget

The Melcher Company produces farm equipment at several plants. The business is seasonal and cyclical in nature. The company has attempted to use budgeting for planning and controlling activities, but the variable nature of the business has caused some company officials to be skeptical about the usefulness of budgeting. The accountant for the Adrian plant has been using a system he calls "flexible budgeting" to help his plant management control operations.

The company president asks him to explain what the term means, how he applies the system at the Adrian plant, and how it can be applied to the company as a whole. The accountant presents the following data as part of his explanation:

Budget Data for 19x3

Normal monthly capacity of the
  plant in direct labor-hours . . . .   10,000 hours
Material costs (6 pounds at $1.50) . . . . $9 per unit
Labor costs (2 hours at $3) . . . . $6 per unit

Overhead estimate at normal monthly capacity:
  Variable (controllable):
    Indirect labor . . . . $ 6,650
    Indirect materials   600
    Repairs   750
      Total variable   8,000

  Fixed (noncontrollable):
    Depreciation   3,250
    Supervision   3,000
      Total fixed   6,250
        Total fixed and variable $14,250

Planned units for January 19x3   4,000
Planned units for February 19x3   6,000

Actual Data for January 19x3

Hours worked   8,400
Units produced   3,800

Costs incurred:
  Material (24,000 pounds) $36,000
  Direct labor   25,200
  Indirect labor   6,000
  Indirect materials   600
  Repairs   1,800
  Depreciation   3,250
  Supervision   3,000
    Total $75,850

Required   *a.* Prepare a budget for January.

b. Prepare a report for January comparing actual and budgeted costs for the actual activity for the month.

c. Can flexible budgeting be applied to the nonmanufacturing activities of the company? Explain your answer.

(AICPA Adapted)

E11–3   **Calculation of Predetermined Overhead Rate Using the High-Low Method, and How It May Be Used by Managers**

Tastee-Treat Company prepares, packages, and distributes six frozen vegetables in two different-size containers. The different vegetables and different sizes are prepared in large batches. The company employs an actual cost job order costing system. Manufacturing overhead is assigned to batches by a predetermined rate on the basis of direct labor-hours. The manufacturing overhead costs incurred by the company during two recent years (adjusted for changes using current prices and wage rates) are presented below:

	Year 1	Year 2
Direct labor-hours worked	2,760,000	2,160,000
Manufacturing overhead costs incurred (adjusted for changes in current prices and wage rates):		
Indirect labor	$11,040,000	$ 8,640,000
Employee benefits.	4,140,000	3,240,000
Supplies	2,760,000	2,160,000
Power	2,208,000	1,728,000
Heat and light	552,000	552,000
Supervision.	2,865,000	2,625,000
Depreciation	7,930,000	7,930,000
Property taxes and insurance	3,005,000	3,005,000
Total overhead costs	$34,500,000	$29,880,000

Required a. Tastee-Treat Company expects to operate at a 2.3 million direct labor-hour level of activity in 19x1. Using the data from two recent years, calculate the rate Tastee-Treat should employ to assign manufacturing overhead to its products.

b. Explain how the company can use the information it developed for calculating the overhead rate for:

(1) Evaluation of product-pricing decisions.

(2) Cost-control evaluation.

(3) Development of budgets.

(CMA Adapted)

E11–4   Preparation of a Flexible Budget for Overhead

The Aberle Company presents you with the following information:

	Activity Levels	
	60,000 DLH	**100,000 DLH**
Indirect materials	$ 13,800	$ 21,000
Indirect labor	39,000	57,000
Power	7,200	12,000
Repairs	17,000	27,000
Maintenance	12,800	18,000
Depreciation of factory equipment	20,000	20,000
Miscellaneous	26,000	38,000
Total	$135,800	$193,000

Required Prepare a flexible budget for activity levels of 70,000 direct labor-hours, 80,000 direct labor-hours, and 90,000 direct labor-hours. Segregate the budget into variable overhead and fixed overhead with subtotals for each. Label your first column *variable cost per unit.* (*Note:* Each item above may appear in both the variable and fixed categories.)

E11–5   **Preparation of a Flexible Budget from a Static Budget**

The Shelton Company presents you with the following budget:

Activity Level	40,000 DLH
Variable overhead:	
Indirect materials	$ 20,000
Indirect labor	9,200
Power	28,000
Repairs	6,000
Miscellaneous	16,800
Total	80,000
Fixed overhead:	
Indirect labor	20,000
Maintenance	12,000
Depreciation of factory equipment	25,000
Superintendence	12,000
Miscellaneous	8,000
Total	77,000
Total overhead	$157,000

Required   Prepare a flexible budget for activity levels of 50,000 direct labor-hours, 55,000 direct labor-hours, and 60,000 direct labor-hours. Label your first column *variable cost per unit*.

E11–6   **Comparison of Actual Data with Budgeted Data Prepared from Flexible Budget**

The Newton Company provides you with the following:

	Activity Levels	
	50,000 DLH	70,000 DLH
Indirect materials	$ 8,500	$ 11,900
Indirect labor	47,000	56,600
Power	27,000	37,800
Repairs and maintenance	29,500	36,500
Depreciation of factory equipment . . .	25,000	25,000
Factory rent	30,000	30,000
Miscellaneous	35,000	43,000
Total	$202,000	$240,800

Actual overhead for the period when 62,000 direct labor-hours were worked is:

Indirect materials	$ 11,780
Indirect labor	53,120
Power	34,100
Repairs and maintenance	30,440
Depreciation of factory equipment	25,000
Factory rent	30,000
Miscellaneous	37,320
Total	$221,760

Actual fixed overhead costs were the same as budgeted fixed overhead costs, except for the following:

1. A factory line supervisor left the employ of the company, and a replacement earns $1,500 less.
2. One maintenance employee was furloughed for two weeks. His salary for that period of time was $1,400.

Required   *a.* Prepare a budget for 62,000 direct labor-hours. Segregate the variable overhead from the fixed overhead and use subtotals for each category. (*Note:* Each item of overhead may appear in both categories.)

b. Alongside the budget for 62,000 direct labor-hours, insert the actual amounts, by category, and indicate the amounts of the differences (labeled *favorable* or *unfavorable*).

E11-7   Computation of Predetermined Overhead Rates and Preparation of Standard Costs from a Flexible Budget

The Rutan Company manufactures only one product and provides you with the following:

	Activity Levels	
	30,000 DLH	**50,000 DLH**
Mixed overhead.	$100,700	$142,900
Fixed overhead	91,200	91,200
Total.	$191,900	$234,100

The company's normal capacity is 40,000 direct labor-hours.

Each unit of product requires three pounds of Tigrin at a standard price of $.90 per pound and two hours of direct labor at a standard rate of $12 per hour.

Required   *a.* Compute predetermined overhead rates per direct labor-hour for variable overhead and fixed overhead.

b. Prepare a standard cost sheet for one unit of product.

E11-8   Preparation of a Flexible Budget for Overhead

The Hendrix Company presents you with the following information:

	Activity Levels	
	30,000 DLH	**40,000 DLH**
Indirect materials	$ 5,100	$ 5,900
Indirect labor	12,800	14,400
Power	7,200	9,600
Repairs	7,400	9,200
Maintenance	4,900	5,200
Depreciation of factory equipment	15,600	20,800
Miscellaneous	11,100	13,800
Total	$64,100	$78,900

Required   Prepare a flexible budget for activity levels of 32,000 direct labor-hours, 34,000 direct labor-hours, 36,000 direct labor-hours, and 38,000 direct labor-hours. Segregate the budget into variable overhead and fixed overhead with subtotals for each. Label your first column *variable cost per unit*. (*Note:* Each item above may appear in both the variable and fixed categories.)

E11–9 Preparation of a Flexible Budget from a Static Budget

The Brown Company presents you with the following budget:

Activity Level	30,000 DLH
Variable overhead:	
Indirect materials	$ 1,620
Indirect labor	10,500
Depreciation of factory equipment	14,400
Power	3,690
Repairs	5,580
Miscellaneous	6,600
Total variable	42,390
Fixed overhead:	
Indirect labor	20,000
Maintenance	12,000
Superintendence	25,000
Miscellaneous	10,000
Total fixed	67,000
Total overhead	$109,390

Required Prepare a flexible budget for activity levels of 32,000 direct labor-hours, 34,000 direct labor-hours, and 36,000 direct labor-hours. Label your first column *variable cost per unit*.

E11–10 Comparison of Actual Data with Budgeted Data Prepared from Flexible Budget

The Newton Company provides you with the following:

	Activity Levels	
	80,000 DLH	**110,000 DLH**
Indirect materials	$ 21,600	$ 29,700
Indirect labor	87,800	104,600
Power	57,600	79,200
Repairs and maintenance	57,600	70,200
Depreciation of factory equipment	35,700	35,700
Factory rent	40,000	40,000
Miscellaneous	93,900	114,000
Total	$394,200	$473,400

Actual overhead for the period when 94,000 direct labor-hours were worked is:

Indirect materials	$ 23,500
Indirect labor	92,605
Power	70,500
Repairs and maintenance	70,270
Depreciation of factory equipment	35,700
Factory rent	40,000
Miscellaneous	98,580
Total	$431,155

Actual fixed costs were the same as budgeted fixed costs, except for the following:

1. A factory line supervisor left the company's employ, and a replacement earns $725 more.

2. An independent repair consultant was hired at a fee of $1,150 to determine the cause of an unusual machine breakdown.

Required *a.* Prepare a budget for 94,000 direct labor-hours. Segregate the variable overhead from the fixed overhead and use subtotals for each category. (*Note:* Each item of overhead may appear in both categories.)

b. Alongside the budget for 94,000 direct labor-hours, insert the actual amounts, by category, and indicate the amounts of the differences (labeled *favorable* or *unfavorable*).

E11–11 Computation from Variances

The Lorton Company provides you with the following information for 19x3:

Total overhead—actual	$362,400
Budgeted overhead	$216,000 plus $1.20 per hour
Overhead application rate	$ 3.60 per hour
Variable spending variance	$ 7,200 U
Volume variance	$ 19,200 F
Fixed spending variance	None

Required *a.* Compute the actual hours worked.
b. Compute the standard hours allowed for good output.
c. Compute the variable efficiency variance.

E11–12 Computation and Analysis of Variances

The Fenton Company manufactures one product and provides you with the following information for the year 19x1:

Normal direct labor-hours	160,000
Standard fixed overhead rate	$ 6.50
Standard fixed overhead cost per unit	$13.00
Units manufactured—actual	96,000
Actual direct labor-hours	188,000
Actual overhead:	
Variable	$ 760,000
Fixed	$1,012,000
Total budgeted overhead	$1,680,000

Required *a.* Compute the variable overhead spending and efficiency variances.
b. Compute the fixed overhead spending and volume variances.
c. Indicate whether each variance is favorable or unfavorable.

E11–13 Computation and Analysis of Variances

The Menton Company manufactures one product and provides you with the following information for the year 19x2:

Normal direct labor-hours	150,000
Standard variable overhead rate	$4.80
Standard variable overhead cost per unit	$9.60
Units manufactured—actual	74,000
Actual direct labor-hours	146,000
Actual overhead:	
Variable	$ 715,000
Fixed	$ 608,000
Total budgeted overhead	$1,320,000

Required *a.* Compute the variable overhead spending and efficiency variances.
b. Compute the fixed overhead spending and volume variances.
c. Indicate whether each variance is favorable or unfavorable.

E11–14   **Computation of Data from Given Variances**

The Horlick Company provides you with the following information for the year 19x3:

Standard variable overhead rate	$4 per DLH
Actual variable overhead	$659,760
Actual fixed overhead	$496,920

	Favorable (F) Unfavorable (U)
Variances:	
Variable spending	$ 1,200 U
Variable efficiency	1,440 F
Fixed spending	7,920 U
Fixed volume	6,000 F

Required   Compute the following (*Hint:* Use the diagrammatic approach):

a. Standard hours allowed.
b. Actual direct labor-hours.
c. Fixed overhead rate.
d. Budgeted fixed overhead.
e. Normal activity in direct labor-hours.
f. Applied overhead to production.

E11–15   **Computation of Selected Data and Variances**

The Winter Company provides you with the following information for the year 19x4:

Standard combined overhead rate	$15 per DLH
Applied fixed overhead	$1,200,000
Standard hours allowed	120,000
Variable overhead efficiency variance . . .	$ 2,500 U
Actual variable overhead	$ 608,700
Budgeted fixed overhead	$1,250,000
Fixed overhead spending variance	$ 6,000 U

Required   Compute the following (*Hint:* Use the diagrammatic approach):

a. Standard fixed overhead rate.
b. Standard variable overhead rate.
c. Applied variable overhead.
d. Actual direct labor-hours.
e. Normal activity in direct labor-hours.
f. Variable overhead spending variance. (Indicate whether it is favorable or unfavorable.)
g. Actual fixed overhead.
h. Fixed overhead volume variance. (Indicate whether it is favorable or unfavorable.)

E11–16   **Computation of Variances for an X ray Lab**

X-Tra Careful X Ray Lab is an X-ray laboratory. The standard time for each set of X rays taken is ¼ hour of direct labor. For the year 19x4, the following information is available:

Normal direct labor-hours	6,000
Standard variable overhead rate	$3.00 per hour
Standard variable overhead cost per set	$0.75
Sets of X rays—actual	23,400
Actual direct labor-hours	5,950
Actual overhead:	
Variable	$20,000
Fixed	$74,000
Total budgeted overhead	$90,000

Required *a.* Compute the variable overhead spending and efficiency variances.

b. Compute the fixed overhead spending and volume variances.

c. Indicate whether each variance is favorable or unfavorable.

E11–17 Computation of Variances for a Word Processing Service

X-Pert Word Processing Company is a word processing service. The standard time for each double-spaced typewritten page is $1/12$ hour of direct labor. For the year 19x3, the following information is available:

Normal direct labor-hours	20,000
Standard variable overhead rate	$2.40 per hour
Standard variable overhead cost per page	$0.20
Pages typed—actual	236,400
Actual direct labor-hours	19,600
Actual overhead:	
Variable	$ 49,600
Fixed	$186,500
Total budgeted overhead	$228,000

Required *a.* Compute the variable overhead spending and efficiency variances.

b. Compute the fixed overhead spending and volume variances.

c. Indicate whether each variance is favorable or unfavorable.

▶ **PROBLEMS** **P11–18 Flexible Budgeting and Comparison Report**

The University of Boyne offers an extensive continuing education program in many cities throughout the state. For the convenience of its faculty and administrative staff and also to save costs, the university operates a motor pool. Prior to February, the motor pool had operated with 20 vehicles. However, an additional automobile was acquired in February this year, increasing the total to 21 vehicles. The motor pool furnishes gasoline, oil, and other supplies for the cars and hires one mechanic, who does routine maintenance and minor repairs. Major repairs are done at a nearby commercial garage. A supervisor manages the operations.

Each year, the supervisor prepares an operating budget for the motor pool. The budget informs university management of the funds needed to operate the pool. Depreciation on the automobiles is recorded in the budget to determine the costs per mile.

The schedule below presents the annual budget approved by the university. The actual costs for March are compared to one twelfth of the annual budget.

UNIVERSITY MOTOR POOL
Budget Report
For March 19x6

	Annual Budget	One-Month Budget	March Actual	Over* Under
Gasoline	$24,000	$2,000	$2,800	$800*
Oil, minor repairs, parts, and supplies	3,600	300	380	80*
Outside repairs	2,700	225	50	175
Insurance	6,000	500	525	25*
Salaries and benefits	30,000	2,500	2,500	—
Depreciation	26,400	2,200	2,310	110*
	$92,700	$7,725	$8,565	$840*
Total miles	600,000	50,000	63,000	
Cost per mile	$.1545	$.1545	$.1359	
Number of automobiles	20	20	21	

The annual budget was constructed on the following assumptions:

1. 20 automobiles in the pool.
2. 30,000 miles per year per automobile.
3. 15 miles per gallon per automobile.
4. $.60 per gallon of gas.
5. $.006 per mile for oil, minor repairs, parts, and supplies.
6. $135 per automobile in outside repairs.

The supervisor is unhappy with the monthly report comparing budget and actual costs for March. He claims it unfairly presents his performance for March. His previous employer used flexible budgeting to compare actual costs to budgeted amounts.

Required   *a.* Employing flexible-budgeting techniques, prepare a report showing budgeted amounts, actual costs, and monthly variation for March.
b. Explain briefly the basis of your budget figure for outside repairs.

(CMA Adapted)

P11–19   Flexible Budget and Performance Report with Analyzed Variances

The Martin Company provides you with the following information for the month of January 19x5:

	Activity Levels	
	120,000 DLH	**150,000 DLH**
Indirect materials	$ 17,700	$ 21,300
Indirect labor	41,000	45,500
Power	37,200	46,500
Repairs and maintenance	46,300	56,500
Depreciation of factory equipment	24,500	24,500
Factory rent	35,000	35,000
Miscellaneous	47,200	56,800
Total	$248,900	$286,100

Actual overhead for the period when 135,000 direct labor-hours were worked is:

	Variable	**Fixed**
Indirect materials.	$ 17,550	$ 3,425
Indirect labor	21,600	23,000
Power.	40,500	—
Repairs and maintenance	47,250	5,250
Depreciation of factory equipment	—	24,500
Factory rent	—	35,000
Miscellaneous	42,525	9,925
Total	$169,425	$101,100

The following additional information is available:

Normal activity	150,000 DLH per month
Units produced	67,000
Standard hours per unit	2

Required   *a.* Prepare a budget for 134,000 direct labor-hours. Segregate the variable overhead from the fixed overhead and use subtotals for each category. (*Note:* Each item of overhead may appear in both categories.)

b. Prepare a performance report for the month of January 19x5. Each item of overhead (both variable and fixed) should be analyzed into appropriate variances labeled *F* or *U* for favorable or unfavorable.

c. The total of all variances for variable overhead is substantially different from the total of all variances for fixed overhead. Explain why this is so. What reasons can you give for the significant volume variances?

P11–20 **Variance Analysis and Performance Report for Direct Materials, Direct Labor, and Manufacturing Overhead**

The Rotor Company manufactures one product and presents you with the following for 19x6:

Standard cost sheet:

Direct material (4 pounds at $3.40)	$ 13.60
Direct labor (5 hours at $11)	55.00
Variable overhead (5 hours at $7)	35.00
Fixed overhead (5 hours at $13)	65.00
Total	$168.60

The following information is also available:

Budgeted total overhead at normal activity	$6,000,000
Units produced.	55,000
Materials purchased and used in production (225,000 pounds at $3.35 per pound)	$ 753,750
Direct labor (270,000 hours at $11.15).	$3,010,500
Actual overhead:	
Variable.	$1,904,500
Fixed	$4,055,300

Required

a. Calculate all appropriate variances for direct materials, direct labor, variable overhead, and fixed overhead.

b. Prepare a performance report for the year, using the following column headings:

(1) Cost per unit.

(2) Budget for 55,000 units.

(3) Actual costs for 55,000 units.

(4) Total variance.

(5) Price (rate, spending) variance.

(6) Quantity (efficiency) variance.

(7) Volume variance.

c. For all variances shown in the performance report, indicate *F* for favorable variances and *U* for unfavorable variances.

P11–21 **Variance Analysis for Direct Materials, Direct Labor, and Overhead**

The Terry Company manufactures a commercial solvent used for industrial maintenance. This solvent is sold by the drum and generally has a stable selling price. Due to a decrease in demand for this product, Terry produced and sold 60,000 drums in December 19x6, which is 50 percent of normal capacity.

The following information is available regarding Terry's operations for the month of December 19x6:

1. Standard costs per drum of product manufactured were as follows:

Materials:

10 gallons of direct material	$20
1 empty drum	1
Total materials	$21

Direct labor:
1 hour $7
Factory overhead (fixed) per direct labor-hour $4
Factory overhead (variable) per direct labor-hour $6

2. Costs incurred during December 19x6 were as follows:

Direct materials	600,000 gallons purchased for $1,150,000
	700,000 gallons used
Empty drums	85,000 drums purchased for $85,000
	60,000 drums used
Direct labor	65,000 hours worked at a cost of $470,000

Factory overhead:
Depreciation of building and
machinery (fixed). $230,000
Supervision and indirect labor
(semivariable) 360,000
Other factory overhead
(variable) . . . . ____76,500
Total factory overhead $666,500

3. The fixed overhead budget for the December level of production was $275,000.
4. In November 19x6, at normal capacity of 120,000 drums, supervision and indirect labor costs were $680,000. All cost functions are linear.

Required Prepare a schedule computing the following variances for the month of December 19x6:

a. Materials price variance (computed at time of purchase).
b. Materials usage variance.
c. Labor rate variance.
d. Labor usage (efficiency) variance.
e. Factory overhead using a four-variance method. Each of the four variances should be appropriately titled.

Indicate whether each variance was favorable or unfavorable.

(AICPA Adapted)

P11–22 **Analysis of Overhead Variances**

The Jason plant of Cast Corporation has been in operation for 15 months. Jason employs a standard cost system for its manufacturing operations. During the first six months, performance was affected by the usual problems associated with a new operation. Since that time, the operations have been running smoothly. Unfortunately, however, the plant has not been able to produce profits on a consistent basis. As the production requirements to meet sales demand have increased, the profit performance has deteriorated.

The plant production manager commented at a staff meeting—in which the plant general manager, the corporate controller, and the corporate budget director were in attendance—that the changing production requirements make it more difficult to control manufacturing costs. She further noted that the budget for the plant, included in the company's annual profit plan, was not useful for judging the plant's performance because of the changes in the operating levels. The meeting resulted in a decision to prepare a report that would compare the plant's actual manufacturing cost performance with a budget of manufacturing cost based on actual direct labor-hours in the plant.

The plant production manager and the plant accountant studied the cost patterns for recent months and volume and cost data from other Cast plants. Then they prepared the following flexible budget schedule for a month with 200,000 planned production-hours, which at standard would result in 50,000 units of output. The corporate controller reviewed and approved the flexible budget.

	Amount	Per Direct Labor-Hour
Manufacturing costs:		
Variable:		
Indirect labor.	$160,000	$ .80
Supplies	26,000	.13
Power	14,000	.07
		$1.00
Fixed:		
Supervisory labor	64,000	
Heat and light	15,000	
Property taxes	5,000	
	$284,000	

The manufacturing cost reports prepared for the first three months after the flexible budget program was approved were pleasing to the plant production manager. They showed that manufacturing costs were in line with the flexible budget allowance. This was also reflected by the report prepared for November, which is presented below, when 50,500 units were manufactured. However, the plant was still not producing an adequate profit because the variances from standard costs were quite large.

JASON PLANT
Manufacturing Costs
November 19x9
(220,000 actual direct labor production-hours)

	Actual Costs	Allowed Costs	(Over) Under Budget
Variable:			
Indirect labor.	$177,000	$176,000	$(1,000)
Supplies	27,400	28,600	1,200
Power	16,000	15,400	(600)
Fixed:			
Supervisory labor	65,000	64,000	(1,000)
Heat and light	15,500	15,000	(500)
Property taxes	5,000	5,000	–0–
	$305,900	$304,000	$(1,900)

Required *a.* Explain the advantages of flexible budgeting over static budgeting for cost-control purposes.

b. Calculate the excess amount over standard spent on manufacturing cost items during November 19x9. Analyze this excess amount into those variances due to:
(1) Efficiency.
(2) Spending.

c. Explain what the management of Jason plant should do to reduce:
(1) The efficiency variance.
(2) The spending variance.

(CMA Adapted)

P11–23   Calculation of Variances and Preparation of a Performance Report

The Fenton Company hired a new factory superintendent at the beginning of 19x2. Under the terms of their employment agreement, the superintendent is to receive a year-end bonus of 20 percent of his annual salary if his performance report for the year shows that costs under his control are equal to, or less than, the standard costs allowed for the year. The superintendent provides you with the following performance report to support his claim that he is entitled to receive the year-end bonus:

Activity	75,000 units	
	Budget	**Actual**
Sales	$2,400,000	$2,400,000
Cost of goods sold at standard cost ($21.55)	1,616,250	1,616,250
Gross margin—standard cost	783,750	783,750
Total variance from standard cost—favorable	—	14,260
Gross margin—actual cost	783,750	798,010
Marketing and administrative costs	290,280	296,360
Operating income before income taxes	493,470	501,650
Provision for income taxes	197,390	200,660
Net income	$ 296,080	$ 300,990

To evaluate the superintendent's claim, you are able to ascertain the following:

1. The company manufactures only one product, and its standard cost sheet consists of the following:

Direct materials (3 pounds at $.15)	$ .45
Direct labor (½ hour at $14 per hour)	7.00
Variable overhead (½ hour at $12.80 per hour)	6.40
Fixed overhead (½ hour at $15.40 per hour)	7.70
Standard cost per unit	$21.55

2. The normal activity for applying overhead to production is 30,000 direct labor hours.
3. Actual costs for the year are:

Direct materials (235,000 pounds at $.18)	$ 42,300
Direct labor (37,800 hours at $14.25)	538,650
Variable overhead	484,998
Fixed overhead	536,042

Required   *a.* Calculate the spending (price, rate) variances and efficiency (quantity) or volume variances for:
(1) Direct materials.
(2) Direct labor.
(3) Variable overhead.
(4) Fixed overhead.

b. Recast the performance report to the format used in the chapter, showing each of the variances you have calculated. Limit your report to costs only (i.e., exclude sales, gross margin, marketing and administrative costs, provision for income taxes, and net income).

c. Write a brief report to the president of the company, explaining your position regarding the superintendent's claim that he is entitled to the bonus.

P11–24 **Calculation of Variances for a Service Business**

Webb & Company is engaged in the preparation of income tax returns for individuals. Webb uses the weighted-average method and actual costs for financial reporting purposes. However, for internal reporting, Webb uses a standard cost system. The standards, based on equivalent performance, have been established as follows:

Labor per return . . . . . . 5 hours at $20 per hour
Overhead per return . . . . . 5 hours at $10 per hour

For March 19x7 performance, budgeted overhead is $49,000 for the standard labor-hours allowed. The following additional information pertains to the month of March 19x7:

Inventory Data

Returns in process, March 1 (25% complete)	200
Returns started in March.	825
Returns in process, March 31 (80% complete)	125

Actual Cost Data

Returns in process March 1:	
Labor	$ 6,000
Overhead	2,500
Labor, March 1 to 31 (4,000 hours)	89,000
Overhead, March 1 to 31.	45,000

Required *a.* Using the weighted-average method, compute the following for each cost element:
    (1) Equivalent units of performance.
    (2) Actual cost per equivalent unit.
  b. Compute the actual cost of returns in process at March 31.
  c. Compute the standard cost per return.
  d. Prepare a schedule for internal reporting analyzing March performance, using the following variances and indicating whether these variances are favorable or unfavorable:
    (1) Total labor.
    (2) Labor rate.
    (3) Labor efficiency.
    (4) Total overhead.
    (5) Overhead volume.
    (6) Overhead budget.

(AICPA Adapted)

P11–25 **Calculation of Variances and Preparation of a Performance Report**

The Lotar Company hired a new factory superintendent at the beginning of 19x2. Under the terms of their employment agreement, the superintendent is to receive a year-end bonus of 20 percent of her annual salary if her performance report for the year shows that costs under her control are equal to, or less than, the standard costs allowed for the year. The superintendent was given the performance report shown below, and she believes something is wrong. She is sure that she was very careful in monitoring all costs under her control, and she believes her report should be favorable. She believes she should get the bonus, despite the unfavorable variance shown in the following report.

Activity . . . . **35,000 units**		
	Budget	**Actual**
Sales	$5,950,000	$5,950,000
Cost of goods sold at standard cost ($87)	3,045,000	3,045,000
Gross margin—standard cost	2,905,000	2,905,000
Total variance from standard cost—unfavorable	—	(12,452)
Gross margin—actual cost	2,905,000	2,892,548
Marketing and administrative costs.	806,950	894,050
Operating income before income taxes	2,098,050	1,998,498
Provision for income taxes	734,320	701,228
Net income	$1,363,730	$1,297,270

To evaluate the superintendent's claim, you are able to ascertain the following:

1. The company manufactures only one product, and its standard cost sheet consists of the following:

Direct materials (4 pounds at $.50)	$ 2.00
Direct labor (2 hours at $20 per hour)	40.00
Variable overhead (2 hours at $10.50 per hour)	21.00
Fixed overhead (2 hours at $12 per hour)	24.00
Standard cost per unit	$87.00

2. The normal activity for applying overhead to production is 100,000 direct labor-hours.

3. Actual costs for the year are:

Direct materials (139,700 pounds at $.47)	$ 65,659
Direct labor (68,500 hours at $19.55)	1,339,175
Variable overhead	714,084
Fixed overhead	938,534

Required *a.* Calculate the spending (price, rate) variances and efficiency (quantity) or volume variances for:

(1) Direct materials.

(2) Direct labor.

(3) Variable overhead.

(4) Fixed overhead.

b. Recast the performance report to the format used in the chapter, showing each variance you have calculated. Limit your report to costs only (i.e., exclude sales, gross margin, marketing and administrative costs, provision for income taxes, and net income).

c. Write a brief report to the president of the company, explaining your position regarding the superintendent's claim that she is entitled to the bonus.

P11–26 ## Computation of Variances—Direct Material, Direct Labor, and Overhead—Process Costing

Salter Division of Fleming Corporation specializes in the manufacturing of computer diskettes. The retail price of these floppy disks ranges from $3 to $140 each, and they are normally sold in boxes of 10. Salter Division has a single department production process and employs a standard process cost system.

Model B, a five-inch multipurpose diskette, is Salter's most popular product. More than 1 million units have been produced and sold in each of the past two years. Demand was expected to continue to increase in 19x4, and 100,000 units were scheduled for production each month.

The quantity, time, and cost standards in effect for the Model B diskette for 19x4 are given below. The direct material is added at the beginning of the process and conversion costs are incurred uniformly throughout the process.

Direct materials (2 oz./diskette at $8/lb)	$1.00
Direct labor (4 DLH/100 diskettes at $18/DLH)	.72
Variable overhead (150 percent of direct labor cost)	1.08
Standard variable cost per diskette	$2.80

The balance of Salter Division's Work in Process Inventory account at the beginning of each month is the standard cost of the incomplete equivalent units still in production. The actual costs incurred during the month for direct materials, direct labor, and variable overhead are entered into the Work in Process Inventory account. The completed units (finished goods) are transferred out at standard. The manufacturing variances are computed and closed out from the Work in Process Inventory account, leaving the account valued at standard for the start of the next month.

The following are data regarding the operations for November 19x4. The variances have not yet been closed out of the Work in Process Inventory account.

		Equivalent Units	
	Total Units	Direct Materials	Conversion Costs
Units completed			
From beginning inventory (40% complete)	14,600	—	8,760
Started and completed	91,800	91,800	91,800
Work in process, November 30 (70% complete)	11,200	11,200	7,840
Total	117,600	103,000	108,400

A summary of costs for November 19x4 is presented below.

Work in process, November 1—at standard	$ 25,112
Direct materials purchased and used—13,000 pounds	98,800
Direct labor—4,390 hours	76,825
Variable overhead	117,675
Total costs to account for	$318,412
Cost of units completed and transferred out—at standard (106,400 units)	297,920
Balance of Work in process, November 30—before closeout of variances	$ 20,492

Required   *a.* The manufacturing variances must be removed from Salter Division's Work in Process Inventory account so that the inventory account will be stated at standard as of November 30, 19x4.

       (1) Determine the standard cost of the Work in Process Inventory account at November 30, 19x4.

       (2) Identify and calculate the applicable direct material, direct labor, and variable overhead variances for November 19x4.

    b. Discuss the benefits of a standard process cost system.

(CMA Adapted)

P11–27   **Calculation of Variances**

Allglow Company is a cosmetics manufacturer specializing in stage makeup. The company's best-selling product is SkinKlear, a protective cream used under the stage makeup to protect the skin from frequent use of makeup. SkinKlear is packaged in three sizes—eight ounces, one pound, and three pounds—and regularly sells for $21 per pound. The standard cost per pound of SkinKlear, based on Allglow's normal monthly production of 8,000 pounds, is as follows.

Cost Item	Quantity	Standard Cost	Total Cost
Direct materials			
Cream base	9.0 oz.	$ .05/oz.	$ .45
Moisturizer	6.5 oz.	.10/oz.	.65
Fragrance	.5 oz.	1.00/oz.	.50
			$ 1.60
Direct labor*			
Mixing	.5 hr.	$4.00/hr.	$ 2.00
Compounding	1.0 hr.	5.00/hr.	5.00
			7.00
Variable overhead†	1.5 hr.	$2.10/hr.	3.15
Total standard cost per pound			$11.75

* Direct labor dollars include employee benefits.

† Applied on the basis of direct labor-hours.

Based on these standard costs, Allglow prepares monthly budgets. Presented below are the budgeted performance and the actual performance for May 19x6 when the company produced and sold 9,000 pounds of SkinKlear.

ALLGLOW COMPANY
Contribution Report for SkinKlear
For the Month of May 19x6

	Budget	Actual	Variance
Units	8,000	9,000	1,000 F
Revenue	$168,000	$180,000	$12,000 F
Direct material	12,800	16,200	3,400 U
Direct labor	56,000	62,500	6,500 U
Variable overhead	25,200	30,900	5,700 U
Total variable costs	94,000	109,600	15,600 U
Contribution margin	$ 74,000	$ 70,400	$ 3,600 U

Barbara Simmons, Allglow's president, was not pleased with these results; despite a sizable increase in the sales of SkinKlear, there was a decrease in the product's contribution to the overall profitability of the firm. Simmons has asked Allglow's cost accountant, Brian Jackson, to prepare a report that identifies the reasons that the contribution margin for SkinKlear has decreased. Jackson has gathered the following information to help in the preparation of the report:

May 19X6 Usage Report for SkinKlear

Cost Item	Quantity	Actual Cost
Direct materials		
Cream base	84,000 oz.	$ 4,200
Moisturizer	60,000 oz.	7,200
Fragrance	4,800 oz.	4,800
Direct labor		
Mixing	4,500 hr.	18,000
Compounding—manual	5,300 hr.	26,500
Compounding—mechanized	2,700 hr.	13,500
Compounding—idle	900 hr.	4,500
Variable overhead		30,900
Total variable cost		$109,600

While doing his research, Jackson discovered that the manufacturing department had mechanized one of the manual operations in the compounding process on an experimental basis. The mechanized operation replaced manual operations that represented 40 percent of the compounding process.

The workers' inexperience with the mechanized operation caused increased usage of both the cream base and the moisturizer; however, Jackson believed these inefficiencies would be negligible if mechanization became a permanent part of the process and the workers' skills improved. The idle time in compounding was traceable to the fact that fewer workers were required for the mechanized process. During this experimental period, the idle time was charged to direct labor rather than overhead. The excess workers could either be reassigned or laid off in the future. Jackson also was able to determine that all of the variable manufacturing overhead costs over standard could be traced directly to the mechanization process.

Required   *a.* Prepare an explanation of the $3,600 unfavorable variance between the budgeted and actual combination margin for SkinKlear during May 19x6 by calculating the following variances:
(1) Material price variance.
(2) Material quantity variance.
(3) Labor efficiency variance.
(4) Variable overhead efficiency variance.
(5) Variable overhead spending variance.
b. Allglow Company must decide whether or not the compounding operation in the SkinKlear manufacturing process that was mechanized on an experimental basis should continue to be mechanized. Calculate the variable cost savings that can be expected in the future from the mechanization. Explain your answer.

(CMA Adapted)

P11–28   (Appendix 11-A) Journal Entries for Recording Standard Costs and Variances
Use the information provided in Problem 11–23, and assume 75,000 units were sold at $32.

Required   *a.* Prepare summary journal entries to record all transactions during the year 19x6. Where needed, credit Wages Payable or Accounts Payable, and so on.
b. Prepare the entries to close the applied overhead accounts and set up overhead variances.
c. Prepare the closing entry(s) to close all variances at year-end.

P11–29   (Appendix 11-A) Journal Entries for Recording Standard Costs and Variances
The Dryer Company manufactures one product and presents you with the following for 19x6:

Standard cost sheet:
Direct material (2 pounds at $9)	$18
Direct labor (1 hour at $21)	21
Variable overhead (1 hour at $6)	6
Fixed overhead (1 hour at $18)	18
Total	$63

The following information is also available:

Budgeted total overhead at normal activity . . . . $ 864,000
Materials purchased and used in production (76,500 pounds at
 $8.85 per pound) . . . . $ 677,025
Direct labor (38,300 hours at $21.30) . . . . $ 815,790

Actual overhead:
 Variable . . . . $ 235,545
 Fixed . . . . $ 660,000
Sales (35,000 units at $150) $5,250,000
Units produced   38,000

Required
a. Prepare summary journal entries to record all transactions during the year 19x6. Where needed, credit Wages Payable or Accounts Payable, and so on.
b. Prepare the entries to close the applied overhead accounts and set up overhead variances.
c. Prepare the closing entry(s) to close all variances at year-end.

P11-30 **(Appendix 11-B) Preparation of Standard Costs Using Alternative Capacity Levels**

The standards committee of the Robert Company is in the process of preparing standards for a new product. All of the needed information is now available; however, there is a difference of opinion regarding which capacity level to use. Some members prefer the normal capacity, and other members prefer the expected capacity to compute the predetermined overhead rate used to apply overhead to production. You have been asked to help the committee reach a decision as to which capacity level to use.

The committee provides you with the following:

1. The estimated production for the ensuing business cycle is:

	Units
19x3	130,000
19x4	110,000
19x5	90,000

2. Estimates for materials, labor, and overhead are:

Direct materials	4 yards at $7 per yard
Direct labor	1 hour at $18 per hour
Variable overhead	1 hour at $14 per DLH
Fixed overhead	$660,000 per annum

3. The company uses direct labor-hours to apply overhead to production.
4. The company wishes to price the product to yield a profit before income taxes of 50 percent of cost, exclusive of marketing and administrative costs. The fixed costs of $660,000 are incremental costs and pertain entirely to the new product.

Required
a. Prepare a standard cost sheet using the normal-capacity level, and compute the selling price per unit at this level.
b. Prepare a standard cost sheet using the expected-capacity level for 19x3, and compute the selling price per unit at this level.
c. Draft a memorandum to the standards committee explaining the differences between (a) and (b). Indicate the advantages and disadvantages of each level and your preference for one level, if you have one.

P11–31   **(Appendix 11-B) Facility Capacities and Overhead Variances**

Nolton Products developed its overhead application rate from the current annual budget. The budget is based on an expected actual output of 720,000 units requiring 3,600,000 direct labor-hours (DLH). The company is able to schedule production uniformly throughout the year.

A total of 66,000 units requiring 315,000 DLH was produced during May. Actual overhead costs for May amounted to $375,000. The actual cost as compared to the annual budget and one twelfth of the annual budget are shown below.

| | Annual Budget | | | | Actual |
	Total Amount	Per Unit	Per DLH	Monthly Budget	Costs for May 19x3
Variable					
Indirect labor	$ 900,000	$1.25	$ .25	$ 75,000	$ 75,000
Supplies	1,224,000	1.70	.34	102,000	111,000
Fixed					
Supervision	648,000	.90	.18	54,000	51,000
Utilities	540,000	.75	.15	45,000	54,000
Depreciation	1,008,000	1.40	.28	84,000	84,000
Total	$4,320,000	$6.00	$1.20	$360,000	$375,000

Required   a. Define each of the following production facility capacity measures:
   (1) Theoretical capacity.
   (2) Practical capacity.
   (3) Normal capacity.
   (4) Expected actual or master budget level of activity.
   b. Calculate the following amounts for Nolton Products for May 19x3:
   (1) Absorbed overhead costs.
   (2) Variable overhead spending variance.
   (3) Fixed overhead spending variance.
   (4) Variable overhead efficiency variance.
   (5) Volume variance.

Be sure to identify each variance as favorable (F) or unfavorable (U).

(CMA Adapted)

▶ **CASE**   C11–32   **Calculation of Variances from Incomplete Data**

Your friend registered for a correspondence course in managerial accounting, and he is required to submit a completed solution to Lesson 15. However, in reviewing the information provided by the school for Lesson 15, your friend finds that he has misplaced one sheet of data for this lesson. If your friend writes to the school for the missing sheet, his answer will be delayed, and points are deducted for late answers to lessons. Knowing that you are studying managerial accounting in college, your friend asks you to assist him in solving the problem for Lesson 15.

The following information is available:

POLY COMPANY
Partial Trial Balance
January 31, 19x3

	Debits	Credits
Accounts payable		$335,050
Wages payable—direct labor		279,980
Manufacturing overhead control—variable	$102,000	
Manufacturing overhead control—fixed	206,000	

The company manufactures a solvent for use in its customers' manufacturing operations. The company's standard cost for one container of solvent is:

3 gallons of direct materials at $6 per gallon . . .	$18
1 hour of direct labor at $15 per hour	15
1 hour of overhead at $15 per hour	15
Total	$48

All of the company's accounts payable are paid currently, and the amount shown in the partial trial balance consists of one invoice for direct materials used in production in January 19x3. No other direct materials were used in January, and there were no direct materials inventories at the beginning or end of January 19x3. Wages are paid on the first day of the month following the period when the direct labor is incurred. All other salaries are paid on the last day of the month in which the salaries are incurred.

The company's purchasing agent had difficulty securing the direct materials from the normal source of supply. Consequently, the agent was forced to pay 10 percent more than the standard price per gallon.

On January 15, 19x3, the company signed a new labor agreement with the union for the company's employees. The employees were granted a 5 percent wage increase retroactive to January 1, 19x3. This wage increase is reflected in the January payroll but not in the standard cost per hour.

Your friend remembers two items from the missing sheet: (1) an unfavorable labor efficiency variance of $6,600 for the month of January and (2) the annual capacity of 240,000 containers per year.

The firm charges its customers a $25 deposit for each container, which is refunded when the containers are returned to the company. Thus, the reusable shipping containers are not included as part of the standard cost per unit because the containers are used again.

The standard cost per unit for overhead has a composition of one-third variable costs and two-thirds fixed costs.

Required   Your friend asks you to help him compute the following:

a. The labor rate variance.
b. The number of direct labor-hours worked.
c. The standard hours allowed.
d. The number of units produced.
e. The materials price variance.
f. The materials quantity variance.
g. The variable overhead spending variance.
h. The variable overhead efficiency variance.

i. The fixed overhead spending variance.

j. The fixed overhead volume (denominator) variance.

► **ETHICAL BEHAVIOR CASE**   C11–33   Tom Savin has recently been hired as a cost accountant by Offset Press Company, a privately held company that produces a line of offset printing presses and lithograph machines. During his first few months on the job, Savin discovered that Offset has been underapplying factory overhead to the Work in Process account, while overstating costs through the General and Administrative account. This practice has been going on since the start of the company, which is in its sixth year of operation. The effect in each year has been favorable, having a material impact on the company's tax position. No internal audit function exists at Offset, and the external auditors have not yet discovered the underapplied factory overhead.

Prior to the sixth-year audit, Savin had pointed out the practice and its effect to Mary Brown, the corporate controller, and had asked her to let him make the necessary adjustments. Brown directed him not to make the adjustments but to wait until the external auditors had completed their work and see what they uncovered.

The sixth-year audit has now been completed, and the external auditors have once more failed to discover the underapplication of factory overhead. Savin again asked Brown if he could make the required adjustments and was again told not to make them. Savin, however, believes that the adjustments should be made and that the external auditors should be informed of the situation.

Since there are no established policies at Offset Press Company for resolving ethical conflicts, Savin is considering following one of the three alternative courses of action listed below.

1. Follow Brown's directive and do nothing further.
2. Attempt to convince Brown to make the proper adjustments and to advise the external auditors of her actions.
3. Tell the audit committee of the board of directors about the problem and give them the appropriate accounting data.

Required   *a.* For each of the three alternative courses of action that Tom Savin is considering, explain whether or not the action is appropriate. Refer to specific standards of *Statements on Management Accounting Number 1C* (SMA 1C), "Standards of Ethical Conduct for Management Accountants," to support your answer.

b. Without prejudice to your answer in part *(a)*, assume that Savin again approaches Brown to make the necessary adjustments and is unsuccessful. Describe the steps that Savin should take in proceeding to resolve this situation. Use SMA 1C to support your answer.

(CMA Adapted)

► **ANSWERS TO SELF-TEST**

True or False

1. False	2. True	3. True	4. True	5. True	6. False
7. True	8. False	9. False	10. True		

Multiple Choice

1. *c.* $1,610,000 − (764,000 × $2) = $82,000 U
2. *a.* 764,000 hours − (250,000 × 3 hours) = 14,000 hours × $2 = $28,000 U
3. *a.* Total budgeted overhead of $2,000,000 ÷ 800,000 budgeted hours = POR of $2.50

Fixed overhead rate = $2.50 − variable rate of $2 = $.50/DLH.

Budgeted fixed overhead (800,000 × $.50) $400,000
Less: Actual fixed overhead   392,000
Fixed overhead spending variance . . . . $ 8,000 F

4. *b.* Budgeted hours.   800,000
        Standard hours (250,000 × 3)   750,000
        Unfavorable variance (in hours)   50,000

Volume variance = 50,000 hours × $.50 = $25,000 U

12

Variable-Costing and Contribution Approach to Segment Reporting

---

▶ **LEARNING OBJECTIVES**

After reading this chapter, you should be able to:

1. Differentiate between absorption costing and variable costing.
2. Explain why variable costing is superior to absorption costing for management decision making.
3. Prepare an income statement using the variable-costing approach.
4. Reconcile the difference in net income between absorption costing and variable costing when there is an inventory buildup or an inventory liquidation.
5. Prepare a segmented income statement using either absorption costing or variable costing.
6. Explain the difference between direct fixed costs and common fixed costs and how a direct fixed cost for a particular segment may become a common fixed cost when that segment is further disaggregated.
7. Discuss the problems associated with allocating common costs, including why segmented reports may lead to incorrect decision making.
8. Explain how segmented income statements are used.

Q. *Have you ever used a segment reporting system from the "bottom up" to prepare a firm's corporate report? If not, what method have you used? Have you had an occasion to disaggregate a division's income statement into segments, such as geographic areas? If so, how did you treat common corporate overhead, and how did you use the disaggregated data?*

A. At PepsiCo, I have had extensive experience working with a reporting system that generates segment reports from the "bottom up." These reports are prepared by each of our divisions and are then used to prepare the consolidated PepsiCo report. Since each division consists of a separate product line, these reports are extremely useful for decision making when evaluating the profitability of each division against its performance targets. The reports are also useful in comparing a division's performance against its competitors.

Common corporate overhead is not allocated to the divisions. PepsiCo's philosophy regarding this practice is that a division president should be held accountable only for costs directly incurred by that division. Charging a division with allocated corporate overhead that a division president is unable to control could create distortions when evaluating the financial performance of a particular division. Further, division presidents would resent being charged for a portion of corporate overhead over which they have no control.

On several occasions, it has been necessary to disaggregate a division's segmented report into geographic areas. Although one of our international divisions may be meeting its income plan, it is sometimes necessary to see how particular foreign operations are contributing to that division's overall profitability. Thus, disaggregating a division's operating results by geographic areas has pointed out opportunities for profit enhancement. Disaggregation of a division's operating results has been helpful when making decisions, such as whether to eliminate parts of a division, expand sales promotion activities, and alter cost-volume-profit strategies, and in detecting a portion of a division's operating results that may not be contributing a sufficient margin in accordance with our objectives.

▶ Traditional costing for external reporting purposes, known as **absorption costing** or *full costing,* is a method of assigning manufacturing costs to production so that *both* variable and fixed manufacturing costs are included in inventories and cost of goods sold. Although this type of costing is also required for income tax reporting, it is rarely relevant for managerial decision making and can lead to incorrect decisions. In contrast, **variable costing,** also known as **direct costing** or **marginal costing,** is a method of assigning manufacturing costs to production so that *only* variable manufacturing costs are included in inventories and cost of goods sold. Variable costing provides useful information for a variety of managerial decisions, such as:

1. Entering a new market.
2. Discontinuing a product.
3. Making or buying component parts.
4. Expanding or contracting production of an existing product.
5. Taking special orders at less than full cost.

Its data also enhance cost-volume-profit analysis. Because variable costing plays such a vital role in decision making, managers need to know how it differs from absorption costing and how it is used to prepare financial statements and reports.

Variable costing is also useful in the preparation of segmented reports. When a firm has multiple product lines and/or operates in different geographic territories, a companywide income statement may mask some serious problems. For example, the profits from a successful product may mask the losses from an unsuccessful product, or the profits from one geographic area may mask the losses of another. Segmented income statements that show profits and losses separately for each product or geographic location provide managers with the more detailed information they need to evaluate, monitor, and reach appropriate decisions about an individual segment's operations.

Segmented income statements should be prepared using variable costing. Absorption-costing income statements, prepared for each segment, may not provide managers with all the information they need.   ◀

▶ VARIABLE COSTING VERSUS ABSORPTION COSTING

L.O. 1

A business firm often faces a dilemma when making decisions about its record-keeping requirements. On the one hand, it may prefer to keep its records on an absorption-costing basis to generate the information needed for external reporting and income tax preparation. When this approach is used, however, the data generated by the firm's management information system will require conversion to the variable-costing approach before they will be useful to managers. On the other hand, if the firm decides to keep its records on a variable-costing basis so that managers can use its reports without adjustment, the variable-costing data will have to be converted to absorption costing when information is needed for external reporting or income tax preparation.

L.O. 2
Superiority of variable costing

In this author's opinion, the variable-costing method is preferable, because the need to convert variable cost data to absorption costing may occur only quarterly, when reports must be issued to stockholders. On the other hand, reports for managers are usually prepared monthly or, in many cases, weekly. Thus, based on frequency alone, it seems preferable for a firm to keep its books and records on a variable-costing basis.

Variable Costing—No Beginning or Ending Inventories

The term *direct costing* is firmly ingrained in accounting literature despite the fact that it is a misnomer. When used to mean variable costing, it is used incorrectly because some fixed costs are also direct costs. At the same time, variable overhead costs are not always direct costs to a product, yet variable overhead is included as a product cost when variable costing is used. In Chapter 2, we noted that a *direct cost* is any cost traceable to a single cost objective. Many fixed costs, in addition to variable costs, fall into this category. Despite this incongruity, accountants refer to variable costing as direct costing and are likely to continue this practice in the foreseeable future. Hence, managers should be familiar with both the correct terminology and the terminology used in everyday practice.

When variable costing is used, inventoriable costs consist of direct materials, direct labor, and *variable* manufacturing overhead. Fixed overhead is *not* inventoried; instead, it is charged to income as a period cost, as are marketing and administrative costs.

Variable costing may be used in conjunction with standard costing, as is the case for most large firms. Alternatively, it may also be used with normal costing—actual direct materials, actual direct labor, and estimated overhead.

To illustrate the concept, assume the Charles River Company manufactures one product and its variable manufacturing costs for the four years 19x2, 19x3, 19x4, and 19x5 are as follows:

Direct materials	$7.20
Direct labor	8.00
Variable overhead	3.80

For the year 19x2, we will assume the following:

Normal activity	20,000 units
Selling price per unit	$40 per unit
Salespersons' commissions	4 % of sales
Fixed marketing costs	$80,000
Administrative costs—all fixed	$100,000
Fixed manufacturing overhead	$100,000

To simplify our presentation, we will also assume that actual production equals 20,000 units (normal activity), sales are also 20,000 units, and there is no beginning or ending inventory of finished goods or work in process.

L.O. 3
Variable costing income statement

The data generated by variable costing can be easily incorporated into a contribution format income statement. A **contribution format income statement** is prepared for managerial use and is classified into fixed and variable cost categories instead of the functional categories of a traditional income statement. *Instead of including fixed manufacturing overhead in cost of goods manufactured, it is shown as a period cost* after *contribution margin.* The variable marketing costs (such as commissions) are shown *before* contribution margin but after variable cost of goods sold. This flow of costs may be diagramed as shown in Illustration 12-1. The Charles River Company's income statement using variable costing is presented in Illustration 12-2.

To illustrate the significance of variable costing, we will compare the results achieved by this method to the results achieved by absorption costing.

▲ ILLUSTRATION 12-1   Income and Cost Flow for Variable Costing

• Inventories are carried at only variable manufacturing cost.

CHARLES RIVER COMPANY
Contribution Format Income Statement
For the Year Ended December 31, 19x2

Sales (20,000 units × $40)		$800,000
Variable cost of goods sold:		
Beginning inventory, finished goods	$ –0–	
Direct materials (20,000 units × $7.20)	144,000	
Direct labor (20,000 units × $8)	160,000	
Variable manufacturing overhead (20,000 × $3.80)	76,000	
Variable cost of goods available	380,000	
Less: Ending inventory, finished goods	–0–	
Variable cost of goods sold		380,000
Variable cost manufacturing margin		420,000
Salespersons' commissions (4% × $800,000).		32,000
Contribution margin		388,000
Less: Fixed costs:		
Fixed manufacturing overhead.	100,000	
Fixed marketing costs	80,000	
Fixed administrative costs.	100,000	
Total fixed costs		280,000
Operating income before income taxes		$108,000

Absorption Costing—No Beginning or Ending Inventories

When absorption costing is used to prepare a traditional income statement, both fixed and variable manufacturing costs are included in the cost of goods manufactured. The cost and income flows for absorption costing may be diagramed as shown in Illustration 12-3.

To contrast the preparation of variable-costing statements with absorption-costing statements, the data from Illustration 12-2 were used to prepare the income statement using absorption costing shown in Illustration 12-4.

A comparison of Illustrations 12-2 and 12-4 discloses that:

1. The operating income of $108,000 is the same for both variable costing and absorption costing.
2. The cost of goods manufactured differs by $100,000, the amount of the fixed manufacturing overhead.
3. The variable salespersons' commissions are deducted from the variable cost manufacturing margin in Illustration 12-2 to arrive at the contribution margin; while in Illustration 12-4, the commissions are deducted as a period cost, *after* the gross margin is derived.
4. The fixed manufacturing overhead is shown as a period cost when variable costing is used (see Illustration 12-2), and the fixed manufacturing overhead is shown as a manufacturing cost when absorption costing is used (see Illustration 12-4).

Although the operating income is the same in both illustrations, this is not always the case. This occurred because Charles River's beginning and ending finished goods inventories for 19x2 were identical. Whenever there is a difference between a firm's beginning and ending finished goods inventories (which reflects the difference between the number of units produced and the

▲ ILLUSTRATION 12-3   Income and Cost Flow for Absorption Costing

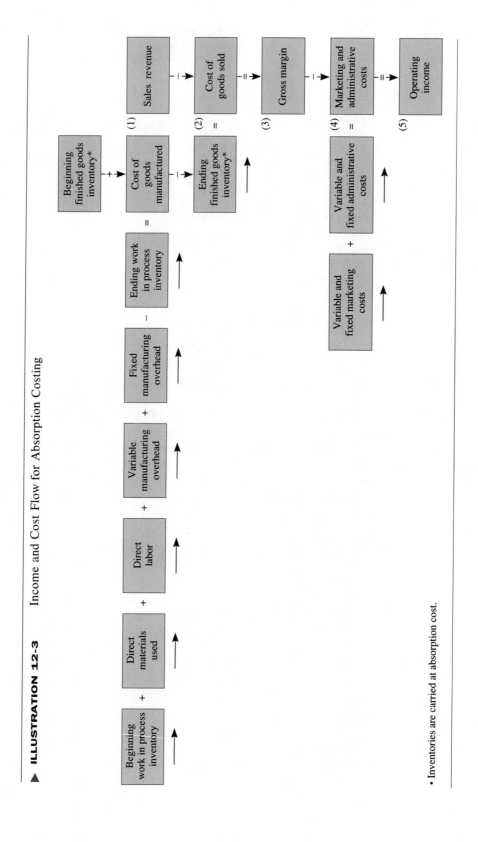

• Inventories are carried at absorption cost.

▶ **ILLUSTRATION 12-4**

CHARLES RIVER COMPANY
Income Statement Using Absorption Costing
For the Year Ended December 31, 19x2

Sales (20,000 units × $40)		$800,000
Cost of goods sold:		
Beginning inventory, finished goods	$ –0–	
Direct materials (20,000 units × $7.20)	144,000	
Direct labor (20,000 units × $8)	160,000	
Variable manufacturing overhead (20,000 × $3.80)	76,000	
Fixed manufacturing overhead	100,000	
Cost of goods available	480,000	
Less: Ending inventory, finished goods	–0–	
Cost of goods sold		480,000
Gross margin		320,000
Marketing and administrative costs:		
Marketing costs	112,000*	
Administrative costs	100,000	212,000
Operating income before income taxes		$108,000

* Variable + Fixed = $32,000 + $80,000 = $112,000.

number sold), variable and absorption costing will produce different net incomes. This case is now considered.

Variable Costing versus Absorption Costing—Beginning and Ending Inventories of Finished Goods

Inventory buildup occurs when a firm's ending inventory is greater than its beginning inventory for any accounting period. The reverse condition, **inventory liquidation,** occurs when a firm's ending inventory is less than its beginning inventory for any accounting period. Under either condition, the net incomes produced by variable costing and absorption costing will differ by the amount of fixed overhead included in the inventories of the absorption-costing income statement.

Let us expand the information for the Charles River Company to include the following:

	19x3	19x4	19x5
Beginning inventory in units . . .	–0–	10,000	10,000
Units manufactured*	20,000	30,000	10,000
Available for sale	20,000	40,000	20,000
Ending inventory in units	10,000	10,000	–0–
Units sold	10,000	30,000	20,000

* The normal activity is assumed to be 20,000 units (20,000 + 30,000 + 10,000 = 60,000 ÷ 3 years = 20,000 units. See Chapter 5 for a discussion of normal activity).

The income statements for the three years using variable costing appear in Illustration 12-5, while the income statements using absorption costing appear in Illustration 12-6.

CHARLES RIVER COMPANY
Income Statements Using Variable Costing
For the Years Ended December 31

	19x3	19x4	19x5
Sales (10,000 units, 30,000 units, and 20,000 units at $40)	$400,000	$1,200,000	$800,000
Variable cost of goods sold:			
Beginning inventory, finished goods	–0–	190,000	190,000
Direct materials (20,000 units, 30,000 units, and 10,000 units at $7.20).	144,000	216,000	72,000
Direct labor (at $8)	160,000	240,000	80,000
Variable overhead (at $3.80)	76,000	114,000	38,000
Cost of goods available	380,000	760,000	380,000
Less: Ending finished goods inventory (10,000 units, 10,000 units, and 0 units at $19)	190,000	190,000	–0–
Variable cost of goods sold.	190,000	570,000	380,000
Variable cost manufacturing margin	210,000	630,000	420,000
Salespersons' commissions (4% of sales).	16,000	48,000	32,000
Contribution margin	194,000	582,000	388,000
Less: Fixed costs:			
Fixed manufacturing overhead	100,000	100,000	100,000
Fixed marketing costs	80,000	80,000	80,000
Fixed administrative costs	100,000	100,000	100,000
Total fixed costs	280,000	280,000	280,000
Operating income (loss) before income taxes	$ (86,000)	$ 302,000	$108,000

CHARLES RIVER COMPANY
Income Statements Using Absorption Costing
For the Years Ended December 31

	19x3	19x4	19x5
Sales (10,000 units, 30,000 units, and 20,000 units at $40)	$400,000	$1,200,000	$800,000
Cost of goods sold:			
Beginning inventory, finished goods	–0–	240,000	240,000
Direct materials (20,000 units, 30,000 units, and 10,000 units at $7.20)	144,000	216,000	72,000
Direct labor (at $8)	160,000	240,000	80,000
Variable overhead (at $3.80)	76,000	114,000	38,000
Fixed overhead (at $5)	100,000	150,000	50,000
Cost of goods available—*at normal cost*	480,000	960,000	480,000
Less: Ending finished goods inventory (10,000 units, 10,000 units, and 0 units at $24)	240,000	240,000	–0–
Cost of goods sold—*at normal cost*	240,000	720,000	480,000
Add (deduct) under/overapplied manufacturing fixed overhead	–0–	(50,000)	50,000
Cost of goods sold—*at actual cost*	240,000	670,000	530,000
Gross margin—*at actual cost*.	160,000	530,000	270,000
Marketing and administrative costs:			
Marketing costs*	96,000	128,000	112,000
Administrative costs	100,000	100,000	100,000
Total marketing and administrative costs	196,000	228,000	212,000
Operating income (loss) before income taxes	$ (36,000)	$ 302,000	$ 58,000

* $80,000 + 4% of sales.

In comparing Illustrations 12-5 and 12-6, note that:

1. Sales in units, gross margin, and contribution margin for the three years are tabulated as follows:

Year	Sales in Units	Gross Margin		Contribution Margin	
		Total	**Per Unit**	**Total**	**Per Unit**
19x3	10,000	$160,000	$16.00	$194,000	$19.40
19x4	30,000	530,000	17.67	582,000	19.40
19x5	20,000	270,000	13.50	388,000	19.40

When there is no change in selling price and costs, a manager can expect profit margin to be a function of units sold. Contribution margin meets this objective, as can be seen from the following:

Year	Sales in Units	Contribution Margin
19x3	10,000	$194,000
19x4	3 × 10,000 = 30,000	3 × $194,000 = $582,000
19x5	2 × 10,000 = 20,000	2 × $194,000 = $388,000

The same analysis is not true for gross margin. This can be observed from the following:

Year	Sales in Units	Projected Gross Margin Based on Linear Relationship	Actual Gross Margin	Difference More (Less)
19x3 . . .	10,000	$160,000	$160,000	$ –0–
19x4 . . .	3 × 10,000	3 × $160,000 = $480,000	530,000	50,000
19x5 . . .	2 × 10,000	2 × $160,000 = $320,000	270,000	(50,000)

Thus, when a firm's information system uses absorption costing, the reports generated must first be converted to variable costing for use in CVP analysis, as discussed in Chapter 4. Also, information based on absorption costing may lead to wrong conclusions when used in the decision-making situations noted at the beginning of this chapter. For example, consider the following results of operations for the Hudson Manufacturing Company for the year 19x3:

HUDSON MANUFACTURING COMPANY
Income Statement Using Absorption Costing
For the Year Ended December 31, 19x3

Sales (50,000 units at $10)	$500,000
Cost of goods sold (50,000 at $6)	300,000
Gross margin	200,000
Marketing and administrative costs—all fixed	160,000
Operating income	$ 40,000

The cost of goods sold includes $4 of variable costs and $2 of fixed costs per unit. For 19x4, the company expects sales volume to decrease by 20 percent and all cost-behavior patterns to remain unchanged. Given the forecasted falling demand for their product, Hudson Manufacturing's board of directors has announced that unless the company will operate at the breakeven point or at a profit in the coming year, they will cease operations. Accurate CVP analysis is thus important. Using the absorption-costing data as submitted, a manager might compute the reduction in profit as 20 percent multiplied by the gross margin of $200,000, or $40,000. This indicates the company would reach its breakeven point and operations should continue.

Such an analysis is faulty, however, because it assumes a 20 percent reduction in fixed overhead, which is at odds with the given information. The correct analysis would be an expected loss of $20,000. This amount may be readily obtained from an income statement prepared using the contribution margin format, as follows:

HUDSON MANUFACTURING COMPANY
Income Statement Using the Contribution Margin Format
For the Year Ended December 31, 19x3

Sales (50,000 at $10)		$500,000
Variable cost of goods sold (50,000 at $4)		200,000
Contribution margin.		300,000
Marketing and administrative costs—all fixed . . .	$160,000	
Fixed overhead.	100,000	
Total fixed costs		260,000
Operating income.		$ 40,000

To consider the effect of the anticipated decrease in sales, a manager would multiply the contribution margin by the expected 20 percent decline. The resulting $60,000 reduction in operating income (.20 × $300,000) would produce a loss of $20,000, indicating the firm should cease operations under the given conditions.

L.O. 4
Reconciliation of the difference in net income using variable costing versus absorption costing

2. The differences in operating incomes for the three years may be analyzed as follows:

Year	Operating Income (Loss)		Difference VC Higher (AC Higher)
	Variable Costing	**Absorption Costing**	
19x3	$ (86,000)	$ (36,000)	$(50,000)
19x4	302,000	302,000	–0–
19x5	108,000	58,000	50,000
Total for three years	$324,000	$324,000	$ –0–

For 19x3, 20,000 units were manufactured and only 10,000 units were sold, resulting in an *inventory buildup* of 10,000 units. Thus, at a standard fixed overhead cost of $5 per unit, the difference between variable costing and absorption costing amounts to $50,000 for the year. When there is an inventory buildup, absorption costing produces a higher operating income because the fixed overhead in the closing inventory (10,000 units × $5 per unit, or $50,000) is deferred and shifted into the next accounting period as part of that beginning inventory. This can be seen by looking at the closing inventories for 19x3 in Illustrations 12-5 and 12-6 (AC = $240,000 and VC = $190,000), which become the opening inventories for 19x4. Thus, for absorption costing, an extra $50,000 of inventory valuation is shifted to 19x4 and becomes part of cost of goods sold in that year.

For 19x4, there is no inventory buildup or liquidation—that is, the beginning and ending inventories are the same. Hence, there is no difference in the operating incomes of $302,000 shown in the two income statements.

For 19x5, there is an *inventory liquidation* of 10,000 units, so at a normal fixed overhead cost of $5 per unit, the difference between variable-costing and absorption-costing amounts to $50,000 for the year. When there is an inventory liquidation, variable costing produces the higher operating income.

3. For the three years together, there is neither inventory buildup nor inventory liquidation, because the beginning inventory for 19x3 and the ending inventory for 19x5 are both zero. Consequently, it is not surprising that the total operating income for the three-year period, $324,000, is the same for both methods.

If a firm wishes to prepare its income statement using one method (either variable or absorption costing) but also wishes to determine its operating income under the other method, it does not need to prepare a second income statement. Instead, it can compute the operating income using the following generalized formulas:

1. Inventory Buildup (Absorption-Costing Income Is Higher)

Inventory buildup = Number of units in ending inventory
− Number of units in beginning inventory

ACOI = VCOI + (Inventory buildup × Fixed overhead per unit) **(1)**[1]

or

VCOI = ACOI − (Inventory buildup × Fixed overhead per unit) **(2)**

where

ACOI = Absorption-costing operating income
VCOI = Variable-costing operating income

2. Inventory Liquidation (Variable-Costing Income Is Higher)

Inventory liquidation = Number of units in beginning inventory
− Number of units in ending inventory

ACOI = VCOI − (Inventory liquidation × Fixed overhead per unit)

(3)

---

[1] Equations 1, 2, 3, and 4 can be used only with standard or normal costing. When actual costing is used, the fixed overhead per unit will usually fluctuate between the beginning and ending inventories, so each unit cost would have to be considered separately.

or

$$VCOI = ACOI + (\text{Inventory liquidation} \times \text{Fixed overhead per unit})$$
(4)

For 19x3, the Charles River Company's operating income using variable costing is a *loss* of $86,000 (see Illustration 12-5). Instead of preparing an income statement as shown in Illustration 12-6, a manager could compute the firm's operating income under absorption costing by using equation 1, as follows:

$$ACOI = \$(86,000) + (10,000 \text{ units} \times \$5 \text{ per unit})$$
$$ACOI = \$(86,000) + \$50,000$$
$$ACOI = \$(36,000)$$

When there is an inventory liquidation as in 19x5, the Charles River Company could use Equation 3 to compute its ACOI from Illustration 12-5, as follows:

$$ACOI = \$108,000 - (10,000 \text{ units} \times \$5 \text{ per unit})$$
$$ACOI = \$108,000 - \$50,000$$
$$ACOI = \$58,000$$

▶ Summary of Inventory Relationships

If Sales = Production, Income under absorption = Income under variable (year 19x4) if Production > Sales, Income under absorption > Income under variable (year 19x3) (*Note:* Loss is less is the same as income is greater.) If Production < Sales, Income under absorption < Income than variable (year 19x5).

The reconciliation of incomes may be computed as follows:

Absorption income	$ XX
+ Fixed overhead in beginning inventory	XX
− Fixed overhead in ending inventory	(XX)
Variable Income	$ XX
Variable income	$ XX
− Fixed overhead in beginning inventory	(XX)
+ Fixed overhead in ending inventory	XX
Absorption Income	$ XX

There is considerable controversy regarding the difference in net income between absorption costing and variable costing. Some accountants believe variable costing should be accepted for external reporting and income tax purposes in addition to being used for internal reporting. But the Internal Revenue Service, with rare exceptions, offers no hope for its acceptance in the near future, and independent auditors doubt that change is likely. Thus, despite its limited use in decision making, managers should understand absorption costing because of its importance in financial reporting to shareholders and its effect on the amount of income tax that a firm pays.

Management accounting should be based on the information that will be most useful to managers, and in such cases, variable costing is clearly superior. When a firm keeps its books and records on this basis, it can open T accounts like the following to convert its books for external reporting and income tax preparation:

Fixed Overhead in Inventory	Income Summary
19x3 *(a)* 50,000	19x3 *(a)* 50,000

Each year, the Fixed Overhead in Inventory account is adjusted in accordance with the generalized formulas for inventory buildup or inventory liquidation. When a firm has both finished goods and work in process inventories, it is customary to use separate T accounts for each.

▶ **PROGRESS CHECK**

1. Are variable-costing statements sometimes more useful than absorption-costing statements? If so, under what circumstances is this the case?
2. Is there a difference in the format of variable-costing statements and absorption-costing statements? If so, describe the difference.
3. What can be said about the difference in net income between a variable-costing statement and an absorption-costing statement when there are no beginning or ending inventories? Why is this the case?
4. What can be said about the difference in net income between a variable-costing statement and an absorption-costing statement when the year's sales and the year's production are the same? Why is this the case?
5. If you are given an income statement prepared using the variable-costing approach, is it possible to compute the absorption-costing net income without preparing a complete income statement? If so, how can this be done?
6. If there is inventory buildup in any year, will variable-costing net income be higher than absorption-costing net income? Explain. ◀

▶ **SEGMENT REPORTING**

A companywide income statement does not provide individual managers with the information they need to effectively plan, coordinate, and control their operations because it merely indicates whether the company as a whole showed a profit or a loss during an accounting period. It does not indicate which product lines, sales territories, and divisions contributed profits or losses to the firm's overall operations. It is quite conceivable that a particular product, division, or sales territory may be suffering an undetected loss that is masked by the profits of another product, division, or territory. To ferret out the needed information, it is necessary to use a **segmented reporting system** that breaks the companywide income statement into segments starting with the largest sections, such as divisions, and continuing with smaller and smaller units, such as product lines and then particular products. Two possible methods of segmentation are diagramed in Illustrations 12-7 and 12-8. The configurations and degrees of segmentation vary among firms and are based on managers' needs for specific kinds of information. Examples are product-line, geographic, and functional segmentation and combinations of these.

▶ **ILLUSTRATION 12-7**   Analysis of Income Statement Data into Segments Based on Product Lines

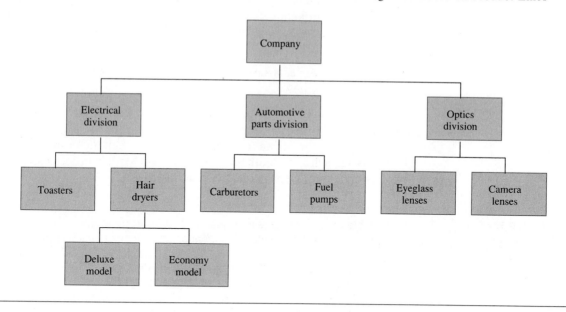

▶ **ILLUSTRATION 12-8**   Analysis of Income Statement Data into Segments Based on Sales Territories

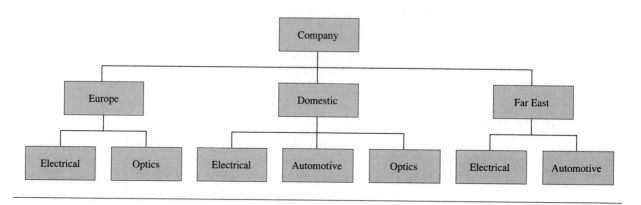

The Format of Segmented Income Statements

L.O. 5

The format of a firm's segmented income statements depends on whether it uses absorption costing or variable costing in its information system.

Absorption Costing   When a firm uses absorption costing, its segmented income statement follows the format of its traditional external reporting counterpart. For example, the Conglomerate Company may prepare its segmented income statement as shown in Illustration 12-9.

Only one product is manufactured in each line of business, and sales (in units) are 40,000, 10,000, and 40,000, respectively, for electrical, automotive, and optics. All marketing and administrative costs are fixed. Information about the Conglomerate Company's unit costs is presented in Illustration 12-10.

▶ **ILLUSTRATION 12-9**

CONGLOMERATE COMPANY
Income Statement—Absorption Costing
For the Year Ended December 31, 19x3

	Total	Electrical	Automotive	Optics
Sales	$1,000,000	$400,000	$300,000	$300,000
Cost of goods sold:				
Direct materials	100,000	40,000	20,000	40,000
Direct labor	200,000	80,000	40,000	80,000
Manufacturing overhead	200,000	60,000	60,000	80,000
Cost of goods sold	500,000	180,000	120,000	200,000
Gross margin	500,000	220,000	180,000	100,000
Marketing and administrative costs:				
Marketing costs	100,000	40,000	30,000	30,000
Administrative costs	200,000	60,000	60,000	80,000
Total marketing and administrative costs	300,000	100,000	90,000	110,000
Operating income (loss) before income taxes	$ 200,000	$120,000	$ 90,000	$(10,000)

▶ **ILLUSTRATION 12-10**

CONGLOMERATE COMPANY
Supplementary Data per Unit

Per Unit	Electrical	Automotive	Optics
Selling price	$10.00	$30	$7.50
Direct materials	1.00	2	1.00
Direct labor	2.00	4	2.00
Variable overhead	.50	4	1.00
Fixed overhead	1.00*	2†	1.00‡

* $40,000 ÷ 40,000 units = $1 per unit.
† $20,000 ÷ 10,000 units = $2 per unit.
‡ $40,000 ÷ 40,000 units = $1 per unit.

If a Conglomerate manager decided to eliminate the optics division based on the income statement shown in Illustration 12-9, the decision most probably would be faulty. The reason for the error would be that although the optics division shows an operating loss of $10,000 before income taxes, the loss arises after the deduction of fixed overhead, marketing, and administrative costs. It is highly probable that some of these fixed costs would continue; and if they exceeded $10,000 for 19x3, then the optics division contributed to the overall profitability of the company, and its elimination would cause company operating income to fall below the current $200,000. The fixed costs not eliminated by the discontinuance of the optics division must be absorbed by the two remaining lines of business, thereby decreasing their operating income. Thus, when an absorption-costing income statement is used to decide whether to discontinue a product, product line, or division, fixed costs must be analyzed to determine which will be eliminated and which will continue. Those that are eliminated when a particular cost objective is discontinued or eliminated are called **avoidable costs.** All fixed costs other than avoidable costs must be absorbed by the remaining segments.

For example, if all fixed costs for the optics division are classified as direct and indirect, the analysis might appear as shown in Illustration 12-11.

▶ **ILLUSTRATION 12-11**

CONGLOMERATE COMPANY
Analysis of Fixed Costs for Optics Division
For the Year Ended December 31, 19x3

	Total	Direct (Avoidable)	Indirect
Fixed manufacturing overhead ($1 × 40,000 units)	$ 40,000	$30,000	$10,000
Marketing costs	30,000	25,000	5,000
Administrative costs	80,000	10,000	70,000
Total	$150,000	$65,000	$85,000

A decision to eliminate the optics division would result in a decrease in operating income before income taxes from $200,000 to $125,000, as the following analysis shows:

Electrical operating income (from Illustration 12-9)	$120,000
Automotive operating income	90,000
Subtotal	210,000
Less: Indirect fixed overhead and other costs from optics division to be absorbed by the remaining divisions	85,000
Overall company operating income	$125,000

The same result may also be achieved by the following calculation:

Present company operating income	$200,000
Less: Common costs that must be absorbed by the remaining segments	85,000
Subtotal	115,000
Add: Elimination of optics' loss	10,000
Projected overall company operating income	$125,000

Hence, the elimination of the optics business would cause a $75,000 diminution of the company's operating income before taxes, a result not evident from the absorption income statement shown in Illustration 12-9.

Instead of using the format shown in Illustration 12-9, it is possible to use a contribution margin format that shows a segment margin for each line of business. When this kind of income statement is used, there is no need to adjust operating income as there is with absorption costing. The information needed to decide whether to discontinue a segment is readily available on the contribution margin income statement.

Segment Margin Segment margin, an important managerial concept, is a segment's sales revenue minus its direct variable and direct fixed costs. Stated differently, it is the sales revenue minus the directly traceable costs of a cost objective. Thus, segment margin is the amount of profit a line of business contributes to the overall profitability of a company. When this measure of margin is used, a manager can directly assess a segment's profitability from a segment margin income statement.

Segment Margin Income Statement A **segment margin income statement** is a contribution format income statement that breaks down total operating results by reportable segment, such as a division, product line, or sales territory. Each segment's direct fixed costs are deducted from its contribu-

► **ILLUSTRATION 12-12**

CONGLOMERATE COMPANY
Segment Margin Income Statement—Contribution Format
For the Year Ended December 31, 19x3

	Total	Electrical	Automotive	Optics
Sales	$1,000,000	$400,000	$300,000	$300,000
Variable cost of goods sold:				
Direct materials	100,000	40,000	20,000	40,000
Direct labor	200,000	80,000	40,000	80,000
Variable overhead*	100,000	20,000	40,000	40,000
Variable cost of goods sold	400,000	140,000	100,000	160,000
Contribution margin	600,000	260,000	200,000	140,000
Less: *Direct* fixed overhead and other costs:				
Fixed overhead.	70,000	25,000	15,000	30,000
Marketing costs	55,000	20,000	10,000	25,000
Administrative costs	35,000	15,000	10,000	10,000
Total direct fixed costs	160,000	60,000	35,000	65,000
Segment margin	440,000	$200,000	$165,000	$ 75,000
Less: *Indirect* fixed overhead and other costs (common costs):				
Fixed overhead.	30,000	($200,000 − $100,000 − $70,000)		
Marketing costs	45,000	($100,000 − $55,000)		
Administrative costs	165,000	($200,000 − $35,000)		
Total common costs	240,000			
Operating income before income taxes	$ 200,000			

* Electrical—40,000 units at $.50 per unit = $20,000.
  Automotive—10,000 units at $4 per unit = $40,000.
  Optics—40,000 units at $1 per unit = $40,000.

tion margin to arrive at the segment margin. **Common costs**—costs that cannot be traced to a single cost objective but may be allocated through the use of a logical allocation base—are usually not allocated in a segment margin income statement. Instead, they are deducted only in the total column to arrive at operating income before income taxes. Using the data given for the Conglomerate Company in Illustrations 12-9, 12-10, and 12-11, a segment margin income statement may be prepared as shown in Illustration 12-12. The direct and indirect fixed overhead and other costs for the electrical and automotive businesses are assumed.

In studying Illustration 12-12, note that:

1. Only the fixed costs that are *directly traceable* to a segment are deducted to arrive at segment margin.
2. The fixed costs that are common to more than one segment appear only in the total (companywide) column. Allocating these costs to particular segments is based on arbitrary assumptions and may provide misleading information to managers.
3. The contribution and segment margins provide useful information to managers. For example, the optics division shows a segment margin (or profitability) of $75,000. This amount agrees with the earlier analysis, which indicated that overall company operating income would be $125,000 without the optics business and $200,000 (as shown in Illustration 12-9) with it. The $10,000 operating loss for the optics

division shown in Illustration 12-9 is faulty for this kind of decision making because it is based on arbitrary allocations of common fixed costs. This does not mean common fixed costs should be ignored.

In the long run, a firm must recover all costs—variable, direct fixed, and common fixed. Despite the need to earn sufficient profits in the long run to recover all costs, including common costs, the allocation of common costs for decision making could lead to wrong decisions, and the practice is avoided by many firms.

Differentiation between Direct Fixed Costs and Common Costs

L.O. 6

Direct fixed costs are usually easily identified because they can be traced to a single cost objective. For example, line supervisors who work exclusively for the Conglomerate Company's optics division are not likely to be retained if that segment ceases to operate. It is also unlikely that these people supervise workers in more than one segment, such as in both the optics and the automotive divisions. Thus, the costs of maintaining the optics division's supervisors are relatively easy to classify as direct fixed.

Another easily classified fixed cost is advertising. An advertisement for one of the firm's optical products is not likely to be combined with an advertisement for an automotive or electrical product. Thus, such an ad would be a direct fixed cost. On the other hand, an advertisement extolling the company's programs to promote environmental protection, that was placed for the purpose of enhancing the general corporate image, would be classified as a common cost. Direct fixed costs may be further classified into those that are controllable by a segment manager and those that are controllable by others. When this distinction is used, two segment margins may be used, one called *controllable* and the other called *noncontrollable*.

Most common costs are also easily classified. The salaries of line personnel are not likely to be considered a common cost, but the manufacturing vice president's salary would be. Certainly most, if not all, staff functions (as discussed in Chapter 1) would be considered common costs.

Common Costs and the Allocation Problem

L.O. 7

Any allocation of a common cost to a particular segment is based on somewhat arbitrary assumptions. Even when the chosen assumptions appear quite logical, a difference of opinion regarding their use is possible. For example, occupancy costs (rent, real estate taxes, and the like) are usually allocated to segments on the basis of square feet occupied, an apparently logical base. Yet, if a retail department store occupies a 10-story building, with its perfumes and toiletries department occupying the entire 1st floor and its furniture department occupying the entire 10th floor, many accountants and managers might question the appropriateness of allocating equal amounts of rent to the two departments. Many might argue that the perfumes and toiletries department should bear a larger share of occupancy costs, because all customers must pass through it and thus may be tempted to do some impulse purchasing on the way to a department on another floor.

Similar debates may arise over any base used to allocate common costs. As a solution, some accountants suggest that the sales revenues provided by each segment may provide an equitable base. Others maintain that contribution margin is a superior base to sales revenue, because one of a firm's objectives is to maximize contribution margin rather than sales revenue.

When the contribution margin ratios of two segments are the same, the maximization of sales revenue in each segment also maximizes contribution margin and vice versa.

The use of sales revenue as an allocation base can lead to distortions in the analysis of a division's operating results. For example, if a firm has two divisions, A and B, with the same sales revenues and contribution margins, and if they occupy the same square footage of space, then the cost of rent would be allocated 50 percent to each division. The operating results of the two divisions might appear as follows:

	Division A	Division B	Total
Sales	$100,000	$100,000	$200,000
Variable costs	40,000	40,000	80,000
Contribution margin	60,000	60,000	120,000
Rent and other common fixed costs	40,000	40,000	80,000
Operating income	$ 20,000	$ 20,000	$ 40,000

Now let us assume that in the following year, all cost patterns remain unchanged and that Division A manages to increase its sales revenue to $400,000. If common costs are again allocated on the basis of sales revenue, the operating results for that year would appear as follows:

	Division A	Division B	Total
Sales	$400,000	$100,000	$500,000
Variable costs	160,000*	40,000	200,000
Contribution margin	240,000	60,000	300,000
Rent and other common fixed costs	64,000†	16,000‡	80,000
Operating income	$176,000	$ 44,000	$220,000

* $400,000 × 40% = $160,000.
† $400,000/$500,000 × $80,000 = $64,000.
‡ $100,000/$500,000 × $80,000 = $16,000.

Note that Division B's operating income automatically grew from $20,000 to $44,000—not because Division B increased its sales, but because Division A increased its sales. And due to its improved sales volume, Division A was also charged with an additional $24,000 of common fixed costs. These results can lead to problems.

First, the manager of Division A might resent the increased charge to her division and the windfall to Division B. Second, the two divisions' performances may be misinterpreted by people who do not understand the pitfalls of using sales revenue as the base for allocating common fixed costs.

Although some common costs may be allocated with somewhat realistic results, other common costs present stubborn allocation problems that are not easily solved. Because allocated common costs can produce arbitrary allocated net incomes, many firms prefer not to allocate common costs to individual segments in internal reports. Instead, they deduct the total common costs from the total segment margins, as shown in Illustration 12-12. This approach is used throughout the remainder of this chapter.

▶ **ILLUSTRATION 12-13**

MULTYPRODUCT COMPANY
Income Statement Segmented by Division—Contribution Format
For the Year Ended December 31, 19x3
(in thousands of dollars)

	Total	Automotive	Electronics
Sales.	$945,000	$400,000	$545,000
Variable cost of goods sold	416,000	160,000	256,000
Variable cost manufacturing margin	529,000	240,000	289,000
Variable marketing costs	28,350	12,000	16,350
Contribution margin	500,650	228,000	272,650
Less: *Direct* fixed overhead and other costs:			
Fixed overhead	130,000	50,000	80,000
Marketing costs	40,000	20,000	20,000
Administrative costs	40,000	20,000	20,000
Total direct fixed costs	210,000	90,000	120,000
Divisional segment margin	290,650	$138,000	$152,650
			(See Illustration 12-14)
Less: *Indirect* fixed overhead and other costs (common costs):			
Fixed overhead	40,000		
Marketing costs	30,000		
Administrative costs	50,000		
Total common costs	120,000		
Operating income before income taxes	$170,650		

Preparing Segmented Income Statements

The segmentation of a firm's income statement may be accomplished in different ways. Illustrations 12-7 and 12-8 indicate some of the possibilities. The segmented report may begin with product lines, with each product line subdivided into products and ultimately into models. Alternatively, the income statement may be segregated by sales territories. The disaggregation may also start with divisions, followed by product lines and then by sales territories, a blending of Illustrations 12-7 and 12-8. Essentially, the segmentation may take whatever form a firm finds useful. Large firms often build their income statements from the bottom up by combining the income statements of their divisions into the income statement for the entire firm.

The Multyproduct Company has two divisions—automotive and electronics. The automotive division manufactures spark plugs, electronic ignition modules, and various relay switches, and the electronics division manufactures automobile radios and digital clock radios. The firm's segmented income statement by divisions for the year 19x3 appears in Illustration 12-13.

The steps needed to prepare segmented statements reflecting segment margins by divisions, products, models, and territories may be summarized as follows:

Step 1

Prepare the income statement for the firm as a whole and analyze all income statement data between divisions, excluding common costs that can only be assigned to a division by using an allocation formula. The analysis should include all variable costs and direct fixed costs (see Illustration 12-13).

▶ **ILLUSTRATION 12-14**

MULTYPRODUCT COMPANY
Electronics Division Income Statement Segmented by Product—
Contribution Format
For the Year Ended December 31, 19x3
(in thousands of dollars)

	Total	Electronics Auto Radios	Clock Radios
Sales	$545,000	$310,000	$235,000
Variable cost of goods sold	256,000	136,000	120,000
Variable cost manufacturing margin	289,000	174,000	115,000
Variable marketing costs	16,350	9,300	7,050
Contribution margin	272,650	164,700	107,950
Less: *Direct* fixed overhead and other costs:			
Fixed overhead	60,000	20,000	40,000
Marketing costs	18,000	3,000	15,000
Administrative costs	10,000	2,000	8,000
Total direct fixed costs	88,000	25,000	63,000
Product segment margin	184,650	$139,700	$ 44,950
			(See Illustration 12-15)
Less: *Indirect* fixed overhead and other costs (common costs):			
Fixed overhead	20,000		
Marketing costs	2,000		
Administrative costs	10,000		
Total common costs	32,000	($120,000 − $88,000)	
Divisional segment margin	$152,650		

Step 2

Repeat step 1 *for each division,* analyzing the data by product (see Illustration 12-14).

Step 3

Repeat step 1 for each product, analyzing the data by model (see Illustration 12-15).

Step 4

Repeat step 1 for each model, analyzing the data by sales territory (see Illustration 12-16).

Analysis of Common Costs   Different levels of segmentation have different direct costs, as indicated in Illustrations 12-13 through 12-16. Some examples that explain the differences are:

1. The president's salary is a common administrative cost in Illustration 12-13, while the divisional managers' salaries are direct fixed administrative costs to their respective divisions.
2. The divisional manager's salary is a common administrative cost in Illustration 12-14 (electronics division), while the product supervisors' salaries are direct fixed overhead costs to their respective products.
3. The product supervisor's salary is a common fixed overhead cost in Illustration 12-15 (models), while the line supervisors' salaries are direct fixed overhead costs to their respective models.

MULTYPRODUCT COMPANY
Clock Radio Income Statement Segmented by Model—
Contribution Format
For the Year Ended December 31, 19x3
(in thousands of dollars)

		Clock Radios	
			Model
	Total	Deluxe	Regular
Sales.	$235,000	$160,000	$75,000
Variable cost of goods sold	120,000	72,000	48,000
Variable cost manufacturing margin	115,000	88,000	27,000
Variable marketing costs	7,050	4,800	2,250
Contribution margin	107,950	83,200	24,750
Less: *Direct* fixed overhead and other costs:			
Fixed overhead	30,000	15,000	15,000
Marketing costs	14,000	2,000	12,000
Administrative costs	6,000	2,500	3,500
Total direct fixed costs	50,000	19,500	30,500
Model segment margin (loss)	57,950	$ 63,700	$(5,750)
			(See Illustration 12-16)
Less: *Indirect* fixed overhead and other costs (common costs):			
Fixed overhead	10,000		
Marketing costs	1,000		
Administrative costs	2,000		
Total common costs	13,000	($63,000 − $50,000)	
Product segment margin	$ 44,950		

MULTYPRODUCT COMPANY
Regular Clock Radio Income Statement Segmented by Territory—
Contribution Format
For the Year Ended December 31, 19x3
(in thousands of dollars)

	Regular Clock Radios		
	Total	Domestic	Foreign
Sales.	$75,000	$50,000	$25,000
Variable cost of goods sold	48,000	32,000	16,000
Variable cost manufacturing margin	27,000	18,000	9,000
Variable marketing costs	2,250	1,500	750
Contribution margin	24,750	16,500	8,250
Less: *Direct* fixed overhead and other costs:			
Fixed overhead	13,000	8,000	5,000
Marketing costs	11,500	2,500	9,000
Administrative costs	2,500	1,000	1,500
Total direct fixed costs	27,000	11,500	15,500
Territorial segment margin (loss)	(2,250)	$ 5,000	$(7,250)
Less: *Indirect* fixed overhead and other costs (common costs):			
Fixed overhead	2,000		
Marketing costs	500		
Administrative costs	1,000		
Total common costs	3,500	($30,500 − $27,000)	
Model segment margin (loss)	$(5,750)		

A similar case can be made for machinery and equipment. The depreciation for equipment used by the electronics division would be a direct fixed cost (if the straight-line method were used) to the division in Illustration 12-13; but it would be a common fixed cost in Illustration 12-14, if the equipment were used for both automobile radios and clock radios.

In interpreting Illustrations 12-13 through 12-16, one might conclude that:

1. The company as a whole is profitable, as are the automotive and electronics divisions (see Illustration 12-13).
2. Auto radios and clock radios are both profitable (see Illustration 12-14).
3. Deluxe clock radios are profitable, and regular clock radios appear unprofitable. Sales revenues of regular clock radios are sufficient to cover variable costs but not direct fixed costs. If a managerial analysis of regular clock radios were based on Illustration 12-15 alone, a decision might be made to eliminate the manufacture of regular clock radios.
4. Regular clock radios sold in the United States are profitable, and foreign sales are unprofitable (see Illustration 12-16). The sales revenues of regular clock radios are sufficient to cover their variable costs. The problem appears to be in the direct fixed marketing costs. On investigation, a manager may determine that the foreign sales representative may be compensated partially on a fixed salary, or that advertising costs may be disproportionate to the amount of sales expected from the advertising, or a combination of both. In any event, Illustration 12-16 points to a problem that might remain undetected if segmented reports are not prepared.
5. Although the deluxe clock radio appears profitable (see Illustration 12-15), a statement segmented by territory may reveal a similar condition to that of the regular clock radio. Thus, regardless of whether a segment is profitable or unprofitable, additional segmentation (for example, by territory) may reveal an unprofitable condition or a potential trouble spot.

In addition to revealing trouble spots and unprofitable conditions, contribution segmented reports may be extremely useful for CVP analysis. They may point out products or territories where additional sales efforts, such as advertising and other forms of sales promotion, may yield the greatest contribution to profit.

▶ USES OF SEGMENT DATA

L.O. 8

Firms vary widely in their use of segment data. An important consideration in the preparation of segment data is the cost-benefit rule. Obviously, the benefit derived from the use of segment data should exceed the cost of obtaining them. Thus, a firm with a substantial amount of foreign sales would probably want a statement segmented by geographic areas, and a firm with mostly localized sales might not prepare such a statement.

Among the more important uses of segmented reports are:

1. Detecting segments operating at a loss.
2. Pinpointing the source of a loss, such as the failure to cover variable

costs or the coverage of variable costs but the failure to cover direct fixed costs.

3. Deciding whether to continue operating a particular segment.

4. Analyzing CVP relationships—altering a segment's selling price, cost, and volume for the purpose of increasing its contribution to profit.

5. Analyzing the potential results of altering marketing strategies (such as advertising, salespersons' visits to customers, and brochure mailings) to increase contribution to profit.

6. Evaluating managerial performance and implementing or amending incentive compensation plans, such as rewarding managers with a profit percentage of a segment's margin.

7. Identifying a particular practice that is producing superior performance in one operating division and then applying this practice to other divisions when appropriate.

Detecting Segments Operating at a Loss

In many cases, a profitable firm may have one or more segments that produce a loss for the firm. Sometimes the segment producing a loss is obvious; other times, the loss is masked when the segment's operations are combined with a similar segment that operates at a profit. Unmasking a losing segment may occasionally be a tricky process. A particular product, or even one model of a product, may show profits even though a particular sales territory where it is sold produces losses. A careful choice of levels of segmentation should reveal all actual or potential loss producers.

The mere fact that a product or territory produces a loss does not mean it should be eliminated. First, the loss may be an isolated or temporary event. In this case, the trend of the loss producer should be monitored, possibly for a period of one or two years, before a conclusion is reached that the loss will continue. Second, a trend analysis of any item contributing to the loss condition should be made to establish if the problem can be corrected. Third, marketing strategies should be examined to determine if a change in strategies might cure the condition. Only when it becomes clear that the loss condition is likely to be permanent, and corrective action is not likely to cure it, should a decision be made to abandon a loss producer. However, care must be exercised in reaching the decision to close a division. The shutting down of a division can directly or indirectly affect the operating results of other divisions. These effects must be factored into the decision to close down a division.

Pinpointing the Source of a Loss

Even when it is obvious that a segment is operating at a loss, the contribution format segmented statement provides useful information not found in absorption-costing income statements. A segment's contribution margin indicates whether its sales revenues are sufficient to cover its variable costs. A case in which sales revenues are insufficient to cover variable costs is much more serious than a case in which revenues fail to cover direct fixed costs. When variable costs are not covered by sales revenue, *every additional sale increases the amount of the loss* and, thus, additional sales volume will only exacerbate the loss. The only solutions to the problem are either an increase in selling price without a loss in sales volume or a reduction in the variable cost per unit.

On the other hand, a segment may be covering its variable costs but not its direct fixed costs. The remedies for this condition might include:

1. Raising selling prices, if possible, without a significant loss of sales volume (CVP analysis would be used here).
2. Reducing the variable cost per unit without a significant loss in volume (CVP analysis would be used here too).
3. Reducing direct fixed costs, if possible.
4. Implementing an aggressive marketing campaign to increase sales volume and produce an increase in contribution margin that is greater than the cost of the marketing campaign (once again, CVP analysis would be used).

Continuing the Operations of a Segment

In addition to helping detect and analyze segments operating at a loss, a segmented report may assist managers in assessing whether to continue operating profitable segments. Profitability does not automatically justify a segment's continued existence. A profitable segment must continually demonstrate that its profits compare favorably with a target return based on the firm's investment of assets in that segment. Because a firm is always faced with scarce resources, it must channel them into those segments that produce the greatest profit in accordance with overall objectives. Thus, it is quite conceivable that a firm may choose to discontinue a profitable segment in favor of another segment that may produce a greater profit. Segmented statements provide the information needed to make these kinds of decisions.

Cost-Volume-Profit Analysis

For a multiproduct firm, reliable CVP analysis can be accomplished only with segmented data. As noted in Chapter 4, CVP analysis for two products produces an average contribution margin and is valid only if the product mix remains unchanged. If a change in mix occurs, the contribution margin must be recomputed. Thus, an average may be used for very limited cases, usually two or three products. A diversified firm would have to use segmented data for CVP analysis, because figures based on a product mix of spark plugs, automotive radios, and household clock radios would be meaningless. A product mix of deluxe clock radios and regular clock radios might be used for CVP analysis, but even in this case, more informative results would probably be obtained through separate analyses for each radio.

Altering Marketing Strategies

The same problems that affect multiproduct CVP analyses arise when a company considers changing its strategies. Changes in marketing strategies can be effective only when a manager knows which products require a change and why they are not adequately profitable. Segmented statements highlight problem areas and provide managers with the information they need to make proper decisions.

Evaluating and Rewarding Managerial Performance

Studies in organizational behavior have shown that incentive compensation motivates most managers in a fashion that maximizes their income while maximizing the firm's income. On the other hand, when compensation is fixed and based on time worked, employees' goals may conflict with company goals. Thus, by instituting an incentive compensation program that gives employees a percentage of profits, a company may be able to lessen goal conflict.

Sales revenue, despite its widespread use in the computation of salespeople's commissions, is not an effective base for incentive compensation. Its deficiency stems from the fact that increases in sales volume do not necessarily guarantee maximum contribution margins. As a result, it is possible for a salesperson to maximize sales revenue by selling low-profit merchandise and thereby maximize her incentive compensation without maximizing profit to the firm.

Contribution margin makes a better base for profit-sharing than does sales revenue, but it suffers from some of the same drawbacks. As shown in Illustration 12-16, a segment may simultaneously have a positive contribution margin and a negative segment margin. Thus, when profit-sharing is based on contribution margin, a manager may receive incentive pay even though his segment is contributing a loss to overall company profitability.

Segment margin makes the best base for evaluating a manager's performance for a number of reasons. First, a maximization of segment margin generally maximizes a firm's overall profitability. Thus, if employees wish to maximize their incentive compensation when this base is used, their goal and the firm's goal will coincide. Second, because only direct costs are deducted to arrive at segment margin, the inequities of common cost allocations are avoided. Third, managers usually feel that segment margin is a fair base, because most—and usually all—costs deducted to arrive at segment margin are theoretically under their control, and they can accept responsibility for the costs' incurrence.

▶ **SUMMARY**

For external reporting and the preparation of income tax returns, firms must use **absorption costing.** When this method of costing is used, both fixed and variable manufacturing overhead are assigned to production and thus included in finished goods inventories. Despite its widespread use, absorption costing is not particularly suited to managerial decision making.

In contrast, with **variable costing,** also known as **direct costing** and **marginal costing,** only variable manufacturing costs are assigned to production and inventoried. Fixed manufacturing overhead is charged to income, as are marketing and administrative costs. The difference between the two methods of costing is that fixed manufacturing overhead is included in inventories with absorption costing and omitted from inventories with variable costing. Because the results are "purer," managers prefer to base their decisions on variable-costing data.

When the beginning and ending finished goods inventories are the same in any year, operating income is the same for both variable and absorption costing. Operating income under the two approaches will differ, however, when there is either an **inventory buildup** or an **inventory liquidation.** The difference in operating income between the two methods may be computed by multiplying the number of units built up—or liquidated—by the fixed cost per unit.

Segment reporting is an extremely important component of a management reporting system when used in conjunction with **contribution format income statements.** A **segment margin income statement** is prepared by showing the contribution margin for each reportable segment, such as a division, product line, or sales territory, and then deducting each segment's **direct fixed costs**

to arrive at **segment margin.** In essence, all **avoidable costs** for a segment are deducted from its sales to produce its margin. **Common costs** should not be allocated to each segment; instead, they should be deducted from the total of all segment margins to arrive at operating income.

Segmented income statements are extremely useful because they can reveal segments that are contributing losses to a firm's overall profitability. In income statements that report companywide results, one segment's losses may be masked by another segment's profits, so that loss-producing segments may go undetected for long periods of time.

In addition to unmasking loss-producing segments, segmented reports are useful for determining the possible reasons for the losses, deciding whether to continue operating both loss-producing and profitable segments, analyzing CVP relationships, altering market strategies, and the implementing or amending of incentive compensation plans.

▶ **GLOSSARY OF KEY TERMS**

Absorption costing (full costing)   A method of assigning manufacturing costs to production so that *both* variable and fixed manufacturing costs are included in inventories and cost of goods sold.   (p. 586)

Avoidable cost   Costs eliminated when a particular cost objective is discontinued or altered.   (p. 599)

Common cost   A cost that cannot be traced to a single cost objective but may be allocated through the use of a logical allocation base.   (p. 601)

Contribution format income statement   An income statement classified into fixed and variable cost categories instead of into the functional categories of a traditional income statement. Instead of including fixed manufacturing overhead in cost of goods manufactured, it is shown as a period cost after contribution margin.   (p. 587)

Direct costing   See **variable costing.**   (p. 586)

Direct fixed cost   A fixed cost that can be traced to a single cost objective.   (p. 602)

Inventory buildup   The excess that occurs when a firm's ending finished goods inventories are greater than its beginning inventories for any accounting period.   (p. 591)

Inventory liquidation   The decrease that occurs when a firm's ending inventories are less than its beginning inventories for any accounting period.   (p. 591)

Marginal costing   See **variable costing.**   (p. 586)

Segment margin   Sales revenue minus variable and fixed costs that would not be incurred (that is, avoidable costs) if the line of business ceased to operate. It is the amount of profit that a line of business contributes to the overall profitability of a company.   (p. 600)

Segment margin income statement   A contribution format income statement that breaks down total operating results by reportable segment, such as division, product line, or sales territory. Each segment's direct fixed costs are deducted from its contribution margin to arrive at the segment margin. Common costs are then deducted in the total column to determine operating income before taxes.   (p. 600)

Segmented reporting system   A management reporting system that breaks companywide income statements into segments, starting with the largest sections, such as divisions, and continuing with smaller and smaller units, such as product lines and then particular products.   (p. 597)

Variable costing   A method of assigning manufacturing costs to production so that *only* variable manufacturing costs are included in inventories and cost of goods sold.   (p. 586)

▶ **REVIEW PROBLEM
(A)**

Preparation of Variable-Costing Income Statements and Reconciliation with Absorption-Costing Income Statements

The Midland Corporation manufactures and sells a single product. The absorption-costing income statements for the Midland Corporation for 19x7 and 19x8 are shown below:

MIDLAND CORPORATION
Income Statement—Absorption Costing
For the Years Ending December 31,

	19x7	19x8
Sales.	$120,000	$120,000
Less: Cost of goods sold	66,000	63,000
Gross margin	54,000	57,000
Marketing and administrative costs	51,600	51,600
Operating income before income taxes.	$ 2,400	$ 5,400

Sales and production data are as follows:

	19x7	19x8
Units sold	3,000	3,000
Units produced	3,000	4,000

Fixed overhead is allocated to production on the number of units produced. Variable and fixed production costs are:

	19x7	19x8
Variable production cost per unit . . .	$ 18	$ 18
Fixed manufacturing overhead	12,000	12,000

Marketing and administrative costs:

Variable marketing costs	8% of sales
Fixed marketing costs	$10,800
Fixed administrative costs . . .	31,200

Variable production cost per unit:

Direct materials	$6
Direct labor	9
Variable manufacturing overhead.	3

Required   *a.* Determine the cost of a single unit of product under absorption costing and variable costing for both 19x7 and 19x8.
b. Prepare variable-costing income statements for the Midland Corporation for both 19x7 and 19x8.
c. Reconcile the absorption-costing and variable-costing operating income figures for 19x8.

d. Explain why the operating income for 19x8 is higher than the operating income for 19x7 although the number of units sold in each year is the same.

▶ **SOLUTION TO REVIEW PROBLEM (A)**

a.

19x7

Absorption Costing		Variable Costing	
Direct materials	$ 6	Direct materials	$ 6
Direct labor.	9	Direct labor	9
Variable overhead	3	Variable overhead	3
Fixed overhead			
($12,000 ÷ 3,000 units)	4		
Total cost per unit	$22	Total cost per unit	$18

19x8

Absorption Costing		Variable Costing	
Direct materials	$ 6	Direct materials	$ 6
Direct labor.	9	Direct labor	9
Variable overhead	3	Variable overhead	3
Fixed overhead			
($12,000 ÷ 4,000 units)	3		
Total cost per unit	$21	Total cost per unit	$18

b.

MIDLAND CORPORATION
Income Statement—Variable Costing
For the Years Ended December 31

	19x7	19x8
Sales.	$120,000	$120,000
Variable cost of goods sold (3,000 units at $18)	54,000	54,000
Variable cost manufacturing margin	66,000	66,000
Variable marketing costs	9,600	9,600
Contribution margin	56,400	56,400
Fixed costs:		
Fixed overhead	12,000	12,000
Marketing costs	10,800	10,800
Administrative costs	31,200	31,200
Total fixed costs	54,000	54,000
Operating income before income taxes.	$ 2,400	$ 2,400

c.

Variable costing operating income—19x8	$2,400
Add: Fixed manufacturing overhead deferred in closing inventory under absorption costing (1,000 units at $3)	3,000
Absorption-costing operating income	$5,400

d. The operating income in 19x8 is higher because $3,000 of fixed manufacturing overhead is deferred until the inventory is sold. Thus, the cost of goods sold is lower and operating income is higher.

The absorption-costing income for 19x8 is higher than in 19x7 because in 19x7, the firm produced the same number of units it sold; hence no fixed overhead was deferred to 19x8. For 19x8, the firm produced 4,000 units but only sold 3,000 units. Thus, $3,000 (1,000 units × $3) of fixed overhead was deferred to 19x9, and the 19x8 income is higher by this amount.

Preparation of a Segmented Income Statement and Analysis of Results

An absorption-costing income statement for 19x7 is shown below for the Garrin Drug Company. The Garrin Drug Company sells aspirin and cough syrup in two sales territories—northwest and northeast.

GARRIN DRUG COMPANY
Absorption-Costing Income Statement
For the Year Ended December 31, 19x7

	Total	Northwest	Northeast
Sales.	$470,000	$240,000	$230,000
Cost of goods sold.	320,270	171,135	149,135
Gross margin	149,730	68,865	80,865
Marketing and administrative costs	146,630	76,765	69,865
Operating income (loss) before income taxes	$ 3,100	$ (7,900)	$ 11,000

A company manager notices the loss in the northwest territory and orders an investigation of that territory to determine whether it should be eliminated. You are provided with the following information:

1. Sales by product and variable costs:

	Aspirin	Cough Syrup
Sales	$320,000	$150,000
Ratio of variable manufacturing costs to sales . . .	45%	64%
Ratio of variable marketing costs to sales	8%	3%

2. Sales of product by region:

Product	Northwest	Northeast
Aspirin	$140,000	$180,000
Cough syrup	100,000	50,000
Total	$240,000	$230,000

3. The total fixed manufacturing overhead amounts to $80,270, of which $37,210 is direct to the northwest region, $29,210 is direct to the northeast region, and the balance is common and allocated 50 percent to each region.
4. The total fixed marketing costs amount to $58,580, of which $22,040 is direct to the northwest region, $24,290 is direct to the northeast region, and the balance is common and allocated 50 percent to each region.
5. The total fixed administrative costs amount to $57,950, of which $30,025 is direct to the northwest region, $19,175 is direct to the northeast region, and the balance is common and allocated 50 percent to each region.

Required   *a.* Prepare a segmented contribution income statement showing segment margin by territory for the Garrin Drug Company.

b. Do you recommend eliminating the northwest territory, which is operating
under a loss? Support your conclusion.

► **SOLUTION TO
REVIEW PROBLEM
(B)**

a.

GARRIN DRUG COMPANY
Segmented Income Statement—Contribution Approach
For the Year Ended December 31, 19x7

	Total	Northwest	Northeast
Sales	$470,000	$240,000	$230,000
Variable costs:			
Cost of goods sold	240,000	127,000*	113,000‡
Variable marketing costs	30,100	14,200†	15,900§
Total variable costs.	270,100	141,200	128,900
Contribution margin	199,900	98,800	101,100
Fixed costs:			
Manufacturing overhead	66,420	37,210	29,210
Marketing	46,330	22,040	24,290
Administrative	49,200	30,025	19,175
Total fixed costs	161,950	89,275	72,675
Territorial segment margin	37,950	$ 9,525	$ 28,425
Less: Common fixed costs:			
Manufacturing overhead	13,850‖		
Marketing	12,250#		
Administrative	8,750**		
Total common costs	34,850		
Operating income before income taxes	$ 3,100		

* ($140,000 × 45%) + ($100,000 × 64%) = $127,000.
† ($140,000 × 8%) + ($100,000 × 3%) = $14,200.
‡ ($180,000 × 45%) + ($50,000 × 64%) = $113,000.
§ ($180,000 × 8%) + ($50,000 × 3%) = $15,900.
‖ $80,270 − $66,420 = $13,850.
$58,580 − $46,330 = $12,250.
** $57,950 − $49,200 = $8,750.

b. No. It is not operating at a loss. The loss was due to the allocation of common
costs to the individual territories. The segment margin is positive.

► **LIBRARY
ASSIGNMENT**

Read the following:

Ajinkya, Bipin, Rowland Atiase, and Linda Smith Bamber. "Absorption versus
Direct Costing: Income Reconciliation and Cost-Volume-Profit Analysis." *Issues
in Accounting Education,* Fall 1986, pp. 268–281.

Cooper, Robin, and Robert S. Kaplan. "How Cost Accounting Distorts Product
Costs." *Management Accounting,* April 1988, pp. 20–27.

Fremgen, James M. "The Direct Costing Controversy—An Identification of the
Issues." *The Accounting Review,* January 1964, pp. 43–51.

Schiff, Michael. "A Closer Look at Variable Costing." *Management Accounting,*
February 1987, pp. 36–39.

Treacy, John E. "For Direct Costing in the Steel Industry." *Management Accounting,* June 1977, pp. 44–46.

▶ **SELF-TEST**

True or False

1. Absorption costing should be used by managers for decision-making purposes even though variable costing must be used for external reporting.
2. When using variable costing, a firm does not include fixed manufacturing overhead costs in the cost of finished goods inventories.
3. Variable marketing costs are shown after contribution margin but before manufacturing margin.
4. Operating income under absorption costing is the same as operating income under variable costing provided that the number of units sold equals the number of units manufactured for any year.
5. Whenever there is an inventory liquidation, absorption-costing income will be lower than income under variable costing.
6. A segment margin statement can be prepared only when variable costing is used.
7. Direct fixed costs should not be allocated to a segment in order to compute segment margin.
8. An avoidable cost is one that can be avoided by using variable costing instead of absorption costing.
9. A common cost may sometimes be an avoidable cost and other times it may be an unavoidable cost, depending on the particular segment the cost relates to.
10. When a segment is covering its variable costs but is not covering its direct fixed costs, a possible management action to alleviate this condition might be to switch the method of depreciation so that less depreciation appears as a direct fixed cost.

Multiple Choice

Strutmatter Company has two divisions, the electrical division and the automotive parts division. Operating results for the year ended December 31, 19x2, are as follows:

	Division	
	Electrical	**Automotive**
Sales	$400,000	$800,000
Direct materials	60,000	200,000
Direct labor	50,000	90,000
Variable overhead	80,000	120,000
Direct fixed overhead.	60,000	100,000
Allocated fixed overhead	30,000	80,000
Variable marketing and administrative costs.	20,000	40,000
Allocated fixed marketing and administrative costs.	45,000	75,000

1. The contribution margin for the electrical division is
   a. $130,000.
   b. $190,000.
   c. $145,000.
   d. $210,000.

2. The contribution margin for the automotive division is
   a. $350,000.
   b. $175,000.
   c. $275,000.
   d. $390,000.

3. The gross margin for the electrical division is
   a. $180,000.
   b. $240,000.
   c. $130,000.
   d. $120,000.

4. The segment margin for the electrical division is
   a. $130,000.
   b. $190,000.
   c. $145,000.
   d. $210,000.

5. The segment margin for the automotive division is
   a. $350,000.
   b. $270,000.
   c. $250,000.
   d. $390,000.

▶ **QUESTIONS**

1. How does absorption costing differ from variable costing?
2. Explain why variable costing is superior to absorption costing in making managerial decisions. In which kinds of decisions is variable costing especially useful?
3. Are variable marketing costs inventoriable when variable costing is used? Why?
4. Are variable marketing costs deducted to arrive at contribution margin? Why?
5. What is inventory buildup? Inventory liquidation? Do they play any role in the amount of reported net income when absorption costing is used? Explain.
6. When the number of units sold equals the number of units manufactured, does absorption costing or variable costing produce the higher net income? Explain.
7. How is fixed manufacturing overhead shifted into a subsequent accounting period when absorption costing is used? Use an example to demonstrate the concept.
8. Is it possible to increase net income under absorption costing without increasing sales volume? Explain.
9. Is it possible for a firm to keep its reporting system on a variable-costing basis and still satisfy the firm's independent auditors and the Internal Revenue Service? Explain.
10. What is a segment? Use examples of segments in your answer.
11. Is it possible to prepare a segmented income statement using absorption costing? If so, what are the limitations of using such a statement for managerial decision making?
12. What are avoidable costs? How should they be used?
13. What is segment margin? How is a contribution format segmented income statement used?
14. What is a common cost? Give some examples of common costs.
15. Is a contribution format segmented income statement preferable to one prepared using absorption costing? Why?
16. What is the difference between contribution margin and segment margin?
17. Should common costs be allocated to segments? Why?
18. Is it possible for the same cost to be a direct cost in one segmented income statement and a common cost in another segmented income statement? Explain.

▶ **EXERCISES**   E12–1   **Variable-Costing and Absorption-Costing Calculations**

The following data apply to items 1 through 4.

Denham Company began operations on January 3, 19x3. Standard costs were established in early January, assuming a normal production volume of 160,000 units.

However, Denham produced only 140,000 units of product and sold 100,000 units at a selling price of $180 per unit during 19x3. Variable costs totaled $7 million, of which 60 percent were manufacturing and 40 percent were marketing. Fixed costs totaled $11.2 million, of which 50 percent were manufacturing and 50 percent were marketing. Denham had no direct materials or work in process inventories at December 31, 19x3. Actual input prices per unit of product and actual input quantities per unit of product were equal to standard.

1. Denham's cost of goods sold at standard cost for 19x3 using full absorption costing is
   a. $8.2 million.
   b. $7.2 million.
   c. $6.5 million.
   d. $7 million.
   e. Some amount other than those given above.
2. The value assigned to Denham's December 31, 19x3, inventory using variable (direct) costing is
   a. $2.8 million.
   b. $1.2 million.
   c. $2 million.
   d. $3 million.
   e. Some amount other than those given above.
3. Denham's manufacturing overhead volume variance in 19x3 using full absorption costing is
   a. $800,000 unfavorable.
   b. $800,000 favorable.
   c. $700,000 unfavorable.
   d. $700,000 favorable.
   e. Some amount other than those given above.
4. Denham's 19x3 income from operations using variable (direct) costing is
   a. $3.4 million.
   b. $1.8 million.
   c. $2.6 million.
   d. $1 million.
   e. Some amount other than those given above.

(CMA Adapted)

E12–2 Variable-Costing and Absorption-Costing Calculations

The Penney Corporation produces and sells one item. The following information on the company for 19x6 is available:

Direct materials	$288,000
Direct labor	$336,000
Variable overhead	$192,000
Fixed overhead	$240,000
Units produced	15,000 units
Units sold	12,500 units
Units in beginning inventory	–0–
Salespersons' commissions	$120,000
Fixed marketing costs	$134,400
Fixed administrative costs	$112,000

There are no work in process inventories.

Required a. Compute the ending finished goods inventory using absorption costing.
b. Compute the ending finished goods inventory using variable costing.

c. Does absorption costing or variable costing show a higher operating income for 19x6? By how much?

E12–3   **Absorption-Costing Income Statement Converted to Variable-Costing Income Statement**

The Praline Company provides you with the following income statement:

PRALINE COMPANY
Income Statement Using Absorption Costing
For the Year Ended December 31, 19x2

Sales			$504,000
Cost of goods sold:			
Beginning inventory—finished goods	$ –0–		
Direct materials	84,000		
Direct labor	147,000		
Manufacturing overhead.	168,000		
Cost of goods manufactured	399,000		
Less: Ending inventory—finished goods	79,800		
Cost of goods sold			319,200
Gross margin.			$184,800
Marketing and administrative costs:			
Marketing	$ 67,200		
Administrative	84,000		151,200
Operating income before income taxes			$ 33,600

During 19x2, the company manufactured only one product. The number of units produced was 50,000, and there were no work in process inventories.

The variable overhead is $1.26 per unit. Variable marketing costs amount to $20,160. The administrative costs are all fixed.

Required   a. How many units are in the ending finished goods inventory?
b. How much is the fixed overhead per unit?
c. How much fixed overhead is in the ending finished goods inventory?
d. Prepare an income statement using the variable-costing format.
e. Explain the difference between your operating income before income taxes and the $33,600 shown in the above income statement.

E12–4   **Variable-Costing Income Statement Converted to Absorption-Costing Income Statement**

The Polly Company manufactures only one product, and during 19x2 it manufactured 60,000 units. There were no work in process inventories at the beginning and end of 19x2.

The company's variable-costing income statement for 19x2 appears below:

POLLY COMPANY
Income Statement Using Variable Costing
For the Year Ended December 31, 19x2

Sales		$432,000
Variable cost of goods sold:		
Beginning inventory—finished goods	$ –0–	
Direct materials	72,000	
Direct labor	96,000	
Variable manufacturing overhead.	48,000	
Variable cost of goods manufactured	216,000	
Less: Ending inventory—finished goods	21,600	
Variable cost of goods sold		194,400
Variable cost manufacturing margin		237,600
Salespersons' commissions		18,000
Contribution margin		219,600
Less: Fixed costs:		
Fixed manufacturing overhead	96,000	
Fixed marketing costs.	36,000	
Fixed administrative costs.	60,000	
Total fixed costs		192,000
Operating income before income taxes		$ 27,600

Required   a. Prepare an absorption-costing income statement for 19x2.

           b. Reconcile your operating income before income taxes with the $27,600 shown above.

E12–5 Preparation of Absorption-Costing and Variable-Costing Income Statements

The Real Corporation manufactures and sells packaged, custom-designed decks of playing cards. The following information on the company is available for 19x3.

Units produced.	25,000 units
Units sold	20,000 units
Selling price per unit	$30
Variable costs per unit:	
Direct materials	$5.00
Direct labor	2.50
Variable manufacturing overhead.	7.50
Variable marketing costs	6.50
Fixed costs:	
Manufacturing overhead.	$25,000
Marketing costs	26,500
Administrative costs	10,500
Beginning inventory.	–0–

There are no work in process inventories and no variable administrative costs.

Required   a. What is the cost of a unit of product using absorption costing? Using variable costing?

           b. Prepare income statements for 19x3, first using absorption costing and then variable costing.

           c. Reconcile the difference between the two income statements.

E12–6   **Preparation of a Variable-Costing Income Statement from an Absorption-Costing Income Statement**

Dublin, Inc., was organized on January 1, 19x5. The absorption-costing income statement for the year ending December 31, 19x5, is shown below.

DUBLIN, INC.
Income Statement—Absorption Costing
For the Year Ending December 31, 19x5

Sales (8,000 units × $90)		$720,000
Cost of goods sold:		
Beginning inventory	$ –0–	
Direct materials (10,000 units × $20)	200,000	
Direct labor (10,000 units × $12)	120,000	
Variable manufacturing overhead (10,000 units × $6)	60,000	
Fixed manufacturing overhead (10,000 units × $22)	220,000	
Goods available for sale	600,000	
Less: Ending inventory—finished goods		
(2,000 units × $60)	120,000	
Cost of goods sold		480,000
Gross margin.		240,000
Marketing and administrative costs:		
Marketing	96,000	
Administrative	100,000	196,000
Operating income before income taxes		$ 44,000

There are no work in process inventories. The total marketing costs of $96,000 consist of variable marketing costs of $36,000 and fixed marketing costs of $60,000. There are no variable administrative costs.

Required   *a.* Prepare another income statement for Dublin, Inc., this time using variable costing.

b. Is there a difference in operating income between the absorption-costing and variable-costing income statements? Explain any difference.

E12–7   **Computation of Variable-Costing Operating Income from Selected Data with an Inventory Buildup and an Inventory Liquidation**

The Progress Company manufactures one product. Selected data for 19x1 and 19x2 are as follows:

	19x1	19x2
Absorption-costing operating income	$250,000	$200,000
Fixed manufacturing overhead	$500,000	$525,000
Units manufactured	62,500	43,750
Units sold	50,000	50,000
Beginning finished goods inventory—in units	6,000	?
Fixed overhead costs in beginning inventory	$ 51,000	?

There are no work in process inventories, and the company uses a FIFO cost flow. Marketing and administrative costs are all fixed.

Required   *a.* How many units are in ending finished goods inventory for 19x1? For 19x2?

b. How much fixed overhead is in the ending finished goods inventory for 19x1? For 19x2?

c. How much is the variable-costing operating income for 19x1? For 19x2?

E12–8 **Computation of Absorption-Costing Operating Income from Selected Data with an Inventory Buildup and an Inventory Liquidation**

The Regress Company manufactures one product. Selected data for 19x1 and 19x2 are as follows:

	19x1	19x2
Variable-costing operating income.	$288,000	$324,000
Fixed manufacturing overhead	$540,000	$612,000
Units manufactured	72,000	48,000
Units sold	60,000	68,000
Beginning finished goods inventory—in units	12,000	?
Fixed overhead costs in absorption-costing beginning inventory	$ 84,000	?

There are no work in process inventories, and the company uses a FIFO cost flow. Marketing and administrative costs are all fixed.

Required
a. How many units are in ending finished goods inventory for 19x1? For 19x2?
b. How much fixed overhead is in the absorption-costing ending finished goods inventory for 19x1? For 19x2?
c. How much is the absorption-costing operating income for 19x1? For 19x2?

E12–9 **Reasons for Using Variable Costing for Internal Reporting**

Grisp Company, a manufacturer with heavy investments in property, plant, and equipment, is presently using absorption costing for both its external and internal reporting. The management of Grisp Company is considering using the variable-costing method for internal reporting only.

Required
a. What is the rationale for using the variable-costing method for internal reporting?
b. Assuming the quantity of ending inventory is higher than the quantity of beginning inventory, would operating income using variable costing differ from operating income using absorption costing? If so, specify if it would be higher or lower. Discuss the rationale for your answer.

(AICPA Adapted)

E12–10 **Absorption Costing and Variable Costing from Partial Information**

The Compact Company prepared condensed comparative income statements for 19x1 and 19x2. During the two years, there were *no changes* in costs or selling price of the company's single product, and the company does not have any work in process inventories. The condensed income statements are as follows:

	19x2	19x1
Sales.	$540,000	$360,000
Cost of goods sold.	324,000	216,000
? margin	216,000	144,000
Other costs	108,000	108,000
Operating income before income taxes	$108,000	$ 36,000

Marketing and administrative costs are all fixed. Fixed overhead for each year amounted to $54,000.

The company began operating on January 1, 19x1, and during 19x1, it produced 13,500 units. Sales for 19x1 amounted to 9,000 units. There was no finished goods inventory on December 31, 19x2.

Required
a. Are the above income statements prepared in accordance with absorption costing? Explain the reasons for your conclusion.

b. Recast the condensed income statements into condensed income statements of the other format (i.e., variable costing if they are absorption costing, or absorption costing if they are variable costing).

E12–11 **Strategy Changes and the Preparation of a Segmented Income Statement**

The Relaxation Company manufactures Aspirin and Relaxaid. A segmented income statement for 19x3 is as follows:

	Total	Aspirin	Relaxaid
Sales	$675,000	$300,000	$375,000
Variable costs	300,000	150,000	150,000
Contribution margin	375,000	150,000	225,000
Direct fixed costs.	135,000	60,000	75,000
Product segment margin.	240,000	$ 90,000	$150,000
Common costs	90,000		
Operating income before income taxes	$150,000		

Cost-behavior patterns are not expected to change during 19x4.

Required
a. A $9,000 advertisement for either product is expected to produce a 5 percent increase in sales volume. Would you recommend the advertisement for Aspirin? For Relaxaid? Why?

b. Prepare a projected segmented income statement for 19x4 if Aspirin sales are expected to increase by 10 percent and Relaxaid sales are expected to increase by 20 percent. Fixed costs are expected to increase by 10 percent.

E12–12 **Segmented Income Statement**

The Burns Company has two divisions: clothing and jewelry. The firm's segmented income statement by divisions for the year 19x5 appears below:

BURNS COMPANY
Segmented Income Statement—Contribution Format
For the Year Ended December 31, 19x5

	Total	Clothing	Jewelry
Sales.	$690,000	$480,000	$210,000
Variable cost of goods sold	196,500	144,000	52,500
Variable cost manufacturing margin	493,500	336,000	157,500
Variable marketing costs	49,425	38,400	11,025
Contribution margin	444,075	297,600	146,475
Less: Direct fixed overhead and other costs:			
Fixed overhead	106,500	67,500	39,000
Marketing costs	19,500	12,000	7,500
Administrative costs	10,875	5,625	5,250
Total direct fixed costs	136,875	85,125	51,750
Divisional segment margin	307,200	212,475	94,725
Less: Indirect fixed overhead and costs (common costs):			
Fixed overhead	45,000		
Marketing costs	65,775		
Administrative costs	123,225		
Total common costs	234,000		
Operating income before income taxes	$ 73,200		

Required   a. Compute the change in operating income if the clothing division increases sales by 12 percent.

b. Compute the change in operating income if the jewelry division increases sales by 12 percent.

c. If you had a choice of increasing sales by 12 percent in the clothing division or by 12 percent in the jewelry division, which would you prefer? Why? What is the contribution margin ratio of each division? Did you select the one with the higher ratio? Explain.

E12–13 Preparation of a Segmented Income Statement

The Fairway Company manufactures two products: automobile heater hose and hose clamps. During 19x3, the company sold 500,000 feet of hose and 200,000 clamps. The selling price of hose is $2 per foot, and clamps sell for $1.50 each.

Costs during the year were as follows:

	Hose	Clamps
Variable costs	$ .80 per foot	$ .60 each
Direct fixed costs	175,000	90,000

Common fixed costs amounted to $150,000.

Required   Prepare an income statement segmented by product using the contribution format.

E12–14 Cost-Volume-Profit Strategies for Segments

Collins Company manufactures two products: blankets and pillows. The firm's income statement segmented by products for the year 19x4 appears below:

COLLINS COMPANY
Segmented Income Statement—Contribution Format
For the Year Ended December 31, 19x4

	Total	Blankets	Pillows
Sales	$570,000	$270,000	$300,000
Variable cost of goods sold	201,000	81,000	120,000
Variable cost manufacturing margin	369,000	189,000	180,000
Variable marketing costs	66,000	54,000	12,000
Contribution margin	303,000	135,000	168,000
Less: Direct fixed overhead and other costs:			
Fixed overhead	72,000	33,000	39,000
Marketing costs	29,775	17,250	12,525
Administrative costs	25,875	5,625	20,250
Total direct fixed costs	127,650	55,875	71,775
Product segment margin	175,350	$ 79,125	$ 96,225
Less: Indirect fixed overhead and costs (common costs)	81,150		
Operating income before income taxes	$ 94,200		

Collins Company intends to spend $7,500 in a direct-mail campaign for either the blankets or the pillows. If the $7,500 is spent on either product, sales of that product will increase by $75,000. Cost-behavior patterns will be unchanged by the direct-mail cost.

Required   a. For which of the two products should Collins Company spend the $7,500 direct-mail campaign funds? Show the computations made to arrive at your decision.

b. Instead of a direct-mail campaign, Collins Company may spend the $7,500 on direct advertising for either the blankets or the pillows. If it is spent on the pillows, sales of pillows will increase by $30,000, but if the $7,500 is spent on the blankets, sales of blankets will increase by $45,000. Should Collins Company spend the $7,500 in direct advertising on the pillows or blankets? Show the computations made to arrive at your decision.

E12–15   **Preparation of a Segmented Income Statement**

The condensed income statement shown below demonstrates a loss for the Palmar Company for 19x2:

Sales		$680,000
Variable costs*		376,000
Contribution margin		304,000
Fixed costs:		
Fixed overhead	$146,400	
Marketing.	72,000	
Administrative.	97,600	
Total fixed costs		316,000
Net income (loss)		$(12,000)

* There are no variable marketing costs.

The Palmar Company produces greeting cards, posters, and stationery. A manager of the company has ordered a segmented income statement by product to trace the loss. The following data are also available:

	Greeting Cards	Posters	Stationery
Sales	$320,000	$200,000	$160,000
Contribution margin ratio	65%	20%	35%
Direct fixed overhead and other costs:			
Fixed overhead	$ 13,600	$ 29,600	$ 10,400
Marketing	14,400	15,200	22,400
Administrative	8,000	23,200	11,200
Total direct fixed costs	$ 36,000	$ 68,000	$ 44,000

Required   a. Prepare a segmented income statement showing segmented margin by product.

b. The manager believes the sales of posters would increase by 40 percent if the direct-mail campaign funds were increased by $20,000. Would you advise an increased direct-mail campaign? Show the computations made to arrive at your answer.

E12–16   **Strategy Changes and the Preparation of a Segmented Income Statement**

The Clark Company manufactures two products: A and B. A segmented income statement for 19x3 is as follows:

	Total	Product A	Product B
Sales	$480,000	$360,000	$120,000
Variable costs	288,000	240,000	48,000
Contribution margin.	192,000	120,000	72,000
Direct fixed costs.	156,000	60,000	96,000
Product segment margin.	36,000	$ 60,000	$ (24,000)
Common costs	48,000		
Operating loss before income taxes	$ (12,000)		

Cost-behavior patterns are not expected to change during 19x4.

Required *a.* If the company expects no change in volume for 19x4, should the company cease to operate? Explain the reasons for your conclusions.

b. The company believes spending $15,000 for advertising product A would increase its sales by 20 percent *or* spending $10,000 for advertising product B would increase its sales by 50 percent. Which course of action would you recommend? Explain.

c. Prepare a segmented income statement using your recommendation from part *(b)*.

E12–17 Segmented Income Statement

The Crum Company has two divisions: C and D. The firm's segmented income statement by division for the year 19x5 appears below:

CRUM COMPANY
Segmented Income Statement—Contribution Format
For the Year Ended December 31, 19x5

	Total	Division C	Division D
Sales	$600,000	$240,000	$360,000
Variable cost of goods sold	204,000	60,000	144,000
Variable cost manufacturing margin.	396,000	180,000	216,000
Variable marketing costs	66,000	48,000	18,000
Contribution margin.	330,000	132,000	198,000
Fixed costs	300,000	150,000	150,000
Operating income (loss) before income taxes.	$ 30,000	$(18,000)	$ 48,000

The president of the company is considering whether to cease operating Division C. She asks you to analyze the fixed costs and prepare a segmented income statement suitable for reaching a conclusion regarding the future operations of Division C. An analysis of the company's fixed costs provides you with the following:

	Total	Division C	Division D
Direct fixed costs.	$180,000	$60,000	$120,000
Common fixed costs	120,000		
Total	$300,000		

For 19x6, the company anticipates sales volume for Division C to increase by 5 percent while its direct fixed costs increase by 20 percent. Division D's sales volume is expected to increase by 10 percent while its direct fixed costs increase by 30 percent. Common fixed costs are expected to increase by 10 percent.

Required   Prepare a projected segmented income statement showing segment margin for 19x6 suitable for decision making.

E12–18   **Preparation of a Segmented Income Statement**

The condensed income statement shown below demonstrates a loss for the Poma Company for 19x2:

Sales		$2,100,000
Variable costs*		1,065,000
Contribution margin		1,035,000
Fixed costs:		
Fixed overhead	$525,000	
Marketing.	300,000	
Administrative.	285,000	
Total fixed costs		1,110,000
Net income (loss)		$ (75,000)

* There are no variable marketing costs.

The Poma Company produces two products: G and H. A manager of the company has ordered a segmented income statement by product to trace the loss. The following data are available:

	Product G	Product H
Sales	$1,200,000	$900,000
Contribution margin ratio	60%	35%
Direct fixed overhead and other costs:		
Fixed overhead	$ 195,000	$225,000
Marketing	135,000	75,000
Administrative	120,000	90,000
Total direct fixed costs	$ 450,000	$390,000

Required   *a.* Prepare a segmented income statement showing segment margin by product.

b. The manager believes the sales of product H would increase by 30 percent if direct-mail campaign funds were increased by $52,500. Would you advise an increased direct-mail campaign? Show the computations used to arrive at your conclusion.

▶ **PROBLEMS**   **P12–19**   **Preparation of Absorption-Costing and Variable-Costing Income Statements**

The Lafayette Company was organized on January 1, 19x4. The company produces and sells one product. The cost data for that product are as follows:

Manufacturing costs:		
Variable cost per unit:		
Direct materials.		$45
Direct labor		15
Variable overhead.		18
Fixed overhead costs		$135,000
Marketing and administrative costs:		
Salespersons' commissions.		8% of sales
Fixed marketing costs		$660,000
Fixed administrative costs		$810,000

Production and sales data for 19x4 and 19x5 are as follows:

	Units Produced	Units Sold
19x4.	60,000	55,000
19x5.	60,000	65,000

The selling price is $140 per unit.

Required
a. Prepare income statements for 19x4 and 19x5 using the absorption-costing approach.
b. Prepare income statements for 19x4 and 19x5 using the variable-costing method.
c. Reconcile the variable-costing and absorption-costing figures for operating income.
d. Compute the cost of a single unit of the product under absorption costing and under variable costing.

P12–20 **Preparation of Variable-Costing Income Statements and Reconciliation with Absorption-Costing Income Statements**

The Cancun Corporation manufactures and sells a single product. Cancun Corporation's absorption-costing income statements for 19x7 and 19x8 are shown below:

CANCUN CORPORATION
Income Statement—Absorption Costing
For the Years Ending December 31

	19x7	19x8
Sales	$176,000	$176,000
Less: Cost of goods sold	70,400	66,880
Gross margin	105,600	109,120
Marketing and administrative costs.	68,800	68,800
Operating income before income taxes	$ 36,800	$ 40,320

Sales and production data are as follows:

	19x7	19x8
Units sold	4,000	4,000
Units produced.	4,000	5,000

Fixed overhead is allocated to production on the number of units produced.

	19x7	19x8
Variable and fixed production costs:		
Variable production cost per unit	$13.20	$13.20
Fixed manufacturing overhead	$17,600	$17,600
Marketing and administrative costs:		
Variable marketing costs	8% of sales	
Fixed marketing costs	$14,400	
Fixed administrative costs	40,320	
Variable production cost per unit:		
Direct materials	$ 3.00	
Direct labor	6.00	
Variable manufacturing overhead	4.20	
Total variable production costs	$13.20	

Required

a. Determine the cost of a single unit of product under absorption costing and variable costing for both 19x7 and 19x8.

b. Prepare variable-costing income statements for the Cancun Corporation for both 19x7 and 19x8.

c. Reconcile the absorption-costing and variable-costing operating income figures for 19x8.

d. Explain why the operating income for 19x8 is higher than the operating income for 19x7 although the number of units sold in each year is the same.

P12–21   Preparation of Variable-Costing and Absorption-Costing Income Statements

The cost and revenue data for the Reincort Company for 19x6 are as follows:

Beginning inventory	–0–
Production in units	8,000
Sales in units	6,000
Sales price per unit	$30
Marketing and administrative costs:	
Salesperson's commissions	8% of sales
Fixed marketing costs	$4,000
Fixed administrative costs	6,000
Production costs per unit:	
Direct materials	$ 2.40
Direct labor	10.00
Variable overhead	6.60
Fixed overhead	4.50

Required

a. Prepare an income statement for the Reincort Company for 19x6 using absorption costing. Compute the cost per unit of product.

b. Prepare an income statement for 19x6 using variable costing. Compute the cost per unit of product.

c. Compute the value of the ending inventory using absorption costing and variable costing.

d. Explain any difference in the ending inventory under the two costing approaches. Explain any difference in operating income between the two approaches.

P12–22   **Preparation of Variable-Costing Income Statements and Comparison with Absorption-Costing Income Statements**

The absorption-costing income statements for the Royale Company's first two years of operation for its only product are shown below:

	19x2	19x3
Sales	$225,000	$525,000
Cost of goods sold:		
Opening inventory	–0–	80,000
Cost of goods manufactured (at $20)	200,000	200,000
Goods available for sale.	200,000	280,000
Less: Ending inventory (at $20)	80,000	–0–
Cost of goods sold	120,000	280,000
Gross margin	105,000	245,000
Marketing and administrative costs.	60,000	76,000
Operating income before income taxes	$ 45,000	$169,000

The cost of goods manufactured per unit of product is computed as follows:

Direct materials	$ 8
Direct labor	4
Variable manufacturing overhead	3
Fixed manufacturing overhead	5
Total cost per unit	$20

Production and sales data:

	19x2	19x3
Units produced	10,000	10,000
Units sold	6,000	14,000

Marketing and administrative costs:

	19x2	19x3
Variable marketing costs	$12,000	$28,000
Fixed marketing costs.	18,000	18,000
Fixed administrative costs	30,000	30,000
Total	$60,000	$76,000

There are no work in process inventories.

Required   a. Prepare income statements for the Royale Company for each year using the variable-costing method.

b. Reconcile the absorption-costing and variable-costing operating incomes for each year.

c. Which income statement format is more suitable for managerial decision making? Incorporate in your discussion the income statements you prepared.

P12–23   **Preparation of Variable-Costing Income Statements**

The absorption-costing income statements for the Marlin Company's first two years of operation for its only product are shown below:

	19x5	19x6
Sales	$180,000	$360,000
Cost of goods sold:		
Opening inventory	–0–	50,000
Cost of goods manufactured	200,000	225,000
Goods available for sale	200,000	275,000
Less: Ending inventory	50,000	–0–
Cost of goods sold	150,000	275,000
Gross margin	30,000	85,000
Marketing and administrative costs	30,000	45,000
Operating income before income taxes	$ –0–	$ 40,000

The cost of goods manufactured per unit of product is computed as follows for 19x5:

Direct materials	$1.00
Direct labor	1.00
Variable manufacturing overhead	.50
Fixed manufacturing overhead	2.50
Total cost per unit	$5.00

The total dollar amount of fixed overhead costs for 19x5 is unchanged for 19x6. Variable manufacturing costs per unit and the selling price of the company's product are also unchanged for 19x6.

Production and sales data:

	19x5	19x6
Units produced	40,000	50,000
Units sold	30,000	60,000

Marketing and administrative costs:

	19x5	19x6
Variable marketing costs	$15,000	$30,000
Fixed marketing costs	5,000	5,000
Fixed administrative costs	10,000	10,000
Total	$30,000	$45,000

There are no work in process inventories.

Required *a.* Prepare income statements for the company for each year using the variable-costing method.

b. Reconcile the absorption-costing and variable-costing operating incomes for each year.

c. The company's management accountant calculated Marlin's breakeven sales as:

$$\frac{\$115,000}{(\$5.50 - \$2.50)} = 38,333 \text{ units} \times \$5.50 = \$210,833$$

For 19x5, the income statement provided above shows sales of $180,000 and a breakeven ($0 operating income). Is the $210,833 breakeven wrong? Explain.

P12–24   **Preparation of Variable-Costing and Absorption-Costing Income Statements: Comparisons with Breakeven Sales**

Julian, Inc., was organized on January 1, 19x1. Sales and production data are as follows:

Units produced	6,000
Units sold	4,200
Selling price per unit	$36.00
Production costs:	
Direct materials per unit	$ 7.95
Direct labor per unit.	4.25
Variable overhead per unit	3.00
Fixed overhead per annum	54,000
Marketing and administrative costs:	
Variable marketing costs.	15,000
Fixed marketing costs	10,800
Fixed administrative costs	12,000

Required   a. Determine the cost of a single unit of product under absorption costing and variable costing.
b. Prepare income statements for 19x1 using absorption costing and variable costing.
c. Reconcile the absorption-costing and variable-costing figures for operating income.
d. Compute the company's breakeven sales in dollars. How does your calculation of breakeven sales compare with your income statement prepared under absorption costing? Explain your comparison.

P12–25   **Preparation of Variable-Costing Income Statements**

The absorption-costing income statements for the Maxim Company's first two years of operation for its only product are shown below:

	19x5	19x6
Sales	$240,000	$360,000
Cost of goods sold:		
Opening inventory	–0–	61,000
Cost of goods manufactured	244,000	235,600
Goods available for sale.	244,000	296,600
Less: Ending inventory	61,000	18,600
Cost of goods sold	183,000	278,000
Gross margin	57,000	82,000
Marketing and administrative costs.	36,000	42,000
Operating income before income taxes	$ 21,000	$ 40,000

The cost of goods manufactured per unit of product is computed as follows for 19x5:

Direct materials	$1.60
Direct labor	1.10
Variable manufacturing overhead	1.50
Fixed manufacturing overhead	1.90
Total cost per unit	$6.10

The total dollar amount of fixed overhead costs for 19x5 is unchanged for 19x6. Variable manufacturing costs per unit and the selling price of the company's product are also unchanged for 19x6.

Production and sales data:

	19x5	19x6
Units produced	40,000	38,000
Units sold	30,000	45,000

Marketing and administrative costs:

	19x5	19x6
Variable marketing costs	$12,000	$18,000
Fixed marketing costs	6,000	6,000
Fixed administrative costs	18,000	18,000
Total	$36,000	$42,000

There are no work in process inventories.

Required
a. Prepare income statements for the company for each year using the variable-costing method.
b. Reconcile the absorption-costing and variable-costing operating incomes for each year.
c. The president of the company notes that sales revenue in 19x6 increased by 50 percent, while the gross margin for 19x6 using absorption costing only increased by 43.8 percent. How do you explain this?

P12–26 **Cost-Volume-Profit Decision Making for Product Lines**

The officers of Bradshaw Company are reviewing the profitability of the company's four products and the potential effect of several proposals for varying the product mix. An excerpt from the income statement and other data follow:

	Totals	Product P	Product Q	Product R	Product S
Sales	$62,600	$10,000	$18,000	$12,600	$22,000
Cost of goods sold	44,274	4,750	7,056	13,968	18,500
Gross profit	18,326	5,250	10,944	(1,368)	3,500
Operating costs	12,012	1,990	2,976	2,826	4,220
Income before income taxes	$ 6,314	$ 3,260	$ 7,968	$ (4,194)	$ (720)
Units sold		1,000	1,200	1,800	2,000
Sales price per unit		$10.00	$15.00	$7.00	$11.00
Variable cost of goods sold per unit		$ 2.50	$ 3.00	$6.50	$ 6.00
Variable operating costs per unit		$ 1.17	$ 1.25	$1.00	$ 1.20

Each of the following proposals is to be considered independently of the other proposals. Consider only the product changes stated in each proposal; the activity of other products remains stable. Ignore income taxes.

a. If product R is discontinued, the effect on income will be
   (1) $900 increase.
   (2) $4,194 increase.
   (3) $12,600 decrease.
   (4) $1,368 increase.
   (5) None of the above.

b. If product R is discontinued and a consequent loss of customers causes a decrease of 200 units in sales of Q, the total effect on income will be
   (1) $15,600 decrease.
   (2) $2,866 increase.
   (3) $2,044 increase.
   (4) $1,250 decrease.
   (5) None of the above.

c. If the sales price of R is increased to $8 with a decrease in the number of units sold to 1,500, the effect on income will be
   (1) $2,199 decrease.
   (2) $600 decrease.
   (3) $750 increase.
   (4) $2,199 increase.
   (5) None of the above.

d. The plant in which R is produced can be utilized to produce a new product, T. The total variable costs per unit of T are $8.05, and 1,600 units can be sold at $9.50 each. If T is introduced and R is discontinued, the total effect on income will be
   (1) $2,600 increase.
   (2) $2,320 increase.
   (3) $3,220 increase.
   (4) $1,420 increase.
   (5) None of the above.

e. Part of the plant in which P is produced can easily be adapted to the production of S, but changes in quantities may make changes in sales prices advisable. If production of P is reduced to 500 units (to be sold at $12 each) and production of S is increased to 2,500 units (to be sold at $10.50 each), the total effect on income will be
   (1) $1,765 decrease.
   (2) $250 increase.
   (3) $2,060 decrease.
   (4) $1,515 decrease.
   (5) None of the above.

f. Production of P can be doubled by adding a second shift, but higher wages must then be paid, increasing variable cost of goods sold to $3.50 for each additional unit. If the 1,000 additional units of P can be sold at $10 each, the total effect on income will be
   (1) $10,000 increase.
   (2) $5,330 increase.
   (3) $6,500 increase.
   (4) $2,260 increase.
   (5) None of the above.

(AICPA Adapted)

P12–27   Preparation of Segmented Income Statements and Analysis of Results

The Summar Company manufactures two products: televisions and clock radios. They are sold in two markets: European and Asian. The condensed income statement for the Summar Company is shown below:

SUMMAR COMPANY
Income Statement—Contribution Format
For the Year Ended December 31, 19x5

Sales		$1,152,000
Variable manufacturing costs		288,000
Contribution margin		864,000
Fixed costs:		
Fixed overhead	$315,440	
Marketing costs	216,160	
Administrative costs	156,000	
Total fixed costs		687,600
Operating income before		
income taxes		$ 176,400

There are no variable marketing costs.

A sales manager is convinced that a problem exists in the Asian territory and has instructed you to find it. You are provided with the following information:

1. Two thirds of the Summar Company's sales are from the European territory. Fifty percent of the variable manufacturing costs are traceable to each territory.
2. The fixed costs are traced to each territory as follows:
   a. Fixed overhead of $117,400 and $88,800 to the European and Asian territories, respectively.
   b. Marketing costs of $109,600 and $51,800 to the European and Asian territories, respectively.
   c. Administrative costs of $67,440 and $43,400 to the European and Asian territories, respectively.
3. Seventy-five percent of the Asian territory's sales are attributable to televisions. The contribution margin ratio is 70 percent for televisions and 40 percent for clock radios.
4. The fixed costs for each product within the Asian territory are as follows:
   a. Fixed overhead is $28,000 for televisions and $23,200 for clock radios.
   b. Marketing costs are $7,200 and $21,600 for the televisions and clock radios, respectively.
   c. Administrative costs are $33,000 for televisions and $5,400 for clock radios.

Required   a. You are to prepare segmented income statements, first by territory and then by product within the Asian sales territory.
   b. Describe the problem in the Asian sales territory and how you would advise solving it.

P12–28   Preparation of a Segmented Income Statement and Analysis of Results

An absorption-costing income statement for 19x7 is shown below for the Edent Drug Company. The Edent Drug Company sells an antacid and a beta blocker in two sales territories: northwest and northeast.

EDENT DRUG COMPANY
Absorption-Costing Income Statement
For the Year Ended December 31, 19x7

	Total	Northwest	Northeast
Sales	$564,000	$288,000	$276,000
Cost of goods sold	384,324	205,362	178,962
Gross margin	179,676	82,638	97,038
Marketing and administrative costs.	175,956	92,118	83,838
Operating income (loss) before income taxes	$ 3,720	$ (9,480)	$ 13,200

A company manager notices the loss in the northwest territory and orders an investigation of that territory to determine whether it should be eliminated. You are provided with the following information:

1. Sales by product and variable costs:

	Antacid	Beta Blocker
Sales.	$384,000	$180,000
Ratio of variable manufacturing costs to sales	45%	64%
Ratio of variable marketing costs to sales	8%	3%

2. Sales of product by region:

Product	Northwest	Northeast
Antacid	$168,000	$216,000
Beta blocker.	120,000	60,000
Total	$288,000	$276,000

3. The total fixed manufacturing overhead amounts to $96,324, of which $44,652 is direct to the northwest region, $35,052 is direct to the northeast region, and the balance is common and allocated 50 percent to each region.
4. The total fixed marketing costs amount to $70,296, of which $26,448 is direct to the northwest region, $29,148 is direct to the northeast region, and the balance is common and allocated 50 percent to each region.
5. The total fixed administrative costs amount to $69,540, of which $36,030 is direct to the northwest region, $23,010 is direct to the northeast region, and the balance is common and allocated 50 percent to each region.

Required
a. Prepare a segmented contribution income statement showing segment margin by territory for the Edent Drug Company.
b. Do you recommend eliminating the northwest territory, which is operating under a loss? Support your conclusion.

P12–29 **Preparation of Segmented Income Statement and Analysis of Results**
The Bobbin Company's segmented income statement by territory for 19x5 is shown below:

BOBBIN COMPANY
Segmented Income Statement—Contribution Format
For the Year Ended December 31, 19x5

	Total	European	Domestic
Sales.	$720,000	$252,000	$468,000
Variable cost of goods sold.	324,000	113,360	210,640
Contribution margin	396,000	138,640	257,360
Less: Direct fixed overhead and other costs:			
Fixed overhead	112,000	64,000	48,000
Marketing costs.	105,600	36,800	68,800
Administrative costs.	80,000	60,000	20,000
Total direct fixed costs.	297,600	160,800	136,800
Territorial segment margin	98,400	$ (22,160)	$120,560
Less: Indirect fixed overhead			
and other costs (common costs):			
Fixed overhead	24,000		
Marketing costs.	19,200		
Administrative costs.	27,200		
Total common costs	70,400		
Operating income before income taxes.	$ 28,000		

The Bobbin Company produces two items: sewing machines and calculators. The company's president wants to study the loss incurred by the European sales territory. An investigation of company records reveals the following:

1. In the European territory, $160,000 of total sales are traceable to calculators. The contribution margin ratios are:

> Calculators 51%
> Sewing machines . . . 62%

2. In the European territory, $56,000 of the total fixed overhead is traceable to direct fixed overhead, and the remainder is traceable to common fixed overhead. Of the $56,000 direct fixed overhead, $30,400 is traceable to sewing machines, and the remainder is traceable to calculators. In addition, $32,800 of the total fixed marketing costs are direct fixed costs, and $24,800 of these are traceable to sewing machines. Finally, $54,400 of the total administrative costs are direct costs, and $42,400 of these are traceable to sewing machines.

Required *a.* Prepare for the company president a segmented income statement by product within the European territory.

b. Discuss any problems you find in the European territory. Make recommendations to the company's president for correcting the existing problems.

P12–30 **Preparation of Segmented Income Statements**

The Klug Corporation produces and sells three products. The three products, A, B, and C, are sold in two markets: east and west. At the end of the first year, the following income statement was prepared:

	Total	East	West
Sales	$700,000	$520,000	$180,000
Cost of goods sold	430,000	304,000	126,000
Gross margin	270,000	216,000	54,000
Marketing costs	51,400	32,000	19,400
Administrative costs	108,000	60,000	48,000
Total marketing and administrative costs	159,400	92,000	67,400
Operating income (loss) before taxes	$110,600	$124,000	$(13,400)

Management has expressed concern with the west market because of the $13,400 loss.

In attempting to decide whether to eliminate the west market, the following information has been gathered:

	Product		
	A	**B**	**C**
Sales	$320,000	$260,000	$120,000
Variable manufacturing costs as a percentage of sales	40%	50%	60%
Variable marketing costs as a percentage of sales.	5%	3%	4%

	Sales by Market	
Product	**East**	**West**
A	$240,000	$80,000
B	200,000	60,000
C	80,000	40,000

All administrative costs and fixed manufacturing costs are common to the three products and the two markets and are fixed for the period. The fixed marketing costs are direct costs and are separable by market. All fixed costs are based on a prorated yearly amount.

Required a. Prepare an income statement showing contribution margins and segment margins by markets.

b. Assuming there are no alternative uses for the corporation's present capacity, would you recommend dropping the west market? Why or why not?

c. Prepare an income statement showing contribution margins and segment margins by products.

P12–31 **Preparation of Segmented Income Statements**

The Krew Corporation produces and sells three products. The three products, A, B, and C, are sold in two markets: east and west. At the end of the first year, the following income statement was prepared:

	Total	East	West
Sales	$960,000	$360,000	$600,000
Cost of goods sold	584,000	216,000	368,000
Gross margin	376,000	144,000	232,000
Marketing costs.	129,600	71,200	58,400
Administrative costs.	180,000	80,000	100,000
Total marketing and administrative	309,600	151,200	158,400
Operating income (loss) before taxes	$ 66,400	$ (7,200)	$ 13,600

Management has expressed concern with the east market because of the $7,200 loss.

In attempting to decide whether to eliminate the east market, the following information has been gathered:

	Product		
	A	**B**	**C**
Sales	$320,000	$240,000	$400,000
Variable manufacturing costs as a percentage of sales	50%	35%	30%
Variable marketing costs as a percentage of sales.	4%	2%	3%

Product	Sales by Market	
	East	**West**
A	$120,000	$200,000
B	80,000	160,000
C	160,000	240,000

Direct fixed costs by market:

	East	West
Manufacturing	$56,000	$72,000
Marketing	40,000	24,000
Administrative	60,000	70,000

Administrative costs are all fixed.

Required
a. Prepare an income statement showing contribution margins and segment margins by markets.
b. Assuming there are no alternative uses for the corporation's present capacity, would you recommend dropping the east market? Why or why not?
c. Prepare an income statement showing contribution margins and segment margins by products.

▶ **CASES**

C12–32 **Preparation of Variable-Costing Income Statements and Analysis of Income Statement Differences**

The Kircus Company was organized on January 1, 19x7. Absorption-costing income statements for the first three years are given below:

	19x7	19x8	19x9
Sales	$450,000	$360,000	$450,000
Less: Cost of goods sold:			
Beginning inventory	–0–	–0–	120,000
Cost of goods produced	315,000	360,000	270,000
Goods available for sale	315,000	360,000	390,000
Less: Ending inventory	–0–	120,000	67,500
Cost of goods sold	315,000	240,000	322,500
Gross margin	135,000	120,000	127,500
Marketing and administrative costs	84,000	76,800	84,000
Operating income (loss) before income taxes	$ 51,000	$ 43,200	$ 43,500

Sales and production data:

	19x7	19x8	19x9
Units sold	30,000	24,000	30,000
Units produced	30,000	36,000	24,000

Marketing and administrative costs:

Variable marketing costs	8% of sales
Fixed marketing costs	$21,000
Fixed administrative costs	27,000

Fixed overhead is charged to production on the basis of *each year's production.* The company uses FIFO in valuing its inventories.

Required *a.* Prepare income statements for each of the three years using the variable-costing approach.

b. Reconcile the absorption-costing and variable-costing figures for operating income for each year. (*Hint:* Use the high-low method to determine the fixed overhead.)

c. Explain why the 19x9 operating income under absorption costing differs from the 19x7 operating income although the same number of units were sold in both years, fixed costs for the two years were unchanged, and variable costs per unit were also unchanged.

d. Given that the fixed costs for the three years are the same and the variable cost per unit is also the same in each year, why is the operating income in 19x9 only $300 more than the operating income in 19x8 despite an increase in sales of 25 percent?

C12–33 **Preparation of Segmented Income Statement for a Service Organization and Discussion of Allocation Strategies**

Music Teachers, Inc., is an educational association for music teachers that had 20,000 members during 19x5. The association operates from a central headquarters but has local membership chapters throughout the United States. Monthly meetings are held by the local chapters to discuss recent developments on topics of interest to music teachers. The association's journal, *Teachers' Forum,* is issued monthly with features about recent developments in the field. The association publishes books and reports and sponsors professional courses that qualify for continuing professional education credit. The statement of revenues and costs for the current year is presented below:

MUSIC TEACHERS, INC.
Statement of Revenues and Costs
For the Year Ended November 30, 19x5
($000 omitted)

Revenues	$3,275
Costs:	
Salaries	$ 920
Personnel costs	230
Occupancy costs	280
Reimbursement to local chapters	600
Other membership services	500
Printing and paper	320
Postage and shipping	176
Instructors' fees	80
General and administrative	38
Total costs	$3,144
Excess of revenues over costs	$ 131

The board of directors of Music Teachers, Inc., has requested that a segmented statement of operations be prepared showing the contribution of each revenue center (i.e., membership, magazine subscriptions, books and reports, and continuing education). Mike Doyle has been assigned this responsibility and has gathered the following data prior to statement preparation.

1. Membership dues are $100 per year, of which $20 is considered to cover a one-year subscription to the association's journal. Other benefits include membership in the association and chapter affiliation. The portion of the dues covering the magazine subscription ($20) should be assigned to the magazine subscriptions revenue center.
2. One-year subscriptions to *Teachers' Forum* were sold to nonmembers and libraries at $30 each. A total of 2,500 of these subscriptions were sold. In addition to subscriptions, the magazine generated $100,000 in advertising revenue. The costs per magazine subscription were $7 for printing and paper and $4 for postage and shipping.
3. A total of 28,000 technical reports and professional texts were sold by the books and reports department at an average unit selling price of $25. Average costs per publication were as follows:

Printing and paper	$4
Postage and shipping . . .	2

4. The association offers a variety of continuing education courses to both members and nonmembers. The one-day courses cost $75 each and were attended by 2,400 students in 19x5. A total of 1,760 students took two-day courses at a cost of $125 for each course. Outside instructors were paid to teach some courses.
5. Salary and occupancy data are as follows:

	Salaries	**Square Footage**
Membership.	$210,000	2,000 sq. ft.
Magazine subscriptions	150,000	2,000
Books and reports	300,000	3,000
Continuing education	180,000	2,000
Corporate staff	80,000	1,000
	$920,000	10,000 sq. ft.

The books and reports department also rents warehouse space at an annual cost of $50,000. Personnel costs are 25 percent of salaries.

6. Printing and paper costs other than for magazine subscriptions and books and reports relate to the continuing education department.

7. General and administrative costs include all other costs incurred by the corporate staff to operate the association.

Doyle has decided he will assign all revenues and costs to the revenue centers that can be:

1. Traced directly to a revenue center.
2. Allocated on a reasonable and logical basis to a revenue center.

The costs that can be traced or assigned to corporate staff as well as any other costs that cannot be assigned to revenue centers will be grouped with the general and administrative costs and not allocated to the revenue centers. Doyle believes allocations tend to be arbitrary and are not useful for management reporting and analysis. He believes any further allocation of the general and administrative costs associated with the operation and administration of the association would be arbitrary.

Required   *a.* Prepare a segmented statement of revenues and costs that presents the contribution of each revenue center and includes the common costs of the organization that are not allocated to the revenue centers.

b. If segmented reporting is adopted by the association for continuing usage, discuss the ways the information provided by the report can be utilized by the association.

c. Mike Doyle decided not to allocate some indirect or nontraceable costs to revenue centers because he believes allocations tend to be arbitrary.

(1) Besides the arbitrary argument, what reasons are often presented for not allocating indirect or nontraceable costs to revenue centers?

(2) Under what circumstances might the allocation of indirect or nontraceable costs to revenue centers be acceptable?

(CMA Adapted)

▶ **ANSWERS TO SELF TEST**

True or False

1. False	2. True	3. False	4. True	5. True	6. False
7. False	8. False	9. True	10. False		

Multiple Choice

1. *b.* Sales $400,000

Less:

Direct materials	$ 60,000	
Direct labor	50,000	
Variable overhead	80,000	
Variable marketing and administrative costs	20,000	210,000
Contribution margin		$190,000

2. *a.* Sales. $800,000
    Less:
        Direct materials $200,000
        Direct labor. 90,000
        Variable overhead 120,000
        Variable marketing and administrative costs 40,000   450,000
          Contribution margin $350,000

3. *d.* Sales. $400,000
    Less:
        Direct materials . . . . $ 60,000
        Direct labor 50,000
        Variable overhead 80,000
        Direct fixed overhead 60,000
        Allocated fixed overhead 30,000   280,000
          Gross margin $120,000

4. *a.* Sales. $400,000
    Less:
        Direct materials . . . . $ 60,000
        Direct labor. 50,000
        Variable overhead 80,000
        Direct fixed overhead 60,000
        Variable marketing and administrative costs 20,000   270,000
          Segment margin $130,000

5. *c.* Sales. $800,000
    Less:
        Direct materials $200,000
        Direct labor. 90,000
        Variable overhead 120,000
        Direct fixed overhead 100,000
        Variable marketing and administrative costs 40,000   550,000
          Segment margin $250,000

Selecting Relevant Data for Decision Making and Product Pricing

---

▶ **LEARNING OBJECTIVES**

After reading this chapter, you should be able to:

1. Distinguish between relevant and irrelevant data and explain why this distinction is important to the decision-making process.
2. Identify two kinds of irrelevant costs and explain why they are irrelevant.
3. Cite the differences between differential analysis and the comparative income approach and the data that each requires.
4. Identify and analyze the relevant costs and revenues when deciding whether to:
   a. Purchase new labor-saving equipment.
   b. Replace existing equipment with newer equipment.
   c. Enter a market with a new product.
   d. Accept a special order at less than full cost.
   e. Make or buy component parts.
5. Analyze the relevant data and correctly decide whether to sell a joint product at the splitoff point or process it further.
6. Assess various pricing strategies and prepare schedules to assist managers in pricing their firm's products.
7. Analyze a product's contribution margin for the purpose of allocating scarce resources.
8. Formulate the objective function and constraint inequalities needed to solve a linear programming problem. (Appendix 13-A)
9. Prepare a graphical solution to a linear programming problem. (Appendix 13-A)

▶ **INTERVIEW**

Lawrence J. Hoffman
Corporate Controller
AAMCO Transmissions,
Inc.

Q. *Have you participated in a firm's pricing decisions? If so, what pricing strategy was employed and what factors influenced the selection of this pricing strategy?*

A. My participation in pricing decisions indicates that a firm will not use one strategy in isolation. Rather, a primary strategy will be adopted for each product line, and the validity of that strategy will be tested by a comparison to pricing generated by other strategies.

I have used various pricing strategies for the company's different product lines and for the same product line under different conditions.

▶ For a secondary business that is viewed as a support to the primary business, competition-based pricing is used as the primary strategy. The validity check is to mark up pricing, using only variable costs. The competition-based pricing is accepted if the secondary business covers all variable costs and makes a contribution to the company-wide fixed overhead.

▶ For a primary business, mark-up pricing using full absorption costing is employed. The validity check is competition-based pricing to ensure that the calculated price is realistic in the market place.

▶ For another primary business, demand-oriented pricing is used. As the brand name increased in recognition, the price was increased. The validity check was mark-up pricing using only variable costs.

▶ For a business opportunity that was viewed as new, incremental, and noncannibalizing, mark-up pricing using only variable costs was employed. Later, when that opportunity was viewed as ongoing, competition-based pricing was the primary strategy with mark-up pricing as the validity check.

The factor that determines what primary strategy to employ is how the company views the business. The factors that influence this view are these:

▶ The stage of the product life cycle, new or established.
▶ The strategic nature of the product, primary or secondary.
▶ The nature of the opportunity, base or incremental, permanent or temporary.
▶ The company philosophy, leader or follower.
▶ The information available, the accuracy of the costing system, and the knowledge of competitors.

▶ A significant portion of a manager's time is spent on decision making. When a firm has a sophisticated management information system, the amount of information available to its managers is almost infinite. Thus, managers must be selective in requesting specific kinds of information if they wish to avoid being inundated in a sea of data. The key to limiting the flow of data is to request only relevant information.

Different decisions require different types of data. An important part of any decision is its cost. Most of us are constantly faced with decisions about items and their costs that run the gamut from what to purchase in a supermarket to which brand of automobile to buy. Managers are often faced with a variety of decisions that rely on cost data. Examples of these decisions are whether to (1) purchase new equipment, (2) replace existing equipment, (3) enter a market with a new product, (4) take special orders at less than full cost, (5) make or buy component parts, and (6) sell multiple products from a common direct material at the splitoff point or process them further. In addition, cost information is needed for (7) product-pricing decisions and (8) the allocation of scarce resources to particular products. To arrive at correct decisions, managers need certain cost and revenue information referred to as *relevant costs and relevant revenues.* ◀

Relevant Data

L.O. 1

This chapter focuses on identifying which information is pertinent, or relevant, to decision making. Techniques that assist decision makers in separating the relevant information from the irrelevant are identified. By focusing on pertinent information only, managers are able to use their time efficiently and to make more appropriate decisions. In the decision-making process, any future cost that differs among alternatives and will influence the outcome is a **relevant cost.** Similarly, a **relevant revenue** is any future revenue that differs among alternatives and will influence the final outcome. Because a decision applies to future actions, relevant costs are *future costs* rather than *historical costs.* (*Note:* In Chapter 2, we discussed a variety of basic cost concepts and terms. Because many of those terms and concepts are used in this chapter, readers may wish to refer to Chapter 2 to refresh their memories.)

Irrelevant Costs

L.O. 2

Before proceeding to the selection and identification of relevant costs, it is useful to identify the **irrelevant costs** that will not affect the decision. They fall into two main groups: (1) sunk costs and (2) costs that are the same for each alternative.

Sunk Costs A **sunk cost** is a cost that has already been incurred and cannot be changed by any future action. Thus, a sunk cost cannot affect the decision-making process. For example, if a firm purchased a special-purpose machine for $50,000, this is a sunk cost that will not affect any future decisions regarding the machine. If the machine has a 10-year useful life and after one year of use a new, more efficient machine is available at a cost of $60,000, the decision whether to purchase the newer machine should be based on the cost savings of the newer machine compared to its net cost ($60,000 minus the sales proceeds from selling the older machine). Both the original cost of the machine ($50,000) and its current book value (the original cost of the machine minus any depreciation) are sunk costs and will not affect the decision except for any tax savings that a tax-deductible loss may bring.

Future Costs that Are the Same for Each Alternative When deciding between two alternatives, the difference in their costs must be considered. However, if the costs are the same, they may be ignored *provided it has already been decided that one of the alternatives will be selected.* For example, if a decision *has already been made* to purchase one of two new cars and their costs are the same, the choice will be based on each car's reputation, features, styling, and so on, *not on its price.* However, if a decision is to be made about whether to purchase a new car, then price will obviously play an important role.

Using Costs in Decision Making

L.O. 3
Differential versus comparative income approaches

As noted in Chapter 4, two different approaches may be used to solve problems for decision-making purposes. The comprehensive comparative income approach includes both relevant and irrelevant costs, while the simpler differential analysis includes only relevant costs. When the **comparative income approach** is used, the net operating income for each alternative is computed and compared. All revenues and costs are considered—even those that are the same for each alternative. On the other hand, in **differential analysis,** only revenues and costs that differ among the alternatives are considered. The end result—a correct decision—will be the same regardless of which method is used.

Sentimentality and financial accounting conventions should never be allowed to cloud the reasoning behind a decision. Many of us have heard someone state that although his shares of X Corporation stock have declined in market value, he has not incurred a loss because he has not sold the shares. Managers should not use this type of reasoning. The cost of the shares is a *sunk cost,* and even though the failure to sell an investment may postpone the recognition of a loss on a firm's financial statements (a bookkeeping convention), the decision to retain an investment must be based on what *the market value is today* and what the future cash inflows are likely to be. If a larger profit can be made by holding the investment instead of selling it and reinvesting the proceeds, then retention is indicated.

Another way of viewing this decision is to realize that whenever a manager decides not to sell an investment, a decision is really being made to reinvest in the same investment. Thus, the criterion for retention should be the same as overt investment—a comparison of current cost (not the sunk cost) with the expected future cash inflows. Too often, managers are concerned with the book value of an existing investment in a product, machine, and so forth, and its effects on the firm's income statement when a loss must be recognized for financial accounting purposes. Instead, managers should recognize that it may be to the firm's advantage—and eventually to the manager's advantage—to bite the bullet now in favor of a new product, machine, and so on, that will enhance future profits more than will the immediate write-off of book values. Book values should not color a manager's thinking or decision making despite their use in calculating gains and losses for financial accounting purposes.

Once a manager recognizes which costs are not relevant for decision-making purposes, he or she is ready to begin analyzing data.

▶ EQUIPMENT DECISIONS

The selection of relevant data—revenues and costs—will depend on the kind of decision to be made. Although all eight kinds of decisions mentioned at the beginning of this chapter have a common thread, the data needed to arrive at the correct choice for each varies to some degree. We will now examine these decisions one by one, focusing on the information that is relevant to each. To simplify our discussion, we will defer income tax considerations to Chapter 15 and the time value of money (interest) to Chapters 14 and 15.

**Purchasing
New Equipment**

L.O. 4a

The data that are relevant to the purchase of new equipment that will not replace existing equipment are simpler to identify than the relevant data for other kinds of decisions. Thus far, our emphasis has been on costs. However, costs often entail allocations to more than one time period, such as depreciation. Decision making focuses on *cash flows.* Hence, the process entails identifying the *net cash inflows* and the *net cash outflows* for the useful life of the equipment and then comparing the two. The net cash outflows may be grouped and referred to as the *net investment,* which consists of deducting the salvage value, if any, from the sum of (1) the cash purchase price of the machine, (2) the cost of insurance during shipment from the vendor, and (3) freight in.

The cash inflows are grouped together and referred to as the cash operating advantage. The **cash operating advantage** is the cash effect of the difference in revenues minus the cash effect of the difference in cash operating costs as a result of a contemplated change in a firm's operations. In this case, the change in operations is the purchase of a new machine. The decision whether to purchase the machine is then based on a comparison of the net investment with the cash operating advantage for the useful life of the machine.

The Automated Manufacturing Company is contemplating the purchase of a piece of sophisticated machinery. The following information is available:

Purchase price of new machine $90,000
Useful life of machine . . . .   5 years
Salvage value at the end of five years . . . $ 5,000

Annual Operating Information

	With New Machine	Without New Machine
Sales	$500,000	$500,000
Direct materials cost	95,000	100,000
Direct labor	46,000	60,000
Variable overhead	32,200	42,000
Fixed overhead	100,000	100,000
Depreciation	17,000	–0–

The differential analysis of the relevant data may be organized as shown in Illustration 13-1.

▶ **ILLUSTRATION 13-1**

AUTOMATED MANUFACTURING COMPANY
Calculation of Net Investment and Cash Operating Advantage
For the Purchase of a New Machine
Differential Income Approach

Net investment:	
Purchase price of machine	$ 90,000
Less: Salvage value	5,000
Net investment	$ 85,000
Cash operating advantage:	
Savings in direct materials cost ($100,000 − $95,000)	$ 5,000
Savings in direct labor cost ($60,000 − $46,000)	14,000
Savings in variable overhead ($42,000 − $32,200)	9,800
Cash operating advantage—one year	28,800
Useful life of machine	× 5
Cash operating advantage—five years	$144,000
Net advantage in favor of purchasing	$ 59,000

Ignoring income taxes and the time value of money, the purchase of the new machine appears to be a favorable investment. A net cash outflow of $85,000 will result in a cash inflow of $144,000 over the five-year period for a net advantage in favor of purchasing the machine. The fixed overhead of $100,000 was ignored in this calculation because it would be unchanged by the decision and is thus an irrelevant cost.

The depreciation of $17,000 is also ignored because the recording of *depreciation* is a bookkeeping convention that *has no effect on cash* when taxes are ignored, as can be seen from the following entry:

Depreciation	17,000	
Accumulated Depreciation		17,000

($90,000 − $5,000 salvage = $85,000) ÷ 5 years = $17,000.

The investment decision should be based on the cash effects of the decision over the estimated life of the machine. The cash effects over the five years may be summarized as follows:

	Cash Inflow (Outflow)
Savings in variable costs ($28,800 × 5)—also the cash operating advantage	$144,000
Cost of machine	(90,000)
Salvage value at the end of five years	5,000
Net cash inflow for five years	$ 59,000

When differential analysis is used, as above, depreciation is ignored because the focus is on *cash flows*. If depreciation of $90,000 were considered, the $90,000 would be counted twice—as a cash outflow and as depreciation. The investment decision is based on the difference between the net cash inflows and the net cash outflows.

The decision whether to replace an existing machine with a newer, more efficient machine is similar to the decision whether to purchase a new machine, except additional relevant data must be considered.

▶ **ILLUSTRATION 13-2**

MATURE PRODUCTS COMPANY
Machine Replacement Data

Original cost of the present machine.	$ 40,000
Less: Accumulated depreciation	30,000
Book value	$ 10,000
Purchase price of new machine	$100,000
Useful life of new machine	5 years
Remaining useful life of old machine	2 years
Overhaul of old machine extending its useful life to a total of 5 years.	$ 10,000
Salvage value of new machine	–0–
Market value of old machine, if sold	$ 4,000

	Old Machine	New Machine
Annual operating information:		
Sales	$400,000	$400,000
Direct materials cost	90,000	90,000
Direct labor cost	80,000	60,000
Variable overhead	48,000	36,000
Fixed overhead exclusive of depreciation	100,000	100,000
Depreciation:		
Old machine—2 years at $5,000 per year	10,000	
New machine—5 years at $20,000 per year		100,000

Replacing Existing Equipment

L.O. 4b

The relevant data needed for a decision whether to replace existing equipment is similar to that for whether to purchase a new machine, except the sales value of the old machine must be considered. Although the sales value of the old equipment is a cash inflow, it is customarily shown as a reduction of the investment to arrive at the net investment.

The Mature Products Company is contemplating replacing one of its present machines with a faster machine. The older machine is nearing the end of its economic useful life, but its life can be extended by a major overhaul. The available information is shown in Illustration 13-2.

Care must be taken to select only the data that are relevant to the decision. As noted for the purchase of new equipment, depreciation is not relevant. And when considering replacement, the book value of the old equipment is not relevant either. This can be seen by comparing Illustration 13-3, which indicates the net income for each alternative (old machine versus new machine), with Illustration 13-4, which is prepared on a net cash flow basis. Regardless of which method is used, the net cash advantage will *always be the same.*

After comparing Illustration 13-3 with Illustration 13-4, you should conclude that the following items are not relevant when the differential analysis is used:

1. *Sales revenue* because it is the same for both alternatives.
2. *Direct materials* because it is the same for both alternatives.
3. *Fixed overhead* because it is the same for both alternatives.
4. *Depreciation of the old machine* because it is a sunk cost that has no effect on cash flow.

▶ **ILLUSTRATION 13-3**

MATURE PRODUCTS COMPANY
Comparative Income Statements for
Retaining Old Machine or Purchasing New Machine
For the Five-Year Useful Life of the New Machine

	Keep Old Machine	Purchase New Machine	Effect on Net Income— Increase (Decrease)
Sales revenue (5 × $400,000).	$2,000,000	$2,000,000	$ –0–
Costs:			
Direct materials (5 × $90,000) . . . , ...	450,000	450,000	–0–
Direct labor (5 × $80,000; 5 × $60,000)	400,000	300,000	100,000
Variable overhead (5 × $48,000; 5 × $36,000)	240,000	180,000	60,000
Fixed overhead (5 × $100,000)	500,000	500,000	–0–
Depreciation: Old machine (2 × $5,000); new machine (5 × $20,000) . . .	10,000	100,000	(90,000)
Overhaul of old machine.	10,000	–0–	10,000
Total costs.	1,610,000	1,530,000	
Operating income	390,000	470,000	
Other income or (loss):			
Sales proceeds from old machine		4,000	4,000
Book value of old machine.		(10,000)	(10,000)
Loss on sale of old machine		(6,000)	
Income before income tax	$ 390,000	$ 464,000	$ 74,000
Net cash advantage in favor of replacing old machine.			$ 74,000 ◄

▶ **ILLUSTRATION 13-4**

MATURE PRODUCTS COMPANY
Analysis of Decision to Retain
Old Machine or Replace with New Machine
For the Five-Year Useful Life of the New Machine
Differential Income Approach

Net investment:		
Purchase price of new machine		$100,000
Less: Sales proceeds from old machine		4,000
Net investment.		96,000
Cash operating advantage:		
Direct labor savings	$100,000	
Variable overhead savings. . . , ...	60,000	
Old machine overhaul savings	10,000	170,000
Net cash advantage in favor of replacing old machine		$ 74,000 ◄

From Illustration 13-4, it can be seen that only the following items are relevant:

1. *The purchase price of the new machine* because it is a cash outflow.
2. *The sales proceeds from the sale of the old machine* because it is a cash inflow.
3. *The cash inflow from the savings in direct labor costs and variable overhead* because these costs would differ if the new machine were purchased.
4. *The cost of overhauling the old machine* because this represents the avoidance of a cash outflow (equivalent to a cash inflow).

▶ ENTERING A MARKET WITH A NEW PRODUCT

L.O. 4c

When deciding whether to introduce a new product, a firm must consider several other relevant costs in addition to those already discussed. These usually include advertising, incremental marketing costs, salespersons' commissions, and incremental administrative costs. Furthermore, the company must consider the amount of working capital that will be tied up in inventories and accounts receivable because this cash will not be available for other uses until the end of the product's life, perhaps in the far distant future. Even when the end of a product's life is foreseeable, the working capital released at its termination may differ from that invested due to losses on obsolete merchandise or the bargain sale of merchandise remaining on hand.

The Physico Company plans to enter the physical fitness market with a treadmill for gymnasium and home use. Based on a market survey and cost estimates provided by the firm's engineering and accounting departments, Physico's accounting department compiled the information shown in Illustration 13-5.

The analysis of the relevant data for deciding whether to enter the new market may be organized as shown in Illustration 13-6.

Ignoring income taxes and the time value of money, the decision favors entering the new market because a net investment of $930,000 should bring a 10-year net cash operating inflow of $2,950,000. The depreciation of the new machine is not factored into the calculations because, as mentioned previously, it stems from a bookkeeping convention that has no effect on cash flow.

▶ **PROGRESS CHECK**

1. What is the difference between relevant costs and irrelevant costs?
2. Assume that you are contemplating the purchase of a new machine to replace an older machine. The present cost of direct labor is $100,000; the cost of the direct labor will be $30,000 if the new machine is purchased. If you are using the comparative income statement approach for your analysis of whether or not to purchase the new machine, will you use both the $100,000 and the $30,000? Explain. Would your answer be different if you were using the differential income approach? Explain.
3. Is depreciation on machinery a relevant cost when making a decision to purchase a new machine if the effect of income taxes is to be ignored? Explain.
4. Is the salvage value of an old machine relevant when making a decision to replace an existing machine with a new one? Explain. What about the salvage value of the new machine? Explain.
5. When working capital is invested in a project of entering a new market, is the amount invested relevant to the decision? Explain.   ◀

The numerous kinds of decisions a manager must make always have some relevant data in common, but each decision usually involves some relevant costs that pertain to it alone. For example, when deciding whether to accept special orders at less than full cost, managers must base their decision on some data that are not relevant when deciding whether to introduce a new product.

▶ ILLUSTRATION 13-5

PHYSICO COMPANY
Data for Entering a New Market

Sales (10,000 at $250)	$2,500,000

Incremental costs:

Direct materials (10,000 at $60)	$600,000
Direct labor (10,000 at $50).	$500,000
Variable overhead (10,000 at $38)	$380,000
Fixed overhead exclusive of new machinery noted below	$400,000
Salespersons' commissions.	5% of sales
Fixed marketing and administrative costs	$200,000
Purchase of machinery needed for manufacturing this product	$900,000
Useful life of machinery	10 years
Salvage value of machinery	$20,000
Working capital needed at inception.	$400,000
Working capital returned at end of 10 years when the demand for this product is expected to be nil.	$350,000
Depreciation of machinery ($1,000,000 − $20,000 = $980,000 × 10%) = ...	$98,000

▶ ILLUSTRATION 13-6

PHYSICO COMPANY
Calculation of Cash Outflows and Cash Inflows
For Entering a New Market for the
10-Year Useful Life of the Product
Differential Income Approach

	Inflow (Outflow)
Net investment:	
Purchase price of the machinery.	$ (900,000)
Salvage value of machine.	20,000
Working capital at inception	(400,000)
Release of working capital at the end of 10 years	350,000
Net investment	$ (930,000)
Cash operating advantage:	
Sales per annum.	$2,500,000
Variable costs per annum:	
Direct materials	(600,000)
Direct labor	(500,000)
Variable overhead	(380,000)
Commissions (5% × $2.5 million)	(125,000)
Fixed costs per annum:	
Manufacturing overhead	(400,000)
Marketing and administrative costs	(200,000)
Cash operating advantage per annum	295,000
Life of product	× 10
Cash operating advantage for 10 years	$2,950,000
Net cash advantage of entering a new market.	$2,020,000

▶ ACCEPTING SPECIAL ORDERS AT LESS THAN FULL COST

L.O. 4d   At first glance, it may appear that accepting a special order at less than full cost can only contribute a loss to a firm's overall profitability. This is not necessarily the case. Under certain conditions, a special order at less than full cost may, in fact, increase a firm's overall profitability. The necessary conditions are:

1. The firm has some unused capacity, usually of a seasonal or temporary nature.
2. The special order is for a *segmented market that does not compete with the firm's regular sales*. The special order may be packaged under a private label that does not compete with the firm's brand name, or it may be sold in a foreign market where the firm's product is not sold.
3. Although the price offered may be less than the firm's total cost per unit (including fixed costs), the price must be high enough to cover the firm's variable costs, any special costs associated with producing and shipping the special order, and some contribution margin.

The Glossy Soap Company manufactures liquid soap and markets it under its brand name. Although the firm is profitable and its product enjoys a good reputation, it is only operating at 80 percent of capacity. Glossy plans to expand into foreign markets in the future, but the unused capacity of 20 percent will not be used during the remainder of 19x3. A soap wholesaler in Mexico wishes to expand its business by marketing liquid soap, which it presently does not sell. The Mexican wholesaler has approached the Glossy Soap Company with an offer to purchase 10,000 cases of soap at a price of $20 per case.

The condensed income statement for the Glossy Soap Company appears in Illustration 13-7. The variable costs for this special order will be the same as those for the firm's normal operations. In addition, Glossy Soap will be required to ship the merchandise FOB destination at a freight charge of $1,400. The sales manager would like to assess the effects on net income of accepting the order at $20 per case even though the company's cost per case is $27 ($5 + $6 + $6 + $10).

The company's income statement with and without the special order is shown in Illustration 13-8. Note that the special order would add $20,020 of net income to the company's overall profitability, provided it does not intrude on regular sales. If the special order could compete with the firm's normal sales and if normal sales decreased by 10,000 cases, the firm's profitability would decrease by $210,980 instead of increase by $20,020. This can be seen from the following:

Normal sales (10,000 × $50)	$500,000
Special order (10,000 × $20)	200,000
Net decrease in sales revenue	300,000
Add freight out*	1,400
	301,400
Income tax at 30%	90,420
Decrease in net income	$210,980

* Other variable and fixed costs are unaffected because the same number of units (80,000 cases) will be produced both with and without the order.

Because of the potential danger of competition, a firm must be certain that a special order will not undermine its regular sales. If Glossy is uncertain of the effects of the special order, it should probably forgo the additional net income of $20,020 and not risk the alternative of a $210,980 decrease in net income.

It is not necessary to compare full income statements to determine the effects of a special order. In fact, by recognizing and using only those reve-

▶ **ILLUSTRATION 13-7**

GLOSSY SOAP COMPANY
Income Statement
For the Six Months Ended June 30, 19x3

Sales (80,000 cases at $50)		$4,000,000
Cost of goods sold:		
Direct materials (80,000 cases at $5)	$400,000	
Direct labor (80,000 cases at $6)	480,000	
Variable overhead (80,000 cases at $6)	480,000	
Fixed overhead (80,000 cases at $10)	800,000	2,160,000
Gross margin.		1,840,000
Marketing and administrative costs—all fixed		800,000
Operating income before income taxes		1,040,000
Provision for income taxes at 30%		312,000
Net income		$ 728,000

▶ **ILLUSTRATION 13-8**

GLOSSY SOAP COMPANY
Income Statements
Without and with a Special Order
For the Six Months Ended June 30, 19x3

	Without Order	With Order	Difference
Sales	$4,000,000	$4,200,000	$200,000*
Cost of goods sold:			
Direct materials	400,000	450,000	50,000†
Direct labor	480,000	540,000	60,000‡
Variable overhead	480,000	540,000	60,000§
Fixed overhead	800,000	800,000	–0–
Total cost of goods sold	2,160,000	2,330,000	170,000
Gross margin	1,840,000	1,870,000	30,000
Marketing and administrative costs—			
all fixed	800,000	800,000	–0–
Freight out	–0–	1,400	1,400
Total marketing and administrative costs . . .	800,000	801,400	1,400
Operating income before income taxes	1,040,000	1,068,600	28,600
Provision for income taxes at 30%.	312,000	320,580	8,580
Net income	$ 728,000	$ 748,020	$ 20,020

* 10,000 units at $20 per unit.
† 10,000 units at $5 per unit.
‡ 10,000 units at $6 per unit.
§ 10,000 units at $6 per unit.

nues and costs that are relevant, it is possible to achieve the desired result much more efficiently. The relevant costs and revenues are those that change. Thus, the fixed overhead and the fixed marketing and administrative costs may be ignored. The analysis may be prepared as shown in Illustration 13-9.

By concentrating only on relevant costs, Glossy's managers can focus more sharply on the items involved in the decision. The inclusion of items that have no effect on the decision may confuse the issue, especially if the

▶ **ILLUSTRATION 13-9**

GLOSSY SOAP COMPANY
Analysis of Relevant Costs and Revenues for Special Order
Differential Income Approach

Revenue (10,000 × $20)		$200,000
Less: Incremental costs:		
Direct materials (10,000 × $5).	$50,000	
Direct labor (10,000 × $6)	60,000	
Variable overhead (10,000 × $6).	60,000	
Freight out	1,400	171,400
Increase in operating income before income tax		28,600
Income tax at 30%.		8,580
Increase in net income		$ 20,020

original offer of $20 per case can be renegotiated or if the relevant costs (variable costs and freight out) can be altered.

Another decision that managers must often make is whether to purchase component parts from other firms or manufacture them internally. Although the selection of the relevant data for taking a special order at less than full cost is very similar to the selection of relevant data for the make-or-buy decision, some additional concepts must be introduced.

▶ MAKING OR BUYING COMPONENT PARTS

L.O. 4e

The make-or-buy decision cannot be reduced to mere quantitative factors. Quantitative considerations are important and may be the deciding factor, but a manager would be remiss if he or she failed to also weigh the relevant qualitative factors. Among the qualitative considerations that must be evaluated are:

1. *The supplier's reliability.*   An interruption in the delivery of a component part may totally shut down a firm's operations.
2. *The supplier's quality control.*   A defective component part may damage the reputation and reliability of the firm's product.
3. *The supplier's labor-management relations.*   Frequent or wildcat strikes may produce an erratic delivery schedule.
4. *Whether a supplier's low price* (an order for less than full cost) *is stable.*   A low price may be available only for the period of a supplier's idle capacity, and prices may increase at a later date. A contract for a long period of time (one to two years) may help avoid this problem.
5. *How long it would take to start manufacturing the part again if the supplier fails to deliver as promised.*   Retraining and rehiring of personnel may be an important consideration.

The quantitative relevant costs are the purchase price versus the component part's variable and avoidable fixed costs. However, it may also be necessary to consider the opportunity cost of any plant capacity that can be converted to an alternative use if it is released from manufacturing the component part. For example, freed plant capacity may be used to manufacture a new product or expand production of an existing product, or it may be sublet to another firm. In any case, the income that could be earned from any of these alternatives is an opportunity cost and must be factored into the quantitative analysis.

The Electric Motor Company manufactures electric motors for use in machinery. Although it currently manufactures its own armatures, it is considering purchasing them from a vendor. The armatures can be purchased from a reliable vendor for a two-year period at a price of $20 each. The firm's standard cost sheet for the armature is:

Direct materials	$ 6
Direct labor	5
Variable overhead	4
Fixed overhead	10
Total	$25

An analysis of the fixed overhead indicates that $3 is direct fixed overhead and $7 is common fixed overhead. The company uses 30,000 armatures per annum. If it decides to purchase the armatures, it can sublet for $30,000 a year the part of its plant where the armatures are now manufactured.

The cost analysis may be organized as follows:

Avoidable Costs	**Cost per Unit**	**Annual Usage**	**Total**
Direct materials	$6	30,000	$180,000
Direct labor	5	30,000	150,000
Variable overhead	4	30,000	120,000
Direct fixed overhead	3	30,000	90,000
Out-of-pocket costs to make			540,000
Add: Opportunity cost:			
Rental income forgone when armatures are manufactured			30,000
Total costs to make			570,000
Deduct: Purchase of part (30,000 × $20)			600,000
Advantage of making the part			$ 30,000

If the company can use the vacated premises for another purpose, the decision may differ. For example, if a new product can be manufactured in place of the armature and if the firm is able to earn a segment margin of $100,000 a year on the new product, the decision would be in favor of buying:

Out-of-pocket costs to make	$540,000
Add: Opportunity cost:	
Segment margin on new product forgone when armatures are manufactured	100,000
Total cost to make	640,000
Deduct: Purchase of part (30,000 × $20)	600,000
Advantage of buying the part	$ 40,000

Therefore, it is important for a manager to understand how to select all the costs that are relevant to a decision whether to make or buy component parts. These relevant costs are usually all of the variable costs, the direct fixed costs, and any opportunity costs that can be identified, using the greatest amount of forgone income from the alternatives available. Common fixed costs that continue when the part is purchased are *irrelevant and do not influence the decision.*

Thus far, we have seen that there is much overlapping of relevant costs and revenues among the kinds of decisions that managers must make. The decision whether to sell a product from a common direct material at its splitoff point or to process it further is no exception. However, when making this kind of decision, an additional concept of relevance must be examined.

▶ JOINT PRODUCT DECISIONS

Allocated Costs and Decision Making

Recall from Chapter 8 that *joint product costs* must be allocated to specific units of inventory for the purpose of inventory valuation. However, the use of allocated costs for inventory valuation should not be confused with their use for decision making. For example, if a furniture manufacturer cuts lumber into the parts used in its production process, it is bound to have ends and other pieces of wood left over. These leftover pieces can be further processed into sawdust for use as sweeping compound. Let us assume the cost of such further processing is $4 per bag and the compound can be sold for $10 per bag. The firm's accountants determine that the allocated cost of the leftover lumber, using a cost-per-board-foot basis, amounts to $7 per bag. If the total of the allocated cost per bag plus the additional processing cost per bag—$11—were used for decision making, management would elect to throw the leftover pieces away because a loss per bag would be predicted, as follows:

		Per Bag
Selling price		$10
Costs:		
Allocated cost	$7	
Additional processing	4	11
Loss		$ (1)

Such a decision process would be faulty, however, because the allocated cost of the leftovers is a sunk cost and is thus irrelevant. The proper analysis, using relevant data, is:

	Per Bag
Selling price	$10
Less: Additional processing cost	4
Profit	$ 6

Sell at Splitoff Point or Process Further

L.O. 5
Sell at splitoff point or process further

The relevant data for a sell-at-splitoff-point-or-process-further decision are the additional revenue earned by further processing and the separable costs.

For example, the Rink Company uses a common direct material R that has a joint product cost of $16,000 and yields 6,000 pounds of product X selling for $3 per pound and 4,000 pounds of product Y selling for $3.50 per pound. Product X can be processed further at an additional cost of $8,000, and product Y can be processed further at an additional cost of $6,000. The new products, XP and YP, can then be sold for $4 and $6 per pound, respectively. The relevant data needed for the decision may be summarized and analyzed as follows:

Product XP:

Sales revenue (6,000 × $4)	$24,000
Less: Sales value at splitoff point (6,000 × $3)	18,000
Additional sales revenue	6,000
Less: Separable costs	8,000
(Loss) on processing further	$(2,000)

Product YP:

Sales revenue (4,000 × $6)	$24,000
Less: Sales value at splitoff point (4,000 × $3.50)	14,000
Additional sales revenue	10,000
Less: Separable costs	6,000
Advantage of processing further	$ 4,000

From this analysis, a manager would correctly conclude that product X should be sold at the splitoff point and product Y should be processed into product YP. The joint product cost of $16,000 should not be used to reach this decision. Rather, the analysis should be limited to the difference between the incremental revenue and the incremental (separable) cost.

▶ PRICING DECISIONS

L.O. 6

Another important decision is the determination of the best price for a product. Although a pricing decision must include consideration of competitive market factors, it must also be based on future relevant costs to avoid long-run profitability and survival problems.

In some industries, firms must price their products to compete with the prices already established by others in the market. Examples are the agriculture industry, in which farmers either price their products at the established market prices or they do not produce, and the automobile industry, in which a price leader sets the price and others must follow if they wish to participate in the market. Members of such industries must concentrate on their costs to be sure they can earn a reasonable profit, or else they must leave the market.

In contrast, firms that have some control over the prices they can charge may use various strategies and pricing policies. Firms vary considerably in their pricing techniques, and some of the more popular approaches are (1) skimming, (2) market penetration, (3) markup pricing, (4) target-return pricing, (5) demand-oriented pricing, and (6) competition-based pricing.

1. Skimming Certain kinds of products, such as new electric appliances, toys, games, and home computers, lend themselves to a pricing strategy known as **skimming the market.** When a firm decides to skim the market, it initially sets the price of a new product quite high so that it will attract only a small number of consumers. The company then gradually lowers the price to eventually capture more and more of the market. This pricing strategy provides manufacturers with a cushion against high risk when introducing a new product. By setting a higher than normal initial price, they can more quickly recover a greater portion of their start-up costs. Then, if the product is successful and they want to expand production, they systematically lower the price to attract more consumers. As a result, the firm will earn a higher revenue for the same number of units sold while limiting demand to match its production capabilities.

A skimming strategy is most effective when it is difficult for competitors to enter the market—as when a company holds the patent on some crucial technology. But when entering the market is easy, competitors will be attracted by the potential profits, and the higher than normal price will be difficult to maintain.

Skimming the market has been used many times. For example, consider the *original* prices of instant cameras, calculators, electronic typewriters, and videocassette recorders and compare them to their prices today.

2. Market Penetration   When it is very easy to enter a market, a firm may prefer to penetrate the market rather than skim it. In **market-penetration pricing,** a company sets the initial price of a new product low enough to immediately capture a large share of the market. A firm may also prefer penetration pricing when it believes entering a market at $4 and lowering the price to $2 a month or two later may not enhance the firm's image in the marketplace. In such a case, the firm may wish to penetrate the market with the $2 price per unit at the outset. This might be especially true for firms that have a very high fixed cost with a low variable cost. If the company can penetrate the market with a high volume and a low price, the fixed cost per unit will decrease rapidly, and overall profitability will increase *because of the large sales volume.* Of course, it should be remembered that fixed costs are constant and therefore not relevant. The larger sales volume, however, is relevant.

3. Markup Pricing   In **markup pricing,** a predetermined percentage is included in a product's cost to cover the seller's operating costs, income taxes, and a reasonable profit. For example, a women's clothing store may set a 100 percent markup on the dresses it sells. Thus, if the shop pays $60 for a dress, it will resell it for $120, with the $60 markup going to cover operating costs, income taxes, and profit. The amount added is usually a percentage of either the item's cost to the seller or its final selling price. This is referred to as the *markup percentage* or sometimes, *profit margin.* When using this approach, managers must be careful to specify whether the markup percentage is based on cost or selling price, because the results are quite different. A markup percentage based on cost is simple to compute. For example, if a dress shop owner wishes to use a markup of 75 percent based on cost, the calculation would be:

Cost of dress	$ 60
Markup on cost—75%	45
Selling price	$105

On the other hand, if the markup of 75 percent is based on selling price, then:

Selling price	100%
Markup	75
Cost	25%

Therefore the calculation is:

$60 cost = .25 selling price

$$\frac{\$60 \text{ cost}}{.25} = \$240$$

or

$60 × 4 = $240

Proof:

		Percent
Selling price	$240	100
Cost	60	25
Markup (gross margin)	$180	75

Most retailers use a markup percentage based on cost—a method known as **cost-plus pricing.** The term *cost-plus pricing* is used to distinguish markup pricing based on cost from markup pricing based on selling price.

Manufacturers who wish to use markup pricing face an additional problem. Before the markup percentage can be computed, the base cost must be determined. Some firms use absorption (full) costing, and others use variable costing.

Absorption Costing When a manufacturing firm uses markup pricing, managers must clearly understand which costs are included in the cost base and which costs are to be recovered in the markup percentage. If a firm uses absorption costing, then direct materials, direct labor, variable overhead, and fixed overhead are included in the cost base, and the markup percentage should include amounts for variable and fixed marketing and administrative costs, income taxes, and profit.

The Morson Company plans to manufacture cabinets and wishes to establish a selling price. The standard cost sheet for the product is:

Direct materials (10 bd. ft. of oak at $.95 per bd. ft.)	$ 9.50
Direct labor (4 hours at $7 per hour)	28.00
Variable overhead (4 hours at $4 per hour)	16.00
Fixed overhead (4 hours at $6 per hour)	24.00
Total standard cost	$77.50

The fixed overhead of $24 is based on an annual volume of 10,000 units, or 40,000 hours of direct labor. In addition, variable marketing costs are 5 percent of sales, fixed marketing costs are $100,000, administrative costs are $150,000, income taxes are 40 percent of operating income before income taxes, and a profit after income taxes of $240,000 is desired. The markup percentage on cost may be computed as follows:

Step 1

Convert the desired profit after income taxes to a before-tax amount:

$$\$240,000 \div (1 - \text{Tax rate}) =$$
$$\$240,000 \div (1 - .4) \quad =$$
$$\$240,000 \div .6 \quad\quad\quad = \$400,000$$

Step 2

Add the marketing and administrative fixed costs plus the before-tax profit to the total product costs for the year:

Fixed marketing costs	$ 100,000
Fixed administrative costs	150,000
Profit before income taxes	400,000
Subtotal	650,000
Product costs (10,000 × $77.50).	775,000
Total.	$1,425,000

Step 3

Compute the sales volume by dividing the total in step 2 by (1 − Variable marketing cost percentage):

$$\$1,425,000 \div (1 - .05) =$$
$$\$1,425,000 \div .95 \qquad = \$1,500,000$$

Step 4

Compute the unit selling price:

$$\$1,500,000 \div 10,000 \text{ units} = \$150 \text{ per unit}$$

Step 5

Compute the markup percentage on cost:

$$\$150.00 - \$77.50 = \$72.50 \text{ markup}$$

$$\text{Markup percentage} = \frac{\$Markup}{\$Product\ cost} = \frac{\$72.50}{\$77.50} = .9355 = 93.55\%$$

The percentage may be used as follows:

Standard product cost	$ 77.50
Markup (93.55% × $77.50).	72.50
Selling price	$150.00

The proof of the selling price would be:

Sales (10,000 at $150)	$1,500,000
Cost of goods sold (10,000 × $77.50)	775,000
Gross margin	725,000
Marketing and administrative costs:	
Variable marketing (5% × $1,500,000)	75,000
Fixed marketing.	100,000
Fixed administrative	150,000
Total marketing and administrative costs	325,000
Operating income before income taxes	400,000
Income taxes at 40%.	160,000
Net income	$ 240,000

Variable Costing   If the Morson Company used variable costing instead of absorption costing, the procedure for computing a markup percentage would be:

Step 1

Compute the firm's variable manufacturing costs:

Direct materials	$ 9.50 × 10,000 =	$ 95,000
Direct labor	28.00 × 10,000 =	280,000
Variable overhead . . .	16.00 × 10,000 =	160,000
Total	$53.50	$535,000

Step 2

Compute the firm's fixed costs:

Manufacturing overhead (10,000 × $24) . . .	$240,000
Marketing costs	100,000
Administrative costs	150,000
Total fixed costs.	$490,000

Step 3

Convert the after-tax desired net income of $240,000 to before-tax operating income:

(See step 1 for absorption costing) . . . $400,000

Step 4

Combine the amounts computed in steps 1, 2, and 3:

($535,000 + $490,000 + $400,000) . . . $1,425,000

Step 5

Compute the selling price per unit:

(See steps 3 and 4 for absorption costing) . . . $150 per unit

Step 6

Compute the markup percentage:

$$\$150.00 - \$53.50 = \$96.50 \text{ markup}$$

$$\text{Markup percentage} = \frac{\$96.50}{\$53.50} = 1.8037 = 180.37\%$$

The proof of the percentage and its use is:

Variable manufacturing costs	$ 53.50
Markup (180.37% × $53.50).	96.50
Selling price.	$150.00

Although the selling price is the same for both accounting systems, the markup percentages differ because the starting points—product costs—are different.

A close relative of markup pricing is target-return pricing.

4. Target-Return Pricing **Target-return pricing** bases price on a specified return on investment (ROI) in place of the desired dollar profit used in markup pricing. Thus, in place of the $240,000 of net income used in the previous example, a predetermined ROI is employed. A problem arises with the term *investment,* however. Investment may be either *net* assets (assets minus liabilities) or *total assets* (without deductions for liabilities). In practice, each firm chooses its preferred definition, but the definition must be clearly stated if ROI-based pricing is to be used effectively.

If the Morson Company requires a 12 percent after-tax ROI instead of the $240,000 profit after taxes stated earlier, and if the ROI is to be based on net assets of $2 million, the computations would be:

Step 1

Convert the after-tax ROI to a before-tax rate:

$$\text{Before-tax ROI} = \frac{\text{After-tax ROI}}{(1 - \text{Tax rate})} = \frac{12\%}{(1 - .40)} = 20\%$$

Step 2

Multiply the before-tax rate by the assets (total or net, as indicated) employed:

$2,000,000 \times 20\% = \$400,000$ targeted income before income taxes

The remaining steps are the same as those noted for markup pricing.

Some firms apply target-return pricing for short intervals and adjust their prices often to reflect changes in costs and net assets. Others, like General Motors, use long-term pricing and attempt to keep their prices stable for long periods, such as a year or more. When long-term target pricing is used, the firm focuses on the average long-term ROI, even if the short-term ROIs do not reflect the desired returns.

5. Demand-Oriented Pricing   Firms like restaurants and hotels may charge different prices for the same item in response to changes in demand. For example, a hotel usually charges more for rooms and meals during its busy season than it does during its off-season. Similarly, the same restaurant meal may cost more at dinner than it does at lunch. The practice of pricing a firm's product by using a higher price when the demand is high and a lower price when demand is low is known as **demand-oriented pricing.**

Manufacturers who use this form of pricing must be careful not to violate the Robinson-Patman Act, however. The act prohibits price discrimination among *the same class of customers* (all lunch-time diners, all wholesalers, all retailers) unless it can be justified by cost differentials. Cost differentials must be found among the marketing and administrative costs and *not* in manufacturing costs. Thus, a manufacturer cannot charge one customer for full manufacturing costs including overhead and charge another customer *in the same class* for only direct materials and labor.

6. Competition-Based Pricing   When a firm uses a **competition-based pricing** strategy, it prices a product to compete with a competitor's price and then assesses whether the product can be manufactured at a cost that will yield a satisfactory profit. The price may be the same as the competitor's, or it might be slightly higher or lower. When competition-based pricing is used, a firm may not be able to realize its normal markup or target-return percentage. In such a case, the firm must decide if it is preferable (1) to not enter the market, (2) to cut the cost of the product, if possible, so that the normal percentage may be realized, or (3) to settle for less than the normal percentage and later reevaluate its decision to enter the market.

The Starlight Company would like to enter the market with a solid brass lamp that other companies sell for $90. For competitive purposes, Starlight also wants to price the lamp at $90. Marketing and administrative costs are each expected to amount to $100,000 at a volume of 15,000 per year, and the company would like a 20 percent before-tax ROI on its investment in net assets amounting to $2 million. The calculations to assess the amount available for manufacturing costs are:

Estimated sales (15,000 × $90)		$1,350,000
Less:		
Marketing and administrative costs		
($100,000 + $100,000)	$200,000	
ROI (20% × $2 million)	400,000	600,000
Amount available for manufacturing costs		$ 750,000

Per-unit amount = $750,000 ÷ 15,000 units = $50 per unit

The engineering, accounting, and purchasing departments must now determine if the product can be made for $50 per unit. If not, the firm must decide whether to forgo entering the market, cut the cost of manufacturing, or accept a lower ROI.

In many cases, managers face pricing decisions without constraints. In other cases, alternative products may be competing for scarce resources, such as capital, material, and labor. Then, in addition to pricing, managers must decide how to allocate scarce resources to particular products in ways that maximize the company's objectives.

► ALLOCATING SCARCE RESOURCES

L.O. 7

Due to scarce resources, a firm must sometimes select one product or several products to emphasize while downplaying other products. When one of the firm's goals is to maximize profits, linear programming or mathematical models may be used to reach an optimal solution. Linear programming is especially useful when multiple constraints exist. It is discussed in Appendix 13-A. However, when it is simply a matter of choosing the best way to allocate resources, the decision maker may use a less complex technique based on the contribution margin per limiting factor. The **contribution margin per limiting factor** is the contribution margin per unit of a firm's product expressed in terms of a production-limiting factor, such as available machine-hours or direct labor-hours. With this approach, management determines the contribution margin per limiting factor for each product and selects the product(s) with the highest contribution margin as the one(s) to produce.

The Shamrin Company manufactures two products. Their selling prices and variable costs are:

	Product A		Product B	
Selling price per unit.		$20		$10
Variable costs:				
Direct materials	$2		$2	
Direct labor.	4		1	
Variable overhead	3		2	
Variable marketing costs	1	10	1	6
Contribution margin		$10		$ 4

If the firm has no production-limiting factors, the firm should produce *both A and B* to the extent that they *can be sold* in the marketplace.

On the other hand, if the number of units that can be produced is limited, managers must decide which product(s) to produce and in what amount(s). Production limitations may relate to (1) labor-hours of capacity for a labor-intensive product, (2) machine-hours of capacity for a machine-intensive product, or (3) units of direct materials available from suppliers. These limiting factors are referred to as **constraints.** It is possible for production to be limited by more than one constraint.

If product A requires 1 hour of direct labor and product B requires one-fourth hour of direct labor, and the Shamrin Company has only 100,000 hours of direct labor capacity available, management must decide how many of each product to produce. The firm estimates that it can sell 100,000 units of product A and 200,000 units of product B for the coming year without changing the selling prices of the products.

Normally, a firm should choose to emphasize the product with the largest contribution margin. In this case, at $10 per unit, product A has the larger contribution margin. However, a manager should compute the contribution margin per limiting factor, in this case direct labor-hours, to make the appropriate decision. The computations are:

	Product A	Product B
Contribution margin per unit	$10	$ 4
Contribution margin per direct labor-hour:		
Product A ($10 ÷ 1 hour)	$10	
Product B ($4 ÷ ¼ hour)		$16

The results indicate that it is possible to produce four units of product B for every unit of product A. Thus, product B can earn $16 in the same amount of direct labor time as product A earns $10. For this reason, product B should be emphasized over product A. The capacities of production may be calculated as follows:

Capacity of product A:

$$100,000 \div 1 \text{ direct labor-hour} = 100,000 \text{ units}$$

Capacity of product B:

$$100,000 \div \text{¼ direct labor-hour} = 400,000 \text{ units}$$

The contribution margins at the limits of production and sales are:

Produce and sell at product A's limit:		
Production and market limitation of 100,000 units at $10 contribution margin.		$1,000,000
Produce and sell at product B's limit:		
Market limitation of 200,000 units at $4 contribution margin		$ 800,000
Balance of production capacity assigned to product A:		
Total direct labor-hour capacity	100,000 hours	
Less: Used by product B (200,000 × ¼ hour).	50,000 hours	
Balance available	50,000 hours	
Sales of product A:		
50,000 hours ÷ 1 hour = 50,000 units × $10 contribution margin		500,000
Total contribution margin.		$1,300,000

This analysis indicates that producing 200,000 units of product B and 50,000 units of product A will cause the firm's contribution margin to be $300,000 ($1,300,000 − $1,000,000) greater than if the firm produced only 100,000 units of product A.

► RECAPITULATION

A recapitulation of the kinds of decisions managers make and the relevant data needed to arrive at correct conclusions appears in Illustration 13-10.

► **ILLUSTRATION 13-10**   Managerial Decisions and Corresponding Relevant Data

Kind of Decision	Relevant Data Needed
1. Purchasing new labor-saving equipment	Cost of equipment; salvage value; useful life of machine; *changes in* sales, direct material costs, direct labor costs, variable overhead, and fixed overhead; and cost of repairs to new machine.
2. Replacing old equipment with newer equipment	Cost of new equipment; useful life of new equipment; remaining life of old equipment; salvage value of new equipment; present resale value of old equipment; needed repairs to old equipment; repairs to new equipment; *changes in* sales, direct material costs, direct labor costs, variable overhead, and fixed overhead.
3. Entering a new market with a new product	Cost of equipment; salvage value; useful life of project; investment of working capital; release of working capital; anticipated sales revenue, direct material costs, direct labor costs, variable overhead, fixed overhead, marketing, and administrative costs.
4. Taking an order at less than full cost	The effect on the company's regular sales volume, the price offered, the variable costs of producing the order, the incremental costs incurred as a result of taking the order.
5. Making or buying component parts	*Qualitative considerations,* such as supplier's reliability, supplier's quality control, supplier's labor problems, supplier's price stability, and start-up costs to renew making the component. *Quantitative considerations,* including cost per unit to manufacture for direct materials, direct labor, variable overhead, total direct fixed overhead, the purchase price from the vendor, the annual usage, and the opportunity cost of the resources used to manufacture the component.
6. Selling products from a common direct material at the splitoff point or processing further	The difference in revenue between selling the product at the splitoff point and at the end of additional processing compared with the costs of additional processing.
7. Pricing: *a.* Skimming	The variable cost to manufacture the product, the elasticity of the product's demand function.
b. Market penetration	Same as for skimming.
c. Markup pricing	For *merchandisers,* the cost of a product and its markup percentage. For *manufacturers,* either the variable cost to manufacture or the full (absorption) cost to manufacture and the respective markup percentages for each.

▶ **ILLUSTRATION 13-10**   *(concluded)*

Kind of Decision	Relevant Data Needed
d. Target-return pricing	The desired return on investment, whether to use net assets or total assets, and the firm's tax rate. The remainder of the information needed is the same as for markup pricing.
e. Demand-oriented pricing	Demand patterns over time periods, such as seasons, special hours, or special days (weekend or weekdays); elasticity of demand functions for each pattern; variable cost of product or service.
f. Competition-based pricing	The competitor's price, the desired profit, marketing and administrative costs, and costs to manufacture.
8. Allocating scarce resources to particular products	A limiting factor, such as direct labor-hours, machine-hours, or direct materials; contribution margin per unit; and contribution margin per limiting factor.
9. Cost-volume-profit	Present variable costs, fixed costs, sales revenues and proposed variable costs, fixed costs, and sales revenues. (See Chapter 4.)
10. Discontinuing a product or segment	The product's or segment's sales revenues, variable costs, direct fixed costs, and allocated common costs. (See Chapter 12.)

▶ **SUMMARY**

As part of their decision-making responsibilities, managers have access to large amounts of data. To improve the decision-making process, managers must decide which data are relevant. **Relevant costs** and **relevant revenues** are those costs and revenues that differ among alternatives and will influence the outcome of the decision-making process. Because decision making is future oriented, relevant data consist of future costs and revenues. Past costs, called **sunk costs,** do not affect the outcomes of decisions to be made and are therefore **irrelevant costs,** as are all other costs and revenues that will remain unchanged among the alternatives being considered.

Different decisions require different relevant data. Thus, managers must be familiar with the most common kinds of business decisions and the specific data needed for each. The required data depend on whether the decision maker will use (1) **differential analysis,** in which only the differences in cash flows among the alternatives are considered or (2) the **comprehensive comparative income approach,** in which all costs and revenues are considered.

The decisions most often made by managers are (1) whether to purchase new labor-saving equipment, (2) whether to replace existing equipment with newer equipment, (3) whether to introduce a new product, (4) whether to take a special order at less than full cost, (5) whether to make or buy component parts, (6) whether to sell joint products at the splitoff point or process them further, (7) what prices to charge for the firm's products, and (8) how to allocate scarce resources to particular products. Selecting the relevant data needed for each of these decisions is the key to reaching a correct conclusion.

A manager most often examines **cash operating advantage** when deciding whether to purchase a new machine, replace an existing machine, or introduce a new product. When considering the acceptance of a special order at less than full cost, a manager must analyze overall profitability both with the order and without. The decision of whether to make or buy component parts hinges on the price at which the parts can be made compared to the costs that can be avoided by purchasing them. The opportunity cost of the space used to make the parts must also be factored into the calculation.

Managers must often decide whether to sell joint products at their splitoff point or process them further. The costs of the common direct material and processing up to the splitoff point are joint product costs, and the costs of additional processing after the splitoff point are separable costs. To decide whether further processing is desirable, the decision maker must compare the product's separable costs with the increased revenue that will result from additional processing.

Businesses use a variety of pricing strategies. Among the most common are **skimming, market-penetration pricing, markup pricing** (one form of which is **cost-plus pricing**), **target-return pricing, demand-oriented pricing,** and **competition-based pricing.** When pricing a product, decision makers must consider competitive market factors as well as future relevant costs to avoid long-run profitability and survival problems.

When a firm has limited capacity or materials, it should allocate its resources to yield the optimum contribution margin. One means of accomplishing this is to emphasize those products with the highest **contribution margin per limiting factor.** A limiting factor is called a **constraint.**

▶ **APPENDIX 13-A**   **Linear Programming**

Linear programming is a mathematical technique that shows managers how to allocate scarce resources to maximize profits or minimize costs. The maximization or minimization of some quantity is an important basic property of all linear programming problems. For example, a manager's goal may be to maximize the use of direct materials that can only be purchased in limited quantities. Or he may want to make maximum use of direct labor-hours or machine-hours that are limited due to the size of his firm's manufacturing facilities. Sometimes a linear programming problem is based on the number of units of a product that *can be produced* exceeds the number of units that can be sold. All of these factors restrict a company from the unlimited pursuit of its goals. In linear programming, these factors are called *constraints*. A constraint is a limiting factor under which the firm must operate, such as a shortage of direct materials, limited plant capacity (labor-hours and/or machine-hours), and limited market demand for a product.

Linear programming is based on five assumptions:

1. The revenue functions and cost functions of a firm's products are linear; hence, a firm's contribution margin is a linear function.
2. A firm's time and material usage rates and limitations are linear.

3. Because negative production is impossible, it is not permissible in solutions to linear programming problems (although this may seem obvious).
4. Fractional units of production are permitted because units not finished in one period can be finished in a succeeding period. (All functions are continuous.)
5. All parameters are known with certainty.

Functional Relationships

The solution to a linear programming problem requires that certain relationships be shown in functional format. The needed functions are (1) the objective function and (2) the constraint functions. The **objective function** is a relationship that sets the goal to be achieved by the linear programming solution, such as the maximization of contribution margin or the minimization of costs. The **constraint functions** are relationships that set the limitations under which the firm must operate, such as material shortages, limited labor-hours, limited machine-hours, and limited market demand for the product.

To see how linear programming works, we will study the Thaxton Company, which produces two products: X and Y. Each product passes through two departments: cutting and finishing. Product X requires six hours of cutting and five hours of finishing; product Y requires four hours of cutting and four hours of finishing. The cutting department has three machines that can operate 8 hours per day for a total of 24 hours per day. The finishing department also has three machines that operate a total of 24 hours per day, but the machines have to be stopped for cleaning, which reduces the capacity of the finishing department to 22 hours per day. Product X sells for $60 per unit and has a variable cost of $20 per unit, resulting in a contribution margin of $40 per unit. Product Y sells for $50 per unit and has a variable cost of $20 per unit, resulting in a contribution margin of $30 per unit. There are no material shortages, and the company can sell all of its output.

L.O. 8
Objective function

Stating the Objective Function   The objective function should set forth the goal to be achieved. In this example, a maximization problem, the goal is to produce a product mix that will produce the maximum contribution margin possible. This may be represented by the following equation:

$$\text{Max } Z = \$40X + \$30Y \tag{1}$$

where

Z = Total contribution margin
X = Number of units of X to be produced and sold
Y = Number of units of Y to be produced and sold

L.O. 8
Constraint functions

Stating the Constraint Functions   The constraint functions should set the time requirement (in machine-hours) for each product in each department. Because the number of units to be produced is unknown and less than the maximum capacity may be utilized, it is necessary to use inequalities in place of equations. Recall that product X requires six hours of cutting and product Y requires four hours of cutting. Thus, the constraint inequality for the cutting department's 24 hours of capacity would be expressed as:

$$6X + 4Y \leq 24 \tag{2}$$

Because product X requires 5 hours of finishing and product Y requires 4 hours of finishing, the constraint inequality for the finishing department's 22 hours of capacity may be expressed as:

$$5X + 4Y \leq 22 \qquad (3)$$

Although the following constraints are understood, because negative production is not possible, they are included for completeness.

$$X \geq 0 \qquad (4)$$
$$Y \geq 0 \qquad (5)$$

The Graphical Solution to a Maximization Problem

The graphical solution to a maximization problem requires the following steps:

L.O. 9

1. Plot the constraint inequalities on a graph. (*Note:* Although the inequalities are technically not equations, in this case they are treated as if they were equations. The mathematics needed to bridge this gap is *not* shown. Thus, = signs will be substituted for the ≤ signs.)
2. Determine the area of feasible (possible) solutions.
3. Locate the corner points of the area of feasible solutions. The optimal solution will be at one of these corner points.
4. For each solution at a corner point, insert the contribution margin per unit for each product in the candidate solution and sum the contribution margin. Select the solution with the highest total contribution margin.

1. Plot the Constraints Starting with Equation 2, first assume only product X and no product Y will be manufactured. This produces the following:

$$
\begin{aligned}
6X + 4Y &\leq 24 \qquad (2)\\
6X + 4(0) &= 24\\
6X &= 24\\
X &= 4
\end{aligned}
$$

Then, assume only product Y and no product X will be produced. This produces the following:

$$
\begin{aligned}
6X + 4Y &\leq 24 \qquad (2)\\
6(0) + 4Y &= 24\\
4Y &= 24\\
Y &= 6
\end{aligned}
$$

It is now possible to plot the constraint for the cutting department as ($X = 4$, $Y = 0$) and ($X = 0$, $Y = 6$) on the graph. This line serves as the boundary or limit for the finishing department. This may be seen in Illustration 13-11.

The same procedure is applied to Equation 3. The results are:

$$
\begin{aligned}
5X + 4Y &\leq 22 \qquad (3)\\
5X + 4(0) &= 22\\
5X &= 22\\
X &= 4\tfrac{2}{5}
\end{aligned}
$$

▶ **ILLUSTRATION 13-11**   Graphical Solution for Maximizing Contribution Margin—Two Constraints *(Area of Feasible Solutions)*

and

$$5X + 4Y \leq 22 \tag{3}$$
$$5(0) + 4Y = 22$$
$$4Y = 22$$
$$Y = 5\tfrac{1}{2}$$

The constraint for the finishing department can now be plotted as ($X = 4\tfrac{2}{5}$, $Y = 0$) and ($X = 0$, $Y = 5\tfrac{1}{2}$). This line represents the limiting condition for the cutting constraint and may be seen in Illustration 13-11.

2. Area of Feasible Solutions   The **area of feasible solutions** for a maximization problem is the area on a linear programming graph that lies beneath the boundaries of *all* of the constraint inequalities. This area is shaded in Illustration 13-11. Remember that *any point* within this area represents a *possible* production combination.

3. Locating the Corner Points   Because any point, including the origin ($X = 0$, $Y = 0$), within the feasible solutions area is a possible solution, the objective of the linear programming solution is to find the point furthest from the origin that will produce the greatest total contribution margin. For this reason, the optimal solution lies at one of the corner points of the feasible solutions area other than the origin. In Illustration 13-12, the corner points are circled. The point of intersection of the cutting and finishing department

▶ **ILLUSTRATION 13-12**   Graphical Solution for Maximizing Contribution Margin—Two Constraints
(Corner Points of the Feasible Solutions Area)

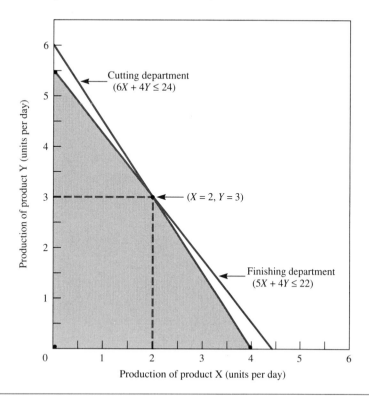

constraints may be obtained by drawing a perpendicular line from the intersection and reading it from the X axis. In this case, it is $X = 2$, shown as a dotted line in Illustration 13-12. As shown in the same illustration, a horizontal line may also be drawn to obtain the value of $Y = 3$.

4. *Determine Contribution Margins at the Corner Points*   The contribution margin for each corner point may be obtained by performing the operations dictated by the objective function. Thus, for each corner point shown in Illustration 13-12, the quantities of products X and Y will be inserted into the objective function (Max $Z = \$40X + \$30Y$) to arrive at the total contribution margin as follows:

Corner Point		Objective Function	Total Contribution Margin
X	**Y**		
0	0	$40(0) + $30(0) =	$ 0
4	0	$40(4) + $30(0) =	160
2	3	$40(2) + $30(3) =	170
0	5½ . . .	$40(0) + $30(5½) =	165

Computer Solution for Maximizing Contribution Margin Using Linear Programming

```
***************************
*                         *
*   LINEAR PROGRAMMING     *
*         ANALYSIS         *
*                         *
***************************
    **       INFORMATION       **
NUMBER OF CONSTRAINTS            2
NUMBER OF VARIABLES             2
NUMBER OF <= CONSTRAINTS         2
NUMBER OF  = CONSTRAINTS         0
NUMBER OF >= CONSTRAINTS         0

MAXIMIZATION PROBLEM
    40 X 1       + 30 X 2

SUBJECT TO
    6 X 1      + 4 X 2        <=24
    5 X 1      + 4 X 2        <=22

    ** RESULTS **

                 VARIABLE     ORIGINAL
VARIABLE          VALUE        COEFF.
    X 1             2            40
    X 2             3            30

CONSTRAINT      ORIGINAL
NUMBER            RHS
    1              24
    2              22

OBJECTIVE FUNCTION VALUE : 170

    ** END OF ANALYSIS **
```

The optimal solution is to produce two units of product X and three units of product Y per day to produce a total contribution margin of $170 per day.

Although this solution is relatively simple, linear programming problems may become quite complex, especially when more than two variables (products) are involved. A more rigorous solution to linear programming problems is the *simplex method,* which can be used to solve any linear programming problem, especially those with three or more variables (products). The procedure used to solve a simplex programming problem may be found in advanced managerial and linear programming texts. However, most firms that use linear programming to solve business problems use a computer.

Computer Solutions to Linear Programming Problems

The Thaxton Company problem can also be solved using a computer to achieve a direct optimal solution without having to test the corner points. The computer solution appears in Illustration 13-13.

Although the optimal solution to this problem lies where the constraints intersect ($X = 2$, $Y = 3$), it would be wrong to assume this is always the case. Different contribution margins may cause the optimal solution to be a different corner point.

Alternative Contribution Margins in the Objective Function

Using the same constraint inequalities and thus the same corner points shown in Illustration 13-12, let us assume the objective function is now changed to contribution margins of $10 for product X and $50 for product Y. The new objective function would be:

$$\text{Max } Z = \$10X + \$50Y \tag{6}$$

The total contribution margin using Equation 6 may be computed as:

Corner Point		Objective Function	Total Contribution Margin
X	**Y**		
0	0	$10(0) + $50(0) =	$ 0
4	0	$10(4) + $50(0) =	40
2	3	$10(2) + $50(3) =	170
0	5½ . . .	$10(0) + $50(5½) =	275

Note how the optimal solution is now $X = 0$, $Y = 5\frac{1}{2}$ because the contribution margin per unit of product Y is five times that of product X, whereas in Equation 1, the contribution margin of product X was slightly more than that of product Y. If the objective function were to shift so that the contribution margin of product X became five times that of product Y, the optimal solution would be $X = 4$, $Y = 0$. (You may wish to verify this by using an objective function of Max $Z = \$50X + \$10Y$.)

Increased Constraints

The graphical solution may still be used effectively with three or even four constraints if the variables (products) are limited to two. Consider the following example:

$$\text{Max } Z = \$30X + \$70Y \tag{7}$$

subject to

$$3X + 2Y \leq 15 \tag{8}$$
$$2X + 4Y \leq 18 \tag{9}$$

In addition, material shortages will prevent the production of more than 4 units of product X per day, while the market demand for product Y cannot exceed 3.5 units per day. Thus, there are now two additional constraints, as follows:

$$X \leq 4 \tag{10}$$
$$Y \leq 3.5 \tag{11}$$

The points for plotting Inequality 8 may be obtained as follows:

$$3X + 2Y = 15 \tag{8}$$
$$3X + 2(0) = 15$$
$$X = 5$$

and

$$3(0) + 2Y = 15$$
$$Y = 7\frac{1}{2}$$

▶ **ILLUSTRATION 13-14**   Graphical Solution for Maximizing Contribution Margin—Four Constraints *(Area of Feasible Solutions)*

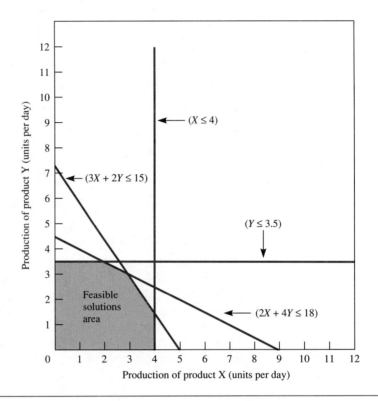

Therefore, the line ($X = 5$, $Y = 0$) and ($X = 0$, $Y = 7\frac{1}{2}$) can now be plotted on a graph. Using the same procedure for Inequality 9, the points ($X = 9$, $Y = 0$) and ($X = 0$, $Y = 4\frac{1}{2}$) can also be plotted along with $X = 4$ for Inequality 10 and $Y = 3.5$ for Inequality 11. These lines all appear in Illustration 13-14 with the feasible solutions area.

As before, the corner points may be ascertained by drawing perpendicular and horizontal lines as shown by the dotted lines in Illustration 13-15. The corner points and the computations of the contribution margins are:

Corner Point		Objective Function		Total Contribution Margin
X	Y			
0	0	$30(0) + $70(0)	=	$ 0
0	3½ . . .	$30(0) + $70(3½)	=	245
2	3½ . . .	$30(2) + $70(3½)	=	305
3	3	$30(3) + $70(3)	=	300
4	1½ . . .	$30(4) + $70(1½)	=	225
4	0	$30(4) + $70(0)	=	120

Note how the demand constraint of 3.5 units of product Y coincides with the optimal solution.

▶ **ILLUSTRATION 13-15**   Graphical Solution for Maximizing Contribution Margin—Four Constraints
(Corner Points of the Feasible Solutions Area)

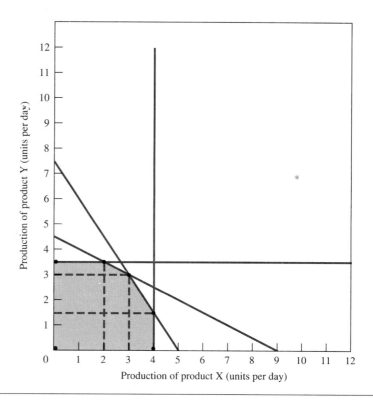

Minimization Problems

Thus far, we have seen that maximization problems are concerned with maximizing contribution margin. Minimization problems are similar to maximization problems, except that instead of using contribution margin as the focal point, the emphasis is now on *minimizing costs*. Some typical minimization problems might involve achieving certain nutritional combinations in food at the least cost, blending ingredients in foods and candies at least cost, and combining ingredients in livestock feed at least cost.

The Besta Pasta Company uses two main ingredients in preparing its pasta. Ingredient A contains 36 units of protein and 12 units of carbohydrate per pound; ingredient B contains 12 units of protein and 24 units of carbohydrate per pound. Each carton of pasta must contain at least 108 units of protein and 96 units of carbohydrate. The cost of ingredient A is 18 cents per pound, and the cost of ingredient B is 30 cents per pound.

The objective function for a minimization problem is similar to that of a maximization problem, except the coefficients of the variables *(A, B)* are costs instead of contribution margins. The objective of the firm is to minimize costs *(C)* given that the costs of ingredients A and B are 18 cents and 30 cents, respectively. The objective function may be stated as:

$$\text{Min } C = \$.18A + \$.30B \qquad \textbf{(12)}$$

▶ **ILLUSTRATION 13-16**   Graphical Solution for Minimizing Costs—Two Constraints *(Area of Feasible Solutions)*

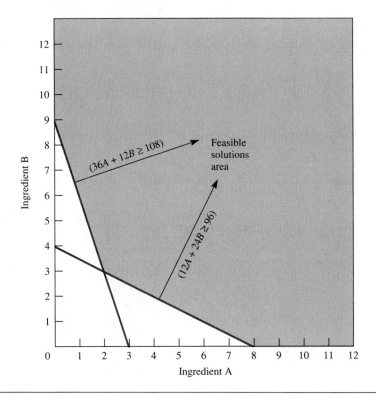

The constraint inequalities for a minimization problem are also similar to the constraints previously discussed, except instead of using *equal to or less than,* the inequalities are stated in terms of *equal to or greater than.*

For protein, the inequality is stated as:

$$36A + 12B \geq 108 \tag{13}$$

For carbohydrates, the inequality is stated as:

$$12A + 24B \geq 96 \tag{14}$$

The graphical solution can now proceed as before. Using Inequality 13, the points of the line may be calculated as follows:

$$
\begin{aligned}
36A \;+\; 12B &\geq 108 \tag{13}\\
36(0) \;+\; 12B &= 108\\
12B &= 108\\
B &= 9
\end{aligned}
$$

and

$$
\begin{aligned}
36A \;+\; 12(0) &= 108\\
36A &= 108\\
A &= 3
\end{aligned}
$$

▶ **ILLUSTRATION 13-17**   Graphical Solution for Minimizing Costs—Two Constraints *(Corner Points of the Feasible Solutions Area)*

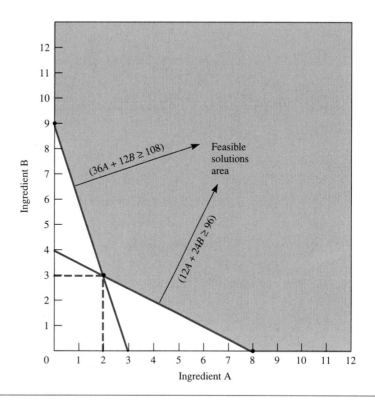

The points to locate Inequality 14 may be calculated as:

$$12A + 24B \geq 96 \tag{14}$$
$$12(0) + 24B = 96$$
$$24B = 96$$
$$B = 4$$

and

$$12A + 24(0) = 96$$
$$12A = 96$$
$$A = 8$$

The lines for these constraints are shown in Illustration 13-16 together with the feasible solutions area. Compare this feasible solutions area with the one in Illustration 13-11. Note that because this is a minimization problem, the feasible solutions area is *above* the intersecting lines, the exact opposite of a maximization problem.

Again, the optimal solution will lie at one of the corner points. Only this time, the task is to *get as close to the origin as possible* because the objective is to minimize costs within the constraints given. The corner points bounding the feasible solutions area are shown in Illustration 13-17.

The determination of the costs at each of the corner points is similar to that for a maximization problem. The calculation of costs is:

Corner Point A	B	Objective Function	Total Cost
0	9 . . .	$.18(0) + $.30(9) =	$2.70
2	3 . . .	$.18(2) + $.30(3) =	1.26
8	0 . . .	$.18(8) + $.30(0) =	1.44

The optimal solution is to use two pounds of ingredient A and three pounds of ingredient B for each carton of pasta manufactured. It might be interesting to see how many units of protein and carbohydrate would be used at each corner point. This may be calculated as:

Corner Point A	B	Units of Protein per Pound	Units of Carbohydrate per Pound	Total Protein	Total Carbohydrate
0	9.	(B) 12	24	108*	216†
2	3.	(A) 36	12	108‡	96§
		(B) 12	24		
8	0.	(A) 36	12	288‖	96#

* 9 × 12 = 108.
† 9 × 24 = 216.
‡ (2 × 36) + (3 × 12) = 108.
§ (2 × 12) + (3 × 24) = 96.
‖ 8 × 36 = 288.
8 × 12 = 96.

Note that all three solutions equal or exceed the minimum requirements of 108 units of protein and 96 units of carbohydrate, but only the optimal solution meets the requirements exactly. This may not always be the case, however.

▶ **GLOSSARY OF KEY TERMS**

Area of feasible solutions*   For a maximization linear programming problem, it is the area on a linear programming graph that lies beneath the boundaries of *all* of the constraint inequalities. For a minimization problem, it is the area that lies above the constraint inequalities.   (p. 672)

Cash operating advantage   The cash effect of the difference in revenues minus the cash effect of the difference in cash operating costs as a result of a contemplated change in a firm's operations.   (p. 648)

Comparative income approach   A method of assessing the effect on profit of a contemplated change in operations in which the net operating income for each

---

* Denotes a glossary term from the chapter appendix.

alternative is computed and compared. All revenues and costs are considered—even those that are the same for each alternative.   (p. 647)

Competition-based pricing   Pricing a product to compete with a competitor's price and then assessing whether the product can be manufactured at a cost that will yield a satisfactory profit.   (p. 664)

Constraint   A limiting factor, such as available machine-hours, available direct labor-hours, or available materials, that limits the amount of production and/or a limited market demand for a product.   (p. 665)

Constraint function*   An equation that sets forth the limitations under which a firm must operate, such as material shortages, limited labor-hours, limited machine-hours, and limited market demand for the product.   (p. 670)

Contribution margin per limiting factor   The contribution margin per unit of a firm's product expressed in terms of a production-limiting factor, such as available machine-hours or available direct labor-hours.   (p. 665)

Cost-plus pricing   A form of markup pricing in which a predetermined percentage of a product's cost is included in its selling price to cover the seller's operating costs, income taxes, and a reasonable profit.   (p. 661)

Demand-oriented pricing   Pricing a product by using a higher price when demand is high and a lower price when the demand is low.   (p. 664)

Differential analysis   A method of assessing the effect on profit of a contemplated change in operations. Only revenues and costs that differ among the alternatives are considered.   (p. 647)

Irrelevant costs   Costs that do not affect a decision to be made, such as sunk costs and costs that are the same for each alternative under consideration.   (p. 646)

Linear programming*   A mathematical technique that shows managers how to allocate scarce resources to maximize profits or minimize costs.   (p. 669)

Market-penetration pricing   Setting the initial price of a new product low enough to immediately capture a large share of the market.   (p. 660)

Markup pricing   The inclusion of a predetermined percentage in a product's price to cover the seller's operating costs, income taxes, and a reasonable profit. The markup percentage may be based on either the item's cost or its final selling price.   (p. 660)

Objective function*   An equation that sets forth the goal to be achieved by a linear programming solution, such as the maximization of contribution margin or the minimization of costs.   (p. 670)

Relevant cost   Any cost that differs among alternatives and will influence the outcome of the decision-making process.   (p. 646)

Relevant revenue   Any revenue that differs among alternatives and will influence the outcome of the decision-making process.   (p. 646)

Skimming the market   Setting the price of a product high enough to get a small share of the market initially, and then lowering the price to attract more consumers for a larger share of the market.   (p. 659)

Sunk cost   A previously incurred cost that cannot be changed by any future action.   (p. 646)

Target-return pricing   Setting the price of a product so that a predetermined amount will be earned as a return on the investment.   (p. 663)

▶ **REVIEW PROBLEM (A)**

Replacement of Equipment

The Nebraska Corporation is presently using a machine, K–1, in its production process. It is contemplating the purchase of a newer, more efficient machine, K–9. The following information is available:

	K–1	**K–9**
Purchase price	$65,000	$100,000
Useful life	12 years	8 years
Salvage value	$ 5,000	$ 4,000
Accumulated depreciation ($60,000 ÷ 12 years = $5,000; $5,000 × 8 years)	40,000	–0–
Depreciation per annum.	5,000	12,000
Sales revenue	50,000	60,000
Direct materials cost	10,000	12,000
Direct labor	12,000	9,000
Variable overhead	6,000	4,500
Fixed overhead	10,000	11,000
Cost to overhaul K–1 to extend its remaining life by 4 years for a total of 8 years	15,000	–0–

The time value of money and income taxes are to be ignored.

Required

a. Using the comparative income approach, compute the following:
  (1) The net investment of purchasing K–9.
  (2) The cash operating advantage of K–9 for the eight-year period.
  (3) The net cash flow for the eight-year period.

b. Assume K–1 can be sold for $30,000. Compute the following for K–1:
  (1) The net investment of K–1. (*Hint:* Use opportunity cost.)
  (2) The cash operating advantage of K–1 for the eight-year life of the machine.
  (3) The net cash flow for the eight-year period.

c. Should K–9 be purchased? Why?

▶ **SOLUTION TO REVIEW PROBLEM (A)**

a. (1) *Net Investment:*

Purchase price of K–9	$100,000
Less: Salvage value of K–9	4,000
Net investment.	$ 96,000

(2) *Total Cash Operating Advantage:*

Sales revenue/year	$ 60,000
Less: Manufacturing cost/year	36,500
Cash operating advantage/year	$ 23,500
Useful life of K–9 (years)	× 8
Total cash operating savings	$188,000

(3) *Net Cash Flow:*

Total cash operating savings	$188,000
Less: Net investment	96,000
Net cash flow	$ 92,000

b. (1) *Net Investment of K–1:*

Opportunity cost of not selling now	$30,000
Less: Ultimate salvage value	5,000
Net investment	$25,000

(2) *Total Cash Operating Advantage:*

Differential sales revenue/year	$50,000
Less: Cash manufacturing costs	38,000
Cash operating advantage/year	$12,000
Useful life (years)	× 8
	$96,000
Less: Required overhaul	15,000
Total cash operating advantage	$81,000

(3) *Net Cash Flow.*

Total cash operating advantage	$81,000
Less: Net investment of K–1	25,000
Net cash flow	$56,000

c. Net cash flow, keep	$56,000
Net cash flow, replace	92,000
Advantage in favor of purchasing new machine	$36,000

▶ **REVIEW PROBLEM (B)**

Entering a New Market

The Aromatic Company, which produces inexpensive automatic coffeemakers, is thinking of introducing a new line of expensive automatic coffeemakers that will both grind the coffee beans and then brew the coffee. A market survey indicates that because of its high cost, there is only a limited market for this product and the survey estimates that after five years there will be no market at all.

The following annual information about the new product is available to you:

Estimated sales (15,000 × $50)	$750,000
Cost of direct materials and direct labor	250,000
Variable overhead	70,000
Variable marketing costs	37,500
Fixed overhead, marketing, and administrative costs	150,000

Additional information is as follows:

Price of new machinery	$750,000
Salvage value at the end of 5 years	10,000
Working capital needed at inception	70,000
Working capital returned at the end of 5 years	65,000
Depreciation of new machinery per annum	48,000

Required

a. Which of the above data is relevant to you in recommending whether it is advantageous for Aromatic to enter this new market?

b. Using relevant data only, determine if it is advantageous for Aromatic to enter this new market.

▶ **SOLUTION TO REVIEW PROBLEM (B)**

a. All data except for annual depreciation are relevant because they are future items (costs/revenues) that differ between the decision alternatives.

b. *Net Investment:*

Price of new machine	$(750,000)
Salvage value of new machine	10,000
Working capital needed at inception	(70,000)
Release of working capital	65,000
Net investment	$(745,000)

Five-Year Total Cash Operating Advantage:

Incremental sales/year	$ 750,000
Less: Incremental cash costs/year	(507,500)
	242,500
Useful life in years	× 5
Total cash operating advantage	$1,212,500

Net Cash Flow:

Total cash operating advantage	$1,212,500
Less: Net investment	(745,000)
Net cash flow	$ 467,500

Invest, because net cash flow is positive.

▶ **REVIEW PROBLEM (C)**

Accepting an Order at Less than Full Cost

The Mason Company manufactures one product—toolboxes—and is operating at 60 percent of its normal capacity. It sells the toolboxes at $10 each. An income statement for the first six months of 19x5 is as follows:

MASON COMPANY
Income Statement
For the Six Months Ended June 30, 19x5

Sales (60,000 at $10)		$600,000
Cost of goods sold:		
Direct materials (60,000 at $2)	$120,000	
Direct labor (60,000 at $3)	180,000	
Variable overhead (60,000 at $.50)	30,000	
Fixed overhead (60,000 at $1.50)	90,000	420,000
Gross margin		180,000
Marketing and administrative costs—all fixed		80,000
Operating income before income taxes		$100,000

A major retailer has offered to purchase 40,000 toolboxes modified to the retailer's specifications. The toolboxes will differ significantly from Mason's design, and the retailer will market the toolboxes under its own private label. Thus, these toolboxes will not compete with Mason's regular toolboxes.

The retailer has offered Mason $5.50 per toolbox. Direct labor and overhead will be at the same unit cost as Mason's regular toolboxes. Direct materials will amount to $1.50 per unit. Shipping costs, to be borne by Mason, will amount to 10 cents per unit.

Required
a. Should Mason accept the order for the remainder of 19x5? Why?
b. Prepare a projected income statement for the remaining six months of 19x5, assuming Mason accepts the order and the sales and costs of the regular toolboxes are the same as for the first six months.

▶ **SOLUTION TO REVIEW PROBLEM (C)**

a. Incremental revenue ($5.50 × 40,000) $220,000

Less: Incremental costs:
   Variable manufacturing costs ($5) . . . . (200,000)
   Variable shipping costs ($.10) . . . . (4,000)

Incremental profit . . . . $ 16,000

Yes. Mason will increase operating income by $16,000.

b.

MASON COMPANY
Projected Income Statement
July 1, 19x5–December 31, 19x5

Sales ($600,000 + $220,000)		$820,000
Cost of goods sold:		
Direct materials ($120,000 + $60,000)	$180,000	
Direct labor ($180,000 + $120,000)	300,000	
Variable overhead ($30,000 + $20,000)	50,000	
Fixed overhead	90,000	620,000
Gross margin		$200,000
Marketing and administrative costs:		
Fixed	$ 80,000	
Variable	4,000	84,000
Operating income before taxes		$116,000

▶ **REVIEW PROBLEM (D)**

Make-Or-Buy Decision

The Distinctive Coat Company makes its own cloth-covered buttons for the coats and jackets it manufactures. It is considering purchasing these buttons from a very reliable manufacturer of buttons. If it does so, it can rent the part of the loft it would no longer need to a small dress manufacturer for $12,000 per annum. The company uses 120,000 buttons per annum. The following information is available from the standard cost sheet for the buttons:

	Per 100
Direct materials	$ 6
Direct labor	4
Variable overhead	3
Fixed overhead, direct	3
Fixed overhead, common	5
Total	$21

The button manufacturer has offered to make the buttons for $26 per 100 buttons, or 26 cents per button.

Required   a. Should the offer be accepted? Why?

b. Instead of renting out the extra space, Distinctive may decide to manufacture skirts to coordinate with the jackets. These skirts would generate a segment margin of $20,000 per annum. Under these conditions, would you recommend that Distinctive stop making its own buttons? Why?

▶ **SOLUTION TO REVIEW PROBLEM (D)**

a. Relevant cost to buy ($.26 × 120,000 buttons) $31,200

Less: Relevant cost to produce:

Avoidable variable costs ($.13)	$15,600	
Avoidable fixed costs (direct overhead)	3,600	
Opportunity cost (rent income forgone)	12,000	$31,200
Net advantage of buying		$ –0–

(Decision requires analysis of qualitative factors.)

b. Yes. Distinctive should stop making its own buttons in favor of making skirts. The opportunity cost of not taking this action is $8,000, and total profits will increase by $8,000.

▶ **REVIEW PROBLEM (E)**

Sell at Splitoff Point or Process Further

The Flavor Company produces three products, A, B, and C, from a joint process. Each product may be sold at the splitoff point or processed further into a packaged health food. The cost of producing all three products is $56,000. The process produces 10,000 gallons each of A and B and 8,000 gallons of C.

The following information is available to you:

Product	Sales Value at Splitoff Point	Costs to Process Further	Sales Value after Processing
A	$40,000	$25,000	$80,000
B	35,000	20,000	50,000
C	25,000	15,000	45,000

Required   Which products would you recommend that Flavor sell at the splitoff point and which should Flavor process further? Show your calculations.

▶ **SOLUTION TO REVIEW PROBLEM (E)**

Product	Incremental Revenues	−	Incremental Costs	=	Incremental Profit
A	$40,000	−	$25,000	=	$15,000*
B	15,000	−	20,000	=	(5,000)
C	20,000	−	15,000	=	5,000*

* Decision should be to process further.

▶ **REVIEW PROBLEM (F)**

Pricing and Markup Percentages

The Harlan Company is in the process of setting a selling price for one of its products. The accounting department provides you with the following:

	Per Unit
Direct materials.	$2
Direct labor	4
Variable overhead.	1
Fixed overhead ($300,000	
÷ 100,000 units)	3
Variable marketing costs.	2
Fixed marketing and administrative	
costs ($400,000 ÷ 100,000 units).	4

The company computed a markup percentage, based on absorption costing, of 110 percent. This percentage is sufficient to cover marketing and administrative costs and income tax.

Required   *a.* Compute the selling price if the markup percentage is to be based on absorption costing.

           b. Compute the markup percentage if the firm wishes to base its selling price—computed in part *(a)*—on variable manufacturing costing.

           c. Compute the markup percentage if the firm wishes to base its selling price—computed in part *(a)*—using the contribution approach. Is your answer the same as in part *(b)*? Why?

► **SOLUTION TO REVIEW PROBLEM (F)**

a.

$$\text{Selling price} = \text{Absorption cost} + 1.1 \,(\text{Absorption cost})$$
$$= \$10 + 1.1\,(\$10)$$
$$= \$21 \text{ per unit}$$

b.

$$\text{Markup percentage} = (\text{Selling price} - \text{Variable manufacturing cost})$$
$$\div \text{Variable manufacturing cost}$$
$$= (\$21 - \$7) \div \$7$$
$$= 200\%$$

c. Answer is different because markup is also calculated on variable marketing cost.

$$\text{Markup percentage} = (\text{SP} - \text{Total VC}) \div \text{Total VC}$$
$$= (\$21 - \$9) \div \$9$$
$$- 133\tfrac{1}{3}\%$$

► **LIBRARY ASSIGNMENT**

Read the following:

Campbell, Robert J. "Pricing Strategy in the Automotive Glass Industry." *Management Accounting,* July 1989, pp. 26–34.

Chow, Chee W., Howard R. Toole, and Adrian Wong-Boren. "Make Better Decisions: Divide and Conquer." *Management Accounting,* August 1986, pp. 41–45.

Dudick, Thomas S. "Pricing Strategies for Manufacturers." *Management Accounting,* November 1989, pp. 30–37.

► **SELF-TEST**

True or False

1. Irrelevant costs for decision-making purposes fall into two main categories—sunk costs and past costs—that are the same for each alternative under consideration.

2. When a decision is to be made whether or not to purchase new equipment, it

is safe to ignore depreciation of the equipment if income taxes are to be ignored.

3. When a decision is to be made whether or not to replace old equipment with new equipment, it is safe to ignore the book value of the old equipment if income taxes are to be ignored.

4. When a decision is to be made whether or not to enter a market with a new product, it is safe to ignore the investment of working capital if income taxes are to be ignored.

5. When a firm is considering an offer from a customer to purchase one of the firm's products at a price less than full cost, the firm's net profit will be greater than it would be without the special order, provided the price offered is greater than the firm's variable costs of producing the special order.

6. When a decision is to be made whether to continue to make a component part or to purchase it from a vendor, the fixed costs allocated to the cost of manufacturing the part must be factored into the decision-making process.

7. When making the decision of whether to sell a joint product, product X, at the splitoff point or to process it further, the allocated joint product cost to product X may be safely ignored.

8. *Skimming the market* is a pricing strategy that is most effective when the barriers for competitors to enter the market are low.

9. Market penetration is an effective pricing strategy when a firm has high variable costs and low fixed costs.

10. Markup pricing is a pricing strategy by which a predetermined percentage is added to a product's cost to cover income taxes and a reasonable profit. This strategy may be used both by firms that use absorption costing or variable costing.

11. Target-return pricing is a pricing strategy that bases selling prices on a desired return on investment rather than a desired amount of dollar profit based on a percentage of cost.

12. Demand-oriented pricing is a pricing strategy that varies selling prices in accordance with the demand of the product or service.

13. Competition-based pricing is a pricing strategy that sets prices of a firm's products at the prices of the firm's competitors without regard to the cost of manufacturing the products.

14. When allocating scarce resources, such as factory capacity or material shortages, a firm will normally emphasize those products that produce the largest dollar amount of contribution margin.

Multiple Choice

1. When video cassette recorders (VCRs) were first marketed, the selling price was about $1,000. Today, a VCR can be purchased for around $200. This pricing strategy is typical of:
   a. Target-return pricing
   b. Skimming the market
   c. Demand-oriented pricing
   d. Markup pricing

2. Gasoline prices tend to rise in the summer when people do more driving. This pricing strategy is an example of:
   a. Target-return pricing
   b. Skimming the market
   c. Demand-oriented pricing
   d. Market-penetration pricing

3. Tango Company manufactures two products, A and B, and currently is operating at 70 percent of capacity of 100,000 units. It has received an offer from a foreign government to manufacture 10,000 units of product A at $3 each. Normal selling price is $5 each. Fixed costs are $2 each and variable costs are $1.50 each. The units are priced FOB shipping point. What would be the effect on net income if the order is accepted?

   a. Increase by $30,000
   b. Increase by $15,000
   c. Decrease by $20,000
   d. Decrease by $5,000

4. Beach Fashions sells exotic clothing. The company received a shipment of original dresses that cost $750 each. If Beach uses a markup pricing technique of 50 percent of cost, what is the selling price of the dresses?

   a. $1,500
   b. $1,125
   c. $1,000
   d. $875

5. A clothier uses a pricing technique of marking up items 60 percent of selling price. What will be the selling price of a coat that cost $56?

   a. $140.00
   b. $89.60
   c. $$78.40
   d. $120.00

The following information should be used to answer questions 6 and 7.

Burr Co. is contemplating the purchase of a new machine. The machine will be used to manufacture a new product. Burr has assembled the following information:

Purchase price of machine	$770,000
Useful life in years	12
Salvage value	$ 50,000
Annual depreciation.	$ 60,000
Budgeted annual sales.	$260,000
Budgeted annual variable costs.	$156,000
Budgeted annual fixed costs	$ 30,000

6. The net investment in the machine is:

   a. $770,000
   b. $720,000
   c. $660,000
   d. $50,000

7. The cash operating advantage over the machine's life is:

   a. $74,000
   b. $118,000
   c. $168,000
   d. $888,000

▶ **QUESTIONS**

1. What are relevant costs in the decision-making process? Use examples to illustrate them.
2. What are irrelevant costs in the decision-making process? Use examples to illustrate them.
3. What is the differential income approach to decision making? What are its advantages?

4. What is the comparative income approach to decision making? What are its advantages and disadvantages?
5. Are variable costs always relevant costs? Explain.
6. Are fixed costs always irrelevant costs? Explain.
7. Identify the relevant costs needed to reach a decision regarding the purchase of new equipment.
8. What is the cash operating advantage? How is it used?
9. Identify the relevant costs needed to reach a decision on whether to replace existing equipment. Is the needed information the same as that needed for purchasing new equipment? Explain.
10. Name the relevant costs for entering a new market.
11. Is it possible for a firm to increase its net income by sometimes accepting an order at a price less than its full cost? Explain.
12. What does the make-or-buy decision consist of? What are the relevant costs for this kind of decision?
13. What is an opportunity cost? For what kinds of decisions is it relevant? Explain.
14. What is a common direct material? A joint product cost?
15. Are allocated joint product costs useful? If so, for what purposes? If not, explain.
16. What information is needed for the process-further-or-sell-at-splitoff-point decision? Are allocated joint product costs useful for this decision? Explain.
17. Firms often use different pricing strategies. Name some of these pricing strategies and indicate the relevant information needed to implement them.
18. Linear programming is often used to solve complex scarce resource allocation problems. However, simpler allocation problems may be solved without using linear programming. How may this be accomplished? Under what conditions may this method be used?

(For Appendix 13-A)

19. What kinds of business problems are especially suitable for linear programming solutions? Be specific.
20. What is an objective function? A constraint inequality?
21. What is the area of feasible solutions? Why is it important?
22. A firm has two constraints, both relating to machine capacity. The firm manufactures two products: R and S. The objective function is Max $Z = \$16\,R + \$18\,S$. There is no market limitation. For the coming year, the contribution margin for product S is expected to be only $3. Would you expect the firm to continue its present product mix for the coming year? Why?
23. Your boss has a son who is studying linear programming in college. The son provides you with his formulation of a linear programming problem. Is it correct? If not, help him correct it. His formulation is:

$$\text{Max } Z = 6X + 3Y$$

subject to

$$\$3X + \$2Y \geq \$20$$
$$\$6X + \$2Y \geq \$26$$

► **EXERCISES**   **E13–1**   **Purchasing a New Machine and Replacing an Existing Machine**

The Montana Corporation is presently using a machine, M–1, in its production process. It is contemplating the purchase of a newer, more efficient machine, M–2. The following information is available:

	M–1	M–2
Purchase price	$240,000	$480,000
Useful life	15 years	10 years
Salvage value	$ 15,000	$ 24,000
Accumulated depreciation ($225,000 ÷ 15 years =		
$15,000; $15,000 × 5 years)	75,000	–0–
Depreciation per annum	15,000	45,600
Sales revenue	264,000	288,000
Direct materials cost	42,000	52,800
Direct labor	72,000	60,000
Variable overhead	43,200	37,200
Fixed overhead	33,000	42,000

Income taxes and the time value of money are to be ignored.

Required   *a.* Assume the Montana Corporation is contemplating the purchase of M–2 and intends to keep M–1. There is a sufficient market for the firm's output from both machines. Prepare schedules to compute:
(1) The net investment of M–2.
(2) The cash operating advantage of M–2 for the 10-year life of the machine.
(3) The net cash flow for the 10-year period.

b. Assume market conditions are such that the corporation can sell the output from either M–2 or M–1 but not both. Thus, if M–2 is purchased, M–1 will be sold for $30,000. Using differential analysis, prepare schedules to compute:
(1) The net investment of M–2.
(2) The cash operating advantage of M–2 for the 10-year life of the machine.
(3) The net cash flow for the 10-year period. Should M–2 be purchased?

E13–2   Replacement of Equipment

The Newton Corporation is presently using a machine, FG–1, in its production process. It is contemplating the purchase of a newer, more efficient machine, FG–3. The following information is available:

	FG–1	FG–3
Purchase price	$156,000	$240,000
Useful life	12 years	8 years
Salvage value	$ 12,000	$ 9,600
Accumulated depreciation ($144,000 ÷ 12 years =		
$12,000; $12,000 × 8 years)	96,000	–0–
Depreciation per annum	12,000	28,800
Sales revenue	120,000	144,000
Direct materials cost	24,000	28,800
Direct labor	28,800	21,600
Variable overhead	14,400	10,800
Fixed overhead	24,000	26,400
Cost to overhaul FG–1 to extend its remaining life by		
4 years for a total of 8 years	36,000	–0–

The time value of money and income taxes are to be ignored.

Required   *a.* Using the comparative income approach, compute the following:
(1) The net investment of purchasing FG–3.
(2) The cash operating advantage of FG–3 for the eight-year period.
(3) The net cash flow for the eight-year period.

    b. Assume FG–1 can be sold for $72,000. Compute the following for FG–1:

       (1) The net investment of FG–1. (*Hint:* Use opportunity cost.)

       (2) The cash operating advantage of FG–1 for the eight-year life of the machine.

       (3) The net cash flow for the eight-year period.

    c. Should FG–3 be purchased? Why?

E13–3   Entering a New Market

The Moreken Company, which produces vacuum cleaners, is thinking of introducing a new line of expensive vacuum cleaners that are more powerful than any presently on the market. A market survey indicates that there is only a limited market for this product because of its high cost and estimates that after five years there will be no market at all.

    The following annual information about the new product is available to you:

Estimated sales (15,000 × $200)	$3,000,000
Cost of direct materials and direct labor	1,000,000
Variable overhead	280,000
Variable marketing costs	150,000
Fixed overhead, marketing, and administrative costs	600,000

    Additional information is as follows:

Price of new machinery	$3,000,000
Salvage value at the end of 5 years	40,000
Working capital needed at inception	280,000
Working capital returned at the end of 5 years	260,000
Depreciation of new machinery per annum	592,000

Required   *a.* Which of the above data is relevant to you in recommending whether it is advantageous for Moreken to enter this new market?

    b. Using relevant data only, determine if it is advantageous for Moreken to enter this new market.

E13–4   Accepting a Special Order at Less than Full Price

The Fancy Cosmetics Company produces and sells in the United States an antichapping lip liner that also prevents lipstick from smearing. The demand for this product is much higher in the winter, and at times the company could produce more than it sells. The Icelandic Company has offered to buy 15,000 cases of Fancy lip liners, which it will sell under its own name. Although Fancy sells its lip liners at $15 per case in the United States, the Icelandic Company has offered to pay $7.50 per case and has agreed to take shipment whenever Fancy has the unused capacity to produce the lip liners.

    The following information is available to you:

Cost of direct materials	$125,000
Cost of direct labor	187,500
Variable overhead	112,500
Fixed overhead	200,000
Fixed marketing and administrative costs	250,000
Freight-out to Iceland	3,750
Annual sales in units	100,000 units

Required   *a.* In determining whether to recommend acceptance of this order, which items would be relevant to your decision? Should the order be accepted? Why?

    b. If instead of being sold to the Icelandic firm these lip liners were to be sold to one of Fancy's U.S. competitors, would different items be considered relevant? Explain. Your answer should include consideration of qualitative matters, if they are appropriate for reaching this decision.

E13–5 Accepting an Order at Less than Full Cost

The Catchem Company manufactures one product—fishing rods—and is operating at 60 percent of its normal capacity. It sells the fishing rods at $15 each. An income statement for the first six months of 19x5 is as follows:

CATCHEM COMPANY
Income Statement
For the Six Months Ended June 30, 19x5

Sales (60,000 at $15)		$900,000
Cost of goods sold:		
Direct materials (60,000 at $3)	$180,000	
Direct labor (60,000 at $4.50)	270,000	
Variable overhead (60,000 at $.75)	45,000	
Fixed overhead (60,000 at $2.25)	135,000	630,000
Gross margin		270,000
Marketing and administrative costs—all fixed		120,000
Operating income before income taxes		$150,000

A major retailer has offered to purchase 40,000 fishing rods modified to the retailer's specifications. The fishing rods will differ significantly from Catchem's design, and the retailer will market the fishing rods under its own private label. Thus, these fishing rods will not compete with Catchem's regular fishing rods.

The retailer has offered Catchem $8.25 per fishing rod. Direct labor and overhead will be at the same unit cost as Catchem's regular fishing rods. Direct materials will amount to $2.25 per unit. Shipping costs, to be borne by Catchem, will amount to $.15 cents per unit.

Required
a. Should Catchem accept the order for the remainder of 19x5? Why?
b. Prepare a projected income statement for the remaining six months of 19x5, assuming Catchem accepts the order and the sales and costs of the regular fishing rods are the same as for the first six months.

E13–6 Make-Or-Buy Decision

The management accountant of the Met Company prepared the following summary of costs for Part A70, used in the manufacture of its only product:

Direct materials	$ 64,000
Direct labor	256,000
Variable overhead	96,000
Direct fixed overhead:	
Supervisory salaries	64,000
Depreciation of equipment	48,000
Common fixed overhead—allocated . . .	160,000
Total	$688,000

The firm uses 20,000 units of Part A70 each year. The Cascade Company offered to supply Part A70 to the Met Company at a cost of $26 per unit.

The depreciation of $48,000 per annum is on special-purpose equipment that cannot be used for any other purpose except to manufacture Part A70. The equipment has no resale value.

Required
a. Assume the space used to manufacture Part A70 cannot be used for any other purpose, nor can it be sublet to another firm. Should the Met Company accept Cascade's offer? Why?

b. If the space could be sublet, would you recommend accepting Cascade's offer if the annual rental income is:
(1) $30,000.
(2) $40,000.
(3) $100,000.
For each answer, show your computations and give the reasons that you have taken the position you recommend.

E13–7 **Make-Or-Buy Decision**
The Viggs and Strutt Company makes its own pistons for use in the small gasoline engines it manufactures. It is considering purchasing these pistons from a very reliable manufacturer of pistons. If it does so, it can rent the part of the factory it would no longer need to a small manufacturer of tools for $18,000 per annum. The company uses 120,000 pistons per annum. The following information is available from the standard cost sheet for the pistons:

	Per Unit
Direct materials.	$ 4.50
Direct labor	3.00
Variable overhead.	2.25
Fixed overhead, direct.	2.25
Fixed overhead, common	3.75
Total	$15.75

The piston manufacturer has offered to make the pistons for $12.50 each.

Required *a.* Should the offer be accepted? Why?
b. Instead of renting out the extra space, Viggs and Strutt may decide to use the space to manufacture a new engine that would generate a segment margin of $90,000 per annum. Under these conditions, would you recommend that Viggs and Strutt stop making its own pistons? Why?

E13–8 **Sell at Splitoff Point or Process Further**
1. Helen Corporation manufactures products W, X, Y, and Z from a joint process. Additional information is as follows:

Product	Units Produced	Sales Value at Splitoff	If Processed Further Additional Costs	If Processed Further Sales Value
W	6,000	$ 80,000	$11,500	$ 90,000
X	5,000	60,000	6,000	70,000
Y	4,000	40,000	4,000	50,000
Z.	3,000	20,000	12,500	30,000
	18,000	$200,000	$34,000	$240,000

Each product may be sold at the splitoff point or processed further. The maximum amount that can be earned from further processing is
a. $6,000.
b. $40,000.
c. $12,500.
d. $10,000.

2. Pendall Company manufactures products Dee and Eff from a joint process. Product Dee has been allocated $2,500 of total joint costs of $20,000 for the 1,000 units produced. Dee can be sold at the splitoff point for $3 per unit, or it can be processed further with additional costs of $1,000 and sold for $5 per unit. If Dee is processed further and sold, the result would be

   a. A breakeven situation.
   b. An additional gain of $1,000 from further processing.
   c. An overall loss of $1,000.
   d. An additional gain of $2,000 from further processing.

(AICPA Adapted)

E13–9   Sell at Splitoff Point or Process Further

The Sweet Company produces three products, A, B, and C, from a joint process. Each product may be sold at the splitoff point or processed further into a packaged confection. The cost of producing all three products is $98,000. The process produces 10,000 gallons each of A and B and 8,000 gallons of C. You must decide which products to sell at the splitoff point and which to process further. The following information is available to you:

Product	Sales Value at Splitoff Point	Costs to Process Further	Sales Value after Processing
A	$ 80,000	$50,000	$120,000
B	60,000	70,000	140,000
C	100,000	60,000	180,000

Required   Which products would you recommend that Sweet sell at the splitoff point? Which should Sweet process further? Show your calculations.

E13–10   Pricing Decision: Skimming versus Market Penetration

The Biltmore Electronics Company plans to market a new product. The firm's marketing research department completed a marketing survey and determined that the product's demand function is:

$$Q = 12 - P$$

where

Q = The quantity demanded (in millions)
P = Price of the product

In tabular form, the demand function appears as follows:

Price	Quantity (in millions)	Total Revenue
$12.	0	$ –0–
11.	1	11,000,000
10.	2	20,000,000
9.	3	27,000,000
8.	4	32,000,000
7.	5	35,000,000
6.	6	36,000,000
5.	7	35,000,000

The variable cost of the product is $4 per unit, and there are no incremental fixed costs associated with the product.

The firm believes the maximum number of units that can be sold is 7 million.

Biltmore does not believe its image will be affected if it uses a skimming-the-market pricing policy. On the other hand, it is also considering a market-penetration pricing policy.

Required
a. If Biltmore wishes to penetrate the market, what price should it charge? Why?
b. If instead of penetrating the market, the firm wishes to maximize its income by skimming the market, what strategy would you recommend? Show your computations to justify your solution.

E13–11 Pricing and Markup Percentages

The Benis Company is in the process of setting a selling price for one of its products. The accounting department provides you with the following:

	Per Unit
Direct materials.	$ 6
Direct labor	12
Variable overhead.	3
Fixed overhead ($900,000 ÷ 100,000 units).	9
Variable marketing costs.	6
Fixed marketing and administrative costs ($900,000 ÷ 100,000 units)	9

The company computed a markup percentage based on absorption costing of 110 percent. This percentage is sufficient to cover marketing and administrative costs and income tax.

Required
a. Compute the selling price if the markup percentage is to be based on absorption costing.
b. Compute the markup percentage if the firm wishes to base its selling price—computed in part (a)—on variable manufacturing costing.
c. Compute the markup percentage if the firm wishes to base its selling price—computed in part (a)—using the contribution approach. Is your answer the same as in part (b)? Why?

E13–12 Computation of Markup Percentage for Pricing Products

The controller for the Sundam Corporation prepared the following standard cost sheet:

Direct materials (8 yards at $2 per yard)	$16
Direct labor (5 hours at $14 per hour)	70
Variable overhead (5 hours at $4 per hour).	20
Fixed overhead (5 hours at $8 per hour)	40
Total.	$146

The fixed overhead of $8 per hour is based on a volume of 150,000 hours per annum. Variable marketing costs are 3 percent of sales, and fixed marketing and administrative costs are $240,000 per annum. The firm's income tax rate is 30 percent.

Required
a. Compute the markup percentage using absorption costing if Sundam is to earn a $840,000 net income (after income tax). What selling price would produce the desired net income?

    b. Compute the markup percentage using the variable manufacturing cost approach.

    c. Compute the markup percentage using the contribution margin approach.

E13–13   Target-Return Pricing

The Welsh Company wishes to earn a target return on one of its product lines. The following information is available:

Variable manufacturing costs per unit	$48
Fixed manufacturing costs per unit	
($560,000 ÷ 80,000 units)	7
Total manufacturing costs.	$55
Fixed marketing and administrative costs	$ 860,000
Investment in assets for this product line	$3,000,000
Desired rate of return.	18%
Income tax rate	40%

Required   *a.* Compute the markup percentage, assuming the firm uses absorption costing as the basis for its markup.

    b. What is the selling price? Prove it is correct.

E13–14   Target-Return Pricing

The Griffin Company wishes to earn a target return on one of its product lines. The following information is available:

Variable manufacturing costs per unit	$50
Fixed manufacturing costs per unit	
($600,000 ÷ 60,000 units)	10
Total manufacturing costs	$60
Variable marketing costs.	$ 240,000
Fixed marketing and administrative costs . . .	$ 520,000
Investment in assets for this product line . . .	$4,000,000
Desired rate of return	24%
Income tax rate.	25%

Required   *a.* (1) Compute the markup percentage, assuming the firm uses variable manufacturing cost as the basis for its markup.

       (2) What is the selling price? Prove it is correct.

    b. Repeat (*a*1) and (*a*2), assuming the firm uses the contribution margin approach.

E13–15   Target-Return Pricing

The Yates Company is introducing a new product and wishes to earn a target return on it. The following information is available:

Variable manufacturing costs per unit	$12
Variable marketing costs per unit	$ 2
Fixed manufacturing costs	$1,200,000
Fixed marketing and administrative costs.	$ 400,000
Investment in assets for this product.	$5,000,000
Desired rate of return	15%
Income tax rate	25%

    The firm is uncertain how many units can be sold each year. However, the director of marketing believes the number of units sold will depend on the selling price. Initially, the director would like to know what the selling price would be at different levels of projected sales volume.

    The firm uses a markup percentage based on absorption costing.

Required   a. Compute the selling prices for each of the following projected sales volumes:
(1) 40,000 units.
(2) 50,000 units.
(3) 80,000 units.
b. For each of the above sales volumes, compute the markup percentage based on absorption costing.

E13–16   **Optimum Allocation of Scarce Resources**

The Good Health Baking Company produces a salt-free, whole-grain bread (B) and a carob-chip cookie (C). The demand for B and C from health-food stores is exceeding Good Health's production capacity. It only has 80,000 direct labor-hours available, and a case of B requires 0.5 direct labor-hour while a case of C requires 1 direct labor-hour. The company estimates it can sell 60,000 cases of B and 80,000 cases of C in the next year.

As the production manager, you must decide what quantities of B and C to produce. You have the following information available:

	B	C
Selling price per case	$60	$120
Variable costs per case:		
Direct materials.	15	30
Direct labor	2	10
Variable overhead.	8	25
Variable marketing costs	5	5

Required   a. What is the contribution margin per case and per direct labor-hour for B and C?
b. Calculate how many cases of B and C the corporation should produce in the next year to achieve the maximum total contribution margin.

E13–17   **Allocating Scarce Machine-Hours to Manufacturing for Optimum Cost Savings**

Items 1 and 2 are based on the following information.

Standard costs and other data for two component parts used by Griffon Electronics are presented below:

	Part A4	Part B5
Direct material	$ .40	$ 8.00
Direct labor	1.00	4.70
Factory overhead	4.00	2.00
Unit standard cost	$5.40	$14.70
Units needed per year	6,000	8,000
Machine-hours per unit	4	2
Unit cost if purchased	$5.00	$15.00

In past years, Griffon has manufactured all of its required components; however, in 19x4, only 30,000 hours of otherwise idle machine time can be devoted to the production of components. Accordingly, some of the parts must be purchased from outside suppliers. In producing parts, factory overhead is applied at $1 per standard machine-hour. Fixed capacity costs, which will not be affected by any make-or-buy decision, represent 60 percent of the applied overhead.

1. The 30,000 hours of available machine time are to be scheduled such that Griffon realizes maximum potential cost savings. The relevant unit production costs to consider in the decision to schedule machine time are
   a. $5.40 for A4 and $14.70 for B5.
   b. $5 for A4 and $15 for B5.
   c. $1.40 for A4 and $12.70 for B5.
   d. $3 for A4 and $13.50 for B5.
2. If the allocation of machine time is based on potential cost savings per machine-hour, then Griffon should produce
   a. 3,500 units of A4 and 8,000 units of B5.
   b. 6,000 units of A4 and 8,000 units of B5.
   c. 6,000 units of A4 and 3,000 units of B5.
   d. No units of A4 and 8,000 units of B5.

(AICPA Adapted)

E13–18   **(For Appendix 13-A) Linear Programming: Maximization Problem**
The Eden Company manufactures two products: X and Y. The contribution margins are $18 for product X and $12 for product Y. The products move through two departments: machining and polishing. The time requirements and limits for each department are as follows:

	Machining	Polishing
Product X	4	2
Product Y	2	2
Hours available.	32	18

Required   a. Formulate the objective function and the constraint inequalities.
b. Use the graphical solution to determine the optimum number of X and Y to produce. Show your computations.

E13–19   **(For Appendix 13-A) Linear Programming: Maximization Problem**
The Garnet Company manufactures two products: X and Y. The contribution margins are $150 for product X and $100 for product Y. The products move through two departments: machining and polishing. The time requirements and limits for each department are as follows:

	Machining	Polishing
Product X	2	4
Product Y	1	1
Hours available.	28	40

Required   a. Formulate the objective function and the constraint inequalities.
b. Use the graphical solution to determine the optimum number of X and Y to produce. Show your computations.

E13–20   **(For Appendix 13-A) Linear Programming: Maximization Problem**
The Bruce Company manufactures two products: S and T. Each product must pass through two departments: cutting and painting. The time requirements and limits of each department are as follows:

Department	Product S	Product T	Daily Capacity Limit
Cutting	2	4	24
Painting.	1	4	20

The contribution margin of S is $100 per unit, and the contribution margin of T is $80 per unit.

Market demand will limit the sales of S to 10 units per day.

Required *a.* Formulate the objective function and the constraint inequalities.
b. Use the graphical solution to determine the optimum quantities of S and T to produce. Show all computations.

E13–21 **(For Appendix 13-A) Linear Programming: Maximization Problem**

The Gautner Company manufactures two products: X and Y. Each product must pass through two departments: cutting and finishing. The time requirements and limits of each department are as follows:

Department	Product X	Product Y	Daily Capacity Limit
Cutting	16	10	240
Finishing	10	10	180

The contribution margin of X is $130 per unit, and the contribution margin of Y is $50 per unit.

Market demand will limit the sales of X to 12 units per day.

Required *a.* Formulate the objective function and the constraint inequalities.
b. Use the graphical solution to determine the optimum quantities of X and Y to produce. Show all computations.

E13–22 **(For Appendix 13-A) Linear Programming: Maximization Problem**

The Hobbs Company manufactures two products: X and Y. Each product must pass through two departments: cutting and finishing. The time requirements and limits of each department are as follows:

Department	Product X	Product Y	Daily Capacity Limit
Cutting	6	10	120
Finishing	4	10	90

The contribution margin of X is $30 per unit, and the contribution margin of Y is $70 per unit.

Market demand will limit the sales of X to eight units per day.

Required *a.* Formulate the objective function and the constraint inequalities.
b. Use the graphical solution to determine the optimum quantities of X and Y to produce. Show all computations.

E13–23 **(For Appendix 13-A) Linear Programming: Maximization Problems**

1. The Hale Company manufactures products A and B, each of which requires two processes: polishing and grinding. The contribution margin is $3 for product A and $4 for product B. The graph shows the maximum number of units of each product that may be processed in the two departments.

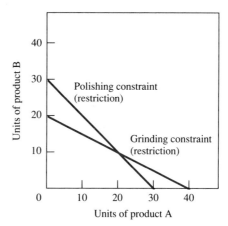

Considering the constraints (restrictions) on processing, which combination of products A and B maximizes the total contribution margin?

a. 0 units of A and 20 units of B.

b. 20 units of A and 10 units of B.

c. 30 units of A and 0 units of B.

d. 40 units of A and 0 units of B.

2. The Pauley Company plans to expand its sales force by opening several new branch offices. Pauley has $10.4 million in capital available for new branch offices. Pauley will consider opening only two types of branches: 20-person branches (type A) and 10-person branches (type B). Expected initial cash outlays are $1.3 million for a type A branch and $670,000 for a type B branch. Expected annual cash inflow, net of income taxes, is $92,000 for a type A branch and $36,000 for a type B branch. Pauley will hire no more than 200 employees for the new branch offices and will not open more than 20 branch offices. Linear programming will be used to help decide how many branch offices should be opened.

In a system of equations for a linear programming model, which of the following equations would *not* represent a constraint (restriction)?

a. $A + B \leq 20$.

b. $20 A + 10 B \leq 200$.

c. $\$92,000 A + \$36,000 B \leq \$128,000$.

d. $\$1,300,000 A + \$670,000 B \leq \$10,400,000$.

(AICPA Adapted)

E13–24 **(For Appendix 13-A) Linear Programming: Minimization Problem**

The Laurence Company manufactures one product, which uses direct materials L and M. Material L costs $100 per pound, and material M costs $150 per pound. Material L has four units of alloy and four units of precious metal. Material M has three units of alloy and eight units of precious metal. The minimum requirements in each unit of product are 30 units of alloy and 40 units of precious metal.

Required   a. Formulate the objective function and the constraint inequalities.

b. Use the graphical solution to determine the optimum quantities of L and M to use in manufacturing. Show all computations.

▶ **PROBLEMS**   **P13–25**   **Purchasing a New Machine and Replacing an Existing Machine**

The Oregon Corporation is presently using two machines, K–1 and K–2, in its production process. It is contemplating the purchase of an automated, more efficient machine, K–5. The following information is available:

	K–1	**K–2**	**K–5**
Purchase price	$120,000	$168,000	$360,000
Useful life	10 years	7 years	5 years
Salvage value.	$ 12,000	$ 16,800	$ 36,000
Accumulated depreciation:			
K–1 ($108,000 ÷ 10 years =			
$10,800 per annum; $10,800 × 5 years)	54,000		
K–2 ($151,200 ÷ 7 years =			
$21,600 per annum; $21,600 × 2 years)		43,200	
Depreciation per annum	10,800	21,600	64,800
Sales revenue.	960,000	960,000	960,000
Direct materials cost.	192,000	192,000	192,000
Direct labor	240,000	240,000	144,000
Variable overhead.	96,000	96,000	57,600
Fixed overhead	192,000	192,000	240,000

At present, the company uses the K–2 machine as its principal machine, while the K–1 machine is only used when the K–2 is down for repairs and maintenance. Occasionally, the K–1 machine is also used when the firm is very busy and must add a special shift of employees. The K–1 and K–2 machines are similar, except the K–1 is older and better constructed. Actually, the K–1 is in better condition in some respects. At the present time, they both have the same resale value of $72,000.

The supervisor of the department where the machines are used asked the accounting department to furnish him with the book values of K–1 and K–2. He then prepared the following:

	K–1	**K–2**
Original cost.	$120,000	$168,000
Accumulated depreciation.	54,000	43,200
Book value	66,000	124,800
Resale value.	72,000	72,000
Gain (loss) on sale	$ 6,000	$(52,800)

Income taxes and the time value of money are to be ignored.

Required   a. Assume the Oregon Corporation is contemplating the purchase of K–5 and also intends to keep both K–1 and K–2. There is a sufficient market for the firm's output from all machines. Prepare schedules to compute:

(1) The net investment of K–5.

(2) The cash operating advantage of K–5 for the five-year life of the machine.

(3) The net cash flow for the five-year period.

b. Assume market conditions are such that the corporation can sell the output from K–5 or K–2 but not both. Thus, if K–5 is purchased, either K–1 or K–2 will be sold, and the one not sold will be used as a spare for K–5. Using differential analysis, prepare schedules to compute:

(1) The net investment of K–5.

(2) The cash operating advantage of K–5 for the five-year life of the machine.

(3) The net cash flow for the five-year period. Should K–5 be purchased?

c. Assume your answer in part (*b*3) is that K–5 should be purchased. The factory supervisor informs you that although K–1 is in better condition than K–2, he intends to sell K–1 because it would show a gain of $6,000 on the sale whereas a sale of K–2 would show a loss of $52,800, and he does not want that loss to appear on his performance report. Draft a response to his argument.

P13–26 **Entering a New Market, Competition Pricing, and Targeted Return on Investment (ROI)**

The Whole Person Company has learned of the success the Good Health Company is having with its bread and has decided to enter the market to compete with Good Health's bread. The Good Health bread sells for $1.50 a loaf. Whole Person knows that to compete it must charge the same price. In addition, Whole Person's company policy is to have a 12 percent ROI on its investment of net assets of $1.35 million. Whole Person's income tax rate is 40 percent.

The company estimates it can sell 1 million loaves of bread annually and its marketing and administrative costs will be $300,000. Of this amount, $60,000 is expected to be variable costs, and the balance ($240,000) is expected to be fixed.

The investment of $1.35 million consists of the following:

Working capital	$ 150,000
Machinery and equipment with a useful life of	
10 years and no salvage value	1,200,000
Total.	$1,350,000

The annual cost of the 1 million loaves of bread is expected to be:

Direct materials	$150,000
Direct labor	?
Variable overhead	150,000
Fixed overhead—in addition to	
the machinery and equipment	300,000

The investment of $150,000 in working capital is expected to be released at the end of 10 years.

Required *a.* Compute the amount the firm can pay for direct labor.

b. Assume the firm estimates the direct labor needed can be obtained for $300,000, including all payroll fringes. Would you recommend that Whole Person go ahead with the project? Explain.

c. Compute the net investment.

d. Compute the cash operating advantage for the 10-year period.

P13–27 **Expanding a Product Line**

Helene's, a high-fashion women's dress manufacturer, is planning to market a new cocktail dress for the coming season. Helene's supplies retailers in the east and mid-Atlantic states.

Four yards of material are required to lay out the dress pattern. Some material remains after cutting, which can be sold as remnants.

The leftover material could also be used to manufacture a matching cape and handbag. However, if the leftover material is to be used for the cape and handbag, more care will be required in the cutting, which will increase the cutting costs.

The company expected to sell 1,250 dresses if no matching cape or handbag were available. Helene's market research reveals that dress sales will be 20 percent higher if a matching cape and handbag are available. The market research indicates that the cape and/or handbag will not be sold individually but only as accessories with the dress. The various combinations of dresses, capes, and handbags that are expected to be sold by retailers are as follows:

	Percent of Total
Complete sets of dress, cape, and handbag.	70
Dress and cape	6
Dress and handbag	15
Dress only	9
Total	100

The material used in the dress costs $12.50 a yard, or $50 for each dress. The cost of cutting the dress if the cape and handbag are not manufactured is estimated at $20 a dress, and the resulting remnants can be sold for $5 for each dress cut out. If the cape and handbag are to be manufactured, the cutting costs will be increased by $9 per dress. There will be no salable remnants if the capes and handbags are manufactured in the quantities estimated.

The selling prices and the costs to complete the three items once they are cut are presented below:

	Selling Price per Unit	Unit Cost to Complete (Excludes Cost of Material and Cutting Operation)
Dress	$200.00	$80.00
Cape	27.50	19.50
Handbag	9.50	6.50

Required
a. Calculate Helene's incremental profit or loss from manufacturing the capes and handbags in conjunction with the dresses.
b. Identify any nonquantitative factors that could influence Helene's management in its decision to manufacture the capes and handbags.

(CMA Adapted)

P13–28   **Accepting a Special Order at Less than Full Cost**

The Burr Electronics Company normally produces 150,000 units of K–9 per year. Due to an economic downturn, the company has some idle capacity. K–9 sells for $24 per unit.

The firm's production, marketing, and administrative costs at its normal capacity are:

	Per Unit
Direct materials	$ 2.00
Direct labor	3.20
Variable overhead	2.00
Fixed overhead ($720,000 ÷ 150,000 units)	4.80
Variable marketing costs	1.68
Fixed marketing and administrative costs ($336,000 ÷ 150,000 units).	2.24
Total	$15.92

Required   *a.* Compute the firm's operating income before income taxes if the firm sold 110,000 units in 19x4.

b. For 19x5, the firm expects to sell the same number of units as it sold in 19x4. However, in a trade newspaper, the firm noticed an invitation to bid on selling K–9 to a state government. There are no marketing costs associated with the order if Burr is awarded the contract. The company wishes to prepare a bid for 40,000 units at its full manufacturing cost plus 20 cents per unit. How much should the company bid? If Burr succeeds in getting the contract, what would be the effect on operating income?

c. Assume the company is awarded the contract on January 2, 19x5. In addition, it receives an order from a foreign vendor for 40,000 units at the regular price of $24 per unit. The foreign shipment will require the firm to incur its normal marketing costs. The government contract contains a 10-day escape clause (i.e., the firm can reject the contract within 10 days without any penalty). If the firm accepts the government contract, overtime pay at one and a half times the straight-time rate will be paid on the 40,000 units. In addition, fixed overhead will increase by $100,000. Variable overhead will behave in its normal pattern. Decide the following:

(1) Should the firm accept the foreign order? Show the effect on operating income of accepting the order.

(2) Assuming the foreign order is accepted, should the firm accept the government order? Show the effect on operating income of accepting the government order.

P13–29   Relevant Costs for Accepting a Special Order

George Jackson operates a small machine shop. He manufactures one standard product that is available from many other similar businesses, and he also manufactures products to customer order. His accountant prepared the annual income statement shown below:

	Custom Sales	Standard Sales	Total
Sales	$50,000	$25,000	$75,000
Costs:			
Material	10,000	8,000	18,000
Labor	20,000	9,000	29,000
Depreciation	6,300	3,600	9,900
Power	700	400	1,100
Rent	6,000	1,000	7,000
Heat and light	600	100	700
Other	400	900	1,300
Total costs	44,000	23,000	67,000
Net income	$ 6,000	$ 2,000	$ 8,000

The depreciation charges are for machines used in the respective product lines. The power charge is apportioned on the estimate of power consumed. The rent is for the building space, which has been leased for 10 years at $7,000 per year. The rent and heat and light are apportioned to the product lines based on amount of floor space occupied. All other costs are current costs identified with the product line causing them.

A valued custom parts customer has asked Mr. Jackson if he would manufacture 5,000 special units for him. Mr. Jackson is working at capacity and would have to give up some other business to take this business. He cannot renege on custom orders already agreed to, but he could reduce the output of his standard product by about one half for one year while producing the specially requested custom part. The customer is willing to pay $7 for each part. The material cost will be about $2 per unit, and the labor will be $3.60 per unit. Mr. Jackson will have to spend $2,000 for a special device that will be discarded when the job is done.

Required
a. Calculate and present the following costs related to the 5,000-unit custom order:
   (1) The incremental cost of the order.
   (2) The full cost of the order.
   (3) The opportunity cost of taking the order.
   (4) The sunk costs related to the order.

b. Should Mr. Jackson take the order? Explain your answer with computations supporting your position.

(CMA Adapted)

P13–30   **Make-Or-Buy Decision**

The Good-4-U Salad Dressing Company produces four varieties of salad dressing. A major ingredient of each salad dressing is low-fat yogurt, which the company produces itself. A well-known, long-established dairy has offered to make this yogurt for Good-4-U and sell it for $20 a case.

You are asked to advise the president whether to accept this offer. It has been determined that Good-4-U would require 20,000 cases of yogurt per year. You have compiled the following information concerning the company's cost of making the yogurt:

	Per Case
Direct materials	$ 5
Direct labor.	4
Variable overhead	5
Fixed overhead	18*

* $8 is direct fixed overhead, and $10 is common fixed overhead.

Required
a. Assume the facilities now used to produce the yogurt can be used for storage instead of using the warehouse, for which the company is now paying $40,000 a year as rent. Would you recommend accepting the dairy's offer? Show your computations.

b. (1) Aside from the calculations in part (a), should any qualitative factors be considered in your decision? If so, discuss them.
   (2) Would your recommendation in part (a) be different if the president told you he planned to keep the yogurt-producing premises intact in the event the dairy is unable to deliver as promised? Show your computations.

c. Assume if the company were no longer producing yogurt, it would use the facilities to produce a new line of diet salad dressings. It is estimated that the new product would generate a segment margin of $70,000. Should the offer be accepted? Show your calculations.

P13–31   **Make-Or-Buy Decision and Accepting a Special Order**

The Sonic Company manufactures electric pencil sharpeners. At present, the company fabricates and manufactures all of the parts required to produce the product. The sharpeners sell for $30 each, and the standard cost for a sharpener consists of:

Direct materials	$ 6.00
Direct labor	4.50
Manufacturing overhead:	
Variable	1.50
Fixed ($720,000 ÷ 200,000 units)	3.60
Total cost	$15.60

The company received an offer from an electric motor manufacturer to manufacture the motors used in the sharpeners for a price of $3 each. If the company accepts the offer, direct materials will decrease by 20 percent, direct labor and variable overhead will decrease by 15 percent, and fixed overhead will decrease by $144,000.

Required   a. Should Sonic purchase the motors from an outside firm if the space occupied by the motor-manufacturing department has no alternative use and the salvage value of the department's equipment is equal to the cost of dismantling the equipment? Show computations.

b. A foreign purchaser approached Sonic with an offer to purchase 50,000 sharpeners at a price of $16. Sonic has sufficient capacity to manufacture the additional 50,000 units, except for the electric motors. Sonic is considering the following actions:
  (1) Subcontracting the manufacture of all of the electric motors and accepting the foreign order.
  (2) Subcontracting the manufacture of 50,000 motors at $3 each and accepting the foreign order.
  (3) Rejecting the foreign order.
  Calculate the effect of each alternative on the company's operating income. Show all computations. Which alternative would you select? Why?

c. Would your answer in part *(a)* be different if the firm could sublet the vacated space for $30,000 per annum? For $160,000 per annum? Explain.

d. What qualitative factors must also be considered before a firm buys components from another manufacturer?

P13–32   **Sell or Process Further**

The Copper Mining Company produces copper, gold, and silver from its mines. The gold and silver are sold to jewelry fabricators; the copper is sold by the pound, but it can be manufactured into soft copper tubing by additional processing.

If the copper is sold by the pound, the firm's profit per pound is computed as follows:

Selling price	$1.80
Less: Allocated joint product cost	1.00
Profit per pound	$ .80

A roll of tubing sells for $22 and requires $6 of additional processing costs and eight pounds of copper.

Required   a. Should the company process the copper into tubing? Show your computations.

b. What is the profit per pound of additional processing?

c. Assume the price of copper increases to $2 per pound, and the additional processing costs rise to $8. What price will the company require before it is willing to process copper into tubing?

P13–33   **Sell at Splitoff Point or Process Further**

The Healthful Extract Company uses a common direct material, CG9, to produce three joint products, AX6, BJ7, and JT8. The cost of each batch of CG9 processed is:

125,000 pounds of CG9.	$200,000
Direct labor	80,000
Overhead	120,000
Total per batch	$400,000

The yield per batch and the selling prices of each product are:

Product	Pounds	Selling Price per Pound
AX6	50,000	$6.00
BJ7	30,000	5.60
JT8.	40,000	4.30

There is a loss of 5,000 pounds per batch in processing.

Each product can be sold to other producers, or it can be processed further into another product. The additional processing costs and the selling prices after additional processing are:

Product	Separable Costs per Batch	Selling Price per Pound after Additional Processing
AX6	$50,000	$6.75
BJ7.	15,000	6.30
JT8	20,000	5.10

Required   *a.* Would you recommend that any of the products be processed further? Show your computations to support your position.

b. Assume the joint product cost of $400,000 is allocated to each product as follows:

AX6	$187,500
BJ7	105,000
JT8	107,500
Total	$400,000

(1) Prepare a schedule showing the gross profit for each product and the total for the batch, assuming the three products are sold at the splitoff point.

(2) Prepare a schedule showing the gross profit for each product and the total for the batch, assuming the three products are processed and sold as you recommended in part *(a)*.

P13–34   **Pricing Decision: Skimming versus Market Penetration**

The Crescent Electronics Company plans to market a new product. The firm's marketing research department completed a marketing survey and determined that the product's demand function is:

$$Q = 40 - 4P$$

where

Q = The quantity demanded (in millions)
P = Price of the product

In tabular form, the demand function appears as follows:

Price	Quantity (in millions)	Total Revenue
$10.	0	$ –0–
9.	4	36,000,000
8.	8	64,000,000
7.	12	84,000,000
6	16	96,000,000
5.	20	100,000,000
4.	24	96,000,000
3.	28	84,000,000

The variable cost of the product is $4 per unit, and there are no incremental fixed costs associated with the product.

The firm believes the maximum number of units that can be sold is 28 million.

Crescent does not believe its image will be affected if it uses a skimming-the-market pricing policy. On the other hand, it is also considering a market-penetration pricing policy.

Required   *a.* If Crescent wishes to penetrate the market, what price should it charge? Why?

b. If instead of penetrating the market, the firm wishes to maximize its income by skimming the market, what strategy would you recommend? Show your computations to justify your solution.

c. If instead of skimming the market, the firm wishes to use a strategy of initially offering the product at one price and then penetrating the market, what should the initial price and the subsequent price be? Show your computations.

P13–35   **Pricing and Markup Percentages**

The Primer Company is in the process of setting a selling price for one of its products. The accounting department provides you with the following for 19x3:

	50,000 Units
Sales	$1,500,000
Cost of goods sold	600,000
Gross margin	900,000
Marketing and administrative costs.	300,000
Operating income before income taxes . . . . . ,	600,000
Income taxes	240,000
Net income	$ 360,000

Cost of goods sold includes $225,000 of fixed overhead, and the $300,000 of marketing and administrative costs consists of $75,000 of variable marketing costs, with the remainder fixed.

For 19x4, the firm is contemplating the manufacture of a competing product marketed under a different label with some design modifications. However, costs and the selling price are expected to parallel the existing product. The firm wishes to earn the same net income in 19x4.

Required   *a.* What should the selling price be?

b. Compute the markup percentage if the firm wishes to base its selling price on absorption costing.

c. Recast the 19x3 income statement into a variable-costing format.

d. Compute the markup percentage if the firm wishes to base its selling price—computed in part *(a)*—on variable manufacturing costing.

e. Compute the markup percentage if the firm wishes to base its selling price—computed in part *(a)*—using the contribution approach. Is your answer the same as in part *(d)*? Why?

P13–36   **Markup Pricing**

E. Berg and Sons build custom-made pleasure boats that range in price from $10,000 to $250,000. For the past 30 years, Mr. Berg, Sr., has determined the selling price of each boat by estimating the costs of material, labor, a prorated portion of overhead, and adding 20 percent to these estimated costs.

For example, a recent price quotation was determined as follows:

Direct materials.	$ 5,000
Direct labor	8,000
Overhead.	2,000
	15,000
Plus 20%	3,000
Selling price	$18,000

The overhead figure was determined by estimating total overhead costs for the year and allocating them at 25 percent of direct labor.

If a customer rejected the price and business was slack, Mr. Berg, Sr., would often be willing to reduce his markup to as little as 5 percent over estimated costs. Thus, average markup for the year is estimated at 15 percent.

Mr. Ed. Berg, Jr., has just completed a course on pricing and believes the firm could use some of the techniques discussed in the course. The course emphasized the contribution margin approach to pricing, and Mr. Berg, Jr., feels such an approach would be helpful in determining the selling prices of their custom-made pleasure boats.

Total overhead, which includes marketing and administrative costs for the year, has been estimated at $150,000, of which $90,000 is fixed and the remainder is variable in direct proportion to direct labor.

Required   *a.* Assume the customer in the example rejected the $18,000 quotation and also rejected a $15,750 quotation (5 percent markup) during a slack period. The customer countered with a $15,000 offer.
  (1) What is the difference in net income for the year between accepting or rejecting the customer's offer?
  (2) What is the minimum selling price Mr. Berg, Jr., could have quoted without reducing or increasing net income?
b. What advantages does the contribution margin approach to pricing have over the approach used by Mr. Berg, Sr.?
c. What pitfalls are there, if any, to contribution margin pricing?

(CMA Adapted)

P13–37   **Target-Return Pricing and Accepting a Special Order**

The Roberts Company wishes to earn a target return on one of its product lines. The following information is available:

Variable manufacturing costs per unit		$60
Fixed manufacturing costs per unit		
($1,800,000 ÷ 60,000 units)		30
Total manufacturing costs.		$90
Variable marketing costs	$ 120,000	
Fixed marketing and administrative costs	$ 600,000	
Investment in assets for this product line	$6,000,000	
Desired rate of return		15%
Income tax rate		25%

Required   *a.* (1) Compute the markup percentage, assuming the firm uses absorption costing as the basis for its markup.

(2) What is the selling price? Prove it is correct.

b. (1) Compute the markup percentage, assuming the firm uses variable manufacturing cost as the basis for its markup.

(2) What is the selling price? Prove it is correct.

c. Repeat (*b*1) and (*b*2), assuming the firm uses the contribution margin approach.

d. It appears that the firm will sell only 40,000 units next year. A foreign purchaser has offered to purchase 20,000 units at $68 per unit. These units will not compete with the firm's regular sales. There will be no variable marketing costs associated with the order. Should the order be accepted? Why? What effect would the acceptance of this order have on the firm's operating income?

P13–38   **Target-Return Pricing**

The Graybar Company is introducing a new product and wishes to earn a target return on it. The following information is available:

Variable manufacturing costs per unit	$30
Variable marketing costs per unit	$ 6
Fixed manufacturing costs	$1,200,000
Fixed marketing and administrative costs.	$ 900,000
Investment in assets for this product.	$3,000,000
Desired rate of return	18%
Income tax rate	40%

The firm is uncertain how many units can be sold each year. However, the director of marketing believes the number of units sold will depend on the selling price. Initially, the director would like to know what the selling price would be at different levels of projected sales volume.

Required   *a.* Compute the selling prices for each of the following projected sales volumes:

(1) 40,000 units.

(2) 50,000 units.

(3) 80,000 units.

b. For each of the above sales volumes, compute the markup percentage based on absorption costing.

c. Repeat part *(b)*, using a markup percentage based on variable manufacturing costs.

d. Repeat part *(b)*, using a markup percentage based on the contribution margin approach.

e. Write a brief explanation of why the selling prices and markup percentages are different at different operating levels.

P13–39   **Optimum Allocation of Scarce Resources**

The Custom Jewelry Company manufactures selected designs of gold jewelry. The company's business has been expanding during the past few years. Previously, it was able to manufacture sufficient quantities to supply all of its customers, but the company is projecting that it will be unable to fill all of its orders for the coming year.

The company prepared the following estimated data for the next year:

Product	Estimated Demand in Units	Selling Price	Direct Materials	Direct Labor
Earrings	8,000	$ 45	$ 6	$ 9
Lockets	4,000	180	30	30
Pendants.	12,000	240	36	24
Bracelets.	10,000	600	90	84
Rings	15,000	450	60	66

The following information is also available:

1. Variable overhead is 40 percent of direct labor cost.
2. Fixed overhead is $2.4 million per annum, and fixed marketing and administrative costs are $1.8 million annually. There are no variable marketing and administrative costs.
3. The direct labor rate is $30 per hour, and the factory has a capacity of 60,000 hours. The company has no plans to operate a second shift or seek additional plant capacity.
4. Competition will prevent the firm from increasing its prices.

Required

a. Compute the contribution margin per unit for each product.
b. Compute the direct labor time required per unit for each product.
c. Compute the contribution margin per direct labor-hour for each product.
d. Compute the total amount of plant capacity needed to produce the estimated demand for the coming year.
e. Prepare a schedule showing how to allocate the 60,000 hours of plant capacity to produce optimum profits for the company.
f. Excluding plant expansion and a second shift, is there any way to obtain additional capacity? If so, how? What problems may be encountered if the additional capacity is obtained?

P13–40 **Allocation of Scarce Resources**

Sportway, Inc., is a wholesale distributor supplying a wide range of moderately priced sporting equipment to large chain stores. About 60 percent of Sportway's products are purchased from other companies while the remainder of the products are manufactured by Sportway. The company has a Plastics Department that is currently manufacturing molded fishing tackle boxes. Sportway is able to manufacture and sell 8,000 tackle boxes annually, making full use of its direct labor capacity at available work stations. Presented below are the selling price and costs associated with Sportway's tackle boxes.

Selling price per box.		$86.00
Costs per box		
Molded plastic	$ 8.00	
Hinges, latches, handle.	9.00	
Direct labor ($15/hr.)	18.75	
Manufacturing overhead	12.50	
Marketing and administrative cost	17.00	65.25
Profit per box		$20.75

Because Sportway believes it could sell 12,000 tackle boxes if it had sufficient manufacturing capacity, the company has looked into the possibility of purchasing the tackle boxes for distribution. Maple Products, a steady supplier of quality products, would be able to provide up to 9,000 tackle boxes per year at a price of $68 per box delivered to Sportway's facility.

Bart Johnson, Sportway's product manager, has suggested that the company could make better use of its Plastics Department by manufacturing skateboards. To support his position, Johnson has a market study that indicates an expanding market for skateboards and a need for additional suppliers. Johnson believes that Sportway could expect to sell 17,500 skateboards annually at a price of $45 per skateboard. Johnson's estimate of the costs to manufacture the skateboards is presented below.

Selling price per skateboard		$45.00
Costs per skateboard		
Molded plastic	$5.50	
Wheels, hardware	7.00	
Direct labor ($15/hr.)	7.50	
Manufacturing overhead	5.00	
Marketing and administrative cost	9.00	34.00
Profit per skateboard		$11.00

In the Plastics Department, Sportway uses direct labor hours as the application base for manufacturing overhead. Included in the manufacturing overhead for the current year is $50,000 of factory-wide, fixed manufacturing overhead that has been allocated to the Plastics Department. For each unit of product that Sportway sells, regardless of whether the product has been purchased or is manufactured by Sportway, there is an allocated $6 fixed overhead cost per unit for distribution that is included in the selling and administrative cost for all products. Total selling and administrative costs for the purchased tackle boxes would be $10 per unit.

Required   To maximize the company's profitability, prepare an analysis based on the data presented that will show which product or products Sportway, Inc., should manufacture and/or purchase and will show the associated financial impact. Support your answer with appropriate calculations.

(CMA Adapted)

▶ **CASES**   **C13–41   Relevant Costs; Purchase of a New Machine**

The Happiness Corporation purchased a machine three years ago at a cost of $200,000. It had a useful life of 10 years with no salvage value and is depreciated using the straight-line method. However, it can be overhauled at a cost of $50,000, which will increase its useful life by five years.

The president has heard about a new machine that performs the same work as this machine and costs $300,000. Because it uses newer technology, it would cut direct labor costs by $12,000 a year and variable overhead by $8,000 a year.

This new machine has a useful life of 12 years and a salvage value of $37,500. If the new machine is purchased, the old machine can be sold for $75,000.

The president has asked her son, who is working with the controller for the summer, to determine whether the new machine should be purchased or the old machine overhauled. The son has prepared the following analysis:

Savings using new machine ($20,000 × 12 years)		$ 240,000
Cost of new machine:		
Price	$300,000	
Loss on old machine (Cost −		
Resale value − Depreciation)	65,000	365,000
Net disadvantage of purchasing new machine		$(125,000)

On the basis of his analysis, the son explained to his mother that the purchase of the new machine, which looked attractive because of the annual savings, would actually cause the business to incur a loss.

Variable overhead is $20,000 per year, direct materials are $20,000 per year, and direct labor costs are $30,000 per year. Sales are expected to remain at $150,000 per year.

Required   a. Prepare comparative income statements for retaining the old machine and purchasing a new machine for the 12-year useful life of the new machine.
   b. Using only relevant costs, analyze whether it is desirable to purchase the new machine or whether you would agree with the president's son (differential income approach).
   c. Comment on the president's son's analysis.

C13–42   Accepting a Special Order

Sommers Company, located in southern Wisconsin, manufactures a variety of industrial valves and pipe fittings that are sold to customers in nearby states. Currently, the company is operating at about 70 percent capacity and is earning a satisfactory return on investment.

Management has been approached by Glascow Industries Ltd. of Scotland with an offer to buy 120,000 units of a pressure valve. Glascow Industries manufactures a valve that is almost identical to Sommers' pressure valve; however, a fire in Glascow Industries' valve plant has shut down its manufacturing operations. Glascow needs the 120,000 valves over the next four months to meet commitments to its regular customers; the company is prepared to pay $19 each for the valves, FOB shipping point.

Sommers' product cost, based on current attainable standards, for the pressure valve is

Direct materials	$ 5
Direct labor	6
Manufacturing overhead	9
Total cost	$20

Manufacturing overhead is applied to production at the rate of $18 per standard direct labor-hour. This overhead rate is made up of the following components.

Variable factory overhead	$ 6
Fixed factory overhead—direct	8
Fixed factory overhead—allocated	4
Applied manufacturing overhead rate	$18

Additional costs incurred in connection with sales of the pressure valve include sales commissions of 5 percent and freight of $1 per unit. However, the company does not pay sales commissions on special orders that come directly to management.

In determining selling prices, Sommers adds a 40 percent markup to product cost. This provides a $28 suggested selling price for the pressure valve. The marketing department, however, has set the current selling price at $27 to maintain market share.

Production management believes that it can handle the Glascow Industries order without disrupting its scheduled production. The order would, however, require additional fixed factory overhead of $12,000 per month in the form of supervision and clerical costs.

If management accepts the order, 30,000 pressure valves will be manufactured and shipped to Glascow Industries each month for the next four months. Shipments will be made in weekly consignments, FOB shipping point.

Required
a. Determine how many additional direct labor-hours would be required each month to fill the Glascow Industries order.
b. Prepare an incremental analysis showing the impact of accepting the Glascow Industries order.
c. Calculate the minimum unit price that Sommers' management could accept for the Glascow Industries order without reducing net income.
d. Identify the factors, other than price, that Sommers Company should consider before accepting the Glascow Industries order.

(CMA Adapted)

▶ **ETHICAL BEHAVIOR CASE** C13–43 Adam Williams was recently hired as assistant controller of GroChem, Inc., which processes chemicals for use in fertilizers. Williams was selected for this position because of his past experience in the chemical processing field. During his first month on the job, Williams made a point of getting to know the people responsible for the plant operations and learning how things are done at GroChem.

During a conversation with the plant supervisor, Williams asked about the company procedures for handling toxic waste materials. The plant supervisor replied that he was not involved with the disposal of wastes and suggested that Williams might be wise to ignore this issue. This response strengthened Williams's determination to probe this area further to be sure that the company was not vulnerable to litigation.

Upon further investigation, Williams discovered evidence that GroChem was using a nearby residential landfill to dump toxic wastes. It appeared that some members of GroChem's management team were aware of this situation and may have been involved in arranging for this dumping; however, Williams was unable to determine whether his superior, the controller, was involved.

Uncertain how he should proceed, Williams began to consider his options by outlining the following three alternative courses of action.

▶ Seek the advice of his superior, the controller.
▶ Anonymously release the information to the local newspaper.
▶ Discuss the situation with an outside member of the board of directors with whom he is acquainted.

Required
a. Discuss why Adam Williams has an ethical responsibility to take some action in the matter of GroChem, Inc., and the dumping of toxic wastes. Refer to the specific standards (competence, confidentiality, integrity, and/or objectivity) of *Statements on Management Accounting Number 1C (SMA 1C),* "Standards of Ethical Conduct for Management Accountants," to support your answer.
b. For each of the three alternative courses of action that Williams has outlined, explain whether or not the action is appropriate. Use *SMA 1C* to support your answer.
c. Without prejudice to your answer in Requirement part (b), assume that Williams sought the advice of his superior, the controller, and discovered that the controller was involved in the dumping of toxic wastes. Using *SMA 1C* to support your answer, describe the steps that Williams should take to resolve this situation.

(CMA Adapted)

▶ **ANSWERS TO SELF-TEST**

True or False

1. False	2. True	3. True	4. False	5. True
6. False	7. True	8. False	9. False	10. True
11. True	12. True	13. False	14. False	

Multiple Choice

1. *b.*   2. *c.*   3. *b.*   4. *b.*   5. *a.*   6. *b.*   7. *d.*

14

Capital Budgeting

▶ **LEARNING
OBJECTIVES**

After reading this chapter, you should be able to:

1. Explain the role of capital budgeting in financial decisions.
2. Discuss why screening and preference selection are key phases of the capital-budgeting process.
3. Use the net present value method to evaluate the profitability of investing in new equipment.
4. Compute the net present value for equipment-replacement and new market-entry decisions using both the differential income and comparative income approaches.
5. Compute a project's internal rate of return and explain how it is used for screening and preference selection.
6. Compute a project's profitability index, describe how it is used, and explain under what conditions it is superior to the net present value and the internal rate of return for preference selection.
7. Explain the need for a follow-up of capital-budgeting decisions.
8. Compute payback and the accounting rate of return, explain how they are used, and describe their shortcomings.

▶ **INTERVIEW**

Manuel D. Fernandes
Vice President for Finance
Iona College

Q. *Have you ever had to evaluate a purchase versus lease decision? If so, what method did you use to reach your decision?*

A. The question of whether to purchase or lease assets needs to be viewed in light of many variables. Although some are financial in nature, other variables require analyses that are qualitative, such as technology, obsolescence, and so on. In the end, all variables have a financial impact, but that of the qualitative factors is more difficult to measure.

The financial questions usually are easier to solve since the data required are readily available. The required analyses are mathematical, and the results are clear. It either costs more or it costs less to lease assets than to buy them.

The purchase versus lease decisions requiring quantitative and qualitative choices are more difficult to make. These usually involve the question of technology, obsolescence, and other considerations. How does one measure the financial impact of changing technologies and obsolescence? The fact is that it is very difficult. In cases in which developing and changing technologies could render a purchased asset obsolete and your firm uncompetitive, a decision to lease may be wise even if the quantitative analysis indicates a purchase to be financially advantageous.

Some years ago, in the early stages of computer technology, I participated in a proposal to buy or lease an up-to-date mainframe computer system with a high purchase price. The lease costs were very high as well. The financial analyses employed were the discounted cash flows for the lease payments and the debt payments required if the asset was purchased. To prepare the discounted cash flows comparison, a determination of the technological state of the art useful life was necessary. At the time, a 10-year life appeared to be reasonable, and the financial analyses were prepared on that basis. The asset was purchased based on a 10-year expected useful life. At the end of 5 years, it became obvious that the 10-year assumption was inappropriate. Computer technology changed at a faster rate than anticipated, and the asset became obsolete in approximately 7 years. Had the analyses been made on the basis of a 7-year life, the decision to buy would not have been made.

This case demonstrates the intricacies of the qualitative factors affecting the purchase versus lease decision. In cases in which changing technology is a serious consideration, a conservative useful life must be used in the decision to purchase or lease assets.

L.O. 1
Role of capital budgeting

▶ **Capital budgeting** is concerned with the planning and financing of a firm's long-term investment decisions. The most frequent capital-budgeting decisions are (1) whether to purchase new labor-saving equipment to perform operations presently performed manually, a cost-reduction decision; (2) whether to replace existing equipment with more efficient, newer equipment, also a cost-reduction decision; and (3) whether to enter a new market by developing a new product or purchasing an existing business already in that market, a profit-expansion decision. These long-term decisions are likely to affect a firm's operations for many years to come, in contrast to short-term decisions, such as investments in small hand and power tools, which may affect the firm's operations for only one or two years.

All firms have limited amounts of available capital, and most firms have more investment opportunities than they can satisfy with their available resources. Thus, a firm must commonly decide which investment opportunities to reject and which to accept to satisfy its operational objectives.

L.O. 2
Screening and
preference selection

The selection process of capital budgeting may be broken down into two phases. In the initial phase, **screening,** a specific cutoff criterion is used to eliminate unprofitable and/or high-risk investment proposals. Projects that fail to satisfy the screening criterion are rejected, and the remaining projects are subjected to further analysis. In the second phase, **preference selection,** the surviving projects are subjected to a ranking criterion, which results in the selection of the most favorable projects for any given amount of capital to be invested.

Not all firms use the same screening tests. However, most firms use one or more of the most popular ones, which are (1) the discounted cash flow model, (2) payback, and (3) the accounting rate of return (simple rate of return). The discounted cash flow model is conceptually superior to the other screening tests and, thus, is most widely used.

In this chapter, the income tax effects on discounted cash flow capital-budgeting decisions are ignored, but they are considered in the next chapter.   ◀

▶ DISCOUNTED CASH FLOW MODELS

The discussion that follows presumes a knowledge of compound-interest and present value concepts. Students who are not already familiar with these topics or who would like some review should consult Appendix 14-A at the end of this chapter.

A **discounted cash flow model** is a technique used to evaluate investment projects that applies the time value of money to all cash inflows and outflows by discounting them to their present values. The two most commonly used discounted cash flow models are:

1. The net present value method (NPV).
2. The internal rate of return method (IRR), also called the *time-adjusted rate of return* (TARR).

**Net Present
Value Method**

L.O. 3

In the **net present value method** of evaluating investment projects, all future cash inflows and outflows are discounted to their present values using an appropriate interest rate. The total of the present values of the cash outflows is subtracted from the total of the present values of the cash inflows to arrive at the project's net present value. If the result is positive, the investment promises more than the interest rate used to evaluate the proposal. If the amount is negative, the opposite is true and the project should be rejected because the required rate of return will not be earned. The interest rate used to find the present value of a future cash flow is called the **discount rate.**

▶ **ILLUSTRATION 14-1**

AUTOMATED MANUFACTURING COMPANY
Calculation of Net Investment and Cash Operating Advantage
For the Purchase of a New Machine
Differential Analysis

Net investment:
Purchase price of machine	$ 90,000	
Less: Salvage value	5,000	
Net investment	$ 85,000	

Cash operating advantage:
Savings in direct materials cost ($100,000 — $95,000).	$ 5,000
Savings in direct labor cost ($60,000 − $46,000)	14,000
Savings in variable overhead ($42,000 − $32,200)	9,800
Cash operating advantage—one year	28,800
Useful life of machine	× 5
Cash operating advantage—five years	$144,000

When making short-term investment decisions, a manager may ignore the time value of money without serious consequences to the firm, but this is not the case for long-term investments (those spanning more than one year). The reason for this is that the time value of money would have a negligible effect on the decision when the time frame is less than one year. However, the consequences of failing to recognize the time value of money become more serious as the life of an investment increases.

Consideration of the time value of money can materially alter the attractiveness of an investment opportunity. To illustrate the use of NPV in evaluating the purchase of a new labor-saving machine, we will return to the Automated Manufacturing Company, first introduced in Chapter 13. The basic data given in Chapter 13 are reproduced below, and the analysis of relevant data using the differential income approach is reproduced in Illustration 14-1.

Purchase price of new machine	$90,000
Useful life of machine	5 years
Salvage value at the end of five years	$5,000

Annual Operating Information

	With New Machine	Without New Machine
Sales	$500,000	$500,000
Direct materials cost	95,000	100,000
Direct labor	46,000	60,000
Variable overhead	32,200	42,000
Fixed overhead	100,000	100,000

Net Present Value Using the Differential Income Approach The steps needed to compute net present value when the differential income approach is used are:

Step 1

Prepare a tabulation of the net investment (cash outflows) as in Illustration 14-1.

▶ **ILLUSTRATION 14-2**

AUTOMATED MANUFACTURING COMPANY
Calculation of Net Present Value
Purchase of New Equipment
Differential Income Approach

Item	Value in Present Dollars	Present Value Factor	Time Period					
			0	1	2	3	4	5
Cash operating advantage:								
Net cash inflow from operations.	$ 86,130	2.99061*		$28,800	$28,800	$28,800	$28,800	$28,800
Total	$ 86,130							
Net investment:								
Purchase price	$(90,000)	1.00000	$(90,000)					
Salvage value	2,009	.40188†						5,000
Total	(87,991)							
Net present value	$ (1,861)							

* From Table 4 in Appendix 14-B, $n = 5$, $i = 20\%$.
† From Table 2 in Appendix 14-B, $n = 5$, $i = 20\%$.

Step 2

Prepare a tabulation of the cash operating advantage (cash inflows) as in Illustration 14-1.

Step 3

Assign a present value factor of 1 to all cash flows *on the investment date.* Assign all other cash flows appropriate present value factors from Tables 2 and 4 in Appendix 14-B. Based on a desired discount rate of 20 percent, Automated Manufacturing's accountants would use the following present value factors:

	Factor
Purchase price of $90,000	1.00000
Salvage value of $5,000, from Table 2 for $n = 5$, $i = 20\%$	.40188
Cash operating advantage of $28,800, from Table 4 for $n = 5$, $i = 20\%$	2.99061

The cash flows and their corresponding present value factors are listed in Illustration 14-2.

Step 4

Perform the arithmetic operations of multiplication and summation. Thus, in Illustration 14-2, the cash inflow from operations of $28,800 is multiplied by the present value factor of 2.99061 for a present value of $86,130. The purchase price of $90,000 is multiplied by the present value factor of 1 for a present value of $90,000. And the salvage value of $5,000 is multiplied by the present value factor of 0.40188 for a present value of $2,009. The present values are then added if they are cash inflows and subtracted if they are cash outflows to produce a cash-operating-advantage present value of $86,130 and a net-investment present value of $87,991. The net investment is then subtracted from the cash operating advantage. *If the result* (net present value) *is positive,* the *investment yields a rate greater*

▶ **ILLUSTRATION 14-3**   Amortization Schedule: Investment at a 10 Percent Return

End of Year	Annual Cash Inflow	Return on Investment at 10 Percent	Recovery of Investment	Balance of Investment
Initial date				$37,908
First	$10,000	$ 3,791*	$ 6,209†	31,699‡
Second.	10,000	3,170	6,830	24,869
Third	10,000	2,487	7,513	17,356
Fourth	10,000	1,735	8,265	9,091
Fifth	10,000	909	9,091	–0–
Total	$50,000	$12,092	$37,908	

* $37,908 × 10% = $3,791.
† $10,000 − $3,791 = $6,209.
‡ $37,908 − $6,209 = $31,699.

than the discount rate and is favorable. *If the result is negative,* the investment *yields a rate less than* the discount rate, which means it is unfavorable and should be rejected. In this case, because the net present value is −$1,861, the project should be rejected.

Note how consideration of the time value of money affected the attractiveness of this investment opportunity. From Illustration 14-1, it appears that a net investment of $85,000 will return $144,000 in cost savings, a net return of $59,000. However, when the time value of money is factored into the calculations, the use of a discount rate of 20 percent converts what appeared to be a profitable investment into an unprofitable one, as shown in Illustration 14-2. The negative net present value means that the investment will earn *less than 20 percent,* which is inadequate to finance it. Thus, investment analysis for decision making should consider the time value of money to avoid incorrect conclusions.

It is important to remember that the net present value method of analyzing investment proposals provides for two things—a return on the net investment at the specified discount rate and the recovery of the investment itself over the life of the investment period.

Let us assume an investment of $37,908 will provide a firm with an annual cash operating advantage of $10,000 each year for five years and the required discount rate is 10 percent. The present value of the cash operating advantage may be computed as follows:

Cash operating advantage	$10,000
Present value factor*	× 3.79079
Present value in dollars	$37,908

* From Table 4, Appendix 14-B, $n = 5$, $i = 10\%$.

Because the net investment and the present value of the cash operating advantage are the same—$37,908—the net present value is zero. Thus, the investment will earn exactly 10 percent. An amortization table, as shown in Illustration 14-3, demonstrates that the investment will earn 10 percent and also recover the initial cash outflow of $37,908.

Note that of the $50,000 cash inflow for the five-year period, $12,092 represents the return *on* investment and $37,908 represents the return *of*

▶ **ILLUSTRATION 14-4**

MATURE PRODUCTS COMPANY
Relevant Data for Replacing a Machine

Original cost of the present machine	$ 40,000	
Less: Accumulated depreciation	30,000	
Book value (undepreciated cost)	$ 10,000	
Purchase price of new machine.	$100,000	
Useful life of new machine.	5 years	
Remaining useful life of old machine	2 years	
Overhaul of old machine will extend its useful life by 3 years for a total of 5 years at a cost of	$ 10,000	
Salvage value of new machine	–0–	
Market value of old machine, if sold now	$ 4,000	

	Old Machine	New Machine
Annual operating information:		
Sales	$400,000	$400,000
Direct materials cost	90,000	90,000
Direct labor cost	80,000	60,000
Variable overhead	48,000	36,000
Incremental out-of-pocket fixed overhead exclusive of depreciation	100,000	100,000

investment. Because the cost of the investment is recovered, it is not necessary to consider depreciation when using discounted cash flow analysis.

The Cost of Capital Discount Rate   The discount rate used in computing NPV is usually either the firm's cost of capital or a rate based on its cost of capital. Although the calculation of a firm's cost of capital is not an easy matter and is usually discussed in detail in finance courses, it nevertheless is used by firms in their capital-budgeting decisions. The cost of capital varies from firm to firm; however, it usually falls into a narrow range. For most firms the *before-income-tax* cost of capital is between 15 percent and 20 percent, while the *after-income-tax* cost of capital is between 10 percent and 14 percent.

All investment decisions should be based on after-tax figures. For ease of presentation, however, income tax considerations are deferred until the next chapter, and income taxes are ignored for all present value investment decisions in this chapter.

L.O. 4
Net present value—differential income approach

Replacing Existing Equipment—The Differential Income Approach   When deciding whether to replace existing equipment, the NPV analysis is similar to that for purchasing a new machine, except additional factors must be considered. Among these are the proceeds from selling the old machine and the cost of overhauling the old machine.

We will use the example of the Mature Products Company from Chapter 13 to illustrate the use of NPV in analyzing the replacement of existing equipment. Recall that the company is contemplating the replacement of one of its present machines with a faster machine. The older machine is nearing the end of its economic useful life, but its life can be extended by a major overhaul. Illustration 14-4 presents data relevant to the decision whether to replace the older machine with a newer one.

▶ **ILLUSTRATION 14-5**

MATURE PRODUCTS COMPANY
Differential Analysis of Decision to Retain Old Machine
or Replace with a New Machine
For the Five-Year Useful Life of the New Machine

Net investment:		
Purchase price of new machine.		$100,000
Less: Sales proceeds for old machine		4,000
Net investment		96,000
Cash operating advantage:		
Direct labor savings.	$100,000	
Variable overhead savings	60,000	
Old machine overhaul savings	10,000	170,000
Net cash advantage in favor		
of replacing old machine		$ 74,000

▶ **ILLUSTRATION 14-6**

MATURE PRODUCTS COMPANY
Calculation of Net Present Value
Retaining Old Machine or Purchasing a New Machine
Differential Income Approach

Item	Present Value in Dollars	Present Value Factor	Time Period					
			0	1	2	3	4	5
Cash operating advantage:								
Direct labor savings. . . .	$ 59,812	2.99061*		$20,000	$20,000	$20,000	$20,000	$20,000
Variable overhead savings	35,887	2.99061		12,000	12,000	12,000	12,000	12,000
Savings of old machine								
overhaul	6,944	.69444†			10,000			
Total	$ 102,643							
Net investment:								
Purchase price of new								
machine	$(100,000)	1.00000	$(100,000)					
Sales proceeds of old								
machine	4,000	1.00000	4,000					
Net investment.	(96,000)							
Net present value.	$ 6,643							

* From Table 4 in Appendix 14-B, $n = 5$, $i = 20\%$.
† From Table 2 in Appendix 14-B, $n = 2$, $i = 20\%$.

To simplify the solution to this problem, we will assume all cash flows occur at the end of the year, except the purchase of the new machine and the sale of the old machine, which occur at the beginning of the year. The differential analysis of the relevant data appears in Illustration 14-5, and the computation of the net present value, using a discount rate of 20 percent, is shown in Illustration 14-6.

Illustration 14-6 indicates that the replacement of the old machine will yield a positive net present value of $6,643; thus, the 20 percent discount rate will be earned with a modest amount to spare. Note that the positive cash flow of $74,000 derived in Illustration 14-5 is reduced to $6,643 once the time value of money is factored in.

▶ **ILLUSTRATION 14-7**

MATURE PRODUCTS COMPANY
Calculation of Net Present Value
Retaining Old Machine or Purchasing a New Machine
Comparative Income Approach
Calculation of Net Cash Inflow from Operations

	Keep Old Machine		Purchase New Machine	
Sales revenue		$400,000		$400,000
Less:				
Direct materials	$ 90,000		$ 90,000	
Direct labor	80,000		60,000	
Variable overhead	48,000		36,000	
Fixed overhead	100,000	318,000	100,000	286,000
Net cash inflow from operations		$ 82,000		$114,000

Item	Present Value in Dollars	Present Value Factor	Time Period					
			0	1	2	3	4	5
Keep old machine:								
Net cash inflow from operations.	$ 245,230	2.99061		$ 82,000	$ 82,000	$ 82,000	$ 82,000	$ 82,000
Opportunity cost of keeping old machine—market value proceeds forgone	(4,000)	1.00000	$ (4,000)					
Overhaul of old machine at the end of 2nd year	(6,944)	.69444			(10,000)			
Net present value . . .	$ 234,286							
Purchase new machine:								
Net cash inflow from operations.	$ 340,929	2.99061		114,000	114,000	114,000	114,000	114,000
Purchase price of new machine	(100,000)	1.00000	(100,000)					
Net present value . . .	$ 240,929							

Recapitulation

Net present value of purchasing new machine	$240,929
Net present value of keeping old machine	234,286
Net present value in favor of new machine	$ 6,643

L.O. 4
Replacing existing equipment—comparative income approach

Replacing Existing Equipment—The Comparative Income Approach The solution shown in Illustration 14-6 may also be obtained with the comparative income approach. Instead of using only the differences in cash flow between the old machine and the new machine, the cash flows of each alternative may be discounted to their respective present values and then compared for the purpose of selecting the most favorable outcome. The solution using the comparative income approach appears in Illustration 14-7.

Although the comparative income and differential income approaches to capital budgeting produce the same result, the differential income approach requires less effort and is used more often.

▶ **ILLUSTRATION 14-8**

PHYSICO COMPANY
Calculation of Cash Outflows and Cash Inflows
For Entering a New Market for the
10-Year Useful Life of the Product
Differential Income Approach

	Inflow (Outflow)
Net investment:	
Purchase price of the machinery	$ (900,000)
Salvage value of machine	20,000
Working capital at inception	(400,000)
Release of working capital at the end of 10 years	350,000
Net investment	$ (930,000)
Cash operating advantage:	
Sales per annum	$2,500,000
Variable costs per annum:	
Direct materials	(600,000)
Direct labor	(500,000)
Variable overhead	(380,000)
Commissions (5% × $2.5 million)	(125,000)
Incremental out-of-pocket fixed cost per annum:	
Manufacturing overhead	(400,000)
Marketing and administrative costs	(200,000)
Cash operating advantage per annum	295,000
Life of product	× 10
Cash operating advantage for 10 years	$2,950,000

L.O. 4
Entering a new market—differential income approach

Entering a New Market—The Differential Income Approach

When entering a new market, working capital is an important element of capital budgeting. As noted in Chapter 13, working capital is normally invested in accounts receivable and inventories for the entire time the firm is in the new market. Because a long period of time is involved, the time value of money must be factored into the calculation for the investment and release of working capital, even when the investment and the release are the same. During this period of investment, the firm incurs its cost of capital on the invested funds, so the cost must be earned back for the investment to be feasible. Failure to consider the time value of money on invested working capital may lead a manager to think an investment is profitable when in fact it is not.

As first mentioned in Chapter 13, the Physico Company plans to enter the physical fitness market with a treadmill for gymnasium and home use. Based on a market survey and cost estimates provided by the firm's engineering and accounting departments, the following information is available:

Sales (10,000 at $250 each)	$2,500,000
Incremental costs:	
Direct materials (10,000 at $60)	$600,000
Direct labor (10,000 at $50)	$500,000
Variable overhead (10,000 at $38)	$380,000
Fixed overhead exclusive of new machinery noted below	$400,000
Variable marketing costs	5% of sales
Fixed marketing and administrative costs	$200,000
Purchase of machinery needed for manufacturing this product	$900,000

▶ **ILLUSTRATION 14-9**

PHYSICO COMPANY
Calculation of Net Present Value
Entering a New Market
Differential Income Approach

Calculation of Net Cash Inflow from Operations

Sales revenue.		$2,500,000
Less:		
Direct materials.	$600,000	
Direct labor	500,000	
Variable overhead.	380,000	
Variable marketing costs.	125,000	
Fixed overhead	400,000	
Fixed marketing and administrative costs	200,000	2,205,000
Net cash inflow from operations		$ 295,000

Item	Present Value in Dollars	Present Value Factor	Time Period				
			0	1	2	. . .	10
Cash operating advantage:							
Net cash inflow from operations . . .	$ 1,236,779	4.19247*		$295,000	$295,000	. . .	$295,000
Net investment:							
Purchase price of machine	$ (900,000)	1.00000	$(900,000)				
Salvage value of machine	3,230	.16151†					20,000
Investment of working capital	(400,000)	1.00000	(400,000)				
Release of working capital at end	56,529	.16151†					350,000
Net investment	$(1,240,241)						
Net present value	$ (3,462)						

* From Table 4 in Appendix 14-B, $n = 10$, $i = 20\%$.
† From Table 2 in Appendix 14-B, $n = 10$, $i = 20\%$.

Useful life of machinery	10 years
Salvage value of machinery.	$20,000
Working capital needed at inception.	$400,000
Working capital returned at end of 10 years when the demand for this product is expected to be nil	$350,000

The analysis of the relevant data for the decision whether to enter the new market may be organized as shown in Illustration 14-8, and the tabulation for net present value analysis using a 20 percent discount rate appears in Illustration 14-9.

Illustration 14-9 indicates that this investment is not feasible because it will produce a negative net present value of $3,462, and the 20 percent discount rate will not be earned. This result should be compared to the outcome predicted in Illustration 14-8, where the investment of $930,000 yields a profit of $2,020,000 (cash operating advantage of $2,950,000 minus the investment of $930,000). The results change dramatically when the time value of money is factored into the calculations.

The importance of including both the investment and release of working capital in the calculation is highlighted by this example. What appears to be a $50,000 ($400,000 − $350,000) loss of working capital becomes a $343,471 ($400,000 − $56,529) loss once the time value of money is applied to both the investment and the release. Even if the full $400,000 of invested working capital would be released at the end of the project, it would have a net present value of only $64,604 ($400,000 × .16151), a diminution in present value of $335,396.

The failure to include the investment and release of working capital in this investment's analysis might have led a manager to make an incorrect decision in favor of accepting the project when, in fact, it should have been rejected.

Internal Rate of Return

Many managers wish to know not only the net present value of a project but also the discounted cash flow (DCF) percentage of return. The size of this percentage, called the *internal rate of return,* is important in helping managers to choose among projects once a proposal passes the screening phase of the capital-budgeting decision.

L.O. 5

The **internal rate of return (IRR),** also known as the *time-adjusted rate of return,* is the rate of interest that produces a zero net present value when a project's discounted cash operating advantage is netted against its discounted net investment. In essence, the IRR is a calculation that indicates the rate of return earned by a particular project. Some managers prefer to use the IRR when screening competing investment projects. They first establish a **cutoff rate,** which is the minimum rate of return that an investment must promise before the firm will commit its resources. Only those projects whose IRRs exceed the cutoff rate (sometimes called the *target rate* or *hurdle rate*) receive further consideration. Managers then rank the surviving projects in descending order by their promised internal rates of return and select the projects with successively lower rates until the capital available for investment is exhausted.

Calculating the Internal Rate of Return—Even Cash Flows The IRR can be computed by dividing the net investment by the *annual* cash operating advantage to find the investment's present value factor. It is then necessary to turn to Table 4 and scan across the interest rate columns that correspond to the length of the investment until that present value factor (or its closest approximation) is reached. The IRR will be the percentage at the top of the column. For example, if the Belair Company is contemplating the purchase of a machine for $35,999 with no salvage value and if the annual cash operating advantage is $9,176 for the 10-year life of the machine, the IRR may be computed as follows:

$$\frac{\text{Net investment in project}}{\text{Annual cash operating advantage}} = \text{Present value factor}$$

$$\frac{\$35,999}{\$9,176} = 3.92317 = 22\%$$

Another manufacturer offers a more advanced machine with a 10-year life for $53,999 that will produce a cash operating advantage of $12,880. Its IRR may be calculated as follows:

$$\frac{\$53,999}{\$12,880} = 4.19247 = 20\%$$

Even if the firm's cutoff rate is 18 percent, the $35,999 machine should still be purchased because it promises a higher IRR.

Linear Interpolation When the present value factor falls between two figures shown in Table 4, a proportional (fractional) calculation called **linear interpolation** is made to estimate the internal rate of return. For example, if the incremental investment of the more advanced machine ($53,999 − $35,999 = $18,000) is compared to the annual incremental cash operating advantage ($12,880 − $9,176 = $3,704), the present value factor on the increments may be computed as usual:

$$\frac{\$18,000}{\$3,704} = 4.85961$$

Because this PV factor falls between the factors for 15 and 16 percent, linear interpolation is necessary as follows:

Rate	Present Value Factor	
15%.	5.01877	
?	4.85961	5.01877 − 4.83323 = .18554
16%.	4.83323	

Linear interpolation:

$$15\% + \frac{5.01877 - 4.85961}{.18554} \times (1\%) = 15.86\%$$

or

$$16\% - \frac{4.85961 - 4.83323}{.18554} \times (1\%) = 15.86\%$$

The incremental investment promises an IRR of only 15.86 percent, which is below the cutoff rate of 18 percent. Thus, the cheaper machine is the better investment, as indicated by the initial IRR calculation of 22 percent.

Internal Rate of Return—Uneven Cash Flows For many capital-budgeting decisions, cash inflows and outflows vary. This is especially likely if both revenues and costs are involved, as when entering a new market. In such cases, and also when salvage value is expected at the end of the project's life, the internal rate of return is found through a trial-and-error approach using the NPV method. The goal of this technique is to find the discount rate that will yield an NPV of zero. A discount rate is selected, such as 15 percent, and the net present value is computed. If the NPV is positive, a higher rate that will produce a negative NPV is selected. The two rates are then interpolated to see if that rate will yield a zero NPV. If the result is other than zero, other discount rates are tried until a zero NPV is derived. Most large firms use computers to calculate the IRR for investment decisions. A sufficient variety of IRR software packages is available to enable most firms to avoid using the manual trial-and-error approach. Also available are sophisticated business analyst calculators, such as the Hewlett-Packard 12C, that are capable of calculating the IRR when cash flows are uneven.

▶ PROJECT SELECTION

When net present value is used to evaluate competing projects, it is often misleading to use the results to rank and select the most profitable choices. For this reason, managers normally use a profitability index instead.

The Profitability Index

L.O. 6

When two or more competing projects have positive net present values, the project with the highest NPV may not necessarily be the best investment. To obtain further information, the amount of net present value should be examined in relation to the *amount of the investment* needed to produce it. One way to do this is by determining each project's **profitability index (PI),** which is computed by dividing an investment's discounted cash inflows (cash operating advantage) by the required net investment. The resulting ratios can then be used to rank the projects by profitability: the higher the profitability index, the more desirable the project.

The Markon Company is using a cutoff rate of 12 percent to evaluate two competing projects, both with five-year useful lives. The projects' net investments and cash inflows are summarized below:

	Project C	Project D
Investment	$90,000	$22,500
Annual cash operating advantage	27,487	7,857

The net present values of the projects may be calculated as follows:

		Project C	Project D
Annual cash operating advantage	(a)	$27,487	$ 7,857
Present value factor—$n = 5$, $i = 12\%$.	(b)	3.60478	3.60478
Present value of cash operating advantage—(a) × (b). . . .		$99,085	$28,323
Less: Net investment		90,000	22,500
Net present value.		$ 9,085	$ 5,823

Although project C has a higher net present value than project D, it may not be the better choice. The analysis should include the calculation of the two projects' profitability indexes, as follows:

$$\text{Profitability index (PI)} = \frac{\text{Discounted cash inflows}}{\text{Net investment}}$$

Project C:

$$\text{PI} = \frac{\$99,085}{\$90,000} = 1.10$$

Project D:

$$\text{PI} = \frac{\$28,323}{\$22,500} = 1.26$$

▶ **ILLUSTRATION 14-10**   Comparison of Projects with Unequal Lives Using Profitability Indexes and IRR

Net Present Value

	Project F	Project G
Discounted cash inflow:		
Project F: $20,000 × 2.40183*.	$48,037	
Project G: $10,000 × 5.65022†		$56,502
Less: Net investment	40,845	44,941
Net present value	$ 7,192	$11,561

Profitability Index

$$\text{Project F} = \frac{\$48,037}{\$40,845} = 1.176$$

$$\text{Project G} = \frac{\$56,502}{\$44,941} = 1.257$$

Internal Rate of Return

$$\text{Project F} = \frac{\$40,845}{\$20,000} = 2.04225 = 22\%$$

$$\text{Project G} = \frac{\$44,941}{\$10,000} = 4.49410 = 18\%$$

* From Table 4 in Appendix 14-B, $n = 3$, $i = 12\%$.

† From Table 4 in Appendix 14-B, $n = 10$, $i = 12\%$.

If these projects are mutually exclusive (that is, if only one can be selected), a manager should select project D over project C on the basis of PI.

The use of profitability indexes for preference decisions usually leads to the correct decision. However, one caveat should be observed: the difference in the projects' costs must be invested at a certain minimum rate. In our example, the $67,500 ($90,000 − $22,500) not invested because project D is chosen over project C must be invested at an IRR of approximately 14 percent (the computation of this rate is complex and thus is not shown) or greater if project D is to be preferred. If the $67,500 cannot be invested at 14 percent or greater, project C would be a better choice.

Profitability indexes are also useful for evaluating projects with unequal lives. If a manager is unsure of what investment opportunities will be available when the cash flows are released at the end of a shorter project's life, profitability indexes will lead to the correct decision, while the NPV and IRR may not. For example, if project F promises an annual cash operating advantage of $20,000 for *3 years* and requires a net investment of $40,845, while project G promises an annual cash operating advantage of $10,000 for *10 years* and requires a net investment of $44,941, the analyses of the two projects using a 12 percent cost of capital may appear as shown in Illustration 14-10.

The results show that the IRR and the net present value approaches can send conflicting signals when competing projects have unequal lives. The profitability index points to the correct decision, however, and is preferable under these circumstances.

1. What is a discounted cash flow model?
2. How does the net present value method differ from the internal rate of return method?
3. When using the net present value method to evaluate an investment decision, is the differential income approach or the comparative income approach easier to use? Why?
4. When using the internal rate of return method to evaluate an investment decision when the cash flows are even, how is the rate of return computed? If the computation falls between two rates and linear interpolation is desired, how is this accomplished?
5. When using the net present value method to evaluate an investment decision, is the project with the highest amount of present value always the preferable investment? If not, explain which preference selection technique would provide the decision maker with the correct choice and why this is so.   ◀

Thus far, we have assumed that all cash inflows and outflows could be accurately predicted. In the real world this is not the case, and managers must deal with data that are subject to varying degrees of uncertainty.

▶ DEALING WITH UNCERTAINTY

Most of the data used for capital-budgeting decisions are estimated. Some of the estimates may be categorized as ''hard'' data, while others are considered ''soft.'' **Hard data** consist of information that may be ascertained with a high degree of precision and for which uncertainty is either small or nonexistent; **soft data** consist of information subject to a high degree of uncertainty. Examples of hard data are the cost of a new machine, freight in, insurance during transit, investment of working capital, and direct labor cost savings in the earlier years of a project's life. Examples of soft data are repairs to machinery, savings on variable overhead, revenues when entering a new market (especially after the first year or two), and the rate of inflation during the life of the project.

Hard Data

Some capital-budgeting data qualify as hard data for two reasons. First, some of the data, such as the cost of a new machine, are fixed-price quotations. Second, some items, such as working capital invested, occur at the outset when it is possible to estimate them with a high degree of precision. In either case, hard data present few problems, if any, to managers concerned with capital budgeting.

Soft Data

Generally, soft data fall into two categories: (1) data from segment managers who deliberately overstate revenues and understate costs in the hope that their projects will be selected and (2) data that require projection into the future, often 10 or more years, for which precise estimates are impossible.

Segment managers may be tempted to estimate data in ways that enhance the chance of having their projects accepted. A manager's worth to a firm and, therefore, his or her compensation usually correspond to the relative size of the segment managed. Thus, growth through capital-budgeting projects may be an important goal. For example, consider the following condensed income statement for a firm with two product lines:

	Automotive Division	Percent	Electronics Division	Percent
Sales revenue	$20,000,000	100	$1,000,000	100
Costs and income taxes. . .	17,000,000	85	800,000	80
Net income	$ 3,000,000	15	$ 200,000	20

Although the electronics division earns 20 percent on its revenues and the automotive division earns only 15 percent, the automotive division is more valuable to the firm because its $3 million of net income accounts for the bulk (94 percent) of the firm's net income. Accordingly, the manager of the automotive division would have a much higher compensation package, and if the manager of the electronics division wishes similar compensation, she will try to expand her division.

Managers who evaluate capital-budgeting proposals should be aware of this tendency and carefully scrutinize all estimates of soft data. Segment managers who consistently distort soft data will ultimately be exposed when the actual results of their projects are compared to their original proposals. However, there may be a significant time lag before this occurs, and the firm may be harmed in the meantime.

In most cases, managers can compensate for the second kind of soft data—uncertain predictions—by using a probability distribution approach that yields expected values.

Another approach can be taken in coping with uncertainty about the effect of inflation on a capital-budgeting decision. The solution is to adjust *both* the estimated cash flows and the cutoff rate by the expected rate of inflation over the life of the project. Because both the cash flows and the cutoff rate are adjusted for the effects of inflation, the net effect of the adjustments on NPV is zero. Thus, many firms choose not to adjust for inflation. For an expanded discussion of the effects of inflation on capital-budgeting decisions, you may wish to consult Appendix 14-C at the end of this chapter.

Auditing Capital-Budgeting Decisions

L.O. 7
Follow-up of capital-budgeting decisions

Most management decisions should be subjected to follow-up evaluations to determine the effectiveness of the decision-making process. This is especially true for capital-budgeting decisions. In an **audit of capital-budgeting projects,** the actual results of an investment project are compared with its expected results. Such an audit is used both for control purposes and for decision making during the project when modifications can be made. This process enables management to (1) detect troublesome projects in their early stages, when they can be either altered or terminated to avoid large losses; (2) detect projects that are performing better than anticipated to see if increased investment will lead to even greater returns; (3) evaluate the investment proposal process to determine its effectiveness; and (4) deter segment managers who may be tempted to submit proposals that contain inflated returns.

If credibility is to be maintained, the audit must use the same investment criteria employed to evaluate the investment proposal. Changing the rules in the middle of the game is unfair to the segment manager submitting the investment proposal.

▶ INVESTING AND FINANCING DECISIONS—LEASING VERSUS PURCHASING

When a decision is contemplated regarding the acquisition of property, the first step should be to decide whether to invest in the property. Then, if the decision is made to acquire the property, a further discounted cash flow analysis should be made regarding the method of financing the acquisition (i.e., whether to purchase the property or to lease it).

Although there may be a temptation to combine the investment and financing decisions, doing this could often result in an incorrect decision. For example, some people are tempted to compare the present value of lease payments for a piece of equipment with the present value of cash inflows to compute their net present value. It is quite possible that such a comparison may make an investment attractive when in fact the investment should be rejected. The reason for this is that lease payments are predicated on using an *interest rate* instead of the hurdle rate which should be used for all of the firm's investments. This hurdle rate is based on the firm's *cost of capital* and is higher than a firm's borrowing rate.

To understand cost of capital, let us consider the case of a firm that has outstanding common stock, preferred stock, and debt in its capital structure. If the firm's debt has an interest rate of 10 percent and the firm is in the 40 percent income tax bracket, the net cost of interest is 6 percent because interest is deductible on the firm's tax return in computing taxable income. A 12 percent dividend rate for the firm's preferred stock would have a cost to the firm of 12 percent because the dividend is not allowed as a deduction on the firm's tax return. A higher rate normally applies to preferred stock because a preferred stock investment carries an increased risk when compared to debt. The cost of capital for common stock is highest because of the still higher risk. When considering an investment proposal, a manager should consider the cost of these three components when evaluating all investment decisions. The hurdle rate used should be based on the firm's **cost of capital,** which is a weighted average of the cost of these three components. If not, a manager may use the firm's borrowing rate of 6 percent as the basis of comparison when contemplating acquiring property purchased with borrowed funds, such as acquiring a building purchased with a mortgage loan from a bank. If this were done, a return of 8 percent would indicate to a manager that the project should be accepted even though the firm's cost of capital might be 14 percent, clearly an incorrect decision. Similarly, if a firm's cost of capital for common stock is 18 percent, and a project promised a return of 16 percent this project would be rejected if the 18 percent hurdle rate were used. A firm could thus be placed in the untenable position of accepting an 8 percent return and rejecting a 16 percent return because different hurdle rates were used to evaluate competing projects.

If a manager rejects a project when the project's cash inflows and its cash outflows for purchasing fail to pass the firm's hurdle rate (cost of capital), no further analysis should be made. On the other hand, if a project passes the investment decision, a manager may then wish to compare the net present value of the cash outflows for purchasing the equipment with the net present value of the cash outflows for leasing the equipment. The one with the lowest cash outflow would be the way to finance the acquisition of the property. Note that a project's cash *inflows* are used to evaluate the investment decision, but only the cash *outflows* of the two different methods of financing are used to evaluate the financing decision.

▶ OTHER CAPITAL-BUDGETING TECHNIQUES

Not all firms use the discounted cash flow (DCF) model for investment decisions. Some firms prefer a simpler method or one that is more compatible with the way they keep their accounting records. These simpler methods generally suffer from several conceptual defects, the principal one being the failure to consider the time value of money.

Managers who prefer capital-budgeting evaluation methods that are simpler than the discounted cash flow model most typically use two other techniques—the payback method and the accounting rate of return. Some firms use either or both of these methods in place of the DCF model, while others use either or both to supplement the DCF model. Although the payback method and the accounting rate of return are conceptually inferior to the DCF model, their wide usage makes it imperative that managers know how to compute and use them.

The Payback Method

L.O. 8

Simply stated, **payback** is the period of time, stated in years, that it will take a firm to recoup its investment in a project. It is very simple to compute. When the cash flows are uniform and no salvage value or release of working capital is involved, the computation is:

$$\text{Payback} = \frac{\text{Net investment}}{\text{Cash inflow per annum}}$$
$$\text{(Cash operating advantage)}$$

For example, if the Automated Manufacturing Company is contemplating the purchase of a new machine for $90,000 with expected cash inflow of $28,800 per year for a period of five years, the calculation of the payback for this machine would be:

$$\frac{\$90,000}{\$28,800} = 3.125 \text{ years}$$

This machine will have its cash outlay returned to the firm in 3⅛ years.

Uses and Limitations of the Payback Method The payback method suffers from two deficiencies—it fails to consider the time value of money, and it provides no indication of whether the investment will be profitable. To determine profitability, further analysis is necessary, and at a minimum, the payback should be compared with the project's total life to make sure that the life is the greater of the two. Although such a comparison does not prove a project is profitable, it should eliminate any project whose life is *shorter* than its payback.

▶ **ILLUSTRATION 14-11**   Cash Flows and Payback for Projects K and L

		Years							
Project	Total	1	2	3	4	5	6	7	8
K.	$200,000	$50,000	$50,000	$50,000	$50,000	—	—	—	—
L.	200,000	25,000	25,000	25,000	25,000	$25,000	$25,000	$25,000	$25,000

The payback for each project is:

$$\text{Project K} = \frac{\$100,000}{\$50,000} = 2 \text{ years}$$

$$\text{Project L} = \frac{\$100,000}{\$25,000} = 4 \text{ years}$$

▶ **ILLUSTRATION 14-12**   Calculation of Net Present Value for Projects K and L

Project K:

$50,000 × 2.58873* = $129,437 − $100,000 = $29,437

Project L:

$25,000 × 3.83716† = $95,929 − $100,000 = $(4,071)

* From Table 4 in Appendix 14-B, $n = 4$, $i = 20\%$.
† From Table 4 in Appendix 14-B, $n = 8$, $i = 20\%$.

Despite payback's shortcomings, managers use it extensively as an initial screening tool. Projects that have high paybacks tend to be less profitable than projects with shorter paybacks. For example, consider competing projects K and L. Each requires a net investment of $100,000, will return $200,000 over its useful life, and has cash inflows as shown in Illustration 14-11. Using a discount rate of 20 percent, the net present values for projects K and L are shown in Illustration 14-12.

The calculations show that project K, with a two-year payback, has a much higher net present value than project L, which has a four-year payback, even though the two projects' total cash inflows are the same. An interesting result in this case—although it is not true in all cases—is that project K has a significantly high net present value (a favorable project for a 20 percent cutoff rate), while project L has a negative net present value (an unacceptable project). Thus, a higher payback may indicate lower profitability on a present value basis.

Users of payback generally employ it to weed out projects that have high risk and low profitability. Thus, a payback cutoff point, such as six years, may be used to screen all incoming projects, with those that survive then subjected to the more rigorous discounted cash flow tests.

Uneven Cash Flows   When a project's cash flows are uneven, the simple calculation approach to payback cannot be used. Instead, it becomes necessary to start with the unrecovered investment balance, deduct each year's cash inflow, and add further outflows until the balance is zero. The amount of time necessary to reach the zero balance is the payback period.

▶ **ILLUSTRATION 14-13**   Computation of Payback for Investment Proposal

Year	(1) Cash Outflow	(2) Cash Inflow	Unrecovered Investment (1) − (2)
Initial investment	$72,000		$72,000
1		$19,000	53,000
2		18,000	35,000
3		16,000	19,000
4	10,000	20,000	9,000
4.5*		9,000	–0–

* The 5th year's inflow of $18,000 is prorated by using the unrecovered investment balance as a percent of the total inflows for the year (i.e., $9,000 ÷ $18,000 = 50%). Hence, one half of a year is added to the 4 preceding years for a payback of 4.5 years.

The Lorton Company is considering the purchase of a machine for $72,000. The machine has an eight-year useful life and no salvage value. The estimated cash flows are:

End of Year	Inflows	Major Repair— Outflow
1	$19,000	
2	18,000	
3	16,000	
4	20,000	$10,000
5	18,000	
6	16,000	
7	18,000	
8	20,000	

The payback may be calculated as shown in Illustration 14-13. Lorton would use the results in the same manner discussed previously.

The Accounting Rate of Return

L.O. 8

Another evaluation method that managers often use, the **accounting rate of return (ARR),** also known as the *simple rate of return,* is computed by dividing accounting net income for a project (revenues minus costs *including depreciation* and income taxes) by the average net investment (ANI) in the project. If there are no revenues but a reduction in costs, the calculation becomes:

$$\text{ARR}_{\text{ANI}} = \frac{\text{Cost savings} - \text{Depreciation} - \text{Income taxes}}{\text{Average net investment}}$$

The accounting rate of return has two shortcomings. First, because it fails to consider the time value of money, the ARR treats the net income (or operating advantage) for each year during a project's life as having no interest cost. Thus, a net income of $10,000 in year 1 is considered equivalent to a net income of $10,000 in year 10. The second deficiency is that users of ARR disagree about the amount that should be used as the net investment in the denominator. Because the numerator is decreased by depreciation each year, the denominator should also be adjusted for the sake of consistency.

The disagreement is over just how the adjustment in the denominator should be made. Two approaches are used: (1) the average net investment or (2) the original net investment (ONI).

The Landy Company has analyzed its expected cost savings from the use of a new machine it plans to purchase. The analysis indicates that (1) the cash savings before income taxes amount to $33,500 per annum, (2) the cost of the new machine is $90,000, (3) the company's income tax on this project is $2,000 annually, (4) there is no salvage value for the machine, and (5) the machine is expected to last five years. The numerator may be calculated as:

$$\$33,500 - \frac{\$90,000}{5 \text{ years}} - \$2,000 = \$13,500$$

▶ **ILLUSTRATION 14-14**   Methods and Techniques Used for Capital-Budgeting Decisions

Method or Technique	Principal Use	Required Data	Assumptions and Limitations
Discounted cash flow model:			
a. Net present value	To screen investment proposals to determine their profitability.	Cash inflows, cash outflows, a hurdle or discount rate—either a firm's cost of capital or a modified rate based on cost of capital.	Cash inflows as they are released from a project *are reinvested at the discount rate used* to evaluate the project. Both profitability and the time value of money are considered.
b. Internal rate of return	To screen investment proposals to determine their profitability, to rank the proposals for preferability.	Cash inflows, cash outflows, a hurdle or discount rate—either a firm's cost of capital or a modified rate based on cost of capital.	Cash inflows as they are released from a project *are reinvested at the computed internal rate of return.* Both profitability and the time value of money are considered.
Profitability index	To convert the present values of competing projects to an index ranking for the purpose of making a preference selection. Especially useful for competing projects with unequal lives or unequal net investments.	The discounted net investment and discounted cash inflows for each competing investment.	When used for competing projects with unequal net investments, care must be exercised in selecting the project with the higher profitability index. In some cases, the project with the lower profitability index may be preferable if a suitable alternative investment is not available for the funds not invested when the project with the lower net investment is selected.
Payback	As an initial screening device to weed out high-risk, low-return proposals, to be followed by another evaluation method.	Cash inflows and net investment.	Its principal shortcomings are that it fails to consider the time value of money and gives no indication of whether the project is profitable.
Accounting rate of return	To screen investment proposals to determine their profitability, to rank the proposals for profitability.	Incremental revenues minus incremental costs including depreciation, and net investment. For cost-reduction projects, cost savings minus depreciation is used together with the net investment.	The concept is based on accounting net income. The time value of money is *not* considered. The investment base may be either the average investment or the original investment.

Using the *average* net investment, the accounting rate of return is then computed as:

$$\text{ARR}_{\text{ANI}} = \frac{\$13,500}{(\$90,000 + \$0) \div 2} = \frac{\$13,500}{\$45,000} = .3 = 30\%$$

Using the *original* net investment, the ARR may also be calculated as:

$$\text{ARR}_{\text{ONI}} = \frac{\$13,500}{\$90,000} = .15 = 15\%$$

Note that the ARR_{ANI} of 30 percent is exactly twice the ARR_{ONI} of 15 percent. Despite this difference in results, both methods are commonly used. The choice depends on management's perception of which rate is more useful rather than on the formula's degree of sophistication. Once the ARR is computed, it is used for screening and preference in the same manner as the IRR.

Advocates of the accounting rate of return believe it is useful because its calculation is compatible with the way accounting net income is calculated from the company's books and records. There is some truth in this thinking, but not a lot. In this author's opinion, ARR's shortcomings far outweigh its small advantage over the discounted cash flow methods.

▶ RECAPITULATION

A recapitulation of the various methods and techniques managers use in reaching investment decisions appears in Illustration 14-14.

▶ **SUMMARY**

Managers must often make **capital-budgeting** decisions about cost reductions, such as whether to invest in new labor-saving equipment or whether to replace an existing machine with a newer, more efficient model. They also must make decisions about expanding profits, such as whether to market a new product or whether to purchase an existing business. The capital-budgeting process usually consists of two phases—**screening** and **preference selection.** Evaluation techniques for screening range from the simplistic payback method, which merely indicates the amount of time it takes for a firm to recoup its investment, to the sophisticated **discounted cash flow models,** known as *the net present value method* and the *internal rate of return.*

The **net present value method** requires discounting the cash inflows by an appropriate **discount rate,** usually the firm's **cost of capital** or a variant of it, and comparing them to the present value of the net investment. If the present value of the cash inflows exceeds the present value of the net investment—a positive net present value—the discount rate will be earned. If the reverse is true and the discounted net investment exceeds the discounted cash inflows, the net present value is negative, and the proposal should be rejected because the discount rate will not be earned.

The **internal rate of return** also makes use of present value concepts. It is the discount rate at which the present value of a project's cash inflows equals the present value of the net investment so that the project's net present value is zero. In essence, the IRR is a calculation that indicates the rate of return earned by a particular project. Most firms use computers to calculate the IRR of investment decisions, but when calculations are performed manually, **linear interpolation** is often necessary. The resulting internal rate of return is then compared to the firm's cost of capital or some other hurdle or **cutoff rate.** If the internal rate of return is greater than the cutoff rate, the project is favorable. Otherwise, the project should be rejected.

When projects must compete for scarce resources (capital), the internal rate of return can be used as a ranking tool. Competing projects evaluated by the net present value method may also be ranked by converting the present values of the cash inflows and the net investment to a **profitability index.** This index is especially suitable for competitive projects that have unequal lives or unequal net investments.

The data used in the discounted cash flow models are subject to a considerable amount of uncertainty. Much of the data are estimated amounts that can be classified as either **hard data,** which involve little or no uncertainty, or **soft data,** which involve estimates far into the future and are thus far less certain than hard data.

Capital-budgeting proposals are most often prepared by a firm's segment managers. An important control device to monitor a manager's effectiveness is the **audit of capital-budgeting projects.** In such an audit, the actual results of an investment project are compared with the estimates prepared by the manager responsible for the project's proposal.

Due to its simplicity, the **payback method** is a popular screening tool among managers. Although payback fails to consider the time value of money (interest), it is an effective indicator of the time it will take for a firm to recover its investment in a project. A long payback may indicate a greater than normal risk. Many firms have a cutoff point for payback. Only those projects with paybacks that are lower than the cutoff point are given further consideration and then subjected to discounted cash flow analysis.

Another screening method that managers use is the **accounting rate of return.** Like payback, this method lacks the sophistication of the discounted cash flow model because it does not consider the time value of money. Managers also disagree over whether to use a project's average investment or gross investment when computing this rate. Despite the ARR's shortcomings, some managers prefer to use it because of its similarity to the way in which accounting net income is derived from the firm's books and records.

Regardless of their differences, all of these evaluation techniques share a common handicap: All are subject to considerable uncertainty when cash inflows and outflows must be estimated well into the future.

▶ **APPENDIX 14-A**   **Compound Interest and Present Value**

All of us have been exposed to the concept of interest at one time or another. From interest received on savings accounts to interest paid on credit card balances, installment loans, and home mortgages, our experiences have likely included both simple interest and compound interest.

There is general agreement that an individual or a business would prefer having a dollar today rather than receiving a dollar at a later date, such as one year from today. The reason is that the dollar received today can be invested to earn interest, say, 10 percent. In one year, the value of that dollar would increase to $1.10 (the original dollar plus the interest of 10 percent of $1). In contrast, a dollar received one year from now would be worth only its face value—$1.

Uncertainty and inflation also influence the preference for collecting money today instead of in the future. Despite a debtor's promise to pay a dollar in the future, a creditor can never be sure the debt will actually be paid. Furthermore, a dollar received in the future may have less purchasing power than a dollar received today. Thus, considering all factors, it is preferable to receive a dollar sooner rather than later.

Given that a dollar received today can be invested to earn interest, it is clear that time can affect the value of money. The **time value of money** is measured by the amount of interest that is (or can be) earned on an investment for a given period of time. The time value of money may be computed in two different ways. One method uses simple interest, and the other uses compound interest.

Simple Interest

Simple interest is computed by multiplying the *principal (P)*, also called the *investment,* by the *interest rate (R)* and the *time period (T)*. The interest amount is computed only on the principal, *not* on the interest earned. The equation is usually shortened to:

$$\text{Interest} = P \times R \times T$$

Assume Harry Jones borrowed $1,000 from his aunt for a period of three years at the simple-interest rate of 10 percent per annum. The maturity value of the loan may be computed as follows:

$$\text{Interest} = \$1,000 \times \frac{10}{100} \times \frac{3}{1} = \$300$$

$$\text{Maturity value} = \$1,000 + \$300 \text{ interest} = \$1,300$$

The computations needed for compound interest are somewhat more complex.

Compound Interest

Compound interest differs from simple interest in its calculation of maturity value—**compound interest** is calculated on both the principal and the previous interest earned. Thus, if Harry Jones were to pay his aunt compound interest, the time period of three years would be broken into shorter time periods, such as three one-year periods. The number of times compounding takes place within *one year* is referred to as the *frequency of compounding*. Thus, compounding that occurs once per year is considered *annual compounding*.

The computation of maturity value using simple interest can be completed in one step; however, the computation of the maturity value using compound interest requires the same number of steps as the frequency of compounding. For example, for a three-year period with annual compounding, three separate steps would be required. Interest for the first compounding period is computed in the same way as simple interest. The next step is to compute the interest on the *principal plus the interest computed in the preceding step*. The process is repeated, each time adding on the previously computed interest, until the full period of time is reached—in this case, three years.

Future Value If Harry Jones's loan were compounded annually, its maturity value would be computed as follows:

First year:

$$\text{Interest} = \$1,000 \times \frac{10}{100} \times \frac{1}{1} = \$100$$

$$\text{Interim value} = \$1,000 + \$100 = \$1,100$$

Second year:

$$\text{Interest} = \$1,100 \times \frac{10}{100} \times \frac{1}{1} = \$110$$

$$\text{Interim value} = \$1,100 + \$110 = \$1,210$$

Third year:

$$\text{Interest} = \$1,210 \times \frac{10}{100} \times \frac{1}{1} = \$121$$

$$\text{Maturity value} = \$1,210 + \$121 = \$1,331$$

The total compound interest for the three-year period is $331 ($1,331 − $1,000), as compared to the $300 simple interest computed earlier.

The same result may be achieved by performing the following multiplication:

$$\$1,000[(1 + i) \times (1 + i) \times (1 + i)] = \$1,000(1 + i)^3$$

Inserting the 10 percent interest rate, it becomes:

$$\$1,000[(1 + .10) \times (1 + .10) \times (1 + .10)] =$$
$$\$1,000[1 + .10]^3 = \$1,000[1.331] = \$1,331$$

The loan's maturity value of $1,331 may also be referred to as its *future value*. **Future value** is the amount that a single payment invested at interest rate i will amount to at the end of the investment period, including interest accumulated for n periods. A generalized formula for the expression of the future value of $1 compounded for n periods at interest rate i may be expressed as:

$$f = (1 + i)^n$$

where

   f = Future value of $1
   i = Interest rate per period
   n = Number of periods

Fortunately, to save time, tables are available that present the future value factors for different interest rates and different periods of n. A sample is Table 1 in Appendix 14-B. Our previous calculation of 1.331 for $(1 + 0.10)^3$ can be verified by consulting Table 1 under the column for 10 percent and across the row for three periods ($n = 3$). The figure 1.33100 indicates the amount that $1 will amount to in three years at $i = 10$ percent. Thus, it is a simple matter to multiply this factor by the amount of Harry Jones's loan ($1,000) to arrive at the maturity value:

$$\$1,000(1.33100) = \$1,331$$

When compounding occurs more than once a year, the compound-interest equation is adjusted by dividing i and multiplying n by the frequency of compounding. For example, if the Harry Jones loan provides for semiannual compounding, the equation would be adjusted as follows:

$$f = \left(1 + \frac{i}{2}\right)^{n \cdot 2} = \left(1 + \frac{.10}{2}\right)^{3 \cdot 2} = (1.05)^6$$

Referring again to Table 1, the needed factor is found under the column for 5 percent and across the row for six periods ($n = 6$)—1.34010. So the maturity value of the loan would be:

$$\$1,000(1.34010) = \$1,340.10$$

The maturity value of the loan increases by $9.10 ($1,340.10 − $1,331.00) as a result of the semiannual compounding. Tables with fractional interest rates may be obtained when the frequency of compounding necessitates their use.

Thus far, we have considered only the future value of an amount for n periods at interest rate i. For many kinds of business problems, however, the future value is already known, and there is a need to determine how much must be invested now to have that amount available when needed. This concept is known as *present value*.

Present Value   The concept of present value is closely related to future value. **Present value** is the estimated worth today of an amount to be received in the future. The amount to be received is adjusted by deducting interest at a rate of i for n interest periods. The present value is always *less* than the amount to be received in the future. Its formula is the reciprocal of the future value formula and is stated as:

$$p = (1 + i)^{-n} = \frac{1}{(1 + i)^n}$$

There are many uses for present value. For example, assume a firm plans to give an employee a $10,000 bonus five years from now, at the time of her retirement. In preparation, the company would like to immediately invest the required amount of money at 10 percent per annum compounded annually. How much must the company invest today to have $10,000 five years from today? The amount can be determined using Table 2. The present value factor corresponding to $i = 10$ percent and $n = 5$ is multiplied by the desired future value to arrive at the present value:

$$\$10,000(.62092) = \$6,209$$

Thus, if $6,209 is deposited today at an interest of 10 percent compounded annually, it will amount to $10,000 in five years. This can be proved by using the factor for $i = 10$ percent, $n = 5$, from Table 1 and multiplying it by $6,209, as follows:

$$\$6,209(1.61051) = \$10,000$$

The Future Value of an Annuity   A series of uniform payments is often required in a transaction, such as an annual payment each year for a period of 10 years. A series of uniform payments for a specified period of time is called an **annuity.** When a series of uniform payments is deposited into a fund, it is possible to use Table 1 to compute the future value of each deposit.

For example, if John Fallon expects to deposit $2,000 into an individual retirement arrangement (IRA) for a period of 10 years and each deposit is made on the *last* day of each year, Table 1 may be used to compute the future value of each payment separately. The maturity values are then totaled to compute the balance in the fund. (*Note:* Only nine payments earn interest. The last payment earns no interest because it is deposited on the last day of the 10th year.)

However, this procedure may entail more arithmetic than necessary. The same results may be obtained using Table 3, which is constructed from Table 1. Table 3 is a table of cumulative values—an annuity—except it assumes the first payment is made on the *last* day of each year, while Table 1 assumes the payments are made on the *first* day of the year. A series of uniform periodic payments made on the last day of each year (period) is called an **ordinary annuity.**

Returning to our IRA example, John Fallon is interested in knowing how much his fund will amount to at the end of 10 years, assuming each $2,000 payment will earn 10 percent per annum compounded annually. Based on Table 3, the factor for $n = 10$, $i = 10$ is 15.93742, so the calculation would be:

$$\text{Future value} = \$2,000(15.93742) = \$31,875$$

The accumulation of the future value of an annuity may be visualized as shown in Illustration 14-15.

Like the present value of a single payment, the present value of an annuity also has many business applications.

The Present Value of an Annuity   The **present value of an annuity** is the estimated value today of a series of uniform periodic payments to be received in the future. The amounts to be received are adjusted by deducting interest at the rate of i for n periods. When a series of uniform payments is expected to be received for a certain number of years into the future, such as from a retirement pension, the recipient may be interested in knowing how much to accept as a lump-sum payment in lieu of the periodic payments. Table 4 provides the factors needed to compute the present value of an ordinary annuity.

James Stinton, at 70 years of age, is retiring from his job. He must choose between receiving $10,000 per annum for a guaranteed period of 15 years or accepting a lump-sum payment of $80,000. Stinton believes he can invest the $80,000 at a 10 percent return, compounded annually, and he will withdraw $10,000 each year for his personal use. Should he accept the lump sum of $80,000 or the annual payments of $10,000 for 15 years?

Table 4 provides the needed factor. Using the 10 percent column for $n = 15$, the factor is 7.60608, so:

$$\text{Present value} = \$10,000(7.60608) = \$76,061$$

▶ **ILLUSTRATION 14-15**   Future Value of an Ordinary Annuity at 10 Percent per Annum

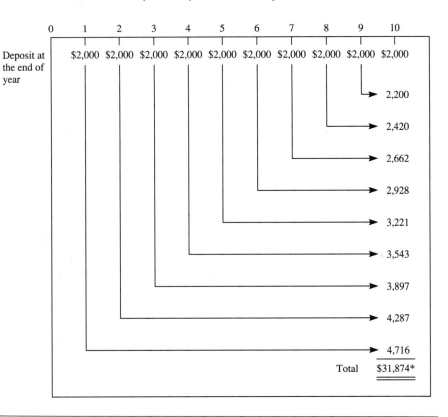

* Difference of $1 due to rounding.

If Stinton were offered $76,061 as a lump sum, he should be indifferent, because a periodic payment of $10,000 per annum for 15 years is the same as $76,061 today, when interest is 10 percent per annum compounded annually. He should accept the lump-sum payment of $80,000, however, because this amount is greater than $76,061. The present value of an ordinary annuity may be visualized as shown in Illustration 14-16.

When annual periodic payments are not uniform, the present value of the payments must be computed individually using Table 2.

Present value concepts can be applied to a variety of business situations. Businesses must frequently budget for cash outlays that will bring in cash receipts for years after the outlays are made. To properly equate a current cash outlay with the cash receipts it will generate in the future, a firm must convert the expected receipts to their present value at the time of the expenditure. The process of adjusting future cash receipts to reflect their present value is known as **discounting.** A firm will not normally invest in a project unless its expected discounted future cash receipts exceed the initial cash outlay. A variety of business problems that require the use of discounting is discussed in this chapter.

A summary of the four compound-interest tables appears in Illustration 14-17.

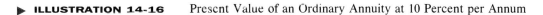

▶ **ILLUSTRATION 14-16**   Present Value of an Ordinary Annuity at 10 Percent per Annum

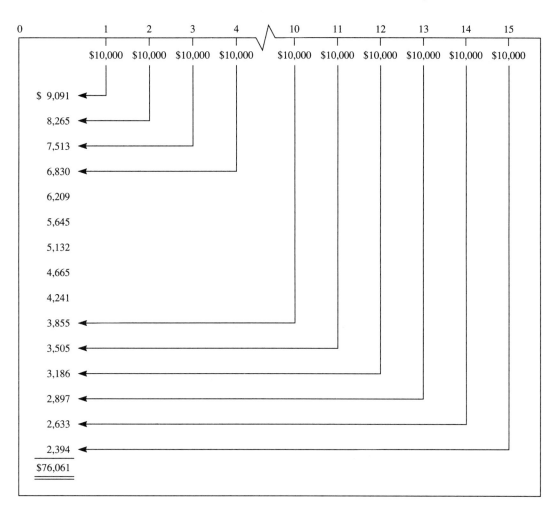

▶ **ILLUSTRATION 14-17**   Summary of Compound-Interest Tables

Table Number		Use
1		Future value of a *single* payment at the *beginning* of the *first* year
2		Present value of a *single* payment at the *end* of the *nth* year
3		Future value of an annuity with each year's payment occurring at the *end* of each year
4		Present value of an annuity with each year's payment occurring at the *end* of each year

▲ TABLE 1   Future Value of 1, $f = (1 + i)^n$

Periods	2%	2½%	3%	4%	5%	6%	7%	8%	9%	10%
1	1.02000	1.02500	1.03000	1.04000	1.05000	1.06000	1.07000	1.08000	1.09000	1.10000
2	1.04040	1.05063	1.06090	1.08160	1.10250	1.12360	1.14490	1.16640	1.18810	1.21000
3	1.06121	1.07689	1.09273	1.12486	1.15763	1.19102	1.22504	1.25971	1.29503	1.33100
4	1.08243	1.10381	1.12551	1.16986	1.21551	1.26248	1.31080	1.36049	1.41158	1.46410
5	1.10408	1.13141	1.15927	1.21665	1.27628	1.33823	1.40255	1.46933	1.53862	1.61051
6	1.12616	1.15969	1.19405	1.26532	1.34010	1.41852	1.50073	1.58687	1.67710	1.77156
7	1.14869	1.18869	1.22987	1.31593	1.40710	1.50363	1.60578	1.71382	1.82804	1.94872
8	1.17166	1.21840	1.26677	1.36857	1.47746	1.59385	1.71819	1.85093	1.99256	2.14359
9	1.19509	1.24886	1.30477	1.42331	1.55133	1.68948	1.83846	1.99900	2.17189	2.35795
10	1.21899	1.28008	1.34392	1.48024	1.62889	1.79085	1.96715	2.15892	2.36736	2.59374
11	1.24337	1.31209	1.38423	1.53945	1.71034	1.89830	2.10485	2.33164	2.58043	2.85312
12	1.26824	1.34489	1.42576	1.60103	1.79586	2.01220	2.25219	2.51817	2.81266	3.13843
13	1.29361	1.37851	1.46853	1.66507	1.88565	2.13293	2.40985	2.71962	3.06580	3.45227
14	1.31948	1.41297	1.51259	1.73168	1.97993	2.26090	2.57853	2.93719	3.34173	3.79750
15	1.34587	1.44830	1.55797	1.80094	2.07893	2.39656	2.75903	3.17217	3.64248	4.17725
16	1.37279	1.48451	1.60471	1.87298	2.18287	2.54035	2.95216	3.42594	3.97031	4.59497
17	1.40024	1.52162	1.65285	1.94790	2.29202	2.69277	3.15882	3.70002	4.32763	5.05447
18	1.42825	1.55966	1.70243	2.02582	2.40662	2.85434	3.37993	3.99602	4.71712	5.55992
19	1.45681	1.59865	1.75351	2.10685	2.52695	3.02560	3.61653	4.31570	5.14166	6.11591
20	1.48595	1.63862	1.80611	2.19112	2.65330	3.20714	3.86968	4.66096	5.60441	6.72750
21	1.51567	1.67958	1.86029	2.27877	2.78596	3.39956	4.14056	5.03383	6.10881	7.40025
22	1.54598	1.72157	1.91610	2.36992	2.92526	3.60354	4.43040	5.43654	6.65860	8.14027
23	1.57690	1.76461	1.97359	2.46472	3.07152	3.81975	4.74053	5.87146	7.25787	8.95430
24	1.60844	1.80873	2.03279	2.56330	3.22510	4.04893	5.07237	6.34118	7.91108	9.84973
25	1.64061	1.85394	2.09378	2.66584	3.38635	4.29187	5.42743	6.84848	8.62308	10.83471

Periods	11%	12%	14%	15%	16%	18%	20%	22%	24%	25%
1	1.11000	1.12000	1.14000	1.15000	1.16000	1.18000	1.20000	1.22000	1.24000	1.25000
2	1.23210	1.25440	1.29960	1.32250	1.34560	1.39240	1.44000	1.48840	1.53760	1.56250
3	1.36763	1.40493	1.48154	1.52088	1.56090	1.64303	1.72800	1.81585	1.90662	1.95313
4	1.51807	1.57352	1.68896	1.74901	1.81064	1.93878	2.07360	2.21533	2.36421	2.44141
5	1.68506	1.76234	1.92541	2.01136	2.10034	2.28776	2.48832	2.70271	2.93163	3.05176
6	1.87041	1.97382	2.19497	2.31306	2.43640	2.69955	2.98598	3.29730	3.63522	3.81470
7	2.07616	2.21068	2.50227	2.66002	2.82622	3.18547	3.58318	4.02271	4.50767	4.76837
8	2.30454	2.47596	2.85259	3.05902	3.27841	3.75886	4.29982	4.90771	5.58951	5.96046
9	2.55804	2.77308	3.25195	3.51788	3.80296	4.43545	5.15978	5.98740	6.93099	7.45058
10	2.83942	3.10585	3.70722	4.04556	4.41144	5.23384	6.19174	7.30463	8.59443	9.31323
11	3.15176	3.47855	4.22623	4.65239	5.11726	6.17593	7.43008	8.91165	10.65709	11.64153
12	3.49845	3.89598	4.81790	5.35025	5.93603	7.28759	8.91610	10.87221	13.21479	14.55192
13	3.88328	4.36349	5.49241	6.15279	6.88579	8.59936	10.69932	13.26410	16.38634	18.18989
14	4.31044	4.88711	6.26135	7.07571	7.98752	10.14724	12.83918	16.18220	20.31906	22.73737
15	4.78459	5.47357	7.13794	8.13706	9.26552	11.97375	15.40702	19.74229	25.19563	28.42171
16	5.31089	6.13039	8.13725	9.35762	10.74800	14.12902	18.48843	24.08559	31.24259	35.52714
17	5.89509	6.86604	9.27646	10.76126	12.46768	16.67225	22.18611	29.38442	38.74081	44.40892
18	6.54355	7.68997	10.57517	12.37545	14.46251	19.67325	26.62333	35.84899	48.03860	55.51115
19	7.26334	8.61276	12.05569	14.23177	16.77652	23.21444	31.94800	43.73577	59.56786	69.38894
20	8.06231	9.64629	13.74349	16.36654	19.46076	27.39303	38.33760	53.35764	73.86415	86.73617
21	8.94917	10.80385	15.66758	18.82152	22.57448	32.32378	46.00512	65.09632	91.59155	108.42022
22	9.93357	12.10031	17.86104	21.64475	26.18640	38.14206	55.20614	79.41751	113.57352	135.52527
23	11.02627	13.55235	20.36158	24.89146	30.37622	45.00763	66.24737	96.88936	140.83116	169.40659
24	12.23916	15.17863	23.21221	28.62518	35.23642	53.10901	79.49685	118.20502	174.63064	211.75824
25	13.58546	17.00006	26.46192	32.91895	40.87424	62.66863	95.39622	144.21013	216.54199	264.69780

▲ **TABLE 2**

Present Value of 1, $p = \dfrac{1}{(1 + i)^n}$

Periods	2%	2½%	3%	4%	5%	6%	7%	8%	9%	10%
1	.98039	.97561	.97087	.96154	.95238	.94340	.93458	.92593	.91743	.90909
2	.96117	.95181	.94260	.92456	.90703	.89000	.87344	.85734	.84168	.82645
3	.94232	.92860	.91514	.88900	.86384	.83962	.81630	.79383	.77218	.75131
4	.92385	.90595	.88849	.85480	.82270	.79209	.76290	.73503	.70843	.68301
5	.90573	.88385	.86261	.82193	.78353	.74726	.71299	.68058	.64993	.62092
6	.88797	.86230	.83748	.79031	.74622	.70496	.66634	.63017	.59627	.56447
7	.87056	.84127	.81309	.75992	.71068	.66506	.62275	.58349	.54703	.51316
8	.85349	.82075	.78941	.73069	.67684	.62741	.58201	.54027	.50187	.46651
9	.83676	.80073	.76642	.70259	.64461	.59190	.54393	.50025	.46043	.42410
10	.82035	.78120	.74409	.67556	.61391	.55839	.50835	.46319	.42241	.38554
11	.80426	.76214	.72242	.64958	.58468	.52679	.47509	.42888	.38753	.35049
12	.78849	.74356	.70138	.62460	.55684	.49697	.44401	.39711	.35553	.31863
13	.77303	.72542	.68095	.60057	.53032	.46884	.41496	.36770	.32618	.28966
14	.75788	.70773	.66112	.57748	.50507	.44230	.38782	.34046	.29925	.26333
15	.74301	.69047	.64186	.55526	.48102	.41727	.36245	.31524	.27454	.23939
16	.72845	.67362	.62317	.53391	.45811	.39365	.33873	.29189	.25187	.21763
17	.71416	.65720	.60502	.51337	.43630	.37136	.31657	.27027	.23107	.19784
18	.70016	.64117	.58739	.49363	.41552	.35034	.29586	.25025	.21199	.17986
19	.68643	.62553	.57029	.47464	.39573	.33051	.27651	.23171	.19449	.16351
20	.67297	.61027	.55368	.45639	.37689	.31180	.25842	.21455	.17843	.14864
21	.65978	.59539	.53755	.43883	.35894	.29416	.24151	.19866	.16370	.13513
22	.64684	.58086	.52189	.42196	.34185	.27751	.22571	.18394	.15018	.12285
23	.63416	.56670	.50669	.40573	.32557	.26180	.21095	.17032	.13778	.11168
24	.62172	.55288	.49193	.39012	.31007	.24698	.19715	.15770	.12640	.10153
25	.60953	.53939	.47761	.37512	.29530	.23300	.18425	.14602	.11597	.09230

Periods	11%	12%	14%	15%	16%	18%	20%	22%	24%	25%
1	.90090	.89286	.87719	.86957	.86207	.84746	.83333	.81967	.80645	.80000
2	.81162	.79719	.76947	.75614	.74316	.71818	.69444	.67186	.65036	.64000
3	.73119	.71178	.67497	.65752	.64066	.60863	.57870	.55071	.52449	.51200
4	.65873	.63552	.59208	.57175	.55229	.51579	.48225	.45140	.42297	.40960
5	.59345	.56743	.51937	.49718	.47611	.43711	.40188	.37000	.34111	.32768
6	.53464	.50663	.45559	.43233	.41044	.37043	.33490	.30323	.27509	.26214
7	.48166	.45235	.39964	.37594	.35383	.31393	.27908	.24859	.22184	.20972
8	.43393	.40388	.35056	.32690	.30503	.26604	.23257	.20376	.17891	.16777
9	.39092	.36061	.30751	.28426	.26295	.22546	.19381	.16702	.14428	.13422
10	.35218	.32197	.26974	.24718	.22668	.19106	.16151	.13690	.11635	.10737
11	.31728	.28748	.23662	.21494	.19542	.16192	.13459	.11221	.09383	.08590
12	.28584	.25668	.20756	.18691	.16846	.13722	.11216	.09198	.07567	.06872
13	.25751	.22917	.18207	.16253	.14523	.11629	.09346	.07539	.06103	.05498
14	.23199	.20462	.15971	.14133	.12520	.09855	.07789	.06180	.04921	.04398
15	.20900	.18270	.14010	.12289	.10793	.08352	.06491	.05065	.03969	.03518
16	.18829	.16312	.12289	.10686	.09304	.07078	.05409	.04152	.03201	.02815
17	.16963	.14564	.10780	.09293	.08021	.05998	.04507	.03403	.02581	.02252
18	.15282	.13004	.09456	.08081	.06914	.05083	.03756	.02789	.02082	.01801
19	.13768	.11611	.08295	.07027	.05961	.04308	.03130	.02286	.01679	.01441
20	.12403	.10367	.07276	.06110	.05139	.03651	.02608	.01874	.01354	.01153
21	.11174	.09256	.06383	.05313	.04430	.03094	.02174	.01536	.01092	.00922
22	.10067	.08264	.05599	.04620	.03819	.02622	.01811	.01259	.00880	.00738
23	.09069	.07379	.04911	.04017	.03292	.02222	.01509	.01032	.00710	.00590
24	.08170	.06588	.04308	.03493	.02838	.01883	.01258	.00846	.00573	.00472
25	.07361	.05882	.03779	.03038	.02447	.01596	.01048	.00693	.00462	.00378

▲ TABLE 3

Future Value of Annuity of n Rents of 1 Each (ordinary), $F_0 = \dfrac{(1+i)^n - 1}{i}$

Periodic Rents (n)	2%	2½%	3%	4%	5%	6%	7%	8%	9%	10%
1	1.00000	1.00000	1.00000	1.00000	1.00000	1.00000	1.00000	1.00000	1.00000	1.00000
2	2.02000	2.02500	2.03000	2.04000	2.05000	2.06000	2.07000	2.08000	2.09000	2.10000
3	3.06040	3.07563	3.09090	3.12160	3.15250	3.18360	3.21490	3.24640	3.27810	3.31000
4	4.12161	4.15252	4.18363	4.24646	4.31013	4.37462	4.43994	4.50611	4.57313	4.64100
5	5.20404	5.25633	5.30914	5.41632	5.52563	5.63709	5.75074	5.86660	5.98471	6.10510
6	6.30812	6.38774	6.46841	6.63298	6.80191	6.97532	7.15329	7.33593	7.52333	7.71561
7	7.43428	7.54753	7.66246	7.89829	8.14201	8.39384	8.65402	8.92280	9.20043	9.48717
8	8.58297	8.73612	8.89234	9.21423	9.54911	9.89747	10.25980	10.63663	11.02847	11.43589
9	9.75463	9.95452	10.15911	10.58280	11.02656	11.49132	11.97799	12.48756	13.02104	13.57948
10	10.94972	11.20338	11.46388	12.00611	12.57789	13.18079	13.81645	14.48656	15.19293	15.93742
11	12.16872	12.48347	12.80780	13.48635	14.20679	14.97164	15.78360	16.64549	17.56029	18.53117
12	13.41209	13.79555	14.19203	15.02581	15.91713	16.86994	17.88845	18.97713	20.14072	21.38428
13	14.68033	15.14044	15.61779	16.62684	17.71298	18.88214	20.14064	21.49530	22.95338	24.52271
14	15.97394	16.51895	17.08632	18.29191	19.59863	21.01507	22.55049	24.21492	26.01919	27.97498
15	17.29342	17.93193	18.59891	20.02359	21.57856	23.27597	25.12902	27.15211	29.36092	31.77248
16	18.63929	19.38022	20.15688	21.82453	23.65749	25.67253	27.88805	30.32428	33.00340	35.94973
17	20.01207	20.86473	21.76159	23.69751	25.84037	28.21288	30.84022	33.75023	36.97370	40.54470
18	21.41231	22.38635	23.41444	25.64541	28.13238	30.90565	33.99903	37.45024	41.30134	45.59917
19	22.84056	23.94601	25.11687	27.67123	30.53900	33.75999	37.37896	41.44626	46.01846	51.15909
20	24.29737	25.54466	26.87037	29.77808	33.06595	36.78559	40.99549	45.76196	51.16012	57.27500
21	25.78332	27.18327	28.67649	31.96920	35.71925	39.99273	44.86518	50.42292	56.76453	64.00250
22	27.29898	28.86286	30.53678	34.24797	38.50521	43.39229	49.00574	55.45676	62.87334	71.40275
23	28.84496	30.58443	32.45288	36.61789	41.43048	46.99583	53.43614	60.89330	69.53194	79.54302
24	30.42186	32.34904	34.42647	39.08260	44.50200	50.81558	58.17667	66.76476	76.78981	88.49733
25	32.03030	34.15776	36.45926	41.64591	47.72710	54.86451	63.24904	73.10594	84.70090	98.34706

Periodic Rents (n)	11%	12%	14%	15%	16%	18%	20%	22%	24%	25%
1	1.00000	1.00000	1.00000	1.00000	1.00000	1.00000	1.00000	1.00000	1.00000	1.00000
2	2.11000	2.12000	2.14000	2.15000	2.16000	2.18000	2.20000	2.22000	2.24000	2.25000
3	3.34210	3.37440	3.43960	3.47250	3.50560	3.57240	3.64000	3.70840	3.77760	3.81250
4	4.70973	4.77933	4.92114	4.99338	5.06650	5.21543	5.36800	5.52425	5.68422	5.76563
5	6.22780	6.35285	6.61010	6.74238	6.87714	7.15421	7.44160	7.73958	8.04844	8.20703
6	7.91286	8.11519	8.53552	8.75374	8.97748	9.44197	9.92992	10.44229	10.98006	11.25879
7	9.78327	10.08901	10.73049	11.06680	11.41387	12.14152	12.91590	13.73959	14.61528	15.07349
8	11.85943	12.29969	13.23276	13.72682	14.24009	15.32700	16.49908	17.76231	19.12294	19.84186
9	14.16397	14.77566	16.08535	16.78584	17.51851	19.08585	20.79890	22.67001	24.71245	25.80232
10	16.72201	17.54874	19.33730	20.30372	21.32147	23.52131	25.95868	28.65742	31.64344	33.25290
11	19.56143	20.65458	23.04452	24.34928	25.73290	28.75514	32.15042	35.96205	40.23787	42.56613
12	22.71319	24.13313	27.27075	29.00167	30.85017	34.93107	39.58050	44.87370	50.89495	54.20766
13	26.21164	28.02911	32.08865	34.35192	36.78620	42.21866	48.49660	55.74591	64.10974	68.75958
14	30.09492	32.39260	37.58107	40.50471	43.67199	50.81802	59.19592	69.01001	80.49608	86.94947
15	34.40536	37.27971	43.84241	47.58041	51.65951	60.96527	72.03511	85.19221	100.81514	109.68684
16	39.18995	42.75328	50.98035	55.71747	60.92503	72.93901	87.44213	104.93450	126.01077	138.10855
17	44.50084	48.88367	59.11760	65.07509	71.67303	87.06804	105.93056	129.02009	157.25336	173.63568
18	50.39594	55.74971	68.39407	75.83636	84.14072	103.74028	128.11667	158.40451	195.99416	218.04460
19	56.93949	63.43968	78.96923	88.21181	98.60323	123.41353	154.74000	194.25350	244.03276	273.55576
20	64.20283	72.05244	91.02493	102.44358	115.37975	146.62797	186.68800	237.98927	303.60062	342.94470
21	72.26514	81.69874	104.76842	118.81012	134.84051	174.02100	225.02560	291.34691	377.46477	429.68087
22	81.21431	92.50258	120.43600	137.63164	157.41499	206.34479	271.03072	356.44323	469.05632	538.10109
23	91.14788	104.60289	138.29704	159.27638	183.60138	244.48685	326.23686	435.86075	582.62984	673.62636
24	102.17415	118.15524	158.65862	184.16784	213.97761	289.49448	392.48424	532.75011	723.46100	843.03295
25	114.41331	133.33387	181.87083	212.79302	249.21402	342.60349	471.98108	650.95513	898.09164	1054.79118

▶ TABLE 4

Present Value of Annuity of n Rents of 1 Each (ordinary), $P_o = \dfrac{1 - \dfrac{1}{(1 + i)^n}}{i}$

Periodic Rents (n)	2%	2½%	3%	4%	5%	6%	7%	8%	9%	10%
1	.98039	.97561	.97087	.96154	.95238	.94340	.93458	.92593	.91743	.90909
2	1.94156	1.92742	1.91347	1.88609	1.85941	1.83339	1.80802	1.78326	1.75911	1.73554
3	2.88388	2.85602	2.82861	2.77509	2.72325	2.67301	2.62432	2.57710	2.53129	2.48685
4	3.80773	3.76197	3.71710	3.62990	3.54595	3.46511	3.38721	3.31213	3.23972	3.16987
5	4.71346	4.64583	4.57971	4.45182	4.32948	4.21236	4.10020	3.99271	3.88965	3.79079
6	5.60143	5.50813	5.41719	5.24214	5.07569	4.91732	4.76654	4.62288	4.48592	4.35526
7	6.47199	6.34939	6.23028	6.00205	5.78637	5.58238	5.38929	5.20637	5.03295	4.86842
8	7.32548	7.17014	7.01969	6.73274	6.46321	6.20979	5.97130	5.74664	5.53482	5.33493
9	8.16224	7.97087	7.78611	7.43533	7.10782	6.80169	6.51523	6.24689	5.99525	5.75902
10	8.98259	8.75206	8.53020	8.11090	7.72173	7.36009	7.02358	6.71008	6.41766	6.14457
11	9.78685	9.51421	9.25262	8.76048	8.30641	7.88687	7.49867	7.13896	6.80519	6.49506
12	10.57534	10.25776	9.95400	9.38507	8.86325	8.38384	7.94269	7.53608	7.16073	6.81369
13	11.34837	10.98318	10.63496	9.98565	9.39357	8.85268	8.35765	7.90378	7.48690	7.10336
14	12.10625	11.69091	11.29607	10.56312	9.89864	9.29498	8.74547	8.24424	7.78615	7.36669
15	12.84926	12.38138	11.93794	11.11839	10.37966	9.71225	9.10791	8.55948	8.06069	7.60608
16	13.57771	13.05500	12.56110	11.65230	10.83777	10.10590	9.44665	8.85137	8.31256	7.82371
17	14.29187	13.71220	13.16612	12.16567	11.27407	10.47726	9.76322	9.12164	8.54363	8.02155
18	14.99203	14.35336	13.75351	12.65930	11.68959	10.82760	10.05909	9.37189	8.75563	8.20141
19	15.67846	14.97889	14.32380	13.13394	12.08532	11.15812	10.33560	9.60360	8.95011	8.36492
20	16.35143	15.58916	14.87747	13.59033	12.46221	11.46992	10.59401	9.81815	9.12855	8.51356
21	17.01121	16.18455	15.41502	14.02916	12.82115	11.76408	10.83553	10.01680	9.29224	8.64869
22	17.65805	16.76541	15.93692	14.45112	13.16300	12.04158	11.06124	10.20074	9.44243	8.77154
23	18.29220	17.33211	16.44361	14.85684	13.48857	12.30338	11.27219	10.37106	9.58021	8.88322
24	18.91393	17.88499	16.93554	15.24696	13.79864	12.55036	11.46933	10.52876	9.70661	8.98474
25	19.52346	18.42438	17.41315	15.62208	14.09394	12.78336	11.65358	10.67478	9.82258	9.07704

Periodic Rents (n)	11%	12%	14%	15%	16%	18%	20%	22%	24%	25%
1	.90090	.89286	.87719	.86957	.86207	.84746	.83333	.81967	.80645	.80000
2	1.71252	1.69005	1.64666	1.62571	1.60523	1.56564	1.52778	1.49153	1.45682	1.44000
3	2.44371	2.40183	2.32163	2.28323	2.24589	2.17427	2.10648	2.04224	1.98130	1.95200
4	3.10245	3.03735	2.91371	2.85498	2.79818	2.69006	2.58873	2.49364	2.40428	2.36160
5	3.69590	3.60478	3.43308	3.35216	3.27429	3.12717	2.99061	2.86364	2.74538	2.68928
6	4.23054	4.11141	3.88867	3.78448	3.68474	3.49760	3.32551	3.16692	3.02047	2.95142
7	4.71220	4.56376	4.28830	4.16042	4.03857	3.81153	3.60459	3.41551	3.24232	3.16114
8	5.14612	4.96764	4.63886	4.48732	4.34359	4.07757	3.83716	3.61927	3.42122	3.32891
9	5.53705	5.32825	4.94637	4.77158	4.60654	4.30302	4.03097	3.78628	3.56550	3.46313
10	5.88923	5.65022	5.21612	5.01877	4.83323	4.49409	4.19247	3.92318	3.68186	3.57050
11	6.20652	5.93770	5.45273	5.23371	5.02864	4.65601	4.32706	4.03540	3.77569	3.65640
12	6.49236	6.19437	5.66029	5.42062	5.19711	4.79322	4.43922	4.12737	3.85136	3.72512
13	6.74987	6.42355	5.84236	5.58315	5.34233	4.90951	4.53268	4.20277	3.91239	3.78010
14	6.98187	6.62817	6.00207	5.72448	5.46753	5.00806	4.61057	4.26456	3.96160	3.82408
15	7.19087	6.81086	6.14217	5.84737	5.57546	5.09158	4.67547	4.31522	4.00129	3.85926
16	7.37916	6.97399	6.26506	5.95423	5.66850	5.16235	4.72956	4.35673	4.03330	3.88741
17	7.54879	7.11963	6.37286	6.04716	5.74870	5.22233	4.77463	4.39077	4.05911	3.90993
18	7.70162	7.24967	6.46742	6.12797	5.81785	5.27316	4.81219	4.41866	4.07993	3.92794
19	7.83929	7.36578	6.55037	6.19823	5.87746	5.31624	4.84350	4.44152	4.09672	3.94235
20	7.96333	7.46944	6.62313	6.25933	5.92884	5.35275	4.86958	4.46027	4.11026	3.95388
21	8.07507	7.56200	6.68696	6.31246	5.97314	5.38368	4.89132	4.47563	4.12117	3.96311
22	8.17574	7.64465	6.74294	6.35866	6.01133	5.40990	4.90943	4.48822	4.12998	3.97049
23	8.26643	7.71843	6.79206	6.39884	6.04425	5.43212	4.92453	4.49654	4.13708	3.97639
24	8.34814	7.78432	6.83514	6.43377	6.07263	5.45095	4.93710	4.50700	4.14281	3.98111
25	8.42174	7.84314	6.87293	6.46415	6.09709	5.46691	4.94759	4.51393	4.14742	3.98489

▶ **APPENDIX 14-C** **Capital Budgeting and Inflation**

Logic might seem to dictate that the effects of inflation should be factored into any capital-budgeting decision. The effects of inflation are not as important to capital budgeting as they might appear, however, due to the nature of the adjustments that must be made. To account for inflationary effects, it is necessary to adjust both the expected cash inflows and outflows and the discount rate for the expected rates of inflation. As a result, the adjustments cancel each other, and the net present value is the same as the unadjusted net present value.

Let us assume the Eyecor Manufacturing Company is contemplating the purchase of a new machine at a cost of $25,000. The machine will not have any salvage value at the end of its three-year useful life, and the firm expects a cash operating advantage of $15,000 during each year of the machine's operation. The firm's cutoff rate for this kind of decision is 12 percent. The unadjusted net present value would be:

Cash operating advantage.	$15,000
Factor, Table 4, $i = 12\%$, $n = 3$	× 2.40183
Present value of cash receipts	36,027
Less: Net investment	25,000
Net present value	$11,027

Let us also assume the inflation rate is expected to be 10 percent each year for the next three years. The necessary adjustment of the cash operating advantage would be:

First year, $15,000 × 110%	$16,500
Second year, $16,500 × 110%. . . .	18,150
Third year, $18,150 × 110%	19,965

The discount rate must be adjusted for two factors—the 10 percent of expected inflation and the combined effect of the inflation and the discount rate (12% × 10% = 1.2%). The adjusted discount rate would then be:

	Rate
Discount rate.	12.0%
Inflation rate	10.0
Combined effect	1.2
Total adjusted rate . . .	23.2%

The adjusted net present value would then be computed as:

Year	Adjusted Cash Operating Advantage	Adjusted Discount Rate	Present Value
1	$16,500	.8117*	$13,393
2	18,150	.6588†	11,957
3	19,965	.5348‡	10,677
Total present value			36,027
Less: Net investment			25,000
Net present value			$11,027

* $1/(1.232)$.

† $1/(1.232)^2$.

‡ $1/(1/232)^3$.

Note that the adjusted and unadjusted net present values are the same. For this reason, many firms do not adjust for inflation in this manner.

Problems may arise, however, if no adjustment is made for inflation, because the postaudit comparisons may provide misleading results. For example, let us assume the cash operating advantage in the first year is, in fact, the projected $16,500, which includes the actual inflation. When this amount is compared to the original $15,000 used in the budget proposal, the project may appear more favorable than it really is. A simple method to correct for this is to take the actual cash advantage of $16,500 and divide it by 110 percent (100% + 10% inflation) to arrive at the amount exclusive of inflation—$15,000 ($16,500 ÷ 110% = $15,000). The amount for the second year would also be $15,000. It would be computed using a 21 percent inflation rate [10% + (10% of 110%) = 21%] and would be calculated as $18,150 ÷ 121% = $15,000. This method has the advantage of using an actual rate of inflation for the audit comparison instead of the assumed rate of inflation used earlier.

▶ **GLOSSARY OF KEY TERMS**

Accounting rate of return (ARR)   A measure used to evaluate investment proposals that is computed by dividing accounting net income for a project (revenues minus costs, including depreciation and income taxes) by the average net investment in the project. Also called the *simple rate of return*. (p. 736)

Annuity*   A series of uniform payments for a specified period of time. (p. 743)

Audit of capital-budgeting projects   The follow-up practice of comparing the actual results of an investment project with its expected results. It is used for control purposes and for decision making during the project when modifications may be indicated. (p. 732)

Capital budgeting   The planning and financing of long-term investments, such as buying equipment and introducing new products. (p. 718)

Compound interest*   Interest calculated on both the principal amount and the previous interest earned. (p. 740)

Cost of capital   The combined weighted-average rate of cost that a firm incurs on its long-term debt, preferred stock, and common stock. (p. 733)

Cutoff rate   The minimum rate of return that an investment must promise before a firm will commit its resources to the investment. Also called the *hurdle rate* or *target rate of return*. (p. 726)

Discount rate   The interest rate used to find the present value of a future cash flow. (p. 718)

Discounted cash flow model (DCF)   A technique used to evaluate investment projects that applies the time value of money to all cash inflows and outflows by discounting them to their present values. The two most commonly used discounted cash flow models are the net present value (NPV) method and the internal rate of return (IRR) method. (p. 718)

Discounting*   The process of adjusting future cash receipts to reflect their present value. (p. 744)

Future value*   The amount that a single payment invested at interest rate *i* will amount to at the end of the investment period, including interest accumulated for *n* periods. (p. 741)

Hard data   Information that may be ascertained with a high degree of precision and for which uncertainty is either small or nonexistent. (p. 731)

Internal rate of return (IRR)   The rate of interest that produces a zero net present value when a project's discounted cash operating advantage is netted against its discounted net investment. (p. 726)

---

*Denotes a glossary term from Appendix 14-A.

Linear interpolation A proportional (fractional) calculation made to estimate a project's internal rate of return when the present value factor falls between two figures shown in the present value tables. (p. 728)

Net present value method (NPV) The amount available after subtracting the discounted net investment from the discounted cash inflows. If the amount is positive, the investment promises more than the discount rate used to evaluate the proposal. If the amount is negative, the reverse is true, and the project should be rejected. (p. 718)

Ordinary annuity* A series of uniform periodic payments made on the last day of the period. (p. 743)

Payback The amount of time, stated in years, that it will take a firm to recoup its investment in a project. (p. 734)

Preference selection The second phase of capital budgeting, in which investment projects that survive the screening process are subjected to a ranking criterion, which results in the selection of the most favorable projects for any given amount of capital to be invested. (p. 718)

Present value* The estimated value today of an amount to be received in the future. The amount to be received is adjusted by deducting interest at a rate of i for n interest periods. (p. 742)

Present value of an annuity* The estimated value today of a series of uniform periodic payments to be received in the future. The amounts to be received are adjusted by deducting interest at the rate of i for n periods. (p. 743)

Profitability index (PI) The ratio obtained by dividing an investment's discounted cash inflow by the required net investment. Competing projects may be ranked by their profitability indexes: the higher the profitability index, the more desirable the project. (p. 729)

Screening The initial phase of capital budgeting, in which a specific cutoff criterion is used to eliminate unprofitable and/or high-risk investment proposals. (p. 718)

Simple interest* Computed by multiplying the principal (P), also called the *investment*, by the interest rate (R) and the time period (T). The interest amount is computed only on the principal and not on the interest earned. (p. 740)

Soft data Information that is subject to a high degree of uncertainty. (p. 731)

Time value of money* The amount of interest that is (or can be) earned on an investment for a given period of time. (p. 740)

► **GLOSSARY OF SYNONYMS**

Hurdle rate See **cutoff rate.**

Simple rate of return See **accounting rate of return.**

Target rate of return See **cutoff rate.**

Time-adjusted rate of return See **internal rate of return.**

► **REVIEW PROBLEM**

The management of Handy Pin Company is contemplating the purchase of a new machine (at a cost of $100,000) capable of producing 192,000 units per year. This machine can be sold for $20,000 and would replace a machine capable of producing 130,000 units per annum. The contribution margin per unit from operating the new machine is $.125, while it is $.10 per unit from operating the old machine.

The useful life of the old machine was 10 years when it was purchased 2 years ago. The useful life of the new machine is eight years. The new machine has a salvage value of $20,000, while the old machine's salvage value is zero. The old machine will require an overhaul at the end of two years from today at a cost of $10,000. The new machine will require an overhaul at the end of the fourth year at a cost of $8,000.

The firm's cutoff rate for investment decisions is 10 percent. Income taxes are to be ignored.

Required   *a.* Using the comparative income approach and net present value analysis, determine if the old machine should be replaced.

b. Redo part *(a),* using the differential income approach to reach your decision.

▶ **SOLUTION TO REVIEW PROBLEM**

a. Keep Old Machine:

Cash flow from operations (130,000 × $.10 × 5.33493)	$ 69,354
Opportunity cost of keeping old machine	(20,000)
Overhaul of machine—end of 2 years ($10,000 × .82645)	(8,264)
Net present value	$ 41,090

Purchase New Machine:

Cash flow from operations (192,000 × $.125 × 5.33493)	$ 128,038
Less: Purchase price of new machine	(100,000)
Overhaul—end of four years ($8,000 × .68301)	(5,464)
Plus: Salvage ($20,000 × .46651).	9,330
Net present value	$ 31,904

No. The old machine should be kept because its NPV is higher than that of the new machine.

b. Cash Operating Advantage:

Inflow from operations	
[(192,000 × $.125) − (130,000 × $.10)] × 5.33493	$ 58,684
Plus: Differential overhaul cost ($8,264 − $5,464)	2,800
	$ 61,484

Net investment:	
Purchase price of new machine	$(100,000)
Less: Proceeds from sale of old machine	20,000
	$ (80,000)
Incremental salvage value of new machine	
[($20,000 − $0) × .46651]	9,330
	$ (70,670)
Net present value ($61,484 − $70,670)	$ (9,186)

Because the return on investment in the new machine will be less than the firm's cutoff rate, the project should be rejected.

▶ **LIBRARY ASSIGNMENT**

Read the following:

Bavishi, Vinod B. "Capital Budgeting Practices at Multinationals." *Management Accounting,* August 1981, pp. 32–35.

Fremgen, James M. "Capital Budgeting Practices: A Survey." *Management Accounting,* May 1973, pp. 19–25.

Gordon, Lawrence A., and Mary D. Myers. "Postauditing Capital Projects." *Management Accounting,* January 1991, pp. 39–42.

Kim, Suk H., and Edward J. Farragher. "Current Capital Budgeting Practices." *Management Accounting,* June 1981, pp. 26–30.

Roth, Harold P., and Robert M. Brown. "Post-Auditing Capital Investments Using IRR and NPV Models." *Management Accounting,* February 1982, pp. 29–33.

Sale, J. Timothy, and Robert W. Scapens. "The Control of Capital Investment in Divisionalized Companies." *Management Accounting,* October 1982, pp. 24–29.

▸ **SELF-TEST**

True or False

1. The internal rate of return is a discounted cash flow technique.
2. When the NPV amount is zero, the project should be adopted because it is yielding a rate higher than the cost of capital.
3. When the NPV amount is negative, the project should not be adopted because the project is yielding a rate that is lower than the cost of capital.
4. Present value of an annuity is the summation of a series of future cash flows which have been restated into today's dollars.
5. Another name for the accounting rate of return is the internal rate of return.
6. The cutoff rate is the minimum rate of return that an investment must yield before the firm will adopt it.
7. The project with the highest positive NPV is always the best project to be adopted.
8. Hard data consist of information that is subject to a relative low degree of uncertainty.
9. The cost of a new asset is an example of soft data.
10. Payback measures the discounted cash inflows of a project.

Multiple Choice

1. What discount rate will result in the lowest net present value for a project?
   a. Any rate greater than the cost of capital.
   b. The highest rate used to evaluate the proposal.
   c. The lowest rate used to evaluate the proposal.
   d. Any rate lower than the cost of capital.
2. Suppose the net present value (NPV) of a project is calculated using the internal rate of return instead of the original discount rate. The NPV of the project would be
   a. Equal to the NPV computed using the original discount rate.
   b. Less than the NPV computed using the original discount rate.
   c. Greater than the NPV computed using the original discount rate.
   d. Equal to zero.
3. If the internal rate of return is less than the discount rate used to obtain the net present value of a project, then the net present value is
   a. Positive.
   b. Negative.
   c. Zero.
   d. Either positive or negative.
4. One reason for using preference selection to rank projects is
   a. To select the most profitable projects in terms of accounting income.
   b. To eliminate projects with an internal rate of return greater than the cost of capital.
   c. To eliminate unprofitable or high-risk investments.
   d. Because firms do not have unlimited capital to invest.
5. If annual cash flows are uniform, payback is equal to
   a. Net investment divided by discounted annual cash flow.
   b. Annual cash flow divided by net investment.
   c. Discounted net investment divided by annual cash flow.
   d. Net investment divided by annual cash flow.

Use the following information to answer questions 6–8.

McSweeney Co. is planning to purchase a computer for a computer-integrated manufacturing process. Information on two acceptable models is presented below:

	FRP290		GKA430		
Cost of mainframe and software	$120,000		$180,000		
Annual maintenance costs	10,000		4,000		
One-time training cost	15,000		0		
Salvage value	25,000		50,000		
Annual cost savings	70,000		70,000		
Useful life	6 years		6 years		

	8%	9%	10%	11%	12%
Present value of $1 in 6 years	0.63017	0.59627	0.56447	0.53464	0.50663
Present value of an annuity of $1 for 6 years	4.62288	4.48592	4.35526	4.23054	4.11141

McSweeney's cost of capital is 10 percent and income tax effects are not considered for capital budgeting decisions.

6. The NPV of Model FRP290 is
   a. $140,427.
   b. $227,530.
   c. $380,427.
   d. $410,427.
7. The NPV of Model GKA430 is
   a. $107,450.
   b. $135,671.
   c. $287,450.
   d. $495,670.
8. The payback period for Model FRP290 is
   a. 1.93 years.
   b. 2.00 years.
   c. 2.25 years.
   d. 2.33 years.

► **QUESTIONS**

1. What is capital budgeting?
2. What is the difference between the screening and preference-selection decisions associated with capital budgeting?
3. What is the discounted cash flow model?
4. What is the net present value approach to capital budgeting?
5. What is the internal rate of return approach to capital budgeting? How does it differ from the net present value approach?
6. What is a firm's cost of capital?
7. What is a cutoff rate? How is it used?
8. When the net present value method is used, the answer may be positive, zero, or negative. Explain what each one means.
9. When a firm is contemplating the purchase of a piece of equipment and the vendor offers the firm a financing rate of 12 percent, should the firm use this rate if it differs from its cost-of-capital rate? Why?
10. What is the underlying assumption of the net present value method?
11. What is the underlying assumption of the internal rate of return? How does it differ from that associated with the net present value method?
12. Explain how the profitability index is computed and used. Are there limitations associated with this method? Discuss.
13. When dealing with uncertainty, managers must often evaluate both hard data and soft data. Discuss.

14. Is it important to audit capital-budgeting results? Why?

15. What is the payback method? How is it computed? Does it have any severe limitations? If so, what are they?

16. The payback method is a popular screening method. How do you explain its popularity?

17. What is the accounting rate of return method? How is it computed? Does it have any serious limitations? Discuss.

18. The accounting rate of return takes depreciation into account, but the discounted cash flow methods do not. Therefore, the discounted cash flow methods are inferior to the accounting rate of return method. Discuss.

▸ **EXERCISES**   E14–1   **Calculating the Present Value of a Machine Purchase**

The Mayfair Company purchased a machine that has an estimated useful life of six years and is expected to have a salvage value of $6,500 at the end of that time. Mayfair expects to save $8,000 in operating costs each year by using the new machine. The internal rate of return promised by the machine's vendor is 16 percent.

Required   *a.* Compute the cost of the machine.

b. Should the machine have been purchased if the firm's cost of capital is
(1) 14 percent? Why?
(2) 16 percent? Why?
(3) 18 percent? Why?

E14–2   **Present Value Computations**

1. Tracy Corporation is planning to invest $80,000 in a three-year project. Tracy's expected rate of return is 10 percent. The present value of $1 at 10 percent for one year is .909, for two years is .826, and for three years is .751. The cash flow, net of income taxes, will be $30,000 for the first year (present value of $27,270) and $36,000 for the second year (present value of $29,736). Assuming the rate of return is exactly 10 percent, what will the cash flow, net of income taxes, be for the third year?
   a. $17,268.
   b. $22,000.
   c. $22,994.
   d. $30,618.

2. Hilldale Company purchased a machine for $480,000. The machine has a useful life of six years and no salvage value. Straight-line depreciation is to be used. The machine is expected to generate cash flow from operations, net of income taxes, of $140,000 in each of the six years. Hilldale's desired rate of return is 14 percent. Information on present value factors is as follows:

Period	Present Value of $1 at 14 Percent	Present Value of Ordinary Annuity of $1 at 14 Percent
1.	.877	0.877
2.	.769	1.647
3.	.675	2.322
4.	.592	2.914
5.	.519	3.433
6.	.456	3.889

What would be the net present value?
a. $63,840.
b. $64,460.

     c. $218,880.

     d. $233,340.

3. Hamilton Company invested in a two-year project having an internal rate of return of 12 percent. The project is expected to produce cash flow from operations, net of income taxes, of $60,000 in the first year and $70,000 in the second year. The present value of $1 for one period at 12 percent is 0.893 and for two periods at 12 percent is 0.797. How much will the project cost?

     a. $103,610.

     b. $109,370.

     c. $116,090.

     d. $122,510.

4. Kipling Company invested in an eight-year project. It is expected that the annual cash flow from the project, net of income taxes, will be $20,000. Information on present value factors is as follows:

> Present value of $1 at 12% for 8 periods. 0.404
> Present value of an ordinary annuity of $1 at 12%
>   for 8 periods 4.968

     Assuming Kipling based its investment decision on an internal rate of return of 12 percent, how much did the project cost?

     a. $160,000.

     b. $99,360.

     c. $80,800.

     d. $64,640.

5. Scott, Inc., is planning to invest $120,000 in a 10-year project. Scott estimates that the annual cash inflow, net of income taxes, from this project will be $20,000. Scott's desired rate of return on investments of this type is 10 percent. Information on present value factors is as follows:

	At 10 Percent	At 12 Percent
Present value of $1 for 10 periods.	0.386	0.322
Present value of an annuity of $1 for 10 periods	6.145	5.650

     Scott's expected rate of return on this investment is

     a. Less than 10 percent, but more than 0 percent.

     b. 10 percent.

     c. Less than 12 percent, but more than 10 percent.

     d. 12 percent.

(AICPA Adapted)

E14–3   **Net Present Value Analysis for Competing Investments and Profitability Index**

Central State University has decided that to remain competitive with other local colleges and universities, it must expand and update its computer science department. State is convinced that to accomplish this, it must purchase a new central processing unit (CPU). Officials of the school have been negotiating with two main-frame manufacturers, JCN Corporation and CNR Technologies. The representative of JCN Corporation has advised State that its model ZIPPY 1000 would be appropriate for the school's needs. The cost of the machine would be $1.3 million. In 10 years, the machine would be obsolete, at which time it would have a disposal value of

$130,000. After a detailed study, the representative has convinced State that additional student revenues and savings from administrative costs would provide a net cash inflow of $260,000 annually.

The representative of CNR Technologies is offering State its model SPEEDY 250 at a cost of $1.95 million. The SPEEDY 250 would also be obsolete in 10 years but would have a disposal value of $325,000. Net cash inflow from this machine would be $325,000 per year.

Required   *a.* Assuming Central State desires a 12 percent return on its investment, use the net present value concept to determine which machine the school should purchase.

          b. Compute the profitability index for each investment. Is your answer the same as in part *(a)*? Is this always true? Explain.

E14–4   Net Present Value and Internal Rate of Return

The Marlow Auto Repair Company is contemplating the purchase of electronic testing equipment, which will enable the firm to perform emission-control inspections. The equipment has a useful life of 10 years, no salvage value, and can be purchased at a cost of $83,849.

Marlow estimates that revenues from inspections will be $60,000 per annum and direct labor and variable overhead costs will be $40,000 per annum.

Required   *a.* Compute the internal rate of return for this investment.

          b. Compute the net present value for each of the following discount rates, and indicate whether the investment should be made at that rate:

            (1) 18 percent.

            (2) 20 percent.

            (3) 22 percent.

          c. Reconsider the net present value computed in part *(b2)*. What is the significance of that net present value?

E14–5   Competing Investments and Net Present Value

The Driscoll Company has $300,000 to invest. The plant superintendent has suggested purchasing a new, more efficient machine. On the other hand, the financial vice president would like the firm to purchase a competing firm's customer list, which is for sale. The machine has a useful life of five years, and the customer list is also expected to yield cash flows for a five-year period. Neither investment is expected to have any residual value.

The projected cash advantage per annum for each investment is:

Year	Machine	Customer List
19x1	$180,000	$ 60,000
19x2	150,000	120,000
19x3	120,000	150,000
19x4	90,000	180,000
19x5	60,000	210,000
Total.	$600,000	$720,000

Required   *a.* Using a cutoff rate of 22 percent, calculate the net present value of each investment. If only one investment can be made, which would you choose? Why?

          b. Redo part *(a)*, but this time use a cutoff rate of 18 percent. Does your answer differ from that in part *(a)*? Explain.

E14–6   Net Present Value and Internal Rate of Return

The Building Corporation, a heavy-construction business, is interested in replacing one of its backhoes with a new model. The new equipment costs $325,000 and has an expected useful life of 10 years. At the end of its useful life, the equipment will have a salvage value of $20,000. Due to increased efficiency, the company expects to save 1,000 hours per year in labor costs. A backhoe operator earns $50 per hour, including fringe benefits.

The manufacturer is offering a $40,000 trade-in allowance on the old equipment, which has a current book value of $195,000 and a zero disposal value at the end of its useful life in 10 years. Building Corporation desires a return of at least 14 percent on its investments.

Required   *a.* Using net present value analysis, determine whether Building Corporation should purchase the equipment.

b. Compute the internal rate of return for this investment, interpolating to the nearest two decimal places.

E14–7   Calculation of Present Value and Future Value

Crown Corporation has agreed to sell some used computer equipment to Bob Parsons, one of the company's employees, for $5,000. Crown and Parsons have been discussing alternative financing arrangements for the sale and the present and future values of each alternative. The following information is pertinent to these discussions.

1. Crown Corporation has offered to accept a $1,000 down payment and set up a note receivable for Bob Parsons that calls for four $1,000 payments at the end of each of the next four years. If Crown uses a 6 percent discount rate, the present value of the note receivable would be
   a. $3,960.
   b. $3,168.
   c. $4,212.
   d. $3,465.
   e. $4,465.
2. Bob Parsons has agreed to the immediate down payment of $1,000 but would like the note for $4,000 to be payable in full at the end of the fourth year. Because of the increased risk associated with the terms of this note, Crown Corporation would apply an 8 percent discount rate. The present value of this note would be
   a. $2,940.
   b. $3,312.
   c. $3,940.
   d. $3,675.
   e. $3,852.
3. If Bob Parsons borrowed the $5,000 at 8 percent interest for four years from his bank and paid Crown Corporation the full price of the equipment immediately, Crown could invest the $5,000 for three years at 7 percent. The future value of this investment (rounded) would be
   a. $6,297.
   b. $6,125.
   c. $6,553.
   d. $6,803.
   e. $5,902.

(CMA Adapted)

E14–8   **Simplified Internal Rate of Return**

The Commerce Company is contemplating the purchase of two machines, X–1 and X–2. The cost of X–1 is $128,649, and the cost of X–2 is $307,800. The useful life of X–1 is 7 years, and the useful life of X–2 is 10 years; neither machine will have a salvage value. The cash operating advantages (cash inflows) are $30,000 per annum for X–1 and $66,000 per annum for X–2.

Interpolation should be carried to two decimal places.

Required   *a.* Compute the internal rate of return for machine X–1, using the simplified method.

b. Compute the internal rate of return for machine X–2, using the simplified method.

E14–9   **Profitability Index**

The Mandrin Company is considering four different projects that are mutually exclusive (i.e., only one project will be selected). All four projects have the same useful life, eight years, and no salvage value. The investments and the promised cash inflows are:

	Project			
	G	**H**	**J**	**K**
Investment.	$52,000	$39,000	$45,500	$58,500
Cash inflow per annum . . .	13,975	9,100	11,700	15,600

The firm's cost of capital is 15 percent.

Required   *a.* Calculate and rank the net present value for each project. Which project would you select on the basis of this ranking?

b. Calculate and rank the profitability index for each project. Which project would you select on the basis of this ranking? Is the answer the same as in part *(a)*? If not, explain the reason for the difference.

E14–10   **Auditing Capital-Budgeting Results**

Firms generally use capital-budgeting evaluation techniques for (1) purchasing new equipment, (2) replacing existing equipment, and (3) entering a new market. Failure to follow up a capital-budgeting project after its implementation may have negative short-run and long-run implications for a firm.

Required   *a.* What benefits could a company derive from a postimplementation audit?

b. What difficulties are likely to be encountered in accumulating the data needed to conduct a postimplementation audit?

E14–11   **Payback and Net Present Value**

The Patron Company is contemplating an investment in one of three possible projects. All three require the same amount of investment, $225,000, and none of the three has a salvage value. The useful life of five years is the same for all three projects.

The cash operating advantages (cash inflows) for the three projects are as follows:

	Project		
Year	L	M	N
19x1	$ 90,000	$ 30,000	$(15,000)
19x2	90,000	60,000	75,000
19x3	90,000	90,000	135,000
19x4	90,000	225,000	300,000
19x5	90,000	150,000	90,000
Total . . .	$450,000	$555,000	$585,000

The firm's cost of capital is 18 percent.

Required *a.* Calculate the payback period for each project. Rank them using payback.
b. Calculate the net present value for each project. Rank them by using net present value.
c. Is there a relationship between payback and net present value for these three projects? Explain.

E14–12 **Payback and Net Present Value**

The Edward Company is contemplating an investment in one of three possible projects. All three require the same amount of investment, $120,000, and none of the three has a salvage value. The useful life of five years is the same for all three projects.

The cash operating advantages (cash inflows) for the three projects are as follows:

	Project		
Year	A	B	C
19x1	$ 60,000	$ 40,000	$ 25,000
19x2	60,000	80,000	50,000
19x3	60,000	80,000	90,000
19x4	60,000	50,000	125,000
19x5	60,000	50,000	60,000
Total . . .	$300,000	$300,000	$350,000

The firm's cost of capital is 12 percent.

Required *a.* Calculate the payback period for each project. Rank them using payback.
b. Calculate the net present value for each project. Rank them by using net present value.
c. Is there a relationship between payback and net present value for these three projects? Explain.

E14–13 **Accounting Rate of Return and Payback**

1. The Herb Company acquired a new machine for $16,000 that it will depreciate on a straight-line basis over a 10-year period. A full year's depreciation was taken in the year of acquisition. The accounting (book value) rate of return is expected to be 12 percent on the initial increase in required investment. If we

assume a uniform cash inflow, the annual cash flow from operations, net of income taxes, will be

a. $320.
b. $1,728.
c. $1,920.
d. $3,520.

2. The Fudge Company is planning to purchase a new machine that it will depreciate on a straight-line basis over a 10-year period with no salvage value. A full year's depreciation will be taken in the year of acquisition. The new machine is expected to produce cash flow from operations, net of income taxes, of $66,000 a year in each of the next 10 years. The accounting (book value) rate of return on the initial investment is expected to be 12 percent. How much will the new machine cost?

a. $300,000.
b. $550,000.
c. $660,000.
d. $792,000.

3. Saratoga Company is planning to purchase a new machine for $600,000. The new machine will be depreciated on the straight-line basis over a six-year period with no salvage, and a full year's depreciation will be taken in the year of acquisition. The new machine is expected to produce cash flow from operations, net of income taxes, of $150,000 a year in each of the next six years. The accounting (book value) rate of return on the initial investment is expected to be

a. 8.3 percent.
b. 12.0 percent.
c. 16.7 percent.
d. 25.0 percent.

(AICPA Adapted)

E14–14 **Accounting Rate of Return**

Boyle Industries uses the accounting rate of return to evaluate its investments in fixed assets. The following data regarding three alternative projects under consideration are available:

Project	Initial Investment	Annual Cash Inflow	Useful Life	Income Taxes
A.	$105,000	$25,500	7 years	$4,200
B.	96,000	21,750	8	3,900
C.	108,000	27,000	6	3,600

Required Using the average investment, determine which project would yield the highest return.

E14–15 **(Appendix 14-A) Using Future Value Compound-Interest Tables**

1. James Martin borrowed $15,000 from his employer for a period of four years. Compute the maturity value of the loan if the interest rate is 12 percent and the compounding is calculated

a. Annually.
b. Semiannually.
c. Quarterly.

2. Mitchell Lawrence plans to retire in 10 years. He plans to deposit $6,000 per annum into a pension plan. How much will he have at retirement if he can earn 10 percent annually and the compounding is calculated
   a. Annually?
   b. Semiannually? (Assume the deposit of $6,000 will be made in two installments of $3,000 each.)

E14–16   **(Appendix 14-A) Using Present Value Compound-Interest Tables**

1. Linda Brooke expects to retire in five years. At that time, she would like to take an extensive trip estimated to cost $30,000. She believes she can earn 12 percent interest during the five-year period. How much money should she deposit today to have the $30,000 available if interest is compounded
   a. Annually?
   b. Semiannually?
   c. Quarterly?
2. Marshall Burton plans to retire in 10 years. At that time, he would like to purchase an annuity from an insurance company that will provide him with $80,000 annually for a period of 12 years. How much will he have to deposit 10 years from now if the interest rate allowed by the insurance company is 10 percent per annum and it is compounded
   a. Annually?
   b. Semiannually? (Assume the $80,000 will be paid twice per annum at $40,000 per payment.)

E14–17   **(Appendix 14-A) Using Compound-Interest Tables**

1. Charles Philip plans to retire in 10 years. At that time, he would like to have $300,000 available to purchase a home in a retirement community. How much should he deposit at the end of each year for the next 10 years to have the $300,000 if he can earn interest at 11 percent compounded annually?
2. Rita Sutton has a 10-year-old daughter. The mother expects her daughter to attend college in eight years. It is estimated that college tuition will then be $40,000 per annum for the four years. How much should the mother deposit at the end of each year during the next eight years to provide for the college tuition if the fund can earn interest at the rate of 12 percent per annum compounded annually? (*Hint:* Consider the annual tuition of $40,000 as one part of the solution and the amount to contribute to the fund as the other part of the solution.)

E14–18   **(Appendix 14-A) Using Compound-Interest Tables**

1. Ronald Samuels entered a giveaway contest and won first prize. The winner can elect to receive the prize in one of four ways. They are
   a. $300,000 in one sum today.
   b. $480,000 at the end of five years.
   c. $78,000 at the end of each year for five years, the first payment commencing one year from now.
   d. $48,000 at the end of each year for 10 years, the first payment commencing 1 year from now.
      Assume Samuels can earn 10 percent interest per annum compounded annually. Income tax considerations are to be ignored. Which option should Samuels take? Why?
      Would your answer be different if the first payment in options *(c)* and *(d)* were to commence today? Why?
2. Gabriel Shane won a lottery. The lottery advertises a jackpot of $10 million. Payments are made at the rate of $500,000 per annum for 20 years. If money

can be invested at 12 percent and the payments are made at the end of each year, how much did Shane really win?

E14–19   **(Appendix 14-A) Using Compound-Interest Tables**

Ralph Hunter is contemplating the purchase of a $50,000 bond that matures in 15 years (i.e., the face value of $50,000 will be paid at maturity). The bond pays interest annually, at the end of each year. The amount of the interest paid is $4,000. Hunter wishes to earn 10 percent on his investment.

Required   *a.* How much should Hunter pay for the bond to earn 10 percent?

b. Using the same procedure you used in part *(a),* calculate the price Hunter should pay for the bond if he is willing to earn only 8 percent on his investment. How do you explain your answer?

▶ **PROBLEMS**   **P14–20**   **Net Present Value Analysis for Purchasing a New Machine and Replacing an Existing Machine**

The Montana Corporation is presently using a machine, M–1, in its production process. It is contemplating the purchase of a newer, more efficient machine, M–2. The following information is available:

	M–1	M–2
Purchase price	$750,000	$1,500,000
Useful life	15 years	10 years
Salvage value	$ 75,000	$ 120,000
Sales revenue	750,000	1,050,000
Direct materials cost	135,000	160,000
Direct labor	225,000	194,000
Variable overhead	135,000	120,000
Direct fixed overhead	105,000	135,000

Income taxes are to be ignored. The firm's cutoff rate for investments is 18 percent.

Required   *a.* Assume the Montana Corporation is contemplating the purchase of M–2 and also intends to keep M–1. There is a sufficient market for the firm's output from both machines. Prepare schedules to compute:

(1) The net investment of M–2.

(2) The cash operating advantage of M–2.

(3) The net present value to determine if M–2 should be purchased. Should M–2 be purchased? Why?

b. Assume market conditions are such that the corporation can sell the output from M–2 or M–1 but not both. Thus, if M–2 is purchased, M–1 will be sold for $200,000. Using differential analysis, prepare schedules to compute

(1) The net investment of M–2.

(2) The cash operating advantage of M–2.

(3) The net present value to determine if M–1 should be replaced. Should M–1 be replaced? Why?

P14–21   **Discussion of Net Present Value, IRR, Payback, and Profitability Index**

Franklin Industries comprises four divisions, each operating in a different industry. The divisions are currently preparing their capital expenditure budgets for the coming year. Caledonia Division, located in the northeast United States, manufactures home appliances that it distributes nationally. The manufacturing and marketing departments of Caledonia have proposed six capital expenditure projects for next year. The division manager must now analyze these investment proposals and select those projects that will be included in the capital budget to be submitted to Franklin Industries for approval. The proposed projects are listed below and are considered to have the same degree of risk.

▶ *Project A*: Redesign and modify an existing product that is currently scheduled to be dropped. The enhanced model would be sold for six more years.
▶ *Project B*: Expand a line of cookware that has been produced on an experimental basis for the past year. The expected life of the cookware line is eight years.
▶ *Project C*: Reorganize the plant's distribution center, including the installation of computerized equipment for tracking inventory. This project would benefit both administration and marketing.
▶ *Project D*: Add a new product, a combination bread and meat slicer. In addition to new manufacturing equipment, a significant amount of introductory advertising would be required. If this project is implemented, Project A would not be feasible due to limited capacity.
▶ *Project E*: Automate the packaging department that would result in cost savings over the next six years.
▶ *Project F*: Construct a building wing to house offices presently located in an area that could be used for manufacturing. The change would not add capacity for new lines but would alleviate crowded conditions that currently exist, making it possible to improve the productivity of two existing product lines that have been unable to meet market demand.

Franklin Industries has established a hurdle rate of 12 percent for capital expenditures for all four divisions. Additional information about each of the proposed projects is presented below.

CALEDONIA DIVISION
Proposed Capital Projects

Required Investment and Operating Cash Flows by Project

	Project A	Project B	Project C	Project D	Project E	Project F
Capital investment	$106,000	$200,000	$140,000	$160,000	$144,000	$130,000
Operating Cash Flows						
Year 1	$ 50,000	$ 20,000	$ 36,000	$ 20,000	$ 50,000	$ 40,000
Year 2	50,000	40,000	36,000	30,000	50,000	40,000
Year 3	40,000	50,000	36,000	40,000	50,000	40,000
Year 4	40,000	60,000	36,000	50,000	20,000	40,000
Year 5	30,000	60,000	36,000	60,000	20,000	40,000
Year 6	40,000	60,000		70,000	11,600	40,000
Year 7		40,000		80,000		40,000
Year 8		44,000		66,000		42,000
Total cash flows	$250,000	$374,000	$180,000	$416,000	$201,600	$322,000
Additional Project Information						
Present value of operating cash flow at 12%	$175,683	$223,773	$129,772	$234,374	$150,027	$199,513
Net present value at 12%	$ 69,683	$ 23,773	$(10,228)	$ 74,374	$ 6,027	$ 69,513
Present value index (profitability index)	1.66	1.12	.93	1.46	1.04	1.53
Internal rate of return	35%	15%	9%	22%	14%	26%
Payback period	2.2 years	4.5 years	3.9 years	4.3 years	2.9 years	3.3 years
Economic life	6 years	8 years	5 years	8 years	6 years	8 years

Required   *a.* Explain how each of the following techniques is used in evaluating capital expenditure proposals and what it is designed to measure.

1. Net present value.
2. Internal rate of return.
3. Payback.
4. Profitability index.

b. If Caledonia Division has no budget restrictions for capital expenditures and has been told to maximize the value to the company, identify the capital investment projects that should be included in the Division's capital budget submitted to Franklin Industries. Explain the basis for your selection.

c. Without prejudice to your response to part (b), assume that Franklin Industries has restricted Caledonia Division to a maximum of $450,000 for capital expenditures and that Caledonia should select projects that maximize the value to the company. Further, assume that any budget not spent on the identified projects will be invested at the hurdle rate. Identify the capital investment projects Caledonia should include in its capital expenditures budget submitted to Franklin in this situation, and explain the basis for your selection.

d. Discuss the propriety of using the same hurdle rate for all four divisions of Franklin Industries.

(CMA Adapted)

P14–22 Net Present Value Analysis for Replacing Equipment—Comparative Income Approach

The Nebraska Corporation is presently using a machine purchased eight years ago, K–1, in its production process. It is contemplating the purchase of a newer, more efficient machine, K–9. The following information is available:

	K–1	K–9
Purchase price	$156,000	$240,000
Useful life	12 years	8 years
Salvage value	$ 12,000	$ 10,000
Present resale value.	72,000	
Sales revenue	120,000	145,000
Direct materials cost	24,000	29,000
Direct labor	29,000	22,000
Variable overhead	14,000	11,000
Direct fixed overhead	24,000	26,000
Cost to overhaul K–1 to extend its remaining life of 4 years by 4 additional years, for a total of 8 years.	36,000	

Income taxes are to be ignored. The firm's cutoff rate for investments is 14 percent.

Required a. Using the comparative income approach, compute the following:
  (1) The net investment of purchasing K–9.
  (2) The cash operating advantage of K–9.
  (3) The net present value to determine if K–9 should be purchased.

b. Using the comparative income approach, compute the following:
  (1) The net investment of retaining K–1. (*Hint:* Use K–1's opportunity cost.)
  (2) The cash operating advantage of K–1.
  (3) The net present value to determine if K–1 should be retained.

c. Should K–9 be purchased and K–1 sold? Why?

P14–23 Comparative Income and Differential Income Approaches to Net Present Value Analysis of Replacing a Machine

The management of Universal Technical Systems is contemplating the purchase of a new machine (at a cost of $300,000) that is capable of producing 288,000 units per year. This machine can be sold for $60,000 and would replace a machine capable of producing 195,000 units per annum. The contribution margin per unit from operating the new machine is $.25, and it is $.20 per unit from operating the old machine.

The useful life of the old machine was 10 years when it was purchased 2 years ago. The useful life of the new machine is eight years. The new machine has a salvage value of $60,000, and the old machine's salvage value is zero. The old machine will require an overhaul at the end of two years from today at a cost of $30,000. The new machine will require an overhaul at the end of the fourth year at a cost of $24,000.

The firm's cutoff rate for investment decisions is 10 percent. Income taxes are to be ignored.

Required   *a.* Using the comparative income approach and net present value analysis, determine if the old machine should be replaced.

b. Redo part *(a),* using the differential income approach to reach your decision.

P14–24   **Comparative Income and Differential Income Approaches to Net Present Value Analysis of Replacing a Machine**

Carmel Company purchased a machine two years ago at a cost of $2.4 million. At that time, the equipment had a useful life of 12 years and a salvage value of $320,000. At the end of the fifth year (three years from now), the equipment is due for a $240,000 overhaul. Estimated cash inflow from the equipment is $112,000 per year. The company is considering the purchase of newer equipment as a replacement. The cost of the new equipment would be $4.16 million. The equipment manufacturer is offering a trade-in allowance of $480,000 for the old equipment. The new equipment represents state-of-the-art technology, and the company expects productivity savings of $608,000 per year over the old equipment. The new equipment will have a useful life of 10 years and a disposal value of $800,000. The company considers a return of less than 12 percent on investments unacceptable.

Required   *a.* Using the comparative income approach and net present value analysis, determine if the old machine should be replaced.

b. Redo part *(a),* using the differential income approach to reach your decision.

P14–25   **Differential Income Approach and Net Present Value Analysis for Purchasing a New Machine and Replacing an Existing Machine**

The Oregon Corporation is presently using two machines, K–1 and K–2, in its production process. It is contemplating the purchase of an automated, more efficient machine, K–5. The following information is available:

	K–1	K–2	K–5
Purchase price	$ 160,000	$ 224,000	$ 480,000
Useful life	10 years	7 years	5 years
Salvage value	$ 16,000	$ 22,400	$ 48,000
Accumulated depreciation:			
K–1 ($144,000 ÷ 10 years = $14,400 per annum; $14,400 × 5 years).	72,000		
K–2 ($201,600 ÷ 7 years = $28,800 per annum; $28,800 × 2 years).		57,600	
Depreciation per annum	14,400	28,800	86,400
Sales revenue	1,280,000	1,280,000	1,280,000
Direct materials cost	256,000	256,000	256,000
Direct labor.	360,000	360,000	192,000
Variable overhead	128,000	128,000	76,800
Direct fixed overhead	256,000	256,000	320,000

At present, the company uses the K–2 machine as its principal machine, while the K–1 machine is used only when the K–2 is down for repairs and maintenance. The K–1 machine is occasionally used when the firm is very busy and must add a special shift of employees. The K–1 and K–2 machines are similar, except the K–1 is older and better constructed. Actually, the K–1 is in better condition in some respects. At the present time, they both have the same resale value of $96,000.

Income taxes are to be ignored. The firm's cutoff rate on investments is 16 percent.

Required   *a.* Assume the Oregon Corporation is contemplating the purchase of K–5 and also intends to keep both K–1 and K–2. There is a sufficient market for the firm's output from all machines. Prepare schedules to compute:
   (1) The net investment of K–5.
   (2) The cash operating advantage of K–5.
   (3) The net present value to determine if K–5 should be purchased. Should K–5 be purchased? Why?

   b. Assume market conditions are such that the corporation can sell the output from K–5 or K–2 but not both. Thus, if K–5 is purchased, either K–1 or K–2 will be sold, and the one not sold will be used as a spare for K–5. Using the differential income approach, prepare schedules to compute:
   (1) The net investment of K–5.
   (2) The cash operating advantage of K–5.
   (3) The net present value to determine if K–5 should be purchased and either K–1 or K–2 sold. Should K–5 be purchased? Why?

P14–26   **Comparative Income and Differential Income Approaches to Net Present Value Analysis of Replacing a Machine**

The Canals Company is considering the purchase of a new piece of equipment (machine B) to use in its manufacturing process as a replacement for an old machine (machine A). Operating costs for machine A have been running at an average annual rate of $90,000. At the end of its useful life, five years from now, machine A will have a disposal value of $9,000. Three years from now, machine A will be due for a complete overhaul at a cost of $22,500. The market value of this machine is currently $54,000. It was purchased five years ago and is being depreciated by the straight-line method.

Machine B will cost the company $90,000 and have a disposal value of $7,000 at the end of its five-year useful life. The operating costs for this machine are estimated to be $60,000 annually.

Income taxes are to be ignored, and the company uses a cutoff rate of 18 percent for this kind of investment.

Required   *a.* Using the comparative income approach, compute the net present value to determine if machine A should be replaced. Should machine A be replaced? Why?

   b. Redo part *(a),* using the differential income approach to reach your decision.

P14–27   **Net Present Value Analysis for Entering a New Market**

The Aromatic Company, which produces inexpensive automatic coffeemakers, is thinking of introducing a new line of expensive automatic coffeemakers that will both grind the coffee beans and brew the coffee. A market survey indicates that there is only a limited market for this product because of its high cost and estimates that after five years, there will be no market at all.

The following annual information about the new product is available to you:

Estimated sales (15,000 × $80)	$1,200,000
Cost of direct materials and direct labor	400,000
Variable overhead	112,000
Variable marketing costs	60,000
Direct fixed overhead, marketing, and administrative costs	240,000

Additional information:

Price of new machine	$1,200,000
Salvage value at the end of 5 years	16,000
Working capital needed at inception	112,000
Working capital returned at the end of 5 years	104,000
Depreciation of new machinery per annum	76,800

Income taxes are to be ignored. The firm's cutoff rate is 14 percent.

Required   *a.* Which of the above data is relevant to you in recommending whether Aromatic should enter this new market?

b. Using net present value analysis, determine if it is advantageous for Aromatic to enter this new market.

P14–28   **Purchasing an Existing Business, Net Present Value Analysis**

Sparky Little is working in the accounting department of a large corporation. It appears that Little's progress is blocked, and he would like to try something else. Several evenings each week, Little visits a tavern called Archer's Place. One evening when Little was feeling very discouraged, he learned that the tavern was for sale, and in the conversation that followed, Archer offered to sell the tavern to Little.

Archer has a 10-year assignable lease of the property. Little hired an engineering consultant to evaluate the equipment, and it was determined that the refrigeration unit would require an overhaul at a cost of $12,000 in five years.

Archer is asking $240,000 for the leasehold and equipment. The equipment should be worth about $48,000 at the end of the 10-year lease.

Little engaged the services of a CPA to review the tavern's records. The CPA is confident that the tavern will yield $48,000 in cash flow for the coming year. Little is equally confident that he can increase cash flow each year by 10 percent over the preceding year's cash flow. Working capital of $36,000 will be needed during the 10 years of operation and will be released at the end of the lease.

Income taxes are to be ignored. Little will only purchase the tavern if it yields a return of 18 percent or more.

Required   Using net present value analysis at the 18 percent cutoff rate, determine if Little should purchase the tavern.

P14–29   **Simplified Calculation of Internal Rate of Return**

The Berry Company is considering the purchase of one of two machines. The following information regarding each machine is available:

	Machine X	Machine Y
Cost	$360,000	$480,000
Useful life	15 years	20 years
Annual production	420,000 units	570,000 units
Contribution margin per unit	30 cents	32 cents
Direct annual fixed costs	$ 72,000	$108,000
Salvage value	–0–	–0–

The company is capable of selling all of the output produced by either machine. Income taxes are to be ignored.

Required   *a.* Calculate the internal rate of return within two decimal places for each machine. Which machine should be purchased if the firm's cutoff rate is 12 percent?

b. The machines have different useful lives. What assumption is implicit when competing projects have unequal lives and the internal rate of return is used to evaluate the projects?

P14–30 **Profitability Index**

The Booker Company is evaluating several investment projects. The following information is available:

	Project			
	N	**O**	**P**	**Q**
Net investment	$300,000	$360,000	$240,000	$450,000
Net present value	$147,681	$123,675	$ 97,815	$225,360
Life of project in years	8	10	7	12
Internal rate of return	25%	20%	24%	22%

The company's cutoff rate is 12 percent. The maximum amount that the company plans to invest is $450,000.

Required
a. Compute the profitability index for each project.
b. Rank the projects according to
  (1) Net present value.
  (2) Internal rate of return.
  (3) Profitability index.
c. Explain why the rankings produce different preferences.
d. Which ranking is preferable? Why?

P14–31 **Payback, IRR, Net Present Value, and Profitability Index**

Spara Corp. is considering the various benefits that may result from shortening its product cycle by changing from the company's present manual system to a computer-aided design/computer-aided manufacturing (CAD/CAM) system. The proposed system can provide productive time equivalency close to the 20,000 hours currently available with the manual system. The incremental annual out-of-pocket costs of maintaining the manual system are $20 per hour.

The incremental annual out-of-pocket costs of maintaining the CAD/CAM system are estimated to be $250,000, with an initial investment of $480,000 in the proposed system. The estimated useful life of this system is six years. Spara requires a minimum return of 20 percent on projects of this type. Full capacity will be utilized.

Required
a. Compute the relevant annual cash flows related to the CAD/CAM project.
b. Based on the computation in part *(a)* above, compute the following:
  1. Payback period for recovery of investment.
  2. Internal rate of return.
  3. Net present value.
  4. Excess present value index (profitability index).

(AICPA Adapted)

P14–32 **Lease or Purchase**

The T&K Trucking Company's business is expanding, and the firm's management has decided that an additional truck is needed. The firm must decide whether to purchase or lease the truck.

Information regarding the purchase of the truck is as follows:

Purchase price	$96,000
Annual operating costs for maintenance, licenses, and fees	6,400
Annual repairs:	
Year 1	1,600
2	3,200
3	4,800
4	16,000
5	6,400
6	8,000
Useful life	6 years
Salvage value	$12,000

The truck can be leased for six years at an annual rental of $28,000 plus 30 cents per mile driven. The lessor will be responsible for repairs, maintenance, licenses, and fees. At the end of the lease term, the truck will be returned to the lessor.

The lessee is responsible for insurance and gasoline usage in either case. T&K normally uses the truck at the rate of 25,000 miles annually. Any damage to the truck is the responsibility of the lessee. The lessor requires a deposit of $12,000, which will be refunded at the end of the lease term if the truck is returned undamaged.

The cost of capital for T&K is 12 percent. Income taxes may be ignored.

Required   *a.* Using present value analysis, compute the cost of purchasing the truck.

b. Using present value analysis, compute the cost of leasing the truck for six years.

c. What choice do you recommend? Why?

P14–33   **Lease or Purchase**

The Sellmore Company hired an additional traveling sales rep. Because the firm's policy is to provide every salesperson with an automobile, Sellmore must decide whether to purchase or lease an automobile for the new sales rep.

Information regarding the purchase of the auto is as follows:

Purchase price	$20,000
Annual operating costs for maintenance, licenses, and fees	1,000
Annual repairs:	
Year 1	500
2	1,600
3	3,000
4	3,600
Useful life	4 years
Salvage value	$ 5,000

The automobile can be leased for four years at an annual rental of $7,000 plus 20 cents per mile driven in excess of 60,000 miles. The lessor will be responsible for repairs, maintenance, licenses, and fees. At the end of the lease term, the auto will be returned to the lessor, and the lessee will pay the excess mileage charge at that time.

The lessee is responsible for insurance and gasoline usage in either case. Sellmore expects its sales rep to use the automobile at the rate of 20,000 miles annually. Any damage to the auto is the responsibility of the lessee. The lessor requires a deposit of $5,000, which will be refunded at the end of the lease term if the auto is returned undamaged.

The cost of capital for Sellmore is 12 percent. Income taxes may be ignored.

Required   *a.* Using present value analysis, compute the cost of purchasing the automobile.
    b. Using present value analysis, compute the cost of leasing the automobile for four years.
    c. What choice do you recommend? Why?

P14–34   **Discontinuing a Segment of a Business and Net Present Value Analysis**

The Crum Company has two divisions: C and D. The firm's segmented income statement by divisions for the year 19x5 appears below:

CRUM COMPANY
Segmented Income Statement—Contribution Format
For the Year Ended December 31, 19x5

	Total	Division C	Division D
Sales	$1,500,000	$ 600,000	$900,000
Variable cost of goods sold	510,000	150,000	360,000
Variable cost manufacturing margin	990,000	450,000	540,000
Variable marketing costs	255,000	210,000	45,000
Contribution margin	735,000	240,000	495,000
Fixed costs	750,000	375,000	375,000
Operating income (loss) before income taxes	$ (15,000)	$(135,000)	$120,000

The president of the company is considering whether to cease operating Division C. She asks you to analyze the operations of the division so she can reach a decision regarding its future.

The following information is available for your analysis:

1. Division C's fixed costs consist of

Direct fixed costs	$225,000
Common costs	105,000
Depreciation of machinery	45,000
Total	$375,000

2. If Division C is discontinued, Division D can be expanded. The marketing department is fairly certain that Division D's sales can be increased by 30 percent. Variable costs at this level are expected to maintain their existing relationship.
3. The machinery used by Division C cannot be adapted to Division D's production. Thus, it must be sold in the secondhand market. Its resale value is $5,000.
4. New equipment will be required by Division D. Its cost is expected to amount to $510,000, with a useful life of 10 years. Salvage value at that time is projected at $45,000.
5. Division C has $60,000 of working capital, which will be released to Division D. An additional $15,000 of working capital will be required, for a total of $75,000. This amount will be released at the end of this expansion phase 10 years hence.

Income taxes are to be ignored. The firm's cutoff rate for investments is 14 percent.

Required   *a.* Using the differential income approach, compute
    (1) The net investment.
    (2) The cash operating advantage.

b. Using net present value analysis, determine if Division C should be discontinued and Division D should be expanded.

P14–35 **Payback, Net Present Value, Internal Rate of Return, Profitability Index, and Accounting Rate of Return**

The president of Carmel Company has asked you to evaluate an investment she is considering. Two machines, R and S, are under consideration. Only one machine will be purchased.

Information concerning the machines is as follows:

	Machine R	Machine S
Investment.	$320,000	$350,000
Annual cash operating advantage.	80,000	70,000
Useful life	10 years	15 years
Salvage value	–0–	–0–

Income taxes are to be ignored. The firm's cost of capital is 14 percent. The company uses straight-line depreciation.

Required *a.* For each machine, compute
(1) Payback.
(2) The net present value.
(3) The internal rate of return to two decimal places.
(4) The profitability index.
(5) The accounting rate of return using the gross investment as the base.
b. For each calculation in part *(a),* indicate your preference. Are they all consistent? Do they have to be consistent? Explain.

P14–36 **Payback, Net Present Value, Internal Rate of Return, Profitability Index, and Accounting Rate of Return**

The president of Camden Company has asked you to evaluate an investment he is considering. Two machines, T and V, are under consideration. Only one machine will be purchased.

Information concerning the machines is as follows:

	Machine T	Machine V
Investment.	$560,000	$700,000
Annual cash operating advantage.	140,000	135,000
Useful life	8 years	15 years
Salvage value	–0–	–0–

Income taxes are to be ignored. The firm's cost of capital is 14 percent. The company uses straight-line depreciation.

Required *a.* For each machine, compute
(1) Payback.
(2) The net present value.
(3) The internal rate of return to two decimal places.
(4) The profitability index.
(5) The accounting rate of return, using the gross investment as the base.
b. For each calculation in part *(a),* indicate your preference. Are they all consistent? Do they have to be consistent? Why?

P14–37 **Payback, Accounting Rate of Return, and Internal Rate of Return**

The Crest Service Station sells gasoline at the retail level and is contemplating the acquisition of an automatic car wash.

The following information is relevant to the acquisition of the car wash:

1. The cost of the car wash is $192,000.
2. The anticipated revenue from the car wash is $120,000 per annum.
3. The useful life of the car wash is 10 years.
4. Annual operating costs are expected to be:

Salaries	$36,000
Utilities	11,520
Water usage	5,280
Supplies	7,200
Repairs and maintenance . . .	12,000

5. The firm uses straight-line depreciation.
6. The salvage value for the car wash is zero.
7. The company's cutoff points are as follows:

Payback	3 years
Accounting rate of return	18%
Internal rate of return	18%

Ignore income taxes.

Required *a.* Compute the cash operating advantage.
b. Compute accounting operating income.
c. Compute payback.
d. Compute the accounting rate of return, using the gross investment as the base.
e. Compute the internal rate of return to the nearest two decimal places.
f. Should the car wash be purchased? Explain your answer.

P14–38 **Payback, Accounting Rate of Return, and Internal Rate of Return**

The operator of a self-service gasoline filling station is contemplating the addition of a convenience food store to the premises. The landlord has agreed to construct an addition to the building to house the food mart. The additional rent cost would amount to $72,000 per year.

Additional information is as follows:

1. Fixtures, refrigerators, and shelves would cost $375,000, with a useful life of eight years.
2. The expected sales are $1.5 million per annum, on which the contribution margin ratio is 30 percent.
3. Annual operating fixed costs are expected to be:

Salaries	$ 90,000
Utilities	27,000
Supplies	30,000
Repairs and maintenance	18,000
Other costs	120,000

4. The salvage value of the fixtures is expected to be zero, and straight-line depreciation is used.
5. The operator of the food mart plans to retire at the end of eight years.
6. The company's cutoff points are as follows:

Payback	4 years
Accounting rate of return	16%
Internal rate of return	16%

Ignore income taxes.

Required
a. Compute the cash operating advantage.
b. Compute accounting operating income.
c. Compute payback.
d. Compute the accounting rate of return, using the gross investment as the base.
e. Compute the internal rate of return to the nearest two decimal places.

▶ **CASE**   C14–39   ### Replacing Equipment—Purchase or Lease

Middleton University is a state-supported, tax-exempt institution. The university has decided to replace the computer used for Middleton's financial and administrative applications. The current computer is more than eight years old and can no longer serve the university's needs adequately.

Donald Abel, vice president of finance, prepared the analysis of the proposed computer that was submitted to Middleton's Board of Regents. The analysis indicated that the new computer would provide the university with annual cost savings of $400,000, excluding the computer's maintenance and insurance. The proposed computer would cost $1 million and have an economic life of five years. The vendor has assured Abel that the computer could be sold for $100,000 after five years. The annual maintenance and insurance costs are estimated to be $50,000.

Abel and the Board of Regents are convinced that the proposed computer is justified. The new computer will provide substantial cost savings. Furthermore, it will meet the university's needs and provide other benefits that cannot be quantified. How to finance the computer acquisition is the only decision left to be made on this project.

Abel has narrowed the financing decision down to two alternatives. The first financing alternative available to Abel is to borrow the money from a commercial bank. Commerce Bank would give Middleton a five-year $1 million loan at an annual interest rate of 15 percent. The bank would require the interest to be paid annually at the end of each year, with the principal amount due at maturity.

The second financing alternative Abel is considering is a proposal from DataBit, a computer leasing company. DataBit would lease the proposed computer to Middleton under a five-year operating lease arrangement. The lease arrangement calls for rental payments at the beginning of each year, starting with $340,000 at the beginning of the first year and decreasing by $40,000 in each of the subsequent four years.

Regardless of its decision to borrow or lease, Middleton would be responsible for paying the maintenance and insurance on the new computer. Abel believes the university's opportunity investment rate is 20 percent, and the current risk-free interest rate is 12 percent.

Required
a. Prepare a financial analysis showing which computer financing arrangement—borrowing from Commerce Bank or leasing from DataBit—will be better for Middleton University.
b. Identify factors other than the cost of financing that Middleton University should consider when making the lease-versus-borrow decision.

(CMA Adapted)

▶ **ANSWERS TO SELF-TEST**

True or False

1. True 2. False 3. True 4. True 5. False 6. True
7. False 8. True 9. False 10. False

Multiple Choice

1. *b.* 2. *d.* 3. *a.* 4. *a.* 5. *d.* 6. *a.* 7. *b.* 8. *c.*

15

Income Tax Effects on Capital-Budgeting Decisions

After reading this chapter, you should be able to:

1. Discuss why it is necessary to consider the income tax effect on revenues and costs when making business decisions.
2. Calculate the after-tax amount of a revenue or cost.
3. Explain why depreciation does not affect a capital-budgeting decision, but the tax shield from depreciation does.
4. Calculate the tax savings from the depreciation tax shield.
5. Explain why MACRS depreciation produces a higher net present value than does straight-line depreciation.
6. Use both differential analysis and the comparative income approach to prepare after-tax analyses for capital-budgeting decisions concerned with:
   a. Reducing costs by replacing an older machine with a newer, more efficient machine.
   b. Expanding profits by entering a new market or introducing a new product.

▶ **INTERVIEW**

E. Joseph Vellone
Vice President and
Divisional Controller
Citibank—Corporate
Securities

Q. *In the course of your work, have you had an occasion to evaluate a capital-budgeting proposal? If so, was the proposal prepared on a pre-tax basis or an after-tax basis? What factors prompted the preparer of the proposal to use this basis?*

A. I have had occasion to review several capital-budgeting proposals. In each case, the proposal was prepared on an after-tax basis because our company is a for-profit firm. The types of proposals reviewed involved real estate development, aircraft purchases, acquisitions of vessels and barges, and leveraged leasing of satellites.

▶ The purpose of using an after-tax capital-budgeting proposal is to determine the after-tax cash flow results. Because U.S. tax rules differ from accounting rules, these differences should be factored in when calculating the after-tax cash flow of a proposal. Some examples of areas affected by book/tax differences include depreciation, salvage value, interest, amortization, and credits to income taxes.

In most capital investment cases, management is interested in payback periods and return on investment. By utilizing an after-tax capital-budgeting model, the financial team provides alternatives predicated on current accounting and tax risks governed by the respective jurisdiction.

Q. *Is it important to factor in a tax shield, such as depreciation or a tax loss, when evaluating a capital-budgeting proposal? Why?*

A. To determine the practical economics of a capital investment, it is essential to measure the effects of tax shields. Both depreciation and tax losses inherent in a capital-budgeting proposal should be quantified and factored into the proposal's results to obtain the true economic reality of the project. Depreciation is a means for a firm to recover the cost of a purchased asset, over time, through periodic deductions or offsets to income. Depreciation is considered a tax benefit because the deductions cause a reduction in taxable income, thereby lowering a firm's tax liability. Tax loss is a measure of the difference between selling price and the property's tax basis (which is greater) including liabilities. In some cases, using book depreciation and book loss may be sufficient to obtain an estimate of a proposal. However, due to the number of significant book/tax differences that exist today under the present accounting and tax rules, it is very possible that the anticipated book results could change quite significantly.

Another tool often used in capital-budgeting proposals to determine the true economics of a proposal is the use of an appraisal. Investors often complement their financial models with appraised values.

▶ Assume you won $1 million in a lottery, payable at $50,000 a year for a period of 20 years. It would certainly be exciting to learn that you had won $1 million. However, after the initial surprise, you would have to decide how much of each annual payment you would like to save, how much you would like to spend, and what items you would like to buy. In doing so, you would not base your decisions on the gross annual amount of $50,000 but rather on the amount that would remain after you paid the required income taxes. Thus, your decision would be based on your *after-tax* disposable income. The same concept applies to capital-budgeting decisions. For a capital-budgeting decision to be correct, it must be made on an *after-tax basis.* ◀

▶ DECISION MAKING AND INCOME TAXES

L.O. 1

Income taxes affect all facets of decision making, and the failure to consider them may lead to incorrect decisions. For example, assume a firm has some seasonally idle cash to invest and is considering investing $1 million in either U.S. government notes paying 10 percent and maturing in six months or municipal bonds of the same risk paying 8 percent and also maturing in six months. The interest received on the municipal bonds will be exempt from federal income taxation; assume the firm's income tax rate is 40 percent. If the decision were based on the gross amount of interest received, the firm would favor the U.S. government securities, because it would receive $50,000 ($1 million $\times \frac{10}{100} \times \frac{6}{12}$ = $50,000) from this investment and only $40,000 ($1 million $\times \frac{8}{100} \times \frac{6}{12}$ = $40,000) from the municipal bonds. However, given the firm's 40 percent income tax rate, this decision would be incorrect. The analysis should be made as follows:

	U.S. Government Notes	Municipal Bonds
Interest income	$50,000	$40,000
Less: Income tax at 40%	20,000	–0–
Disposable income after income tax	$30,000	$40,000

L.O. 2
After-tax revenues or costs

By considering the income tax effect on income, the firm would reach the correct decision and purchase the municipal bonds instead of the U.S. government notes.

The analysis may be simplified considerably by converting the gross revenues directly into after-tax revenues. Any revenue or cost may be converted into its after-tax equivalent as follows:

After-tax cash flow = Before-tax cash − (Tax rate × Before-tax cash)

and

After-tax cash flow = Before-tax cash × (1 − Tax rate)

Thus, an after-tax revenue may be computed as:

After-tax revenue = Revenue × (1 − Tax rate)   **(1)**

When the interest on the U.S. government note is inserted into equation 1, the result is:

$$\$50,000(1 - .40) = \$30,000$$

The after-tax revenue of $30,000 may then be compared directly with competing after-tax revenues for the purpose of selecting the largest.

The same procedure may be applied to compute an after-tax cost. For example, if a firm is contemplating a direct-mail campaign that is expected to cost $20,000, its after-tax cost, using a 40 percent tax rate, would be:

$$\text{After-tax cost} = \$20,000(1 - .40) = \$12,000$$

An essential ingredient of capital-budgeting decisions is the present value of the cash operating advantage. Nonprofit hospitals, schools, and governmental units pay no income taxes; thus, their capital-budgeting decisions may be based on the analysis presented in Chapter 14. However, for-profit firms must pay income taxes, and the managers of these firms must use after-tax cash flows for present value analysis if their decisions are to be valid.

After-Tax Cash Flows for Capital-Budgeting Analysis

L.O. 3
Depreciation tax shield

An **after-tax cash flow** is the value of a cash inflow or outflow after giving effect to income taxes. The computation of the after-tax cash operating advantage is very similar to the technique used to compute cash operating advantage in Chapter 14, except the before-tax amount must be reduced by the amount of income tax to be paid.

Tax Shields   A **tax shield** is any *deduction on a firm's income tax return* that does *not* require an outlay of cash in *that* period. Although depreciation is not a relevant cost for capital-budgeting decisions, *it is deductible for income tax purposes* and thus has an effect on the amount of income taxes that a firm pays. In essence, depreciation "shields" income from being taxed. The same is true for the book value (the tax basis) of a machine that is to be sold at a loss or scrapped when newer equipment is bought to replace it. The most common tax shields are depreciation and losses on the disposal of assets. The computation of the tax saving resulting from a tax shield is:

$$\text{Tax saving} = \text{Tax shield} \times \text{Tax rate}$$

The Mayfair Company is planning to purchase a new machine for $90,000 and expects to save direct labor costs of $40,000 per annum for a period of six years, the useful life of the machine. Mayfair's income tax rate is 40 percent, and, for ease of presentation, we will ignore salvage value. The after-tax cash operating advantage may be computed as shown in Illustration 15-1. It is important to note that depreciation is deducted to arrive at the amount of income subject to income tax but that the depreciation must be added back to the after-tax net income because it is *not a cash outflow* and does not affect cash. It merely affects the amount of income tax that the firm pays.

The results may be verified by the following:

Annual direct labor cost savings	$40,000
Less: Income tax	10,000
Cash operating advantage after income tax	$30,000

▶ **ILLUSTRATION 15-1**

MAYFAIR COMPANY
Calculation of After-Tax Cash Operating Advantage

Annual direct labor cost savings	$40,000
Less: Depreciation ($90,000 ÷ 6 years)	15,000
Operating advantage before income tax	25,000
Less: Income tax at 40%	10,000
Net income	15,000
Add: Depreciation*	15,000
Cash operating advantage after income tax	$30,000

* Depreciation must be added back to net income to arrive at the cash inflow because it is *not a cash outflow* but is deductible on the firm's income tax return.

L.O. 4
Tax savings from tax shield

An alternative method of determining the after-tax cash operating advantage is to compute the after-tax direct labor cost savings and then add the tax savings of the depreciation to the result. Using its depreciation of $15,000, the Mayfair Company would compute its tax savings from depreciation as:

$$\text{Tax savings} = \$15,000 \times 40 \text{ percent} = \$6,000$$

Then its cash operating advantage after taxes could be computed as:

After-tax savings of direct labor [$40,000(1 − .40)]	$24,000
Add: Income tax savings from depreciation tax shield ($15,000 × .40)	6,000
Cash operating advantage after income tax	$30,000

Notice that the after-tax cash flow from the saving of direct labor is computed using 1 minus the tax rate (60 percent), while the saving from the depreciation tax shield is computed using the tax rate itself (40 percent). The 60 percent rate is applied to cash inflows because the objective is to compute how much is left for the firm after *paying* income tax on the cash inflow. The 40 percent rate is applied to tax shields because the objective is to compute how much income tax the firm is *not paying* as a result of using a tax shield.

For tax purposes, the **adjusted tax basis** (original cost less depreciation allowed) of old equipment that will be sold or scrapped if new equipment is purchased may also be a tax shield. Because a *loss* on the sale of old equipment is deductible on an income tax return and no cash for the loss is disbursed (cash may, in fact, be *received*), a firm will have the equivalent of a cash receipt equal to the income tax saved. The calculation of the tax shield is similar to that for depreciation, except the adjusted tax basis of the old equipment must be reduced by the expected sales proceeds.

The Saybrook Company is contemplating the replacement of an existing machine with a newer, more efficient machine. The old machine has an adjusted tax basis of $20,000 and can be sold for $4,000. The tax shield would be $16,000 ($20,000 − $4,000), and the tax savings, using a 40 percent tax rate, would be:

$$\text{Tax savings} = \$16,000 \times 40 \text{ percent} = \$6,400$$

A tax shield can sometimes make the difference in whether a project is profitable or not profitable. For example, the Taylor Company is considering two competing projects. The projects have the same useful life, the same net investment, the same cash operating advantage before income taxes, and the same income tax rates. The only difference is that the net investment in project A may be depreciated over its useful life for tax purposes. The net investment in project B cannot be depreciated but must be carried at its original amount until the company is either sold or liquidated, at which time the original amount may be deducted in full on the firm's final tax return. An example of such an investment would be the goodwill acquired in a business merger. Here are the relevant data for the two projects:

	Project A	**Project B**
Net investment.	$100,000	$100,000
Useful life	10 years	10 years
Annual cash operating advantage		
before income tax	$ 30,000	$ 30,000
Income tax rate	40%	40%
After-tax discount rate	14%	14%

Each project's cash operating advantage after income tax may be computed as follows:

Project A:

Annual after-tax cash inflow [$30,000(1 − .40)]	$18,000
Add: Tax savings on depreciation tax shield	
($100,000 ÷ 10 years = $10,000 × 40%).	4,000
Cash operating advantage after income tax	$22,000

Project B:

After-tax cash inflow [$30,000(1 − .40) = $18,000]	
(also cash operating advantage after income tax)	$18,000

The net present value of each project would be:

Project A:

Present value of cash inflow	
($22,000 × 5.21612*)	$114,755
Less: Net investment at present value	
($100,000 × 1.00000)	100,000
Net present value	$ 14,755

Project B:

Present value of cash inflow	
($18,000 × 5.21612*)	$ 93,890
Less: Net investment at present value	
($100,000 × 1.00000)	100,000
Net present value	$ (6,110)

* From Table 4 in Appendix 14-B, $n = 10$, $i = 14\%$.

This analysis indicates that project A passes the cutoff rate but project B does not. In effect, the depreciation tax shield may be the difference that makes a project acceptable. The present value of the tax shield for project B is ignored because the present value of its tax benefit is very small and thus would not alter the decision. For example, if it is anticipated that the company will be sold or liquidated more than 25 years into the future, the present value of the tax savings from the net investment in project B would be *less than $3,779,* computed as follows:

$$\text{Present value} = \$100,000 \times .03779^* = \$3,779$$

* From Table 2 in Appendix 14-B, $n = 25$, $i = 14\%$.

A longer time horizon, such as 50 years, would produce a present value of $100 ($100,000 × 0.001—from another table). In either case, the present value of the tax savings does not affect the outcome of this decision, and for most other cases, the decision might be unchanged as well.

Like the depreciation tax shield, the choice of depreciation method, when a choice is available, may also alter a capital-budgeting decision. Thus, managers must understand how different depreciation methods affect after-tax income.

Depreciation Methods and Their Effects on Capital-Budgeting Decisions

Prior to 1981, taxpayers could choose one of several depreciation methods: the straight-line, sum-of-the-years'-digits, declining-balance, and units-of-production methods. These methods may still be used under certain conditions; thus, managers should be familiar with their computations, which are thoroughly discussed in most financial accounting textbooks.

By law, the choice of depreciation methods has been narrowed for years after 1980. Congress legislated a new approach, the accelerated cost recovery system (ACRS)—modified by the Tax Reform Act of 1986 (TRA 1986) and now referred to as the modified accelerated cost recovery system (MACRS)—and taxpayers must now use either the MACRS or the straight-line method in computing their taxes.

The Modified Accelerated Cost Recovery System Federal tax laws require taxpayers to use MACRS unless they choose the straight-line method of depreciation. The **modified accelerated cost recovery system** is a depreciation method used for income tax purposes that classifies property into one of eight groupings without considering the property's actual useful life. The percentage of depreciation that may be claimed in each year an asset is owned is explained below. Prior to MACRS, one taxpayer could estimate a delivery van's useful life at three years, and another taxpayer could estimate it at five years, depending on the number of miles driven per year. This is no longer possible because MACRS requires all taxpayers to use the same useful life for similar property. The MACRS classifications of property are presented in Illustration 15-2.

The salvage value of equipment does not affect the amount of depreciation allowed because it is ignored for the purpose of calculating depreciation. However, the purchase date of equipment may affect the amount of depreciation allowed in a particular year. The reason for this is that MACRS depreciation is subject to the following averaging conventions:

1. Half-Year Convention. Other than 27.5-year or 31.5-year property, it is assumed that all property (other than property subject to the mid-quarter convention discussed below) is placed in service at the mid-point of the year, and one half of a year's depreciation is taken in the year the property is placed in service.

2. Mid-Quarter Convention. When a taxpayer places more than 40 percent of a year's acquired property into service in the last three months of that tax year, the property is subject to a mid-quarter convention. That is, all

▶ **ILLUSTRATION 15-2**   Classification by Recovery Period of Property Used in a Trade or Business

Recovery Period	Kind of Property
3-year.	Race horses older than 2 years or other horses older than 12 years
5-year.	Automobiles, light general-purpose trucks, research and experimentation equipment, semiconductor manufacturing equipment, and qualified technological equipment
7-year.	Railroad track, single-purpose agricultural structures, and property not otherwise classified
10-year.	Property with a useful life of 16 to 20 years
15-year.	Municipal waste treatment plants and telephone distribution plants
20-year.	Municipal sewers
27.5-year.	Residential rental property
31.5-year.	Nonresidential real property

property for that year is treated as if it were placed into service at the mid-point of the quarter in which the property is actually placed in service.

3. **Mid-Month Convention.** Real property—both residential and nonresidential—is considered placed in service at the middle of the month in which the property is actually placed in service. That is, one half of a month's depreciation is taken in the month the property is placed in service.

Depreciation Calculations   Under MACRS, the amount of depreciation allowed for 3-year, 5-year, 7-year, and 10-year properties is an amount of depreciation computed at twice the straight-line method on the unrecovered balance of cost. This method is identical to the double-declining-balance method (DDB) discussed in financial accounting texts. However, the MACRS requires a modification of this method. Under the straight-line method, when the depreciation for a year produces a higher amount of depreciation than DDB, straight-line depreciation is required. Assume a firm purchases an asset for $100,000 in 19x1, and that asset is 5-year property. The MACRS method produces the following allowable depreciation:

Year	Depreciation	Accumulated Depreciation	Unrecovered Balance
			$100,000
19x1.	$20,000[a]	$ 20,000	80,000[b]
19x2.	32,000[c]	52,000	48,000[d]
19x3.	19,200[e]	71,200	28,800[f]
19x4.	11,520[g]	82,720	17,280[h]
19x5.	11,520[i]	94,240	5,760
19x6.	5,760[j]	100,000	–0–

a. $100,000 × (20% × 2) = $40,000 × ½ year.

b. $100,000 − $20,000 = $80,000.

c. $80,000 × 40% = $32,000.

d. $80,000 − $32,000 = $48,000.

e. $48,000 × 40% = $19,200.

f. $48,000 − $19,200 = $28,800.

g. $28,800 × $40% = $11,520 for DDB; $28,800 ÷ 2½ years = $11,520 for straight-line. Use the higher of the two. In this case, they are the same.

h. $28,800 − $11,520 = $17,280.

i. $11,520 straight-line.

j. $11,520 × ½ year.

▶ **ILLUSTRATION 15-3**   Allowable MACRS Depreciation Deductions

Taxable Year	Applicable Percentage for the Class of Property					
	3-Year	**5-Year**	**7-Year**	**10-Year**	**15-Year**	**20-Year**
1	33.333	20.000	14.286	10.000	5.000	3.750
2	44.444	32.000	24.490	18.000	9.500	7.219
3	14.815*	19.200	17.493	14.400	8.550	6.677
4	7.408	11.520*	12.494	11.520	7.695	6.177
5		11.520	8.925*	9.216	6.926	5.713
6		5.760	8.925	7.372	6.233	5.285
7			8.925	6.554*	5.905*	4.888
8			4.462	6.554	5.905	4.522
9				6.554	5.905	4.462*
10				6.554	5.905	4.462
11				3.276	5.905	4.462
12					5.905	4.462
13					5.905	4.462
14					5.905	4.462
15					5.904	4.461
16					2.952	4.461
17						4.461
18						4.461
19						4.461
20						4.461
21						2.231

* Change to straight-line depreciation.

The amounts of depreciation computed above in dollars can be converted into percentages by dividing the dollar amount of depreciation by the cost of the property placed in service. For example, in 19x1 the percentage of cost allowable as depreciation would be 20 percent ($20,000 ÷ $100,000), and the allowable depreciation for 19x2 would be 32 percent ($32,000 ÷ $100,000). A table that shows the percentages of depreciation allowable for all property other than residential and nonresidential realty appears in Illustration 15-3.

Fifteen-year and 20-year properties also require the use of a form of declining-balance depreciation, except the rate is 150 percent instead of 200 percent of straight-line depreciation. Except for this difference, the procedure is the same as the treatment for DDB discussed above.

Taxpayers may choose to use straight-line depreciation instead of declining-balance depreciation. If a taxpayer chooses MACRS-straight-line depreciation, the investment property is classified using the categories shown in Illustration 15-2.

Residential rental property and nonresidential real property are depreciated using the straight-line method over the respective periods of 27.5 and 31.5 years.

Optional Straight-Line Method   Under MACRS, the taxpayer may choose the straight-line method. However, the taxpayer must select MACRS-straight-line depreciation for all property in that class for that year, and this selection cannot be changed. Both MACRS and MACRS straight line are subject to the half-year convention. When MACRS straight line is chosen, the amount of depreciation allowed for a five-year asset is as follows:

Year	Percent of Depreciation Allowed
1.	10
2.	20
3.	20
4.	20
5.	20
6.	10
Total.	100

Salvage value is ignored for both approaches to depreciation, as discussed later.

Selecting a Depreciation Method   Whenever there is a choice, the objective of a capital-budgeting decision should be to accelerate as many cash inflows as possible to the earliest years of the project. Also, an attempt should be made to have larger inflows in the earlier years and smaller inflows in the later years. Because the earlier years have higher present value factors than do the later years, these strategies will cause a higher net present value for a project and make the project more favorable to the firm. A dollar received today is worth more than a dollar received five years from now, and a tax shield that can be accelerated is worth more than one of an equivalent amount that cannot be accelerated.

The Estar Company is thinking about purchasing a new machine for $100,000. The machine is five-year property, Estar Company's income tax rate is 40 percent, and it wants to use an after-tax discount rate of 15 percent. The present values of the income tax savings using both the MACRS table from Illustration 15-3 and the straight-line method are shown in Illustration 15-4.

The comparison shows that when a choice exists, the MACRS-DDB rates are usually more advantageous than the straight-line method because the straight-line method produces smaller present value tax savings. However, a company must have sufficient taxable income to absorb the MACRS depreciation before it is beneficial. When a company is operating at a loss, it may prefer the straight-line method.

Once the depreciation strategy is selected, it is possible to apply it to the decisions managers must make when they receive investment proposals.

▶ **PROGRESS CHECK**

1. Is it important to evaluate an investment decision on an after-tax basis? Explain.

2. What is an after-tax cash flow? How is it calculated?

3. What is a tax shield? Give some examples of tax shields. How is a tax shield computed?

4. What is the MACRS method of computing depreciation? Is a firm required to use MACRS? Explain.

5. What is the half-year convention? Is a firm required to use the half-year convention? Explain.

6. Although the amount of depreciation taken in any one year is different under the straight-line and MACRS methods, the total depreciation taken over the life of an asset is the same for both methods. Would you expect the present values of the tax shields to be different? If so, which would have a higher present value? Why? ◀

▶ **ILLUSTRATION 15-4**

ESTAR COMPANY
Computation of Present Values of Income Tax Savings
Using Alternative Depreciation Methods

MACRS Five-Year Method

(1) Year	(2) Depreciation*	(3) Income Tax Savings (2) × 40%	(4) Present Value of 15 Percent— From Table 2†	(5) Present Value (3) × (4)
1	$ 20,000	$ 8,000	.86957	$ 6,957
2	32,000	12,800	.75614	9,679
3	19,200	7,680	.65752	5,050
4	11,520	4,608	.57175	2,635
5	11,520	4,608	.49718	2,291
6	5,760	2,304	.43233	996
Total	$100,000	$40,000		$27,608

Straight-Line Method

(1) Year	(2) Percent	(3) Depreciation	(4) Income Tax Savings (3) × 40%	(5) Present Value of 15 Percent— From Table 2†	(6) Present Value (4) × (5)
1	10	$ 10,000	$ 4,000	.86957	$ 3,478
2	20	20,000	8,000	.75614	6,049
3	20	20,000	8,000	.65752	5,260
4	20	20,000	8,000	.57175	4,574
5	20	20,000	8,000	.49718	3,977
6	10	10,000	4,000	.43233	1,729
Total	100	$100,000	$40,000		$25,067

* Calculated by using the percentages from Illustration 15-3.
† Table 2 in Appendix 14-B.

▶ **AFTER-TAX CAPITAL BUDGETING**

L.O. 5
Higher net present value for MACRS

The most common capital-budgeting decisions usually involve cost-reduction decisions (such as purchasing new labor-saving equipment or replacing an existing machine with a newer, more efficient machine) or profit-expansion decisions (such as entering a new market or introducing a new product). Because most of the after-tax capital-budgeting computations are the same for both the purchase of a new machine and the replacement of an existing machine, our discussion focuses on a single cost-reduction example—the replacement of an existing machine. We will then examine the after-tax capital-budgeting procedures used when entering a new market.

Purchasing New or Replacement Equipment—Additional Tax Considerations

In Chapter 13, we discussed how to calculate the before-tax *net investment* and *cash operating advantage* when purchasing equipment. To be more accurate, however, these calculations should be made on an *after-tax basis,* because income taxes affect these cash flows just as they affect any other cash inflow or outflow.

Salvage Value

When evaluating a project's profitability, besides the depreciation tax shield, a firm must consider the salvage value of the machine and its after-tax effect on the net investment. Under MACRS, salvage value is not taken into account when computing the annual deduction for depreciation; but when the property is fully depreciated for tax purposes, its *adjusted tax basis*—the amount used to calculate a taxable gain—is zero. Thus, the proceeds from the sale of fully depreciated property at the end of its useful life would be subject to income tax. The after-tax cash inflow of $5,000 from the sale of a fully depreciated machine using a 40 percent tax rate may be calculated as follows:

$$\text{After-tax cash inflow} = (\text{Sales proceeds} - \text{Adjusted tax basis})$$
$$\times (1 - t) \tag{2}$$
$$\text{After-tax cash inflow} = (\$5,000 - \$0) \times (1 - .40) = \$3,000$$

The Book Value of an Existing Machine

We noted earlier that book value is not relevant to the decision to replace an old machine with a newer machine if differential analysis is used. However, if the old machine is sold when the new machine is purchased, the adjusted tax basis of the existing machine must be used to calculate the tax consequences of its sale.

If a *taxable gain* results from the old machine's sale, the income tax due is a *cash outflow*. If a *taxable loss* results from the sale, the income tax saved is a *cash inflow*. The income tax consequences may be calculated as follows if the adjusted tax basis of the old equipment is $10,000, the sales proceeds are $4,000, and the tax rate is 25 percent:

$$\text{Income tax savings} = (\text{Adjusted tax basis} - \text{Sales proceeds}) \times \text{Tax rate}$$
$$\text{Income tax savings} = (\$10,000 - \$4,000) \times .25 = \$1,500 \tag{3}$$

If a gain is anticipated, the equation may be modified to:

$$\text{Income tax due} = (\text{Sales proceeds} - \text{Adjusted tax basis}) \times \text{Tax rate} \tag{4}$$

▶ Recapitulation of Tax-Shield Equations

(1) After-tax revenue = Revenue × (1 − Tax rate)
   After-tax cost = Cost × (1 − Tax rate)

(2) After-tax cash inflow = (Sales proceeds − Adjusted tax basis) × (1 − Tax rate)

(3) Income tax savings = (Adjusted tax basis − Sales proceeds) × Tax rate

(4) Income tax due = (Sales proceeds − Adjusted tax basis) × Tax rate

---

Differences in Tax Shields   Another factor that must be considered when replacing existing equipment is the *difference* in the depreciation tax shields between the old machine and the new machine. When *differential analysis* is used, the difference is arrived at by netting the two. When the *comparative income approach* is used, each depreciation tax shield is considered separately.

We will now expand our machine-replacement example from Chapter 13 to include the salvage value for the new machine. Remember that the Mature Products Company may replace one of its old machines with a faster machine. The older machine is nearing the end of its economic useful life, but its life can be extended by a major overhaul. The information needed to evaluate the replacement decision is presented in Illustration 15-5.

▶ **ILLUSTRATION 15-5**

MATURE PRODUCTS COMPANY
Information for the Replacement of a Machine

Original cost of the present machine $40,000
    Less: Accumulated depreciation. 30,000*
Book value (adjusted tax basis) $10,000

Purchase price of new machine $95,000
Useful life of new machine . . . . 5 years
Remaining useful life of old machine. 2 years
Overhaul of old machine will extend its 2-year remaining useful
    life by 3 years, for a total of 5 years at a cost of. . . . . $10,000†
Salvage value of new machine 6,000
Market value of old machine, if sold 4,000

	Old Machine	New Machine
Annual operating information:		
Sales	$400,000	$400,000
Direct material cost	90,000	90,000
Direct labor cost	80,000	60,000
Variable overhead	48,000	36,000
Fixed overhead exclusive of depreciation	100,000	100,000

* Straight-line depreciation was used. The half-year convention was not employed because it was assumed that the equipment was purchased prior to the enactment of TRA 1986.

† This will be deducted on the tax return in full in the year paid.

In addition, the Mature Products Company estimates that its after-tax cost of capital is 14 percent and its income tax rate is 25 percent. The company uses its cost of capital as the cutoff rate for capital-budgeting decisions.

L.O. 6a
Differential analysis for replacing a machine

Differential Analysis The steps needed to analyze the relevant data for a capital-budgeting decision using differential analysis are:

Step 1
Convert the before-tax annual cash operating advantage items to an after-tax basis, using Equation 1:

After-tax annual direct labor savings = $20,000(1 − .25) = $15,000
After-tax annual variable overhead savings = $12,000(1 − .25) = $9,000
After-tax old machine overhaul = $10,000(1 − .25) = $7,500*

* Under current income tax law, the cost of the machine overhaul is fully deductible in the year of the expenditure.

Step 2
Convert the salvage value of the new machine to an after-tax basis:

After-tax salvage value = $6,000(1 − .25) = $4,500

Step 3
Using Equation 3, compute the income tax savings on the book loss created when the old machine is sold:

Income tax savings = ($10,000 − $4,000) × .25 = $1,500

Step 4
Compute the differences in the amounts of depreciation allowable for tax purposes between the old machine and the new machine and convert them

▶ **ILLUSTRATION 15-6**

MATURE PRODUCTS COMPANY
Computation of the Income Tax Savings Resulting
from the Difference between the Depreciation Tax Shields
of Two Machines

	Amount ×	Tax Rate =	Income Tax Savings
New machine:			
Cost of 5-year property	$95,000		
Depreciation allowable:			
First year (20% × $95,000)	$19,000 ×	.25 =	$4,750
Second year (32% × $95,000)	30,400 ×	.25 =	7,600
Third year (19.2% × $95,000)	18,240 ×	.25 =	4,560
Fourth year (11.52% × $95,000)	10,944 ×	.25 =	2,736
Fifth year (11.52% × $95,000)	10,944 ×	.25 =	2,736
Sixth year (5.76% × $95,000)	5,472 ×	.25 =	1,368
Total depreciation	$95,000		
Old machine:			
First year (10,000 book value ÷ 2 years)	$ 5,000 ×	.25 =	$1,250
Second year	5,000 ×	.25 =	1,250
Third year	0 ×	.25 =	0
Fourth year	0 ×	.25 =	0
Fifth year	0 ×	.25 =	0
Sixth year	0 ×	.25 =	0
Total depreciation	$10,000		

Income Tax Savings

	New Machine	Old Machine	Differential Amount
Comparison:			
First year	$4,750	$1,250	$3,500
Second year	7,600	1,250	6,350
Third year.	4,560	0	4,560
Fourth year	2,736	0	2,736
Fifth year	2,736	0	2,736
Sixth year.	1,368	0	1,368

to the amount of tax savings for each year. The old machine is being depreciated on the straight-line basis. This analysis and computation appear in Illustration 15-6.

Step 5
Using the amounts computed in steps 1 through 4 and the sales proceeds from the old machine and the investment, prepare the present value analysis needed to reach an investment decision, as shown in Illustration 15-7.

From Illustration 15-7, note the following:

1. The direct labor savings, variable overhead savings, and machine overhaul savings are all used on an *after-tax* basis.
2. The purchase price of the new machine is *not* adjusted for income taxes. The deduction for tax purposes of this cash outlay is recouped by the depreciation tax shield.

▶ **ILLUSTRATION 15-7**

MATURE PRODUCTS COMPANY
Calculation of Net Present Value on an After-Tax Basis
Retaining Old Machine or Purchasing a New Machine
Differential Analysis

Item	Present Value in Dollars	Present Value Factor	Time Period 0	1	2	3	4	5	6
Cash operating advantage:									
Direct labor savings . .	$ 51,496‡	3.43308*		$15,000	$15,000	$15,000	$15,000	$15,000	
Variable overhead savings	30,898	3.43308		9,000	9,000	9,000	9,000	9,000	
Savings of old machine overhaul.	5,771	.76947†				7,500			
Depreciation tax shield	3,070	.87719†		3,500					
	4,886	.76947†			6,350				
	3,078	.67497†				4,560			
	1,620	.59208†					2,736		
	1,421	.51937†						2,736	
	623	.45559†							1,368
Total	$102,863								
Net investment:									
Purchase price of new machine	$ (95,000)	1.00000	$(95,000)						
Sales proceeds of old machine	4,000	1.00000	4,000						
Tax shield from loss on sale of old machine . .	1,500	1.00000	1,500						
Salvage value of new machine	2,337§	.51937†						4,500	
Net investment	(87,163)								
Net present value	$ 15,700‖								

* From Table 4 in Appendix 14-B.
† From Table 2 in Appendix 14-B.
‡ $15,000 × 3.43308 = $51,496.
§ $4,500 × .51937 = $2,337.
‖ The present value of the cash operating advantage minus the present value of the net investment ($102,863 − $87,163).

3. The sales proceeds from the old machine are *not* adjusted for income taxes, and the *loss on the sale of the old machine* is recouped as a tax savings on a net-tax basis. The rationale for this treatment is that the book value (tax basis) of $10,000 may be viewed as consisting of two parts. The first part is the $4,000 of cost that is recovered from the machine's sale, and no tax effects should occur when something is sold for the exact amount of its cost. The second part is the remaining $6,000, which will not be recovered and is lost. This loss is deductible on the firm's tax return, and at a 25 percent tax rate, the firm will save $1,500 ($6,000 × .25) in taxes.

L.O. 6a
Comparative income analysis for replacing a machine

The Comparative Income Approach   The comparative income approach can lead to the same results as differential analysis if present values are computed separately for each alternative—that is, keeping the old machine and purchasing the new machine. The steps needed to prepare the comparative income analysis are:

▶ **ILLUSTRATION 15-8**

MATURE PRODUCTS COMPANY
Computation of Income Tax Savings
Difference between the Depreciation Tax Shields of Two Machines

	Amount	×	Tax Rate	=	Income Tax Savings
New machine:					
Cost of 5-year property	$95,000				
Depreciation allowable:					
First year (20% × $95,000)	$19,000	×	.25	=	$4,750
Second year (32% × $95,000)	30,400	×	.25	=	7,600
Third year (19.2% × $95,000)	18,240	×	.25	=	4,560
Fourth year (11.52% × $95,000)	10,944	×	.25	=	2,736
Fifth year (11.52% × $95,000)	10,944	×	.25	=	2,736
Sixth year (5.76% × $95,000)	5,472	×	.25	=	1,368
Total depreciation	$95,000				
Old machine:					
First year (10,000 book value ÷ 2 years)	$ 5,000	×	.25	=	$1,250
Second year	5,000	×	.25	=	1,250
Third year	0	×	.25	=	0
Fourth year	0	×	.25	=	0
Fifth year	0	×	.25	=	0
Sixth year	0	×	.25	=	0
Total depreciation	$10,000				

Step 1

Convert all revenues and costs to an after-tax basis for each alternative using Equation 1. For example, sales revenue may be converted as follows:

$$\text{After-tax sales revenue} = \$400,000(1 - .25) = \$300,000$$

Step 2

Convert the salvage value of the new machine to an after-tax basis:

$$\text{After-tax salvage value} = \$6,000(1 - .25) = \$4,500$$

Step 3

Using Equation 3, compute the income tax savings on the book loss created when the old machine is sold:

$$\text{Income tax savings} = (\$10,000 - \$4,000) \times .25 = \$1,500$$

Step 4

Compute the amounts of depreciation allowable for tax purposes for the old machine and the new machine and convert them to the amounts of tax savings for each year. This analysis and computation appear in Illustration 15-8.

Step 5

Using the amounts computed in steps 1 through 4 together with the sales proceeds from the old machine and the investment, prepare the present value analysis needed to reach an investment decision, as shown in Illustration 15-9.

MATURE PRODUCTS COMPANY
Calculation of Net Present Value on an After-Tax Basis
Retaining Old Machine or Purchasing a New Machine
Comparative Income Approach

Item	Present Value in Dollars	Present Value Factor	0	1	2	3	4	5	6
Keep old machine:									
Net cash inflow from operations . . .	$211,134	3.43308*		$61,500‡	$61,500	$61,500	$61,500	$61,500	
Depreciation tax shield . . .	1,096	.87719†		1,250	1,250				
	962	.76947†							
Opportunity cost of forgoing tax loss on the sale of the old machine . . .	(1,500)	1.00000	(1,500)						
Opportunity cost of keeping old machine—market value proceeds forgone . . .	(4,000)	1.00000	(4,000)						
Overhaul of old machine at the end of second year . . .	(5,771)	.76947†			(7,500)				
Net present value . . .	$201,921								
Purchase new machine:									
Net cash inflow from operations . . .	$293,528	3.43308*		$85,500§	$85,500	$85,500	$85,500	$85,500	
Depreciation tax shield . . .	4,166	.87719†		4,750					
	5,848	.76947†			7,600				
	3,078	.67497†				4,560			
	1,620	.59208†					2,736		
	1,421	.51937†						2,736	
	623	.45559†							1,368
Salvage value . . .	2,337	.51937†						4,500	
Purchase price of new machine . . .	(95,000)	1.00000	(95,000)						
Net present value . . .	$217,621								

Recapitulation:

Net present value of purchasing new machine . . .	$217,621
Net present value of keeping old machine . . .	201,921
Net present value in favor of new machine . . .	$ 15,700

SCHEDULE 1
Keep Old Machine—
Net Cash Inflow from Operations

Sales revenue—$400,000(1 − .25)	$300,000
Direct materials—$90,000(1 − .25)	(67,500)
Direct labor—$80,000(1 − .25)	(60,000)
Variable overhead—$48,000(1 − .25)	(36,000)
Fixed overhead—$100,000(1 − .25)	(75,000)
Net cash inflow from operations after income taxes	$ 61,500

SCHEDULE 2
Purchase New Machine—
Net Cash Inflow from Operations

Sales revenue—$400,000(1 − .25)	$300,000
Direct materials—$90,000(1 − .25)	(67,500)
Direct labor—$60,000(1 − .25)	(45,000)
Variable overhead—$36,000(1 − .25)	(27,000)
Fixed overhead—$100,000(1 − .25)	(75,000)
Net cash inflow from operations after income taxes	$ 85,500

* From Table 4 in Appendix 14-B.
† From Table 2 in Appendix 14-B.
‡ See Schedule 1 above.
§ See Schedule 2 above.

In Illustration 15-9, note the following:

1. All inflows and outflows resulting in the net cash inflow from operations are computed on an *after-tax* basis.
2. If the old machine is kept, two items are given up: the sales proceeds from the sale of the old machine ($4,000) and the tax loss of $6,000, which is deductible on the firm's tax return. Both are opportunity costs that must be considered as costs of keeping the old machine. (To review why the $4,000 is not adjusted for tax effects while the $6,000 is, see item 3 of the discussion preceding Illustration 15-7.)

The analyses in Illustrations 15-7 and 15-9 both indicate that it is favorable to replace the old machine with the new one. However, the comparative income approach (Illustration 15-9) requires much greater effort than the differential analysis approach (Illustration 15-7). Of course, many firms have the computer capability to generate both analyses easily.

Entering a new market or introducing a new product requires after-tax analyses similar to those for purchasing a new machine and replacing existing equipment. However, several additional after-tax concepts are needed.

Entering a New Market or Introducing a New Product—Additional Tax Considerations

Working Capital   Entering a new market or introducing a new product requires a firm to invest working capital in accounts receivable and inventories. This working capital is then unavailable for other uses and must be treated like any other investment for capital-budgeting purposes. However, the investment in working capital *does not provide a tax shield* similar to that provided by depreciation when there is an investment in equipment. The difference occurs because an investment in equipment is partially consumed each year until the end of its useful life, when only salvage value remains, while an investment in working capital is usually maintained and returned at the end of the project. Thus, because there is no diminution of the working capital investment, there is no income tax deduction. In some cases, a portion of working capital may not be recovered because of obsolete inventory that has to be sold at a loss. This portion would be a tax shield at the time of the loss. Such an event is difficult to foresee and quantify, however, and it will probably occur so far into the future that it may safely be ignored because of its small present value factor.

The release of working capital at the end of a project also has no income tax effects. Because the investment of working capital is not deductible for tax purposes, its release is also free from taxes.

L.O. 6b
Differential analysis for entering a new market

Differential Analysis   To illustrate the after-tax analysis for introducing a new product, we will continue with the example from Chapter 13 with one alteration. In this case, the release of working capital is the same as the amount invested. Recall that the Physico Company plans to enter the physical fitness market with a treadmill for gymnasium and home use. Based on a market survey and cost estimates provided by the firm's engineering and accounting departments, the information presented in Illustration 15-10 was derived.

▶ **ILLUSTRATION 15-10**

PHYSICO COMPANY
Information for Entering the Treadmill Market

Sales (10,000 at $250 each)	$2,500,000
Incremental costs:	
Direct materials (10,000 at $60)	$600,000
Direct labor (10,000 at $50)	$500,000
Variable overhead (10,000 at $38)	$380,000
Fixed overhead exclusive of new machinery noted below	$400,000
Variable marketing costs	5% of sales
Fixed marketing and administrative costs	$200,000
Purchase of machinery needed for manufacturing	
this product	$950,000
Useful life of machinery	10 years
Salvage value of machinery.	$ 20,000
Working capital needed at inception	$400,000
Working capital returned at end of 10 years when the demand for	
this product is expected to be nil	$400,000

▶ **ILLUSTRATION 15-11**

PHYSICO COMPANY
Calculation of Cash Outflows and Cash Inflows
For Entering a New Market
Differential Income Approach

	(Outflow) Inflow
Net investment:	
Purchase price of machinery.	$ (950,000)
Salvage value of machine	20,000
Working capital at inception	(400,000)
Release of working capital at the end of 10 years	400,000
Net investment.	$ (930,000)
Cash operating advantage:	
Sales per annum	$2,500,000
Variable costs per annum:	
Direct materials	(600,000)
Direct labor	(500,000)
Variable overhead	(380,000)
Marketing costs (5% × $2.5 million)	(125,000)
Fixed costs per annum:	
Manufacturing overhead.	(400,000)
Marketing and administrative costs.	(200,000)
Cash operating advantage per annum	$ 295,000

The analysis of the relevant data for deciding whether to enter the new market may be organized on a *before-tax basis,* as shown in Illustration 15-11.

In addition, the Physico Company estimates that its income tax rate will be 25 percent and its after-tax cost of capital is 14 percent. It wishes to use its cost of capital as the cutoff rate. The steps needed to compute the net present value on an *after-tax basis* are as follows:

PHYSICO COMPANY
Calculation of Income Tax Savings from
the Depreciation Tax Shield

	Amount ×	Tax Rate =	Income Tax Savings
Cost of 5-year property	$950,000		
Depreciation allowable:			
First year (20% × $950,000)	$190,000 ×	.25 =	$47,500
Second year (32% × $950,000)	304,000 ×	.25 =	76,000
Third year (19.2% × $950,000)	182,400 ×	.25 =	45,600
Fourth year (11.52% × $950,000)	109,440 ×	.25 =	27,360
Fifth year (11.52% × $950,000)	109,440 ×	.25 =	27,360
Sixth year (5.76% × $950,000)	54,720 ×	.25 =	13,680
Total depreciation	$950,000		

Step 1

Convert the annual before-tax cash operating items to an after-tax basis by multiplying them by $(1 - t)$:

After-tax sales	$= \$2,500,000(1 - .25) = \$1,875,000$	
Less:		
After-tax direct materials	$= 600,000(1 - .25) =$	(450,000)
After-tax direct labor	$= 500,000(1 - .25) =$	(375,000)
After-tax variable overhead	$= 380,000(1 - .25) =$	(285,000)
After-tax variable marketing costs	$= 125,000(1 - .25) =$	(93,750)
After-tax fixed manufacturing overhead	$= 400,000(1 - .25) =$	(300,000)
After-tax fixed marketing and administrative costs	$= 200,000(1 - .25) =$	(150,000)
After-tax cash operating advantage		$ 221,250

Step 2

Convert the salvage value to an after-tax basis:

$$\text{After-tax salvage value} = \$20,000(1 - .25) = \$15,000$$

Step 3

Translate the depreciation tax shield into the amounts of income tax saved each year. The computation appears in Illustration 15-12.

Step 4

Using the information from steps 1, 2, and 3 together with the investment of $950,000, and the investment and release of the working capital of $400,000, prepare an after-tax net present value computation, as shown in Illustration 15-13.

Based on this analysis, management could assume that the investment is favorable because the positive net present value of $76,562 indicates that the after-tax cutoff rate of 14 percent will be earned. Of course, if there are competing projects, this investment must be ranked for preference selection.

▶ **ILLUSTRATION 15-13**

PHYSICO COMPANY
Calculation of After-Tax Net Present Value for Entering a New Market
Differential Analysis

Item	Present Value in Dollars	Present Value Factor	Time Period						
			0	1	2	3	4	5	6 . . . 10
Cash operating advantage:									
Net cash inflow from operations	$ 1,154,067	5.21612*		$221,250	221,250	221,250	221,250	. . . .	221,250
Depreciation tax shield	41,667	.87719†		47,500					
	58,480	.76947			76,000				
	30,779	.67497				45,600			
	16,199	.59208					27,360		
	14,210	.51937						27,360	
	6,232	.45559							13,680
Total	$ 1,321,634								
Net investment:									
Purchase price of machine	$ (950,000)	1.00000	(950,000)						
Salvage value of machine	4,046	.26974†							15,000
Investment of working capital . .	(400,000)	1.00000	(400,000)						
Release of working capital at end . . .	107,896	.26974†							400,000
Net investment . . .	(1,238,058)								
Net present value	$ 83,576								

* From Table 4 in Appendix 14-B.

† From Table 2 in Appendix 14-B.

▶ **SUMMARY**

Because income taxes affect all facets of business, a manager's failure to consider them when making decisions may have a serious impact on a firm's profitability. Decisions should therefore be made on an after-tax basis.

To be effective, capital-budgeting decisions must not only be based on **after-tax cash flows** but must also recognize the effects of **tax shields.** Two common tax shields are the realized loss on the sale of old equipment when new equipment is purchased and the amount of tax-deductible depreciation that will result from an investment decision.

The selection of a particular depreciation method can have a significant impact on an investment decision and may, in some cases, be the *determining factor that makes an investment decision profitable.* For tax purposes, only two depreciation methods may be used: the **modified accelerated cost recovery system (MACRS)** and straight-line. Because larger deductions in the earlier years of a project's life provide greater tax savings on a present value basis, *the MACRS method generally provides more favorable results than straight-line depreciation.*

The net present value analysis needed to make an investment decision should be prepared by converting cash inflows and outflows to an after-tax basis. This may be accomplished by multiplying each cash inflow or outflow by 1 minus the tax rate. Tax shields, such as depreciation, should be converted into tax savings by *multiplying the shield by the tax rate*. The NPV analysis is then prepared as discussed in Chapter 14.

▶ **GLOSSARY OF KEY TERMS**

Adjusted tax basis   Acquisition cost less allowable depreciation.   (p. 784)

After-tax cash flow   The value of a cash inflow or outflow after giving effect to income taxes.   (p. 783)

Half-year convention   For property other than 27.5-year or 31.5-year property, it is assumed that all property (other than property subject to the mid-quarter convention) is placed in service at the mid-point of the year. One half of a year's depreciation is taken in the year the property is placed in service.   (p. 786)

Mid-month convention   Real property—both residential and nonresidential—is deemed to be placed in service at the middle of the month in which the property is actually placed in service. That is, one half of a month's depreciation is taken in the month the property is placed in service.   (p. 787)

Mid-quarter convention   When a taxpayer places more than 40 percent of a year's acquired property into service in the last three months of that tax year, the property is subject to a mid-quarter convention. That is, all property for that year is treated as if it were placed into service at the mid-point of the quarter in which the property is actually placed in service.   (p. 786)

Modified accelerated cost recovery system (MACRS)   A method of depreciation used for income tax purposes that classifies depreciable property into one of eight groupings without regard to the property's actual useful life.   (p. 786)

Tax shield   Any deduction on a firm's income tax return that does not require an outlay of cash in that period.   (p. 783)

▶ **REVIEW PROBLEM**

The management of Boot Stamping Company is contemplating the purchase of a new machine, at a cost of $80,000, that is capable of producing 180,000 units per year. This machine can be sold for $20,000 and would replace a machine capable of producing 130,000 units per annum. The contribution margin per unit from operating the new machine is $.125, and it is $.10 per unit from operating the old machine.

The useful life of the old machine was 10 years when it was purchased for $25,000 two years ago. The useful life of the new machine is eight years. The new machine has a salvage value of $20,000, and the old machine's salvage value is zero. The old machine will require an overhaul at the end of two years from today at a cost of $10,000. The new machine will require an overhaul at the end of the fourth year at a cost of $8,000. The old machine is depreciated using the straight-line method.

The firm's after-tax cutoff rate for investment decisions is 14 percent. The property qualifies as five-year-MACRS property. Income taxes are at the rate of 20 percent.

Required

a. Using the comparative income approach and net present value analysis, determine if the old machine should be replaced.

b. Redo part *(a),* using the differential income approach to reach your decision.

▶ **SOLUTION TO**
REVIEW PROBLEM

a. Keep Old Machine:

	Amount	Present Value Factor	Present Value in Dollars
After-tax cash from operations ($.10 × 130,000 units × .80)	$ 10,400	4.63886	$ 48,244
Depreciation tax shield ($25,000 ÷ 5 years = $5,000 per year)*			
Year 1 ($5,000 × .20)	1,000	.87719	877
Year 2 ($5,000 × .20)	1,000	.76947	769
Year 3 ($5,000 × .20)	1,000	.67497	675
Year 4 (½ year) ($2,500 × .20)	500	.59208	296
Machine overhaul ($10,000 × .80)	(8,000)	.76947	(6,156)
Opportunity cost of keeping machine	(20,000)	1.00000	(20,000)
Net present value			$ 24,705

* Note: Depreciation was previously taken for 1½ years.

Buy New Machine:

	Amount	Present Value Factor	Present Value in Dollars
Purchase price	$(80,000)	1.00000	$(80,000)
After-tax cash from operations (180,000 × $.125 × .80)	18,000	4.63886	83,499
Depreciation tax shield:			
Year 1 ($80,000 × .20 × .20)	3,200	.87719	2,807
Year 2 ($80,000 × .32 × .20)	5,120	.76947	3,940
Year 3 ($80,000 × .192 × .20)	3,072	.67497	2,074
Year 4 ($80,000 × .1152 × .20)	1,843	.59208	1,091
Year 5 ($80,000 × .1152 × .20)	1,843	.51937	957
Year 6 ($80,000 × .0576 × .20)	922	.45559	420
Salvage value ($20,000 × .80)	16,000	.35056	5,609
Machine overhaul ($8,000 × .80)	(6,400)	.59208	(3,789)
Net present value			$ 16,608

The present value of cash inflows for the old machine exceeds that of the new machine by $8,097. Therefore, the new machine should not be purchased.

b. Net Investment:

	Amount	Present Value Factor	Present Value in Dollars
Purchase price of new machine	$(80,000)	1.00000	$(80,000)
Sales proceeds of old machine	20,000	1.00000	20,000
Salvage value of new machine	16,000	.35056	5,609
Present value			$(54,391)

Cash Operating Advantage:

	Amount	Present Value Factor	Present Value in Dollars
Incremental cash flow ($18,000 − $10,400) . . .	$ 7,600	4.63886	$ 35,255
Incremental tax shield:			
Year 1 ($3,200 − $1,000)	2,200	.87719	1,930
Year 2 ($5,120 − $1,000)	4,120	.76947	3,170
Year 3 ($3,072 − $1,000)	2,072	.67497	1,399
Year 4 ($1,843 − $500)	1,343	.59208	795
Year 5 ($1,843 − $0)	1,843	.51937	957
Year 6 ($922 − $0)	922	.45559	420
Machine overhaul:			
Old machine	8,000	.76947	6,156
New machine	(6,400)	.59208	(3,789)
Present value			46,293
Net present value			$ (8,098)

Because the net present value is negative, do not purchase the new machine.

▶ **LIBRARY ASSIGNMENT**

Read the following:

Singhvi, Surendra S., and Robert J. Lambrix. "Investment versus Financing Decisions." *Management Accounting,* March 1984, pp. 54–56.

Van Breda, Michael F. "Capital Budgeting Using Terminal Values." *Management Accounting,* July 1981, pp. 42–48.

Wolk, Harry I., Gary A. Porter, and Daniel E. Vetter. "Net Working Capital Investment and Capital Budgeting Analysis: Some Pedagogical Insights." *Journal of Accounting Education,* Fall 1989, pp. 253–62.

▶ **SELF-TEST**

True or False

1. Capital budgeting decisions are identical regardless of whether they are based on before-tax or after-tax considerations.
2. To adjust a cash inflow for tax effect, the cash inflow is multiplied by the tax rate.
3. To adjust a cash outflow for tax effect, the cash outflow is multiplied by 1 minus the tax rate.
4. Depreciation is adjusted for tax effects in capital budgeting analysis.
5. The tax savings resulting from depreciation charges are found by multiplying the depreciation by 1 minus the tax rate.
6. An automobile is classified as a three-year property for tax purposes.
7. The purchase date of equipment does affect the amount of depreciation allowed in a year.
8. Under MACRS, salvage value is taken into consideration for computing depreciation.
9. When a taxable gain results from the sale of an asset, the net cash inflow equals the product of the gain multiplied by 1 minus the tax rate.

10. When differential analysis is used, the difference in the depreciation tax shields is arrived at by adding the two depreciation amounts.
11. When comparative analysis is used, the difference in the depreciation tax shields is arrived at by netting the two depreciation amounts.
12. An investment in working capital does not provide a tax shield.
13. When working capital is released from a project, it is not adjusted for tax effects.
14. An investment in inventory provides a tax shield because it is a cash outflow.
15. If a company with a 30 percent tax rate elects straight-line depreciation for its $20,000 computer (five year property), the tax shield in the first year would equal $600.

Multiple Choice

1. Shireburk purchased 20 percent of the outstanding capital stock of Hebert Corporation for $275,000 on May 1, 19x4. Hebert declares a dividend of $100,000 to be distributed among the capital stock owners on December 30, 19x4. If Shireburk has a marginal tax rate of 30 percent, the cash flow (disposable income) is
   a. $6,000.
   b. $14,000.
   c. $20,000.
   d. $70,000.
2. The after-tax cash flow of a revenue item is
   a. Revenue × (1 + tax rate).
   b. Revenue × (tax rate).
   c. Revenue × (1 − tax rate).
   d. None of the above.
3. The after-tax cash flow of a cost item is
   a. Cost × (1 + tax rate).
   b. Cost × (tax rate).
   c. Cost × (1 − tax rate).
   d. Cost.
4. The after-tax cash flow of depreciation cost is
   a. Depreciation × (1 + tax rate).
   b. Depreciation × (tax rate).
   c. Depreciation × (1 − tax rate).
   d. Depreciation.
5. Gros plans to purchase 10 Kaos bonds that mature in 10 years from today for $10,000. The stated rate of interest on the bonds is 10 percent semiannually. Gros requires a 6 percent after-tax rate of return on all investments. If Gros has a marginal income tax rate of 40 percent, what is the maximum investment amount it should be willing to pay?
   a. $9,642.83.
   b. $9,024.88.
   c. $10,000.00
   d. $9,263.95.
6. In 19x5, Ventura, Inc., purchased an 18-wheel delivery truck for $80,000. The truck is classified as five-year MACRS property. If Ventura has a 40 percent tax rate and if it requires a 10 percent after-tax rate of return, what is the present value of the tax shield in year 1?
   a. $4,364.
   b. $5,818.
   c. $6,545.
   d. $8,727.

► **QUESTIONS**

1. Is it necessary to consider the effects of income taxes when making a capital-budgeting decision? Why?
2. What is an after-tax cost? How is it computed?
3. What is after-tax cash flow? How is it computed?
4. What is a tax shield? Why is it important for capital-budgeting decisions?
5. If an investment in a machine has an estimated useful life of eight years and it is five-year MACRS property, how is the difference between eight and five years treated in a capital-budgeting analysis?
6. What is the half-year convention?
7. If a firm has a choice between MACRS and straight-line depreciation, which method should the firm use on its income tax return if it is operating at a profit? Why?
8. Depreciation has no effect on cash flow. Discuss the validity of this statement if:
   a. Income taxes *are not* considered when making a capital-budgeting decision.
   b. Income taxes *are* considered when making a capital-budgeting decision.
9. The book value of a machine that is being replaced with a newer machine has no effect on a firm's cash flow. Discuss the validity of this statement if:
   a. Income taxes *are not* considered when making a capital-budgeting decision.
   b. Income taxes *are* considered when making a capital-budgeting decision.
10. When a firm sells an old machine at a taxable gain, it has both an inflow and an outflow; but if the machine is sold at a taxable loss, only cash inflows result. Explain.
11. A firm plans to spend $30,000 for an advertisement, and its income tax bracket is 40 percent. What is the after-tax cost of the advertisement?
12. A firm plans to purchase a machine for $60,000. The machine is five-year MACRS property. Calculate the tax shield if the firm is in the 30 percent income tax bracket.
13. A firm is evaluating the purchase of a machine that has a cost of $90,000 and a useful life of six years. The firm plans to use straight-line depreciation, and the machine has a zero salvage value. The machine is expected to earn revenues of $80,000 in the second year of its useful life, and variable costs are expected to be $30,000 in that year. There are no direct fixed costs associated with the machine. The firm's income tax rate is 40 percent. Compute the firm's after-tax cash inflow from the machine in the second year of its useful life.

► **EXERCISES**

E15–1 **Net Present Value—MACRS Depreciation**

The Newton Auto Repair Company is contemplating the purchase of electronic testing equipment that will enable the firm to perform emission-control inspections. The equipment has a useful life of 10 years, no salvage value, and can be purchased at a cost of $24,000.

Newton estimates that revenues from inspections will be $24,000 per annum and direct labor and variable overhead costs will be $18,000 per annum.

The property qualifies as five-year MACRS property. The company's income tax rate is 25 percent.

Required Compute the net present value for each of the following after-tax discount rates, and indicate whether the investment should be made at that rate:
a. 18 percent.
b. 20 percent.

E15–2 **Net Present Value—Straight-Line Depreciation**

Use the information provided in Exercise 15-1 except that the company elects not to use MACRS.

The property is to be depreciated using the straight-line method over the shortest period possible for five-year property. The company's income tax rate is 25 percent.

Required Compute the net present value for each of the following after-tax discount rates, and indicate whether the investment should be made at that rate:

a. 18 percent.

b. 20 percent.

E15–3 Net Present Value Analysis for Competing Investments and Profitability Index—MACRS Depreciation

Brown Business School has decided that to remain competitive with other local business schools, it must expand and update its computer science department. Brown is convinced that to accomplish this, it must purchase a new central processing unit (CPU). Officials of the school have been negotiating with two mainframe manufacturers, JCN Corporation and CNR Technologies. The representative of JCN Corporation has advised Brown that its model ZIPPY 1000 would be appropriate for the school's needs. The cost of the machine would be $1.6 million. In 10 years, the machine would be obsolete, at which time it would have a disposal value of $160,000. After a detailed study, the representative has convinced Brown that additional student revenues and savings from administrative costs would provide a net cash inflow of $320,000 annually.

The representative of CNR Technologies is offering Brown its model SPEEDY 250 at a cost of $2.4 million. The SPEEDY 250 would also be obsolete in 10 years but would have a disposal value of $400,000. Net cash inflow from this machine would be $400,000 per year.

The property qualifies as five-year MACRS property. The school's income tax rate is 25 percent. Salvage value is not taken into account when computing MACRS depreciation.

Required *a.* Assuming the school desires a 12 percent after-tax return on its investment, use the net present value concept to determine which machine the school should purchase.

b. Compute the profitability index for each investment. Is your answer the same as in part *(a)*? Is this always true? Explain.

E15–4 Net Present Value Analysis for Competing Investments and Profitability Index—Straight-Line Depreciation

Use the information provided in Exercise 15–3 except that the school elects not to use MACRS.

The school elects to take straight-line depreciation over the shortest period possible for five-year property. The school's income tax rate is 25 percent.

Required *a.* Assuming the school desires a 12 percent after-tax return on its investment, use the net present value concept to determine which machine the school should purchase.

b. Compute the profitability index for each investment. Is your answer the same as in part *(a)*? Is this always true? Explain.

E15–5 Competing Investments and Net Present Value

The Driscoll Company has $300,000 to invest. The plant superintendent has suggested purchasing a new, more efficient machine. On the other hand, the financial vice president would like the firm to purchase a competing firm's customer list, which is for sale. The machine has a useful life of five years, and the customer list is also expected to yield cash flows for a five-year period. Neither investment is expected to have any residual value.

The projected cash advantage per annum for each investment is:

Year	Machine	Customer List
19x1	$240,000	$ 81,000
19x2	201,000	159,000
19x3	159,000	201,000
19x4	120,000	240,000
19x5	81,000	279,000
Total.	$801,000	$960,000

The machine qualifies as five-year MACRS property. The company's income tax rate is 25 percent.

The customer list is not MACRS property. However, it will qualify for straight-line depreciation. The half-year convention does not apply to the customer list.

Required
a. Using an after-tax cutoff rate of 22 percent, calculate the net present value of each investment. If only one investment can be made, which would you choose? Why?

b. Redo part (a), but this time use an after-tax cutoff rate of 10 percent. Does your answer differ from the answer to part (a)? Explain.

E15–6   Competing Investments and Net Present Value

The Burton Company has $600,000 to invest. The plant superintendent has suggested purchasing a new, more efficient machine. On the other hand, the financial vice president would like the firm to purchase a competing firm's customer list, which is for sale. The machine has a useful life of five years, and the customer list is also expected to yield cash flows for a five-year period. Neither investment is expected to have any residual value.

The projected cash advantage per annum for each investment is:

Year	Machine	Customer List
19x1	$ 360,000	$ 160,800
19x2	280,800	240,000
19x3	240,000	400,800
19x4	199,200	360,000
19x5	240,000	360,000
Total.	$1,320,000	$1,521,600

The machine qualifies as five-year MACRS property. The company's income tax rate is 40 percent.

The customer list is not MACRS property. However, it will qualify for straight-line depreciation. The half-year convention does not apply to the customer list.

Required
a. Using an after-tax cutoff rate of 16 percent, calculate the net present value of each investment. If only one investment can be made, which would you choose? Why?

b. Redo part (a), but this time use an after-tax cutoff rate of 10 percent. Does your answer differ from the answer to part (a)? Explain.

E15–7   **Net Present Value (Extension of Exercise 14–6)—MACRS Depreciation**

The Building Corporation, a heavy-construction business, is interested in replacing one of its backhoes with a new model. The new equipment costs $325,000 and has an expected useful life of 10 years. At the end of its useful life, the equipment will have a salvage value of $20,000. Due to increased efficiency, the company expects to save 1,000 hours per year in labor costs. A backhoe operator earns $50 per hour, including fringe benefits.

The manufacturer is offering a $40,000 trade-in allowance on the old equipment, which has a current book value of $195,000 and a zero disposal value at the end of its useful life in 10 years. Building Corporation desires an after-tax return of at least 14 percent on its investments.

The property qualifies as five-year MACRS property. The company's income tax rate is 25 percent.

Required   Using net present value analysis, determine whether Building Corporation should purchase the equipment.

E15–8   **Net Present Value (Extension of Exercise 14–6)—Straight-Line Depreciation**

Use the information provided in Exercise 15-7 except that Building elects not to use MACRS.

The company elects to take straight-line depreciation over the shortest period possible for five-year property. The company's income tax rate is 25 percent.

Required   Using net present value analysis, determine whether Building Corporation should purchase the equipment.

E15–9   **Net Present Value—Straight-Line Depreciation**

The Boise Company, an electronics manufacturer, is interested in replacing one of its machines with a new model. The new equipment costs $360,000 and has an expected useful life of 10 years. At the end of its useful life, the equipment will have a salvage value of $24,000. Due to increased efficiency, the company expects to save 5,000 hours per year in labor costs. A machine operator earns $24 per hour, including fringe benefits.

The old machine can be sold for $48,000 and has a current book value of $120,000. Its disposal value at the end of its useful life in 10 years is zero. Boise desires an after-tax return of at least 16 percent on its investments.

The company elects to take straight-line depreciation over the shortest period possible for five-year property. The company's income tax rate is 30 percent.

Required   Using net present value analysis, determine whether Boise should purchase the equipment.

▶ **PROBLEMS**   P15–10   **Net Present Value Analysis for Purchasing a New Machine and Replacing an Existing Machine (Extension of Problem 14–20)—Straight-Line Depreciation**

The Montana Corporation is presently using a machine, M–1, in its production process. It is contemplating the purchase of a newer, more efficient machine, M–2. The following information is available:

	M–1	M–2
Purchase price	$750,000	$1,500,000
Useful life	15 years	10 years
Salvage value	$ 75,000	$ 120,000
Accumulated depreciation ($675,000 ÷ 15 years = $45,000; $45,000 × 5 years)	225,000	–0–
Depreciation per annum	45,000	?
Sales revenue	750,000	1,050,000
Direct materials cost.	135,000	160,000
Direct labor.	225,000	194,000
Variable overhead	135,000	120,000
Direct fixed overhead	105,000	135,000

The property is to be depreciated by the straight-line method over the shortest period possible for five-year property. The company's income tax rate is 25 percent. The after-tax cutoff rate for investments is 14 percent.

Required *a.* Assume the Montana Corporation is contemplating the purchase of M–2 and also intends to keep M–1. There is a sufficient market for the firm's output from both machines. Prepare schedules to compute:

(1) The net investment of M–2.

(2) The cash operating advantage of M–2.

(3) The net present value to determine if M–2 should be purchased. Should M–2 be purchased? Why?

b. Assume market conditions are such that the corporation can sell the output from M–2 or M–1 but not both. Thus, if M–2 is purchased, M–1 will be sold for $150,000. Using differential analysis, prepare schedules to compute:

(1) The net investment of M–2.

(2) The cash operating advantage of M–2.

(3) The net present value to determine if M–1 should be replaced. Should M–1 be replaced? Why?

P15–11 **Net Present Value Analysis for Purchasing a New Machine and Replacing an Existing Machine (Extension of Problem 14–20)— MACRS Depreciation**

Use the information provided in Problem 15–10 except that Montana elects to use MACRS.

The property qualifies as five-year MACRS property. The company's income tax rate is 25 percent. The after-tax cutoff rate for investments is 14 percent.

Required *a.* Assume the Montana Corporation is contemplating the purchase of M–2 and also intends to keep M–1. There is a sufficient market for the firm's output from both machines. Prepare schedules to compute:

(1) The net investment of M–2.

(2) The cash operating advantage of M–2.

(3) The net present value to determine if M–2 should be purchased. Should M–2 be purchased? Why?

b. Assume market conditions are such that the corporation can sell the output from M–2 or M–1 but not both. Thus, if M–2 is purchased, M–1 will be sold for $200,000. Using differential analysis, prepare schedules to compute:

(1) The net investment of M–2.

(2) The cash operating advantage of M–2.

(3) The net present value to determine if M–1 should be replaced. Should M–1 be replaced? Why?

P15–12   **Net Present Value Analysis for Replacing Equipment (Extension of Problem 14–22)—Comparative Income Approach, MACRS Depreciation**

The Nebraska Corporation is presently using a machine, K–1, in its production process. It is contemplating the purchase of a newer, more efficient machine, K–9. The following information is available:

	K–1	K–9
Purchase price	$156,000	$240,000
Useful life	12 years	8 years
Salvage value	$ 12,000	$ 10,000
Present resale value	72,000	
Sales revenue	120,000	145,000
Direct materials cost	24,000	29,000
Direct labor	29,000	22,000
Variable overhead	14,000	11,000
Direct fixed overhead	24,000	26,000
Cost to overhaul K–1 to extend its remaining life of 4 years by 4 additional years, for a total of 8 years	36,000	

The property qualifies as five-year MACRS property. The company's income tax rate is 25 percent. The firm's after-tax cutoff rate for investments is 14 percent.

Required   *a.* Using the comparative income approach, compute the following:
(1) The net investment of purchasing K–9.
(2) The cash operating advantage of K–9.
(3) The net present value to determine if K–9 should be purchased.
b. Using the comparative income approach, compute the following:
(1) The net investment of retaining K–1. (*Hint:* Use K–1's opportunity cost.)
(2) The cash operating advantage of K–1.
(3) The net present value to determine if K–1 should be retained.
c. Should K–9 be purchased and K–1 sold? Why?

P15–13   **Net Present Value Analysis for Replacing Equipment (Extension of Problem 14–22)—Differential Income Approach, MACRS Depreciation**

The Nebraska Corporation is presently using a machine, K–1, in its production process. It is contemplating the purchase of a newer, more efficient machine, K–9. Use the information provided in Problem 15–12.

The property qualifies as five-year MACRS property. The company's income tax rate is 25 percent. The firm's after-tax cutoff rate for investments is 14 percent.

Required   Using the differential income approach, compute the following:

a. The net investment of replacing K–1.
b. The cash operating advantage of replacing K–1.
c. The net present value to determine if K–1 should be replaced. Should K–1 be replaced? Why?

P15–14   **Payback, Accounting Rate of Return, Net Present Value, Profitability Index, and Internal Rate of Return—Straight-Line Depreciation**

Hazman Company plans to replace an old piece of equipment that is obsolete and expected to be unreliable under the stress of daily operations. The equipment is fully depreciated, and no salvage value can be realized on its disposal.

One piece of equipment being considered would provide annual cash savings of $7,000 before income taxes. The equipment would cost $18,000 and have an estimated useful life of five years. No salvage value would be used for depreciation purposes because the equipment is expected to have no value at the end of five years.

Hazman uses the straight-line depreciation method on all equipment for tax purposes. The company is subject to a 40 percent tax rate. Hazman has an after-tax cost of capital of 14 percent.

Required   *a.* For Hazman Company's proposed investment in new equipment, calculate the after-tax:
   (1) Payback period.
   (2) Accounting rate of return.
   (3) Net present value.
   (4) Profitability (present value) index.
   (5) Internal rate of return.
   Assume all operating revenues and costs occur at the end of the year.

   b. Identify and discuss the issues Hazman Company should consider when deciding which of the five decision models identified in part *(a)* it should employ to compare and evaluate alternative capital-investment projects.

(CMA Adapted)

P15–15   Comparative Income and Differential Income Approaches to Net Present Value Analysis of Replacing a Machine—MACRS Depreciation

The management of Yates Stamping Company is contemplating the purchase of a new machine, at a cost of $190,000, that is capable of producing 180,000 units per year. The old machine can be sold for $48,000 and is capable of producing 130,000 units per annum. The contribution margin per unit from operating the new machine is $.30, and it is $.24 per unit from operating the old machine.

The useful life of the old machine was 10 years when it was purchased for $60,000 two years ago. The useful life of the new machine is eight years. The new machine has a salvage value of $48,000, and the old machine's salvage value is zero. The old machine will require an overhaul at the end of two years from today at a cost of $24,000. The new machine will require an overhaul at the end of the fourth year at a cost of $19,000. The old machine is depreciated using the straight-line method.

The firm's after-tax cutoff rate for investment decisions is 14 percent. The property qualifies as five-year MACRS property. Income taxes are at the rate of 20 percent.

Required   *a.* Using the comparative income approach and net present value analysis, determine if the old machine should be replaced.

   b. Redo part *(a)*, using the differential income approach to reach your decision.

P15–16   Comparative Income and Differential Income Approaches to Net Present Value Analysis of Replacing a Machine—Straight-Line Depreciation

Carmel Company purchased a machine two years ago at a cost of $1.2 million. At that time, the equipment had a useful life of 12 years and a salvage value of $160,000. At the end of the fifth year (three years from now), the equipment is due for a $120,000 overhaul. Estimated cash inflow from the equipment is $56,000 per year. The company is considering the purchase of newer equipment as a replacement. The cost of the new equipment would be $2.2 million. The equipment manufacturer is willing to purchase the old equipment for $400,000. The new equipment represents state-of-the-art technology, and the company expects productivity savings of $465,000 per year over the old equipment. The new equipment will have a useful life of 10 years and a disposal value of $400,000. The company elects straight-line depreciation on all assets of this type and considers an after-tax return of less than 12 percent on investments unacceptable. The company's income tax rate is 30 percent.

Required   *a.* Using the comparative income approach and net present value analysis, determine if the old machine should be replaced.

   b. Redo part *(a)*, using the differential income approach to reach your decision.

P15–17 **Comparative Income and Differential Income Approaches to Net Present Value Analysis of Replacing a Machine (Extension of Problem 14–26)—MACRS Depreciation**

The Canals Company is considering the purchase of a new piece of equipment (machine B) to use in its manufacturing process as a replacement for an old machine (machine A). Operating costs for machine A have been running at an average annual rate of $90,000. At the end of its useful life, five years from now, machine A will have a disposal value of $9,000. Three years from now, machine A will be due for a complete overhaul at a cost of $22,500. The market value of this machine is currently $54,000. It was purchased five years ago for $75,000 and is being depreciated by the straight-line method.

Machine B will cost the company $90,000 and have a disposal value of $7,000 at the end of its five-year useful life. The operating costs for this machine are estimated to be $60,000 annually.

The property qualifies as five-year MACRS property. The company's income tax rate is 25 percent. The firm's after-tax cutoff rate for this kind of investment is 18 percent.

Required *a.* Using the comparative income approach, compute the net present value to determine if machine A should be replaced. Should machine A be replaced? Why?

b. Redo part *(a)*, using the differential income approach to reach your decision.

P15–18 **Net Present Value for Entering a New Market— Straight-Line Depreciation**

The Gambel Company is considering whether to market a newly developed dishwashing compound. The following information is available:

1. A mixing and packaging machine would be required at a cost of $1.2 million. The machine would have a useful life of 10 years. The company uses straight-line depreciation for tax purposes. At the end of 10 years, the machine would have a salvage value of $48,000.
2. At the end of the fifth year, the machine would require an overhaul at a cost of $192,000. This amount would be deductible on the company's income tax return in that year.
3. Working capital required at the beginning of the first year would amount to $120,000. At the end of the third year, another $48,000 will be required. The full $168,000 will be released at the end of the 10-year period, at which time the firm expects to drop this product and market a replacement product.
4. The firm will launch the marketing with an advertising blitz at a cost of $192,000. This will occur at the beginning of the first year and is in addition to the regular recurring advertising.
5. The operating cash inflows before income taxes are expected to be:

Years	Amount
1–3	$324,000
4–6	432,000
7–10	288,000

The company's after-tax cutoff rate is 14 percent. Income taxes are 30 percent.

Required *a.* Using net present value analysis, prepare schedules to compute the net present value of the project.

b. Should the firm go ahead with the project? Why?

P15–19   **Net Present Value for Entering a New Market—MACRS Depreciation**

The Gambel Company is considering whether to market a newly developed dishwashing compound. Use the information provided in Problem 15–18 except that Gambel elects to use MACRS.

The company's after-tax cutoff rate is 14 percent. Income taxes are 30 percent.

Required   *a.* Using net present value analysis, prepare schedules to compute the net present value of the project.

b. Should the firm go ahead with the project? Why?

P15–20   **Net Present Value Analysis for Entering a New Market (Extension of Problem 14–27)—MACRS Depreciation**

The Aromatic Company, which produces inexpensive automatic coffeemakers, is thinking of introducing a new line of expensive automatic coffeemakers that will both grind the coffee beans and brew the coffee. A market survey indicates that there is only a limited market for this product because of its high cost and estimates that after five years, there will be no market at all.

The following annual information about the new product is available to you:

Estimated sales (15,000 × $80)	$1,200,000
Cost of direct materials and direct labor	400,000
Variable overhead	112,000
Variable marketing costs.	60,000
Direct fixed overhead, marketing, and administrative costs . . .	240,000

Additional information:

Price of new machine	$1,200,000
Salvage value at the end of 5 years	16,000
Working capital needed at inception	112,000
Working capital returned at the end of 5 years	104,000
Depreciation of new machinery	MACRS

The firm's after-tax cutoff rate for investments of this type is 14 percent. The property qualifies as five-year MACRS property. The company's income tax rate is 25 percent.

Required   *a.* Which of the above data is relevant to you in recommending whether Aromatic should enter this new market?

b. Using net present value analysis, determine if it is advantageous for Aromatic to enter this new market.

P15–21   **Purchasing an Existing Business and Net Present Value Analysis (Extension of Problem 14–28)—Straight-Line Amortization of Leasehold**

Sparky Little is working in the accounting department of a large corporation. It appears that Little's progress is blocked, and he would like to try something else. Several evenings each week, Little visits a tavern called Archer's Place. One evening when Little was feeling very discouraged, he learned that the tavern was for sale, and in the conversation that followed, Archer offered to sell the tavern to Little.

Archer has a 10-year assignable lease of the property. Little hired an engineering consultant to evaluate the equipment, and it was determined that the refrigeration unit would require an overhaul at a cost of $12,000 in five years.

Archer is asking $240,000 for the leasehold and equipment. The equipment should be worth about $48,000 at the end of the 10-year lease.

Little engaged the services of a CPA to review the tavern's records. The CPA is confident that the tavern will yield $48,000 in cash flow for the coming year. Little is equally confident that he can increase cash flow each year by 10 percent over the preceding year's cash flow. Working capital of $36,000 will be needed during the 10 years of operation and will be released at the end of the lease.

Little will only purchase the tavern if it yields an after-tax return of 18 percent.

Required Using net present value analysis, determine if Little should purchase the tavern.

P15–22 **Lease or Purchase (Extension of Problem 14–32)—MACRS Depreciation**

The T&K Trucking Company's business is expanding, and the firm's management has decided that an additional truck is needed. The firm must decide whether to purchase or lease the truck.

Information regarding the purchase of the truck is as follows:

Purchase price	$96,000
Annual operating costs for maintenance, licenses, and fees	6,400
Annual repairs:	
Year 1	1,600
2	3,200
3	4,800
4	16,000
5	6,400
6	8,000
Useful life	6 years
Salvage value	$12,000

The truck can be leased for six years at an annual rental of $28,000 plus 30 cents per mile driven. The lessor will be responsible for repairs, maintenance, licenses, and fees. At the end of the lease term, the truck will be returned to the lessor.

The lessee is responsible for insurance and gasoline usage in either case. T&K normally uses the truck at the rate of 25,000 miles annually. Any damage to the truck is the responsibility of the lessee. The lessor requires a deposit of $12,000, which will be refunded at the end of the lease term if the truck is returned undamaged.

If the truck is purchased, it will qualify as five-year property for MACRS purposes, which will be used on the firm's income tax return. The firm's income tax rate is 30 percent. The after-tax cost of capital for T&K is 12 percent.

Required a. Using present value analysis, compute the cost of purchasing the truck.
b. Using present value analysis, compute the cost of renting the truck for six years.
c. What choice do you recommend? Why?

P15–23 **Lease or Purchase (Extension of Problem 14–33)—MACRS Depreciation**

The Sellmore Company hired an additional traveling sales rep. Because the firm's policy is to provide every salesperson with an automobile, Sellmore must decide whether to purchase or lease an automobile for the new sales rep.

Information regarding the purchase of the auto is as follows:

Purchase price	$20,000
Annual operational costs for maintenance, licenses, and fees	1,000
Annual repairs:	
Year 1	500
2	1,600
3	3,000
4	3,600
Useful life	4 years
Salvage value	$ 5,000

The automobile can be leased for four years at an annual rental of $7,000 plus 20 cents per mile driven in excess of 60,000 miles. The lessor will be responsible for repairs, maintenance, licenses, and fees. At the end of the lease term, the auto will be returned to the lessor, and the lessee will pay the excess mileage charge at that time.

The lessee is responsible for insurance and gasoline usage in either case. Sellmore expects its sales rep to use the automobile at the rate of 20,000 miles annually. Any damage to the auto is the responsibility of the lessee. The lessor requires a deposit of $5,000, which will be refunded at the end of the lease term if the auto is returned undamaged.

If the automobile is purchased, it will qualify as five-year property for MACRS purposes, which will be used on the firm's income tax return. The firm's income tax rate is 30 percent. The after-tax cost of capital for Sellmore is 12 percent.

Required
a. Using present value analysis, compute the cost of purchasing the automobile.
b. Using present value analysis, compute the cost of renting the automobile for four years.
c. What choice do you recommend? Why?

► **CASE**   **C15–24**   **Computations of Contribution Margin, Standard Overhead Rate, and Net Present Value for Investing in a New Machine**

The Oilers Company makes a microcomputer desk that it sells for $20 under a contract to a large computer retailer. The company operates one shift in its Ohio plant. The annual normal capacity is 100,000 units.

Direct labor is paid at the rate of $4 per hour. An employee can produce a desk in four hours. Eight board feet of hardboard costing $.25 per board foot are used in each desk. Indirect manufacturing costs (manufacturing overhead) at normal capacity of 100,000 units are described by the following budget line:

Total costs = Fixed costs + Variable cost per unit
Total costs = $25,000 + $.30 per unit

Some years ago, the Oilers Company installed a saw that presently has a carrying value (book value) of $20,000 and is being depreciated $2,000 a year. At the time of installation, it was estimated that the saw would have no scrap value at the end of its useful life because the scrap value would equal its dismantling costs.

At present, a sales agent from the Whalers Company is encouraging the Oilers Company to replace the old saw, currently in operation, with its new computer-controlled saw. An advantage of the new machine is that it will cut direct labor time substantially; the time required to produce one desk will fall from four hours to two hours. However, because the new saw is more powerful than the present machine, utility costs are expected to increase by $.10 per unit.

The new saw will cost $100,000, including installation charges and transportation. The estimated useful life of the new saw is 10 years; it will be depreciated by the straight-line method. At the end of 10 years, the salvage value is estimated to be $10,000.

The Whalers Company agrees that if Oilers will buy the new saw, it will buy the old saw for $4,000 with no dismantling costs to be charged to Oilers. The income tax rate is 50 percent. The Oilers Company management expects a return on investment of 15 percent. For income tax purposes, the loss on trade-in of the old machine is allowable as a tax deduction.

Required   As financial analyst for the Oilers Company, you are charged with analysis of the purchase of the new equipment. In the preparation of a report for the president, you will need to determine for consideration by management:

a. The contribution margin per unit, under current operating conditions.

b. The standard overhead rate (applied rate) per unit under current operating conditions.

c. The budget line for indirect manufacturing costs (manufacturing overhead), assuming the new saw is purchased and installed.

d. The manufacturing overhead standard rate (applied rate) of the new machine if normal capacity of 100,000 units is expected to remain the same.

e. The contribution margin per unit, assuming the sales price remains unchanged, if the new saw is purchased and installed.

f. The net additional investment of the machine, assuming the Oilers Company decides to install the new saw.

g. The expected net additional cash flow per year if the new saw is installed—assume the company sells all that it produces.

h. The present value index (profitability index) of the new equipment.

i. Comment on the importance of the profitability index.

[Prepared by Professor Nabil Hassan of Wright State University, Dayton, Ohio. Adapted with the permission of the Institute of Management Accountants (IMA).]

▶ **ANSWERS TO SELF-TEST**

True or False

1. False	2. False	3. True	4. True	5. False
6. False	7. False	8. False	9. True	10. False
11. False	12. True	13. True	14. False	15. True

Multiple Choice

1. *b.*   2. *c.*   3. *c.*   4. *b.*   5. *c.*   6. *b.*

16

Decentralized Operations and Transfer Pricing

After reading this chapter, you should be able to:

1. Differentiate between a cost center, a revenue center, a profit center, and an investment center.
2. Discuss the advantages and disadvantages of decentralized operations.
3. Prepare an organization chart showing the lines of authority for responsibility centers.
4. Explain how the building block approach is used to prepare performance reports for responsibility centers.
5. Describe the different approaches used to evaluate cost centers and revenue centers.
6. Prepare performance reports for revenue centers.
7. Describe the different approaches used to evaluate profit centers and investment centers.
8. Compute return on investment and residual income.
9. Prepare performance reports for investment centers.
10. Compute an appropriate transfer price between responsibility centers of an organization such that the firm's contribution margin is optimized under a condition of full capacity or idle capacity.

► **INTERVIEW**

John Harriott
Management Associate of
Economics and
Management
Manhattanville College

Q. *In the course of your work, have you had an occasion to work with a responsibility center, such as a cost center, a revenue center, a profit center, or an investment center? If so, with which ones have you worked? What was the rationale for the selection of that particular center?*

A. I have worked with cost centers, profit centers, and investment centers to provide managers with tools for decision making and performance evaluation.

A properly designed hierarchical structure of cost centers, profit centers, and investment centers provides a mechanism for planning and control of all aspects of a business. This hierarchy allows for a "bottom up" approach to construction of the corporate or investment center's financial or profit plan. The hierarchy also provides the means for interim evaluation of performance for mid-course correction.

Using a decentralized approach that allows each cost center manager to determine the resources he or she needs to accomplish the requirements, the center places ownership at the level to which it belongs. The more an individual is involved in creating and controlling his or her destiny the better performance will be.

However, the decentralized approach requires significantly more time for analysis and evaluation in the planning process because of the natural tendency of managers to project costs higher than necessary. One method that I have found useful in counteracting this tendency is to use the "zero base" budget technique for all significant line items required by the center, primarily for salaries, travel and entertainment, consulting services, and similar expenses.

This technique can also be used for profit centers by determining revenues from forecasted sales of products assigned to the center. All other costs can be derived from this projected volume and compared to historical data for reasonableness.

When accepting the decentralized system of control, however, be prepared to experience higher operating costs because of the need for duplicate functions. Arguments can be made that the increased costs are more than offset by the savings that a hands-on decentralized approach can generate.

▶ Controlling a firm's operations is a vital part of a manager's duties. The management by exception principle, discussed in Chapter 10 in conjunction with standard costing and performance reporting, is but one aspect of the controlling function. A senior manager must also delegate authority and the responsibility for making decisions to others. The amount of authority delegated varies widely among companies.

To monitor managers to whom authority has been delegated, many firms incorporate responsibility accounting into their performance reporting system. As discussed in Chapter 2, *responsibility accounting* is a reporting system in which a cost is charged to the lowest level of management that has responsibility for it. In this chapter, this concept is expanded to include not only costs but also, in certain cases, revenues. The reporting system begins with a performance report at the lowest level of management responsibility. This report is then included in the next level of management responsibility, and the process is repeated until the top level of management is reached.

Different criteria are used to evaluate the performance of responsibility centers. The choice depends on the extent of authority delegation and a manager's preference for a particular criterion. The most commonly used criterion by investment centers is return on investment (ROI) or a variation of it.   ◀

▶ RESPONSIBILITY ACCOUNTING

Chapter 1 discussed the functions of management. One function, the delegation of authority, is often used in the largest companies, and these firms are referred to as *decentralized firms*. **Decentralization** is the delegation of a great deal of authority to the lowest level of management responsibility that can make important decisions. On the other hand, a **centralized organization** is one in which little authority is delegated to lower-level managers.

When a firm is highly decentralized, it must have a control mechanism that effectively monitors and motivates employees to behave in ways that will help the firm meet its objectives. Although the bottom line—profit maximization—should be one of a firm's goals, other goals, and the manner in which they are achieved, are equally important. Thus, there may be different routes for achieving a specific objective, and the route taken should be compatible with the company's image. To ensure control, the firm's objectives, which may include targeted profits, market leadership, excellent employee relations, social consciousness, and quality of products, should be clearly delineated together with the routes by which the goals are to be achieved. In addition, some form of incentive compensation is apt to motivate managers to behave in accordance with organizational goals. One way in which decentralized firms can delegate authority yet retain control and monitor managers' performance is to structure the organization into responsibility centers.

Responsibility Centers

A **responsibility center** is a segment of an organization whose managers have the authority to incur and control costs, earn revenues, and invest funds in assets. A responsibility center may be responsible for all three functions or for only one function. A responsibility center may be a cost center, a revenue center, a profit center, or an investment center.

L.O. 1
Cost, revenue, profit, and investment centers

Cost Center   A **cost center** is a segment of an organization whose managers have the authority to incur and control costs. An example of a cost center is a fabricating department in a manufacturing firm. The department would have no revenues if *all of its production is part of the production process.*

However, the department's manager would be responsible for the department's variable costs and direct fixed costs.

Revenue Center   A **revenue center** is a segment of an organization whose managers are responsible only for the *revenues* the center earns. Typically, the manager of a revenue center is responsible for marketing a product or product line. However, a revenue center normally has some costs, even if they are only salaries and occupancy costs. Thus, a revenue center is responsible primarily for revenues and only incidentally for some costs, usually not product costs. In that way, a revenue center differs from a cost center, which has primary responsibility for product costs, and a profit center, which has primary responsibility for both revenues and product costs.

Profit Center   A **profit center** is a segment of an organization whose managers have the authority to incur and control costs and to control the revenues the center earns. A typical profit center would be a specific product line. The manager of a profit center has the ability to control the center's variable and direct fixed costs. In addition, he or she can decide how many units to produce and thus control the revenues earned. A profit center manager also has the ability to control some of the investments in assets, but not all. By controlling revenues and costs, the manager is also able to *control profits*.

Investment Center   An **investment center** is a segment of an organization whose managers have the authority to incur and control costs, earn revenues, and control investments in assets. An investment center is an autonomous company, except for its linkage to an overall corporate headquarters. An example of an investment center might be an automobile product line that is manufactured on its own premises and whose manager has complete autonomy as long as the operations are compatible with overall corporate objectives.

Most organizations have cost centers, and many have profit centers. The use of investment centers depends on the degree of decentralization desired, the preferences of top management, and the perceived benefits derived from decentralization.

Advantages and Disadvantages of Decentralization

L.O. 2

The terms *decentralization* and *centralization* refer to two extremes. Although most firms operate somewhere between these two extremes, the question of how much decentralization is optimal will depend on a company's individual circumstances.

The advantages of decentralization are that:

1. Top-level managers are relieved of making routine decisions and can concentrate on making important and difficult decisions.
2. Employee morale is higher because lower-level managers become involved in the decision-making process instead of having a title with little or no authority.
3. Lower-level managers are better equipped for promotion to upper-level positions because they gain valuable knowledge about the company's operations through their involvement in the decision-making process.
4. Decision making becomes more effective because the person most familiar with the circumstances of the decision, the lower-level manager, has the final say.

▶ **ILLUSTRATION 16-1**   Universal Motor Car Company: Organization Chart by Product Line

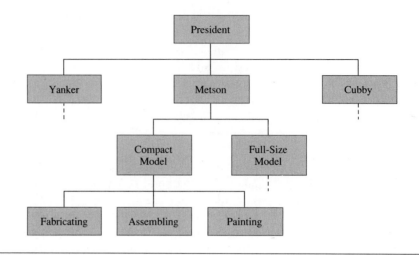

The disadvantages of decentralized operations are that:

1. Upper-level managers lose some control.
2. The lack of goal congruence between the firm and the employee may introduce dysfunctional consequences.
3. There may be duplication of effort.
4. Managers lose touch with daily operations.

The amount of decentralization employed by a firm should be periodically reviewed for its effectiveness, and adjustments should be made when necessary.

Reporting System for Responsibility Accounting

L.O. 3
Organization chart

L.O. 4
Performance reports for responsibility centers

As noted in Chapters 10 and 11, performance reports generally contain columns for budgeted and actual data, a variance column, and a space for explanations of variances. These performance reports are prepared for cost centers, revenue centers, profit centers, and investment centers starting at the lowest level. That report is then incorporated into the next level and so on until the president's report is prepared. To ensure the success of this process, it is extremely important for the levels of management responsibility to be clearly delineated, a task that can be easily accomplished by an organization chart showing responsibility centers and lines of authority. An organization chart for the Universal Motor Car Company appears in Illustration 16-1. The company manufactures three product lines—the Yanker, the Metson, and the Cubby—and each product line manufactures different models.

Each responsibility center requires a performance report. Starting with the reports for the lowest level—that is, the cost centers of fabricating, assembling, and painting—the reports are incorporated into the next level's report—compact model—and so on until the president's report is prepared. Sample reports may be seen in Illustration 16-2.

▶ **ILLUSTRATION 16-2**

UNIVERSAL MOTOR CAR COMPANY
Sample Performance Reports
(in thousands of dollars)

	Budget	Actual	Variance
President's report:			
President's office	$(15,000)	$(16,000)	$1,000(U)
Yanker vice president.	310,000	315,000	5,000(F)
Metson vice president.	203,000	205,420	2,420(F)◄┐
Cubby vice president	220,000	221,000	1,000(F) │
Operating income before			│
income taxes	$718,000	$725,420	$7,420(F) │
Metson vice president's report:			│
Vice president's office	$(10,000)	$(10,500)	$ 500(U) │
Compact model . . . . →133,000	134,420	1,420(F) │
Full-size model.	80,000	81,500	1,500(F) │
Operating income before			│
income taxes	$203,000	$205,420	$2,420(F) ─┘
Supervisor's report for compact			
model:			
Revenue.	$300,000	$305,000	$5,000(F)
Costs:			
Fabricating	72,000	73,780	1,780(U)◄┐
Assembling	60,000	61,000	1,000(U) │
Painting	15,000	14,800	200(F) │
Other direct costs	20,000	21,000	1,000(U) │
Total costs.	167,000	170,580	3,580(U) │
Operating income before			│
income taxes . . . . └$133,000	$134,420	$1,420(F) │
Supervisor's report for fabricating			│
department:			│
Direct materials	$ 10,000	$ 10,500	$ 500(U) │
Direct labor	20,000	20,800	800(U) │
Variable overhead	12,000	12,480	480(U) │
Direct fixed overhead	30,000	30,000	–0– │
Total direct costs	$ 72,000	$ 73,780	$1,780(U) ─┘

By following the arrows in Illustration 16-2, you can see that the reporting system starts with the fabricating department's performance report, which shows an unfavorable variance of $1,780,000. The totals on this line are carried forward to the supervisor's report for the compact model. The totals of the compact model supervisor's report are then carried forward to the Metson vice president's report, and his totals are then carried forward to the president's report. Note that each responsibility center has direct costs that are *not allocated* to a lower-level manager's report.

The fabricating, assembling, and painting departments are cost centers. If the supervisor of the compact model had control of revenues (as shown in Illustration 16-2), the responsibility center would be a profit center. The responsibility center for the vice president of the Metson product line would be an investment center if the vice president controlled the investment in assets for Metson. If not, the center would be a profit center. Of course, the company as a whole would be an investment center.

Evaluating Performance Reports

Cost Centers Cost centers may be subdivided into **standard cost centers,** in which a clear relationship exists between standard inputs and standard outputs, and **discretionary cost centers,** in which costs are clearly specified but outcomes are not directly related to inputs. Typical standard cost centers would be the fabricating and assembling departments shown in Illustration 16-1. Typical discretionary cost centers would be the research and development department of a manufacturing firm and the administrative departments, such as marketing and accounting, in any company.

L.O. 5
Evaluation of cost centers

Cost centers are expected to perform within an area of targeted costs, usually budgeted or standard costs. A standard cost center's actual costs are compared to the standard costs allowed for a period of time, and the variances between the two are computed and explained to the extent possible. Illustration 10-5 (on page 486) shows a responsibility performance report for a standard cost center. Discretionary cost centers are usually assigned a budgeted amount of costs for a period of time. The performance report should compare the center's actual costs with the budgeted amounts, and any unusual variances should be investigated by senior managers. Because there is little cause and effect between output and costs, managers of research and development discretionary cost centers must be evaluated using such criteria as patentable discoveries, process improvements, and new production designs.

L.O. 5
Evaluation of revenue centers

Revenue Centers A revenue center is normally responsible for generating a portion of a firm's sales revenue. As such, the performance report for a revenue center should contain the budgeted sales for the center segregated by products and analyzed as discussed in Chapter 12. The budgeted sales should be compared to the actual sales, and any variances should be computed and analyzed. If the revenue center manager has the authority to set prices, she should be accountable for *price variances, volume variances,* and the *standard contribution margin* resulting from those variances. Otherwise, her performance should be evaluated on the basis of volume variances only.

To illustrate variance analysis, let us assume the Bobbie Company manufactures a variety of toys and has a revenue center for its doll division. The division manager has the authority to set prices. For 19x2, the center's *budget* is:

Dolls:	
500,000 units at $3 per unit	$1,500,000
Clothing:	
1 million units at $2 per unit	2,000,000
Budgeted sales	$3,500,000

Actual results for 19x2 are:

Dolls:	
600,000 units at $2.95 per unit	$1,770,000
Clothing:	
1.1 million units at $2.10 per unit . . .	2,310,000
Actual sales	$4,080,000

The *standard variable costs* for manufacturing are $1 per unit for dolls and $.80 per unit for clothing. Standard variable costs (or budgeted costs per unit) rather than *actual* costs should be used in the evaluation of revenue centers. The difference between actual and standard costs is chargeable to the cost center manufacturing the product.

A responsibility performance report may be prepared by isolating and analyzing the variances from budgeted sales as follows:

Step 1

Compare the budgeted units of a product with the actual sales in units and multiply the difference by the budgeted price per unit. The result is the *volume variance,* which may be expressed as:

Volume variance = (Actual units − Budgeted units) × Budgeted price

Step 2

Multiply the actual units sold by the difference in price between the budgeted price and the actual price. The result is the *price variance,* which may be expressed as:

Price variance = (Actual price − Budgeted price) × Actual units sold

Step 3

Compute the *standard contribution margin* effects from the variances computed in steps 1 and 2 and prepare the performance report.

L.O. 6
Performance report for revenue center

The revenue center performance report for the Bobbie Company appears in Illustration 16-3.

In evaluating the revenue center's performance, note that:

1. Although the sales revenue from dolls increased by $270,000 ($1,770,000 − $1,500,000), there was a price reduction of 5 cents per unit. Thus, for 600,000 units, a price reduction of $30,000 resulted. For this reason, it is important to look at the *increase in standard contribution margin* rather than the increase in sales revenue. It is usually possible to increase sales volume by reducing selling prices. In an extreme case, it is possible for *sales revenue to increase dramatically with a concomitant reduction in contribution margin.* If a manager received a reward for the increase in sales revenue in such a case, the reward would be improper because a penalty should have been invoked. Thus, in the Bobbie Company case, the manager should be evaluated on the basis of the $170,000 increase in the contribution margin for dolls and *not* on the $270,000 increase in doll sales revenue.

2. The manager's performance regarding clothing is positive for both volume and price, because both increased. This may be seen more clearly by comparing the sales revenue increases for dolls and clothing with their respective increases in contribution margins as follows:

	Dolls	Clothing	Excess of Clothing over Dolls
Increase in sales revenue (from recapitulation)	$270,000	$310,000	$40,000
Increase in contribution margin (from recapitulation)	170,000	230,000	60,000

► **ILLUSTRATION 16-3**

BOBBIE COMPANY
Performance Report for the Doll Revenue Center
Sales

Product	Actual Sales	Budgeted Sales	Variance (F) = Favorable (U) = Unfavorable
Dolls	$1,770,000	$1,500,000	$270,000(F)
Clothing	2,310,000	2,000,000	310,000(F)
Total sales	$4,080,000	$3,500,000	$580,000(F)

Standard Variable Cost of Sales

Dolls (600,000 × $1) and (500,000 × $1).	$ 600,000	$ 500,000	$100,000
Clothing (1.1 million × $.80) and (1 million × $.80)	880,000	800,000	80,000
Total standard costs	$1,480,000	$1,300,000	$180,000

Recapitulation

	Dolls	Clothing	Total
Increase in sales revenue	$270,000	$310,000	$580,000(F)
Increase in standard variable costs	100,000	80,000	180,000
Increase in standard contribution margin	$170,000	$230,000	$400,000(F)

Analysis of Variances

Volume:	
Increase in sales of dolls (600,000 units − 500,000 units) × $3	$300,000(F)
Increase in sales of clothing (1.1 million units − 1 million units) × $2	200,000(F)
Total volume variance	500,000(F)
Price:	
Decrease in the price of dolls ($2.95 − $3.00) × 600,000 units	30,000(U)
Increase in the price of clothing ($2.10 − $2.00) × 1.1 million units	110,000(F)
Total price variance	80,000(F)
Total sales revenue variance.	$580,000(F)

Although the increase in clothing sales revenue exceeded that of dolls by $40,000, the contribution margin increase was $60,000. An increase in sales revenue *may* increase a firm's profitability, but it is the contribution margin that affects a firm's profitability when fixed costs remain unchanged. Thus, the performance of clothing is preferred to that of dolls. Nonetheless, rewards are indicated for the performance of both because both added to the contribution margin.

L.O. 7
Evaluation of profit centers

Profit Centers   For profit centers, performance evaluation hinges on segmented income statements, as discussed in Chapter 12. The responsibility reporting system should provide management with (1) budgeted income statements showing targeted segment margins by profit center, (2) actual income statements showing segment margins by profit center, and (3) any variances between the two. A manager of a profit center is usually rewarded when his center's segment margin is equal to or greater than his targeted segment margin. The reward system is usually a function of the amount by which the actual segment margin exceeds the targeted margin—that is, the greater the excess, the greater the reward. Conversely, sanctions are usually applied in cases where actual margins are less than targeted margins, unless the condition was not controllable by the manager of the profit center.

L.O. 7
Evaluation of investment centers

L.O. 8
Return on investment

Investment Centers   A performance report for an investment center contains data on its revenues and costs and on its assets employed to earn the center's segment margin. A common measurement used to evaluate the performance of an investment center is return on investment. Return on investment is consistent with the measurement of targeted income for a responsibility center. **Return on investment (ROI)** is a measure of profitability computed by dividing the amount of operating income earned by the average investment in operating assets required to earn the income. If an investor purchases a certificate of deposit for $100,000 and receives $12,000 annually as interest income, ROI may be computed as:

$$ROI = \frac{\text{Operating income}}{\text{Investment in average operating assets}}$$

$$ROI = \frac{\$12,000}{\$100,000} = .12 = 12\%$$

The ROI concept is similar to the accounting rate of return, discussed in Chapter 14.

▶ EVALUATING A MANAGER'S PERFORMANCE USING THE ROI MODEL

Operating Income and Operating Assets

A clear understanding of the ROI model is needed for it to be used effectively in evaluating an investment center's performance.

Chapters 14 and 15 discuss the evaluation techniques used when acquiring operating assets, such as equipment and machinery. If the assets are acquired by borrowing the necessary funds, the firm will incur interest costs. On the other hand, if the firm uses cash or sells capital stock, no interest cost will appear on its income statement. Thus, interest costs are related to the means by which assets *are acquired* but not to how effectively assets *are used*. Because the ROI model measures how effectively assets are used to earn income, interest costs should not be included. Thus, the numerator of the ROI formula should exclude interest costs.

The income taxes that a firm pays are influenced by many factors. Among these are the depreciation method used (MACRS, straight-line, etc.), gains and losses on investments in stocks and bonds, foreign tax credits, and the results of sophisticated tax-planning techniques. Obviously, these factors should not influence how effectively assets are employed to earn income.

Therefore, income taxes are normally excluded from the numerator of the ROI formula. However, some firms use income *after* income taxes when a manager is given the responsibility to make decisions that affect the amount of income taxes a firm will pay.

The numerator of the ROI formula is sometimes referred to as *EBIT* (earnings before interest and taxes). In previous chapters, the term *operating income before income taxes* has been used. This term is now shortened to *operating income*.

Because the numerator is limited to income earned from operating activities, the denominator should also be limited to operating assets. Thus, if idle operating cash is invested in stocks, bonds, and real estate not used by the firm in its operations, these assets are excluded from the denominator. Hence the denominator is referred to as *investment in average operating assets*. Because operating income is earned throughout a period of time, such as a year, it is necessary to use the *average* assets for the year rather than the assets on any particular day. If the period of time in which the operating income is earned is less than a year, the average assets for that period of time are used as the denominator. The term *investment in average operating assets* is now shortened to *average operating assets*. Average operating assets are usually an average of a firm's beginning and ending amounts for a particular year.

Analysis of the ROI Formula

It is important for managers to understand how ROI can be influenced. For example, an increase in the numerator (operating income) could increase ROI. However, a decrease in the denominator (average operating assets) could also increase ROI. If an investment center's operating income for 19x1 amounted to $100,000 and its average operating assets amounted to $1 million, its ROI would be:

$$\text{ROI} = \frac{\$100,000}{\$1,000,000} = .10 = 10\%$$

If in 19x2 its operating income increased to $125,000 while its average operating assets remained at $1 million, its ROI would be 12.5 percent. The calculation would be:

$$\text{ROI} = \frac{\$125,000}{\$1,000,000} = .125 = 12.5\%$$

This increase in ROI would be considered a favorable condition for the firm, provided that a 12.5 percent ROI is greater than the firm's cost of capital (discussed in Chapter 14).

It is also possible to increase ROI by lowering average operating assets. If in 19x2 operating income remained at $100,000 but average operating assets were reduced to $800,000, ROI would also be 12.5 percent:

$$\text{ROI} = \frac{\$100,000}{\$800,000} = .125 = 12.5\%$$

This condition may be favorable, but it may also be unfavorable. Further analysis is required before a manager could reach a conclusion. To aid in analysis, managers should break ROI into its two component parts: the operating margin percentage and asset turnover. This analysis was pioneered by the E. I. du Pont de Nemours Company (Du Pont).

Operating Margin Percentage   The **operating margin percentage** may be defined as operating income divided by sales revenue. If a firm has an investment center with sales revenue of $10 million and an operating income of $1.5 million, its operating margin percentage (OMP) may be computed as:

$$\text{OMP} = \frac{\text{Operating income}}{\text{Sales revenue}} = \frac{\$1,500,000}{\$10,000,000} = .15 = 15\%$$

This measurement indicates the percentage of sales dollars available to cover interest costs, income taxes, and profit. The higher the percentage, the greater the amount of profit per dollar of sales available to the firm. This measurement enables top managers to:

1. Compare an investment center's percentage over a period of years to determine whether it is constant, increasing, or decreasing. Managers usually become concerned if the percentage is decreasing. The percentage may be increased by increasing selling prices, reducing costs, or a combination of both.
2. Compare profit centers where margin percentages are low with other profit centers. A low-percentage profit center may require greater scrutiny by top-level managers to determine if the percentage can be increased.
3. Compare their percentage with competitors' percentages when available. The competitors' information may be available from published financial statements and financial reporting services, such as Dun & Bradstreet and Financial Research Associates.

Asset Turnover   **Asset turnover** may be defined as sales revenue divided by average operating assets. A simple example of the turnover concept would be the case of a firm selling one VCR and earning an operating income of $35. If the firm's investment in the VCR is $315 and the firm sells one VCR per year, its turnover is 1 and it will earn $35 on an investment of $315. On the other hand, if the firm sells two VCRs per year, it will earn $70 ($35 × 2) on the same investment of $315, and its turnover would be 2. Thus, the higher the turnover, the more the company will earn per dollar of investment in operating assets. Our discussion of the turnover concept in this chapter is limited to operating asset turnover. Asset turnovers for individual assets, such as accounts receivable and inventories, are also useful management tools, but in another context. These turnover concepts are discussed in Chapter 18.

If a firm has sales revenue of $10 million and its average operating assets are $5 million, its asset turnover may be computed as:

$$\text{Asset turnover} = \frac{\text{Sales revenue}}{\text{Operating assets}} = \frac{\$10,000,000}{\$5,000,000} = 2$$

We would expect different investment centers to have different turnover ratios. For example, we all hope a fresh fruit and vegetables market would have a very high turnover, possibly 150. Alternatively, heavy industrial equipment would have a much lower turnover, possibly 5 or less.

Asset turnover is also useful for evaluating an investment center. Depending on its pattern, asset turnover may indicate potential trouble or convey other useful information. For example:

1. A decreasing turnover trend may indicate that the center is carrying unneeded plant assets, experiencing increased collection time for receivables, carrying obsolete inventories, and/or experiencing diminished sales revenues. A decreasing turnover trend may also mean a diminished ROI and lower profits to the firm.

2. A higher turnover trend may signal a shift away from owning plant assets and toward leasing them. By leasing plant assets, the manager of an investment center is able to decrease the denominator and thereby increase asset turnover without necessarily increasing the effective utilization of plant assets. Because neither rental costs nor ownership costs associated with plant assets appear in the asset turnover ratio, it is possible to increase this ratio by renting equipment instead of purchasing it. Although the operating margin percentage *may* be affected by rental costs if they exceed ownership costs, the increase in the turnover ratio may more than offset the decrease in the operating margin percentage.

ROI may be obtained by multiplying its component parts as follows:

$$\text{Operating margin percentage} \times \text{Asset turnover} = \text{ROI}$$

Therefore, using the previous calculations, ROI may be computed as:

$$\text{ROI} = 15\% \times 2 = 30\%$$

or

$$\text{ROI} = \frac{\$1,500,000}{\$10,000,000} \times \frac{\$10,000,000}{\$5,000,000} = 30\%$$

Notice that the sales revenue appears in both fractions and that, in fact, they cancel each other:

$$\frac{\$1,500,000}{\cancel{\$10,000,000}} \times \frac{\cancel{\$10,000,000}}{\$5,000,000} = \frac{\$1,500,000}{\$5,000,000} = 30\%$$

The final fraction after the cancellation of sales revenue is the basic ROI equation of:

$$\text{ROI} = \frac{\text{Operating income}}{\text{Operating assets}}$$

When ROI changes from one period to the next, it is important to know the cause. The change in the operating margin percentage and/or the change in the asset turnover ratio provide the answers. For example, jewelry stores typically have high margins and low turnover; the reverse is true for discount stores.

Using ROI

ROI is a more effective evaluation tool than the mere comparison of an investment center's actual operating income with its targeted amount. Managers generally agree that the ROI concept is superior to many other measurements because it relates operating income to the assets employed to earn that income.

Investment center managers should be rewarded when their ROI performance warrants it. This reward should be correlated to the magnitude of the ROI improvement. Improvements in ROI can be achieved by:

1. Increasing sales revenue.
2. Reducing costs.
3. Reducing operating assets.

Consider the following information for the Pluto Investment Center for 19x2:

Sales revenue $6,000,000
Operating income   720,000
Operating assets, January 1, 19x2 2,800,000
Operating assets, December 31, 19x2. 3,200,000

The operating margin percentage for 19x2 would be:

$$\text{OMP} = \frac{\text{Operating income}}{\text{Sales revenue}} = \frac{\$720,000}{\$6,000,000} = .12 = 12\%$$

The asset turnover for 19x2 would be:

$$\text{Asset turnover} = \frac{\text{Sales revenue}}{\text{Average operating assets}}$$

$$= \frac{\$6,000,000}{\frac{1}{2}\,(\$2,800,000 + \$3,200,000)}$$

$$= \frac{\$6,000,000}{\$3,000,000} = 2$$

The ROI for 19x2 would be:

$$\text{OMP} \times \text{Asset turnover} = 12\% \times 2 = 24\%$$

Calculating ROI for an Increase in Sales   The manager of Pluto believes he can increase sales in 19x3 by 15 percent. The 19x2 variable cost ratio of 40 percent is expected to stay the same for 19x3. No increase in fixed costs for 19x3 is anticipated, and average operating assets for 19x3 are also expected to remain unchanged at $3 million. Recall that an increase in sales will affect both the operating margin percentage and the asset turnover. The calculation would be:

$$\text{ROI} = \frac{\$1,260,000^*}{\$6,900,000\dagger} \times \frac{\$6,900,000\dagger}{\$3,000,000}$$

$$\text{ROI} = \quad 18.26\% \quad \times \quad 2.3 \quad = 42\%$$

* $6,000,000 × 15% = $900,000 − (40% × $900,000) = $540,000 + $720,000 = $1,260,000.

† $6,000,000 + 15% ($6,000,000) = $6,900,000.

Note how a 15 percent increase in sales caused the operating margin ratio to increase from 12 percent to 18.26 percent *and* caused the asset turnover ratio to increase from 2 to 2.3. The net effect on ROI was an increase from 24 percent to 42 percent.

Calculating ROI for a Reduction in Costs   If instead of an expected increase in sales, the manager of Pluto concentrated on cost reduction, and the only change expected in 19x3 was a savings of fixed costs of $300,000, the ROI would be calculated as:

$$\text{ROI} = \frac{\$720,000 + \$300,000}{\$6,000,000} \times \frac{\$6,000,000}{\$3,000,000}$$

$$\text{ROI} = \qquad 17\% \qquad \times \qquad 2 \qquad = 34\%$$

The savings in fixed costs of $300,000 will cause the operating margin percentage to increase from 12 percent to 17 percent while the asset turnover ratio remains unchanged at 2. Thus, ROI will increase from 24 percent to 34 percent. Note how the separate components of ROI—the increase in operating margin percentage and the unchanged asset turnover—provide more information than would be available if only the change in ROI were shown.

Calculating ROI for a Reduction in Operating Assets   The third possibility for increasing ROI is to decrease the average investment in operating assets. Let us assume the only change anticipated for 19x3 is a decrease in operating assets on December 31, 19x3, to $1.8 million. The calculation of ROI would be:

$$\text{ROI} = \frac{\$720,000}{\$6,000,000} \times \frac{\$6,000,000}{\$2,500,000^*}$$

$$\text{ROI} = \qquad 12\% \qquad \times \qquad 2.4 \qquad = 28.8\%$$

* ($3,200,000 + $1,800,000) ÷ 2 = $2,500,000.

The increase in asset turnover caused the ROI to increase from 24 percent to 28.8 percent. Thus, it is important for the manager of an investment center to control asset turnover when trying to increase the ROI for his center.

Controlling Asset Turnover   Managers have always been aware of operating margins and have tried to improve them with increased sales and cost reductions. However, they gave asset turnover scant attention when interest rates and cost-of-capital rates were relatively low. With the advent of near double-digit interest rates, however, managers began to pay a great deal of attention to asset turnover. When working capital is needlessly invested in assets, a firm sacrifices a part of its ROI, which may place it at a competitive disadvantage.

As firms showed increased attention to asset turnover, they began to tighten lax collection policies for delinquent accounts receivable. Many firms also had their customers' payments delivered to a lockbox, with the firm's bank depositing the checks on receipt and the firm doing the accounts receivable bookkeeping at a later date. Previously, the process was reversed, with a correspondingly greater investment in accounts receivable.

Similarly, little attention had been paid to excessive inventories. But sophisticated techniques are now used to minimize investment in inventories without interrupting production or sales practices. This subject is discussed more fully in Chapter 7 and in Appendix 9-A.

Overzealous investment center managers may attempt to lower their investments in operating assets by leasing them instead of purchasing them. For example, consider the operating results of a firm's two divisions, as shown in Illustration 16-4. Presently, they both have an investment in aver-

▶ **ILLUSTRATION 16-4**

BAGLEY COMPANY
Segmented Income Statements
For the Year Ended December 31, 19x3

	Division A	Division B
Sales	$4,000,000	$4,000,000
Variable costs	1,200,000	1,200,000
Contribution margin	2,800,000	2,800,000
Direct fixed costs	1,000,000	1,000,000
Segment margin	$1,800,000	$1,800,000

age operating assets of $9 million. Their ROIs are the same and may be computed as:

$$\text{ROI} = \frac{\$1,800,000}{\$9,000,000} = .2 = 20\%$$

For 19x4, both divisions expect to replace equipment that originally cost $3 million with new equipment expected to cost $3 million. The new equipment is expected to last 10 years. Division A plans to purchase the equipment, and Division B plans to lease the equipment for only five years. To simplify the ROI calculations, let us assume the cost of leasing is approximately the same as owning the equipment. The results of operations for 19x5 are expected to be the same as that for 19x3. The projected ROIs for 19x5 are:

$$\text{Division A ROI} = \frac{\$1,800,000}{\$9,000,000} = .2 = 20\%$$

$$\text{Division B ROI} = \frac{\$1,800,000}{\$9,000,000 - \$3,000,000} = .3 = 30\%$$

Because Division B plans to replace $3 million of equipment with leased equipment, its average operating assets will decrease by $3 million and its ROI will increase from 20 percent to 30 percent; Division A's ROI will remain at 20 percent. To prevent individuals from employing this device to the detriment of the company, investment center managers should be permitted the latitude of purchasing or leasing assets as long as the decision can be justified by net present value analysis, discussed in Chapters 14 and 15.

When a manager decides to lease equipment instead of purchasing it, a control mechanism should be in place such that the manager justifies the leasing using the purchase versus lease decision discussed in Chapter 14. If not, a manager could lease equipment and permit the lessor to recoup the resale value of the equipment at the end of the lease term. Very often, this resale value could be significant and be the deciding factor when the firm decides whether to purchase property instead of leasing it. For example, suppose a manager leases a truck that has a useful life of six years and has a purchase price of $50,000. If the lease term is for six years and the resale value is $5,000, it might be advantageous for the firm to purchase the truck. However, the investment center manager will ignore the advantage to the firm and continue to lease the truck if the removal of $50,000 from the investment base improves ROI, as would be the case when the costs to

▶ **ILLUSTRATION 16-5**

LATUR COMPANY
Investment Center Performance Report
For the Year Ended December 31, 19x5
(in thousands of dollars)

	Budget	Actual	Variance— Favorable (F) Unfavorable (U)
Sales	$5,000	$5,400	$400(F)
Variable costs	1,500	1,600	100(U)
Contribution margin	3,500	3,800	300(F)
Direct fixed costs.	1,200	1,250	50(U)
Segment margin	2,300	2,550	250(F)
Allocated common costs	800	825	25(U)
Operating income	$1,500	$1,725	$225(F)
Average operating assets:			
Cash	$ 300	$ 350	$ 50
Receivables	800	825	25
Inventories	900	925	25
Plant assets, net of accumulated			
depreciation	4,000	4,200	200
Total	$6,000	$6,300	$300
ROI.	25%	27.38%	2.38%

operate the truck are approximately equal to the cost of leasing the truck. Because operating income would be approximately the same under either alternative and the investment base would be smaller when the truck is leased, ROI would increase. By leasing, the firm might not benefit from the resale value of the truck if the truck were purchased and then sold at the end of its useful life. The purchase versus lease decision discussed in Chapter 14 factors in the resale value of equipment when the lease term ends and offers the manager the correct decision.

Allocated Common Costs

Although an investment center is theoretically an autonomous business, this is not always the case. There may still be some centralized services that the investment center may use or benefit from. Examples are computer services, printing services, legal and accounting services, and management consulting. If these services were not available from corporate headquarters, the investment center would be obligated to acquire them from outsiders. Thus, it is reasonable to allocate their costs to the investment center. The allocation should be based on usage, possibly employing an hourly rate or a competitive rate charged by outsiders and not an arbitrary allocation formula. For this reason, operating income (after the allocated common costs) is used to evaluate investment centers instead of segment margin (before allocated common costs), which is used to evaluate profit centers.

Investment Center Performance Report

L.O. 9

Comparisons using ROI can be useful, but upper-level managers should make their decisions based on more detailed and informative investment center performance reports. These reports should contain budgeted data, actual data, and a column showing the difference between the two. Such a report appears in Illustration 16-5.

▶ **ILLUSTRATION 16-6**

MUTAK COMPANY
Performance Report for Investment Centers—ROI

	Investment Center X		Investment Center Y	
	19x3	**19x4**	**19x3**	**19x4**
Operating income	$ 6,000,000	$ 7,200,000	$100,000	$125,000
Average operating assets	$40,000,000	$40,000,000	$500,000	$500,000
ROI	15%	18%	20%	25%

Despite its popularity and superiority over a targeted segment margin for a profit center, ROI can be less than optimal as an evaluation technique for investment centers. Some firms prefer a variation of ROI called *residual income*.

Residual Income

L.O. 8

Residual income, a performance parameter similar to ROI, is also consistent with the targeted-income evaluation of responsibility centers. **Residual income** is the amount of investment center operating income left after deducting a desired rate of return on the average operating assets employed by the investment center. The minimum desired rate of return may be viewed as similar to the cutoff rate (cost of capital) used in net present value analysis.

For the Pluto Investment Center with its 19x2 operating income of $720,000 together with its average operating assets of $3 million, the residual income, using a minimum desired rate of return of 16 percent, would be calculated as:

Operating income	$720,000
Less: Desired return on average operating assets (16% × $3 million)	480,000
Residual income	$240,000

Advantages of Residual Income

Incentive compensation for an investment center's manager would normally be a function of the amount of residual income. The residual income evaluation concept has certain advantages over the ROI method. In particular, it eliminates (1) false signals generated by using a rate of return and failing to consider dollar amounts and (2) distortions that may result when a manager's objectives conflict with organizational objectives.

Eliminating False Signals   The importance of individual investment centers may be obscured by using ROI and failing to consider the dollar amounts involved. To demonstrate the concept, consider the information presented in Illustration 16-6 for two investment centers at the Mutak Company.

If the evaluation of the investment centers is based solely on ROI, the conclusions reached might be as follows:

1. Investment center Y is more valuable to the firm because its ROI for 19x3 was 20 percent while investment center X's ROI was only 15 percent.
2. The manager of investment center Y should receive a greater reward than the manager of X because he increased his ROI from 20 percent

▶ **ILLUSTRATION 16-7**

MUTAK COMPANY
Performance Report for Investment Centers
Residual Income

	Investment Center X		Investment Center Y	
	19x3	19x4	19x3	19x4
Average operating assets	$40,000,000	$40,000,000	$500,000	$500,000
Operating income	$ 6,000,000	$ 7,200,000	$100,000	$125,000
Less: Desired return (14% × Average operating assets)	5,600,000	5,600,000	70,000	70,000
Residual income	$ 400,000	$ 1,600,000	$ 30,000	$ 55,000

to 25 percent, which is greater than X's increase from 15 percent to 18 percent.

Of course, by looking at dollar amounts, Y's increase in operating income from 19x3 to 19x4 is only $25,000, while X's increase is $1.2 million for the same period. Thus, residual income may enable an upper-level manager to have a clearer picture of each center's performance. Using a desired rate of return of 14 percent, the analysis using residual income appears in Illustration 16-7.

Note how the signal given by residual income differs from that given by ROI. Each center's relative value to the firm is clearly evident in 19x3, as is the magnitude of each center's improvement in 19x4.

Eliminating Conflicting Objectives   When ROI is used as the reward criterion, a manager's objective is usually to increase ROI and thereby increase his or her reward. Normally, the firm benefits from an increased ROI and, therefore, the goals of the manager and the firm are congruent. However, this is not always the case. Reconsider investment center Y's performance for 19x3, shown in Illustration 16-6. For that year:

$$\text{ROI} = \frac{\$100,000}{\$500,000} = .2 = 20\%$$

Suppose it is possible to expand the center by investing $300,000 in operating assets, on which $48,000 of operating income can be earned. On this investment:

$$\text{ROI} = \frac{\$48,000}{\$300,000} = .16 = 16\%$$

The manager of Y would normally reject this project because it would lower his ROI. The computations are:

$$\text{ROI} = \frac{\$100,000 + \$48,000}{\$500,000 + \$300,000} = .185 = 18.5\%$$

However, this may not be the correct decision for the firm. Because the firm's desired rate of return is 14 percent, a 16 percent return would be

▶ **ILLUSTRATION 16-8**

MUTAK COMPANY
Effect of Accepting an Expansion Project
for Investment Center Y

	19x3	Expansion Project	Combined
Operating assets	$500,000	$300,000	$800,000
Operating income	$100,000	$ 48,000	$148,000
Less: Desired return (14% × Operating assets)	70,000	42,000	112,000
Residual income	$ 30,000	$ 6,000	$ 36,000

▶ **ILLUSTRATION 16-9**

SUNSET COMPANY
Performance Report for Investment Centers
Residual Income

	R	S
Average operating assets	$500,000	$1,500,000
Operating income	$110,000	$ 262,500
Less: Desired return (14% × Average operating assets).	70,000	210,000
Residual income	$ 40,000	$ 52,500

favorable. Residual income would increase if the project were accepted. The calculation is shown in Illustration 16-8.

From this analysis, it is clear that an investment center manager is likely to reject a project that would lower his or her ROI even if the project will enhance the company's profitability. This condition does not exist when residual income is used to evaluate managerial performance.

Relying exclusively on residual income may also present an incorrect signal, however. When investment centers are different sizes, residual income, used by itself, may cause an investment center manager to be treated unfairly.

For example, assume the Sunset Company has two investment centers, R and S, and their operating results are as shown in Illustration 16-9. The firm uses residual income to evaluate the managers.

If residual income were to be used exclusively, then investment center S would be considered the winner, and its manager would be rewarded more handsomely than R's manager. However, when the operating assets are factored into the calculations, S produced only $12,500 ($52,500 − $40,000) of additional residual income even though its investment in operating assets is three times that of R. Stated differently, a $500,000 investment in R produced $40,000 of residual income, but an extra $1 million ($1,500,000 − $500,000) of investment in S produced only an extra $12,500 of residual income. Thus, top-level managers should be aware of this limitation of residual income and, when faced with a situation similar to that shown in Illustration 16-9, should analyze the results by comparing the returns on operating assets.

1. What are the differences between a cost center, a revenue center, a profit center, and an investment center?

2. What are the advantages and disadvantages of decentralization?

3. What is responsibility accounting?

4. What is ROI? What are the separate components of the calculation? Why is it important to use the components separately? Evaluate this statement: "When two firms have the same ROI, it is not necessary to look at the individual components of their ROIs."

5. What is *residual income*? Are there advantages to using residual income in place of ROI? Discuss.   ◀

▶ TRANSFER PRICES

L.O. 10

Many firms have responsibility centers manufacturing products that may be sold both to outsiders and to other responsibility centers within the firm. An example would be a center that produces spark plugs, transfers them to another center for use in the manufacture of automobiles, and also sells them to retailers of automotive supplies. When a firm has these kinds of responsibility centers, special problems arise if ROI or residual income is used to evaluate a center's performance. An important issue is the **transfer price**— the price charged by one responsibility center for goods and services transferred to another responsibility center. Transfer prices can be especially problematical when the entire output of a center is "sold" to another responsibility center or when there is no market for an intermediate product that must be transferred to another center. The major oil companies, which are usually vertically integrated in that they extract crude oil, refine it, wholesale it, and even retail it as gasoline and petroleum products, make great use of transfer prices.

The determination of an appropriate transfer price can be difficult. In many cases, manufacturers of intermediate products find that a well-defined market exists for their products and, thus, external market prices may be used to gauge transfer prices. In other cases, the markets may be thin, and, although market prices are available, they may not be relevant for large purchases. In still other cases, there may be no market for the intermediate product and, hence, no external market price.

The most commonly used transfer prices generally fall into five categories:

1. Variable cost (incremental cost).
2. Full cost (variable plus fixed costs).
3. Cost plus a markup.
4. External market price.
5. Negotiated price (internal market price).

Variable Cost

In the context of transfer pricing, *variable cost* is generally used synonymously with *incremental cost*. Occasionally, it may be necessary to incur an additional fixed cost when manufacturing an intermediate product, and, when this is the case, incremental cost should be used instead of variable cost.

▶ **ILLUSTRATION 16-10**

DECORATIVE LAMP COMPANY
Contribution Margin Statement
For the Year Ended December 31, 19x2

	Sockets (200,000 Units)	Assembling (100,000 Units)	Total
Sales (50 cents per socket and $25 per lamp)	$100,000	$2,500,000	$2,600,000
Variable costs:			
Sockets (20 cents and 35 cents, respectively)	40,000	35,000	75,000
Other parts ($10 each)		1,000,000	1,000,000
Total variable costs	40,000	1,035,000	1,075,000
Contribution margin	$ 60,000	$1,465,000	$1,525,000

Some problems are associated with the use of variable cost as a transfer price. First, if a responsibility center charges only its variable costs, it will not recover its fixed costs and, thus, not show a profit. The manager of such a responsibility center could not be evaluated using ROI or residual income, and the responsibility center would be restricted to the role of cost center. Second, if costs could be passed on to another responsibility center without limit, the cost center manager would lack any incentive to control costs, which consequently might escalate. In addition, the purchasing center's manager would probably object to the cost center's inefficiencies being passed along as part of the variable costs billed to her. Therefore, in fairness to both parties, *standard* variable costs should be used as a transfer price in this situation.

Under certain conditions, variable cost should be used as a transfer price to maximize overall company profits. If a lamp manufacturer manufactures its own lamp sockets in its socket responsibility center and the socket center sells both to outsiders and to the company's assembly center, a condition may arise in which variable cost, or one slightly above it, is the best transfer price. The preference for variable cost depends on whether the socket center can sell all of its output to outsiders or if it has idle capacity. The situation is analogous to accepting a special order at less than full cost, discussed in Chapter 13. Recall that a firm with idle capacity can increase contribution margin by accepting an order at less than full cost as long as the price exceeds variable (incremental) cost.

Consider the present operating results of the two responsibility centers shown in Illustration 16-10. In this case, the socket center is capable of selling all of its output to outsiders, and the assembly center purchases its sockets at the special price of 35 cents each from an outsider.

Now let us assume that for 19x3, the socket center will be able to sell only 100,000 sockets to outsiders. Should the assembling center continue to purchase the sockets externally at 35 cents if the socket center insists on getting 50 cents for its sockets? When the only alternative is an internal transfer price of 50 cents, the answer is to purchase externally. However, this is not the best solution for the firm. Assume all factors are expected to be the same for 19x3, except the projected reduction in the sales volume of sockets. The

► **ILLUSTRATION 16-11**

DECORATIVE LAMP COMPANY
Budgeted Contribution Margin Statement
For the Year Ended December 31, 19x3

	Sockets (100,000 Units)	Assembling (100,000 Units)	Total
Sales (50 cents per socket and $25 per lamp)	$50,000	$2,500,000	$2,550,000
Variable costs:			
Sockets (20 cents and 35 cents, respectively)	20,000	35,000	55,000
Other parts ($10 each)		1,000,000	1,000,000
Total variable costs	20,000	1,035,000	1,055,000
Contribution margin	$30,000	$1,465,000	$1,495,000

► **ILLUSTRATION 16-12**

DECORATIVE LAMP COMPANY
Budgeted Contribution Margin Statement
For the Year Ended December 31, 19x3

	Sockets (200,000 Units)	Assembling (100,000 Units)	Total
Sales:			
Sales to outsiders (100,000 at 50 cents and 100,000 at $25)	$50,000	$2,500,000	$2,550,000
Sales to assembling (100,000 at 20 cents)	20,000		20,000
Total sales	70,000	2,500,000	2,570,000
Variable costs:			
Sockets (20 cents)	40,000	20,000	60,000
Other parts ($10 each)		1,000,000	1,000,000
Total variable costs	40,000	1,020,000	1,060,000
Contribution margin	$30,000	$1,480,000	$1,510,000

budgeted contribution margin statement for 19x3 appears in Illustration 16-11.

To fully appreciate the impact of the decision to purchase the sockets externally, Illustration 16-11 should be compared with the results obtainable if the socket division were to sell its idle capacity output of 100,000 sockets at a transfer price of 20 cents, its variable cost. This budgeted statement appears in Illustration 16-12.

By comparing Illustration 16-12 to Illustration 16-11, we can see that the firm would gain $15,000 ($1,510,000 − $1,495,000) if the socket center were to sell to assembling. Note that the socket center has a contribution margin of $30,000 in either case and, therefore, should be willing to sell to assembling for the benefit of the firm. Of course, the manager of assembling could offer to pay a small amount above variable cost, say, 25 cents. Therefore, both centers would be the beneficiaries—sockets would earn a contribution margin of 5 cents per socket, and assembling would still save 10 cents per socket over purchasing from outsiders. *The firm would be in the same posi-*

tion regardless of the transfer price as long as the sockets are purchased internally. In fact, for external reporting purposes, the purchase and sale cancel each other and do not appear in the firm's published income statement.

Transfer prices higher than variable cost and lower than market price are discussed in the section about *negotiated price*.

Full Cost

The problems associated with a transfer price at variable cost also apply to a transfer price at full cost. Thus, if full cost is used, it should also be at *standard* cost or normal cost rather than at actual cost. This transfer price is normally used by cost centers. Normal cost transfers were discussed in Chapter 5 for job order cost systems and in Chapter 6 for process cost systems. Standard cost transfers were discussed in Chapters 10 and 11.

Cost Plus a Markup

When a transfer price will include a markup, standard cost should be used as the base. Such a transfer price permits a responsibility center to earn a profit, which is not the case when the transfer price is either variable cost or full cost. Therefore, when cost plus a markup is used, the selling responsibility center could be a profit center or an investment center, which permits the use of ROI or residual income for evaluation purposes. The problem with using this transfer price is that it does not reflect the competitive spirit of the marketplace. And to the extent that the standard cost may be biased, the markup compounds the bias. Nevertheless, when there is no market for an intermediate product, cost plus a markup may be used effectively.

External Market Price

When a division manager has complete freedom to sell internally or externally, an external market price is the most effective transfer price between profit or investment centers. Such a price reflects the arm's-length nature of parties doing business as strangers. If a purchasing center is able to purchase externally at a specific price and the selling center has no idle capacity, each manager is free to conduct business with outsiders or insiders without detriment to the firm.

In some cases, a transfer price based on market price may require an adjustment for quantity discounts and/or cost savings that arise from selling internally. Among the costs that may be saved and thus should be considered are shipping costs, selling commissions, bookkeeping costs for customers' ledgers, and credit and collection costs. Although the selling center may not have a quantity discount policy, a discount may have to be factored into the transfer price. In most situations, if the buying center were an external customer, the selling center would offer a volume discount, so a similar discount should be offered as part of the transfer price. Thus, although the transfer price is based on the market price, the two may differ significantly.

The Eastern Electronics Company manufactures toaster ovens. One of its responsibility centers manufactures timers that can be used in the ovens. This center is presently operating at full capacity and selling its entire output to outsiders. Fifty percent of its output is sold to one customer at a price of $1.80 per unit, which is 10 percent less than its regular price of $2 per unit. The cost of shipping and sales commissions amount to 20 cents per unit on regular business and 18 cents per unit for its large customer. The operating results for 19x1, the first year of operations, appear in Illustration 16-13.

▶ **ILLUSTRATION 16-13**

EASTERN ELECTRONICS COMPANY
Contribution Margin Statement
For the Year Ended December 31, 19x1

	Timers (400,000 Units)	Toasters (200,000 Units)	Total
Sales:			
($2 × 200,000)	$400,000		$ 400,000
($1.80 × 200,000).	360,000		360,000
($20 × 200,000)		$4,000,000	4,000,000
Total sales.	760,000	4,000,000	4,760,000
Variable costs:			
Timers ($.88 × 200,000).	176,000		176,000
($.90 × 200,000).	180,000		180,000
($2 × 200,000).		400,000	400,000
Other costs ($6 × 200,000)		1,200,000	1,200,000
Total variable costs.	356,000	1,600,000	1,956,000
Contribution margin	$404,000	$2,400,000	$2,804,000

The contribution margin statement shown in Illustration 16-13 is suboptimal for the company because the toaster center paid $2 for timers while the timer center sold them at $1.80 in large quantities. Furthermore, the timer center incurred costs of 18 cents per timer that could have been avoided if the timers were sold to the toaster center.

Let us assume that for 19x2, the toaster center would like to purchase the timers internally because it encountered some minor quality and delivery problems during 19x1. What price would be fair to both centers? One approach would be to pay the timer center for its variable costs per unit plus the per-unit contribution margin it would lose by giving up its large customer. As a generalized equation, we might state that the minimum transfer price is:

Minimum transfer price = Incremental cost outlay + Opportunity cost

Stated differently, the equation would be:

Minimum transfer price = Variable cost per unit + Contribution margin per unit lost on outside sales

First, we would compute the contribution margin per unit:

	Per Unit
Selling price	$1.80
Less: Variable costs	.88
Contribution margin	$ .92

Then, the out-of-pocket cost to produce the timers for sale to the toaster center is computed as:

	Per Unit
Total variable cost	$.88
Less: Freight and commissions	.18
Net variable cost	$.70

▶ **ILLUSTRATION 16-14**

EASTERN ELECTRONICS COMPANY
Budgeted Contribution Margin Statement
For the Year Ended December 31, 19x2

	Timers (400,000 Units)	Toasters (200,000 Units)	Total
Sales:			
($2 × 200,000)	$400,000		$ 400,000
($1.62 × 200,000).	324,000		324,000
($20 × 200,000)		$4,000,000	4,000,000
Total sales.	724,000	4,000,000	4,724,000
Variable costs:			
Timers ($.70 × 200,000).	140,000		140,000
($.90 × 200,000).	180,000		180,000
($1.62 × 200,000)		324,000	324,000
Other costs ($6 × 200,000)		1,200,000	1,200,000
Total variable costs.	320,000	1,524,000	1,844,000
Contribution margin	$404,000	$2,476,000	$2,880,000

So the price to be charged, according to the generalized equation, is:

$$\text{Transfer price} = \$.70 + \$.92 = \$1.62$$

For 19x2, the *only change* in operations anticipated is the internal purchase of timers. The budgeted contribution margin statement for 19x2 appears in Illustration 16-14.

The budgeted contribution margin statement shown in Illustration 16-14 is optimal from the company's perspective. In comparing Illustrations 16-13 and 16-14, note that:

1. The 19x2 contribution margin is $76,000 more than the 19x1 contribution margin ($2,880,000 − $2,804,000). This amount consists of:

Difference between the price paid by the toaster center and the price received by the timer center ($2.00 − $1.80 = $.20 × 200,000 units)	$40,000
Savings in freight and commissions ($.18 × 200,000)	36,000
Total company savings	$76,000

2. The variable cost for timers sold to the toaster center is 70 cents.
3. The contribution margin shown by the timer center is $404,000 in both illustrations. Thus, the timer center manager will receive the same reward whether she sells to an outsider or to the toaster center.
4. The sale and purchase of timers in the amount of $324,000 could have been canceled in the companywide column.

This example highlights the value of managers being team players. As long as the manager of timers is not sacrificing any contribution margin, she should be willing to sell the timers to the toaster centers.

The generalized equation also applies to centers that have idle capacity. In the case of the Decorative Lamp Company (Illustrations 16-11 and 16-12), in which the socket center had idle capacity of 100,000 units, we concluded that the transfer price should be at variable cost. Using the generalized equation, the transfer price would be:

$$\text{Transfer price} = \text{Variable cost per unit} + \text{Contribution margin lost on outside sales}$$
$$\text{Transfer price} = \$.20 + \$0 = \$.20$$

Thus, the generalized formula produces optimal results for the company by recommending a transfer price at variable cost when idle capacity is present.

Negotiated Price

Typically, a transfer price is negotiated when there is no market for an intermediate product manufactured by a responsibility center. An example would be a center that produces circuit boards for a radio manufacturer. Circuit boards are custom tailored to a manufacturer's specifications. Normally, a center that produced circuit boards for internal use only would be a cost center, and a transfer price would not be needed. However, suppose the center manufactures circuit boards for an external television manufacturer as well as for the internal radio center. In this case, the center would normally be a profit or investment center, and a negotiated transfer price would be needed because there is no external market for the radio circuit board.

The generalized equation may be used to set the negotiated transfer price. For example, the circuit board center devotes 40 percent of its capacity to manufacturing the television circuit boards. The television circuit boards are sold for $10 each and have a variable cost of $3 each. Sales for 19x2 amounted to 200,000 units. Because the radio circuit boards are smaller and simpler to make, the center is able to manufacture 600,000 circuit boards, as needed by the radio center. Variable costs are 80 cents each.

The circuit board center could sell its entire output to the television manufacturer if it did not make the circuit boards for the radio center. Thus, the opportunity cost of making radio circuit boards is the income given up by not making television circuit boards.

The negotiated transfer price may be set as follows:

	Per Unit
Contribution margin forgone:	
Selling price	$ 10
Variable cost	3
Contribution margin	$ 7

	Units
Number of units forgone:	
Factory capacity (200,000 ÷ .40).	500,000
Less: Units sold	200,000
Units forgone	300,000
Contribution margin forgone (300,000 × $7).	$2,100,000

The contribution margin needed is $3.50 ($2.1 million ÷ 600,000) per unit. Adding the $3.50 to the variable cost of $.80 per unit produces a negotiated transfer price of $4.30 per unit. The proof of the calculation is:

Entire output sold externally:	
500,000 × $7 contribution margin.	$3,500,000

Output sold internally and externally:	
200,000 × $7	$1,400,000
600,000 × $3.50	2,100,000
Total contribution margin	$3,500,000

▶ **ILLUSTRATION 16-15**   Transfer-Pricing Diagram

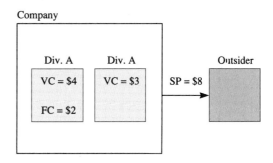

The transfer price of $4.20 is fair to both parties and should be accepted by both, provided they understand the managerial and cost concepts as just illustrated.

A negotiated transfer price may also be used in place of variable cost when a center has idle capacity. When variable cost is used, the selling center neither gains nor loses by selling at variable cost. On the other hand, the buying center acquires the product at a substantial amount below market price because fixed costs and profits are omitted from the transfer price. Under such circumstances, using a negotiated transfer price in place of variable cost would provide an incentive to the selling center, and the buying center would still pay less than it would to an outside supplier.

When a transfer-pricing problem that contains complex relationships is encountered, it is possible to diagram the problem to clarify the complexities. A sample diagram appears in Illustration 16-15.

Behavioral Aspects of Transfer Pricing

Ideally, managers of responsibility centers should be free to make decisions without fear of being vetoed by top management. Occasionally, a center manager, believing he is acting in the best interest of both his center and the company, may make a decision that is detrimental to the company as a whole. And, on rare occasions, a manager may stubbornly stick to a decision, knowing it is wrong for the company. Whatever the reason, if a manager's decision is overturned by top management, the firm is closer to centralization than to decentralization. To achieve the benefits of decentralization, top management must sit back and allow the consequences of the wrong decision to materialize. In the process, center managers will learn to trust the system and probably make fewer poor decisions.

Education is the key to encouraging center managers to make correct decisions for the firm as a whole. Center managers should be encouraged to be team players. As a team player, a center manager should recognize that sometimes a decision must be made for the benefit of the company, such as when idle capacity exists, and that when needed, the center manager can expect reciprocity. Furthermore, all managers should have a thorough understanding of their center's cost-behavior patterns and cost structure so that when it is necessary for them to sell at variable cost, they will understand they are not being hurt. They should also understand that if they make many wrong decisions, they will be held accountable.

▶ **SUMMARY**

Practically all large firms have some form of **decentralization.** A highly decentralized firm delegates a great deal of authority for making important decisions to lower-level managers, and a **centralized organization** delegates little authority.

A decentralized firm is usually divided into **responsibility centers**—individual segments whose managers have control over their own costs and/or revenues. A segment that controls only costs is a **cost center,** and a segment that controls only revenues is a **revenue center.** A segment that controls both costs and revenues but not investments in its assets is a **profit center,** and a segment that controls costs, revenues, and its investments in assets is an **investment center.** Regardless of its kind, a responsibility center's performance should be evaluated according to specified criteria. To accomplish this, most firms make use of responsibility accounting, which requires performance reports to be prepared for each segment, starting with the lowest level of authority. Each report is incorporated into the next level's report and builds to the president's report, which then includes the entire company's operating results.

Standard costs are used to evaluate the performance of cost centers. For this purpose, cost centers are normally divided into two categories. In **standard cost centers,** there is a high correlation between inputs and outputs, as there is in producing departments. In **discretionary cost centers,** only inputs can be controlled, as is the case in research and development centers.

Budgeted contribution margin is used to evaluate revenue centers, and budgeted segment margin is used to assess profit centers. Investment centers are often judged by **return on investment (ROI),** which may be broken into its component parts of **operating margin percentage** multiplied by **asset turnover.** Because ROI may be increased in different ways, the component parts provide more information about an investment center than does ROI alone. In some cases, a manager may be tempted to use ROI to further his own goals, although it would be detrimental to the firm. For this reason, many firms, such as Du Pont, prefer to use a variant of ROI known as **residual income.** This evaluation technique requires a charge for the assets used by a segment to be deducted from its operating income to arrive at residual income.

Many firms transfer goods and services among segments. The price at which the goods are transferred is known as the **transfer price.** Depending on the circumstances, the transfer price may be based on variable cost, full cost, or cost plus a markup. As another alternative, many managers prefer to use the market price if a market for the product exists. If there is no market, then a negotiated transfer price may be used. The transfer price used depends on the degree of autonomy granted to the firm's segments and whether the selling segment is operating at full capacity or limited capacity.

▶ **GLOSSARY OF**
  KEY TERMS

Asset turnover   Sales revenue divided by average operating assets.   (p. 829)

Centralized organization   A firm in which little authority is delegated to lower-level managers.   (p. 820)

Cost center   A segment of an organization whose managers have the authority to incur and control costs.   (p. 820)

Decentralization   The delegation of a great deal of authority to the lowest level of management responsibility that is capable of making important decisions. (p. 820)

Discretionary cost center   A segment of a firm in which costs are clearly specified but outcomes are not clearly related to inputs, as in a research and development center. (p. 824)

Investment center   A segment of an organization whose managers have the authority to incur and control costs, earn revenues, and control investments in assets. (p. 821)

Operating margin percentage   Operating income divided by sales revenue. (p. 829)

Profit center   A segment of an organization whose managers have the authority to incur and control costs and to control the revenues the center earns. (p. 821)

Residual income   The amount of investment center operating income left after deducting a desired rate of return on the average operating assets employed by the investment center. (p. 835)

Responsibility center   A segment of an organization whose managers have the authority to incur and control costs, earn revenues, and invest funds in assets. It is possible for a responsibility center to be responsible for all three functions or for only one function. (p. 820)

Return on investment (ROI)   A measure of profitability computed by dividing the amount of operating income earned by the average investment in operating assets required to earn the income. (p. 827)

Revenue center   A segment of an organization whose managers are responsible only for the revenues the center earns. (p. 821)

Standard cost center   A segment of a firm in which there is a clear relationship between standard inputs and standard outputs, as in a producing department. (p. 824)

Transfer price   The price charged by one responsibility center for goods or services transferred to another responsibility center. (p. 838)

▶ **REVIEW PROBLEM**   The Westman Company has a lens division that is operated as an investment center. The division is operating at only 60 percent of capacity. The results of operations for 19x3 are:

WESTMAN COMPANY
Lens Division
Statement of Operating Income
For the Year Ended December 31, 19x3

Sales (120,000 × $10)	$1,200,000
Variable costs (at $4)	480,000
Contribution margin	720,000
Direct fixed costs	300,000
Segment margin.	420,000
Invoiced common costs for services from other divisions	180,000
Operating income	$ 240,000
Operating assets—January 1, 19x3	$ 460,000
Operating assets—December 31, 19x3	500,000

The company's minimum desired rate of return for residual income purposes is 15 percent.

Required   *a.* Compute:

(1) The operating margin percentage.

(2) Asset turnover.

(3) ROI.

b. Compute residual income.

c. For 19x4, the lens division expects its operations to be unchanged from 19x3. However, it has an opportunity to accept a special order from an outsider for 80,000 lenses at a price of $6. The order will not affect its regular sales and will require an additional outlay of $100,000 for direct fixed costs. Additional operating assets will be needed at a cost of $150,000. Calculate the following for the *special order only:*

(1) ROI.

(2) Residual income.

Would you expect the manager of the lens division to accept the order if the parameter used for evaluation were ROI? Why? Would your answer be different if the parameter used were residual income? Why?

d. The Westman Company is planning to market a new product, binoculars. The lenses manufactured by the lens division could be used in the binoculars. Assume the offer in part *(c)* was withdrawn. Thus, the lens division will still have the idle capacity. The manager in charge of producing the binoculars learned that he could purchase externally the 80,000 lenses he needs for $9 each. What price should the lens division quote for the lenses, assuming no increase in fixed costs and no additional investment will be needed by the lens division? Why?

e. Assume the same facts as in part *(d)*, except the lens division has a customer who is willing to purchase the 80,000 lenses in 19x4 for $10 each. The lenses will not require any shipping costs or sales commissions. What price should the lens division now quote to the binocular division? What should the binocular manager's reaction be to the prices quoted? Why?

f. Assume the same facts as in part *(e)*, except shipping costs and sales commissions amount to $2 per unit on the 80,000 lenses. What price should be quoted? What should the binocular manager do? Why?

g. Assume the lens division can only sell 120,000 lenses in 19x4 and its budgeted statement of operating income for 19x4 is the same as that for 19x3. The binocular division expects to use 200,000 lenses and thus would require all of the output of the lens division. There are no shipping costs or sales commissions listed in the statement of operating income. What price should be charged by the lens division? What should the binocular manager do if he can purchase the lenses externally at $8.50 per lens? Why?

▸ **SOLUTION TO REVIEW PROBLEM**

a. (1)
$$\text{OMP} = \frac{\$240,000}{\$1,200,000} = .2 = 20\%$$

(2)
$$\text{Asset turnover} = \frac{\$1,200,000}{\frac{1}{2}(\$460,000 + \$500,000)} = \frac{\$1,200,000}{\$480,000} = 2.5$$

(3)
$$\text{ROI} = 20\% \times 2.5 = 50\%$$

b. Residual Income:

Operating income	$240,000
Less: Desired return $\left(15\% \times \dfrac{\$460,000 + \$500,000}{2}\right)$	72,000
Residual income.	$168,000

c. (1) *Operating Income:*

Sales (80,000 × $6).	$480,000
Variable costs (at $4)	320,000
Contribution margin	160,000
Direct fixed costs.	100,000
Operating income	$ 60,000
Average operating assets*.	$150,000

* The $150,000 will be expended at the *beginning* of the year. Thus, the average is $150,000.

ROI:

$$ROI = \frac{\$60,000}{\$150,000} = .4 = 40\%$$

(2) *Residual Income:*

Operating income	$60,000
Less: Desired return	
(15% × $150,000)	22,500
Residual income.	$37,500

The manager of the lens division would probably reject the special order because it only produces an ROI of 40 percent, which will lower his present ROI of 50 percent. He would accept the special order if residual income is used to evaluate his performance because the order produces an additional $37,500 of residual income.

d. The minimum price in this case should be $4, the variable cost. Using the generalized formula, the price may be computed as:

$$\text{Transfer price} = \text{Variable cost per unit}$$
$$+ \text{ Lost contribution margin per unit}$$
$$\text{Transfer price} = \$4 + \$0 = \$4$$

The binocular manager may be willing to pay more than $4 but less than $9 so that the lens division would have an incentive to sell internally and the binocular division could still purchase the lenses for less than the external price.

e. Using the generalized formula, the price would be $10, computed as follows:

$$\text{Transfer price} = \$4 + \$6 = \$10$$

The binocular manager should purchase the lenses externally because $9 is less than the internal price of $10. If the lens division were to quote a $9 price, the firm would lose $80,000 (80,000 lenses × $1).

f. The contribution margin is:

		Per Unit
Selling price.		$10
Less:		
Variable manufacturing cost	$4	
Shipping and sales commissions.	2	6
Contribution margin		$ 4

The transfer price should be $8 and may be computed, using the generalized formula, as follows:

$$\text{Transfer price} = \$4 + \$4 = \$8$$

The binocular manager should purchase internally because $8 is less than $9.

g. The contribution margin of $720,000 presently earned will be sacrificed, and thus it must be spread over the expected 200,000 lenses as follows:

$$\frac{\$720,000}{200,000} = \$3.60 \text{ per unit}$$

Using the generalized formula, the transfer price is $7.60, computed as follows:

$$\text{Transfer price} = \$4.00 + \$3.60 = \$7.60$$

The lenses should be purchased internally because $7.60 is less than $8.50.

▶ **LIBRARY ASSIGNMENT**

Read the following:

Agami, Abdel M. "How to Choose Transfer Prices for FSCs." *Management Accounting,* May 1986, pp. 48–50.

Beard, Larry H., and Charles W. Caldwell. "Transfer Pricing Can Improve Sales and Credit Cooperation." *Management Accounting,* March 1984, pp. 60–65.

Benke, Ralph L., and James Don Edwards. "Should You Use Transfer Pricing to Create Pseudo-Profit Centers?" *Management Accounting,* February 1981, pp. 36–39, 43.

Hoshower, Leon B., and Robert B. Crum. "Straightening the Tortuous—and Treacherous—ROI Path." *Management Accounting,* December 1986, pp. 41–45.

Lesser, Frederic E. "Does Your Transfer Pricing Make Cents?" *Management Accounting,* December 1987, pp. 43–47.

▶ **SELF-TEST**

True or False

1. The minimum transfer price is the sum of the variable cost per unit and the contribution margin per unit lost on outside sales.
2. A firm in which authority to make decisions is retained by upper management is a centralized organization.
3. A highly decentralized firm does not require control mechanisms to monitor employees.
4. An investment center is a cost center with the added ability to control investments.
5. A revenue center is responsible only for the revenues it earns.
6. A performance report is rarely useful if it clearly delineates the level of management responsibility.
7. Two types of cost centers are centralized and decentralized.
8. A standard cost center is one in which a clear relationship between standard inputs and standard outputs exists.
9. Cost centers perform within an area of targeted costs.
10. A revenue center performs within a transfer price range.
11. In ROI, the operating income includes the deductions for interest costs and income taxes.
12. The operating margin percentage measures the percentage of sales that are available to cover income taxes and profit but not interest costs.

13. ROI is improved by increasing sales revenue.
14. ROI is improved by increasing costs.
15. A decrease in costs results in a higher ROI, a higher operating margin, and an unchanged asset turnover ratio.

Multiple Choice

1. The marketing department of a firm is likely to be a
    a. Responsibility center.
    b. Profit center.
    c. Revenue center.
    d. Cost center.
2. One disadvantage of decentralization is that
    a. Top management is relieved of routine decision making.
    b. There may be duplication of efforts.
    c. Employee morale is improved.
    d. Decision making often becomes more effective.
3. One advantage of decentralization is that
    a. Lower-level managers are better equipped for promotion.
    b. Upper-level managers lose some control.
    c. There may be duplication of effort.
    d. Employee goals may conflict with company goals.
4. A cost center in which costs are clearly specified but outcomes are not directly related to inputs is a (an)
    a. Discretionary cost center.
    b. Investment center.
    c. Standard cost center.
    d. Profit center.
5. A major difficulty in analyzing variances for discretionary cost centers is that
    a. Total costs are difficult to calculate.
    b. Lack of cause and effect makes evaluation difficult.
    c. Standard costs are difficult to assign.
    d. Cost assignment tends to be arbitrary.
6. Return on investment (ROI) is computed as operating income divided by
    a. Total assets.
    b. Ending operating assets.
    c. Average operating assets.
    d. Average total equity.
7. A decreasing trend in asset turnover may indicate any of the following except
    a. Receivable collection time is increasing.
    b. Inventories are obsolete.
    c. Company has unneeded assets.
    d. The trend is toward leasing assets.
8. If there is no outside market for a component product, the best transfer price is
    a. The external market price.
    b. A negotiated price.
    c. Full cost.
    d. Variable cost.

▶ **QUESTIONS**

1. What does decentralization mean? Which kinds of firms employ the concept? Why?
2. What is a responsibility center? Why is it important for decentralized firms to use responsibility centers?

3. Distinguish between a cost center, a revenue center, a profit center, and an investment center.
4. What are the advantages and disadvantages of decentralized operations?
5. Describe the operation of a reporting system for a decentralized firm that uses responsibility accounting.
6. What parameter is generally used to evaluate cost centers? What is the difference between a standard cost center and a discretionary cost center? Are they evaluated differently? Explain.
7. What parameter is used to evaluate a revenue center? Are actual costs or standard costs used in the evaluation process? Why? Is it possible for the sales revenue of a revenue center to increase and yet be considered a negative performance by the center's manager? Explain.
8. Are different parameters used to evaluate profit centers and investment centers? Explain.
9. Is ROI a superior measurement over a targeted operating income? Why?
10. Is there more than one way to compute ROI? If so, which do you prefer? Why?
11. What is the operating margin percentage? Why is it important?
12. What is asset turnover? Why is it important?
13. Could the use of ROI result in a manager's performance that may be detrimental to the firm? Explain.
14. What is residual income? It has a certain advantage over ROI. Explain. There may be a disadvantage encountered when using residual income. Explain.
15. What is a transfer price? Why is it needed?
16. What are the three cost-based transfer prices? When should each be used?
17. Why is the external market price for an intermediate product preferred as a transfer price?
18. When should a negotiated transfer price be used?
19. Is it important for a responsibility center manager to be a team player? Explain.

▶ **EXERCISES**   E16–1   **ROI and Residual Income**

The Burns Company has two investment centers: clothing and jewelry. Selected information for each segment follows:

	Clothing	Jewelry
Sales	$520,000	$950,000
Operating income	98,800	209,000
Operating assets—January 1, 19x2	170,000	480,000
Operating assets—December 31, 19x2.	230,000	520,000

The firm's minimum desired rate of return for investment center evaluation is 20 percent. All calculations for percentages should be carried to one decimal place.

Required a. Calculate the following for each segment:
  (1) Operating margin percentage.
  (2) Asset turnover.
  (3) ROI.
  (4) Residual income.
  b. Which segment appears to be performing better on the basis of
  (1) ROI? Explain by examining the components of ROI.
  (2) Residual income? Explain.

E16–2   ROI and Residual Income

The Collins Company has two investment centers: blankets and pillows. Selected information for each segment follows:

	Blankets	Pillows
Sales	$500,000	$800,000
Operating income	70,000	88,000
Operating assets—January 1, 19x3	200,000	240,000
Operating assets—December 31, 19x3	216,666	293,333

The firm's minimum desired rate of return for investment center evaluation is 18 percent.

Required   *a.* Calculate the following for each segment:
  (1) Operating margin percentage.
  (2) Asset turnover.
  (3) ROI.
  (4) Residual income.
b. Which segment appears to be performing better on the basis of
  (1) ROI? Explain by examining the components of ROI.
  (2) Residual income? Explain.

E16–3   Responsibility Centers

1. A segment of an organization is referred to as a *profit center* if it has
   a. Authority to make decisions affecting the major determinants of profit, including the power to choose its markets and sources of supply.
   b. Authority to make decisions affecting the major determinants of profit, including the power to choose its markets and sources of supply and significant control over the amount of invested capital.
   c. Authority to make decisions over the most significant costs of operations, including the power to choose the sources of supply.
   d. Authority to provide specialized support to other units within the organization.
   e. Responsibility for combining the direct materials, direct labor, and other factors of production into a final output.
2. A segment of an organization is referred to as an *investment center* if it has
   a. Authority to make decisions affecting the major determinants of profit, including the power to choose its markets and sources of supply.
   b. Authority to make decisions affecting the major determinants of profit, including the power to choose its markets and sources of supply and significant control over the amount of invested capital.
   c. Authority to make decisions over the most significant costs of operations, including the power to choose the sources of supply.
   d. Authority to provide specialized support to other units within the organization.
   e. Responsibility for developing markets for and selling the output of the organization.
3. A segment of an organization is referred to as a *service center* if it has
   a. Responsibility for developing markets for and selling the output of the organization.

      b. Responsibility for combining the direct materials, direct labor, and other factors of production into a final output.

      c. Authority to make decisions affecting the major determinants of profit, including the power to choose its markets and sources of supply.

      d. Authority to provide specialized support to other units within the organization.

      e. Authority to make decisions over the most significant costs of operations, including the power to choose the sources of supply.

4. A segment of an organization is referred to as a *cost center* if it has

      a. Responsibility for developing markets for and selling the output of the organization.

      b. Authority to make decisions affecting the major determinants of profit, including the power to choose its markets and sources of supply.

      c. Authority to make decisions over the most significant costs of operations, including the power to choose the sources of supply.

      d. Authority to provide specialized support to other units within the organization.

      e. Responsibility for combining the direct materials, direct labor, and other factors of production into a final output.

(CMA Adapted)

E16–4   Residual Income

1. The basic objective of the residual income approach of performance measurement and evaluation is to have a division maximize its

      a. Return on investment rate.

      b. Imputed interest rate charge.

      c. Cash flows.

      d. Cash flows in excess of a desired minimum amount.

      e. Income in excess of a desired minimum return.

2. The imputed interest rate used in the residual income approach for performance measurement and evaluation can best be characterized as the

      a. Historical weighted-average cost of capital for the company.

      b. Marginal after-tax cost of new equity capital.

      c. Average return on investment that has been earned by the company over a particular time period.

      d. Target return on investment set by management.

      e. Average prime lending rate for the year being evaluated.

3. Which one of the following items would most likely *not* be incorporated into the calculation of a division's investment base when using the residual income approach for performance measurement and evaluation?

      a. Fixed assets employed in divisional operations.

      b. Vacant land being held by the division as a potential site for a new plant.

      c. Divisional inventories when division management exercises control over the inventory levels.

      d. Divisional accounts payable when division management exercises control over the amount of short-term credit utilized.

      e. Divisional accounts receivable when division management exercises control over credit policy and credit terms.

(CMA Adapted)

E16–5   ROI and Residual Income

Fill in the missing data in the following cases:

	Investment Center		
	A	**B**	**C**
Sales.	$456,000	$?	$?
Operating income	?	240,000	157,500
Average operating assets.	?	?	250,000
Operating margin percentage	?	?	21%
Asset turnover	2.4	3	?
ROI	42%	30%	?
Minimum desired rate of return percentage	16%	?	?
Residual income	?	128,000	122,500

E16–6 **ROI and Residual Income**

Fill in the missing data in the following cases:

	Investment Center		
	D	**E**	**F**
Sales.	$?	$500,000	$900,000
Operating income	?	?	?
Average operating assets.	180,000	250,000	?
Operating margin percentage	?	10%	16%
Asset turnover	2.4	?	?
ROI	36%	?	25%
Minimum desired rate of return percentage	20%	?	?
Residual income	?	10,000	63,360

E16–7 **Costs for Investment Centers**

For each item listed below, indicate whether the cost should be deducted on an investment center's income statement to arrive at operating income, and give a brief explanation of your position.

1. The cost of fuel pumps purchased from another investment center at the price sold in the intermediate market.
2. Computer services billed by the computer service center at a competitive hourly rate per hour used.
3. The corporate president's salary and other corporate costs at 2 percent of sales revenue.
4. Industrial psychology service cost, which is billed by allocating the department's costs over the firm's number of employees.
5. The factory cafeteria's operating loss allocated over the number of factory employees.

E16–8 **Transfer Pricing**

The Masterson Electric Company manufactures electric motors and electric hair dryers. The electric motors are sold for $24 each and have a variable cost of $9 each. Direct fixed costs are $6 each at a capacity of 200,000 motors. The hair dryer division uses 50,000 motors per annum, which are purchased externally at $21 each. The motors used by the hair dryer division are similar to those manufactured by the electric motor division.

Required   *a.* Assume 200,000 electric motors are sold externally at $24. What transfer price should be quoted to the hair dryer division if the 50,000 motors are to be purchased internally? Will the internal purchase and sale take place? Explain.

b. Assume that for the following year, only 150,000 electric motors can be sold externally. What transfer price should be quoted to the hair dryer division for the 50,000 motors, assuming no change in costs? Will the internal purchase and sale take place? Explain.

E16-9 Transfer Pricing

The Fabric Manufacturing Company manufactures piece goods suitable for manufacture into men's and ladies' suits. The company also manufactures men's suits. The piece goods division sells a particular fabric for $45 per yard. For 19x3, the piece goods division operated at full capacity of 1 million yards, all sold externally. Variable costs amounted to $12 per yard, and direct fixed costs amounted to $15 per yard, or $15 million annually.

The men's suits division purchased all of its fabric needs externally during 19x3. For 19x4, the suit division expects to enter a different men's suit market, which will require 500,000 yards of fabric similar to that manufactured by the piece goods division. Checking with other piece goods manufacturers, the suit division was able to ascertain that it could purchase the needed fabric at $45 per yard less a quantity discount of 8 percent.

The piece goods division pays a commission of 4 percent of sales to its salespeople. In addition, it pays shipping costs at an average of 60 cents per yard. These two costs would not be incurred if the piece goods are sold to the suit division.

Required

a. If the suit division wishes to purchase the piece goods internally, what transfer price should be quoted if the piece goods division expects to operate at full capacity in 19x4? Will the internal sale and purchase take place? Explain.

b. If the piece goods division expects to operate at 50 percent of capacity in 19x4, what transfer price should it quote to the suit division? Will the internal sale and purchase take place? Explain.

E16-10 Transfer Pricing

The Brass Fabricating Company's brass tubing division manufactures brass tubing used in the manufacture of lamps. For 19x3, the division operated at 70 percent of capacity, which is expected to continue for 19x4. Its contribution margin income statement for 19x3 is as follows:

BRASS FABRICATING COMPANY
Brass Tubing Division
Contribution Margin Income Statement
For the Year Ended December 31, 19x3

Sales (8 million ft. at 60¢ per ft.)	$4,800,000
Less: Variable costs (at 22¢ per ft.).	1,760,000
Contribution margin.	$3,040,000

The company plans to manufacture lamps during 19x4. The lamps will sell for $40 each and will have variable costs as follows:

Brass tubing—2 ft. at 60¢	$ 1.20
Other variable costs	14.80
Total variable costs	$16.00

The company believes it can sell 1 million lamps in 19x4. No change is expected in sales of brass tubing to outsiders in 19x4. Variable cost patterns are also expected to be unchanged.

a. Prepare a contribution margin income statement for each division, assuming the tubing is purchased internally at 60 cents per foot. Also prepare a combined contribution margin statement. Use three columns, labeled *Tubing*, *Lamps*, and *Combined*. (Show the internal purchase and sale separately in the individual and combined columns.)

b. Redo part *(a)*, this time using a transfer price of 22 cents per foot for tubing. What conclusion can you reach regarding the transfer price charged for internal sales when idle capacity exists in the selling division?

E16–11   **Transfer Pricing**

1. The blade division of Dana Company produces hardened steel blades. One third of the blade division's output is sold to Dana's lawn products division; the remainder is sold to outside customers. The blade division's estimated sales and standard cost data for the fiscal year ending June 30, 19x1, are as follows:

	Lawn Products	Outsiders
Sales	$15,000	$40,000
Variable costs	(10,000)	(20,000)
Fixed costs	(3,000)	(6,000)
Gross margin.	$ 2,000	$14,000
Unit sales	10,000	20,000

The lawn products division has an opportunity to purchase 10,000 identical quality blades from an outside supplier at a cost of $1.25 per unit on a continuing basis. Assume the blade division cannot sell any additional products to outside customers. Should Dana allow its lawn products division to purchase the blades from the outside supplier? Why?

a. Yes, because buying the blades would save Dana Company $500.

b. No, because making the blades would save Dana Company $1,500.

c. Yes, because buying the blades would save Dana Company $2,500.

d. No, because making the blades would save Dana Company $2,500.

2. Mar Company has two decentralized divisions, X and Y. Division X has always purchased certain units from Division Y at $75 per unit. Because Division Y plans to raise the price to $100 per unit, Division X desires to purchase these units from outside suppliers for $75 per unit. Division Y's costs follow:

Y's variable costs per unit	$70
Y's annual fixed costs	$15,000
Y's annual production of these units for X	1,000 units

If Division X buys from an outside supplier, the facilities Division Y uses to manufacture these units would remain idle. What would be the result if Mar enforces a transfer price of $100 per unit between Divisions X and Y?

a. It would be suboptimization for the company because X should buy from outside suppliers at $75 per unit.

b. It would provide lower overall company net income than a transfer price of $75 per unit.

c. It would provide higher overall company net income than a transfer price of $75 per unit.

d. It would be more profitable for the company than allowing X to buy from outside suppliers at $75 per unit.

(AICPA Adapted)

► **PROBLEMS**   **P16–12**   **ROI, Residual Income, and CVP Analysis**

The manager of an investment center presents you with her division's operating results for the year just completed, 19x4, as follows:

STONES INVESTMENT CENTER
Operating Income Statement
For the Year Ended December 31, 19x4

Sales (400,000 at $25).	$10,000,000
Variable costs (at $10)	4,000,000
Contribution margin	6,000,000
Direct fixed costs	4,500,000
Operating income	$1,500,000

Operating assets on January 1, 19x4, amounted to $6 million, and on December 31, 19x4, they amounted to $6.5 million.

The minimum desired rate of return for residual income is 16 percent.

Required   a. Compute:
  (1) The operating margin percentage.
  (2) Asset turnover.
  (3) ROI.
  (4) Residual income.
  b. Each of the following is to be considered independently:
  (1) For 19x5, the manager would like the division to increase its operating margin percentage to 18 percent. This can be accomplished by fixed cost savings. How much would operating income have to increase to reach this goal?
  (2) If in part (b1) the goal is to be achieved by an increase in sales instead of cost savings, how much increased sales would be needed to reach the goal, assuming no increase in direct fixed costs and no change in the variable cost ratio? (*Hint*: Use an algebraic equation to solve the problem.)
  (3) For 19x5, the manager would like to increase the asset turnover to 2. By how much would operating assets have to decrease on December 31, 19x5, to accomplish this objective?
  (4) If in part (b3) the objective is to be achieved by an increase in sales instead of a reduction in operating assets, how much would sales have to increase to reach this objective? Assume operating assets will remain unchanged during 19x5.
  (5) If the selling price were increased by 15 percent in 19x5, sales volume would decrease by 10 percent. Assuming no change in operating assets for 19x5, determine what effect this action would have on:
   (i) The operating margin percentage.
   (ii) Asset turnover.
   (iii) ROI.
   (iv) Residual income.

P16–13   **ROI, Residual Income, and CVP Analysis**

The manager of an investment center presents you with his division's operating results for the year just completed, 19x4, as follows:

SILVER INVESTMENT CENTER
Operating Income Statement
For the Year Ended December 31, 19x4

Sales (400,000 at $24)	$9,600,000
Variable costs (at $12)	4,800,000
Contribution margin	4,800,000
Direct fixed costs	3,648,000
Operating income	$1,152,000

Operating assets on January 1, 19x4, amounted to $6.2 million, and on December 31, 19x4, they amounted to $6.6 million.

The minimum desired rate of return for residual income is 14 percent.

Required   a. Compute:
   (1) The operating margin percentage.
   (2) Asset turnover.
   (3) ROI.
   (4) Residual income.
   b. Each of the following is to be considered independently:
   (1) For 19x5, the manager would like the division to increase its operating margin percentage to 14 percent. This can be accomplished by fixed cost savings. How much would operating income have to increase to reach this goal?
   (2) If in part (b1) the goal is to be achieved by an increase in sales instead of cost savings, how much increased sales would be needed to reach the goal, assuming no increase in direct fixed costs and no change in the variable cost ratio?
   (3) For 19x5, the manager would like to increase the asset turnover to 1.8. By how much would operating assets have to decrease on December 31, 19x5, to accomplish this objective?
   (4) If in part (b3) the objective is to be achieved by an increase in sales instead of a reduction in operating assets, how much would sales have to increase to reach this objective? Assume operating assets will remain unchanged during 19x5.
   (5) If the selling price were decreased by 10 percent in 19x5, sales volume would increase by 20 percent. Assuming no change in operating assets for 19x5, determine what effect this action would have on:
      (i) The operating margin percentage.
      (ii) Asset turnover.
      (iii) ROI.
      (iv) Residual income.

P16–14   ROI and Residual Income

The Mango Company has three divisions, which are operated as investment centers. For residual income calculations, the firm requires a minimum desired rate of return of 16 percent.

Selected information for the three divisions follows:

	Division		
	X	**Y**	**Z**
Sales	$2,400,000	$1,440,000	$800,000
Operating income	264,000	144,000	96,000
Average operating assets	1,090,908	576,000	347,826

Required a. For each division, compute the following:
    (1) The operating margin percentage.
    (2) Asset turnover.
    (3) ROI.
    (4) Residual income.
  b. Select the division that is doing the best job for the company. Explain why you selected the division that is the best and why you rejected the other two.
  c. Division Z has some idle capacity. It has the opportunity to earn an additional $32,000 of operating income, which will require an additional investment of $128,000. Would you expect the division manager to accept the additional project if the evaluation parameter were ROI? Explain. Suppose that instead of ROI, the company uses residual income to evaluate its managers. Would you expect the manager of Division Z to accept the project? Explain.

P16–15 **Transfer Pricing**

The Portable Electric Company has several divisions. One division manufactures small electric motors used in the manufacture of electric hand tools. The motors are sold for $24 each in the intermediate market. During 19x5, the division sold externally 600,000 motors, its full capacity. The variable cost per motor was $6 each, while the direct fixed costs amounted to $12 per motor at the 600,000 capacity.

For the coming year, 19x6, the company plans to market electric drills. The company estimates it can market 200,000 drills annually at a price of $72 each. The expected costs to manufacture are:

Variable costs:	
Electric motor	$21.60
Other costs	12.00
Direct fixed costs	18.00
Total costs	$51.60

Required a. An external electric motor manufacturer quoted a price of $24 less a quantity discount of 10 percent. If the motor division can sell its entire output (600,000 units) externally, what transfer price should be quoted to the drill division for the 200,000 motors? Will the internal sale and purchase take place? Explain. What is the difference in company income of purchasing internally?
  b. If the motor division expects to sell only 400,000 motors in 19x6, what transfer price should be quoted to the drill division for the 200,000 motors? Will the internal sale and purchase take place? Explain. What is the difference in company income of purchasing internally?
  c. If the motor division can sell its entire output externally but can save $1.80 per unit in shipping costs and sales commissions for units sold internally, what transfer price should be quoted? Will the internal sale and purchase take place? Explain. What is the difference in company income of purchasing internally?
  d. If the motor divison can only sell 500,000 motors in 19x6 and the drill division must purchase at least 200,000 motors to get the 10 percent quantity discount off the regular price of $24, what transfer price should be quoted? Will the internal sale and purchase take place? Explain. What is the difference in company income of purchasing internally?

P16–16 **Transfer Pricing**

The Diversified Company has a chemical division that manufactures product A, which is sold externally for $12 per pound. It has a variable cost of $3 per pound and a direct fixed cost of $1 per pound at its present maximum capacity of 1 million pounds per year.

The company also has a fertilizer division that uses product B in its formula. Product B has been purchased externally, but the fertilizer division received a notice that this supplier will be discontinuing the manufacture of product B. The company cannot locate another manufacturer of product B. However, Diversified's chemical division can manufacture product B. The variable costs of manufacturing product B amount to $2 per pound. No change in direct fixed costs will occur if product B is manufactured.

The fertilizer division requires 500,000 pounds of product B per annum. If product B is manufactured by the chemical division, it will only be able to manufacture 600,000 pounds of product A.

The fertilizer division normally produces 10 million pounds of fertilizer per year at a sales price of $.50 per pound. The costs for the fertilizer last year at the 10-million-pound-capacity level were:

	Per Hundred Pounds
Product B—5 pounds at $4 per pound	$ 20
Other ingredients	5
Direct fixed costs	1
Total per 100 pounds	$ 26
Cost per pound—$26/100 pounds	$.26

Required *a.* Prepare a contribution margin income statement for the preceding year for the chemical division, the fertilizer division, and combined for the two divisions, assuming sales at full capacity for both divisions.

b. What transfer price should the chemical division charge for product B, assuming there is a market for all of its output (1 million pounds) of product A? Using this transfer price for product B and assuming the transfer takes place, prepare a budgeted contribution margin income statement for the coming year, using the same format you used in part *(a)*. Compare your result for the chemical division with its result in part *(a)*. Explain.

c. Prepare a contribution margin income statement for the preceding year for the chemical division, the fertilizer division, and combined for the two divisions, assuming sales of 600,000 pounds of product A and full capacity for the fertilizer division.

d. What transfer price should the chemical division charge for product B, assuming it can only sell 600,000 pounds of product A for the coming year? Using this transfer price for product B and assuming the transfer takes place, prepare a budgeted contribution margin income statement for the coming year, using the same format you used in part *(c)*. Compare your result for the chemical division with its result in part *(c)*. Explain.

P16–17   Profit Center Evaluation and Transfer Prices

A. R. Oma, Inc., manufactures a line of men's perfumes and after-shaving lotions. The manufacturing process is basically a series of mixing operations with the addition of certain aromatic and coloring ingredients; the finished product is packaged in a company-produced glass bottle and packed in cases containing six bottles.

A. R. Oma believes the sale of its product is heavily influenced by the appearance and appeal of the bottle and has therefore devoted considerable managerial effort to the bottle-production process. This has resulted in the development of certain unique bottle-production processes in which management takes considerable pride.

The two areas (i.e., perfume production and bottle manufacture) have evolved over the years in an almost independent manner; in fact, a rivalry has developed between management personnel as to "which division is the more important" to A. R. Oma. This attitude is probably intensified because the bottle manufacturing plant was purchased intact 10 years ago and no real interchange of management personnel or ideas (except at the top corporate level) has taken place.

Since the acquisition, all bottle production has been absorbed by the perfume manufacturing plant. Each area is considered a separate profit center and evaluated as such. As the new corporate controller, you are responsible for the definition of a proper transfer value to use in crediting the bottle-production profit center and in debiting the packaging profit center.

At your request, the bottle division general manager has asked certain other bottle manufacturers to quote a price for the quantity and sizes demanded by the perfume division. These competitive prices are:

Volume	Total Price	Price per Case
2 million equivalent cases*.	$ 4 million	$2.00
4 million	7 million	1.75
6 million	10 million	1.67

* An equivalent case represents six bottles each.

A cost analysis of the internal bottle plant indicates it can produce bottles at these costs:

Volume	Total Price	Cost per Case
2 million equivalent cases.	$3.2 million	$1.60
4 million	5.2 million	1.30
6 million	7.2 million	1.20

(Your cost analysts point out that these costs represent fixed costs of $1.2 million and variable costs of $1 per equivalent case.)

These figures have given rise to considerable corporate discussion as to the proper value to use in the transfer of bottles to the perfume division. This interest is heightened because a significant portion of a division manager's income is an incentive bonus based on profit center results.

The perfume-production division has the following costs in addition to the bottle costs:

Volume	Total Cost	Cost per Case
2 million cases.	$16.4 million	$8.20
4 million	32.4 million	8.10
6 million	48.4 million	8.07

After considerable analysis, the marketing research department has furnished you with the following price-demand relationships for the finished product:

Sales Volume	Total Sales Revenue	Sales Price per Case
2 million cases.	$25.0 million	$12.50
4 million	45.6 million	11.40
6 million	63.9 million	10.65

Required   *a.* The A. R. Oma Company has used market price transfer prices in the past. Using the current market prices and costs and assuming a volume of 6 million cases, calculate the income for

(1) The bottle division.

(2) The perfume division.

(3) The corporation.

b. Is this production and sales level the most profitable volume for

(1) The bottle division?

(2) The perfume division?

(3) The corporation?

Explain your answer.

(CMA Adapted)

P16–18   **Transfer Pricing**

The Southern Company has two divisions: S and T. Division S manufactures product C, which is also used by Division T. Presently, Division T is purchasing product C externally for $12 per pound. The following information is available:

	Product C	Division T
Selling price per unit	$14	$50
Costs:		
Product C	$ 0	$12
Other variable costs.	4	10
Direct fixed costs	3	6
Total costs	$ 7	$28
Capacity	60,000 pounds	40,000 pounds

Required   *a.* Assume Division S is selling its entire output (60,000 pounds) externally at $14 per pound. It pays its salespeople a commission of 5 percent of sales, which could be avoided by selling to Division T. Shipping costs amount to 30 cents per pound. What transfer price should Division S quote to Division T? Would you expect the internal sale to take place? Explain.

b. Division T would like to alter the formula of its product and use product D in place of product C. Product D is presently unavailable in the intermediate market. The variable cost of producing product D, exclusive of commissions and shipping costs, is $2 per pound. If Division S produces 40,000 pounds of product D—the annual requirement by Division T—it will still be able to produce 40,000 pounds of product C for sale externally. No change in direct fixed costs would be necessary if product D is produced. What transfer price should be quoted for product D? Explain.

P16–19   **Transfer Pricing, ROI, and Residual Income**

The Northern Company has a switch division operated as an investment center. The division is operating at only 80 percent of capacity. The result of operations for 19x3 are shown below:

NORTHERN COMPANY
Switch Division
Statement of Operating Income
For the Year Ended December 31, 19x3

Sales (80,000 × $9)	$720,000
Variable costs (at $4.50)	360,000
Contribution margin	360,000
Direct fixed costs	270,000
Segment margin	90,000
Billed common costs for services from other divisions	25,200
Operating income	$ 64,800
Operating assets—January 1, 19x3	$380,000
Operating assets—December 31, 19x3	417,500

The company's minimum desired rate of return to be used for residual income is 12 percent.

Required

a. Compute the following:
   (1) The operating margin percentage.
   (2) Asset turnover.
   (3) ROI.
b. Compute residual income.
c. For 19x4, the switch division expects its operations to be unchanged from 19x3. However, it has an opportunity to accept a special order from an outsider for 20,000 switches at a price of $6. The order will not affect its regular sales and will require an additional outlay of $15,000 for direct fixed costs. Additional operating assets will be needed at a cost of $110,000. Calculate the following for the combined operations, assuming that the order is accepted:
   (1) ROI.
   (2) Residual income.
   Would you expect the manager of the switch division to accept the order if the parameter used for evaluation were ROI? Why? Would your answer be different if the parameter used were residual income? Why?
d. The Northern Company is planning to market a new product. The switches manufactured by the switch division could be used in the new product. Assume the offer in part (c) was withdrawn. Thus, the switch division will still have the idle capacity. The manager in charge of producing the new product learned that he could purchase the 20,000 switches externally for $7.50 each. What price should the switch division quote for the switch, assuming no increase in fixed costs and no additional investment will be needed by the switch division? Why?
e. Assume the same facts as in part (d), except the switch division has a customer willing to purchase the 20,000 switches in 19x4 for $8.25 each. The switches will not require any shipping costs or sales commissions. What price should the switch division now quote to the purchasing division? What should the purchasing manager's reaction be to the price quoted? Why?
f. Assume the same facts as in part (e), except shipping costs and sales commissions amount to $1.50 per unit on the 20,000 switches. What price should be quoted? What should the purchasing manager do? Why?
g. Assume the switch division can only sell 80,000 switches (80 percent of capacity) in 19x4 and its budgeted statement of operating income for 19x4 is the same as that shown for 19x3. The purchasing division expects to use

100,000 switches and thus would require all of the switch division's output. There are no shipping costs or sales commissions in the income statement for 19x3. What price should be charged by the switch division? What should the purchasing manager do if she can purchase the switches externally at $7.88 per switch? Why?

P16–20   Transfer Pricing

National Industries is a diversified corporation with separate and distinct operating divisions. Each division's performance is evaluated on the basis of total dollar profits and return on division investment.

The WindAir division manufactures and sells air conditioner units. The coming year's budgeted income statement, based on a sales volume of 15,000 units, appears below:

	Per Unit	Total (in thousands)
NATIONAL INDUSTRIES		
WindAir Division		
Budgeted Income Statement		
For the 19x8–x9 Fiscal Year		
Sales revenue	$400	$6,000
Manufacturing costs:		
Compressor	70	1,050
Other direct materials.	37	555
Direct labor	30	450
Variable overhead	45	675
Fixed overhead	32	480
Total manufacturing costs.	214	3,210
Gross margin	186	2,790
Operating costs:		
Variable marketing	18	270
Fixed marketing	19	285
Fixed administrative	38	570
Total operating costs	75	1,125
Net income before taxes	$111	$1,665

WindAir's division manager believes sales can be increased if the unit selling price of the air conditioners is reduced. A market research study conducted by an independent firm at the request of the manager indicates that a 5 percent reduction ($20) in the selling price would increase sales volume 16 percent, or 2,400 units. WindAir has sufficient production capacity to manage this increased volume with no increase in fixed costs.

At the present time, WindAir uses in its units a compressor that it purchases from an outside supplier at a cost of $70 per compressor. The division manager of WindAir has approached the manager of the compressor division regarding the sale of a compressor unit to WindAir. The compressor division currently manufactures and sells exclusively to outside firms a unit that is similar to the unit used by WindAir. The specifications of the WindAir compressor are slightly different, which would reduce the compressor division's direct material cost by $1.50 per unit. In addition, the compressor division would not incur any variable marketing costs in the units sold to WindAir. The WindAir manager wants all of the compressors it uses to come from one supplier and has offered to pay $50 for each compressor unit.

The compressor division has the capacity to produce 75,000 units. The coming year's budgeted income statement for the compressor division is shown below and is based on a sales volume of 64,000 units without considering WindAir's proposal.

NATIONAL INDUSTRIES
Compressor Division
Budgeted Income Statement
For the 19x8–x9 Fiscal Year

	Per Unit	Total (in thousands)
Sales revenue	$100	$6,400
Manufacturing costs:		
Direct materials	12	768
Direct labor	8	512
Variable overhead	10	640
Fixed overhead	11	704
Total manufacturing costs.	41	2,624
Gross margin	59	3,776
Operating costs:		
Variable marketing	6	384
Fixed marketing	4	256
Fixed administrative	7	448
Total operating costs	17	1,088
Net income before taxes	$ 42	$2,688

Required *a.* Should WindAir division institute the 5 percent price reduction on its air conditioner units even if it cannot acquire the compressors internally for $50 each? Support your conclusion with appropriate calculations.

b. Without prejudice to your answer to part *(a)*, assume WindAir needs 17,400 units. Should the compressor division be willing to supply the compressor units for $50 each? Support your conclusions with appropriate calculations.

c. Without prejudice to your answer to part *(a)*, assume WindAir needs 17,400 units. Would it be in the best interest of National Industries for the compressor division to supply the compressor units at $50 each to the WindAir division? Support your conclusions with appropriate calculations.

(CMA Adapted)

P16–21 **ROI and Residual Income**

Raddington Industries produces tool and die machinery for manufacturers. The company expanded vertically in 19x4 by acquiring one of its suppliers of alloy steel plates, Reigis Steel Company. To manage the two separate businesses, the operations of Reigis are reported separately as an investment center.

Raddington monitors its divisions on the basis of both unit contribution and return on average investment (ROI), with investment defined as average operating assets employed. Management bonuses are determined on ROI. All investments in operating assets are expected to earn a minimum return of 11 percent before income taxes.

Reigis' cost of goods sold is considered to be entirely variable, and the division's administrative costs are not dependent on volume. Selling costs are a mixed cost with 40 percent attributed to sales volume. Reigis' ROI has ranged from 11.8 to 14.7 percent since 19x4. During the fiscal year ended November 30, 19x9, Reigis contemplated a capital acquisition with an estimated ROI of 11.5 percent; however, division management decided against the investment because it believed that the investment would decrease Reigis' overall ROI.

The 19x9 operating statement for Reigis is presented below. The division's operating assets employed were $15,750,000 at November 30, 19x9, a 5 percent increase over the 19x8 year-end balance.

REIGIS STEEL DIVISION
Operating Statement
For the Year Ended November 30, 19x9
(in thousands)

Sales revenue		$25,000
Less costs:		
Cost of goods sold	$16,500	
Administrative costs	3,955	
Selling costs	2,700	23,155
Income from operations before		
income taxes		$1,845

Required

a. Calculate the unit contribution for Reigis Steel Division if 1,484,000 units were produced and sold during the year ended November 30, 19x9.

b. Calculate the following performance measures for 19x9 for Reigis Steel Division.
   (1) Pretax return on average investment in operating assets employed (ROI).
   (2) Residual income calculated on the basis of average operating assets employed.

c. Explain why the management of Reigis Steel Division would have been more likely to accept the contemplated capital acquisition if residual income rather than ROI had been used as a performance measure.

d. Reigis Steel Division is a separate investment center within Raddington Industries. Identify several items that Reigis should control if it is to be evaluated fairly by either the ROI or residual income performance measures.

(CMA Adapted)

P16–22   **ROI and Residual Income**

The Heron Company has a motor division that manufactures small electric motors. The division is operated as an investment center and is operating at only 50 percent of capacity. The results of operations for 19x3 are shown below:

HERON COMPANY
Motor Division
Statement of Operating Income
For the Year Ended December 31, 19x3

Sales (100,000 × $3.60).	$360,000
Variable costs (at $1.20)	120,000
Contribution margin	240,000
Direct fixed costs	150,000
Segment margin	90,000
Billed common costs for services from other divisions	18,000
Operating income	$ 72,000
Operating assets—January 1, 19x3	$288,000
Operating assets—December 31, 19x3	312,000

The company's minimum desired rate of return for residual income is 14 percent.

Required *a.* Compute the following:
   (1) The operating margin percentage.
   (2) Asset turnover.
   (3) ROI.
b. Compute residual income.
c. For 19x4, the division expects its operations to be unchanged from 19x3. However, it has an opportunity to accept a special order from a foreign manufacturer for 80,000 motors at a price of $1.80 per unit. The order will not affect its regular sales and will require an additional outlay of $24,000 for direct fixed costs. Additional operating assets will be needed at a cost of $120,000. Calculate the following for 19x4, if the special order is accepted (combine the special order with the regular operations):
   (1) The operating margin percentage.
   (2) Asset turnover.
   (3) ROI.
   (4) Residual income.
   Would you expect the manager of the motor division to accept the order if the parameter used for evaluation were ROI? Why? Would your answer be different if the parameter used were residual income? Why?

▶ **CASE**   C16–23   **Discussion of a Performance Evaluation Program**

The ATCO Company purchased the Dexter Company three years ago. Prior to the acquisition, Dexter manufactured and sold plastic products to a wide variety of customers. Dexter has since become a division of ATCO and now only manufactures plastic components for products made by ATCO's Macon division. Macon sells its products to hardware wholesalers.

ATCO's corporate management gives the Dexter division management a considerable amount of authority in running the division's operations. However, corporate management retains authority for decisions regarding capital investments, price setting of all products, and the quantity of each product to be produced by the Dexter division.

ATCO has a formal performance evaluation program for the managements of all its divisions. The performance evaluation program relies heavily on each division's return on investment. The income statement of Dexter division presented below provides the basis for the evaluation of Dexter's divisional management.

The financial statements for the divisions are prepared by the corporate accounting staff. The corporate general services costs are allocated on the basis of sales dollars, and the computer department's actual costs are apportioned among the divisions on the basis of use. The net division investment includes division fixed assets at net book value (cost less depreciation), division inventory, and corporate working capital apportioned to the divisions on the basis of sales dollars.

ATCO COMPANY
Dexter Division
Income Statement
For the Year Ended October 31, 19x0
(in thousands)

Sales.		$4,000
Costs:		
Product costs:		
Direct materials	$ 500	
Direct labor.	1,100	
Factory overhead	1,300	
Total.	2,900	
Less: Increase in inventory.	350	2,550
Engineering and research.		120
Shipping and receiving		240
Division administration:		
Manager's office.	210	
Cost accounting	40	
Personnel.	82	332
Corporate costs:		
Computer.	48	
General services.	230	278
Total costs		3,520
Divisional operating income		$ 480
Net plant investment.		$1,600
Return on investment		30%

Required *a.* Discuss the financial reporting and performance evaluation program at ATCO Company as it relates to the responsibilities of the Dexter division.

b. Based on your response to part *(a)*, recommend appropriate revisions of the financial information and reports used to evaluate the performance of Dexter's divisional management. If revisions are not necessary, explain why not.

(CMA Adapted)

▶ **ANSWERS TO SELF-TEST**

True or False

1. True	2. True	3. False	4. False	5. True
6. False	7. False	8. True	9. True	10. False
11. False	12. False	13. False	14. False	15. True

Multiple Choice

1. *c.*   2. *b.*   3. *a.*   4. *a.*   5. *b.*   6. *c.*   7. *d.*   8. *b.*

PART
▶

3

Additional Selected Topics

17 Statement of Cash Flows

18 Analysis of Financial Statements

Statement of Cash Flows

▶ **LEARNING OBJECTIVES**

After reading this chapter, you should be able to:

1. Describe the significance and purpose of the statement of cash flows.
2. List the major sources and uses of cash.
3. Analyze the sources and uses of cash and classify them into operating, investing, and financing activities.
4. Describe a noncash exchange transaction and explain how it appears on a statement of cash flows.
5. Prepare a statement of cash flows using the indirect approach.
6. Prepare a statement of cash flows using the direct approach.

▶ **INTERVIEW**

Robert Ripp
Vice President
and Treasurer
International Business
Machines Corporation

Q. *In terms of importance to users of financial statements, does the income statement or the statement of cash flows provide more useful information? Explain.*

A. The usefulness of a financial statement depends on the information needs of the user. Income statements are indispensable to a financial analyst preparing a gross profit margin report; on the other hand, the statement of cash flows is invaluable to a treasury analyst in projecting the future cash balance of a company. One could continue a point-counterpoint debate as to which statement is indeed more useful, and in the end, such a discussion would be decided based on the user's perspective.

The vast majority of experienced and novice users of financial statements have a built-in bias, believing that the income statement is more useful. This bias is due in part to greater familiarity (understanding) and greater educational experience with income statements. Generally, financial managers at large corporations have concentrated on income statements and have not concerned themselves with cash. Now, financial managers are increasingly asked to understand the cash dynamics of their businesses. In the past, only small business managers and managers in countries with hyperinflation shared this focus on cash.

Today, financial managers should use cash flow statements as illustrated below.

Cash Flow from Operating Activities

▶ Reveals whether current operations are generating or consuming cash.
▶ Highlights whether cash is needed to fund working capital (short-term financing).
▶ Shows the cash flow impact of accounts receivable and inventory management initiatives.

Cash Used in Investing Activities

▶ Shows the level of long-term funds required to support future capital expenditures.
▶ When netted with cash from operations, the result reveals the level of cash generated or consumed.

  Positive cash flow can be used to pay dividends, repurchase shares, retire debt, or invest.
  Negative cash flow must be funded by cash from financing activities.

Cash from Financing Activities

▶ Shows how financing activities are used to balance the cash generated or consumed by operations and investing activities.

▶ When a firm issues financial statements for external use, three statements are presented: (1) an income statement, (2) a balance sheet, and (3) a statement of cash flows. The last statement, mandated by *SFAS No. 95*,[1] is important because cash is universally acknowledged as the most liquid of assets. Also, cash is used to repay loans to lenders and pay dividends to stockholders. Cash is ultimately needed for a business to remain viable operationally. For example, it is needed to replace inventories that are sold and to replace plant and equipment a firm uses in its operations.[2]

Cash is the beginning as well as the end of an operating cycle. Thus, cash is converted into inventories, which are then sold and converted into accounts receivable. When these accounts are ultimately collected from the firm's customers, the collected cash enters the operating cycle again and the process is repeated. The firm's objective, then, is that more cash will be returned to the firm at the end of an operating cycle than is used at the beginning of the cycle.

Users of financial statements have long recognized that accrual-based net income may hide a firm's real cash flows from operations. It is not surprising then that the Financial Accounting Standards Board (FASB) requires firms to include a statement of cash flows in their set of financial statements.   ◀

▶ SIGNIFICANCE AND PURPOSE

L.O. 1

The ability of an enterprise to meet its obligations on time and its ability to expand and grow depend on adequate levels of cash. The valid measurement of an enterprise's cash inflows and outflows is an important indicator of a firm's short-term liquidity, long-term solvency, and operating performance.

Although fragmentary information on sources and uses of cash is obtained from comparative balance sheets and income statements, a comprehensive picture of this area of activity is found only on a statement of cash flows. A **statement of cash flows (SCF),** classified into operating activities, investing activities, and financing activities, provides information about the sources and uses of cash over a period of time. **Operating activities** include all the earning-related activities of producing goods and services for customers. Thus they include all the cash inflows and outflows entering into the determination of net income.[3] **Investing activities** include the making and collecting of loans to *other* enterprises, the purchase and sale of equity instruments (stocks) of *other* enterprises, and the purchase and sale of the firm's property, plant, and equipment.[4] **Financing activities** include the sale and purchase of a firm's *own* capital stock, the borrowing of cash, the repayment of debt, and the payment of dividends to a firm's stockholders.[5]

However, a case can be made for considering interest and dividend income as a cash receipt from investing activities. The FASB chose to consider these items as cash receipts from operating activities. The FASB perceived a widespread support for the notion that operating cash flows should

---

[1] FASB, *Statement of Financial Accounting Standards No. 95*, "Statement of Cash Flows" (Stamford, Conn., November 1987), par. 3.

[2] The author is grateful to Professor Leopold A. Bernstein for permission to abstract portions of his book, *Financial Statement Analysis,* published by Richard D. Irwin, Inc., 1989. Those who are interested in a definitive treatment of this subject matter should refer to Chapter 13 of that book.

[3] *SFAS 95*, par. 21.

[4] Ibid., par. 15–17.

[5] Ibid., par. 18–20.

articulate closely with reported net income. Also, because interest and dividend income are reflected in a firm's income statement, these cash flows should be classified as operating income.[6]

The importance of the SCF is growing because the statement provides information on such questions as:

1. What amount of cash was generated by operations?
2. What use was made of cash provided by operations?
3. What was the source of cash invested in new plant and equipment?
4. What use was made of cash derived from a new bond issue or the sale of stock?
5. How was it possible to continue the regular dividend despite an operating loss?
6. How was the debt repayment achieved, or what was the source of cash used to redeem the preferred stock?
7. How was the increase in investments financed?
8. Why, despite record profits, is the cash position lower than last year?

▶ WHAT IS CASH FLOW?

Cash flow is a term that is widely used but poorly understood. Standing alone and unqualified, the term *cash flow* is meaningless. A company can experience cash *inflows* (i.e., cash receipts) and cash *outflows* (i.e., cash disbursements). Moreover, these cash inflows and outflows can relate to a variety of activities (e.g., the profit-directed activities that are called *operations,* or financing activities, or investing activities). We can also identify the difference between the inflows and outflows of cash for each of these activities and for all combined activities of the enterprise. These are referred to as *net inflows* or *net outflows* of cash. Thus, a net inflow of cash reconciles to an *increase* in the cash balance for the period, and a net outflow corresponds to a *decrease* of the cash balance for the period. To avoid confusion, the type of cash flow referred to should be specifically described. When using the term *cash flow,* users of financial reports mean cash generated by operations. However, cash flow is also used to describe other concepts of generated cash, such as the net change in the cash balance. These uses of the term depend on the needs and objectives of the users.

▶ EVOLUTION OF THE ACCOUNTING FOR CASH FLOWS

Historically, accountants have recognized the need to explain changes in funds, however defined, from period to period. However, not until 1971 did *APB Opinion No. 19,* "Reporting Changes in Financial Position," require that a statement of changes in financial position be presented as a basic financial statement and that it explain changes in either working capital or cash.

Sophisticated users of financial statements have also recognized that the most useful focus is on the change in *cash* rather than on any other measure of liquidity. Because financial statements are prepared on an accrual basis

---

[6] Ibid., par. 90.

and many important analytical objectives focus on an entity's ability to meet cash obligations (such as interest, principal repayment, capital outlays, and dividends), the financial statement user needs to know the cash consequences of the entity's operating, financing, and investing activities.

In 1976, the FASB began to formulate a "conceptual framework" of accounting and reporting. As part of its work on the conceptual framework, in December 1980 the FASB issued a *Discussion Memorandum,* "Reporting Funds Flow, Liquidity, and Financial Flexibility," which discussed funds flow reporting issues. The major issues discussed were the concepts of which funds should be adopted for the funds flow statement and the form of presentation of funds flow information. Feedback received by the FASB in connection with the conceptual framework project indicated an overall consensus among users of financial statements that a cash flow statement would be more useful than any other funds flow statement.

In December 1983, as part of its study on recognition and measurement concepts, the board issued an *Exposure Draft,* "Recognition and Measurement in Financial Statements of Business Enterprises," which discussed the role of the cash flow statement. This exposure draft led to the issuance of *Statement of Financial Accounting Concepts No. 5* (1984), which states that a *full* set of financial statements for a reporting period should show "cash flows during the period."

Following the issuance of an exposure draft of a proposed SFAS, "Statement of Cash Flows" in 1986, the FASB issued *SFAS No. 95,* "Statement of Cash Flows," which requires a statement of cash flows as part of a full set of financial statements of all business entities. Thus, the SCF replaced the statement of changes in financial position.

▶ STATEMENT FORMAT

Although the FASB sanctions two formats for the presentation of the statement of cash flows, its preference is the direct method. The **direct method** of preparing a statement of cash flows consists of reporting the major classes of gross cash receipts, less gross cash payments, and their arithmetic sum— that is, the net cash flow from operating activities.[7] *SFAS No. 95* also permits the presentation of a statement of cash flows using the indirect method. The **indirect method** of preparing a statement of cash flows consists of presenting net income and then reporting the effects of deferrals and accruals that do not affect cash. Therefore, the result reports the net cash flow from operating activities.[8] This chapter illustrates both approaches.

▶ DEFINITION OF CASH AND CASH EQUIVALENTS

A statement of cash flows explains the change in cash and cash equivalents for the period of the statement. **Cash and cash equivalents** include cash, demand deposits, and short-term, highly liquid investments. These investments are both readily convertible to known amounts of cash and so near to maturity that no significant risk is present for a change in market values from

---

[7] Ibid., par. 27.

[8] Ibid., par. 28.

▶ **ILLUSTRATION 17-1**   Summary of Sources of Cash

Operating Activities
1. Net income.
2. Reduction of Accounts Receivable balance (collections in excess of sales for the period).
3. Reduction of Inventory balance (more inventory sold than purchased during the period).
4. Reduction of Prepaid Costs balance (more prepaid costs, such as prepaid insurance, written off than purchased during the period).
5. Increase in Accounts Payable balance (payments are less than costs incurred during the period).
6. Increases in other current liabilities, such as wages payable, arising from operating activities during the period.

Investing Activities
1. Proceeds from the sale of property, plant, and equipment.
2. Proceeds from the sale of investments in the capital stock or bonds of *other* corporations.
3. Collections of loans made to other companies.

Financing Activities
1. Proceeds from the sale of a firm's own capital stock (common or preferred).
2. Proceeds from the issuance of short-term or long-term notes, loans, bonds, or mortgages payable.
3. Proceeds from the sale of a firm's treasury stock (stock previously issued and then reacquired by the firm).

their face values.[9] For short-term purposes, only securities with an *original* maturity of three months or less qualify. Thus, a security with an *original* maturity of greater than three months but with a remaining maturity of less than three months remaining from the date of the firm's balance sheet *would not* qualify as a cash equivalent. The amount reconciled as cash and cash equivalents should be the same amount shown as the *change* in cash and cash equivalents between the firm's balance sheets as of the beginning of the period and the end of the period covering the statement of cash flows. Ambiguous terms like *funds* should be avoided in a statement of cash flows,[10] despite their sanctioned use in the statement of changes in financial position required prior to the issuance of *SFAS No. 95*.

▶ SOURCES AND USES OF CASH

It is important to include the reasons for the changes in cash on a financial statement. The principal reasons for changes in cash are divided into (1) sources of cash and (2) uses of cash.

Sources of Cash

L.O. 2 and 3

The sources of cash are divided into three categories: (1) cash provided by operations, (2) cash provided by investing activities, and (3) cash provided by financing activities.

Illustration 17-1 summarizes the principal sources of cash, classified into operating, investing, and financing activities.

---
[9] Ibid., par. 7–8.
[10] Ibid., par. 7.

▶ **ILLUSTRATION 17-2**   Summary of Uses of Cash

Operating Activities

1. Net loss.
2. Increase in Accounts Receivable balance.
3. Increase in Inventory balance.
4. Increase in Prepaid Costs balance.
5. Reduction in Accounts Payable balance.
6. Reduction in other current liabilities, such as wages payable, arising from operating activities during the period.

Investing Activities

1. Purchases of property, plant, and equipment.
2. Purchases of investments in the capital stock or bonds of *other* corporations.
3. Lending money to other companies.

Financing Activities

1. Payments of short-term or long-term notes, loans, bonds, or mortgages payable.
2. Purchases of a firm's treasury stock (stock previously issued and then reacquired by the firm).
3. Payment of dividends.

Uses of Cash
L.O. 2 and 3

Illustration 17-2 summarizes the principal uses of cash, classified into operating, investing, and financing activities.

▶ GROSS CASH FLOWS VERSUS NET CASH FLOWS

When the indirect method (starting with net income) is used, the net cash flows of the reconciling items, such as the changes in accounts receivable, inventory, or accounts payable, are generally reported on a net basis.[11] A **net cash flow** is the netting of the cash inflow and outflow of the same grouping, such as the net change in inventory. Thus, if the activity in an inventory account has a beginning balance of $200,000, purchases of $1.3 million, cost of goods sold of $1.2 million, and a closing balance of $300,000, only the $100,000 increase in inventory is shown in the operating section of the statement of cash flows as a cash outflow. When the direct method is used, then the gross cash flows are shown. A **gross cash flow** is the showing of both the cash inflow and cash outflow of the same grouping, such as the borrowing and repayment of debt. For example, if the activity in a notes payable account has a beginning balance of $200,000, borrowings of $1 million, repayments of $1.1 million, and a closing balance of $100,000, both the borrowings of $1 million and the repayment of $1.1 million must be shown as a source and a use, respectively, in the financing activities section of the statement of cash flows.[12] Therefore, the gross cash inflows for sales revenue are shown. The gross cash flow for revenue is the revenue shown on an income statement plus the beginning balance of Accounts Receivable minus the ending balance of Accounts Receivable. The gross cash outflows for cost of goods sold and other costs are deducted to arrive at the net cash flow from operating activities. Under either method, the gross cash flows concerning investing and financing activities are generally shown.

---

[11] Ibid., par. 28.

[12] Ibid., par. 31.

► NONCASH EXCHANGE TRANSACTIONS FOR INVESTING AND FINANCING ACTIVITIES

L.O. 4

Firms often have noncash transactions. A **noncash exchange transaction** is a transaction of an investing or financing activity where cash is not involved. Examples include acquiring a building by incurring a mortgage or issuing capital stock for the building and exchanging bonds payable for common stock. The transaction is reported either in a narrative form or in a related, summarized schedule appended to the statement of cash flows.[13]

► CASH FLOW PER SHARE

A cash flow per share statistic cannot appear on any financial statement.[14] The only permissible per-share amount that appears on financial statements is the earnings per share statistic discussed in Chapter 18.

► OTHER DISCLOSURES

When the indirect method (starting with net income) is used to prepare a statement of cash flows, the total amount of interest paid (less the amount of capitalized interest) and the total amount of income taxes paid must be disclosed separately as an addendum to the statement.[15] This disclosure will automatically appear in the statement of cash flows when the direct method is used. With this approach, all gross revenues and gross costs arrive at the net cash flow from operations. The interest and income taxes would appear individually as part of the cash outflows in the costs section of the operating activities.

► PREPARATION OF THE STATEMENT OF CASH FLOWS—INDIRECT METHOD

L.O. 5

To focus on changes in cash, let us study two condensed balance sheets divided into sections disclosing (1) cash and (2) all other balance sheet accounts:

	Dr. (Cr.)	
	Year-End 1	Year-End 2
Cash:		
Cash and cash equivalents	$ 3,000	$ 5,000
Other balance sheet accounts:		
Current assets (other than cash)	$ 9,000	$ 11,000
Noncurrent assets	6,000	8,000
Current liabilities	(8,000)	(10,000)
Long-term liabilities.	(3,000)	(5,000)
Equity accounts	(7,000)	(9,000)
Net cash.	$(3,000)	$(5,000)

[13] Ibid., par. 32.
[14] Ibid., par. 33.
[15] Ibid., par. 29.

Although the above sections are not a conventional form of balance sheet presentation, they provide a very useful framework for understanding the interactions between cash and all other balance sheet accounts. Observe that the net change in cash from year-end 1 to year-end 2 (a debit change of $2,000) is matched exactly by the $2,000 change in the other balance sheet accounts between these two year-ends (an increase in net credits). Because assets must always equal liabilities plus capital, a change in one sector of the balance sheet must be matched by an equal change in the rest of the accounts.

Cash Provided by Operations   When operations are profitable, cash normally increases but not usually by the amount of net income shown on the income statement. Some charges and credits used in the income statement to arrive at net income do not affect cash. Thus, some of them must be reversed on the SCF when the statement is prepared using the indirect method and net income as the starting point. Consider the following entry for depreciation:

(a)

Depreciation xxx
    Accumulated Depreciation xxx

This depreciation entry reduces a firm's income, yet it does not reduce cash. Because cash is *not* reduced by depreciation, it must be added back to net income to arrive at the cash provided by operations. Compare the above entry with the following entry for material costs:

(b)

Material Cost xxx
    Cash xxx

Note that material cost also reduces income, but it also affects cash in entry *(b)*. Therefore, material cost is not added back to net income because *both income and cash are reduced* by material cost.

Stock Dividends   Recall that a stock dividend does not alter a firm's assets or liabilities; it is merely a bookkeeping entry that transfers a dollar amount from Retained Earnings to Common Stock (and possibly Additional Paid-In Capital). The firm does not disburse any assets, nor do the recipients of the stock dividend receive any assets. The recipients merely have more shares of the company, but their percentages of ownership of the firm remain unchanged. Because there are no financing or investing activities involved in a stock dividend, no disclosure of this item is required in the SCF. The same treatment applies to stock splits, which are similar to stock dividends because the number of outstanding shares are increased. The difference between a stock dividend and a stock split is in bookkeeping; in substance they are the same.

To more fully understand the preparation of the SCF, focus on the following simple illustration.

▶ **ILLUSTRATION 17-3**

WIDGET CORPORATION
Condensed Balance Sheets
(in thousands)

	December 31		Changes during 19x2*			
			Operating Activity	Investing Activity	Financing Activity	Noncash Transactions
	19x1	19x2				
1. Cash	$ 120	$ 100				
2. Accounts receivable.	200	145	$ 55			
3. Inventories.	150	175	(25)			
4. Fixed assets	660	874		$(214)		
5. Accumulated depreciation	(200)	(244)	64	(20)		
6. Intangible assets	150	100	50			
Total assets	$1,080	$1,150				
7. Accounts payable.	$ 150	$ 130	(20)			
8. Long-term debt.	420	400			$ (10)	$(10)
9. Capital stock and paid-in capital	250	300			40	10
10. Retained earnings.	260	320	180		(120)	
Total liabilities and equity . . .	$1,080	$1,150				
Totals			$304	$(234)	$ (90)	$–0–

* Items in parentheses reflect *decreases* in cash or noncash resources.

Simple Illustration of Preparation of Statement of Cash Flows

To illustrate the preparation of a statement of cash flows (SCF), the condensed comparative balance sheets at two consecutive year-ends (shown in Illustration 17-3) will be used. These balance sheets are condensed here for convenience of illustration. The preparation of the SCF requires additional information about account changes, and the supplementary data are as follows:

1. The $20 decrease in cash is the change that the SCF sets out to explain. It is explained through the changes in all other balance sheet accounts.
2. The decrease in accounts receivable is a positive (cash inflow) adjustment to income in arriving at cash from operations. It means cash was received this accounting period from sales made in a previous accounting period.
3. The increase in inventories is a negative (cash outflow) adjustment to income because cash outlays for inventory exceeded accrual-basis purchases included in cost of sales.
4. The T account below summarizes the changes in the Fixed Asset account:

Fixed Assets	
Balance 660	
Additions 314	Disposals 100
Balance 874	

Both the additions and the disposals are part of investing activities. Although each event is shown separately in the SCF, here they net out to $214 ($314 − $100).

5. The T account below summarizes the change in the Accumulated Depreciation account:

Accumulated Depreciation

Accumulated depreciation on assets disposed of	20	Balance	200
		Depreciation for period	64
		Balance	244

As discussed above, depreciation ($64) is a noncash item. It represents an internal change in Group B—a debit to income (retained earnings) and a credit to Accumulated Depreciation. It is, thus, added back to income to arrive at cash from operations. The $20 in Accumulated Depreciation relates to the $100 (original cash) of fixed assets disposed of. The assets were sold at book value (i.e., $100 − $20 = $80). The $20 of accumulated depreciation adjusts the $100 amount included in the investing activity (see line 5 of Illustration 17-3).

6. The decline of $50 in intangible assets represents amortization. Amortization is a noncash item similar to depreciation. Therefore, it is added back to income in the operating activity column.

7. The decrease in accounts payable is a negative (cash outflow) adjustment to income, because amounts due to suppliers for preceding periods were not paid in preceding periods but were paid this period in cash.

8. The decrease of $20 in long-term debt represents $10 in repayment (classified as a financing outflow) and a $10 reduction due to conversion of debt into equity (classified as a noncash transaction).

9. The increase of $50 in capital stock represents the sale of capital stock of $40 (a financing inflow) and $10 in stock issued by conversion of debt (a noncash transaction).

10. The change in retained earnings is summarized in the T account below:

Retained Earnings

		Balance	260
Dividends paid	120	Net income	180
		Balance	320

The net income of $180 is the figure that, after adjustments, becomes the source of cash from operations of $304. The dividend of $120 is a financing cash outflow.

To summarize, the change in cash is explained as follows:

	($000)
Net cash flow from operations	$ 304
Cash flows for investing activities	(234)
Cash flows for financing activities	(90)
Decrease in cash	$ (20)

Illustration 17-4 presents these results in a formal and more detailed statement of cash flows.

► **ILLUSTRATION 17-4**

WIDGET CORPORATION
Statement of Cash Flows—Indirect Method
For the Year Ended December 31, 19x2

Net cash flow from operating activities:		
Net income	$180,000	
Adjustments to reconcile net income to net		
cash provided by operating activities:		
Depreciation	64,000	
Amortization of intangibles	50,000	
Decrease in accounts receivable	55,000	
Increase in inventory	(25,000)	
Decrease in accounts payable.	(20,000)	
Net cash flow from operating activities		$304,000
Cash flows from investing activities:		
Purchase of fixed assets	(314,000)	
Sale of fixed assets	80,000	
Net cash used in investing activities		(234,000)
Cash flows from financing activities:		
Sale of capital stock	40,000	
Payment of dividends	(120,000)	
Repayment of long-term debt	(10,000)	
Net cash used in financing activities		(90,000)
Net increase (decrease) in cash		$ (20,000)
Schedule of noncash investing and financing activities:		
Common stock issued in conversion of long-term debt. . . .		$ 10,000

Note: The amounts paid for interest and income taxes must also be disclosed.

In the illustration of Widget Corporation, the SCF was constructed directly from the comparative balance sheets and information given. When financial statements need more detail and complexity, a more structured and systematic method of preparation is used. In the sections that follow, we will illustrate the T account technique for the systematic preparation of an SCF. We shall also discuss and elaborate on the computation of cash flow from operations (CFO).

► **PROGRESS CHECK**

1. What kinds of information may be obtained from a statement of cash flows (SCF) that cannot be obtained from an income statement or balance sheet?
2. What are cash and cash equivalents?
3. The SCF is broken down into three sections. What are they? What items may be found in each section?
4. What is the difference between a net cash flow and a gross cash flow? Which is used in the SCF?
5. What is a noncash exchange? Does this appear in an SCF? If so, how is it shown? If not, should it be shown? Why?   ◄

Illustration of T Account Technique

The simple illustration above showed some of the more common steps involved in the preparation of the SCF. These and other steps found in more complex examples are:

1. Analyzing net changes based on further detail and information.
2. Reversing or eliminating transactions internal to noncash accounts.

▶ **ILLUSTRATION 17-5**

THE VATTER COMPANY
Comparative Balance Sheets
As of December 31, 19x1, and 19x2

Assets	19x1	19x2	Increase (Decrease)
Current assets:			
Cash	$ 240,000	$ 120,000	$ (120,000)
Accounts Receivable	360,000	450,000	90,000
Inventories	750,000	1,053,000	303,000
Total current assets	1,350,000	1,623,000	273,000
Fixed assets.	4,500,000	6,438,000	1,938,000
Less: Accumulated depreciation	(1,500,000)	(1,740,000)	(240,000)
Investments in marketable securities	1,000,000	1,050,000	50,000
Intangibles	950,000	980,000	30,000
Total assets	$6,300,000	$8,351,000	$2,051,000
Liabilities and Capital			
Accounts payable	$ 360,000	$ 590,000	$ 230,000
Bonds payable.	300,000	700,000	400,000
Deferred income taxes payable	240,000	260,000	20,000
Common stock	2,400,000	3,200,000	800,000
Paid-in capital	900,000	1,300,000	400,000
Retained earnings	2,100,000	2,301,000	201,000
Total liabilities and capital	$6,300,000	$8,351,000	$2,051,000

3. Regrouping and reconstructing transactions in the noncash group that affect, and hence explain, the changes in cash.

The methods used to implement these adjustments vary from elaborate, multicolumn worksheets to summarized adjustments that are performed mentally. One of the most direct and most flexible methods uses the reconstruction of summarized T accounts. This method, developed by Professor W. J. Vatter, is illustrated below.

The basic objective of the T account method is to reconstruct in *summary fashion,* by means of T accounts, all balance sheet accounts and the transactions reflected in them during the period reported on. If the reconstructed transaction reveals it was a source of or a use of cash, it is posted to the summary cash T account. If the transaction has no effect on cash and does not have a significant investing or financing nature, it is reversed among the applicable noncash T accounts.

Illustration 17-5 presents the comparative balance sheets, and Illustration 17-6 presents the income statement of the Vatter Company.

The following additional information also is available:

1. On March 1, 19x2, the company bought for $510,000 cash fixed assets with a value of $450,000 and intangible assets with a value of $60,000.
2. Old machinery was sold for $18,000; it originally cost $36,000, and $20,000 of depreciation was accumulated to date of sale.
3. In April, the company acquired $100,000 in fixed assets by issuing bonds with $100,000 par value.
4. In June, the company received $1 million in cash for a new issue of

▶ **ILLUSTRATION 17-6**

THE VATTER COMPANY
Income Statement
For the Year Ended December 31, 19x2

Sales		$19,950,000
Cost of goods sold (includes $360,000 depreciation)		11,101,000
Gross profit		8,849,000
Marketing and administrative costs.	$7,000,000	
Amortization of intangibles	30,000	7,030,000
		1,819,000
Investment income		50,000
Gain on sale of fixed assets		2,000
Income before taxes		1,871,000
Income taxes:		
Current	900,000	
Deferred	20,000	920,000
Net income		$ 951,000

capital stock with a par value of $600,000. Two hundred thousand dollars of convertible bonds were converted into capital stock, par value $200,000. Long-term bonds were also sold for $500,000 (at par).
5. Fully depreciated assets of $100,000 were written off.
6. Dividends paid were $750,000.
7. Marketable securities were acquired for cash in the amount of $50,000.
8. Marketing and administrative costs include interest paid in the amount of $50,000.
9. There were no unpaid liabilities for income taxes at the beginning and end of 19x2.

Use the following steps to prepare a statement of cash flows:

Step 1

Compute the net change in the cash and cash equivalents for the period of the statement. This step is done by comparing the balances of these items at the beginning of the period (year) with their balances at the end of the year. This amount represents the target figure to which the statement must reconcile.

Step 2

Compute the net changes from the beginning of the period (year) to the end of the period for each item other than cash and cash equivalents that appears on the comparative balance sheets for the period.

Step 3

For each item computed in step 2, determine the reasons for the changes in the account. An effective way to accomplish this is to use a T account to reconstruct each group of changes that occurred in the account during the period (year). Thus, set up a T account for each noncash account appearing in the comparative balance sheet. The opening and closing balance of the account is posted to the T account as follows:

Fixed Assets

B*	4,500	
B†	6,438	

* Signifies opening balance.
† Signifies closing balance.

The difference between the ending balance of $6,438 and the beginning balance of $4,500, or $1,938, is explained by fixed asset acquisitions, sales, retirements, or a combination of them.

Step 4

a. Open a cash T account, divided into four sections: Operations, Investing Activities, Financing Activities, and Noncash Transactions. Post all reconstruction entries to the appropriate section of this T account.

b. Based on information supplied and inferences drawn from the changes in the noncash accounts, the balance in the T account is reconstructed by:
   1. Debiting or crediting items of income or loss, as well as items converting them to the cash basis, to the Operations section.
   2. Debiting or crediting all remaining items to the other three sections to which they relate.

c. When the process is completed, the cash T account will contain the detail necessary for the preparation of the SCF.

Step 5

Prepare the statement of cash flows by starting with net income. Then make the necessary reconciling adjustments to arrive at the cash flow from operating activities, investing activities, and financing activities. The total of all these amounts should agree with the amount of change in cash and cash equivalents computed in step 1. Disclose any noncash investing and financing activities in a separate schedule to the statement.

Determining Cash Flow from Operations

Cash may also be increased because of changes in the components of working capital. **Working capital** is a firm's current assets minus its current liabilities. It includes cash, temporary investments in marketable securities, accounts receivable, inventories, and prepaid costs, minus its accounts payable, short-term maturities of notes and mortgages payable, and other liabilities payable within one year.

Following are examples of items that may appear in the income statement and have no effect on cash:

Income Statement Item	Related to the Following Noncash Balance Sheet Item
Amortization of bond premium	Unamortized bond premium
Amortization of bond discount	Unamortized bond discount
Warranty cost	Provision for warranty costs (noncurrent)
Amortization of leasehold improvements	Leasehold improvements
Subscription income	Deferred subscription income (noncurrent portion)

This concept can also be summarized as follows:

Income Statement Item	Related to Contra Account	Effect on Cash from Operations
Debit cost or loss	Credit to cash	Use of cash
	Credit to noncash account	Add back—not using cash
Credit income, or gain, or cost	Debit to cash	Source of cash
	Debit to noncash account	Deduct—not providing cash

The gain on sale of fixed assets will receive separate consideration. It is removed from income because the total cash received on the sale (including the gain) is classified as part of investing activities. Thus, if the gain on sale of the fixed assets is not removed from income, the total proceeds from the sale of the fixed assets ($18,000) will be found in *two* places: (1) recovery of book value of fixed assets of $16,000 ($36,000 − $20,000) and (2) gain on sale in net income.

Also note that some current accounts do not relate to operations and are classified by type of activity to which they relate. For example:

Account	Type of Activity
Loans Receivable (e.g., from officers)	Investing
Current Portion of Long-Term Debt.	Financing
Notes Payable to Bank	Financing
Dividends Payable	Financing

In the illustration of Vatter Company, there are no nonoperating current accounts.

The T accounts and explanation of transactions are as follows:

T Accounts (Dollars in Thousands)

Cash

B*	240	

Operations

Depreciation	(g)	360	Gain on sale of property, plant, and equipment	(b)	2
Deferred income taxes	(k)	20	Increase in receivables	(q)	90
Net income	(m)	951	Increase in inventories	(r)	303
Intangibles amortization	(o)	30			
Increase in accounts payable	(s)	230			

Investing Activities

Sale of property, plant, and equipment	(b)	18	Acquisition of fixed assets	(a)	450
			Acquisition of intangibles	(a)	60
			Acquisition of fixed assets	(f)	1,524
			Acquisition of marketable securities	(p)	50

Financing Activities

Bonds sold	(h)	500	Dividends paid	(n)	750
Sale of stock	(l)	1,000			

Noncash Transactions

Bonds issued to acquire fixed assets	*(d)*	100	Fixed assets acquired with bonds	*(c)*	100
Stock issued in conversion	*(j)*	200	Bond conversion to stock	*(i)*	200
B†		120			

Accounts Receivable

B*	360	
(q)	90	
B†	450	

Inventories

B*	750	
(r)	303	
B†	1,053	

Accounts Payable

	B*	360
	(s)	230
	B†	590

Fixed Assets

B*	4,500			
(a)	450	*(b)*	36
(c)	100	*(e)*	100
(f)	1,524		
B†	6,438		

Accumulated Depreciation

			B*	1,500
(b)	20	*(g)*	360
(e)	100		
		B†	1,740

Investment in Marketable Securities

B*	1,000	
(p)	50	
B†	1,050	

Intangibles

B*	950		
(a)	60	*(o)*	30
B†	980		

Bonds Payable

		B*	300
(i)	200	*(d)*	100
		(h)	500
		B†	700

Deferred Income Taxes Payable

	B*	240
	(k)	20
	B†	260

Capital Stock

		B*	2,400
		(j)	200
		(l)	600
		B†	3,200

Additional Paid-In Capital

	B*	900
	(l)	400
	B†	1,300

Retained Earnings

		B*	2,100
(n)	750	*(m)*	951
		B†	2,301

▶ RECONSTRUCTION OF TRANSACTIONS

Fixed Assets   The acquisition of the going concern is reconstructed as follows:

(a)

Fixed Assets	450,000	
Intangible Assets	60,000	
Cash—Investing.		510,000

In the statement of cash flows, the acquisition is treated as an investing activity. It represents the acquisition of productive assets that are expected to generate revenue over a long period of time.

The transaction for the sale of equipment is as follows:

(b)

Cash—Investing.	18,000	
Accumulated Depreciation	20,000	
Fixed Assets		36,000
Cash—Operations		2,000

The entire proceeds of $18,000 are debited to Cash from Investing Activities. In the statement of cash flows, the sale of property, plant, and equipment represents an investing activity.

Cash from Operations is credited to remove the gain on the sale of equipment from net income. This gain must be removed from net income to link it with the recovery of book value of $16,000 and to show the entire proceeds as part of cash from investing activities.

The statement of cash flows requires all significant investing and financing activities to be disclosed whether or not cash is directly affected. Therefore, the following entries are necessary to account for the acquisition of fixed assets through the issuance of debt:

(c)

Fixed Assets	100,000	
Noncash Transactions		100,000

(d)

Noncash Transactions	100,000	
Bonds Payable		100,000

The write-off of depreciated assets does not affect cash. Also, it does not represent an important investing or financing activity. Therefore, it is not reflected in the statement of cash flows. The transaction is reconstructed as follows:

(e)

Accumulated Depreciation	100,000	
Fixed Assets		100,000

All known transactions except for fixed assets acquired were posted to the Fixed Asset account. To arrive at the ending balance, it is necessary to debit the account for $1,524,000, the amount of fixed assets acquired.

(f)

Fixed Assets.	1,524,000	
Cash—Investing		1,524,000

Accumulated Depreciation

To balance the Accumulated Depreciation account, a credit of $360,000 is needed. This amount represents the depreciation found on the income statement.

(g)

Cash—Operations (Noncash Adjustment)	360,000	
Accumulated Depreciation		360,000

Depreciation is added back to income because it is an item not using cash.

Bonds Payable

The issuance of bonds is a financing activity in a statement of cash flows. The entry for the issuance of bonds is as follows:

(h)

Cash—Financing	500,000	
Bonds Payable		500,000

The conversion of bonds into common stock does not affect cash. As a significant financing activity, however, it must be disclosed in a separate schedule of the SCF.

(i)

Bonds Payable	200,000	
Noncash Transactions		200,000

(j)

Noncash Transactions	200,000	
Capital Stock		200,000

Deferred Income Taxes

The charge for deferred income taxes does not require the use of cash. It is an add-back to net income as an item not requiring cash.

(k)

Cash—Operations (Noncash Adjustment)	20,000	
Deferred Income Taxes Payable		20,000

Capital Stock and Paid-In Capital

The sale of stock is a financing activity in a statement of cash flows. The entry for the sale of stock is as follows:

(l)

Cash—Financing	1,000,000	
Capital Stock		600,000
Additional Paid-In Capital		400,000

Retained Earnings

Net income of $951,000 is the starting number that is adjusted for items needed to convert it to a cash basis.

(m)

Cash—Operations	951,000	
Retained Earnings		951,000

Cash dividends paid to stockholders are a financing activity in the statement of cash flows. Cash dividends paid amounted to $750,000.

(n)

Retained Earnings	750,000	
Cash—Financing		750,000

▶ **ILLUSTRATION 17-7**

THE VATTER COMPANY
Statement of Cash Flows—Indirect Method
For the Year Ended December 31, 19x2
(in thousands)

Cash flows from operating activities:		
Net income	$ 951	
Add (deduct) adjustments to cash basis:		
Depreciation	360	
Amortization of intangibles	30	
Deferred income taxes	20	
Gain on sale of equipment	(2)	
Increase in receivables	(90)	
Increase in inventories	(303)	
Increase in accounts payable	230	
Net cash provided by operating activities.		$ 1,196
Cash flows from investing activities:		
Purchase of fixed assets	(1,974)	
Purchase of intangibles	(60)	
Sale of property, plant, and equipment	18	
Acquisition of marketable securities	(50)	
Net cash used by investing activities		(2,066)
Cash flows from financing activities:		
Net proceeds from sale of bonds	500	
Sale of capital stock	1,000	
Payment of dividends	(750)	
Net cash provided by financing activities		750
Net decrease in cash		$ (120)
Supplemental disclosure of cash flow information:		
Interest paid during the year		$ 50
Income taxes paid during the year		$ 900
Schedule of noncash investing and financing activities:		
Bonds issued to acquire fixed assets		$ 100
Stock issued in conversion of bonds		$ 200

Intangibles Amortization

The income statement shows $30,000 of amortization of intangibles. Because this charge to income does not require cash, it is added back to net income.

(*o*)

Cash—Operations (Noncash Adjustment)	30,000	
Intangibles		30,000

Investment in Marketable Securities

Marketable securities were acquired for $50,000. This amount is a cash outflow of an investing activity.

(*p*)

Investment in Marketable Securities	50,000	
Cash—Investing.		50,000

Accounts Receivable

The change in accounts receivable should be reflected in arriving at "cash flows from operating activities" to convert income from an accrual basis to a cash basis. An increase in accounts receivable indicates that some sales were not collected in cash. In this case, the $90,000 increase in accounts receivable reduces CFO by an adjustment to income.

(q)

Accounts Receivable.	90,000	
Cash—Operations		90,000

Inventories

The change in inventories affects cash flows from operating activities. An increase in inventories indicates that purchases exceeded the cash outlays reflected in cost of goods sold. Thus, an adjustment reducing CFO is needed.

(r)

Inventories	303,000	
Cash—Operations		303,000

Accounts Payable

The change in accounts payable should also be reflected in arriving at cash flows from operating activities. An increase in accounts payable indicates that some purchases were not yet paid for in cash. Thus, costs exceed cash outlays, requiring an adjustment that increases cash from operations.

(s)

Cash—Operations	230,000	
Accounts Payable		230,000

Now that all the transactions were reconstructed, a comprehensive statement of cash flows can be developed from the Cash T account. This statement appears in Illustration 17-7.

The adjustments to convert Vatter Company's net income to the cash basis are also explained as follows:

Item	Amount ($000)	Explanation
Net income, accrual basis	$ 951	Starting point.
Add (deduct) adjustments to cash basis:		
Depreciation	360	Add back because item has no cash outflow.
Amortization of intangibles	30	Add back because item has no cash outflow.
Deferred income taxes payable	20	Add back because item has no cash outflow.
Gain on sale of equipment	(2)	Remove gain so that total cash inflow is shown as cash from investing activities.
Increase in receivables	(90)	Deduct because cash flow from sales is *less* than accrual sales revenue.
Increase in inventories	(303)	Deduct because cash outflows for inventory *exceeds* accrual-basis inventory cost included in cost of goods sold.
Increase in accounts payable	230	Add because cash outflows for purchases (included in cost of goods sold) is *less* than accrual purchase cost.
CFO (Illustration 17-7)	$1,196	

► PREPARATION OF THE STATEMENT OF CASH FLOWS—DIRECT METHOD

L.O. 6

As noted earlier, the FASB expressed a preference for the direct method. This method of statement presentation involves listing (1) the gross collections of cash from customers, (2) the gross cash collections from interest and dividend income, and (3) all cash payments for operating activities to arrive at the cash flow from operations. This approach provides statement users with certain useful information not found in a statement prepared using the indirect approach. That is, it contains the cash inflows from sales and the cash outflows of costs to produce those sales. The *net* cash flows are shown in both methods of statement preparation. However, a statement user likes to know the amount of cash provided from sales to make a projection of the future cash inflows. The indirect method of statement preparation does not give that information.

Under the direct method, an enterprise must provide a reconciliation of net income to CFO in a separate schedule. Minimally, it must also report on the following cash receipts and payments:

1. Cash collected from customers, including lessees, licensees, and the like.
2. Interest and dividends received.
3. Other operating cash receipts, if any.
4. Cash paid to employees and other suppliers of goods or services, including suppliers of insurance, advertising, and the like.
5. Interest paid.
6. Income taxes paid.
7. Other operating cash payments, if any.

Also, enterprises should provide further details of operating receipts and payments. However, as noted earlier, they must disclose, under either method, the amount of interest paid (net of amounts capitalized) and income taxes paid.

Statement Preparation Procedures

It is important to note that the parts of the statement pertaining to investing and financing activities are identical for either method. Thus, the procedures illustrated above for these parts are not repeated. The focus, therefore, is on the operating activities part of the statement.

Because the income statement provides accrual-based information, it is necessary to convert this information to a cash basis. An effective method for this conversion is to use the T account reconstruction method shown above. However, under the indirect method, the starting point is net income. Recall that noncash charges, such as depreciation, were deducted to arrive at net income. Therefore, it was necessary to add these noncash charges back to negate their effect. Under the direct method, the starting point is gross cash receipts minus gross cash payments, and it is thus not necessary to add any noncash items back because they are not deducted. The only items that appear in the operating section of the statement are those items that appear in the income statement *and* have an effect on cash flow.

T Account Reconstruction

The illustration of the direct method is based on the data presented in Illustrations 17-5 and 17-6.

The steps needed to prepare the operating activities section of the statement are:

Step 1

Cash collections from customers: Open a T account for Accounts Receivable. Insert the beginning and ending balances as was done previously. If a separate account is given for Allowance for Doubtful Accounts, do the same for this account. If not, then ignore the latter account. Open blank accounts for Cash and Sales. Then debit Accounts Receivable and credit Sales for the net amount of sales shown on the income statement. Credit Accounts Receivable for the amount needed to balance the account and debit Cash for this amount. This amount represents the cash collections from customers. This procedure is modified when a separate Allowance for Doubtful Accounts account is used. This account is adjusted through the Accounts Receivable account in the same manner as that account.

Step 2

Open T accounts for Accounts Payable and Inventories. Insert beginning and ending balances. Also open blank T accounts for Cost of Goods Sold, Marketing and Administrative Costs, and Cash. Using the same procedures as noted in step 1, reconstruct all accounts until the amount of cash payments is arrived at. Remember to exclude any depreciation or amortization from Cost of Goods Sold and Marketing and Administrative Costs if they are included in either of these costs.

Step 3

Use the same procedures to compute the amounts of income taxes paid and interest (less amount capitalized) paid. The amount of income taxes paid may be merely the current portion on the income statement if the deferred portion on the income statement is equal to the net change in deferred income taxes on the balance sheet *and* there is no change in the Income Taxes Payable account, as is the case in this example. Note that in this case, there are no unpaid income taxes at the beginning or end of the year.

Step 4

Using the amounts of cash payments computed in the preceding steps, prepare the operating activities section of the statement. Show the cash collections from customers, from interest income, and from dividend income. Deduct the cash payments to suppliers, for income taxes, and for interest to arrive at the cash flow from operations.

Step 5

Complete the statement using the cash flows computed for investing activities and financing activities.

Illustration of T Accounts   The T accounts are as follows:

Cash Collections

Accounts Receivable

B*	360	Collections	(b) 19,860
Sales	(a) 19,950		
B†	450		

Sales

	(a) 19,950

Cash

Collections	(b) 19,860

Cash Payments

Accounts Payable

Cash payments	(f) 17,764	B*	360
		Cost of goods sold	(c) 10,741
		Increase in inventories	(d) 303
		Marketing and administrative	(e) 6,950
		B†	590

Inventories

B*	750	
Increase	(d) 303	
B†	1,053	

Cost of Goods Sold

(c) 10,741	

Marketing and Administrative Costs

(e) 6,950	

Interest Paid

(g) 50	

Cash

	Payments	(f) 17,764
	Interest paid	(g) 50

Explanations The explanations of the reconstruction entries (in thousands of dollars) are as follows:

(a)

Accounts Receivable.	19,950	
Sales.		19,950

This entry reconstructs the sales for the year. The Sales account agrees with the year-end balance shown on the income statement.

(b)

Cash.	19,860	
Accounts Receivable.		19,860

This entry is the plugged amount necessary to convert the beginning balance of Accounts Receivable to the ending balance.

(c)

Cost of Goods Sold	10,741	
Accounts Payable		10,741

Although the balance of Cost of Goods Sold on the income statement is $11,101, only $10,741 is used because the $11,101 includes $360 of depreciation that did not require a cash outflow. After making this reconstruction entry, account for the total amount of cash outflows for cost of goods sold.

(d)

Inventories.	303	
Accounts Payable.		303

Inventories increased by $303. Thus, this amount of merchandise must have been purchased in excess of that appearing in cost of goods sold. This amount must be recorded as a reconstruction entry so that the ending balance shown in Inventories will agree with the amount appearing on Vatter's balance sheet.

(e)

Marketing and Administrative Costs.	6,950	
Accounts Payable		6,950

Only $6,950 of Marketing and Administrative Costs is reconstructed because these costs include $50 of interest that must be reported separately. Also, the amortization of intangibles is shown as a separate item on the income statement. Therefore, $6,950 must have required cash outflows for goods and services.

(f)

Accounts Payable	17,764	
Cash.		17,764

This entry is the plugged amount necessary to convert the beginning balance of Accounts Payable to the ending balance.

(g)

Interest Paid.	50	
Cash		50

This entry reconstructs the amount of interest paid.

The statement of cash flows for the Vatter Company, prepared under the direct method, appears in Illustration 17-8.

▶ **ILLUSTRATION 17-8**

THE VATTER COMPANY
Statement of Cash Flows—Direct Method
For the Year Ended December 31, 19x2
(in thousands)

Cash flows from operating activities:		
Cash received from customers	$ 19,860	
Cash paid to suppliers and employees.	(17,764)	
Interest paid	(50)	
Income taxes paid	(900)	
Investment income	50	
Net cash provided by operating activities		$ 1,196
Cash flows from investing activities:		
Purchase of fixed assets	(1,974)	
Purchase of intangibles	(60)	
Sale of property, plant, and equipment	18	
Acquisition of marketable securities.	(50)	
Net cash used by investing activities		(2,066)
Cash flows from financing activities:		
Net proceeds from sale of bonds	500	
Sale of capital stock.	1,000	
Payment of dividends	(750)	
Net cash provided by financing activities		750
Net decrease in cash		$ (120)
Schedule of noncash investing and financing activities:		
Stock issued in conversion of bonds		$ 200
Bonds issued to acquire fixed assets		$ 100
Reconciliation of net income to net cash provided by		
operating activities:		
Net income		$ 951
Add (deduct) adjustments to cash basis:		
Depreciation		360
Amortization of intangibles		30
Deferred income taxes.		20
Gain on sale of equipment		(2)
Increase in receivables		(90)
Increase in inventories		(303)
Increase in accounts payable.		230
Net cash flow from operating activities		$ 1,196

▶ PUBLISHED STATEMENT OF CASH FLOWS

Notice in Illustration 17-9, a published statement of cash flows for PepsiCo, Inc., that PepsiCo's cash and cash equivalents increased in 1988 to $142.7 million from the $79.3 million in 1987, an increase of $63.4 million. Although *operating activities* generated $1.895 billion of cash, *investing activities* consumed $2.051 billion of cash. A principal consumption of cash was for acquisitions and investments in equity securities in the amount of $1.416 billion. The notes to the financial statements indicate that these investments were for franchised soft drink bottlers. An important part of the *financing* for these acquisitions was the issuance of long-term debt in the amount of $475 million.

For 1989, cash and cash equivalents fell from $142.7 million to $76.2 million, a decrease of $66.5 million. Note that PepsiCo invested $3.297 billion of cash in acquisitions and equity investments and that these were

▶ **ILLUSTRATION 17-9**

PEPSICO, INC. AND SUBSIDIARIES
Consolidated Statement of Cash Flows
Fifty-Two Weeks Ended December 30, 1989, Fifty-three Weeks Ended December 31, 1988,
and Fifty-Two Weeks Ended December 26, 1987
(in millions)

	1989	1988	1987
Cash flows from continuing operations:			
Income from continuing operations	$ 901.4	$ 762.2	$ 605.1
Adjustments to reconcile income from continuing operations to net cash generated by continuing operations:			
Depreciation and amortization.	772.0	629.3	563.0
Deferred income taxes	71.2	20.1	59.0
Other noncash charges and credits—net	128.4	213.4	105.4
Changes in operating working capital:			
Notes and accounts receivable	(149.9)	(50.1)	(95.6)
Inventories	(50.1)	13.8	4.1
Prepaid expenses, taxes, and other current assets .	6.5	37.8	39.7
Accounts payable	134.9	138.2	(76.9)
Income taxes payable	80.9	55.1	23.3
Other current liabilities.	(9.4)	74.7	107.4
Net change in operating working capital	12.9	269.5	2.0
Net cash generated by continuing operations	1,885.9	1,894.5	1,334.5
Cash flows from investing activities:			
Acquisitions and equity investments	(3,296.6)	(1,415.5)	(371.5)
Purchases of property, plant, and equipment	(943.8)	(725.8)	(770.5)
Proceeds from sales of property, plant, and equipment.	69.7	67.4	98.6
Proceeds from sales of businesses	—	283.2	161.6
Other short-term investments—by original maturity:			
Three months or less—net	667.0	(411.1)	(736.1)
More than three months—purchases.	(2,131.1)	(692.6)	(1,311.8)
More than three months—sales	1,476.4	902.0	1,526.2
Other, net.	(97.9)	(58.7)	(72.9)
Net cash used for investing activities	(4,256.3)	(2,051.1)	(1,476.4)
Cash flows from financing activities:			
Proceeds from issuances of long-term debt	71.7	475.3	598.3
Payments of long-term debt	(405.4)	(190.0)	(113.4)
Short-term borrowings—by original maturity:			
Three months or less—net	2,292.2	306.7	114.7
More than three months—proceeds	1,109.5	292.0	547.9
More than three months—payments	(476.2)	(367.4)	(1,157.0)
Proceeds from nonrecourse obligation	—	0.1	299.3
Cash dividends paid	(241.9)	(199.0)	(172.0)
Purchases of treasury stock	—	(71.8)	(18.6)
Other, net.	(28.9)	(24.5)	(38.8)
Net cash generated by financing activities	2,321.0	221.4	60.4
Effect of exchange rate changes on cash and cash equivalents	(17.1)	(1.4)	(8.0)
Net increase (decrease) in cash and cash equivalents .	(66.5)	63.4	(89.5)
Cash and cash equivalents—beginning of year	142.7	79.3	168.8
Cash and cash equivalents—end of year	$ 76.2	$ 142.7	$ 79.3

financed by cash from operating activities and from short-term borrowings. The notes to the financial statements indicate that these investments were for franchised soft drink bottlers including the soft drink operations of General Cinema Corporation. Clearly, PepsiCo was expanding its operations during the years 1988–1989.

The statement of cash flows is used by managerial accountants to determine what the effects of expansion would be on a company's cash and cash equivalents and how to finance acquisitions. The information provided in the statement of cash flows is not available in a company's income statement or its balance sheet.

▶ **SUMMARY**

A firm must present a **statement of cash flows** whenever it prepares a set of financial statements for the public's use. The statement is important because it helps users assess future cash inflows and outflows, short-term liquidity, long-term solvency, and operating performance. Also, it contains information not found in a firm's income statement.

The statement's format contains three sections: (1) **operating activities,** (2) **investing activities,** and (3) **financing activities.** The preferred method of preparing the operating activity section is the **direct method.** With this method, a firm's gross collections from customers—its **gross cash flows**—are shown together with the cash collections from interest income and dividend income. From the total of these items, the cash payments to suppliers and employees are deducted together with the cash payments for income taxes and the cash payments for interest to arrive at the **net cash flow** from operations. An alternate method is the **indirect method,** which starts with net income. Then noncash reconciling items, such as depreciation and amortization, are added back to arrive at the net cash flow from operations. Regardless of which method is used, the net cash flow from operations is the same in both formats, as are the sections dealing with investing activities and financing activities. Occasionally, firms have **noncash exchange transactions,** such as the acquisition of a plant asset in exchange for a firm's capital stock. These items are disclosed separately in an addendum to the statement of cash flows.

A firm may temporarily invest its idle cash in short-term investments for three months or less and earn a return on the invested cash. This type of investment is a cash equivalent. Because *SFAS No. 95* requires the statement to reconcile to **cash and cash equivalents,** it is important to understand that they consist of cash, demand deposits, and investments with original maturities of three months or less. Prior to the issuance of *SFAS No. 95,* it was acceptable to prepare a statement reconciling to **working capital.**

The cash flows statement can be prepared using different procedures, such as a worksheet or making mental calculations to compute the needed data. However, a useful and methodical procedure is to use the T account reconstruction method. When this method is used, beginning balances are inserted in balance sheet accounts; and the necessary entries that occurred during the year are posted to these accounts and the related income statement accounts. Therefore, the end result is the ending balances in the balance sheet accounts. The Cash account is subdivided into sections for operating, investing, and financing activities. When completed, this Cash account provides the information needed to prepare the statement.

▶ **GLOSSARY OF KEY TERMS**

Cash and cash equivalents   Cash, demand deposits, and short-term, highly liquid investments that are both readily convertible to known amounts of cash and so near to maturity that no significant risk is present for a change in market values from their face values.   (p. 876)

Direct method   A method of preparing a statement of cash flows that consists of reporting the major classes of gross cash receipts, less the gross cash payments, and their arithmetic sum—that is, the net cash flow from operating activities.   (p. 876)

Financing activities   Activities of a firm that include the sale and purchase of a firm's *own* capital stock, the borrowing of cash, and the payment of dividends to a firm's stockholders.   (p. 874)

Gross cash flow   The showing of both the cash inflow and cash outflow of the same grouping, such as the borrowing and repayment of debt.   (p. 878)

Indirect method   A method of preparing a statement of cash flows consisting of presenting net income and then reporting the effects of deferrals and accruals that do not affect cash so the result reports the net cash flow from operating activities.   (p. 876)

Investing activities   Activities of a firm that include the making and collecting of loans to *other* enterprises, the purchase and sale of equity instruments (stocks) of *other* enterprises, and the purchase and sale of the firm's property, plant, and equipment.   (p. 874)

Net cash flow   The netting of the cash inflow and outflow of the same grouping, such as the net change in inventory.   (p. 878)

Noncash exchange transaction   Transactions of investing or financing activities where cash is not involved, such as acquiring a building by incurring a mortgage or issuing capital stock for the building, or exchanging bonds payable for common stock. These are reported either in a narrative form or in a related, summarized schedule appended to the statement of cash flows.   (p. 879)

Operating activities   Activities of a firm that encompass all the earning-related activities of producing goods and services for customers. They include all the cash inflows and outflows entering into the determination of net income.   (p. 874)

Statement of cash flows (SCF)   A required financial statement classified into operating activities, investing activities, and financing activities and providing information about the sources and uses of cash over a period of time.   (p. 874)

Working capital   A firm's current assets minus its current liabilities. It includes cash, temporary investments in marketable securities, accounts receivable, inventories, and prepaid costs, minus its accounts payable, short-term maturities of notes and mortgages payable, and other liabilities payable within one year.   (p. 886)

▶ **REVIEW PROBLEM**   **Preparation of SCF—Indirect Method and Direct Method**

Brett Company presents you with the following data:

	December 31	
Debits	**19x5**	**19x4**
Accounts receivable—net	$ 480,000	$ 520,000
Cash.	$ 160,000	$ 200,000
Inventory	260,000	220,000
Prepaid marketing and administrative costs	20,000	18,000
Property, plant, and equipment	1,040,000	960,000
Treasury stock	540,000	–0–
Total debits.	$2,500,000	$1,918,000
Credits		
Accumulated depreciation	$ 480,000	$ 420,000
Accounts payable.	240,000	160,000
Long-term notes payable.	350,000	200,000
Common stock	800,000	600,000
Additional paid-in capital.	210,000	160,000
Retained earnings	420,000	378,000
Total credits	$2,500,000	$1,918,000

An analysis of the company's Retained Earnings account produced the following:

Retained earnings—January 1, 19x5	$378,000
Add: Net income	202,000
Subtotal	580,000
Less: Cash dividends	160,000
Retained earnings—December 31, 19x5 . . .	$420,000

BRETT COMPANY
Income Statement
For the Year Ended December 31, 19x5

Sales	$3,000,000
Cost of goods sold	1,800,000
Gross margin	1,200,000
Marketing and administrative costs	900,000
Income before income taxes	300,000
Income taxes	98,000
Net income	$ 202,000

Marketing and administrative costs include $26,000 paid for interest. There were no sales, trade-ins, or disposals of any property, plant, and equipment.

Required   *a.* Prepare an SCF using the indirect method.
b. Prepare an SCF under the direct method.

► SOLUTION TO
REVIEW PROBLEM

a.

BRETT COMPANY
Statement of Cash Flows
For the Year Ended December 31, 19x5

Net cash flow from operating activities:

Net income	$202,000	
Noncash costs, revenues, losses, and gains included in income:		
Depreciation	60,000	
Decrease in accounts receivable	40,000	
Increase in inventory	(40,000)	
Increase in prepaid costs	(2,000)	
Increase in accounts payable	80,000	
Net cash flow from operating activities		$340,000
Cash flows from investing activities:		
Cash outflows for property, plant and equipment	(80,000)	
Net cash used in investing activities		(80,000)
Cash flows from financing activities:		
Proceeds from issuance of long-term notes	150,000	
Proceeds from sale of common stock	250,000	
Purchases of treasury stock	(540,000)	
Payments for cash dividends	(160,000)	
Net cash used for financing activities		(300,000)
Net increase (decrease) in cash		$(40,000)

Supplemental disclosure of cash flow information:

Interest paid during the year	$ 26,000
Income taxes paid during the year	98,000

b.

BRETT COMPANY
Statement of Cash Flows
For the Year Ended December 31, 19x5

Cash flows from operating activities:

Cash received from customers (Schedule No. 1)		$3,040,000
Cash paid to suppliers and employees (Schedule No. 2)	$2,576,000	
Interest paid	26,000	
Income taxes paid	98,000	
Cash disbursed for operating activities		2,700,000
Net cash flow from operating activities		340,000
Cash flows from investing activities:		
Purchases of property, plant and equipment	(80,000)	
Net cash used in investing activities		(80,000)
Cash flows from financing activities:		
Issuance of long-term note	150,000	
Purchase of treasury stock	(540,000)	
Proceeds from sale of common stock	250,000	
Dividends paid	(160,000)	
Net cash used for financing activities		(300,000)
Net increase (decrease) in cash		$ (40,000)

Reconciliation of net income to net cash provided by operations:

Net income		$ 202,000
Noncash costs, revenues, losses, and gains included in income:		
Depreciation	60,000	
Decrease in accounts receivable	40,000	
Increase in inventory	(40,000)	
Increase in prepaid costs	(2,000)	
Increase in accounts payable	80,000	
Net cash flow from operating activities		$ 340,000

Schedule No. 1

Cash Collections

Accounts Receivable

B*		520,000	3,040,000 *(b)* Collections
Sales	*(a)*	3,000,000	
B†		480,000	

Sales

	3,000,000	*(a)*

Cash

Collections	*(b)* 3,040,000	

Schedule No. 2

Cash Payments

Accounts Payable

Cash payments	*(g)* 2,576,000	160,000	B*
		1,740,000 *(c)* Cost of goods sold	
		40,000 *(d)* Increase in inventories	
		876,000 *(e)* Marketing and administrative	
		240,000	B†

Inventories

B*		220,000	
Increase	*(d)*	40,000	
B†		260,000	

Cost of Goods Sold

($1,800,000 − $60,000 depreciation)	*(c)* 1,740,000	

Marketing and Administrative Costs

($900,000 − $26,000 interest + $2,000 prepaid costs)	*(e)* 876,000	2,000 *(f)*

Prepaid Marketing and Administrative

B*	18,000	
	(f) 2,000	
B†	20,000	

Cash

	2,576,000 *(g)* Payments—Accounts payable	

► **LIBRARY ASSIGNMENT**

Read the following:

Bracken, Robert M., and Ara G. Volkan. "Cash Flows: New Reporting Format for Turbulent Times." *Management Accounting,* January 1988, pp. 38–41.

Giacomino, Don E., and David E. Mielke. "Using the Statement of Cash Flows to Analyze Performance." *Management Accounting,* May 1988, pp. 54–57.

Kronquist, Stacey L., and Nancy Newman-Limata. "Reporting Corporate Cash Flows." *Management Accounting,* July 1990, pp. 31–36.

Moskowitz, Jerald I. "What's Your Business Worth?" *Management Accounting,* March 1988, pp. 30–34.

Seed, Allen H. III. "Improving Cost Management." *Management Accounting,* February 1990, pp. 27–30.

Zega, Cheryl Ann. "The New Statement of Cash Flows." *Management Accounting,* September 1988, pp. 54–59.

► **SELF-TEST**

True or False

1. A noncash exchange transaction is reported either in a narrative form or in a schedule appended to the statement of cash flows.
2. A SCF shows an analysis of working capital accounts in a separate schedule.
3. A set of comparative balance sheets and an income statement provide a financial statement user only fragmented information on the firm's sources and uses of cash.
4. The statement of cash flows provides a comprehensive picture of the sources and uses of cash.
5. The operating activities section of the SCF includes the purchase and sale of plant, property, and equipment.
6. In a SCF, net income or net loss is found in the operating activities section when the indirect method is used.
7. The investing activities section of a SCF includes the making and collecting of loans to other enterprises.
8. Interest and dividend income of a corporation is listed in the investing section category of the SCF.
9. One reason for the growing importance of the SCF is that the statement provides information about the cash generated by the operation.
10. The SCF provides information on how debt repayment was achieved.
11. The SCF does not provide any information on how this year's investments were financed.
12. A decrease in the cash balance for a period indicates a cash outflow.
13. The SCF can be prepared either by the direct method or by the indirect method.
14. Accounts receivable are included in the definition of cash and cash equivalents.
15. A short-term note payable with an original maturity of 60 days qualifies as a cash equivalent.

Multiple Choice

1. Operating activities include the
   a. Purchase and sale of equipment.
   b. Payment of cash dividends.
   c. Earning-related activities of products sold.
   d. None of the above.

2. The paying of cash dividends is a (an)
   a. Operating activity.
   b. Investing activity.
   c. Financing activity.
   d. Supplemental disclosure.

3. Making or collecting loans to/from other corporations is included in the
   a. Operating activity.
   b. Investing activity.
   c. Financing activity.
   d. Supplemental disclosure.

4. A noncash exchange transaction not involving cash is a transaction of a (an)
   a. Operating activity.
   b. Investing activity.
   c. Financing activity.
   d. Either *b* or *c*.

5. When the direct method is used to prepare a SCF, the total amount of interest paid less any capitalized interest is disclosed in the
   a. Operating activities section.
   b. Investing activities section.
   c. Financing activities section.
   d. Addendum to the SCF.

6. Given the following information, determine the net cash flow from investing activities for the period.

Net income	$155,000
Depreciation of fixed assets	15,000
Common stock issued	100,000
Gain on sale of fixed assets	5,000
Proceeds from sale of fixed assets	40,000
Cash dividends paid	45,000

   a. $60,000.
   b. $45,000.
   c. $40,000.
   d. $ 5,000.

7. Given the following information, what was the net cash flow from financing activities?

Net income	$ 75,000
Depreciation of fixed assets	25,000
Proceeds from the sale of bonds for the purchase of fixed assets	150,000
Cash dividends paid	10,000
Proceeds from sale of treasury stock	60,000

   a. $300,000.
   b. $220,000.
   c. $210,000.
   d. $200,000.

► **QUESTIONS**

1. What is the significance and purpose of the statement of cash flows?
2. The statement of cash flows is divided into three sections. What are they? What does each section contain?
3. What information can the user of financial statements obtain from the SCF?
4. What is cash flow?
5. There are two different formats for the statement of cash flows. What are they? How do they differ? Is one format preferred? If so, which one?

6.   What is "cash and cash equivalents"?

7.   Are there any charges (or credits) to the income statement that do not affect cash? If so, give an example and explain why it has no effect on cash.

8.   What is the difference between a gross cash flow and a net cash flow? Explain when it is appropriate to use each one.

9.   What is a noncash exchange transaction? Where is it shown?

10.   Is cash flow per share permitted to be shown on the financial statements? Explain.

11.   What disclosures must be made if they are not already shown on the SCF?

12.   Is there more than one procedure to use to prepare the SCF? What are the more popular ones? Explain how the T account method is used.

► **EXERCISES**   **E17–1**   **Preparation of Cash Flow from Operations—Indirect Method**

The Aster Company presents you with the following data:

	December 31	
	19x4	**19x3**
Current assets:		
Cash.	$ 30,123	$ 32,815
Accounts receivable.	507,647	526,083
Inventory	632,543	406,250
Prepaid costs	67,456	68,780
Total current assets	$1,237,769	$1,033,928
Current liabilities:		
Accounts payable.	$ 516,775	$ 411,635
Wages payable	118,012	102,250
Income taxes payable	98,029	76,879
Total current liabilities.	$ 732,816	$ 590,764

ASTER COMPANY
Income Statement
For the Year Ended December 31, 19x4

Sales.		$3,973,216
Cost of goods sold		1,585,144
Gross margin		2,388,072
Marketing and administrative costs		965,910
Operating income before income taxes.		1,422,162
Interest cost		120,000
Income before income taxes		1,302,162
Income taxes—Current	$ 509,881	
Deferred	70,000	579,881
Net income.		$ 722,281

Additional information:

1. Cost of goods sold includes depreciation in the amount of $215,000.

2. Marketing and administrative costs include amortization of intangibles in the amount of $45,000.

3. Interest paid during 19x4 amounted to $120,000.

Required   Using the indirect method, prepare a partial SCF showing the cash flow from operations.

E17-2   Preparation of Cash Flow from Operations—Direct Method

Refer to the data provided in Exercise 17–1.

Required   Using the direct method, prepare a partial SCF showing the cash flow from operations.

E17-3   Preparation of SCF—Indirect Method

The Doreen Company presents you with the following data:

	December 31	
Debits	**19x2**	**19x1**
Cash.	$ 352,000	$ 320,000
Accounts receivable.	440,000	304,000
Inventory	144,000	192,000
Prepaid costs	24,000	16,000
Property, plant, and equipment	1,579,000	1,280,000
Intangibles	640,000	640,000
Total.	$3,179,000	$2,752,000

Credits		
Accumulated depreciation—property, plant, and equipment	$ 368,000	$ 320,000
Accumulated amortization—intangibles	96,000	64,000
Accounts payable.	344,000	368,000
Wages payable	24,000	48,000
Income taxes payable	80,000	64,000
Bonds payable	400,000	400,000
Premium on bonds payable.	43,000	48,000
Preferred stock	320,000	320,000
Common stock	640,000	480,000
Additional paid-in capital—common stock	32,000	–0–
Retained earnings.	832,000	640,000
Total.	$3,179,000	$2,752,000

An analysis of the company's Retained Earnings account produced the following:

Retained earnings—January 1, 19x2	$640,000
Add: Net income.	240,000
Subtotal.	880,000
Less: Cash dividends	48,000
Retained earnings—December 31, 19x2.	$832,000

Interest paid amounted to $32,000; income taxes paid amounted to $160,000. There were no sales, trade-ins, or disposals of any property, plant, and equipment.

Required   Prepare an SCF using the indirect method.

E17-4   SCF

The statement of cash flows is normally a required basic financial statement for each period for which an earnings statement is presented.

Required   What effect, if any, would each of the following have on the preparation of a statement of cash flows prepared in accordance with generally accepted accounting principles?

a. Accounts receivable—trade.
b. Inventory.

  c. Depreciation.
  d. Deferred income tax payable from interperiod allocation.
  e. Issuance of long-term debt in payment for a building.
  f. Payoff of current portion of debt.
  g. Sale of a fixed asset resulting in a loss.

(AICPA Adapted)

E17–5　**Effects of Transactions on SCF**

For each of the following transactions, indicate the effect of the transaction on an SCF, using the following designations:

  (SCO)　Source of cash from operating activities
  (UCO)　Use of cash for operating activities
  (SCI)　Source of cash from investing activities
  (UCI)　Use of cash for investing activities
  (SCFA)　Source of cash from financing activities
  (UCFA)　Use of cash for financing activities
  (NCEX)　Noncash exchange transaction
  (NE)　No effect on SCF

  1. Purchased inventory on account for $100,000.
  2. Purchased treasury stock for $150,000 cash.
  3. Paid for the merchandise in (1).
  4. Purchased equipment for $50,000 by issuing a one-year note payable.
  5. Purchased land by issuing common stock in the amount of $200,000.
  6. Collected $150,000 of accounts receivable.
  7. Declared a cash dividend of $80,000 but did not pay it.
  8. Declared a stock split by issuing to stockholders one additional share for each share held (a 2-for-1 split).
  9. Paid the cash dividend in (7).
  10. Amortized bond discount for $2,000.
  11. Refinanced $1 million of bonds payable by issuing a like amount at a lower interest rate.
  12. Sold equipment with a book value of $10,000 for $6,000 cash.
  13. Interest cost of $40,000 was recorded as payable but not paid.
  14. Recorded depreciation of $210,000.
  15. Exchanged a piece of heavy-duty machinery for three delivery trucks.

Required　For each number (1 through 15), insert a parenthetical designation. A transaction may require more than one designation.

E17–6　**Preparation of SCF—Indirect Method**

The Batter Company presents you with the following data:

Debits	December 31	
	19x2	**19x1**
Accounts receivable	$ 330,000	$ 265,000
Cash	220,000	175,000
Inventory	176,000	200,000
Prepaid costs	11,000	9,000
Property, plant, and equipment	1,760,000	1,232,000
Intangibles	264,000	264,000
Total	$2,761,000	$2,145,000

	December 31	
Credits	**19x2**	**19x1**
Accumulated depreciation—property, plant, and equipment	$ 396,000	$ 265,000
Accumulated amortization—intangibles	88,000	65,000
Income taxes payable	33,000	45,000
Notes payable—current	22,000	65,000
Accounts payable	33,000	30,000
Bonds payable	440,000	440,000
Premium on bonds payable	77,000	85,000
Preferred stock	220,000	220,000
Common stock	550,000	220,000
Additional paid-in capital—common stock	66,000	45,000
Retained earnings	836,000	665,000
Total	$2,761,000	$2,145,000

An analysis of the company's Retained Earnings account produced the following:

Retained earnings—January 1, 19x2	$665,000
Add: Net income	261,000
Subtotal	926,000
Less: Cash dividends	90,000
Retained earnings—December 31, 19x2	$836,000

Interest paid amounted to $70,000; income taxes paid amounted to $180,000. There were no sales, trade-ins, or disposals of any property, plant, and equipment.

Required   Prepare an SCF using the indirect method.

E17–7   Preparation of SCF—Indirect Method
The Cuter Company presents you with the following data:

	December 31	
Debits	**19x2**	**19x1**
Accounts receivable	$ 190,000	$ 240,000
Cash	210,000	295,000
Inventory	310,000	260,000
Prepaid costs	15,000	25,000
Property, plant, and equipment	1,400,000	1,150,000
Intangibles	240,000	240,000
Total	$2,365,000	$2,210,000

Credits		
Accumulated depreciation—property, plant, and equipment	$ 435,000	$ 240,000
Accumulated amortization—intangibles	90,000	70,000
Income taxes payable	15,000	50,000
Notes payable—current	–0–	200,000
Accounts payable	190,000	140,000
Bonds payable	240,000	240,000
Discount on bonds payable	(25,000)	(30,000)
Preferred stock ($20 par value)	120,000	240,000
Common stock	500,000	350,000
Additional paid-in capital—common stock	120,000	80,000
Retained earnings	680,000	630,000
Total	$2,365,000	$2,210,000

An analysis of the company's Retained Earnings account produced the following:

Retained earnings—January 1, 19x2	$630,000
Add: Net income	250,000
Subtotal	880,000
Less: Cash dividends	200,000
Retained earnings—December 31, 19x2 . . .	$680,000

Additional information:

1. Preferred stock was redeemed at par value.
2. Interest paid amounted to $25,000; income taxes provided were $150,000. (*Hint*: Compute payments.)
3. There were no sales, trade-ins, or disposals of any property, plant, and equipment.

Required Prepare an SCF using the indirect method.

E17–8   **Preparation of Cash Flow from Operations—Indirect Method**

The Master Company presents you with the following data:

	December 31	
	19x4	**19x3**
Current assets:		
Cash	$340,000	$ 285,000
Accounts receivable	185,000	200,000
Inventory	180,000	166,000
Prepaid costs	26,000	22,000
Total current assets	$731,000	$ 673,000
Current liabilities:		
Accounts payable	$210,000	$ 175,000
Wages payable	45,000	54,000
Income taxes payable	32,000	22,000
Total current liabilities	$287,000	$ 251,000

MASTER COMPANY
Income Statement
For the Year Ended December 31, 19x4

Sales		$2,000,000
Cost of goods sold		800,000
Gross margin		1,200,000
Marketing and administrative costs		450,000
Operating income before income taxes		750,000
Interest cost		70,000
Income before income taxes		680,000
Income taxes—Current	$300,000	
Deferred	25,000	325,000
Net income		$ 355,000

Additional information:

1. Cost of goods sold includes depreciation in the amount of $110,000.
2. Marketing and administrative costs include amortization of intangibles in the amount of $25,000.
3. Interest paid during 19x4 amounted to $70,000.

Required Using the indirect method, prepare a partial SCF showing the cash flow from operations.

E17–9   **Preparation of Cash Flow from Operations—Direct Method**
Refer to the data provided in Exercise 17-8.

Required   Using the direct method, prepare a partial SCF showing the cash flow from operations.

E17–10   **Preparation of Cash Provided from Operating Activities**
The following data were taken from the accounting records of Lexi Corporation and subsidiaries for 19x1:

	($000)
Income before extraordinary items	$10,000
Extraordinary items (net of tax) (gain involving cash)	2,400
Depreciation, depletion, and amortization	16,600
Major disposals of property, plant, and equipment (book value) for cash	2,000
Deferred income taxes for 19x1 (noncurrent)	400
Amortization of discount on bonds payable	40
Amortization of premium on bonds payable	60
Decrease in noncurrent assets	2,600
Cash proceeds from exercise of stock options	400
Increase in accounts receivable	1,600
Increase in accounts payable	1,200
Decrease in inventories	1,000
Increase in dividends payable	600

Required   Determine the amount of cash provided by operations in 19x1.

E17–11   **Effects of Transactions**
A simplified schematic statement of cash flows for a company for the year is shown below. The company closes its books once each year, on December 31.

The titles of the lines in the schematic shown below are given labels (letters). For each of the activities listed, identify which of these lines is affected and by *how much*. Each activity is separate and unrelated to other activities. Do not consider subsequent activities. Use the labels (letters) shown below. Do not indicate the effect on any line not given a label. If a transaction has no effect, write *none*. In indicating the effect for lines Y and C, use a "+" to indicate an increase and a "−" to indicate a decrease.

Note: Every activity with an effect affects at least two lines (equal debits and credits). A journal entry is helpful in arriving at a solution.

Schematic Statement of Cash Flows of the Company for the Year

Sources of Cash:

(Y)	Net income	_____(Y)
(YA)	Additions or addbacks for costs, losses, etc., not using cash	_____(YA)
(YS)	Subtractions for revenues, gains, etc., not generating cash	_____(YS)
	Changes in current assets and current liabilities related to operations	
(CC)	Add credit changes	_____(CC)
(DC)	Deduct debit changes	_____(DC)
(NC)	Add (deduct) changes in noncurrent accounts related to operations	_____(NC)
	Cash flow from operations Y + YA − YS + CC − DC + or − NC	
(DE)	Proceeds of debt and equity issues	_____(DE)
(IL)	Increase in nonoperating current liabilities	_____(IL)
(AD)	Proceeds of long-term asset dispositions	_____(AD)
(OS)	Other sources of cash	_____(OS)
	Total sources of cash	_____

Uses of Cash:

(ID)   Income distributions . . . . _____(ID)
(R)   Retirements of debt and equity. . . . . _____(R)
(DL)   Decreases in nonoperating current liabilities .. . . _____(DL)
(AA)   Long-term asset acquisitions . . . . _____(AA)
(OU)   Other uses of cash . . . . _____(OU)
       Total uses of cash . . . . _____
(C)   Increase (decrease) in cash . . . . _____(C)

Schedule of Noncash Investing and Financing Activities

(NDE) Issue of debt or equity . . . . _____(NDE)
(NCR) Other noncash generating credits . . . . _____(NCR)
(NAA) Acquisitions of assets . . . . _____(NAA)
(NDR) Other noncash requiring debits . . . . _____(NDR)

Illustration:

0.   Sales of $10,000 are made on account.
00.   Dividends of $4,000 are paid.
000.   Entered into long-term capital lease obligation (present value $60,000).

Answer:

0.	(DC)	10,000	+Y	10,000
00.	(ID)	4,000	−C	4,000
000.	(NAA)	60,000	NDE	60,000

1. Inventories originally costing $50,000 have been used by production departments in producing finished goods that have been sold for $70,000 in cash and $10,000 in accounts receivable.
2. Accounts receivable of $16,000 are written off. There was an Allowance for Doubtful Accounts balance of $10,000 only.
3. The company acquired a long-lived asset for $200,000 in cash on January 1. The company decided to depreciate $40,000 each year.
4. A machine costing $30,000 with an accumulated depreciation of $12,000 is sold for $16,000 in cash.
5. Treasury stock with a cost of $14,000 is retired and canceled.
6. The company has 50,000 shares of common stock outstanding with par value of $2. The company declared a 20 percent stock dividend at the end of the year when the stock was selling for $32 a share.
7. Inventory costing $24,000 has been destroyed by fire. The insurance company paid only $20,000 for that loss, although the market value of the inventory was $30,000.
8. Provision for bad debts of $22,000 for the year was included in marketing costs.
9. Depreciation of $32,000 was charged to cost of goods sold.
10. A building was acquired by issuance of a long-term mortgage note for $200,000, the first payment of $20,000 being due 10 months from now.

Required   For each of the 10 transactions, analyze each one as shown in the illustration.

E17–12   Preparation of SCF—Indirect Method

The following financial statements and data relate to Debbie Dress Shops, Inc.

DEBBIE DRESS SHOPS, INC.
Balance Sheets

	December 31	
Assets	**19x1**	**19x0**
Current assets:		
Cash.	$ 300,000	$ 200,000
Accounts receivable—net	840,000	580,000
Merchandise inventory.	660,000	420,000
Prepaid costs	100,000	50,000
Total current assets	1,900,000	1,250,000
Long-term investments	80,000	—
Land, buildings, and fixtures	1,130,000	600,000
Less: Accumulated depreciation	110,000	50,000
	1,020,000	550,000
Total assets.	$3,000,000	$1,800,000

Equities		
Current liabilities:		
Accounts payable	$ 530,000	$ 440,000
Accrued liabilities	140,000	130,000
Dividends payable.	70,000	—
Total current liabilities.	740,000	570,000
Note payable—due 19x3	500,000	—
Stockholders' equity:		
Common stock	1,200,000	900,000
Retained earnings	560,000	330,000
	1,760,000	1,230,000
Total liabilities and stockholders' equity	$3,000,000	$1,800,000

DEBBIE DRESS SHOPS, INC.
Income Statements

	Year Ended December 31	
	19x1	**19x0**
Net credit sales	$6,400,000	$4,000,000
Cost of goods sold	5,000,000	3,200,000
Gross profit.	1,400,000	800,000
Other costs (including income taxes)	1,000,000	520,000
Net income.	$ 400,000	$ 280,000

Additional information included the following:

1. All accounts receivable and accounts payable relate to trade merchandise. Accounts payable are recorded net and always are paid to take all of the discount allowed. The allowance for doubtful accounts at the end of 19x1 was the same as at the end of 19x0; no receivables were charged against the allowance during 19x1.
2. The proceeds from the note payable were used to finance a new store building. Capital stock was sold to provide additional working capital.

3. Other costs for 19x1 include the following:
    a. Income taxes—$200,000.
    b. Interest—$30,000.
    There were no unpaid income taxes and interest at the beginning or ending of 19x1.
4. There were no sales, trade-ins, or exchanges of land, buildings, and fixtures, except for the note payable transaction noted above.

Required Prepare an SCF using the indirect method.

(AICPA Adapted)

E17–13 Preparation of SCF—Direct Method
Refer to the data contained in Exercise 16–12.

Required Prepare an SCF using the direct method.

E17–14 Preparation of SCF—Indirect Method
The Frederick Company's balance sheets are shown below (in thousands of dollars).

FREDERICK COMPANY
Balance Sheets

Assets	December 31 19x8	December 31 19x7
Current assets:		
Cash	$ 31,948	$ 46,216
Accounts receivable	200,891	174,522
Inventory	161,990	148,768
Prepaid costs	16,896	15,299
Total current assets	411,725	384,805
Property, plant, and equipment:		
Land	8,136	8,136
Building	75,112	72,574
Machinery and equipment	146,978	127,494
Total	230,226	208,204
Less: Accumulated depreciation	97,262	83,222
Total property, plant, and equipment	132,964	124,982
Total assets	$544,689	$509,787

Liabilities and Stockholders' Equity

Current liabilities:		
Accounts payable	$ 96,792	$ 89,906
Wages payable	10,232	8,331
Income taxes payable	12,836	10,111
Total current liabilities	119,860	108,348
Long-term liabilities:		
Bonds payable	100,000	90,000
Premium on bonds payable	4,790	5,320
Total long-term liabilities	104,790	95,320
Stockholders' equity:		
Common stock	82,000	70,000
Additional paid-in capital	111,760	98,120
Retained earnings	126,279	137,999
Total stockholders' equity	320,039	306,119
Total liabilities and stockholders' equity	$544,689	$509,787

An analysis of the company's Retained Earnings account produced the following:

Retained earnings—January 1, 19x8	$137,999
Add: Net income	5,500
Subtotal	143,499
Less: Cash dividends	17,220
Retained earnings—December 31, 19x8 . . .	$126,279

Interest paid for 19x8 amounted to $8,000; income taxes paid in 19x8 amounted to $2,750 (both in thousands of dollars). There were no sales, trade ins, or disposals of any property, plant, and equipment. Bonds sold during the year were sold at par.

Required   Prepare an SCF using the indirect method.

E17–15   **Preparation of SCF—Indirect Method**

The Garrett Company presents you with the following data:

	December 31	
Debits	**19x5**	**19x4**
Accounts receivable—net	$ 288,000	$ 312,000
Cash.	96,000	120,000
Inventory	156,000	132,000
Prepaid marketing and administrative costs	12,000	10,000
Property, plant, and equipment	624,000	576,000
Treasury stock	324,000	–0–
Total debits.	$1,500,000	$1,150,000
Credits		
Accumulated depreciation	$ 288,000	$ 252,000
Accounts payable	144,000	96,000
Long-term notes payable	210,000	120,000
Common stock	480,000	360,000
Additional paid-in capital.	126,000	96,000
Retained earnings	252,000	226,000
Total credits	$1,500,000	$1,150,000

An analysis of the company's Retained Earnings account produced the following:

Retained earnings—January 1, 19x5	$226,000
Add: Net income	121,000
Subtotal	347,000
Less: Cash dividends	95,000
Retained earnings—December 31, 19x5 . . .	$252,000

Interest paid for 19x5 amounted to $20,000; income taxes paid in 19x5 amounted to $60,000. There were no sales, trade-ins, or disposals of any property, plant, and equipment.

Required   Prepare an SCF using the indirect method.

E17–16 **Preparation of SCF—Direct Method**

The Garrett Company's income statement for 19x5 is as follows:

GARRETT COMPANY
Income Statement
For the Year Ended December 31, 19x5

Sales	$1,800,000
Cost of goods sold	1,080,000
Gross margin	720,000
Marketing and administrative costs.	539,000
Income before income taxes	181,000
Income taxes	60,000
Net income	$ 121,000

Marketing and administrative costs include $20,000 paid for interest.

Required   Using the information provided in Exercise 17–15 together with the above income statement, prepare an SCF under the direct method.

► **PROBLEMS**   E17–17 **Preparation of SCF—Direct Method**

Spoke Company, a major retailer of bicycles and accessories, operates several stores and is a publicly traded company. The comparative statement of financial position as of May 31, 19x2 and 19x1, and income statement for Spoke for the years ended May 31, 19x1 and 19x2, are shown below. The company is preparing its statement of cash flows to comply with *Statement of Financial Accounting Standards (SFAS) No. 95,* "Statement of Cash Flows."

SPOKE COMPANY
Comparative Statement of Financial Position
As of May 31, 19x2, and May 31, 19x1

	May 31, 19x2	May 31, 19x1
Current assets		
Cash	$ 43,250	$ 20,000
Accounts receivable	70,000	50,000
Merchandise inventory	210,000	250,000
Prepaid costs	9,000	7,000
Total current assets	332,250	327,000
Plant assets		
Plant assets	600,000	510,000
Less: Accumulated depreciation	150,000	125,000
Net plant assets	450,000	385,000
Total assets	$782,250	$712,000

	May 31, 19x2	May 31, 19x1
Current liabilities		
Accounts payable	$123,000	$115,000
Salaries payable	47,250	72,000
Interest payable	27,000	25,000
Total current liabilities	197,250	212,000
Long-term debt		
Bonds payable	70,000	100,000
Total liabilities	267,250	312,000
Shareholders' equity		
Common stock, $10 par	370,000	280,000
Retained earnings	145,000	120,000
Total shareholders' equity	515,000	400,000
Total liabilities and shareholders' equity	$782,250	$712,000

SPOKE COMPANY
Income Statement
For the Year Ended May 31, 19x2

Sales	$1,255,250
Cost of merchandise sold	712,000
Total contribution	543,250
Administrative and other costs:	
Salary	252,100
Interest	75,000
Other costs	8,150
Depreciation	25,000
Total	360,250
Operating income	183,000
Income tax	43,000
Net income	$ 140,000

The following is additional information concerning Spoke's transactions during the year ended May 31, 19x2.

▶ All sales during the year were made on account.
▶ All merchandise was purchased on account, and consisted of the total Accounts Payable account.
▶ Plant assets costing $90,000 were purchased by paying $40,000 in cash and issuing 5,000 shares of stock.
▶ The "other costs" are related to prepaid items.
▶ All income taxes incurred during the year were paid during the year.
▶ To supplement its cash, Spoke issued 4,000 shares of common stock at par value.
▶ There were no penalties assessed for the retirement of bonds.
▶ Cash dividends of $115,000 were declared and paid at the end of the fiscal year.

Required *a.* Compare and contrast the direct method and the indirect method for reporting cash flows from operating activities, as prescribed by *SFAS No. 95.*

b. Prepare a statement of cash flows for Spoke Company for the year ended May 31, 19x2, using the direct method. Be sure to support the statement with appropriate calculations. (A reconciliation of net income to net cash is not required.)

c. Using the indirect method, calculate only the net cash flow from operating activities for Spoke Company for the year ended May 31, 19x2.

(CMA Adapted)

P17–18 **Preparation of SCF—Indirect Method**

The following is a balance sheet of Zero Corporation for 19x1 and 19x2 (amounts are in thousands of dollars):

Assets			19x2		19x1
Cash			$ 1,200		$1,506
Accounts receivable			2,064		1,320
Inventories			2,244		1,890
Prepaid costs			60		—
Total current assets			5,568		4,716
Patents	$ 336				
Amortization	24		312		—
Plant and equipment	6,360			$4,680	
Less: Accumulated depreciation	1,440		4,920	1,220	3,460
Other assets	480			420	
Less: Accumulated depreciation	72		408	60	360
Total noncurrent assets			5,640		3,820
Total assets			$11,208		$8,536
Liabilities and Equity					
Accounts payable			$ 1,272		$1,200
Deferred income tax			137		100
Other current liabilities			204		161
Total current liabilities			1,613		1,461
Long-term debt			4,000		2,600
Common stock, $2 par			5,000		4,000
Retained earnings			595		475
Total long-term debt and equity			9,595		7,075
Total liabilities and equity			$11,208		$8,536

The following information is also available:

1. Net income for 19x2 was $380,000, and for 19x1 it was $300,000.
2. Cash dividends paid during 19x2 were $260,000; during 19x1, they were $240,000.
3. Depreciation costs charged to income during 19x2 were $232,000.
4. During 19x2, the company purchased patents for $336,000 in cash. Amortization of patents during the year amounted to $24,000.
5. Deferred income tax for 19x2 amounted to $37,000, and for 19x1 it amounted to $30,000.

Required   *a.* Prepare a statement of cash flows for 19x2 using the indirect method. (Use T accounts.)

b. Explain the significant discrepancy between net income and ''cash from operations.'' What are the major reasons?

P17–19   Preparation of SCF—Indirect Method

The James Company provides you with the following:

JAMES COMPANY
Income Statement
For the Year Ended December 31, 19x6

Sales.		$4,160,000
Cost of goods sold		1,600,000
Gross margin		2,560,000
Marketing and administrative costs		1,440,000
Income before income taxes		1,120,000
Income taxes—Current	$ 416,000	
Deferred	34,000	450,000
Net income.		$ 670,000

JAMES COMPANY
Post-Closing Trial Balances

	December 31	
Debits	**19x6**	**19x5**
Accounts receivable, net.	$ 288,000	$ 400,000
Cash.	120,000	360,000
Intangibles	464,000	480,000
Inventory	288,000	416,000
Investment in affiliate	1,000,000	–0–
Prepaid marketing and administrative costs	20,000	24,000
Property, plant, and equipment.	2,180,000	1,120,000
Total.	$4,360,000	$2,800,000

Credits		
Accumulated depreciation	$ 448,000	$ 330,000
Accounts payable.	164,000	136,000
Deferred income tax.	128,000	94,000
Long-term notes payable.	40,000	200,000
Common stock	800,000	480,000
Additional paid-in capital.	1,380,000	500,000
Retained earnings	1,400,000	1,000,000
Wages payable	–0–	60,000
Total.	$4,360,000	$2,800,000

An analysis of the company's Retained Earnings account produced the following:

Retained earnings—January 1, 19x6		$1,000,000
Add: Net income.		670,000
Subtotal.		1,670,000
Less:		
Cash dividends.	$ 70,000	
Stock dividend.	200,000	270,000
Retained earnings—December 31, 19x6.		$1,400,000

Interest paid during 19x6 amounted to $8,000 and is included in marketing and administrative costs. There were no sales, trade-ins, or disposals of any property, plant, and equipment.

The changes in the Common Stock and Additional Paid-In Capital accounts arose from the acquisition of shares of stock in an affiliate and the payment of the stock dividend. There were no sales of common stock.

The company president, Rita Duggan, is concerned about the decrease in cash to below $200,000, as well as an apparent decrease in working capital. She believes the company had a satisfactory year from its operations, earning $670,000 after income taxes and only paying a cash dividend of $70,000. Taking into account the depreciation charge to income that does not require cash and the fact that the acquisition of the affiliate's shares did not affect the cash, she would like an explanation of why cash decreased during 19x6.

Required   *a.* Prepare an SCF using the indirect method.
b. Write a brief report to the president, explaining why cash decreased.

P17–20   Preparation of SCF—Direct Method

Refer to the data contained in Problem 17–19.

Required   Prepare an SCF using the direct method.

P17–21   Preparation of SCF—Indirect Method

The Kenneth Company's accounts reflect the following:

KENNETH COMPANY
Balance Sheets
December 31, 19x3, and 19x2

Assets	19x3	19x2
Current assets:		
Cash.	$ 300,000	$ 180,000
Accounts receivable, net.	375,000	300,000
Inventory	420,000	390,000
Prepaid marketing and administrative costs	15,000	30,000
Total current assets	1,110,000	900,000
Investment in marketable securities	575,000	540,000
Property, plant, and equipment	1,425,000	1,380,000
Less: Accumulated depreciation	570,000	450,000
Net property, plant, and equipment.	855,000	930,000
Patent	540,000	630,000
Total assets.	$3,080,000	$3,000,000

Liabilities and Stockholders' Equity

	19x3	19x2
Current liabilities:		
Accounts payable	$ 315,000	$ 285,000
Notes payable	105,000	160,000
Accrued liabilities	125,000	120,000
Total current liabilities.	545,000	565,000
Long-term liabilities:		
Bonds payable	900,000	600,000
Premium on bonds payable.	180,000	135,000
Total long-term liabilities.	1,080,000	735,000
Stockholders' equity:		
Preferred stock	150,000	–0–
Common stock	990,000	900,000
Additional paid-in capital.	255,000	225,000
Retained earnings	60,000	575,000
Total stockholders' equity	1,455,000	1,700,000
Total liabilities and stockholders' equity	$3,080,000	$3,000,000

KENNETH COMPANY
Income Statement
For the Year Ended December 31, 19x3

Sales.	$6,000,000
Cost of goods sold.	3,300,000
Gross margin	2,700,000
Marketing and administrative costs . . .	3,000,000
Operating loss.	(300,000)
Add: Investment income	40,000
Net loss	$ (260,000)

An analysis of the company's Retained Earnings account produced the following:

Retained earnings—January 1, 19x3		$575,000
Net loss		(260,000)
Subtotal		315,000
Less:		
Cash dividends	$135,000	
Stock dividend	120,000	255,000
Retained earnings—December 31, 19x3 . . .		$ 60,000

No income taxes were paid in 19x3, and $90,000 of interest was shown as a *cost* included in marketing and administrative costs.

There were no sales, trade-ins, or disposals of any property, plant, and equipment. There were no sales of common stock. The change in the Common Stock and Additional Paid-In Capital accounts stems from the stock dividend.

During the year, bonds payable with a face value of $300,000 were sold at a premium of $60,000 for a total of $360,000.

A relative of yours received a copy of the Kenneth Company's financial statements and wonders how a company that pays a cash dividend of $135,000 and has a net loss of $260,000 can show an increase in cash and an increase in working capital.

Required a. Prepare an SCF using the indirect method. (Use T accounts.)
b. Write a brief report for your relative, explaining the increase in cash.

P17–22 ### Preparation of SCF—Direct Method
Refer to the data contained in Problem 17–21.

Required Prepare an SCF using the direct method. (Use T accounts.)

P17–23 ### Preparation of SCF—Indirect Method
An investor concerned by the decline in both cash and working capital of the Fluid Corporation hands you the following data:

FLUID CORPORATION
Comparative Balance Sheets
As of December 31, 19x3, and 19x2
(in thousands of dollars)

Assets	19x3	19x2
Current assets:		
Cash	$ 75	$ 675
Accounts receivable	1,500	1,125
Inventories	750	675
Prepaid costs	450	525
Total current assets	2,775	3,000
Property, plant, and equipment	6,000	4,875
Less: Accumulated depreciation	(1,275)	(825)
Patents	300	450
Total assets	$7,800	$ 7,500

Liabilities and Stockholders' Equity	19x3	19x2
Current liabilities:		
Accounts payable	$ 750	$ 600
Notes payable	375	375
Accrued liabilities	600	525
Total current liabilities	1,725	1,500
Bonds payable	1,500	2,100
Common stock	4,050	3,450
Retained earnings	525	450
Total liabilities and stockholders' equity	$7,800	$ 7,500

FLUID CORPORATION
Income Statement
For the Year Ended December 31, 19x3

Sales		$30,000
Cost of goods sold		22,500
Gross profit		7,500
Depreciation ($600) and patent amortization ($150)	$ 750	
Marketing and administrative costs	3,975	
Other costs	2,550	7,275
Income from operations		225
Add: Gain on sale of equipment ($300) net of loss on land		150
		375
Interest cost		225
Pre-tax income		150
Income taxes (50%)		75
Net income		$ 75

Additional information:

1. Equipment originally costing $750,000 was sold for $900,000.
2. Land with an original cost of $375,000 was sold for $225,000.
3. There were no accrued liabilities for interest and income taxes at the beginning and end of 19x3.
4. Convertible bonds in the amount of $600,000 were converted into $600,000 of common stock.

Required   Prepare a statement of cash flows using the indirect method. (Use the T account method.)

P17—24   **Preparation of SCF—Direct Method**

Refer to the data contained in Problem 17—23.

Required   Prepare an SCF using the direct method. (Use the T account method.)

► **CASE**   **C17—25**   **Reconstruction of a Balance Sheet from an SCF**

While on an urgent assignment, you discover to your dismay that you have left behind the balance sheet of Zoro Corporation as of January 1, 19x0. You realize you do have the following data on that company:

ZORO COMPANY
Post-Closing Trial Balance
December 31, 19x0

Debit Balances

Cash.	$ 150,000
Accounts receivable.	180,000
Inventory	195,000
Property, plant, and equipment.	825,000
Other noncurrent investments	300,000
Total debits	$1,650,000

Credit Balances

Accounts payable	$ 150,000
Current portion of long-term debt.	120,000
Accumulated depreciation	405,000
Long-term debt	300,000
Common stock	450,000
Retained earnings.	225,000
Total credits	$1,650,000

ZORO CORPORATION
Statement of Cash Flows
For the Year Ended December 31, 19x0

Cash from operations:		
Net income		$225,000
Add (deduct) adjustments to cash basis:		
Depreciation	$128,000	
Loss on sale of equipment	7,000	
Gain on sale of noncurrent investments . . .	(75,000)	
Increase in accounts receivable	(45,000)	
Increase in inventories	(30,000)	
Increase in accounts payable	60,000	45,000
Cash from operations.		270,000
Investing activities:		
Additions to property and equipment.	(225,000)	
Sale of equipment	15,000	
Sale of investments	140,000	
Cash used for investing activities		(70,000)
Financing activities:		
Issuance of common stock	15,000	
Additions to long-term debt $25,000		
Decrease in current portion of		
long-term debt. . . . . (45,000)	(20,000)	
Cash dividends	(120,000)	
Cash used for financing activities		(125,000)
Increase in cash		$ 75,000

The equipment that has been sold had accumulated depreciation of $75,000.

Required   Reconstruct the T accounts of Zoro Corporation, using the above data and information. Use the T accounts to prepare the balance sheet of Zoro Corporation as of January 1, 19x0, that you so urgently need.

▸ **ANSWERS TO SELF-TEST**

True or False

1. True	2. False	3. True	4. True	5. False
6. True	7. True	8. False	9. True	10. True
11. False	12. True	13. True	14. False	15. False

Multiple Choice

1. *c.*   2. *c.*   3. *b.*   4. *d.*   5. *a.*   6. *c.*   7. *d.*

Analysis of Financial Statements

After reading this chapter, you should be able to:

1. Explain how different groups of financial statement users depend on financial statement analysis.
2. Discuss the principal tools used by analysts of financial statements.
3. Prepare comparative financial statements showing year-to-year changes in absolute dollars and in percentages and indicate how these statements are used.
4. Convert selected financial statement data into an index-number trend series and interpret the results of the data.
5. Transform absolute-dollar financial statements into common-size financial statements and explain how the results help financial statement users.
6. Compute the ratios used to determine the status of a firm's short-term liquidity and explain their significance.
7. Calculate the ratios that determine a firm's capital structure and long-term solvency and discuss how the ratios are used.
8. Illustrate the ratios used for return-on-investment analysis.
9. Compute various market ratios and measures and indicate their importance to users of financial statements.

▶ **INTERVIEW**

Sheila Leonard
Tax Accountant
Ernst & Young

Q. *Describe methods used in analyzing financial statements.*
A. Many different methods are used in analyzing financial statements. A couple of examples would be the debt to equity ratio and the quick ratio. The outcome of the analysis is usually done from the prior year to the current year. This analysis may show why sales have increased or decreased. The financials may also be tested for reasonableness in the industry. The client may compare his financials with those of similar companies (if the other companies' financials are available to the public) to give a better indication of whether or not the earnings are above or below the standard in the industry.

Q. *In measuring a firm's long-term solvency, do you find ratio analysis satisfies all your needs? If not, what other tools do you employ before you feel that you can reach a conclusion about a firm's long-term solvency?*
A. Ratio analysis alone does not satisfy all my needs when measuring a firm's long-term solvency. Before reaching a conclusion about a firm's long-term solvency, issues of fact and circumstance must be considered about the individual company. Factors such as the economic conditions of the market, competition, and the condition of the economy as a whole (for example, coming into a recession or recovery from a recession) influence predicting the conclusion of a company's long-term solvency. Ratio analysis plays a major role in measuring a firm's long-term solvency, but other factors should also be considered.

▶ Managers, stockholders, potential investors, creditors, financial analysts, employees, and their representatives are the major users of a firm's financial statements. Because financial statements are prepared using a historical cost framework, the statements represent a summary of past transactions. Although external users may be interested in historical results to evaluate the company's past performance, their main focus is future oriented (i.e., how well the company will perform in the future). Management's concerns are also future oriented. Thus, statement users must use various analytical tools to make inferences from historical financial statements regarding a firm's future expected performance. The inferences assist users in their decision making.

The principal analytical tools of financial statement analysis consist of comparisons of year-to-year changes, trend analysis, structural analysis, ratio analysis, and other specialized analyses.   ◀

▶ REASONS FOR FINANCIAL STATEMENT ANALYSIS

L.O. 1
Users' needs for financial statement analysis

All user groups are concerned with the future course a company will probably take. Managers are concerned with the firm's future operating results and its ability to attract capital. Satisfactory profits are needed to keep stockholders satisfied and to preserve their tenure as managers. Sufficient cash must be generated for the firm to continue operating and pay dividends. Stockholders are concerned with a firm's operating performance and its profits. Dividend payments and the stock market price of a firm's shares are usually a function of the firm's profit performance. Potential stockholders have similar concerns. Creditors are concerned that interest and principal payments will be paid when due. Normally, a sufficient cash flow must be generated to provide for these payments. Financial analysts provide advisory services to other users, and their recommendations depend on their ability to make satisfactory predictions regarding a firm's future operations and financial condition. Employees and their collective bargaining representatives are concerned with negotiating increases in wages and benefits without forcing the firm into bankruptcy. Essentially, a firm's employees are interested in securing a "fair share of the pie," so they need analysts to project what the size of the pie will be in the future. Thus, they must also project what the firm's future results of operations will probably be.

Although financial statement analysis by itself cannot provide all the answers to the concerns of the decision makers noted above, it can assist them in their deliberations. Other factors that may assist the decision makers, such as forecasting techniques, are discussed in Chapter 9 in the section on budgeting.

▶ THE PRINCIPAL TOOLS OF FINANCIAL STATEMENT ANALYSIS

L.O. 2

In the analysis of financial statements, a statement user has a variety of tools available from which she can choose those best suited to her specific purpose. The principal tools of analysis are:

1. Comparative financial statements.
   a. Year-to-year changes.
2. Index-number trend series.

3. Common-size financial statements.
   a. Structural analysis.
4. Ratio analysis.
5. Specialized analyses.
   a. Cash forecasts.
   b. Analysis of changes in financial position.
   c. Statement of variation in gross margin.
   d. Breakeven analysis.

Comparative Financial Statements

L.O. 3

The comparison of financial statements is done by setting up balance sheets, income statements, or statements of cash flows (SCF), side by side, and reviewing the changes that have occurred in individual categories from year to year and over the years.

The most important factor shown by comparative financial statements is trend. **Trend** is the general direction of financial data expressed in terms of a base period (usually one year). The comparison of financial statements over a number of years will also reveal the velocity of trend. The **velocity of trend** is the rate of movement of financial data in a general direction.[1]

Further analysis can be done to compare the trends in related items. For example, a year-to-year increase in sales of 10 percent accompanied by an increase in freight-out costs of 20 percent requires an investigation and explanation of the reasons for the difference. Similarly, an increase in accounts receivable of 15 percent during the same period would also warrant an investigation into the reasons for the difference in the rate of increase of sales as against that of receivables.

Year-to-Year Change   A comparison of financial statements over two to three years can be undertaken by computing the *year-to-year change* in absolute amounts and in terms of percentage changes. When a two- or three-year comparison is attempted, such presentations are manageable and can be understood by the reader. These comparisons present changes in terms of absolute dollar amounts as well as in percentages. Both have to be considered because the dollar size of the different bases on which percentage changes are computed may yield large percentage changes that are out of proportion to their real significance. For example, in the same financial statements, a 50 percent change from a base figure of $1,000 is less significant than the same percentage change from a base of $100,000. Thus, reference to the dollar amounts involved is always necessary to retain the proper perspective and to reach valid conclusions regarding the relative significance of the changes disclosed by this type of analysis.

The computation of year-to-year changes is simple. However, a few clarifying rules should be remembered. When a negative amount appears in the base year and a positive amount in the following year, or vice versa, no meaningful percentage change can be computed. When an item has a value in a base year and none in the following period, the decrease is 100 percent.

---

[1] The author is grateful to Professor Leopold A. Bernstein for permission to abstract portions of his book, *Financial Statement Analysis*, published by Richard D. Irwin, Inc., in 1989. Those who are interested in a definitive treatment of this subject matter should refer to the fourth edition of his book.

▶ **ILLUSTRATION 18-1**

FREDER COMPANY
Comparative Balance Sheets
December 31, 19x7, and 19x8

Assets	19x8	19x7	Change Increase (Decrease) Amount	Change Increase (Decrease) Percent
Current assets:				
Cash	$ 14,522	$ 20,962	$ (6,440)	(30.7)
Accounts receivable	91,314	79,328	11,986	15.1
Inventory	73,632	67,622	6,010	8.9
Prepaid costs	7,680	6,954	726	10.4
Total current assets	187,148	174,866	12,282	7.0
Property, plant, and equipment:				
Land	3,698	3,698	–0–	–0–
Building	34,142	32,988	1,154	3.5
Machinery and equipment	66,808	57,952	8,856	15.3
Total	104,648	94,638	10,010	10.6
Less: Accumulated depreciation	44,210	37,828	6,382	16.9
Total property, plant, and equipment	60,438	56,810	3,628	6.4
Total assets	$247,586	$231,676	$15,910	6.9

Liabilities and Stockholders' Equity

	19x8	19x7	Change Increase (Decrease) Amount	Change Increase (Decrease) Percent
Current liabilities:				
Accounts payable	$ 42,716	$ 40,490	$ 2,226	5.5
Wages payable	4,651	3,787	864	22.8
Income taxes payable	7,198	4,596	2,602	56.6
Total current liabilities	54,565	48,873	5,692	11.6
Long-term liabilities:				
Bonds payable	45,000	40,000	5,000	12.5
Premium on bonds payable	2,180	2,420	(240)	(9.9)
Total long-term liabilities	47,180	42,420	4,760	11.2
Total liabilities	101,745	91,293	10,452	11.4
Stockholders' equity:				
Preferred stock—$100 par, 10%	20,000	20,000	–0–	–0–
Common stock—$5 par	37,500	32,500	5,000	15.4
Additional paid-in capital	30,800	24,600	6,200	25.2
Retained earnings	57,541	63,283	(5,742)	(9.1)
Total stockholders' equity	145,841	140,383	5,458	3.9
Total liabilities and stockholders' equity	$247,586	$231,676	$15,910	6.9

Where there is no figure for the base year, no percentage change can be computed. The following summary will illustrate this:

Item	19x1	19x2	Change Increase (Decrease) Amount	Change Increase (Decrease) Percent
Net income (loss)	$ (4,500)	$ 1,500	$ 6,000	—
Tax cost	2,000	(1,000)	(3,000)	—
Notes payable	—	8,000	8,000	—
Notes receivable	10,000	—	(10,000)	(100)

▶ **ILLUSTRATION 18-2**

FREDER COMPANY
Comparative Income Statements
For the Years Ended December 31, 19x7, and 19x8

	19x8	19x7	Change Increase (Decrease) Amount	Percent
Sales.	$720,860	$676,080	$44,780	6.6
Cost of goods sold.	453,178	414,554	38,624	9.3
Gross margin	267,682	261,526	6,156	2.4
Marketing and administrative:				
Marketing costs.	129,939	124,382	5,557	4.5
Administrative costs.	122,730	116,996	5,734	4.9
Total marketing and administrative	252,669	241,378	11,291	4.7
Operating income	15,013	20,148	(5,135)	(25.5)
Interest cost	5,000	4,500	500	11.1
Income before income taxes	10,013	15,648	(5,635)	(36.0)
Income tax provision (40%).	4,005	6,259	(2,254)	(36.0)
Net income	$ 6,008	$ 9,389	$(3,381)	(36.0)

▶ **ILLUSTRATION 18-3**

FREDER COMPANY
Retained Earnings Statements
For the Years Ended December 31, 19x7, and 19x8

	19x8	19x7
Retained earnings, January 1	$63,283	$64,344
Add: Net income	6,008	9,389
Subtotal	69,291	73,733
Deduct dividends:		
Preferred stock	2,000	2,000
Common stock	9,750	8,450
Total deductions	11,750	10,450
Retained earnings, December 31 . . .	$57,541	$63,283

Comparative financial statements can also be presented so that the cumulative total for the period for each item under study and the average for that period are shown.

The value of comparing yearly amounts with an average covering a number of years is that unusual factors in any one year are highlighted. Averages smooth out erratic or unusual fluctuations in data.

An example of comparative balance sheets and income statements for the Freder Company showing the absolute and percentage changes is shown in Illustrations 18-1 and 18-2. These statements will also be used for further analysis throughout this chapter.

Comparative statements of retained earnings appear in Illustration 18-3.

Index-Number Trend Series

L.O. 4

When a comparison of financial statements for more than three years is undertaken, the year-to-year method of comparison may become too cumbersome. The best way to make such longer-term trend comparisons is by means of index numbers. An **index number** is a measure used to indicate qualities common to a group of items. The computation of a series of index numbers requires the choice of a base year that will, for all items, have an index amount of 100. Because such a base year represents a frame of reference for all comparisons, it is best to choose a year that, in a business conditions sense, is as typical or normal as possible. If the earliest year in the series compared cannot fulfill this function, another year is chosen.

As is the case with the computation of year-to-year percentage changes, certain changes, such as those from negative to positive amounts, cannot be expressed by means of index numbers. All index numbers are computed by reference to the base year.

Let us assume that in the base year at 12/31/19xA, there is a cash balance of $12,000. Based on an index number of 100 for 19xA, if the cash balance in the following year (at 12/31/19xB) is $18,000, then the index number will be

$$\frac{\$18,000}{\$12,000} \times 100 = 150$$

On 12/31/19xC, the cash balance is $9,000; the index will be 75, arrived at as follows:

$$\frac{\$9,000}{\$12,000} \times 100 \left(\frac{\text{Balance in current year}}{\text{Balance in base year}} \times 100 \right)$$

When using index numbers, percentage changes cannot be read off directly except by reference to the base year. Thus, the change of the cash balance between 19xA and 19xB is 50 percent (index 150 − index 100), which can be read off directly from the index numbers. The change from 19xB to 19xC, however, is not 75 percent (150 − 75), as a direct comparison may suggest, but rather 50 percent (i.e., $9,000/$18,000), which involves computing the 19xB to 19xC change by reference to the amount at 19xB. The percentage change can, however, be computed by use of the index numbers only (for example, 75/150 = .5, or a change of 50 percent).

In planning an index-number trend comparison, it is not necessary to include all the items in the financial statements. Only the most significant items need to be included in such a comparison.

Care should be exercised in the use of index-number trend comparisons because such comparisons have weaknesses as well as strengths. Thus, in trying to assess changes in the current financial condition, the analyst may use comparative statements of changes in financial position to advantage. On the other hand, the index-number trend comparison is well suited to a comparison of the changes in the *composition* of working capital items over the years.

Let us extend the Freder Company data to include the following:

	19x8	19x7	19x6	19x5	19x4
Sales	$720,860	$676,080	$592,290	$478,447	$465,895
Cost of goods sold	453,178	414,554	357,839	287,379	276,699
Gross margin	267,682	261,526	234,451	191,068	189,196
Marketing costs	129,939	124,382	108,945	90,470	89,520
Administrative costs	122,730	116,996	103,815	79,120	78,225
Net income	6,008	9,389	10,015	9,887	9,871

▶ **ILLUSTRATION 18 4**

FREDER COMPANY
Income Statement Data
Converted into an Index-Number Trend Series
For the Years Ended December 31

	19x8	19x7	19x6	19x5	19x4
Sales	158	145	127	103	100
Cost of goods sold	164	150	129	104	100
Gross margin	141	138	124	101	100
Marketing costs	145	139	122	101	100
Administrative costs	157	149	132	101	100
Net income	61	95	101	100	100

Note that sales, cost of goods sold, gross margin, marketing costs, and administrative costs all increased when compared to the respective item in the preceding year. However, net income increased in 19x5 and 19x6, while it decreased in 19x7 and 19x8. To assess the reasons for these results, a statement user would find it difficult to reach a conclusion if the absolute data are used as given. The reasons become readily apparent when the data are converted into an index-number trend series, as shown in Illustration 18-4.

Note in Illustration 18-4 that although sales increased each year, cost of goods sold increased at a faster rate, thus causing gross margin to increase at a slower rate. In addition, marketing costs and administrative costs generally increased at a more rapid rate than that for gross margin. Net income remained relatively static for 19x5, 19x6, and 19x7 and then declined at a rapid rate in 19x8. With this analysis, a manager can determine where the problem areas are and attempt to implement corrective action. Trend analysis is often referred to as **horizontal analysis.**

Common-Size Financial Statements

L.O. 5

A **common-size statement** is one in which each component of the statement is shown as a percentage instead of in dollar amounts. In the analysis of financial statements, it is often helpful to find out the proportion that a single item represents of a total group or subgroup. In a balance sheet, the assets as well as the liabilities and capital are each expressed as 100 percent, and each item in these categories is expressed as a percentage of the respective totals. Similarly, in the income statement, net sales are set at 100 percent, and every other item in the statement is expressed as a percent of net sales. Because the totals always equal 100 percent, these statements are referred to as ''common size.'' Similarly, following the eye as it reviews the common-size statement is referred to as **vertical analysis.**

Structural Analysis   The analysis of common-size financial statements may be described as an analysis of the internal structure of the financial statements. In the analysis of a balance sheet, this structural analysis focuses on two major aspects:

1. The sources of capital of the enterprise, that is, the distribution of equities between current liabilities, long-term liabilities, and equity capital.
2. The amount of capital from all sources, the distribution of assets (current, fixed, and other) in which it is invested. Stated differently,

▶ **ILLUSTRATION 18-5**

FREDER COMPANY
Comparative Balance Sheets
December 31, 19x7, and 19x8

Assets	19x8	19x7	Common-Size Percentages 19x8	Common-Size Percentages 19x7
Current assets:				
Cash	$ 14,522	$ 20,962	5.9	9.0
Accounts receivable	91,314	79,328	36.9	34.3
Inventory	73,632	67,622	29.7	29.2
Prepaid costs	7,680	6,954	3.1	3.0
Total current assets	187,148	174,866	75.6	75.5
Property, plant, and equipment:				
Land	3,698	3,698	1.5	1.6
Building	34,142	32,988	13.8	14.2
Machinery and equipment	66,808	57,952	27.0	25.0
Total	104,648	94,638	42.3	40.8
Less: Accumulated depreciation	44,210	37,828	17.9	16.3
Total property, plant, and equipment	60,438	56,810	24.4	24.5
Total assets	$247,586	$231,676	100.0	100.0
Liabilities and Stockholders' Equity				
Current liabilities:				
Accounts payable	$ 42,716	$ 40,490	17.2	17.5
Wages payable	4,651	3,787	1.9	1.6
Income taxes payable	7,198	4,596	2.9	2.0
Total current liabilities	54,565	48,873	22.0	21.1
Long-term liabilities:				
Bonds payable	45,000	40,000	18.2	17.3
Premium on bonds payable	2,180	2,420	.9	1.0
Total long-term liabilities	47,180	42,420	19.1	18.3
Total liabilities	101,745	91,293	41.1	39.4
Stockholders' equity:				
Preferred stock—$100 par, 10%	20,000	20,000	8.1	8.7
Common stock—$5 par	37,500	32,500	15.2	14.0
Additional paid-in capital	30,800	24,600	12.4	10.6
Retained earnings	57,541	63,283	23.2	27.3
Total stockholders' equity	145,841	140,383	58.9	60.6
Total liabilities and stockholders' equity	$247,586	$231,676	100.0	100.0

the mix of assets with which the enterprise has chosen to conduct its operations.

The common-size balance sheet analysis can be extended to an examination of what proportion of a subgroup, rather than the total, an item is. Thus, in assessing the liquidity of current assets, it may be interesting to know not only what proportion of total assets is invested in inventories but also what proportion of current assets is represented by this asset.

With the income statement, common-size statement analysis is a useful tool that may even be more important than the analysis of the balance sheet. The income statement lends itself to an analysis because each item is related to a central quantum (that is, sales). With some exceptions, the level of each

▶ **ILLUSTRATION 18-6**

FREDER COMPANY
Comparative Income Statements
For the Years Ended December 31, 19x7, and 19x8

	19x8	19x7	Common-Size Percentages 19x8	19x7
Sales	$720,860	$676,080	100.0	100.0
Cost of goods sold	453,178	414,554	62.9	61.3
Gross margin	267,682	261,526	37.1	38.7
Marketing and administrative:				
Marketing costs	129,939	124,382	18.0	18.4
Administrative costs	122,730	116,996	17.0	17.3
Total marketing and administrative	252,669	241,378	35.0	35.7
Operating income	15,013	20,148	2.1	3.0
Interest cost	5,000	4,500	.7	.7
Income before income taxes	10,013	15,648	1.4	2.3
Income tax provision (40%).	4,005	6,259	.6	.9
Net income	$ 6,008	$ 9,389	.8	1.4

cost item is affected by the level of sales, and thus it is helpful to know what proportion of the sales dollar is absorbed by the various costs incurred by the enterprise.

Comparisons of common-size statements of a single enterprise over the years are valuable because they show the changing proportions of components within groups of assets, liabilities, costs, and other financial statement categories. However, care must be exercised in interpreting such changes and the trend they disclose. For example, the table below shows the amount of land and total assets of an enterprise over three years:

	19x3	19x2	19x1
Land	$ 50,000	$ 50,000	$ 50,000
Total assets	1,000,000	750,000	500,000
Land as a percentage of total assets	5%	6.67%	10%

Although the amount of land remained unchanged, the increase in total assets made this item a progressively smaller proportion of total assets. Because this proportion can change with either a change in the absolute amount of the item or a change in the total of the group of which it is a part, the interpretation of a common-size statement comparison requires an examination of the actual figures and the basis on which they are computed.

Comparative balance sheets and income statements for the Freder Company, showing the common-size percentages, are given in Illustrations 18-5 and 18-6.

Following are observations about Illustrations 18-5 and 18-6:

1. Although stockholders' equity increased in absolute dollars in 19x8, its common-size percentage decreased (see Illustration 18-5). Therefore, the firm is relying on a greater use of borrowed funds relative to equity

funds. This concept is discussed in the section about debt-to-equity ratio.

2. Illustration 18-2 shows that both sales and cost of goods sold in absolute dollars increased in 19x8. However, cost of goods sold increased at a faster rate in 19x8, and although gross margin increased in absolute dollars in 19x8, its common-size percentage decreased (see Illustration 18-6). This implies that either (1) increases in costs were *not* proportionately passed on to the firm's customers, or (2) the firm lowered its selling prices to increase its volume without a proportionate reduction in its costs, or (3) a combination of the two. In each case, the policy of the firm may partially explain the reduction in net income for 19x8. If this policy continues, the firm may operate at a loss in the future.

3. Marketing costs and administrative costs (see Illustration 18-6) increased at a rate slightly less than that for sales. Normally, when sales increase, marketing and administrative costs also increase, but not proportionately to sales; these costs should increase at a significantly slower rate than sales because many marketing and administrative costs are fixed. In 19x8, these costs occupy about the same common-size percentage as in 19x7, which indicates these costs may be a troublesome area that should be investigated by the managers who control them.

▶ RATIOS

Ratio Analysis

Ratios are among the best known and most widely used tools of financial analysis. At the same time, their function is often misunderstood, and consequently their significance may easily be overrated.

A **ratio** expresses the mathematical relationship between two quantities. The ratio of 200 to 100 is expressed as 2:1, or as 2. The computation of a ratio involves a simple arithmetical operation, but its interpretation is a more complex matter.

The ratio must express a relationship that has significance. Thus, there is a clear, direct, and understandable relationship between the sales price of an item and its cost. As a result, the ratio of cost of goods sold to sales is significant. On the other hand, there is no a priori or understandable relationship between freight costs incurred and the marketable securities held by an enterprise; hence, a ratio of one to the other has no significance.

Ratios are tools of analysis that provide clues and symptoms of underlying conditions. Ratios properly interpreted can also identify areas requiring further investigation and inquiry. The analysis of a ratio can disclose relationships as well as bases of comparison that reveal conditions and trends that cannot be detected by an inspection of the individual components of the ratio.

Interpretation of Ratios

Ratios should always be interpreted carefully because factors affecting the numerator may correlate with those affecting the denominator. Thus, it is possible to improve the ratio of operating costs to sales by reducing costs that act to stimulate sales. If the cost reduction results in a loss of sales or share of market, such a seeming improvement in profitability may, in fact, have an overall detrimental effect on the future prospects of the enterprise and must be interpreted accordingly. Also, many ratios have important variables in common with other ratios, so they can vary and be influenced by the same factors. Consequently, there is no need to use all available ratios to diagnose a given condition.

Ratios, like most other relationships in financial analysis, are not significant in themselves and can be interpreted only by comparison with (1) past ratios of the same enterprise, or (2) some predetermined standard, or (3) ratios of other companies in the industry. The range of a ratio over time is also significant, as is the trend of a given ratio over time. Appendix 18-A contains sources of information on financial and operating ratios.

▶ ILLUSTRATION OF RATIO COMPUTATIONS

Many ratios can be developed from the items included in an enterprise's financial statements. Some ratios have general application in financial analysis, and others have specific uses in certain circumstances or in specific industries. Discussed below are some of the more significant ratios that can be applied generally to business situations. They are grouped by major objectives of financial analysis.

▶ SHORT-TERM LIQUIDITY

L.O. 6

The short-term liquidity of an enterprise is measured by the degree to which it can meet its short-term obligations. Liquidity implies the ready ability to convert assets into cash or to obtain cash. The short term is conventionally viewed as a time span up to a year, although it is sometimes also identified with the normal operating cycle of a business (that is, the time span that is the buying-producing-selling and collecting cycle of an enterprise).

The importance of short-term liquidity can best be measured by examining the repercussions that stem from a lack of ability to meet short-term obligations.

A lack of liquidity may mean the enterprise cannot take advantage of favorable discounts and profitable business opportunities as they arise. At this stage, a lack of liquidity implies a lack of freedom of choice as well as constraints on management's freedom of movement.

A more serious lack of liquidity means the enterprise is unable to pay its current debts and obligations. This can cause the forced sale of long-term investments and assets and, in its most severe form, insolvency and bankruptcy.

One of the most widely used measures of liquidity is working capital. In addition to its importance as a pool of liquid assets that provides a safety cushion to creditors, net working capital is also important because it provides a liquid reserve with which to meet contingencies and the ever-present uncertainty regarding an enterprise's ability to balance the outflow of funds with an adequate inflow of funds.

Working Capital

Basically, **working capital** is the excess of current assets over current liabilities. That excess is sometimes referred to as *net working capital* because some businesses consider current assets as working capital. A working capital deficiency exists when current liabilities exceed current assets.

The most common categories of current assets are:

1. Cash.
2. Cash equivalents (i.e., temporary investments).
3. Accounts and notes receivable.
4. Inventories.
5. Prepaid costs.

Current liabilities are obligations that would, generally, require the use of current assets for their discharge or, alternatively, the creation of other current liabilities. The most common categories of current liabilities are:

1. Accounts payable.
2. Notes payable.
3. Short-term bank and other loans.
4. Tax and other accruals.
5. Current portion of long-term debt.

The absolute amount of working capital has significance only when related to other variables such as sales, total assets, and so forth. It has limited value for comparison purposes and for judging the adequacy of working capital. This can be illustrated as follows:

	Company A	Company B
Current assets	$300,000	$1,200,000
Current liabilities	100,000	1,000,000
Working capital	$200,000	$ 200,000

Although both companies have an equal amount of working capital, a cursory comparison of the relationship of current assets to current liabilities suggests that Company A's current condition is superior to that of Company B. This example illustrates the need for further analysis, discussed later in the current-ratio section.

The working capital for the Freder Company may be computed as follows:

	19x8	19x7
Current assets	$187,148	$174,866
Current liabilities	54,565	48,873
Working capital	$132,583	$125,993

The analysis of working capital by itself is insufficient to reach a conclusion regarding a firm's short-term liquidity. Four ratios should be used in conjunction with working capital to reach an opinion about a firm's short-term liquidity position. These ratios are the (1) current ratio, (2) acid-test ratio, (3) average-accounts-receivable-turnover ratio, and (4) inventory-turnover ratio.

▶ **ILLUSTRATION 18-7**

$$\frac{\text{Current assets}}{\text{Current liabilities}} = \frac{\text{Cash and cash equivalents} + \text{Accounts receivable} + \text{Inventories}}{\text{Current liabilities}}$$

Current Ratio

The **current ratio** is a firm's current assets divided by its current liabilities and is often expressed as:

$$\text{Current ratio} = \frac{\text{Current assets}}{\text{Current liabilities}} \qquad \textbf{(1)}$$

The current ratios for the Freder Company for 19x8 and 19x7 are:

19x8	19x7
$\dfrac{\$187,148}{\$54,565} = 3.42 \text{ to } 1$	$\dfrac{\$174,866}{\$48,873} = 3.58 \text{ to } 1$

Note that the current ratio deteriorated to 3.42 : 1 in 19x8 from 3.58 : 1 despite an increase in working capital in 19x8 of $6,590 ($132,583 − $125,993). This highlights the importance of analyzing data in more than one approach (i.e., by using absolute dollars and relative relationships).

Some of the reasons for the widespread use of the current ratio as a measure of liquidity are:

1. It measures the degree to which current assets cover current liabilities. The higher the amount of current assets in relation to current liabilities, the greater the assurance that these liabilities can be paid out of such assets.
2. The excess of current assets over current liabilities provides a buffer against losses that may be incurred in the disposition or liquidation of the current assets other than cash. The more substantial such a buffer is, the better for creditors. Thus, the current ratio measures the margin of safety available to cover any possible shrinkage in the value of current assets. However, an excessive current ratio may indicate that excess funds are invested in short-term assets when they might earn a higher return if invested in long-term assets.
3. It measures the reserve of liquid funds in excess of current obligations that is available as a margin of safety against uncertainty and the random shocks to which the flows of funds in an enterprise are subject. Random shocks, such as strikes or extraordinary losses, can temporarily and unexpectedly stop or reduce the inflow of funds.

Limitations of the Current Ratio   The first step in our examination of the current ratio as a tool of liquidity and short-term solvency analysis is to examine the components normally included in the ratio shown in Illustration 18-7.

Disregarding, for purposes of this evaluation, prepaid costs and similar unsubstantial items entering the computation of the current ratio, we have the following four major elements that compose this ratio:

1. Cash and cash equivalents.
2. Accounts receivable.
3. Inventories.
4. Current liabilities.

If we define liquidity as the ability to balance required cash outflows with adequate inflows, including an allowance for unexpected interruptions of inflows or increases in outflows, we must ask: Does the relationship of these four elements at a given point in time—

1. Measure and predict the pattern of future fund flows?
2. Measure the adequacy of future fund inflows in relation to outflows?

The answer to these questions is negative. The current ratio is a static or "stock" concept of what resources are available at a given time to meet obligations at that moment. The existing reservoir of net funds does not have a logical or causative relationship to the future funds that will flow through it. And yet, the future flows are the subject of our greatest interest in the assessment of liquidity. These flows depend on elements *not* included in the ratio itself, such as sales, profits, and changes in business conditions. To elaborate, let us examine more closely the four elements of the ratio.

Cash and Cash Equivalents The amount of cash held by a well-managed enterprise is a precautionary reserve, intended to take care of short-term imbalances in cash flows. In cases of a business downturn, sales may fall more rapidly than outlays for purchases and other costs. Because cash is a nonearning asset and cash equivalents are usually low-yielding securities, the investment in such assets is kept at a safe minimum. To consider this minimum balance as available for payment of current debts would require the dropping of the going-concern assumption underlying accounting statements. Even though the balance of cash has some relation to the existing level of activity, such a relationship is not strong, nor does it contain predictive implications regarding the future. In fact, some enterprises may use cash substitutes, such as open lines of credit, that do not enter into the computation of the current ratio.

The important link between cash and solvency is illustrated by the well-known fact that a shortage of cash, more than any other factor, is the element that can clinch the insolvency of an enterprise.

Accounts Receivable The major determinant of the level of accounts receivable is sales. The size of accounts receivable in relation to sales is governed by terms of trade and credit policy. Changes in receivables will correspond to changes in sales, though not necessarily on a directly proportional basis.

When we look at accounts receivable as a source of cash, we must, except in the case of liquidation, recognize the revolving nature of the asset with the collection of one account replaced by the extension of fresh credit. Thus, the level of receivables is not an index to future net inflows of cash.

Inventories As is the case with accounts receivable, the main determinant of the size of inventories is the level of sales, or expected sales, rather than the level of current liabilities. Given that the level of sales is a measure of the level of demand, scientific methods of inventory management (economic order quantities, safety stock levels, and reorder points) generally establish that inventory increments vary not in proportion to demand but rather with the *square root* of demand.

The relationship of inventories to sales is further accented by the fact that sales is the one essential element that starts the conversion of inventories to cash. Moreover, the determination of future cash inflows through the sale of inventories depends on the profit margin that can be realized because inventories are generally stated at the lower of *cost* or market. The current ratio, while including inventories, does not recognize the sales level or profit margin, both of which are important elements entering into the determination of future cash inflows.

Current Liabilities   The level of current liabilities, the safety of which the current ratio is intended to measure, is also largely determined by the level of sales.

Current liabilities are a source of funds in the same sense that receivables and inventories tie up funds. Because purchases, which give rise to accounts payable, are a function of the level of activity (i.e., sales), these payables vary with sales. As long as sales remain constant or are rising, the payment of current liabilities is essentially a refunding operation. The components of the current ratio give little, if any, recognition to these elements and their effects on the future flow of funds. Nor do the current liabilities that enter into the computation of the current ratio include prospective outlays, such as commitments under construction contracts, loans, leases, or pensions, all of which affect the future outflow of funds.

The Use of Rules-Of-Thumb Standards   A currently popular belief is that the current ratio can be evaluated by means of *rules of thumb*. Thus, if the current ratio is 2 : 1 (or 200 percent), it is sound; anything below that norm is bad, while the higher above that figure the current ratio is, the better.

The 2 : 1 standard means there are $2 of current assets available for each dollar of current liabilities, or the value of current assets can, on liquidation, shrink by 50 percent before it will be inadequate to cover the current liabilities. A current ratio much higher than 2 : 1, while implying a superior coverage of current liabilities, may also mean a wasteful accumulation of liquid resources that do not "carry their weight" by earning an appropriate return for the enterprise.

The evaluation of the current ratio in terms of rules of thumb is a technique of dubious validity for two major reasons:

1. The quality of the current assets, as well as the composition of the current liabilities that make up this ratio, are the most important determinants in an evaluation of the quality of the current ratio. Thus, two companies that have identical current ratios may be in quite different current financial condition due to variations in the quality of the working capital components.
2. The need of an enterprise for working capital varies with industry conditions as well as with the length of its own particular *net trade cycle*.

The following assumed data concerning the Brace and Hall Companies illustrate two companies that have identical current ratios but different positions of short-term liquidity.

	Brace Company	Hall Company
Current assets:		
Cash	$100,000	$ 10,000
Accounts receivable, net	80,000	30,000
Merchandise inventory	120,000	260,000
Total current assets	$300,000	$300,000
Current liabilities	$150,000	$150,000
Current ratio	2 : 1	2 : 1

The short-term liquidity of the Brace Company is preferable to that of the Hall Company, notwithstanding the fact that they both have the same current ratio.

Another short-term liquidity measure, the acid-test ratio, helps users differentiate preferable short-term liquidity in cases like this.

Acid-Test Ratio

The most liquid of current assets is cash, which is the standard of liquidity. A close second to cash is "temporary investments" that are usually highly marketable and relatively safe temporary repositories of cash. These are, in effect, considered "cash equivalents" and usually earn a modest return. Accounts receivable are only one step removed from cash and are normally converted into cash within a relatively short period of time (usually 30 to 60 days). Thus, accounts receivable is also considered a relatively liquid asset. Although inventories are current assets, they are not nearly as liquid as accounts receivable. They must first be sold before they become liquid assets in the form of accounts receivable. During periods of economic recession, inventories may not be immediately salable in the normal course of business. Therefore, users of financial statements also use a more stringent test than the current ratio to evaluate a firm's liquidity. Prepaid costs and inventories are excluded from the numerator of this test because prepaid costs are not normally converted into cash and inventories must first be sold. The stringent test, the **acid-test ratio,** consists of a numerator composed of cash, short-term marketable securities, and accounts (and short-term notes) receivable divided by the denominator of current liabilities. The acid-test ratio, also known as the *quick ratio,* may be expressed as:

$$\text{Acid-test ratio} = \frac{\text{Cash} + \text{Short-term marketable securities} + \text{Current receivables}}{\text{Current liabilities}} \quad (2)$$

As with the current ratio where a popular rule-of-thumb standard exists, the acid-test ratio also has a standard. Although the standard has dubious validity, many users of financial statements feel that the acid-test ratio should be a minimum of 1 : 1. A ratio of 1 : 1 implies that a sufficient amount of liquid assets is available to meet the demands of the firm's present current liabilities, but it does not imply that the condition is likely to continue in the future, nor does the ratio factor in different requirements for different industries.

The calculations of the ratio for the Freder Company for 19x8 and 19x7 are:

	19x8	19x7
Cash.	$ 14,522	$ 20,962
Accounts receivable	91,314	79,328
Total quick assets	$105,836	$100,290
Current liabilities	$ 54,565	$ 48,873
Acid-test ratio	1.94 : 1	2.05 : 1

Even though the acid-test ratios for the Freder Company are in excess of the rule-of-thumb standard, it should be noted that the ratio decreased in 19x8. This may be a sign that the company's trend of short-term liquidity is weakening.

Average-Accounts-Receivable-Turnover Ratio

In most enterprises that sell on credit, accounts and notes receivable are a significant part of working capital. In assessing the quality of working capital and of the current ratio, it is important to get some measure of the quality and the liquidity of the receivables.

Both the quality and liquidity of accounts receivable are affected by their rate of turnover. Quality means the likelihood of collection without loss. An indicator of this likelihood is the degree to which receivables are within the terms of payment set by the enterprise. Experience has shown that the longer receivables remain outstanding beyond the date on which they are due, the lower is the probability of their collection in full. Turnover is an indicator of the age of the receivables, particularly when it is compared with an expected turnover rate determined by credit terms granted.

The measure of liquidity is concerned with the speed with which accounts receivables will, on average, be converted into cash. Here again, turnover is among the best measures to use.

The **accounts-receivable-turnover ratio** is computed by dividing net credit sales by the average accounts receivable. Average accounts receivable may be computed by adding the beginning and ending balances of accounts receivable and then dividing the sum by 2. The ratio may be expressed as:

$$\text{Accounts receivable turnover} = \frac{\text{Net sales on credit}}{\text{Average accounts receivable}} \quad \textbf{(3)}$$

Notes receivable arising from normal sales should be included in the accounts receivable figure in computing the turnover ratio. Discounted notes receivable that are still outstanding should also be included in the accounts receivable total.

The sales figure used in computing the ratio should be that of credit sales only, because cash sales do not generate receivables. Because published financial statements rarely disclose the division between cash and credit sales, the external analyst may have to compute the ratio under the assumption that cash sales are insignificant. If they are not insignificant, then a degree of distortion may occur in the ratio. However, if the proportion of cash sales to total sales remains relatively constant, the year-to-year comparison of changes in the receivables-turnover ratio may nevertheless be validly based.

The average-receivables-turnover figure indicates how many *times,* on average, the receivables revolve (that is, are generated and collected during the year). Comparative turnover ratios are also used to detect meaningful trends.

The accounts-receivable-turnover ratio for the Freder Company is:

$$\frac{\$720,860}{(\$79,328 + \$91,314) \div 2} = \frac{\$720,860}{\$85,321} = 8.4 \text{ times}$$

Although the turnover figure furnishes a sense of the speed of collections and is valuable for comparison purposes, it is not directly comparable to the terms of trade that the enterprise normally extends. Such comparison is best made by converting the turnover into days of sales tied up in receivables.

Collection Period for Accounts Receivable

The **collection period for accounts receivable,** also known as *days' sales in accounts receivable,* measures the number of days it takes, on average, to collect accounts (and notes) receivable. The number of days can be obtained by dividing the average-accounts-receivable-turnover ratio discussed above into 360, the approximate round number of days in the year. Thus,

$$\text{Collection period} = \frac{360}{\text{Average accounts receivable turnover}} \qquad \textbf{(4)}$$

Using the figures of the preceding example, the collection period is:

$$\frac{360}{8.4} = 43 \text{ days}$$

Accounts-receivable-turnover rates or collection periods can be compared to industry averages (see Appendix 18-A) or to the credit terms granted by the enterprise.

When the collection period is compared with the terms of sale allowed by the enterprise, the degree to which customers are paying on time can be assessed. Thus, if the average terms of sale in the illustration used above are 30 days, then an average collection period of 43 days reflects either some or all of the following conditions:

1. A poor collection job.
2. Difficulty in obtaining prompt payment from customers in spite of diligent collection efforts.
3. Customers in financial difficulty.

The first conclusion calls for remedial managerial action, while the last two reflect on both the quality and the liquidity of the accounts receivable.

An *average* figure may not be representative of the receivables population. Thus, it is possible that the 43-day average collection period does not represent an across-the-board payment tardiness on the part of customers but rather is caused by the excessive delinquency of one or two substantial customers.

The best way to further investigate an excessive collection period is to *age* the accounts receivable so that the distribution of each account by the number of days past due is clearly apparent. An aging schedule in a format like the one given below will show whether the problem is widespread or concentrated.

Accounts Receivable Aging Schedule

		Days Past Due			
	Current	**0–30**	**31–60**	**61–90**	**Over 90**
Accounts receivable					

The age distribution of the receivables will, of course, lead to better informed conclusions regarding the quality and liquidity of the receivables as well as the kind of action necessary to remedy the situation. Another dimension of receivables classification is quality ratings by credit agencies like Dun & Bradstreet.

Notes receivable also deserve scrutiny because although they are normally regarded as more negotiable than open accounts, they may be of poorer quality than regular receivables if they originated as an extension device for an unpaid account rather than at the inception of the original sale.

Inventory-Turnover Ratio

In many cases, inventories represent a substantial proportion of the current asset group. This fact has little effect on an enterprise's objective of maintaining adequate levels of liquid funds. Reserves of liquid funds are seldom kept in the form of inventories. Inventories represent investments made to obtain a return. The return is derived from the expected profits that may result from sales. In most businesses, a certain level of inventory must be kept to generate an adequate level of sales. If the inventory level is inadequate, the sales volume will fall below the level otherwise attainable. Excessive inventories, on the other hand, expose the enterprise to such costs as storage costs, insurance, and taxes, as well as to risks of loss of value through obsolescence and physical deterioration. Moreover, excessive inventories tie up funds that can be used more profitably elsewhere.

Due to the risk involved in holding inventories and the fact that inventories are one step further removed from cash than receivables (they have to be sold before they are converted into receivables), inventories are normally considered the least liquid component of the current assets group. However, this generalization is not always true. Certain staple items, such as commodities, direct materials, and standard sizes of structural steel, enjoy broad and ready markets and can usually be sold with little effort, cost, or loss. On the other hand, fashion merchandise, specialized components, or perishable items can lose their value rapidly unless they are sold on a timely basis.

The evaluation of the current ratio, which includes inventories in its computation, must include a thorough evaluation of the quality as well as the liquidity of these assets. Here again, measures of turnover are the best overall tools available for this purpose.

The **inventory-turnover ratio** measures the average rate of speed with which inventories move through and out of the enterprise. It is computed by dividing cost of goods sold by average inventory.

Computation   The computation of the average inventory turnover is as follows:

$$\text{Inventory-turnover ratio} = \frac{\text{Cost of goods sold}}{\text{Average inventory}} \qquad (5)$$

The average inventory figure is most readily obtained as follows:

$$\frac{\text{Opening inventory} + \text{Closing inventory}}{2}$$

Further refinement in the averaging process can be achieved, where possible and necessary, by averaging quarterly or monthly inventory figures.

When an inventory-turnover ratio is computed to evaluate the *level* of inventory at a certain date, such as the year-end inventory, the inventory figure in the denominator should be the figure as of that date rather than an average inventory figure.

The 19x8 inventory turnover for the Freder Company may be computed as follows:

$$\frac{\text{Cost of goods sold}}{\text{Average inventory}} = \frac{\$453,178}{(\$67,622 + \$73,632) \div 2} = \frac{\$453,178}{\$70,627} = 6.4 \text{ times}$$

Comparative turnover ratios are used to detect meaningful trends. For example, a decreasing inventory-turnover trend may be indicative of excessive investment in inventories, obsolete merchandise, or a change in the composition of the inventory.

Days to Sell Inventory   Another measure of inventory turnover that is also useful in assessing purchasing policy is the required number of days to sell inventory. The number of **days to sell inventory** measures the number of days it takes to sell the average inventory and is computed by dividing the number of days in a year (rounded to 360 days) by the average inventory turnover. It may be presented as:

$$\text{Days to sell inventory} = \frac{360 \text{ days}}{\text{Average inventory turnover}} \qquad (6)$$

The Freder Company's days to sell inventory for 19x8 is computed as follows:

$$\frac{360}{6.4 \text{ times}} = 56\frac{1}{4} \text{ days}$$

Interpretation of Inventory-Turnover Ratios   The current ratio computation views its current asset components as sources of funds that can, as a means of last resort, be used to pay off the current liabilities. Viewed this way, the inventory-turnover ratios give us a measure of the quality as well as the liquidity of the inventory component of the current assets.

In practice, a going concern cannot use its investment in inventory for the payment of current liabilities because any drastic reduction in normal inventory levels will cut into the sales volume.

▶ **PROGRESS CHECK**

1. Three tools of financial statement analysis are comparative financial statements, index-number trend series, and common-size financial statements. Describe each tool and the way it is used to assist a user of financial statements.
2. Ratio analysis is a very important tool of financial analysts. What is a ratio and why is it important to financial analysts?
3. What is working capital and why is it important to a financial analyst?
4. The current ratio and the acid-test ratio are similar, yet they are different. What is the difference and why is each ratio important to a financial analyst?
5. Financial analysts use two turnover ratios, the accounts-receivable turnover and the inventory-turnover ratio. How is each ratio computed and how is each one used? ◀

▶ CAPITAL STRUCTURE AND LONG-TERM SOLVENCY RATIOS

L.O. 7

Long-term creditors have two main concerns. In the short run, they are concerned about receiving their annual interest payments; in the long run, they are concerned about receiving the maturity value of their loans when they become due. The ratios discussed below are important to the long-term creditors in assessing long-term solvency, but the ability of a firm to meet its debts when due depends on *earnings*. If a firm is unprofitable in the long run, it will be unable to meet its obligations when they mature and unable to refinance its debts. However, the trend of the ratios discussed below may highlight a deteriorating condition well in advance of a company's impending default on its long-term debt.

The basic ratio measurements of capital structure relate the various components of the capital structure to each other or to their total. Some of these ratios in common use are explained below.

Debt-to-Equity Ratio

The most comprehensive ratio in this area, the **debt-to-equity ratio,** measures the relationship between *total debt* (Current liabilities + Long-term liabilities) to *total stockholders' equity*. The ratio is total debt divided by total stockholders' equity and may be expressed as:

$$\text{Debt-to-equity ratio} = \frac{\text{Total liabilities}}{\text{Total stockholders' equity}} \quad (7)$$

The computation of the debt-to-equity ratio for the years 19x8 and 19x7 for the Freder Company is as follows:

	19x8	19x7
Total current liabilities	$ 54,565	$ 48,873
Total long-term liabilities	47,180	42,420
Total liabilities (A)	$101,745	$ 91,293
Total stockholders' equity (B)	$145,841	$140,383
Debt-to-equity ratio (A) ÷ (B)	.70	.65

This ratio means Freder's total debt in 19x8 is 70 percent of its equity capital, or the creditors advanced 70 cents for every dollar of the company's stockholders' equity. This ratio varies for different types of businesses. For example, traditionally, public utilities have a high debt-to-equity ratio in relation to manufacturing firms because the stability of their revenues allows them to carry more debt. Although a debt-to-equity ratio of .70 may be comfortable for the creditors of Freder, they may feel that the movement from .65 in 19x7 to .70 in 19x8 should be watched. The higher this ratio becomes, the more risk the creditors assume because the stockholders' equity acts as a buffer when operating losses occur. The operating losses are charged against stockholders' equity before any of the losses are assumed by the creditors, and the lower this ratio, the greater the buffer.

Times Interest Earned Ratio

An important measure of protection for the long-term creditor is the number of times interest is earned. The **times interest earned ratio** measures the likelihood that long-term creditors will continue to receive their interest when due. It is computed by dividing the numerator (net income, income taxes, and interest cost) by the firm's interest cost. The ratio may be expressed as:

$$\frac{\text{Times interest}}{\text{earned}} = \frac{\text{Net income} + \text{Income taxes} + \text{Interest cost}}{\text{Interest cost}} \quad (8)$$

For many firms, the numerator will be the same as their operating income. The operating income of the Freder company (see Illustration 18-2) is $15,013 for 19x8, and this amount would be the numerator for this ratio. The computation for 19x8 is as follows:

$$\frac{\$6,008 + \$4,005 + \$5,000}{\$5,000} = \frac{\$15,013}{\$5,000} = 3 \text{ times}$$

Income taxes must be added back to the numerator because income taxes are only paid if profits exist, and interest must be deducted first before profits become subject to income taxes. Interest cost must also be added back to the numerator because this item is measured by the denominator.

Some users of this ratio believe a rule-of-thumb ratio provides a measure of safety for the long-term creditor. More important than a single year's ratio, the trend of the ratio over a period of years provides the long-term creditor with the likelihood that interest payments will be met when due.

▶ RETURN-ON-INVESTMENT RATIOS

L.O. 8
Investment analysis ratios

Performance can be measured by many criteria. Changes in sales, in profits, or in various measures of output are among the criteria frequently used.

None of these measurements by itself is useful as a comprehensive measure of enterprise performance. The reasons for this are easy to grasp. Increases in sales are desirable only if they result in increased profits. The same is true of increases in volume of production. Increases in profits, on the other hand, must be related to the capital that is invested to attain these profits.

Return on Investment (ROI)

The relationship between net income and the capital invested in the generation of that income is one of the most valid and most widely recognized measures of enterprise performance. In relating income to invested capital, the ROI measure allows the analyst to compare it to alternative uses of capital as well as to the return realized by enterprises subject to similar degrees of risk. The investment of capital can always yield some return. If capital is invested in government bonds, the return will be low because of the small risk involved. Riskier investments require higher returns to make them worthwhile. The ROI measure relates income (reward) to the size of the capital needed to generate it.

Economic performance is the first purpose of business enterprise. It is the reason for its existence. The effectiveness of operating performance determines the ability of the enterprise to survive financially, to attract suppliers of funds, and to reward them adequately. ROI is the prime measure of economic performance. The analyst uses it as a tool in three areas of great importance:

1. An indicator of managerial effectiveness.
2. A measure of an enterprise's ability to earn a satisfactory return on investment.
3. A method of projecting earnings.

An Indicator of Managerial Effectiveness   The earning of an adequate or superior return on funds invested in an enterprise depends first on the resourcefullness, skill, ingenuity, and motivation of management. Thus, the longer-term ROI has great interest and importance to the financial analyst because it offers a prime means of evaluating this indispensable criterion of business success: the quality of management.

A Measure of Enterprise Ability to Earn a Satisfactory ROI   Although related to managerial effectiveness, this measure is a far more reliable indicator of long-term financial health than is any measure of current financial strength based only on balance sheet relationships. For this reason, ROI has great importance and interest to longer-term creditors as well as to equity investors.

A Method of Projecting Earnings   A third important function of the ROI measure is that of a means of earnings projection. The advantage of this method of earnings projection is that it links the estimated amount of earnings that an enterprise will earn to the total invested capital. This adds discipline and realism to the projection process.

The rate of the ROI method of earnings projection can be used by the analyst as either the primary method of earnings projection or as a supplementary check on estimates derived from other projection methods.

Basic Elements of ROI

The basic concept of ROI is simple to understand. However, care must be used in determining the elements for its computation, because there is a variety of views, which reflect different objectives, of how these elements should be defined.

The basic formula for computing ROI is as follows:

$$\frac{Income}{Investment}$$

We shall now examine the various definitions of *investment* and of *income*.

There is no generally accepted measure of capital investment on which the rate of return is computed. The different concepts of investment reflect different objectives. Because the term *return on investment (ROI)* covers a multitude of concepts of investment base and income, we need more specific terms to describe the actual investment base used.

Total Assets   Return on total assets is perhaps the best measure of the *operating efficiency* of an enterprise. It measures the return obtained on *all* the assets entrusted to management. *By removing from this computation the effect of the method used in financing the assets,* the analyst can concentrate on the evaluation or projection of operating performance.

In the computation of ROI, the definition of return (income) depends on the definition of the investment base. If the investment base is defined as comprising total assets, then income *before* interest cost is used. The exclusion of interest from income deductions occurs because it is regarded as a payment for the use of money to the suppliers of debt capital in the same way that dividends are regarded as a reward to suppliers of equity capital.

The **return on total assets** measures the effectiveness of asset utilization and is computed by dividing a numerator consisting of a firm's net income plus its after-tax cost of interest by a denominator consisting of the firm's average total assets. The ROI may be expressed as:

$$\frac{\text{Return on}}{\text{total assets}} = \frac{\text{Net income} + \text{Interest cost } (1 - \text{Tax rate})}{\text{Average total assets}} \qquad (9)$$

The calculation of this return for the Freder Company for 19x8 is as follows:

$$\frac{\$6{,}008 + \$5{,}000(1 - 40\%)}{(\$231{,}676 + \$247{,}586) \div 2} = \frac{\$9{,}008}{\$239{,}631} = .038 = 3.8\%$$

By most standards, a 3.8 percent return on total assets would be considered unsatisfactory. In addition to this year's performance, the trend as well as the level of this parameter must be evaluated.

Return on Common Stockholders' Equity   Although a corporation's objectives are varied, the main reason for its existence is to earn a satisfactory return for its common stockholders. The measure used to evaluate this performance is **return on common stockholders' equity** and is computed by dividing a numerator consisting of net income minus preferred dividends by a denominator of average common stockholders' equity. The formula may be expressed as:

$$\frac{\text{Return on common}}{\text{stockholders' equity}} = \frac{\text{Net income} - \text{Preferred dividends}}{\text{Average common stockholders' equity}} \qquad (10)$$

The return on common stockholders' equity for the Freder Company for 19x8 is as follows:

Net income	$ 6,008	
Less: Preferred dividends	2,000	
Net income available to common stockholders	$ 4,008	(A)
Stockholders' equity—January 1, 19x8	$140,383	
Stockholders' equity—December 31, 19x8.	145,841	
Total	$286,224	
Average stockholders' equity ($286,224 ÷ 2).	$143,112	
Less: Average preferred stock	20,000*	
Average common stockholders' equity	$123,112	(B)
Return on common stockholders' equity (A) ÷ (B)	3.3%	

*$20,000 + $20,000 = $40,000 ÷ 2 = $20,000.

▶ **ILLUSTRATION 18-8**

FREDER COMPANY
Analysis of the Cost of Liabilities and Preferred Stock
For the Year Ended December 31, 19x8

Interest cost, net of tax ($5,000 × .60) . . . . $ 3,000
Add: Preferred dividends   2,000

Total cost of interest and preferred dividends . . . . $ 5,000 (C)

Average liabilities and preferred stock:
  Average total assets—computed above
    in conjunction with formula 9 . . . . $239,631
  Less: Average common stockholders' equity—
    computed above in conjunction with
    formula 10 (labeled B).   123,112

  Average liabilities and preferred stock . . . . $116,519 (D)

Average cost of liabilities and preferred stock (C) ÷ (D) 4.3%

Note that the return on common stockholders' equity decreased to 3.3 percent when compared to the return on total assets of 3.8 percent. The reason for this decrease is that the firm's interest cost of liabilities (net of income tax) plus the cost of the preferred stock is greater than the 3.8 percent return on total assets. This analysis is shown in Illustration 18-8.

When the return on total assets is less than the after-tax cost of liabilities and preferred stock, the return on common stockholders' equity is less than the return on total assets. On the other hand, when the after-tax interest cost of liabilities and the cost of preferred stock is less than the return on total assets, the return on common stockholders' equity will be greater than that for total assets. Incurring debt is known as *employing financial leverage.*

Financial Leverage   Using borrowed funds or funds acquired from the sale of preferred stock—both of which require fixed costs for the use of the funds—in place of funds acquired from the sale of common stock is known as **financial leverage.** Financial leverage, also called *trading on the equity,* is normally employed to increase the return to common stockholders, and when successful, the financial leverage is said to be positive. **Positive financial leverage** exists when the cost of borrowed funds (and/or the dividend cost of preferred stock) is less than the return on total assets, and the return on common stockholders' equity exceeds the return on total assets.

Let us assume the Freder Company has an opportunity to enter a new market with an investment of $200,000 that will yield an operating income of $80,000 per year. The firm plans to borrow the $200,000 at an interest rate of 10 percent per annum. The simple return on this investment may be computed as follows:

Operating income $80,000
Less: Interest cost ($200,000 × 10%).   20,000

Income before income taxes.   60,000
Income taxes (40%)   24,000

Net income $36,000

Return on this investment:

$$\frac{\$36,000}{\$200,000} = 18\%$$

We can now modify the previously given data of the Freder Company for 19x8 to see what effect this investment will have on the return of total assets and the return on common stockholders' equity.

Return on Total Assets

Modified net income:
Net income as given . . . . $ 6,008
Add: Net income from the project. 36,000
    Modified net income . . . . $ 42,008

Modified total assets:
Average net assets as given
(See information for formula 9) $239,631
Add: Assets acquired for project 200,000
    Modified total assets $439,631

Using formula 9, the return on total assets would be:

$$\frac{\$42,008 + [\$5,000 + \$20,000 = \$25,000(1 - .40)]}{\$439,631} = \frac{\$57,008}{\$439,631} = 13\%$$

Return on Common Stockholders' Equity

$$\frac{\text{Net income} - \text{Preferred dividends}}{\text{Average common stockholders' equity}} \qquad \textbf{(10)}$$

$$\frac{\$42,008 - \$2,000}{\$123,112^*} = \frac{\$40,008}{123,112} = 32.5\%$$

---

* This amount is unchanged because the project's funds would be all borrowed.

Note that the return on total assets increased from 3.8 percent to 13 percent as a result of factoring in the contemplated project; the return on common stockholders' equity increased more dramatically from 3.3 percent to 32.5 percent. Hence, positive financial leverage may have a profound effect on the return on common stockholders' equity. However, financial leverage may be negative, as in the original data presented for the Freder Company, and when this occurs, the opposite effect is encountered. **Negative financial leverage** exists when the cost of borrowing funds (and/or the dividend cost of preferred stock) is greater than the return on total assets, and the return on common stockholders' equity is less than the return on total assets.

Although borrowed funds and funds from the sale of preferred stock with a fixed yield are both sources of financial leverage, they have different effects on a firm's use of financial leverage.

Effects of Financial Leverage Long-term debt, consisting mainly of bonds payable, notes payable, and lease obligations under capitalized leases, has a fixed interest cost, whether it is stated interest or imputed interest. Short-term debt may have some elements (such as notes payable) that have a fixed interest cost, but other elements (such as accounts payable and accrued wages payable) have no interest cost. Thus, when the return on common stockholders' equity is computed, debt without any interest cost benefits common stockholders.

▶ **ILLUSTRATION 18-9**   Effects of Leverage Using Common Stock, Preferred Stock, and Bonds Payable

	Common Stock	Preferred Stock	Bonds Payable
Operating income	$120,000	$120,000	$120,000
Less: Interest cost (10% × $300,000)	—	—	30,000
Income before income taxes	120,000	120,000	90,000
Income taxes at 40%.	48,000	48,000	36,000
Net income	72,000	72,000	54,000
Less: Preferred dividends (10% × $300,000) . . .	—	30,000	—
Net income available to common stockholders (A)	$ 72,000	$ 42,000	$ 54,000
Common stockholders' equity (B).	$600,000	$300,000	$300,000
Return on common stockholders' equity (A) ÷ (B)	12%	14%	18%

Long-term notes payable and long-term bonds payable benefit common stockholders less than accounts payable but more than preferred stock, because the interest cost associated with long-term debt is deductible for income tax purposes but the dividends paid to preferred stockholders are not.

To illustrate the different effects on the use of leverage, assume a company's stockholders' equity and total assets are $300,000 and consist entirely of common stock. Its earnings before income taxes are $60,000, and its income tax rate is 40 percent. The firm can double its operating income to $120,000 by doubling its total assets to $600,000 by using one of three possible plans: (1) issuing $300,000 of common stock, (2) issuing $300,000 of preferred stock with a 10 percent dividend, or (3) issuing $300,000 of 10 percent bonds payable. The effects of the three plans on the return on common stockholders' equity are shown in Illustration 18-9.

Illustration 18-9 indicates that when financial leverage is positive, the use of long-term debt has the greatest impact on the return on common stockholders' equity, and the use of preferred stock has a lesser impact. Most firms use financial leverage, and the blend of long-term debt, preferred stock, and common stock is usually dictated by market forces and conditions.

Notice that for the Freder Company, the cost of liabilities and preferred stock (see Illustration 18-8) is only 4.3 percent even though the pre-tax interest cost on the bonds payable is greater than 10 percent ($5,000 ÷ $47,180) (from Illustrations 18-1 and 18-2) and the preferred dividend cost is 10 percent (from Illustration 18-1). The reason for this is that current liabilities have a zero cost, while the weighted-average after-tax cost of the bonds payable is 6.7 percent, computed as follows:

Bonds payable—January 1, 19x8	$42,420
Bonds payable—December 31, 19x8.	47,180
Total.	$89,600
Average ($89,600 ÷ 2)	$44,800
Net-of-tax interest = $5,000 (1 − .40)	$ 3,000
After-tax cost of bonds ($3,000 ÷ $44,800)	6.696%

The cost shown in Illustration 18-8 may also be computed as follows:

	(1) Weighted-Average Amount	(2) Percent of Total	(3) Rate Cost	(4) Weighted Rate Cost (2) × (3)
Current liabilities	$ 51,719	44.39	–0–	–0–
Bonds payable	44,800	38.45	6.7%	2.6%
Preferred stock	20,000	17.16	10.0%	1.7%
Total	$116,519	100.00		4.3%

► EARNINGS PER SHARE (EPS)

Earnings per share is a statistic quoted by investment services, stock brokerage reports on specific companies, and various financial publications. Also, it is the statistic most often relied on by investors as the measure of a company's operating performance. **Earnings per share** is computed by dividing the numerator of a firm's net income available to common stockholders by the denominator of the weighted-average number of common shares outstanding for the period. Earnings per share may be expressed as:

$$\frac{\text{Earnings}}{\text{per share}} = \frac{\text{Net income} - \text{Preferred dividends}}{\text{Weighted-average common shares outstanding}} \quad (11)$$

The weighted-average common shares outstanding for the Freder Company is easily calculated. At the beginning of the year (see Illustration 18-1), there were 6,500 ($32,500 ÷ $5 par value) shares outstanding. At the end of the year, there were 7,500 ($37,500 ÷ $5 par value) shares outstanding. If the additional 1,000 shares were sold on April 1, 19x8, the weighted-average number of shares may be calculated as follows:

Date	Shares Outstanding	Months Unchanged	Product
19x8:			
January 1	6,500	3	19,500
April 1	7,500	9	67,500
Total		12	87,000
Weighted average (87,000 ÷ 12)			7,250

The calculation of earnings per share for 19x8 for the Freder Company is:

$$\frac{\$6,008 - \$2,000}{7,250 \text{ shares}} = \frac{\$4,008}{7,250 \text{ shares}} = \$.55 \text{ per share}$$

Although the earnings-per-share statistic is useful when used with the share's market price (discussed later), over a period of years this statistic's trend provides users with its greatest use. Remember net income is derived from accounting practices that permit the selection of various alternatives, such as inventory valuations and depreciation methods. If a firm consistcntly uses the same accounting alternatives from year to year, then its trend of EPS is reliable. However, care must be exercised when comparisons between competing firms are made. These firms may be using different accounting methods, such as for depreciation and inventory valuation. When this is the case, comparisons may still be made if the differences created by the accounting methods are factored into the comparisons.

Another problem in relying on a single EPS number is that a variety of potentially dilutive securities, such as options, warrants, convertible debt, and convertible preferred stock, is not included in the EPS calculation. When a firm has these securities outstanding, it must present additional EPS statistics.

Primary and Fully Diluted Earnings per Share

During the past two decades, there has been an increased tendency for firms to issue bonds payable and preferred stock that can be converted into specific numbers of shares of common stock. When an investor exercises this conversion feature, the bond and/or the preferred stock is surrendered, and common stock is received in its place. Because of the uncertainty regarding the ultimate outcome of conversion, a question arises regarding how these securities should be treated for EPS calculations. In 1970, the Accounting Principles Board of the American Institute of Certified Public Accountants determined that the best approach to disclosing the problems created by potentially dilutive securities is to present two EPS statistics, one similar to that discussed previously[2] and another giving effect to the possible full dilution (lower amount) of EPS. **Fully diluted earnings per share** is computed by dividing the net income available to common shareholders by the weighted-average common shares outstanding and then adjusting both the numerator and denominator for the assumed conversion of all potentially dilutive securities. Computing earnings per share can be quite complex, and, of necessity, the discussion of this topic is limited to the simpler calculations.

Let us assume the Freder Company's preferred stock and bonds payable shown in Illustration 18-1 are convertible into common stock. The preferred stock can be converted into 5,000 shares of common stock, and the bonds can be converted into 10,000 shares of common stock.

The starting point of the calculation is the previously computed earnings-per-share fraction. An important point to remember is that fully diluted EPS *cannot be* greater than the original EPS of 55 cents per share for the Freder Company as a result of the adjustments for potentially dilutive securities. If this amount is greater, a condition known as *antidilution,* then the fully diluted EPS is *not* shown and the presentation is limited to a single presentation, 55 cents per share.

The denominator of the basic fraction is adjusted by the amount of common shares that would be issued for the conversion of the preferred stock and bonds payable. These adjustments assume the preferred stock is no longer outstanding, and therefore the preferred dividend of $2,000 must be added back to the numerator because it would no longer be paid. The same is true for the $5,000 of interest cost for the bonds payable, except it must be

---

[2] When certain dilutive securities called *common stock equivalents* are present in a firm's capital structure, the simple EPS figure is modified by these dilutive securities, and the new EPS figure is called *primary EPS*. This calculation is discussed in intermediate accounting texts.

added back net of tax because interest is deductible on the firm's income statement to arrive at net income. The calculation would be as follows:

$$\text{Fully diluted EPS} =$$

$$\frac{\$4,008 + \$2,000 + \$5,000(1 - .40)}{7,250 + 5,000 + 10,000} = \frac{\$9,008}{22,250} = \$.40 \text{ per share}$$

Because fully diluted EPS is 40 cents per share and is less than 55 cents per share (the original amount), both amounts are shown. The 55-cents-per-share amount is called *primary EPS*.

When a firm has extraordinary items on its income statement, EPS is computed separately for *income before extraordinary items, extraordinary items,* and *net income*. This is done for both primary EPS and fully diluted EPS. Thus, six EPS numbers would be required when a firm has both extraordinary items and potentially dilutive securities outstanding.

▶ MARKET MEASURES

Price-Earnings Ratio

L.O. 9

Investors and potential investors relate a firm's EPS to the market price of its stock. The **price-earnings ratio** is computed by dividing the market price of a firm's share of common stock by the primary earnings per share. The price-earnings ratio (PE ratio) may also be expressed as:

$$\text{Price-earnings ratio} = \frac{\text{Market price per share}}{\text{Earnings per share}} \qquad \textbf{(12)}$$

Assuming a market price of $8 per share for the Freder Company, its PE ratio for 19x8 would be computed as follows:

$$\frac{\$8}{\$.55} = 14.5$$

This means the firm's shares are selling at 14.5 times earnings.

Although investors use PE ratios as a measure of a company's future prospects, the ratio also provides investors with a measurement by which to gauge competing investments in the same industry. PE ratios vary between firms in different industries and between growth companies and well-seasoned companies. The trend of a firm's PE ratio also provides useful information for investors and indicates whether a particular stock is cheap or expensive in relation to competing investments.

Dividend Payout and Yield Ratios

Different stockholders have different investment objectives. Investors who are taxed at relatively low income tax brackets may prefer a high current income in the form of dividends, which are taxed at ordinary income tax rates. They are willing to accept this high current income with a concomitant low amount of capital appreciation. Investors who are taxed at high income tax rates would probably prefer to invest in so-called *growth companies* that pay low dividends and reinvest their earnings for growth potential. These investors are willing to forgo current income in favor of capital appreciation of their stock, which might be taxed at lower tax rates when the investor retires. The dividend payout ratio would help investors determine which company's stock would meet their objectives.

Dividend Payout Ratio   The **dividend payout ratio** is computed by dividing common stock dividends per share by primary earnings per share. This ratio may be shown as follows:

$$\text{Dividend payout ratio} = \frac{\text{Common stock dividends per share}}{\text{Primary earnings per share}} \qquad (13)$$

Assume the common stock dividends per share for the Freder Company are $1.34 for 19x8. The dividend payout ratio for the firm would be:

$$\frac{\$1.34}{\$.55} = 2.436 = 243.6\%$$

Although this ratio is extremely unusual, a company may occasionally pay more dividends than it earns when the reduction in earnings is temporary and the firm wishes to maintain its dividend-paying record. If this payout ratio were maintained for any significant length of time, the company would be engaged in a partial liquidation.

Let us now assume the Hall Company pays a common dividend per share of $1 and its primary earnings per share are $2.50. Its dividend payout ratio would be:

$$\frac{\$1}{\$2.50} = .40 = 40\%$$

This ratio would be considered average, but ratios fluctuate widely. As noted, growth companies with good investment opportunities would have dividend payout ratios considerably less than 40 percent, while firms with limited investment opportunities, such as some public utilities, have dividend payout ratios considerably in excess of 40 percent.

Dividend Yield Ratio   The **dividend yield ratio** is computed by dividing a firm's dividends per share by its market price per share and may be shown as follows:

$$\text{Dividend yield ratio} = \frac{\text{Dividends per share}}{\text{Market price per share}} \qquad (14)$$

Using the assumed dividends per common share of $1.34 and the market price per share of $8 for the Freder Company, the common stock dividend yield ratio for 19x8 would be as follows:

$$\frac{\$1.34}{\$8} = .1675 = 16.75\%$$

When an investor makes this calculation, she should use the *current* market price and not the price she paid for the investment. By continuing to hold this stock, she gives up her right to receive $8 per share (her opportunity cost). The *current dividend* must be related to the *current cost* of purchasing the stock. Otherwise, a meaningless yield ratio may be the result.

Although EPS is an important statistic for investors, they rarely, if ever, actually receive a firm's EPS. Instead, they usually receive an amount each year in the form of dividends and, hopefully, some capital gains when the stock is sold. Therefore, when evaluating an investment (or potential investment), the investor must look to the yield received in the form of dividends.

A tabulation of all of the ratios previously discussed is provided in Illustration 18-10.

▶ **ILLUSTRATION 18-10**   Tabulation of Ratios

	Number	Ratio	Formula
Liquidity Ratios	(1)	Current ratio	$\dfrac{\text{Current assets}}{\text{Current liabilities}}$
	(2)	Acid-test ratio (quick ratio)	$\dfrac{\text{Cash + Short-term marketable securities + Current receivables}}{\text{Current liabilities}}$
	(3)	Accounts-receivable-turnover ratio	$\dfrac{\text{Net sales on credit}}{\text{Average accounts receivable}}$
	(4)	Collection period of receivables	$\dfrac{360}{\text{Average-accounts-receivable-turnover ratio}}$
	(5)	Inventory-turnover ratio	$\dfrac{\text{Cost of goods sold}}{\text{Average inventory}}$
	(6)	Days to sell inventory	$\dfrac{360}{\text{Average inventory turnover}}$
Long-Term Solvency Ratios	(7)	Debt-to-equity ratio	$\dfrac{\text{Total liabilities}}{\text{Total stockholders' equity}}$
	(8)	Times interest earned ratio	$\dfrac{\text{Net income + Income taxes + Interest cost}}{\text{Interest cost}}$
ROI Ratios	(9)	Return on total assets	$\dfrac{\text{Net income + Interest cost } (1 - \text{Tax rate})}{\text{Average total assets}}$
	(10)	Return on common stockholders' equity	$\dfrac{\text{Net income} - \text{Preferred dividends}}{\text{Average common stockholders' equity}}$
	(11)	Earnings per share	$\dfrac{\text{Net income} - \text{Preferred dividends}}{\text{Weighted-average common shares outstanding}}$
Market Measure Ratios	(12)	Price-earnings ratio	$\dfrac{\text{Market price per share}}{\text{Earnings per share}}$
	(13)	Dividend payout ratio	$\dfrac{\text{Common stock dividends per share}}{\text{Primary earnings per share}}$
	(14)	Dividend yield ratio	$\dfrac{\text{Dividends per share}}{\text{Market price per share}}$

Appendix 18-A contains a listing of various sources of published financial and operating ratios classified by the type of source that collects and compiles them.

▶ **SUMMARY**

Financial statements are prepared using an historical basis and thus are based on past transactions. Investors find this information useful from a stewardship viewpoint, but managers and other external users of financial statements are more interested in the future course a company is likely to take. Therefore, financial statements assist users in making inferences about a company's future. Financial statement analysis provides users with the needed information.

The principal tools of financial statement analysis consist of (1) comparative financial statements showing year-to-year changes, (2) index-number trend series, which show the relative changes of the subsequent periods' items compared to a base period, often called **horizontal analysis,** (3) **common-size statements,** also called **vertical analysis,** where each component of a statement is shown as a percentage of the total instead of in absolute dollars, and (4) **ratio analysis,** where a numerical value is shown in relation to another value. An **index number,** which is used to measure a quality that is common to a group of items, has little useful value by itself. When an index number is used as part of a **trend** analysis, which indicates the general direction that the measured attribute is taking, then the index number achieves its greatest usefulness. The **velocity of trend,** which measures the rate of movement in a general direction, is also extremely useful for predicting the future course of a business.

Ratios have various classifications. One group of ratios is the short-term liquidity classification, which is related to **working capital** and includes the **current ratio,** the **acid-test (quick) ratio,** the **average-accounts-receivable turnover ratio,** the **collection period for accounts receivable,** the **inventory-turnover ratio,** and the **days to sell inventory.**

Another group of ratios is the capital structure and long-term solvency ratios, which include the **debt-to-equity ratio** and the **times interest earned ratio.**

A third ratio group is the return-on-investment classification, which includes the **return on total assets ratio** and the **return on common stockholders' equity ratio.** Because a firm is operated primarily to benefit common stockholders, a major objective of most firms is to improve and maintain the return to common stockholders. One method of accomplishing this is to increase earnings. Another method is to make use of **financial leverage,** which is borrowing funds or selling preferred stock, in place of raising additional funds through the sale of common stock. When the fixed cost (in percentage terms) paid to lenders or to the preferred stockholders is less than the return on total assets, **positive financial leverage** is said to exist. When the reverse is true, **negative financial leverage** exists.

The most often quoted statistic that relates to a firm's operating performance is **earnings per share.** This measure indicates the amount of net income available to common stockholders on a per-share basis. When a firm has potentially dilutive securities outstanding, such as options, warrants, convertible bonds payable, or convertible preferred stock, the effects of these securities' *assumed* conversion into common stock are factored into the original EPS and shown as an additional EPS statistic labeled **fully diluted earnings per share.** When this figure is shown, the original EPS is labeled *primary* earnings per share.

Still another grouping of ratios is the market measure ratios classification. This includes the **price-earnings ratio,** the **dividend payout ratio,** and the **dividend yield ratio.** The price-earnings ratio provides investors with a means of comparing competing investments to determine which ones are expensive or inexpensive. The dividend payout ratio and the dividend yield ratio provide investors with data that help them achieve their investment objectives.

Ratios can be potent analytical tools if they are analyzed in conjunction with the trend of each ratio. Although it is important to see a particular relationship at a point in time, it is more important to examine the trend of a ratio and the velocity of the trend for that ratio.

► **APPENDIX 18-A** **Sources of Information on Financial and Operating Ratios**

A good way to achieve familiarity with the wide variety of published financial and operating ratios is to classify them by the type of source that collects or compiles them. The specific sources given under each category are intended to exemplify the type of material available. These are by no means complete lists.

Professional and Commercial Organizations

Dun & Bradstreet, Inc., Business Economics Division, New York, N.Y.
  Key Business Ratios. Important operating and financial ratios in 190 lines.
  Selected operating cost figures for many retailing, wholesaling, manufacturing lines, as well as for contract construction; service/transportation/communication; finance/insurance/real estate; agriculture/forestry/fishing; mining.
  Cost-of-Doing-Business Series. Typical operating ratios for 185 lines of business, showing national averages. They represent a percentage of business receipts reported by a representative sample of the total of all federal tax returns.

Moody's Investor Service, New York, N.Y.
  Moody's Manuals contain financial and operating ratios on individual companies covered.

National Cash Register Company. *Expenses in Retail Business*. Biennial.
  Operating ratios for 35 lines of retail business, as taken from trade associations and other sources, including many from *Barometer of Small Business*.

Robert Morris Associates. *Annual Statement Studies*.
  Financial and operating ratios for about 300 lines of business—manufacturers, wholesalers, retailers, services, and contractors—based on information obtained from member banks of RMA. Data are broken down by company size.

Standard & Poor's Corporation
  Industry Surveys in two parts: (1) Basic Analysis and (2) Current Analysis contains many industry and individual company ratios.
  Analysts Handbook. "Composite corporate per-share data—by industries," for over 90 industries. Statistics and percentages cover 13 components, including sales, operating profits, depreciation, earnings dividends, and the like.
  Industry Surveys. Basic data on 36 important industries, with financial comparisons of the leading companies in each industry. Includes a "Basic Analysis" for each, revised annually. A "Current Analysis" is published quarterly for each industry. A monthly "Trends and Projections" includes tables of economic and industry indicators.

Almanac of Business and Industrial Financial Ratios by Leo Troy. Prentice-Hall, Englewood Cliffs, N.J.

A compilation of corporate performance ratios (operating and financial). The significance of these ratios is explained. All industries are covered in the study; each industry is subdivided by asset size.

The Federal Government

Small Business Administration
Publications containing industry statistics:
Small Marketers Aid
Small Business Management Series
Business Service Bulletins

U.S. Department of Commerce
Census of Business—Wholesale Trade—Summary Statistics. Monthly Wholesale Trade Report. Ratio of operating costs to sales.

U.S. Department of the Treasury
Statistics of Income, Corporation Income Tax Returns. Operating Statistics based on income tax returns.

Federal Trade Commission—Securities and Exchange Commission
Quarterly Financial Report for Manufacturing, Mining, and Trade Corporations. Contains operating ratios and balance sheet ratios as well as the balance sheet in ratio format.

U.S. Internal Revenue Service
Source Book: Statistics of Income: Corporation Income Tax Returns. Washington, D.C.: U.S. Government Printing Office. Annual. "Balance sheet, income statement, tax items by major and minor industries, broken down by size of total assets."
Statistics of Income: Corporation Income Tax Returns. Washington, D.C.: U.S. Government Printing Office. Annual. Balance sheet and income statement statistics from a sample of corporate returns. Includes tables by major industry, by asset size, and so on. Includes historical summaries.

▶ **GLOSSARY OF KEY TERMS**

Common-size statements   A financial statement where each component of the statement is shown as a percentage instead of as dollar amounts. (p. 933)
Financial leverage   Using borrowed funds or funds acquired from the sale of preferred stock—both of which require fixed costs for the use of the funds—in place of funds acquired from the sale of common stock. (p. 951)
Horizontal analysis   See **trend.** (p. 933)
Index number   A measure used to indicate qualities common to a group of items. (p. 931)
Negative financial leverage   When the cost of borrowed funds (and/or the dividend cost of preferred stock) is greater than the return on total assets and the return on common stockholders' equity is less than the return on total assets. (p. 952)
Positive financial leverage   When the cost of borrowed funds (and/or the dividend cost of preferred stock) is less than the return on total assets and the return on common stockholders' equity exceeds the return on total assets. (p. 951)
Ratio   An expression of the mathematical relationship between one quantity and another. (p. 936)
Trend   The general direction of financial data expressed in terms of a base period (usually one year). (p. 929)

Velocity of trend   The rate of movement of financial data in a general direction. (p. 929)

Vertical analysis   See **common-size statements.**   (p. 933)

Working capital   The excess of current assets over current liabilities.   (p. 937)

▶ **GLOSSARY OF KEY RATIOS**

Accounts-receivable-turnover ratio   Computed by dividing net credit sales by the average accounts receivable.   (p. 943)

Acid-test ratio (quick ratio)   A numerator composed of cash, short-term marketable securities, and accounts (and short-term notes) receivable divided by a denominator of current liabilities.   (p. 942)

Collection period for accounts receivable   A measure of the number of days it takes, on average, to collect accounts (and notes) receivable. It is obtained by dividing the average-accounts-receivable-turnover ratio into 360 days.   (p. 944)

Current ratio   A firm's current assets divided by its current liabilities.   (p. 939)

Days to sell inventory   A measure of the number of days it takes to sell the average inventory, computed by dividing the number of days in a year by the average inventory turnover.   (p. 946)

Debt-to-equity ratio   A measure of the relationship between total debt (Current liabilities + Long-term liabilities) to total stockholders' equity, computed by dividing total debt by stockholders' equity.   (p. 947)

Dividend payout ratio   Computed by dividing common stock dividends per share by primary earnings per share.   (p. 957)

Dividend yield ratio   Computed by dividing a firm's dividends per share by its market price per share.   (p. 957)

Earnings per share (primary earnings per share)   Computed by dividing the numerator of a firm's net income available to common stockholders by the denominator of the weighted-average number of common shares outstanding for the period. (p. 954)

Fully diluted earnings per share   Earnings per share adjusted for the assumed conversion of all potentially dilutive securities.   (p. 955)

Inventory-turnover ratio   A measurement of the average speed with which inventories move through and out of the enterprise, computed by dividing cost of goods sold by average inventory.   (p. 945)

Price-earnings ratio   Computed by dividing the market price of a firm's share of stock by the primary earnings per share.   (p. 956)

Return on common stockholders' equity   Computed by dividing a numerator consisting of net income minus preferred dividends by a denominator of average common stockholders' equity.   (p. 950)

Return on total assets   A measure of the effectiveness of asset utilization computed by dividing a numerator consisting of a firm's net income plus its after-tax cost of interest by a denominator consisting of the firm's average assets.   (p. 950)

Times interest earned ratio   A measurement of the likelihood that long-term creditors will continue to receive their interest when due, computed by dividing the numerator consisting of net income, income taxes, and interest cost by the denominator consisting of the firm's interest cost.   (p. 948)

▶ **GLOSSARY OF SYNONYMS**

Days' sales in accounts receivable   See **collection period for accounts receivable.**

Horizontal analysis   See **trend.**

Quick ratio   See **acid-test ratio.**

Trading on the equity   See **financial leverage.**

Vertical analysis   See **common-size statements.**

▶ **LIBRARY ASSIGNMENT**

Read the following:

Brandt, Lloyd, Joseph R. Danos, and J. Herman Brasseaux. "Financial Statement Analysis: Benefits and Pitfalls." Part 1, *Practical Accountant,* May 1989, pp. 34–38, 40, 42, 44, 46–47.

———. "Financial Statement Analysis: Benefits and Pitfalls." Part 2, *Practical Accountant,* June 1989, pp. 68–70, 72–78.

Gibson, Charles H, "How Industry Perceives Financial Ratios." *Management Accounting,* April 1982, pp. 13–19.

O'Donnell, Robert G. "How Users Analyze Financial Statements." *Corporate Accounting,* Summer 1986, pp. 14–18.

Siegel, Joel G. "How Management Can Make Significant Use of Financial Analysis to Evaluate the Health of a Firm." *National Public Accountant,* February 1982, pp. 25–29.

———. "Quality of Earnings Concept—A Survey." *Financial Analysts Journal,* March/April 1982, pp. 60–68.

Yallapragada, RamMohan R., and Arleene P. Breaux. "Financial Statement Analysis—Its Use in Lending Institutions." *National Public Accountant,* January 1989, pp. 32–37.

▶ **SELF-TEST**

True or False

1. A company's debt-to-equity ratio is 1.0 if it has $125,000 of total current liabilities, $275,000 of total noncurrent liabilities, and $400,000 of total stockholders' equity.

2. If net income is $180,000 in 19x4 and $210,000 in 19x5, the absolute dollar and percentage changes are $30,000 increase and 16.7 percent.

3. For the period of 19x4 to 19x6, the accounts receivable balances were $120,000, $150,000, and $180,000, respectively. If 19x4 is the base year, the index trend is 100, 125, and 150 respectively.

4. For the period of 19x4 to 19x6, the accounts payable balances were $120,000, $150,000, and $180,000, respectively. If 19x5 is the base year, the index trend is 100, 125, and 150, respectively.

5. Horizontal analysis tells the user the proportion that a single account represents of a total group or subgroup.

6. Given the data below, the common-size percentages for patents is decreasing.

	Patents		Total Assets
19x3	$150,000	19x3	$1,000,000
19x2	$200,000	19x2	$2,000,000

7. If total current assets exceed total current liabilities, the excess amount is known as *working capital.*

8. The current ratio equals the total current assets divided by the total current liabilities.

9. The current ratio is a measure of short-term solvency.

10. The acid test is a weaker measure than the current ratio because inventory and prepaid assets are removed from the current asset amount.

11. If the average accounts receivable turnover ratio increases, a likely cause is that average accounts receivable have decreased while the net credit sales have remained constant.

12. The collection period for accounts receivable increases when the average account receivables decrease and the net credit sales remain constant.

13. The inventory turnover ratio indicates the average length of time inventory stays on display.
14. The average length of time inventory stays on display is 360 days divided by the inventory-turnover ratio.
15. A comprehensive ratio of a company's capital structure is the debt-to-equity ratio.

Multiple Choice

1. All of the following are principal tools of financial statement analysis except
   a. Trend analysis.
   b. Structural analysis.
   c. Factor analysis.
   d. Ratio analysis.
2. Which of the following is not a short-term liquidity ratio?
   a. Inventory turnover.
   b. Accounts-receivable turnover.
   c. Acid test.
   d. Times interest earned.
3. Which of the following is not a market measure ratio?
   a. Debt to equity.
   b. Price earnings.
   c. Dividend payout.
   d. Dividend yield.
4. The accounts-receivable-turnover ratio is equal to
   a. Sales divided by accounts receivable.
   b. Sales divided by average accounts receivable.
   c. Net credit sales divided by accounts receivable.
   d. Net credit sales divided by average accounts receivable.
5. Which of the following is not used to compute the acid-test ratio?
   a. Accounts receivable.
   b. Inventory.
   c. Cash.
   d. Accounts payable.
6. The inventory-turnover ratio is equal to
   a. Cost of goods sold divided by average inventory.
   b. Average inventory divided by cost of goods sold.
   c. Cost of goods sold divided by 360.
   d. Cost of goods sold divided by ending inventory.
7. Assume that current assets are greater than current liabilities. Which of the following transactions will not increase the current ratio?
   a. Selling inventory on credit for a profit.
   b. Paying accounts payable with cash.
   c. Collecting accounts receivable.
   d. Selling inventory for cash at a profit.
8. When the cost for borrowed funds is greater than the return on total assets, and the return on common stockholders' equity is less than the return on total assets, the result is
   a. Positive financial leverage.
   b. Unprofitable operations.
   c. Securities dilution.
   d. Negative financial leverage.

▶ **QUESTIONS**

1. Give four broad categories of analysis tools.
2. Is the trend of the past a good predictor of the future? Give reasons for your argument.
3. Which is the better indicator of significant change—the absolute amount of change or the change in percentage? Why?
4. What conditions would prevent the computation of a valid percentage change? Give an example.
5. What are some of the criteria to be used in picking out a base year in an index-number comparative analysis?
6. What information can be obtained from trend analysis?
7. What is a common-size financial statement? How do you prepare one?
8. What does a common-size financial statement tell about an enterprise?
9. Do all ratios have significance? Explain.
10. What are some of the limitations of ratio analysis?
11. Give three ratios that can be prepared by use of balance sheet figures only.
12. Give four ratios that require data from both the balance sheet and the income statement.
13. Why is short-term liquidity so significant? Explain from the viewpoint of various parties concerned.
14. The concept of working capital is simple (that is, the excess of current assets over current liabilities). What are some of the factors that make this simple computation complicated in practice?
15. What are cash equivalents? How should an analyst value them in his analysis?
16. Your careful computation of the working capitals of Companies A and B reveals that both have the same amount of working capital. Are you ready to conclude that the liquidity position of both is the same? Explain.
17. What is the current ratio? What does it measure? What are the reasons for its widespread use?
18. What does the average-accounts-receivable-turnover ratio measure?
19. What is the collection period for accounts receivable? What does it measure?
20. A company's collection period is 60 days this year, as compared to 40 days last year. Give three or more possible reasons for this change.
21. What is an accounts receivable aging schedule? What is its use in the analysis of financial statements?
22. What are the repercussions to an enterprise of (a) overinvestment or (b) underinvestment in inventories?
23. What is the rule of thumb governing the expected size of the current ratio? What dangers are there in using this rule of thumb mechanically?
24. What are the dangers for investors who rely on EPS?
25. What is financial leverage?
26. What is the difference between positive financial leverage and negative financial leverage?
27. Assume you are considering the purchase of common stock in a particular firm. As an inducement to speed your contemplated purchase, your stockbroker states that the company has no long-term debt and has never borrowed any funds except in the ordinary course of purchasing its direct materials on account. Comment on your stockbroker's assertion that the company is so sound it never had to borrow funds for any period longer than 30 days.
28. Different firms traditionally have different debt-to-equity ratios. Use examples to explain why this is so.
29. Is there a difference between the positive leverage obtained from long-term debt and preferred stock? Explain.

30. Different firms have different dividend payout ratios. Explain why.
31. Different investors have different investment objectives. Explain.

▸ **EXERCISES**   **E18–1**   **Preparation of Year-to-Year Changes for a Balance Sheet**
Given below are comparative balance sheets for Jem Stores, Inc.:

JEM STORES, INC.
Comparative Condensed Balance Sheets
As of June 30, 19x4, and 19x3

	19x4	19x3
Assets		
Cash	$ 20,000	$ 24,000
Accounts receivable, net	125,000	93,000
Inventory	192,000	80,000
Other current assets	11,000	8,000
Plant and equipment (net)	112,000	95,000
Total assets	$460,000	$300,000
Liabilities and Equity		
Accounts payable	$112,000	$ 48,000
Federal income tax payable	22,000	32,000
Long-term liabilities	111,000	75,000
Common stock.	145,000	110,000
Retained earnings	70,000	35,000
Total liabilities and equity	$460,000	$300,000

Required   *a.* Prepare comparative balance sheets showing the year-to-year changes in *both* dollars and percent. Use 19x3 as the base period.
b. Write a brief report highlighting the changes you consider important.

E18–2   **Preparation of Year-to-Year Changes for an Income Statement**
Given below are comparative income statements for Jem Stores, Inc.:

JEM STORES, INC.
Condensed Income Statements
For the Years Ended June 30, 19x4, and 19x3

	19x4	19x3
Net sales	$1,820,000	$1,400,000
Cost of goods sold	1,120,000	700,000
Gross margin on sales.	700,000	700,000
Marketing and administrative costs	644,000	602,000
Income before federal income tax	56,000	98,000
Income tax	22,000	39,000
Net income	$ 34,000	$ 59,000

Required   *a.* Prepare comparative income statements showing the year-to-year changes in *both* dollars and percent. Use 19x3 as the base period.
b. Write a brief report highlighting the changes you consider important.

E18–3   **Index-Number Trend Series**

The Burrows Company provides you with the following selected data:

	19x8	19x7	19x6	19x5	19x4
Sales	$837,015	$711,083	$594,000	$517,500	$450,000
Cost of goods sold	415,821	320,484	261,012	214,210	180,000
Gross margin	421,194	390,599	332,988	303,290	270,000
Marketing costs	109,850	104,650	83,850	76,050	65,000
Administrative costs	142,206	124,216	111,600	97,200	90,000
Net income	115,525	102,205	93,100	79,800	70,000

Required   *a.* Convert the data into an index-number trend series using 19x4 as the base period.

b. Write a brief explanation of the information revealed by the index-number trend series that is not readily apparent from the given data.

E18–4   **Preparation of Common-Size Balance Sheets**

Refer to the balance sheets given in Exercise 18–1.

Required   *a.* Prepare comparative common-size balance sheets for Jem Stores, Inc.

b. Write a brief report highlighting the changes in 19x4 from 19x3 that you consider important.

E18–5   **Preparation of Common-Size Income Statements**

Refer to the income statements given in Exercise 18–2.

Required   *a.* Prepare comparative common-size income statements for Jem Stores, Inc.

b. Write a brief report highlighting the changes in 19x4 from 19x3 that you consider important.

E18–6   **Calculation of Ratios**

The following data apply to items 1 through 7:

The statement of financial position and income statement for MND Corporation for the 19x0–x1 fiscal year are presented below:

MND CORPORATION
Statement of Financial Position
May 31, 19x1
(in thousands)

Assets

Cash		$ 8,000
Accounts receivable		12,000
Inventory		9,000
Property, plant, and equipment	$48,400	
Less: Allowance for depreciation.	11,900	36,500
Total assets		$65,500

Liabilities and Stockholders' Equity

Accounts payable—trade		$10,700
Notes payable (short-term)		5,300
Mortgage bonds—due in 19x4		9,500
Common stock—$10 par value, 4.5 million shares authorized, 2.5 million shares issued and outstanding		25,000
Paid-in capital in excess of par.		5,000
Retained earnings		10,000
Total liabilities and stockholders' equity . . .		$65,500

MND CORPORATION
Income Statement
For the Year Ended May 31, 19x1
(in thousands)

Cash sales		$10,000
Credit sales		60,000
Total sales		70,000
Cost of sales:		
Inventory of finished goods 6/1/x0	$ 4,000	
Cost of goods manufactured	50,000	
Cost of goods available	54,000	
Inventory of finished goods 5/31/x1	5,000	49,000
Gross margin on sales.		21,000
Operating costs:		
Marketing	3,000	
General and administrative	10,800	13,800
Operating income.		7,200
Interest cost		1,200
Income before federal income tax		6,000
Federal income tax		2,400
Net income		$ 3,600

1. MND's current ratio is
   a. 1.81.
   b. 1.25.
   c. 1.14.
   d. 2.71.
   e. Some amount other than those shown above.
2. The average collection period for accounts receivable is
   a. 5 days.
   b. 61.7 days.

    c. 72 days.

    d. 36 days.

    e. Some amount other than those shown above.

3. The inventory turnover for finished goods for the current fiscal year was

    a. 10.9 times.

    b. 10 times.

    c. 9.8 times.

    d. 11.1 times.

    e. Some amount other than those shown above.

4. The ratio of total debt to stockholders' equity is

    a. .73 : 1.

    b. .64 : 1.

    c. .40 : 1.

    d. .24 : 1.

    e. Some amount other than those shown above.

5. MND's earnings per share for the 19x0–x1 fiscal year is

    a. $.80/share.

    b. $2.40/share.

    c. $1.33/share.

    d. $1.44/share.

    e. Some amount other than those shown above.

6. The return on stockholders' investment is

    a. 15%.

    b. 5.5%.

    c. 9%.

    d. 9.2%.

    e. Some amount other than those shown above.

7. The times interest earned ratio for MND is

    a. 7.9 times.

    b. 3 times.

    c. 5 times.

    d. 6 times.

    e. Some amount other than those shown above.

(CMA Adapted)

E18–7   **Effects of Transactions on Short-Term Liquidity Ratios**

The following data apply to items 1 through 4:

    Depoole Company is a manufacturer of industrial products and employs a calendar year for financial reporting purposes. Items 1 through 4 present several of Depoole's transactions during 19x0. Assume total quick assets exceeded total current liabilities both before and after each transaction described. Further assume Depoole has positive profits in 19x0 and a credit balance throughout 19x0 in its retained earnings account.

1. Payment of a trade account payable of $64,500 would

    a. Increase the current ratio, but the quick ratio would not be affected.

    b. Increase the quick ratio, but the current ratio would not be affected.

    c. Increase both the current and quick ratios.

    d. Decrease both the current and quick ratios.

    e. Have no effect on the current and quick ratios.

2. The purchase of direct materials for $85,000 on open account would

    a. Increase the current ratio.

    b. Decrease the current ratio.

    c. Increase net working capital.

    d. Decrease net working capital.

    e. Increase both the current ratio and net working capital.

3. The collection of a current accounts receivable of $29,000 would

    a. Increase the current ratio.

    b. Decrease the current ratio.

    c. Increase the quick ratio.

    d. Decrease the quick ratio.

    e. Not affect the current or quick ratios.

4. Obsolete inventory of $125,000 was written off during 19x0. This would

    a. Decrease the quick ratio.

    b. Increase the quick ratio.

    c. Increase net working capital.

    d. Decrease the current ratio.

    e. Decrease both the current and quick ratios.

(CMA Adapted)

E18–8 **Calculation of Ratios**

The following data apply to items 1 through 5:

The 19x9 financial statements for Johanson Company are reproduced below:

JOHANSON COMPANY
Statement of Financial Position
December 31, 19x8, and 19x9
(in thousands)

	19x8	19x9
Assets		
Current assets:		
Cash and temporary investments	$ 380	$ 400
Accounts receivable (net)	1,500	1,700
Inventories	2,120	2,200
Total current assets	4,000	4,300
Long-term assets:		
Land	500	500
Building and equipment (net)	4,000	4,700
Total long-term assets	4,500	5,200
Total assets	$8,500	$9,500
Liabilities and Equities		
Current liabilities:		
Accounts payable	$ 700	$1,400
Current portion long-term debt	500	1,000
Total current liabilities	1,200	2,400
Long-term debt	4,000	3,000
Total liabilities	5,200	5,400
Stockholders' equity:		
Common stock	3,000	3,000
Retained earnings	300	1,100
Total stockholders' equity	3,300	4,100
Total liabilities and equities	$8,500	$9,500

JOHANSON COMPANY
Statement of Income and Retained Earnings
For the Year Ended December 31, 19x9
(in thousands)

Net sales		$28,800
Less: Cost of goods sold	$15,120	
Marketing costs.	7,180	
Administrative costs	4,100	
Interest	400	
Income taxes	800	27,600
Net income		1,200
Retained earnings, January 1		300
Subtotal		1,500
Cash dividends declared and paid		400
Retained earnings, December 31		$ 1,100

1. The acid-test ratio for 19x9 for Johanson Company is
   a. 1.1 to 1.
   b. .9 to 1.
   c. 1.8 to 1.
   d. .2 to 1.
   e. .17 to 1.

2. The average number of days' sales outstanding in 19x9 for Johanson Company is
   a. 18 days.
   b. 360 days.
   c. 20 days.
   d. 4.4 days.
   e. 80 days.

3. The times interest earned ratio in 19x9 for Johanson Company is
   a. 3 times.
   b. 1 times.
   c. 72 times.
   d. 2 times.
   e. 6 times.

4. The inventory turnover in 19x9 for Johanson Company is
   a. 13.6 times.
   b. 12.5 times.
   c. .9 times.
   d. 7 times.
   e. 51.4 times.

5. The dividend payout ratio in 19x9 for Johanson Company is
   a. 100%.
   b. 36%.
   c. 20%.
   d. 8.8%.
   e. 33.3%.

(CMA Adapted)

E18–9   **Calculation of Ratios**

The previous year's financial statements for the Zeta Corporation are given below:

ZETA CORPORATION
Income Statement
For the Year Ended December 31, 19x1

Net sales		$1,200,000
Cost of goods sold		480,000
Gross margin		720,000
Depreciation	$ 45,000	
Marketing and administrative costs	300,000	345,000
Income before taxes		375,000
Income taxes (48%)		180,000
Net income		$ 195,000

ZETA CORPORATION
Balance Sheet
As of December 31, 19x1

Assets

Current assets:		
Cash	$ 30,000	
Marketable securities	3,000	
Accounts receivable	67,000	
Inventories	90,000	
Total current assets		$ 190,000
Plant and equipment	870,000	
Less: Accumulated depreciation	270,000	600,000
Total assets		$ 790,000

Liabilities and Equity

Current liabilities:		
Accounts payable	$ 66,000	
Notes payable	32,000	
Total current liabilities		$ 98,000
Long-term debt		142,000
Equities:		
Common stock, $20 par	345,000	
Retained earnings	205,000	550,000
Total liabilities and equity		$ 790,000

The following additional data are available:

1. Balances of selected data at the beginning of the year consist of
   a. Accounts receivable, $60,000.
   b. Inventories, $75,000.
   c. Total assets, $720,000.
   d. Total stockholders' equity, $425,000.
2. The interest cost for the year amounted to $17,400 and is included as part of the administrative costs.
3. Dividends paid during the year were $69,000 at the rate of $4 per share.
4. All sales were credit sales.
5. The market value per share was $55.

Required   Compute the following:

   a. Current ratio.
   b. Acid-test ratio.
   c. Accounts receivable turnover.

d. Collection period of receivables. (Use 360 days.)
e. Inventory turnover.
f. Days to sell inventory. (Use 360 days.)
g. Debt-to-equity ratio.
h. Times interest earned.

E18–10 Calculation of Ratios

Refer to the financial statements and the additional data given in Exercise 18–9.

Required *a.* Compute the following:
 (1) Return on total assets.
 (2) Return on common stockholders' equity.
 (3) Earnings per share.
 (4) Price-earnings ratio.
 (5) Dividend payout ratio.
 (6) Dividend yield ratio.
 b. Was the financial leverage for the year positive or negative? Explain.

E18–11 Interpretation of Ratios

Thorpe Company is a wholesale distributor of professional equipment and supplies. The company's sales have averaged about $900,000 annually for the three-year period 19x3–x5. The firm's total assets at the end of 19x5 amounted to $850,000.

The president of Thorpe Company has asked the controller to prepare a report summarizing the financial aspects of the company's operations for the past three years. This report will be presented to the board of directors at its next meeting.

In addition to comparative financial statements, the controller has decided to present a number of relevant financial ratios that can assist in the identification and interpretation of trends. At the request of the controller, the accounting staff has calculated the following ratios for the three-year period 19x3–x5:

	19x3	19x4	19x5
Current ratio	2.00	2.13	2.18
Acid-test (quick) ratio	1.20	1.10	0.97
Accounts receivable turnover	9.72	8.57	7.13
Inventory turnover	5.25	4.80	3.80
Percent of total debt to total assets	44	41	38
Percent of long-term debt to total assets	25	22	19
Sales to fixed assets (fixed asset turnover)	1.75	1.88	1.99
Sales as a percent of 19x3 sales	1.00	1.03	1.06
Gross margin percentage	40.0	38.6	38.5
Net income to sales	7.8%	7.8%	8.0%
Return on total assets	8.5%	8.6%	8.7%
Return on stockholders' equity	15.1%	14.6%	14.1%

In the preparation of his report, the controller has decided to first examine the financial ratios independently of any other data to determine if the ratios themselves reveal any significant trends over the three-year period.

Required Answer the following questions. Indicate in each case which ratio(s) you used in arriving at your conclusion.

a. The current ratio is increasing while the acid-test (quick) ratio is decreasing. Using the ratios provided, identify and explain the contributing factor(s) for this apparently divergent trend.
b. In terms of the ratios provided, what conclusion(s) can be drawn regarding the company's use of financial leverage during the 19x3–x5 period?

(CMA Adapted)

E18–12   **Completion of Missing Income Statement Data**

Complete the following comparative operating statement of Forward Corporation:

FORWARD CORPORATION
Operating Statement
For Years Ending on December 31
(in thousands of dollars)

	19x4	19x3	19x2	Cumulative Amount	Annual Average Amount
Net sales		4,560	3,996		
Cost of goods sold	3,820				3,840
Gross profit		600			714
Total operating costs					560
Income before taxes	372	50	40		
Net income	186	27	20		

E18–13   **Completion of Missing Balance Sheet Data through the Use of Ratios**

The Rigid Company's balance sheet consists of only the following items:

Cash.	—
Accounts receivable	—
Inventory	$ 80
Fixed assets (net)	—
Current liabilities	—
Common stock	100
Retained earnings	—

The following information is also available:

1. Total assets minus liabilities equals $220.
2. Stockholders' equity equals 2.75 times total debt.
3. Current ratio is 2.25 to 1.
4. Inventory turnover is 14.4 times (based on cost of goods sold and ending inventory).
5. Days' sales in accounts receivable are 15 days (based on a 360-day year).
6. Gross profit is 25 percent of cost of goods sold.

Required   Use the given information to complete the balance sheet.

E18–14   **Preparation of Income Statements from Selected Information and Interpretation of Results**

The following data are available for the Disco Company for 19x1 and 19x2:

	19x2	19x1
Gross profit percentage	40%	35%
Ending accounts receivable	$360,000	$216,000
Number of days' sales in ending accounts receivable	60	50
Income tax rate.	40%	30%
Net income as a percent of sales	7%	8%
Maximum credit allowed to creditors	60 days	30 days

Required   a. Prepare income statements in comparative form for the two years.

b. Comment on the trend in sales volume, gross profit percentage, and net income percentage.

c. Compute the ending accounts-receivable-turnover ratios, and briefly comment on the trend in view of the changing credit terms. All sales are made on credit.

E18–15   Preparation of a Balance Sheet from Selected Ratios and Other Information

The Burnt Company had maintained its records in a safe place for many years. However, a fire destroyed them just before the company's June 19x8 fiscal year-end, leaving only the following information:

Inventory	$ 96,000
Common stock, no par	120,000
Net assets	300,000
Current ratio.	2.5 to 1
Inventory turnover	12
Accounts receivable turnover	20
Gross profit	25%
Ratio of debt (all current) to equity.	1 to 2.5

Additional balance sheet accounts must be computed. There were no prepaid costs or accumulated depreciation at June 30, 19x8.

Required   Prepare a balance sheet in good form. Use a 360-day year in your computations.

E18–16   Effects of Transactions on Ratios

Give the effect of each of the following transactions or events on working capital, current ratio, and the quick ratio (acid test). Assume a current ratio of 3 to 1 and a quick ratio of 1.4 to 1 before any of the transactions that follow. (Effects: I for increase, D for decrease, and N for no effect.)

	Working Capital	Current Ratio	Acid-Test Ratio
1. Company pays $5,000 short-term notes payable in cash.	_____	_____	_____
2. Company sells equipment for $3,000 cash.	_____	_____	_____
3. Company purchases short-term marketable securities for $4,000.	_____	_____	_____
4. Company purchases building by issuing common stock (par value $20) valued at $40,000.	_____	_____	_____
5. Company purchases equipment for $2,000 cash.	_____	_____	_____
6. Company pays long-term bond payable, $5,000.	_____	_____	_____
7. Company collects $2,000 on a long-term note receivable.	_____	_____	_____
8. Company purchases inventory of $5,000 for $2,000 cash plus long-term note payable of $3,000.	_____	_____	_____
9. Company issues short-term note payable and receives $5,000 cash.	_____	_____	_____
10. Fire destroys $4,000 of inventory (no insurance).	_____	_____	_____
11. Obsolete inventory of $3,000 was found and written off.	_____	_____	_____
12. Accounts payable of $10,000 were paid in cash.	_____	_____	_____
13. Land with a book value of $20,000 was sold for $15,000.	_____	_____	_____
14. Merchandise inventory of $2,000 bought on open trade credit.	_____	_____	_____
15. Automobile sold for $2,000 at loss of $6,000.	_____	_____	_____

E18–17   **Computation of ROI and Effects of Financial Leverage**

The Exeter Company makes the following information available:

	Beginning of 19x3	Ending of 19x3
Current assets	$ 450,000	$ 540,000
Property, plant, and equipment—net	1,335,000	1,425,000
Total assets	$1,785,000	$1,965,000
Current liabilities	$ 210,000	$ 240,000
Long-term debt	300,000	300,000
Preferred stock, $20 par value, 12% dividend rate	225,000	225,000
Common stock	450,000	450,000
Retained earnings	600,000	750,000
Total liabilities and stockholders' equity	$1,785,000	$1,965,000

The company had a net income of $290,000, and its income tax rate for 19x3 was 30 percent. Interest cost for the year amounted to $36,000.

Required   *a.* Compute the return on total assets.
b. Compute the return on common stockholders' equity.
c. Was the financial leverage for the year positive or negative? Explain.

E18–18   **Calculation of Short-Term Liquidity Ratios**

Given the following for the Rex Corporation for the years 19x1 and 19x2:

REX CORPORATION
Selected Financial Data

	As of December 31	
	19x2	19x1
Cash	$ 15,000	$120,000
Accounts receivable (net)	75,000	225,000
Merchandise inventory	135,000	225,000
Short-term marketable securities	45,000	15,000
Land and buildings (net)	510,000	540,000
Mortgage payable (no current portion)	405,000	420,000
Accounts payable (trade)	105,000	165,000
Short-term notes payable	300,000	60,000

	Year Ended December 31	
	19x2	19x1
Cash sales	$2,700,000	$2,400,000
Credit sales	750,000	1,200,000
Cost of goods sold	1,500,000	2,100,000

Required   Compute the following:

a. Quick (acid-test) ratio as of December 31, 19x2.
b. Receivable turnover for 19x2.
c. Merchandise inventory turnover for 19x2.
d. Current ratio at December 31, 19x2.

► **PROBLEMS**   P18–19   **Construction of a Balance Sheet from Selected Ratios and Other Data**

It is Sunday, and you have just opened your briefcase to work with Elusive Company's December 31, 19x1, balance sheet. To your dismay, you discover the computer printouts that your assistant stuffed into your briefcase contain only the sketchy information below:

1. Accounts receivable and inventory were the same at the end of the year as at the beginning.
2. Net income, $1,200.
3. Times interest earned is 5 (ignore income taxes). The company has outstanding 5 percent bonds issued at par.
4. Net income to sales, 20 percent; gross margin ratio, 40 percent; inventory turnover, 6.
5. Accounts receivable turnover, 4.
6. Sales to working capital, 5; current ratio, 1.6.
7. Acid-test ratio, 1.0 (exclude prepaid costs).
8. Plant and equipment is one-third depreciated.
9. Dividend paid on 8 percent nonparticipating preferred stock was $80. The effective yield in the current year was 10 percent. These shares were issued two years ago at par.
10. Earnings per common share, $5.60.
11. Common stock has a $20 par value and was issued at a 5 percent premium.
12. Retained earnings at January 1, 19x1, $1,800.

Required   Given the information available, complete the balance sheet as of December 31, 19x1. Also, determine the amount of dividends paid on the common stock in 19x1.

Cash	_____
Accounts receivable	_____
Inventory	_____
Prepaid costs	_____
Plant and equipment (net).	$12,000
Total assets	_____
Current liabilities.	_____
Bonds payable.	_____
Stockholders' equity	_____
Total liabilities and equity. . . .	_____

P18–20   **Comprehensive Ratio Analysis with Industry Comparisons**

Early one morning, even before your coffee break, a senior member of your institution's financial policy committee hurriedly walks into your office and hands you the following data. "This afternoon, our committee will consider the relative merits of Re Company and Flex Company, which are both in the flexible hose manufacturing business," said he, adding, "Please prepare a preliminary ratio analysis and conclusions so as to enable me to give intelligent answers to expected questions."

Balance Sheets
As of December 31, 19x7
(in thousands)

	Re Company	Flex Company
Cash	$ 45	$ 30
Accounts receivable	150	270
Inventory	165	351
Plant and equipment, net	450	720
Total assets	$ 810	$1,371
Current liabilities	$ 171	$ 303
Bonds payable	225	300
Common stock, $15 par	150	210
Retained earnings	264	558
Total liabilities and equity	$ 810	$1,371

Data from Income Statements
For the Year Ending December 31, 19x7
(in thousands)

Sales	$1,500	$2,100
Cost of goods sold	975	1,365
Interest cost	21	24
Income before taxes	180	264
Net income	126	185
Tax rate	30%	30%

Balances at January 1, 19x7
(in thousands)

Accounts receivable	$ 138	$ 258
Inventory	153	339
Total assets	750	1,275

Other Selected Data for 19x7

Dividends paid per share	$ 7.50	$ 7.50
Market price per share at year-end	216	255

Flexible Hose Manufacturing Industry
Averages for 19x7

Current ratio	2.2 to 1
Acid-test ratio	1.2 to 1
Accounts receivable turnover (average)	10 times
Inventory turnover (average)	5.8 times
Times interest earned	8 times
Debt-to-equity ratio	.8 to 1
Dividend yield	3%
Price-earnings ratio	14%
Dividend payout ratio	60%
Return on total assets (average)	9%
Return on common equity	15.5%

Required To satisfy the senior member's request—

a. Compute the following ratios for each company:
  (1) Current ratio.
  (2) Acid-test ratio.
  (3) Average accounts receivable turnover.
  (4) Average collection period for receivables.
  (5) Average inventory turnover.

b. Using the above ratios as well as industry ratios, indicate which company is the better short-term credit risk and why.

c. Compute the following ratios for each company:
   (1) Times interest earned.
   (2) Total debt-to-equity ratio.

d. Using the above ratios, determine which company should be in a better position to take on *additional* long-term debt and why.

e. Compute the following ratios for each company:
   (1) Earnings per share.
   (2) Dividend yield.
   (3) Price-earnings ratio.
   (4) Dividend payout ratio.
   (5) Return on total assets.
   (6) Return on common equity.

f. For each of the companies, indicate whether financial leverage is positive or negative, and explain how you reached this conclusion.

g. Using the above ratios, present preliminary conclusions regarding the relative market standing and attractiveness of both companies.

P18–21   **Computation of Ratios**

The Point Company is listed on the New York Stock Exchange. The market value of its common stock was quoted at $10 per share at December 31, 19x5, and 19x4. Point's balance sheet at December 31, 19x5, and 19x4, and statement of income and retained earnings for the years then ended are presented below:

POINT COMPANY
Balance Sheet
December 31, 19x5, and 19x4
(in thousands)

	December 31	
Assets	**19x5**	**19x4**
Current assets:		
Cash	$ 3,500	$ 3,600
Marketable securities, at cost that approximates market	13,000	11,000
Accounts receivable, net of allowance for doubtful		
accounts	105,000	95,000
Inventories, lower of cost or market	126,000	154,000
Prepaid costs	2,500	2,400
Total current assets	250,000	266,000
Property, plant, and equipment, net of accumulated		
depreciation	311,000	308,000
Investments in marketable securities	2,000	3,000
Long-term receivables	14,000	16,000
Goodwill and patents, net of accumulated amortization	6,000	6,500
Other assets	7,000	8,500
Total assets	$590,000	$608,000

| | December 31 | |
Liabilities and Stockholders' Equity	19x5	19x4
Current liabilities:		
Notes payable	$ 5,000	$ 15,000
Accounts payable	38,000	48,000
Accrued liabilities	24,500	27,000
Income taxes payable	1,000	1,000
Payments due within one year on long-term debt	6,500	7,000
Total current liabilities	75,000	98,000
Long-term debt	169,000	180,000
Estimated product warranty liability	74,000	67,000
Other liabilities	9,000	8,000
Stockholders' equity:		
Common stock, par value $1 per share; authorized 20 million shares; issued and outstanding 10 million shares	10,000	10,000
5% cumulative preferred stock, par value $100 per share; $100 liquidating value; authorized 50,000 shares; issued and outstanding 40,000 shares	4,000	4,000
Additional paid-in capital	107,000	107,000
Retained earnings	142,000	134,000
Total stockholders' equity	263,000	255,000
Total liabilities and stockholders' equity	$590,000	$608,000

POINT COMPANY
Statement of Income and Retained Earnings
For the Years Ended December 31, 19x5, and 19x4
(in thousands)

| | Year Ended December 31 | |
	19x5	19x4
Net sales	$600,000	$500,000
Costs:		
Cost of goods sold	490,000	400,000
Marketing and administrative costs	66,000	60,000
Other, interest.	7,000	6,000
Total costs	563,000	466,000
Income before income taxes	37,000	34,000
Income taxes	16,800	15,800
Net income	20,200	18,200
Retained earnings at beginning of period	134,000	126.000
Dividends on common stock	(12,000)	(10,000)
Dividends on preferred stock	(200)	(200)
Retained earnings at end of period.	$142,000	$134,000

Required   *a.* Based on the above information, compute (for the year 19x5 only) the following:

(1) Current (working capital) ratio.

(2) Quick (acid-test) ratio.

(3) Number of days' sales in average receivables, assuming a business year consisting of 300 days and all sales on account.

(4) Inventory turnover.

(5) Debt-to-equity ratio.

(6) Earnings per share on common stock.

(7) Price-earnings ratio on common stock.

(8) Dividend payout ratio on common stock.
(9) Times interest earned.
(10) Return on total assets.
(11) Return on common stockholders' equity.
(12) Dividend yield ratio.
b. For 19x5, is the financial leverage positive or negative? Explain your answer.

(AICPA Adapted)

P18-22   **Comprehensive Problem—Part 1: Short-Term Liquidity and Creditor Ratios**

The Telly Manufacturing Company was organized five years ago and manufactures toys. Its most recent three years' balance sheets and income statements are presented below:

TELLY MANUFACTURING COMPANY
Comparative Condensed Balance Sheets
As of June 30, 19x5, 19x4, and 19x3

Assets	19x5	19x4	19x3
Cash	$ 19,200	$ 24,000	$ 25,600
Accounts receivable, net.	292,800	128,000	96,400
Inventory	227,200	155,200	83,000
Other current assets.	8,000	9,600	6,000
Plant and equipment (net)	256,000	176,000	112,000
Total assets	$803,200	$492,800	$323,000

Liabilities and Equity			
Accounts payable.	$236,400	$ 80,600	$ 35,000
Federal income tax payable	48,000	23,000	45,000
Long-term liabilities.	192,000	116,800	35,200
Common stock, $10 par value	176,000	176,000	128,000
Retained earnings.	150,800	96,400	79,800
Total liabilities and equity	$803,200	$492,800	$323,000

TELLY MANUFACTURING COMPANY
Condensed Income Statements
For the Years Ended June 30, 19x5, 19x4, and 19x3

	19x5	19x4	19x3
Net sales (all credit)	$2,694,000	$2,000,000	$1,680,000
Cost of goods sold.	1,483,000	1,296,000	819,000
Gross margin on sales	1,211,000	704,000	861,000
Marketing and administrative costs	1,072,000	635,000	748,400
Operating income	139,000	69,000	112,600
Interest cost.	19,000	12,000	3,600
Income before federal income tax	120,000	57,000	109,000
Income tax	48,000	22,800	43,600
Net income	$ 72,000	$ 34,200	$ 65,400

A reconciliation of its retained earnings for the years ended June 30, 19x4, and June 30, 19x5, is as follows:

TELLY MANUFACTURING COMPANY
Statement of Retained Earnings
For the Years Ended June 30, 19x5, and 19x4

	19x5	19x4
Balance, beginning	$ 96,400	$ 79,800
Add: Net income.	72,000	34,200
Subtotal.	168,400	114,000
Deduct: Dividends paid	17,600	17,600
Balance, ending	$150,800	$ 96,400

Additional information is as follows:

1. All sales are on account.
2. Long-term liabilities are owed to the firm's bank.
3. The firm's terms of sale are net 30 days.

You are employed as an assistant to a bank loan officer, and she has asked you to evaluate the firm's request for an additional long-term loan of $150,000.

In the course of evaluating the loan, you ascertain that the following ratios are typical for toy manufacturers:

Current ratio	2.2 : 1
Acid-test ratio	1.2 : 1
Accounts receivable turnover.	14 times
Collection period of receivables.	26 days
Inventory-turnover ratio	8 times
Days to sell inventory	45 days
Debt-to-equity ratio	.75 to 1
Times interest earned	6 times

Required   *a.* Compute the following for 19x4 and 19x5:
   (1) Working capital.
   (2) Current ratio.
   (3) Acid-test ratio.
   (4) Accounts receivable turnover.
   (5) Collection period of receivables.
   (6) Inventory-turnover ratio.
   (7) Days to sell inventory.
   (8) Debt-to-equity ratio.
   (9) Times interest earned.
   b. Using 19x3 as the base year, compute an index-number trend series for
   (1) Sales.
   (2) Cost of goods sold.
   (3) Gross margin.
   (4) Marketing and administrative costs.
   (5) Net income.
   c. Based on your analyses above, would you advise the bank to grant the loan? Write a brief report giving the reasons for your recommendation.

P18–23   **Comprehensive Problem—Part 2: Investor Ratios**
Refer to the data given in Problem 18–22. One of the current shareholders of the Telly Manufacturing Company has approached you with an offer to sell you 4,000 shares of common stock at $32 per share, the current (19x5) market price per share. The market price for 19x4 was $29 per share.

As part of your analysis in evaluating the offer, you are able to ascertain that the following data are typical for investments of this kind:

Return on total assets	10%
Return on common stockholders' equity.	18
Price-earnings ratio	12
Dividend payout ratio	30
Dividend yield ratio	5

Required   *a.* Compute the following for the years 19x4 and 19x5:
  (1) Return on total assets.
  (2) Return on common stockholders' equity.
  (3) Earnings per share.
  (4) Price-earnings ratio.
  (5) Dividend payout ratio.
  (6) Dividend yield ratio.
b. Is the financial leverage positive or negative for 19x5? For 19x4? Explain each answer.
c. Based on your analysis above, do you plan to accept the offer? Explain.

P18–24   **Comprehensive Problem—Part 3: Year-to-Year Changes and Common-Size Statements**

Refer to the data in Problem 18–22. The president of the Telly Manufacturing Company has asked you to assist him in analyzing certain aspects of the firm's 19x4 and 19x5 financial statements.

Required   *a.* For 19x4 and 19x5, prepare the balance sheets and income statements showing the year-to-year changes in both dollars and percent. Use 19x4 as the base period.
b. For 19x4 and 19x5, prepare the balance sheets and income statements in common-size format.
c. Write a brief report summarizing any significant information revealed by your analysis.

P18–25   **Comprehensive Ratio Analysis with Industry Comparisons**

Bedrosian Incorporated has a line of credit from the Belmont National Bank that is due to be renewed February 1, 19x3. The bank has requested the current income statement and comparative statements of financial position for November 30, 19x2 and 19x1, which are presented below.

BEDROSIAN INCORPORATED
Income Statement
Year Ended November 30, 19x2
(thousand omitted)

Revenues:

Net sales	$60,000
Other	4,500
Total revenue	64,500

Costs:

Cost of goods sold	40,500
Marketing and administrative	11,625
Depreciation and amortization	1,875
Interest	1,500
Total costs	55,500
Income before income taxes	9,000
Income taxes	3,600
Net income	5,400
Less: Dividends to common shareholders ($3.86 per share)	2,550
Net income added to retained earnings	2,850
Retained earnings, 12/1/x1	8,550
Retained earnings, 11/30/x2	$11,400
Earnings per share	$8.18

BEDROSIAN INCORPORATED
Statement of Financial Position
November 30, 19x2 and 19x1
(thousands omitted)

Assets	19x2	19x1
Current assets		
Cash and marketable securities	$ 1,950	$ 1,575
Receivables, less allowance for doubtful accounts ($84 in 19x2 and $105 in 19x1)	3,600	3,750
Inventories, at lower of FIFO cost or market	4,875	4,650
Prepaid items and other current assets	375	225
Total current assets	10,800	10,200
Other assets		
Investments, at cost	7,950	7,950
Deposits	750	600
Total other assets	8,700	8,550
Property, plant, and equipment		
Land	900	900
Buildings and equipment, less accumulated depreciation ($9,450 in 19x2 and $9,150 in 19x1)	20,100	18,600
Total property, plant, and equipment	21,000	19,500
Total assets	$40,500	$38,250

Liabilities and Shareholders' Equity	19x2	19x1
Current liabilities		
Short-term loans	$ 1,650	$ 1,800
Accounts payable.	5,400	5,325
Salaries, wages, and other.	1,950	2,025
Total current liabilities	9,000	9,150
Long-term debt.	12,000	12,825
Total liabilities	21,000	21,975
Shareholders' equity		
Common stock, at par	3,300	3,150
Paid-in capital in excess of par.	4,800	4,575
Total paid-in capital.	8,100	7,725
Retained earnings.	11,400	8,550
Total shareholders' equity	19,500	16,275
Total liabilities and shareholders' equity	$40,500	$38,250

The bank has also requested that Bedrosian calculate several ratios and report the latest industry ratios. Bedrosian's ratios have not been calculated for the 19x2 fiscal year. However, the accounting staff has gathered the following industry ratios, which are the latest available.

▶ Net profit margin	3.42%
▶ Return on total assets	6.37%
▶ Return on common shareholders' equity	12.48%
▶ Total asset turnover	2.23
▶ Current ratio	1.86
▶ Quick (acid-test) ratio	.85
▶ Debt/equity ratio	1.23
▶ Times interest earned	7.78
▶ Dividend payout ratio	39.57%

Required

a. Explain why the bank would be interested in the comparative financial statements and the financial ratios given above.

b. Calculate the following financial ratios for 19x2 for Bedrosian Incorporated (round your answer to two decimal places).

1. Net profit margin.
2. Return on total assets.
3. Return on common shareholders' equity.
4. Total asset turnover.
5. Current ratio.
6. Quick (acid-test) ratio.
7. Debt/equity ratio.
8. Times interest earned.
9. Dividend payout ratio.

c. By comparing the ratios calculated in part *(b)* with the industry ratios, evaluate Bedrosian's operations.

(CMA Adapted)

P18–26   **Computation of Primary EPS and Fully Diluted EPS**

The Preston Company showed the following for 19x8:

Income before extraordinary item	$1,800,000
Extraordinary item—casualty loss (net after taxes).	400,000
Net income for period.	$1,400,000

At January 1, 19x8, there were 210,000 shares of common stock outstanding. On October 1, 19x8, an additional 60,000 shares were sold for cash.

In 19x4, 8 percent bonds were issued at par, $5 million. These are convertible into 50,000 shares of common stock. None have been converted.

In 19x2, 45,000 shares of $16 cumulative preferred stock were issued at par, $200. Each preferred share is convertible into four shares of common stock. None have been converted.

Assume an income tax rate of 40 percent.

Required   *a.* Calculate primary earnings per share. (Round to the nearest cent.)

b. Calculate fully diluted earnings per share. (Round to the nearest cent.)

P18–27   Computation of Primary EPS and Fully Diluted EPS

Foster, Inc., showed the following for 19x6:

Income before extraordinary item	$1,600,000
Extraordinary item—casualty loss (net after taxes).	300,000
Net income for period.	$1,300,000

At January 1, 19x6, there were 180,000 shares of common stock outstanding. On October 1, 19x6, an additional 40,000 shares were sold for cash.

In 19x4, 6 percent bonds were issued at par, $3 million. These are convertible into 30,000 shares of common stock. None have been converted.

In 19x2, 25,000 shares of $8 cumulative preferred stock were issued at $180 per share. Each preferred share is convertible into two shares of common stock. None have been converted.

Assume an income tax rate of 40 percent.

Required   *a.* Calculate primary earnings per share. (Round to the nearest cent.)

b. Calculate fully diluted earnings per share. (Round to the nearest cent.)

P18–28   Using Financial Leverage

A newly formed corporation, Katonah Company, was formed with an initial issuance of 30,000 shares of common stock with a par value of $20 per share for a total capitalization (in cash) of $600,000.

The firm will require another $600,000 to commence operations. The three principal stockholders each have a different plan for raising the needed $600,000:

1. Stockholder R believes the firm should sell 30,000 shares of stock to a limited group of individuals for $600,000.
2. Stockholder S believes the firm should sell $600,000 of 12 percent preferred stock.
3. Stockholder T believes the firm should borrow the $600,000 for 10 years at a 12 percent interest rate.

The firm expects to earn $200,000 annually from operations (before interest cost and income taxes). The firm's income tax rate will be 30 percent.

Required   *a.* For each of the three plans, compute:

(1) The net income of the firm.

(2) The return on common stockholders' equity.

b. Write a brief report to the stockholders, indicating which plan you believe they should adopt and explaining why each plan produces a different return on common stockholders' equity.

▶ **CASES**   **C18–29**   **Preparation of Financial Statements from Given Ratios and Selected Miscellaneous Data**

Argo Sales Corporation has in recent prior years maintained the following relationships among the data on its financial statements:

1. Gross profit rate on net sales 40%
2. Net profit rate on net sales 10%
3. Rate of marketing costs to net sales 20%
4. Accounts receivable turnover . . . . 8 per year
5. Inventory turnover . . . . 6 per year
6. Acid-test ratio . . . . 2 to 1
7. Current ratio . . . . 3 to 1
8. Quick-asset composition: 8% cash, 32% marketable securities, 60% accounts receivable
9. Asset turnover (Sales ÷ Total assets) . . . . 2 per year
10. Ratio of total assets to intangible assets . . . . 20 to 1
11. Ratio of accumulated depreciation to cost of fixed assets . . . . 1 to 3
12. Ratio of accounts receivable to accounts payable . . . . 1.5 to 1
13. Ratio of working capital to stockholders' equity . . . . 1 to 1.6
14. Ratio of total debt to stockholders' equity . . . . 1 to 2

The corporation had a net income of $120,000 for 19x8, which resulted in earnings of $5.20 per share of common stock. Additional information includes the following:

1. Capital stock authorized, issued (all in 19x0), and outstanding:
   Common, $10 per share par value, issued at a 10% premium.
   Preferred, 6% nonparticipating, $100 per share par value, issued at a 10% premium.
2. Market value per share of common at December 31, 19x8: $78.
3. Preferred dividends paid in 19x8: $3,000.
4. Times interest earned in 19x8: 33.
5. The amounts of the following were the same at December 31, 19x8, as at January 1, 19x8: inventory, accounts receivable, 5% bonds payable—long term, and total stockholders' equity.
6. All purchases and sales were "on account."

Required   a. Prepare in good form the condensed (1) balance sheet and (2) income statement for the year ending December 31, 19x8, presenting the amounts you would expect to appear on Argo's financial statements (ignoring income taxes). Major captions appearing on Argo's balance sheet are current assets, fixed assets, intangible assets, current liabilities, long-term liabilities, and stockholders' equity. In addition to the accounts divulged in the problem, you should include accounts for prepaid costs, accrued liabilities, and administrative costs.
   b. Compute the following for 19x8 (show your computations):
   (1) Rate of return on common stockholders' equity.
   (2) Price-earnings ratio for common stock.
   (3) Dividends paid per share of common stock.
   (4) Dividends paid per share of preferred stock.
   (5) Dividend yield on common stock.

(AICPA Adapted)

C18–30   **Decision Making and Ratio Analysis**

The management of the Wykagil Corp., a manufacturer of pizza ovens, has decided that the increased demand for its product warrants an expansion of its plant capacity. This expansion has been estimated to cost $3.6 million. The financing choice is between issuing $3.6 million of long-term debt at an interest rate of 10% per annum or issuing 100,000 shares of common stock at a current market price of $36 per share. It is expected that added capacity will increase annual profits by $1,152,000 before interest and taxes. The firm's latest financial statements are presented below.

WYKAGIL CORP.
Balance Sheet
December 31, 19x9

Assets

Current assets:

Cash	$1,200,000	
Accounts receivable	1,800,000	
Inventories	1,200,000	
Total current assets		$ 4,200,000

Property, plant, and equipment:

Property, plant, and equipment—net of accumulated depreciation		14,700,000
Other assets		540,000
Total assets		$19,440,000

Liabilities and Stockholders' Equity

Current liabilities:

Accounts payable	$1,320,000	
Notes payable	240,000	
Miscellaneous current liabilities	120,000	
Total current liabilities		$ 1,680,000

Long-term debt:

Bonds payable—8% due 20x8		4,800,000
Total liabilities		6,480,000

Stockholders' equity:

Common stock issued and outstanding—360,000 shares, par value $10 per share	3,600,000	
Additional paid-in capital	600,000	
Retained earnings	8,760,000	
Total stockholders' equity		12,960,000
Total liabilities and stockholders' equity		$19,440,000

WYKAGIL CORP.
Income Statement
For the Year Ended December 31, 19x9

Sales	$11,088,000
Cost of sales	7,440,000
Gross profit	3,648,000
Marketing and administrative costs	1,608,000
Operating income	2,040,000
Interest cost	384,000
Net income before income taxes	1,656,000
Income taxes (tax rate 35%)	580,000
Net income	$ 1,076,000
Earnings per share	$ 2.99
Current dividends per share	1.80

The firm's objective is to remain within the long-term debt-to-equity range of 39% to 43% and to maintain, also within reason, the current dividend rate.

Required

a. You are asked by the firm to render an opinion regarding its ability to achieve its goals based on the contemplated financing alternatives.

b. Compute the dividend you would expect the firm to pay under each alternative.

c. If you were making the decision, which alternative would you choose? Explain your answer.

(*Hint*: Calculate the new debt ratio using the year-end equity after the assumed payment of dividends.)

C18–31   **Ratio Analysis**

Radatron, Inc., is a manufacturer of highly specialized electronic components used in aircraft and radar installations. The company's financial position is being reviewed by its bank, an important potential customer, and a new supplier of raw materials. As part of the review process, Radatron was required to provide its latest financial statements, along with information on selected financial ratios. A summary of the information provided by Radatron is presented below.

RADATRON, INC.
Statement of Income
For the Year Ended May 31, 19x9
(thousands omitted)

Sales (net)	$20,100
Cost of goods sold	11,060
Marketing and administrative costs	2,340
Depreciation	1,120
Interest	1,200
Income before taxes	4,380
Income taxes	1,760
Net income	$ 2,620

RADATRON, INC.
Statement of Financial Position
As of May 31, 19x9
(thousands omitted)

Cash	$ 450
Accounts receivable (net)	2,050
Inventory	3,300
Total current assets	5,800
Property, plant, and equipment (net)	4,600
Total assets	$10,400
Accounts payable	$ 1,770
Income taxes payable	245
Accrued liabilities	960
Total current liabilities	2,975
Long-term debt	2,720
Total liabilities	5,695
Common stock ($10 par value)	1,800
Paid-in-capital in excess of par	1,250
Retained earnings	1,655
Total stockholders' equity	4,705
Total liabilities and stockholders' equity	$10,400

Selected Financial Ratios

	Radatron, Inc. 19x7	Radatron, Inc. 19x8	Current Industry Average
Current ratio	2.11	2.02	2.16
Times interest earned	3.8	4.9	4.5
Net profit margin	12.1%	13.2%	12.0%
Total debt to net worth.	1.04	1.16	1.10
Total asset turnover	1.98	1.89	2.12

Each of the parties described below must recommend an action based on its evaluation of Radatron's financial position.

▶ Northwest Bank is currently reviewing a request from Radatron for additional financing. Although Northwest has been Radatron's primary bank for the past several years, bank regulations require that Northwest reevaluate a company's financial position before each major transaction.

▶ Wilson Aviation has recently received a substantial government contract and is considering subcontracting a portion of the work to Radatron. The contract would result in a significant increase in Radatron's annual sales over the next three years.

▶ Allied Electronics, a manufacturer of transistors and diodes, has recently been asked by Radatron to bid on a contract requiring the shipment of approximately $10,000 of components per month for 12 months. Allied has not previously done business with Radatron and must decide whether or not to respond to the request for bid, and if the company does respond, what terms it should offer.

Required   a. Explain the analytical use of each of the five ratios presented above.

b. Calculate a new set of ratios for fiscal year 19x9 for Radatron, Inc., based on the financial statements presented above. (Assume total assets were unchanged throughout the year.)

c. For each of the parties reviewing Radatron's financial position
   (1) Select two ratios from those ratios presented that would be most valuable as a basis for its decision regarding Radatron.
   (2) Using the selected financial ratios presented above, explain what the two ratios reveal about Radatron's financial performance.

(CMA Adapted)

▶ **ANSWERS TO SELF-TEST**

True or False

1. True	2. True	3. True	4. False	5. False
6. False	7. True	8. True	9. True	10. False
11. True	12. False	13. False	14. True	15. True

Multiple Choice

1. *c.*   2. *d.*   3. *a.*   4. *d.*   5. *b.*   6. *a.*   7. *c.*   8. *d*

INDEX

►

► A

Abnormal spoilage, 266–68, 275
Absorption costing, 186, 221
  with beginning and ending inventories, 591–97
  conversion for CVP analysis, 593–95
  and markup pricing, 661–62
  no beginning or ending inventories, 589–91
  overview, 586, 610, 611
  versus variable costing, 586–87
Accelerated cost recovery system (ACRS), 786
Account analysis, 87, 95, 100
Accounting, purpose of, 4
Accounting rate of return (ARR), 736–38, 739, 755
Accounts Receivable
  aging schedule, 945
  cash flow, 878
Accounts-receivable-turnover ratio, 943–44, 959, 962
Acid-test ratio, 942–43, 959, 962
Activity accounting, 54, 57. *See also* **Responsibility accounting**
Activity base, 80–82, 95, 100
Activity-based costing (ABC), 311–15, 326, 327. *See also* **Transaction-based costing**
Adjusted tax basis, 784, 802
Administrative cost budget, 408–409, 424, 432
After tax
After-tax cash flow, 783, 801, 802
  net income, 129
  operating income, 127–29
Aggregate cost, 52, 56, 57
Allocated costs, **joint products**, 366–69
  net-realizable-sales-value method, 368–69
  physical-units method, 367
  relative-sales-value method, 367–68
Allocation base, 221
  direct labor cost base, 208–209
  direct labor-hours base, 209–210
  machine-hours base, 210
  materials cost base, 210–11
  normal overhead rate, 212

Allocation base—*Cont.*
  prime cost base, 211
  seasonal and other fluctuations, 211–12
American Institute of Certified Public Accountants (AICPA), 4, 23
Analyzing mixed costs, 86–92
Annual compounding, 740
Annual Statement Studies, Robert Morris Associates, 960
Annual usage, of direct materials, 319
Annuity, 743, 755
Antidilution, 955
APB Opinion No. 19, "Reporting Changes in Financial Position," 875
Applied manufacturing overhead, 208, 221
Area of feasible solutions, 672, 680
Assets, 36, 56. *See also* **Unexpired costs**
Asset turnover, 829–30, 832–34, 846
Assignable product costs, 40, 56, 57. *See also* **Inventoriable costs**
Attainable standards, 477
Audit of capital-budgeting projects, 732–33, 739, 755
Automated systems, 207
Average cost assumption, 254, 268, 275
Average operating assets, 828
Average usage, 431
Avoidable costs, 599, 611

► B

Backflush costing, 324, 327
Balance sheet
  budgeted balance sheet, 417, 424, 432
  for a manufacturing firm, 42–43
  for a merchandising firm, 37
  use in financial reporting, 874
Barometer of Small Business, 960
Bill of materials, 476, 490, 496
Book inventories, 186, 221, 222
Book value, and tax considerations, 791
Bottom up budgeting, 395, 421, 424, 432
Breakeven analysis
  margin of safety, 131
  and sales mix, 147–48

Breakeven analysis—*Cont.*
  using equations, 125–31
  using graphs, 132–34
Breakeven dollar sales, 125–26
Breakeven graph, 132–34, 151, 152
Breakeven sales (BES), 125–27, 151, 152
  limiting assumptions, 130–31
Breakeven units (BEU), 126, 152
Budget committee, 397–98, 424, 432
Budgeted cost, 476, 491, 496
Budgeted income statement, 414–16
Budgets
  administrative cost budget, 408–409
  bottom up, 395, 421
  budget committee, 397–98
  budget slack, 418–19, 432
  capital budget, 397
  cash budget, 394, 409, 410–14
  continuous budget, 397
  direct labor budget, 405–406
  direct materials budget, 403–405
  ending inventory budget, 406–407
  flexible budget, 527–31
  in hospitals, 420–21
  incremental budgeting, 419
  manufacturing overhead budget, 406
  marketing cost budget, 407
  master budget, 394, 398–99
  in not-for-profit organizations, 419–23
  operating budget, 394
  overview, 394–96, 432
  participative budget, 396
  production budget, 400–403
  sales budget, 399–400
  and standard costs, 478
  time frame, 396–97
  zero-base budgeting, 419–20
Budget slack, 418–19, 424
Burden, 39, 57. *See also* **Manufacturing overhead**

► C

Capacity level, 538, 553
  applying overhead, selecting for, 550–53

Capital budget, 397, 424, 433, 718, 738, 755
  after-tax, 790–800
  and inflation, 754–55
Carrying costs, inventory, 425, 433
Cash and cash equivalents, 876–77, 899, 900
  provided by operations, 880
  sources of cash, 877
  stock dividends, 880
  uses of cash, 878
Cash budget, 394, 409, 410–14, 424, 433
Cash flows, 648, 875. *See also* Statement of Cash Flows
  gross versus net, 878
  from operations, 886–89
  per share, 879
  and **working capital**, 886–89
Cash management, 409–10, 424, 433
Cash operating advantage, 648, 669, 680
Cell, 20
Centralized organization, 820, 846
Certified Management Accountant (CMA), 18–19, 23, 24
  program objectives, 18–19
Certified Public Accountant (CPA), 19, 23, 24
Changes in selling price, and CVP analysis, 142–46
Collection period for accounts receivable, 944–45, 959, 962
Committed costs, 83, 95, 100
Common cost. *See also* **Indirect costs**
  allocation to segments, 602–604, 605–607, 611
  and **segment margin income statement**, 601–602
Common-size statement, 933–36, 959, 961
Comparative income approach, 647, 680
  replacing existing equipment, 724
  and tax considerations, 794–95
Comparative income statement approach
  and changes in selling price, 143
  CVP analysis, 140–41, 152
Competence, and management accountants, 21
Competition-based pricing, 664–65, 669, 681
Compound interest, 740–41, 755
Comprehensive comparative income approach, 668
Comptroller, 16, 24. *See also* **Controller**
Computer Aided Manufacturing-International, Inc. (CAM-I), 316
Computer-assisted manufacturing (CAM), 308, 321, 327
Computer-integrated manufacturing (CIM), 20, 23, 24, 321, 327
Confidentiality, 21, 22
Constraint functions, linear programming, 670, 681
Constraints, 665, 669, 681
Continuous budget, 397, 424, 433
Contribution format income statement, 92–95, 95–96, 100

Contribution format income statement— *Cont.*
  preparation of, 93–95
  and variable costing, 587–89, 610, 611
Contribution margin, 92–93, 95–96, 100, 124
Contribution margin approach, CVP analysis, 142, 152
  and changes in selling price, 144–45
Contribution margin per limiting factor, 665–66, 669, 680
Contribution margin per unit (CMPU), 124–25, 127, 151, 153
  and changes in variable unit costs, 145–46
Contribution margin ratio (CMR), 124, 127, 151, 153
  and changes in variable unit costs, 145–46
Contribution margin ratio per mix (CMRM), 146, 152, 153
Controllable cost, 53–54, 57
Controller, 15–17, 23, 24
Controlling, 5, 12–13, 23, 24, 394, 425, 433
Conversion cost, 50, 56, 57
  in just-in-time systems, 324
Corner points, 672–74
Cost accounting, 186, 220, 222
  hospital, 219–20
  job order cost accounting system, 187–88
  for just-in-time systems, 323–25
  law firm, 218–19
  process cost accounting system, 187–88
Cost accounting cycle, 186, 205–207, 220, 222
  and standard costing, 547–49
Cost behavior, 50, 56, 57, 80, 95, 100
  curvilinear, 85–86
Cost-benefit rule, 39
  applied to variance analysis, 486–88
Cost budgets, for hospitals, 422–23
Cost center, 820–21, 846
  discretionary cost centers, 824
  standard cost centers, 824
Cost drivers, 208, 312, 326, 327
Cost-flow assumptions
  activity-based costing, 311–15
  process costing, 254–55
  volume-based approach, 310–11
Cost in Preceding Department, 261
Cost management system, 316, 326, 328
Cost objective, 38–39, 56, 57
Cost of capital, 733, 738, 739, 755
Cost of capital discount rate, 722
Cost-of-Doing-Business Series Moody's Manuals, 960
Cost of goods manufactured, 44–45, 48, 56, 57, 216–17
Cost of goods sold, 45, 48, 56, 57, 203–205, 217–18
Cost of production report, 259, 268, 276
Cost-plus pricing, 661, 669, 681. *See also* **Markup pricing**
  and transfer pricing, 841
Cost recapitulation section, 259, 268, 276

Costs, 34–59
  aggregate cost, 52
  committed costs, 83, 95
  controllable, 53
  conversion, 50
  cost behavior, 50, 95
  definition of, 36
  differential cost, 52
  direct vs. indirect, 51
  discretionary costs, 83, 95
  expired costs, 36
  fixed costs, 51, 82–83, 95
  in a manufacturing firm, 38–42
  marginal costs, 80, 95
  mixed costs, 84–92, 95
  noncontrollable, 53–54
  opportunity cost, 52–53
  prime, 50
  semivariable costs, 84, 95
  for service industries, 54–55
  step-variable costs, 85, 95
  sunk, 53
  unexpired costs, 36
  variable costs, 50–51, 80–82, 95
Cost structure, 135–37, 151, 153
Cost-volume-profit (CVP) analysis, 124, 139–46, 152, 153
  and changes in selling price, 142–46
  comparative income statement approach, 140–41
  contribution margin approach, 142
  and decision making, 668
  differential analysis, 141–42
  incremental analysis, 141–42
  and sales mix, 148–51
  volume changes only, 140
Current assets, 937–38
Current data, 7, 22, 24
Current dividend, 957
Current liabilities, 937–38
Current ratio, 939–42, 959, 962
  limitations of, 939–40
  rules-of-thumb standards, 941–42
Curvilinear cost behavior, 85–86
Cutoff rate, 726, 739, 755

▶ **D**

Days' sales in accounts receivable, 944–45. *See also* **Collection period for accounts receivable**
Days to sell inventory, 946, 959, 962
Debt-to-equity ratio, 947–48, 959, 962
Decentralization, 13, 820, 846, 847
  advantages of, 821
  disadvantages of, 822
Decision making, 6–7, 22, 24, 187
  contribution margin per limiting factor, 665–66
  existing equipment, replacing, 650–51
  and income taxes, 782–90
  joint products, 658–59
  linear programming, 665–66
  make-or-buy, component parts, 656–58
  new equipment, purchasing, 648–50
  new products, 652–53

Decision making—*Cont.*
overview, 646
pricing, 659–65
special orders, less than full cost, 653–56
use of costs, 647–48
Declining balance, depreciation, 786
Defective units, 274, 276
and JIT, 320
Degree of operating leverage, 138–39, 152, 153
Delegation of authority, 14, 23, 24
Demand-oriented pricing, 664, 669, 681
Denominator activity, 538, 553. *See also* **Capacity level**
Denominator variance, 540
Departmental overhead rates, 215–16
Dependent variable, 96, 100
Depreciation, 36
as tax shield, 783
bookkeeping convention, 649
under MACRS, 787–88
methods of, 786–89
optional straight-line method, MACRS, 788–89
selecting a method, 789
Diagnostic-related group (DRG), 56, 57
Diagrammatic approach, variance analysis, 483–84, 491, 496
Differential analysis, 141–42, 152, 153, 647, 668, 681
and changes in selling price, 143–44
Differential cost, 52, 57
Differential income approach
entering a new market, 725–26
net present value calculation, 719–22
replacing existing equipment, 722–24
tax considerations, 791–94
Direct cost, 38–39, 56, 57
Direct costing, 586, 587, 610, 611.
See also **Variable costing**
Direct fixed costs, 602, 610–11
Direct labor, 38, 39, 56, 57
cost accumulation
just-in-time, 324
process system, 256
Direct labor budget, 405–406, 424, 433
standards for, 479
variance analysis for, 484–85
Direct labor cost base, 208–209, 209–10, 221, 222
Direct labor efficiency variance, 484–85, 496
Direct labor-hours base, 222
Direct labor rate variance, 484, 496
Direct materials, 38, 39, 43–44, 48, 56, 58
cost accumulation
process system, 256
just-in-time systems, 323–24
direct materials budget, 403–405, 424, 433
standards for, 478
variance analysis for, 482–83
Direct materials used, 58
Direct method, service department overhead allocation, 352–53, 370, 371

Direct method, statement of cash flow
overview, 876, 899, 900
preparation of, 893–97
Discounted cash flow model, 718, 726, 738, 755
Discounting, 744, 755
Discount rate, 718, 738, 755
Discretionary cost centers, 824, 846, 847
Discretionary costs, 83, 95, 100
Dividend payout ratio, 957, 959, 962
Dividend yield ratio, 957, 962
Dun & Bradstreet, 945, 960

► **E**

E. I. du Pont de Nemours Company (Du Pont), 829
Earnings before interest and taxes, EBIT, 828
Earnings per share, 954–55, 959, 962
Economic order quantity (EOQ), 425–29, 433
Economic production run in units, 429, 433
Effectiveness, 475, 490, 496
Efficiency, 475, 490, 496
Employee groupings, and JIT, 320
Ending inventory budget, 406–407, 424, 433
Engineering cost analysis, 87, 95, 100
Equipment decisions, 648–52, 667
differential income approach, 722–24
Equivalent production
FIFO equivalent production, 269–70
in process costing system, 257–59, 268, 276
Equivalent units, 257. *See also* **Equivalent production**
Estimated costs, 490
Estimated overhead rate. *See* **Predetermined overhead rate**
Ethical standards, and the AICPA, 4
Ethics, 20–23
Even cash flows, IRR, 726–27
Expected usage, 431–32
Expected capacity, 553
Expenses, 36, 56, 58. *See also* **Expired costs**
Expired costs, 36, 56
External market price, transfer pricing, 841–44

► **F**

Factory burden, 39, 58. *See also* **Manufacturing overhead**
Factory expenses, 39, 58. *See also* **Manufacturing overhead**
Factory overhead, 39, 58. *See also* **Manufacturing overhead**
Factory rent, 40
FASB Discussion Memorandum, "Reporting Funds Flow, Liquidity, and Financial Flexibility," 876

FASB Exposure Draft, "Recognition and Measurement in Financial Statements of Business Enterprises," 876
Favorable variance, 481, 491, 496
Federal Trade Commission—Securities and Exchange Commission. Quarterly Financial Report, 961
Feedback, 12, 23, 24
Financial accounting 4–6, 22, 24
Financial Accounting Standards Board (FASB), 4
Financial leverage, 951–54, 959, 961
Financial statements
for a manufacturing firm, 42–50
for a merchandising firm, 37–38
for service businesses, 38
Financial statements analysis
comparative statements, 929–33
overview, 928
principal tools, 928–29
Financing activities, 874, 899, 900
Finished goods, 42, 56, 58
Finished goods inventory ledger, 201–203, 221, 222
First-in, first-out (FIFO) method, 254, 268, 268–73, 276
equivalent production, 269–70
production report, 270–73
Fixed costs, 51, 56–57, 58, 82–83, 95, 100
service department overhead allocations, 358–64
Fixed manufacturing overhead, 537–44
journal entries, 544, 547–49
predetermined overhead rates, 537–38
relationship with fixed costs, 538–39
variance analysis, 539–41, 541–44
Fixed overhead capacity variance, 540, 547, 553. *See also* **Fixed overhead volume variance**
Fixed overhead denominator variance, 553. *See also* **Fixed overhead volume variance**
Fixed overhead production volume variance, 540
Fixed overhead spending variance, 540, 541, 547, 553
Fixed overhead volume variance, 540, 541–42, 547, 553
Flexible budget
overview, 527–28, 547, 553
preparing, 528–31
Flexible budget quantity. *See* **Standard quantity allowed**
Flexible manufacturing cell (FMC), 321, 327, 328
Flexible manufacturing system (FMS), 19–20, 23, 24, 308, 327, 328
and just-in-time, 321–22
Frame of reference, 51
Frequency of compounding, 740
Full costing, 186, 222. *See also* **Absorption costing**
and transfer pricing, 841
Fully diluted earnings per share, 955, 959, 962

Future value, 741–42, 755
Future value of an annuity, 743

▶ **G**

Generally accepted accounting principles
   (GAAP), 4
Generally accepted auditing standards
   (GAAS), 4
Goals, 7, 9, 22, 24
Graphical solution
   fixed overhead variances, 542–44
   maximization problem, 671–74
   minimization problems, 677–80
Gross cash flow, 878, 899, 900
Gross margin, 45, 48, 56, 58, 92, 100
Gross profit, 45, 48, 58. *See also* **Gross
   margin**

▶ **H**

Half-year convention, MACRS, 786, 802
Hard data, 731, 739, 755
Hewlett-Packard 12C, financial calcula-
   tor, 728
High-low graph, 89–90
High-low method, mixed cost analysis,
   87–89, 95, 100
Horizontal analysis, 933, 959, 961. *See
   also* **Trend analysis**
Hospitals
   budgeting for, 420–21
   cost budget for, 422–23
   cost terms, 55–56
   and standard cost accounting, 489
Human factors, budgetary planning and
   control, 417–19
Hurdle rate, 726, 739, 755. *See also*
   Cutoff rate

▶ **I**

Ideal capacity, 550, 554
Ideal standards, 476–77, 491, 496
Idle time, 198, 222
Income statement
   budgeted income statement, 414–16,
     424, 432
   contribution format, 92–95, 95–96
   for a manufacturing firm, 43–48
   for a merchandising firm, 37–38
   segment margin income statement,
     600–602
   segment statements
     format, 598–600
     preparation of, 604–607
   use in CVP analysis, 140–41
   use in financial reporting, 874
   variance presentation, 545–46
Income taxes, 45
   after-tax cash flow, 783
   and decision making, 782–90
   tax shields, 783
Incremental analysis, 141–42, 152, 153
   and changes in selling price, 143–44

Incremental budgeting, 419, 424, 433
Incremental cost. *See* **Variable cost**
Independent variable, 96, 101
Index number, financial statement analy-
   sis, 931–33, 959, 961
Indirect costs, 39, 51, 56, 58
Indirect factory expenses, 40, 58. *See
   also* **Manufacturing overhead**
Indirect labor costs, 39
Indirect manufacturing costs, 39, 58. *See
   also* **Manufacturing overhead**
Indirect material costs, 39
Indirect method, statement of cash flow
   overview, 876, 899, 900
   preparation of, 879–81
Inflation, and capital budgeting, 754–55
Input, 481, 491, 496
Inspection time, 317, 326, 328
Institute of Certified Management Ac-
   countants (ICMA), 18
Institute of Management Accountants
   (IMA), 18
   and ethical behavior, 21–22
Integrated cost accounting system, 186,
   220, 222
Integrity and management accountants,
   22
Interest and dividend income, treatment
   of, 874
Interest rate, 740
Intermediate products, 368, 371
Internal audit function, 16
Internal rate of return method (IRR),
   718, 726, 738, 755
   calculations, even cash flows, 726–27
   uneven cash flows, 728
Inventoriable costs, 40–41, 58. *See also*
   Assignable product cost
Inventory
   ending inventory budget, 406–407, 424,
     433
   inventory carrying costs, 425, 433
   inventory ordering costs, 425, 433
   inventory planning and control, 425–
     32, 433
   in a manufacturing firm, 42
   in merchandisers, 37
Inventory buildup, 591–97, 610, 611
   and income statement preparation,
     595–97
Inventory liquidation, 591–97, 610, 611
   and income statement preparation,
     595–97
Inventory-turnover ratio, 945–46, 959,
   962
Inventory valuation, 186
   joint products, 366–69
   net-realizable-sales-value method, 368–
     69
   physical-units method, 367
   relative-sales-value method, 367–68
   and standard costs, 477–78
Investing activities, 874, 899
   overview, 874, 900
Investment, 740
Investment center, 821, 827, 846,
   847

Investment center—*Cont.*
   allocation of common costs, 834
   performance report, 834–35
Irrelevant costs, 646, 668, 681

▶ **J**

Job, definition of, 187, 222
Job cost sheet, 195, 220, 222
Job order cost accounting system, 187–
   88, 220, 222
   in manufacturing firms, 188–207
Job time ticket, 195–97, 221, 222
Joint product costs, 365, 370, 371
   allocated costs, 366–69
   decision making, 658–59
   inventory valuation, 366–69
   net-realizable-sales-value method, 368–
     69
   physical-units method, 367
   relative-sales-value method, 367–68
Journal entries
   cost of goods sold, 203–205
   finished goods, 202–203
   job time, 197–98
   materials requisition, 193–95
   overhead rates, 199–201
   overhead variances, 544
   price and quantity variances, 492–94
   production orders, 192
   purchase requisition, 189
   receiving report, 190
   standard costs, 492–94, 547–49
   variances
     at time of purchase, 493–94
     at time of use, 492–93
Just-in-time (JIT), 19, 308, 319–23, 326,
   328
   conversion costs, 324
   cost accounting, 323–25
   direct labor job costing, 324
   direct materials inventories, 323–24
   nonvalue-added costs, 324
   process costing, 324–25
   service department costs, 364

▶ **K**

Kanban, and JIT, 320
Key Business Ratios, 960

▶ **L**

Labor-intensive firm, 208, 221, 222
Leading, 5, 11–12, 23, 24
Lead time, 317, 326, 328, 430, 433
Leasing versus purchasing, 733–34
Least-squares method, mixed cost analy-
   sis, 96–100, 101. *See also* **Regression
   line**
   short-cut method, 98–100
Limiting assumptions, of breakeven
   analysis, 130–31
Linear interpolation, 728, 739, 756

Linear programming, 669–80, 681
  area of feasible solutions, 672
  computer solutions, 674
  constraint functions, 670
  corner points, 672–74
  graphical solution, maximization problem, 671–74
  minimization problems, 677–80
  objective function, 670
  overview, 665–66
Line functions, 15, 23, 24
Lines of authority, 15, 23, 24
Long-range profitability, 394
Long-term planning, 397, 424, 433. *See also* **Capital budget; Strategic planning**
Lost units, 266–68, 274–75, 276

► **M**

Machine-hours base, 210, 221, 222
Machine-intensive firm, 208, 221, 222
Machine maintenance, and JIT, 320
Make-or-buy, component parts, 656–58, 667
Management accountants
  and the budget committee, 398
  and competence, 21
  and confidentiality, 22
  and ethics, 21–22
  and integrity, 22
  and objectivity, 22
Management by exception, 13, 23, 24, 474–75, 490, 496
Managerial accounting 4–6, 22, 24
Managers, five basic duties of, 5, 10–13
Manufacturing-cycle efficiency (MCE), 317–19, 326, 328
  and standard costing, 489–90
Manufacturing firm
  financial statements for, 42–50
  job order cost accounting systems, 188–207
Manufacturing overhead, 38, 39–40, 56, 58, 198–201, 207, 222
  activity-based costing, 312–16
  control of, 526
  cost accumulation, process system, 257
  fixed overhead, 537–44
  manufacturing overhead budget, 406, 424, 433
  traditional application, 309–310, 311–12
  variable overhead, 531–37
Manufacturing overhead applied, 222. *See also* **Applied manufacturing overhead**
Marginal cost, 80, 95, 101
Marginal costing, 586, 610, 611. *See also* **Variable costing**
Margin of safety, 131, 151, 153
Marketing costs, 41
  marketing cost budget, 407, 424, 434
Market-penetration pricing, 660, 669, 681

Markup pricing, 660–63, 669, 681
  absorption costing, 661–62
  variable costing, 662–63
Master budget, 394, 398–99, 423, 434
Master plan, 23
Master strategy, 10, 24
Materials cost base, 210–11, 221
Materials ledger cards, 195
Materials requisition, 193–95, 220, 222
Mathematical approach, service department overhead allocation, 355–58, 370, 371
Maturity value, 740
Maximization problem, graphical solution, 671–74
Maximum usage, 431
Medicare, 56
Merchandising firm, financial statements for, 37–38
Method of neglect, 274–75, 276
Mid-month convention, MACRS, 787, 802
Mid-quarter convention, 786–87, 802
Minimization problems, linear programming, 677–80
Mixed costs, 84–92, 95, 101
  account analysis, 87, 95
  analyzing, 86–92
  engineering cost analysis, 87, 95
  high-low graph, used in analysis, 89–90
  high-low method, of analysis, 87–89, 95
  least-squares method, of analysis, 96–100
  scatter diagram, analysis method, 90–92
Modified accelerated cost recovery system (MACRS), 786–87, 801, 802
  depreciation calculations, 787–88
  depreciation method, selecting, 789
  half-year convention, 786
  mid-month convention, 787
  mid-quarter convention, 786–87
  optional straight-line method, 788–89
Move time, 317, 326, 328
Moving average cost assumption, 254
Multiple regression, 96, 101

► **N**

National Association of Accountants (NAA), 18
National Cash Register Company, Expenses in Retail Business, 960
Negative financial leverage, 952, 959, 961
Negotiated price, as transfer price, 844–45
Net cash flow, 648, 878, 899, 900
Net income, 45, 48, 56, 58
Net investment, 648
Net present value method (NPV), 756
  differential income approach, 719–22
  overview, 718–19, 738
  and tax considerations, 801–802
Net-realizable-sales-value method, joint products costing, 368–69, 371

New product, entering a market, 652–53, 667
  differential income approach, 725–26
  tax considerations, 798–801
Noncash exchange transaction, 879, 899, 900
Noncontrollable cost, 53–54, 57, 58
Nonvalue-added cost, 316, 317–19, 326, 328
  and just-in-time, 321, 324
Normal capacity, 551–52, 554
Normal costing, 217, 221, 222
Normal overhead rate, 212, 221, 223
Normal spoilage, 266–68, 275, 276. *See also* **Method of neglect**
Not-for-profit organizations, and budgets, 419–23

► **O**

Objective function, linear programming, 670, 681
Objectives. *See* **Goals**
Objectivity and management accountants, 22
Office rent, 40
Operating activities, 874, 899, 900
Operating budget, 394, 424, 434
Operating income, 828
Operating leverage, 137–39, 152, 153
Operating margin percentage, 829, 846, 847
Operating profit, 45, 48, 56, 58
Opportunity cost, 52–53, 57, 58
Ordering costs, inventory, 425, 433
Ordinary annuity, 743, 756
Organization charts, 13–17, 23, 24
Organizing 5, 10, 23, 25
Output, 481, 491, 496
Overabsorbed overhead, 212, 223. *See also* **Overapplied overhead**
Overapplied overhead, 212, 221, 223
  disposition of, 212–14
Overhead, 39, 58. *See also* **Manufacturing overhead**
Overhead application base, 547, 554
Overhead applied, 223. *See also* **Applied manufacturing overhead**
Overhead departmentalization, 350–58
  direct method, 352–53
  fixed vs. variable costs, 358–64
  for just-in-time systems, 364
  mathematical approach, 355–58
  reciprocal method, 354–55
  step-down method, 353–54
Overhead pool, 39, 58, 326. *See also* **Manufacturing overhead**
Overtime premium, 198, 223

► **P**

Parallel production process, 255, 268, 276
Participative budget, 396, 424, 434
Patient-day, 55, 57

Payback method
overview, 734–35, 739, 756
uneven cash flows, 735–36
Payroll fringes, 214–15, 223
Performance report, 417, 425, 434
for responsibility centers, 822–23, 825–26
and standard costs, 477
and variance analysis
overview, 485–86, 491, 496
for variable overhead, 533–35
Period costs, 41, 56, 58
Perpetual budget, 397. *See also* **Continuous budget**
Physical flow of production, 188, 220, 223, 254–55
Physical-units method, joint products costing, 367, 371
Planning, 5, 23, 25, 186, 394, 423, 434
Plant layout
and just-in-time manufacturing, 321–22
traditional, 308–309
Positive financial leverage, 951–52, 959, 961
Potentially dilutive securities, 955
Practical capacity, 550, 554
Practical standards, 477, 491, 496
Predetermined overhead rate (POR), 199–201, 208, 221, 223
Preference selection, 718, 738, 756
Present value, 742, 756
Present value of an annuity, 743, 756
Pre-tax targeted operating income, 127–29
Price-earnings ratio, 956, 959, 962
Price variance, 482, 491, 496
Pricing decisions, 667–68
competition-based pricing, 664–65
demand-oriented pricing, 664
market-penetration pricing, 660
markup pricing, 660–61
skimming the market, 659–60
target-return pricing, 663–64
Primary earnings per share (EPS), 956, 959, 962
Prime cost, 50, 56, 58
Prime cost base, 211, 221, 223
Principal, 740
Privileged information, 21
Procedural standards, and the FASB, 4
Process cost accounting system, 187–88, 220, 223, 254, 268, 276
cost accumulation, 256–59
cost flow assumptions, 254–55
equivalent production, 257–59
the **FIFO method**, 268–73
and just-in-time systems, 324
Processing centers, 254–55
Process time, 317, 326, 328
Producing department, 350, 370, 371
Product costs. *See also* **Inventoriable cost**
for a merchandising firm, 37
in manufacturing, 38, 56, 58
Production budget, 400–403, 424, 434

Production order, 190–92, 220, 223
and journal entries, 192
Production report, 268, 276
beginning work in process inventory, 264–66
FIFO production report, 270–73
initial department, 259–61
subsequent departments, 261–64
Production volume variance. *See* **Fixed overhead volume variance**
Profitability index (PI), 729–31, 739, 756
Profit center, 821, 827, 846, 847
Profit planning, 394, 423, 434
Profit-volume graph, 134–35, 151, 153
Proration procedure, 213–14, 223
Pull-it-through control, 319, 327, 328
Purchase order, 189, 220, 223
cost, and JIT, 320
Purchase requisition, 188–89, 220, 223
Push-it-through control, 319, 327, 328

▶ **Q**

Qualitative information, 7–9, 22, 25
Quantitative information, 7, 22, 25
Quantity of production report, 258–59, 268, 276
Quantity variance, 482, 491, 496
Queue time, 317, 326, 328
Quick ratio, 942–43, 959, 962. *See also* **Acid-test ratio**

▶ **R**

Ratio, 936, 961
tabulation of, 958
Ratio analysis, 936–37, 959
Raw materials, 39. *See also* **Direct materials**
Receiving report, 189–90, 220, 223
Reciprocal method, service department overhead allocation, 354–55, 370, 371
Redistribution method, service department
overhead allocation, 354–55, 371
Regression analysis, for mixed costs, 96–100
Regression line, 90–92, 101
Relative-sales-value method, joint products costing, 367–68, 371
Relative value unit, 489, 491, 497
Relevant cost, 646, 668, 681
Relevant range, 51, 57, 58, 80, 83, 95, 101
and **flexible budgets**, 528–31
Relevant revenue, 646, 668, 681
Reorder point, 430–32, 434
Repetitive production, and JIT, 320
Replacing existing equipment
comparative income approach, 724
differential income approach, 722–24
tax considerations, 790–98
Residual income, 835–38, 846, 847

Responsibility accounting, 54, 57, 58, 820
Responsibility center, 820, 846, 847
performance reports for, 822–23, 825–26
Return on common stockholders' equity, 950–51, 959, 962
Return on investment (ROI), 827–35, 846, 847
asset turnover, controlling, 832–34
financial statement performance measure, 948–50
increase in sales, calculation for, 831
reduction in operating assets, calculation for, 832
the ROI formula, 828–29
and **target return pricing**, 663–64
using ROI, 830–31
Return on total assets, 950, 959, 962
Revenue budget, for hospitals, 421
Revenue center, 821, 846, 847
evaluation of, 824–27
Robotic technology, 19, 23, 25
Rules-of-thumb standards, 941–42

▶ **S**

Safety stock, 188, 220, 223, 431, 434
Sales budget, 399–400, 424, 434
Sales commissions and targeted-income decisions, 130
Sales forecast, 399–400, 424, 434
Sales mix, 146–51, 152, 153
Sales revenue use as allocation base, 602–604
Salvage value, 790–91
Scatter diagram, 90–92, 101
Scattergraph. *See* **Scatter diagram**
Schedule of Cost of Goods Manufactured, 44–45
Schedule of Direct Materials Used in Production, 43–44
Screening, 718, 738, 756
Securities and Exchange Commission (SEC), 4, 23
Segment reporting
common cost allocation, 602–604, 605–607
income statement
format, 598–600
statement preparation, 604–607
overview, 597–98, 610, 611
segment margin, 600, 611
income statement, 600–602, 610, 611
uses of, 607–10
Self-imposed budget, 396. *See also* **Participative budget**
Sell at splitoff point, 658–59, 667
Semivariable costs, 84, 95, 101
Separable costs, 365, 370, 372
Sequential production process, 254–55, 268, 276
Service businesses
cost definitions and cost concepts, 54–55
cost objectives, 55

Service businesses—*Cont.*
 financial statements, 38
 and standard cost accounting, 489
Service department, 350, 370, 372
SFAS No. 95, "Statement of Cash Flows," 876, 899
Short-cut method of least squares, 98–100, 101
Short-term
 budget, 396–97
 liquidity, 937
Short-term planning, 10, 23, 25, 396–97, 424, 434
Simple interest, 740, 756
Simple rate of return, 736. *See also* **Accounting rate of return**
Simple regression, 96, 101
Skimming the market, 659–60, 669, 681
Slack. *See* **Budgets, budget slack**
Small Business Administration Publications, 961
Soft data, 731–32, 739, 756
Source documents, 188, 220, 223
Sources of cash, 877
Special orders, accepting, 653–56, 667
Splitoff point, 365, 370, 372, 658–59, 667
Spoiled units, 274, 275, 276
Staff functions, 15, 23, 25
Staffing, 5, 10–11, 23, 25
Standard & Poor's, 960
Standard cost centers, 824, 846, 847
Standard costing
 motivating employees, 476–77
 overview, 474, 475, 475–476, 490, 497
 setting standards, 476
 uses of , 477–78
Standard cost of direct labor, 479, 491, 497
Standard cost of direct materials, 478, 491, 497
Standard cost of goods sold, 545, 547, 554
Standard direct labor rate, 479, 491, 497
Standard gross margin, 545, 547, 554
Standard price of direct materials, 478, 491, 497
Standard quantity allowed, 479–81, 491, 497
Standard quantity of direct labor, 479, 491, 497
Standard quantity of direct materials, 478, 491, 497
Standards committee, 476, 490, 497
Standards of Ethical Conduct for Management Accountants, 19
State Board of Licensing, 21
Statement of Cash Flows (SCF)
 direct method
  preparation of, 893–97
  format, 876
 evolution of, 875–76
 indirect method
  format, 876
  preparation, 879–81
 and interest and dividend income, 874
 overview, 874–75, 899, 900

Statement of Cash Flows (SCF)—*Cont.*
 preparation, illustration of, 881–86
 stock dividends, treatment of, 880
 use of T account technique, 883–86
Statement of Financial Accounting Concepts No. 5 (1984), 876
Statement on Management Accounting Number 1C (SMA 1C), 21
Static budget, 526, 546, 554
Step-down method, service department overhead allocation, 353–54, 370, 372
Step-variable costs, 85, 95, 101
Storage time, 317, 326, 328
Straight-line depreciation, 786
Strategic planning, 9–10, 23, 25, 397, 424. *See also* **Long-term planning**
Strategies, 9, 23, 25
Structural analysis, 933–36
Sum-of-the-years'-digits, 786
Sunk costs, 53, 57, 58, 646–47, 668, 681

▶ **T**

T account technique, Statement of Cash Flows, 883–86, 899
 illustrated example, 887–92
Targeted income, 127, 151, 153
Target rate, 726, 755. *See also* **Cutoff rate**
Target-return pricing, 663–64, 669, 681
Tax Reform Act of 1986 (TRA 1986), 786
Tax shield, 783, 801, 802
 adjusted tax basis, 784
 differential analysis, replacement of equipment, 791–94
Throughput, 310, 325, 328
Time-adjusted rate of return (TARR), 718, 726. *See also* **Internal rate of return method**
Time period, 740
Times interest earned ratio, 948, 959, 962
Time value of money, 740, 756
Total debt, 947
Total manufacturing costs in process, 217
Total quality control, 320, 326, 328
Total standard cost, 480–81, 491, 497
Total standard variable overhead cost, 531–32, 554
Total stockholders' equity, 947
Total variance, 482, 491, 497
Trading on equity, 951. *See also* **Financial leverage**
Transaction-based costing, 312, 328. *See also* **Activity-based costing (ABC)**
Transfer price
 behavioral aspects of, 845
 cost plus markup, 841
 external market price, 841–44
 full cost, 841
 negotiated price, 844–45
 overview, 838, 846, 847
 variable cost, 838–41
Transferred-in cost, 261, 268, 276

Transferred-out cost, 261, 268, 276
Treasurer, 15–17, 23, 25
Trend analysis, 929, 959, 961
Troy, Leo, Almanac of Business and Industrial Financial Ratios, 961

▶ **U**

Underabsorbed overhead, 212, 223. *See also* **Underapplied overhead**
Underapplied overhead, 212, 221, 223
 disposition of, 212–14
Uneven cash flows
 IRR calculation, 728
 payback method, 735–36
Unexpired costs, 36, 56, 58
Unfavorable variance, 481, 491, 497
Uninterrupted sources of supply, and JIT, 319–20
Unit costs, 41, 58
 no work in process, 257
U.S. Department of Commerce, Census of Business, 961
U.S. Department of the Treasury. Statistics of Income, 961
U.S. Internal Revenue Service. Statistics of Income, 961
Units-of-production depreciation, 786
Uses of cash, 878

▶ **V**

Value-added cost, 318–19, 326, 328
Variable cost, 50–51, 56, 58, 80–82, 95, 101
 changes in, effect on contribution margin ratios, 145–46
 service department overhead allocations, 358–64
 in transfer pricing, 838–41
Variable costing
 versus absorption costing, 586–87
 with beginning and ending inventories, 591–97
 and markup pricing, 662–63
 no beginning or ending inventories, 587–89
 overview, 586, 610, 611
Variable cost ratio (VCR), 125–26, 151, 153
Variable manufacturing overhead
 application to production, 531–32
 journal entries, 544, 547–49
 selecting the base, 531
 variance analysis, 533–37
Variable overhead efficiency variance, 532, 537, 547, 554
Variable overhead spending variance, 532, 535–36, 547, 554
Variance analysis, 16
 cost/benefit rule applied to investigation of, 486–88
 diagrammatic approach, 483–84
 for direct labor, 484–85
 of direct materials, 482–83

Variance analysis—*Cont.*
  and fixed overhead, 539–41, 541–44
  graphical solution, fixed overhead
    variance, 542–44
  income statement presentation, 545–
    46
  joint price and quantity variance, 494–
    96
  overview, 481–82, 491, 497
  and **performance reports**, 485–86, 533–
    35
  and variable overhead, 533–37
Vatter, Professor W. J., 884

Velocity of trend, 929, 959, 962
Vendor's invoice, 190
Vertical analysis, 933–36, 959, 962. *See
  also* **Common-size statement**
Volume changes, CVP analysis, 140
Volume level, 538. *See also* **Capacity
  level**

▶ **W**

**Weighted contribution margin per mix
  (WCMPM)**, 146, 152, 153

Working capital
  and cash flow, 886–89, 899, 900
  and financial analysis, 937–38, 959, 962
  and taxes, 798
Work in process, 42, 45, 56, 59
  beginning inventory, production re-
    port, 264–66

▶ **Y**

Year-to-year change, 929–31

▶ **Z**

Zero-base budgeting, 419–20, 424, 434